GW01471522

BRITISH CATALOGUE OF MUSIC

Annual Volume ● 2008

ISSN:0068-1407

Published on behalf of
THE BRITISH LIBRARY
by

ProQuest®

Start here.

2009 Proquest

Published by ProQuest
The Quorum
Barnwell Road
Cambridge
CB5 8SW
UK
Tel: +44 (0) 1223 271458
Fax: +44 (0) 1223 215513
http://www.csa.com
ProQuest is part of Cambridge Information Group

ISSN 0068-1407

The *British Catalogue of Music* is compiled within
The British Library
Music Collections
96 Euston Road
London NW1 2DB

Subscription enquiries should be directed to:
ProQuest Journals Division
7200 Wisconsin Avenue
Suite 715
Bethesda
MD 20814
USA
Tel: +1 301 961 6798
Fax: +1 301 961 6799
E-mail: journals@csa.com

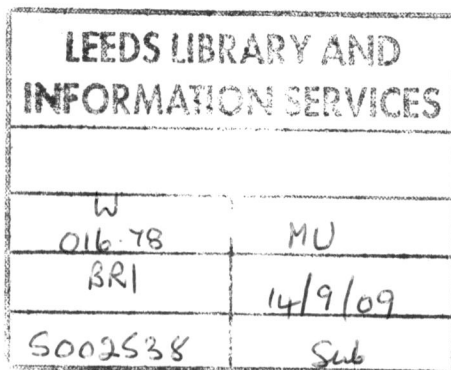

Computer typesetting by Solidus, www.solid-us.com
Printed in Great Britain by Page Bros, Mile Cross Lane, Norwich NR6 6SA

PREFACE

The British Catalogue of Music is the most complete list of current music available. It records:-

(i) new music published in Great Britain,

(ii) new music available in Great Britain through a sole agent.

(iii) Music acquired by the British Library Music Collections from foreign publishers who do not have agents in Great Britain.

The records of (i) and (ii) are derived from copies of the publications deposited at the Legal Deposit Office at the British Library, where all newly published works must be sent by law.

The catalogue is presented in three sections:

The Classified Section
This forms the body of the catalogue and gives full details of each work arranged according to the 22nd edition of the Dewey Decimal Classification. An outline of the classification is given overleaf.

The works are arranged according to the instrument or ensemble for which the work is written. Details for each entry (catalogued by the second edition of the *Anglo-American Cataloguing Rules*) include the name of the composer (as established by the Name Authority List), the title as given in the publication followed by appropriate statements of responsibility, the location and identity of the publisher, year of issue, the collation, a note identifying the series (when required), other information relating to the publication and International Standard Book Number and International Standard Music Number (when given). Each entry also includes the system number of the record as used on the British Library's Integrated Catalogue (*http://catalogue.bl.uk*)

The Composer and Title Index
This is an Index to composers and titles of works given in the main classified section. Arranged alphabetically, entries are given under the composers of works, editors and arrangers.

Entries are also made under the titles of all works having distinctive titles.

The information contained in this index, including publisher, is sufficient to identify the work, but by using the class number given at the end of each entry, you can refer to the full details of the work in the classified section.

The Subject Index
This is an alphabetically arranged guide to the classified section. It lists the principal musical forms and musical characters and indicates the appropriate classification character. For example, under the word Sonatas, the following entries may appear:

Sonatas
For organ   786.5183
For violin   787.2183

As a further example, under the word Violin, the following entries may be found:

Violins
Violins with orchestra   784.272
Violins with string orchestra   784.7272

Here the subject index collocates works for a particular instrument, giving the necessary classification number to locate the items in the classified section.

Books about Music
Records of books about music may be found in the *British National Bibliography* (ISSN 0007-1544). This is a weekly list of new and forthcoming titles published in Britain.

OUTLINE OF THE CLASSIFICATION

Entries in the British Catalogue of Music are classified by the 22nd edition of the Dewey Decimal Classification. The following outline is given for general information only. Users are advised to consult the Subject Index in the annual volume to discover the exact location of required material in the Classified Section.

780	General Collections	786.2	Piano
782	Vocal Music	786.3	Clavichord
782.1	Dramatic Vocal forms	786.4	Harpsichord
782.2	Non-Dramatic Forms	786.5	Organs
782.3	Services (Liturgy and Ritual)	786.6	Mechanical and Aeolian Instruments
782.4	Secular forms	786.7	Electrophones and Electronic Music
782.5	Mixed Voices	786.8	Percussion Instruments
782.6	Female Voices	787	String Instruments
782.7	Children's Voices	787.2	Violin
782.8	Male Voices	787.3	Viola
782.9	Other types of Voices	787.4	Cello
783	Music for Single Voices. The Voice	787.5	Double Bass
783.1	Single Voices in Combination	787.6	Viols and Other Bowed String Instruments
783.2	Solo Voice	787.7	Plectral Instruments
783.3	High Voice	787.8	Lute, Guitar, etc.
783.4	Middle Voice	787.9	Harp
783.5	Low Voice	788	Wind Instruments (Aerophones)
783.6/8	Female's, Child's, Male's Voices	788.2	Woodwind Instruments
783.9	Other Types of Voices	788.3	Flute, Recorder, etc.
784	Instruments and Instrumental Ensembles	788.4	Reed Instruments
784.2	Symphony Orchestra	788.49	Bagpipes
784.3	Chamber Orchestra	788.5	Double Reed Instruments
784.4	Light Orchestra	788.52	Oboe
784.44	School or Amateur Orchestra	788.53	Cor Anglais
784.46	Orchestra with Toy Instruments	788.58	Bassoon
784.48	Dance Bands	788.59	Double Bassoon
784.6	Keyboard, Mechanical Electronic, Percussion Bands	788.6	Single Reed Instruments
		788.62	Clarinet
784.7	String Orchestra	788.65	Bass Clarinet
784.8	Wind Band	788.7	Saxophone
784.9	Brass Band	788.79	Bagpipes
785	Chamber Music	788.8	Free Reeds
785.2	Ensembles with Keyboard	788.82	Mouth Organ
785.3	Ensembles without Electrophones and with Percussion and Keyboard	788.84	Concertina
		788.86	Accordion
785.4	Ensembles without Keyboard	788.9	Brass Instruments
785.5	Ensembles without Keyboard and with Percussion	788.92	Trumpet
		788.93	Trombone
785.6	Keyboard, Electrophone, Percussion Ensembles	788.94	Horn
		788.95	Bugle
785.7	String Ensembles	788.96	Cornet
785.8	Woodwind Ensembles	788.96	Flugelhorn
785.9	Brass Ensembles	788.975	Euphonium, Baritone, etc.
786	Keyboard, Mechanical, Electrophonic, Percussion Instruments	788.98	Tuba
		788.99	Other Brass Instruments

LIST OF ABBREVIATIONS

The following list is a key to abbreviations used in the Classified section and Composer and Title Index.

A	alto	c	copyright	no.	number	s.l.	[sine loco]
ad lib	ad libitum	cm.	centimetres	op.	opus		without place
arr.	arrangement	et al	[et allii]	p.	page(s)	T.	tenor
B.	bass		and others	publ.	publisher's	v.	volume(s)
Bar.	baritone	ill.	illustrated	S.	soprano		

CLASSIFIED SECTION

THIS SECTION CONTAINS ENTRIES UNDER SUBJECTS AND INSTRUMENTS ACCORDING TO A SYSTEM OF CLASSIFICATION, A SYNOPSIS OF WHICH APPEARS IN THE PRELIMINARY PAGES. THE COMPOSER AND TITLE INDEX FOLLOWS THIS SECTION.

780 – GENERAL COLLECTIONS

780

*Anthology for The musician's guide to theory and analysis / [compiled by] Jane Piper Clendinning, Elizabeth West Marvin. — New York : W.W. Norton & Co., c2005. — 1 score (vii, 260 p.) ; 28 cm.
Includes index. — Words of vocal works in English, German, and Italian; non-English words also printed separately for reference with English translations.
ISBN 0393925765
System number: 001312079

*[Antología (Archivo Musical de Moxos)]
Antología / Archivo Musical de Moxos ; [transcrita y editada por] Piotr Nawrot. — 1. ed. — Santa Cruz de la Sierra, Bolivia : Fondo editorial APAC ; Cochabamba, Bolivia : Verbo Divino, c2004. — 1 score (4 v.) : facsims. ; 29 cm. — Monumenta música ; 11-14
Variously for 1-6 voices, 1-2 violins, harp, and continuo. — "Monuménta música in Moxórum reductiónibus Bolíviae." — Latin (chiefly) and Spanish words.
ISBN 9990510962 (v. 1)
ISBN 9990510970 (v. 2)
ISBN 9990510989 (v. 3)
ISBN 9990510997 (v. 4)
System number: 013043834

*Rheinberger, Josef, 1839-1901.
[Vocal music. *Selections*]
Geistliche Gesänge. I : für Solostimmen bzw. Frauenchor mit Begleitung / [Josef Gabriel Rheinberger] ; vorgelegt von Berthold Over. — Stuttgart : Carus, c2005. — 1 score (xlvi, 241 p.) : facsims. ; 33 cm. — (Sämtliche Werke / Josef Gabriel Rheinberger. Abteilung I, Geistliche Vokalmusik ; Bd. 6)
For solo voice, vocal ensemble, or women's chorus with various acc. — Includes alternate versions of several pieces. — Pref. in German with English and French translations; Critical report in German with English and French summaries. — Series under the general editorship of the Josef-Rheinberger-Archiv, Vaduz. — German and/or Latin words.
Publ. no. 50.206
Publ. no. CV 50.206
ISBN 3899480058
ISMN M007087234
System number: 013534196
Also classified at 782

780.9032

Anthology of Baroque music : music in Western Europe, 1580-1750 / edited by John Walter Hill. — New York ; London : W. W. Norton & Co., c2005. — 1 score (xi, 565 p.) ; 22 x 28 cm. — Norton introduction to music history
"This anthology serves as a companion to Baroque Music in the Norton Introduction to music history series"—P. xi. — Vocal selections in Italian, Latin, English, French, German and Spanish; words also printed for reference with English translations following each work.
ISBN 039397801X
ISBN 9780393978018
System number: 013212022

781.2

Kolb, Tom.
Music theory / Tom Kolb. — Milwaukee, WI : Hal Leonard, c2005. — 104 p.: port ; 31 cm. + 1 compact disc. — Hal Leonard guitar method.
In standard and tablature notation.
Publ. no. HL00695790
ISBN 063406651X
System number: 013299202
Primary classification 787.87076

781.65

Essential jazz classics : 10 essential jazz classics / arranged and produced by Mark Taylor. — [S.l.] : Hal Leonard Europe ; London : distributed by Music Sales, [2005?] — 55 p. ; 31 cm. + 1 compact disc — Jazz play along ; v. 12
Lead sheets for B♭, E♭ and C instruments. — Melody lines with chord symbols. — Words printed for reference: p.54-55. — CD contains demonstration and backing tracks.
Publ. no. HLE90002462
ISBN 1846091152
System number: 013357996

Evans, Bill, 1929-1980.
[Selections; *arr.*]
Bill Evans : 10 original compositions / arranged and produced by Mark Taylor. — [S.l.] : TRO The Richmond Organization ; Milwaukee, Wis. : Exclusively distributed by Hal Leonard, c2005. — 71 p. ; 31 cm. + 1 compact disc. — Jazz play along ; v. 37
Lead sheets for B♭, E♭, and C instruments. — Melody lines with chord symbols. — CD contains demonstration and backing tracks.
Publ. no. HL00843033
ISBN 0634081837
System number: 013335910

Great jazz standards : 10 jazz standards / arranged and produced by Mark Taylor. — [S.l.] : Hal Leonard Europe ; London : distributed by Music Sales, c2005. — 88 p. ; 31 cm + 1 compact disc. — Jazz play along ; v. 27
Lead sheets for B♭, E♭ and C instruments. — Melody lines with chord symbols. — Words provided for reference: p.86-88. — CD contains demonstration and backing tracks.
Publ. no. HLE90002352
ISBN 1844498409
System number: 013212159

Hancock, Herbie, 1940-
[Selections; *arr.*]
Herbie Hancock : 9 jazz classics / arranged and produced by Mark Taylor. — [S.l.] : Hal Leonard Europe ; London : distributed by Music Sales, [2005] — 47 p. of music ; 31 cm + 1 sound disc (digital ; 4 3/4 in.) — Jazz play along ; v. 14
Lead sheets for B♭, E♭, and C instruments. — Melody lines with chord symbols. — CD contains demonstration and backing tracks. — Publisher's no.: HLE90002517 (music), CD#63006530 (CD).
Publ. no. HLE90002517
Publ. no. CD#63006530
ISBN 1846091306
System number: 013383268

Rollins, Sonny.
[Selections; *arr.*]
Sonny Rollins : 10 jazz classics / arranged and produced by Mark Taylor. — Milwaukee, Wis. : Hal Leonard, c2005. — 59 p. ; 31 cm. + 1 compact disc. — Jazz play along ; v. 33
Lead sheets for B♭, E♭, and C instruments. — Melody lines with chord symbols. — CD contains demonstration and backing tracks.
Publ. no. HL00843029
ISBN 0634079883
System number: 013335917

Silver, Horace, 1928-
[Selections; *arr.*]
Horace Silver : [10 hard bop classics] / arranged and produced by Mark Taylor. — Milwaukee, Wis. : Hal Leonard, c2005. — 51 p. of music ; 31 cm + 1 sound disc (digital ; 4 3/4 in.) — Jazz play along ; v. 36
Lead sheets for B♭, E♭, and C instruments. — Melody lines with chord symbols. — CD contains demonstration and backing tracks. — Publisher's no.: HL00843032 (music), CD#63007922 (CD).
Publ. no. HL00843032
Publ. no. CD#63007922
ISBN 0634079913
System number: 013381861

781.65076

Rawlins, Robert.
Jazzology : the encyclopedia of jazz theory for all musicians / by Robert Rawlins and Nor Eddine Bahha ; edited by Barrett Tagliarino. — Milwaukee, Wis. : Hal Leonard, c2005. — v, 265 p. ; 31 cm.
Contains instrumental and theoretical excercises, analyses of compositions, and explanations of various topics pertaining to jazz theory, composition, and performance.
Publ. no. HL00311167
ISBN 0634086782
System number: 013358435

781.651643

Bluesy jazz : 10 jazz favorites / [arranged and produced by Mark Taylor] — [S.l.] : Hal Leonard Europe ; London : Distributed by Music Sales, c2005. — 52 p. ; 31 cm. + 1 compact disc. — Jazz play along ; v. 35
Lead sheets for B♭, E♭, and C instruments. — Melody lines with chord symbols. — CD contains demonstration and backing tracks.
Publ. no. HLE90002385
ISBN 1844499987
System number: 013219947

781.654
Best of swing : 10 swing classics / [arranged and produced by Mark Taylor and Jim Roberts] — [S.l.] : Hal Leonard Europe ; London : Exclusive distributors, Music Sales, [2005?] — 64 p. ; 31 cm. + 1 compact disc. — Jazz play along ; v. 32
Lead sheets for B♭, E♭ and C instruments. — Melody lines with chord symbols. — Words printed for reference : p.62-64. — CD contains demonstration and backing tracks.
Publ. no. HLE90002418
ISBN 1846090156
System number: 013323811

782 – VOCAL MUSIC

782

*Rheinberger, Josef, 1839-1901.
[Vocal music. *Selections*]
Geistliche Gesänge. I : für Solostimmen bzw. Frauenchor mit Begleitung / [Josef Gabriel Rheinberger] ; vorgelegt von Berthold Over. — Stuttgart : Carus, c2005. — 1 score (xlvi, 241 p.) : facsims. ; 33 cm. — (Sämtliche Werke / Josef Gabriel Rheinberger. Abteilung I, Geistliche Vokalmusik ; Bd. 6)
For solo voice, vocal ensemble, or women's chorus with various acc. — Includes alternate versions of several pieces. — Pref. in German with English and French translations; Critical report in German with English and French summaries. — Series under the general editorship of the Josef-Rheinberger-Archiv, Vaduz. — German and/or Latin words.
Publ. no. 50.206
Publ. no. CV 50.206
ISBN 3899480058
ISMN M007087234
System number: 013534196
Primary classification 780

782.1 – DRAMATIC VOCAL FORMS

782.1

*Arnold, Samuel, 1740-1802.
Polly : an opera : (1777) / music by Johann Christoph Pepusch ; rearrang'd and new airs compos'd by Samuel Arnold ; libretto by John Gay ; revis'd by George Colman, the elder ; edited by Robert Hoskins. — Wellington, N.Z. : Artaria Editions, c2004. — 1 score (207 p.) ; 30 cm. — (Centre for Eighteenth-Century Music, Massey University. Series 1 ; no. 1)
Source: Harvard University Library (Houghton fMS Mus 97) : "Polly (1729), a ballad opera with tunes harmonized by Johann Christoph Pepusch to a libretto by John Gay, was written as a sequel to The beggar's opera (1728) … in mid 1777 Polly was performed … the libretto was a cut version by the elder George Colman with a completely renovated score by Samuel Arnold"—P. 5.
Pl. no. AE100
ISBN 1877369012
ISBN 9781877369018
ISMN M674519021
System number: 013107352

*Bellini, Vincenzo, 1801-1835.
I Capuleti e i Montecchi / Vincenzo Bellini ; tragedia lirica in due atti di Felice Romani ; a cura di Claudio Toscani. — Partitura. — Milano : Ricordi, c2003. — 1 score (2 v.) : facsims. ; 35 cm. + 1 critical commentary (120 p. : music ; 25 cm.) — (Edizione critica delle opere / di Vincenzo Bellini ; v. 6)
Prefatory material and critical commentary in Italian. — Italian words; also printed separately for reference.
Pl. no. 138469
ISBN 8875927294
ISMN M041384696
System number: 014682330

*Biber, Heinrich Ignaz Franz, 1644-1704.
Chi la dura la vince (Wer ausharrt, siegt) : Dramma musicale in drei Akten / Heinrich Franz Biber ; Text von Francesco Maria Raffaelini (?) ; Einfürhung von Sibylle Dahms. — Salzburg : Selke Verlag, c2004. — 1 facsimile of manuscript score (157 fol.) + 1 commentary volume (107 p.) ; 31 cm. — Denkmäler der Musik in Salzburg. Faksimile-Ausgaben ; Bd. 10.
Facsimile of the full score at shelfmark Hs 560 in the Salzburg Museum Carolino Augusteum. — Title from commentary volume. — Opera ; Italian words. — Libretto attr. to Francesco Maria Rarraelini. — Commentary volume includes historical and critical notes in German and complete libretto in German and Italian.
ISBN 3901353305
System number: 013120293

*Chapí, Ruperto, 1851-1909.
La venta de Don Quijote : comedia lírica en un acto / Ruperto Chapí ; libreto, Carlos Fernández Shaw ; edición crítica Manuel Moreno-Buendia. — Madrid : Instituto Complutense de Ciencias Musicales, c2004. — 1 score (xxxix, 152 p.) : port. ; 30 cm. — (Música hispana. Serie A, Música lírica ; 47)
Pref. in Spanish and English. — Spanish words, also printed separately for reference.
ISBN 8480485590
System number: 014679578

Charpentier, Marc-Antoine, 1643-1704.
Acteon : H. 481 ; Acteon changé en biche, H. 481a / M.-A. Charpentier. — Marandeuil : Éditions des Abbesses, 2006. — 1 score (xli, 152 p.) : facsims. ; 31 cm. — (Les arts florissants / collection dirigée par William Christie ; Série I-A. Musique française. Œuvres pour le théâtre ; 1. M.-A. Charpentier ; vol. 3)
Figured bass unrealized. — Edited by Sébastien Daucé, H. Wiley Hitchcock, Fannie Vernaz, and Benoît Hartoin; series edited by William Christie. — Preface and critical notes in French and English. — French words, also printed separately for reference with English translation, p. xxxi-xxxvi.
Pl. no. EDA 20/00
System number: 013728836

Dokumente und Texte zu "Tannhäuser und der Sängerkrieg auf Wartburg" / herausgegeben von Peter Jost ; Reinschrift des Textbuches mit Varianten herausgegeben von Cristina Urcheuguía. — Mainz : Schott , c2007. — 565 p. : facsims., ill. ; 31 cm. — (Sämtliche Werke / Richard Wagner ; Bd. 25)
Spine title: Tannhäuser und der Sängerkrieg auf Wartburg Dokumente. — Series edited by the Gesellschaft zur Förderung der Richard Wagner-Gesamtausgabe in conjunction with the Bayerischen Akademie der Schönen Künste, München, founded by Carl Dahlhaus, under the general editorship of Egon Voss.
Publ. no. RWA 225
Publ. no. BSS 43722
ISMN M001144223
System number: 013825606

Erkel, Ferenc.
[Hunyadi László]
Hunyadi László : opera négy felvonásban = opera in four acts / [Erkel Ferenc] ; szöveg Benjámin Egressy ; közreadja Katalin Szacsvai-Kim ; bevezetés Tibor Tallián, Katalin Szacsvai-Kim. — Budapest : Rózsavölgyi és Társa kiadása, 2006. — 1 score (3 v. (lxx, 867 p.)) : facsims. ; 34 cm. — (Operák / Erkel Ferenc = Operas / Ferenc Erkel ; 2)
Opera. — Libretto based on a play by Lőrinc Tóth. — Pref. and introd. in Hungarian with English translation; — "The score includes all emendations and insertions added to the work that originate with or were approved by the composer"—P. vii. — "Issued by the Institute for Musicology of the Hungarian Academy of Sciences in association with the National Széchényi Library"—Series t.p. — Hungarian words; libretto printed for reference with English and German translations.
Pl. no. RÉT 020
ISMN M801653208 (Elsö kötet : cl.) :
ISMN M801653215 (Masodik kötet : cl.)
ISMN M801653239 (Harmadik kötet : cl.)
System number: 013688162

Greene, Maurice, 1696-1755.
Phoebe : a pastoral opera / Maurice Greene ; edited by H. Diack Johnstone. — London : Stainer and Bell, 2004. — 1 score (xli, 147 p.) : ill., facsims. ; 34 cm. — Musica Britannica ; 82
Libretto by John Hoadly. — Edited principally from mss. in the Bodleian Library, Oxford (MS Mus. d. 53, ff. 2-121v; MS Mus. d. 35, ff. 97-102v (Overture)). — "Published for the Musica Britannica Trust established by the Royal Musical Association." — Duration: ca. 150:00. — Pref. in English, French, and German; historical, editorial, and performance notes, synopsis, and critical commentary in English.
ISBN 0852498810
ISMN M220221026
System number: 013195981

Halévy, F., 1799-1862.
La fée aux roses : opéra-comique en trois actes / Fromental Halévy ; paroles d'Eugène Scribe et de Henri V. de Saint-Georges ; edité par Peter Kaiser. — Partition d'orchestre. — Weinsberg : Musik-Edition Lucie Galland, c2005. — 1 score (xv, 621 p.) : facsims. ; 30 cm. — (Nouvelle édition d'opéras choisis / Fromental Halevy ; v. 3)
Introd. in German and French; other prefatory material in French. — Includes reproduction of published mise en scène for 1st performace.
Pl. no. L.G3
ISBN 3925934650
System number: 013801715

Lully, Jean Baptiste, 1632-1687.
[Armide. *Vocal score*]
Armide : tragédie en musique / Jean-Baptiste Lully ; édition de Lois Rosow ; réduction clavier-chant, Noam A. Krieger. — Hildesheim : G. Olms, 2006. — 1 score (249 p.) ; 30 cm. — Musica Gallica — (Œuvres complètes. Série III, Opéras / Jean-Baptiste Lully ; v. 14)
French libretto by Philippe Quinault, based on Tasso's Gerusalemme liberata. — Pref. in French, English, and German.
ISBN 3487131331
System number: 013775736

Monteverdi, Claudio, 1567-1643.
[Ritorno d'Ulisse in patria]
Il ritorno di Ulisse in patria : Ms. Wien, partitura / Claudio Monteverdi . — Firenze : Studio per edizioni scelte, 2006. — 1 score (269 p.) : 21 x 28 cm + 1 v. (197 p.). — Archivum musicum. Musica drammatica ; 9
Facsimile edition of a manuscript score from the Österreichische Nationalbibliothek Wien (v. [1]). — Facsimile of librettos and documents: Saggio introduttivo e libretti / a cura di Sergio Vartolo (v. [2]). — Libretto by G. Badoaro after Homer's Odyssey. — Pref. in Italian and English.
Publ. no. AM06MD009
ISBN 9788872428207 (pbk.)
ISBN 8872428203 (pbk.)
System number: 013771133

*Novak, Janez Krstnik, ca. 1756-1833.
Figaro ; Cantate zum Geburts oder Namensfeste einer Mutter / Janez Krstnik Novak ; transkribirala in revidirala = transcription and critical edition by Aleš Nagode (Figaro), Zoran Krstulović (Cantate). — Ljubljana : Slovenska akademija znanosti in umetnosti, 2004. — 1 score (xxxvi, 108 p.) : facsims. ; 28 cm. — Monumenta artis musicae Sloveniae ; 47
For solo voices, chorus (SATB) and orchestra. — Introd. and editorial notes in Slovenian and English. — Edited from mss.in the Narodna in univerzitetna knjižnica v Ljubljani (Figaro) and the Conservatorio Giuseppe Tartini di Trieste (Cantate). — Slovenian words (Figaro, also printed for reference with English translation) and German words (Cantate, also printed separately with English and Slovenian translation).
ISMN M709004140
ISMN 9790709004140
System number: 014663614
Also classified at 783.1448

Offenbach, Jacques, 1819-1880.
[Rheinnixen. *Vocal score*]
Les fées du Rhin = Die Rheinnixen : opéra romantique en 4 actes (1864 / Jacques Offenbach ; livret de Jacques Offenbach et Charles Nuitter ; adaptation allemande par Alfred von Wolzogen ; partition chant-piano [par Jean-Yves Aizic avec la collaboration de Dominik Rahmer, Jean-Christophe Keck] — Berlin : Boosey & Hawkes : Bote & Bock, c2007. — 1 score (557 p.) ; 31 cm. — (Offenbach Edition Keck : kritische Ausgabe / Jean-Christophe Keck)
Orchestral acc. arr. for piano. — Contains all the music for the original version, the intermediate version and the Vienna version. — Pref. in French, German, and English. — German words.
Publ. no. BB3039
ISMN M202530399
System number: 013598594

Paisiello, Giovanni, 1740-1816.
I giuochi d'Agrigento / [libretto di] Alessandro Pepoli ; [musica di] Giovanni Paisiello ; saggio introduttivo a cura di Lorenzo Mattei. — Partitura dell' opera in facsimile. — Milano : Ricordi, c2007. — 1 score (2 v.) ; 23 x 30 cm. — Drammaturgia musicale veneta ; 27
Opera in 3 acts. — Reproduction of "manoscritto conservato presso la Biblioteca Nazionale di Venezia [I-Vnm: Codd. It. IV, 779-780 (=10185-10186)]" — At head of title: Istituto italiano Antonio Vivaldi della Fondazione Giorgio Cini Venezia ; Dipartimento di storia e critica delle arti "Giuseppe Mazzarioli" della Università di Venezia. — Italian words; also printed for reference p. [xxxiii]-li.
ISBN 9788875928278
ISMN M041397870
System number: 013801677

*Pedrell, Felipe, 1841-1922.
Los Pirineus : ópera en tres actos / Felipe Pedrell ; libreto, Victor Balaguer ; edición crítica, Francesc Cortes y Edmon Colomer. — Madrid : Instituto Complutense de Ciencias Musicales, c2004. — 1 score (lxxxvii, 763 p.) : ports. ; 30 cm. — (Música hispana. Series A, Música lírica ; 46)
"Esta edición se estrenó en el Gran Teatre del Liceu de Barcelona el 17 de febrero de 2003"—T.p. — Commentary and critical report in Spanish and English. — Catalan words; also printed separately for reference with Spanish translation.
ISBN 8480485531
System number: 014679497

*Portugal, Marcos Antônio da Fonseca, 1762-1830.
Gli Orazi e i Curiazi : partitura dell'opera in facsimile, edizione del libretto / [libretto di] Simeone Antonio Sografi ; [musica di] Marco Portogallo. Catalogo cronologico degli spettacoli a Venezia (1797-1815) / a cura di Maria Giovanna Miggiani. — Milano : Ricordi, 2003. — 1 score (2 v. (ccclxiii, 541 p.)) : port. ; 23 x 30 cm. — Drammaturgia musicale veneta ; 29
At head of title: Istituto italiano Antonio Vivaldi della Fondazione Giorgio Cini Venezia ; Dipartimento di storia e critica delle arti "Giuseppe Mazzariol" della Università di Venezia. — Based on: Horace / Pierre Corneille. — Reproduces ms. score in the Biblioteca del Conservatorio Luigi Cherubini, Florence (Fondo Basevi, A.394) with modern edition of libretto and a chronological catalogue of theatrical performances in Venice from 1797 to 1815. — Preface in Italian with English summary.
Publ. no. 139095
ISBN 8875927324
ISBN 9788875927325
ISMN M041390956
System number: 014661287

Raff, Joachim, 1822-1882.
[Benedetto Marcello. *Vocal score*]
Bendetto Marcello : (Kunst und Liebe) : lyrische Oper in drei Aufzugen : WoO 46 / Joachim Raff ; Text vom Komponisten ; nach dem Autograph herausgegeben von Volker Tosta ; Klavierauszug. — Stuttgart : Edition Nordstern, c2002. — 1 score (174 p.) ; 30 cm. — (Raff Werke ; Bd. XVIII/2b)
Includes pref. in German with English translation. — Based on the autograph in the Staatsbibliothek zu Berlin - Preussischer Kulturbesitz (Mus. ms. autogr. J.Raff 13). — Limited ed. of 200 copies. — German words.
Pl. no. 01.07.03
ISMN M700164522
System number: 014503175

Rameau, Jean-Philippe, 1683-1764.
Hippolyte et Aricie : tragédie en cinq actes : version 1757 ; version 1742 (compléments) / [musique de Jean Philippe Rameau] ; livret de Simon-Joseph Pellegrin ; édition de Sylvie Bouissou. — Bonneuil-Matours, France : Société Jean-Philippe Rameau ; Kassel : Distribution mondiale, Bärenreiter, c2007. — 1 score (lxxiv, 429 p.) ; 34 cm. — Musica Gallica — (Opera omnia / Jean-Philippe Rameau ; sér. 4, v. 6)
Opera in 4 acts. — Duration: ca. 3:15:00. — Includes pref. in French and English. — French words.
Pl. no. SJPR-OOR IV.6
Publ. no. RCT 43
Publ. no. BA 8853
ISMN M006527892
System number: 013822163

Rameau, Jean-Philippe, 1683-1764.
[Platée. *Vocal score*]
Platée : ballet bouffon en un prologue et trois actes : version 1749, version 1745 (compléments) / [musique de Jean-Philippe Rameau] ; livret de Jacques Autreau ; révisé par Adrien-Joseph Valois d'Orville et Balot de Sovot ; édition de M. Elizabeth C. Barlet ; réduction clavier-chant de François Saint-Yves. — Bonneuil-Matours : Société Jean-Philippe Rameau ; Kassel ; London : Distribution mondiale Bärenreiter, c2005. — 1 score (xii, 352 p.) ; 27 cm. — Musica Gallica — (Opera omnia. Série IV, Musique dramatique / Jean-Philippe Rameau ; v. 10)
Opéra-ballet. — Acc. arr. for keyboard instrument. — Duration: ca.: 3:00:00. — Includes the complete Paris version of 1749 with additional scenes from the Versailles version of 1745. — French words.
Pl. no. OOR IV.10r
Publ. no. BA 8852a
ISMN M006527885
System number: 013376540

Royer, Pancrace, 1705-1755.
Le pouvoir de l'Amour / Pancrace Royer ; édition de Lisa Goode Crawford ; avec la collaboration de Gérard Geay. — Versailles : Éditions du Centre de Musique Baroque, c2006. — 1 score (civ, 266 p.) : facsims. ; 35 cm. — Patrimoine musical français. Anthologies. IV, Musique de scène ; 2
Ballet-héroïque in a prologue and 3 acts. — Figured bass unrealized. — Introduction and critical notes in English and French. — French words, libretto attributed to C. H. Lefebre de Saint-Marc but more likely by C. H. de Fusée, Abbé de Voisenon; also printed for reference with English translation.
Pl. no. CMBV 047
ISMN M707034477
System number: 013825410

*Schubert, Franz, 1797-1828.
Fierrabras / Franz Schubert. — Kassel ; London : Bärenreiter, 2005- — 1 score (- v.) : facsims. ; 33 cm. — (Neue Ausgabe sämtlicher Werke / Franz Schubert. Serie II, Bühnenwerke ; Bd. 8)
Opera. — V. 1 edited by Thomas A. Denny; v. 2 edited by Christine Martin. — Series under the general editorship of the Internationale Schubert-Gesellschaft. — Editorial notes in German. — German words by Josef Kupelwieser.
Publ. no. BA 5557
ISMN M006497225 (v. 1)
ISMN M006497249 (v. 2)
System number: 013777720

*Serrano, José, 1873-1941.
El mal de amores ; La mala sombra : sainetes líricos en un acto / José Serrano ; libretos, Joaquín y Serafín Álvarez Quintero ; edición crítica, Miguel Roa. — Madrid : Instituto Complutense de Ciencias Musicales, c2004. — 1 score (xli, 284 p.) : port. ; 30 cm. — (Música hispana. A, Música lírica ; 45)
Critical notes in Spanish and English. — Spanish words, also printed separately for reference.
ISBN 8480485574
System number: 014679490

Stradella, Alessandro, 1639-1682.
La forza dell'amor paterno / Alessandro Stradella ; a cura di Mariateresa Dellaborra, Carolyn Gianturco. — Pisa : ETS, 2006. — 1 score (cxlix, 356 p.) : facsims. ; 32 cm. — (Opera omnia / Alessandro Stradella ; Ser. II, Musica teatrale, v. 2)
Opera in 3 acts. — Partially figured bass, unrealized. — Pref. in Italian and English; critical commentary in Italian. — Italian libretto by Niccolò Minato, also printed for reference with English translation on p. xxvi-cxxxvii.
ISBN 9788846712653
ISMN M705015133
System number: 013825578

Tippett, Michael, 1905-1998.
[King Priam. *German & English*]
King Priam : opera in three acts : (1958-61) / Michael Tippett ; text by the composer. — New rev. ed. — Study score. — London : Schott, c2005. — 1 score (282 p.) ; 30 cm.
Duration: 125 min. — Words in English and German.
Publ. no. ED 12809
Publ. no. S&Co. 7888
ISMN M220123559
System number: 013382330

Vaughan Williams, Ralph, 1872-1958.
[Riders to the sea. *Vocal score*]
Riders to the sea / [based on the play by] J.M. Synge ; set to music by R. Vaughan Williams. — Oxford : Oxford University Press, [2005?], c1964. — 1 score (60 p.) ; 26 cm. — Oxford operas
Opera in 1 act. — Orchestral acc. arr. for piano. — Reprint. Originally published: London : Oxford University Press, 1936 (copyright renewed 1964).
ISBN 0193850079
System number: 013199387

*Verdi, Giuseppe, 1813-1901.
I masnadieri : a tragic opera (in four acts) = melodramma (in quattro atti) / Giuseppe Verdi ; libretto by Andrea Maffei ; edited by Roberta Montemorra Marvin. — Chicago : University of Chicago Press ; Milano : Ricordi, 2000. — 1 score (lxii, 493 p.) : facsims. ; 38 cm. + 1 critical commentary (vii, 169 p. ; 25 cm.) — (The works of Giuseppe Verdi. Series I, Operas = Le opere di Giuseppe Verdi. Serie I, Opere teatrali ; v. 11)
Based on: Die Räuber by Friedrich Schiller. — Edited principally from the holograph in the archives of Casa Ricordi, Milan. — Appendix includes rejected settings from Act I. — Editorial and critical notes in English, with Italian translation. — Italian words.
ISBN 8875926719 (Ricordi)
ISBN 0226853187 (University of Chicago Press)
ISMN M041385617 (Ricordi)
ISMN M041385662 (University of Chicago Press)
System number: 013122497

*Verdi, Giuseppe, 1813-1901.
Stiffelio / Giuseppe Verdi ; libretto (in three acts) by Francesco Maria Piave ; edited by Kathleen Kuzmick Hansell. — Chicago : University of Chicago Press ; Milano : Ricordi, c2003. — 1 score (lxxv, 423 p., 6 p. of plates) : facsims. ; 38 cm. + critical commentary (viii, 164 p. ; 25 cm.) — (The works of Giuseppe Verdi. Series I, Operas = Le opere di Giuseppe Verdi. Serie I, Opere teatrali ; v. 16)
Based on: Le pasteur, ou, L'évangile et le foyer / Emile Souvestre and Eugène Bourgeois. — Edited principally from the holograph at Villa Verdi, S. Agata. — Prefatory matter in English and Italian; critical commentary in English. — Italian words.
ISBN 0226853195 (University of Chicago Press)
ISBN 8875927065 (Ricordi)
ISMN M041388724 (University of Chicago Press)
ISMN M041360904 (Ricordi)
System number: 013122506

Weill, Kurt, 1900-1950.
Der Protagonist : ein Akt Oper : op. 15 / Musik von Kurt Weill ; Text von Georg Kaiser ; edited by Gunther Diehl and Jürgen Selk. — New York : Kurt Weill Foundation for Music : European American Music, 2006. — 1 score (377 p.) : facsims. ; 38 cm. + 1 critical report (53 p.) ; 29 cm. — (Kurt Weill Edition. Series I, Stage ; vol. 1)
Critical edition of score includes introductory essay, facsimiles, and notes in English. — Accompanied by critical report in English. — German words; libretto follows score.
ISBN 0913574643
ISBN 9780913574645
System number: 013813360

782.10265

*Bartók, Béla, 1881-1945.
[Kékszakállú herceg vára. *English & Hungarian*]
A Kékszakállú herceg vára : opera egy felvonásban szövegét írta Balázs Béla = Duke Bluebeard's castle : opera in one act to the libretto by Béla Balázs / Béla Bartók. — Score. — Homosassa, Fla. : Bartók Records, 2005, c2007. — 1 score (xxii, 210 p.) : ill. ; 29 cm.
Hungarian and English words; English translation by Peter Bartók. — Preface in English and Hungarian; editorial notes in English only. — With errata slip inserted.
Pl. no. BR 610
Publ. no. UE 33085
ISMN M901200180
System number: 014586910

782.12

*Esteve, Pablo.
Los jardineros de Aranjuez : (1768) : zarzuela en dos actos / Pablo Esteve y Grimau ; estudio y edición crítica de Juan Pablo Fernández-Cortés. — Granada : Universidad de Granada, 2005. — 1 score (ciii, 393 p.) ; 30 cm.
Includes biographical notes, critical notes, and libretto.
ISBN 8433834401
EAN 9788433834409
System number: 013335030

*Luna, Pablo, 1879-1942.
El asombro de Damasco : zarzuela en dos actos / Pablo Luna ; libreto, Antonio Paso y Joaquín Abati ; edición crítica, Miguel Roa. — Madrid : Instituto Complutense de Ciencias Musicales, c2004. — 1 score (xxxix, 303 p.) : ports. ; 30 cm. — (Música hispana. Series A, Música lírica ; 48)
Pref. in Spanish and English. — Includes bibliographical references. — Spanish words, also printed separately for reference.
ISBN 8480485639
System number: 014679583

782.14

Linley, Thomas, 1733-1795.
[Robinson Crusoe. *Vocal score*]
The pantomine [or rather, pantomime] of Robinson Crusoe : (1781) / Thomas Linley ; wordbook by Richard Brinsley Sheridan ; edited by Robert Hoskins. — Wellington, N.Z. : Artaria Éditions, c2005. — 1 score (47 p.) : ill., facsims. ; 30 cm. — (Centre for eighteenth-century music, Massey University ; ser. 1, no. 2)
The 1st act of a two-act pantomime, first staged in 1781. — Acc. arr. for piano. — Sources of this edition are Sheridan's wordbook and Linley's piano-vocal score, both copies held at the British Library, shelf marks 11781.bbb.20(1) and E.82.f, respectively. — Includes pref. and Sheridan's wordbook.
Pl. no. AE447
ISBN 1877369160
ISBN 9781877369162
ISMN M674519724
System number: 013750212

Roberts, Jimmy.
[I love you, you're perfect, now change. *Vocal score. Selections*]
I love you, you're perfect, now change : vocal selections / [book and lyrics by Joe Dipietro ; music by Jimmy Roberts ; with Jordan Leeds ... [et al.]] — Expanded ed. — [S.l.] : Williamson Music ; c2005. Milwaukee, Wis. : exclusively distributed by Hal Leonard, — 1 score (80 p.) ; 31 cm.
Acc. arr. for piano.
Publ. no. HL00313140
ISBN 0634009338
System number: 013383297

Rodgers, Richard, 1902-1979.
[Musicals. *Selections; arr.*]
Rodgers & Hart classics : 10 Rodgers & Hart classics / arranged and produced by Mark Taylor. — [S.l.] : Williamson Music ; Milwaukee, Wis. : Hal Leonard, [2003?] — 81 p. ; 31 cm. + 1 compact disc. — Jazz play along ; v. 21
Lead sheets for B♭, E♭ and C instruments. — Music by Richard Rodgers, words by Lorenz Hart. — Words printed for reference: p.76-81. — CD contains demonstration and backing tracks.
Publ. no. HL00843014
ISBN 0634061410
System number: 013323820

Rodgers, Richard, 1902-1979.
[Musicals. *Selections; arr.*]
Rodgers & Hart favorites : 10 Rodgers & Hart favorites / arranged and produced by Mark Taylor. — [S.l.] : Williamson Music ; Milwaukee, Wis. : Hal Leonard, [2003?] — 71 p. ; 31 cm. + 1 compact disc — Jazz play along ; v. 11
Lead sheets for B♭, E♭ and C instruments. — Music by Richard Rodgers, words by Lorenz Hart. — Words printed for reference: p.68-71. — CD contains demonstration and backing tracks.
Publ. no. HL00843004
ISBN 0634053574
System number: 013323827

782.140264

Schönberg, Claude-Michel.
[Misérables. *Vocal score. English. Selections*]
Les Misérables : Boublil and Schönberg's legendary musical : in concert : piano, vocal, guitar / music by Claude-Michel Schönberg. — New York : Alain Boublil Music ; Milwaukee, Wis. : Exclusively distributed by Hal Leonard, [2003?] — 1 score (100 p.) ; 31 cm.
For voice and piano, with chord symbols and guitar chord diagrams. — Original French lyrics by Alain Boublil and Jean-Marc Natel; English lyrics by Herbert Kretzmer. — Based on the novel by Victor Hugo.
Publ. no. HL00313212
ISBN 0634050036
System number: 006936060

782.14083

Brookes, Katherine.
The gunpowder plot : remember, remember the 5th of November. — Kenilworth : Maplewood Education, c2003. — 2 v. : ill. ; 30 cm. + 1 compact disc. — (An Anthony James musical)
"Written by Daniel Dalton. Music & lyrics by Katherine Brookes. Illustrations by Anthony James"- p. [1]
ISBN 1905123205
System number: 013390750

Brookes, Katherine.
Perfect pirates : the story of Anne Bonny & Mary Read. — Kenilworth : Maplewood Education, c2002. — 2 v. : ill. ; 30 cm. + 1 compact disc. — (An Anthony James musical)
"Music & lyrics by Katherine Brookes & Anthony James. Illustrations by Anthony James"-p. [1]
ISBN 1905123167
System number: 013390755

*Brookes, Katherine.
Pompeii : the rain of fire / written by Katherine Brookes ; music by Katherine Brookes. — Kenilworth : Maplewood Education : Educational Musicals, c2005. — 2 v. : ill. ; 30 cm. + 1 compact disc.
Children's musical; includes performance notes and background information. — For treble voices, mainly in unison but occasionally in 2 parts, with piano accompaniment and guitar chord symbols. — "...an Anthony James Musical". — "Illustrations by Anthony James"—P. 1. — CD contains rehearsal and backing tracks.
ISBN 1905123418
System number: 013587134

*Brookes, Katherine.
The Saxon king : the story of Sutton Hoo. — Kenilworth : Maplewood Education : Educational Musicals, c2003. — 2 v. : ill. ; 30 cm. + 1 compact disc.
Children's musical; includes performance notes and background information. — For treble voices, mainly in unison but occasionally in 2 parts, with piano accompaniment and guitar chord symbols. — "An Anthony James Musical". — "Written by Anthony James. Music & lyrics by Katherine Brookes. Illustrations by Anthony James"—P. [1]. — CD contains rehearsal and backing tracks.
ISBN 1905123213
System number: 013587305

*Hewitt, Daniel.
1066 : the Battle of Hastings / written by Daniel Dalton ; music [& lyrics] by Dan Hewitt. — Kenilworth : Educational Musicals, c2005. — 2 v. ill. ; 30 cm. + 1 compact disc.
Children's musical; includes performance notes and background information. — For treble voices, mainly in unison but occasionally in 2-3 parts, with piano accompaniment and guitar chord symbols. — "...an Anthony James Musical". — "Illustrations by Anthony James"—P. [1]. — CD contains rehearsal and performance tracks.
ISBN 1905123469
System number: 013587029

Hewitt, Daniel.
Battle of Britain : a story of the few. — Kenilworth : Maplewood Education, c2000. — 2 v. : ill. ; 30 cm. + 1 compact disc. — (An Anthony James musical)
"Music & lyrics by Daniel Hewitt. Illustrations by Anthony James"-p. 1.
ISBN 1905123116
System number: 013390765

Hewitt, Daniel.
Gettysburg : brothers at war. — Kenilworth : Maplewood Education, c2001. — 2 v. : ill. ; 30 cm. + 1 compact disc. — (An Anthony James musical)
"Written by Daniel Dalton. Music & lyrics by Daniel Hewitt. Illustrations by Anthony James"-p [1]
ISBN 1905123124
System number: 013390730

Hewitt, Daniel.
Henry VIII : the break with Rome. — 2nd ed. — Kenilworth : Maplewood Education, 2002, c2001. — 2 v. : ill ; 30 cm. + 1 compact disc. — (An Anthony James musical)
"Written by Daniel Dalton. Music & lyrics by Daniel Hewitt. Illustrations by Anthony James. Rhymes by Anita Allen"- p. 1.
ISBN 1905123140
System number: 013390722

Hewitt, Daniel.
The Spanish Armada : the invasion of England. — 2nd ed. — Kenilworth : Maplewood Education, 2002, c2000. — 2 v. : ill. ; 30 cm. + 1 compact disc. — (An Anthony James musical)
"Written by Daniel Dalton. Music and lyrics by Daniel Hewitt. Illustrations by Anthony James. Rhymes by Anita Allen"-p. 1.
ISBN 1905123086
System number: 013390715

Hewitt, Daniel.
The Trojan horse : the fall of Troy. — Kenilworth : Maplewood Education, 2002. — 2 v. : ill. ; 30 cm. + 1 compact disc. — (An Anthony James musical)
"Written by Daniel Dalton. Music & lyrics by Daniel Hewitt. Illustrations by Anthony James"-p. [1] — Errata sheet pasted to reverse of cover, v. 1.
ISBN 1905123159
System number: 013390719

Hewitt, Daniel.
The valley of the kings : the power of the Sun God. — 2nd ed. — Kenilworth : Maplewood Education, 2002. — 2 v. : ill. ; 30 cm. + 1 compact disc. — (An Anthony James musical)
Music & lyrics by Daniel Hewitt. Illustrations by Anthony James.
ISBN 1905123183
System number: 013390789

Johnson, Mark (Mark Noel Hugh).
Moving on : a brilliant new musical for primary schools / by Mark and Helen Johnson. — Hersham Green : Out of the Ark Music, c2002. — 1 score (84 p.) : port. ; 30 cm. + 1 compact disc.
Script, and songs for voice(s) and piano, with chord symbols. — Song words printed separately for reference. — "For ages 5-12"—Prelim. — CD contains full performances of the songs, backing tracks and sound effects.
ISBN 190198012X (book & CD pack)
System number: 013277136

Johnson, Mark.
Alice - the musical : a children's musical with up to eighteen songs, in two acts / by Mark and Helen Johnson ; based on the original story of 'Alice's adventures in Wonderland', by Lewis Carroll, retold in song and dance, drama and narrative. — Teacher's book : score and production notes. — Hersham Green : Out of the Ark Music, 2004. — 1 score (96 p.) : ill. ; 30 cm. — (The classic series)
"For children aged 7-14 (KS 2-3). Adaptable for younger children." — For treble voices, mainly unison but occasionally in 2-3 parts, with piano accompaniment and chord symbols. — Includes synopsis, performance notes, and complete lyrics printed for reference.
ISBN 0951911678
System number: 013271525

*Spencer, Tim.
The ancient Olympics : the legend of Callipateira. — Kenilworth : Maplewood Education : Educational Musicals, c2003. — 2 v. : ill. ; 30 cm. + 1 compact disc.
Children's musical; includes performance notes and background information. — For treble voices, mainly unison but occasionally in 2-3 parts, with piano accompaniment and chord symbols. — "An Anthony James Musical". — "Written by Daniel Dalton. Music & lyrics by Tim Spencer. Illustrations by Anthony James. Rhymes by Anita Allen"—P. 1. — CD contains rehearsal and backing tracks.
ISBN 1905123191
System number: 013587294

Spencer, Tim.
The boy king : the legend of Tutankhamun. — 2nd ed. — Kenilworth : Maplewood Education, 2001, c1999. — 2 v. : ill. ; 30 cm. + 1 compact disc. — (An Anthony James musical)
"Music & lyrics by Tim Spencer. Illustrations by Anthony James"-p.[1]
ISBN 1905123051
System number: 013390813

Spencer, Tim.
The golden city : the lost empire of the Aztecs. — 2nd ed. — Kenilworth : Maplewood Education, 2001, c2000. — 2 v. : ill. ; 30 cm. + 1 compact disc. — (An Anthony James musical)
"Music & lyrics by Tim Spencer and Anthony James. Illustrations by Anthony James"-p. [1]
ISBN 1905123094
System number: 013390718

Spencer, Tim.
The lucky Viking : the discovery of America. — 2nd ed. — Kenilworth : Maplewood Education, 2001. — 2 v. : ill. ; 30 cm. + 1 compact disc. — (An Anthony James musical)
Music & lyrics by Tim Spencer. Illustrations by Anthony James"-p.1.
ISBN 1905123043
System number: 013390817

Spencer, Tim.
Monster of the maze : the story of Theseus and the Minotaur. — 2nd ed. — Kenilworth : Maplewood Education, 2001, c1999. — 2 v. : ill. ; 30 cm. + 1 compact disc. — (An Anthony James musical)
"Music & lyrics by Tim Spencer. All illustrations by Anthony James"-p. [1]
ISBN 1905123000
System number: 013390808

Spencer, Tim.
The ship of dreams : the voyage of the RMS Titanic. — Kenilworth : Maplewood Education, c2000. — 2 v. : ill. ; 30 cm. + 1 compact disc. — (An Anthony James musical)
"Music & lyrics by Tim Spencer. Illustrations by Anthony James"- p. 1.
ISBN 1905123025
System number: 013390712

*Spencer, Tim.
Trafalgar : Nelson's finest hour / written by Daniel Dalton ; music [& lyrics] by Tim Spencer. — Kenilworth : Maplewood Education : Educational Musicals, c2005. — 2 v. : ill. ; 30 cm. + 1 compact disc.'
Children's musical; includes performance and background information. — For treble voices, mainly in unison but occasionally in 2 parts, with piano accompaniment and chord symbols. — "...an Anthony James Musical". — "Illustrations by Anthony James"—P. [1] — CD contains rehearsal and backing tracks.
ISBN 190512340X
System number: 013587097

Spencer, Tim.
The Victorian historian : a journey to Victorian Britain. — 2nd ed. — Kenilworth : Maplewood Education, 2001, c1999. — 2 v. : ill. ; 30 cm. + 1 compact disc. — (An Anthony James musical)
"Music & lyrics by Tim Spencer. Illustrations by Anthony James"- p. [1]
ISBN 1905123019
System number: 013390670

Spencer, Tim.
The warrior queen : Boudica and the Romans. — 2nd ed. — Kenilworth : Maplewood Education, 2001, c2000. — 2 v. : ill. ; 30 cm. + 1 compact disc. — (An Anthony James musical)
"Music & lyrics by Tim Spencer. Illustrations by Anthony James"- p. 1.
ISBN 190512306X
System number: 013390707

782.141723083

Brookes, Katherine.
Happy Christmas Tommy : the Christmas miracle of 1914. — Kenilworth : Maplewood Education, c2002. — 2 v. : ill. ; 30 cm. + 1 compact disc. — (An Anthony James musical)
"Music & lyrics by Katherine Brookes. Illustrations by Anthony James"—p. 1.
ISBN 1905123175
System number: 013390785

Davies, Niki.
The bossy king : a new nativity musical / by Niki Davies. — Hersham Green : Out of the Ark Music, 2001, c1999. — 1 score (32 p.) : port. ; 30 cm. + 1 compact disc.
Children's musical; libretto and songs. — For voice(s) and piano, with chord symbols. — "Nursery and infants"—Cover.
ISBN 1901980162 (book & CD pack.)
System number: 013272406

Davies, Niki.
Humph the camel : an amusing new nativity musical / by Niki Davies. — Hersham Green : Out of the Ark Music, c2002. — 1 score (28 p.) : port. ; 30 cm. + 1 compact disc.
Children's musical; libretto and songs. — For voice(s) and piano, with chord symbols. — "3-6's"—Cover.
ISBN 1901980456 (book & CD pack.)
System number: 013272400

Davies, Niki.
Ralph the reindeer : an original Christmas musical / by Niki Davies. — Hersham Green : Out of the Ark Music, c2004. — 1 score (27 p.) ; 30 cm. + 1 compact disc.
Children's musical; libretto and songs. — For voice(s) and piano, with chord symbols. — "4-7's"—Cover. — CD contains full performances of the songs and backing tracks.
ISBN 1901980618 (book & CD pack)
System number: 013272403

Davies, Niki.
The sleepy shepherd : a great new nativity musical / by Niki Davies ; edited by Mark and Helen Johnson. — Hersham Green : Out of the Ark Music, 2003, c2000. — 1 score (31 p.) : port. ; 30 cm. + 1 compact disc.
Children's musical; libretto and songs. — For voice(s) and piano, with chord symbols. — "3-6's"—Cover. — CD contains full vocal and backing tracks.
ISBN 1901980235 (book & cd pack)
System number: 013272373

Davies, Niki.
Snowman at sunset : a delightful new Christmas musical / by Niki Davies ; edited by Mark and Helen Johnson. — Hersham Green : Out of the Ark Music, c2001. — 1 score (31 p.) : port. ; 30 cm. + 1 compact disc.
Children's musical; libretto and 7 songs. — For voice(s) and piano, with chord symbols. — "Nursery and infants"—Cover. — CD contains full performances of the songs and backing tracks.
ISBN 1901980324 (book & cd pack)
System number: 013272426

Davies, Niki.
Toby's Christmas drum: a simple new Christmas musical / by Niki Davies. — Hersham Green : Out of the Ark Music, c2003. — 1 score (28 p.) : port. ; 30 cm. + 1 compact disc.
Children's musical; libretto and songs. — For voice(s) and piano, with chord symbols. — "3-6's"—Cover. — CD contains full performances of the songs and backing tracks.
ISBN 1901980510 (book & cd pack)
System number: 013270981

Davies, Niki.
Whoops-a-daisy angel : a short nativity musical / by Niki Davies ; edited by Mark and Helen Johnson. — Hersham Green : Out of the Ark Music, 2002, c1998. — 1 score (32 p.) : port. ; 30 cm. + 1 compact disc.
Children's musical; libretto and songs. — For voice(s) and piano, with chord symbols. — "3-6's"—Cover.
ISBN 1901980049 (book & CD pack)
System number: 013270971

Hewitt, Daniel.
The magic tree : a story for Christmas. — Kenilworth : Maplewood Education, 2001. — 2 v. : ill. ; 30 cm. + 1 compact disc. — (An Anthony James musical)
"Music & lyrics by Daniel Hewitt. Illustrations by Anthony James"—p. 1.
ISBN 1905123132
System number: 013390726

Hewitt, Daniel.
Saint Nicholas : the real Santa Claus. — 2nd ed. — Kenilworth : Maplewood Education, 2001, c2000. — 2 v. : ill. ; 30 cm. + 1 compact disc. — (An Anthony James musical)
"Music & lyrics by Daniel Hewitt. Illustrations by Anthony James"-p. 1.
ISBN 1905123108
System number: 013390759

Johnson, Mark (Mark Noel Hugh).
Are we nearly there yet-? : another great nativity musical / by Mark and Helen Johnson. — Hersham Green : Out of the Ark Music, c2002. — 1 score (51 p.) : port. ; 30 cm. + 1 compact disc.
Script, and songs for voices and piano, with chord symbols. — Words printed separately for reference. — "5-9's"—Cover. — CD contains full performances of the songs and backing tracks.
ISBN 190198043X (book & CD pack)
System number: 013272448

Johnson, Mark (Mark Noel Hugh).
It's a baby! : 9 new nativity songs for 3-7 year olds / by Mark and Helen Johnson. — Hersham Green : Out of the Ark Music, 2003, c1997. — 1 score (40 p.) : port. ; 30 cm. + 1 compact disc.
For voice(s) and piano, with chord symbols. — "Simple narration/spoken links have been provided to join the songs together into a short play"—Overview, p. 2. — Song words printed separately for reference, with short percussion parts. — CD contains full performances of the songs and backing tracks.
ISBN 1901980103 (book & CD pack)
System number: 013270802
Primary classification 782.7421723

Johnson, Mark (Mark Noel Hugh).
It's a party! : a great new nativity musical / by Mark and Helen Johnson. — Hersham Green : Out of the Ark Music, 2002, c2000. — 1 score (48 p.) : port. ; 30 cm. + 1 compact disc.
Script, and songs for voice(s) and piano, with chord symbols. — Song words printed separately for reference. — "Key Stages 1 and 2"—Cover. — CD contains full performances of the songs and backing tracks.
ISBN 1901980219 (book & CD pack)
System number: 013272440

Spencer, Tim.
The star child : the Christmas story. — 2nd ed. — Kenilworth : Maplewood Education, 2001, c1999. — 2 v. : ill. ; 30 cm. + 1 compact disc. — (An Anthony James musical)
"Music, lyrics & words by Tim Spencer. Illustrations by Anthony James"-p.1.
ISBN 1905123027
System number: 013390742

782.141727083

Hart, Barry.
Jesus is alive! : a simple Easter musical for key stage 1 / O'Gorman & Hart. — Buxhall : Kevin Mayhew, c2004. — 1 score (16 p.) ; 30 cm. — (Sunrise)
Unison songs with piano acc. and chord symbols. — "Text and lyrics: Denis O'Gorman, music: Barry Hart"— caption.
Publ. no. 1500739
ISBN 1844173232
ISMN M570243891
System number: 013159205

782.15

Elgar, Edward, 1857-1934.
The crown of India. — London : Elgar Society Edition Ltd. in association with Novello, c2004. — 1 score (xxxi, 223 p.) : ill., 2 facsims., ill. ; 44 cm. — (Elgar complete edition ; v. 18. Series III, Dramatic works)
Masque, keyboard arrangement (vocal score) of which is the only extant complete version; also includes an aria from the masque for contralto, mixed chorus (SATB) and orchestra, a march from the masque for orchestra, and the suite for orchestra arr. by the composer. — Foreword by Robert Anderson with sources and critical commentary.
Publ. no. NOV730018
ISBN 1904856187
System number: 013173848

782.3 – SERVICES (LITURGY AND RITUAL)

782.3222

Catholic Church.
Tropaire séquentiaire prosaire prosulaire de Moissac : (troisième quart du XIe siècle) : Manuscrit Paris, Bibliothèque nationale de France, n.a.l. 1871 / édition, introduction et index par Marie-Noël Colette ; analyse de l'écriture et de la décoration par Marie-Thérèse Gousset. — Paris : Société Française de Musicologie, 2006. — 116 p., [356] p. of music : col. facsim. ; 32 cm. — Publications de la Société française de musicologie. Première série ; t. 27
Introductory material in French. — Latin words.
ISBN 2853570169
System number: 013822688

*Hildegard, Saint, 1098-1179.
[Symphonia armonie celestium revelationum]
Symphonia harmoniae caelestium revelationum : Dendermonde, St.-Pieters & Paulusabdij, ms. Cod. 9 / Hildegard of Bingen ; introduction, Peter van Poucke. — Peer [Belgium] : Alamire, 1991. — 15 p., p. 153-170 [i.e. 307-340] of music : col. facsims. ; 32 cm. — Facsimile editions of prints and manuscripts
Unacc. melodies (early German neumes). — Reproduces the 12th-cent. ms. — Latin words; prefatory matter in English.
ISBN 9068530518
System number: 014763129

782.324

*Michna z Otradovic, Adam, ca. 1600-1676.
[Officium vespertinum. *Selections*]
Officium vespertinum : Compositiones ad honorem B.M.V. ; Falsi burdoni /
[Adam Michna z Otradovic] ; ed., Vratislav Bělský, Jiří Sehnal. — 1. vyd.
— Praha : Editio Bärenreiter Praha, 2004. — 1 score (xv, 58 p.) ; 31 cm. —
(Compositiones / Adam Michna z Otradovic ; v. 8)
For solo voices (SMzATB), mixed chorus and organ/continuo (figured bass with
realization provided by V. Bělský). — Latin words; includes introduction and
editor's notes in English, Czech and German.
Pl. no. H 7979
ISMN M260103009
System number: 014764427

782.4 – SECULAR FORMS

782.41083

Spencer, Tim.
The dream catcher : the plains indians of North America. — 2nd ed. —
Kenilworth : Maplewood Education, 2001, c1999. — 2 v. : ill. ; 30 cm. + 1
compact disc. — (An Anthony James musical)
"Music & lyrics by Tim Spencer. All illustrations by Anthony James"–p. [1]
ISBN 1905123035
System number: 013390705

782.4184

Escudero, Francisco, 1912-2002.
[Symphonies, no. 5]
Quinta sinfonía : Ultreia / Francisco Escudero. — 1a ed. — Barcelona :
Tritó : Eresbil, 2006, c2002. — 1 score (xxxiv, 151 p.) ; 34 cm. — (Euskal
musikagileak)
Pref. in Basque, Catalan, Spanish and English. — Duration: ca. 25:00.
Publ. no. TR 140
ISMN M692043065
System number: 013710076

782.421660263

Rice, Damien.
O / Damien Rice. — Guitar tab ed. — London : Faber, c2005. — 1 score
(80 p.) : 31 cm.
"Guitar tablature vocal"—Front cover. — 12 songs from Damien Rice's 2003 album
"O".
ISBN 0571524524
System number: 013086203

782.5 – MIXED VOICES

782.5

Body, Jack, 1944-
[Lullabies, voices]
Five lullabies : choir / Jack Body. — Wellington, N.Z. : Waiteata Music
Press, c2005. — 1 score (12 p.) ; 30 cm. — (2005 ; no. 1)
For unaccompanied SATB chorus. — "The words are 'invented languages' and have
no semantic meaning."—P. [2] of cover. — Duration: 14:00. — Prefatory notes on p.
[2] of cover.
System number: 013728819

*Davies, Peter Maxwell, 1934-
Angelus : for mixed chorus, SATB (2003) / Peter Maxwell Davies. —
London : Schott, c2004. — 1 score (14 p.) ; 30 cm. — Choral music of our
time
Settings of texts by Michelangelo and Marsilio Ficino. — Includes piano reduction
for rehearsal only. — Includes composer's note. — Duration: ca. 8:00. — Words in
mixed Italian and Latin; also printed for reference with English translation preceding
score.
Publ. no. ED 12832
Pl. no. S&Co.7803
ISMN M220123191
System number: 013381830

Dvořák, Antonín, 1841-1904.
[Symphonies, no. 9, op. 95, E minor. Largo; *arr.*]
Largo from New World symphony : SSAATTBB / Antonín Dvořák ;
arranged by Jonathan Rathbone. — London : Edition Peters, c2004. — 1
score (5 p.) ; 30 cm. — Kikapust choral series
Publisher's no.: Edition Peters no. 77064.
Publ. no. EP 77064
Publ. no. 77064
ISMN M577085296
System number: 013305848

Furrer, Beat, 1954-
Stimmen : für Chor und 4 Schlagzeuger : 1996 / Beat Furrer. — Partitur. —
Kassel : Bärenreiter, [2007], c1996. — 1 score (68 p.) ; 59 cm.
For double choir (SSSSAAAATTTTBBBB SSSSAAAATTTTBBBB) and
percussion quartet. — Settings of texts by Christine Huber and Leonardo da Vinci.
— Reproduced from holograph. — German and Italian words, also printed for
reference.
Publ. no. BA 7390
System number: 013771069

*Grylls, Richard G.
Epitaph for Grace : for unaccompanied mixed voice choir / by Richard G.
Grylls. — Tewkesbury : Roberton Publications, a part of Goodmusic
Publishing, c2005. — 1 score (11 p.) : ill. ; 26 cm.
For SATB with divisions. — Includes piano reduction for rehearsal only. —
Anon. words from a memorial plaque dated 1636.
Pl. no. 63269
ISMN M222260122
System number: 013373072

*Grylls, Richard G.
A royal nursery muddley : traditional tunes arranged for unaccompanied
mixed voice choir / by Richard G. Grylls. — Tewkesbury : Roberton
Publications, a part of Goodmusic Publishing, c2005. — 1 score (8 p.) ;
26 cm.
Includes piano reduction for rehearsal only.
Pl. no. 63268
ISMN M222260115
System number: 013373074

Hellawell, Piers, 1956-
The Hilliard songbook : (1995) : (in two volumes) / Piers Hellawell ; text:
Treatise upon the art of limning, by Nicholas Hilliard. — Kenley :
Maecenas Music, c1995. — 2 v. of music ; 30 cm.
For unaccompanied voices in various combinations from solo voice to eight
voices.
System number: 013416604

Hoffmann, E. T. A. (Ernst Theodor Amadeus), 1776-1822.
[Vocal music. *Selections*]
Kleine Vokalkompsitionen und Klaviersonaten / E.T.A. Hoffmann ; aus
dem Nachlaß von Friedrich Schnapp und unter Mitarbeit von Gerhard
Allroggen ; herausgegeben von Alexander Erhard und Thomas Kohlhase.
— Mainz ; London : Schott, c2006. — 1 score (xvii, 203 p.) ; 33 cm. —
(Ausgewählte musikalische Werke / E.T.A. Hoffmann ; Bd. 12a)
Most vocal works for vocal ensemble, with or without piano accompaniment. —
Editorial prefaces and critical commentary in German. — Italian or German
words
Publ. no. ETAH 112-10
Publ. no. BSS 43736
System number: 013798962
Primary classification 783

*Lachenmann, Helmut.
[Consolation, no. 2]
Consolation II : (Wessobrunner Gebet) : für 16 Singstimmen / Helmut
Lachenmann. — Singpartitur. — Wiesbaden : Breitkopf & Härtel,
[2003?], 1980. — 1 score (40 p.) ; 33 cm.
For chorus (SSSSAAAATTTTBBBB) unacc. — Includes performance
instructions in German. — Text consists of German words and syllables.
Publ. no. BG 767
Pl. no. HG 767
ISMN M004120705
EAN 979004120705
System number: 014798262

*Lewis, Paul, 1943-
[Rosa Mundi; *arr.*]
Rosa Mundi : a vocalise for vocal sextet or mixed voice choir
(SSATBarB) / by Paul Lewis. — Tewkesbury : Roberton Publications, a
part of Goodmusic Publishing, c2005. — 1 score (8 p.) ; 26 cm.
Arranged by the composer; originally for string orchestra. — Includes programme
and biographical notes. — Wordless.
Pl. no. 63272
ISMN M222263697
System number: 013373054

Mozart, Wolfgang Amadeus, 1756-1791.
[Symphonies, K. 550, G minor. Molto allegro; *arr.*]
Symphony no. 40 : (movement 1) : SSAATTBB : Mozart ; arranged by
Jonathan Rathbone. — London : Edition Peters, c2004. — 1 score
(28 p.) ; 30 cm. — Kikapust choral series
Publisher's no.: Edition Peters no. 77066.
Publ. no. EP 77066
Publ. no. 77066
ISMN M577085395
System number: 013305906

Mozart, Wolfgang Amadeus, 1756-1791.
[Zauberflöte. Ouverture; *arr.*]
Magic flute : overture : SSAATTBB / Mozart ; arranged by Ben Parry. —
London : Edition Peters, c2004. — 1 score (15 p.) ; 30 cm. — Kikapust
choral series
Publisher's no.: Edition Peters no. 77069.
Publ. no. EP 77069
Publ. no. 77069
ISMN M577085425
System number: 013305892

Rossini, Gioacchino, 1792-1868.
[Barbiere di Siviglia. Sinfonia; *arr.*]
Il Barbiere di Siviglia : overture : SSAATTBB / music by Gioachino Rossini ; arranged by Jonathan Rathbone. — London : Edition Peters, c2004. — 1 score (39 p.) ; 30 cm. — Kikapust choral series
"As recorded by the Swingle Singers on Notability." — Publisher's no.: Edition Peters no. 77062.
Publ. no. EP 77062
Publ. no. 77062
ISMN M577085012
System number: 013305815

Schreker, Franz, 1878-1934.
[Choral music]
Chorwerk / Franz Schreker ; Gesamtausgabe herausgegeben von Christopher Hailey, Iris Pfeiffer. — Stuttgart : Carus, c2006. — 1 score (xxii, 154 p.) : facsim. ; 33 cm.
Secular and sacred choral music, some unaccompanied and some accompanied by piano and/or orchestra. — "Urtext." — Pref. in German and English. — German words; also printed for reference in German and English preceding score.
Publ. no. CV 4.103
Pl. no. Carus 4.103
ISMN M007076054
System number: 013565245

Schubert, Franz, 1797-1828.
[Vocal music. *Selections*]
Mehrstimmige Gesänge für gemischte Stimmen. Teil b / [Franz Schubert] ; vorgelegt von Dietrich Berke und Michael Kube. — Kassel ; London : Bärenreiter, 2006. — 1 score (196-456 p.) ; 28 cm. — (Neue Ausgabe sämtlicher Werke / Franz Schubert ; Ser. III, Bd. 2, T. b)
For various solo voices all with piano acc. (except 2nd work unacc.), some including chorus; the 7th work for 2-part mixed chorus and piano. — Commentary in German on sources and versions of all works in both Teil a and Teil b volumes, p. 391-456. — Principally German words, from various sources; some also printed for reference within the editorial notes; the 2nd work with transliterated Hebrew words.
Publ. no. BA 5536
ISMN M006497010
System number: 013798568
Primary classification 783.12

Smetana, Bedřich, 1824-1884.
[Má vlast. Vltava; *arr.*]
Die Moldau : SSAATTBB = Vltava / Bedřich Smetana ; arranged by Jonathan Rathbone. — London : Edition Peters, c2004. — 1 score (30 p.) ; 30 cm. — Kikapust choral series
Text consists of arbitrary syllables.
Publ. no. EP 77061
ISMN M577085418
System number: 013305784

Steele, Douglas, 1910-
[Short songs]
Three short songs : for either solo voice, or unison voices, with piano / Douglas Steele. — Matfield : Encore Publications, c2005. — 1 score (11 p.) ; 26 cm.
Includes biographical note.
System number: 013358905
Primary classification 783.242

*Sviridov, Georgiĭ Vasil'evich, 1915-1998.
[Choral music. *Selections*]
Sochineniïa dlïa khora bez soprovozhdeniïa / Georgiĭ Sviridov ; tom podgotovlen K. A. Titarenko. — Moskva, Sankt-Peterburg : Natsional'nyĭ Sviridovskiĭ Fond, 2003. — 1 score (xviii, 115 p.) : port., facsim. ; 30 cm. — (Polnoe sobranie sochineniĭ ; tom 18)
In 4-13 parts, unaccompanied except for "Osen'" with organ acc.
Pl. no. NSF 002
System number: 014750711

Tann, Hilary.
Wales, our land : for mixed choir (SATB) and flute, with optional piano / Hilary Tann. — [New York] : Oxford University Press, c2004. — 1 score (16 p.) ; 31 cm. — Oxford choral music
The text is a translation by John S. Ellis, of an anonymous poem "Os Ydyw Cymru'n Fach". — Flute part printed separately p.[15]-16. — Includes biographical, performance and programme notes. — Mixed English and Welsh words; words also printed for reference in English, preceding score.
ISBN 0193867451
System number: 013062310

Tchaikovsky, Peter Ilich, 1840-1893.
[Overture "1812". Op. 49; *arr.*]
1812 overture : SSAATTBB / Tchaikovsky ; arranged by Jonathan Rathbone. — London : Edition Peters, c2004. — 1 score (29 p.) ; 30 cm. — Kikapust choral series
Text consists of arbitrary syllables.
Publ. no. EP 77060
ISMN M577085265
System number: 013305764

*Thoresen, Lasse, 1949-
Yá kafi, yá shafi : for two choirs, 1996 / Lasse Thoresen ; text, Bahá'u'lláh. — Adliswil : Pizzicato Verlag, c2004. — 1 score (38 p.) ; 30 cm.
"Op. 27:5"—Caption. — Includes performance instructions in English. — Romanized Arabic words; also printed for reference with English translation.
Publ. no. PVH 1065
System number: 014629755

*Voth, Ellen Gilson.
The circle of time : for unaccompanied mixed choir (SSAATTBB) with solo voices / Ellen Gilson Voth. — [New York] : Oxford University Press, c2005. — 1 score (8 p.) ; 27 cm. — Oxford choral music
Includes piano reduction for rehearsal only. — Words from Ecclesiastes 3:1-8, 11 adapted by the composer. — Errata slip enclosed.
ISBN 9780193868779
ISBN 0193868776
System number: 013472230

782.51552
Hoffmann, E. T. A. (Ernst Theodor Amadeus), 1776-1822.
[Kreuz an der Ostsee]
Zacharias Werners Trauerspiel "Das Kreuz an der Ostsee" : mit der Bühnenmusik von E.T.A. Hoffmann ; Ballettmusik "Arlequin" / E.T.A. Hoffmann ; hrsg. aus dem Nachlaß von Friedrich Schnapp ; unter Mitarbeit von Gerhard Allroggen und Michael Kohlhäufl von Thomas Kohlhase. — Mainz ; London : Schott, c2006. — 1 score (xv, 300 p.) ; 33 cm. — (Ausgewählte musikalische Werke / E.T.A. Hoffmann ; Bd. 9)
Editorial prefaces and critical commentary in German. — 1st work for SSATB soloists, mixed chorus (SSATB) and orchestra; 2nd work for orchestra. — German words in first work.
Publ. no. ETAH 109
Publ. no. BSS 43740
ISMN M001137461
System number: 013798965
Also classified at 784.21556

782.51556
Stravinsky, Igor, 1882-1971.
[Svadebka. *French & Russian*]
Les noces = (Svadebka) : scènes chorégraphiques russes avec chant et musique : for four pianos, percussion and voices in a revised and corrected edition based upon relevant autograph and printed sources / composées par Igor Stravinsky ; French text by C.-F. Ramuz ; edited by Margarita Mazo ; associate editor, Millan Sachania. — Study score. — London : Chester Music, c2005. — 1 score (lv, 135 p.) : facsims., ill. ; 35 cm. — (Chester Stravinsky edition)
Ballet. — 'Dancing Les Noces' by Stephanie Jordan p. xxiv-xxvi. — Pref. includes historical and editorial notes, list of sources and critical commentary. — Words in Russian (in Cyrillic script and transliterated) with French translation. Pronunciation guide, p. liii-lvi.
Publ. no. CH61799
ISBN 1846092809
System number: 013383538

782.51655
Rathbone, Jonathan.
Running wild : ATBarBB / Jonathan Rathbone. — London : Edition Peters, 2004. — 1 score (7 p.) ; 30 cm. — Kikapust choral series
Publisher's no.: Edition Peters no. 77100.
Publ. no. EP 77100
Publ. no. 77100
ISMN M577085340
System number: 013305895

782.522
*Adlgasser, Anton Cajetan, 1729-1777.
Litaniae de venerabili altaris Sacramento : in B-Dur (WV 3/53) : per Soli (SATB), Coro (SATB), Trombone alto solo o Organo solo, 2 Clarini, Timpani, 2 Violini, Basso continuo (Violoncello/Fagotto/Contrabbasso/Organo), 3 Tromboni colla parte voci ad lib. / Anton Cajetan Adlgasser ; herausgegeben von Armin Kircher. — Erstausg. — Partitur. — Stuttgart : Carus, c2005. — 1 score (72 p.) : facsim. ; 30 cm. — (Salzburger Kirchenmusik = Sacred music from Salzburg = Musique sacrée de Salzbourg)
Foreword in German with abridged English and French translations. — Duration: ca. 19:00. — "Editionsreihe des Kirchenmusikreferates der Erzdiözese Salzburg." — Latin words; also printed for reference with German, English and French translations, p. 8-9.
Pl. no. Carus 27.114
Publ. no. CV 27.114
ISMN M007076207
System number: 013353377

Glory to God : Englische Chormusik aus fünf Jahrhunderten / herausgegeben von Hans Wülfing für den Landesverband ev. Kirchenchöre im Rheinland in Zusammenarbeit mit dem Verband ev. Kirchenchöre Deutschlands. — Oxford : Oxford University Press, 2005. — 1 score (xviii, 229 p.) ; 25 cm.
56 anthems, carols, services and psalm settings. — For mixed voices (mostly SATB), some with organ or piano acc. — Pref. in German. — German or Latin words; mostly also with the original English words. The Latin works have German translations printed for reference.
ISBN 019436256
ISBN 9780193436251
System number: 013312902

Gubaĭdulina, Sofia Asgatovna.
Sonnengesang = The canticle of the sun : revidierte Fassung 5/1998 / Sofia Gubaidulina. — Partitur. — Hamburg : Sikorski Musikverlage, [2006?], c1997. — 1 score (62 p.) ; 42 cm.
For chamber choir (SATB) in six parts, violoncello, and 2 percussionists. — Text by St. Francis of Assisi. — Notes on instrumentation and notation signs in German and English precede score. — Reproduced from holograph. — In Italian.
System number: 013688147

The Gyffard partbooks I / transcribed and edited by David Mateer. — London : Published for the British Academy by Stainer and Bell, c2007. — 1 score (xvii, 314 p.) ; 33 cm. — Early English church music ; 48

16th century liturgical music, probably for use in St Paul's Cathedral, London. Also known as the Gyffard Partbook because of its one-time ownership by Philip Gyffard. — Principally for 4 voices, unacc. — Based on British Library Add. MSS 17802-5. — Includes critical commentaries. — Latin words; also printed separately as texts with English translations.
ISBN 9780852498927
ISMN M220221606
System number: 013815039

782.523

Bach, Johann Sebastian, 1685-1750.
[Lobet Gott in seinen Reichen. *English & German*]
Himmelfahrtsoratorium : Lobet Gott in seinen Reichen : BWV 11/BC D 9 : Oratorium Festo Ascensionis Christi : für Soli (SATB), Chor (SATB), 3 Trompeten, Pauken, 2 Traversflöten, 2 Oboen, 2 Violinen, Viola und Basso continuo = Oratorio for Ascension Day : Praise God on high in heaven : for soli (SATB), choir (SATB), 3 trumpets, timpani, 2 flutes, 2 oboes, 2 violins, viola, and basso continuo / Johann Sebastian Bach ; herausgegeben von Ulrich Leisinger ; English version by Henry S. Drinker. — Urtext. — Partitur. — Stuttgart : Carus, c2005. — 1 score (79 p.) : 1 facsim. ; 30 cm. — Stuttgarter Bach-Ausgaben
Edited from holograph score in the Staatsbibliothek zu Berlin—Preussischer Kulturbesitz, Musikabteilung mit Mendelssohn-Archiv (Mus. ms. Bach P 44 adnex 4) and ms. parts in the Bibiloteka Jagiellońska, Kraków (Mus. ms. Bach St 356). — Pref. in English, French, and German; critical report in German.
Pl. no. 31.011
ISMN M007042004
EAN 9790007042004
System number: 013714772

Handel, George Frideric, 1685-1759.
Athalia : oratorio in three parts : HWV 52 / Georg Friedrich Händel ; herausgegeben von Stephan Blaut. — Kassel ; London : Bärenreiter, 2006. — 1 score (2 v.) : facsims. ; 33 cm. — (Hallische Händel-Ausgabe. Serie I, Oratorien und grosse Kantaten ; Bd. 12)
For solo voices (SSSATB), SATB chorus and orchestra. — Text by Samuel Humphreys based on a biblical story and a tragedy by Racine. — English words; also printed as facsims. of the libretto (London : J. Watts, 1733/35) (v. 1, p. xlii-xlvii), German translation (v. 1, p. xlviii-liii), and vocal texts of the appendices I-III in German and English (v. 1, p. liv-lv).
Publ. no. BA 4082
ISMN M006497751
System number: 013772192

Handel, George Frideric, 1685-1759.
[Messiah. *Chorus score*]
Handel's Messiah from scratch / [edited by David Meacock] — Alto ed. — Iver Heath : Artemis Editions, c2002. — 1 chorus score (160 p.) ; 25 cm. + 2 sound discs (digital ; 4 3/4 in.)
Oratorio; chorus parts only, with alto line in larger format. — Performance notes on p. 4-19. — CDs contain orchestral and choral demonstration tracks, performed by the Artemis Chorus & Sinfonia, David Meacock, conductor, with alto part increased in volume; also vocal warm-ups, practice exercises, and slowed down versions of difficult sections.
Publ. no. ART00002
ISBN 1904411010
ISBN 9781904411017
ISMN M570270011
System number: 006920515

Handel, George Frideric, 1685-1759.
[Messiah. *Chorus score*]
Handel's Messiah from scratch / [edited by David Meacock] — Bass ed. — Iver Heath : Artemis Editions, c2002. — 1 chorus score (160 p.) + 2 sound discs (digital ; 4 3/4 in.)
Oratorio; chorus parts only, with bass line in larger format. — Performance notes on p. 4-19. — CDs contain orchestral and choral demonstration tracks, performed by the Artemis Chorus & Sinfonia, David Meacock, conductor, with bass part increased in volume; also vocal warm-ups, practice exercises, and slowed down versions of difficult sections.
Publ. no. ART00004
ISBN 1904411037
ISBN 9781904411031
ISMN M570250035
System number: 006920500

Handel, George Frideric, 1685-1759.
[Messiah. *Chorus score*]
Handel's Messiah from scratch / [edited by David Meacock] — Soprano ed. — Iver Heath : Artemis Editions, c2002. — 1 chorus score (160 p.) ; 25 cm. + 2 sound discs (digital ; 4 3/4 in.)
Oratorio; chorus parts only, with soprano line in larger format. — Performance notes on p. 4-19. — CDs contain orchestral and choral demonstration tracks, performed by the Artemis Chorus & Sinfonia, David Meacock, conductor, with soprano part increased in volume; also vocal warm-ups, practice exercises, and slowed down versions of difficult sections.
Publ. no. ART00001
ISBN 1904411002
ISBN 9781904411000
ISMN M570250004
System number: 006920529

Handel, George Frideric, 1685-1759.
[Messiah. *Chorus score*]
Handel's Messiah from scratch / [edited by David Meacock] — Tenor ed. — Iver Heath : Artemis Editions, c2002. — 1 chorus score (160 p.) ; 25 cm. + 2 sound discs (digital ; 4 3/4 in.)
Oratorio; chorus parts only, with tenor line in larger format. — Performance notes on p. 4-19. — CDs contain orchestral and choral demonstration tracks, performed by the Artemis Chorus & Sinfonia, David Meacock, conductor, with tenor part increased in volume; also vocal warm-ups, practice exercises, and slowed down versions of difficult sections.
Publ. no. ART00003
ISBN 1904411029
ISBN 9781904411024
ISMN M570250028
System number: 006920502

*Handel, George Frideric, 1685-1759.
[Samson. *Vocal score*]
Samson : an oratorio for soloists (3 sopranos, alto, 2 tenors, 2 basses; or soprano, alto tenor and bass), mixed chorus and orchestra / music by George Frideric Handel ; words by Newburgh Hamilton, after John Milton's Samson Agonistes ; edited by Donald Burrows ; vocal score. — London : Novello, c2005. — 1 score (xxi, 300 p.) ; 28 cm. — New Novello choral edition — (Novello Handel Edition)
Acc. arr. for piano. — Includes the music for the 1743 version, together with a subsequent version — Pref. includes notes on sources.
Publ. no. NOV090926
ISBN 184609187X
System number: 013433587

Longueval, Antoine de, fl. 1498-1525.
Passio Domini nostri Jesu Christi : zu 4 Stimmen / Antoine de Longueval ; herausgegeben von Rainer Heyink. — Wolfenbüttel : Möseler, c2006. — 1 score (viii, 19 p.) ; 27 cm. — Chorwerk ; Heft 144
For mixed voices (SATB), unacc. — Transposed one tone higher than the original. — Pref. in German. — Latin words.
Publ. no. 80.144
Publ. no. M 80.144
System number: 013714764

782.5231723

Bach, Johann Sebastian, 1685-1750.
[Weihnachts-Oratorium. *English & German*]
Weihnachtsoratorium : Oratorium tempore nativitatis Christi : BWV 248 : für Soli (SSATB), Chor (SATB), 3 Trompeten, Pauken, 2 Hörner, 2 Querflöten, 2 Oboen/Oboen d'amore, 2 Oboen da caccia, 2 Violinen, Viola und Basso continuo : Urtext = Christmas oratorio : for soli (SSATB), choir (SATB), 3 trumpets, timpani, 2 horns, 2 flutes, 2 oboes/oboes d'amore, 2 oboes da caccia, 2 violins, viola, and basso continuo / Johann Sebastian Bach ; herausgegeben von Klaus Hofmann ; English version by Henry S. Drinker. — Partitur. — Stuttgart : Carus, c2005. — 1 score (ix, 310 p.) ; 33 cm. — Stuttgarter Bach-Ausgaben
"Urtext." — Includes foreword in English, French, and German, and Kritischer Bericht in German following score.
Publ. no. 31.248/50
Pl. no. CV 31.248
System number: 013714886

782.5231726

Haydn, Joseph, 1732-1809.
[Sieben letzten Worte unseres Erlösers am Kreuze. *English. Vocal score*]
Passion : the seven words of our Saviour on the cross / Joseph Haydn ; vocal score. — London : Novello, [2005] — 1 score (81 p.) ; 25 cm.
For SATB soloists, SATB choir and orchestra; acc. arr. for piano. — Pref. by the composer. — Reprint of the ed. published: London : Novello, Ewer & Co., [1876], with English adaptation by H. Clementi-Smith. — English words.
Pl. no. NOV070163
ISBN 0853605963
System number: 013190863

782.524

Bach, Johann Sebastian, 1685-1750.
[Ach Herr, mich armen Sünder (Cantata). *English & German*]
Ach Herr, mich armen Sünder : BWV 135/BC A 100 : Kantate zum 3. Sonntag nach Trinitatis für Soli (ATB), Chor (SATB), Zink, Posaune, 2 oboen, 2 Violinen, Viola und Basso continuo = Ah Lord, spare thou this sinner : cantata for the third Sunday after Trinity for soli (ATB), choir (SATB), cornett, trombone, 2 oboes, 2 violins, viola, and basso continuo / Johann Sebastian Bach ; herausgegeben von Wolfram Ensslin ; English version by Henry S. Drinker. — Urtext. — Partitur. — Stuttgart : Carus, c2005. — 1 score (35 p.) ; 30 cm.
Edited from holograph score in the Bach-Archiv Leipzig and ms. score, dated 1803, in the Staatsbibliothek zu Berlin—Preussischer Kulturbesitz, Musikabteilung mit Mendelssohn-Archiv (Mus. ms. Bach P 52). — Duration: ca. 17:00. — Pref. in German, English, and French; critical report in German.
Pl. no. 31.135
ISMN M007076061
EAN 9790007076061
System number: 013714858

Bach, Johann Sebastian, 1685-1750.
[Gott, der Herr, ist Sonn' und Schild. *English & German*]
Gott der Herr ist Sonn und Schild : BWV 79 / BC 184 : Kantate zum Reformationsfest : für Soli (SAB), Chor (SATB), 2 Hörner, Pauken, 2 Traversflöten ad libitum, 2 Oboen, 2 Violinen, Viola und Basso continuo = God the Lord is sun and shield : cantata for the Reformation Festival : for soli (SAB), choir (SATB), 2 horns, timpani, 2 flutes ad libitum, 2 oboes, 2 violins, viola and basso continuo / Johann Sebastian Bach ; herausgegeben von Uwe Wolf ; English version by Jutta and Vernon Wicker and Catherine Winkworth. — Partitur. — Stuttgart : Carus, c2006. — 1 score (51 p.) ; 30 cm. — Stuttgarter Bach-Ausgaben
"Urtext". — Pref. in German and English. — German words with English translation.
Pl. no. 31.079
ISMN M007045203
EAN 9790007045203
System number: 013714792

Bach, Johann Sebastian, 1685-1750.
[Herr Gott, dich loben wir (Cantata). *English & German*]
Herr Gott, dich loben wir : BWV 16/BC A 23 : Kantate zum Neujahrstag für Soli (ATB), Chor (SATB), Corno da caccia, 2 Oboen, Oboe da caccia (Violetta), 2 Violinen, Viola und Basso continuo = Lord God, Thy praise we sing : cantata for New Year's Day for soli (ATB), choir (SATB), corno da caccia, 2 oboes, oboe da caccia (violetta), 2 violins, viola, and basso continuo / Johann Sebastian Bach ; herausgegeben von Michael Märker ; English version by Henry S. Drinker. — Urtext. — Partitur. — Stuttgart : Carus, c2006. — 1 score (31 p.) ; 30 cm. — Stuttgarter Bach-Ausgaben
Pref. in German with English and French translations; critical report in German.
Publ. no. CV 31.016
Pl. no. 31.016
ISMN M007087623
EAN 9790007087623
System number: 013714778

Bach, Johann Sebastian, 1685-1750.
[Wir müssen durch viel Trübsal in das Reich Gottes eingehen. *English & German*]
Wir müssen durch viel Trübsal in das Reich Gottes eingehen : BWV 146/BC A 70 : Kantate zum Sonntag Jubilate für Soli (SATB), Chor (SATB), Traversflöte, 2 Oboen/Oboen d'amore, Taille, 2 Violinen, Viola, obligate Orgel und Basso continuo = Through bitter tribulation we enter into God's kingdom : cantata for the third Sunday after Easter for soli (STB), choir (SATB), flute, 2 oboes/oboes d'amore, taille, 2 violins, viola, organ obbligato, and basso continuo / Johann Sebastian Bach ; herausgegeben von Anja Morgenstern ; English version by Henry S. Drinker. — Urtext. — Partitur. — Stuttgart : Carus, c2005. — 1 score (78 p.) ; 30 cm. — Stuttgarter Bach-Ausgaben
Edited from copyists' ms. scores in the Staatsbibliothek zu Berlin—Preussischer Kulturbesitz, Musikabteilung mit Mendelssohn-Archiv (Am. B. 538 and Mus. ms. Bach P 48). — Duration: ca. 40:00. — Pref. in German, English, and French; critical report in German.
Pl. no. 31.146
ISMN M007074371
EAN 9790007074371
System number: 013714867

*Bainbridge, Simon, 1952-
Eichá : (Lamentation) : for mezzo-soprano solo, SATB chorus and wind ensemble : (1997) / Simon Bainbridge. — Score. — London : Novello ; Bury St Edmunds : Music Sales [distributor], c2002. — 1 score (66 p.) ; 30 cm.
Wind ensemble: 2 oboes, cor anglais, bassoon, contrabassoon, 2 trumpets, 3 trombones. — Words from Lamentations, I, v.1-2. — Includes pronunciation guide. — Also printed as text with English translation preceding score.
Publ. no. NOV 120923
ISBN 0711995214
System number: 013434131

*Capricornus, Samuel, d. 1665.
Theatrum musicum : quod per duodecim scenas seu sacras cantiones / aperuit Samuel Capricornus. — Stuttgart : Cornetto-Verlag, c2003. — 8 parts ; 21 x 30 cm. — (Faksimile-Edition Capricornus ; Nr. 2)
For solo vioices (ATB), 4 viols, and continuo. — Imprint from last leaf of organ part. — "RISM C 937." — Reproduced from the copy in the Murhardsche Bibliothek der Stadt Kassel und Landesbibliothek. — Reprint. Originally published: Herbipoli, J. Bencard, 1669.
Publ. no. CF134
ISMN M501000487
System number: 013521766

Gurre-Lieder : für Soli, Chor und Orchester : kritischer Bericht / Arnold Schönberg ; [Text] von Jens Peter Jacobsen (deutsch von Robert Franz Arnold) ; herausgegeben von Ulrich Krämer. — Mainz : Schott Musik International ; Wien : Universal Edition, 2006. — xxxvi, 524 p. : facsims. ; 31 cm. — (Sämtliche Werke / Arnold Schönberg. Abt. V, Chorwerke ; Reihe B, Bd. 16, T. 1)
"Contains the critical commentary to the full score of the Gurre-Lieder published in Series A, Vol. 16/1 of the Schoenberg edition. It includes not only a detailed description of the sources used in preparing the edition ... a table listing all the errors, omissions and oversights in the main source ... and the critical notes ..., but also a comparative list of the changes that Schoenberg later made to the main source and to the secondary sources used for this revision ... and a line-by-line comparison between the two versions of Robert Franz Arnold's translation of Jens Peter Jacobsen's poems used the compoer, the verion of the text found in the main source and the version published in the complete edition"—P. vii. — Pref. in German and English; main text in German. — "Unter dem Patronat der Akademie der Künste, Berlin, begründet von Josef Rufer, herausgegeben von Rudolf Stephan"—Series t.p.
Publ. no. AS 1016-21
ISMN M001144277
System number: 013821946

Hertel, Johann Wilhelm, 1727-1789.
Jesu, meine Freude : Kantate für Sopran und Tenor solo, 4 st. gem. Chor SSTB, 2 Trompeten, 2 Hörner, Pauken, 2 Flöten, 2 Oboen, Fagott, Streichorchester und Generalbass / Johann Wilhelm Hertel ; herausgegeben von Norbert Klose. — Erstausg. — Partitur. — Haale : Renaissance Musikverlag, c2005. — 1 score (58 p.) ; 30 cm.
Cantata for soprano and tenor solo, mixed chorus (SATB), 2 trumpets, 2 horns, trombone, 2 flutes, 2 oboes, bassoon, string orchestra, and continuo. — Figured bass not realized. — German words.
Publ. no. 10127/1
ISMN M500658450
System number: 013771121

Herzogenberg, Heinrich von, 1843-1900.
Gott ist gegenwärtig : Choralkantate op. 106 : Gemeindegesang, Chor SATB, 2 Trompeten, 3 Posaunen, Pauken, 2 Violinen, Viola, 2 Violoncelli, Kontrabass, Orgel / Heinrich von Herzogenberg ; Text, Gerhard Tersteegen ; vorgelegt und revidiert von Konrad Klek. — Partitur. — Stuttgart : Carus, [2006, 1900] — 1 score (vii, 73 p.) : facsim. ; 30 cm.
For congregation, chorus (SATB), 2 trumpets, 3 trombones, timpani, strings, and organ. — "Reprint der Erstausg. Leipzig 1900." — Preface in German with English and French translations; critical commentary in German.
Publ. no. 23.001
ISMN M007090197
EAN 9790007090197
System number: 013771126

Loewe, Carl, 1796-1869.
Was Gott tut, das ist wohlgetan : Kantate für Solisten SAB, 4 st. gem. Chor SATB, und Kammerorchester (2 Klarinetten, 2 Fagotti und Streicher) / Carl Loewe ; herausgegeben von Norbert Klose. — Erstausgabe. — Partitur. — Haale : Renaissance Musikverlag, 2005, c2004. — 1 score (31 p.) : port. ; 30 cm.
Edited from a ms. in the Biblioteka Jagiellonska in Krakau. — Pref. in German on p. [2] of cover. — German words.
Publ. no. 10114/1
ISMN M500657484
System number: 013750217

*Romberg, Andreas, 1767-1821.
Der Messias : Kantate in drei Teilen : für Soli, Chor und Orchester, nach Friedrich Gottlieb Klopstocks "Messias" : WoO, zweite Fassung (1802) / Andreas Romberg ; vorgelegt von Karlheinz Höfer und Klaus G. Werner. — Partitur. — Wilhelmshaven : F. Noetzel, 2004. — 1 score (xxiii, 374 p.) : facsim. ; 30 cm. — (Ausgewählte Werke / Andreas Romberg ; Ser. 2, Bd. 6)
For solo voices (STTBarB or SSTBarB), chorus (SATB) and orchestra. — Edited from an autograph manuscript in the Staats- und Universitätsbibliothek Carl von Ossietzky, Hamburg, Handschriftenabteilung (ND VI 395 al). — Pref. in German. — "Kritischer Bericht", p. 363-372. — German words.
Pl. no. AM 7462
ISMN M201974620
System number: 014763138

Telemann, Georg Philipp, 1681-1767.
[Cantatas. *Selections*]
Französischer Jahrgang : Kantaten von Neujahr bis zum Sonntag Sexagesimae und dem Fest Mariae Reinigung / Georg Philipp Telemann ; herausgegeben von Ute Poetzsch-Seban. — Kassel ; London : Bärenreiter, 2006. — 1 score (xlviii, 302 p.) : facsims. ; 33 cm. — (Musikalische Werke / Georg Philipp Telemann ; Bd. 40)
Cantatas, principally with strings and basso continuo. — Figured bass realized by Andreas Köhs. — Editorial, historical and critical notes in German. — German words, also printed as texts, p. xlii-xlviii.
Publ. no. BA 5864
ISMN M006498000
System number: 013798608

Telemann, Georg Philipp, 1681-1767.
Jesu, wirst du bald erscheinen : Kantate zum 26. Sonntag nach Trinitatis, für Sopran-, Tenor- und Bass-Solo, vierstimmigen gemischten Chor, Zink, 3 Posaunen, 2 Oboen, Streicher und Basso continuo, TWV 1:988 / Georg Philipp Telemann ; herausgegeben von Arno Paduch und Eric F. Fiedler. — Frankfurt am Main : Habsburger Verlag, [2004] — 1 score (48 p.) ; 30 cm. — (Frankfurter Telemann-Ausgaben ; 39)
Pl. no. FTA 39
System number: 014655745

*Tunder, Franz, 1614-1667.
Dominus illuminatio mea : (Ps. 27, 1-3) : Geistliches Konzert für Solo (A), Chor (SSATB), 2 Violinen und Basso continuo / Franz Tunder ; herausgegeben von Bernhard Römer. — Salzgitter, Germany : Ostinato, c2004. — 1 score (23 p.) ; 30 cm.
Figured bass realized for organ. — Biographical note in German, p. [2] — Latin words.
Publ. no. os 86.513
System number: 014629772

Vacchi, Fabio, 1949-
Voce d'altra voce : per due recitanti, grande coro misto e orchestra, 2005 / Fabio Vacchi. — Partitura. — Milano : Ricordi, c2005. — 1 score (115 p.) ; 46 cm.
Italian text translated from the Song of Songs, also printed for reference.
Publ. no. 139488
ISMN M041394886
System number: 014053372

782.5241588
***Musik am Meininger Hofe** / herausgegeben von Ulrike Feld und Ulrich Leisinger. — Leipzig : Friedrich Hofmeister, c2003. — 1 score (xxiv, 329 p.) : facsims. ; 31 cm. — Denkmäler mitteldeutscher Barockmusik. Serie 1, Musikalische Zentren in Sachsen, Sachsen-Anhalt und Thüringen ; Bd. 2
Three Pentecost cantatas for solo voices (SATB), mixed chorus (SATB), 2 violins, 2 violas and continuo; Funeral music for Herzog Ernst Ludwig I of Saxe-Coburg-Meiningen for solo voices (SATB), 2 mixed choruses (SATB), oboe, 2 flutes, 2 violins, 2 violas and continuo. — Pref. in German and English by Ulrich Leisinger; Kritische Berichte in German only. — German words, also printed for reference preceding scores.
ISMN M203483526
System number: 014660514
Primary classification 782.52417293

782.5241723
Carol medley : Deck the halls ; I saw three ships ; We wish you a merry Christmas ; The holly and the ivy ; The first nowell ; Past three o'clock : SSAATTBB (with optional organ part) / arranged by Jonathan Rathbone. — London : Edition Peters, c2004. — 1 score (10 p.) ; 30 cm. — Kikapust choral series
"As recorded by the Swingle Singers on The story of Christmas." — No organ part provided. — Publisher's no.: Edition Peters no. 77003.
Publ. no. EP 77003
Publ. no. 77003
ISMN M577084978
System number: 013304437
Also classified at 782.5281723

*Zechner, Georg, 1716-1778.
[Ihr Hirten Bethlehems]
Weihnachtskantate Ihr Hirten Bethlehems : soprano, alto, tenore e basso, 2 corni, 2 violini, 2 viole e basso continuo / Johann Georg Zechner. — Erstausg. / vorgelegt von Leonhard Riedel. — Partitur. — Stuttgart : Carus, c2005. — 1 score (32 p.) ; 30 cm.
For solo voices and chorus (SATB), 2 horns, strings and continuo. — Pref. in German and English and critical notes in German. — Duration: ca. 20:00. — Figured bass not realized. — German words; also printed for reference, p. 5.
Pl. no. CV 10.377
Publ. no. 10.377
ISMN M007077501
System number: 013832409

782.5241727
Bach, Johann Sebastian, 1685-1750.
[Himmel lacht, die Erde jubilieret. *English & German*]
Der Himmel lacht! Die Erde jubilieret : BWV 31 / BC A 55b, Kantate zum ersten Ostertag : für Soli (STB), Chor (SSATB), 3 Trompeten, Pauken, Oboe, 2 Oboen ad lib., Taille ad lib., Fagott ad lib., 2 Violinen, 2 Violen und Basso continuo = The heavens laugh, the earth exults in gladness : cantata for Easter Sunday : for soli (STB), choir (SSATB), 3 trumpets, timpani, oboe, 2 oboes ad lib., taille ad lib., bassoon ad lib., 2 violins, 2 violas and basso continuo / Johann Sebastian Bach ; herausgegeben von Michael Märker ; English version by Henry S. Drinker. — Partitur. — Stuttgart : Carus, c2006. — 1 score (67 p.) ; 30 cm. — Stuttgarter Bach-Ausgaben
"Urtext". — Pref. in German, English, and French. — German words with English translation.
Pl. no. 31.031
ISMN M007084660
EAN 9790007084660
System number: 013714787

782.52417293
***Musik am Meininger Hofe** / herausgegeben von Ulrike Feld und Ulrich Leisinger. — Leipzig : Friedrich Hofmeister, c2003. — 1 score (xxiv, 329 p.) : facsims. ; 31 cm. — Denkmäler mitteldeutscher Barockmusik. Serie 1, Musikalische Zentren in Sachsen, Sachsen-Anhalt und Thüringen ; Bd. 2
Three Pentecost cantatas for solo voices (SATB), mixed chorus (SATB), 2 violins, 2 violas and continuo; Funeral music for Herzog Ernst Ludwig I of Saxe-Coburg-Meiningen for solo voices (SATB), 2 mixed choruses (SATB), oboe, 2 flutes, 2 violins, 2 violas and continuo. — Pref. in German and English by Ulrich Leisinger; Kritische Berichte in German only. — German words, also printed for reference preceding scores.
ISMN M203483526
System number: 014660514
Also classified at 782.5241588

782.525
Bach, Johann Sebastian, 1685-1750.
[Wachet auf, ruft uns die Stimme (Cantata). Wachet auf, ruft uns die Stimme; *arr.*]
Sleepers wake : SSATTBB / J.S. Bach ; arranged by Ben Parry. — London : Edition Peters, c2004. — 1 score (12 p.) ; 30 cm. — Kikapust choral series
Publisher's no.: Edition Peters no. 77065.
Publ. no. EP 77065
Publ. no. 77065
ISMN M577085388
System number: 013305901

Byrd, William, 1542 or 3-1623.
[Psalmes, sonets, and songs]
Psalmes, sonets and songs (1588) / [William Byrd] ; edited by Jeremy Smith. — London : Stainer & Bell, c2004. — 1 score (xliv, 176 p.) : facsims. ; 26 cm. — (The Byrd edition ; v. 12)
35 psalms and part-songs; for superius, medius, contratenor, tenor and bassus. — Words also printed for reference, p. xvi-xxxvi. — Includes editorial notes, notes on the poems, list of extant copies and index of first lines. — Series under the general editorship of Philip Brett. — Words mostly in English; "La virginella" in Italian.
Publ. no. B374
ISBN 0852493746
ISMN M220220432
System number: 013063061
Primary classification 782.542

Byrd, William, 1542 or 3-1623.
[Songs of sundrie natures]
Songs of sundrie natures (1589) / [William Byrd] ; edited by David Mateer. — London : Stainer & Bell, c2004. — 1 score (xxxvii, 274 p.) : facsims. ; 26 cm. — (The Byrd edition ; v. 13)
47 sacred and secular songs for 3-6 parts. unacc. — Words also printed for reference, p. xix-xxxi. — Includes editorial notes, notes on the poems, list of extant copies and index of first lines. — Series under the general editorship of Philip Brett.
Publ. no. B375
ISBN 0852493754
ISMN M220220449
System number: 013201995
Primary classification 782.542

*Davies, Bryan.
[Never weather beaten sail, mixed voices]
Never weather beaten sail / [words by] Thomas Campion ; [setting by] Bryan Davies. — Tewkesbury : Roberton Publications, a part of Goodmusic Publishing, c2005. — 1 score (4 p.) ; 26 cm.
For mixed voices (SATB), unacc. — Includes piano reduction for rehearsal only.
Pl. no. 63271
ISMN M222261457
System number: 013373029

Fanshawe, David, 1942-
[African Sanctus (Musical work). Lord's prayer; *arr.*]
The Lord's prayer : from African sanctus / vocal arrangement by the composer, David Fanshawe ; brass band arrangement by Liz Lane. — Brass band set. — London : Studio Music, [2005?], c1974. — 1 score (28 p.) + 1 set of parts ; 30 cm.
1st version for brass band; 2nd version for brass band with solo voice(s) and/or SATB chorus. — Instrumental parts only; score includes vocal lines for 2nd version.
ISMN M050065968 (set)
ISMN M050065975 (score)
System number: 013382672
Primary classification 784.9

Franklin, Cary John.
A Navaho prayer : SATB a cappella / [music] by Cary John Franklin. — [New York?] : Boosey & Hawkes ; Milwaukee, Wis. : exclusively distributed by Hal Leonard, c2005. — 1 score (4 p.) ; 27 cm. — Cathedral series
Words anonymous. — Includes program and biographical notes.
Publ. no. 48018888
ISMN M051475889
System number: 013361391

*Moeran, E. J. (Ernest John), 1894-1950.
[Choral music. *Selections*]
Collected choral music. Volume five, church music / E.J. Moeran ; edited by John Talbot. — Centenary ed. — London : Thames Publishing, c2003. — 1 score (37 p.) ; 30 cm.
For mixed voices (SATB), mostly with organ acc. — Reprinted from earlier editions. — Editorial notes following score.
System number: 013167658

Música para exequias en tiempo de Felipe IV / estudio y edición, Luis Antonio Gonzáles Marín. — Barcelona : Consejo Superior de Investigaciones Científicas, Institución "Milà i Fontanals, " Departamento de Musicología, 2004. — 1 score (303 p.) : facsims. ; 32 cm. — Monumentos de la música española ; 70
For chorus of mixed voices with continuo; partially figured bass not realized. — Pref. and critical notes in Spanish. — Chiefly Latin words; Fabordón del Miserere and Dioses de Olimpio, venid in Spanish.
ISBN 8400082788
System number: 013812414

Neufeld, Ken.
Veni, Sancte Spiritus : para coro mixto / Kenneth Neufeld. — Valencia : Piles, c2005. — 1 score (14 p.) ; 30 cm.
Latin words; English translation printed for reference.
System number: 014053349

*Rose, Barry, 1934-
Here, O my Lord : SATB and organ / [music by] Barry Rose ; [words by] Horatius Bonar. — London : Novello & Co, [2005?], c2002. — 1 score (3 p.) ; 25 cm.
Caption title.
Publ. no. NOV955812
System number: 013505660

*Rose, Barry, 1934-
Here, O my Lord : unis. with descant & organ / [music by] Barry Rose ; [words by] Horatius Bonar. — London : Novello & Co, c2004. — 1 score (4 p.) ; 25 cm.
Caption title.
Publ. no. NOV955834
System number: 013505667

*Rose, Barry, 1934-
The Lord is risen : (2005) : SATB chorus and organ / Barry Rose. — London : Novello & Co, c2005. — 1 score ([3] p.) ; 25 cm.
Publ. no. NOV955845
System number: 013505682

*Rose, Barry, 1934-
Nation shall speak peace unto nation : SSATBarB / Barry Rose ; words from the Book of Micah. — London : Novello & Co, c2005. — 1 score (7 p.) ; 25 cm.
Includes keyboard reduction for rehearsal only. — Caption title.
Publ. no. NOV955867
System number: 013506278

Roxburgh, Edwin.
The beginning of sorrows : soprano solo, off-stage vocal quartet, divided SATB choir / Edwin Roxburgh. — Waltham Abbey : United Music Publishers, c2005. — 1 score (24 p.) ; 31 cm.
Includes piano reduction for rehearsal only. — Incorporates the four-part chorale "Es ist genug" by J.S. Bach. — Title from cover. — Includes pref. in English. — Words in Latin, German and English ; also printed separately for reference, with English translations of the Latin and German sections.
ISMN M224404692
System number: 013222641

The scarlet cover : SATB a cappella / arranged by Stephen Hatfield. — [New York?] : Boosey & Hawkes ; Milwaukee, Wis. : exclusively distributed by Hal Leonard, c2005. — 1 score (15 p.) ; 27 cm. — (Doreen Rao's choral music experience) — (CME conductor's choice)
16th-century English words. — Includes program, performance and biographical notes.
Publ. no. 48018805
ISMN M051475643
System number: 013243883

*Terzakis, Dimitri.
Visionen : Die Schalen des Zorns : für gemischten Chor und Viola ad libitum = for mixed chorus and viola ad libitum (2004) / Dimitri Terzakis. — Bad Schwalbach : Edition Gravis, c2005. — 1 score (18 p.) + 1 part (2 p.) ; 30 cm.
For speaker, SATB chorus, and optional viola. — Duration: ca. 14:00. — Includes performance instructions in German. — Speaker's part in German; choral part wordless and in German; words also printed for reference with English translation.
Pl. no. EG 942
Publ. no. EG 942a
System number: 014629751

782.5251723

Ledger, Philip.
Lie still and slumber : two lullabies for Christmas : for mixed voices and keyboard / Philip Ledger. — Matfield : Encore Publications, c2005. — 1 score (8 p.) ; 26 cm.
System number: 013382722

Martinson, Joel.
Lions and oxen : for unison voices (with optional divisi), oboe and organ / words by Thomas H. Troeger ; music by Joel Martinson. — [New York] : Oxford University Press, c2004. — 1 score (11 p.) ; 27 cm. — Oxford sacred music
Oboe part printed separately following score. — Duration: 3:50.
ISBN 0193867834
ISBN 9780193867833
System number: 013115654

Rogers, Wayland.
Peace on earth, goodwill to men : SATB a cappella / [music] by Wayland Rogers. — [New York?] : Boosey & Hawkes ; Milwaukee, Wis. : exclusively distributed by Hal Leonard, c2004. — 1 close score (4 p.) ; 27 cm. — (Doreen Rao's choral music experience) — (CME holiday lights)
Words by Douglas LeTell Rights. — Includes program and biographical notes.
Publ. no. 48018847
ISMN M051475377
System number: 013243906

*Smith, Alan, 1930-
There is no rose : SATB, unaccompanied / Alan Smith. — New York : Oxford University Press, c2006. — 1 score (4 p.) ; 27 cm. — Oxford Christmas music
Anonymous 15th century words in mixed English and Latin.
ISBN 0193869780
System number: 013668630

782.5253

All my trials / [arr.] Bob Chilcott. — Oxford : Oxford University Press, c2004. — 1 score (8 p.) ; 26 cm.
For mixed voices (SATB) and piano. — Offprinted from 'Spirituals for choirs', edited by Bob Chilcott, (ISBN 0193435373).
Publ. no. BC77
ISBN 019343329X
System number: 013083866

Feel the spirit. Volume two : twenty-eight arrangements for mixed chorus / by Moses Hogan ; with a foreword by Craig Jessop. — Milwaukee : Hal Leonard, c2005. — 1 score (230 p.) : port. ; 27 cm.
28 spirituals for SATB chorus (partly with soli and divisions), mostly unacc. (5 with piano acc., 1 with optional conga drums, 1 with piano and flute, 1 with piano/organ and 3 trumpets). Instrumental parts printed separately following the relevant spiritual. — Includes piano reductions for some of the unacc. works. — "For worship and concert performance"—Back cover. — Includes biographical note.
Publ. no. 08744710
ISBN 0634096842
System number: 013222168

*Fisherman Peter : a South Carolina spiritual for unaccompanied choir (SATB) / arranged by Robert J. Powell. — [New York] : Oxford University Press, c2005. — 1 score (7 p.) ; 27 cm. — Oxford choral music
Includes piano reduction for rehearsal only. — Includes biographical note about the arranger.
ISBN 9780193868601
ISBN 0193868601
System number: 013472242

I want Jesus to walk with me / [arr.] Roderick Williams. — Oxford : Oxford University Press, c2004. — 1 score (11 p.) ; 26 cm. — (Choral songs ; X455)
For mixed voices (SATB) and piano. — "The bass line of the piano part may also be augmented by a double bass playing pizzicato"—P. [3] — Offprinted from 'Spirituals for choirs', edited by Bob Chilcott (ISBN 0193435373).
Publ. no. X455
ISBN 0193432684
System number: 013083861

Joshua fought the battle of Jericho : SSAATTBB / arranged by Jonathan Rathbone. — London : Edition Peters, c2004. — 1 score (9 p.) ; 30 cm. — Kikapust choral series
Publ. no. EP 77055
ISMN M577085043
System number: 013305728

*Krouwel, Juliet.
Slow down Moses! : for SATB (unaccompanied) / words by Cecily Taylor [based on Exodus 18:13-18] ; music by Juliet Krouwel. — London : Stainer & Bell, c2005. — 1 score (4 p.) ; 26 cm.
Publ. no. W214
ISMN M220221460
System number: 013222612

Nobody knows / Deep river (medley) : soprano solo, TTBB : spiritual / arranged by Jonathan Rathbone. — London : Edition Peters, c2004. — 1 score (5 p.) ; 30 cm. — Kikapust choral series
Publ. no. EP 77057
ISMN M577085180
System number: 013305751

*Peace like a river : for mixed chorus (SATB) and organ / [African-American spiritual ; arranged by] Mack Wilberg. — [New York] : Oxford University Press, c2005. — 1 score (11 p.) ; 27 cm. — Oxford choral music
ISBN 0193868148
System number: 013483999

Swing low, sweet chariot / [arr.] Andrew Pryce Jackman. — Oxford : Oxford University Press, c2004. — 1 score (7 p.) ; 26 cm. — (Choral songs)
For mixed voices (SATB) and piano. — "Offprinted from 'Spirituals for choirs', edited by Bob Chilcott (ISBN 0193435373)"—P. [2]
Publ. no. X454
ISBN 0193432676
ISBN 9780193432673
System number: 013084260

782.526
Aleotti, Raffaella, ca. 1570-ca. 1646.
Sacrae cantiones : quinque, septem, octo & decem vocibus decantandae / Raffaella Aleotti ; edited by C. Ann Carruthers ; introduction by Thomas W. Bridges. — New York : Broude Trust, c2006. — 1 score (xli, 150 p.) : facsim. ; 30 cm. — Music at the courts of Italy ; v. 2
For 5, 6, 8, or 10 unacc. voices. — Pref. in English. — Critical apparatus and bibliography at end. — Latin words; also printed as text with English translation (p. xxxviii-xli).
Pl. no. RA 2
ISBN 0845077023
System number: 013750188

Bertolusi, Vincenzo, ca. 1550-1607 or 8.
[Sacrae cantiones, libro 1o]
Sacrarum cantionum : 1601 / Vincentius Bertholusius ; edgivet af = herausgegeben von = edited by Ole Kongsted. — Copenhagen : Capella Hafniensis Editions, c2005. — 1 score (190 p.) : facsim. ; 31 cm. — (Monumenta musica regionis Balticae = Denkmäler der Musik des Ostseeraums = Monuments of music from the Baltic Sea Area ; vol. 6)
Sacred motets for 6-10 voices, unaccompanied. — Pref. and critical commentary, in Danish, German and English. — Latin words.
Publ. no. CHE A/6
ISMN M706785059
System number: 013581664

Brikner, Eryk, 1705-1760.
[Completorium (RISM A/II 300.033.575)]
Completorium : a canto & basso obligato, alto & tenore ad libitum, due violini con organo ; Hymnus pro festis apostolorum : a canto, alto, tenore, basso con organo / Eryk Brikner ; opracowanie i wstęp Aleksandra Patalas. — Wyd. 1. — [Partytura] — Częstochowa : Klasztor OO. Paulinów Jasna Góra ; Kraków : Polskie Wydawn. Muzyczne, 2006. — 1 score (78 p.) : facsims. ; 31 cm. — (Muzyka Jasnogórska = Musica Claromontana ; 5)
For soprano and bass solo (contralto and tenor ad libitum), 2 violins and organ (Completorium) and for soprano, contralto, tenor, bass and organ (Hymnus pro festis apostolorum). — Figured bass unrealized. — Pref. and critical report in Polish and English. — Latin words, also printed separately for reference with Polish and English translation.
Publ. no. PWM 10 469
ISMN M274002558
System number: 013887063
Also classified at 782.527

*Cantica nova : 18 new motets for choirs. — Oxford : Oxford University Press, 2004. — 1 score (xiv, 153 p.) ; 25 cm. — (New horizons)
For mixed voices, unacc. or with organ. — Unacc. motets include piano reductions for rehearsal only. — Includes composer's notes and liturgical notes. — Latin words; also printed separately for reference with English translations, p.vii-xiii.
ISBN 0193355361
System number: 013062771

Cantiones sacrae : madrigalian motets from Jacobean England / edited by Ross W. Duffin. — Middleton, Wis. : A-R Editions, c2006. — 1 score (xxiii, 128 p.) : facsims. ; 28 cm. — Recent researches in the music of the Renaissance ; 142
Includes introduction and critical report in English. — Latin words, also printed for reference with English translations.
ISBN 9780895795748
ISBN 0895795744
System number: 013379210

The complete motets [of] Orlando di Lasso : afterword, addenda and corrigenda, indexes / edited by Peter Bergquist. — Middleton, Wis : A-R Editions, c2007. — vi, 106 p. ; 23 cm. — Recent researches in the music of the Renaissance, 0486-123X ; 148S — (The complete motets. Supplement / Orlando di Lasso)
ISBN 9780895796097
ISBN 0895796090
System number: 013801796

Guerrero, Francisco, 1528?-1599.
[Motets. *Selections*]
Motetes de tempore et alia : LXXVI-CVII / Francisco Guerrero ; introducción, estudio y transcripción, Josep M. Llorens i Cisteró ; semitonía y estructuras modales, Karl H. Müller-Lancé. — Barcelona : Consejo Superior de Investigaciones Científicas, Institución "Milà i Fontanals", Departamento de Musicología, 2005. — 1 score (301 p.) : port. ; 32 cm. — Monumentos de la música española ; 72 — (Opera omnia / Francisco Guerrero ; v. 14)
For 4-12 voices, unacc. — Editorial, historical and critical commentary in Spanish on p. [13]-119. — Latin words; also printed for reference.
ISBN 8400002245 (set)

ISMN M97832006
System number: 013812163

Guggumos, Gallus, 16th cent.
[Motets, voices (4-6), continuo (1612). *Selections*]
Mottecta, Venedig 1612. Heft 1, Motetten zu vier Stimmen mit b.c. / Gallus Guggumos ; herausgegeben von Leopold Fendt. — Stuttgart : Cornetto-Verlag, c2004. — 1 score (38 p.) + 1 part ; 30 cm. — (Edition Schermar-Bibliothek Ulm ; 2)
"Anhang: Veni sponsa Christi (SSB b.c.)." — The 1st-4th works for 4 voices (cantus, altus, tenor, bassus) and continuo; 5th work for 2 high voices (canti), bass, and continuo. — Figured bass (1st-4th works) unrealized; unfigured bass (5th work) also unrealized. — Foreword in German. — Includes part for continuo. — Latin words, also printed separately for reference.
Publ. no. CP204
ISMN M501001187
System number: 014646420

Guggumos, Gallus, 16th cent.
[Motets, voices (4-6), continuo (1612). *Selections*]
Mottecta, Venedig 1612. Heft 2, Motetten zu fünf Stimmen mit B.c. / Gallus Guggumos ; herausgegeben von Leopold Fendt. — Stuttgart : Cornetto-Verlag, c2004. — 1 score (56 p.) + 1 part ; 30 cm. — (Edition Schermar-Bibliothek Ulm ; 12)
For 5 voices (cantus, quintus, altus, tenor, bassus) and continuo. — Figured bass unrealized. — Foreword in German. — Includes part for continuo. — Latin words, also printed separately for reference.
Publ. no. CP496
ISMN M501004676
System number: 014646432

Hasse, Johann Adolf, 1699-1783.
Ascolta i preghi : (Psalm 42:9, 10) : motet for 2 sopranos and basso continuo / Johann A. Hasse ; edited by Alejandro Garri ; assisted by Kent Carlson. — First ed. — Frankfurt : Garri Editions, 2007. — 1 score (10 p.) + 1 part ; 30 cm. — Canti di cielo ; 108
Edited from a 19th century manuscript copy in the possession of Padre Paolo Bagnoli, Rome. — Preface in English. — Unfigured bass unrealized. — Italian words.
Publ. no. GE 348
System number: 013771092

Josquin, des Prez, d. 1521.
[Motets. *Selections*]
Motets on non-biblical texts. I, De domino Jesu Christo. 1 / Josquin des
Prez ; edited by Bonnie J. Blackburn. — Utrecht : Koninklijke Vereniging
voor Nederlandse Muziekgeschiedenis, c2007. — 1 score (xv, 58 p) ;
34 cm. + 1 critical commentary (xvii, 148 p. ; 23 x 24 cm.). — (New
Josquin edition ; 21) — (Collected works of Josquin des Prez ; v. 21)
For 3, 4, or 6 voices, unacc. — Includes pref. in English. — Three spurious works
listed in contents, but excluded from score : Ave caro Christi cara — Ave verum
corpus : 5v — Ave verum corpus/Ecce panis/Bone pastor/O salutaris hostia—Cf.
pref, p. xi. — Words in Latin; text also printed separately in critical commentary
with English translation.
ISBN 9063750722 (score volume)
ISBN 9063751346 (commentary volume)
ISBN 906375051X (score set)
ISBN 9063751451 (commentary set)
System number: 013949874

Josquin, des Prez, d. 1521.
[Motets. *Selections*]
"Si placet" parts for motets by Josquin and his contemporaries / edited by
Stephanie P. Schlagel. — Madison, Wis : A-R Editions, c2006. — 1 score
(xxix, 216 p.) : facsims. ; 28 cm. — Recent researches in the music of the
Renaissance, 0486-123X ; v. 146
"Si placet writing ... involves the creation of newly composed voices that are added
to an original composition which otherwise remains unaltered; the new part or parts
can be performed si placet (literally "if it pleases") or omitted since the original
composition remains intact"—P. ix. — The complete motets are printed, with the "si
placet" parts highlighted. — Historical, editorial and critical notes in English. —
Latin words, also printed as texts with English translations, p. xxiv-xxix.
ISBN 9780895796028
ISBN 0895796023
System number: 013801801

Lasso, Orlando di, 1532-1594.
[Motets. *Selections.*]
Cantiones quinque vocum (Munich, 1597) / Orlando and Ferdinand di
Lasso. Cantiones sacrae sex vocibus (Munich, 1601) / Orlando and Rudolph
di Lasso ; [both] edited by David Crook. — Middleton, Wis. : A-R Editions,
c2007. — 1 score (xxxviii, 160 p., [8] p. of plates) : facsims. ; 28 cm. —
Recent researches in the music of the Renaissance, 0486-123X ; 147 —
(The complete motets / Orlando di Lasso ; 20)
Historical, editorial and critical notes in English. — Latin words, also printed for
reference with English translations, p. xxix-xxxviii.
ISBN 9780895796073
ISBN 0895796074
System number: 013801776

Lasso, Orlando di, 1532-1594.
[Motets. *Selections*]
Motets for three to twelve voices from Magnum Opus Musicum (Munich,
1604) / Orlando di Lasso ; edited by Peter Bergquist. — Madison, Wis :
A-R Editions, c2006. — 1 score (xxxviii, 360 p.) : facsims. ; 28 cm. —
Recent researches in the music of the Renaissance ; 148 — (The complete
motets / Orlando di Lasso ; 21)
Historical, editorial and critical notes in English. — Latin words; also printed for
reference with English translations, p. xxv-xxxviii.
ISBN 9780895795960
ISBN 0895795965
System number: 013801786

Lasso, Orlando di, 1532-1594.
[Mottetta typis nondum uspiam excusa]
Mottetta, sex vocum, typis nondum uspiam excusa (Munich, 1582) / edited
by Rebecca Wagner Oettinger. — Midddleton, Wis. : A-R Editions, c2005.
— 1 score (xxvii, 160 p.) : ill. ; 29 cm. — Recent researches in the music of
the Renaissance ; v. 141 — (The complete motets / Orlando di Lasso ; 13)
For cantus 1 and 2, altus, tenor 1 and 2, and bassus. — Edited from the 1st ed.
published: Monachii : A. Berg, 1582. — Historical, editorial, and critical notes in
English. — General editor of Lasso motet series: Peter Bergquist. — Latin words;
also printed for reference with English translation.
ISBN 0895795728
System number: 013294495

Leonarda, Isabella, 1620-1704.
Vespro a cappella della Beata Vergine e motetti concertati : opera ottava
(1678) / Isabella Leonarda ; a cura di Paolo Monticelli. — Lucca : Libreria
Musicale Italiana, c2005. — 1 score (xliv, 136 p.) ; 34 cm. — Collana di
musiche a cura della Cappella strumentale del Duomo di Novara
For canto, alto, tenore, basso, organo (unrealized figured bass). — Pref. with critical
commentary in Italian. — Latin words.
ISBN 887096406X
System number: 013739259

Mozart, Wolfgang Amadeus, 1756-1791.
Jubilate Deo : motet for SATB and organ / attributed to W.A.Mozart ; edited
by David Patrick. — [Barnet] : Fitzjohn Music, c2005. — 1 score (4 p.) ;
30 cm.
System number: 013359697

*Palestrina, Giovanni Pierluigi da, 1525?-1594.
[Motets (1563)]
Motecta festorum totius anni cum communi sanctorum quaternis vocibus
/ Giovanni Pierluigi da Palestrina ; edizione critica a cura di Daniele V.
Filippi. — Pisa : ETS, c2003. — 1 score (vi, 280 p.) ; 30 cm. — Diverse
voci ;
For mixed voices (SATB) unacc. — Pref. and critical commentary in Italian. —
At head of title: Università di Pavia, Dipartimento di scienze musicologiche e
paleografico-filologiche. — Latin words.
ISBN 8846706897
ISMN M705015065
System number: 013224013

*Palestrina, Giovanni Pierluigi da, 1525?-1594.
[Motets (1563). Veni sponsa Christi]
Veni sponsa Christi : SATB / Giovanni Pierluigi da Palestrina ;
transcribed and edited by Jon Dixon. — Carshalton Beeches : JOED
Music, 2004, c2003. — 1 score (6 p.) ; 30 cm. — Renaissance
polyphonic choral music
Subtitle in caption: Magnificat antiphon at vespers of the common of Virgins. —
Source: Printed partbooks, published Venice : Angelo Gardano, 1585. —
Duration: 2:40. — Latin words; English translation printed as text preceding
score.
Pl. no. JOED P113
System number: 013498095

*Palestrina, Giovanni Pierluigi da, 1525?-1594.
[Motets (1572). Domine, in virtute tua]
Domine, in virtute tua : (SATB+SATB) / Giovanni Pierluigi da
Palestrina ; transcribed and edited by Jon Dixon. — Carshalton Beeches :
JOED Music, c2004. — 1 score (20 p.) ; 30 cm. — Renaissance
polyphonic choral music
A setting of Psalm 21, v. 1-7. — Source: Printed part books, published Venice :
Girolamo Scotto, 1572. — Cover title. — Duration: 6:42. — Latin words; English
translation printed as text preceding score.
Pl. no. JOED P159
System number: 013498156

*Palestrina, Giovanni Pierluigi da, 1525?-1594.
[Motets (1575). Inclytae Sanctae Virginis Catherinae]
Inclytae Sanctae Virginis Catherinae : SAATB / Giovanni Pierluigi da
Palestrina ; transcribed and edited by Jon Dixon. — Carshalton Beeches :
JOED Music, c2004. — 1 score (8 p.) ; 30 cm. — Renaissance
polyphonic choral music
Votive motet in praise of St. Catherine. — Source: 'Motettorum ... liber 3',
published Venice : erede di Girolamo Scotto, 1575. — Duration: 2:35. — Latin
words; English translation printed as text preceding score.
Pl. no. JOED P153
System number: 013498151

Payen, Nicolas, ca. 1512-ca. 1559.
[Vocal music. *Selections*]
Motets and chansons / Nicolas Payen ; edited by Laura Pollic McDowell.
— Middleton, Wis. : A-R Editions, c2006. — 1 score (xxvi, 160 p., [3] p.
of plates) : facsims. ; 28 cm. — Recent researches in the music of the
Renaissance, 144
Chiefly for 4 mixed voices; Resurrectio Christi and Benedictus Dominus Deus
Israel are for 5 mixed voices. — Texts with English translations: p. xx-xxvi. —
Introduction and critical commentary in English. — Motets have Latin words;
chansons have French words.
ISBN 9780895795939
ISBN 0895795930
System number: 013693493

Pitkin, Jonathan, 1978-
Esto mihi in Deum protectorem : SATB (with divisions) a cappella /
Jonathan Pitkin. — Oxford : Oxford University Press, c2005. — 1 score
(7 p.) : port. ; 26 cm. — (New horizons ; NH25)
Includes keyboard reduction for rehearsal only. — Words from Psalms 31, 71 and
48. — Duration: 2:30. — Includes biographical note. — Latin words; also printed
separately for reference with English translation preceding score.
Publ. no. NH25
ISBN 0193439247
ISBN 9780193439245
System number: 013213412

***Schermar-Bibliothek Ulm Ms. 237 : Brugge? ca. 1515-1540 : unedierte
Stücke und Unikate. Stücke zu 4 Stimmen / herausgegeben von Dieter
Klöckner. — [Stuttgart] : Cornetto, [2004?] — 1 score (ca. 41 p.) +
1 part (ca. 10 p.) ; 30 cm. — (Edition Schermar-Bibliothek Ulm ; Nr. 6)**
Four-voice motets and polyphonic chansons; in part without text. — The part is in
score format, designated "Umblätterseiten", and comprises pages from selected
works in the longer, complete score, provided to facilitate performance with
minimal page-turning. — The texted works with Latin or French words.
Publ. no. CP368
ISMN M501003396
System number: 014766586

*Schermar-Bibliothek Ulm Ms. 237 : Brugge? ca. 1515-1540 : unedierte
Stücke und Unikate. Stücke zu 5 und 6 Stimmen / herausgegeben von
Dieter Klöckner. — [Stuttgart] : Cornetto, [2004 or 2005] — 1 score
(various pagings) + 3 parts ; 30 cm. — Edition Schermar-Bibliothek Ulm ;
Nr. 7
Five- and six-voice motets and polyphonic chansons; in part without text. — Parts
for voices 1 & 2, 3 & 4, and 5 & 6; in score format. — The texted works with Latin
or French words.
Publ. no. CP370
ISMN M501003419
System number: 014766587

*Tallis, Thomas, ca. 1505-1585.
Gaude gloriosa Dei Mater : S(S)A(A)TTBB / Thomas Tallis ; transcribed
and edited by Jon Dixon. — [Rev. ed.] — Carshalton Beeches : JOED
Music, [2005?], c1992. — 1 score (28 p.) ; 30 cm. — Renaissance
polyphonic choral music
Cover title. — Sources: Oxford, ChristChurch mss. 979-983 and Oxford, Bodleian
Library, Ms. Tenbury 810. — Duration: 18:30. — Originally published: 1991, with
the pl. no. JOED T14. — Latin words; English translation printed as text preceding
score.
Pl. no. JOED T13
System number: 013525907

*Tallis, Thomas, ca. 1505-1585.
[Miserere nostri]
Miserere nostri ; & Loquebantur variis linguis : SSAATBB / Thomas Tallis ;
transcribed and edited by Jon Dixon. — Carshalton Beeches : JOED Music,
2004, c1992. — 1 score (14 p.) ; 30 cm. — Renaissance polyphonic choral
music
Sources: Cantiones Sacrae, 1575 (1st work), Oxford, ChristChurch Ms. 979-983 and
London, British Library Baldwin mss (2nd work). — Durations: 1:30 ; 4:05. —
Latin words; English translation printed as text preceding each work.
Pl. no. JOED T15
System number: 013525881

Taverner, John, 1495 (ca.)-1545.
Christe, Jesu, pastor bone / John Taverner ; edited by David Skinner. —
Oxford : Oxford University Press, [2005?], c1994. — 1 score (8 p.) ; 26 cm.
— (Tudor church music ; TCM 84 (revised))
For SATBarB unacc.; keyboard reduction for rehearsal only. — "This edition
presents two texts. The first, the Elizabethan adaptation ...appropriate for church use
... the second ... a hypothetical recostruction ofthe 1526-30 original with references
to St. William and Wolsey, is suitable for concert use"—P. 8. — Latin words;
English translations at the bottom of p. [1]
Publ. no. TCM 84 (revised)
ISBN 0193851024
ISBN 9780193851023
System number: 013424001

Victoria, Tomás Luis de, ca. 1548-1611.
[Masses (1583). Missa O quam gloriosum]
Missa O Quam gloriosum (SATB) ; Motet, O quam gloriosum est regnum
(SATB) / Tomás Luis de Victoria ; transcribed and edited by Andrew Parker.
— London : Novello, c2005. — 1 score (30 p.) ; 26 cm. — (Masses and
motets / Tomás Luis de Victoria)
Includes piano reduction for rehearsal only. — Includes introductory essay "Victoria
and his publications" by the editor. — List of sources and editorial notes on p. 30. —
Latin words.
Publ. no. NOV020713
ISBN 1846091853
System number: 013335998
Primary classification 782.53232

Victoria, Tomás Luis de, ca. 1548-1611.
[Missae, Psalmi, Magnificat, ad Virginem Dei Matrem salutiones, aliaque.
Missa Dum complerentur]
Missa Dum complerentur (SAATTB) ; Motet, Dum complerentur dies
Pentecostes (SSATB) / Tomás Luis de Victoria ; transcribed and edited by
Andrew Parker. — London : Novello, c2005. — 1 score (69 p.) ; 26 cm. —
(Masses and motets / Tomás Luis de Victoria)
Includes piano reduction for rehearsal only. — Includes introductory essay "Victoria
and his publications" by the editor. — List of sources and editorial notes on p. 69. —
Latin words.
Publ. no. NOV020691
ISBN 1846091845
System number: 013335980
Primary classification 782.53232

*Werner, Gregor Joseph, 1695-1766.
[Salve Regina, voices (4), violins (2), organ, B♭ major]
Salve Regina : in B-flat major : for mixed choir, two violins and organ / by
Gregor Joseph Werner ; edited by Alejandro Garri ; assisted by Kent
Carlson. — 1st ed. — [Frankfurt] : Garri Editions, c2005. — 1 score (iv,
9 p.) + 2 parts ; 30 cm. — Chorus angelorum ; v. 15
Figured bass realized. — Based on a manuscript in the Landesbibliothek, Darmstadt
(Mus. ms. 1292). — Pref. in English. — Latin words.
Publ. no. GE 191
System number: 014629781

Zarlino, Gioseffo, 1517-1590.
[Motets. Selections]
Motets from 1549 / Gioseffo Zarlino ; edited by Cristle Collins Judd. —
Middleton, Wis. : A-R Editions, c2006-2007. — 1 score (2 v.) : facsims. ;
28 cm. — Recent researches in the music of the Renaissance ; 145, 149
Motets are for 5 voices, unacc. The Pater noster is for 7 voices. — Edited from
Zarlino's Musici quinque vocum moduli (RISM AI, Z99) and the prints Il primo
libro di motetti a cinque voci (RISM BI, 1549â ·) and Il terzo libro di motetti a
cinque voci di Cipriano de Rore et de altri excellentissimi musici (RISM BI,
1549â). — Includes editorial commentary and critical report in English. —
Latin words, also printed as text with English translations precediing score.
ISBN 9780895795984 (pt. 1)
ISBN 9780895796080 (pt. 2)
ISBN 0895795981 (pt. 1)
ISBN 0895796082 (pt. 2)
System number: 013888152

782.5261722

*Wecker, Georg Kaspar, 1632-1695.
[O Herr hilf]
O Herr hilf! O Herr, laß wohl gelingen! : (1695) : geistliches Konzert
zum 1. Advent für Sopran I, Sopran II (Tenor), Alt, Baß, 2 Violinen, 2
Violen und B.c. / Georg Caspar Wecker ; herausgegeben von Raimund
Schächer. — Erstausg. — Stuttgart : Cornetto-Verlag, c2005. — 1 score
(18 p.) + 1 vocal score + 3 parts ; 30 cm.
Motet for SATB (canto primo, canto secondo o tenore, alto and basso) chorus, 2
violins, 2 violas, and continuo. — Figured bass not realized. — German words.
Publ. no. CP559
ISMN M501005307
System number: 014629780

782.5261723

*Mouton, Jean, d. 1522.
[Noe, noe, noe psallite noe]
Noe, noe, psallite noe : motet for the season of Christmas : SATB / Jean
Mouton. — [Altamonte Springs, FL?] : Anglo-American Music
Publishers, c1998. — 1 score (7 p.) ; 28 cm.
Latin words.
System number: 013594406

*Palestrina, Giovanni Pierluigi da, 1525?-1594.
[Motets (1563). Dies sanctificatus]
Dies sanctificatus : SATB / Giovanni Pierluigi da Palestrina ; transcribed
and edited by Jon Dixon. — Carshalton Beeches : JOED Music, c2002.
— 1 score (5 p.) ; 30 cm. — Renaissance polyphonic choral music
Subtitle in caption: Motet for the thrid mass of Christmas. — Source: Reissue of
'Motecta festorum totius anni cum Communi Sanctorum', published Venice :
Angelo Gardano, 1585. — Cover title. — Duration: 3:05. — Latin words; English
translation printed as text preceding score.
Publ. no. JOED P137
System number: 013498138

*Palestrina, Giovanni Pierluigi da, 1525?-1594.
[Motets (1575). Hodie Christus natus est]
Hodie Christus natus est : (SSAB+ATTB) / Giovanni Pierluigi da
Palestrina ; transcribed and edited by Jon Dixon. — Carshalton Beeches :
JOED Music, 2003, c1991. — 1 score (8 p.) ; 30 cm. — Renaissance
polyphonic choral music
Motet for Christmas day. — Source: 'Mottetorum ... liber tertius', published
Venice : erede di Girolamo Scotto, 1575. — Cover title. — Duration: 2:45. —
Latin words; English translation printed as text preceding score.
Pl. no. JOED P1
System number: 013498063

*Palestrina, Giovanni Pierluigi da, 1525?-1594.
[Motets (1575). Rex pacificus]
Rex pacificus : SAATTB / Giovanni Pierluigi da Palestrina ; transcribed
and edited by Jon Dixon. — Carshalton Beeches : JOED Music, c2002.
— 1 score (6 p.) ; 30 cm. — Renaissance polyphonic choral music
Subtitle in caption: First antiphon at First vespers of the Feast of the Nativity of
Our Lord. — Source: Printed partbooks, published Venice : Apud haeredem
Hieronymi Scoti, 1575. — Cover title. — Duration: 2:46. — Latin words; English
translation printed as text preceding score.
Pl. no. JOED P135
System number: 013498111

782.5261724

*Palestrina, Giovanni Pierluigi da, 1525?-1594.
[Motets (1569). Stella, quam viderant Magi]
Stella quam viderant Magi : SATTB / Giovanni Pierluigi da Palestrina ;
transcribed and edited by Jon Dixon. — Carshalton Beeches : JOED
Music, c2003. — 1 score (8 p.) ; 30 cm. — Renaissance polyphonic
choral music
Motet for the Feast of the Epiphany. — Source: 'Florilegium sacrarum
cantionum', published Antwerp : Phalèse, 1602. — Cover title. — Duration: 3:28.
— Latin words; English translation printed as text preceding score.
Pl. no. JOED P139
System number: 013498144

782.5261727

*Palestrina, Giovanni Pierluigi da, 1525?-1594.
[Motets (1575). Haec dies]
Haec dies : SSATTB / Giovanni Pierluigi da Palestrina ; transcribed and edited by Jon Dixon. — Carshalton Beeches : JOED Music, 2005, c1995. — 1 score (6 p.) ; 30 cm. — Renaissance polyphonic choral music
Subtitle in caption: Antiphon at vespers on Easter Sunday. — Source: 'Motettorum ... liber 3', published Venice : erede di Girolamo Scotto, 1575. — Duration: 1:50. — Latin words; English translation printed as text preceding score.
Pl. no. JOED P41
System number: 013498077

782.5261728

*Palestrina, Giovanni Pierluigi da, 1525?-1594.
[Motets (1572). Ascendo ad Patrem]
Ascendo ad Patrem : (SATTB) / Giovanni Pierluigi da Palestrina ; transcribed and edited by Jon Dixon. — Carshalton Beeches : JOED Music, c2002. — 1 score (12 p.) ; 30 cm. — Renaissance polyphonic choral music
Subtitle in caption: Motet for Ascensiontide. — Source: 'Corollarium cantionum Sacrarum', published Nuremburg : Gerlach, 1590. — Cover title. — Duration: 5:45. — Latin words; English translation printed as text preceding score.
Pl. no. JOED P93
System number: 013526318

782.52617293

*Palestrina, Giovanni Pierluigi da, 1525?-1594.
[Hymni totius anni. Veni Creator Spiritus]
Veni Creator Spiritus : SAT(T)B / Giovanni Pierluigi da Palestrina ; transcribed and edited by Jon Dixon. — Carshalton Beeches : JOED Music, 2003, c2002. — 1 score (11 p.) ; 30 cm. — Renaissance polyphonic choral music
Subtitle in caption: Hymn at second vespers on Whit Sunday. — Source: 'Hymni totius anni', published Venice : Angelo Gardano, 1589. — Cover title. — Duration: 7:36. — Latin words; English translation printed as text preceding score.
Pl. no. JOED P103
System number: 013498084

782.5265

Aston, Peter.
If ye love me : for mixed voices and organ / Peter Aston. — Matfield : Encore Publications, c2005. — 1 score (8 p.) ; 26 cm.
Chorus: SATB. — Words: John 14: 15-18.
System number: 013199443

Baker, Richard, 1972-
To keep a true Lent : SATTBB (with T solo) a cappella / Richard Baker. — Oxford : Oxford University Press, c2005. — 1 score (11 p.) : port. ; 26 cm. — (New horizons ; NH22)
Words by Robert Herrick. — Duration: 2:00. — Includes biographical note.
Publ. no. NH22
ISBN 0193439212
System number: 013213405

Baldwin, Antony, 1957-
God be in my head : for unaccompanied mixed choir (SATB) / Antony Baldwin. — [New York] : Oxford University Press, c2005. — 1 score (3 p.) ; 27 cm. — Oxford church music
Words from a Book of hours (1514).
ISBN 0193868571
ISBN 9780193868571
System number: 013212297

Bingham, Judith.
In nomine : anthem after Taverner for SATB choir unaccompanied : (2005) / Judith Bingham. — Kenley : Maecenas Music, c2005. — 1 score (8 p.) ; 30 cm.
"This anthem is designed to come after the 'Benedictus' of the Taverner 'Missa Gloria Tibi Trinitas' and lead smoothly into the 'Agnus Dei' without a pause"—Composer's note. — Duration: ca. 4:00. — Latin words, also provided for reference with English translation.
System number: 013416593

Bingham, Judith.
Our faith is a light : anthem for SATB and organ : (2004) / Judith Bingham. — Kenley : Maecenas Music, c2004. — 1 score (22 p.) ; 30 cm.
Combines texts of an extract from St. Julian of Norwich's Revelations of Divine Love and the hymn Regina Caeli laetare. — Duration: ca. 6:00. — Includes composer's note. — Words in English and Latin; also printed for reference preceding score.
System number: 013193889

*Blackford, Richard, 1954-
On another's sorrow / words by Willam [sic] Blake ; music by Richard Blackford. — London : Novello & Co, c2004. — 1 score (8 p.) ; 30 cm.
For mixed voices (SATB), unacc. — Includes piano reduction for rehearsal only. — Caption title.
Publ. no. NOV200453
System number: 013582444

*Carey, Paul, 1954-
Behold, I tell you a mystery : for unaccompanied mixed choir (SATB) / Paul Carey. — [New York] : Oxford University Press, c2005. — 1 score (7 p.) ; 27 cm. — Oxford sacred music
Includes piano reduction for rehearsal only. — Words from I Corinthians 15:51-55.
ISBN 0193868660
System number: 013472331

Carey, Paul, 1954-
A million miracles : a Celtic prayer for mixed choir (SATB) and piano / Paul Carey. — [New York] : Oxford University Press, c2004. — 1 score (6 p.) ; 27 cm. — Oxford sacred music
Includes biographical note.
ISBN 0193867354
ISBN 9780193867352
System number: 013324499

*Chilcott, Bob.
The dove and the olive leaf : for mixed choir (SATB), soprano saxophone (or B♭ clarinet) and piano / Bob Chilcott. — [New York] : Oxford University Press, c2005. — 1 score (10 p.) ; 27 cm. — Oxford sacred music
Words: Genesis 8:11. — Saxophone part printed separately on p. 10. — Includes biographical and programme notes. — Macaronic English and Hebrew text.
ISBN 019386908X
System number: 013521812

*Chilcott, Bob.
Now thank we : for mixed choir (SATB), soprano descant, and organ / Bob Chilcott. — [New York] : Oxford University Press, c2005. — 1 score (22 p.) ; 27 cm. — Oxford sacred music
Words from Ecclesiasticus and by Martin Rinkart. — Includes congregational singing of "Now thank we all our God.". — Includes biographical and programme notes.
ISBN 0193869063
System number: 013515526

*Child, William, 1606?-1697.
Sing we merrily : anthem for seven voices (SSAATTBB) with organ accompaniment / William Child. — [s.l.] : Anglo-American Music Publishers, c2006. — 1 score (28 p.) ; 28 cm.
Includes biographical note.
System number: 013594302

Gibbons, Orlando, 1583-1625.
[Song 13; arr.]
With grateful hearts : meditation for Remembrance Sunday : for mixed voices and organ / [Orlando Gibbons ; arr.] Philip Ledger. — Matfield : Encore Publications, c2005. — 1 score (3 p.) ; 26 cm.
Chorus: SATB. — Words by Philip Ledger.
System number: 013225245

Goddard, Mark.
Anthem, The priests of the Lord : for SATB and organ / music by Mark Goddard ; text from Leviticus. — Oxford : Spartan Press, c1990. — 1 score (8 p.) ; 30 cm.
Publ. no. SP117
System number: 013263962

*Goddard, Mark.
Be strong and of good courage : an anthem for St. Barnabas Day : SATB with STB soloists [and organ] / music by Mark Goddard. — Laggan Bridge : Spartan Press, [2005], c1990. — 1 score (12 p.) ; 26 cm.
"Typeset and re-published in the spring of 2005" - Publisher's website (1 June 2006).
Pl. no. SP102
System number: 013482277

Godfrey, Philip, 1964-
Day by day : [a prayer of St. Richard of Chichester] : for mixed voices (SATB) and piano or organ / Philip Godfrey. — Matfield : Encore Publications, c2005. — 1 score (4 p.) ; 26 cm.
System number: 013416377

Godfrey, Philip, 1964-
May the road rise with you : a choral blessing / music: Philip Godfrey ; words: a Gaelic blessing. — Matfield : Encore Publications, c2005. — 1 score (4 p.) ; 26 cm.
For mixed voices (SATB) and organ.
System number: 013416371

*Larsen, Libby.
Is God, our endless day : an anthem for mixed choir (SATB), unaccompanied : for Trinity Sunday (A, B, C), Third Sunday after the Epiphany (A), Last Sunday after the Epiphany (C) / text by Julian of Norwich ; music by Libby Larsen. — [New York] : Oxford University Press, c2001. — 1 score (9 p.) ; 27 cm. — (Libby Larsen liturgical cycle)
Includes piano reduction for rehearsal only. — To complement the Revised Common Lectionary, Years A, B and C. — Includes biographical and programme notes.
ISBN 9780193864092
ISBN 0193864096
System number: 013472561

Lole, Simon.
My beloved is mine / music: Simon Lole ; words: Francis Quarles. —
Matfield : Encore Publications, c2005. — 1 score (4 p.) ; 26 cm.
For mixed voices (SATB with divisions), unacc.
System number: 013416520

Lole, Simon.
A Sarum blessing / Simon Lole ; words: Sarum Breviary. — Matfield :
Encore Publications, c2005. — 1 score (4 p.) ; 26 cm.
For mixed voices (SATB) and organ.
System number: 013416538

*Love divine : a collection of Victorian & Edwardian anthems : for mixed
voice chorus / selected & edited by Barry Rose. — London : Novello,
c2005. — 1 score (xi, 148 p.) ; 26 cm.
20 anthems, for 4-8 vv., mostly with organ acc. — Unacc. works include piano
reductions for rehearsal only. — Includes notes on the music. — Mostly English
words.
Publ. no. NOV032208
ISBN 184449683X
System number: 013201787

*MacMillan, James, 1959-
Chosen : for SAATTB and organ / James MacMillan ; words by Michael
Symmons Roberts. — [S.l.] : Boosey & Hawkes, c2004. — 1 score (12 p.) ;
26 cm.
Duration: 5:00. — English words, also printed for reference with German and
French translations preceding score.
Pl. no. 13870
ISMN M060116407
System number: 013192577

*The Novello short anthems collection : five centuries of anthems for
smaller mixed voice choirs, a cappella or with organ accompaniment /
selected & edited with a preface by David Hill. — London : Novello,
c2005. — 1 score (2 v.) ; 25 cm. — Novello choral programme
English or Latin words. Latin works also have either words in English or an English
translation printed for reference.
Publ. no. NOV032175
Publ. no. NOV032274
ISBN 184609058X (v. 1)
ISBN 1846090598 (v. 2)
System number: 013335704

Rommereim, John Christian.
I look for you early : for mixed choir (SATB), organ and optional alto
saxophone / John Christian Rommereim. — [New York] : Oxford
University Press, c2004. — 1 score (10 p.) ; 27 cm. — Oxford sacred music
Words by Solomon Ibn Gabirol, translated from the Hebrew by Peter Cole. — Words
also printed for reference preceding score. — Includes biographical notes about the
composer and poet. — Saxophone part printed separately following score.
ISBN 0193867435
System number: 013324503

Rutter, John, 1945-
Arise, shine / John Rutter. — Oxford : Oxford University Press, c2003. — 1
score (15 p.) ; 26 cm. — (Anthems ; A471)
For mixed voices (SATB) and organ. — Words from Isaiah 60:1-4, 19.
Publ. no. A471
ISBN 0193505258
ISBN 9780193505254
System number: 013084325

Rutter, John, 1945-
A crown of glory / John Rutter. — Oxford : Oxford University Press, c2004.
— 1 score (15 p.) ; 26 cm. — (Anthems ; A472)
For mixed voices (SATB) and organ. — Text is an Advent prayer from the
Mozarabic liturgy and a prayer by the composer. — Words also printed for reference
preceding score.
Publ. no. A472
ISBN 0193533588
System number: 013084314

Rutter, John, 1945-
[Wings of the morning. *Vocal score*]
Wings of the morning / John Rutter. — Oxford : Oxford University Press,
c2003. — 1 score (15 p.) ; 26 cm. — (Anthems ; A470)
Originally for mixed voices (SATB) and orchestra; acc. arr. for piano. — Words from
Pslam 139.
Publ. no. A470
ISBN 019350524X
System number: 013084308

*Sametz, Steven, 1954-
Alleluia : for mixed choir (SA, TB, or SATB) and handbells with optional
harp or keyboard / Steven Sametz. — [New York] : Oxford University
Press, c2005. — 1 score (9 p.) ; 27 cm. — Oxford sacred music
Handbells part also printed separately p. [8]-9. — Includes biographical note.
ISBN 0193868784
System number: 013472367

*Sanders, John, 1933-2003.
The firmament : anthem for treble soloist, SATB choir & organ / music
by John Sanders. — [Altamonte Springs, FL?] : Anglo-American Music
Publishers : distribution, Worldwide Music International, c2005. — 1
score (20 p.) ; 28 cm.
The words, also printed for reference preceding score, are an ode by Joseph
Addison combined with verses from psalms 19, 96, 121 and the Benedicite (Book
of Common Prayer texts).
System number: 013594323

*Schelat, David.
By your word, O God : for two-part choir and organ / David Schelat. —
[New York] : Oxford University Press, c2005. — 1 score (6 p.) ; 27 cm.
— Oxford sacred music
Words from the Presbyterian Book of Common Worship. — Includes biographical
note.
ISBN 9780193868892
ISBN 019386889X
System number: 013472216

Shephard, Richard, 1949-
Lord, I have loved the habitation of thy house : for mixed voices and
organ / Richard Shephard. — [Matfield?] : Encore Publications, c2005.
— 1 score (8 p.) ; 26 cm.
Chorus: SATB. — Words: Psalm 26:8-10, 84:1-3, and Samuel Crossman.
System number: 013192606

Skempton, Howard, 1947-
Rise up, my love : SATB a cappella / Howard Skempton. — Oxford :
Oxford University Press, c2005. — 1 score (7 p.) : port. ; 26 cm. — (New
horizons ; NH26)
Words from the Song of Solomon. — Duration: 10:00. — Includes biographical
note.
Publ. no. NH26
ISBN 0193439255
ISBN 9780193439252
System number: 013213402

*Stewart, Richard N.
[Just as I am. *Spanish*]
Tal como soy = (Just as I am) : for unaccompanied mixed choir (SATB) /
Richard N. Stewart. — [New York] : Oxford University Press, c2005. —
1 score (11 p.) ; 27 cm. — Oxford church music
Includes piano reduction for rehearsal only. — Words by Charlotte Elliott. —
Includes biographical note. — Spanish words; with non-singing superlinear
English translation (not the original English words).
ISBN 9780193868458
ISBN 0193868458
System number: 013472571

*Stewart, Richard N.
Just as I am : for unaccompanied mixed choir (SATB) / Richard N.
Stewart. — [New York] : Oxford University Press, c2005. — 1 score
(11 p.) ; 27 cm. — Oxford church music
Includes piano reduction for rehearsal only. — Words by Charlotte Elliott. —
Includes biographical note.
ISBN 9780193868441
ISBN 019386844X
System number: 013472140

Tavener, John.
Prayer for the healing of the sick : for SATB chorus and bass solo / John
Tavener. — London : Chester Music, [2003?], c1999. — 1 score (2 p.) ;
25 cm. — Contemporary church music series
Words from the Orthodox Service of Holy Unction.
Publ. no. CH69091
System number: 013190774

Tye, Christopher, 1497?-1572.
Give almes of thy goods / Christopher Tye ; edited by John Milsom. —
Oxford : Oxford University Press, [2005?], c1991. — 1 score (4 p.) ;
27 cm. — (Tudor church music ; TCM 57 (2nd revision))
For SATB unacc.; keyboard reduction for rehearsal only. — The words are the
Offertory sentence (Tobit 4:7). — Includes list of sources and critical
commentary.
Publ. no. TCM 57 (2nd revision)
ISBN 0193851040
ISBN 9780193851047
System number: 013424016

Vaughan Williams, Ralph, 1872-1958.
[Fantasia on Greensleeves; *arr.*]
Greensleeves : or, The king of love : a choral setting for mixed voice
choir and piano or orchestra of "Fantasia on Greensleeves" / by R.
Vaughan Williams ; arranged by Philip Lane. — Tewkesbury : Roberton
Publications, c2004. — 1 score (12 p.) ; 26 cm.
For mixed voices (SATB) with piano or organ acc. Orchestral acc. available
separately. — Words to Greensleeves from "A handfull of pleasant delites", 1584.
Words to The king of love by H.W. Baker.
Publ. no. 63270
ISMN M222260450
System number: 013193252
Primary classification 782.542

*Wilberg, Mack.
Thou gracious God, whose mercy lends : for mixed choir (SATBarB) and piano / [English folk tune ; arranged by] Mack Wilberg. — [New York] : Oxford University Press, c2005. — 1 score (7 p.) ; 27 cm. — Oxford sacred music
Words by Oliver Wendell Holmes.
ISBN 9780193868182
ISBN 0193868180
System number: 013472378

*Wilkinson, fl. 1579-1596.
O Lord, my God : verse anthem for SS/AATB with organ and/or viols / Thomas Wylkinson ; edited by Peter le Huray. — [Altamonte Springs, FL?] : Anglo-American Music Publishers, c2005. — 1 score (12 p.) ; 28 cm.
Words from Psalm 7. — Includes biographical note and critical commentary.
System number: 013594681

*Wilkinson, fl. 1579-1596.
Praise the Lord, O ye his servants : verse anthem for SAATB with organ and/or viols / Thomas Wylkinson ; edited by Peter le Huray. — [Altamonte Springs, FL?] : Anglo-American Music Publishers, c2005. — 1 score (13 p.) ; 28 cm.
Words from Psalm 113. — Includes biographical note and critical commentary.
System number: 013594684

*Wilkinson, fl. 1579-1596.
Preserve me, O Lord : verse anthem for SSATB with organ and/or viols / Thomas Wylkinson ; edited by Peter le Huray. — [Altamonte Springs, FL?] : Anglo-American Music Publishers, c2005. — 1 score (14 p.) ; 28 cm.
Includes biographical note and critical commentary.
System number: 013594691

*Þorkell Sigurbjörnsson, 1938-
Hymn to Mary = (Maríukvæði) / Þorkell Sigurbjörnsson. — Oxford : Oxford University Press, c2005. — 1 score (7 p.) ; 26 cm. — Oxford anthems ; A469
For soprano solo and mixed chorus (SATBB) unacc. — Words attrib. to Jón Arason. — Icelandic words, with English translation by the composer. Words also printed as text in Icelandic with transliteration and pronunciation guide.
Publ. no. A469
ISBN 0193505231
System number: 013359691

782.52651582
*White, Nicholas.
A baptism hymn : for unison choir, soprano descant and keyboard / Nicholas White. — [New York] : Oxford University Press, c2005. — 1 score (6 p.) ; 27 cm. — Oxford church music
First line: Be with us, our Father. — Includes biographical note.
ISBN 9780193868595
ISBN 0193868598
System number: 013472208

782.52651722
*Larsen, Libby.
Lord, before this fleeting season : an anthem for mixed choir (SATB), unaccompanied : for the First Sunday of Advent (A, B, C) / text by MaryAnn Jindra ; music by Libby Larsen. — [New York] : Oxford University Press, c2001. — 1 score (7 p.) ; 27 cm. — (Libby Larsen liturgical cycle)
Includes piano reduction for rehearsal only. — To complement the Revised Common Lectionary, Years A, B and C. — Includes biographical and programme notes.
ISBN 9780193864085
ISBN 0193864088
System number: 013472556

Parry, Ben.
Make we merry : SSAATTBB / Ben Parry. — London : Edition Peters, c2004. — 1 score (8 p.) ; 30 cm. — Kikapust choral series
Publisher's no.: Edition Peters no. 77019. — English words.
Publ. no. EP 77019
Publ. no. 77019
EAN M577085401
System number: 013304583

[Veni Emmanuel.]
O come, o come Emmanuel : SSAATTBB : arranged by Jonathan Rathbone. — London : Edition Peters, c2004. — 1 score (5 p.) ; 30 cm. — Kikapust choral series
15th century French melody. — "As recorded by the Swingle Singers on The story of Christmas." — Publisher's no.: Edition Peters no. 77008. — English words.
Publ. no. EP 77008
Publ. no. 77008
ISMN M577085463
System number: 013304602

782.52651723
*Dicie, Don Michael.
The burning babe : a Christmas anthem for unaccompanied mixed choir (SATB) / Don Michael Dicie. — [New York] : Oxford University Press, c2005. — 1 score (6 p.) ; 27 cm. — Oxford Christmas music
Words by Robert Southwell. — Includes biographical and composer's notes.
ISBN 9780193868939

ISBN 0193868938
System number: 013472523

782.527
Brikner, Eryk, 1705-1760.
[Completorium (RISM A/II 300.033.575)]
Completorium : a canto & basso obligato, alto & tenore ad libitum, due violini con organo ; Hymnus pro festis apostolorum : a canto, alto, tenore, basso con organo / Eryk Brikner ; opracowanie i wstęp Aleksandra Patalas. — Wyd. 1. — [Partytura] — Częstochowa : Klasztor OO. Paulinów Jasna Góra ; Kraków : Polskie Wydawn. Muzyczne, 2006. — 1 score (78 p.) : facsims. ; 31 cm. — (Muzyka Jasnogorska = Musica Claromontana ; 5)
For soprano and bass solo (contralto and tenor ad libitum), 2 violins and organ (Completorium) and for soprano, contralto, tenor, bass and organ (Hymnus pro festis apostolorum). — Figured bass unrealized. — Pref. and critical report in Polish and English. — Latin words, also printed separately for reference with Polish and English translation.
Publ. no. PWM 10 469
ISMN M274002558
System number: 013887063
Primary classification 782.526

Church hymnary. — 4th ed. — Full music. — Norwich : Canterbury Press, 2005. — 1 close score (cxv, unpaged) ; 22 cm.
Contains 825 psalm settings, hymns, worship songs and doxologies.
ISBN 1853116130
System number: 013217828

*Church hymnary. — 4th ed. — Melody [ed.] — Norwich : published on behalf of The Church Hymnary Trust by Canterbury Press, 2005. — 1 v. of music (xix, unpaged) ; 22 cm.
Contains melody lines, with chord symbols where appropriate, for 825 psalm settings, hymns, worship songs and doxologies.
ISBN 1853116149
System number: 013432918

Complete mission praise / compiled by Peter Horrobin and Greg Leavers — Music ed. — London : Collins, 2005. — 1 close score (unpaged) ; 25 cm.
1144 hymns and worship songs. — Includes chord symbols.
ISBN 0007193440
System number: 013028169

Lole, Simon.
For all thy saints, O Lord / music: Simon Lole ; words: Richard Mant. — Matfield : Encore Publications, c2005. — 1 score (4 p.) ; 26 cm.
For mixed voices (SATB) and organ.
System number: 013416381

*Lord of all hopefulness : for SATB chorus and organ / [arranged by] Barry Rose (2002). — London : Novello & Co, [2005?], c2002. — 1 score (5 p.) ; 25 cm.
"Irish trad., arr. Barry Rose" - caption. — Words by Jan Struther.
Publ. no. NOV955856
System number: 013505674

The Missouri harmony : or, a choice collection of psalm tunes, hymns, and anthems / [compiled] by Wings of Song. — 2005 ed. — [Saint Louis, Mo.] : Missouri Historical Society Press ; Distributed by University of Missouri Press, 2005. — 1 score (180 p.) ; 19 x 26 cm.
For mixed voices in 3-4 parts. — Shape-note notation. — Based partly on the early editions compiled by Allen D. Carden.
ISBN 1883982545
System number: 013307548

*Palestrina, Giovanni Pierluigi da, 1525?-1594.
[Hymni totius anni. Conditor alme siderum]
Two hymns for Advent and Christmas / Giovanni Pierluigi da Palestrina ; transcribed and edited by Jon Dixon. — Carshalton Beeches : JOED Music, c2002. — 1 score (22 p.) ; 30 cm. — Renaissance polyphonic choral music
For 6-part mixed chorus. — Source: 'Hymni totius anni', published Venice : Angelo Gardano, 1589. — Duration: 5:50 ; 6:45. — Latin words; English translation printed as text preceding each work.
Pl. no. JOED P129
System number: 013526329

*Polska pieśń wielogłosowa XVI i początku XVII wieku / zebrał i przygotował do druku = edited by Piotr Poźniak ; transkrypcja i opracowanie tekstów staropolskich = old Polish texts transcribed and annotated by Wacław Walecki. — Warszawa : Instytut Sztuki Polskiej Akademii Nauk ; Kraków : Instytut Muzykologii Uniwersytetu Jagiellońskiego : Musica Iagellonica, 2004. — 2 v. (370, 190 p.) : facsims. ; 32 cm. — Monumenta musicae in Polonia. Seria B
Polish polyphonic hymns and secular songs for 3-4 voices. — Introduction and editorial notes in Polish and English.
Pl. no. MI 0028
ISBN 8370991114
System number: 013277659
Also classified at 782.542

A selection of shape-note folk hymns : from Southern United States tune books, 1816-61 / edited by David W. Music. — Middleton, Wis. : A-R Editions, c2005. — 1 score (lvi, 89 p.) : facsims. ; 31 cm. — Recent researches in American music ; 52
Principally for 4 voices (SATB). — Includes pref. and critical report.
ISBN 0895795752
EAN 9780895795755
System number: 014619892

*Sibelius, Jean, 1865-1957.
[Finlandia. Hymni; *arr.*]
Be still, my soul : for mixed choir (SATB) and organ / [Jean Sibelius ; arr. by] Mack Wilberg. — [New York] : Oxford University Press, c2005. — 1 score (10 p.) ; 27 cm. — Oxford sacred music
Originally for mixed chorus (SATB) and orchestra with a secular patriotic text in Finnish; this ed. with a different text by Kathrina von Schelgel, translated into English by Jane Borthwick.
ISBN 0193868792
System number: 013571345

*Steffe, William, ca. 1830-1890.
The battle hymn of the Republic / [attributed to] William Steffe ; arr. John Hearne. — Inverurie : Longship, c2005. — 1 score (12 p.) ; 30 cm.
For SATB divisi with accompaniment of piano and percussion. — Words by Julia Ward Howe & others.
ISMN M900203694
System number: 013440370

Vaughan Williams, Ralph, 1872-1958.
[Old Hundredth Psalm tune; *arr.*]
The Old Hundreth Psalm tune : (All people that on earth do dwell) / R. Vaughan Williams (arr.) ; rescored by Roy Douglas for mixed choir (SATB), congregation, 3 trumpets, organ and optional timpani. — Oxford : Oxford University Press, [2005?], c1969. — 1 score (9 p.) ; 26 cm. + 4 parts ; 31 cm. — Oxford choral music
Originally with orchestral acc. — Words by W. Kethe (Daye's Psalter, 1560-1). — Reprint. Originally published: Oxford : Oxford University Press, c1969.
ISBN 019385029X
ISBN 9780193850293
System number: 013280400

782.52709429
*Y delyn aur : alaw gymreig : [arranged for SATB double chorus] / arr. John Hearne. — Inverurie : Longship, c2004. — 1 score (6 p.) ; 30 cm.
Words by William Williams, Pantycelyn. — Welsh words, also printed for reference with phonetic transcription and with English translation.
ISMN M900203687
System number: 013440356

782.5271727
McDowall, Cecilia.
Regina caeli : SATB (with divisions) a cappella / Cecilia McDowall. — Oxford : Oxford University Press, c2005. — 1 score (10 p.) : port. ; 26 cm. — (New horizons ; NH24)
Eastertide hymn. — Includes piano reduction for rehearsal only. — Includes biographical note. — Latin words.
Publ. no. NH24
ISBN 0193439220
ISBN 9780193439221
System number: 013213418

782.528
Jack Goodison's collection of local & traditional carols / [collected and compiled by Jack Goodison] — 4th ed., fully rev. and augm. — Derbyshire : Forgefolk on behalf of Rolling Stock Company, 2005. — 1 close score (116 p.) ; 30 cm.
88 carols, mainly for Christmas, as sung in the area north of Sheffield. — Arranged for SATB (hymnbook format). — First published 1992. — Includes introduction, historical notes and indexes. — Running title: The red book (Fourth edition)
ISMN M900298515
System number: 013358302

*World carols for choirs : 31 carols for mixed voices / edited and compiled by Bob Chilcott & Susan Knight. — Oxford : Oxford University Press, 2005. — 1 score (xvi, 221 p.) ; 25 cm.
Contains original carols and arrangements. — Mostly unacc.; many pieces have keyboard reductions for rehearsal only. — Pronunciation guide: p. 207-221. — Introduction contains notes on each carol. — Each piece is in the original language with English translation.
ISBN 019353231X
System number: 013334443

782.52815246
Nixon, June.
Harvest carol / text: W. Chatterton Dix ; music: June Dixon. — Matfield : Encore Publications, c2005. — 1 score (7 p.) ; 26 cm.
For mixed voices (SATB) and organ.
System number: 013382725

782.5281722
Ledger, Philip.
Advent carol : for unison voices and keyboard / Philip Ledger. — Matfield : Encore Publications, c2005. — 1 score (3 p.) ; 26 cm.
Words adapted from S. Baring-Gould's The angel Gabriel from heaven came.
System number: 013382713

*Voth, Ellen Gilson, 1972-
An Advent carol : for mixed choir (SATB) and keyboard / Ellen Gilson Voth. — [New York] : Oxford University Press, c2005. — 1 score (7 p.) ; 27 cm. — Oxford Advent music
First line: This Advent moon shines cold and clear. — Words by Christina Rossetti. — Includes biographical note.
ISBN 9780193868755
ISBN 019386875X
System number: 013472156

782.5281723
*The angel Gabriel : for mezzo-soprano with optional tenor solo, mixed choir (SATB) and harp / [Basque traditional ; arranged by] Robert A.M. Ross. — [New York] : Oxford University Press, c2005. — 1 score (11 p.) ; 27 cm. — Oxford church music
Words by Sabine Baring-Gould. — Includes biographical note about the arranger.
ISBN 9780193868700
ISBN 0193868709
System number: 013472203

As Joseph was a-walking : for mixed choir (SATB), oboe and organ / [traditional, arr.] Ian Brentnall. — [New York] : Oxford University Press, c2004. — 1 score (11 p.) ; 27 cm. — Oxford Christmas music
Oboe part printed following score (p. 11). — Includes biographical note.
ISBN 0193867826
System number: 013177896

*Bigler, Dwight.
[All you who are to mirth inclined; *arr.*]
All you who are to mirth inclined : for mixed choir (SATB), brass quintet and piano (with optional percussion) / [traditional English carol, arr.] Dwight Bigler. — [New York] : Oxford University Press, c2004. — 1 score (12 p.) ; 31 cm. — Oxford Christmas music
Original acc.: large brass choir, piano and percussion. — Includes biographical note.
ISBN 0193867753
System number: 013115013

Bingham, Judith.
God would be born in thee : carol for SATB & organ : (2004) / Judith Bingham ; text, Silesius Angelus. — Kenley : Maecenas Music, c2004. — 1 score (15 p.) ; 30 cm.
Duration: ca. 4:00. — Words in English and Latin; also provided for reference preceding score.
System number: 013193696

The boar's head carol : SSAATTBB / English traditional ; arranged by Ben Parry. — London : Edition Peters, c2004. — 1 score (3 p.) ; 30 cm. — Kikapust choral series
Publisher's no.: Edition Peters no. 77001. — English and Latin words.
Publ. no. EP 77001
Publ. no. 77001
ISMN M577085319
System number: 013304423

Carol medley : Deck the halls ; I saw three ships ; We wish you a merry Christmas ; The holly and the ivy ; The first nowell ; Past three o'clock : SSAATTBB (with optional organ part) / arranged by Jonathan Rathbone. — London : Edition Peters, c2004. — 1 score (10 p.) ; 30 cm. — Kikapust choral series
"As recorded by the Swingle Singers on The story of Christmas." — No organ part provided. — Publisher's no.: Edition Peters 77003.
Publ. no. EP 77003
Publ. no. 77003
ISMN M577084978
System number: 013304437
Primary classification 782.5241723

Chilcott, Bob.
And every stone shall cry : SATB unaccompanied / Bob Chilcott. — Oxford : Oxford University Press, c2005. — 1 score (11 p.) ; 26 cm. — Oxford carols
For SATB with divisions. — Includes piano reduction for rehearsal only. — Words by Richard Wilbur.
Publ. no. BC78
ISBN 0193433303
ISBN 9780193433304
System number: 013225229

Chilcott, Bob.
[And peace on earth. Put memory away. *Vocal score*]
Put memory away : SATB and piano / Bob Chilcott. — Oxford : Oxford University Press, c2005. — 1 score (8 p.) ; 26 cm. — Oxford carols
Words by Elizabeth Jennings. — "This is the fourth movement of 'And peace on earth', a Christmas cantata for female vocalist, children's choir, SATB choir, piano, bass, brass ensemble and percussion"—p. [2]
Publ. no. BC79
ISBN 019343370
ISBN 9780193433373
System number: 013225234

Coventry carol : SSAATTBB / arranged by Jonathan Rathbone. — London : Edition Peters, c2004. — 1 score (3 p.) ; 30 cm. — Kikapust choral series
"As recorded by the Swingle Singers on The story of Christmas." — Publisher's no.: Edition Peters no. 77004.
Publ. no. EP 77004
Publ. no. 77004
ISMN M577085326
System number: 013304460

*Cummings, William Hayman, 1831-1915.
[Hark! the herald angels sing ; *arr.*]
Hark! the herald angels sing : for mixed choir (SATB) and organ / [arranged by] Mack Wilberg. — [New York] : Oxford University Press, c2001. — 1 score (15 p.) ; 27 cm.
Music by F. Mendelssohn Bartholdy (from Festgesang), adapted as a carol by W.H. Cummings. — Words by Charles Wesley, altered.
Publ. no. 98.246
ISBN 0193864231
System number: 013515341

Dmitriev, Alexander I., 1961-
[Songs of Mary]
Two songs of Mary : for unaccompanied mixed choir (SATB) / Alexander Dmitriev. — [New York] : Oxford University Press, c2004. — 1 score (11 p.) ; 27 cm. — Oxford Christmas music
Includes piano reduction for rehearsal only. — Anonymous 15th century English words (1st song) and anonymous 17th century English words (2nd song). — Includes biographical note.
ISBN 0193867788
System number: 013177881

Un flambeau, Jeannette, Isabelle : SSAATTBB / French traditional ; arranged by Mark Williams. — London : Edition Peters, c2004. — 1 score (7 p.) ; 30 cm. — Kikapust choral series
"As recorded by the Swingle Singers on The story of Christmas." — Publisher's no.: Edition Peters no. 77014.
Publ. no. EP 77014
Publ. no. 77014
ISMN M577085449
System number: 013304730

Gabriel's message : SSAATTBB / arranged by Jonathan Rathbone. — London : Edition Peters, c2004. — 1 score (4 p.) ; 30 cm. — Kikapust choral series
"As recorded by the Swingle Singers on The story of Christmas." — Publisher's no.: Edition Peters no. 77005.
Publ. no. EP 77005
Publ. no. 77005
ISMN M577085364
System number: 013304479

Gruber, Franz Xaver, 1787-1863.
[Stille Nacht, heilige Nacht; *arr.*]
Silent night : SSAATTBB / Franz Gruber ; arranged by Jonathan Rathbone. — London : Edition Peters, c2004. — 1 score (3 p.) ; 30 cm. — Kikapust choral series
"As recorded by the Swingle Singers on The story of Christmas." — Publisher's no.: Edition Peters no. 77012.
Publ. no. EP 77012
Publ. no. 77012
ISMN M577085227
System number: 013304669

Gruber, Franz Xaver, 1787-1863.
[Stille Nacht, heilige Nacht; *arr.*]
Stille nacht : SATB : [music by Franz Gruber] ; arranged by Jonathan Rathbone. — London : Edition Peters, c2004. — 1 score (3 p.) ; 30 cm. — Kikapust choral series
Publisher's no.: Edition Peters no. 77011. — German words.
Publ. no. EP 77011
Publ. no. 77011
ISMN M577084961
System number: 013304656

He is born : [a setting of "Il est né"] : for mixed choir (SATB) and keyboard, with optional flute and oboe / [traditional French melody arr.] Don Michael Dicie. — [New York] : Oxford University Press, c2004. — 1 score (9 p.) + 2 parts ; 27 cm. — Oxford Christmas music
"The flute and oboe may be substituted with other C instruments"—P. [2] — Instrumental parts printed following score.
ISBN 0193867656
System number: 013177891

Hopkins, John H. (John Henry), 1820-1891.
[We three kings of Orient are; *arr.*]
We three kings : SATB / [words and music by J. H. Hopkins] ; arranged by Jonathan Rathbone. — London : Edition Peters, c2004. — 1 score (5 p.) ; 30 cm. — Kikapust choral series
Publisher's no.: Edition Peters no. 77021.
Publ. no. EP 77021
Publ. no. 77021
ISMN M577085074
System number: 013304743

Il est né le divin enfant : for unaccompanied mixed choir (SATB) / traditional French ; arr. Paul Carey. — [New York?] : Oxford University Press, c2005. — 1 score (13 p.) ; 27 cm. — Oxford Christmas Music
Includes piano reduction for rehearsal only. — Includes performance and biographical notes. — French words; English translation printed for reference preceding score.
ISBN 019386830X
System number: 013212287

[In dulci jubilo]
Good Christian men, rejoice : German carol In dulci jubilo arranged for mixed voices & organ / arranged by Philip Ledger. — Matfield : Encore Publications, [2005?], c1998. — 1 score (8 p.) ; 16 cm.
"Words: J.M. Neale"—Caption.
System number: 013382719

Infant holy, infant lowly : for mixed choir (SATB) and organ / [Polish carol ; arr.] Mack Wilberg. — [New York] : Oxford University Press, c2004. — 1 score (7 p.) ; 27 cm. — Oxford Christmas music
Words translated by Edith M.G. Reed.
ISBN 0193867966
System number: 013126609

It was Christmas to us : carol singing in Bamford through the 20th century / words, music and historical notes researched and transcribed by Joanna and Peter Mackey ; introduction by Ian Russell. — Bamford : Bamford Community Arts and Crafts, 2004. — 1 close score (69 p.) : ill., ports. ; 25 cm.
19 carols and hymns for SATB chorus, including six different settings of "While shepherds watched". — Cover title.
System number: 013178364

Jesus, Jesus, rest your head : for unaccompanied mixed choir (SATB) with baritone solo / [American folk carol ; arranged by] Lester Seigel. — [New York] : Oxford University Press, c2004. — 1 score (7 p.) ; 27 cm. — Oxford Christmas music
Includes piano reduction for rehearsal only.
ISBN 019386780X
ISBN 9780193867802
System number: 013126600

King's Singers Christmas. — Hal Leonard, c2004. [S.l.] : K'S the colour of song ; Milwaukee, Wis. : exclusively distributed by Hal Leonard, c2004. — 1 score (61 p.) ; 27 cm.
For mixed voices (SATB div.), unacc. Most works include piano reductions for rehearsal only. — Words in Latin, English, German or Spanish.
Publ. no. 08744049
ISBN 0634090445
System number: 013222165

Ledger, Philip.
Bethlehem : for unison voices & keyboard [and percussion] / Philip Ledger ; words by Richard Pomfret. — Matfield : Encore Publications, c2005. — 1 score (3 p.) ; 26 cm.
System number: 013225249

*Mason, Lowell, 1792-1872.
[Modern Psalmist. Antioch; *arr.*]
Joy to the world : for mixed choir (SATB) and keyboard / ['Antioch' by Lowell Mason ; arranged by] Mack Wilberg. — [New York] : Oxford University Press, c2001. — 1 score (15 p.) ; 27 cm. — Oxford Christmas music
Words by Isaac Watts. — Includes optional primo part that may be played by a second player up an octave on the same keyboard or in doubled octaves on a second keyboard.
ISBN 9780193864276
ISBN 0193864274
System number: 013472421

Masters in this hall : for two-part choir (equal or unequal voices), flute, oboe and keyboard / [traditional French carol, arr.] Don Michael Dicie. — [New York] : Oxford University Press, c2004. — 1 score (13 p.) + 2 parts ; 27 cm. — Oxford Christmas music
"The two-part choir may be composed with any pairing of voices (SATB)"—P. 2. — Instrumental parts printed following score. — Words by William Morris.
ISBN 0193867664
System number: 013177983

*Masters in this hall : for two-part choir (equal or unequal voices), flute, oboe and strings / [traditional French carol, arr.] Don Michael Dicie. — [New York] : Oxford University Press, c2004. — 1 score (11 p.) + 1 set of parts ; 28 cm. — Oxford Christmas music
"The two-part choir may be composed with any pairing of voices (SATB)"—P. [1] — Words by William Morris.
ISBN 0193867672
System number: 013196381

Mills, Alan, 1964-
The Lord at first did Adam make : for SATB chorus unaccompanied / Alan Mills. — Boston, Mass. : ECS Pub., c2007. — 1 score (12 p.) ; 28 cm.
Includes keyboard line for rehearsal only.
Publ. no. 6515
System number: 014052735

Parry, Ben.
And is it true? : SATB / Ben Parry ; [words by John Betjeman] — London : Edition Peters, c2004. — 1 score (3 p.) ; 30 cm. — Kikapust choral series
Publisher's no.: Edition Peters no. 77000.
Publ. no. EP 77000
Publ. no. 77000
ISMN M577085241
System number: 013304402

Quem pastores laudavere : SSAATTBB / German 14th century ; arranged by Jonathan Rathbone. — London : Edition Peters, c2004. — 1 score (3 p.) ; 30 cm. — Kikapust choral series
"As recorded by the Swingle Singers on The story of Christmas." — Publisher's no.: Edition Peters no. 77010.
Publ. no. EP 77010
Publ. no. 77010
ISMN M577085357
System number: 013304633

Raining bliss and benison : a collection of folk carols arranged for voices / compiled and arranged by Alison Burns ; illustrations by Denise Zygadlo. — Castle Douglas : Little Egg, c2005. — 1 score (42 p.) ; 30 cm.
For mixed chorus in 2-4 parts, with some rounds for equal voices. — Includes historical notes.
ISBN 0954101219
System number: 013383307

Rathbone, Jonathan.
The oxen : SAATTBB / Jonathan Rathbone ; [words by Thomas Hardy] — London : Edition Peters, c2004. — 1 score (3 p.) ; 30 cm. — Kikapust choral series
"As recorded by the Swingle Singers on The story of Christmas." — Publisher's no.: Edition Peters no. 77009.
Publ. no. EP 77009
Publ. no. 77009
ISMN M577085456
System number: 013304621

*Rentz, Earlene.
Lo, how a rose e'er blooming = (Es ist ein' Ros' entsprungen) : for mixed choir (SATB), flute and piano / [from Alte Catholische Geistliche Kirchengesang' (1599) harmonized by Michael Praetorius (1609) ; arranged by] Earlene Rentz. — [New York] : Oxford University Press, c2005. — 1 score (7 p.) ; 27 cm. — Oxford Christmas music
Words are an English translation by Theodore Baker of 15th-cent. German words. — Includes alternative modern words. — Flute part also printed separately following score.
ISBN 9780193868915
ISBN 0193868911
System number: 013472538

*Rutter, John, 1945-
[Carols. *Selections*]
Carols : 10 carols for mixed voices / John Rutter. — Oxford : Oxford University Press, 2005. — 1 score (64 p.) ; 26 cm.
For mixed voices (SATB), mostly with piano or organ acc. — Mostly English words.
ISBN 0193533812
System number: 013382232

Rutter, John, 1945-
[Rejoice and be merry. *Vocal score*]
Rejoice and be merry / John Rutter. — Oxford : Oxford University Press, c2004. — 1 score (12 p.) ; 27 cm.
For mixed voices (SATB), brass ensemble and optional organ and optional handbells; acc. arr. for piano. Vocal score includes the optional handbell part, which is also printed separately on p.12. — Words: English traditional.
Publ. no. X456
ISBN 0193468328
ISBN 9780193468320
System number: 013084320

Swayne, Giles.
[Christmas carols, op. 77]
Four Christmas carols : op. 77 / Giles Swayne. — London : Novello, c2005. — 1 score (21 p.) ; 25 cm. — Novello choral programme
For unison voices and piano (1st-3rd works) or mixed voices (SATB) and piano (4th work). — Includes composer's note. — The first three carols were previously published separately.
Publ. no. NOV050204
ISBN 1846091837
System number: 013336027

*Swayne, Giles.
The Coventry carol : op. 77 no. 4 : (2005) : for SATB chorus and piano / Giles Swayne. — London : Novello & Co, c2005. — 1 score (11 p.) ; 25 cm.
"Words: anon, 16th century" - caption.
Publ. no. NOV050193
System number: 013526387

Three carols for Christmas : for unaccompanied mixed choir (SATB). — [New York] : Oxford University Press, c2004. — 1 score (7 p.) ; 27 cm. — Oxford Christmas music
Words by Christina Rossetti (1st and 3rd works) and Angelus Silesius (2nd work).
ISBN 0193867699
System number: 013177887

*Timmermann, Leni, 1901-
[Weihnachtslieder]
Three Christmas carols = Drei Weihnachtslieder : gemischter Chor und Orgel (Klavier) / Leni Timmermann. — Solingen : Bergischer Musikverlag, [2004?] — 1 score (15 p.) ; 30 cm.
For mixed choir (SATB) and organ or piano. — English and German words; the last work includes version in French.
Pl. no. BM 300
ISMN M500323006
System number: 013019535

Tomorrow shall be my dancing day : SATB and organ / [English trad. arr.] Malcolm Pearce. — Oxford : Oxford University Press, c2005. — 1 score (10 p.) ; 26 cm. — (Christmas carols)
Publ. no. X461
ISBN 0193467755
ISBN 9780193467750
System number: 013225210

Warlock, Peter, 1894-1930.
[Carols, mixed voices, orchestra. *Vocal score*]
Three carols / by Peter Warlock. — New York ; Oxford : Oxford University Press, [2005?], c1923. — 1 score (16 p.) ; 27 cm. — Oxford choral songs ; OCS 251
For mixed voices (SATB). — Orchestral acc. arr. for piano.
Publ. no. OCS 251
ISBN 0193850672
ISBN 9780193850675
System number: 013424586

What child is this? : SSAATTBB / arranged by Jonathan Rathbone. — London : Edition Peters, c2004. — 1 score (8 p.) ; 30 cm. — Kikapust choral series
Publisher's no.: Edition Peters no. 77020.
Publ. no. EP 77020
Publ. no. 77020
ISMN M577085258
System number: 013304755

*Wilberg, Mack.
How far is it to Bethlehem? : for mixed choir (SATB), 2 flutes, and harp or piano / [English carol ; arranged by] Mack Wilberg. — [New York] : Oxford University Press, c2001. — 1 score (10 p.) ; 27 cm. — Oxford Christmas music
Words by Frances Chesterton. — Flute parts also printed separately following score.
ISBN 9780193864252
ISBN 0193864258
System number: 013472428

*Wilberg, Mack.
Masters in this hall : for mixed choir (SATB) and piano / [French carol ; arranged by] Mack Wilberg. — [New York] : Oxford University Press, c2001. — 1 score (19 p.) ; 27 cm. — Oxford Christmas music
Words by William Morris.
ISBN 9780193864290
ISBN 0193864290
System number: 013472417

*Wilberg, Mack.
Whence is that goodly fragrance flowing? : for mixed choir (SATB) and piano / [French carol ; arranged by] Mack Wilberg. — [New York] : Oxford University Press, c2001. — 1 score (11 p.) ; 27 cm. — Oxford Christmas music
English words; translated by A.B. Ramsay.
ISBN 9780193864320
ISBN 0193864320
System number: 013472410

Willcocks, David, 1919-
Starry night : SATB (with divisions) and organ / David Willcocks. — Oxford : Oxford University Press, c2005. — 1 score (11 p.) ; 26 cm. — (Christmans carols)
Words by Anne Willcocks. — Words in mixed English and Latin.
Publ. no. X460
ISBN 0193432722
ISBN 9780193432727
System number: 013243536

782.5294
Elsner, Józef, 1769-1854.
[Vespers, D major]
Nieszpory = Vespers : ex Officio majori Beatae Virginis Mariae ad Vesperas : a canto, alto, tenore, basso, due violini, viola, bassi (violoncello et basso), due flauti, due clarinetti, due corni, due clarini, timpani con organo / Jozef Elsner ; opracowanie Hubert Prochota ; wstęp Remigiusz Pośpiech. — Wyd. 1. — [Partytura] — Częstochowa : Klasztor OO. Paulinów Jasna Góra ; Kraków : Polskie Wydawn. Muzyczne, 2006. — 1 score (158 p.) ; facsims. ; 31 cm. — (Muzyka Jasnogorska = Musica Claromontana ; 6)
Preface and critical report in Polish and English. — Latin words, also printed separately for reference with Polish and English translation.
Publ. no. PWM 10 467
ISMN M274002534

EAN 9790274002534
System number: 013887069
Primary classification 782.5325

Guinjoan, Joan.
In tribulatione mea invocavi Dominum : per a cor i orquestra / Joan
Guinjoan. — 1a ed. — Barcelona : Tritó, 2006, c2000. — 1 score (88 p.) ;
34 cm.
For chorus and orchestra. — Preface and performance instructions in Catalan,
Spanish and English. — Duration: ca. 20:00. — Latin words, also printed for
reference with Catalan, Spanish and English translations.
Publ. no. TR 112
ISMN M692043171
System number: 013711562

*Head, Michael, 1900-1976.
[Psalms. I will lift up mine eyes; *arr.*]
I will lift up mine eyes : Psalm 121 ; for mixed voice choir with organ or
piano / by Michael Head ; arranged by Antonín Tučapský. — Tewkesbury :
Roberton Publications, a part of Goodmusic Publishing, c2005. — 1 score
(8 p.) ; 26 cm.
Originally for solo voice with organ or piano. — Duration: 2:45.
Publ. no. 85190
ISMN M222263222
System number: 013554436

*Head, Michael, 1900-1976.
[Psalms. Make a joyful noise unto the Lord; *arr.*]
Make a joyful noise unto the Lord : Psalm 100 : (SATB) / Michael Head ;
arranged by Antonín Tučapský. — Tewkesbury : Roberton Publications, a
part of Goodmusic Publishing, c2005. — 1 score (8 p.) ; 26 cm.
With piano or organ accompaniment. — Originally for solo voice with organ or
piano.
Publ. no. 85191
ISMN M222263239
System number: 013554372

*Palestrina, Giovanni Pierluigi da, 1525?-1594.
[Motets (1572). Laudate Dominum omnes gentes]
Laudate Dominum omnes gentes : (SATB+SATB) / Giovanni Pierluigi da
Palestrina ; transcribed and edited by Jon Dixon. — Carshalton Beeches :
JOED Music, c2004. — 1 score (10 p.) ; 30 cm. — Renaissance polyphonic
choral music
"A vesper psalm which sets the full text of Psalm 117"—Pref. — Source: Printed
part books, published Venice : Girolamo Scotto, 1572. — Cover title. — Duration:
3:00. — Latin words; English translation printed as text preceding score.
Pl. no. JOED P157
System number: 013526028

*Palestrina, Giovanni Pierluigi da, 1525?-1594.
[Motets (1572). Laudate pueri]
Laudate pueri Dominum : SATB+SATB / Giovanni Pierluigi da Palestrina ;
transcribed and edited by Jon Dixon. — Carshalton Beeches : JOED Music,
c2004. — 1 score (20 p.) ; 30 cm. — Renaissance polyphonic choral music
"A vesper psalm which sets the full text of Psalm 113"—Pref. — Source: Printed
part books, published Venice : Girolamo Scotto, 1572. — Duration: 6:52. — Latin
words; English translation provided for reference preceding score.
Pl. no. JOED P141
System number: 013526040

*Palestrina, Giovanni Pierluigi da, 1525?-1594.
[Motets (1575). Jubilate Deo omnis terra, voices (8)]
Iubilate Deo : SATB+SATB / Giovanni Pierluigi da Palestrina ; transcribed
and edited by Jon Dixon. — Carshalton Beeches : JOED Music, c2005. —
1 score (14 p.) ; 30 cm. — Renaissance polyphonic choral music
Source: 'Mottetorum … liber tertius', published Venice : erede di Girolamo Scotto,
1575. — Cover title. — Duration: 4:00. — Latin words from Psalm 100; English
translation printed as text preceding score.
Pl. no. JOED P165
System number: 013498162

*Piccolo, Anthony, 1946-
O come, let us sing unto the Lord = (Venite, exultemus Domino) / Anthony
Piccolo ; [words], Psalm 95:1-7. — New York ; Oxford : Oxford University
Press, [2005?], c1980. — 1 score (7 p.) ; 27 cm. — Oxford anthems ; A 329
For mixed voices (SATB) and organ. — Reprint. Originally published: London :
Oxford University Press, 1980. — English words.
Publ. no. A 329
ISBN 0193851075
System number: 013441837

*Schütz, Heinrich, 1585-1672.
[Psalmen Davids (1619). 100. Psalm. *Italian & German*]
Salmo 100 : per doppio coro a voci miste o per coro e quartetto di ottoni :
Lodi al Signore = "Jauchzet dem Herren" / Heinrich Schütz ; revisione e
versione italiana di Davide Liani. — Udine, Italy : Pizzicato edizioni
musicali, c2003. — 1 score (10 p.) ; 31 cm.
For 2 SATB choruses, unacc. — Italian and German words also printed for reference.
Publ. no. N. 394
System number: 014766580

Shields, Valerie.
Psalm 124: a song of deliverance : [for unison treble voices, SAB chorus
& piano] / by Valerie Shields. — [New York?] : Boosey & Hawkes ;
Milwaukee : exclusively distributed by Hal Leonard, c2005. — 1 score
(12 p.) ; 27 cm. — (CME conductor's choice) — (Doreen Rao's choral
music experience)
Text adapted by Valerie Shields. — Includes biographical and programme notes.
Publ. no. 48018857
ISMN M051475681
System number: 013312831

*Tallis, Thomas, ca. 1505-1585.
[Psalm tunes]
8 tunes for Archbishop Parker's psalter / Thomas Tallis ; transcribed and
edited by Jon Dixon. — Carshalton Beeches : JOED Music, 2004, c1993.
— 1 score (10 p.) ; 30 cm. — Renaissance polyphonic choral music
For mixed voices (SATB), unacc. — Source: British Library, John Daye's Psalter,
1567. — Duration: 0:50 ; 0:40 ; 0:47 ; 0:54 ; 0:46 ; 0:49 ; 0:39 ; 0:40. — English
words from Matthew Parker's metrical translation of the psalms.
Pl. no. JOED T17
System number: 013525858

*Zelenka, Johann Dismas, 1679-1745.
[Miserere, ZWV 56, D minor]
Misere d-Moll, ZWV 56, für Soli (SATB), Chor (SATB), 2 Oboen, 3
Posaunen, 2 Violinen, 2 Violen und Basso continuo / Jan Dismas
Zelenka ; herausgegeben von Stephan Thamm. — Partitur. — Beeskow :
Ortus, c2005. — 1 score (xxiii, 58 p.) : facsim. ; 30 cm. — Musik aus
der Dresdner Hofkirche ; Bd. 4
For soloists (SATB), chorus (SATB) and instrumental ensemble; with unrealized
figured bass. — Pref. in German with English translation; critical commentary in
German. — Latin words, also printed for reference with German translation.
Publ. no. om 32/1
ISMN M700150839
System number: 013775682

782.5295

Tavener, John.
[Lord's prayer (1982). *Slavonic & English*]
The Lord's prayer : versions in English and Slavonic : (1982) : for SATB
chorus / John Tavener. — London : Chester Music, c2003. — 1 score
(5 p.) ; 25 cm. — Contemporary church music series
Slavonic version has romanized text. Includes pronunciation guide.
Publ. no. CH55782
System number: 013222679

782.52951587

Rutter, John, 1945-
Wedding canticle : (Blessed are all they that fear the Lord) / John Rutter.
— Oxford : Oxford University Press, c2004. — 1 score (16 p.) ; 26 cm.
— (Anthems ; A473)
For mixed voices (SATB) with flute and guitar; includes alternative acc. for piano
(preferably for rehearsal use only). — Words from Psalm 128.
Publ. no. Oxford University Press
ISBN 0193505266
System number: 013122839

782.53232

Altnikol, Johann Christoph, 1719-1759.
[Mass, D minor]
Missa d : Kyrie-Gloria-Messe in d : per soli (SATB), coro (SATB), 2
violini, viola e basso continuo / Johann Christoph Altnickol ;
herausgegeben von Clemens Harasim. — Erstausg. — Partitur. —
Stuttgart : Carus, c2007. — 1 score (56 p.) ; 30 cm.
"Urtext." — Figured bass realized for keyboard instrument. — Duration: ca.
17:00. — Preface in German, with English and French abridged translations;
critical report in German (p. 54-56) — Latin words.
Publ. no. 27.068
Publ. no. CV 27.068
ISMN M007090692
System number: 013887057

*Aston, Hugh, b. ca. 1485.
[Missa Te Deum]
Missa Te deum laudamus / Hugh Aston ; edited by Nick Sandon. —
Moretonhampstead : Antico Edition, [2004], c2001. — 1 score (viii,
48 p.) : facsim. ; 30 cm. — (Renaissance church music ; 27)
For 5-part choir (treble, mean, contratenor, tenor, bass), unacc. — Cover title. —
Pref. includes biographical notes, performance suggestions and critical
commentary. — Latin words.
Pl. no. RCM27
System number: 013087141

Bach, Johann Sebastian, 1685-1750.
[Masses, BWV 232, B minor]
Messe in h-Moll, BWV 232 : mit Sanctus in D-Dur (1724), BWV 232[III] / Johann Sebastian Bach ; commentary by Christoph Wolff. — Limitierte ed. — Kassel ; London : Bärenreiter, c2007. — 1 score (188, 19, xxxvii, [7] p.) ; 36 cm. — (Faksimile-Reihe Bachscher Werke und Schriftstücke / herausgegeben vom Bach-Archiv Leipzig ; n.F., Bd. 2) — (Documenta musicologica. Zweite Reihe, Handschriften-Faksimiles ; Bd. 35)
For solo voices, chorus, and orchestra. — Facsimile reproduction of the autograph score from the Staatsbibliothek zu Berlin - Preussischer Kulturbesitz. Includes facsimile of an early version of the Sanctus in D major and selected pages from the 1924 Leipzig facsimile. — Commentary by Christoph Wolff in German with English and Japanese translations, p. ii-xxxvii. — Publisher's no. from supplier's information slip. — Latin words.
Publ. no. BVK 1911
ISBN 9783761819111
System number: 014048771

Bartoli, Giuseppe, 1739-1801.
Messa a tre voci con stromenti / Giuseppe Bartoli. — Erstausg. / [herausgegeben] von Klaus-Norbert Kremers. — Partitur. — Köln : Dohr, c2007. — 1 score (101 p.) ; 30 cm.
For SAB chorus, 2 violins and cello (continuo). — Preface and critical report in German. — Partially figured bass, unrealized. — Edited from a manuscript in the possession of the editor. — Latin words.
Pl. no. E.D. 27432
ISMN M202014325
System number: 013887060

***Bennett, Richard Rodney.**
Missa brevis / Richard Rodney Bennett. — London : Novello, c2004. — 1 score (30 p.) ; 25 cm.
For mixed voices (SATB), unacc. — Includes piano reduction for rehearsal only. — Latin words.
Publ. no. NOV290711
ISBN 1844497577
System number: 013218330

Bruckner, Anton, 1824-1896.
[Masses, no. 3, F minor]
Messe f-Moll / [Anton Bruckner] — Kritische Neuasgabe / unter Berücksichtigung der Arbeiten von Robert Haas und Leopold Nowak ; vorgelegt von Paul Hawkshaw. — Studienpartitur. — Wien : Musikwissenschaftlicher Verlag der Internationalen Bruckner-Gesellschaft, 2005. — 1 miniature score (xv, 248 p.) ; 23 cm. — (Sämtliche Werke / Anton Bruckner ; Bd. 18)
For solo voices (SATB), chorus (SATB) and orchestra. — Pref. in German and English. — At head of title: Österreichische Nationalbibliothek in Wien. — Series published under the general editorship of the Österreichische Nationalbibliothek and the Internationale Bruckner-Gesellschaft. — The 1893 version, with variants from the 1883 version printed at the bottom of the appropriate pages. — Latin words.
ISMN M500252511
ISMN 979500252511
System number: 014654474

Centorio, Marco Antonio, d. 1638.
Messa a sei voci / Marco Antonio Centorio; a cura di Marco Romagnoli. — Lucca : Libreria Musicale Italiana, c2006. — 1 score (xiv, 53 p.) : facsims. ; 32 cm. — (Corona di delizie musicali : Collana di musiche degli Antichi Stati Sabaudi e del Piemonte ; 8)
For six voices. — Extensive preface and critical report in Italian. — Latin words.
ISBN 9788870964684
ISBN 887096468X
EAN 9788870964684
System number: 013688124

Dicie, Don Michael.
Gloria in excelsis : for unaccompanied mixed choir (SATB) / Don Michael Dicie. — [New York] : Oxford University Press, c2004. — 1 score (7 p) ; 27 cm. — Oxford church music
Includes composer's and biographical notes. — Latin words.
ISBN 0193867648
ISBN 9780193867642
System number: 013115451

***Dvořák, Antonín, 1841-1904.**
[Masses, B. 175, D major. *Vocal score*]
Mass in D major : op. 86 : for soprano, alto, tenor and bass soloists, SATB and organ, or SATB (with optional soloists) and orchestra = Mše D dur / Antonín Dvořák ; edited by Michael Pilkington. — London : Novello, [2005], c2000. — 1 score (vii, 71 p.) : facsim. ; 28 cm. — New Novello choral edition
Acc. arr. for organ. — Supersedes the vocal score published by Novello in 1893 with acc. arr. by Berthold Tours from Dvořák's orchestral version. — "Designed to be used for performance with either the 1887 organ version or the 1892 orchestral version"—Pref. — Pref. and critical commentary in English. — Latin words.
Publ. no. NOV 072491
ISBN 085360990X
System number: 013528269

Eberlin, Johann Ernst, 1702-1762.
Missa septimi toni : für Soli, SATB, Streicher und Orgel / Johann Ernst Eberlin ; herausgegeben von Konrad Führlinger und Friedrich Hägele. — Erstausg. — Partitur. — Sankt Augustin : Butz, 2007. — 1 score (28 p.) ; 30 cm.
Figured bass realized for organ and violoncello. — Foreword in German. — Latin words.
Publ. no. 2034
System number: 013887067

Elsner, Józef, 1769-1854.
[Masses, F major]
Missa F a canto, alto, tenore, basso, due violini, viole, bassi (violoncello et basso), due clarinetti, due corni con organo / Józef Elsner ; opracowanie, Hubert Prochota ; wstęp, Remigiusz Pośpiech ; [redaktor, Irena Stachel] — [Partytura] — Kraków : Polskie Wydawn. Muzyczne ; Częstochowa : Klasztor OO. Paulinów Jasna Góra, 2005. — 1 score (165 p.) : facsims. ; 31 cm. — (Muzyka Jasnogórska = Musica claromontana ; 3)
Edited from a ms. in the Jasna Góra archives (ref. num. III-195). — Includes pref. and critical commentary in English and Polish. — Latin words; also printed separately for reference with English and Polish translations.
Pl. no. PWM 10 436
ISMN M274002152
EAN 9790274002152
System number: 013887068

Fifteenth-century liturgical music V, Settings of the Sanctus and Agnus dei / transcribed and edited by Peter Wright. — London : Published for the British Academy : Stainer and Bell, c2006. — 1 score (167 p.) ; 33 cm. — Early English church music ; 47
ISBN 9780852498842
ISBN 0852498845
ISMN M220221255
System number: 013701476

Guilmant, Alexandre, 1837-1911.
[Masses, mixed voices, organ, no. 3, op. 11, E♭ major]
3me messe solennelle : op. 11 : für Soli, Chor und Orgel / Felix-Alexandre Guilmant ; herausgegeben von Martin Sokoll. — Sankt Augustin : Butz, 2006. — 1 score (87 p.) ; 30 cm.
For solists (STBarB), chorus (SATB) and organ. — Pref. and critical report in German. — Latin words.
Publ. no. 1969
System number: 013887074

Heinichen, Johann David, 1683-1729.
[Masses, S. 5, D major]
Missa Nr. 9 in D : für Soli SATB, Chor SATB, 2 flauti, 2 oboi, fagotto, 2 corni, 2 trombe, timpani, 2 violini, viola, violoncello, contrabasso, organo / Johann David Heinichen. — Erstausg. / herausgegeben von Katrin Bemmann. — Partitur. — Stuttgart : Carus-Verlag, c2005. — 1 score (ix, 159 p.) ; 30 cm.
Preface in German, English and French; critical report in German. — Latin words.
Publ. no. CV 27.048
Pl. no. 27.048
ISMN M007075958
System number: 013635330

***[Lambeth choirbook.]**
The Arundel choirbook : London, Lambeth Palace Library, MS 1 : a facsimile and introduction / introduction by David Skinner. — [Huddersfield] : Roxburghe Club, 2003. — 26 p., [95] leaves of music : col. facsims. ; 43 cm.
Full colour facsimile of the manuscript original in the Lambeth Palace Library. — Contains music by Robert Fayrfax, Nicholas Ludford, and their contemporaries. — Privately typeset, printed and bound for the members of the Roxburghe Club by the Charlesworth Group, Huddersfield. — The facsimile pages, printed on the recto and verso of each leaf, are numbered from 0r to 94v.
ISBN 0954509005
ISBN 9780954509002
System number: 013216740

Leibl, Carl, 1784-1870.
[Masses, no. 3, E♭ major. *Vocal score*]
Messe Nr. 3 Es-Dur / Carl Leibl ; herausgegeben von Eberhard Metternich ; mit einem einführenden Text von Oliver Sperling ; Klavierauszug. — Erstdruck. — Köln : Dohr, 2007. — 1 score (136 p.) ; 27 cm. — Denkmäler rheinischer Musik ; Bd. 29a
Mass for SATB soloists, SATB chorus and orchestra; acc. arr. for piano. — Pref. in German. — Latin words.
Pl. no. E.D. 25287
ISMN M202012871
System number: 013801668

Liberto, Giuseppe.
Missa "Pie Iesu Domine" : in exsequiis Ioannis Pauli PP. II / Giuseppe Liberto. — Città del Vaticano : Libreria editrice vaticana, c2005. — 1 score (46 p.) ; 30 cm. — Collana Liturgica poliphonia ; 5
For SATB chorus, unacc. — Funeral mass for Pope John Paul II. — Includes pref. in Italian. — Latin words.
ISBN 882097757S
ISBN 9788820977573
System number: 013750206

*Ludford, Nicholas, ca. 1490-1557.
[Vocal music. *Selections*]
Five- and six-part Masses ; and, Magnificat / [Nicholas Ludford] ;
transcribed and edited by David Skinner. — London : Published for the
British Academy by Stainer and Bell, c2005. — 1 score (xii, 240 p.) ;
33 cm. — Early English church music, 0424-0359 ; 46 — (Nicholas
Ludford ; 2)
The Magnificat for 6 voices. — Includes editorial notes and critical commentary. —
Latin words.
ISBN 0852498756
ISMN M220220463
System number: 013433942
Also classified at 782.5326

La misa policoral en Cataluña en la segunda mitad del siglo XVII /
introducción, estudio y transcripción, Francesc Bonastre. — Barcelona :
Consejo Superior de Investigaciones Científicas, Institución "Milà i
Fontanals", Departamento de Musicología, 2005. — 1 score (351 p.) ;
33 cm. — Monumentos de la música española ; 73
For 8-15 voices, unacc. — Editorial, historical and critical commentary in Spanish
on p. [13]-119. — Historical commentary in Spanish, Catalan and English on p.
[7]-43; critical commentary and catalogue of works in Spanish on p. [44]-74. —
Latin words.
ISBN 8400083970
ISMN M73442006
System number: 013812474

Mozart, Wolfgang Amadeus, 1756-1791.
[Masses, K. 427, C minor]
Missa in c, KV 427 (417a), per soli (SSTB), coro (SATB), flauto, 2 oboi, 2
fagotti, 2 corni, 2 clarini, 3 tromboni, timpani, 2 violini, viola e basso
continuo (Violoncello / contrabbasso, organo) / Wolfgang Amadeus
Mozart ; ergänzt und herausgegeben von Robert D. Levin. — Partitur = Full
score. — Stuttgart : Carus, c2005. — 1 score (x, 290 p.) ; 33 cm. —
(Stuttgarter Mozart-Ausgaben)
For soloists (SSTB), chorus (SATB), and orchestra. — Foreword and note to edition
by Robert D. Levin in German and English. — Duration: ca. 80:00. — Latin words.
Pl. no. Carus 51.427
Publ. no. 51.427
ISMN M007076122
System number: 013728835

*Palestrina, Giovanni Pierluigi da, 1525?-1594.
[Masses, book 3. Missa de Beata Virgine]
Missa de Beata Virgine : [SSATTB] / Giovanni Pierluigi da Palestrina ;
transcribed and edited by Jon Dixon. — Carshalton Beeches : JOED Music,
c2004. — 1 score (62 p.) ; 30 cm. — Renaissance polyphonic choral music
Source: Third book of masses, published Rome : Eredi di Valerio & Aloysio Dorico,
1570. — Duration: 30:54. — Latin words.
Pl. no. JOED P63
System number: 013498043

*Palestrina, Giovanni Pierluigi da, 1525?-1594.
Missa confitebor tibi Domine : [SATB+SATB] / Giovanni Pierluigi da
Palestrina ; transcribed and edited by Jon Dixon. — Carshalton Beeches :
JOED Music, 2004, c2001. — 1 score (76 p.) ; 30 cm. — Renaissance
polyphonic choral music
Source: part books, published Venice : erede di Girolamo Scotto, 1585. — Duration:
26:20. — Latin words.
Pl. no. JOED P23
System number: 013498037

*Palestrina, Giovanni Pierluigi da, 1525?-1594.
Missa fratres ego enim accepi : [SATB+SATB] / Giovanni Pierluigi da
Palestrina ; transcribed and edited by Jon Dixon. — Carshalton Beeches :
JOED Music, c2005. — 1 score (68 p.) ; 30 cm. — Renaissance polyphonic
choral music
Source: 'Missae quatuor octonis vocibus concinendae', published Venice : Riccardio
Amadino, 1601. — Duration: 26:43. — Latin words.
Pl. no. JOED P97
System number: 013498057

*Palestrina, Giovanni Pierluigi da, 1525?-1594.
Missa Hodie Christus natus est : [SSAB+ATTB] / Giovanni Pierluigi da
Palestrina ; transcribed and edited by Jon Dixon. — Carshalton Beeches :
JOED Music, c2005. — 1 score (52 p.) ; 30 cm. — Renaissance polyphonic
choral music
Source: 'Missae quatuor octonis vocibus concinendae', published Venice : Riccardio
Amadino, 1601. — Duration: 24:20. — Latin words.
Pl. no. JOED P3
System number: 013498024

*Palestrina, Giovanni Pierluigi da, 1525?-1594.
[Missa Laudate Dominum omnes gentes]
Missa Laudate Domine : [SATB+SATB] / Giovanni Pierluigi da Palestrina ;
transcribed and edited by Jon Dixon. — Carshalton Beeches : JOED Music,
c2004. — 1 score (66 p.) ; 30 cm. — Renaissance polyphonic choral music
Source: 'Missae quatuor octonis vocibus concinendae, ' published Venice :
Riccardio Amadino, 1601. — Duration: 29:52. — Latin words.
Pl. no. JOED P95
System number: 013498052

Panufnik, Roxanna, 1968-
Westminster mass : for soprano, mixed choir, tubular bells, harp and
organ : (1997) / Roxanna Panufnik. — Vienna ; London : Universal
Edition, c2003. — 1 score (57 p.) ; 31 cm.
Biographical note on p. [4] of cover. — Mostly English words.
Pl. no. UE 70111
ISBN 9783702432355
ISMN M008078316
System number: 014053350

Rathgeber, Valentin, 1682-1750.
[Missale tum rurale tum civile. Missa brevis, B flat major]
Missa brevis in B : für Soli (SATB), SATB, Streicher und Orgel / Johann
Valentin Rathgeber ; herausgegeben von Friedrich Hägele ; Orgelstimme
von Hermann Angstenberger. — Orchesterpartitur. — Sankt Augustin :
Butz, 2007. — 1 score (40 p.) ; 30 cm.
Latin words. — Preface and biographical notes in German.
Publ. no. 2027
System number: 013953480

Ryba, Jakub Jan, 1765-1815.
[Missa pastoralis, C major]
Missa pastoralis in C : in Nativitate Domini in nocte : per soli SATB, coro
SATB, fagotto solo, clarino solo, 2 violini e basso continuo / Jakub Jan
Ryba ; herausgegeben von Karlheinz Ostermann ; Generalbassaussetzung
von Paul Horn. — Erstausg. — Partitur. — Stuttgart : Carus, c2006. — 1
score (43 p.) ; 30 cm.
For SATB (chorus and soloists) with chamber orchestra. — Figured bass realized
for organ. — Pref. by the editor in English and German, and critical commentary
in German. — Duration: ca. 16:00. — Latin words.
Pl. no. 40.683
Publ. no. CV 40.683
ISMN M007087319
EAN 9790007087319
System number: 013832392

*Tallis, Thomas, ca. 1505-1585.
[Mass, voices (4)]
Mass for four voices / Thomas Tallis ; transcribed and edited by Jon
Dixon. — [Rev. ed.] — Carshalton Beeches : JOED Music, [2004?],
c1994. — 1 score (28 p.) ; 30 cm. — Renaissance polyphonic choral
music
For mixed voices (SATB) unacc. — "Music transposed into modern clefs and up
a fifth to a pitch suitable for modern SATB choirs"—Pref. — A plainsong troped
Kyrie (Kyrie omnipotens Pater) has been included to provide a basis for liturgical
performance. — Source: London, British Library, Add. Mss. 17802-5. —
Duration: 21:50. — Latin words; English translation of Kyrie omnipotens Pater
printed as text at the beginning of it.
Pl. no. JOED T11
System number: 013525964

*Tallis, Thomas, ca. 1505-1585.
[Missa Salve intemerata virgo]
Mass, Salve intemerata / Thomas Tallis ; transcribed and edited by Jon
Dixon. — [Rev. ed.] — Carshalton Beeches : JOED Music, [2005?],
c1991. — 1 score (36 p.) ; 30 cm. — Renaissance polyphonic choral
music
For mixed voices (SATBB) unacc. — Caption title: Missa Salve intemerata. —
Source: Cambridge, Peterhouse mss. 40, 41, 31, 32. — A plainsong troped Kyrie
(Kyrie fons bonitatis) has been included to provide a basis for liturgical
performance. — Duration: 21:50. — Latin words.
Pl. no. JOED T5
System number: 013526358

*Tortamano, Nicola.
[Masses. *Selections*]
Messa a due cori e messe a quattro voci con basso continuo / Nicola
Tortamano ; edizione critica a cura di Alberto Mammarella. — Lucca :
Libreria Musicale Italiana, c2005. — 1 score (135 p.) : facsims. ; 34 cm.
— Didattica della filologia musicale ; 4 — (I testi ; II - 2005)
Figured bass unrealized. — Pref. and critical commentary in Italian. — Latin
words.
ISBN 8870964264
System number: 014629768

Tres missae super "Quem dicunt homines" / edidit Harry Elzinga. —
Middleton, Wis. : American Institute of Musicology, c2006. — 1 score
(xxxiv, 112 p.) ; 35 cm. — Corpus mensurabilis musicae ; 81 — (Opera
omnia / Johannes Richafort ; IV)
Three masses based upon Jean Richafort's motet 'Quem dicunt homines'. — For
4 voices unacc. (1st and 2nd works), or 5 voices unacc. (3rd work). — Editorial
and critical notes in English. — Latin words.
Pl. no. CMM 81-4
ISBN 9781595513496
ISBN 1595513493
System number: 013718230

Victoria, Tomás Luis de, ca. 1548-1611.
[Masses (1583). Missa O quam gloriosum]
Missa O Quam gloriosum (SATB) ; Motet, O quam gloriosum est regnum (SATB) / Tomás Luis de Victoria ; transcribed and edited by Andrew Parker. — London : Novello, c2005. — 1 score (30 p.) ; 26 cm. — (Masses and motets / Tomás Luis de Victoria)
Includes piano reduction for rehearsal only. — Includes introductory essay "Victoria and his publications" by the editor. — List of sources and editorial notes on p. 30. — Latin words.
Publ. no. NOV020713
ISBN 1846091853
System number: 013335998
Also classified at 782.526

Victoria, Tomás Luis de, ca. 1548-1611.
[Missae, Psalmi, Magnificat, ad Virginem Dei Matrem salutiones, aliaque. Missa Dum complerentur]
Missa Dum complerentur (SAATTB) ; Motet, Dum complerentur dies Pentecostes (SSATB) / Tomás Luis de Victoria ; transcribed and edited by Andrew Parker. — London : Novello, c2005. — 1 score (69 p.) ; 26 cm. — (Masses and motets / Tomás Luis de Victoria)
Includes piano reduction for rehearsal only. — Includes introductory essay "Victoria and his publications" by the editor. — List of sources and editorial notes on p. 69. — Latin words.
Publ. no. NOV020691
ISBN 1846091845
System number: 013335980
Also classified at 782.526

Żebrowski, Marcin Józef.
[Masses, D major (RISM A/II 300.033.496)]
Missa ex D a canto, basso, due violini, due clarini ad libitum con organo / Marcin Józef Żebrowski ; opracowanie i wstęp Remigiusz Pośpiech. — Wyd. 1. — [Partytura] — Częstochowa : Klasztor OO. Paulinów Jasna Góra ; Kraków : Polskie Wydawn. Muzyczne, 2006. — 1 score (105 p.) : facsims. ; 31 cm. — (Muzyka Jasnogorska = Musica Claromontana ; 4)
Pref. and critical report in Polish and English. — Latin words, also printed separately for reference with Polish and English translations.
Publ. no. PWM 10 465
ISMN M274002510
System number: 013953492

Żebrowski, Marcin Józef.
Missa pastoralis : a canto, basso, due violini, due clarini con organo / Marcin Józef Żebrowski ; opracowanie i wstęp Remigiusz Pośpiech ; [redaktor, Irena Stachel] — Partytura. — Częstochowa : Klasztor OO. Paulinów Jasna Góra ; Kraków : Polskie Wydawn. Muzyczne, 2005. — 1 score (90 p.) : facsims ; 31 cm. — (Muzyka Jasnogórska = Musica claromontana ; 1)
With unrealized figured bass. — Based on an ms. in the archives of the Paulite Fathers at Jasna Góra (ref. num. III-745). — Program notes by Andrzej Kosowski, Father Nikodem Kilnar and Remigiusz Pośpiech, and critical commentary in English and Polish. — Latin words, also printed for reference with English and Polish translations.
Pl. no. PWM 10 415
ISMN M274002138
EAN 9790274002138
System number: 013953493

*Zechlin, Ruth, 1926-2007.
[Missa in honorem Sancti Stephani]
Missa in honorem Sancti Stephani : für 4 Solisten, 4-16-stimmigen Chor, grosses Orchester und Orgel / Ruth Zechlin. — Manuskript-Edition. — Partitur. — Berlin : Ries & Erler, c2005. — 1 score (104 p.) ; 30 cm.
Preface in German. — Duration: ca. 50:00. — Reproduced from holograph. — Latin words.
ISMN M013511457
System number: 014629795

*Zelenka, Johann Dismas, 1679-1745.
Missa Sanctae Caeciliae : für Soprano, Alt, Tenor, Bass, Chor, 2 Oboen, Fagott, Streicher & B.c. / Jan Dismas Zelenka ; herausgegeben von Martin Kellhuber. — Erstausg. — Magdeburg : Edition Walhall, c2005. — 1 score (xi, 94 p.) ; 31 cm. — Sacri concentus Ratisbonenses
Chorus: SATB. — Figured bass unrealized. — Pref. in German and English. — Duration: ca. 45:00. — Errata slip tipped in. — Latin words, also printed separately for reference, with German translation, p. [ii]-[iii]
Pl. no. EW 409
System number: 013631618

782.53235
*Dvořák, Antonín, 1841-1904.
[Stabat Mater, op. 58, D major]
Stabat mater : für Soli, Chor und Orchester = for soloists, chorus and orchestra : op. 58 / Antonín Dvořák ; herausgegeben von Klaus Döge. — Wiesbaden : Breitkopf & Härtel, c2004. — 1 score (237 p.) ; 32 cm. — (Breitkopf & Härtel Partitur Bibliothek ; Nr. 5361)
For mixed solo voices (SATB), mixed chorus (SATB) and orchestra. — Duration: ca. 1:25:00. — Preface in German and English ; kritischer Bericht in German. — Latin words.
Pl. no. PB 5361
Publ. no. 5361
ISMN M004211441
System number: 013113504

*Tropi proprii missae / editor Hana Vlhova-Wörner. — Praha : Editio Bärenreiter, c2004. — 175 p. of music : facsims. ; 30 cm. — Repertorium troporum Bohemiae medii aevi ; pars 1
Critical edition of tropes for the Proper of the Mass from mainly Bohemian sources. — Unacc. melodies. — Extensive preface and critical report in Czech and English. — Latin words; also printed for reference.
Publ. no. H 7878
ISMN M260103313
System number: 014629770

782.532351722
*Palestrina, Giovanni Pierluigi da, 1525?-1594.
[Offertories, voices (5). *Selections*]
Four offertories for Sundays in Advent / Giovanni Pierluigi da Palestrina ; transcribed and edited by Jon Dixon. — Carshalton Beeches : JOED Music, c2002. — 1 score (24 p.) ; 30 cm. — Renaissance polyphonic choral music
For 5-part mixed chorus. — Source: 'Offertoria totius anni', published Rome : Francesco Coattino, 1593. — Duration: 3:00 ; 3:20 ; 2:45 ; 2:40. — Latin words; English translation printed as text preceding each work.
Pl. no. JOED P131
System number: 013526296

782.532351723
*Palestrina, Giovanni Pierluigi da, 1525?-1594.
[Offertories, voices (5). Tui sunt coeli]
Offertory at the third mass of Christmas : Tui sunt coeli : SATTB / Giovanni Pierluigi da Palestrina ; transcribed and edited by Jon Dixon. — Carshalton Beeches : JOED Music, c2002. — 1 score (6 p.) ; 30 cm. — Renaissance polyphonic choral music
Source: 'Offertoria totius anni', published Rome : Francesco Coattino, 1593. — Cover title. — Duration: 2:40. — Latin words; English translation printed as text preceding score.
Pl. no. JOED P133
System number: 013498103

782.532351726
*Dvořák, Antonín, 1841-1904.
[Stabat Mater, op. 58, D major. *Vocal score*]
Stabat Mater für Soli, Chor und Orchester, op. 58 = for soloists, chorus and orchestra / Antonín Dvořák ; Klavierauszug von Josef Zubatý ; herausgegeben von Klaus Döge. — Wiesbaden : Breitkopf & Härtel, c2004. — 1 score (110 p.) ; 27 cm.
For solo voices (SATB), chorus (SATB), and orchestra; acc. arr. for piano. — "Breitkopf Urtext"—Cover. — Duration: ca. 1:25:00. — Includes pref. in German and English. — Latin words.
Pl. no. EB 8631
Publ. no. 8631
ISMN M004181959
System number: 013111497

Fenaroli, Fedele, 1730-1818.
Stabat mater : for soprano, alto, strings & basso continuo / Fedele Fenaroli ; edited by Alejandro Garri ; assisted by Kent Carlson. — First ed. — Full score. — Frankfurt : Garri Editions, c2007. — 1 score (48 p.) ; 30 cm. — Canti di cielo ; v. 100
Preface in English. — First edition based on a 19th century manuscript in the possession of Padre Paolo Bagnoli, Rome. — "Urtext." — Figured bass unrealized. — Duration: ca. 28:00. — Latin words.
Publ. no. GE 325
System number: 013771081

*Palestrina, Giovanni Pierluigi da, 1525?-1594.
[Stabat Mater, voices (8)]
Stabat Mater dolorosa : SATB+SATB / Giovanni Pierluigi da Palestrina ; transcribed and edited by Jon Dixon. — Carshalton Beeches : JOED Music, 2004, c1995. — 1 score (20 p.) ; 30 cm. — Renaissance polyphonic choral music
Cover title. — Duration: 7:15. — Latin words; English translation printed as text preceding score.
Pl. no. JOED P29
System number: 013526308

782.5323517293
*Palestrina, Giovanni Pierluigi da, 1525?-1594.
[Offertories, voices (5). Confirma hoc Deus]
Confirma hoc Deus : (SATTB) / Giovanni Pierluigi da Palestrina ; transcribed and edited by Jon Dixon. — Carshalton Beeches : JOED Music, c2001. — 1 score (6 p.) ; 30 cm. — Renaissance polyphonic choral music
Subtitle in caption: Offertory at mass on Whit Sunday. — Source: 'Offertoria totius anni', published Rome : Francesco Coattino, 1593. — Cover title. — Duration: 2:37. — Latin words; English translation printed as text preceding score.
Pl. no. JOED P111
System number: 013526326

782.53238

Florentz, Jean-Louis.
Requiem de la vierge : conte liturgique pour l'assomption de Marie : pour soprano, tenor, baryton, chœur d'enfants, chœur mixte et orchestre, opus 7, [1986-1988] / Jean-Louis Florentz. — Paris : Ricordi, 2006. — 1 score (xiv, 154 p.) ; 42 cm.
Performance notes in French. — Duration: ca. 50:00. — Latin words, also printed separately for reference with French translation.
Publ. no. R.2415
ISMN M231202779
System number: 013762688

Haydn, Michael, 1737-1806.
[Missa pro defunctis, MH 838]
Requiem in B-Dur, MH 838 : Faksimile der autographen Partitur aus dem Besitz der Österreichischen Nationalbibliothek ; Faksimile des Partitur-Erstdrucks (Leipzig, Ambros Kühnel) aus dem Besitz der Bayerischen Staatsbibliothek München / Johann Michael Haydn ; vorgelegt und kommentiert von Manfred Hermann Schmid. — München : Strube Verlag, c2006. — 1 score (2 v.) + commentary ; 26 x 35 cm. — Denkmäler der Musik in Salzburg. Faksimile-Ausgaben ; Bd. 12
For vocal soloists, chorus and orchestra. — Facsimiles of the autograph score (Mus. Hs. 34232) in the Österreichische Nationalbibliothek, Wien and the first printed edition: Leipzig : Kühnel, s.d. (1811). — Separate commentary in German. — Latin words.
Publ. no. Edition 7521
ISBN 9783899120936
ISBN 3899120930
System number: 013771097

Moryto, Stanisław, 1947-
Missa brevis pro defunctis : na chór mieszany a cappella / Stanisław Moryto. — [Poland : s.n.], 2005. — 1 score (16 p.) ; 30 cm.
For mixed voices (SATB), unacc., with baritone solo in one movement. — Reproduced from holograph. — Latin words.
System number: 013810172

Rutter, John, 1945-
Requiem : for soprano solo, mixed choir and instrumental ensemble with organ / John Rutter. — Version with ensemble. — Oxford : Oxford University Press, c2004. — 1 score (103 p.) ; 32 cm.
Instrumental ensemble: flute, oboe, violoncello, timpani, glockenspiel, harp, organ. — Includes composer's note. — Duration: ca. 37:00. — Latin words, the Latin with English translations; Latin words from Missa pro defunctis, English portions of Agnus Dei and Lux aeterna from the Burial Service, 1662 Book of common prayer; words with translations also printed for reference preceding score.
ISBN 0193380935
System number: 013122746

Sanders, John, 1933-2003.
Requiem : for unaccompanied mixed voices (SSAATTBB) / John Sanders. — Matfield : Encore Publications, [2005?], c1998. — 1 score (37 p.) ; 26 cm.
"The text is from the 'Missa pro Defunctis', the writings of John Donne, (Bring us O Lord God) and the Russian Contakion of the Departed (Give rest, O Christ)"—Pref. — Duration: ca. 25:00. — Mixed English and Latin text.
System number: 013222726

782.5324

*Allain, Richard.
Salve Regina : for SSAATTBB chorus / Richard Allain. — London : Novello & Co, c2005. — 1 score (15 p.) ; 25 cm.
Includes performance suggestions. — Latin words.
Publ. no. NOV161249
System number: 013360921

Liberto, Giuseppe.
Te Deum laudamus / Giuseppe Liberto. — Città del Vaticano : Libreria Editrice Vaticana, c2004. — 1 score (24 p.) ; 30 cm. — Collana Liturgica poliphonia ; 2
For chorus (SATB), 3 trumpets, horn, trombone, tuba, and organ. — Includes pref. and biographical notes in Italian. — Latin words.
ISBN 8820975769
ISBN 9788820975760
System number: 013750207

*Salieri, Antonio, 1750-1825.
Salve regina : für vierstimmigen gemischten Chor, 2 Violinen, Viola, Bass und Orgel / Antonio Salieri ; revidiert und herausgegeben von Otto Biba ; Continuofassung von Wolfgang Fürlinger. — Erstdruck. — Altötting : Alfred Coppenrath, c2004. — 1 score (7 p.) ; 30 cm. — Kirchenmusik der Wiener Klassik ; Bd. 8
Latin words.
Publ. no. COP 10.008-01
ISMN M202706800
System number: 014666999

782.53241726

*Tallis, Thomas, ca. 1505-1585.
[Lamentations, no. 1]
Lamentations I & II / Thomas Tallis ; transcribed and edited by Jon Dixon. — [Rev. ed.] — Carshalton Beeches : JOED Music, [2004?], c1991. — 1 score (28 p.) ; 30 cm. — Renaissance polyphonic choral music
For SATTB (1st work), SAATB (2nd work). — Sources: British Library, MSS. Add. 17792-6 (1st work), MS. Add. 5059, ff 71-77 (2nd work). — Durations: 5:55 ; 9:35. — Latin words; English translation printed as text preceding each work.
Pl. no. JOED T3
System number: 013525975

782.5325

Elsner, Józef, 1769-1854.
[Vespers, D major]
Nieszpory = Vespers : ex Officio majori Beatae Virginis Mariae ad Vesperas : a canto, alto, tenore, basso, due violini, viola, bassi (violoncello et basso), due flauti, due clarinetti, due corni, due clarini, timpani con organo / Jozef Elsner ; opracowanie Hubert Prochota ; wstęp Remigiusz Pośpiech. — Wyd. 1. — [Partytura] — Częstochowa : Klasztor OO. Paulinów Jasna Góra ; Kraków : Polskie Wydawn. Muzyczne, 2006. — 1 score (158 p.) : facsims. ; 31 cm. — (Muzyka Jasnogorska = Musica Claromontana ; 6)
Preface and critical report in Polish and English. — Latin words, also printed separately for reference with Polish and English translation.
Publ. no. PWM 10 467
ISMN M274002534
EAN 9790274002534
System number: 013887069
Also classified at 782.5294

Furtwängler, Wilhelm, 1886-1954.
Te Deum : für gemischten Chor, 4 Solostimmen und Orchester / Wilhelm Furtwängler ; herausgegeben von George Alexander Albrecht. — Partitur. — Berlin : Ries & Erler, c2004. — 1 score (99 p.) ; 30 cm. — (Wilhelm Furtwängler Gesamtausgabe ; II.1)
For SATB choir and soloists and orchestra.
ISMN M013511327
System number: 014658145

782.5326

*Andreas, Carolus.
Magnificat & Nunc dimittis : faux-bourdon service : SATB / Carolus Andreas. — [s.l.] : Anglo-American Music Publishers, c2005. — 1 score (11 p.) ; 28 cm.
Includes performance note. — English words from the Book of Common Prayer.
System number: 013594264

Jackson, Gabriel, 1962-
Magnificat and Nunc dimittis : (Truro service) : SATB a cappella / Gabriel Jackson. — Oxford : Oxford University Press, c2005. — 1 score (11 p.) : port. ; 26 cm. — (New horizons ; NH23)
Includes keyboard reduction for rehearsal only. — Duration: 7:00. — Includes biographical note. — English words, Book of common prayer text.
Publ. no. NH23
ISBN 0193439239
ISBN 9780193439238
System number: 013213389

Kelly, Bryan.
Kentucky canticles : Magnificat and Nunc dimittis for SATB and organ / Bryan Kelly. — London : Stainer & Bell, c2005. — 1 score (19 p.) ; 26 cm.
English words from the Book of Common Prayer.
Publ. no. W215
ISMN M220221477
System number: 013307559

*Ludford, Nicholas, ca. 1490-1557.
[Vocal music. *Selections*]
Five- and six-part Masses : and, Magnificat / [Nicholas Ludford] ; transcribed and edited by David Skinner. — London : Published for the British Academy by Stainer and Bell, c2005. — 1 score (xii, 240 p.) ; 33 cm. — Early English church music, 0424-0359 ; 46 — (Nicholas Ludford ; 2)
The Magnificat for 6 voices. — Includes editorial notes and critical commentary. — Latin words.
ISBN 0852498756
ISMN M220220463
System number: 013433942
Primary classification 782.53232

O'Regan, Tarik.
Magnificat & Nunc dimittis : variations for choir : [for SATB (divisi) ripieno choir and SATB concertate choir (four or eight soloists) with solo soprano saxophone or violoncello] / Tarik O'Regan. — London : Novello, c2004. — 1 score (44 p.) ; 30 cm.
Includes programme and performance notes by the composer. — Latin words also printed for reference with English translation, p.44.
Publ. no. NOV200310
ISBN 1844499529
System number: 013173392

Rathbone, Jonathan.
Magnificat : SSAATTBB / Jonathan Rathbone. — London : Edition Peters, c2004. — 1 score (7 p.) ; 30 cm. — Kikapust choral series
Publisher's no.: Edition Peters no. 77018. — English words.
Publ. no. EP 77018
Publ. no. 77018
EAN M577085333
System number: 013304565

*Tallis, Thomas, ca. 1505-1585.
[Magnificat, voices (5)]
Magnificat and Nunc dimittis : SAT(T)BB / Thomas Tallis ; transcribed and edited by Jon Dixon. — [Rev. ed.] — Carshalton Beeches : JOED Music, [2004?], c1991. — 1 score (22 p.) ; 30 cm. — Renaissance polyphonic choral music
The editor has reconstructed the missing 5th part. — Source: Oxford, ChristChurch mss. 979-983. — Duration: 10:50. — Originally published: 1991, with pl. no. JOED T8. — Latin words; English translation printed as text preceding each work.
Pl. no. JOED T7
System number: 013525924

*Vann, Stanley.
[Magnificat and Nunc dimittis (Ripon Service)]
Magnificat and Nunc dimittis : (Ripon Cathedral) : SATB with organ / Stanley Vann. — [S.l.] : Anglo-American Music Publishers ; c2005. — 1 score (14 p.) ; 28 cm.
English words from the Book of Common Prayer.
System number: 013594285

*Walton, William, 1902-1983.
Magnificat and Nunc dimittis : SATB / William Walton. — Oxford : Oxford University Press, [2005?], c1976. — 1 score (15 p.) ; 27 cm. — Oxford church services ; S609
With organ acc. — Reprint. Originally published: Oxford : Oxford University Press, 1976. — English words.
Publ. no. S609
ISBN 0193851067
ISBN 9780193851061
System number: 013432739

Whitbourn, James.
[Magnificat and Nunc dimittis (Collegium Regale)]
Magnificat and Nunc dimittis : Collegium regale : for tenor solo, SATB choir, organ and optional tam-tam / James Whitbourn. — London : Chester Music, c2005. — 1 score (31 p.) ; 25 cm. — Contemporary church music series
Words in mixed Latin and English from the Liber usualis and the Book of Common Prayer.
Publ. no. CH69630
System number: 013222158

782.53261722
Chilcott, Bob.
Advent antiphons : for SATB double choir a cappella / Bob Chilcott. — Oxford : Oxford University Press, 2005. — 1 score (48 p.) ; 28 cm.
"The texts … are known as the 'Great O antiphons' … traditionally sung before and after the Magnificat on the seven days preceding Christmas Eve"—Composer's note. — Includes keyboard reduction for rehearsal only. — Duration: ca. 10:00. — Latin words; English translation printed for reference preceding score.
Publ. no. BC78
ISBN 0193433362
System number: 013382226

782.542
[American songs]
Three American songs : SATB / arranged by Jonathan Rathbone. — London : Edition Peters, c2004. — 1 score (15 p.) ; 30 cm. — Kikapust choral series
The second and third songs with occasional divisi in all four parts.
Publ. no. EP 77047
ISMN M577085005
System number: 013304769

Andersson, Benny.
[Mamma mia! *Selections; arr.*]
Mamma mia! : choral highlights : SAB / arranged by Mac Huff. — Milwaukee, Wis. : Hal Leonard, c2005. — 1 score (55 p.) ; 27 cm. — Broadway choral series
A medley of 7 songs from the musical "Mamma mia!" based on ABBA songs. — Arr. for mixed voices (SABar) and piano. — Words and music by Benny Andersson, Björn Ulvaeus and Stig Anderson.
Publ. no. 08621355
System number: 013219992

Andersson, Benny.
[Mamma mia! *Selections; arr.*]
Mamma mia! : choral highlights : SATB / arranged by Mac Huff. — Milwaukee, Wis. : Hal Leonard, c2005. — 1 score (55 p.) ; 27 cm + 1 compact disc. — Broadway choral series
Medley of 7 songs from the musical "Mamma mia!" based on ABBA songs. — Arr. for mixed voices (SATB) and piano. — Words and music by Benny Andersson, Björn Ulvaeus and Stig Anderson. — CD produced in 2004. — CD contains full demonstration and backing tracks.
Publ. no. 08621354
System number: 013219975

The ash grove : SSAATTBB : Welsh traditional / arranged by Jonathan Rathbone. — London : Edition Peters, c2004. — 1 score (6 p.) ; 30 cm. — Kikapust choral series
"As recorded by the Swingle Singers on Around the world."
Publ. no. EP 77030
ISMN M577085111
System number: 013304773

*Bennett, Richard Rodney.
Time : for SAATTBB / Richard Rodney Bennett. — London : Novello, c2005. — 1 score (8 p.) ; 25 cm.
Words by Giles Fletcher, the elder, from Licia (1593). — Includes piano reduction for rehearsal only.
Publ. no. NOV955339
System number: 013497176

Bushes and briars : alto solo, SSATTBB : English traditional / arranged by Ben Parry. — London : Edition Peters, c2004. — 1 score (7 p.) ; 30 cm. — Kikapust choral series
Publ. no. EP 77031
ISMN M577085470
System number: 013304845

Byrd, William, 1542 or 3-1623.
[Psalmes, sonets, and songs]
Psalmes, sonets and songs (1588) / [William Byrd] ; edited by Jeremy Smith. — London : Stainer & Bell, c2004. — 1 score (xliv, 176 p.) : facsims. ; 26 cm. — (The Byrd edition ; v. 12)
35 psalms and part-songs; for superius, medius, contratenor, tenor and bassus. — Words also printed for reference, p. xvi-xxxvi. — Includes editorial notes, notes on the poems, list of extant copies and index of first lines. — Series under the general editorship of Philip Brett. — Words mostly in English ; "La virginella" in Italian.
Publ. no. B374
ISBN 0852493746
ISMN M220220432
System number: 013063061
Also classified at 782.525

Byrd, William, 1542 or 3-1623.
[Songs of sundrie natures]
Songs of sundrie natures (1589) / [William Byrd] ; edited by David Mateer. — London : Stainer & Bell, c2004. — 1 score (xxxvii, 274 p.) : facsims. ; 26 cm. — (The Byrd edition ; v. 13)
47 sacred and secular songs for 3-6 parts. unacc. — Words also printed for reference, p. xix-xxxi. — Includes editorial notes, notes on the poems, list of extant copies and index of first lines. — Series under the general editorship of Philip Brett.
Publ. no. B375
ISBN 0852493754
ISMN M220220449
System number: 013201995
Also classified at 782.525

Carter, Andrew.
O mistress mine / Andrew Carter. — Oxford : Oxford University Press, c2004. — 1 score (7 p.) ; 26 cm. — (Choral songs ; X457)
For mixed voices (SATB), unacc. — Includes keyboard reduction for rehearsal only. — Words from Twelfth Night, Act II, scene ii, by William Shakespeare. — Duration: 2:30.
Publ. no. X457
ISBN 0193432692
ISBN 9780193432697
System number: 013134168

Charlie is my darlin' : SSAATTBB : Scottish traditional / arranged by Ben Parry. — London : Edition Peters, c2004. — 1 score (7 p.) ; 30 cm. — Kikapust choral series
Publ. no. EP 77032
ISMN M577085135
System number: 013304863

Chilcott, Bob.
The isle is full of noises : SAATB with divisions, unaccompanied / Bob Chilcott. — Oxford : Oxford University Press, c2004. — 1 score (12 p.) ; 26 cm.
Includes piano reduction for rehearsal only. — Words from Act III, scene ii, of "The Tempest" by William Shakespeare.
Publ. no. BC80
ISBN 0193355426
ISBN 9780193355422
System number: 013132075

Chilcott, Bob.
You and me : SATB unaccompanied / Bob Chilcott. — Oxford : Oxford University Press, c2005. — 1 score (12 p.) ; 26 cm.
Includes piano reduction for rehearsal only. — Words by Denis Glover (1st movement) and Elizabeth Jennings (2nd movement).
Publ. no. BC67
ISBN 0193433192
ISBN 9780193433199
System number: 013225225

Ciao bella, ciao : SSAATTBB : Italian traditional / arranged by Ben Parry.
— London : Edition Peters, c2004. — 1 score (10 p.) ; 30 cm. — Kikapust
choral series
"As recorded by the Swingle Singers on Around the world."
Publ. no. EP 77050
ISMN M577084985
System number: 013304873

Colahan, Arthur.
Galway Bay : SSAATTBB / Arthur Colohan [sic] ; arranged by Jonathan
Rathbone. — London : Edition Peters, [2004?] — 1 score (8 p.) ; 30 cm. —
Kikapust choral series
Publ. no. EP 77034
ISMN M577085159
System number: 013304928

*Crescenz, Valerie Showers.
Crossing the bar : for mixed chorus (SATB) and piano / Valerie Showers
Crescenz. — [New York] : Oxford University Press, c2005. — 1 score
(11 p.) ; 27 cm. — Oxford choral music
Words by Alfred Tennyson. — Includes biographical note.
ISBN 9780193868670
ISBN 0193868679
System number: 013472291

La cucaracha : SSAATTBB : Mexican traditional / arranged by Jonathan
Rathbone. — London : Edition Peters, c2004. — 1 score (12 p.) ; 30 cm.
— Kikapust choral series
English words.
Publ. no. EP 77035
ISMN M577085081
System number: 013304936

Danny boy : SSAATTBB : Irish traditional / arranged by Jonathan Rathbone.
— London : Edition Peters, c2004. — 1 score (3 p.) ; 30 cm. — Kikapust
choral series
"As recorded by the Swingle Singers on Around the world."
Publ. no. EP 77033
ISMN M577084947
System number: 013304902

David of the white rock : SSAATTBB : Welsh traditional / arranged by Ben
Parry. — London : Edition Peters, c2004. — 1 score (6 p.) ; 30 cm. —
Kikapust choral series
"As recorded by the Swingle Singers on Around the world." — First verse in Welsh;
remainder in English.
Publ. no. EP 77048
ISMN M577085142
System number: 013304919

*David, Jonathan, 1965-
Now sleeps the crimson petal : for unaccompanied mixed chorus
(SSAATTBB) / Jonathan David. — [New York] : Oxford University Press,
c2005. — 1 score (11 p.) ; 27 cm. — Oxford choral music
Words by Alfred Tennyson. — Includes piano reduction for rehearsal only. —
Includes biographical note.
ISBN 9780193868687
ISBN 0193868687
System number: 013472278

*Davies, Peter Maxwell, 1934-
Il rozzo martello : for unaccompanied choir SATB / words by Dante and
Michelangelo ; music by Peter Maxwell Davies. — London : Chester
Music ; Bury St. Edmunds, Suffolk : Exclusive distributor, Music Sales,
c1998. — 1 score (26 p.) ; 30 cm.
Includes piano part for rehearsal only. — Duration: ca. 12:00. — Italian words; also
printed for reference with English translations preceding score.
Publ. no. CH 61506
System number: 006937452

*Davies, Peter Maxwell, 1934-
Sea elegy : for SATB soli, chorus and orchestra : (1998) / Peter Maxwell
Davies ; words by George Mackay Brown. — Study score. — London :
Chester Music, c2005. — 1 miniature score (42 p.) ; 26 cm.
Words also printed for reference preceding score.
Publ. no. CH66253
ISBN 0711998000
System number: 013203926

[Down by the Salley Gardens; arr.]
The Salley Gardens : SATB / Irish traditional ; arranged by Ben Parry ;
[words by W.B. Yeats] — London : Edition Peters, c2004. — 1 score (4 p.) ;
30 cm. — Kikapust choral series
Publisher's no.: Edition Peters no. 77039.
Publ. no. EP 77039
Publ. no. 77039
ISMN M577085210
System number: 013305005

*Ellingboe, Bradley.
Be music, night : for unaccompanied mixed choir (SSAATTBB) / words by
Kenneth Patchen ; music by Bradley Ellingboe. — [New York] : Oxford
University Press, c2005. — 1 score (11 p.) ; 27 cm. — Oxford choral music
Includes piano reduction for rehearsal only. — Words also printed as text preceding
score. — Includes biographical note.
ISBN 9780193868694

ISBN 0193868695
System number: 013472304

Foster, Stephen Collins, 1826-1864.
[Songs. *Selections; arr.*]
Stephen Foster medley : SSAATTBB / music by Stephen Foster ;
arranged by Jonathan Rathbone. — London : Edition Peters, c2004. — 1
score (19 p.) ; 30 cm. — Kikapust choral series
Publisher's no.: Edition Peters no. 77090.
Publ. no. EP 77090
Publ. no. 77090
ISMN M577085166
System number: 013305049

*Hawes, Patrick.
Tres amores : double SATB choir / words by Andrew Hawes ; music by
Patrick Hawes. — London : Novello & Co, c2005. — 1 score (8 p.) ;
25 cm.
For mixed voices (SATBSATB), unacc. — Caption title. — Mixed Latin and
English words.
Publ. no. NOV955042
System number: 013582428

Kesselman, Lee R.
[Nights in armor. No. 1, Merlin's riddle]
Merlin's riddle (no. 1 from "Nights in Armor") / Lee R. Kesselman. —
[S.l.] : Boosey & Hawkes ; Milwaukee, Wis. : Exclusively distributed by
Hal Leonard, c2004. — 1 score (8 p.) ; 27 cm. — (CME conductor's
choice) — (Doreen Rao's choral music experience)
For unacc. chorus (SATB). — Includes piano reduction for rehearsal only. — Text
from "Idylls of the King" by Alfred, Lord Tennyson.
ISMN M051473861
System number: 013213621

Lennon, John, 1940-1980.
[Fool on the hill; *arr.*]
The fool on the hill : [for SAB and piano] / words and music by John
Lennon and Paul McCartney ; recorded by Sergio Mendes ; arranged by
Mac Huff. — Milwaukee, Wis. : Hal Leonard, c2003. — 1 score (12 p.) ;
27 cm. — Vocal jazz series
Publ. no. 08743685
System number: 013211808

Lennon, John, 1940-1980.
[Fool on the hill; *arr.*]
The fool on the hill : [for SATB and piano] / words and music by John
Lennon and Paul McCartney ; recorded by Sergio Mendes ; arranged by
Mac Huff. — Milwaukee, Wis. : Hal Leonard, c2003. — 1 score (12 p.) ;
27 cm. — Vocal jazz series
Publ. no. 08743684
System number: 013211798

Loch Lomond : tenor solo & SSAATTBB : Scottish traditional / arranged
by Jonathan Rathbone. — London : Edition Peters, c2004. — 1 score
(6 p.) ; 30 cm. — Kikapust choral series
Publ. no. EP 77036
ISMN M577085128
System number: 013304945

*McCabe, John, 1939-
The evening watch : for SATB and organ / John McCabe. — London :
Novello & Co, c2003. — 1 score (12 p.) ; 30 cm.
Words by Henry Vaughan; also printed as text preceding score.
Publ. no. NOV078771
System number: 013498327

The miller of Dee : SSAATTBB : English traditional / arranged by Mark
Williams. — London : Edition Peters, c2004. — 1 score (14 p.) ; 30 cm.
— Kikapust choral series
"As recorded by the Swingle Singers on New world."
Publ. no. EP 77049
ISMN M577085029
System number: 013304961

*Moeran, E. J. (Ernest John), 1894-1950.
[Choral music. *Selections*]
Collected choral music. Volume four, unison voices / E.J. Moeran ; edited
by John Talbot. — Centenary ed. — London : Thames Publishing, c2003.
— 1 score (30 p.) ; 30 cm.
5 songs with piano acc. — Reprinted from earlier editions. — Editorial notes
following score.
System number: 013167517

Mozart, Wolfgang Amadeus, 1756-1791.
[Così fan tutte. Aura amorosa; *arr.*]
Un' aura amorosa : from Così fan tutte : T solo & SSAATTBB / Mozart ;
arranged by Jonathan Rathbone. — London : Edition Peters, c2004. — 1
score (3 p.) ; 30 cm. — Kikapust choral series
Publisher's no.: Edition Peters no. 77067.
Publ. no. EP 77067
Publ. no. 77067
ISMN M577085302
System number: 013305913

My love is like a red, red rose : SATB / Scottish traditional ; arranged by Jonathan Rathbone ; words by Robert Burns. — London : Edition Peters, c2004. — 1 score (4 p.) ; 30 cm. — Kikapust choral series
Publisher's no.: Edition Peters no. 77037.
Publ. no. EP 77037
Publ. no. 77037
ISMN M577084954
System number: 013304980

***Polska pieśń wielogłosowa XVI i początku XVII wieku** / zebrał i przygotował do druku = edited by Piotr Poźniak ; transkrypcja i opracowanie tekstów staropolskich = old Polish texts transcribed and annotated by Wacław Walecki. — Warszawa : Instytut Sztuki Polskiej Akademii Nauk ; Kraków : Instytut Muzykologii Uniwersytetu Jagiellońskiego : Musica Iagellonica, 2004. — 2 v. (370, 190 p.) : facsims. ; 32 cm. — Monumenta musicae in Polonia. Seria B
Polish polyphonic hymns and secular songs for 3-4 voices. — Introduction and editorial notes in Polish and English.
Pl. no. MI 0028
ISBN 8370991114
System number: 013277659
Primary classification 782.527

Purcell, Henry, 1659-1695.
[Choral music. *Selections*]
Royal welcome songs. Part II / Henry Purcell ; edited under the supervision of the Purcell Society by Bruce Wood. — [New ed.] — London : Novello, c2005. — 1 score (xxxvii, 223 p.) : facsims. ; 28 cm. — (Works of Henry Purcell ; v. 18)
For solo voices, mixed chorus and string orchestra or orchestra, with continuo. — Words of 1st work by Thomas Flatman; words of other works are anonymous. — Words printed for reference on p. xxxi-xxxvii. — Pref. and list of sources: p. viii-xxvii; critical commentary: p. 213-223.
Publ. no. NOV 151018
ISBN 1844497550
System number: 013213667

Richardson, Michael.
How many bards : [for SATB voices, oboe (or violin) & piano] / Michael Richardson. — [S.l.] : Boosey & Hawkes ; Milwaukee, Wis. : Exclusively distributed by Hal Leonard, c2005. — 1 score (10 p.) 27 cm. — (CME conductor's choice) — (Doreen Rao's choral music experience)
Words by John Keats. — Includes biographical and programme notes.
ISMN M051475575
System number: 013213606

Sakkijarven polkka : SSAATTBB / Finnish traditional ; arranged by Jonathan Rathbone. — London : Edition Peters, c2004. — 1 score (19 p.) ; 30 cm. — Kikapust choral series
"As recorded by the Swingle Singers on Around the world." — Publisher's no.: Edition Peters no. 77038.
Publ. no. EP 77038
Publ. no. 77038
ISMN M577085098
System number: 013304996

***Salonen, Esa-Pekka, 1958-**
[Sånger till text av Ann Jäderlund]
Two songs from Kalender röd : for unaccompanied choir SSAATTBB / Esa-Pekka Salonen ; poems by Ann Jäderlund. — London : Chester Music, c2005. — 1 score (67 p.) ; 30 cm.
Includes piano reduction for rehearsal only. — Parallel title p. [ii]: Two songs from red calendar. — Includes composer's note. — Swedish words, also printed for reference with English translation preceding score.
Publ. no. CH63470
ISBN 0711998922
System number: 013173422

***Samuel, Rhian.**
Pan ddaw ust y nos : i gôr SATB & organ / [alaw] Rhian Samuel ; [geiriau gan] Nesta Wyn Jones. — London : Stainer & Bell, c2005. — 1 score (11 p.) ; 30 cm.
Caption title.
Publ. no. AC222
ISMN M220221491
System number: 013237465

Scarborough Fair : English folk song : arranged for mixed voice choir and piano / by Derek J. Clark. — Tewkesbury : Roberton Publications, c2004. — 1 score (14 p.) ; 26 cm.
Chorus: SATB.
Publ. no. 63251
ISMN M222260733
System number: 013193327

Seeger, Pete, 1919-
Where have all the flowers gone? : for SATB choir & piano / words and music by Pete Seeger ; arranged by Mark G. Sirett. — [New York?] : Boosey & Hawkes ; Milwaukee : exclusively distributed by Hal Leonard , c2005. — 1 score (13 p.) ; 27 cm. — (CME building bridges) — (Doreen Rao's choral music experience)
Includes biographical notes.
Publ. no. 48018867
ISMN M051475407
System number: 013312787

She moved thro' the fair : ATTBarBB / Irish traditional ; arranged by Jonathan Rathbone ; [words by Padraic Colum] — London : Edition Peters, c2004. — 1 score (5 p.) ; 30 cm. — Kikapust choral series
Publisher's no.: Edition Peters no. 77052.
Publ. no. EP 77052
Publ. no. 77052
ISMN M577085289
System number: 013305020

Skempton, Howard, 1947-
The flight of song : SATB a cappella / Howard Skempton. — Oxford : Oxford University Press, c2005. — 1 score (16 p.) ; 26 cm. — (New horizons ; NH27)
In graphic notation (p. [4]-[7]) and standard notation (p. 8-16). — Words by Henry Wadsworth Longfellow and others. — Includes performance instructions.
Publ. no. NH27
ISBN 0193381524
System number: 013243774

Skye boat song : SSAATTBB / Scottish traditional ; arranged by Jonathan Rathbone. — London : Edition Peters, c2004. — 1 score (15 p.) ; 30 cm. — Kikapust choral series
Publisher's no.: Edition Peters no. 77051.
Publ. no. EP 77051
Publ. no. 77051
ISMN M577085036
System number: 013305026

Snyder, Audrey.
The complete history of Western music (abridged) / arranged by Audrey Snyder ; additional words and music by Audrey Snyder. — Milwaukee: Hal Leonard, c2005. — 1 score (14 p.) ; 27 cm.
A medley of themes by Beethoven, Rossini, Bach, Handel, Mozart, Haydn and others. — For 2-part choir and piano.
Publ. no. 08744675
System number: 013221833

Snyder, Audrey.
The complete history of Western music (abridged) / arranged by Audrey Snyder ; additional words and music by Audrey Snyder. — Milwaukee: Hal Leonard, c2005. — 1 score (15 p.) ; 27 cm.
A medley of themes by Beethoven, Rossini, Bach, Handel, Mozart, Haydn and others. — For mixed voices (SATB) and piano.
Publ. no. 08744674
System number: 013221839

Star of the County Down : SSAATTBB / Irish traditional ; arranged by Ben Parry. — London : Edition Peters, c2004. — 1 score (12 p.) ; 30 cm. — Kikapust choral series
Publisher's no.: Edition Peters no. 77040.
Publ. no. EP 77040
Publ. no. 77040
ISMN M577085203
System number: 013305040

Tavener, John.
Exhortation and Kohima : for unaccompanied choir and semichorus SATB/SATB / John Tavener. — London : Chester Music, c2004. — 1 score (7 p.) ; 25 cm. — Contemporary church music series
Words by Laurence Binyon (Exhortation) and John Maxwell Edmonds (Kohima) also printed for reference preceding score. — Includes composer's note.
Publ. no. CH67540
System number: 013201804

***Theile, Johann, 1646-1724.**
[Vocal music. *Selections*]
Weltliche Arien und Canzonetten / Johann Theile ; herausgegeben von Stephan Blaut. — Leipzig : Friedrich Hofmeister, c2004. — 1 score (xxiii, 60 p.) : facsims. ; 31 cm. — Denkmäler mitteldeutscher Barockmusik. Serie 1, Musikalische Zentren in Sachsen, Sachsen-Anhalt und Thüringen ; Bd. 3
For 1-4 solo voices (SATB), strings and continuo; figured bass not realized. — Edited from the 1667 edition held in Universitätsbibliothek Uppsala (Sign.: Utl. vok. mus. tr. 459-465). — Introd. in German with English translation; critical notes in German only. — German words; additional verses printed separately for reference following each song.
ISMN M203483533
System number: 014660605
Primary classification 783.42

Three folk songs : The oak and the ash ; Swing low, sweet chariot ; Nine hundred miles : SATB / arranged by Jonathan Rathbone. — London : Edition Peters, c2004. — 1 score (12 p.) ; 30 cm. — Kikapust choral series
Publisher's no.: Edition Peters no. 77046.
Publ. no. EP 77046
Publ. no. 77046
ISMN M577084992
System number: 013304758

*Unterseher, Reginald.
Live with me, and be my love : for mixed chorus (SATB) and piano / Reginald Unterseher. — [New York] : Oxford University Press, c2005. — 1 score (12 p.) ; 27 cm. — Oxford choral music
Words: Sonnet V from 'Sonnets to sundry notes of music' by William Shakespeare.
ISBN 9780193868731
ISBN 0193868733
System number: 013472311

Vaughan Williams, Ralph, 1872-1958.
[Fantasia on Greensleeves; *arr.*]
Greensleeves : or, The king of love : a choral setting for mixed voice choir and piano or orchestra of "Fantasia on Greensleeves" / by R. Vaughan Williams ; arranged by Philip Lane. — Tewkesbury : Roberton Publications, c2004. — 1 score (12 p.) ; 26 cm.
For mixed voices (SATB) with piano or organ acc. Orchestral acc. available separately. — Words to Greensleeves from "A handfull of pleasant delites", 1584. Words to The king of love by H.W. Baker.
Publ. no. 63270
ISMN M222260450
System number: 013193252
Also classified at 782.5265

Vaughan Williams, Ralph, 1872-1958.
[Song of thanksgiving. *Vocal score*]
A song of thanksgiving : for soprano solo, speaker, chorus and orchestra / R. Vaughan Williams ; vocal score. — London : Oxford University Press, [197-?], c1945. — 1 vocal score (28 p) ; 26 cm.
First published in 1945 with the title "Thanksgiving for victory". — Words from the Bible, Shakespeare, and Kipling. — Duration: 15-16 min.
ISBN 0193394553
System number: 013050462

Vem kan segla förutan vind? : SSAATTBB / Swedish traditional ; arranged by Jonathan Rathbone. — London : Edition Peters, c2004. — 1 score (3 p.) ; 30 cm. — Kikapust choral series
"As recorded by the Swingle Singers on Around the world." — Publisher's no.: Edition Peters no. 77041.
Publ. no. EP 77041
Publ. no. 77041
ISMN M577085104
System number: 013305058

Viel Freuden mit sich bringet : SSAATTBB / German traditional ; arranged by Ben Parry. — London : Edition Peters, c2004. — 1 score (6 p.) ; 30 cm. — Kikapust choral series
Publisher's no.: Edition Peters no. 77042.
Publ. no. EP 77042
Publ. no. 77042
ISMN M577085432
System number: 013305072

Waltzing Matilda : SSAATTBB : Australian traditional / arranged by Jonathan Rathbone. — London : Edition Peters, c2004. — 1 score (11 p.) ; 30 cm. — Kikapust choral series
"As recorded by the Swingle Singers on Around the world."
Publ. no. EP 77043
ISMN M577085067
System number: 013305700

Willcocks, David, 1919-
O mistress mine : SATB a cappella / David Willcocks. — Oxford : Oxford University Press, c2005. — 1 score (4 p.) ; 26 cm. — (Choral songs ; X458)
Words by William Shakespeare from Twelfth Night, Act II, scene iii.
Publ. no. X458
ISBN 0193432706
ISBN 9780193432703
System number: 013243525

782.5421542
Collins, Phil.
[Look through my eyes; *arr.*]
Look through my eyes : from Walt Disney Pictures' Brother Bear : SAB / words and music by Phil Collins ; arranged by Ed Lojeski. — [S.l.] : Walt Disney Music Company ; Milwaukee, WI : Hal Leonard, c2004. — 1 score (16 p.) ; 27 cm.
Piano acc. with chord symbols.
Publ. no. 08744057
System number: 013194161

Collins, Phil.
[Look through my eyes; *arr.*]
Look through my eyes : from Walt Disney Pictures' Brother Bear : SATB / words and music by Phil Collins ; arranged by Ed Lojeski. — [S.l.] : Walt Disney Music Company ; Milwaukee, WI : Hal Leonard, c2004. — 1 score (16 p.) ; 27 cm.
Piano acc. with chord symbols.
Publ. no. 08744056
System number: 013194143

782.5421587
Estonian wedding song : for mixed chorus (SATB) and piano / [Estonian folk song, arr.] Theron Kirk. — [New York] : Oxford University Press, c2004. — 1 score (7 p.) ; 27 cm. — Oxford choral music
Includes biographical note. — English words.
ISBN 0193867508

ISBN 9780193867505
System number: 013324505

782.5421595
What shall we do with the drunken sailor? : SSAATTBB : English traditional / arranged by Jonathan Rathbone. — London : Edition Peters, c2004. — 1 score (11 p.) ; 30 cm. — Kikapust choral series
Publ. no. EP 77044
ISMN M577085197
System number: 013305710

782.54215990973
[Star-spangled banner (Song); *arr.*]
The star-spangled banner : for mixed chorus, unaccompanied / arranged by Jerry Rubino. — [New York] : Oxford University Press, c2002. — 1 score (6 p.) ; 27 cm. — Oxford choral music
For mixed voices (SSAATTBB), unacc. — Includes piano reduction for rehearsal only. — Based on the 'Anacreonitick song' by J.S. Smith. — Words by Francis Scott Key. — Includes biographical note about the arranger.
ISBN 019386584X
System number: 013196283

*Ward, Samuel A., 1847-1903.
[America the beautiful; *arr.*]
America the beautiful : for mixed chorus (SATB) and organ / [Samuel A. Ward ; arranged by] Mack Wilberg. — [New York] : Oxford University Press, c2005. — 1 score (14 p.) ; 27 cm. — Oxford choral music
Words by Katharine Lee Bates. — Includes biographical note about the arranger.
ISBN 9780193868120
ISBN 0193868121
System number: 013472297

782.542162009429
Little cuckoo = (Cwcw fach) : SATB a cappella / arranged by Nigel E. Jones. — [New York?] : Boosey & Hawkes ; Milwaukee, Wis. : exclusively distributed by Hal Leonard, c2005. — 1 score (6 p.) ; 27 cm. — (Doreen Rao's choral music experience) — (CME conductor's choice)
English and traditional Welsh words, also printed for reference. — English translation by Nigel E. Jones. — Includes performance and biographical notes.
Publ. no. 48018831
ISMN M051475933
System number: 013243888

782.5421620094735
*Sviridov, Georgiĭ Vasil'evich, 1915-1998.
[Kurskie pesni]
Kurskie pesni ; Kurskie pesni ; Tri starinnye pesni kurskoĭ gubernii / Georgiĭ Sviridov ; tom podgotovlen P. V. Luk'ĭanchenko. — Partitura. — Moskva, Sankt-Peterburg : Natsional'nyĭ Sviridovskiĭ Fond, 2003. — 1 score (xiv, 161 p.) : port., facsim. ; 30 cm. — (Polnoe sobranie sochineniĭ ; tom 3)
Includes two versions of the first work, one with full orchestra, the other arr. by the composer with keyboards and percussion only.
Pl. no. NSF 0004
System number: 014750500
Primary classification 782.548

782.5421620094796
Aija bernin pupas = [Rock my child in feather down : for SAB chorus & piano : Latvian folk song] / arranged by James Hudson. — [New York?] : Boosey & Hawkes ; Milwaukee, Wis. : exclusively distributed by Hal Leonard, c2005. — 1 score (7 p.) ; 27 cm. — (Doreen Rao's choral music experience) — (CME building bridges)
Latvian and English words, also printed for reference with phonetic transcription. — Includes program and biographical notes.
Publ. no. 48018965
ISMN M051476008
System number: 013361300

782.542162009711
Nootka paddle song : (no. 1 from "Northwest trilogy") : SATB a cappella / arranged by Imant Raminsh. — [New York?] : Boosey & Hawkes ; Milwaukee, Wis. : exclusively distributed by Hal Leonard, c2004. — 1 score (9 p.) ; 27 cm. — (Doreen Rao's choral music experience) — (CME conductor's choice)
Includes piano acc. for rehearsal only. — "Collected by Ida Halpern"—Caption. — Includes program and biographical notes. — Words also printed for reference.
Publ. no. 48018904
ISMN M051476183
System number: 013243880

Sunset : (no. 3 from "Northwest trilogy") : SATB a cappella / arranged by Imant Raminsh. — [New York?] : Boosey & Hawkes ; Milwaukee, Wis. : exclusively distributed by Hal Leonard, c2004. — 1 score (18 p.) ; 27 cm. — (Doreen Rao's choral music experience) — (CME conductor's choice)
Includes piano acc. for rehearsal only. — "Collected by Philip J. Thomas"—Caption. — Includes program and biographical notes. — Words also printed for reference.
Publ. no. 48018910
ISMN M051476206
System number: 013243875

782.54216200981

O sapo : SSATB a cappella : [Brazilian folk song] / arranged by Stephen Hatfield. — [New York?] : Boosey & Hawkes ; Milwaukee, Wis. : exclusively distributed by Hal Leonard, c2005. — 1 score (11 p.) ; 27 cm. — (Doreen Rao's choral music experience) — (CME Latin accents)
With optional percussion. — Portuguese words, also printed separately and with English translation for reference. — Includes pronunciation, performance and biographical notes.
Publ. no. 48018902
ISMN M041476541
System number: 013361311

782.542164

*****Anything goes :** & three other songs / arranged by David Nield. — London : Novello, c2005. — 1 score (46 p.) ; 25 cm. — Novello close harmony popular classics ; bk. 2 Novello choral programme
Arr. for mixed voices (ATBarB). — Includes piano reduction for rehearsal only.
Publ. no. NOV955064
ISBN 1846091640
System number: 013748296

*****A fine romance :** & four other songs / arranged by David Nield. — London : Novello, c2005. — 1 score (42 p.) ; 25 cm. — Novello close harmony popular classics ; bk. 3 Novello choral programme
Arr. for mixed voices (ATBarB). — Includes piano reduction for rehearsal only.
Publ. no. NOV955075
ISBN 1846091659
System number: 013748338

Harris, Jesse, 1969-
[Don't know why; *arr.*]
Don't know why / words and music by Jesse Harris ; arranged by Paris Rutherford ; recorded by Norah Jones. — Milwaukee, Wis. : Hal Leonard, c2004. — 1 score (8 p.) ; 27 cm. — Vocal jazz series
Arr. for mixed voices (SATB) and piano.
Publ. no. 08744062
System number: 013222721

Smoke gets in your eyes : & five other songs / arranged by David Nield. — London : Novello, c2005. — 1 score (42 p.) ; 25 cm. — Novello close harmony popular classics ; bk. 1 Novello choral programme
Arr. for mixed voices (ATBarB). — Includes piano reduction for rehearsal only.
Publ. no. NOV955053
ISBN 1846091632
System number: 013323734

782.542166

Lennon, John, 1940-1980.
[All you need is love; *arr.*]
All you need is love : the 1967 #1 pop hit by The Beatles : [for 2-part and piano] / words and music by John Lennon and Paul McCartney ; arranged by Alan Billingsley. — Milwaukee, Wis. : Hal Leonard, [2005?], c1998. — 1 score (11 p.) ; 27 cm.
Publ. no. 08200937
System number: 013211851

Lennon, John, 1940-1980.
[All you need is love; *arr.*]
All you need is love : the 1967 #1 pop hit by The Beatles : [for SAB and piano] / words and music by John Lennon and Paul McCartney ; arranged by Alan Billingsley. — Milwaukee, Wis. : Hal Leonard, [2005?], c1998. — 1 score (11 p.) ; 27 cm.
Publ. no. 08200936
System number: 013211842

Lennon, John, 1940-1980.
[All you need is love; *arr.*]
All you need is love : the 1967 #1 pop hit by The Beatles : [for SATB and piano] / words and music by John Lennon and Paul McCartney ; arranged by Alan Billingsley. — Milwaukee, Wis. : Hal Leonard, [2005?], c1998. — 1 score (11 p.) ; 27 cm.
Publ. no. 08200935
System number: 013211833

Lennon, John, 1940-1980.
[Songs. *Selections*]
Beatles love songs / words and music by John Lennon and Paul McCartney ; arranged by Ed Lojeski ; recorded by The Beatles. — Milwaukee, Wis. : Hal Leonard, c2004. — 1 score (12 p.) ; 27 cm.
Arr. for mixed voices (SABar) and piano.
Publ. no. 08201687
System number: 013222742

Lennon, John, 1940-1980.
[Songs. *Selections*]
Beatles love songs / words and music by John Lennon and Paul McCartney ; arranged by Ed Lojeski ; recorded by The Beatles. — Milwaukee, Wis. : Hal Leonard, c2004. — 1 score (12 p.) ; 27 cm. + 1 compact disc.
Arr. for mixed voices (SATB) and piano. — CD contains full demonstration and backing tracks.
Publ. no. 08201686
System number: 013220387

Lennon, John, 1940-1980.
[Songs. *Selections*]
Ticket to ride : a collection of Lennon and McCartney arrangements / The Swingle Singers. — Southwest Harbor, Me. : Contemporary A Cappella Publishing ; [Milwaukee, Wis.] : Exclusively distributed by Hal Leonard, c2003. — 1 score (ix, 148 p.) : ill. ; 28 cm.
17 songs, from the repertoire of the Swingle Singers, arranged for mixed voices (various combinations), unacc. — Words and music by John Lennon and Paul McCartney. — Pref. includes performance notes and information about the group.
Publ. no. HL08743854
ISBN 0634060244
System number: 013222593

782.5421723

*****Crescenz, Valerie Showers.**
Christmas in Saint Petersburg : for unaccompanied mixed choir (SSAATTBB) / Valerie Showers Crescenz. — [New York] : Oxford University Press, c2005. — 1 score (14 p.) ; 27 cm. — Oxford Christmas music
Includes piano reduction for rehearsal only. — Words by the composer also printed as text preceding score. — Includes biographical and composer's notes. — Mostly English words; includes one phrase in Russian.
ISBN 9780193868724
ISBN 0193868725
System number: 013472185

*****Pierpont, James, 1822-1893.**
[Jingle bells; *arr.*]
Jingle bells : for two-part or mixed chorus and piano / [James Pierpont ; arranged by] Reginald Unterseher. — [New York] : Oxford University Press, c2004. — 1 score (7 p.) ; 27 cm. — Oxford Christmas music
May be performed by SA or TB or SATB and piano.
ISBN 0193867680
System number: 013515374

Pierpont, James, 1822-1893.
[Jingle bells; *arr.*]
Jingle bells : SATB / arranged by Jonathan Rathbone. — London : Edition Peters, c2004. — 1 score (4 p.) ; 30 cm. — Kikapust choral series
"Words and music by J. Peirpoint [i.e. Pierpont]"—Caption. — Publisher's no.: Edition Peters no. 77006.
Publ. no. EP 77006
Publ. no. 77006
ISMN M577084930
System number: 013304552

Pierpont, James, 1822-1893.
[Jingle bells; *arr.*]
Jingle bells : SSAATTBB / arranged by Ben Parry. — London : Edition Peters, c2004. — 1 score (14 p.) ; 30 cm. — Kikapust choral series
"Words and music by J. Peirpont"—Caption. — "As recorded by the Swingle Singers on The story of Christmas." — Publisher's no.: Edition Peters no. 77007.
Publ. no. EP 77007
Publ. no. 77007
ISMN M577085234
System number: 013304535

Pierpont, James, 1822-1893.
[Jingle bells; *arr.*]
Jingle, bells / J. Pierpont ; arranged by David Blackwell. — Oxford : Oxford University Press, [2004?], c1992. — 1 score (16 p.) ; 27 cm. — Oxford carols ; X367
For mixed voices (SATB), unacc. — Includes piano reduction for rehearsal only.
Publ. no. X367
ISBN 0193850095
System number: 013173829

The twelve days of Christmas : SSAATTBB / arranged by Jonathan Rathbone. — London : Edition Peters, c2004. — 1 score (15 p.) ; 30 cm. — Kikapust choral series
"As recorded by the Swingle Singers on The story of Christmas." — Publisher's no.: Edition Peters no. 77013.
Publ. no. EP 77013
Publ. no. 77013
ISMN M577085050
System number: 013304685

782.54217700941

Muslim songs of the British Isles / arranged for schools by Abdal Hakim Murad [Timothy J. Winter] — London : Quilliam Press, 2005. — 32 p. ; 30 cm.
22 unaccompanied songs, duets, rounds and part-songs. — Includes introduction and historical notes. — Tunes mainly traditional. — Words mostly by Sheikh Abdullah Quilliam or Amherst Tyssen. — English words, also printed for reference beneath each song. Some songs have Arabic refrains.
ISBN 187203814X
System number: 013190270

782.543

Cancionero poético-musical hispánico de Lisboa / introducción y edición crítica de Mariano Lambea y Lola Josa. — Madrid : Sociedad Española de Musicología, 2004- — 1 score (v. -2) : facsims. ; 32 cm. — Música y la poesía en cancioneros polifónicos del siglo XVII ; 3, 5 Publicaciones de la Sociedad Española de Musicología. Sección D, Ediciones de música antigua ; 15-16
Anonymous vocal quartets (for parts designated tiple 1â °, tiple 2â °, alto, and tenor) and continuo. — Ed. prepared from four volumes of music and poetry in the Biblioteca da Ajuda, Lisbon. — Unfigured bass not realized. — Critical notes precede the music in each vol. — Spanish words; also printed for reference preceding music in each volume.
ISBN 8486878845 (obra completa)
ISBN 8486878853 (v. 1)
ISBN 8486878055 (v. 2)
System number: 013647252

*[Codice Rossi 215.]
Il codice rossiano 215 : madrigali, ballate, una caccia, un rotondello / edizione critica e studio introduttivo a cura di Tiziana Sucato. — Pisa : Edizioni ETS, c2003. — 1 score (xv, 202 p.) ; 30 cm. — Diverse voci— ; 1
At head of title: Università di Pavia, Dipartimento di scienze musicologiche e paleografico filologiche, Centro di musicologia Walter Stauffer.
ISBN 8846706005
ISMN M705015058
EAN 9788846706003
System number: 013224000

Crecquillon, Thomas, d. 1557?
[Chansons, voices (4). *Selections*]
Cantiones quatuor vocum / edidit Laura Youens and Barton Hudson ; editrix verborum Mary Beth Winn. — Middleton, Wisc. : American Institute of Musicology, 2005. — 1 score (lxxiii, 127 p.) ; 35 cm. — Corpus mensurabilis musicae ; 63 — (Thomasii Crequillonis opera omnia ; 17)
For 4 voices, unacc. — Chansons no. 90-116. — Critical notes in English (xxviii-lxxiii). — French words; also printed for reference, with English translation, in notes.
Pl. no. CMM 63-XVII
ISBN 1595513256
System number: 013718133

*Giovannelli, Ruggiero, ca. 1560-1625.
[Selections]
Three pieces à 5 : TrTrTTB / Ruggiero Giovannelli ; edited by Virginia Brookes. — [S.l.] : Viola da Gamba Society of Great Britain, c2005. — 1 score (12 p.) + 5 parts ; 30 cm.
For viols (1st and 2nd works) or voices (3rd work). — Cover title. — Sources: London, British Library, Egerton 3665 f. 199, p. 393 (1st work), Egerton 3665 no. 102, p. 492 (2nd work), London, British Library K3.1.14 no. XVIII (3rd work). — Includes critical commentary.
Pl. no. 210
System number: 013441010
Primary classification 785.76195

Ingegneri, Marc Antonio, 1535 or 6-1592.
[Madrigals, voices (5), book 5]
V libro di madrigali a 5 voci / Marc'Antonio Ingegneri ; a cura di Gloria Joriini e Marco Mangani. — Lucca : Libreria musicale italiana, c2006. — 1 score (liii, 84 p.) ; 34 cm. — (Opera omnia / Marc' Antonio Ingegneri ; ser. 2, v. 5)
17 madrigals for mixed voices (SATTB), unacc. — Pref. and critical notes in Italian and English. — Half title: Università degli studi di Pavia, Scuola di paleografia e filologia musicale. — Italian words, also printed for reference in the preface.
ISBN 8870964353
System number: 013707583

Luzzaschi, Luzzasco, d. 1607.
[Madrigals. *Selections*]
Il quarto libro de' madrigali a cinque voci (Ferrara, 1594) ; and, Madrigals published only in anthologies, 1583-1604 / Luzzasco Luzzaschi ; edited by Anthony Newcomb. — Madison, Wis. : A-R Editions, c2004. — 1 score (xli, 163 p.) : ill. ; 28 cm. — (Complete unaccompanied madrigals / Luzzasco Luzzaschi ; pt. 2) — (Recent researches in the music of the Renaissance, 0486-123X ; 139)
Principally for 5 voices, unacc.; includes 2 madrigals for 4 voices and 2 for 6 voices. — Historical, editorial, and critical notes in English. — Appendix includes settings of some of the same texts by Luzzaschi's contemporaries. — Italian words, also printed for reference with English translations.
ISBN 0895795582
System number: 014630289

*Milton, John, ca. 1563-1647.
[If that a sinner's sighs, voices (5)]
Two settings of "If that a sinner's sighs" : à 5, TrTrTTB, fully texted : [and] à 6, TrTrT(with text)TBB / John Milton ; edited by Virginia Brookes. — [S.l.] : Viola da Gamba Society of Great Britain, c2005. — 1 score (12 p.) + 6 parts ; 30 cm.
Edited for viols (with or without voices). — Cover title. — Includes critical commentary.
Publ. no. 204
System number: 013441046
Primary classification 785.76195

Le rossignol musical des chansons : (Antwerp, 1597) / edited by Gerald R. Hoekstra. — Middleton : A-R Editions, c2004. — 1 score (xxxi, 224 p.) : 4 facsims. ; 28 cm. — (Recent researches in the music of the Renaissance, 0486-123X ; 138)
For 4-6 voices, unacc. — Edited from the 1st ed. compiled and published by Pierre Phalèse (RISM B/I, 1597-10). — Includes "Index of first lines." — Introd. includes bibliographic references. — Contains works by S. Bernard, D. Caignet, S. Cornet, E. du Caurroy, N. Faignient, A. Ferabosco, de La Cassaigne, G. de La Hele, C. Le Jeune, J. de Macque, R. del Mel, Mitou, P. de Monte, H. Naich, A. Pevernage, P. Rogier, J.P. Sweelinck, C. Verdonck, and P. van Wilder (cf. RISM B/I, 1597-10). — French words, also printed separately for reference with English translations.
ISBN 0895795558
EAN 9780895795557
System number: 014630302

Striggio, Alessandro, 1536 or 7-1592.
[Madrigals, voices (5), book 1]
Il primo libro de madrigali a cinque voci / Alessandro Striggio ; edited by David Butchart. — Middleton, Wis. : A-R Editions, c2006. — 1 score (xxxi, 181 p., [2] p. of plates) : facsims. ; 28 cm. — Recent researches in the music of the Renaissance ; 143
For mixed voices, unaccompanied. — Italian words; also printed for reference with English translation: p. xxi-xxxi.
ISBN 9780895795892
ISBN 0895795892
System number: 013703139

Wilder, Philip van, d. 1553.
[Chansons. *Selections*]
3 chansons à 4 & à 5 : (TrTr/TTB with text) / Philip Van Wilder ; edited by John Bryan. — [S.l.] : Viola da Gamba Society of Great Britain, c2004. — 2 scores (8, 4 p.) + 5 parts ; 30 cm.
May be performed by voices, viols or a combination. — Source: York Minster Library, Music Manuscript M 91 (S). — French words; English translation printed for reference on verso of front cover.
Pl. no. 201a—201b
Publ. no. 201
System number: 013382531
Also classified at 785.76194; 785.76195

782.548

*McCabe, John, 1939-
[Songs of the garden. *Vocal score*]
Songs of the garden : [for SATB soloists, SATB choir, brass quintet and organ : (2004)] / John McCabe ; [vocal score] — London : Novello, c2004. — 1 score (93 p.) ; 25 cm.
Acc. arr. for piano. — Includes composer's note. — Words also printed for reference, p. 90-93.
Publ. no. NOV078826
ISBN 1844499499
System number: 013202052

*Sviridov, Georgiĭ Vasil'evich, 1915-1998.
[Kurskie pesni]
Kurskie pesni ; Kurskie pesni ; Tri starinnye pesni kurskoĭ gubernii / Georgiĭ Sviridov ; tom podgotovlen P. V. Luk'ianchenko. — Partitura. — Moskva, Sankt-Peterburg : Natsional'nyĭ Sviridovskiĭ Fond, 2003. — 1 score (xiv, 161 p.) : port., facsim. ; 30 cm. — (Polnoe sobranie sochineniĭ ; tom 3)
Includes two versions of the first work, one with full orchestra, the other arr. by the composer with keyboards and percussion only.
Pl. no. NSF 0004
System number: 014750500
Also classified at 782.5421620094735

782.6 – FEMALE VOICES

782.625

Giordani, Giuseppe, 1751-1798.
Veni sponsa Christi : antifona / Giuseppe Giordani (Giordaniello) ; edizione critica a cura di Ugo Gironacci et Italo Vescovo. — Lucca : Libreria Musicale Italiana, c2004. — 1 score (xxiv, 19 p.) : facsims. ; 32 cm. — (Opera omnia / Giuseppe Giordani ; serie 2 ; vol. 1)
For women's voices (SA) and orchestra. — Preface and introd. in Italian and English; critical comments in Italian. — Latin words, also printed for reference with Italian translation, p. xvii.
ISBN 8870964582
ISBN 9788870964585
System number: 013949593

*Hughes, Arwel, 1909-1988.
[Dewi Sant. O dyred, Dewi. *Vocal score. English & Welsh*]
O dyred, Dewi : cytgan i leisiau SSA allan o'r oratorio Dewi Sant = Come hither, David : chorus for SSA voices from the oratorio Saint David / Arwel Hughes. — St. Bride's Major : Aureus, 2004. — 1 score (14 p.) ; 26 cm.
Orchestral acc. arr. for piano. — Words by Aneirin Talfan Davies. — Words in Welsh with English translation.
Publ. no. A.P.59
System number: 013173362

782.6251723
*Meyer, Lesley Hopwood.
[Nunc gaudet Maria ; *arr.*]
Nunc gaudet Maria : for upper voices (SSAA), harp and drum / Lesley
Hopwood Meyer ; arranged by Robert A.M. Ross. — [New York] : Oxford
University Press, c2005. — 1 score (4 p.) ; 27 cm. — Oxford sacred music
15th century words translated by the composer. — Drum is optional. — Mixed
English and Latin words.
ISBN 0193868741
System number: 013472173

782.626
*Handl, Jacob, 1550-1591.
[Musicum opus, 2. tomus. Ascendit Deus in iubilatione]
Ascendit Deus : motet for the Feast of Ascension : SSSAA / Jakob Handl.
— [Altamonte Springs, FL?] : Anglo-American Music Publishers :
distributed by Worldwide Music International, c2005. — 1 score (4 p.) ;
28 cm.
Includes biographical note. — Latin words.
System number: 013594209

Lole, Simon.
Ubi caritas et amor / Simon Lole. — Matfield : Encore Publications, c2005.
— 1 score (4 p.) ; 26 c m.
For two soprano voices and organ. — Words attributed to St. Paulinus of Aquileia.
System number: 013416531

*Palestrina, Giovanni Pierluigi da, 1525?-1594.
[Motets (1584 : Voices (4)). *Selections*]
Alma redemptoris ; Ave Regina ; and, Salve Regina : SSSA / Giovanni
Pierluigi da Palestrina ; transcribed and edited by Jon Dixon. — Carshalton
Beeches : JOED Music, 2001, c1994. — 1 score (20 p.) ; 30 cm. —
Renaissance polyphonic choral music
"The music has been transposed into modern clefs at a pitch suitable for women's
voices"—Pref. — Source: Later editions of the second book of motets for 4 voices,
published Venice: Angelo Gardano, 1598 and 1604. — Cover title. — Duration:
5:00 ; 4:40 ; 4:40. — Latin words; English translation printed as text preceding each
work.
Pl. no. JOED P27h
System number: 013498068

782.6265
Cousins, Mervyn.
Be joyful! : for sopranos (with divisions) and piano (or organ) / Mervyn
Cousins. — Matfield : Encore Publications, c2005. — 1 score (8 p.) ;
26 cm.
"Words: from Psalms 100 and 47, with an Eisteddfod reference!"—Caption.
System number: 013299044

Ledger, Philip.
Gift of love : for solo, upper voices (SSA) & keyboard / Philip Ledger &
David Miller ; words by Richard Pomfret. — Matfield : Encore
Publications, c2003. — 1 score (4 p.) ; 26 cm.
System number: 013220448

Parnell, Andrew.
Dear Lord and father of mankind : for two-part upper voices and organ /
Andrew Parnell. — Matfield : Encore Publications, c2005. — 1 score
(4 p.) ; 26 cm.
Words by J.G. Whittier.
System number: 013220445

Tadman-Robins, Hilary.
Loving shepherd : for soprano solo, two-part upper voices and organ or
piano / Hilary Tadman-Robins. — Matfield : Encore Publications, c2005. —
1 score (7 p.) ; 26 cm.
Words by Jane E. Leeson.
System number: 013382732

Vaughan Williams, Ralph, 1872-1958.
[Fantasia on Greensleeves ; *arr*]
Greensleeves : or, The king of love : a choral setting for female voice choir
and piano or orchestra of "Fantasia on Greensleeves" / by R. Vaughan
Williams ; arranged by Philip Lane. — Tewkesbury : Roberton Publications,
c2004. — 1 score (12 p.) ; 26 cm.
For women's voices (SSA) with piano or organ acc. Orchestral acc. available
separately. — Words to Greensleeves from "A handfull of pleasant delites", 1584.
Words to The king of love by H.W. Baker.
Publ. no. 75479
ISMN M222261358
System number: 013193259
Primary classification 782.642

782.627
Hughes, John, 1873-1932.
[Cwm Rhondda ; *arr.*]
Cwm Rhondda : i leisiau merched a phiano = for female voices and piano /
John Hughes (Llanilltud Faerdref) ; trefnwyd gan Arwel Hughes. — St.
Bride's Major : Aureus Publishing, [2005?], c1994. — 1 score (6 p.) ;
30 cm.
For three-part female chorus (SSA). — Welsh and English words.
Publ. no. A.P. 38
System number: 013382379

*Rose, Barry, 1934-
Watts's cradle hymn : SSA and organ / Barry Rose. — London : Novello
& Co, [2005?], c1999. — 1 score (3 p.) ; 25 cm.
Words by Isaac Watts.
Publ. no. NOV955922
System number: 013506274

Wondrous love : SSA a capella [sic] / arr. by Betty Bertaux. — [U.S.A.] :
Boosey & Hawkes ; Milwaukee, Wis. : exclusively distributed by Hal
Leonard, c2005. — 1 score (iii, 6 p.) : facsim. ; 27 cm. — (Betty
Bertaux series)
"Early American Sacred Harp hymn (Christopher)"—Caption. — Includes
program notes for the arranger.
Publ. no. 48018909
ISMN M051475865
System number: 013243922

782.628
*Boyle, Rory.
Flower of all : a carol of the Incarnation : SSAA chorus / Rory Boyle ;
text, John Audelay, c.1426 (adapted). — London : Novello Publishing,
c2005. — 1 score (4 p.) ; 25 cm.
Includes piano reduction for rehearsal only. — Caption title.
Publ. no. NOV161381
System number: 013434226

782.6281722
*People, look east : upper-voices and organ / Besançon melody arr.
Barry Rose ; [words by] Eleanor Farjeon. — London : Novello & Co,
[2005?], c1999. — 1 score (3 p.) ; 25 cm.
Publ. no. NOV955878
System number: 013506279

*Voth, Ellen Gilson, 1972-
An Advent carol : for upper voices (SSA) and keyboard / Ellen Gilson
Voth. — [New York] : Oxford University Press, c2005. — 1 score (7 p.) ;
27 cm. — Oxford Advent music
First line: This Advent moon shines cold and clear. — Words by Christina
Rossetti. — Includes biographical note.
ISBN 9780193868762
ISBN 0193868768
System number: 013472165

782.6281723
*The angel Gabriel : for soprano solo, upper voices (SSAA) and harp /
[Basque traditional ; arranged by] Robert A.M. Ross. — [New York] :
Oxford University Press, c2005. — 1 score (11 p.) ; 27 cm. — Oxford
church music
Words by Sabine Baring-Gould. — Includes biographical note about the arranger.
ISBN 9780193868717
ISBN 0193868717
System number: 013472190

Ar gyfer heddiw'r bore'n faban bach = For us this Christmas morning :
traditional Welsh folk-song arranged for SSAA choir and piano / by
Jayne Davies ; English text by Rhian Davies. — Tewkesbury :
Roberton Publications, c2004. — 1 score (11 p.) ; 26 cm.
Words in Welsh and English.
Publ. no. 75457
ISMN M222252288
System number: 013193235

Chilcott, Bob.
The angel Gabriel / Bob Chilcott. — Oxford : Oxford University Press,
c2004. — 1 score (7 p.) : port. ; 26 cm. — Oxford carols
For womens' voices (SS) and piano. — Words by Sabine Baring-Gould. —
Includes biographical note.
Publ. no. BC73
ISBN 0193433257
ISBN 9780193433250
System number: 013084329

*Lewis, Paul, 1943-
Child's carol : for two-part choir or two solo voices with piano or harp /
words by Helen Cresswell ; music by Paul Lewis. — Tewkesbury :
Roberton Publications, a part of Goodmusic Publishing, c2005. — 1
score (8 p.) ; 26 cm.
Pl. no. 75477
ISMN M222261280
System number: 013373065

*Rentz, Earlene.
Lo, how a rose e'er blooming = (Es ist ein' Ros' entsprungen) : for upper
voices (SA), flute and piano / [from Alte Catholische Geistliche
Kirchengesang' (1599) harmonized by Michael Praetorius (1609) ;
arranged by] Earlene Rentz. — [New York] : Oxford University Press,
c2005. — 1 score (7 p.) ; 27 cm. — Oxford Christmas music
Words are an English translation by Theodore Baker of fifteenth-century German
words. — Includes alternative modern words. — Flute part also printed separately
following score.
ISBN 9780193868908
ISBN 0193868903
System number: 013472544

*Still, still, still : for SAA chorus and organ / [arranged by] Barry Rose
(1999). — London : Novello & Co, [2005?], c1999. — 1 score (5 p.) ;
25 cm.
"Trad. German arr. Barry Rose" - caption. — German words.
Publ. no. NOV955911
System number: 013506277

The Virgin Mary had a baby boy / [West Indian] ; arranged by Michael
Neaum for three-part female voice choir and piano. — Tewkesbury :
Roberton Publications, a part of Goodmusic Publishing, c2004. — 1 score
(7 p.) ; 26 cm.
First line: De Virgin Mary had a baby boy.
Pl. no. 75464
ISMN M222258938
System number: 013192676

Wiggins, Christopher.
I sing of a maiden : SSA and organ / Christopher Wiggins. — Oxford :
Oxford University Press, c2005. — 1 score (8 p.) ; 26 cm. — (Christmas
carols)
Words: anonymous 15th century.
Publ. no. X459
ISBN 0193432714
System number: 013243540

782.62921722
*Rose, Barry, 1934-
An Advent responsory : I look from afar : for SSAA chorus / Barry Rose. —
London : Novello & Co, [2005?], c1999. — [3] p. of music ; 25 cm.
Words translated from an early rite of the Office of Matins for Advent Sunday.
Publ. no. NOV955790
System number: 013506231

782.6294
Goode, David, organist.
Like as the hart : for sopranos (with solo parts) and organ / David Goode. —
Matfield : Encore Publications, c2005. — 1 score (11 p.) ; 26 cm.
Mixed Latin and English words from Psalm 42, v.1-3.
System number: 013182240

782.632231587
Jackman, Jeremy.
Wedding responses : for upper voices (divisi) / by Jeremy Jackman. —
London : Stainer & Bell, c2005. — 1 score (4 p.) ; 26 cm.
For 4-part women's chorus. — Words from the Book of Common Prayer.
Publ. no. W216
ISMN M220221514
System number: 013307563

782.6326
Parnell, Andrew.
Preces and responses / words, The Book of common prayer ; music, Andrew
Parnell. — Matfield : Encore Publications, c2005. — 1 score (4 p.) ; 26 cm.
For women's voices (SSA), unacc. — Caption title.
System number: 013220461

782.642
Andersson, Benny.
[Mamma mia! *Selections; arr.*]
Mamma mia! : choral highlights : SSA / arranged by Mac Huff. —
Milwaukee, Wis. : Hal Leonard, c2005. — 1 score (48 p.) ; 27 cm. —
Broadway choral series
Medley of 7 songs from the musical "Mamma mia!" based on ABBA songs. — Arr.
for women's voices (SSA) and piano. — Words and music by Benny Andersson,
Björn Ulvaeus and Stig Anderson.
Publ. no. 08621356
System number: 013220010

Carey, Paul, 1954-
A cradle song : for upper voices (SA) and piano or harp / Paul Carey. —
[New York] : Oxford University Press, c2005. — 1 score (9 p.) ; 27 cm. —
Oxford music for upper voices
Words by William Blake, also printed for reference preceding score. — Includes
biographical note.
ISBN 0193868296
System number: 013174157

De Wald, Frank K.
If you were coming in the fall : 2-part treble / [music] by Frank K. DeWald.
— [New York?] : Boosey & Hawkes ; Milwaukee, Wis. : exclusively
distributed by Hal Leonard, c2005. — 1 score (10 p.) ; 27 cm. — (Doreen
Rao's choral music experience) — (CME in high voice)
"For two-part treble voices [in fact, soprano and alto], horn (or cello) &
piano"—Caption. — Parts for horn in F and cello also printed separately on p. 9-10.
— Words by Emily Dickinson, also printed for reference. — Includes program and
biographical notes.
Publ. no. 48018968
ISMN M051475605
System number: 013361318

DeWald, Frank K.
Summer's farewell : [for SSA voices, viola or horn & piano] / by Frank
K. DeWald. — [New York?] : Boosey & Hawkes ; Milwaukee :
exclusively distributed by Hal Leonard, c2005. — 1 score (6 p.) ; 27 cm.
— (CME in high voice) — (Doreen Rao's choral music experience)
Words by Emily Dickinson. — Parts for viola and horn p. 7-8. — Includes
biographical and programme notes.
Publ. no. 48018967
ISMN M051475612
System number: 013312827

Hind, John, 1916-
[Shakespearean songs]
Two Shakespearean songs : for SSA and piano / by John Hind. —
London : Novello, [2005?], c1958. — 1 score (8 p.) ; 25 cm.
Publ. no. NOV510617
System number: 013173213

*Larsen, Libby.
A young nun singing : for unaccompanied upper voices (SSA) / Libby
Larsen. — [New York] : Oxford University Press, c2005. — 1 score
(27 p.) ; 27 cm. — Oxford music for upper voices
Includes piano reduction for rehearsal only. — Words by various authors; also
printed as text p.26-27. — Includes biographical and programme notes.
ISBN 9780193868557
ISBN 0193868555
System number: 013472566

The last rose of summer : for upper voices (SSA), flute and piano / [Irish
air ; arr.] Earlene Rentz. — [New York] : Oxford University Press,
c2004. — 1 score (9 p.) ; 27 cm. — Oxford music for upper voices
Flute part printed separately following score. — Includes biographical note.
ISBN 0193867397
ISBN 9780193867390
System number: 013050493

Lennon, John, 1940-1980.
[Fool on the hill; *arr.*]
The fool on the hill : [for SSA and piano] / words and music by John
Lennon and Paul McCartney ; recorded by Sergio Mendes ; arranged by
Mac Huff. — Milwaukee, Wis. : Hal Leonard, c2003. — 1 score (12 p.) ;
27 cm. — Vocal jazz series
Publ. no. 08743686
System number: 013211827

*Moeran, E. J. (Ernest John), 1894-1950.
[Choral music. *Selections*]
Collected choral music. Volume two, female (and treble) voices / E.J.
Moeran ; edited by John Talbot. — Centenary ed. — London : Thames
Publishing, c2003. — 1 score (63 p.) ; 26 cm.
Mostly two-part songs (SS or SA) with piano acc.; includes 2 three-part songs,
unacc. — Mostly reprinted from earlier editions. — Editorial notes following
score.
System number: 012965821

*Neaum, Michael.
Japanese lullaby : for choir of female voices with soloists and piano
accompaniment / [traditional] ; arranged by Michael Neaum. —
Tewkesbury : Roberton Publications, a part of Goodmusic Publishing,
c2005. — 1 score (7 p.) ; 26 cm.
Duration:2:00. — Romanized Japanese words; approximate English translation
also provided for reference.
Pl. no. 75470
ISMN M222258990
System number: 013373016

Portman, Rachel.
[Little prince. Birds; *arr.*]
The birds : from The little prince : for SSA and piano / Rachel Portman ;
[arr. by Richard Allain] — London : Chester Music c2003. — 1 score
(9 p.) ; 25 cm.
Song from the opera based on Antoine de Saint-Exupery's "Le petit prince." —
Words by Nicholas Wright.
Publ. no. CH69553
ISBN 1846090504
System number: 013213576

Portman, Rachel.
[Little prince. Lamplighters; *arr.*]
The lamplighters : from The little prince ; for SSA and piano / Rachel
Portman ; [arr. by Richard Allain] — London : Chester Music, c2003. —
1 score (19 p) ; 25 cm.
Song from the opera based on Antoine de Saint-Exupery's "Le petit prince". —
Words by Nicholas Wright.
Publ. no. CH69531
ISBN 1846090482
System number: 013213662

Portman, Rachel.
[Little prince. Look at the stars; *arr.*]
Look at the stars : from The little prince ; for SSA and piano / Rachel Portman ; [arr. by Richard Allain] — London : Chester Music, c2003. — 1 score (12 p) ; 25 cm.
Song from the opera based on Antoine de Saint-Exupery's "Le petit prince". — Words by Nicholas Wright.
Publ. no. CH69542
ISBN 1846090490
System number: 013213587

Portman, Rachel.
[Little prince. Roses; *arr.*]
The roses : from The little prince : for SSA and piano / Rachel Portman ; [arr. by Richard Allain] — London : Chester Music c2003. — 1 score (11 p.) ; 25 cm.
Song from the opera based on Antoine de Saint-Exupery's "Le petit prince." — Words by Nicholas Wright.
Publ. no. CH69520
ISBN 1846090474
System number: 013213598

Portman, Rachel.
[Little prince. Stars; *arr.*]
The stars : from The little prince ; for SSA and piano / Rachel Portman ; [arr. by Richard Allain] — London : Chester Music, c2003. — 1 score (17 p) ; 25 cm.
Song from the opera based on Antoine de Saint-Exupery's "Le petit prince". — Words by Nicholas Wright.
Publ. no. CH69564
ISBN 1846090512
System number: 013213592

Richardson, Michael.
How many bards : SSA / [music by] Michael Richardson. — [New York?] : Boosey & Hawkes ; Milwaukee, Wis. : exclusively distributed by Hal Leonard, c2005. — 1 score (10 p.) ; 27 cm. — (Doreen Rao's choral music experience) — (CME in high voice)
For SSA voices, oboe (or violin) & piano. — Oboe or violin part also printed separately on p. 10. — Words by John Keats, also printed for reference with interpretation by the composer. — Includes program and biographical notes.
Publ. no. 48018787
ISMN M051475568
System number: 013243892

Rosseter, Philip, 1567 or 8-1623.
[What then is love but mourning?; *arr.*]
What, then, is love but mourning? / by Philip Rosseter ; arranged for unaccompanied female voice choir (SSA) by Michael Neaum. — Tewkesbury : Roberton Publications, c2005. — 1 score (3 p.) ; 26 cm.
Originally for solo voice and lute.
Publ. no. 75468
ISMN M222258976
System number: 013193607

Scarborough Fair : English folk song : arranged for female voice choir and piano / by Derek J. Clark. — Tewkesbury : Roberton Publications, c2004. — 1 score (14 p.) ; 26 cm.
Chorus: SSAA.
Publ. no. 75431
ISMN M222260740
System number: 013193334

She's like the swallow : traditional Newfoundland song for SSAA choir and piano / arranged by Michael Neaum. — Tewkesbury : Roberton Publications, a part of Goodmusic Publishing, c2005. — 1 score (8 p.) ; 26 cm.
Pl. no. 75467
ISMN M222258969
System number: 013193600

Vaughan Williams, Ralph, 1872-1958.
[Fantasia on Greensleeves; *arr*]
Greensleeves : or, The king of love : a choral setting for female voice choir and piano or orchestra of "Fantasia on Greensleeves" / by R. Vaughan Williams ; arranged by Philip Lane. — Tewkesbury : Roberton Publications, c2004. — 1 score (12 p.) ; 26 cm.
For women's voices (SSA) with piano or organ acc. Orchestral acc. available separately. — Words to Greensleeves from "A handfull of pleasant delites", 1584. Words to The king of love by H.W. Baker.
Publ. no. 75479
ISMN M222261358
System number: 013193259
Also classified at 782.6265

Zhou, Long, 1953-
Four seasons : for unaccompanied treble chorus (SSAA) / Zhou Long. — [New York] : Oxford University Press, c2004. — 1 score (15 p.) ; 27 cm. — Oxford music for upper voices
Includes piano reduction for rehearsal only. — Includes biographical note. — English words translated from the Chinese by the composer; words also printed for reference in Chinese and English preceding score.
ISBN 0193867796
System number: 013115222

782.64216200944
J'ai vû le loup : SSA a cappella / arranged by Stephen Hatfield. — [New York?] : Boosey & Hawkes ; Milwaukee, Wis. : exclusively distributed by Hal Leonard, c2004. — 1 score (7 p.) ; 27 cm. — (Doreen Rao's choral music experience) — (CME in high voice)
Medieval French words, also printed for reference with phonetic transcription and English translation for reference. — Includes program, performance and biographical notes.
Publ. no. 48018832
ISMN M051475636
System number: 013243898

782.64216209415
My love's an arbutus : traditional Irish melody arranged for SSA choir, solo voice and piano / by Michael Neaum. — Tewkesbury : Roberton Publications, c2005. — 1 score (7 p.) ; 26 cm.
Publ. no. 75469
ISMN M222258983
System number: 013193614

Oft in the stilly night : traditional Irish song for female voice choir (SSA), solo voice and piano / words by Thomas Moore ; arranged by Michael Neaum. — Tewkesbury : Roberton Publications, c2004. — 1 score (7 p.) ; 26 cm.
Publ. no. 75466
ISMN M222258952
System number: 013192689

782.64216209429
Bugeilio'r gwenith gwyn = Watching the white wheat : traditional Welsh folk-song arranged for SSA choir, solo voice and piano / by Jayne Davies ; English text by Rhian Davies. — Tewkesbury : Roberton Publications, c2004. — 1 score (14 p.) ; 26 cm.
Words in Welsh and English.
Publ. no. 75454
ISMN M222252257
System number: 013193376

Deryn y bwn o'r banna' = The bittern : traditional Welsh folk-song arranged for SSAA choir, solo voice and piano and bottle (optional) / by Jayne Davies ; English text by Rhian Davies. — Tewkesbury : Roberton Publications, c2004. — 1 score (14 p.) ; 26 cm.
Includes note on the bittern and performance note. — Words in Welsh and English.
Publ. no. 75453
ISMN M222252240
System number: 013193361

Y gelynnen = The holly : traditional Welsh folk-song arranged for female voice choir and piano / by Jayne Davies ; English text by Rhian Davies. — Tewkesbury : Roberton Publications, c2004. — 1 score (10 p.) ; 26 cm.
Chorus: SA with divisions. — Words in Welsh and English; includes pronunciation guide.
Publ. no. 75456
ISMN M222252271
System number: 013193204

Y g'loman = The dove : traditional Welsh folk-song arranged for SSAA choir, solo voice, flute and piano / by Jayne Davies ; English text by Rhian Davies. — Tewkesbury : Roberton Publications, c2004. — 1 score (11 p.) ; 26 cm.
Words in Welsh and English.
Publ. no. 75452
ISMN M222252233
System number: 013193354

Lisa Lân = Lisa fair : traditional Welsh folk-song arranged for SSAA choir and piano / by Jayne Davies ; English text by Rhian Davies. — Tewkesbury : Roberton Publications, c2004. — 1 score (11 p.) ; 26 cm.
Words in Welsh with English translation.
Publ. no. 75455
ISMN M222252264
System number: 013193393

782.6421620944
Two French folksongs : for female voice choir (SSA), soloists and piano / arranged by Michael Neaum. — Tewkesbury : Roberton Publications, c2005. — 1 score (15 p.) ; 26 cm.
French words.
Publ. no. 75465
ISMN M222258945
System number: 013193595

782.64216209729l
*Neaum, Michael.
Duerme negrito : traditional Cuban song arranged for SSAA choir and soloist with piano / by Michael Neaum. — Tewkesbury : Roberton Publications, a part of Goodmusic Publishing, c2005. — 1 score (11 p.) ; 26 cm.
Duration: 2:45. — Spanish words; English translation provided for reference p. [2]
Pl. no. 75471
ISMN M222259003
System number: 013373083

782.642164

Rodgers, Richard, 1902-1979.
[Sound of music. My favorite things; *arr.*]
My favorite things : from The sound of music : SSA / lyrics by Oscar Hammerstein II ; music by Richard Rodgers ; arranged by Mac Huff. — [S.l.] : Williamson Music ; Milwaukee, Wis. : exclusively distributed by Hal Leonard, c2004. — 1 score (15 p.) ; 27 cm. — SSA showcase
For 3-part female chorus with piano acc., including chord symbols.
Publ. no. 08621338
System number: 013424061

782.6625

Bach, Johann Sebastian, 1685-1750.
[Weihnachts-Oratorium. Bereite dich Zion, mit zärtlichen Trieben; *arr. English & German*]
Prepare thyself, Zion : unison treble / J. S. Bach ; arranged by B. Wayne Bisbee. — [New York?] : Boosey & Hawkes ; Milwaukee, Wis. : exclusively distributed by Hal Leonard, c2005. — 1 score (6 p.) ; 27 cm. — (Doreen Rao's choral music experience) — (CME beginning repertoire)
For unison voices & piano. — "Text attributed to Christian Fredrich [sic] Henrici ... English version by Rev. John Troutbeck"—Caption. — Includes program and biographical notes, and words printed for reference.
Publ. no. 48018853
ISMN M051475797
System number: 013243843

Sadler, Kathryn.
LAWA : (Love Art Wisdom Adventure) : 4-part treble voices a cappella / [words & music by] Kathryn Sadler. — [New York?] : Boosey & Hawkes ; Milwaukee, Wis. : exclusively distributed by Hal Leonard, c2005. — 1 score (8 p.) ; 27 cm. — (Doreen Rao's choral music experience) — (CME in high voice)
Consists of four melodic parts accompanied by a four-part chordal chorale, which "can be adapted for guitar, piano or string quartet". — Includes program and biographical notes. — Words also printed for reference.
Publ. no. 48018827
ISMN M051475988
System number: 013324488

782.6642

Bisbee, B. Wayne.
Night song : 2-pt treble / [music by] B. Wayne Bisbee. — [New York?] : Boosey & Hawkes ; Milwaukee, Wis. : exclusively distributed by Hal Leonard, c2005. — 1 score (7 p.) ; 27 cm. — (Doreen Rao's choral music experience) — (CME intermediate repertoire)
For two-part treble voices, piano & triangle or finger cymbals. — Text by Peggy Leavitt. — Includes program and biographical notes, and words printed for reference.
Publ. no. 48004995
ISMN M051473175
System number: 013243862

782.6642162009429

Lullaby = (Suo-gân) : 3-part treble / arranged by Nigel E. Jones. — [New York?] : Boosey & Hawkes ; Milwaukee, Wis. : exclusively distributed by Hal Leonard, c2005. — 1 score (4 p.) ; 27 cm. — (Doreen Rao's choral music experience) — (CME Celtic voices)
English and traditional Welsh words, also printed for reference. — English translation by Nigel E. Jones. — Includes performance and biographical notes.
Publ. no. 48018830
ISMN M051475940
System number: 013243902

782.6647

Ramsey, Andrea.
From a river's edge : treble voices / [words & music by] Andrea Ramsey. — [New York?] : Boosey & Hawkes ; Milwaukee, Wis. : exclusively distributed by Hal Leonard, c2005. — 1 score (7 p.) ; 27 cm. — (Doreen Rao's choral music experience) — (CME intermediate repertoire)
With piano acc. — Includes performance and biographical notes.
Publ. no. 48018803
ISMN M051475599
System number: 013243914

782.7 – CHILDREN'S VOICES

782.7

*Brookes, Katherine.
[Pompeii. *Selections*]
Pompeii : escape from the cloud : assembly pack / written by Katherine Brookes ; music by Katherine Brookes. — Kenilworth : Educational Musicals, c2005. — 1 score ([13] p.) : ill. ; 30 cm. + 1 compact disc.
Shorter, simpler version of the childrenâ ™s musical of the same title, for use in school assembly; 3 songs with libretto and performance notes. — For treble voices, with piano accompaniment and guitar chord symbols. — "...an Anthony James Musical". — "Illustrations by Anthony James"—P. [1] — CD contains rehearsal and performance tracks.
ISBN 1905123485
System number: 013587016

*Brookes, Katherine.
[Pompeii. *Selections*]
Pompeii : life in a Roman town : assembly pack / written by Katherine Brookes ; music by Katherine Brookes. — Kenilworth : Educational Musicals, c2005. — 1 score ([32] p.) ; 30 cm. + 1 compact disc.
Shorter, simpler version of the childrenâ ™s musical of the same title, for use in school assembly; 3 songs with libretto and performance notes. — For treble voices, with piano accompaniment and guitar chord symbols. — "...an Anthony James Musical". — CD contains rehearsal and performance tracks.
ISBN 1905123477
System number: 013587020

*Hewitt, Daniel.
[Battle of Britain. *Selections*]
The Battle of Britain : their finest hour : assembly pack / written by Anthony James ; music [& lyrics] by Dan[iel] Hewitt. — Kenilworth : Maplewood Education : Educational Musicals, c2005. — 1 score ([25] p.) : ill. ; 30 cm. + 1 compact disc.
Shorter, simpler version of the childrenâ ™s musical of the same title, for use in school assembly; 3 songs with libretto and performance notes. — For treble voices, with piano accompaniment and guitar chord symbols. — "...an Anthony James Musical". — "Illustrations by Anthony James"—P. [1] — CD contains rehearsal tracks.
ISBN 1905123434
System number: 013587396

*Hewitt, Daniel.
[Christopher Columbus. *Selections*]
Christopher Columbus : voyage to the end of the world : assembly pack / written by Daniel Dalton ; music [& lyrics] by Dan Hewitt. — Kenilworth : Maplewood Education : Educational Musicals, c2004. — 1 score ([32] p.) : ill. ; 30 cm. + 1 compact disc.
Shorter, simpler version of the childrenâ ™s musical of the same title, for use in school assembly; 3 songs with libretto and performance notes. — For treble voices, with piano accompaniment and guitar chord symbols. — "...an Anthony James Musical". — "Illustrations by Anthony James"—P. [1] — CD contains rehearsal and performance tracks.
ISBN 1905123396
System number: 013587439

*Hewitt, Daniel.
[Henry VIII. *Selections*]
Henry VIII : Henry and Anne Boleyn : assembly pack / written by Daniel Dalton ; music [& lyrics] by Dan Hewitt. — Kenilworth : Educational Musicals, c2005. — 1 score ([27] p.) : ill. ; 30 cm. + 1 compact disc.
Shorter, simpler version of the childrenâ ™s musical of the same title, for use in school assembly; 3 songs with libretto and performance notes. — For treble voices, with piano accompaniment and guitar chord symbols. — "...an Anthony James Musical". — "Illustrations by Anthony James"—P. [1] — CD contains rehearsal and backing tracks.
ISBN 1905123507
System number: 013587013

*Hewitt, Daniel.
[Henry VIII. *Selections*]
Henry VIII : the break with Rome : assembly pack / written by Daniel Dalton ; music [& lyrics] by Dan Hewitt. — Kenilworth : Maplewood Education : Educational Musicals, c2003. — 1 score ([26] p.) : ill. ; 30 cm. + 1 compact disc.
Shorter, simpler version of the childrenâ ™s musical of the same title, for use in school assembly; 3 songs with libretto and performance notes. — For treble voices, with piano accompaniment and guitar chord symbols. — "...an Anthony James Musical". — "Illustrations by Anthony James. Rhymes by Anita Allen"—P. 1. — CD contains rehearsal and performance tracks.
ISBN 1905123264
System number: 013587425

*Hewitt, Daniel.
[Spanish Armada. *Selections*]
The Spanish Armada : the invasion of England : assembly pack. — Kenilworth : Maplewood Education : Educational Musicals, c2003. — 1 score ([28] p.) : ill. ; 30 cm. + 1 compact disc.
Shorter, simpler version of the children's musical of the same title, for use is school assembly; 3 songs with libretto and performance notes. — For treble voices, with piano accompaniment and guitar chord symbols. — "An Anthony James Musical". — "Written by Daniel Dalton. Music & lyrics by Daniel Hewitt. Illustrations by Anthony James. Rhymes by Anita Allen"—P. 1. — CD contains rehearsal and performance tracks.
System number: 013587402

*Hewitt, Daniel.
[Trojan horse. *Selections*]
The Trojan horse : the fall of Troy : assembly pack. — Kenilworth ; Maplewood Education : Educational Musicals, c2003. — 1 score ([38] p.) : ill. ; 30 cm. + 1 compact disc.
Shorter, simpler version of the children's musical of the same title, for use in school assembly; 3 songs with libretto and performance notes. — For treble voices, with piano accompaniment and guitar chord symbols. — "An Anthony James Musical". — "Written by Daniel Dalton. Music & Lyrics by Daniel Hewitt. Illustrations by Anthony James. Rhymes by Anita Allen"—P. 1. — CD contains rehearsal and performance tracks.
ISBN 1905123329
System number: 013587435

*Spencer, Tim.
[Ancient Olympics. *Selections*]
The ancient Olympics : the Olympic traditions : assembly pack. —
Kenilworth : Maplewood Education : Educational Musicals, c2004. — 1
score ([30] p.) : ill. ; 30 cm. + 1 compact disc.
Shorter, simpler version of the children's musical of the same title, for use in school
assembly; 3 songs with libretto and performance notes. — For treble voices, with
piano accompaniment and chord symbols. — "An Anthony James Musical". —
"Written by Daniel Dalton. Music by Tim Spencer. Ilustrations by Anthony
James. Rhymes by Anita Allen"—P. 1. — CD contains rehearsal and performance
tracks.
ISBN 1905123353
System number: 013586998

*Spencer, Tim.
[Ancient Olympics. *Selections*]
The ancient Olympics : the story of Callipateira : assembly pack / written by
Daniel Dalton ; music [& lyrics] by Tim Spencer. — Kenilworth :
Educational Musicals, c2005. — 1 score ([33] p.) : ill. ; 30 cm. + 1 compact
disc.
Shorter, simpler version of the children's musical of the same title, for use in school
assembly; 3 songs with libretto and performance notes. — For treble voices, with
piano accompaniment and chord symbols. — "...an Anthony James Musical". —
"Illustrations by Anthony James"—P. 1. — CD contains rehearsal and performance
tracks.
ISBN 1905123493
System number: 013587006

*Spencer, Tim.
[Boy king. *Selections*]
The boy king : the legend of Tutankhamun : assembly pack / written by
Anthony James ; music [& lyrics] by Tim Spencer. — Kenilworth ;
Maplewood Education : Educational Musicals, c2003. — 1 score ([26] p.) :
ill. ; 30 cm. + 1 compact disc.
Shorter, simpler version of the children's musical of the same title, for use in school
assembly; 3 songs with libretto and performance notes. — For treble voices and
piano. — "...an Anthony James Musical". — "Illustrations by Anthony
James"—P.1. — CD contains rehearsal and performance tracks.
ISBN 1905123272
System number: 013587415

*Spencer, Tim.
[Dream catcher. *Selections*]
The dream catcher : the Plains Indians of North America : assembly pack.
— Kenilworth : Maplewood Education : Educational Musicals, 2003. — 1
score ([28] p.) : ill. ; 30 cm. + 1 compact disc.
Shorter, simpler version of the childrenâ ™s musical of the same title, for use in
school assembly; 3 songs with libretto and performance notes. — For treble voices,
with piano accompaniment and guitar chord symbols. — "An Anthony James
Musical". — "Written by Anthony James. Music & lyrics by Tim Spencer.
Illustrations by Anthony James"—P. [1] — CD contains rehearsal and performance
tracks.
System number: 013587532

*Spencer, Tim.
[Lucky Viking. *Selections*]
The lucky Viking : the discovery of America : assembly pack / written by
Anthony James ; music [& lyrics] by Tim Spencer. — Kenilworth :
Educational Musicals, 2005. — 1 score ([18] p.) : ill. ; 30 cm. + 1 compact
disc.
Shorter, simpler version of the childrenâ ™s musical of the same title, for use in
school assembly; 3 songs with libretto and performance notes. — For treble voices,
with piano accompaniment. — "...an Anthony James Musical". — "Illustrations by
Anthony James"—P. [1] — CD contains rehearsal and performance tracks.
ISBN 1905123310
System number: 013587391

*Spencer, Tim.
[Monster of the maze. *Selections*]
Monster of the maze : the story of Theseus and the Minotaur : assembly
pack. — Kenilworth Maplewood Education : Educational Musicals, c2003.
— 1 score ([31] p.) : ill. ; 30 cm. + 1 compact disc.
Shorter, simpler version of the children's musical of the same title, for use in school
assembly; 3 songs with libretto and performance notes. — For treble voices, with
piano accompaniment. — "An Anthony James Musical". — "Written by Anthony
James. Music & Lyrics by Tim Spencer. Illustrations by Anthony James"—P. 1. —
CD contains rehearsal and performance tracks.
ISBN 1905123248
System number: 013587420

*Spencer, Tim.
[Trafalgar. *Selections*]
Trafalgar : Napolean's navy : assembly pack / written by Daniel Dalton ;
music [& lyrics] by Tim Spencer. — Kenilworth : Educational Musicals,
c2005. — 1 score ([28] p.) : ill. ; 30 cm. + 1 compact disc.
Shorter, simpler version of the children's musical of the same title, for use in
school assembly; 3 songs with libretto and performance notes. — For treble voices,
with piano accompaniment and chord symbols. — "...an Anthony James Musical".
— "Illustrations by Anthony James. Narration by Anita Allen"—P. [1] — CD
contains rehearsal and performance tracks.
ISBN 1905123450
System number: 013586933

*Spencer, Tim.
[Trafalgar. *Selections*]
Trafalgar : Nelson's finest hour : assembly pack / written by Daniel
Dalton ; musc [& lyrics] by Tim Spencer. — Kenilworth : Maplewood
Education : Educational Musicals, c2005. — 1 sccore ([29] p.) : ill. ;
30 cm. + 1 compact disc.
Shorter, simpler version of the children's musical of the same title, for use in
school assembly; 3 songs with libretto and performance notes. — For treble
voices, with piano accompaniment. — "...an Anthony James Musical". —
"Illustrations by Anthony James. Rhymes by Anita Allen"—P. [1] — CD contains
rehearsal and backing tracks.
ISBN 1905123426
System number: 013587002

*Spencer, Tim.
[Victorian historian. *Selections*]
The Victorian historian : history is boring? : assembly pack / written by
Anthony James ; music [& lyrics] by Tim Spencer. — Kenilworth :
Maplewood Education : Educational Musicals, c2004. — 1 score ([24]
p.) : ill. ; 30 cm. + 1 compact disc.
Shorter, simpler version of the childrenâ ™s musical of the same title, for use in
school assembly; 3 songs with libretto and performance notes. — For treble
voices, with piano accompaniment and guitar chord symbols. — "...an Anthony
James Musical". — "Illustrations by Anthony James"—P. 1. — CD contains
rehearsal and performance tracks.
ISBN 1905123388
System number: 013587074

*Spencer, Tim.
[Victorian historian. *Selections*]
The Victorian historian : rogues, railways & royalty: assembly pack. —
Kenilworth : Maplewood Education : Educational Musicals, c2004. — 1
score ([22] p.) : ill. ; 30 cm. + 1 compact disc.
Shorter, simpler version of the childrenâ ™s musical of the same title, for use in
school assembly; 3 songs with libretto and performance notes. — For treble
voices, with piano accompaniment and guitar chord symbols. — "An Anthony
James Musical". — "Written by Anthony James. Music & lyrics by Tim Spencer.
Illustrations by Anthony James"—P. 1. — CD contains rehearsal and performance
tracks.
ISBN 190512337X
System number: 013587081

*Spencer, Tim.
[Warrior queen. *Selections*]
The warrior queen : Boudica and the Romans : assembly pack. —
Kenilworth : Maplewood Education : Educational Musicals, c2004. — 1
score ([27] p.) : ill. ; 30 cm. + 1 compact disc.
Shorter, simpler version of the childrenâ ™s musical of the same title, for use in
school assembly; 3 songs with libretto and performance notes. — For treble
voices, with piano accompaniment. — "An Anthony James Musical". — "Written
by Anthony James. Music & lyrics by Tim Spencer. Illustrations by Anthony
James"—P. [1] — CD contains rehearsal and backing tracks.
ISBN 1905123361
System number: 013587444

*Spencer, Tim.
[Warrior queen. *Selections*]
The warrior queen : the Romans in Britannia : assembly pack / written by
Anthony James ; music [& lyrics] by Tim Spencer. — Kenilworth :
Educational Musicals, c2000. — 1 score ([26] p.) : ill. ; 30 cm. + 1
compact disc.
Shorter, simpler version of the childrenâ ™s musical of the same title, for use in
school assembly; 3 songs with libretto and performance notes. — For treble
voices, with piano accompaniment. — "...an Anthony James Musical". —
"Illustrations by Anthony James"—P. 1. — CD contains rehearsal and backing
tracks.
ISBN 1905123302
System number: 013586988

782.71542
Coulais, Bruno.
[Choristes. *Vocal score. Selections*]
Les choristes : piano, chant (choeurs), paroles. — [France?] : Éditions
Galatée : Bookmakers International : Paul Beuscher, distribution
exclusive, c2004. — 1 score (64 p.) : col. ill. ; 31 cm.
Music from the 2004 film "Les choristes." — Music by Bruno Coulais and
Christophe Barratier. — Mostly for boy's voices (SA or SSA) and piano.
'Pépinot' is for piano solo. 'Fond-de-l'Etang' is an unaccompanied melody for
sopranos. — "Jacques Perrin présente Les choristes." — Words in French or
Latin, also printed for reference after each song.
Publ. no. AG 06 02 82 01
System number: 013376913

782.725
Hardwick, John.
Come on let's celebrate! : 20 songs and talks for all occasions / John
Hardwick. — Buxhall : Kevin Mayhew, 2004. — 71 p. : music, port. ;
30 cm. + 1 CD.
Songs arranged for keyboard, with chord symbols and interlinear text. — "All
songs by John Hardwick, except: 'Baby, Jesus' by Rachel Munoz Hardwick and
'God loves you when' by Joy Howell"—t.p. verso.
Publ. no. 1400372
ISBN 1844173267
ISMN M570243907
System number: 013173251

Johnson, Mark (Mark Noel Hugh).
Songs for every assembly : 15 great new songs for the whole year through / by Mark and Helen Johnson. — Hersham Green : Out of the Ark Music, 2004, c1998. — 1 score (60 p.) ; 30 cm. + 1 compact disc.
For voice(s) and piano, with chord symbols. — "5-11s"—Cover. — Words also printed separately for reference. — CD contains full performances of the songs and backing tracks.
ISBN 0951911635 (book & CD pack)
System number: 013272453

Junior praise / compiled by Phil Burt, Peter Horrobin and Greg Leavers. — Combined music ed. — London : Collins, 2004. — 1 score ([989] p.) ; 24 cm.
"The bestselling collection of songs for young people"—cover. — Melodies with piano acc. and guitar chord symbols. — Includes list of copyright holders' addresses, notes for guitarists, and indexes. — Previous ed.: 1997.
ISBN 0007184670
System number: 012878554

*Rose, Barry, 1934-
God be with you till we meet again : unis. voices & org. / Barry Rose. — London : Novello & Co, c2004. — 1 score (4 p.) ; 25 cm.
For unison children's voices with descant, optional flute part and piano or organ acc. — Words by Jeremiah Eames Rankin.
Publ. no. NOV955801
System number: 013506226

782.742
Children's songs : piano, vocal, guitar. — Milwaukee, Wis. : Hal Leonard, [2004?] — 1 score (31 p.) ; 31 cm. + 1 compact disc. — Hal Leonard piano play-along v. 9
7 songs arranged for voice and piano, with chord symbols and guitar chord diagrams, and 1 piano piece with chord symbols. — Words and music by various songwriters. — CD contains full performances and backing tracks.
Publ. no. HL00311080
ISBN 0634069098
System number: 013219922

Diamond, Eileen.
Let's make music fun. The blue songbook / Eileen Diamond. — London : International Music Publications, c2004. — 1 score (73 p.) ; 31 cm + 2 sound discs (digital ; 4 3/4 in.)
"A selection of familiar and new songs including action songs, part songs, story songs, instrumental songs and rounds"—T.p. — With piano acc. and chord symbols. — For pre-school, key stage one and key stage two. — Includes teaching ideas and performance notes. — CDs contain full performances and backing tracks.
Publ. no. 10075A
ISBN 1843287757
ISMN M570217755
System number: 013039915

Diamond, Eileen.
Let's make music fun. The green songbook / Eileen Diamond. — London : International Music Publications, c2004. — 1 score (71 p.) ; 31 cm + 2 sound discs (digital ; 4 3/4 in.)
"A selection of familiar and new songs including action songs, part songs, story songs, instrumental songs and rounds"—T.p. — With piano acc. and chord symbols. — For pre-school, key stage one and key stage two. — Includes teaching ideas and performance notes. — CDs contain full performances and backing tracks.
Publ. no. 10077A
ISBN 1843287773
ISMN M570217779
System number: 013039917

Diamond, Eileen.
Let's make music fun. The red songbook / Eileen Diamond. — London : International Music Publications, c2004. — 1 score (73 p.) ; 31 cm + 2 sound discs (digital ; 4 3/4 in.)
"A selection of familiar and new songs including action songs, part songs, story songs, instrumental songs and rounds"—T.p. — With piano acc. and chord symbols. — For pre-school, key stage one and key stage two. — Includes teaching ideas and performance notes. — CDs contain full performances and backing tracks.
Publ. no. 10074A
ISBN 1843287749
ISMN M570217755
System number: 013039914

Diamond, Eileen.
Let's make music fun. The yellow songbook / Eileen Diamond. — London : International Music Publications, c2004. — 1 score (83 p.) ; 31 cm + 2 sound discs (digital ; 4 3/4 in.)
"A selection of familiar and new songs including action songs, part songs, story songs, instrumental songs and rounds"—T.p. — With piano acc. and chord symbols. — For pre-school, key stage one and key stage two. — Includes teaching ideas and performance notes. — CDs contain full performances and backing tracks.
Publ. no. 10076A
ISBN 1843287765
ISMN M570217762
System number: 013039916

Elgar, Edward, 1857-1934.
[Rapid stream, voices (2)]
The rapid stream ; The woodland stream / Edward Elgar ; edited by David Patrick. — [Barnet] : Fitzjohn Music Publications, c2005. — 1 score (6 p.) ; 30 cm.
For two voices (SA) and piano. — Words by Charles Mackay.
System number: 013214639

The fantastic big book of children's songs. — Milwaukee, Wis. : Hal Leonard, [2004]. — 1 score (238 p.) ; 31 cm.
67 songs for voice and piano, with guitar chord symbols.
Publ. no. HL00311062
ISBN 0634068202
System number: 013129773

*Hewitt, Daniel.
Greek selection 1 : a collection of songs from Educational Musicals' Greek shows / [music & lyrics by Daniel Hewitt & Tim Spencer] — Kenilworth : Maplewood Education : Educational Musicals, c2003. — 1 score ([80] p.) ; 30 cm. + 1 compact disc. — (Sing a-long songbooks)
10 songs from the children's musicals 'The Trojan horse' and 'Monster of the maze'. — For treble voices, with piano accompaniment and guitar chord symbols. — CD contains rehearsal and backing tracks.
System number: 013587341

*Hewitt, Daniel.
Tudor selection 1 : a collection of songs from Educational Musicals' Tudor shows / [music and lyrics by Daniel Hewitt] — Kenilworth : Maplewood Education : Educational Musicals, c2003. — 1 score ([60]p.) ; 30 cm. + 1 compact disc. — (Sing a-long songbooks)
10 songs from the children's musicals 'The Spanish armada' and 'Henry VIII'. — For treble voices, with piano accompaniment and chord symbols. — CD contains rehearsal and backing tracks.
System number: 013587323

*Hewitt, Daniel.
World wars I & II : a collection of wars songs from Educational Musicals shows / [music & lyrics by Daniel Hewitt & Katherine Brookes] — Kenilworth : Maplewood Education : Educational Musicals, c2003. — 1 score ([74] p.) ; 30 cm. + 1 compact disc. — (Sing a-long songbooks)
10 songs from the childrenâ ™s musicals 'Battle of Britain' and 'Happy Christmas Tommy'. — For treble voices, with piano accompaniment and guitar chord symbols. — CD contains rehearsal and backing tracks.
System number: 013587347

*Musgrave, Thea.
Going north : for children's chorus and two clarinets / Thea Musgrave. — Vocal score. — London : Novello, c2004. — 1 score (19 p.) ; 30 cm. — Transient glory
For two-part children's chorus (SA). — Words by John Keats; also printed for reference preceding score.
Publ. no. NOV955273
ISBN 184609318X
System number: 013383451

People who help us : 12 original songs from Out of the Ark Music. — Hersham Green : Out of the Ark Music, c2004. — 1 score (43 p.) : ports. ; 30 cm. + 1 compact disc. — My world (Out of the Ark Music)
With piano acc. and chord symbols. — Words and music by various songwriters. — Includes teacher's notes and lyric sheets: p.4-15. — "Developed specifically for pre-school and reception aged children"—Introduction. — CD contains full performances and backing tracks.
System number: 013269312

*Spencer, Tim.
Egyptian selection 1 : a collection of songs from Educational Musicals' Egyptian shows / [music & lyrics by Tim Spencer and Daniel Hewitt] — Kenilworth : Maplewood Education : Educational Musicals, c2003. — 1 score ([68] p.) ; 30 cm. + 1 compact disc. — (Sing a-long songbooks)
10 songs from the children's musicals 'Valley of the kings' and 'The boy king'. — For treble voices, with piano accompaniment. — CD contains rehearsal and backing tracks.
System number: 013587354

782.7421723
*Brookes, Katherine.
[Happy Christmas Tommy. *Selections*]
Happy Christmas Tommy : the Christmas miracle of 1914 : assembly pack. — Kenilworth : Maplewood Education : Educational Musicals, c2003. — 1 score ([26] p.) : ill. ; 30 cm. + 1 compact disc.
Shorter, simpler version of the childrenâ ™s musical of the same title, for use in school assembly; 3 songs with libretto and performance notes. — For treble voices, with piano accompaniment and guitar chord symbols. — "An Anthony James Musical". — "Written by Anthony James. Music & lyrics by Katherine Brookes. Illustrations by Anthony James"—P. 1. — CD contains rehearsal and performance tracks.
System number: 013587523

*Christmas selection 1 : a collection of songs from Educational Musicals' Christmas shows. — Kenilworth : Maplewood Education : Educational Musicals, c2003. — 1 score ([72] p.) ; 30 cm. + 1 compact disc. — (Sing a-long songbooks)
10 songs from four children's musicals; 'The Magic tree', 'The Star child', 'Saint Nicholas' and 'Happy Christmas Tommy'. — For treble voices, with piano accompaniment and chord symbols. — "Music & lyrics by Tim Spencer, Daniel Hewitt & Katherine Brookes"—Cover verso. — CD contains rehearsal and backing tracks.
System number: 013587517

*Christmas selection 2 : a collection of songs from our Christmas shows. —
Kenilworth : Maplewood Education : Educational Musicals, c2003. — 1
score ([68] p.) ; 30 cm. + 1 compact disc. — (Sing a-long songbooks)
10 songs from four children's musicals; 'The Magic tree', 'The Star child', 'Saint
Nicholas' and 'Happy Christmas Tommy'. — For treble voices, mainly in unison but
occasionally in 2 parts, with piano accompaniment and guitar chord symbols. —
"Music & lyrics by Tim Spencer, Daniel Hewitt & Katherine Brookes"—Cover
verso. — CD contains rehearsal and backing tracks.
System number: 013587493

*Hewitt, Daniel.
[Magic tree. Selections]
The magic tree : a story for Christmas : assembly pack. — Kenilworth :
Maplewood Education : Educational Musicals, c2003. — 1 score ([32] p.) :
ill. ; 30 cm. + 1 compact disc.
Shorter, simpler version of the children's musical of the same title, for use in school
assembly; 3 songs with libretto and performance notes. — For treble voices, with
piano accompaniment and guitar chord symbols. — "An Anthony James Musical".
— "Written by Daniel Dalton. Music & lyrics by Daniel Hewitt. Illustrations by
Anthony James. Rhyme by Anita Allen"—P. 1. — CD contains rehearsal and
performance tracks.
ISBN 1905123345
System number: 013587069

*Hewitt, Daniel.
[Saint Nicholas. Selections]
Saint Nicholas : the real Santa Claus : assembly pack. — Kenilworth :
Maplewood Education : Educational Musicals, c2003. — 1 score ([24] p.) :
ill. ; 30 cm. + 1 compact disc.
Shorter, simpler version of the children's musical of the same title; 3 songs with
libretto and performance notes. — For treble voices, with piano accompaniment and
guitar chord symbols. — "An Anthony James Musical". — "Written by Anthony
James. Music & lyrics by Daniel Hewitt. Illustrations by Anthony James"—P. 1. —
CD contains rehearsal and performance tracks.
System number: 013587060

Johnson, Mark (Mark Noel Hugh).
It's a baby! : 9 new nativity songs for 3-7 year olds / by Mark and Helen
Johnson. — Hersham Green : Out of the Ark Music, 2003, c1997. — 1
score (40 p.) : port. ; 30 cm. + 1 compact disc.
For voice(s) and piano, with chord symbols. — "Simple narration/spoken links have
been provided to join the songs together into a short play"—Overview, p. 2. — Song
words printed separately for reference, with short percussion parts. — CD contains
full performances of the songs and backing tracks.
ISBN 1901980103 (book & CD pack)
System number: 013270802
Also classified at 782.141723083

782.76196
*Milton, John, ca. 1563-1647.
[If that a sinner's sighs, voices (5)]
Two settings of "If that a sinner's sighs" : à 5, TrTrTTB, fully texted : [and]
à 6, TrTrT(with text)TBB / John Milton ; edited by Virginia Brookes. —
[S.l.] : Viola da Gamba Society of Great Britain, c2005. — 1 score (12 p.) +
6 parts ; 30 cm.
Edited for viols (with or without voices). — Cover title. — Includes critical
commentary.
Publ. no. 204
System number: 013441046
Primary classification 785.76195

782.76265
*Gordon, Andrew, composer.
An evening prayer : for unison treble choir and organ / Andrew Gordon. —
[New York] : Oxford University Press, c2005. — 1 score (5 p.) ; 27 cm. —
Oxford sacred music
Words from the Book of Common Prayer. — Includes biographical note.
ISBN 0193868652
System number: 013525131

782.7642
Bisbee, B. Wayne.
I never ate a cloud : unison treble [voices & piano] / by B. Wayne Bisbee —
[New York?] : Boosey & Hawkes ; Milwaukee : exclusively distributed by
Hal Leonard, c2005. — 1 score (8 p.) ; 27 cm. — (Doreen Rao's choral
music experience) — (CME beginning repertoire)
Words by Peggy Leavitt. — Includes biographical and programme notes.
Publ. no. 48018885
ISMN M051475773
System number: 013312813

Brunner, David L., 1953-
Painted memories : 2-pt treble / [music by] David L. Brunner. — [New
York?] : Boosey & Hawkes ; Milwaukee, Wis. : exclusively distributed by
Hal Leonard, c2005. — 1 score (16 p.) ; 27 cm. — (Doreen Rao's choral
music experience) — (CME intermediate repertoire)
For two-part treble voices, piano & oboe. — Includes separate oboe part (p. 15-16).
— Words by Bill Worrell. — Includes program and biographical notes.
Publ. no. 48018859
ISMN M051475735
System number: 013243919

Larsen, Libby.
Eine kleine Snailmusik : for upper voices and contrabass / Libby Larsen.
— [New York] : Oxford University Press, c2001. — 1 score (10 p.) ;
27 cm. — Oxford music for upper voices
For 3-part choir and double bass. — Includes piano reduction for rehearsal only.
— Words by May Sarton. — Double bass part printed separately following score.
— Includes biographical note.
Publ. no. 95.440
ISBN 0193864355
System number: 013196364

Nursery songs for young choirs : unison treble / arranged by B. Wayne
Bisbee. — [New York?] : Boosey & Hawkes ; Milwaukee, Wis. :
exclusively distributed by Hal Leonard, c2005. — 1 score (17 p.) ;
27 cm. — (Doreen Rao's choral music experience) — (CME beginning
repertoire)
"For unison voices, piano & percussion"—Caption. — Includes separate
percussion part, in score with vocal line (p.14-17). — Includes program and
biographical notes.
Publ. no. 48018886
ISMN M051475780
System number: 013243822

Seeger, Pete, 1919-
Where have all the flowers gone? : three part treble voices & piano /
words and music by Pete Seeger ; arranged by Mark G. Sirett. — [New
York?] : Boosey & Hawkes ; Milwaukee : exclusively distributed by Hal
Leonard, c2005. — 1 score (14 p.) ; 27 cm. — (CME building bridges)
— (Doreen Rao's choral music experience)
Includes biographical notes.
Publ. no. 48018855
ISMN M051476299
System number: 013312821

782.7642162009429
As I went with Tom to Tywyn = [Wrth fynd efo Deio i Dywyn : for
unison treble voices & piano] / arranged by Nigel E. Jones. — [New
York?] : Boosey & Hawkes ; Milwaukee, Wis. : exclusively distributed
by Hal Leonard, c2005. — 1 score (7 p.) ; 27 cm. — (Doreen Rao's
choral music experience) — (CME Celtic voices)
English and traditional Welsh words, also printed for reference. — English
translation by Nigel E. Jones. — Includes performance notes, pronunciation guide
and biographical note.
Publ. no. 48018877
ISMN M051475957
System number: 013361287

782.8 – MALE VOICES

782.8
Mozart, Wolfgang Amadeus, 1756-1791.
[Concertos, horn, orchestra, K. 495, E♭ major. Rondo; arr.]
Horn concerto, rondo : TTBB / Mozart ; arranged by Jonathan Rathbone.
— London : Edition Peters, c2004. — 1 score (39 p.) ; 30 cm. —
Kikapust choral series
Publisher's no.: Edition Peters no. 77063.
Publ. no. EP 77063
Publ. no. 77063
ISMN M577085272
System number: 013305805

782.825
*Davies, Bryan.
[Never weather beaten sail, men's voices]
Never weather beaten sail / [words by] Thomas Campion ; [setting by]
Bryan Davies. — Tewkesbury : Roberton Publications, a part of
Goodmusic Publishing, c2005. — 1 score (4 p.) ; 26 cm.
For men's voices (TTBB), unacc. — Includes piano reduction for rehearsal only.
Pl. no. 53094
ISMN M222261334
System number: 013373045

782.8253
Moore, William, d. 1825.
[Sweet rivers; arr.]
Sweet rivers : for lower voices (TBB) and piano / William Moore ; arr.
Reginald Unterseher. — [New York] : Oxford University Press, c2005.
— 1 score (7 p.) ; 27 cm. — Oxford music for lower voices
Words by John Adam Granade. — Includes biographical note about the arranger.
ISBN 019386827X
System number: 013196353

My Lord, what a mornin' : TTBB : spiritual / arranged by Mark
Williams. — London : Edition Peters, c2004. — 1 score (3 p.) ; 30 cm.
— Kikapust choral series
Publ. no. EP 77056
ISMN M577085173
System number: 013305738

Tippett, Michael, 1905-1998.
[Child of our time. *Selections; arr.*]
Five spirituals : from A child of our time / Michael Tippett ; arr. by Edward
Milner for male voice choir. — London : Schott, c2004. — 1 score (27 p.) ;
30 cm. — Choral music of our time
Originally for SATB choir. — Includes piano reduction for rehearsal only. —
Includes arranger's note. — English words with German translation; words also
printed for reference preceding score.
Pl. no. S&Co.7958
Publ. no. ED 12812
ISMN M220123177
System number: 013173808

782.827
*Dicie, Don Michael.
[Nineteenth-century hymns. Marching to Zion]
Three nineteenth-century hymns. 3, Marching to Zion : for lower voices
(TTBB) and piano / [arranged by] Don Michael Dicie. — [New York] :
Oxford University Press, c2005. — 1 score (7 p.) ; 27 cm. — Oxford sacred
music
An arrangement of the hymn by Robert Lowry. — Words by Isaac Watts. — Includes
biographical note about the arranger.
ISBN 9780193868830
ISBN 0193868830
System number: 013472346

*Dicie, Don Michael.
[Nineteenth-century hymns. My faith looks up to Thee]
Three nineteenth-century hymns. 1, My faith looks up to Thee : for lower
voices (TTBB) and piano / [arranged by] Don Michael Dicie. — [New
York] : Oxford University Press, c2005. — 1 score (7 p.) ; 27 cm. — Oxford
sacred music
An arrangement of the hymn by Lowell Mason. — Words by Ray Palmer. —
Includes biographical note about the arranger.
ISBN 9780193868816
ISBN 0193868814
System number: 013472357

*Dicie, Don Michael.
[Nineteenth-century hymns. The church in the wildwood]
Three nineteenth-century hymns. 2, The church in the wildwood : for lower
voices (TTBB) and piano / [arranged by] Don Michael Dicie. — [New
York] : Oxford University Press, c2005. — 1 score (7 p.) ; 27 cm. — Oxford
sacred music
An arrangement of the hymn by William S. Pitts. — Includes biographical note
about the arranger.
ISBN 9780193868823
ISBN 0193868822
System number: 013472351

White, B. F. (Benjamin Franklin), 1800-1879.
[O when shall I see Jesus; *arr.*]
The morning trumpet : for unaccompanied lower voices / B.F. White ; arr.
Mack Wilberg. — [New York] : Oxford University Press, c2005. — 1 score
(7 p.) ; 27 cm. — Oxford choral music
For men's voices (TTBB), unacc. — Words by John Leland. — Includes
biographical note about the arranger.
ISBN 0193868288
System number: 013196342

782.8281723
*Gruber, Franz Xaver, 1787-1863.
[Stille Nacht, heilige Nacht; *arr.*]
Silent night : for tenor solo and men's choir (TTBB), unaccompanied /
[Franz Gruber ; arranged by] Mack Wilberg. — [New York] : Oxford
University Press, c2001. — 1 score (7 p.) ; 27 cm. — Oxford Christmas
music
Words are an English translation by John F. Young of the original German words by
Joseph Mohr. — Includes piano reduction for rehearsal only.
ISBN 9780193864313
ISBN 0193864312
System number: 013472433

Hopkins, John H. (John Henry), 1820-1891.
[We three kings of Orient are; *arr.*]
We three kings : TTBB / John Henry Hopkins ; arranged by Jonathan
Rathbone. — London : Edition Peters, c2004. — 1 score (6 p.) ; 30 cm. —
Kikapust choral series
"As recorded by the Swingle Singers on The story of Christmas." — Publisher's no.:
Edition Peters no. 77015.
Publ. no. EP 77015
Publ. no. 77015
ISMN M577085371
System number: 013304747

782.8326
*Vann, Stanley.
[Lichfield Service]
Magnificat and Nunc dimittis : (the Lichfield Service) : for men's voices
(ATB divisi) / Stanley Vann. — [S.l.] : Anglo-American Music Publishers ;
Altamonte Springs, FL : distributed by Worldwide Music International,
c2004. — 1 score (7 p.) ; 28 cm.
English words from the Book of Common Prayer.
System number: 013196878

782.842
Cliff, Tony.
The wreck of the Anson : male voice choir (TTBB) with piano
accompaniment / [lyrics and music] Tony Cliff. — [Falmouth] : Tony
Cliff Music, c2005. — 1 score (6 p.) ; 30 cm.
ISMN M900211408
System number: 013216375

*Davies, Bryan.
Kolokolchik = The little bell : Russian folk song for tenor solo and male
voice choir with balalaikas (opotional) and tubular bell / arranged by
Bryan Davies ; [English words by Leon Wiltshire] — Tewkesbury :
Roberton Publications, a part of Goodmusic Publishing, c2005. — 1
score (8 p.) ; 26 cm.
Includes piano reduction for rehearsal only.
Pl. no. 53095
ISMN M222261341
System number: 013486514

*Drake, Ervin.
[I believe; *arr.*]
I believe : arranged for male voice choir (TTBB) with piano
accompaniment and optional string bass / Words & music by Ervin Drake
… [et al.] ; arranged by Bryan Davies. — Tewkesbury : Roberton
Publications, a part of Goodmusic Publishing, 2005, c1953. — 1 score
(8 p.) ; 26 cm.
Duration: 2:30.
Publ. no. 53140
ISMN M222261327
System number: 013373024

*Moeran, E. J. (Ernest John), 1894-1950.
[Choral music. *Selections*]
Collected choral music. Volume three, male voices / E.J. Moeran ; edited
by John Talbot. — Centenary ed. — London : Thames Publishing, c2003.
— 1 score (40 p.) ; 26 cm.
For men's voices, mostly (TTBB), some with piano acc. — Unacc. songs include
piano reduction for rehearsal only. — Mostly reprinted from earlier editions. —
Editorial notes following score.
System number: 012965820

Scarborough Fair : English folk song : arranged for male voice choir and
piano / by Derek J. Clark. — Tewkesbury : Roberton Publications,
c2004. — 1 score (14 p.) ; 26 cm.
Chorus: TTBarB.
Publ. no. 53164
ISMN M222260726
System number: 013193324

*The white cockade : Jacobite song arranged for male voice choir with
accompaniment of snare drum and two piccolos / by Bryan Davies. —
Tewkesbury : Roberton Publications, a part of Goodmusic Publishing,
c2005. — 1 score (12 p.) ; 26 cm.
Words by Robert Burns.
Pl. no. 53169
ISMN M222263925
System number: 013486508

782.8421723
Cliff, Tony.
Crackers at Christmas : male voice choir (TTBB) with piano
accompaniment / [lyrics & music] Tony Cliff. — [Falmouth] : Tony Cliff
Music, c2005. — 1 score (10 p.) ; 30 cm.
ISMN M900211415
System number: 013216368

783 – MUSIC FOR SINGLE VOICES. THE VOICE

783
Hoffmann, E. T. A. (Ernst Theodor Amadeus), 1776-1822.
[Vocal music. *Selections*]
Kleine Vokalkompsitionen und Klaviersonaten / E.T.A. Hoffmann ; aus
dem Nachlaß von Friedrich Schnapp und unter Mitarbeit von Gerhard
Allroggen ; herausgegeben von Alexander Erhard und Thomas Kohlhase.
— Mainz ; London : Schott, c2006. — 1 score (xvii, 203 p.) ; 33 cm. —
(Ausgewählte musikalische Werke / E.T.A. Hoffmann ; Bd. 12a)
Most vocal works for vocal ensemble, with or without piano accompaniment. —
Editorial prefaces and critical commentary in German. — Italian or German
words
Publ. no. ETAH 112-10
Publ. no. BSS 43736
System number: 013798962
Also classified at 782.5; 786.2183

783.1 – SINGLE VOICES IN COMBINATION

783.12

Gorb, Adam, 1958-
Weimar : (2000) : for large ensemble / Adam Gorb. — Kenley : Maecenas
Music, [2005?] — 1 score (95 p.) ; 30 cm.
For flute/piccolo, oboe, 2 clarinets, tenor saxophone, bassoon, horn, trumpet,
trombone, percussion kit, piano, harp, 2 wordless sopranos (1 plays whistle, 2 plays
tambourine and rattle), 2 violins, viola, cello, double bass. — "Although the work is
performable with solo strings, the composer much prefers that a larger body be
used". — Duration: ca. 18:00.
System number: 013422553
Primary classification 785.32199

Schubert, Franz, 1797-1828.
[Vocal music. *Selections*]
Mehrstimmige Gesänge für gemischte Stimmen. Teil b / [Franz Schubert] ;
vorgelegt von Dietrich Berke und Michael Kube. — Kassel ; London :
Bärenreiter, 2006. — 1 score (196-456 p.) ; 28 cm. — (Neue Ausgabe
sämtlicher Werke / Franz Schubert ; Ser. III, Bd. 2, T. b)
For various solo voices all with piano acc. (except 2nd work unacc.), some including
chorus; the 7th work for 2-part mixed chorus and piano. — Commentary in German
on sources and versions of all works in both Teil a and Teil b volumes, p. 391-456.
— Principally German words, from various sources; some also printed for reference
within the editorial notes; the 2nd work with transliterated Hebrew words.
Publ. no. BA 5536
ISMN M006497010
System number: 013798568
Also classified at 782.5

783.1225

Hasse, Johann Adolf, 1699-1783.
[Salve regina, soprano, alto, orchestra, E♭ major]
Salve regina Es-Dur für Sopran, Alt und Instrumente, 1766 : Facsimile nach
der Handschrift des Komponisten / Johann Adolph Hasse. —
Niedernhausen : Edition Kemel, 2006. — 1 score (48 p.) ; 30 cm.
Reproduced from holograph. — "075879 1 87"—Label, p. [3] of cover.
Publ. no. LR232
System number: 013887075

783.1226

*Jeffreys, George, ca. 1610-1685.
[Duets, soprano, bass, continuo]
Three dialogues : for soprano, bass and continuo / George Jeffreys. —
Richmond : Green Man Press, c2001. — 3 scores + 1 part (8 p.) ; 30 cm.
One score contains keyboard realization of continuo part, the other two have figured
bass only. — Includes continuo part for bass instrument. — Edited from British
Library, Add. MS 10338. — Introduction and editorial notes by Cedric Lee. —
English (1st and 2nd works) or Latin (3rd work) words; also printed for reference
with English translation where appropriate p. 3.
Publ. no. Jef 8
Pl. no. Jef 8-1—Jef 8-2
System number: 013597274
Primary classification 783.1242

*Porpora, Nicola, 1686-1768.
[Duetti latini per la passione di Gesù Cristo]
Sei duetti latini sulla passione di nostro signore Gesù Cristo ; Motetti per
Angiola Moro / Nicola Antonio Porpora ; edizione critica a cura di Stefano
Aresi. — Pisa : ETS, c2004. — 1 score (xii, 233 p.) : facsims. ; 30 cm. —
Diverse voci— ; 5
For soprano and alto with continuo (1st work); alto, strings and continuo (2nd work).
— Figured bass unrealized. — Historical and critical notes in Italian. — At head of
title: Università di Pavia, Dipartimento di scienze musicologiche e
paleografico-filologiche. — Latin words, also printed for reference with Italian
translation p. 40-41 (1st work) and p. 135-137 (2nd work).
ISBN 8846710266
System number: 013224213
Also classified at 783.6826

783.1242

*Jeffreys, George, ca. 1610-1685.
[Duets, soprano, bass, continuo]
Three dialogues : for soprano, bass and continuo / George Jeffreys. —
Richmond : Green Man Press, c2001. — 3 scores + 1 part (8 p.) ; 30 cm.
One score contains keyboard realization of continuo part, the other two have figured
bass only. — Includes continuo part for bass instrument. — Edited from British
Library, Add. MS 10338. — Introduction and editorial notes by Cedric Lee. —
English (1st and 2nd works) or Latin (3rd work) words; also printed for reference
with English translation where appropriate p. 3.
Publ. no. Jef 8
Pl. no. Jef 8-1—Jef 8-2
System number: 013597274
Also classified at 783.1226

*Purcell, Henry, 1659-1695.
[Soft notes and gently rais'd accent]
Two songs with flutes : from Orpheus Britannicus / Henry Purcell. —
Richmond : Green Man Press, c2001. — 3 scores + 3 parts ; 30 cm.
1st work for soprano, bass, 2 recorders and continuo; 2nd work for soprano,
baritone, 2 recorders and continuo. — One score includes keyboard realization of
continuo part, the others have figured bass only. — Introduction and editorial notes
by Cedric Lee. — Words also printed for reference preceding each song.
Publ. no. Pur 6
System number: 013589523

*Purcell, Henry, 1659-1695.
[Vocal music. *Selections*]
4 duets from Orpheus Britannicus : for soprano and bass with basso
continuo / Henry Purcell. — Richmond : Green Man Press, c2000. — 3
scores + 1 part ; 30 cm.
One score includes keyboard realization of continuo part, the others have figured
bass only. — Includes continuo part for bass instrument. — Introduction and
editorial notes by Cedric Lee. — Words also printed for reference preceding
realized score.
Publ. no. Pur 5
System number: 013589515

*Webern, Anton, 1883-1945.
[Songs. *Selections*]
The Anton Webern collection : early vocal music, 1899-1909 / [Anton
Webern] ; ed. by Matthew R. Shaftel. — New York : Carl Fischer, c2004.
— xxxvi, 92 p. of music : facsim. ; 30 cm. — (The masters collection)
German words, printed for reference with English translations, p. xvi-xx. —
Introductory essay and critical notes in English by Matthew R. Shaftel.
Pl. no. VF10
ISBN 0825856590
ISBN 9780825856594
System number: 014688074
Primary classification 783.242

783.1242162009411

*Haydn, Joseph, 1732-1809.
[Songs, violin, continuo acc. *Selections*]
Volksliedbearbeitungen Nr. 269-364 : Schottische und Walisische Lieder
für George Thomson / Joseph Haydn ; herausgegeben von Marjorie
Rycroft in Verbindung von Warwick Edwards und Kirsteen McCue. —
München : G. Henle, 2004. — 1 score (xxiii, 327 p.) : facsims. ; 33 cm.
— (Werke / Joseph Haydn. Reihe 32 ; Bd. 4)
For one or two voices, violin, and continuo. — "Kritischer Bericht" in German: p.
[257]-327. — English words; also printed for reference following each selection.
System number: 014710566
Primary classification 783.242162009411

783.1242164

*Dynamic duos : the best duets ever! : the most memorable vocal duets
of all time. — London : Wise, c2005. — 1 score (160 p.) ; 31 cm.
29 vocal duets with piano acc. and guitar chord symbols.
Publ. no. AM84302
ISBN 9780711926028
ISBN 0711926026
System number: 013432696

783.1248

*Bernier, Nicolas, 1665-1734.
[Cantates françoises, 2e livre. Diane et Endimion]
Diane et Endimion : cantata for soprano, bass & continuo / Nicolas
Bernier. — Richmond : Green Man Press, c2000. — 3 scores + 1 part ;
30 cm.
Introduction and editorial notes by Cedric Lee. — One score includes keyboard
realization of continuo part, the others have figured bass only. — Includes
continuo part for bass instrument. — French words by Louis Fuzelier; also
printed for reference with English translation preceding score.
Publ. no. Ber 1
System number: 013596964

*Montéclair, Michel Pignolet de, 1667-1737.
[Cantatas, book 3. Tircis et Climene]
Tircis et Climene : cantata for soprano, bass, violin/flute & continuo / M
P de Montéclair. — Richmond : Green Man Press, c2004. — 3 scores +
3 parts ; 30 cm.
One score includes keyboard realization of continuo part, the others have figured
bass only. — Includes continuo part for bass instrument. — Introduction and
editorial notes by Cedric Lee. — French words, also printed for reference with
English translation preceding score.
Publ. no. Mon 1
System number: 013596837

783.126625

*Mazzocchi, D. (Domenico), 1592-1665.
[Musiche sacre, e morali. Cangia mio cor]
Cangia mio cor : si dee fuggire il diletto dannoso / Domenico
Mazzocchi ; [words by] Abbate Bentivogli. — Richmond : Green Man
Press, c2004. — 3 scores (7 p. each) ; 30 cm. — Vocal concerti series ;
VC 4
For 2 sopranos and continuo. — Edited by Cedric Lee. — Comprises 3 identical
scores with unfigured bass. — From Mazzocchi's Musiche sacre e morali, 1640.
— Italian words.
Publ. no. VC 4
System number: 013613877

*Mazzocchi, D. (Domenico), 1592-1665.
[Musiche sacre, e morali. Colombella, che di latte]
Colombella, che di latte : sopra Maria, e Giesù / Domenico Mazzocchi ;
[words by] Monsignor Ciampoli. — Richmond : Green Man Press,
c2004. — 3 scores (5 p. each) ; 30 cm. — Vocal concerti series ; VC 5
For 2 sopranos and continuo. — Editorial notes on p. 5. — Edited by Cedric Lee.
— Comprises 3 identical scores with partially figured bass, unrealized. — From
Mazzocchi's Musiche sacre e morali, 1640. — Italian words.
Publ. no. VC 5
System number: 013613882

*Mazzocchi, D. (Domenico), 1592-1665.
[Musiche sacre, e morali. Piangete occhi, piangete]
Piangete occhi, piangete : dovemo piangere la Passione di N. S. / Domenico
Mazzocchi ; [words by] Girolamo Preti. — Richmond : Green Man Press,
c2004. — 3 scores (7 p. each) ; 30 cm. — Vocal concerti series ; VC 2
For 2 sopranos and continuo. — Edited by Cedric Lee. — Comprises 3 identical
scores with unrealized figured bass. — From Mazzocchi's Musiche sacre e morali,
1640. — Italian words.
Publ. no. VC 2
System number: 013613855

*Mazzocchi, D. (Domenico), 1592-1665.
[Musiche sacre, e morali. Signor, non sotto l'ombra]
Signor, non sotto l'ombra : eccitamento alle virtù / Domenico Mazzocchi ;
[words by] Torquato Tasso. — Richmond : Green Man Press, c2004. — 3
scores (7 p. each) ; 30 cm. — Vocal concerti series ; VC 3
For 2 sopranos and continuo. — Edited by Cedric Lee. — Comprises 3 identical
scores with unfigured bass. — From Mazzocchi's Musiche sacre e morali, 1640. —
Italian words.
Publ. no. VC 3
System number: 013613872

783.126648

Buxtehude, Dietrich, 1637-1707.
[Laudate pueri]
Laudate pueri Dominum : chiaccona für 2 Soprane, 6 Gamben (oder andere
Streicher) und B.c., BuxWV 69 = chiaconna for 2 sopranos, 6 viols (or other
strings) and b.c. / Dieterich Buxtehude ; Generalbassaussetzung von
Dankwart von Zadow ; herausgegeben von Günter und Leonore Zadow. —
Heidelberg : Edition Güntersberg, c2007. — 1 score (19 p.) + 9 parts ;
30 cm.
Latin words, also printed separately for reference with German and English
translation. — Preface in German and English. — Unfigured bass, realized for
keyboard instrument.
Publ. no. G123
ISMN M501741236
System number: 013887064

783.128925

*Jeffreys, George, ca. 1610-1685.
[With notes that are both loud and sweet]
Two duets for basses : for voices and basso continuo / Jeffreys & Purcell. —
Richmond : Green Man Press, c2001. — 3 scores + 1 part ; 30 cm.
One score contains keyboard realization of continuo part, the other two have figured
bass only. — Includes continuo part for bass instrument. — Introduction and
editorial notes by Cedric Lee. — Words also printed for reference, p. 3.
Publ. no. Jef 7
Pl. no. Jef 7-1—Jef 7-2
System number: 013597245

783.1326

Herbst, Johann Andreas, 1588-1666.
Lobet, ihr Knechte des Herrn : (Psalm 113) : motet for tenor, baritone, bass,
2 violins & basso continuo / Johann Andreas Herbst ; edited by Alejandro
Garri ; assisted by Kent Carlson. — 1st ed. — Full score & 3 parts. —
[Muehlheim am Main, Germany] : Garri Editions, c2005. — 1 score (27 p.)
+ 3 parts ; 30 cm. — Canti di cielo ; v. 72
Edited from a ms. housed at the Stadt- und Universitätsbibliothek, Frankfurt am
Main (Ms. Ff. Mus. 24). — Includes pref. in English. — Duration: ca. 6:30. —
German words.
Publ. no. GE 242
System number: 013771119

783.1342

*Mazzocchi, D. (Domenico), 1592-1665.
[Musiche sacre, e morali. Battaglia per espugnare Amore]
Battaglia per espugnare Amore : concerto à 3 : for two sopranos, bass and
basso continuo / Domenico Mazzocchi. — Richmond : Green Man Press,
c2002. — 4 scores (11 p. each) + 1 part ([2] p.) ; 30 cm.
Includes 1 score with figured bass realized for keyboard instrument; 3 scores with
figured bass unrealized; and part for bass instrument. — Pref. and editorial note by
Cedric Lee. — Italian words; also printed for reference with English translation, p.3.
Publ. no. Maz 3
System number: 013597082

783.1343

*Puliti, Gabriello, b. ca. 1575.
Ghirlanda odorifera : (1612) / Gabriello Puliti ; transkribiral in revidiral =
transcription and revision by Ivano Cavallini. — Ljubljana : Slovenska
akademija znanosti in umetnosti, 2004. — 1 score (xxvi, 44 p.) : facsims. ;
28 cm. — Monumenta artis musicae Sloveniae ; 46
Introduction and editorial notes in Slovenian and English. — Italian words.
ISMN M709004157
ISMN 9790709004157
System number: 014663578

783.136642

*Mazzocchi, D. (Domenico), 1592-1665.
[Musiche sacre, e morali. Folle cor]
Folle cor : breve è la vita nostra : aria a tre soprani / Domenico
Mazzocchi ; [words by] Ottavio Tronsarelli. — Richmond : Green Man
Press, c2004. — 4 scores (4 p. each) ; 30 cm. — Vocal concerti series ;
VC 1
For 3 sopranos and continuo. — From Mazzocchi's Musiche sacre e morali, 1640.
— Edited by Cedric Lee. — Comprises 4 identical scores with partially figured
bass. — Italian words.
Publ. no. VC 1
System number: 013613865

783.136643

*Luzzaschi, Luzzasco, d. 1607.
[Madrigali per cantare et sonare. O dolcezze]
O dolcezze amarissime d'amore : a tre soprani / Luzzasco Luzzaschi. —
Richmond, : Green Man Press, c2004. — 4 scores (8 p. each) ; 30 cm. —
Vocal concerti series ; VC 6
For 3 sopranos and continuo. — Edited by Cedric Lee. — Comprises 4 identical
scores with figured bass realized for keyboard instrument. — From Luzzaschi's
Madrigali per cantare et sonare a uno, e doi, e tre soprani, Roma, 1601. — Italian
words.
Publ. no. VC 6
System number: 013613916

783.1448

*Novak, Janez Krstnik, ca. 1756-1833.
Figaro ; Cantate zum Geburts oder Namensfeste einer Mutter / Janez
Krstnik Novak ; transkribirala in revidirala = transcription and critical
edition by Aleš Nagode (Figaro), Zoran Krstulović (Cantate). —
Ljubljana : Slovenska akademija znanosti in umetnosti, 2004. — 1 score
(xxxvi, 108 p.) : facsims. ; 28 cm. — Monumenta artis musicae
Sloveniae ; 47
For solo voices, chorus (SATB) and orchestra. — Introd. and editorial notes in
Slovenian and English. — Edited from mss. in the Narodna in univerzitetna
knjižnica v Ljubljani (Figaro) and the Conservatorio Giuseppe Tartini di Trieste
(Cantate). — Slovenian words (Figaro, also printed for reference with English
translation) and German words (Cantate, also printed separately with English and
Slovenian translation).
ISMN M709004140
ISMN 9790709004140
System number: 014663614
Primary classification 782.1

783.1642

Sciarrino, Salvatore.
Cantare con silenzio : per voci, flauto, risonanze e percussori, 1999 /
Salvatore Sciarrino. — Partitura. — Milano : Ricordi, [2007], c1999. —
1 score (145 p.) ; 46 cm.
For flute in C, live electronics, six voices (SMzATBarB) and two percussionists.
— Composer's note and performance notes in Italian. — Italian words by various
authors, also printed for reference.
Publ. no. 138428
ISMN M041384283
System number: 014053365

783.188

Lachenmann, Helmut.
Nun : Musik für Flöte, Posaune, Männerstimmen und Orchester :
Neufassung 2003 = Music for flute, trombone, male voices, and
orchestra : revised version 2003 / Helmut Lachenmann. —
Studienpartitur. — Wiesbaden : Breitkopf & Härtel, [2003?], c2002. — 1
score (xxvi, 119 p.) ; 31 cm. — Partitur-Bibliothek ; 5420
For flute, trombone, 8 male vocalists and orchestra. — Reproduced from
holograph. — Duration: ca. 38:00. — Performance instructions in German and
English precede score. — Arbitrary syllables for reference.
ISMN M004211830
EAN 9790004211830
System number: 014457020

783.2 – SOLO VOICE

783.21423

Kember, John.
Sight-singing 2 : a fresh approach = Déchiffrage pour le chant 2 :
nouvelle approche = Vom-Blatt-Singen 2 : eine erfrischend neue Methode
/ John Kember. — London : Schott, c2005. — 1 score (60 p.) ; 31 cm.
No words. — Contains 95 solo/2-part exercises and 16 solos with piano acc. —
"Useful for Grade 6+ Aural" — Back cover. — Pref. and instructions in English,
French and German.
Publ. no. ED 12790
ISBN 1902455223
ISMN M220123153
System number: 013191850

783.242

Church, Charlotte, 1986-
Selections from Prelude : the best of Charlotte Church. — London : Chester Music, c2005. — 1 score (86 p.) : ports ; 31 cm.
16 songs (sacred, popular, operatic and traditional) from Charlotte Church's 2002 album "Prelude." — For voice(s) and piano, with guitar chord symbols. — Words in English, Latin, French or Italian.
Publ. no. CH70257
ISBN 1846091500
System number: 013312897

*Fesch, Willem de, 1687-1761.
[Songs. *Selections*]
Matthew Prior songs : for voice and basso continuo : 1741 / Willem de Fesch ; based on 'Lyric Poems' by Matthew Prior ; edited by Robert L. Tusler. — Amsterdam : Donemus, 2004, c2003. — 1 score (v, 13 p.) ; 30 cm.
Figured bass realized for keyboard instrument.
System number: 014747680

*Fesch, Willem de, 1687-1761.
Temple of love : for voice, two obligato instruments and basso continuo : 1753 / Willem de Fesch ; edited by Robert L. Tusler. — Amsterdam : Donemus, 2004, c2003. — 1 score (v, 52 p.) ; 30 cm.
Songs. — Partially figured bass realized for keyboard instrument. — Edited from "The Temple of love / Mr Defesch's songs / sung at / Marybon-Gardens / Printed for J. Walsh [London: J. Walsh, No 546, 1753]" — Pref. in English.
System number: 014747725

Schulz, J. A. P. (Johann Abraham Peter), 1747-1800.
Lieder im Volkston / Johann Abraham Peter Schulz ; herausgegeben von Walther Dürr und Stefanie Steiner unter Mitarbeit von Michael Kohlhäufl. — München : Henle, 2006. — 1 score (xxvii, 224 p.) : facsims. ; 34 cm. — Erbe deutscher Musik ; 105 Erbe deutscher Musik. Abteilung Frühromantik ; Bd. 4
125 songs for voice(s) and piano. — Preface and critical report in German. — German words.
System number: 013801647

Shostakovich, Dmitriĭ Dmitrievich, 1906-1975.
[Vocal music. *Selections*]
Dve basni I.A. Krylova, dlia metsso-soprano, zhenskogo khora (metsso-soprano) i orkestra, soch. 4 ; Shest' romansov na slova iaponskikh poėtov, dlia tenora s orkestrom, soch. 21 ; Tri romansa na slova A.S. Pushkina, dlia basa i kamernogo orkestra, soch. 46a / Dmitriĭ Shostakovich ; obshchaia redaktsiia i poiasnitel'naia stat'ia Manashira IAkubova. — Partitura. — Moskva : Izd-vo "DSCH", 2006. — 1 score (140 p.) ; 30 cm. — (Novoe sobranie sochineniĭ / Dmitriĭ Shostakovich ; t. 87. Ser. 8, Sochineniia dlia golosa s orkestrom = New collected works / Dmitri Shostakovich ; 87th v. 8th series, Compositions for solo voice(s) with orchestra)
Title on parallel English t.p.: Two fables by Ivan Krylov, for mezzo-soprano, female chorus (mezzo-sopranos) and orchestra, op. 4 ; Six romances on Japanese poems, for tenor and orchestra, op. 21 ; Three romances on poems by Alexander Pushkin, for bass and chamber orchestra, op. 46a. — Editorial, historical and critical notes in Russian and English.
System number: 013821897

Steele, Douglas, 1910-
[Short songs]
Three short songs : for either solo voice, or unison voices, with piano / Douglas Steele. — Matfield : Encore Publications, c2005. — 1 score (11 p.) ; 26 cm.
Includes biographical note.
System number: 013358905
Also classified at 782.5

*Sviridov, Georgiĭ Vasil'evich, 1915-1998.
[Songs. *Selections*]
Romansy i pesni : dlia golosa i fortepiano / Georgiĭ Sviridov ; tom podgotovlen K. A. Titarenko. — Moskva, Sankt-Peterburg : Natsional'nyĭ Sviridovskiĭ Fond, 2003. — 1 score (xxxii, 123 p.) : port., facsim. ; 30 cm. — (Polnoe sobranie sochineniĭ ; tom 10)
Pl. no. NSF 003
System number: 014750606

Thomson, Mr. (George), 1757-1851.
[Select collection of original Scotish airs]
Scottish songs : for George Thomson : 32 schottische Lieder für 1-2 Singstimmen, Violine, Violoncello und Klavier / [music by] Ignaz Pleyel] ; [edited by] Marjorie Rycroft. — Erstdruck. — Wien : Doblinger, 2007. — 1 score and 2 parts (2 v.) ; 30 cm. — (Diletto musicale ; Nr. 1414-1415)
Parts for violin and violoncello. Violoncello parts by Leopold Kozeluch. — English words.
Pl. no. D. 19 774
Pl. no. D. 19 775
Publ. no. DM 1414
Publ. no. DM 1415
ISBN 9790012197744
ISBN 9790012197751
ISMN M012197744
ISMN M012197751
System number: 014050890

Ullmann, Viktor.
[Songs]
Sämtliche Lieder für Singstimme und Klavier = Complete songs for voice and piano / Viktor Ullmann ; herausgegeben von Axel Bauni und Christian Hoesch. — Mainz ; London : Schott, c2004. — 1 score (243 p.) : facsim. ; 31 cm.
Pref. in German, English and French; critical report in German. — Chiefly German words.
Publ. no. ED 8199
ISMN M001120357
System number: 013887077

*Webern, Anton, 1883-1945.
[Songs. *Selections*]
The Anton Webern collection : early vocal music, 1899-1909 / [Anton Webern] ; ed. by Matthew R. Shaftel. — New York : Carl Fischer, c2004. — xxxvi, 92 p. of music : facsim. ; 30 cm. — (The masters collection)
German words, printed for reference with English translations, p. xvi-xx. — Introductory essay and critical notes in English by Matthew R. Shaftel.
Pl. no. VF10
ISBN 0825856590
ISBN 9780825856594
System number: 014688074
Also classified at 783.1242

783.242094137

The Hawick songs : a complete collection / edited by Ian W. Seeley. — Rev. and enl. [ed.] — Hawick : Hawick Callants' Club, 2001. — 1 score (ix, 109 p.) ; 30 cm.
With piano acc. — Includes indexes, glossary and subscribers' list. — Words partly Lowland Scots.
System number: 013201857

783.2421542

The all-time greatest film songs : [26 of the best songs from the silver screen : arranged for piano and voice with guitar chord boxes] — London : Wise, c2005. — 1 score (128 p.) ; 31 cm.
Publ. no. AM92045
ISBN 0711941750
System number: 013326341

Collins, Phil.
Brother bear : piano, vocal, guitar / [words and music by Phil Collins] — [S.l.] : Walt Disney Music Co. ; Milwaukee, Wis. : Distributed by Hal Leonard, c2003. — 1 score (56 p.) : col. ill. ; 31 cm.
At head of title: Disney presents. — For voice and piano, with chord symbols and guitar chord diagrams.
Publ. no. HL00313257
ISBN 0634068369
System number: 006906655

Essential film songs : the ultimate modern-day movie songbook. Take 2. — London : Wise Publications, c2004. — 1 score (128 p.) ; 31 cm.
23 songs from contemporary films arranged for voice and piano, with chord symbols and guitar chord diagrams. — Compiled by Nick Crispin ; music arranged by Derek Jones & Paul Honey.
Publ. no. AM980782
ISBN 1844496481
System number: 013169092

Piglet's big movie / featuring new songs by Carly Simon. — [S.l.] : Walt Disney Music Co. : Wonderland Music Co. ; Milwaukee, WI : Distributed by Hal Leonard, c2003. — 1 score (48 p.) : col. ill. ; 31 cm.
For voice and piano, with guitar chord symbols. — Words and music mostly by Carly Simon. — At head of title: Walt Disney Pictures presents.
Publ. no. HL00313242
ISBN 0634059750
System number: 006914468

Pooh's heffalump movie / [featuring new songs by Carly Simon] — [S.l.] : Disneytoon studios : c2005. Walt Disney Music Company : Wonderland Music Company ; Milwaukee, Wis. : distributed by Hal Leonard, — 1 score (39 p.) : col. ill., col. port. ; 31 cm.
For voice and piano, with chord symbols and guitar chord diagrams. — Words and music mostly by Carly Simon. — At head of title: Walt Disney Pictures presents.
Publ. no. HL00313295
ISBN 0634099175
System number: 013376143

783.2421546

TV classics : piano, vocal, guitar. — Milwaukee, Wis. : Hal Leonard, [2004?] — 1 score (31 p.) ; 31 cm. + 1 compact disc. — Hal Leonard piano play-along v. 16
6 songs arranged for voice and piano, with chord symbols and guitar chord diagrams, and 2 piano pieces. — Words and music by various songwriters. — CD contains full performances and backing tracks.
Publ. no. HL00311147
ISBN 0634083937
System number: 013220396

783.242162009411
Haydn, Joseph, 1732-1809.
[Songs, violin, continuo acc. *Selections*]
Volksliedbearbeitungen Nr. 269-364 : Schottische und Walisische Lieder für George Thomson / Joseph Haydn ; herausgegeben von Marjorie Rycroft in Verbindung von Warwick Edwards und Kirsteen McCue. — München : G. Henle, 2004. — 1 score (xxiii, 327 p.) : facsims. ; 33 cm. — (Werke / Joseph Haydn. Reihe 32 ; Bd. 4)
For one or two voices, violin, and continuo. — "Kritischer Bericht" in German: p. [257]-327. — English words; also printed for reference following each selection.
System number: 014710566
Also classified at 783.1242162009411

783.242162009415
The big book of Irish songs. piano, vocal, guitar. — Milwaukee, Wis. : Hal Leonard ; c2003. — 1 score (192 p.) ; 31 cm.
For voice and piano, with chord symbols and guitar chord diagrams. — English words.
Publ. no. HL00310981
ISBN 0634058479
System number: 012874857

783.242164
100 of the greatest love songs ever : piano, vocal, guitar. — London : Wise, c2005. — 1 score (488 p.) ; 31 cm.
For voice and piano, with guitar chord symbols.
Publ. no. AM92241
ISBN 0711943664
System number: 013374970

Audition sourcebook : female singers : a collection of 22 songs covering eight different vocal styles : arranged for piano, voice and guitar, with sound-alike backing tracks on 2 CDs. — London : Wise Publications, c2005. — 1 score (128 p.) ; 31 cm + 2 sound discs (digital ; 4 3/4 in.)
Mostly English words; one song in French with English translation.
Publ. no. AM90116
ISBN 0711931828
System number: 013281431

Audition sourcebook : male singers : a collection of 22 songs : covering seven different vocal styles : arranged for piano, voice and guitar, with sound-alike backing tracks on 2 CDs. — London : Wise, c2005. — 1 score (127 p.) ; 31 cm + 2 sound discs (digital ; 4 3/4 in.)
Publ. no. AM90133
ISBN 071193195X
System number: 013374888

The big book of piano songs : piano, vocal, guitar. — [S.l.] : Hal Leonard Europe ; London : exclusive distributor, Music Sales, c2005. — 1 score (254 p.) ; 31 cm.
45 songs arranged for voice and piano, with guitar chord symbols.
Publ. no. HLE90002440
ISBN 1846090946
System number: 013358425

Buckley, Jeff, 1966-1997.
[Songs. *Selections*]
Jeff Buckley : arranged for piano [sic] — London : Wise, c2005. — 1 score (78 p.) ; 31 cm.
13 songs arranged for piano, with guitar chord symbols. — Words and music by Jeff Buckley and others.
Publ. no. AM983840
ISBN 9781846092473
ISBN 1846092477
System number: 013441950

Careless love / Madeleine Peyroux. — London : Wise, c2005. — 1 score (48 p.) ; 31 cm.
12 songs from Madeleine Peyroux's 2004 album "Careless love." — For voice and piano, with guitar chord symbols. — Words and music by various songwriters. — Mostly English words, 1 song in French.
Publ. no. AM984115
ISBN 9781846092725
ISBN 1846092728
System number: 013376154

Charles, Ray, 1930-2004.
[Songs. *Selections*]
Ray : essential piano songs : transcribed for piano, voice & guitar. — London : Wise, c2005. — 1 score (80 p.) ; 31 cm.
12 songs from the film "Ray" arranged for voice and piano, with guitar chord symbols. — Words and music by Ray Charles and others.
Publ. no. AM91977
ISBN 0711940932
System number: 013199575

Darin, Bobby.
[Songs. *Selections*]
The best of Bobby Darin : [a selection of his biggest hits, arranged for piano, voice and guitar] — London : Wise Publications, c2005. — 1 score (80 p.) ; 31 cm.
For voice and piano, with chord symbols and guitar chord diagrams. — Words and music by Bobby Darin and others. — Includes biographical note.
Publ. no. AM92017
ISBN 0711941246
System number: 013220435

Darin, Bobby.
[Songs. *Selections*]
Bobby Darin : 15 timeless classics : piano/vocal arrangements with guitar chord boxes. — London : International Music Publications, 2005. — 1 score (71 p.) ; 31 cm. — (Budget series)
Words and music by Bobby Darin and others.
Publ. no. 10086A
ISBN 1843287889
ISMN M570217885
System number: 013226555

Doris Day : 15 timeless classics : piano/vocal arrangements with guitar chord boxes. — London : International Music Publications, 2005. — 1 score (64 p.) ; 31 cm. — Budget series
15 songs from the repertoire of Doris Day. — Words and music by various songwriters.
Publ. no. 10127A
ISBN 184328846X
ISMN M570218462
System number: 013226543

Essential piano songs. Book 2 : [a superb collection of 22 exceptional songs by some of the world's greatest songwriters] — London : Wise, c2005. — 1 score (128 p.) ; 31 cm.
For voice and piano, with guitar chord symbols.
Publ. no. AM92046
ISBN 0711941769
System number: 013292865

Favorite standards : piano, vocal, guitar. — Milwaukee, Wis. : Hal Leonard, [2004?] — 1 score (32 p.) ; 31 cm. + 1 compact disc. — Hal Leonard piano play-along v. 15
8 songs arranged for voice and piano, with chord symbols and guitar chord diagrams. — Words and music by various songwriters. — CD contains full performances and backing tracks.
Publ. no. HL00311146
ISBN 0634083910
System number: 013219842

Goldrich, Zina.
[Songs. *Selections*]
Songbook : volume 1 / Goldrich and Heisler ; lyrics by Marcy Heisler ; music by Zina Goldrich. — 2nd ed. — New York : Marcy and Zina Co. ; Milwaukee, Wis : Exclusively distributed by Hal Leonard, 2004, c2003. — 1 score (318 p.) ; 31 cm.
For voice and piano, with guitar chord symbols. Includes some duets.
Publ. no. HL00313288
ISBN 0634093770
UPC 073999252095
EAN 9780634093777
System number: 013212015

Kander, John.
[Kiss of the spider woman. *Vocal score. Selections*]
Kiss of the spider woman : the musical : [vocal selections] / book by Terrence McNally ; music by John Kander ; lyrics by Fred Ebb ; based on the novel by Manuel Puig. — [New York, N.Y.] : Carlin America ; Milwaukee, Wis. : Exclusively distributed by Hal Leonard, [200-?] — 1 score (104 p.) ; 31 cm.
Acc. arr. for piano.
Publ. no. HL00313277
ISBN 0634084763
System number: 013381892

Legend, John.
Get lifted / John Legend ; piano/vocal arrangements by John Nicholas. — New York : Cherry Lane Music Company ; Milwaukee, Wis. : distributed by Hal Leonard, c2005. — 1 score (86 p.) : port. ; 31 cm.
14 songs from John Legend's 2004 album "Get lifted." — For voice and piano with guitar chord symbols. — Words and music by John Stephens (real name of John Legend) and others. — "A Milton Okun publication"—Cover. — Biographical note: p. [3-6]
Publ. no. 02500822
ISBN 1575608235
System number: 013359497

Liza Minnelli : 15 timeless classics : piano/vocal arrangements with guitar chord boxes. — London : International Music Publications, 2005. — 1 score (96 p.) ; 31 cm. — Budget series
15 songs from the repertoire of Liza Minnelli. — Words and music by various songwriters.
Publ. no. 10085A
ISBN 1843287870
ISMN M570217878
System number: 013226564

Lloyd Webber, Andrew, 1948-
[Musicals. *Selections; arr.*]
Andrew Lloyd Webber favorites. — Milwaukee, Wis. : Hal Leonard, [2005] — 1 score (47 p.) ; 31 cm + 1 sound disc (digital ; 4 3/4 in.) — Hal Leonard piano play-along v. 26
8 songs arranged for voice and piano, with guitar chord symbols. — CD contains full performances and backing tracks. — Publisher's no.: HL00311178 (score), CD#63008795 (CD).
Publ. no. HL00311178

Publ. no. CD#63008795
ISBN 0634089641
System number: 013383285

Love songs : piano, vocal, guitar. — Milwaukee, Wis. : Hal Leonard, [2004] — 1 score (36 p.) ; 31 cm. + 1 compact disc. — Hal Leonard piano play-along v. 7
8 songs arranged for voice and piano, with chord symbols and guitar chord diagrams. — Words and music by various songwriters. — CD contains full performances and backing tracks.
Publ. no. HL00311078
ISBN 0634069071
System number: 013219936

The most beautiful songs ever : piano, vocal, guitar. — [S.l.] : Hal Leonard Europe ; London : Distributed by Music Sales, c2005. — 1 score (576 p.) ; 31 cm.
150 songs arranged for voice and piano, with chord symbols and guitar chord diagrams.
Publ. no. HLE90002341
ISBN 1844498395
System number: 013220402

*****The new crooners** : [22 spectacular songs from the greatest male vocalists of the 21st century : arranged for piano, voice & guitar] — London : Wise, c2005. — 1 score (128 p.) ; 31 cm.
For voice and piano with chord symbols and guitar chord diagrams.
Publ. no. AM983686
ISBN 9781846092220
ISBN 1846092221
System number: 013432776

Play piano with— Ray Charles. — London : Wise, c2005. — 1 score ([64] p.) ; 31 cm + 1 sound disc (digital ; 4 3/4 in.)
"Authentic piano transcriptions for eight hit songs [recorded by Ray Charles], includes vocal line, full lyrics and chord boxes"—Cover. — Words and music by various song writers. — Compiled by Nick Crispin; music arranged by Paul Honey. — CD contains full performances and backing tracks. — Publisher's no., AM91964.
Publ. no. AM91964
ISBN 0711940800
System number: 013201608

Popular sheet music hits : easy piano ; arranged by Dan Coates. — London : International Music Publications, 2004. — 101 p. : 31 cm.
24 popular songs arranged for voice and piano, with chord symbols.
Publ. no. 10056A
ISBN 1843287552
ISMN M570217557
System number: 013046772

Rodgers, Richard, 1902-1979.
[Musicals. *Vocal scores. Selections*]
Bewitched : the greatest songs of Rodgers & Hart. — [S.l.] : Chappell/Intersong ; Milwaukee, Wis. : Exclusively distributed by Hal Leonard, [2005?] — 1 score (128 p.) : ill., ports. ; 31 cm.
34 songs with music by Richard Rodgers and words by Lorenz Hart. — Acc. arr. for piano, with chord symbols.
Publ. no. HL00312354
System number: 013323785

Rodgers, Richard, 1902-1979.
[Musicals. *Vocal scores. Selections*]
Rodgers and Hart : a musical anthology : piano-vocal. — Milwaukee, Wis. : Hal Leonard, c1995. — 1 score (288 p.) ; 31 cm.
73 songs, nearly all from musicals, arr. for voice and piano, with chord symbols. — Music by Richard Rodgers, words by Lorenz Hart. — Foreword by Dorothy Rodgers.
Publ. no. HL00307940
ISBN 0881883379
System number: 013323664

Rodgers, Richard, 1902-1979.
[Sound of music. *Vocal score. Selections; arr.*]
The sound of music / Rodgers and Hammerstein. — [S.l.] : Williamson Music ; Milwaukee, Wis. : exclusively distributed by Hal Leonard, c2005. — 1 score (45 p.) ; 31 cm + 1 sound disc (digital ; 4 3/4 in.) — Hal Leonard piano play-along v. 25
8 songs arranged for voice and piano, with guitar chord symbols. — CD contains full performances and backing tracks. — Publisher's no.: HL00311175 (score), CD#63008648 (CD).
Publ. no. HL00311175
Publ. no. CD#63008648
ISBN 0634088343
System number: 013382301

Sedaka, Neil.
[Songs. *Selections*]
Neil Sedaka : 15 timeless classics : piano/vocal arrangements with guitar chord boxes. — London : International Music Publications, 2005. — 1 score (64 p.) ; 31 cm. — Budget series
Words and music by Neil Sedaka and others.
Publ. no. 10126A
ISBN 1843288451
ISMN M570218455
System number: 013226509

Simon, Paul, 1941-
[Songs. *Selections*]
The definitive Paul Simon songbook. — New York ; London : Amsco, c2005. — 555 p. of music ; 30 cm.
"Over 150 songs drawn from every period in the unique career of this master songwriter. Each song includes melody, guitar chords and complete lyrics"—Cover.
Publ. no. PS 11594
ISBN 0825633230 (US)
ISBN 1844496457 (UK)
System number: 013265854

Songbird : chord songbook. — London : Wise Publications, c2004. — 96 p. ; 25 cm.
40 songs from the 2004 compilation album "Songbird." — Words and chord symbols. — Words and music by various songwriters. — Music arranged by James Dean.
Publ. no. AM91730
ISBN 0711938466
System number: 013085454

Under Filk Wood : a songbook created for Interaction, the 2005 World Science Fiction Convention, held in Glasgow, Scotland / compiled by Alison Richards. — Harold Wood, Essex : Beccon Publications, c2005. — 128 p. : ill ; 30 cm.
Contains 71 songs. Some have melody lines with chord symbols, other have words only and the name of the tune. — Words and music by various songwriters.
ISBN 1870824539
System number: 013280373

West End hit songs : twenty-nine hit songs from London's most successful stage musicals : arranged for piano, voice and guitar, complete with lyrics and chord symbols. — London : Wise, c2005. — 1 score (160 p.) ; 31 cm.
Publ. no. AM91554
ISBN 0711937818
System number: 013312999

West End love songs : thirty-four of the best romantic songs from London's most successful stage musicals : arranged for piano, voice and guitar, complete with lyrics and chord symbols. — London : Wise, c2005. — 1 score (160 p.) ; 31 cm.
Publ. no. AM91665
ISBN 0711938024
System number: 013307269

West End show hits. — London : Wise, c2005. — 1 score (160 p.) ; 31 cm.
"Thirty hit songs from London's most successful stage musicals. Arranged for piano, voice and guitar, complete with lyrics and chord symbols"—Cover.
Publ. no. AM982872
ISBN 1846090571
System number: 013307364

783.2421640264
Mitchell, Joni.
[Songs. *Selections*]
The very best of Joni Mitchell. — London : Wise Publications, c2005. — 1 score (96 p.) ; 31 cm.
For voice and piano, with guitar chord symbols. — 20 songs from various albums by Joni Mitchell.
Publ. no. AM91734
ISBN 0711938504
System number: 013222822

783.2421643
*****Audition songs for male singers.** R&B anthems : ten great songs ideal for auditions. — London : Wise, c2005. — 1 score (63 p.) ; 31 cm + 1 sound disc (digital ; 4 3/4 in.)
"CD+music pack specially developed for male singers auditioning for shows, revues and bands"—Back cover. — For voice and piano, with guitar chord symbols. — CD contains backing tracks.
Publ. no. AM91979
ISBN 0711940959
System number: 013434068

Blues rock. — Milwaukee, WI : Hal Leonard, [2003?] — 1 score (80 p.) ; 31 cm + 1 compact disc. — Hal Leonard guitar play-along ; 14
8 songs for voice and guitar in standard and tablature notation, with chord symbols. — Words and music by various songwriters. — CD contains full demonstration and backing tracks.
Publ. no. HL00699582
ISBN 0634056344
System number: 013191100
Primary classification 787.871643

Blues : Guitar play-along. — Milwaukee, WI : Hal Leonard, [2003] — 1 score (53 p.) ; 31 cm + 1 sound disc (digital ; 4 3/4 in.) — Hal Leonard guitar play-along ; 7
7 songs and 1 instrumental piece for voice and guitar in standard and tablature notation, with chord symbols. — Words and music by various songwriters. — CD contains full demonstration and backing tracks.
Publ. no. HL00699575
ISBN 0634056271
System number: 013191092
Also classified at 787.871643

Johnson, Robert, d. 1938.
Robert Johnson complete : piano, vocal, guitar. — Milwaukee, Wis. : Hal Leonard ; [2003?] — 1 score (216 p.) ; 31 cm.
For voice and piano, with chord symbols and guitar chord diagrams.
Publ. no. HL00306507
ISBN 0634056565
System number: 006936059

783.242165
You're the voice : Billie Holliday. — London : International Music Publications, 2004. — 1 score (40 p.) ; 31 cm. + 1 sound disc (digital ; 4 3/4 in.)
For voice and piano, with chord symbols and guitar chord diagrams. — "Ten timeless classics arranged for voice, piano, and guitar, as performed and recorded by the legendary Billie Holliday"—Cover.
Publ. no. 10039A
ISBN 1843287374
ISMN M570217373
System number: 013086205

783.242166
101 songs for easy guitar. Book 5. — London : Wise Publications, c2005. — 237 p. ; 31 cm.
Melody lines with words and chord symbols.
Publ. no. AM982883
ISBN 184609061X
System number: 013297793
Also classified at 787.87166

21st century rock : [vol. 5] / compiled by Nick Crispin ; music arranged by Matt Cowe. — Guitar tab ed. — London : Wise Publications, c2004. — 1 score (176 p.) ; 31 cm.
"Twenty-four great songs ... arranged for guitar tab with standard notation, chord symbols and full lyrics"—Back cover.
Publ. no. AM981409
ISBN 1844498182
System number: 013172321

The all-time greatest million-selling singles. — London : Wise, c2005. — 1 score (159 p.) ; 31 cm.
31 songs arranged for voice and piano, with guitar chord symbols.
Publ. no. AM92338
ISBN 9780711944145
ISBN 0711944148
System number: 013382742

Alter Bridge (Musical group).
One day remains / Alter Bridge. — Milwaukee, WI : Hal Leonard, [2004] — 1 score (111 p.) : port. ; 31 cm. — (Guitar recorded versions)
11 songs from Alter Bridge's 2004 album "One day remains." — For voice and guitar(s) in standard and tablature notation, with chord symbols. — Words and music mostly by Mark Tremonti. — Music transcriptions by Pete Billmann.
Publ. no. HL00690755
ISBN 0634091441
System number: 013191642

Amos, Tori.
The beekeeper / Tori Amos. — New York ; Amsco Publishing, c2005. London : — 1 score (139 p.) : col. ports ; 31 cm.
20 songs from Tori Amos' 2005 album "The beekeeper." — For voice and piano, with guitar chord symbols. — Words and music by Tori Amos. — Words also printed for reference preceding score.
Publ. no. AM982454
ISBN 0825634059
System number: 013323485

Archer, Richard, 1976 or 7-
Stars of CCTV : guitar tab edition / Hard-Fi. — London : Wise Publications, c2005. — 1 score (79 p.) ; 31 cm.
11 songs from Hard-Fi's 2005 album "Stars of CCTV." — For voice and guitar(s) in standard and tablature notation, with chord symbols. — Words and music by Richard Archer.
Publ. no. AM983488
ISBN 9781846092107
ISBN 1846092108
System number: 013383492

Athlete (Musical group).
Tourist / Athlete. — London : Wise Publications, c2005. — 1 score (56 p.) ; 31 cm.
11 songs from Athlete's 2005 album "Tourist." — For voice and piano, with chord symbols and guitar chord diagrams. — Words and music by members of the group.
Publ. no. AM91968
ISBN 0711940843
System number: 013382614

*Beatles.
[Songs. *Selections*]
The Beatles : note-for-note. — London : Wise, c2005. — 1 score (64 p.) ; 31 cm.
"Fourteen Beatles classics transcribed from the original recordings ... Includes note-for-note piano accompaniment with complete piano solos, lyrics, melody line and guitar chord voicings"—Back cover. — Words and music by John Lennon and Paul McCartney.
Publ. no. NO91113
ISBN 9781846093128

ISBN 1846093120
System number: 013432684

Beatles.
[Songs. *Selections*]
Play bass with— The Beatles. — London : Wise Publications, c2005. — 1 score (48 p.) ; 31 cm. + 1 compact disc
10 rock songs for voice and 4 or 5-string bass guitar (in standard and tablature notation), with chord symbols. — Words and music by John Lennon and Paul McCartney. — CD contains full instrumental performances and backing tracks.
Publ. no. NO90904
ISBN 0711992703
System number: 013190805

Beck.
Guero / Beck ; music transcriptions by Pete Billmann, Addi Booth and David Stocker. — Milwaukee, Wis. : Hal Leonard, c2005. — 1 score (77 p.) ; 31 cm. — (Guitar recorded versions)
13 songs from Beck's 2005 album "Guero." — For voice and guitar(s) in standard and tablature notation, with chord symbols. — Words and music by Beck and others.
Publ. no. HL00690792
ISBN 1423400062
System number: 013383507

Beck.
Sea change / Beck ; music transcriptions by Andrew Moore, David Stocker, and Jeff Story. — Milwaukee, Wis. : Hal Leonard, [2002?] — 102 p. ; 31 cm. — (Guitar recorded versions)
"Authentic transcriptions with notes and tablature." — For voice and guitar with chord symbols, in standard and tablature notation.
Publ. no. HL00690632
ISBN 063406309X
System number: 006906656

Bedingfield, Natasha.
Unwritten / Natasha Bedingfield. — London : International Music Publications, 2004. — 1 score (73 p.) ; 31 cm.
13 songs from Natasha Bedingfield's 2004 album "Unwritten." — For voice and piano, with chord symbols and guitar chord diagrams. — Words and music by Natasha Bedingfield and others.
Publ. no. 10087A
ISBN 1843287897
ISMN M570217892
System number: 013185871

Bee Gees.
[Songs. *Selections*]
Number ones : piano, vocal, guitar / Bee Gees. — Milwaukee, Wis. : Hal Leonard, [2005?] — 1 score (80 p.) ; 31 cm.
19 songs from the Bee Gees' 2004 album "Number ones." — For voice and piano, with chord symbols and guitar chord diagrams. — Words and music by members of the group.
Publ. no. HL00306710
ISBN 0634096915
System number: 013222066

The best acoustic guitar songs ever. — [S.l.] : Hal Leonard Europe ; London : exclusive distributors, Music Sales, c2005. — 1 score (239 p.) ; 31 cm. — (Guitar recorded versions)
30 songs for voice and guitar(s), in standard and tablature notation, with chord symbols.
Publ. no. HLE90002451
ISBN 1846090954
System number: 013408007
Also classified at 787.87166

The best of 1000 UK number one hits. Early years : [from 1952 to 1974 : arranged for piano, voice and guitar] — London : Wise Publications, c2004. — 1 score (160 p.) ; 31 cm.
37 songs or instrumental pieces for voice and piano, with guitar chord symbols. — Compiled by Nick Crispin ; music arranged by Derek Jones. — English words, with one song in French.
Publ. no. AM91479
ISBN 0711937168
System number: 013129814

The big guitar chord songbook. Classic rock. — London : Wise Publications, c2005. — 192 p. ; 25 cm.
"Over 70 rock classics, complete with lyrics, chord symbols and guitar boxes"—Cover. — Compiled by Nick Crispin; music arrangements by Paul Carr and Jason Broadbent.
Publ. no. AM979979
ISBN 1844494772
System number: 013203906

Blues rock. — Milwaukee, WI : Hal Leonard, [2003?] — 1 score (80 p.) ; 31 cm + 1 compact disc. — Hal Leonard guitar play-along ; 14
8 songs for voice and guitar in standard and tablature notation, with chord symbols. — Words and music by various songwriters. — CD contains full demonstration and backing tracks.
Publ. no. HL00699582
ISBN 0634056344
System number: 013191100
Primary classification 787.871643

Bon Jovi (Musical group).
Have a nice day / Bon Jovi. — Guitar tab ed. — London : Wise, c2005. — 1 score (103 p.) ; 31 cm.
14 songs from Bon Jovi's 2005 album "Have a nice day." — For voice and guitar(s) in standard and tablature notation, with chord symbols. — Words and music by members of the group and others.
Publ. no. AM984368
ISBN 9781846092992
ISBN 184609299X
System number: 013395868

Carlton, Vanessa.
Harmonium : piano, vocal, guitar / Vanessa Carlton. — Milwaukee, Wis. : Hal Leonard, c2004. — 1 score (80 p.) ; 31 cm.
10 songs from Vanessa Carlton's 2004 album "Harmonium." — For voice and piano with chord symbols and guitar chord diagrams. — Words and music by Vanessa Carlton or Vanessa Carlton and Stephan Jenkins.
Publ. no. HL00306700
ISBN 0634095188
System number: 013335640

Clapton, Eric.
[Songs. *Selections*]
Eric Clapton : guitar play-along. — Milwaukee, WI : Hal Leonard, [2004?] — 1 score (56 p.) ; 31 cm + 1 compact disc. — Hal Leonard guitar play-along ; 24
8 songs arranged for voice and guitar in standard and tablature notation, with chord symbols. — Words and music by Eric Clapton and others. — With errata sheet inserted. — CD contains full demonstration and backing tracks.
Publ. no. HL00699649
ISBN 0634080172
System number: 013219768
Primary classification 787.87166

Clapton, Eric.
[Songs. *Selections*]
Play guitar with— Eric Clapton. — London : Wise, [2005], c1997. — 1 score (56 p.) ; 31 cm + 1 sound disc (digital ; 4 3/4 in.) + 1 video disc (digital ; 4 3/4 in.)
Rocks songs with guitar acc. (in tablature and standard notation). — Words and music by Eric Clapton. — CD contains full instrumental performances and backing tracks. — "Includes DVD guitar lesson"—Sticker on cover. — DVD features the song "Layla." — Publisher's no.: AM950862 (t.p.), AM983664 (sticker on back cover).
Publ. no. AM950862
Publ. no. AM983664
ISBN 1846092205 (sticker on back cover)
System number: 013374869
Also classified at 787.87166

*Clash (Musical group).
[Songs. *Selections*]
Play guitar with— The Clash. — London : Wise, c2005. — 1 score (55 p.) ; 31 cm + 1 sound disc (digital ; 4 3/4 in.)
8 songs arranged for voice and guitar(s) in standard and tablature notation, with chord symbols. — Words and music by members of the group; music arrangements by Arthur Dick. — CDs contain full instrumental performances and backing tracks.
Publ. no. AM983103
ISBN 9781846091032
ISBN 1846091039
System number: 013432677

Coldplay (Musical group).
Coldplay live 2003. — London : Wise, c2004. — 1 score (111 p.) : ports ; 31 cm.
18 songs from Coldplay's 2003 album "Coldplay live 2003." — For voice and piano, with guitar chord symbols. — Words and music by members of the group.
Publ. no. AM979770
ISBN 1844494209
System number: 013297924

Coldplay (Musical group).
[X&Y; *arr.*]
Play guitar with— Coldplay : X&Y. — London : Wise, c2005. — 1 score (104 p.) ; 31 cm + 2 sound discs (digital ; 4 3/4 in.)
13 songs from Coldplay's 2005 album "X&Y." — For voice and guitar(s) in standard and tablature notation, with chord symbols. — Words and music by members of the group; music arrangements by Arthur Dick and Martin Shellard. — CDs contain full instrumental performances and backing tracks.
Publ. no. AM92351
ISBN 071194427X
System number: 013371830

Coldplay (Musical group).
X&Y : [piano/vocal transcriptions] / Coldplay. — London : Wise Publications, c2005. — 1 score (96 p.) : ports. ; 31 cm.
13 songs from Coldplay's 2005 album "X&Y." — For voice and piano, with chord symbols and guitar chord diagrams. — Words and music by members of the group.
Publ. no. AM92113
ISBN 9780711942394
ISBN 0711942390
System number: 013226469

Coldplay (Musical group).
X&Y : guitar tab edition / Coldplay. — London : Wise Publications, c2005. — 1 score (104 p.) : ports. ; 31 cm.
13 songs from Coldplay's 2005 album "X&Y." — For voice and guitar(s), in standard and tablature notation with guitar chord symbols. — Words and music by members of the group.
Publ. no. AM92346
ISBN 9780711944220
ISBN 0711944229
System number: 013226461

Cure (Musical group).
The Cure : guitar tab edition / The Cure. — London : Wise Publications, c2005. — 1 score (104 p.) : ill. ; 31 cm.
11 songs from The Cure's 2004 album "The Cure" plus 2 bonus tracks, 'Truth, goodness and beauty" and "Going nowhere." — For voice and guitar(s) in standard and tablature notation, with chord symbols. — Words and music by members of the group.
Publ. no. AM981321
ISBN 1844497992
System number: 013185954

Doves (Musical group).
Some cities / Doves. — Guitar tab ed. — London : International Music Publications, 2005. — 1 score (112 p.) ; 31 cm.
11 songs from Doves' 2005 album "Some cities." — For voice and guitar(s) in standard and tablature notation, with chord symbols. — Words and music by members of the group.
Publ. no. 10150A
ISBN 1843288699
ISMN M570218691
System number: 013299322

Elvis Presley greats. — Milwaukee, Wis. : Hal Leonard, c2005. — 1 score (27 p.) ; 31 cm + 1 sound disc (digital ; 4 3/4 in.) — Hal Leonard piano play-along v. 36
8 songs from the repertoire of Elvis Presley, arranged for voice and piano, with guitar chord symbols. — Words and music by various songwriters. — CD contains full performances and backing tracks. — Publisher's no.: HL00311231 (score), CD#63009377 (CD).
Publ. no. HL00311231
Publ. no. CD#63009377
ISBN 0634077309
System number: 013383571

Embrace (Musical group).
Out of nothing / Embrace. — Guitar tab ed. — London : International Music Publications, 2005. — 1 score (84 p.) : col. ports ; 31 cm.
10 songs from Embrace's 2005 album "Out of nothing." — For voice and guitar(s) in standard and tablature notation, with chord symbols. — Words and music mostly by Daniel McNamara and Richard McNamara.
Publ. no. 10111A
ISBN 1843288192
ISMN M570218196
System number: 013158969

The essential nü metal playlist. — London : Wise Publications, c2005. — 1 score (135 p.) ; 31 cm.
18 songs for voice and guitar in standard and tablature notation, with chord symbols. — Compiled by Nick Crispin ; music arranged by Matt Cowe and Arthur Dick. — English words, with one song in German.
Publ. no. AM980991
ISBN 1844497224
System number: 013139688

Father and son : + 9 smash hits. — London : Wise Publications, c2004. — 1 score (56 p.) ; 31 cm.
For voice and piano, with chord symbols and guitar chord diagrams. — Words and music by various songwriters.
Publ. no. AM91916
ISBN 0711940320
System number: 013178698

Feeder (Musical group).
Pushing the senses / Feeder. — Guitar tab ed. — London : Wise, c2005. — 1 score (103 p.) ; 31 cm.
10 songs from Feeder's 2005 album "Pushing the senses." — For voice and guitars in standard and tablature notation, with chord symbols. — Words and music by Grant Nicholas (wrongly printed as Nicholas Grant in the score).
Publ. no. AM91966
ISBN 0711940827
System number: 013201234

Filthy/Gorgeous : + 9 smash hits. — London : Wise Publications, c2005. — 1 score (56 p.) ; 31 cm.
For voice and piano, with chord symbols and guitar chord diagrams. — Words and music by various songwriters.
Publ. no. AM92013
ISBN 0711941203
System number: 013201212

Folds, Ben, 1966-
Songs for Silverman : piano transcriptions, vocal / Ben Folds. — [S.l.] :
BMG Publications ; Milwaukee, Wis. : Hal Leonard, c2005. — 1 score
(133 p.) : ill. ; 31 cm.
11 songs from Ben Folds' 2005 album "Songs for Silverman." — For voice and
piano, with guitar chord symbols. — Words and music by Ben Folds.
Publ. no. HL00306720
ISBN 0634099108
System number: 013383512

Folk rock : guitar play-along. — Milwaukee, Wis. : Hal Leonard, [2003?] —
1 score (56 p.) ; 31 cm. + 1 compact disc. — Guitar play-along ; v. 13
8 songs for voice and guitar in standard and tablature notation, with chord symbols.
— Words and music by various songwriters. — CD contains full demonstration and
backing tracks.
Publ. no. HL00699581
ISBN 0634056336
System number: 013222766

Foo Fighters (Musical group).
In your honor / Foo Fighters ; music transcriptions by Pete Billmann and
David Stocker. — London : Wise, c2005. — 1 score (157 p.) ; 31 cm. —
(Guitar recorded versions)
20 songs from Foo Fighter's 2005 album "In your honor." — For voice and guitar(s)
in standard and tablature notation, with chord symbols. — Words and music by
members of the group.
Publ. no. AM984423
ISBN 184609304X
System number: 013395944

***Franz Ferdinand (Musical group).**
You could have it so much better / [Franz Ferdinand] — Guitar tab ed. —
London : Wise Publications. — 1 score (88 p.) ; 31 cm.
13 songs from Franz Ferdinand's 2005 album "You could have it so much better." —
For voice and guitar(s) in standard and tablature notation, with chord symbols. —
Words and music by members of the group.
Publ. no. AM984379
ISBN 9781846093005
ISBN 1846093007
System number: 013440051

Gray, David, 1970-
Life in slow motion / David Gray. — London : Wise Publications, c2005. —
1 score (64 p.) : ports ; 31 cm.
10 songs from David Gray's 2005 album "Life in slow motion." — For voice and
piano, with guitar chord symbols. — Words and music by David Gray and others.
Publ. no. AM983741
ISBN 1846092388
System number: 013371790

Great songs of the 60s for guitar : [thirty songs that defined an era] —
[S.l.] : Hal Leonard Europe ; London : distributed by Music Sales, c2004.
— 1 score (200 p.) ; 31 cm. — Guitar recorded versions
For voice and guitar(s) in standard and tablature notation with chord symbols.
Publ. no. HLE90002209
ISBN 1844495809
System number: 013130716

Great songs of the 70s : for guitar : [thirty songs that defined an era] —
[S.l.] : Hal Leonard Europe ; London : distributed by Music Sales, c2004.
— 1 score (230 p.) ; 31 cm. — Guitar recorded versions.
For voice and guitar(s) in standard and tablature notation with chord symbols.
Publ. no. HLE90002220
ISBN 1844495817
System number: 013130717

Guitar tab : white pages : now! volume 2 : [a giant collection of authentic
guitar transcriptions] — [s.l.] : Hal Leonard Europe ; London : exclusive
distributors, Music Sales, c2005. — 1 score (1040 p.) ; 28 cm.
150 songs for voice and guitar(s) in standard and tablature notation, with chord
symbols. — Spine title: Guitar tab 2 : white pages.
Publ. no. HLE90002297
ISBN 184449814X
System number: 013197181
Also classified at 787.87166

Happy songs : twenty-three of the greatest feel-good songs of all time :
arranged for piano, voice and guitar. — London : Wise Publications,
c2005. — 1 score (128 p.) ; 31 cm.
For voice and piano, with guitar chord boxes.
Publ. no. AM92233
ISBN 0711943583
ISBN 9780711943582
System number: 013371778

Harrison, George, 1943-2001.
[Songs. *Selections*]
The Dark Horse years : 1976-1992 / George Harrison. — Milwaukee, Wis. :
Hal Leonard, [2004?] — 1 score (312 p.) : ports (some col.), ill. (some
col.) ; 31 cm.
55 songs from George Harrison's 2004 eight-album boxed set "The Dark Horse
years, 1976-1992." — For voice and piano, with guitar chord symbols. — Words and
music mostly by George Harrison.
Publ. no. HL00306703
ISBN 0634095595
System number: 013383584

Hendrix, Jimi.
Blue wild angel : live at the Isle of Wight / Jimi Hendrix ; music
transcriptions Andy Aledort. — [S.l.] : Experience Hendrix ; Milwaukee,
Wis. : exclusively distributed by Hal Leonard, [2005?] — 1 score
(230 p.) ; 31 cm. — (Guitar recorded versions)
17 songs and one instrumental piece performed by Jimi Hendrix at the 1970 Isle
of Wight festival and released as an album in 2002. — For voice and guitar in
standard and tablature notation, with chord symbols. — Includes Hendrix's
spoken introductions. — Words and music by Jimi Hendrix and others.
Publ. no. HL00690608
ISBN 0634057286
System number: 013382751

John, Elton.
[Songs. *Selections*]
The piano transcriptions / Elton John. — London : Wise, 2005. — 1
score (92 p.) ; 31 cm.
15 songs for voice and piano, with guitar chord symbols. — "Transcribed from
the original recordings as performed by Elton John"—Back cover. — Words and
music mostly by Elton John and Bernie Taupin.
Publ. no. AM92020
ISBN 0711941270
System number: 013326340

Johnson, Jack, 1975-
In between dreams / Jack Johnson ; transcribed by Jeff Jacobson. — New
York : Cherry Lane Music ; Milwaukee, Wis. : distributed by Hal
Leonard, c2005. — 1 score (64 p.) : port. ; 31 cm. — Play it like it is.
Guitar
14 songs from Jack Johnson's 2005 album "In between dreams." — For voice and
guitar(s) in standard and tablature notation, with chord symbols. — Words and
music mostly by Jack Johnson. — Includes biographical note.
Publ. no. 02500831
ISBN 1575608308
System number: 013382270

Just classic rock real book. — C edition fakebook. — London :
International Music Publications, 2004. — 548 p. of music ; 31 cm.
"Songs from the '60s, '70s, '80s and '90s … Classic rock, pop, heavy rock, new
wave, metal and much more"—Cover. — Melody lines, words and chord symbols
for over 220 rock songs. — Includes indexes.
Publ. no. 9998A
ISBN 1843286440
ISMN M570216444
System number: 013189085

Kaiser Chiefs (Musical group).
Employment : guitar tab ed. / Kaiser Chiefs. — London : Wise
Publications, c2005. — 1 score (104 p.) ; 31 cm.
12 songs from Kaiser Chiefs' 2005 album "Employment." — For voice and
guitar(s) in standard and tablature notation, with chord symbols. — Words and
music by members of the group.
Publ. no. AM982938
ISBN 1846090806
System number: 013297794

Keane (Musical group).
[Hopes and fears; *arr.*]
Play piano with — Keane : Hopes and fears. — London : Wise, c2004.
— 1 score (94 p.) ; 31 cm + 2 sound discs (digital ; 4 3/4 in.)
12 songs from Keane's 2004 album "Hopes and fears" plus 3 bonus tracks. — For
voice and piano, with guitar chord symbols. — Words and music by members of
the group, arranged by Paul Honey. — CD contains full performances and
backing tracks.
Publ. no. AM91698
ISBN 071193813X
System number: 013193365

Killers (Musical group).
Hot fuss / The Killers. — Guitar recorded versions. — London : Wise
Publications, 2004. — 1 score (87 p.) ; 31 cm.
11 songs from The Killers' 2004 album "Hot fuss." — For voice and guitar(s) in
standard and tablature notation, with chord symbols. — Words and music by
members of the group.
Publ. no. AM981420
ISBN 1844498190
System number: 013169025

Kiss (Musical group).
[Songs. *Selections*]
Kiss. — Milwaukee, WI : Hal Leonard, [2005] — 1 score (48 p.) ; 31 cm
+ 1 sound disc (digital ; 4 3/4 in.) — Hal Leonard guitar play-along ; v.
30
8 songs for voice and guitar in standard and tablature notation, with chord
symbols. — Words and music by members of the group. — CD contains full
demonstration and backing tracks.
Publ. no. HL00699644
ISBN 0634079247
System number: 013383477
Also classified at 787.87166

Lennon, John, 1940-1980.
[Songs. *Selections*]
Lennon & McCartney : guitar play-along. — Milwaukee, WI : Hal Leonard, [2004] — 1 score (46 p.) ; 31 cm + 1 sound disc (digital ; 4 3/4 in.) — Hal Leonard guitar play-along ; 25
8 songs arranged for voice and guitar in standard and tablature notation, with chord symbols. — CD contains full demonstration and backing tracks.
Publ. no. HL00699642
ISBN 0634079220
System number: 013191084
Also classified at 787.87166

Lostprophets (Musical group).
Start something / Lostprophets ; music transcriptions by Addi Booth and David Stocker. — Milwaukee, Wis. : Hal Leonard, c2004. — 1 score (110 p.) ; 31 cm. — Guitar recorded versions
12 songs from Lostprophets' 2004 album "Start something." — For voice and guitar(s) in standard and tablature notation, with chord symbols. — Words and music by members of the group.
Publ. no. HL00690720
ISBN 0634083708
System number: 013169064

Maroon 5 (Musical group).
1.22.03.Acoustic : guitar recorded versions / Maroon 5 ; music transcriptions by Addi Booth. — Milwaukee, Wis. : Hal Leonard, [2005?] — 1 score (54 p.) ; 31 cm.
7 songs from Maroon 5's 2004 ablum "1.22.03.Acoustic." — For voice and guitar(s) in standard and tablature notation, with chord symbols. — Words and music by members of the band and others.
Publ. no. HL00690748
ISBN 0634089420
System number: 013383808

McFly (Musical group).
Room on the 3rd floor / McFly. — London : Wise Publications, c2005. — 1 score (79 p.) ; 31 cm.
13 songs from McFly's 2004 album "Room on the 3rd floor." — For voice and piano, with chord symbols and guitar chord diagrams. — Words and music by members of the group and others.
Publ. no. AM91976
ISBN 0711940924
System number: 013190707

McFly (Musical group).
Wonderland / McFly. — London : Wise, c2005. — 1 score (71 p.) ; 31 cm.
12 songs from McFly's 2005 album "Wonderland." — For voice and piano, with guitar chord symbols. — Words and music by members of the group and others.
Publ. no. AM984214
ISBN 9781846092824
ISBN 1846092825
System number: 013374982

Metallica (Musical group).
[Songs. *Selections*]
Play guitar with— Metallica. — London : Wise, [2005], c1997. — 1 score (64 p.) ; 31 cm + 1 sound disc (digital ; 4 3/4 in.) + 1 video disc (digital ; 4 3/4 in.)
6 songs with guitar acc., in tablature and standard notation. — Words and music by members of the group. — CD contains full instrumental performances and backing tracks. — "Includes DVD guitar lesson"—Sticker on cover. — DVD features the song "Enter sandman." — Publisher's no.: AM92559 (inside back cover), AM983642 (sticker on back cover).
Publ. no. AM92559
Publ. no. AM983642
ISBN 1846092183

ISBN 1846092183 (sticker on back cover)
System number: 013374852
Also classified at 787.87166

Metallica (Musical group).
St Anger / Metallica ; arranged by Jeff Jacobson. — New York, NY : Cherry Lane Music Company ; Milwaukee, WI : exclusively distributed by Hal Leonard, c2004. — 1 score (80 p.) : port., ill.; 31 cm.
11 songs from the Metallica 2003 album "St. Anger." — "EZ guitar with riffs, with tab"—Cover. — For voice and guitar, in standard and tablature notation with chord symbols. — Words and music by members of the group. — Includes discography.
Publ. no. 02500641
ISBN 1575606852
System number: 012875197

Modest Mouse (Musical group).
Good news for people who love bad news : guitar recorded versions / by Modest Mouse ; music transcriptions by Pete Billmann, Addi Booth and Jeff Story. — Milwaukee, Wis. : Hal Leonard, c2004. — 1 score (101 p.) ; 31 cm.
14 songs and 1 guitar piece from Modest Mouse's 2004 album "Good news for people who love bad news." — For voice and guitar(s) in standard and tablature notation, with chord symbols. — Words and music by members of the group.
Publ. no. HL00690769
ISBN 0634093037
System number: 013222187

Mraz, Jason.
Waiting for my rocket to come / Jason Mraz ; transcribed by Paul Pappas. — New York : Cherry Lane Music Co. ; Milwaukee : exclusively distributed by Hal Leonard, c2005. — 1 score (127 p.) : port. 31 cm. — Play it like it is. Guitar
12 songs from Jason Mraz's 2002 album "Waiting for my rocket to come." — For voice and guitar(s) in standard and tablature notation, with chord symbols. — Words and music by Jason Mraz and others. — Includes interview with Jason Mraz, p. 2-6. — "A Milton Okun publication"—Cover.
Publ. no. 02500765
ISBN 1575607867
System number: 013382309

Mudvayne (Musical group).
The end of all things to come / Mudvayne ; transcribed by Danny Begelman, Bill LaFleur and Greg Tribbett. — [S.l.] : Zomba Music ; Milwaukee, Wis. : Hal Leonard, [2005?], c2003. — 1 score (99 p.) : col. ill. ; 31 cm. — (Guitar recorded versions)
12 songs from Mudvayne's 2002 album "The end of all things to come." — For voice and guitar(s) in standard and tablature notation. — Words and music by the group.
Publ. no. HL00690786
ISBN 0634099930
System number: 013376127

Muse (Musical group : Great Britain).
[Songs. *Selections*]
The best of Muse. — Guitar tab ed. — London : Wise, c2005. — 1 score (79 p.) ; 31 cm.
12 songs from Muse's albums "Showbiz" (2000), "Origin of symmetry" (2001) and "Hullabaloo soundtrack" (2002). — For voice and guitar, in standard and tablature notation, with chord symbols. — Words and music mostly by Matthew Bellamy.
Publ. no. AM982905
ISBN 1846090644
System number: 013221817

Muse (Musical group : Great Britain).
[Songs. *Selections*]
Play bass with— Muse. — London : Wise, c2004. — 1 score (55 p.) ; 31 cm + 1 sound disc (digital ; 4 3/4 in.)
9 rock songs for voice and bass guitar (in standard and tablature notation), with chord symbols. — Words and music mostly by Matthew Bellamy. — CD contains full instrumental performances and backing tracks.
Publ. no. AM981354
ISBN 1844498050
System number: 013173839

Muse (Musical group : Great Britain).
[Songs. *Selections*]
Play guitar with— Muse : Stockholm syndrome and other great songs. — London : Wise, [2005], c2004. — 1 score (39 p.) ; 31 cm + 1 sound disc (digital ; 4 3/4 in.) + 1 video disc (digital ; 4 3/4 in.)
5 songs for voice and guitar, in standard and tablature notation, with chord symbols. — Words and music mostly by Matthew Bellamy. — CD contains full instrumental performances and backing tracks. — "Includes DVD guitar lesson"—Sticker on cover. — DVD features the song "Plug in baby." — Publisher's no.: AM981002 (t.p. verso), AM983653 (sticker on back cover).
Publ. no. AM981002
Publ. no. AM983653
ISBN 1844497232 (t.p. verso)
ISBN 1846092191 (sticker on back cover)
System number: 013374879
Also classified at 787.87166

Oasis (Musical group).
Don't believe the truth / Oasis. — Guitar tab ed. — London : Wise Publications, c2005. — 1 score (71 p.) ; 31 cm.
11 songs from Oasis' 2005 album "Don't believe the truth." — For voice & guitar, in standard and tablature notation, with chord symbols. — Words and music by members of the group.
Publ. no. AM983224
ISBN 1846091438
System number: 013390011

Oasis (Musical group).
Don't believe the truth / Oasis. — London : Wise Publications, c2005. — 1 score (56 p.) ; 31 cm.
11 songs from Oasis' 2005 album "Don't believe the truth." — For voice and piano, with guitar chord symbols. — Words and music by members of the group.
Publ. no. AM92240
ISBN 0711943656
System number: 013383522

Play guitar with— 20 rock classics. — London : Wise, c2005. — 1 score (143 p.) ; 31 cm + 2 sound discs (digital ; 4 3/4 in.)
20 rock songs for voice and guitar (in standard and tablature notation), with chord symbols. — CDs contain full instrumental performances and backing tracks.
Publ. no. AM92108
ISBN 071194234X
System number: 013299265

Play guitar with— Velvet Revolver, U2, Jeff Buckley, the Killers, Jet and Razorlight. — London : Wise Publications, c2005. — 1 score (63 p.) ; 31 cm. + 1 compact disc.
7 rock songs for voice and guitar (in tablature and standard notation), with chord symbols. — CD contains full instrumental performances and backing tracks.
Publ. no. AM91957
ISBN 0711940738
System number: 013191043

*Play piano with— John Lennon ... [et al.] — London : Wise, c2005. — 1 score (56 p) ; 31 cm + 1 sound disc (digital ; 4 3/4 in.)
8 songs for voice and piano, with piano parts taken from the original recordings. — Includes guitar chord symbols. — CD contains backing tracks. — Publisher's no.: AM92009 (score), OM33528 (CD)
Publ. no. AM92009
ISBN 0711941157
System number: 013432731

Presley, Elvis, 1935-1977.
[Songs. *Selections*]
Elvis : guitar play-along. — Milwaukee, WI : Hal Leonard, [2004] — 1 score (38 p.) ; 31 cm + 1 sound disc (digital ; 4 3/4 in.) — Hal Leonard guitar play-along ; 26
8 songs arranged for voice and guitar in standard and tablature notation, with chord symbols. — Words and music by Elvis Presley and others. — CD contains full demonstration and backing tracks. — Publisher's no.: HL00699643 (score), 63007869 (CD).
Publ. no. HL00699643
Publ. no. 63007869
ISBN 0634079239
System number: 013219807
Also classified at 787.87166

Red Hot Chili Peppers (Musical group).
[Songs. *Selections*]
Red Hot Chili Peppers : guitar chord songbook : [50 songs : includes complete lyrics, chord symbols & guitar chord diagrams] — Milwaukee, Wis. : Hal Leonard, [2005?] — 141 p. ; 23 cm.
Words and music mostly by members of the group.
Publ. no. HL00699710
ISBN 0634096486
System number: 013336122

Scissor Sisters.
Scissor Sisters. — London : International Music Publications, 2005. — 1 score (62 p.) ; 31 cm.
11 songs from Scissor Sisters' 2004 album "Scissor Sisters." — For voice and piano, with chord symbols and guitar chord diagrams. — Words and music mostly by members of the group.
Publ. no. 10037A
ISBN 1843287358
ISMN M570217359
System number: 013265863

Seal (Musician).
[Songs. *Selections*]
Seal best : 1991-2004. — London : Wise Publications, c2004. — 1 score (96 p.) ; 31 cm.
14 songs from Seal's 2004 album "Seal best : 1991-2004." — For voice and piano, with chord symbols and guitar chord diagrams. — Words and music by Seal and others.
Publ. no. AM91779
ISBN 0711939020
System number: 013178685

Seger, Bob.
[Songs. *Selections*]
Bob Seger. — Milwaukee, WI : Hal Leonard, [2005] — 1 score (64 p.) ; 31 cm + 1 compact disc. — Hal Leonard guitar play-along ; 29
8 songs for voice and guitar in standard and tablature notation, with chord symbols. — CD contains full demonstration and backing tracks.
Publ. no. HL00699647
ISBN 063407931X
System number: 013299275
Primary classification 787.87166

Six chord songbook : hits collection. — London : Wise Publications, c2004. — 128 p. ; 25 cm.
Words and guitar chord symbols for 54 rock songs.
Publ. no. AM91106
ISBN 0711934371
System number: 013185211

Smiths (Musical group).
[Songs]
The Smiths : complete chord songbook : every song recorded by The Smiths. — London : Wise Publications, c2005. — 185 p. ; 25 cm.
Words and guitar chord symbols for 72 songs. — Words and music mostly by Morrissey and Johnny Marr. — Includes discography.
Publ. no. AM92011
ISBN 0711941181
System number: 013359293

Smiths (Musical group).
[Songs. *Selections*]
Play guitar with— The Smiths. — London : Wise, c2005. — 1 score (46 p.) ; 31 cm + 1 sound disc (digital ; 4 3/4 in.)
6 songs for voice and guitar(s), in tablature and standard notation with chord symbols. — Words and music by Morrissey and Johnny Marr. — CD contains full instrumental performances and backing tracks.
Publ. no. AM983180
ISBN 1846091179
System number: 013336526

Smiths (Musical group).
[Songs. *Selections*]
The singles collection / The Smiths. — London : Wise, c2005. — 1 score (143 p.) ; 31 cm.
"19 of The Smith's most popular single releases"—Cover. — For voice and guitar(s) in standard and tablature notation, with chord symbols. — Words and music by Morrissey and Johnny Marr.
Publ. no. AM983092
ISBN 1846091020
System number: 013383555

Snow Patrol (Musical group).
Final straw / Snow Patrol. — Guitar tab ed. — London : International Music Publications, 2005. — 1 score (112 p.) ; 31 cm.
12 songs from Snow Patrol's 2004 album "Final straw", plus two bonus tracks, "We can run away now they're all dead and gone" and "Half the fun". — For voice and guitar(s) in standard and tablature notation, with chord symbols. — Words and music by members of the group.
Publ. no. 10094A
ISBN 184328796X
ISMN M570217960
System number: 013262486

Stereophonics.
Language, sex, violence, other? / Stereophonics. — Guitar tab ed. — London : Wise, c2005. — 1 score (79 p.) ; 31 cm.
11 songs from Sterophonics' 2005 album "Language. Sex. Violence. Other?" — For voice and guitar(s) in standard and tablature notation, with chord symbols. — Words and music by Kelly Jones.
Publ. no. AM92025
ISBN 0711941327
System number: 013297754

Sting (Musician).
[Songs. *Selections*]
Sting for guitar tab / [Compiled by Peter Evans]; [words & music by Sting] — London : Wise Publications, c1994. — 1 score (80 p.) ; 31 cm.
"Ten great songs in easy-to-read guitar tablature & standard notation, including chord symbols, melody line & lyrics"—Cover.
Publ. no. AM90259
ISBN 0711933154
System number: 013202148

System of a Down (Musical group).
Mezmerize / System of a Down ; music transcriptions by Pete Billmann and David Stocker. — [S.l.] : Sony/ATV Music Publishing ; Milwaukee, Wis. : exclusively distributed by Hal Leonard, c2005. — 1 score (87 p.) ; 31 cm. — (Guitar recorded versions)
11 songs from System of a Down's 2005 album "Mezmerize." — For voice and guitar(s) in standard and tablature notation, with chord symbols. — Words and music by members of the group.
Publ. no. HL00690799
ISBN 142340145X
System number: 013376891
Also classified at 787.87166

Top of the charts. — London : International Music Publications, 2005. — 1 score (110 p.) ; 31 cm.
20 rock songs arranged for voice and piano, with guitar chord symbols.
Publ. no. 10148A
ISBN 1843288672
ISMN M570218677
System number: 013307375

Train (Musical group).
[Songs. *Selections*]
Best of Train / music transcriptions by David Stocker. — Guitar recorded versions. — Milwaukee, WI : Hal Leonard, [2004?] — 1 score (124 p.) ; 31 cm.
12 songs from Train's 2003 album "My private nation", 2001 album "Drops of Jupiter" and 1998 album "Train." — For voice and guitar(s) in standard and tablature notation with chord symbols. — Words and music by members of the group.
Publ. no. HL00690654
ISBN 0634067990
System number: 013167704

Tunstall, KT.
Eye to the telescope / KT Tunstall. — London : Wise Publications c2005. — 1 score (72 p.) ; 31 cm.
12 songs from KT Tunstall's 2005 album "Eye to the telescope." — For voice and piano with guitar chord symbols. — Words and music mostly by KT Tunstall.
Publ. no. AM92234
ISBN 0711943591
System number: 013326342

Twain, Shania.
Greatest hits / Shania Twain. — London : Wise Publications, c2004. — 1 score (143 p.) : 31 cm. ports.
21 songs from Shania Twain's 2004 album "Greatest hits." — For voice and piano with guitar chord symbols. — Words and music mostly by Shania Twain and Robert J. Lange.
Publ. no. AM91902
ISBN 0711940185
System number: 013167493

U2 (Musical group).
[Songs. *Selections*]
Play guitar with— U2 : (1984-1987). — London : Wise, c2004. — 1 score (62 p.) ; 31 cm + 1 sound disc (digital ; 4 3/4 in.)
7 songs for voice and guitar(s) in standard and tablature notation, with chord symbols. — Words and music by members of the group. — CDs contain full instrumental performances, and backing tracks without guitar.
Publ. no. AM980804
ISBN 1844496627
System number: 013190592

U2 (Musical group).
[Songs. *Selections*]
U2 : the piano collection : twenty hit songs from one of the world's best rock bands specially arranged for piano, voice and guitar. — London : Wise Publications, c2005. — 1 score (128 p.) ; 31 cm.
For voice and piano, with chord symbols and guitar chord diagrams. — Words and music mostly by U2.
Publ. no. AM91965
ISBN 9780711940819
ISBN 0711940819
System number: 013395771

Usher.
[Confessions. *Selections*]
Selections from Confessions : piano/vocal/guitar / Usher. — [S.l.] : EMI Music Publishing ; Milwaukee : exclusively distributed by Hal Leonard, [2004] — 1 score (104 p.) : port. ; 31 cm.
13 songs from Usher's 2004 album "Confessions." — For voice and piano, with guitar chord symbols. — Words and music by Usher and others.
Publ. no. HL00306644
ISBN 0634084534
System number: 013191618

Vai, Steve.
Eat 'em and smile / David Lee Roth ; music transcriptions by Addi Booth. — Milwaukee, Wis. : Hal Leonard, [2005?] — 1 score (104 p.) ; 31 cm. — (Guitar recorded versions)
10 songs from David Lee Roth's 1986 album "Eat 'em and smile." — For voice and guitar(s) in standard and tablature notation, with chord symbols. — Words mostly by David Lee Roth, music mostly by Steve Vai.
Publ. no. HL00690685
ISBN 0634078518
System number: 013222589

Verve (Musical group).
[Songs. *Selections*]
This is music : the singles 92-98 / The Verve. — Guitar tab ed. — London : International Music Publications, 2004. — 1 score (103 p.) ; 31 cm.
14 songs from The Verve's 2004 compilation album "This is music: the singles 92-98." — For voice and guitar(s) in standard and tablature notation with chord symbols and guitar chord diagrams. — Words and music mostly by Richard Ashcroft and other members of the group.
Publ. no. 10109A
ISBN 1843288176
ISMN M570218172
System number: 013172276

Williams, Robbie.
Intensive care : piano, vocal, guitar / Robbie Williams. — London : Wise, c2005. — 1 score (76 p.) : ports. ; 31 cm.
12 songs from Robbie Williams' 2005 album "Intensive care." — For voice and piano, with guitar chord symbols. — Words and music by Robbie Williams and Stephen Duffy.
Publ. no. AM984533
ISBN 9781846093173
ISBN 1846093171
System number: 013395834

The world's greatest artists and bands : chord songbook : a selection of fifty-five songs from the album. — London : Wise Publications, c2005. — 160 p. ; 25 cm.
Words and guitar chord symbols.
Publ. no. AM91967
ISBN 0711940835
System number: 013265847

783.2421660264
Sting (Musician).
[Songs. *Selections*]
The singles collection / Sting. — London : Wise Publications, c2005. — 1 score (112 p.) ; 31 cm.
"18 of Sting's most popular releases"—Back cover. — For voice and piano, with guitar chord symbols. — Words and music by Sting.
Publ. no. AM984104
ISBN 184609271X
System number: 013383548

783.3 – HIGH VOICES

783.342
Beach, H. H. A., Mrs., 1867-1944.
[Song of liberty; *arr.*]
A song of liberty : for high voice and piano, op. 49 / by Amy Beach. — Boca Raton, Fla. : Masters Music Publications, [2005?] — 1 score (7 p.) ; 31 cm. — Master vocal series
For high voice and piano; originally for mixed chorus and orchestra. — Text by Frank L. Stanton.
Publ. no. M 3913
System number: 014497795

Duparc, Henri, 1848-1933.
[Songs]
Complete songs : with texts in English, German and French : high voice = Hohe Stimme = voix élevées / Henri Duparc ; edited by Roger Nichols. — London : Edition Peters, c2005. — 1 score (xviii, 123 p.) ; 31 cm.
With piano accompaniment. — 'La fuite' is a duet. — Pref. in English, French and German; critical commentary in English. — "Urtext"—Cover. — Publisher's no.: Edition Peters no. 7778a. — French words; also printed for reference with English and German translations p.xi-xviii.
Publ. no. EP 7778a
ISMN M577085517
System number: 013312852

*Fesch, Willem de, 1687-1761.
[English songs]
VI English songs : for soprano, violins, flutes and basso continuo : 1748 / Willem de Fesch ; edited by Robert L. Tusler. — Amsterdam : Donemus, 2004, c2003.
Figured bass realized for keyboard instrument.
System number: 014747718

Jackson, William, 1730-1803.
[Songs, op. 16. When fond, you Damon's charms recite]
When fond, you Damon's charms recite : op. 16 no. 7 (c. 1793) : song with obbligato viola da gamba / William Jackson ; edited by David J. Rhodes. — [S.l.] : Viola da Gamba Society of Great Britain, c2003. — 1 score (3 p.) + 2 parts ; 30 cm.
For voice and continuo, with obligato viola da gamba. — Score contains partially figured bass realized for piano. Includes unrealized bass part for violoncello. — Edited from the printed ed.: London, Longman & Broderip, [1793?] — Includes biographical note and critical commentary.
Pl. no. 192
System number: 013382414

*Purcell, Henry, 1659-1695.
[Fairy queen. *Selections*]
The four seasons in the Fairy queen : for soprano, alto, tenor, and bass solos, strings and continuo : from Orpheus Britannicus / Henry Purcell. — Richmond : Green Man Press, c2002. — 5 scores + 4 parts ; 30 cm.
Includes 1 score with figured bass realized for keyboard instrument; 4 scores with figured bass unrealized; and parts for 2 violins, viola and bass instrument. — "In the Orpheus Britannicus version the first three songs have a treble (G2) clef, but they can be sung by a soprano, alto and tenor respectively"—P. 2. — First 3 songs for high voice, 2 violins and continuo; 4th song for bass voice, 2 violins, viola and continuo. — Pref. and editorial notes in English by Cedric Lee. — English words, also printed for reference on p. 2 of score.
Publ. no. Pur 11
Pl. no. Pur 11-1—Pur 11-2
System number: 013597526
Also classified at 783.542

*Purcell, Henry, 1659-1695.
[Vocal music. *Selections*]
Three songs with hautboys : from Orpheus Britannicus / Henry Purcell. — Richmond : Green Man Press, c2001. — 2 scores + 3 parts ; 30 cm.
1st work for soprano/tenor, 2 oboes and continuo; 2nd and 3rd works for bass, 2 oboes and continuo. — One score includes keyboard realization of continuo part, the other has figured bass only. — Introduction and editorial notes by Cedric Lee. — Words also printed for reference preceding score.
Publ. no. Pur 7
System number: 013597487
Also classified at 783.8942

*Samuel, Rhian.
Trinity : three songs for high voice, flute and piano / to texts by Anne Stevenson ; by Rhian Samuel. — London : Stainer & Bell, c2005. — 1 score (23 p.) + 1 part (10 p.) ; 30 cm.
Words also printed for reference preceding score.
Publ. no. AC220
ISMN M220221422
System number: 013213374

*Vaughan Williams, Ralph, 1872-1958.
[Blake songs]
Ten Blake songs : for voice and oboe / Ralph Vaughan Williams. — [New York] : Oxford University Press, [2004?], c1958. — 1 score (14 p.) ; 31 cm. — Oxford vocal music
Reprint. Originally published: 1958.
ISBN 0193850265
System number: 013094158

*Warlock, Peter, 1894-1930.
[Songs. *Selections*]
Songs 1923-1928 : high voice / Peter Warlock ; edited by Michael
Pilkington. — [Norwich] : Thames Publishing, in association with the Peter
Warlock Society, c2004. — 1 score (63 p.) ; 30 cm. — (New Peter Warlock
critical edition ; v. 5)
With piano acc. — Includes editorial notes.
System number: 013173999

783.3420945

*A selection of Italian arias, c.1600-c.1800. Volume II / edition prepared
by Damian Cranmer ; English translations by Dorothy Richardson ;
edition supervised by Michael Pilkington. — High voice. — London :
Associated Board of the Royal Schools of Music, c2005. — 1 score
(80 p.) ; 31 cm.
For voice and piano; some accompaniments realized from figured bass or reduced
from orchestral acc. — Includes source notes. — Italian and English words.
Pl. no. AB 2729
ISBN 9781860961007
ISBN 1860961002
System number: 013307384

783.348

*Pepusch, John Christopher, 1667-1752.
[English cantatas. *Selections*]
Five cantatas with recorder : for soprano or tenor, recorder and continuo /
J.C. Pepusch. — Richmond : Green Man Press, c2003. — 2 scores +
2 parts ; 30 cm.
One score includes keyboard realization of continuo part, the other has figured bass
only. — Includes continuo part for bass instrument. — Words also printed for
reference preceding score. — Introduction and editorial notes by Cedric Lee.
Publ. no. Pep 1
System number: 013590950

Stanley, John, 1712-1786.
[Cantatas, op. 8]
Six cantata's, for a voice and instruments / set to musick by John Stanley. —
Alston : JPH Publications, c2004. — 1 score (45 p.) ; 30 cm.
For solo voice and continuo (figured bass) with various combinations of other
instruments. — Facsim. of publication held in the British Library (H.1217),
originally published: London : Printed for John Stanley…, 1748. — Words by J.
Hawkins.
ISMN M708029397
System number: 013312779

783.4 – MIDDLE VOICE

783.42

*Theile, Johann, 1646-1724.
[Vocal music. *Selections*]
Weltliche Arien und Canzonetten / Johann Theile ; herausgegeben von
Stephan Blaut. — Leipzig : Friedrich Hofmeister, c2004. — 1 score (xxiii,
60 p.) : facsims. ; 31 cm. — Denkmäler mitteldeutscher Barockmusik. Serie
1, Musikalische Zentren in Sachsen, Sachsen-Anhalt und Thüringen ; Bd. 3
For 1-4 solo voices (SATB), strings and continuo; figured bass not realized. —
Edited from the 1667 edition held in Universitätsbibliothek Uppsala (Sign.: Utl. vok.
mus. tr. 459-465). — Introd. in German with English translation; critical notes in
German only. — German words; additional verses printed separately for reference
following each song.
ISMN M203483533
System number: 014660605
Also classified at 782.542

783.42709438

Pieśni i hymny Piwnicy pod Baranami / [wybór piosenek Piotr Ferster,
Marek Pacuła] — Kraków : Piwnica pod Baranami ; Polskie
Wydawnictwo Muzyczne, c2006. — 1 score (144 p.) : ill. ; 31 cm.
For voice and piano. — Accompanying material in Polish. — Polish words.
Pl. no. PWM 10 445
ISMN M274002695
System number: 013739029
Also classified at 783.44209438

783.442

D'Amico, Matteo, 1955-
The entertainment of the senses : cabaret musicale per voce e strumenti
(2005) / Matteo D'Amico ; su testi di W.H. Auden and Ch. Kallman. —
Partitura. — Milano : Ricordi, [2006], c2005. — 1 score (136 p.) ; 30 cm.
For medium voice with flute, oboe, clarinet, horn, bassoon, and piano. — English
words.
Publ. no. 139553
ISMN M041395531
System number: 013688128

*Duparc, Henri, 1848-1933.
[Songs]
Complete songs : with texts in English, German and French :
medium/low voice = Mittlere/Tiefe Stimme = voix moyennes/graves /
Henri Duparc ; edited by Roger Nichols. — London : Edition Peters,
c2005. New York : — 1 score (xviii, 123 p.) ; 31 cm.
With piano accompaniment. — 'La fuite' is a duet. — Pref. in English, French
and German; critical commentary in English. — "Urtext"—Cover. — Publisher's
no.: Edition Peters no. 7778b. — French words, also printed for reference with
English and German translations.
Publ. no. EP 7778b
ISMN M577085654
EAN 9790577085654
System number: 013643025
Also classified at 783.542

*Tann, Hilary.
Wings of the grasses : for voice and oboe (or other melody instrument) /
words by Menna Elfyn ; music by Hilary Tann. — [New York] : Oxford
University Press, c2004. — 1 score (7 p.) ; 31 cm. — Oxford vocal music
Words also printed for reference preceding score. — Includes composer's note.
ISBN 019386777X
ISBN 9780193867772
System number: 013114973

Ullmann, Viktor.
[Herbst]
Drei Lieder : für Singstimme und Streichtrio = for voice and string trio
(1943) / Viktor Ullmann ; nach Texten von Georg Trakl und Albert
Steffen. — Mainz ; London : Schott, c2005. — 1 score (13 p.) + 3 parts ;
31 cm.
Foreword in German, English and French; critical report in German at end.
Pl. no. 48 195
Publ. no. ED 8284
ISMN M001120395
System number: 013510089

*Warlock, Peter, 1894-1930.
[Songs. *Selections*]
Songs 1920-1923 : medium voice / Peter Warlock ; edited by Michael
Pilkington. — [Norwich] : Thames Publishing, in association with the
Peter Warlock Society, c2004. — 1 score (68 p.) ; 30 cm. — (New Peter
Warlock critical edition ; v. 4)
With piano acc. — Includes editorial notes.
System number: 013173934

*Warlock, Peter, 1894-1930.
[Songs. *Selections*]
Songs 1923-1926 : medium voice / Peter Warlock ; edited by Michael
Pilkington. — [Norwich] : Thames Publishing, in association with the
Peter Warlock Society, c2004. — 1 score (56 p.) ; 30 cm. — (New Peter
Warlock critical edition ; v. 6)
With piano acc. — Includes editorial notes.
System number: 013173995

*Warlock, Peter, 1894-1930.
[Songs. *Selections*]
Songs 1927-1928 : medium voice / Peter Warlock ; edited by Michael
Pilkington. — [S.l.] : Thames Publishing, in association with the Peter
Warlock Society, c2005. — 1 score (51 p.) ; 30 cm. — (New Peter
Warlock critical edition ; VII)
With piano acc. — Includes editorial notes.
System number: 013214749

*Warlock, Peter, 1894-1930.
[Songs. *Selections*]
Songs 1928-1930 : medium voice / Peter Warlock ; edited by Michael
Pilkington. — [S.l.] : Thames Publishing, in association with the Peter
Warlock Society, c2005. — 1 score (56 p.) ; 30 cm. — (New Peter
Warlock critical edition ; v. 8)
With piano acc. — Includes editorial notes.
System number: 013214763

783.44209438

Pieśni i hymny Piwnicy pod Baranami / [wybór piosenek Piotr Ferster,
Marek Pacuła] — Kraków : Piwnica pod Baranami ; Polskie
Wydawnictwo Muzyczne, c2006. — 1 score (144 p.) : ill. ; 31 cm.
For voice and piano. — Accompanying material in Polish. — Polish words.
Pl. no. PWM 10 445
ISMN M274002695
System number: 013739029
Primary classification 783.42709438

783.5 – LOW VOICE

783.542

*Duparc, Henri, 1848-1933.
[Songs]
Complete songs : with texts in English, German and French : medium/low voice = Mittlere/Tiefe Stimme = voix moyennes/graves / Henri Duparc ; edited by Roger Nichols. — London : Edition Peters, c2005. New York : —
1 score (xviii, 123 p.) ; 31 cm.
With piano accompaniment. — 'La fuite' is a duet. — Pref. in English, French and German; critical commentary in English. — "Urtext"—Cover. — Publisher's no.: Edition Peters no. 7778b. — French words, also printed for reference with English and German translations.
Publ. no. EP 7778b
ISMN M577085654
EAN 9790577085654
System number: 013643025
Primary classification 783.442

*Purcell, Henry, 1659-1695.
[Fairy queen. *Selections*]
The four seasons in the Fairy queen : for soprano, alto, tenor, and bass solos, strings and continuo : from Orpheus Britannicus / Henry Purcell. — Richmond : Green Man Press, c2002. — 5 scores + 4 parts ; 30 cm.
Includes 1 score with figured bass realized for keyboard instrument; 4 scores with figured bass unrealized; and parts for 2 violins, viola and bass instrument. — "In the Orpheus Britannicus version the first three songs have a treble (G2) clef, but they can be sung by a soprano, alto and tenor respectively"—P. 2. — First 3 songs for high voice, 2 violins and continuo; 4th song for bass voice, 2 violins, viola and continuo. — Pref. and editorial notes in English by Cedric Lee. — English words, also printed for reference on p. 2 of score.
Publ. no. Pur 11
Pl. no. Pur 11-1—Pur 11-2
System number: 013597526
Primary classification 783.342

783.5420945

*A selection of Italian arias, c.1600-c.1800. Volume II / edition prepared by Damian Cranmer ; English translations by Dorothy Richardson ; edition supervised by Michael Pilkington. — London : Associated Board of the Royal Schools of Music, c2005. — 1 score (80 p.) ; 31 cm.
For low voice and piano; some accompaniments realized from figured bass or reduced from orchestral acc. — Includes source notes. — Italian and English words.
Pl. no. AB 2730
ISBN 9781860961014
ISBN 1860961010
System number: 013307377

783.6 – FEMALE'S, CHILD'S, MALE'S VOICES

783.6

Febel, Reinhard, 1952-
Die Masken des Pierrot : für Frauenstimme und Klavier, 2003 / Reinhard Febel. — München : Ricordi, c2004. — 1 score (13 p.) ; 30 cm. + 1 score (13 leaves) ; 43 cm.
For woman's voice and piano. — Text comprises nonsense syllables. — Performance notes in German. — Reproduced from holograph.
Publ. no. SY 3703
ISMN M204237036
System number: 013771078

783.642

Lloyd Webber, Andrew, 1948-
[Musicals. *Selections; arr.*]
Andrew Lloyd Webber audition songbook : ten great show songs, ideal for auditions. — Female ed. — London : Wise, c2005. — 1 score (56 p.) ; 31 cm + 1 sound disc (digital ; 4 3/4 in.)
Arr. for voice and piano, with guitar chord symbols. — CD contains backing tracks.
Publ. no. AM982630
ISBN 1846090148
System number: 013222757

*Schönberg, Claude-Michel.
[Musicals. *Vocal scores. Selections*]
The Boublil-Schönberg collection : show hits : twelve great show songs, ideal for auditions. — Female ed. — London : Wise, c2005. — 1 score (54 p.) ; 31 cm + 1 sound disc (digital ; 4 3/4 in.)
Arr. for voice and piano, with guitar chord symbols. — Music by Claude-Michel Schönberg, words by Alain Boublil. — CD contains backing tracks. — Mostly English words; "Quatre saisons pour un amour" is in French.
Publ. no. AM983719
ISBN 9781846092305
ISBN 1846092302
System number: 013432817

783.642164

Great women! Great songs! [36 classic hits from some of the greatest female artists of all time! : arranged for piano, voice and guitar, complete with lyrics and guitar chord boxes] — London : Wise, c2005. — 1 score (160 p.) ; 31 cm.
Publ. no. AM91111
ISBN 0711934428
System number: 013220473

*The new divas : [22 stunning songs from the greatest female vocalists of the 21st century : arranged for piano, voice & guitar] — London : Wise Publications, c2005. — 1 score (128 p.) ; 31 cm.
For voice and piano, with chord symbols and guitar chord diagrams.
Publ. no. AM983796
ISBN 1846092426
System number: 013432793

783.6421643

*Audition songs for female singers. R&B anthems : nine great songs ideal for auditions. — London : Wise, c2005. — 1 score (63 p.) ; 31 cm + 1 sound disc (digital ; 4 3/4 in.)
"CD+music pack specially developed for female singers auditioning for shows, revues and bands"—Back cover. — For voice and piano, with guitar chord symbols. — CD contains backing tracks.
Publ. no. AM978340
ISBN 9781844492176
ISBN 1844492176
System number: 013441494

783.642166

Audition songs. Number one hits. — London : Wise Publications, c2005. — 1 score (112 p.) 31 cm. + 2 compact discs
20 songs for female voice and piano with chord symbols and guitar chord diagrams. — Words and music by various songwriters. — Compiled by Lucy Holliday. — CDs contain full backing tracks for each song.
Publ. no. AM91540
ISBN 0711937621
System number: 013268771

The big acoustic guitar chord songbook. Female. — London : Wise Publications, c2003. — 192 p. ; 25 cm.
Words and guitar symbols for 76 songs [performed] by female artists. — Compiled by Nick Crispin ; arranger Frank Moon & Jason Broadbent.
Publ. no. AM975315
ISBN 0711996482
System number: 006914459

783.6624

Hellawell, Piers, 1956-
Quem quæritis : (1995) : [cantata] for soprano and five players : clarinet in B♭, bass clarinet, viola, 'cello and double bass / Piers Hellawell. — Kenley : Maecenas Music, c1998. — 1 score (14 p.) ; 30 cm.
"Text: Extract from the mediaeval mystery play Quem Quæritis O Christicolæ". — Duration: ca. 6:00. — Latin words, also printed for reference with English translation.
System number: 013422567

783.6642

Bayford, Frank.
Echoes from a golden time : opus 95 : seven songs to poems from the Greek Anthology : for soprano and piano / translated by Forrest Reid ; [music by] Frank Bayford. — Enfield : Modus Music, 2005. — 1 score (16 p.) ; 30 cm.
Publ. no. MM 323
System number: 013373629

Beavers, Kevin, 1971-
[Wandlebury Ring. *Vocal score*]
Wandlebury Ring : for voice and string quartet / words by Andrew Sofer ; music by Kevin E. Beavers. — New York : Oxford University Press, c2004. — 1 score (16 p.) + 4 parts ; 31 cm. — Oxford vocal music
Words also printed for reference preceding score. — Includes composer's and biographical notes.
ISBN 0193867117
System number: 013115468

Cipullo, Tom.
Another reason why I don't keep a gun in the house : songs on poems of Billy Collins : for voice and piano / Tom Cipullo. — [New York] : Oxford University Press, c2004. — 1 score (23 p.) ; 31 cm. — Oxford vocal music
Words also printed for reference following score.
ISBN 0193867184
System number: 013115549

*Croft, William, 1678-1727.
By purling streams : (a song with hautboy) : for soprano, oboe/flute and continuo / William Croft. — Richmond : Green Man Press, c2002. — 2 scores + 2 parts ; 30 cm.
Words also printed separately for reference. — One score contains keyboard realization of continuo part, the other has figured bass only. — Includes continuo part for bass instrument. — Edited from Oxford, Bodleian Library, MS. Tenbury 1232. — Introduction and editorial notes by Cedric Lee.
Publ. no. Cro 3
Pl. no. Cro 3-1—Cro 3-2
System number: 013430526

Dicie, Don Michael.
Songs of comfort : for high voice and keyboard / Don Michael Dicie. — [New York] : Oxford University Press, c2004. — 1 score (7 p.) ; 31 cm. — Oxford vocal music
Includes biographical note.
ISBN 0193868008
System number: 013115541

*Fesch, Willem de, 1687-1761.
[Canzonettas, violin, continuo acc.]
Miss Ashe canzonettas : for soprano, violin or flute, mandoline and basso
continuo : c.1734 / Willem de Fesch ; on poems by Paolo Rolli, Pietro
Metastasio and others ; edited by Robert L. Tusler. — Amsterdam :
Donemus, 2004, c2003. — 1 score (iii, 25 p.) ; 30 cm.
Figured bass realized for keyboard instrument. — Italian words.
System number: 014747661

*Fesch, Willem de, 1687-1761.
[Canzonette ed arie, violin, continuo acc.]
Lady Erskine canzonettas : for soprano, violin or flute and basso continuo :
c.1730 / Willem de Fesch ; on poems by Paolo Rolli and others ; edited by
Robert L. Tusler. — Amsterdam : Donemus, 2004, c2003. — 1 score (v,
23 p.) ; 30 cm.
Figured bass realized for keyboard instrument. — Italian words.
System number: 014747651

*Fesch, Willem de, 1687-1761.
[New English songs]
VI new English songs : for soprano, violin or flute and basso continuo :
1749 / Willem de Fesch ; edited by Robert L. Tusler. — Amsterdam :
Donemus, 2004, c2003. — 1 score (v, 16 p.) ; 30 cm.
Figured bass realized for keyboard instrument.
System number: 014747723

*Fesch, Willem de, 1687-1761.
[Songs. *Selections*]
Miscellaneous songs : for soprano, violin or flute, and basso continuo :
1748-53 / Willem de Fesch ; edited by Robert L. Tusler. — Amsterdam :
Donemus, 2004, c2003. — 1 score (v, 21 p.) ; 30 cm.
Figured bass realized for keyboard instrument.
System number: 014747925

*Fesch, Willem de, 1687-1761.
[Tempest]
The Tempest songs, or, The enchanted island : for soprano, small ensemble
and basso continuo, 1745 / Willem de Fesch ; edited by Robert L. Tusler. —
Amsterdam : Donemus, 2004, c2003. — 1 score (iii, 17 p.) ; 30 cm.
Incidental music to Shakespeare's 'The Tempest'. Some of the texts set are not by
Shakespeare. — Figured bass unrealized.
System number: 014747698

Foster, Stephen Collins, 1826-1864.
[Songs. *Selections; arr.*]
Seven songs of Stephen Foster : for voice and piano / in versions by Warren
Michel Swenson. — [New York] : Oxford University Press, 2004. — 1
score (19 p.) ; 31 cm. — Oxford vocal music
Includes biographical notes about the composer and arranger.
ISBN 0193867176
System number: 013103270

Gilmore, Bernard, 1937-
[Folksongs]
Five folk songs : for soprano and symphonic wind band : (1966) / Bernard
Gilmore. — Kenley : Maecenas Music, c2002. — 1 score (89 p.) ; 30 cm.
— Millennium series for wind bands & ensembles
Edited by Thomas Stone. — Words in English, Greek, Spanish or Yiddish.
Publ. no. MC0072
System number: 013192859
Also classified at 784.8

Grange, Philip.
As it was : (1985) / Philip Grange ; words, Edward Thomas. — Kenley :
Maecenas Music, [2002?], c1991. — 1 score (17 p.) ; 30 cm.
For soprano, 2 clarinets (doubling bass clarinets) and piano. — Reproduced from
holograph. — Duration: ca. 11:00. — Words also printed for reference preceding
score.
Publ. no. MM0011
System number: 013422451

*Handel, George Frideric, 1685-1759.
Languia di bocca lusinghiera : (HWV 123) : recitative and aria for soprano,
oboe, violin and basso continuo / G.F. Handel. — 2nd ed. — Richmond :
Green Man Press, c2003. — 2 scores + 3 parts ; 30 cm.
One score contains keyboard realization of continuo part, the other has figured bass
only. — Includes continuo part for bass instrument. — Introduction and editorial
notes by Cedric Lee. — Italian words; also printed for reference with English
translation on p. 3.
Publ. no. Han 5 A
Pl. no. Han 5-1A—Han 5-2A
System number: 013597586

Hedges, Anthony, 1931-
[Contemplations]
Three contemplations : op. 149 : for soprano, flute, cello & piano / Anthony
Hedges. — Beverley : Westfield Music, c2003. — 1 score (15 p.) ; 30 cm.
Texts from poems by Jay Appleton.
System number: 013188532

Kaye, Ernest.
[Songs. *Selections*]
Five songs : for voice and piano / Ernest Kaye. — [New York] : Oxford
University Press, c2004. — 1 score (18 p.) ; 31 cm. — Oxford vocal
music
Includes composer's notes.
ISBN 0193867192
System number: 013434221

Larsen, Libby.
My Ántonia : seven songs for high voice and piano / Libby Larsen ;
based on the novel by Willa Cather ; text adapted by Libby Larsen. —
[New York] : Oxford University Press, c2004. — 1 score (28 p.) ; 31 cm.
— Oxford vocal music
Words also printed for reference following score. — Includes biographical note.
ISBN 0193867214
System number: 013062653

*Monteverdi, Claudio, 1567-1643.
[Lamento d'Arianna (Aria)]
Lamento d'Arianna, and addendum : for soprano & basso continuo /
Claudio Monteverdi ; edited by Barbara Sachs. — Richmond : Green
Man Press, c2001. — 2 scores (16, 11 p.) ; 30 cm.
1st score with figured bass realized for keyboard instrument; 2nd score with
figured bass unrealized. — "A critical performing edition." — Includes Pref.,
editorial remarks, and critical commentary in English. — Addendum with
sections of other versions, p. 15. — Italian words by Ottavio Rinuccini; also
printed for reference with English translation by Barbara Sachs, p. 5-7.
Publ. no. Mv 1
System number: 013589497

*Pepusch, John Christopher, 1667-1752.
[Death of Dido. Oh I feel the friendly blow]
Aria, Oh I feel the friendly blow : from The death of Dido : for soprano,
recorder, strings and continuo / J.C. Pepusch. — Richmond : Green Man
Press, c2003. — 2 scores + 5 parts ; 30 cm.
From the masque "The death of Dido", words by Barton Booth. — One score
includes keyboard realization of continuo part, the other has unfigured bass only.
— Includes continuo part for bass instrument. — Words also printed separately
for reference. — Introduction and editorial notes by Cedric Lee.
Publ. no. Pep 2
System number: 013589506

*Purcell, Henry, 1659-1695.
[Fairy queen. Plaint]
O, O let me weep! : for soprano, oboe (or recorder) and continuo : from
Orpheus Britannicus / Henry Purcell. — Richmond : Green Man Press,
c2001. — 2 scores (8, 7 p.) + 2 parts ; 30 cm.
1st score with figured bass realized for keyboard instrument; 2nd score with
figured bass unrealized; parts for oboe (or recorder) and bass clef instrument. —
Words also printed for reference on p. 2. — Pref. and editorial notes by Cedric
Lee.
Publ. no. Pur 10
System number: 013597510

783.6647
*Terteryan, A. (Avet), 1929-
[Rodina. *Russian & Armenian*]
Heimat : vokalsinfonischer Zyklus für Sopran, Bariton und Orchester
(1957) / Awet Terterjan. — Hamburg : Sikorski, [2005?, c1964] — 1
score (65 p.) ; 30 cm.
Baritone is soloist in 1st and 4th movements, soprano in 2nd, 3rd and 5th
movements. — Words by Hovhannes Shiraz. — Reprint of the edition: Moskva :
Sovetskiĭ kompozitor, 1964. — "Autorisierte Kopie"—Stamp on p. 5. —
Armenian and Russian words.
Pl. no. c 2727 k
System number: 014629740
Also classified at 783.8847

783.6648
*Bouvard, François, 1683-1760.
La feste de Cloris : cantata for soprano, violin, flute, oboe, bassoon &
continuo / François Bouvard. — Richmond : Green Man Press, c2004. —
2 scores + 4 parts ; 30 cm.
One score includes keyboard realization of continuo part, the other has figured
bass only. — Includes continuo part for bass instrument. — Introduction and
editorial notes by Cedric Lee. — French words, also printed for reference with
English translation preceding score.
Publ. no. Bou 1
Pl. no. Bou 1-2
System number: 013596823

*Chi sà dove è speranza? : cantata for soprano, oboe or recorder and
continuo : an anonymous cantata from a manuscript in the Santini
collection, Münster / attrib. A.D. Lignani. — Richmond : Green Man
Press, c2006. — 2 scores + 2 parts ; 30 cm.
One score contains keyboard realization of continuo part, the other has figured
bass only. — Includes continuo part for bass instrument. — Introduction and
editorial notes by Cedric Lee. — Italian words, also printed for reference with
English translation, p. 3.
Publ. no. Anon 1
Publ. no. Anon 1A
Pl. no. Anon 1A-1—Anon 1A-2
System number: 013596854

*Clérambault, Louis-Nicolas, 1676-1749.
[Cantates françoises, livre 2. Léandre et Héro]
Leandre et Hero : cantata for soprano, flute, violin & continuo /
Louis-Nicolas Clérambault. — Richmond : Green Man Press, c2004. — 2
scores + 4 parts ; 30 cm.
One score contains keyboard realization of continuo part, the other has figured bass
only. — Includes continuo part for bass instrument (viol). — Introduction and
editorial notes by Cedric Lee. — French words; also printed for reference with
English translation, p. 2-3.
Publ. no. Cle 2
Pl. no. Ces 2-1—Ces 2-2
System number: 013596908

*Handel, George Frideric, 1685-1759.
[Cantatas. *Selections*]
Four cantatas from Rome, 1707 : for soprano and basso continuo / G.F.
Handel. — Richmond : Green Man Press, c2003. — 2 scores + 1 part
(15 p.) ; 30 cm.
One score contains keyboard realization of continuo part, the other has figured bass
only. — Includes continuo part for bass instrument. — Edited principally from
British Library, Royal Music Collection, R.M.20.d.11 and British Library, Egerton
2942. — Introduction and editorial notes by Cedric Lee. — Italian words; also
printed for reference with English translation, p. 3-5.
Publ. no. Han 4
Pl. no. Han 4-1—Han 4-2
System number: 013597568

*Scarlatti, Alessandro, 1660-1725.
[Cantatas. *Selections*]
Three cantatas with recorders : for soprano, two recorders & continuo /
Alessandro Scarlatti ; edited by Barbara Sachs. — Richmond : Green Man
Press, c2004. — 2 scores + 3 parts ; 30 cm.
One score includes figured bass realized for keyboard instrument, the other has
unrealized figured bass; includes separate part for bass instrument. — Edited from
manuscripts in the Diözesanbibliothek Münster. — Italian words; also printed for
reference with English translations, p. 4-5 of realized score.
Publ. no. Sca 2
System number: 013612380

783.6724
Biber, Heinrich Ignaz Franz, 1644-1704.
O dulcis Jesu : geistliches Konzert : canto solo, violino discordato e basso
continuo / Heinrich Ignaz Franz Biber? ; herausgegeben von Wolfram
Steude. — Erstausg. — Stuttgart : Carus, 2007. — 1 score (19 p.) + 2 parts ;
30 cm. — (Die Kantate : Eine Sammlung geistlicher Musik für
Singstimmen und Instrumente)
For medium-high voice, scordatura violin and continuo. — Attribution to Biber
doubtful; cf. foreword. — Figured bass realized for keyboard instrument. — Preface
in German, English and French; critical report in German only. — Latin words; also
printed for reference with English, French, and German translations.
Publ. no. CV 10.362
Pl. no. 10.362
ISMN M007091224
System number: 013771073

783.6742
Heider, Werner, 1930-
[Gedichte von Günter Grass]
Drei Gedichte von Günter Grass : (2003) : für mittlere Stimme
(Mezzosopran/Bariton) und Klavier = for medium voice
(mezzo-soprano/baritone) and piano / Werner Heider. — Bad Schwalbach :
Edition Gravis, c2004. — 1 score (12 p.) ; 30 cm.
Reproduced from holograph. — Duration: ca. 7:30. — German words by Günter
Grass, also printed separately for reference preceding score.
Publ. no. EG 928
System number: 013771099
Also classified at 783.8842

Henze, Hans Werner, 1926-
El rey de Harlem : imaginäres Theater I : für Mezzosopran und kleines
Ensemble = imaginary theatre I : for mezzo soprano and small ensemble /
Hans Werner Henze ; Dichtung von Federico Garcia Lorca. —
Studienpartitur. — Mainz ; London : Schott, c2000. — 1 score (81 p.) ;
30 cm. — (Musik unserer Zeit = Music of our time = Musique de notre
temps)
For mezzo-soprano with clarinet (doubling bass clarinet and saxophones), trumpet,
trombone, percussion (1 player), electric guitar (doubling banjo and bass guitar),
celeste (doubling harmonium and piano) viola, and violoncello. — Duration: ca.
30:00. — Explanation of signs in German and English. — Spanish words.
Publ. no. ED 9128
ISMN M001126328
ISMN 9790001126328
System number: 014406572

783.6824
Hasse, Johann Adolf, 1699-1783.
Ave Regina coelorum : Marian antiphon for alto, 2 oboes, strings & basso
continuo / Johann A. Hasse ; edited by Alejandro Garri ; assisted by Kent
Carlson. — 1st ed. — Full score. — Frankfurt : Garri Editions, c2007. — 1
score (23 p.) ; 30 cm. — (Canti di cielo ; v. 113
Edited from the manuscript held in the Sächsische Landesbibliothek, Dresden (Mus.
2477-E-11). — Figured bass unrealized. — Duration: ca. 9:00. — Preface in
English. — Latin words.
Publ. no. GE 372
System number: 013771093
Primary classification 783.8624

783.68241723
*Zelenka, Johann Dismas, 1679-1745.
[O magnum mysterium]
Motetto pro nativitate I, ZWV 171 : Dormi nate, dormi Deus : per alto
solo, 2 flauti traversi o flauti a becco (ad lib.), 2 violini, viola e basso
continuo / Jan Dismas Zelenka ; Erstausgabe herausgegeben von Thomas
Kohlhase. — Partitur. — Stuttgart : Carus, c2005. — 1 score (20 p.) ;
30 cm.
For contralto, 2 flutes or recorders, 2 violins, viola, and continuo. — Preface and
translations of the text in German, English, and French and critical commentary in
German. — Latin words.
Publ. no. CV 40.764
Pl. no. 40.764
ISMN M007074289
System number: 013641968

783.6826
*Porpora, Nicola, 1686-1768.
[Duetti latini per la passione di Gesù Cristo]
Sei duetti latini sulla passione di nostro signore Gesù Cristo ; Motetti per
Angiola Moro / Nicola Antonio Porpora ; edizione critica a cura di
Stefano Aresi. — Pisa : ETS, c2004. — 1 score (xii, 233 p.) : facsims. ;
30 cm. — Diverse voci— ; 5
For soprano and alto with continuo (1st work); alto, strings and continuo (2nd
work). — Figured bass unrealized. — Historical and critical notes in Italian. —
At head of title: Università di Pavia, Dipartimento di scienze musicologiche e
paleografico-filologiche. — Latin words, also printed for reference with Italian
translation p. 40-41 (1st work) and p. 135-137 (2nd work).
ISBN 8846710266
System number: 013224213
Primary classification 783.1226

783.6842
*Bach, Johann Sebastian, 1685-1750.
[Himmelskönig, sei willkommen. Leget euch dem Heiland unter]
Aria, Leget euch dem Heiland unter : from cantata BWV 182 : for alto,
recorder (or flute) and continuo / J.S. Bach. — Richmond : Green Man
Press, c2003. — 2 scores + 2 parts ; 30 cm.
One score contains keyboard realization of continuo part, the other has figured
bass only. — Includes continuo part for bass instrument and individual parts for
both recorder and flute. — Introduction and editorial notes by Cedric Lee. —
German words; also printed for reference with English translation on p. 2.
Publ. no. Bach 2
Pl. no. Bac 2-1—Bac 2-2
System number: 013597019
Also classified at 783.8642

*Sing solo contralto / edited by Constance Shacklock ; general editor,
John Carol Case. — Rev. ed. — Oxford : Oxford University Press,
[2005?] — 1 score (44 p.) ; 31 cm. — Oxford vocal music
11 songs with piano acc. — Reprint of rev. ed. of 1986 (first published, 1985). —
English, Italian or German words with English translations where appropriate.
ISBN 0193850168
System number: 013173224

783.6848
*Caldara, Antonio, 1670-1736.
[Clori, mia bella Clori]
Cantata, Clori, mia bella Clori : for contralto, flute, oboe & basso
continuo / Antonio Caldara ; edited by Gail Hennessy. — Richmond :
Green Man Press, c2003. — 2 scores + 3 parts ; 30 cm.
One score includes keyboard realization of continuo part, the other has unfigured
bass only. — Includes continuo part for bass instrument. — Edited from a
non-autograph manuscript score in the Royal Academy of Music, London (Ms.
48/2). — Italian words, also printed for reference with English translation
preceding score.
Publ. no. Cal 1
System number: 013589459

*Fesch, Willem de, 1687-1761.
[Apis amata]
Two solo cantatas / Willem de Fesch ; edited by Robert L. Tusler. —
Amsterdam : Donemus, 2004, c2003. — 1 score (v, 17 p.) ; 30 cm.
Partially figured bass realized for keyboard instrument. — Italian words; also
printed for refernece with English translation p.iii-iv.
System number: 014747929

*Greber, Jakob, 1691-1731.
Fuori di sua capanna : cantata for alto, recorder & continuo ; Sinfonia a
flauto solo : symphony for recorder and continuo / Jakob Greber. —
Richmond : Green Man Press, c2004. — 2 scores + 2 parts ; 30 cm.
One score contains keyboard realization of continuo part, the other has figured
bass only. — Includes continuo part for bass instrument. — Edited from
manuscripts in the Santini collection in the Diözesanbibliothek, Münster. —
Introduction and editorial notes by Cedric Lee. — Cantata has Italian words, also
printed for reference with English translation p. 3.
Publ. no. Gre 1
Pl. no. Gre 1-1—Gre 1-2
System number: 013596869
Also classified at 788.36

*Scarlatti, Alessandro, 1660-1725.
Bella dama di nome santa : Tu sei quella : cantata for alto, recorder, two violins and continuo / Alessandro Scarlatti ; edited by Derek Harrison. — Richmond : Green Man Press, c2004. — 2 scores + 4 parts ; 30 cm.
One score includes figured bass realized for keyboard instrument, the other has unrealized figured bass; includes separate part for bass instrument. — Edited from the manuscript in the Biblioteca del Conservatorio di Musica San Pietro a Majella, Naples. — Italian words; also printed for reference with English translation on p. 3 of realized score.
Publ. no. Sca 1
System number: 013612367

783.8 – FEMALE'S, CHILD'S, MALE'S VOICES

783.8

*Davies, Peter Maxwell, 1934-
[Songs for a mad king. *Vocal score*]
Eight songs for a mad king : music-theatre work for male voice and ensemble / Peter Maxwell Davies ; text by Randolph Stow and George III ; vocal score. — [S.l.] : Boosey & Hawkes, c2005. — 1 score (35 p.) ; 31 cm.
Acc. arr. for piano. — Words also printed for reference preceding score. — Composer's note, librettist's note and performance note in English, French and German. — Duration: 33:00.
Publ. no. 03024
ISMN M060116575
System number: 013194613

783.842

Lloyd Webber, Andrew, 1948-
[Musicals. *Selections; arr.*]
Andrew Lloyd Webber audition songbook : ten great show songs, ideal for auditions. — Male ed. — London : Wise, c2005. — 1 score (63 p.) ; 31 cm + 1 sound disc (digital ; 4 3/4 in.)
Arr. for voice and piano, with guitar chord symbols. — CD contains backing tracks.
Publ. no. AM982619
ISBN 184609013X
System number: 013220095

*Schönberg, Claude-Michel.
[Musicals. *Vocal scores. Selections*]
The Boublil-Schönberg collection : show hits : twelve great show songs, ideal for auditions. — Male ed. — London : Wise, c2005. — 1 score (62 p.) ; 31 cm + 1 sound disc (digital ; 4 3/4 in.)
Arr. for voice and piano, with guitar chord symbols. — Music by Claude-Michel Schönberg, words by Alain Boublil. — CD contains backing tracks.
Publ. no. AM983708
ISBN 9781846092299
ISBN 1846092299
System number: 013432662

783.842164

*Audition songs for male singers. The rat pack : Frank Sinatra, Dean Martin, Sammy Davis, jr. : ten great songs ideal for auditions. — London : Wise, c2005. — 1 score (64 p.) ; 31 cm + 1 sound disc (digital ; 4 3/4 in.)
"CD+music pack specially developed for male singers auditioning for shows, revues and bands"—Back cover. — 10 songs from the repertoire of The rat pack. — Words and music by various songwriters. — For voice and piano, with guitar chord symbols. — CD contains backing tracks. — Publisher's no.: AM980089 (score), OM31372 (CD).
Publ. no. AM980089
Publ. no. OM31372
ISBN 9781844494989
ISBN 1844494985
System number: 013441477

783.8624

Hasse, Johann Adolf, 1699-1783.
Ave Regina coelorum : Marian antiphon for alto, 2 oboes, strings & basso continuo / Johann A. Hasse ; edited by Alejandro Garri ; assisted by Kent Carlson. — 1st ed. — Full score. — Frankfurt : Garri Editions, c2007. — 1 score (23 p.) ; 30 cm. — Canti di cielo ; v. 113
Edited from the manuscript held in the Sächsische Landesbibliothek, Dresden (Mus. 2477-E-11). — Figured bass unrealized. — Duration: ca. 9:00. — Preface in English. — Latin words.
Publ. no. GE 372
System number: 013771093
Also classified at 783.6824

783.8642

*Bach, Johann Sebastian, 1685-1750.
[Himmelskönig, sei willkommen. Leget euch dem Heiland unter]
Aria, Leget euch dem Heiland unter : from cantata BWV 182 : for alto, recorder (or flute) and continuo / J.S. Bach. — Richmond : Green Man Press, c2003. — 2 scores + 2 parts ; 30 cm.
One score contains keyboard realization of continuo part, the other has figured bass only. — Includes continuo part for bass instrument and individual parts for both recorder and flute. — Introduction and editorial notes by Cedric Lee. — German words; also printed for reference with English translation on p. 2.
Publ. no. Bach 2
Pl. no. Bac 2-1—Bac 2-2
System number: 013597019
Primary classification 783.6842

*Boyd, Anne, 1946-
Meditations on a Chinese character : for ensemble / Anne Boyd. — York : University of York Music Press, [2004?], c1996. — 1 score (29 p.) ; 21 x 30 cm.
For countertenor, piccolo, flute, shakahachi, cello, harp, 2 pianos, glockenspiel, percussion. — Reproduced from ms.
ISMN M570200658
System number: 013430714

783.87241723

*Zelenka, Johann Dismas, 1679-1745.
[Pro quos criminis]
Motetto pro nativitate II, ZWV 172 : Dormi, Deus incarnate : per tenore solo, 2 flauti a becco, 2 flauti traversi, 2 violini, viola e basso continuo / Jan Dismas Zelenka ; herausgegeben von Thomas Kohlhase. — Erstausg. — Partitur. — Stuttgart : Carus, c2005. — 1 score (24 p.) ; 30 cm.
For tenor, 2 recorders, 2 flutes, 2 violins, viola, and continuo. — Preface and translations of the text in German, English, and French and critical commentary in German. — Latin words.
Publ. no. CV 40.765
Pl. no. 40.765
ISMN M007074296
EAN 9790007074296
System number: 013641972

783.8742

*Previn, André, 1929-
[Songs (2004)]
Four songs : for tenor and piano / André Previn ; texts by Philip Larkin and William Carlos Williams. — New York : G. Schirmer ; Milwaukee, Wis. : distributed by Hal Leonard, 2005, c2004. — 1 score (12 p.) ; 31 cm.
Words also printed for reference preceding score. — Duration: 9:00.
Publ. no. ED 4258
Publ. no. HL50486045
ISBN 1423402472
System number: 013376711

Russian operatic arias for tenor : 19th and 20th century repertoire complete with translations and guidance on pronunciation / selected and edited by David Fanning ; singing translations by Alexander Wells. — London : Edition Peters, c2004. — 1 score (xxix, 110 p.) ; 31 cm.
Pref. in English, French and German; critical remarks in English. — Publisher's no.: Edition Peters no. 7582. — Russian words, in both Cyrillic and transliterated versions, with English translations. Transliterated words also printed for reference with English, French and German translations, p. x-xxix.
Publ. no. EP 7582
ISMN M577084053
EAN 9790577084053
System number: 013191206

*Sing solo tenor / edited by Robert Tear ; general editor, John Carol Case. — Rev. ed. — Oxford : Oxford University Press, [2004?] — 1 score (39 p.) ; 31 cm. — Oxford vocal music
11 songs with piano acc. — Reprint of rev. ed. of 1986 (first published, 1985). — English, German or Italian words with English translations where appropriate.
ISBN 0193850176
System number: 013172270

783.8824

Telemann, Georg Philipp, 1681-1767.
[Wo soll ich fliehen hin?, TVWV 1:1724]
Wo soll ich fliehen hin? : Kantate zum 22. Sonntag nach Trinitatis für Bariton-Solo, Flauto traverso, Oboe, Fagotto, Violine, Viola und Basso continuo, TVWV 1:1724 / Georg Philipp Telemann ; herausgegeben von Eric F. Fiedler. — Frankfurt am Main : Habsburger Verlag, [2005] — 1 score (23 p.) ; 30 cm. — (Frankfurter Telemann-Ausgaben ; 40)
Pref in German and English. — German words, also printed separately for reference.
Pl. no. FTA 40
System number: 014655646

783.88294

Herbst, Johann Andreas, 1588-1666.
Erbarm' dich mein, o Herre Gott : (Psalm 51) : Miserere for baritone or bass, strings & basso continuo ; edited by Alejandro Garri, assited by Kent Carlson. — 1st ed. — Full score & 4 parts. — [Mühlheim am Main, Germany] : Garri Editions, c2005. — 1 score (16 p.) + 4 parts ; 30 cm. — Canti di cielo ; v. 79
Figured bass unrealized. — Includes editor's notes in English. — Edited from a manuscript in the Stadt- und Universitätsbibliothek, Frankfurt am Main (Ms. Ff. Mus. 9). — Duration: ca. 4:00. — German words.
Publ. no. GE 264
System number: 013771118
Also classified at 783.89294

783.8842

Heider, Werner, 1930-
[Gedichte von Günter Grass]
Drei Gedichte von Günter Grass : (2003) : für mittlere Stimme
(Mezzosopran/Bariton) und Klavier = for medium voice
(mezzo-soprano/baritone) and piano / Werner Heider. — Bad Schwalbach :
Edition Gravis, c2004. — 1 score (12 p.) ; 30 cm.
Reproduced from holograph. — Duration: ca. 7:30. — German words by Günter
Grass, also printed separately for reference preceding score.
Publ. no. EG 928
System number: 013771099
Primary classification 783.6742

Russian operatic arias for baritone : 19th and 20th-century repertoire :
complete with translations and guidance on pronunciation / selected and
edited by David Fanning ; singing translations by Martin Pickard. —
London : Edition Peters, c2005. — 1 score (xxix, 103 p.) ; 31 cm.
For baritone voice and piano. — Pref. in English, French and German. — Russian
words, in both Cyrillic and transliterated versions, with English translations.
Transliterated words also printed for reference with English, French and German
translations.
Publ. no. EP 7583
ISMN M577084060
System number: 013335808

783.8847

*Terteryan, A. (Avet), 1929-
[Rodina. *Russian & Armenian*]
Heimat : vokalsinfonischer Zyklus für Sopran, Bariton und Orchester
(1957) / Awet Terterjan. — Hamburg : Sikorski, [2005?, c1964] — 1 score
(65 p.) ; 30 cm.
Baritone is soloist in 1st and 4th movements, soprano in 2nd, 3rd and 5th
movements. — Words by Hovhannes Shiraz. — Reprint of the edition: Moskva :
Sovetskiĭ kompozitor, 1964. — "Autorisierte Kopie"—Stamp on p. 5. — Armenian
and Russian words.
Pl. no. c 2727 k
System number: 014629740
Primary classification 783.6647

783.8848

*Vaughan Williams, Ralph, 1872-1958.
[Willow-wood. *Vocal score*]
Willow-wood : cantata for baritone solo, soprano and alto chorus (ad lib.)
and orchestra / by Ralph Vaughan Williams. — London : Stainer & Bell,
2005. — 1 score (24 p.) ; 26 cm.
Acc. arr. for piano. — Words by Dante Gabriel Rossetti also printed for reference
preceding score.
Publ. no. D90
ISMN M220221378
System number: 013190675

783.8925

*Bach, Johann Sebastian, 1685-1750.
[Liebster Jesu, mein Verlangen. Hier in meines Vaters Stätte]
Aria, Hier in meines Vaters Stätte : from cantata BWV 32 : for bass, violin
and basso continuo / J.S. Bach. — Richmond : Green Man Press, c2002. —
2 scores + 2 parts ; 30 cm.
One score contains keyboard realization of continuo part, the other has figured bass
only. — Includes continuo part for bass instrument. — Introduction and editorial
notes by Cedric Lee. — German words; also printed for reference with English
translation on p. 2.
Publ. no. Bach 1
Pl. no. Bac 1-1—Bac 1-2
System number: 013596985

*Jeffreys, George, ca. 1610-1685.
[Songs. *Selections*]
Three devotional songs : solo bass with bass continuo / George Jeffreys. —
Richmond : Green Man Press, 2000. — 2 scores + 1 part ; 30 cm.
One score includes keyboard realization of continuo part, the other has figured bass
only. — Includes continuo part for bass instrument. — Introduction and editorial
notes by Cedric Lee. — English and Latin words, also printed for reference with
English translation p. 4.
Publ. no. Jef 6
System number: 013597217

783.8926

Leonarda, Isabella, 1620-1704.
[Motets, bass, continuo. *Selections*]
Ausgewählte Bassmotetten für Bass und B.c. = Selected bass motets for
bass and b.c. / Isabella Leonarda ; [edited by Dragan Karolic] — Moderne
kritische Ed. — Kassel : Furore, c2005. — 1 score (38 p.) + 2 parts ; 30 cm.
Prefatory notes in English and German with critical commentary in German only. —
Figured bass realized for keyboard instrument (in the score); parts have unrealized
figured bass. — Publisher's no.: Furore-Edition 6780. — Latin words.
Publ. no. 6780
Publ. no. fue 6780
ISMN M500126782
System number: 013623496

783.89294

Herbst, Johann Andreas, 1588-1666.
Erbarm' dich mein, o Herre Gott : (Psalm 51) : Miserere for baritone or
bass, strings & basso continuo ; edited by Alejandro Garri, assited by
Kent Carlson. — 1st ed. — Full score & 4 parts. — [Mühlheim am Main,
Germany] : Garri Editions, c2005. — 1 score (16 p.) + 4 parts ; 30 cm. —
Canti di cielo ; v. 79
Figured bass unrealized. — Includes editor's notes in English. — Edited from a
manuscript in the Stadt- und Universitätsbibliothek, Frankfurt am Main (Ms. Ff.
Mus. 9). — Duration: ca. 4:00. — German words.
Publ. no. GE 264
System number: 013771118
Primary classification 783.88294

783.8942

*Croft, William, 1678-1727.
[How charming is beauty]
Songs with violins : for bass, two violins and basso continuo / William
Croft. — Richmond : Green Man Press, 2003. — 2 scores + 3 parts ;
30 cm.
Words also printed separately for reference. — One score contains keyboard
realization of continuo part, the other has figured bass only. — Includes continuo
part for bass instrument. — Edited from Oxford, Bodleian Library, MS. Tenbury
1232. — Introduction and editorial notes by Cedric Lee.
Publ. no. Cro 2
Pl. no. Cro 2-1—Cro 2-2
System number: 013597294

*Croft, William, 1678-1727.
[Musicus apparatus academicus. With noise of cannon. With noise of
cannon]
With noise of cannon : from the ode : for bass, two violins and basso
continuo / William Croft. — Richmond : Green Man Press, c2002. — 2
scores + 3 parts ; 30 cm.
The opening vocal number from the ode "With noise of cannon." — Words by
Joseph Trapp also printed for reference. — One score contains keyboard
realization of continuo part, the other has figured bass only. — Includes continuo
part for bass instrument. — Introduction and editorial notes by Cedric Lee.
Publ. no. Cro 3
Pl. no. Cro 1-1—Cro 1-2
System number: 013430857

*Handel, George Frideric, 1685-1759.
[Acis and Galatea. O ruddier than the cherry]
O ruddier than the cherry : recitative and aria from Acis and Galatea
(HWV 49a) : for bass, recorder, two violins & continuo / G.F. Handel. —
Richmond : Green Man Press, c2004. — 2 scores + 4 parts ; 30 cm.
One score includes keyboard realization of continuo part, the other has unfigured
bass only. — Includes continuo part for bass instrument. — Edited from the
autograph ms. in the British Library. — Introduction and editorial notes by Cedric
Lee.
Publ. no. Han 6
System number: 013597596

*Legrenzi, Giovanni, 1626-1690.
[Cantate e canzonette. *Selections*]
A cantata & two canzonettas : for bass and basso continuo / Giovanni
Legrenzi. — Richmond : Green Man Press, 2002, c2001. — 2 scores +
1 part ; 30 cm.
One score includes keyboard realization of continuo part, the other has figured
bass only. — Includes continuo part for bass instrument. — Introduction and
editorial notes by Cedric Lee. — Italian words; also printed for reference with
English translation, preceding score.
Publ. no. Leg 2
System number: 013597373
Primary classification 783.8948

*Mazzocchi, D. (Domenico), 1592-1665.
[Songs. *Selections*]
Three songs for solo bass / Domenico Mazzocchi. — Richmond : Green
Man Press, c2001. — 2 scores + 1 part ; 30 cm.
For bass voice and continuo. — 1st and 2nd work from Musiche sacre, e morali
(1640), 3rd work from Dialoghi e sonetti (1638). — One score includes keyboard
realization of continuo part, the other has figured bass only. — Includes continuo
part for bass instrument. — Introduction and editorial notes by Cedric Lee. —
Italian words; also printed for reference with English translation.
Publ. no. Maz 1
System number: 013597053

*Purcell, Henry, 1659-1695.
[Songs. *Selections*]
Songs for bass solo : from Orpheus Britannicus / Henry Purcell. —
Richmond : Green Man Press, c2002. — 2 scores (23, 18 p.) + 1 part
(11 p.) ; 30 cm.
For bass voice and continuo. — 1st score with figured bass realized for keyboard
instrument; 2nd score with figured bass unrealized; includes part for bass clef
instrument. — Words also printed for reference on p. 3. — Pref. and editorial
notesby Cedric Lee.
Publ. no. Pur 12
System number: 013590938

*Purcell, Henry, 1659-1695.
[Vocal music. *Selections*]
Three songs with hautboys : from Orpheus Britannicus / Henry Purcell. — Richmond : Green Man Press, c2001. — 2 scores + 3 parts ; 30 cm.
1st work for soprano/tenor, 2 oboes and continuo; 2nd and 3rd works for bass, 2 oboes and continuo. — One score includes keyboard realization of continuo part, the other has figured bass only. — Introduction and editorial notes by Cedric Lee. — Words also printed for reference preceding score.
Publ. no. Pur 7
System number: 013597487
Primary classification 783.342

783.8948

*Campra, André, 1660-1744.
[Cantates françoises, livre 1. Femmes]
Les femmes : cantata for bass, two violins & continuo / André Campra. — Richmond : Green Man Press, c2000. — 2 scores + 3 parts ; 30 cm.
One score includes keyboard realization of continuo part, the other has figured bass only. — Introduction and editorial notes by Cedric Lee. — French words; also printed for reference with English translation preceding score.
Publ. no. Cam 1
System number: 013597179

*Cesti, Antonio, 1623-1669.
[Cantatas, bass, continuo. *Selections*]
Four cantatas for bass / Antonio Cesti ; a critical performing edition edited by Barbara Sachs. — Richmond : Green Man Press, c2003. — 2 scores + 1 part (11 p.) ; 30 cm.
With continuo acc. — One score contains keyboard realization of continuo part, the other has figured bass only. — Includes continuo part for bass instrument. — Sources: Bayerische Staatsbibliothek, Munich, Mus.Ms. 1527, nos. 3, 5, 15 and 16 and Modena, Biblioteca Estense, Mus.F.1350 and Mus.F.252. — Introduction and editorial notes by Barbara Sachs. — Italian words; also printed for reference with English translation, p. 3-5.
Publ. no. Ces 1
Pl. no. Ces 1-1—Ces 1-2
System number: 013597096

*Clérambault, Louis-Nicolas, 1676-1749.
[Cantates françoises, livre 3. Mort d'Hercule]
La mort d'Hercule : cantata for bass, violin & continuo / Louis-Nicolas Clérambault. — Richmond : Green Man Press, 2002, c2000. — 2 scores + 2 parts ; 30 cm.
One score includes keyboard of continuo part, the other has figured bass only. — Introduction and editorial notes by Cedric Lee. — French words; also printed for reference with English translation preceding score.
Publ. no. Cle 1
System number: 013596900

*Handel, George Frideric, 1685-1759.
[Cuopre tal volta il cielo]
Cuopre tal volto il cielo : (HWV 98) : Italian cantata for bass, 2 violins and basso continuo / G.F. Handel. — Richmond : Green Man Press, c2002. — 2 scores + 3 parts ; 30 cm.
One score contains keyboard realization of continuo part, the other has figured bass only. — Includes continuo part for bass instrument. — Edited from British Library, Royal Music Collection, R.M.20.e.5. — Introduction and editorial notes by Cedric Lee. — Italian words; also printed for reference with English translation on p. 3.
Publ. no. Han 1
Pl. no. Han 1-1—Han 1-2
System number: 013589492

*Handel, George Frideric, 1685-1759.
[Nell' Africane selve]
Nell' Africane selve (HWV 136a) ; Dalla guerra amorosa (HWV 102[a]) : Italian cantatas for bass and basso continuo / G.F. Handel. — Richmond : Green Man Press, c2003. — 2 scores + 1 part (8 p.) ; 30 cm.
One score contains keyboard realization of continuo part, the other has figured bass only. — Includes continuo part for bass instrument. — Edited from British Library, Royal Music Collection, R.M.20.d.11 and British Library, Egerton 2942 (1st work) and British Library, Royal Music Collection, R.M.19.e.7 and British Library, Egerton 2942 (2nd work). — Introduction and editorial notes by Cedric Lee. — Italian words; also printed for reference with English translation, p. 3-4.
Publ. no. Han 3
Pl. no. Han 3-1—Han 3-2
System number: 013597552

*Handel, George Frideric, 1685-1759.
Spande ancor a mio dispetto : (HWV 165) : Italian cantata for bass, 2 violins and basso continuo / G.F. Handel. — Richmond : Green Man Press, c2003. — 2 scores + 3 parts ; 30 cm.
One score includes keyboard realization of continuo part, the other has figured bass only. — Includes continuo part for bass instrument. — Edited from British Library, Royal Music Collection, R.M.20.e.2. — Introduction and editorial notes by Cedric Lee. — Italian words; also printed for reference with English translation on p. 3.
Publ. no. Han 2
Pl. no. Han 2-1—Han 2-2
System number: 013597541

*Legrenzi, Giovanni, 1626-1690.
[Cantate e canzonette. *Selections*]
A cantata & two canzonettas : for bass and basso continuo / Giovanni Legrenzi. — Richmond : Green Man Press, 2002, c2001. — 2 scores + 1 part ; 30 cm.
One score includes keyboard realization of continuo part, the other has figured bass only. — Includes continuo part for bass instrument. — Introduction and editorial notes by Cedric Lee. — Italian words; also printed for reference with English translation, preceding score.
Publ. no. Leg 2
System number: 013597373
Also classified at 783.8942

*Legrenzi, Giovanni, 1626-1690.
[Cantate e canzonette. *Selections*]
Three cantatas for bass and basso continuo / Giovanni Legrenzi. — Richmond : Green Man Press, 2002, c2001. — 2 scores + 1 part ; 30 cm.
One score includes keyboard realization of continuo part, the other has figured bass only. — Includes continuo part for bass instrument. — Introduction and editorial notes by Cedric Lee. — Italian words; also printed for reference with English translation, preceding each cantata.
Publ. no. Leg 1
System number: 013597308

*Legrenzi, Giovanni, 1626-1690.
[Dal calore agitato]
Two cantatas from the Munich ms. : for bass and basso continuo / Giovanni Legrenzi ; edited by Barbara Sachs. — Richmond : Green Man Press, c2002. — 2 scores (18, 18 p.) + 1 part (8 p.) ; 30 cm.
1st score with figured bass realized for keyboard instrument; 2nd score with figured bass unrealized; part for bass clef instrument. — Pref. with editorial note by Barbara Sachs. — Italian words; also printed for reference with English translation, p. 3-5.
Publ. no. Leg 3
System number: 013597388

*Rameau, Jean-Philippe, 1683-1764.
Aquilon et Orithie : cantata : for bass, violin & basso continuo / Jean-Philippe Rameau. — Richmond : Green Man Press, c2002. — 2 scores (23, 17 p.) + 2 parts ; 30 cm.
1st score with figured bass realized for keyboard instrument; 2nd score with figured bass unrealized; includes parts for violin and for bass clef instrument. — Pref. and editorial note by Cedric Lee. — French words, also printed for reference with English translation preceding score.
Publ. no. Ram 1
System number: 013596876

*Rameau, Jean-Philippe, 1683-1764.
Thétis : cantata for bass, violin & basso continuo / Jean-Philippe Rameau. — Richmond : Green Man Press, c2002. — 1 score (21, 16 p.) + 2 parts ; 30 cm.
1st score with figured bass realized for keyboard instrument; 2nd score with figured bass unrealized; includes parts for violin and for bass clef instrument. — Pref. and editorial note by Cedric Lee. — French words, also printed for reference with English translation preceding score.
Publ. no. Ram 2
System number: 013596888

783.9 – OTHER TYPES OF VOICES

783.96

*Fibich, Zdeněk, 1850-1900.
[Štědrý den. *Polyglot*]
Štědrý den ; Vodník : melodramy = Der Heilige Abend ; Der Wassermann : Melodramen = Christmas eve ; The water sprite : melodramas : recitazione e piano / Zdeněk Fibich ; text Karel Jaromír Erben ; deutsche Übersetzung Marie Kwaysser und Eduard Albert ; English translation Judith Mabary. — Praha : Amos Editio, 2003. — 1 score (59 p.) ; 31 cm.
The 1st work for narrator & piano; the 2nd work for narrator & orchestra (orch. acc. arr. for piano by the composer). — Czech, German and English words; also printed as text. — Pref. in Czech, German and English.
Pl. no. AM 0009
ISMN M660570333
System number: 013114862

Morricone, Ennio.
Neodiscanto : per voce recitante, pianoforte e percussioni / Ennio Morricone ; [testo di Sergio Miceli] — Milano : Edizioni Curci, c2005. — 1 score (18 p.) ; 30 cm. — Campi sonori
Includes performance notes. — Italian words, also printed separately for reference.
Pl. no. EC.11530
ISBN 8848506372
EAN 9798848506372
System number: 014050067

Waterhouse, Graham, 1962-
Der Handschuh : Ballade von Friedrich Schiller : für Sprechstimme und
Violoncello = The glove : a ballad by Friedrich Schiller : for speaking voice
and violoncello / Graham Waterhouse. — Wilhelmshaven : Heinrichshofen,
c2007. — 1 score (24 p.) ; 31 cm.
In 2 versions, German and English. — Preface and biographical notes in German and
English.
Pl. no. N 2614
ISMN M204426140
System number: 013953489

*Zhou, Long, 1953-
[Wild grass; *arr.*]
Wild grass : for viola / Zhou Long. — [New York] : Oxford University
Press, c2004. — 3 p. of music ; 31 cm. — Oxford music for viola
Originally for violoncello; arranged by the composer for viola. — "The music is
based on the foreword to the poem "Wild Grass" by the father of contemporary
Chinese literature, Lu Hsun"—Pref. — Includes an English translation of the poem's
foreword that may be recited concurrently with the music. — Includes biographical
note.
ISBN 0193868024
System number: 013196402
Primary classification 787.3

783.9618945
*Terzakis, Dimitri.
Hero und Leander : 2002/03 : Rapsodia für 1 Sprecher, Viola, Klavier und
Tonband / Dimitri Terzakis ; nach Texten von Ovid und Friedrich Schiller.
— Partitur. — Bad Schwalbach : Edition Gravis, c2003. — 1 score (26 p.) ;
30 cm.
Pl. no. EG 857
System number: 013015978

784 – INSTRUMENTS AND INSTRUMENTAL ENSEMBLES

784
Música instrumental en las catedrales españolas en la época ilustrada :
conciertos, versos y sonatas, para chirimía, oboe, flauta y bajón—con
violines y/u órgano—, de La Seo y El Pilar de Zaragoza / estudio y
edición, Antonio Ezquerro Esteban. — Barcelona : Consejo Superior de
Investigaciones Científicas, Institución "Milà i Fontanals, " Departamento
de Musicología, 2004. — 1 score (303 p.) : facsims. ; 32 cm. —
Monumentos de la música española ; 69
Essay and critical notes in Spanish. — Includes several anonymous versets for
various woodwind instruments with organ.
ISBN 840008277X
System number: 013796771

784.18846165
Jazz in three : 9 jazz waltzes / arranged and produced by Mark Taylor. —
[S.l.] : Hal Leonard Europe ; London : Distributed by Music Sales, [2005]
— 80 p. ; 31 cm. + 1 compact disc. — Jazz play along ; v. 31
Lead sheets for B♭, E♭ and C instruments. — Melody lines with chord symbols. —
Words printed for reference: p.78-80. — CD contains demonstration and backing
tracks.
Publ. no. HLE90002374
ISBN 1846090024
System number: 013335922

784.2 – SYMPHONY ORCHESTRA

784.2
*Adès, Thomas, 1971-
Asyla : for large orchestra, op. 17 (1997) / Thomas Adès. — London : Faber
Music, 1999. — 1 score ([v], 86 p.) ; 38 cm.
Duration: ca. 25:00.
ISBN 057151863X
System number: 006891421

*Adès, Thomas, 1971-
Asyla : for orchestra (1997) / Thomas Adès. — London : Faber Music,
c1997. — 1 score (106 p.) ; 30 cm.
Duration: ca. 20:00-25:00. — "Faber Music Hire Library"—Cover. — Reproduced
from holograph.
System number: 014482452

Bingham, Judith.
The temple at Karnak : (1996) : [for orchestra] / Judith Bingham. —
Kenley : Maecenas, Music, c1996. — 1 score (66 p.) ; 30 cm.
Duration: ca. 13:00.
System number: 013193680

Body, Jack, 1944-
[Melodies, orchestra]
Melodies for orchestra / Jack Body. — Wellington, N.Z. : Waiteata Music
Press, c2005. — 1 score (86 p.) ; 30 cm. — (2005 ; no. 11)
Based on melodies from Greece, West Sumatra, and India. — "Commissioned by the
New Zealand Symphony Orchestra in 1982 to celebrate the centenary of the
University of Auckland"—Program note. — Duration: 14:00. — Program note on p.
[2] of cover.
ISBN 1877381136
ISBN 9781877381133
System number: 013728860

Börtz, Daniel, 1943-
[Adagio, orchestra]
Adagio per orchestra (1999) / Daniel Börtz. — Partitura. — Stockholm :
Gehrmans Musikförlag, 2002, c1999. — 1 score (20 p.) ; 30 cm.
Duration: 11:00 — Includes notes in Swedish.
Pl. no. CG 7660
ISMN M661520016
UPC 9790661520016
System number: 014457005

Davies, Peter Maxwell, 1934-
Spinning Jenny : a portrait of Leigh, Lancashire c.1948 : for orchestra /
Peter Maxwell Davies. — London : Chester Music, c2005. — 1 score
(57 p.) ; 19 cm.
Includes composer's note.
Publ. no. CH69036
ISBN 1846090059
System number: 013281644

Henze, Hans Werner, 1926-
[Botschaften für die Königin von Saba]
Fünf Botschaften für die Königin von Saba = Five messages for the
Queen of Saba : (2004) / Hans Werner Henze. — [Full score] —
London : Chester Music, c2005. — 1 score (65 p.) ; 35 cm.
For orchestra. — Notes on instrumentation in English and German.
Publ. no. CH67881
ISBN 1846091217
System number: 013323716

Lilburn, Douglas, 1915-2001.
A birthday offering : orchestra / Douglas Lilburn. — Wellington :
Waiteata Music Press, c2005. — 1 score (45 p.) ; 36 cm. — (2005 ; no. 5)
Duration: 11:15.
System number: 013731870

Lim, Liza, 1966-
Ecstatic architecture : for large orchestra, 2002-2004 / Liza Lim. —
Partitura. — Milano : Ricordi, c2004. — 1 score (108 p.) ; 46 cm.
Reproduced from ms. — Duration: ca. 26:00. — Performance notes in English.
Publ. no. 139202
ISMN M041392028
System number: 013771131

*Puccini, Giacomo, 1858-1924.
[Capriccio sinfonico]
Capriccio sinfonico / Giacomo Puccini ; a cura di Pietro Spada. —
Roma : Boccaccini & Spada, c2003. — 1 score (62 p.) : port. ; 32 cm. —
(Tutte le composizioni per orchestra / Giacomo Puccini ; 3)
For orchestra. — Pref. in Italian, English, French, and German. — Duration: 8:00.
Pl. no. BS. 1647
System number: 014694866

*Rachmaninoff, Sergei, 1873-1943.
[Orchestra music. *Selections*]
Symphonic dances ; 5 études-tableaux ; Vocalise [2 versions] / Serge
Rachmaninoff. — London : Boosey & Hawkes, 2005. — 1 score (xii,
276 p.) ; 31 cm. — Boosey & Hawkes masterworks library
For orchestra. 5 études-tableaux originally for piano; Vocalise originally for voice
and piano. — Vocalise is wordless. — Pref. by Malcolm MacDonald in English,
French and German. — Reprinted from plates of earlier editions.
ISBN 0851624642
ISMN M060115882
System number: 013194634

Routh, Francis.
Capriccio : op. 62 (1995) / Francis Routh. — Full score. — London :
Redcliffe Edition, [2004?], c1995. — 1 score (81 p.) ; 42 cm.
For orchestra.
ISMN M708045328
System number: 013175818

Vacchi, Fabio, 1949-
Canti d'ombre : per grande orchestra, 2004 / Fabio Vacchi. — Partitura.
— Milano : Ricordi, c2004. — 1 score (89 p.) ; 46 cm.
Duration: ca. 25:00.
Publ. no. 139349
ISMN M041393490
System number: 014053371

784.21556
Escudero, Francisco, 1912-2002.
El sueño de un bailarín : poema coreográfico / Francisco Escudero. — 1a
ed. — Barcelona : Tritó : Eresbil, 2006, c2002. — 1 score (xxxiv, 82 p.) ;
35 cm. — (Euskal musikagileak)
Ballet, for orchestra. — Pref. in Basque, Catalan, Spanish and English. —
Duration: ca. 15:00.
Publ. no. TR 142
ISMN M692043270
System number: 013710053

Hoffmann, E. T. A. (Ernst Theodor Amadeus), 1776-1822.
[Kreuz an der Ostsee]
Zacharias Werners Trauerspiel "Das Kreuz an der Ostsee" : mit der
Bühnenmusik von E.T.A. Hoffmann ; Ballettmusik "Arlequin" / E.T.A.
Hoffmann ; hrsg. aus dem Nachlaß von Friedrich Schnapp ; unter Mitarbeit
von Gerhard Allroggen und Michael Kohlhäufl von Thomas Kohlhase. —
Mainz ; London : Schott, c2006. — 1 score (xv, 300 p.) ; 33 cm. —
(Ausgewählte musikalische Werke / E.T.A. Hoffmann ; Bd. 9)
Editorial prefaces and critical commentary in German. — 1st work for SSATB
soloists, mixed chorus (SSATB) and orchestra; 2nd work for orchestra. — German
words in first work.
Publ. no. ETAH 109
Publ. no. BSS 43740
ISMN M001137461
System number: 013798965
Primary classification 782.51552

Lambert, Constant, 1905-1951.
Prize fight : (1924 rev. '27) : ballet in one act for small orchestra / Constant
Lambert. — Kenley : Maecenas Music, [ca. 2001] — 1 score (40 p.) ;
30 cm.
Reproduced from holograph.
System number: 013193732

Peçi, Aleksandër, 1951-
Kecat dhe ujku : Ballet : symphony orchestra / Aleksandër Peçi. — Tirana :
Aelfior Editions, [2006] — 1 score (224 p.) ; 30 cm.
Reproduced from holograph.
Publ. no. AED 32106
System number: 014053352

*Verdi, Giuseppe, 1813-1901.
[Macbeth. Ballo]
Macbeth. Ballet : (1865) / [Giuseppe Verdi] ; a cura di Pietro Spada. —
Pavona di Albano Laziale, Roma : Boccaccini & Spada, c2001. — 1 score
(72 p.) ; 32 cm. — (Tutti i balletti / Giuseppe Verdi ; 4)
Prefatory material in English, Italian, French, and German. — Edited from the
autograph ms. in the Bibliothèque Nationale de France. — Duration: 10:35.
Pl. no. B.S. 1640
System number: 014876376

784.21825

*Davies, Peter Maxwell, 1934-
Swinton jig : on a nineteenth century Lancashire fiddle tune : for orchestra /
Peter Maxwell Davies. — London : Chester Music, c2005. — 1 miniature
score (38 p.) ; 19 cm.
Includes composer's note. — Duration: ca. 15:00.
Publ. no. CH63723
ISBN 0711991243
System number: 013213654

Leyendecker, Ulrich, 1946-
Pensées sur un prélude : Debussy-Variationen : für Orchester =
Debussy-variations : for orchestra / Ulrich Leyendecker. — Hamburg : H.
Sikorski, c2005. — 1 score (viii, 56 p.) ; 30 cm. — (Exempla nova ; 332)
Includes an orchestral arrangement of Debussy's Prélude nr. 6, Des pas sur la neige,
on which Pensées was based. — Duration: 13:00-14:00 (without the prelude);
16:00-17:00 (with the prelude). — Includes performance instructions in English and
German. — Publisher's no.: Edition Sikorski 8532.
Publ. no. 8532
Pl. no. H.S. 8532
ISMN M003034058
System number: 013750198

784.2184

*Brahms, Johannes, 1833-1897.
[Symphonies, no. 3, op. 90, F major]
Symphonie Nr. 3, F-Dur, Opus 90 / Johannes Brahms ; herausgegeben von
Robert Pascall. — München : G. Henle, 2005. — 1 score (xxix, 215 p.) :
facsim. ; 33 cm. — (Neue Ausgabe sämtlicher Werke. Serie I,
Orchesterwerke / Johannes Brahms ; Bd. 3)
Pref. and introd. in German on p. [vii]-xxix; kritischer Bericht on p. 139-215.
Publ. no. HN 6007
ISMN M201860077
System number: 013428349

Bruckner, Anton, 1824-1896.
[Symphonies, no. 2, C minor]
II. Symphonie, C-Moll : Fassung von 1872 / Anton Bruckner ; vorgelegt
von William Carragan. — Studienpartitur. — Wien :
Musikwissenschaftlicher Verlag der Internationalen Bruckner-Gesellschaft,
2005. — 1 score (xv, 191 p.) ; 23 cm. — (Sämtliche Werke / Anton
Bruckner ; Bd. 2/1)
Series published under the general editorship of the Österreichische
Nationalbibliothek and the Internationale Bruckner-Gesellschaft. — Pref. in German
and English.
ISMN M500251804
System number: 013622832

*Clementi, Muzio, 1752-1832.
[Symphonies, T. 35, D major]
Sinfonia n. 4 in re maggiore, op-sn 37 (WO 35) / [Muzio Clementi] ; a
cura di Manuel De Col e Massimiliano Sala. — Bologna, Italia : Ut
Orpheus, c2004. — 1 score (xiii, 164 p.) : facsim. ; 32 cm. — (Opera
omnia / Muzio Celementi ; v. 59)
"Urtext." — Critical matter in Italian. Preface to series in Italian and English.
Pl. no. MC 59A
ISMN M215309067
EAN 9790215309067
System number: 014748291

Davies, Peter Maxwell, 1934-
[Symphonies, no. 7]
Symphony no. 7 / Peter Maxwell Davies. — [London] : Boosey &
Hawkes, c2004. — 1 score (150 p.) ; 27 cm.
Pref. by the composer in English, French and German. — Duration: 45:00.
Pl. no. 12721
Publ. no. HPS 1374
ISMN M060115585
System number: 013194597

*Dvořák, Antonín, 1841-1904.
[Symphonies, no. 8, op. 88, G major]
Symphonie Nr. 8, G dur, op. 88 = Symphony no. 8 in G major, op. 88 /
Antonín Dvořák ; herausgegeben von Klaus Döge. — Wiesbaden :
Breitkopf & Härtel, c2004. — 1 score (vi, 142, [4] p.) ; 32 cm. —
(Breitkopf & Härtel Partitur-Bibliothek ; Nr. 5291)
Accompanying text in English and German.
Pl. no. PB 5291
Publ. no. 5291
ISMN M004211472
System number: 013113516

Furtwängler, Wilhelm, 1886-1954.
[Symphonies, no. 1, B minor]
Sinfonie Nr. 1, H-Moll / Wilhelm Furtwängler ; herausgegeben von
George Alexander Albrecht. — Partitur. — Berlin : Ries & Erler, c2002.
— 1 score (ii, 384 p.) ; 31 cm. + 1 critical commentary. —
(Gesamtausgabe / Wilhelm Furtwängler. Werkgruppe I, Werke für
Orchester ; Band I)
Duration: ca. 84:00. — Preface including biographical material in German.
Publ. no. 51115
ISMN M013511150
System number: 014655929

Furtwängler, Wilhelm, 1886-1954.
[Symphonies, no. 2, E minor]
Sinfonie Nr. 2 E-moll / Wilhelm Furtwängler ; herausgegeben von
George Alexander Albrecht.   Partitur. — Berlin : Ries & Erler, c2005.
— 1 score (341 p.) ; 30 cm. + 1 critical commentary. — (Wilhelm
Furtwängler Gesamtausgabe ; Bd. I.II)
Duration: ca. 80:00. — Pref. in German.
Publ. no. 51148
ISMN M013511488
System number: 013570939

Furtwängler, Wilhelm, 1886-1954.
[Symphonies, no. 3, C sharp minor]
Sinfonie Nr. 3 cis-moll / Wilhelm Furtwängler ; herausgegeben von
George Alexander Albrecht. — Partitur. — Berlin : Ries & Erler, c2003.
— 1 score (293 p.) ; 30 cm. — (Wilhelm Furtwängler Gesamtausgabe.
Werkgruppe I, Werke für Orchester ; Bd. III)
Pref. in German.
Publ. no. 51119
ISMN M013511198
System number: 013599651

*Haydn, Joseph, 1732-1809.
[Symphonies. *Selections.*]
Londoner Sinfonien. 1. Folge / Joseph Haydn ; herausgegeben von
Robert von Zahn und Gernot Gruber. — München : G. Henle, 2005. — 1
score (xv, 176 p.) : facsim. ; 33 cm. — (Werke / Joseph Haydn ; Reihe 1,
Bd. 15)
Critical commentary in German.
System number: 013581255

Lindblad, Adolf Fredrik, 1801-1878.
[Symphonies, no. 2, D major]
Symfoni D-dur = Symphony, D major / Adolf Fredrik Lindblad ; utgiven
av Owe Ander. — Stockholm : Edition Reimers, 2004. — 1 score (xix,
272 p.) : facsims. ; 32 cm. — Monumenta musicae Svecicae ; 21
For orchestra. — Pref. in Swedish and English; critical commentary in English.
Publ. no. ER 107031
ISMN M661533245
System number: 014619868

Mozart, Wolfgang Amadeus, 1756-1791.
[Symphonies, K. 551, C major]
Sinfonie in C, KV 551 : "Jupiter" / Wolfgang Amadeus Mozart ; Ulrich Konrad, commentary. — Kassel ; London : Bärenreiter, c2005. — 1 score (48 leaves, 64 p.) : ill. ; 24 x 32 cm.
Facsimile of the autograph manuscript, Mus. ms. autogr. W. A Mozart 551, held in the Staatsbibliothek zu Berlin - Preussischer Kulturbesitz Musikabteilung mit Mendelssohn-Archiv. — "Bärenreiter Facsimile." — Commentary in English, German, and Japanese.
ISBN 3761818246
System number: 014491849

*Ordoñez, Carlos d', 1734-1786.
[Symphonies. *Selections*]
Sinfonías ; Concierto para violín en re mayor / Carlos Ordóñez ; edición crítica Miguel Simarro Grande [y] Ángel Oliver. — Madrid : Instituto Complutense de Ciencias Musicales, c2004. — 1 score (xxi, 417 p.) ; 30 cm. — (Música hispana. Serie B, Música instrumental ; 26)
Mostly for orchestra. 6th, 7th and 10th works for string orchestra. — Pref. in Spanish with English translation.
ISBN 8480485620
System number: 014679359
Also classified at 784.7184; 784.272186

Peçi, Aleksandër, 1951-
[Symphonies, no. 1]
Symphonie no. 1 / Aleksander Peçi. — Tirana : Aelfior Editions, [2006] — 1 score (186 p.) : port. ; 30 cm.
Reproduced from holograph. — Biographical notes and worklist in English.
System number: 014053357

Rachmaninoff, Sergei, 1873-1943.
[Symphonies, no. 3, op. 44, A minor]
Symphony no.3, op. 44 / Serge Rachmaninoff. — London : Boosey & Hawkes, c2003. — 1 score (viii, 206 p.) : port. ; 31 cm. — Boosey & Hawkes masterworks library
Reprinted from the plates of the ed.: New York, Charles Foley, 1939. — Pref. in English, French and German by Malcolm MacDonald. — Duration: 42:00.
ISBN 0851624634
ISMN M060115905
System number: 013095150

*Schnittke, Alfred, 1934-1998.
[Concerti grossi, no. 4]
Concerto grosso Nr. 4— Sinfonie Nr. 5 = Concerto grosso no. 4— Symphony no. 5 / Alfred Schnittke. — Partitur. — Hamburg : Hans Sikorski, c2005. — 1 score (162 p.) ; 30 cm. — (Exempla nova ; 329)
'Concerto grosso Nr. 4— Sinfonie Nr. 5' is a single work. — For orchestra with soloists (violin, oboe and harpsichord/spinet in first movement ; violin, viola and cello in second movement). — Duration: ca. 39:00. — Performance notes in English and German.
Pl. no. H.S. 8529
Publ. no. 8529
ISMN M003033815
System number: 013571403

*Terteryan, A. (Avet), 1929-
[Symphonies, no. 4]
Sinfonie Nr. 4 für grosses Sinfonieorchester = Symphony no. 4 for full symphony orchestra (1976) / Awet Terterjan. — Partitur. — Hamburg : Sikorski, [2005] — 1 score (77 p.) ; 30 cm.
Duration: ca. 16:00. — "Autorisierte Kopie"—Stamp on p. 5.
System number: 014629741

*Terteryan, A. (Avet), 1929-
[Symphonies, no. 7]
Sinfonie Nr. 7 für grosses Sinfonieorchester = Symphony no. 7 for full symphony orchestra (1987) / Awet Terterjan. — Partitur. — Hamburg : Sikorski, [2005], c1999. — 1 score (64 p.) ; 30 cm.
Duration: 28:00. — "Autorisierte Kopie"—Stamp on p. [3] — Performance instructions in German.
System number: 014629742

*Wilms, J. W. (Johann Wilhelm), 1772-1847.
[Symphonies, no. 5, op. 52, D major]
Sinfonie D-Dur, op. 52 / Johann Wilhelm Wilms ; herausgegeben von Bert Hagels. — Partitur. — Berlin : Ries & Erler, c2005. — 1 score (vii, 182 p.) ; 30 cm. — (Sinfonik : 19. Jahrhundert = 19th century)
"Ed.: ca. 1814-19." — Foreword and critical report in Gemrna (p. [1]-vii).
Publ. no. 51140
ISMN M013511402
System number: 014629783

*Zimmermann, Anton, 1741-1781.
[Symphonies. *Selections*]
Four symphonies / Anton Zimmermann ; edited by János Bali and Péter Halász ; introduced by Péter Halász. — Budapest : Magyar Tudományos Akadémia Zenetudományi Intézet, 2004. — 1 score (301 p.) ; facsims. ; 29 cm. — Musicalia Danubiana ; 20
Pref. and critical notes in English and Hungarian.
ISBN 9637074872
System number: 014629804

784.21843
Escudero, Francisco, 1912-2002.
Poème symphonique / Francisco Escudero. — 1a ed. — Barcelona : Tritó : Eresbil, 2006, c2002. — 1 score (xxxiv, 79 p.) ; 34 cm. — (Euskal musikagileak)
For orchestra. — Pref. in Basque, Catalan, Spanish and English. — "Op. 3"—Cover. — Duration: ca. 20:00.
Publ. no. TR 139
ISMN M692043218
System number: 013710090

784.21858
*Schnittke, Alfred, 1934-1998.
Gogol-Suite : Suite aus der Bühnenmusik zum Schauspiel "Die Revisionsliste" von Nikolai Gogol = Suite from the music to a production of "The dead souls register" by Nikolai Gogol / Alfred Schnittke ; Zusammenstellung, Gennadi Rozhdestvensky. — Partitur. — Hamburg : Sikorski, [2004?], c1990. — 1 score (136 p.) ; 30 cm. — (Exempla nova ; 237)
For orchestra.
Pl. no. H.S. 1937
Publ. no. 1937
ISMN M003029252
System number: 013577535

784.2186
Schulhoff, Ervín, 1894-1942.
[Concertos, string quartet, band]
Konzert pro smyčcovy kvartet a dechový orchestr = Konzert für Streichquartett und Bläser-Ensemble = Concerto for string quartet and wind ensemble : 1930 / Erwin Schulhoff. — Studijní partitury. — Mainz ; Praha : Panton, [2004], c1961. — 1 score (79 p.) ; 30 cm. — Musik unserer Zeit
Pl. no. P 5038
ISMN M205007300
System number: 013953483

784.218844
Strauss, Johann, 1825-1899.
[Nachtigall-Polka ; *arr.*]
Nachtigall-Polka : op. 222 / Johann Strauss (Sohn) ; [herausgegeben von] Isabella Sommer. — Partitur. — Wien : Doblinger, c2004. — 1 score (22 p.) : facsim. ; 30 cm. — (Diletto musicale ; DM 1024) — (Doblingers Johann Strauss Gesamtausgabe)
Originally for piano; this edition for orchestra based on a score by Georg Kraus. — Series and vol. numbering in the Gesamtausgabe supplied from Harrassowitz web site. — Pref. in English and German; "Revisionsbericht" in German.
Publ. no. DM 1024
Pl. no. D.18 420
ISMN M012405054
System number: 013587599

784.218885
Serebrier, José, 1938-
Tango in blue = Tango in azul : for orchestra / José Serebrier. — New York : PeerMusic Classical, c2005. — 1 score (16 p.) ; 31 cm.
Duration: 3:00. — Includes composer's note.
Publ. no. 62103-856
System number: 014457045

784.218926
Martinez, Marianne, 1744-1812.
[Isacco, figura del Redentore. Ouverture]
Overture to the oratorio Isacco figura del Redentore (1782) / by Marianna Martines ; edited by Shirley Bean. — Score. — Fayetteville, AR : ClarNan Editions, c2004. — 1 score (v, 75 p.) ; 29 cm.
For orchestra. — Edited from the manuscript in the Gesellschaft der Musikfreunde, Vienna. — Biographical, editorial and performance notes in English.
Publ. no. CN50
System number: 014457029

Mendelssohn-Bartholdy, Felix, 1809-1847.
[Overtures. *Selections*]
Ouvertüren I / Felix Mendelssohn Bartholdy ; herausgegeben von Christian Martin Schmidt. — Wiesbaden : Breitkopf & Härtel, 2006. — 1 score (xxxi, 330 p.) : facsims. ; 33 cm. — (Leipziger Ausgabe der Werke von Felix Mendelssohn Bartholdy. Serie I, Orchesterwerke ; Bd. 8)
For orchestra. — Series "herausgegeben von der Sächsischen Akademie der Wissenschaften zu Leipzig." — Pref. in German and English; critical commentary in German.
Publ. no. SON 420
ISMN M004802700
System number: 013798492

Rott, Hans, 1858-1884.
[Vorspiele, orchestra, E major]
Orchestervorspiel E-Dur / Hans Rott ; herausgegeben von Johannes Volker Schmidt. — Partitur. — Berlin : Ries & Erler, 2007. — 1 score (xv, 13 p.) ; 30 cm. — (19. Jahrhundert Sinfonik = 19th century)
"Erstausgabe"—P. iv. — Preface and critical report in German.
Publ. no. 51171
ISMN M013511716
System number: 013953482

784.218928

Escudero, Francisco, 1912-2002.
Evocación en Ícíar : preludio matinal / Francisco Escudero. — 1a ed. —
Barcelona : Tritó : Eresbil, 2006, c2002. — 1 score (xxxiii, 16 p.) ; 34 cm.
— (Euskal musikagileak)
For orchestra. — Pref. in Basque, Catalan, Spanish and English. — Duration: ca.
7:00.
Publ. no. TR 136
ISMN M692043294
System number: 013710068

Escudero, Francisco, 1912-2002.
[Prelude, orchestra]
Preludio / Francisco Escudero. — 1a ed. — Barcelona : Tritó : Eresbil,
2006, c2002. — 1 score (xxx, 17 p.) ; 34 cm. — (Euskal musikagileak)
For orchestra. — Pref. in Basque, Catalan, Spanish and English. — Duration: ca.
3:00.
Publ. no. TR 150
ISMN M692043256
System number: 013710105

784.21894

Franckenstein, Clemens von, 1875-1942.
[Fantasien, orchestra, op. 15]
Fantasie : Nachtstimmung / Clemens von Franckenstein. Symphonische
Phantasie über ein Gedicht von Edgar Steiger : ("Ibsen-Phantasie") / August
Reuss. Nachtstück / Felix vom Rath ; herausgegeben von Stephan Hörner.
— Wiesbaden : Breitkopf & Härtel, 2005. — 1 score (xliii, 180 p.) : ill.,
facsims. ; 34 cm. — (Denkmäler der Tonkunst in Bayern ; neue Folge, Bd.
17)
Symphonic poems. — Pref. in German.
Pl. no. SON 247
ISMN M004802571
EAN 9790004802571
System number: 014620316

784.218964

Raff, Joachim, 1822-1882.
[Elegy, orchestra, WoO 48, C minor]
Elegie für grosses Orchester WoO 48, urpsrünglicher, dritter Satz aus der
Symphonie Nr. 10 "Zur Herbstzeit, " op. 213 / Joachim Raff ; Erstausgabe
nach dem Autograph des Komponisten herausgegeben von Volker Tosta. —
Partitur. — Stuttgart : Edition Nordstern, c2003. — 1 score (viii, 29 p.) ;
30 cm. — (Werke / Joachim Raff ; Bd. XVII/1)
Pref. in English and German. — Limited ed. of 200 copies.
Publ. no. 0110-1923
Pl. no. 13.05.03
ISMN M700164379
System number: 014503139

784.218966

Escudero, Francisco, 1912-2002.
[Nocturne, orchestra]
Nocturno / Francisco Escudero. — 1a ed. — Barcelona : Tritó : Eresbil,
2006, c2002. — 1 score (xxxiii, 15 p.) ; 35 cm. — (Euskal musikagileak)
For orchestra. — Pref. in Basque, Catalan, Spanish and English. — Duration: ca.
4:00.
Publ. no. TR 148
ISMN M692043232
System number: 013710094

784.24

Hellawell, Piers, 1956-
Inside story : violin & viola soli and orchestra (1999) / Piers Hellawell. —
Kenley, Surrey : Maecenas Music, c1999. — 1 score (87 p.) ; 30 cm.
Duration: 22:00.
System number: 013416609

*Rosetti, Antonio, ca. 1750-1792.
[Simphonie concertante, M. C14, D major]
Sinfonia concertante für zwei Violinen und Orchester in D-Dur RWV C14 =
Sinfonia concertante for two violins and orchestra in D major / Antonio
Rosetti ; herausgegeben von Johannes Moesus. — Winterthur,
Schweiz : Amadeus, 2004. — 1 score (23 p.) ; 31 cm. — (Werke / Antonio
Rosetti. Reihe C: Konzerte ; Bd. 5 = Works / Antonio Rosetti. Series C:
Concertos ; v. 5)
Includes pref. in English and German.
Publ. no. BP 1293
System number: 014764138

Sciarrino, Salvatore.
Graffito sul mare : per trio e orchestra, 2003 / Salvatore Sciarrino. —
Partitura. — Milano : Ricordi, c2003. — 1 score (60 p.) ; 46 cm.
For piano, soprano saxophone and percussion solo and orchestra. — Performance
notes in Italian, preceding score.
Publ. no. 139086
ISMN M041390864
System number: 014053366

784.24186

Gudmundsen-Holmgreen, Pelle.
[Concerto grosso]
Concerto grosso (1990, rev. 2006) : for strygekvartet og symfonisk
ensemble / Pelle Gudmundsen-Holmgreen. — Copenhagen : Samfundet
til udgivelse af dansk musik, c2006. — 1 score (129 p.) ; 43 cm.
Duration: 30:00. — Pref. in Danish; performance instructions in English.
Publ. no. No. 0424
System number: 013711552

Routh, Francis.
Double concerto : for violin, violoncello and orchestra : op. 19 (1970) /
Francis Routh. — Full score. — London : Redcliffe Edition, [2004?] — 1
score (106 p.) ; 42 cm.
The copyright date (c 1976) has been added in the composer's autograph at foot
of p. 1.
ISMN M708045076
System number: 013174254

784.262186

Chopin, Frédéric, 1810-1849.
[Concertos, piano, orchestra, no. 1, op. 11, E minor]
Koncert e-moll op. 11 na fortepian i orkiestrę : wersja historyczna =
Concerto in E minor op. 11 for piano and orchestra : historical version /
Fryderyk Chopin ; [redakcja tomu, Jan Ekier, Paweł Kamiński] —
Partytura . — Warszawa : Fundacja Wydania Narodowego Dzieł
Fryderyka Chopina, 2005. — 1 score (107 p.) ; 31 cm. + 1 commentary
(12 p. : music) — (Wydanie narodowe dzieł Fryderyka Chopina ; 18.
Seria A, Utwory wydane za życia Chopina ; t. 15b)
Edition compiled from the parts of the 1st editions. — Pref. in Polish and English;
commentary pamphlet in English.
Pl. no. FWN 18 A XVb
ISBN 8392036549
ISMN M901332843
System number: 014490802

Chopin, Frédéric, 1810-1849.
[Concertos, piano, orchestra, no. 1, op. 11, E minor]
Koncert e-moll op. 11 na fortepian i orkiestrę = Concerto in E minor
op. 11 for piano and orchestra / Fryderyk Chopin ; [redakcja tomu, Jan
Ekier, Paweł Kamiński] — Partytura, wersja koncertowa = Score, concert
version. — Warszawa : Polskie Wydawnictwo Muzyczne, 2005. — 1
score (107 p.) ; 31 cm. + 1 commentary (15 p. : music) — (Wydanie
narodowe dzieł Fryderyka Chopina ; 33. Seria B, Utwory wydane
pośmiertnie ; t. 8a)
Pref. in English and Polish; commentary pamphlet in English.
Pl. no. FWN 33 B VIIIa
ISBN 8392036530
ISMN M901332836
System number: 014490787

Chopin, Frédéric, 1810-1849.
[Concertos, piano, orchestra, no. 2, op. 21, F minor]
Koncert f-moll op. 21 na fortepian i orkiestrę : wersja historyczna =
Concerto in F minor op. 21 for piano and orchestra : historical version /
Fryderyk Chopin ; [redakcja tomu, Jan Ekier, Paweł Kamiński] —
Warszawa : Fundacja Wydania Narodowego Dzieł Fryderyka Chopina,
2005. — 1 score (79 p.) ; 31 cm. + 1 commentary (11 p. : music) —
(Wydanie narodowe dzieł Fryderyka Chopina ; 21. Seria A, Utwory
wydane za życia Chopina ; t. 15e)
Edition based on the semi-autograph and the parts from the 1st editions. — Pref.
in English and Polish; commentary pamphlet in English.
Pl. no. FWN 21 A XVe
ISBN 8392036522
ISMN M901332829
System number: 014490807

Chopin, Frédéric, 1810-1849.
[Concertos, piano, orchestra, no. 2, op. 21, F minor]
Koncert f-moll op. 21 na fortepian i orkiestrę = Concerto in F minor
op. 21 for piano and orchestra / Fryderyk Chopin ; [redakcja tomu, Jan
Ekier, Paweł Kamiński] — Partytura, wersja koncertowa = Score, concert
version. — Warszawa : Wydanie Narodowe, 2005. — 1 score (79 p.) ;
31 cm. + 1 commentary (15 p. : music) — (Wydanie narodowe dzieł
Fryderyka Chopina ; 34. Seria B, Utwory wydane pośmiertnie ; t. 8b)
Pref. in English and Polish; commentary pamphlet in English.
Pl. no. FWN 34 B VIIIb
ISBN 8392036514
ISMN M901332812
System number: 014490798

*Clementi, Muzio, 1752-1832.
[Concerto, piano, orchestra, C major]
Concerto in do maggiore, op-sn 30, per clavicembalo (pianoforte) e
orchestra = for harpsichord (piano) and orchestra / [Muzio Clementi] ; a
cura di Luca Sala. — Bologna, Italy : Ut Orpheus, c2004. — 1 score (x,
65 p.) 32 cm. — (Opera omnia / Muzio Clementi ; v. 60)
"Ms. Johann Schenk, 1796." — "Urtext." — Critical matter in Italian. Preface to
series in Italian and English.
Pl. no. MC 60A
ISMN M215309074
EAN 9790215309074
System number: 014748297
Also classified at 784.264186

Furtwängler, Wilhelm, 1886-1954.
[Symphonisches Konzert]
Sinfonisches Konzert für Klavier und Orchester / Wilhelm Furtwängler ;
herausgegeben von George Alexander Albrecht. — Partitur. — Berlin : Ries
& Erler, c2004. — 1 score (252 p.) ; 30 cm. — (Wilhelm Furtwängler
Gesamtausgabe ; Bd. I.IV)
Duration: ca. 80:00. — Pref. in German.
ISMN M013511303
System number: 014658035

Lindberg, Magnus, 1958-
[Concertos, piano, orchestra, no. 1]
Piano concerto, 1990, revised 1994 : for piano and orchestra / Magnus
Lindberg. — Full score. — Helsinki : Edition Wilhelm Hansen, c2005. — 1
score (111 p.) ; 42 cm.
Duration: ca. 24:00.
Publ. no. 021105
System number: 013750211

Peçi, Aleksandër, 1951-
[Concertos, piano, orchestra, no. 1]
Concerto pour piano et orchestre no. 1 / Aleksander Peci. — Tirana : Aelfior
Editions, [2006] — 1 score (136 p.) : port. ; 30 cm.
Biographical notes in English. — Reproduced from holograph.
System number: 014053351

784.2621894

Debussy, Claude, 1862-1918.
[Fantaisie, piano, orchestra]
Fantaisie pour piano et orchestre (2e version) / Claude Debussy ; édition de
Jean-Pierre Marty ; avec la collaboration de Denis Herlin et Edmond
Lemaître. — Paris : Durand, c2007. — 1 score (xix, 223 p.) : col. facsims. ;
35 cm. — Musica Gallica — (Œuvres complètes de Claude Debussy. Série
V, Œuvres pour orchestre ; v. 2 bis)
Version based on the composer's corrections possibly from 1902-1903 and
1916-1917 to the original work from 1890. — Foreword and critical notes in French
and English. — Publisher no. and ISMN from dustjacket.
Pl. no. D. & F. 15575
Publ. no. DB 15575
ISMN M044080618
System number: 013801751

784.264186

*Clementi, Muzio, 1752-1832.
[Concerto, piano, orchestra, C major]
Concerto in do maggiore, op-sn 30, per clavicembalo (pianoforte) e
orchestra = for harpsichord (piano) and orchestra / [Muzio Clementi] ; a
cura di Luca Sala. — Bologna, Italy : Ut Orpheus, c2004. — 1 score (x,
65 p.) 32 cm. — (Opera omnia / Muzio Clementi ; v. 60)
"Ms. Johann Schenk, 1796." — "Urtext." — Critical matter in Italian. Preface to
series in Italian and English.
Pl. no. MC 60A
ISMN M215309074
EAN 9790215309074
System number: 014748297
Primary classification 784.262186

784.265186

Rheinberger, Josef, 1839-1901.
[Instrumental music. *Selections*]
Orgelkonzerte / [Josef Gabriel Rheinberger] ; vorgelegt von Wolfgang
Hochstein. — Stuttgart : Carus, c2007. — 1 score (xxxvi, 195 p.) :
facsims. ; 33 cm. — (Sämtliche Werke / Josef Gabriel Rheinberger.
Abteilung V, Orchestermusik, Orgelkonzerte ; Bd. 28)
Prefatory matter and critical report in German with English and French translations;
includes bibliographical references. — The 3rd work originally for violin, cello and
organ, arr. by the composer for violin, cello, organ and string orchestra.
Publ. no. 50.228
ISBN 9783899480276
ISBN 3899480279
ISMN M007091842
System number: 013836215

784.268

*Takemitsu, Tōru.
From me flows what you call time : for five percussionists and orchestra /
Tōru Takemitsu. — [Tokyo] : Schott Japan, c2004. — 1 score (41 p.) ;
37 cm.
Title page and performance instructions in English and Japanese. — Duration:
31:00.
Publ. no. SJ 1148
ISBN 4890664483
ISMN M650011976
EAN 9790650011976
System number: 013015917

784.2721858

Raff, Joachim, 1822-1882.
[Suites, violin, orchestra, op. 180, G minor]
Suite für Violine und Orchester g-Moll, op. 180 / Joachim Raff ; nach der
Erstausgabe neu herausgegeben von Volker Tosta. — Partitur. —
Stuttgart : Edition Nordstern, c2005. — 1 score (xiv, 118 p.) ; 30 cm. —
(Raff Werke ; Bd. XVI/3a)
Pref. in German with English translation; critical notes in German. — Limited ed.
of 200 copies.
Publ. no. 0116-1800
ISMN M700164720
System number: 014503121

784.272186

*Brahms, Johannes, 1833-1897.
[Concertos, violin, orchestra, op. 77, D major]
Violinkonzert D-Dur Opus 77 / Johannes Brahms ; herausgegeben von
Linda Correll Roesner und Michael Struck. — München : G. Henle
Verlag, 2004. — 1 score (xxvi, 307 p.) : facsims. ; 33 cm. — (Neue
Ausgabe sämtlicher Werke. Serie I, Orchesterwerke / Johannes Brahms ;
Bd. 9)
"Herausgegeben von der Johannes Brahms Gesamtausgabe ... Editionsleitung
Kiel in Verbindung mit der Gesellschaft der Musikfreunde in Wien." — Pref.,
introd., and critical report (p. [197]-307) in German.
System number: 013474479

*Clement, Franz, 1780-1842.
[Concertos, violin, orchestra, D major]
Violin concerto in D major : (1805) / Franz Clement ; edited by Clive
Brown. — Middleton, Wis. : A-R Editions, c2005. — 1 score (184 p.) :
facsims. ; 31 cm. + + 1 piano score (71 p.) + 1 part (31 p.) ; 28 cm. —
Recent researches in the music of the nineteenth and early twentieth
centuries, 0193-5364 ; 41
Edited from 2 copies of a lithographed edition housed at the British Library,
London (GB-Lbl:i100.uu.) and at the Österreichische Nationalbibliothek, Vienna
(A-Wn: MS.36456). — Editorial, historical and critical notes in English.
ISBN 0895795698
System number: 013350825
Also classified at 787.2186

Fedele, Ivan.
[Concertos, violin, orchestra, (1999)]
Concerto per violino e orchestra, 1998/99 / Ivan Fedele. — Milano :
Edizioni Suvini Zerboni, [2007] — 1 score (125 p.) ; 46 cm.
For violin and orchestra.
Publ. no. S. 11499 Z.
System number: 013771080

Maw, Nicholas.
[Concertos, violin, orchestra]
Violin concerto / Nicholas Maw. — London : Faber Music, c1999. — 1
score (171 p) ; 30 cm.
"The Violin concerto was written for Joshua Bell at the request of Roger
Norrington for the Orchestra of St Luke's, New York." — t.p. verso. — Duration:
42:00.
ISBN 057151796X
System number: 006914457

*Ordoñez, Carlos d', 1734-1786.
[Symphonies. *Selections*]
Sinfonías ; Concierto para violín en re mayor / Carlos Ordóñez ; edición
crítica Miguel Simarro Grande [y] Ángel Oliver. — Madrid : Instituto
Complutense de Ciencias Musicales, c2004. — 1 score (xxi, 417 p.) ;
30 cm. — (Música hispana. Serie B, Música instrumental ; 26)
Mostly for orchestra. 6th, 7th and 10th works for string orchestra. — Pref. in
Spanish with English translation.
ISBN 8480485620
System number: 014679359
Primary classification 784.2184

784.2814

*Rosetti, Antonio, ca. 1750-1792.
[Symphonies, M. A21, D major]
Sinfonie Nr. 26 in D-dur = Symphony no. 26 in D major : RWV A21 /
Antonio Rosetti ; herausgegeben von Johannes Moesus. —
Winterthur/Schweiz : Amadeus : B. Päuler, 2004. — 1 score (44 p.) ;
30 cm. — (Werke / Antonio Rosetti. Reihe A, Sinfonien ; Bd. 2)
Pref. in English and German.
Publ. no. BP 1292
System number: 014763892

784.2832

*Davies, Peter Maxwell, 1934-
Temenos, with mermaids and angels : for flute and orchestra / Peter
Maxwell Davies. — London : Chester Music, c2005. — 1 miniature
score (47 p.) ; 19 cm.
Includes composer's note.
Publ. no. CH61596
ISBN 1844493423
System number: 013190880

*Hurel, Philippe, 1955-
[Phonus]
Phonus, ou, La voix du faune : pour flûte et orchestre / Philippe Hurel. —
Partition d'orchestre. — Paris : Lemoine, c2004. — 1 score (87 p.) ; 30 cm.
Performance instructions in French with some English.
Pl. no. 28182 H.L.
ISMN 9790230981828
System number: 014835204

784.2836
Börtz, Daniel, 1943-
Pipor och klockor / Daniel Börtz. — Stockholm : Gehrmans, 2004, c2002.
— 1 score (28 p.) ; 30 cm.
For recorder and orchestra. — Duration: ca. 17:00.
Publ. no. GE 10309
ISMN M070103091
System number: 014457007

784.2843186
Alderete Acosta, Igmar.
[Concertos, marimba, orchestra (2004)]
Concierto no. 1 para marimba y orquesta / Igmar Alderete Acosta. —
Granada : Junta de Andalucía, Consejería de Cultura, [2007] — 1 score
(73 p.) ; 34 cm.
Concerto for marimba and orchestra.
ISMN M901311978
System number: 014053148

784.2862
Donizetti, Gaetano, 1797-1848.
Piccola composizione : per clarinetto ed orchestra / Gaetano Donizetti ; a
cura di Pietro Spada. — Partitura. — Roma : Boccaccini & Spada, c2006.
— 1 score (17 p.) ; 31 cm.
First ed. based on a manuscript from the Biblioteca Civica di Bergamo. — Includes
pref. in Italian, English, French and German.
Pl. no. BS. 1418
System number: 013771075

784.3 – CHAMBER ORCHESTRA

784.3
Hindemith, Paul, 1895-1963.
[Kammermusik, no. 1]
Konzertante Kammermusiken I / Paul Hindemith ; herausgegeben von
Giselher Schubert. — Mainz : Schott, 2007. — 1 score (xxxix, 313 p.) :
facsims. ; 39 cm. — (Sämtliche Werke / Paul Hindemith ; Bd. IV, 1)
Pref. and kritische Berichte (p. 287-313) in German.
Pl. no. 43 654
Publ. no. BSS 43654
Publ. no. PHA 401
ISMN M001138000
System number: 013822607

784.31556
Lully, Jean Baptiste, 1632-1687.
[Ballets. *Vocal scores. Selections*]
Ballet des saisons ; Les amours déguisés ; Ballet royal de Flore /
Jean-Baptiste Lully ; édition [par Ballet des saisons] de James P. Cassaro ;
édition [par Les amours déguisés] de James R. Anthony et Rebecca
Harris-Warrick ; édition [par Ballet royal de flore] d'Albert Cohen ;
réduction clavier-chant, Noam A. Krieger. — Hildesheim : G. Olms, 2004.
— 1 score (156 p.) ; 30 cm. — Musica Gallica — (Œuvres complètes /
Jean-Baptiste Lully ; sér. 1, v. 6)
Pref. in English, French, and German. — French words.
ISBN 3487125552
System number: 013775846

Lully, Jean Baptiste, 1632-1687.
[Monsieur de Pourceaugnac. *Vocal score*]
Monsieur de Pourceaugnac : (Le divertissement de Chambord) ; Le
bourgeois gentilhomme : comédie-ballet / Jean-Baptiste Lully/Molière ;
[Monsieur de Pourceaugnac] édition de Jérôme de La Gorce ; [Le bourgeois
gentilhomme] édition de Herbert Schneider ; réduction clavier-chant, Noam
A. Krieger. — Hildesheim ; New York : Georg Olms, 2007. — 1 score
(211 p.) : facsims. ; 30 cm. — Musica Gallica — (Œuvres complètes. Série
II, Comédies-ballets et autres divertissements / Jean-Baptiste Lully ; v. 4)
Pref. in French with English and German translations. — French words.
ISBN 9783487132464
System number: 013949776

784.3184
Kalsons, Romualds.
[Symphonies, chamber orchestra, no. 1]
Sinfonie für Kammerorchester, 1981 / Romualds Kalsons. — Hamburg :
Sikorski, 2007. — 1 score (85 p.) ; 42 cm.
For chamber orchestra. — Reproduced from holograph.
System number: 013762794

Martinez, Marianne, 1744-1812.
[Symphony, C major]
Sinfonia in C major, (Ouverture), (1770) / by Marianna Martines ; edited
by Shirley Bean and Karen Fremar. — Fayetteville, AR : ClarNan
Editions, c2002. — 1 score (x, 81 p.) ; 28 cm.
For chamber orchestra. — Includes pref. and critical notes. — Edited from the
autograph ms. in the Gesellschaft der Musikfreunde, Vienna.
Publ. no. CN44
System number: 014457030

784.31894
Wegener, Margaret, 1920-
[Down Hilo; *arr.*]
Down Hilo : fantasy for small orchestra based on two sea-shanties /
Margaret Wegener. — Manchester : Da Capo Music, c2005. — 1 score
(23 p.) ; 30 cm.
Originally for piano; arr. for chamber orchestra by the composer. — Duration: ca.
8:00. — Includes biographical notes.
Pl. no. DC 638
System number: 013351570

784.3262186
Lambert, Constant, 1905-1951.
[Concertos, piano, instrumental ensemble, (1924)]
Concerto (1924), for piano solo, 2 trumpets, strings and timpani /
Constant Lambert ; edited, arranged and orchestrated from the
composer's original 2 piano score by Edward Shipley and Giles
Easterbrook. — Kenley : Maecenas Music, [2005?] — 1 score (44 p.)
30 cm.
Duration: ca. 20:00.
System number: 013422549

Martinez, Marianne, 1744-1812.
[Concertos, harpsichord, orchestra, G major]
Concerto in G major for piano and orchestra / by Marianna Martines ;
edited by Shirley Bean. — Score. — Fayetteville, Ark. : ClarNan
Editions, c2005. — 1 score (vi, 160 p.) ; 28 cm.
Edited from the autograph manuscript in the Gesellschaft der Musikfreunde,
Vienna. — Biographical, editorial, and performance notes in English.
Publ. no. CN55
System number: 014457031

**784.60 – KEYBOARD, MECHANICAL ELECTRONIC,
PERCUSSION BANDS**

784.680834
Bartlett, Keith.
Cossack capers / Keith Bartlett. — Waltham Abbey : United Music
Publishers, c2005. — 1 score (7 p.) + 9 parts : ill. ; 31 cm. + 1 compact
disc. — Crash bang wallop!
"Easy percussion music for the whole class (with piano accompaniment)". —
Performance notes in English, French, German, Spanish and Japanese.
ISMN M224404951
System number: 013416287

Bartlett, Keith.
Jingle jangle jungle / Keith Bartlett. — Waltham Abbey : United Music
Publishers, c2005. — 1 score (6 p.) + 9 parts : ill. ; 31 cm. + 1 compact
disc. — Crash bang wallop!
"Easy percussion music for the whole class (with piano accompaniment)". —
Performance notes in English, French, German, Spanish and Japanese.
ISMN M224404937
System number: 013416318

Bartlett, Keith.
Viva Mexico / Keith Bartlett. — Waltham Abbey : United Music
Publishers, c2005. — 1 score (10 p.) + 9 parts : ill. ; 31 cm. + 1 compact
disc. — Crash bang wallop!
"Easy percussion music for the whole class (with piano accompaniment)". —
Performance notes in English, French, German, Spanish and Japanese.
ISMN M224404968
System number: 013416308

784.68188417230834
Bartlett, Keith.
Christmas cancan / Keith Bartlett. — Waltham Abbey : United Music
Publishers, c2005. — 1 score (7 p.) + 9 parts : ill. ; 31 cm. + 1 compact
disc. — Crash bang wallop!
"Easy percussion music for the whole class (with piano accompaniment)". —
Performance notes in English, French, German, Spanish and Japanese.
ISMN M224404920
System number: 013416246

784.6818880834
Bartlett, Keith.
Sing a song o' conga / Keith Bartlett. — Waltham Abbey : United Music
Publishers, c2005. — 1 score (14 p.) + 8 parts : ill. ; 31 cm. + 1 compact
disc. — Crash bang wallop!
"Easy percussion music for the whole class (with piano accompaniment)". —
Performance notes in English, French, German, Spanish and Japanese.
ISMN M224404944
System number: 013416191

784.6818970834
Bartlett, Keith.
Mystical march / Keith Bartlett. — Waltham Abbey : United Music
Publishers, c2005. — 1 score (9 p.) + 9 parts : ill. ; 31 cm. + 1 compact disc.
— Crash bang wallop!
"Easy percussion music for the whole class (with piano accompaniment)". —
Performance notes in English, French, German, Spanish and Japanese.
ISMN M224404975
System number: 013416262

784.7 – STRING ORCHESTRA

784.7
Bayliss, Colin.
Epilogue : for string orchestra : [B139] / Colin Bayliss. — Manchester : Da
Capo Music, c2005. — 1 score (9 p.) ; 30 cm.
Duration: ca. 6:00. — Includes biographical and programme notes.
Pl. no. DC 645
System number: 013351513

Peçi, Aleksandër, 1951-
Motor motus : string orchestra / Aleksandër Peçi. — Tirana : Aelfior
Editions, c2006. — 1 score (19 p.) ; 31 cm.
Pl. no. AED.1206
System number: 014053355

Peçi, Aleksandër, 1951-
Pizzicato brillante : string orchestra / Aleksandër Peçi. — Tirana : Aelfior
Editions, 2006. — 1 score (31 p.) ; 31 cm.
Pl. no. AED.1406
Publ. no. AED 1506
System number: 014053356

Poole, Geoffrey, 1949-
Fragments : (1974 rev. '98) : for 14 solo strings (44321) or multiples /
Geoffrey Poole. — Kenley : Maecenas Music, c1998. — 1 score (36 p.) ;
30 cm.
Duration: ca. 5:00.
System number: 013422512
Primary classification 785.7199

Sewell, Dominic.
[Adagios, string orchestra, op. 23]
Adagio : opus 23 / Dominic Sewell. — Dover : Broadbent & Dunn, c2003.
— 1 score (4 p.) ; 30 cm.
For string orchestra.
Publ. no. B&D 13404
System number: 013167651

Vine, Carl, 1954-
Prologue & canzona : for string orchestra (1985-6) / Carl Vine. — London :
Faber Music, c1999. — 1 score (31 p.) ; 30 cm.
Duration: 14:00. — Program note by composer.
ISBN 057151913X
ISBN 9780571519132
System number: 006915011

*Zhou, Long, 1953-
Chinese folk songs : for string orchestra / Zhou Long. — [New York] :
Oxford University Press, c2004. — 1 score (16 p.) + 5 parts ; 31 cm. —
Oxford music for string orchestra
Includes composer's and biographical notes. — Duration: 15:00.
ISBN 0193867893 (score)
ISBN 0193867907 (violin 1)
ISBN 0193867915 (violin 2)
ISBN 0193867923 (viola)
ISBN 0193867931 (cello)
ISBN 019386794X (double bass)
System number: 013115382

784.7184
*Ordoñez, Carlos d', 1734-1786.
[Symphonies. *Selections*]
Sinfonías ; Concierto para violín en re mayor / Carlos Ordóñez ; edición
crítica Miguel Simarro Grande [y] Ángel Oliver. — Madrid : Instituto
Complutense de Ciencias Musicales, c2004. — 1 score (xxi, 417 p.) ;
30 cm. — (Música hispana. Serie B, Música instrumental ; 26)
Mostly for orchestra. 6th, 7th and 10th works for string orchestra. — Pref. in
Spanish with English translation.
ISBN 8480485620
System number: 014679359
Primary classification 784.2184

784.71858
Dall'Abaco, Evaristo Felice, 1675-1742.
[Concerti da chiesa]
Concerti a quattro da chiesa, cioè due violini, alto viola, violoncello e basso
continuo, opera seconda : Amsterdam s.d. / Evaristo Felice Dall'Abaco. —
Firenze : Studio per edizioni scelte, 2006. — 5 parts ; 35 cm. — Monumenta
musicae revocata ; 33
Facsimile edition. — Reprint. Originally published: Amsterdam : Estienne Roger &
Le Cene, between 1710 and 1714. — Pref. by Marco Materassi and Laura Och, in
Italian with English translation.
ISBN 9788872428184

ISBN 8872428181
System number: 013688127

Grieg, Edvard, 1843-1907.
[Piano music. *Selections; arr.*]
A Grieg suite : 3 movements based on Grieg's 'Lyric pieces' arranged for
school string ensemble / arranged by Chris Allen. — Laggan : Spartan
Press, c2001. — 1 score (8 p.) + 1 set of parts ; 31 cm.
For five-part string ensemble. — "Grades 3-5."
Pl. no. SP578
ISMN M579995784
System number: 013482658

*Sculthorpe, Peter, 1929-
Little suite for strings : for string orchestra : (1983) / Peter Sculthorpe. —
London : Faber Music, c1983. — 1 score (12 p.) ; 30 cm.
Duration: 10:00.
ISBN 0571557430
System number: 013555388

784.724
Bach, Carl Philipp Emanuel, 1714-1788.
[Fantasien, violin, keyboard instrument, H. 536, F minor; *arr.*]
I sentimenti di Carl Philipp Emanuel Bach : (1982) : trascrizione per
flauto, arpa ed archi della Clavier-Fantasie con accompagnamento di un
violino (1787) = Transkription für Flöte, Harfe und Streicher der
Clavier-Fantasie mit Begleitung einer Violine (1787) = transcription for
flute, harp, and strings of the Clavier-Fantasie with violin accompaniment
(1787) / [composed by C.P.E. Bach ; arr. by] Hans Werner Henze. —
Studienpartitur. — Mainz ; Schott, c2000. New York : — 1 score (34 p.) ;
30 cm. — (Musik unserer Zeit = Music of our time)
Originally composed by C.P.E. Bach for keyboard and violin, transcribed by
Henze for flute, harp, and string orchestra. — Duration: ca. 17:00.
Publ. no. ED 9130
Publ. no. 49659
ISBN 9790001126342
ISMN M001126342
EAN 9790001126342
System number: 014457017

*Shchedrin, Rodion Konstantinovich, 1932-
[Vologodskie svireli]
Shepherd's pipes of Vologda : for oboe, cor anglais, horn and string
orchestra = Hirtenklänge aus Wologda : für Oboe, Englisch Horn, Horn
und Streichorchester : Hommage à Bartók (1995) / Rodion Shchedrin. —
Study score. — Mainz ; London : Schott, c2003. — 1 score (20 p.) ;
30 cm. — (Musik unserer Zeit = Music of our time)
Pl. no. 49 045
Publ. no. ED 8678
ISMN M001121033
System number: 013587082

784.724186
*Fesch, Willem de, 1687-1761.
[Concertos, violins (2), string orchestra]
Concerto in A minor à 4 stromenti, c.1710 / Willem de Fesch ; edited by
Robert L. Tusler. — Amsterdam : Donemus, 2004, c2003. — 1 score (iii,
12 p.) ; 30 cm.
For 2 solo violins, tutti violins in 3 parts and basso continuo. — Unfigured bass
unrealized.
System number: 014747956

784.7264186
Galuppi, Baldassare, 1706-1785.
[Concertos, harpsichord, string orchestra, C minor]
Concerti per cembalo n. 5 e n. 6 per clavicembalo, violino I, violino II,
viola e basso / Baldassare Galuppi, detto il Buranello ; a cura di Rita
Peiretti ; prefazione di Alberto Iesuè. — Bologna : Associazione
clavicembalistica bolognese, 2006. — 1 score (xi, 37 p.) ; 34 cm. —
(Collana editoriale. Seconda serie / Associazione clavicembalistica
bolognese ; n. 4)
Edited from ms. D 3998 (Bibliothèque nationale, Paris) in which concertos for
harpsichord attributed to Galuppi are numbered 1-6. — Preface and critical notes
in Italian with English translations.
ISMN M705002225
System number: 013647815

784.727
Gorb, Adam, 1958-
Diaspora : 2003 : for string ensemble (33221 players) / Adam Gorb. —
Kenley : Maecenas Music, c2003. — 1 score (32 p.) ; 30 cm.
For 2 solo violins, solo double bass and string ensemble or string orchestra. —
Commissioned by the Goldberg Ensemble. — Duration: ca. 16:00.
System number: 013416719
Primary classification 785.7199

784.72741827
Routh, Francis.
[Chaconnes, violoncello, string orchestra, op. 51]
Ciacona : (romance) : for violoncello and string orchestra : op. 51 (1989)
/ Franis Routh. — Full score. — London : Redcliffe Edition, [2004?] —
1 score (26 p.) ; 42 cm.
ISMN M708045274
System number: 013176950

784.72765186

Graun, Johann Gottlieb, 1702 or 3-1771.
[Concertos, viola da gamba, string orchestra, A major]
Concerto in A major for viola da gamba, strings & basso continuo / Johann
Gottlieb Graun ; edited by Alejandro Garri ; assisted by Kent Carlson. —
1st ed. — Full score. — Frankfurt am Main : Garri Editions, c2006. — 1
score (66 p.) ; 30 cm. — Instrumental treasures ; v. 31
Edited from a ms. score in the Landesbibliothek, Darmstadt (Mus. ms. 355). — Pref.
in English.
Publ. no. GE 291
System number: 013750191

784.72832186

*Boyd, Anne, 1946-
[Concertos, flute, string orchestra]
Concerto for flute and strings / Anne Boyd. — York : University of York
Music Press, c1997. — 1 score (51 p.) ; 21 x 30 cm.
Reproduced from holograph.
ISMN M570200566
System number: 013430702

Porpora, Nicola, 1686-1768.
[Concertos, flute, string orchestra, D major]
Concerto per flauto ed archi / Niccolò Porpora ; a cura di Pietro Spada. —
Partitura. — Roma : Boccaccini & Spada, c2006. — 1 score (18 p.) ; 31 cm.
Unfigured bass unrealized. — Preface in Italian, English, French and German.
Pl. no. BS. 1717
System number: 014053358

Quantz, Johann Joachim, 1697-1773.
[Concertos, flute, string orchestra, QV 5:149, F major]
Flötenkonzert in F : Concerto QV 5:149, per flauto traverso, 2 violini, viola
e basso continuo (violoncello, contrabbasso, cembalo) / Johann Joachim
Quantz ; Generalbassaussetzung von Siegfried Petrenz. — Erstausg. /
herausgegeben von Horst Augsbach. — Partitur. — Stuttgart : Carus, c2007.
— 1 score (44 p.) ; 30 cm.
Figured bass realized for keyboard instrument. — Duration: ca. 16:00. — Preface in
German, English and French. — Critical report in German on p. 41-44.
Publ. no. CV 17.011
Pl. no. 17.011
ISMN M007090647
System number: 013953478

784.72852186

*Bach, Carl Philipp Emanuel, 1714-1788.
[Concertos, oboe, string orchestra, H. 466, B♭ major]
Oboe concertos / Carl Philipp Emanuel Bach ; edited by Janet K. Page. —
Los Altos, Calif. : Packard Humanities Institute, 2006. — 1 score (xv p.,
5 p. of plates, 83, [2] p.) : facsims. ; 33 cm. — (Complete works. Series III,
Orchestral music / Carl Philipp Emanuel Bach ; v. 5)
Issued in cooperation with the Bach-Archiv Leipzig, the Sächsische Akademie der
Wissenschaften zu Leipzig, and Harvard University. — Includes prefaces,
introduction, plates, list of abbreviations, critical report, commentary, and appendix,
in English.
ISBN 1933280174
ISBN 9781933280172
System number: 013810205

784.72853

Brumby, Colin.
Scena : for cor anglais and strings / by Colin Brumby. — Lancaster :
Phylloscopus Publications, c2004. — 1 score (17 p.) + 6 parts ; 30 cm.
"Although conceived for solo and chamber orchestra, the piece can be performed
with one string player to each part ..."—Pref.
Publ. no. PP530
ISMN M570166619
System number: 013188736
Also classified at 785.44196

784.72862

Peçi, Aleksandër, 1951-
Klitheu tragjik : clarinet, string orchestra / Aleksandër Peçi. — Tirana :
Aelfior Editions, c2006. — 1 score ([29] p.) ; 31 cm.
Pl. no. AED.13006
System number: 014053353

784.728941896

LeFanu, Nicola.
Amores : (2003) : 5 songs without words for horn and strings (33221
players min) / Nicola LeFanu. — Kenley : Maecenas Music, c2003. — 1
score (44 p.) ; 30 cm.
Duration: ca. 20:00. — Composer's note in English.
System number: 013193882

784.8 – WIND BAND

784.8

Binney, Malcolm.
Civitas / Malcolm Binney. — Kenley : Maecenas Music, c1997. — 1
score (88 p.) ; 30 cm. — Millennium series for wind bands & ensembles
For wind band. — "A musical portrait reflecting Bradford's industrial
past"—Pref. — Movements may be played separately. — Duration: ca. 19:00.
Publ. no. MC0037
System number: 013422238

Binney, Malcolm.
Emerald breeze : for wind orchestra / Malcolm Binney. — Kenley :
Maecenas Music, c1994. — 1 score (10 p.) ; 30 cm. — Millennium series
for wind bands & ensembles
Publ. no. MC0003
System number: 013192940

*Brooker, Gary.
[Whiter shade of pale; arr.]
A whiter shade of pale : grade 3 / Gary Brooker ; arr. Kit Turnbull. —
Wind band set. — London : Studio Music, [2005?], c1967. — 1 score
(15 p.) + 1 set of parts ; 30 cm. — (Simply classics)
Arr. for wind band. — Duration: 3:45.
ISMN M050066415 (wind band set)
ISMN M050066422 (score)
System number: 013359070

Carroll, Fergal.
Song of Lir : [2004] : for symphonic wind band / Fergal Carroll. —
Kenley : Maecenas Music, [2004] — 1 score (14 p.) ; 30 cm. —
Millennium series for wind bands & ensembles
Includes program notes. — Duration: ca. 6:00-7:00.
Publ. no. MC0086
System number: 013192951

Debussy, Claude, 1862-1918.
[Children's corner. Little shepherd; arr.]
The little shepherd : from Children's corner : grade 3 / Claude Debussy ;
arr. Rodney Newton. — Wind band set. — London : Studio Music,
c2005. — 1 score (11 p.) + 1 set of parts ; 30 cm. — (Simply classics)
Arr. for wind band. — Duration: 3:00.
ISMN M050066477 (wind band set)
ISMN M050066484 (score)
System number: 013382631

Early one morning : grade 1.5 / traditional ; arr. Duncan Stubbs. — Wind
band set. — London : Studio Music, c2005. — 1 score (11 p.) + 1 set of
parts ; 30 cm. — (Simply classics)
For wind band. — Duration: 1:50.
ISMN M050066057 (set)
ISMN M050066064 (score)
System number: 013358958

Ellerby, Martin, 1957-
Paris sketches : homages for band : [1994 rev. 2004] / Martin Ellerby. —
10th anniversay ed. — Kenley : Maecenas Music, 2004. — 1 score
(63 p.) ; 30 cm. — Millennium series for wind bands & ensembles
For wind band. — "Each movement pays homage to some part of the French
capital and to other composers who lived, worked or passed through
it"—Composer's note. — Duration: ca. 14:00-15:00.
Publ. no. MC0028
System number: 013193019

Gilmore, Bernard, 1937-
[Folksongs]
Five folk songs : for soprano and symphonic wind band : (1966) /
Bernard Gilmore. — Kenley : Maecenas Music, c2002. — 1 score
(89 p.) ; 30 cm. — Millennium series for wind bands & ensembles
Edited by Thomas Stone. — Words in English, Greek, Spanish or Yiddish.
Publ. no. MC0072
System number: 013192859
Primary classification 783.6642

Gorb, Adam, 1958-
Awayday : (1996) / Adam Gorb. — Kenley : Maecenas Music, 1996. —
1 score (52 p.) ; 30 cm. — Millennium series for wind bands &
ensembles
For wind band, including percussion and piano. — Duration: 7:00.
Publ. no. MC0036
System number: 013193029

Gorb, Adam, 1958-
Over hill, over dale / Adam Gorb. — Kenley : Maecenas Music, [199-?]
— 1 score (34 p.) ; 30 cm. — Millennium series for wind bands &
ensembles
For wind band. — Duration: ca. 6:00.
Publ. no. MC0039
System number: 013193107

Gorb, Adam, 1958-
Towards Nirvana : (2002) : for wind orchestra / Adam Gorb. — Kenley : Maecenas Music, c2002 — 1 score (76 p.) ; 30 cm. — International series for wind bands & ensembles
For wind band, with harp, piano, string bass and percussion. — Includes composer's programme note. — Duration: ca. 20:00.
Publ. no. MC0074
System number: 013422427

Grainer, Ron.
[Tales of the unexpected. Theme; arr.]
Tales of the unexpected : grade 1.5 / Ron Grainer ; arr. Rodney Newton. — Wind band set. — London : Studio Music, [2005?] — 1 score (11 p.) + 1 set of parts ; 30 cm. — (Simply classics)
Arr. for wind band. — Duration: 1:50.
ISMN M050066170 (set)
ISMN M050066187 (score)
System number: 013359115

Lloyd Webber, Andrew, 1948-
[Jesus Christ superstar. I don't know how to love him; arr.]
I don't know how to love him : grade 2 / Tim Rice & Andrew Lloyd Webber ; arr. Rob Wiffin. — Wind band set. — London Studio Music, [2005?], c1970. — 1 score (11 p.) + 1 set of parts ; 30 cm. — (Simply classics)
Arr. for wind band. — Duration: 2:25.
ISMN M050066262 (set)
ISMN M050066279 (score)
System number: 013376747

*Marshall, Christopher, 1956-
Aue! : for wind orchestra / Christopher Marshall. — Kenley : Maecenas Music, c2001. — 1 score (39 p.) ; 30 cm. — Millennium series for wind bands & ensembles
Duration: ca. 6:00-7:00. — Includes composer's notes.
Publ. no. MM0061
System number: 013422114

*McAlister, Clark.
Canovacci : [2002] : commedia for winds / Clark McAlister. — Kenley, UK : Maecenas, c2003. — 1 score (50 p.) ; 30 cm. — Millennium series for wind bands & ensembles
Includes program notes. — Duration: ca. 6:00-7:00.
Publ. no. MC0085
System number: 013422223

McNeff, Stephen.
Moving parts : (1991 rev. 2003) : for concert band / Stephen McNeff. — Kenley : Maecenas Music, c2003. — 1 score (51 p.) ; 30 cm. — Millennium series for wind bands & ensembles
Duration: ca. 10:00.
Publ. no. MC0075
System number: 013193087

McNeff, Stephen.
Rant! : [2002] : for concert band / Stephen McNeff. — Kenley : Maecenas Music, c2002. — 1 score (37 p.) ; 30 cm. — Millennium series for wind bands & ensembles
Duration: ca. 5:00.
Publ. no. MC0073
System number: 013192983

McNeff, Stephen.
Wasteland wind music 2 : (2001) : for concert band / Stephen McNeff. — Kenley : Maecenas Music, c2001. — 1 score (63 p.) ; 30 cm. — Millennium series for wind bands & ensembles
Includes compoer's note. — Duration: ca. 12:00.
Publ. no. MC0064
System number: 013193003

Men of Harlech : grade 1.5 / traditional ; arr. Rodney Newton. — Wind band set. — London : Studio Music, c2005. — 1 score (7 p.) + 1 set of parts ; 30 cm. — (Simply classics)
For wind band. — Duration: 1:50.
ISMN M050066149 (set)
ISMN M050066156 (score)
System number: 013359131

Parry, C. Hubert H. (Charles Hubert Hastings), 1848-1918.
[Jerusalem; arr.]
Jerusalem / Hubert Parry ; arranged for wind band by Rob Wiffin. — Wind band set. — London : Studio Music, c2005. — 1 score (7 p.) + 1 set of parts ; 30 cm. — Studio Music programme series
With optional vocal part.
ISMN M050065845 (score)
ISMN M050065838 (set)
System number: 013390607

Saint-Saëns, Camille, 1835-1921.
[Carnaval des animaux. Cygne; arr.]
The swan : from Carnival of the animals : grade 2 / Saint-Saëns ; arr. Darrol Barry. — Wind band set. — London : Studio Music, c2005. — 1 score (11 p.) + 1 set of parts ; 30 cm. — (Simply classics)
Arr. for wind band. — Duration: 2:10.
ISMN M050066385 (set)
ISMN M050066392 (score)
System number: 013359053

Townsend, Declan.
Dreamworld = Taidhreamh : [1994]/ Declan Townsend. — Kenley : Maecenas Music, c1999. — 1 score (29 p.) ; 30 cm. — Millennium series for wind bands & ensembles
For wind orchestra. — Composer's note preceding score. — Duration: 8:00.
Publ. no. MM0054
System number: 013192918

*Wengler, Marcel, 1946-
Versuche über einen Marsch : (1981 rev. '98) : for wind orchestra / Marcel Wengler. — Kenley : Maecenas Music, [2005?] — 1 score (86 p.) ; 30 cm. — International series for wind bands & ensembles
Duration: ca. 17:00.
Publ. no. MC0087
System number: 013422366

Whitten, Danny.
[I don't want to talk about it; arr.]
I don't want to talk about it : grade 1.5 / Danny Whitten ; arr. Kit Turnbull. — Wind band set. — London : Studio Music, [2005?], c1971. — 1 score (10 p.) + 1 set of parts ; 30 cm. — (Simply classics)
Arr. for wind band. — Duration: 2:20.
ISMN M050066088 (set)
ISMN M050066095 (score)
System number: 013359661

Wiffin, R. K. (Rob K.).
Here's a health / Rob Wiffin. — Wind band set. — London : Studio Music, c2004. — 1 score (21 p.) + 1 set of parts ; 30 cm. — Studio Music programme series
"A concert prelude based on an old English tune by Jeremy Savile"—Score cover. — For wind band. — Duration: 3:31.
ISMN M050062547 (set)
ISMN M050062554 (score)
System number: 013416628

Wiffin, R. K. (Rob K.).
The White Russian / Rob Wiffin. — Wind band set. — London : Studio Music, c2005. — 1 score (16 p.) + 1 set of parts ; 30 cm. — Studio Music programme series
For wind band.
ISMN M050064619 (score)
ISMN M050064602 (set)
System number: 013390561

*Wood, Gareth.
[Mexican pictures. Spanish]
Spanish picture : from Three Mexican pictures / Gareth Wood. — Score. — Kenley : Maecenas Music, [2005?] — 1 score (22 p.) ; 30 cm. — Millennium series for wind bands & ensembles
For band.
Publ. no. MC0091
System number: 013422274

784.81824
*Mozart, Wolfgang Amadeus, 1756-1791.
[Concertos, horn, orchestra, K. 495, E♭ major. Rondo; arr.]
Rondo from Horn concerto in E flat (K.495) : grade 3 / Mozart ; arr. Michael McDermott. — Wind band set. — London : Studio Music, c2005. — 1 score (27 p.) + 1 set of parts ; 30 cm. — (Simply classics)
Arr. for wind band. — Duration: 3:00.
ISMN M050066545 (score)
ISMN M050066538 (wind band set)
System number: 013390596

784.81858
*Binney, Malcolm.
Charivari / Malcolm Binney. — Full score. — Kenley : Maecenas Music, [199-], c1981. — 1 score (48 p.) ; 30 cm. — Millennium series for wind bands & ensembles
For wind band. — Duration: ca. 12:00. — Includes program notes.
Publ. no. MC0021
Publ. no. MB0021
System number: 013421618

Gorb, Adam, 1958-
Bridgewater breeze : [1996] / Adam Gorb. — Kenley : Maecenas Music, 1996. — 1 score (42 p.) ; 30 cm. — Millennium series for wind bands & ensembles
"This work is a transcription by the composer of his Suite for winds (MC0007)"—Prelim. — For wind band. — Items may be performed separately. — Duration: ca. 10:00.
Publ. no. MC0035
System number: 013193076

*Wood, Gareth.
Legends of the bear : for wind orchestra / Gareth Wood. — Kenley :
Maecenas Music, c2004. — 1 score (58 p.) ; 30 cm. — Millennium series
for wind bands & ensembles
Duration: ca. 18:00. — Includes composer's notes.
Publ. no. MC0088
System number: 013422589

784.8186

Martin, Frank, 1890-1974.
[Ouverture et foxtrot, pianos (2); *arr.*]
Concerto pour les instruments à vent et le piano (1924) / Frank Martin ;
edition realized by Bastiaan Blomhert. — Score. — Den Haag, The
Netherlands : Floricor Editions, c2004. — 1 score (iv, 60 p.) ; 30 cm.
For piccolo, flute, E♭ clarinet, B♭ clarinet, alto saxophone, 2 bassoons, 2
trumpets, trombone, bass trombone, timpani, percussion, and "honky-tonk" piano. —
Originally written as incidental music for a puppet theatre, arr. by the composer as a
concert work. — Duration: 10:00. — Pref. in English by Bastiaan Blomhert.
Pl. no. F.E. 0420 A
EAN M6940004000420
System number: 014406581

784.818835

Pezold, Christian, 1677-1733.
[Suites, harpsichord, G major. Menuet alternativement; *arr.*]
Minuet : from the Anna Magdalena notebook : grade 1 / J.S. Bach [or rather,
Christian Pezold] ; arr. Kit Turnbull. — Wind band set. — London : Studio
Music, c2005. — 1 score (7 p.) + 1 set of parts ; 30 cm. — (Simply classics)
Arr. for wind band. — Duration: 1:40.
ISMN M050065999 (set)
ISMN M050066002 (score)
System number: 013359647

784.818926

Binney, Malcolm.
Brasser : an overture / Malcolm Binney. — Kenley : Maecenas Music,
c1997. — Millennium series for wind bands & ensembles
For wind band. — "Written to mark the 125th anniversay of Marlborough College
Wind Orchestra, or 'Brasser' as it is known"—Pref. — Duration: ca. 5:00-6:00.
Publ. no. MC0038
System number: 013422221

Binney, Malcolm.
Overture Saturnalia / Malcolm Binney. — Kenley : Maecenas Music,
c1992. — 1 score (39 p.) ; 30 cm. — Millennium series for wind bands &
ensembles
"Saturnalia was commissioned by Alan Hutt and the Kent Youth Wind Orchestra and
was completed in the spring of 1992"—Pref. — Duration: ca. 6:30.
Publ. no. MC0025
System number: 013192992

784.81897

Binney, Malcolm.
London pageant : a British concert march for the millennium / Malcolm
Binney. — Kenley : Maecenas Music, c1999. — 1 score (26 p.) ; 30 cm. —
Millennium series for wind bands & ensembles
For wind band. — Duration: 7:00.
Publ. no. MM0051
System number: 013192902

Sparke, Philip.
Skyrider : [concert march] / by Philip Sparke. — Wind band set. —
London : Studio Music, c2005. — 1 score (15 p.) + 1 set of parts ; 30 cm. —
Studio Music prestige series
Arr. for wind band; originally for brass band.
ISMN M050078593 (score)
ISMN M050078586 (set)
System number: 013407857

784.82852

Debussy, Claude, 1862-1918.
[Rêverie (Piano work); *arr.*]
Rêverie / Debussy ; arranged for oboe solo and wind band by Rob Wiffin.
— Wind band set. — London : Studio Music, c2004. — 1 score (15 p.) + 1
set of parts ; 30 cm. — Studio Music programme series
ISMN M050064541 (set)
ISMN M050064558 (score)
System number: 013359017

784.82862186

*Grange, Philip.
[Concertos, clarinet, band]
Concerto Shēng Shēng Bù Shí : for solo clarinet radical & symphonic wind
band / Philip Grange. — Kenley : Maecenas Music, c2000. — 1 score
(114 p.) ; 30 cm. — International series for wind bands & ensembles
Duration: ca. 20:00. — Includes composer's notes.
Publ. no. MC0057
System number: 013422379

784.89

Gorb, Adam, 1958-
Battle symphony : for woodwind ensemble including saxophones / Adam
Gorb. — Kenley : Maecenas Music, c1999. — 1 score (65 p.) ; 30 cm. —
Millennium series for wind bands & ensembles
"Op.26 (1997)"—Prelim. — For woodwind "ensembles of quite a wide size
range, form one player per part to significantly larger groups."—Prelim. —
Duration: 10:00.
Publ. no. MC0053
System number: 013193057
Also classified at 785.8199

784.9 – BRASS BAND

784.9

Fanshawe, David, 1942-
[African Sanctus (Musical work). Lord's prayer; *arr.*]
The Lord's prayer : from African sanctus / vocal arrangement by the
composer, David Fanshawe ; brass band arrangement by Liz Lane. —
Brass band set. — London : Studio Music, [2005?], c1974. — 1 score
(28 p.) + 1 set of parts ; 30 cm.
1st version for brass band; 2nd version for brass band with solo voice(s) and/or
SATB chorus. — Instrumental parts only; score includes vocal lines for 2nd
version.
ISMN M050065968 (set)
ISMN M050065975 (score)
System number: 013382672
Also classified at 782.525

Richards, Goff.
Mythic Trevithick! / by Goff Richards. — London : Studio Music, c2004.
— 1 score (23 p.) + 1 set of parts ; 30 cm.
For brass band. — Composed in 2001 to mark the 200th anniversary of Richard
Trevithick's first journey in his steam locomotive.
ISMN M050063384 (set)
ISMN M050063391 (score)
System number: 013190979

784.91858

Walker, Robert, 1946-
A South Yorkshire suite / Robert Walker. — Kenley : Maecenas Music,
c2004. — 1 score (62 p.) ; 30 cm. — Maecenas brass
For brass band.
System number: 013193564

784.928971723

A Christmas lullaby / arranged for flugel horn and brass band by Darrol
Barry. — London : Studio Music, c2005. — 1 score (8 p.) + 27 parts ;
30 cm.
Arr. of the traditional Czech Rocking carol.
ISMN M050078203 (score)
ISMN M050078197 (set)
System number: 013376806

784.928975

Mozart, Wolfgang Amadeus, 1756-1791.
[Ave verum corpus; *arr.*]
Ave verum corpus / Mozart ; arranged for four euphoniums and brass
band by Philip Sparke. — London : Studio Music, c2005. — 1 score
(7 p.) + 17 parts ; 30 cm.
"All cornets and percussion - tacet"—Back cover.
ISMN M050078470 (set)
ISMN M050078487 (score)
System number: 013376831

785 – CHAMBER MUSIC

785

*Cunliffe, Simon.
Blueberry blues / Simon Cunliffe. — Laggan Bridge : Spartan Press,
c2005. — 1 score (8 p.) + 1 set of parts ; 31 cm. — (Flexible little
big-band series)
For 3-part ensemble plus piano/keyboard, bass and drums. — Includes parts in C,
B♭ and E♭. — Approximate grading 2-6"—Cover. — Includes biographical note.
Pl. no. SP762
ISMN M579997627
System number: 013516041

*Cunliffe, Simon.
Let's rumba / Simon Cunliffe. — Laggan Bridge : Spartan Press, c2005.
— 1 score (12 p.) + 1 set of parts ; 31 cm. — (Flexible little big-band
series)
For 3-part ensemble plus piano/keyboard, bass and drums. — Includes parts in C,
B♭ and E♭. — Approximate grading 2-6"—Cover. — Includes biographical note.
— Cover title.
Pl. no. SP761
ISMN M579997610

System number: 013516079

Rheinberger, Josef, 1839-1901.
[Chamber music. *Selections*]
Kammermusik V / [Josef Gabriel Rheinberger] ; vorgelegt von Astrid
Bauer. — Stuttgart : Carus-Verlag, 2007. — 1 score (xxii, 160 p.) :
facsims. ; 33 cm. — (Sämtliche Werke / Josef Gabriel Rheinberger ; Bd. 33)
Works for solo instruments and organ. First two pieces originally for solo organ. —
Pref. in German, English, and French; critical report in German.
Publ. no. 50.233
Publ. no. CV 50.233
ISBN 9783899480320
System number: 013949572

*Vierdanck, Johann, ca. 1605-1646.
[Capricci, Canzoni und Sonaten]
Capricci, Canzoni und Sonaten : [mit 2, 3, 4 und 5 Instrumenten ohne und
mit dem Basso continuo], Rostock 1641 / Johann Vierdanck ; trascrizione a
cura di Alessandro Bares. — Albese con Cassano : Musedita ; Stuttgart :
Cornetto, gedruckt in Lizenz von Musedita, c1999. — 1 score (2 v.) +
6 parts ; 30 cm.
Figured bass not realized. — Editorial notes in Italian, English and French.
Publ. no. CM535
ISMN M501005062
System number: 014599831

785.13

*Haydn, Joseph, 1732-1809.
[Divertimenti, H. IV, 1-11.]
Trios für Blas- und Streichinstrumente / Joseph Haydn ; herausgegeben von
Andreas Friesenhagen. — München : G. Henle, 2004. — 1 score (xii,
96 p.) : facsims. ; 33 cm. — (Werke / Joseph Haydn ; Reihe 9)
"Herausgegeben vom Joseph Haydn-Institut, Köln"—Series t.p. — Editorial notes in
German on preliminary pages; kritischer Bericht in German on p. 78-96. — Includes
thematic index.
System number: 014730851

785.14

Cavaccio, Giovanni, ca. 1556-1626.
[Music, voices (4)]
Musica a quattro voci : Venezia 1597 / Giovanni Cavaccio ; a cura di
Daniele Salvatore. — Bologna : Ut Orpheus, c2004. — 1 score (vi, 70 p.) ;
30 cm. — Ricercare capriccio fantasia ; 19A
Includes two works with Italian texts underlaid; words also printed for reference. —
Pref. in Italian.
Pl. no. RCF 19A
ISMN M215309296
System number: 014167958

785.151882

*Praetorius, Bartholomeus, ca. 1590-1623.
[Newe liebliche Paduanen und Galliarden]
Pavans and galliards in five parts = Newe liebliche Paduanen und
Galliarden mit fünff Stimmen, 1616 / Bartholomeus Praetorius ;
[Bearbeitung und Herausgabe, Richard Carter] — Stuttgart : Cornetto,
Lizenzausgabe von Oriana, c2005. — 1 score (v, 31 p.) + 5 parts ; 30 cm.
Cover title. — For 5 unspecified Renaissance instruments. — Preface, biographical
notes and critical report in English and German.
Publ. no. COM582
ISMN M501005536
System number: 014629729

785.2 – ENSEMBLES WITH KEYBOARD

785.22183

*Schmelzer, Johann Heinrich, ca. 1623-1680.
Sacro-profanus concentus musicus : fidium aliorumque instrumentorum : 13
sonate a 2, 4, 5, 6, 7, e 8 strumenti, Nürnberg, 1662 / Johann Heinrich
Schmelzer ; a cura di Alessandro Bares. — Albese con Cassano, Italia :
Musedita ; Stuttgart : Gedruckt in Lizenz von Cornetto-Verlag, c2003. — 1
score (2 v.) + 12 parts ; 30 cm.
Variously for violins, violas, cornetti, trumpets, trombones and continuo. — Figured
bass not realized. — Pref. in Italian, English and French.
Publ. no. CM528
ISMN M501004997
System number: 014766573

785.22195

*Vaughan Williams, Ralph, 1872-1958.
[Quintets, piano, clarinet, horn, violin, violoncello, D major]
Quintet in D major (1898), for clarinet, horn, violin, cello and piano / Ralph
Vaughan Williams. — Piano score and parts. — London : Faber Music,
2002. — 1 score (82 p.) + 4 parts ; 32 cm. — (The early works / Ralph
Vaughan Williams)
Prepared for publication by Bernard Benoliel, from the autograph manuscript held in
the British Library. — Includes editorial note.
ISBN 0571519830
System number: 013126445

785.22196

Routh, Francis.
[Concertos, instrumental ensemble, no. 3, op. 55]
Concerto for ensemble III : op. 55 (1991) / Francis Routh. — Full score.
— London : Redcliffe Edition, [2004?] — 1 score (35 p.) ; 42 cm.
For clarinet, horn, piano, violin, viola and violoncello.
ISMN M708045601
System number: 013176186

Routh, Francis.
[Concertos, instrumental ensemble, no. 4, op. 67]
Concerto for ensemble IV : suite for Tblisi : op. 67 (1997/2002) / Francis
Routh. — Full score. — London : Redcliffe Edition, [2004?], c2002. — 1
score (32 p.) ; 42 cm.
For clarinet, trumpet, piano, violin, viola and violoncello.
ISMN M708045670
System number: 013176282

785.22197

*Ziani, Pietro Andrea, 1616-1684.
[Sonatas, trumpet, strings, continuo, D major]
Sonata à 6 für Trompete, 2 Violinen, 3 Violen & B.c. / Pietro Andrea
Ziani ; [herausgegeben von] Konrad Ruhland. — Erstausg. —
Magdeburg : Edition Walhall, c2005. — 1 score (10 p.) + 8 parts ; 30 cm.
— (Collection Monarca della tromba : Musik der Fürstenhöfe)
Based on a ms. at the Christ Church Library in Oxford: SONATA Con V-V e
Tromba à 6 (shelfmark Mus. 711). — Here attributed to Ziani; Grove gives
probable attribution to Tomaso Albinoni. — Pref. in German and English.
Pl. no. EW 511
System number: 014629801

785.22198

*St.-Lubin, Léon de.
[Octet, op. 33, E minor]
Grand octetto op. 33 : for flute, clarinet in A, horn in E, D & G (part in F
included), bassoon, viola, cello, double bass and piano / by Léon de
Saint-Lubin ; [edited by Chris & Frances Nex] — Lancaster :
Phylloscopus Publications, c2005. — 1 score (95 p.) + 8 parts ; 30 cm.
Publ. no. PP565
ISMN M570166978
System number: 013561009

785.22199

Turnage, Mark-Anthony.
Eulogy : for solo viola and eight instruments / Mark-Anthony Turnage.
— London : Boosey & Hawkes, 2005. — 1 score (40 p.) ; 19 cm.
Accompanying ensemble: cor anglais, clarinet in B♭, horn in F, piano, harp, violin,
violoncello, double bass.
Pl. no. 13739
Publ. no. HPS 1384
ISMN M060116735
System number: 013213736

785.24193

Andre, Mark, 1964-
—als— I : für Bassklarinette, Violoncello und Klavier, 2001 / Mark
André. — Studienpartitur. — München : Ricordi, c2004. — 1 score
(52 p.) ; 30 cm.
Includes graphic notation. — Performance notes in French and German.
Publ. no. Sy. 3630/08
ISMN M204236305
System number: 013771071

Lewis, Paul, 1943-
Spring suite : flute, optional 'cello and piano or harmonica and piano /
Paul Lewis. — Dover : Broadbent & Dunn, c2003. — 1 score (20 p.) +
2 parts ; 30 cm.
Pl. no. B&D 13205
System number: 013374699
Primary classification 788.321858

785.24194

*Buchner, Philipp Friedrich, 1614-1669.
Harmonia instrumentalis : 12 sonate per 2 violini, fagotto e basso
continuo, op. 5, Würzburg 1664 / Philipp Friedrich Buchner ; trascrizione
a cura di Alessandro Bares. — [Albese con Cassano] : Musedita ;
Stuttgart : Cornetto, gedruckt in Lizenz von Musedita, c2004. — 1 score
(48 p.) + 4 parts ; 30 cm.
For 2 violins, bassoon and continuo. — Figured bass not realized.
Publ. no. CM692
ISMN M501006618
System number: 014599810

Carbonell i Saurí, Albert, 1972-
Seqüències : sis petites peces per a clarinet, violí, violoncel i piano /
Albert Carbonell i Saurí. — Valencia : Institució Alfons el Magnànim :
Piles, 2004. — 1 score (29 p.) + 3 parts ; 31 cm. — Col·lecció partitures ;
6
ISMN M801210029
System number: 014457010

785.2419418885

Waterhouse, Graham, 1962-
Tango Toulouse : for violin, clarinet in B♭, violoncello and piano = für Violine, Klarinette in B, Violoncello und Klavier / Graham Waterhouse. — Leipzig : Hofmeister, c2007. — 1 score (12 p.) + 3 parts ; 30 cm.
Preface and biographical notes in English and German.
Pl. no. FH 3224
ISMN M203432241
System number: 013953490

785.24195

***Cooke, Arnold.**
[Divertimenti, piano, flute, oboe, violin, violoncello]
Divertimento for flute, oboe, violin, cello and piano / Arnold Cooke. — Altamonte Springs, FL : Anglo-American Music Publishers, 2005, c1989. — 1 score (74 p.) + 4 parts ; 28 cm.
Cover title. — Includes biographical note.
System number: 013593668

785.24196

Routh, Francis.
[Concertos, instrumental ensemble, no. 1, op. 41]
Concerto for ensemble I : op. 41 (1981) / Francis Routh. — Full score. — London : Redcliffe Edition, [2004?] — 1 score (38 p.) ; 42 cm.
For clarinet, guitar, piano, violin, viola and violoncello.
ISMN M708045496
System number: 013176131

Routh, Francis.
[Concertos, instrumental ensemble, no. 2, op. 44]
Concerto for ensemble II : op. 44 (1983) / Francis Routh. — Full score. — London : Redcliffe Edition, [2004?] — 1 score (52 p.) ; 42 cm.
For clarinet, guitar, piano, violin, viola and violoncello.
ISMN M708045533
System number: 013176159

785.25193

Brouwer, Leo, 1939-
Pictures at another exhibition : for horn, violin and piano / Leo Brouwer. — London : Chester Music, c2004. — 1 score (6 v.) + 2 parts (6 v.) ; 30 cm.
The movements may be performed in any order.
Publ. no. CH67452
ISBN 184449926X
System number: 013182227

Ganassi, Giacomo, fl. 1625-1637.
[Vespertina psalmodia (1637) Selections]
13 canzoni strumentali a due e a quattro strumenti con il basso per l'organo : estratte da: Vespertina psalmodia in totius anni solemnitates— : Venezia, 1637 / Giacomo Ganassi ; trascrizione a cura di Alessandro Bares. — Albese con Cassano : Musedita ; Stuttgart : Cornetto, gedruckt in Lizenz von Musedita, c2005. — 1 score (2 v.) + 5 parts ; 30 cm.
For 2 (violin and trombone, or, violin and viola) or 4 instruments and continuo. — Edited from 5 part-books, preserved in the Biblioteka Universytezka, Wroclaw. — Prefatory remarks in Italian, English and French.
Publ. no. CM 508
ISMN M501004799
System number: 013688132
Also classified at 785.28193

785.25199183

***Dolar, Janez Krstnik, ca. 1620-1673.**
[Sonatas, trumpet, instrumental ensemble, C major]
Sonata à 10 : (Natur-) Trompete C/B, 3 Posaunen, 2 Violinen, 3 Violen, Violoncello, Orgel (Cembalo) / Johannes Babtist Tolar ; edited & arranged by Wolfgang G. Haas. — Köln : W.G. Haas-Musikverlag, c2004. — 1 score (23 p.) ; 30 cm. — (Tschechische Barockmusik = Czech Baroque Music ; Nr. 74)
Original 4th viola part given here for violoncello. — Figured bass realized for organ or harpsichord by the editor. "Europäische Musik: Tschechien, Kremsler"— Cover. — Duration: 6:50. — Includes critical notes in German.
ISMN M205405458
System number: 014629766

785.26193

Barton, David, 1983-
[Pieces, piano, flutes (2) (2004)]
Two pieces for flute duet and piano / David Barton. — Manchester : Da Capo Music, c2005. — 1 score (8 p.) ; 30 cm.
Includes programme and biographical notes.
Pl. no. DC 631
System number: 013351600

Finnissy, Michael.
Keroiylu : oboe, bassoon and piano = Oboe, Fagott und Klavier, 1981 / Michael Finnissy. — Karlsruhe : Tre Media, c2007. — 1 score (14 p.) ; 30 x 42 cm.
Reproduced from holograph. — Duration: ca. 8:00. — Performance notes in English.
Pl. no. TM 864 E
ISMN M500015383
System number: 013771082

785.26194

Stulick, Matthäus Nikolaus.
[Concertino, woodwinds, continuo, B♭ major]
Concertino a 4 stromenti, für Oboe, Klarinette (B), Fagott und Basso continuo = Concertino a 4 stromenti, for oboe, clarinet (B♭), bassoon and basso continuo / Matthäus Nicolaus Stulick ; herausgegeben von Hans-Peter Vogel. — Erstdruck = 1st ed. — Planegg : Thomi-Berg, c2007. — 1 score (26 p.) + 4 parts ; 30 cm. — Werkreihe für Bläser
Based on a ms. set of parts from the Universitätsbibliothek Rostock. — Unfigured bass realized for harpsichord. — Pref. in German and English.
Pl. no. TB 967
ISMN M202300671
System number: 014053369

785.261951858

Cowles, Colin, .
[Suites, harpsichord, saxophones (4)]
Suite for harpsichord and saxophone quartet / by Colin Cowles. — Laggan Bridge : Spartan Press, c2004. — 1 score (63 p.) + 4 parts ; 30 cm.
Pl. no. SP750
ISMN M579997504
System number: 013169102

785.281723

Pott, Francis, 1957-
Lullay, my liking : for SATB chorus / Francis Pott. — London : Novello, c2005. — 1 score (16 p.) ; 25 cm.
Includes keyboard reduction for rehearsal only. — Anonymous 15th century words also printed for reference preceding score.
Publ. no. NOV161293
System number: 013313841

Sutton, Tim, composer.
Quittez, pasteurs : for SATB chorus and organ / Tim Sutton. — London : Novello, c2005. — 1 score (14 p.) ; 25 cm.
French words; also printed for reference preceding score.
Publ. no. NOV161282
System number: 013313838

785.28193

***Andrée, Elfrida, 1841-1929.**
[Trios, piano, strings, C minor]
Two chamber works / Elfrida Andrée ; edited by Katherine L. Axtell. — Middleton, Wis. : A-R Editions, c2004. — 1 score (xv, 121 p., 5 p. of plates) : facsims. ; 31 cm. + 5 parts ; 28 cm. — (Recent researches in the music of the nineteenth and early twentieth centuries, 0193-5364 ; 40)
Edited from mss. in the Statens musikbibliotek, Stockholm. — Includes introd. and critical report.
ISBN 0895795566
EAN 9780895795564
System number: 014746024
Also classified at 785.28194

[Beggar's opera. *Selections; arr.*]
Six songs from John Gay's The beggar's opera / arranged for piano trio by Nancy O'Neill Breth and Jean Goberman ; edited by J. Mark Baker. — Milwaukee, Wis. : Hal Leonard, c2005. — 1 score (32 p.) + 2 parts ; 31 cm. + 1 compact disc. — Hal Leonard student piano library. Beginning chamber music
"Early intermediate level"—T.p. — Pref. contains advice on setting up chamber music groups. — CD contains demonstration tracks.
Publ. no. HL00296585
ISBN 0634096265
System number: 013220496

Davies, Peter Maxwell, 1934-
[Trio, piano, strings]
Piano trio : a voyage to Fair Isle : for violin, cello and piano / Peter Maxwell Davies. — London : Chester Music, c2005. — 1 score (35 p.) + 2 parts ; 30 cm.
Includes composer's note.
Publ. no. CH66264
ISBN 1846091187
System number: 013346047

Ganassi, Giacomo, fl. 1625-1637.
[Vespertina psalmodia (1637) Selections]
13 canzoni strumentali a due e a quattro strumenti con il basso per l'organo : estratte da: Vespertina psalmodia in totius anni solemnitates— : Venezia, 1637 / Giacomo Ganassi ; trascrizione a cura di Alessandro Bares. — Albese con Cassano : Musedita ; Stuttgart : Cornetto, gedruckt in Lizenz von Musedita, c2005. — 1 score (2 v.) + 5 parts ; 30 cm.
For 2 (violin and trombone, or, violin and viola) or 4 instruments and continuo. — Edited from 5 part-books, preserved in the Biblioteka Universytezka, Wroclaw. — Prefatory remarks in Italian, English and French.
Publ. no. CM 508
ISMN M501004799
System number: 013688132
Primary classification 785.25193

*Larsen, Libby.
[Trios, piano, strings]
Trio for violin, cello and piano / Libby Larsen. — [New York] : Oxford University Press, c2004. — 1 score (24 p.) + 2 parts ; 31 cm. — Oxford chamber music
Includes biographical note. — Duration: 19:00.
ISBN 0193866951
System number: 013324497

Mozart, Wolfgang Amadeus, 1756-1791.
[Sinfonie concertanti, violin, viola, orchestra, K. 364, E♭ major; *arr.*]
Sinfonia concertante für Violine, Viola und Orchester, Es-dur, KV 364 = Sinfonia concertante in E♭ major for violin, viola and orchestra, K. 364 / Wolfgang Amadeus Mozart ; herausgegeben von Wolf-Dieter Seiffert ; Klavierauszug von Siegfried Petrenz ; Fingersatz und Strichbezeichnung von Frank Peter Zimmermann [und] Tabea Zimmermann ; piano reduction. — München : G. Henle ; Wiesbaden : Breitkopf & Härtel, 2006. — 1 score (59 p.) + 3 parts ; 31 cm.
Acc. arr. for piano. — Includes edited and unedited parts for viola. — "Urtext." — Pref. in German, English and French ; critical comments in German and English.
Publ. no. HN 798
Publ. no. EB 10798
ISMN M201807980
System number: 013945442

Thistle & minuet : 16 easy pieces from the Scottish Baroque for violin (or flute or oboe), keyboard, and optional cello (or bassoon) = 16 einfache Stücke aus der schottischen Barockzeit für Violine (oder Flöte oder Oboe), Tasteninstrument und Cello (oder Fagott) ad libitum = 16 pièces faciles du Baroque écossais pour violon (ou flûte ou hautbois), clavier et violoncelle (ou basson) facultatif / edited by David Johnson. — London : Schott, c2005. — 1 score (32 p.) + 2 parts ; 31 cm + 1 sound disc (digital ; 4 3/4 in.) — Baroque around the world
Some pieces have an optional part for a second melody instrument. — Pref., biographical and historical notes in English, French and German. — CD contains full demonstrations and backing tracks.
Publ. no. ED 12773
ISBN 1902455193
ISMN M220122965
System number: 013192325
Primary classification 787.2

Ward, John, 1571-1638.
[Chamber music. *Selections*]
Consort music of four parts / John Ward ; transcribed and edited by Ian Payne. — London : Stainer and Bell, 2005. — 1 score (xxxviii, 106 p.) : facsims. ; 34 cm. — Musica Britannica ; 83
Fantasias and In nomines for 4 viols, and 6 ayres for 2 bass viols and organ. — Edited from Bibliothèque nationale de France, Fonds du Conservatoire, MS Réserve F.770 (In nomines and "Paris" fantasias), and other sources. — "Published for the Musica Britannica Trust established by the Royal Musical Association." — Pref. in English, French and German; introduction and critical commentary in English only.
ISBN 0852498853
ISMN M220221323
System number: 013216320
Primary classification 785.76194

Ward, John, 1571-1638.
[Fantasias, viols (4), Meyer 1-6. *Parts*]
Oxford fantasias : and, two-part ayres : for viols and organ / John Ward ; edited by Ian Payne. — London : Stainer & Bell, c2005. — 7 parts ; 30 cm.
"Set for four string parts for the Oxford fantasias corresponding with Musica Britannica, volume LXXXIII, 21-26, and two bass viol and organ parts for the ayres corresponding with Musica Britannica, volume LXXXIII, 27-32"—Cover.
Publ. no. AC221
ISMN M220221484
System number: 013307456
Primary classification 785.761941876

*Warshauer, Meira, 1949-
Aecha = Lamentations : for violin, cello and piano / Meira Warshauer. — [New York] : Oxford University Press, c2004. — 1 score (20 p.) + 2 parts ; 31 cm. — Oxford chamber music
Includes composer's and biographical notes.
ISBN 0193866854
System number: 013062978

Ye, Xiaogang.
Colorful sutra banner : for piano trio, opus 58 (2006) / Xiaogang Ye. — Mainz : Schott, c2006. — 1 score (28 p.) + 2 parts ; 31 cm.
Title also in Chinese. — Pref. in English and Chinese.
Publ. no. ED 20178
ISMN M001147262
System number: 013953491

785.28193183
*Philarmonica, Mrs.
[Sonatas, violins (2), violoncello, continuo]
12 Triosonaten für 2 Violinen und B.c. (1715) = 12 trio sonatas for 2 violins and b.c. (1715) / by Mrs. Philarmonica ; edited by Elke Martha Umbach. — Kassel : Furore Verlag, c2004. — 1 score (2 v.) + 4 parts (2 v.) ; 30 cm.
Edited from a score in the British Library (shelfmark g.1032.). — Figured bass unrealized. — Includes separate parts for violoncello and basso continuo. — Pref. in German and English; critical matter in German.
Publ. no. fue 448
Publ. no. fue 449

Publ. no. 448
Publ. no. 449
Pl. no. fue-Nr. 448
Pl. no. fue-Nr. 449
ISMN M500129486
ISMN M500129493
System number: 013031307
Primary classification 785.28194183

*Schmelzer, Johann Heinrich, ca. 1623-1680.
[Trio sonatas, violin, viola da gamba, continuo, D minor]
Sonata â due für Violine, Viola da gamba & B.c. / Johann Heinrich Schmelzer ; herausgegeben von Christian Zincke. — Erstausg. — Magdeburg : Edition Walhall, c2004. — 1 score (7 p.) + 3 parts (2 p. each) ; 30 cm. — (Musik für Viola da gamba / herausgegeben von Konrad Ruhland)
Trio sonata for violin, viola da gamba, and continuo; figured bass unrealized. — Introductory notes in German and English by Konrad Ruhland.
Publ. no. EW 487
System number: 014766574

785.28194
*Andrée, Elfrida, 1841-1929.
[Trios, piano, strings, C minor]
Two chamber works / Elfrida Andrée ; edited by Katherine L. Axtell. — Middleton, Wis. : A-R Editions, c2004. — 1 score (xv, 121 p., 5 p. of plates) : facsims. ; 31 cm. + 5 parts ; 28 cm. — (Recent researches in the music of the nineteenth and early twentieth centuries, 0193-5364 ; 40)
Edited from mss. in the Statens musikbibliotek, Stockholm. — Includes introd. and critical report.
ISBN 0895795566
EAN 9780895795564
System number: 014746024
Primary classification 785.28193

*Sculthorpe, Peter, 1929-
[From Nourlangie; *arr.*]
From Nourlangie : for piano quartet / Peter Sculthorpe. — [London] : Faber Music, c1993. — 1 score (7 p.) ; 30 cm. + 4 parts ; 36 cm.
Originally for string quartet. — Reproduced from ms.
System number: 006917878

Telemann, Georg Philipp, 1681-1767.
[Concertos, violins (2), viola, continuo, TWV 43:G8, G major]
Concerto in G-Dur für 2 Violinen, Viola und Basso continuo = Concerto in G major for 2 violins, viola and basso continuo, TWV 43:G8 / Georg Philipp Telemann ; herausgegeben von Bernhard Päuler ; Continuo-Aussetzung von Wolfgang Kostujak. — Erstdruck. — Winterthur : Amadeus, 2006. — 1 score (15 p.) + 4 parts ; 31 cm. — Aurea Amadeus ; Nr. 237
First edition based on a manuscript (Mus. ms. 1033/90) kept in the Hessische Landes- und Hochschulbibliothek, Darmstadt. — Unfigured bass realized for keyboard instrument. — Pref. in German and English.
Publ. no. BP 1990
System number: 013953485

*Torelli, Giuseppe, 1658-1709.
[Concerto da camera]
Concerto da camera per due violini, violone e clavicembalo, op. 2 : Bologna, 1686 / Giuseppe Torelli ; trascizione a cura di Pasquale Spiniello. — Albese con Cassano : Musedita ; Stuttgart : Cornetto, gedruckt in Lizenz von Musedita, c2005. — 1 score (50 p.) + 4 parts ; 30 cm.
For 2 violins, violone and harpsichord. — Figured bass not realized.
Publ. no. CM709
ISMN M501006786
System number: 014456961

785.281941
*Samuel, Rhian.
[Light and water]
Quartet : light and water : for piano and strings / Rhian Samuel. — London : Stainer & Bell, c2003. — 1 score (33 p.) + 3 parts ; 30 cm.
For violin, viola, violoncello and piano. — Includes programme note.
Publ. no. AC211
ISMN M220221217
System number: 013050614

785.28194183
*Philarmonica, Mrs.
[Sonatas, violins (2), violoncello, continuo]
12 Triosonaten für 2 Violinen und B.c. (1715) = 12 trio sonatas for 2 violins and b.c. (1715) / by Mrs. Philarmonica ; edited by Elke Martha Umbach. — Kassel : Furore Verlag, c2004. — 1 score (2 v.) + 4 parts (2 v.) ; 30 cm.
Edited from a score in the British Library (shelfmark g.1032.). — Figured bass unrealized. — Includes separate parts for violoncello and basso continuo. — Pref. in German and English; critical matter in German.
Publ. no. fue 448
Publ. no. fue 449
Publ. no. 448
Publ. no. 449
Pl. no. fue-Nr. 448
Pl. no. fue-Nr. 449
ISMN M500129486

ISMN M500129493
System number: 013031307
Also classified at 785.28193183

785.281941858

*Schmelzer, Johann Heinrich, ca. 1623-1680.
[Ballets. *Selections*]
Balletti à 4 für 2 Violinen, Violetta (Viola), Violone & B.c. / Johann
Heinrich Schmelzer. — Erstausg. — Magdeburg, Germany : Edition
Walhall, c2004. — 1 score (21 p.) : ill. ; 30 cm. — (Musica speciosa /
herausgegeben von Konrad Ruhland)
Suites of dance music selected from ballet interludes composed for other composers'
operas; for 2 violins, viola, and continuo (harpsichord and violone). — Figured bass
unrealized. — Includes pref. in German by Konrad Ruhland with English translation.
Pl. no. EW 365
System number: 014766568

785.28195

Onslow, Georges, 1784-1853.
[Quintets, piano, violin, viola, violoncello, double bass, op. 70, B minor]
Quintet in B minor, opus 70 : for piano, violin, viola, cello & double
bass/cello / George Onslow. — Cambridge : SJ Music, c2005. — 1 score
(83 p.) + 5 parts ; 30 cm. — Chamber music series (Cambridge, England)
Cover title. — Includes alternative parts for double bass and cello II. — "This
edition … was transcribed from a 19th century edition. Minor editing, mainly
harmonization of the phrasing and occasional correction of accidentals, has been
carried out" - note on back cover.
Pl. no. SJ Q2005-2
ISMN M708807797
System number: 013394887

*Vaughan Williams, Ralph, 1872-1958.
[Quintets, piano, violin, viola, violoncello, double bass, C minor]
Piano quintet in C minor (1903), for violin, viola, cello, double bass and
piano / Ralph Vaughan Williams. — Piano score and parts. — London :
Faber Music, c2002. — 1 score (80 p.) + 4 parts ; 32 cm. — (The early
works / Ralph Vaughan Williams)
Prepared for publication by Bernard Benoliel, from the autograph manuscript held in
the British Library. — Introductory note by Michael Kennedy. — Includes editorial
note. — Duration: ca. 30:00.
ISBN 0571519539
System number: 013126521

785.281951858

*Jenkins, John, 1592-1678.
[Fantasia-suites, organ, viols (4). *Selections*]
Fantasia-suites : for two trebles (violins), two basses (viols) and organ /
John Jenkins ; edited by Andrew Ashbee. — London : Stainer & Bell,
c2005. — 4 parts ; 30 cm.
"Set of four string parts corresponding with Musica Britannica, Volume XXVI,
33-40, and for use in conjunction with the organ part printed in that
volume"—Cover. — Includes editorial note.
Publ. no. AC218
ISMN M220221347
System number: 013182170

*Schmelzer, Johann Heinrich, ca. 1623-1680.
[Ballets. *Selections*]
Balletti à 5 für 2 Violinen, 3 Violen & B.c. / Johann Heinrich Schmelzer. —
Erstausg. — Magdeburg : Edition Walhall, c2004. — 1 score (19 p.) +
1 part ; 30 cm. — (Musica speciosa / herausgegeben von Konrad Ruhland)
Suites of dance music from ballets, selected from opera interludes; for 2 violins, 2
violas (or viols), and continuo (harpsichord and violoncello or viola da gamba). —
Figured bass unrealized. — From sources in the Archiepiscopal Music Archive in
Kremsier. — Includes pref. in German with English translation. — Viola II line is in
tenor clef in the score, alto clef in the part.
Pl. no. EW 366
System number: 014766569

785.2819518885

Bayliss, Colin.
Anglo tango : for tango band : (violin, double bass, guitar, bandoneon and
piano) : [B126] / Colin Bayliss. — Manchester : Da Capo Music, c2003. —
1 score (12 p.) ; 30 cm.
Duration: ca. 5:00. — Includes biographical and programme notes.
Pl. no. DC 576
System number: 013351688

785.28196

*Schmelzer, Johann Heinrich, ca. 1623-1680.
[Sonatas, violins (2), viols (3), continuo, (1676)]
Duae sonatae a 5 für 2 Violinen, 3 Violen & B.c. / Johann Heinrich
Schmelzer. — Erstausg. — Magdeburg : Walhall, c2004. — 1 score (10 p.)
+ 7 parts ; 30 cm. — Musica speciosa
For 2 violins, 2 viols/violas, viola da gamba, and continuo. — Edited from ms. in the
Archiepiscopal Music Archive Kremsier (shelfmark: Br.IV/91 = A 537 = SP 611). —
Pref. in German and English. — Figured bass unrealized.
Pl. no. EW 472
System number: 014766570

785.2998193

Globokar, Vinko, 1934-
Métamorphoses parallèles : für Viola, Klavier und Live-Elektronik, 2005
/ Vinko Globokar. — Studienpartitur. — München : Ricordi, c2005. — 1
score (20 p.) ; 21 x 30 cm.
Reproduced from holograph. — Performance notes in German and French.
Pl. no. Sy. 3160/08
ISMN M204231607
System number: 013771088

785.3 – ENSEMBLES WITHOUT ELECTROPHONES AND WITH PERCUSSION AND KEYBOARD

785.32199

Gorb, Adam, 1958-
Weimar : (2000) : for large ensemble / Adam Gorb. — Kenley :
Maecenas Music, [2005?] — 1 score (95 p.) ; 30 cm.
For flute/piccolo, oboe, 2 clarinets, tenor saxophone, bassoon, horn, trumpet,
trombone, percussion kit, piano, harp, 2 wordless sopranos (1 plays whistle, 2
plays tambourine and rattle), 2 violins, viola, cello, double bass. — "Although the
work is performable with solo strings, the composer much prefers that a larger
body be used". — Duration: ca. 18:00.
System number: 013422553
Also classified at 783.12

*Harrison, Sadie, 1965-
Architechtonia : for solo violoncello and ensemble / Sadie Harrison. —
York : University of York Music Press, c2002. — 1 score (32 p.) ; 21 x
30 cm.
For solo cello, flute/piccolo, oboe, clarinet in B flat/bass clarinet, bassoon, horn in
F, trumpet in C, bass trombone, percussion (2 players), piano, mandolin, 2 violins,
viola and double bass. — Reproduced from holograph.
ISMN M570201518
System number: 013433162

Lindberg, Magnus, 1958-
Corrente : for chamber ensemble : 1992 / Magnus Lindberg. — London :
Chester Music, c2005. — 1 score (iv, 65 p.) ; 31 cm.
For flute/alto flute, oboe/cor anglais, clarinet in Bb, bassoon, 2 horns in F, trumpet
in C, trombone, percussion, harp, piano, 2 violins, viola, 'cello, double bass. —
Includes programme note.
Publ. no. CH67683
ISBN 1846090792
System number: 013222829

*Woolrich, John.
From the shadows : five pieces for chamber ensemble of eleven players
(1994) / John Woolrich. — London : Faber Music, [2005?] c1994. — 1
score (34 p.) ; 30 cm.
For flute/piccolo/alto flute, clarinet in Bb/clarinet in Eb/bass clarinet, soprano
saxophone, horn, trumpet, percussion (1 player), violin, viola, violoncello and
double bass. — Reproduced from holograph. — Duration: 7:00.
ISBN 0571554695
System number: 013243713

785.321991858

*Gorb, Adam, 1958-
Elements : (1998) : suite for solo percussion and wind ensemble / Adam
Gorb. — Kenley : Maecenas Music, [2005?] — 1 score (133 p.) ; 30 cm.
— International series for wind bands & ensembles
For solo percussionist with ensemble of woodwind, brass, harp, piano, percussion
(3 players), and string bass. — "This work is conceived to be performed by one
player to a part." — Duration: ca. 30:00.
Publ. no. MC0050
System number: 013422352

785.34194

Martinaitis, A. (Algirdas), 1950-
Paskutinių sodų muzika : obojui, violončelei, fortepijonui ir
mušamiesiems = Music of the last gardens : for oboe, cello, piano and
percussion : 1979 / Algirdas Martinaitis ; leidinį redagavo Julius
Andrejevas. — Vilnius : Muzikos informacijos ir leidybos centras, 2006.
— 1 score (42 p.) + 3 parts ; 30 cm.
Duration: ca. 13:00. — Preface in Lithuanian and English.
Publ. no. MILC 059
ISMN M599990745
System number: 013771132

785.34196

*Davies, Peter Maxwell, 1934-
[Glasses of wine]
Two glasses of wine : for instrumental ensemble / Peter Maxwell Davies.
— London : Chester Music, c2004. — 1 score (26 p.) ; 19 cm.
For flute, clarinet in A, marimba, piano, violin doubling viola, and violoncello. —
The movements were first performed as separate works.
Publ. no. CH65791
ISBN 1844494950
System number: 013190640

785.39192
Duddell, Joe, 1972-
Parallel lines : for tuned percussion and piano : (1999) / Joe Duddell. —
London : Schott, c2004. — 1 score (25 p.) + 1 part (14 p.) ; 31 cm.
Percussion: marimba, vibraphone, crotales. — Duration: 10:00.
Publ. no. ED 12682
Publ. no. S&Co.7908
ISMN M220121784
System number: 013173234

785.4 – ENSEMBLES WITHOUT KEYBOARD

785.420991858
***Rosetti, Antonio, ca. 1750-1792.**
[Partitas, woodwinds, horns (3), violone, M. B18, F major]
Partita in F-Dur für 2 Flöten, 2 Oboen, 2 Klarinetten, 3 Hörner, 2 Fagotte
und Kontrabass, RWV B18 = Partita in F major for 2 flutes, 2 oboes, 2
clarinets, 3 horns, 2 bassoons and double-bass / Antonio Rosetti ;
herausgegeben von Eberhard Buschmann. — Partitur und Stimmen. —
Winterthur, Schweiz : Amadeus, 2004. — 1 score (36 p.) + 12 parts ; 31 cm.
— (Werke / Antonio Rosetti. Reihe B: Partiten, Serenaden, Notturni ; Bd.
11)
Includes pref. in English and German.
Publ. no. BP 1288
System number: 014763916

785.4219318966
***Kurpiński, Karol, 1785-1857.**
[Nocturnes, bassoon, horn, viola, op. 16]
Nocturne, op. 16 : for viola, horn in F and bassoon / by C. Kurpinsky. —
Lancaster : Phylloscopus Publications, c2005. — 1 score (5 p.) + 3 parts ;
30 cm.
Edited by Chris and Frances Nex. — New version, replaces PP6 (M570160068).
Publ. no. PP557
ISMN M570166893
System number: 013472925

785.42197
***Cooke, Arnold.**
[Septets, bassoon, clarinet, horn, violin, viola, violoncello, double bass]
Septet for clarinet, horn, bassoon, violin, viola, violoncello and contrabass /
Arnold Cooke. — Altamonte Springs, Fla. : Anglo-American Music
Publishers ; [s.l.] : distribution, Worldwide Music Services International,
c2005. — 1 score (63 p.) + 7 parts ; 28 cm.
Cover title.
System number: 013440636

785.42198
***Cooke, Arnold.**
[Octet, woodwinds, horn, strings]
Octet : (Passacaglia & fugue) / Arnold Cooke. — [s.l.] : Anglo-American
Music Publishers, c2005. — 1 score (17 p.) + 8 parts ; 28 cm.
For flute, clarinet, bassoon, horn, violin, viola, violoncello and double bass. —
Cover title. — Includes biographical note.
System number: 013593949

785.42199
Badings, Henk, 1907-1987.
Azioni musicali : per duodeci strumenti, TWEC: HHB-1, 1980 / Henk
Badings. — Den Haag : Floricor Editions, c2005. — 1 score (iv, 62 p.) ;
30 cm.
Printed and revised edition. — For 2 flutes, 2 oboes, 2 clarinets, 2 bassoons, 2 horns,
violoncello and double bass. — Duration: ca. 24:00. — Preface and critical notes in
English.
Pl. no. F.E. 0413 A
System number: 014599804

***Waterhouse, Graham, 1962-**
Jacobean salute : op. 34 : für Bläserquintett, Streichquartett und
Kontrabass = for wind quintet, string quartet and double bass / Graham
Waterhouse. — Frankfurt : R. Lienau, c2003. — 1 score (23 p.) ; 30 cm.
For flute (piccolo), oboe, clarinet, horn, bassoon, violins (2), viola, violoncello and
double bass. — Duration: ca. 13:00. — Preface and biographical notes in German,
English and French.
Pl. no. RL 40840
ISMN M011408407
System number: 013176618

***Waterhouse, Graham, 1962-**
[Nonet, woodwinds, horn, strings, op. 30]
Nonett, op. 30, für Flöte (Piccolo), Oboe, Klarinette, Horn, Fagott, Violine,
Viola, Violoncello, Kontrabass = for flute (piccolo), oboe, clarinet, horn,
bassoon, violin, viola, violoncello, double bass / Graham Waterhouse. —
Partitur. — Frankfurt : R. Lienau, c2003. — 1 score (36 p.) ; 30 cm.
Duration: ca. 13:00. — Preface and biographical notes in German, English and
French.
Pl. no. RL 40830
ISMN M011408308
EAN 9790011408308
System number: 013176633

785.42199184
***Gorb, Adam, 1958-**
[Symphonies, no. 1, C]
Symphony no. 1 in C : for 12 wind & double bass / Adam Gorb. —
Kenley : Maecenas Music, c2000. — 1 score (82 p.) ; 30 cm. —
Millennium series for wind bands & ensembles
For 2 flutes, 2 oboes, 2 clarinets, 2 bassoons, 4 horns, and double bass. —
Duration: ca. 16:00.
Publ. no. MM0056
System number: 013422267

785.4219918846
Spohr, Louis, 1784-1859.
Erinnerung an Marienbad : (waltz, op. 89) : for flute, clarinet 1 in A (or
oboe), clarinet 2 in A, horns 1 & 2 in D (or in F), bassoon, violins 1 & 2,
viola and bassi / by Louis Spohr. — Lancaster : Phylloscopus
Publications, c2004. — 1 score (15 p.) + 13 parts ; 30 cm.
Edited by Chris and Frances Nex. — Includes biographical and editorial notes.
Publ. no. PP539
ISMN M570166718
System number: 013173883

785.43
Michael, David Moritz, 1751-1827.
[Wind music]
Complete wind chamber music / David Moritz Michael ; edited by Nola
Reed Knouse. — Middleton, Wis. : Published for the American
Musicological Society by A-R Editions, c2006. — 1 score (l, 386 p., 4 p.
of plates) + parts : facsims. ; 31 cm. — Recent researches in American
music, 0147-0078 ; v. 59 Music of the United States of America ; v. 16
Suites; for 2 clarinets, 2 horns, and 2 bassoons (1st work and Parthia III-VI, X,
and XII); 2 clarinets, 2 horns, and bassoon (2nd work and Parthia VII-IX and
XIII-XIV); trumpet, 2 clarinets, 2 horns, and bassoon (Parthia I); flute, 2 clarinets,
2 horns, and bassoon (Parthia II); trumpet, 2 clarinets, 2 horns, and 2 bassoons
(Parthia XI). — Edited from parts (copyists' mss. and holographs) in the
collections of the Moravian Music Foundation, Bethlehem, Pa. and
Winston-Salem, N.C. — "David Michael Moritz and the music of the
Moravians": p. xiii-l; critical commentary: p. 371-382.
ISBN 089579599X
ISBN 9780895795991
System number: 013802028

785.43195
Carr, Paul.
Diverting Sundays : for wind quintet / by Paul Carr. — Lancaster :
Phylloscopus Publications, c2004. — 1 score (16 p.) + 5 parts ; 30 cm.
For flute, oboe, clarinet, bassoon and horn. — Includes biographical and
programme notes.
Publ. no. PP517
ISMN M570166473
System number: 013188715

Grange, Philip.
Bacchus bagatelles : (1993) : six short pieces for wind quintet / Philip
Grange. — Kenley : Maecenas Music, [2004?], c1993. — 1 score
(25 p.) ; 30 cm.
For flute (doubling piccolo), oboe (doubling cor anglais), clarinet, horn and
bassoon. — Reproduced from holograph. — Duration: ca. 12:00.
System number: 013422538

***Hearne, John, 1937-**
[Ghostwatch ; arr.]
Ghostwatch : [originally] for brass quintet : arranged for wind quintet /
John Hearne. — Score. — Inverurie : Longship, [2005?], c1995. — 1
score (17 p.) ; 30 cm.
"Bass clarinet should be used wherever possible. An alternative B♭ clarinet part is
available"—Composer's note.
ISMN M900203670
System number: 013440381

McAlister, Clark.
The lion and the mouse : for narrator and woodwind [sic] quintet / music
by Clark McAlister ; text by A.J. Wood. — Kenley : Maecenas Music,
c1996. — 1 score (17 p.) ; 30 cm. — (Chamber series for wind bands &
ensembles)
For narrator, flute, oboe, clarinet, horn and bassoon. — "An Æsop
fable"—Caption. — English words.
Publ. no. MC0041
System number: 013193651

***Mengal, Martin-Joseph, 1784-1851.**
[Quintets, winds, no. 2]
Wind quintet after Mozart : for flute, oboe, clarinet in B♭, horn in E♭ & F
and bassoon / by Martin Joseph Mengal (l'aîné). — New, rev. ed. —
Lancaster : Phylloscopus Publications, c2005. — 1 score (20 p.) +
5 parts ; 30 cm.
"Mengal uses themes from Mozart violin sonatas … Allegro (from K.304), an
Adagio (K.306), Minuet (K.304) and Finale (K.379)."—Horn part. — Edited by
Chris and Frances Nex. — Edition, replaces PP7 (ISMN M570160075). — Horn
part includes biographical and editiorial notes.
Publ. no. PP555
ISMN M570166879
System number: 013472984

Sor, Fernando, 1778-1839.
[Encouragement. *Selections; arr.*]
Andante, theme & variations [from] (Duo for guitars, op. 34) / by Fernando Sor; arranged for wind quintet by David B. Johnson. — Lancaster : Phylloscopus Publications, c2004. — 1 score (8 p.) + 5 parts ; 30 cm.
Publ. no. PP542
ISMN M570166749
System number: 013173919

Wolstenholme, W. (William), 1865-1931.
[Quintets, winds]
Quintet for flute, oboe, clarinet, horn & bassoon / William Wolstenholme. — Ampleforth : Emerson Edition, c2004. — 1 score (25 p.) + 5 parts ; 28 cm.
Includes biographical note. — Duration: 16:30.
Publ. no. 420
Publ. no. E420
ISMN M570404889 (score)
ISMN M570404940 (set of parts)
System number: 013360897

785.43198
Dodgson, Stephen, 1924-
Pieces of eight : [1997] : for wind octet : two oboes, two clarinets in B♭, two horns in F and two bassoons / by Stephen Dodgson. — Lancaster : Phylloscopus Publications, c2004. — 1 score (18 p.) + 8 parts ; 30 cm.
Publ. no. PP552
ISMN M570166848
System number: 013173888

Harrison, Pamela, 1915-1990.
Octetto pastorale : for wind octet (2 oboes, 2 clarinets in A, 2 horns in F and 2 bassoons) / by Pamela Harrison. — Lancaster : Phylloscopus Publications, c2004. — 1 score (19 p.) + 8 parts ; 30 cm.
Publ. no. PP543
ISMN M570166756
System number: 013173924

McAlister, Clark.
Forest music : [1991] : for wind octet / Clark McAlister. — Full score. — Kenley : Maecenas Music, c1992. — 1 score (41 p.) ; 30 cm. — (Chamber series for wind bands & ensembles)
For 2 oboes, 2 clarinets, 2 horns and 2 bassoons. — Duration: 15:00.
System number: 013193628

Righini, Vincenzo, 1756-1812.
[Partita, woodwinds, horns (2), E♭ major]
Serenade Es-Dur für zwei Oboen, zwei Klarinetten in B, zwei Hörner in Es (F) und zwei Fagotte / Vincenzo Righini ; Herausgeber, Alexander Maschat. — Erstausg. — Warngau : Accolade, c2007. — 1 score (23 p.) + 10 parts ; 30 cm.
Pref. in German and English.
Pl. no. ACC.1183
ISMN M501355136
System number: 013953481

785.431981852
Gál, Hans, 1890-1987.
[Divertimenti, winds, op. 22]
Divertimento, op. 22, octet for woodwind and brass / Hans Gál. — Set of parts and score. — Kenley : Maecenas Contemporary Composers, [2005], c1927. — 1 score (39 p.) + 8 parts ; 30 cm. — Maecenas contemporary composers elite edition
For flute, oboe, 2 clarinets, trumpet, 2 horns, and bassoon. — Originally published: Leipzig : F.E.C. Leuckart, 1927.
Publ. no. MM0007
System number: 013322060

785.43199
*Dodgson, Stephen, 1924-
Windbag : five occasional pieces for ten occasional players (2 flutes, 2 oboes, 2 clarinets in B♭, 2 horns in F and 2 bassoons / by Stephen Dodgson. — Lancaster : Phylloscopus Publications, c2005. — 1 score (35 p.) + 9 parts ; 30 cm.
Publ. no. PP568
ISMN M570167005
System number: 013561027

*Gilbert, Anthony.
Unrise : for ten wind (2001) / Anthony Gilbert. — Full score. — York : University of York Music Press, c2001. — 1 score (89 p.) ; 21 x 30 cm.
For flute/piccolo, oboe, English horn, clarinet, bass clarinet/clarinet, bassoon, trumpet, flügelhorn/trumpet, horn and tenor trombone. — Duration: ca. 16:00. — Brief program notes by the composer precede score.
ISMN M570201433
System number: 013430756

Lindberg, Magnus, 1958-
Gran duo : for woodwind and brass / Magnus Lindberg. — London : Boosey & Hawkes, 2005, c2001. — 1 score (77 p.) ; 30 cm.
Publisher's note in English, French and German.
Pl. no. 12671

Publ. no. HPS 1354
ISMN M060116629
System number: 013214771

McAlister, Clark.
Jeux d'été : [1989 rev. 1990] : for ten wind instruments / Clark McAlister. — Kenley : Maecenas Music, c1991. — 1 score (61 p.) ; 30 cm. — (Chamber series for wind bands & ensembles)
For 2 flutes (1 doubling piccolo), oboe, cor anglais, 2 clarinets, 2 bassoons and 2 horns. — Duration: 12:00.
System number: 013193616

785.431991832
*Dvořák, Antonín, 1841-1904.
[Sonatina, violin, piano, op. 100, G major; *arr.*]
Sonatina in G, op. 100 / by Anton Dvořák ; arranged for flute, two oboes, two clarinets in B♭, two horns in F and two bassoons by David King. — Lancaster : Phylloscopus Publications, c2005. — 1 score (35 p.) + 9 parts ; 30 cm.
Publ. no. PP549
ISMN M570166817
System number: 013472992

785.431991852
*Lorriman, Howard.
[Divertimenti, winds (2005)]
Divertimento for wind nonet : (flute, 2 oboes, 2 clarinets in B♭, 2 horns in F & 2 bassoons) / by Howard Lorriman. — Lancaster : Phylloscopus Publications, c2005. — 1 score (28 p.) + 9 parts ; 30 cm.
Publ. no. PP571
ISMN M570167036
System number: 013561727

785.431991854
Dodgson, Stephen, 1924-
[Partitas, winds (1994)]
Partita for ten wind instruments : flute 1, flute 2 & piccolo, 2 oboes, 2 clarinets in B♭, 2 horns in F and 2 bassoons / by Stephen Dodgson. — Lancaster : Phylloscopus Publications, c2004. — 1 score (39 p.) + 10 parts ; 30 cm.
Publ. no. PP548
ISMN M570166800
System number: 013188929

785.43199186
*Bailey, Judith, 1941-
[Concertos, wind ensemble, op. 20]
Concerto for ten wind instruments, op. 20 : for two flutes, two oboes, two clarinets in B♭, two bassoons and two horns in F / by Judith Bailey. — Lancaster : Phylloscopus Publications, c2005. — 1 score (24 p.) + 10 parts ; 30 cm.
Publ. no. PP554
ISMN M570166862
System number: 013472741

785.44192
Bayliss, Colin.
[Grumpy tunes; *arr.*]
Grumpy tunes : arranged for recorder and guitar : [B79a] / Colin Bayliss. — Manchester : Da Capo Music, c2004. — 1 score (10 p.) ; 30 cm.
Acc. originally for piano; arrangement by the composer. — Duration: ca. 10:00. — Includes biographical and programme notes.
Pl. no. DC 612
System number: 013351677

Giardini, Felice, 1716-1796.
[Duets, viola, bassoon]
3 Duetti à fagotto e viola concerta / Felice de Giardini ; herausgegeben von Helge Bartholomäus. — Erstdruck. — Leipzig : Hofmeister, c2006. — 1 score (14 p.) + 2 parts ; 31 cm.
Biographical notes in German and English.
Pl. no. FH 2876
ISMN M203428763
System number: 013887073

Riehm, Rolf, 1937-
Adieu, Marie, mon amour : drei Liebeslieder in den Tod : nach Klavierstücken von Johann Sebastian Bach : für Bratsche und Akkordeon, 2002-2003 / Rolf Riehm. — Spielpartitur. — München : Ricordi, c2005. — 1 score ([13] leaves) ; 36 cm. in folder 43 cm.
Preface in German. — Duration: 15:00. — Reproduced from ms.
Pl. no. Sy. 3583
ISMN M204235834
System number: 014053359

785.44192183

*Cooke, Arnold.
[Sonatas, flute, harp]
Sonata for flute and harp : (1988) / Arnold Cooke. — Altamonte Springs,
Fla. : Anglo-American Music Publishers ; [s.l.] : distribution, Worldwide
Music Services International, [2005?], c1989. — 1 score (23 p.) + 1 part
(9 p.) ; 28 cm.
Cover title.
System number: 013440553

785.44193

*Devienne, François, 1759-1803.
[Trios, flutes, violoncello, op. 19. No. 1]
Trio op. 19 no. 1, for flute, flute or violin, and cello or bassoon / by François
Devienne. — Lancaster : Phylloscopus Publications; c2005. — 1 score
(6 p.) + 3 parts ; 30 cm.
Edited by Chris and Frances Nex. — New version, replaces PP13 (M570160143).
Publ. no. PP564
ISMN M570166961
System number: 013561743
Also classified at 785.8193

*Molino, Francesco, 1768-1847.
[Grand trio concertant, no. 1]
Grand trio concertant, op. 30 : for flute or violin, viola, and guitar /
Francesco Molino ; edited by Brian Jeffery. — London : Tecla Editions,
2005. — 1 score (21 p.) + 3 parts ; 31 cm.
Includes editorial notes.
Pl. no. TECLA 0235
ISBN 0948607661 (cased)
ISBN 0948607653 (pbk.)
System number: 013334497
Also classified at 785.7193

Neubauer, Franz Christoph, 1750-1795.
[Trios, flute, violin, viola, op. 14. No. 1]
Trio op. 14, no. 1, for flute, violin or flute and viola / by Franz Christoph
Neubauer. — Lancaster : Phylloscopus Publications, c2004. — 1 score
(8 p.) + 3 parts ; 30 cm.
Edited by Chris and Frances Nex.
Publ. no. PP536
ISMN M570166688
System number: 013188891

785.441931852

Lewis, Paul, 1943-
Divertimento : flute, viola & harp / by Paul Lewis. — Dover : Broadbent &
Dunn, c2003. — 1 score (23 p.) + 2 parts ; 30 cm.
Pl. no. B&D 13203
System number: 013167535

785.44193186

Backofen, Johann Georg Heinrich, 1768-1839.
[Concertantes, basset horn, harp, violoncello, op. 7, F major]
Concertante, op. 7/8, per arpa, corno di bassetto (o viola) e violoncello ad
libitum = for harp, basset-horn (or viola) and violoncello and libitum /
Heinrich Backofen ; a cura di Anna Pasetti. — Bologna : Ut Orpheus,
c2007. — 1 score (vi, 19 p.) + 2 parts ; 31 cm. — Magadis ; 192
Basset horn part not playable by viola; notated for instrument in F only. — Edition
based on two different printings from Breitkopf & Härtel, the basset horn version
(op. 7) and the viola version (op. 8). — Preface in Italian and English.
Pl. no. MAG 192
ISMN M215314580
System number: 013887059

785.44194

Graf, Friedrich Hartmann, 1727-1795.
[Favourite quartettos. No. 5]
Quartetto V for bassoon (or cello), violin 1 (or oboe) violin 2 and cello / by
Friedrich Hartmann Graf. — Lancaster : Phylloscopus Publications, c2004.
— 1 score (11 p.) + 4 parts ; 30 cm.
Edited by C.M.M. Nex and F.H. Nex.
Publ. no. PP537
ISMN M570166695
System number: 013188895

Graf, Friedrich Hartmann, 1727-1795.
[Quartets, bassoon, violin, viola, violoncello, B♭ major]
Quartetto VI for bassoon (or cello), violin (or oboe), viola and cello / by
Friedrich Hartmann Graf. — Lancaster : Phylloscopus Publications, c2004.
— 1 score (11 p.) + 4 parts ; 30 cm.
Edited by Chris and Frances Nex.
Publ. no. PP538
ISMN M570166701
System number: 013188898
Also classified at 785.7194

Küchler, Johann, 1738-1790.
[Quartets, clarinet, bassoon, violin, viola, op. 1. No. 2]
Quatuor concertant op. 1, no. 2, for clarinet in B♭ or oboe, violin, viola
and bassoon or cello / by Johann Küchler. — Lancaster : Phylloscopus
Publications, c2004. — 1 score (7 p.) + 5 parts ; 30 cm.
Edited by Chris and Frances Nex.
Publ. no. PP534
ISMN M570166664
System number: 013189015

785.44195

*Cooke, Arnold.
[Divertimenti, recorder, string quartet]
Divertimento for treble recorder and string quartet / Arnold Cooke. —
[Altamonte Springs, FL] : Anglo-American Music Publishers, c2005. —
1 score (19 p.) + 5 parts ; 28 cm.
Cover title. — Includes biographical note.
System number: 013593661

*Cooke, Arnold.
[Quintets, clarinet, flute, harp, violin, violoncello]
Quintet for harp, flute, clarinet, violin and violoncello / Arnold Cooke. —
Altamonte Springs, Fla. : Anglo-American Music Publishers ; [s.l.] :
distribution, Worldwide Music Services International, c2005. — 1 score
(82 p.) + 5 parts ; 28 cm.
Cover title.
System number: 013440594

Kreutzer, Rodolphe, 1766-1831.
[Quintets, oboe, violins, viola, violoncello, C major]
Grand quintette : for oboe, two violins, viola and cello / by Rodolphe
Kreutzer. — Lancaster : Phylloscopus Publications, c2004. — 1 score
(18 p.) + 5 parts ; 30 cm.
Edited by Chris and Frances Nex.
Publ. no. PP535
ISMN M570166671
System number: 013188886

*Wranitzky, Paul, 1756-1808.
[Quintets, flute, oboe, violas, violoncello, op. 3. No. 1]
Quintet in F, op. III no. 1 : for flute, oboe, two violas and cello / by Paul
Wranitzky. — Lancaster : Phylloscopus Publications, c2005. — 1 score
(12 p.) + 5 parts ; 30 cm.
Edited by Chris and Frances Nex.
Publ. no. PP556
ISMN M570166886
System number: 013472931

785.44196

Brumby, Colin.
Scena : for cor anglais and strings / by Colin Brumby. — Lancaster :
Phylloscopus Publications, c2004. — 1 score (17 p.) + 6 parts ; 30 cm.
"Although conceived for solo and chamber orchestra, the piece can be performed
with one string player to each part ..."—Pref.
Publ. no. PP530
ISMN M570166619
System number: 013188736
Primary classification 784.72853

Tippett, Michael, 1905-1998.
In memoriam magistri : for flute, clarinet and string quartet : (1971) /
Michael Tippett. — London : Schott, c2005. — 1 score ([1] p.) ; 31 cm.
Clarinet in C. — Duration: 1:00.
Publ. no. ED 12852
ISMN M220123566
System number: 013381848

785.44197

*Serei, Zsolt.
L'ombre sur les structures pliées : hommage à Pierre Boulez : pour deux
clarinettes et cinq instruments à cordes = for two clarinets and five strings
/ Serei Zsolt. — Partitura. — Budapest : Editio Musica, c2004. — 1 score
(28 p.) ; 30 cm. — (EMB contemporary music)
For 2 clarinets, 3 violins, viola, and violoncello. — Duration: ca. 16:00. —
Includes performance instructions in English and Hungarian.
Pl. no. Z. 14 394
ISMN M080143940
System number: 014766582

785.45195

*Cooke, Arnold.
Arioso and scherzo : for French horn & strings (violin, 2 violas & cello) /
Arnold Cooke. — Altamonte Springs, Florida : Anglo-American Music
Publishers, c1999. — 1 score (16 p.) + 5 parts ; 28 cm.
Duration: 9:00.
System number: 013593736

785.5 – ENSEMBLES WITHOUT KEYBOARD AND WITH PERCUSSION

785.56192
*Gilbert, Anthony.
Os : for oboe and vibraphone : [2002 revision] / Anthony Gilbert. — York : University of York Music Press, [2003?], c2000. — 1 score (27 p.) ; 21 x 30 cm.
Program notes by the composer precede score. — Duration: ca. 15:42.
ISMN M570201358
System number: 013430853

785.57
Richards, Goff.
À la carte : brass band ensemble / by Goff Richards. — Brass band instrument edition — London : Studio Music, c2005. — 1 score (32 p.) + 12 parts ; 30 cm. — (Studio Music brass ensemble series.)
"A separate set of parts for orchestral brass instruments (M050064275) is also available. Please note: The two sets are not interchangeable"—Back cover. — For 3 cornets, flugel horn, E flat horn, baritone, 2 trombones, euphonium, E flat bass and 2 percussion.
ISMN M050063841 (set)
ISMN M050063858 (score)
System number: 013188557
Also classified at 785.9

Richards, Goff.
À la carte : orchestral brass ensemble / Goff Richards. — Orchestral brass instrument edition. — London : Studio Music, c2005. — 1 score (32 p.) + 11 parts ; 30 cm. — (Studio Music brass ensemble series)
"A separate set of parts for brass band instruments (M050063841) is also available. Please note: The two sets are not interchangeable"—Back cover. — For 4 trumpets, horn, 3 trombones, tuba and 2 percussion.
ISMN M050064275 (set)
ISMN M050064282 (score)
System number: 013188547

785.5719518924
*Cooke, Arnold.
Fanfare : four trumpets [and timpani] / Arnold Cooke. — [s.l.] : Anglo-American Music Publishers, c2005. — 1 score (3 p.) + 5 parts ; 28 cm.
Cover title. — Includes biographical note.
System number: 013593963

785.58192
Gilbert, Anthony.
Moonfaring : for cello and percussion (1983-1986) / Anthony Gilbert. — Mainz : Schott, c2007. — 1 score (25 p.) + 2 parts ; 31 cm.
Duration: ca. 19:30. — Composer's note in English.
Publ. no. ED 13071
Pl. no. S&Co.8290
ISMN M001146906
System number: 013771084

785.594195
Andersson, Benny.
[Mamma mia! Selections; arr.]
Mamma mia! : choral highlights : instrumental pak / arranged by Mac Huff. — Milwaukee, Wis. : Hal Leonard, c2005. — 5 parts ; 28 cm.
Medley of 7 songs from the musical "Mamma mia!" based on ABBA songs. — Words and music by Benny Andersson, Björn Ulvaeus and Stig Anderson. — Parts for tenor saxophone, synthesizer, guitar, bass and drums for use with the various choral arrangements published by Hal Leonard.
Publ. no. 08621357
System number: 013220029

785.6 – KEYBOARD, ELECTROPHONE, PERCUSSION ENSEMBLES

785.62192
Brady, Deborah.
The toymaker's workshop : for one piano, four hands / by Deborah Brady ; edited by J. Mark Baker. — Milwaukee, Wis. : Hal Leonard, c2004. — 31 p. of music : port. ; 31 cm. — Hal Leonard student piano library. Composer showcase
"One piano, four hands - late elementary level"—T.p. — Poem by the composer, "The toymaker's workshop", precedes score. — Includes biographical note. — Durations: 0:45; 1:26; 0:38; 1:45; 1:15.
Publ. no. HL00296513
ISBN 0634080415
System number: 013376406

Czerny, Carl, 1791-1857.
[Ouverture charactéristique et brillante]
Ouverture brillante : piano duet, (op. 54) / Carl Czerny ; edited by David Patrick. — Barnet : Fitzjohn Music Publications, c2005. — 27 p. of music ; 21 x 30 cm.
For piano, 4 hands.
System number: 013214605

Double act : duets for piano / popular melodies arranged by Marian Hellen. — Buxhall : Kevin Mayhew, 2004. — 45 p. ; 30 cm.
Publ. no. 3611839
ISMN M570243846
System number: 013201432

*Hall, Pauline, 1924-
Mixed doubles : piano time duets. Book 2 / Pauline Hall. — New ed. — Oxford : Oxford University Press, 2005. — 1 score (48 p.) ; 32 cm.
22 duets for piano (4 hands).
ISBN 0193727544
ISBN 9780193727540
System number: 013190557

Kember, John.
On the lighter side : duet collection : 10 pieces for piano duet in Latin, spiritual and jazz styles / John Kember. — London : Schott, c2005. — 55 p. of music ; 31 cm + 1 sound disc (digital ; 4 3/4 in.)
For piano (4 hands). — Mostly in teacher/pupil format. — Taken from previously published works: 9 pieces for piano duet, Latin pieces for piano duet and 12 spirituals for piano solo and duet. — Notes on pieces in English, French and German. — CD contains full demonstrations and teacher's part for pupils to play along to.
Publ. no. ED 12842
ISMN M220123313
System number: 013192400

*Rachmaninoff, Sergei, 1873-1943.
[Symphonic dances; arr.]
Symphonic dances, op. 45 : 2 pianos, 4 hands / Serge Rachmaninoff. — Definitive ed. — London : Boosey & Hawkes, 2005. — 2 scores (89 p. each) ; 31 cm.
Originally for orchestra; arr. by the composer. — Pref. in English, French and German. — Duration: 37:00.
Pl. no. 13939
ISMN M060116520
System number: 013312836

Samuel, Rhian.
Gaslight Square II : for piano duet / Rhian Samuel. — London : Stainer & Bell, c2005. — 1 score (19 p.) ; 30 cm.
Publ. no. AC223
ISMN M220221521
System number: 013280257

*Samuel, Rhian.
Serenade duo : for two pianos / Rhian Samuel. — London : Stainer & Bell, c2005. — 1 score (18 p.) ; 30 cm.
Includes composer's note.
Publ. no. AC219
ISMN M220221415
System number: 013213368

*Wagner, Richard, 1813-1883.
[Meistersinger von Nürnberg. Vorspiel; arr.]
Die Meistersinger von Nürnberg : (Vorspiel) = (Prelude) / Richard Wagner ; in einer Transkription für Klavier zu zwei Händen oder für zwei Klaviere zu vier Händen von Glenn Gould ; herausgegeben von Carl Morey. — Mainz ; London : Schott, c2003. — 1 score (28 p.) ; 31 cm. — (The virtuoso piano transcription series ; 6)
The full version is for 2 pianists but "the musical essentials of the transcription may be played by a solo pianist who might incorporate material from the secondo part according to individual technique and imagination"—Pref. — Pref. in English with French and German translations.
Publ. no. ED 9547
ISMN M001133715
EAN 9790001133715
System number: 013176594

*Walton, William, 1902-1983.
Duets for children / William Walton ; edited by Michael Aston. — Oxford : Oxford University Press, 2004. — 1 score (39 p.) ; 32 cm.
For piano, 4 hands.
ISBN 0193683237
ISBN 9780193683235
System number: 013174177

*Wildman, Peter, 1957-
Rock study duets : educational duets in pop styles for piano or keyboard / music by Peter Wildman. — Laggan Bridge : Spartan Press, c2005. — 2 v. ; 30 cm + 2 compact discs.
CDs contain demonstration and backing tracks. — Pl. no.: SP795 (v. 1), SP796 (v. 2). — Publisher's no.: SP795/797 (CD v. 1), SP796/798 (CD v. 2).
Pl. no. SP795
Pl. no. SP796
Publ. no. SP795/797
Publ. no. SP796/798
ISMN M579997955 (v. 1)
ISMN M579997962 (v. 2)
System number: 013376539

785.62192186
Beethoven, Ludwig van, 1770-1827.
[Concertos, violin, orchestra, op. 61, D major; *arr.*]
Klavierkonzert Opus 61a : nach dem Violinkonzert Opus 61 = Piano
concerto op. 61a : after the Violin concerto op. 61 / Ludwig van Beethoven ;
herausgegeben von Hans-Werner Küthen ; Fingersatz von Klaus Schilde ;
Klavierauszug von Jürgen Sommer ; Kadenzen von Komponisten. —
München : G. Henle, c2005. — 1 score (xi, 79 p.) ; 32 cm.
Originally for violin and orchestra; arr. for 2 pianos. — "Urtext"—Cover. —
Includes pref. in German, English, and French and critical commentary in German
and English.
Publ. no. HN 815
Publ. no. 815
ISMN M201808154
EAN 9790201808154
System number: 013364364

785.6219218846
Gavrilin, V. (Valerii).
[Selections]
Val'sy dlia fortepiano i fortepiano v 4 ruki = Waltzes for piano and piano in
four hands / V. Gavrilin. — St. Petersburg : Kompozitor, 2005, c2001. —
87 p. of music ; 30 cm.
Some works are arrangements of orchestral pieces.
Pl. no. c 3086 k
System number: 013637528
Primary classification 786.418846

785.6219218947
Uspenskii, Vladislav Aleksandrovich.
Tokkata-fantaziia : na temu M.I. Glinki : dlia dvukh fortepiano v vosem'
ruk = Toccata-fantasy : to M.I. Glinka : for two pianos in eight hands /
Vladislav Uspenskii. — Sankt-Peterburg : Kompozitor, 2005, c2004. — 1
score (20 p.) ; 30 cm. — (Pedagogicheskii repertuar = Pedagogical
repertoire)
Publ. no. 3802
Pl. no. s 3802 k
System number: 013887081

785.6519218945
Hakim, Naji, 1955-
[Rhapsody, organs (2)]
Rhapsody for organ duet / Naji Hakim. — Waltham Abbey : United Music
Publishers, c2005. — 1 score (34 p.) ; 31 cm. — UMP organ repertoire
series ; no. 46
Includes biographical and programme notes in English and French.
ISMN M224404982
System number: 013383464

785.68194
*Sculthorpe, Peter, 1929-
[Djilile, percussion]
Djilile : arranged for percussion ensemble : (1981/90) / Peter Sculthorpe. —
London : Faber Music, c1999. — 1 score (7 p.) ; 30 cm.
Version for percussion (4 players): vibraphone, 2 marimbas, tam-tam, thunder sheet,
2 rain sticks. — Reproduced from ms. — Duration: 7:00.
ISBN 0571555969
System number: 013555083

785.7 – STRING ENSEMBLES

785.7192
*Cooke, Arnold.
[Duet, violin, viola]
Duo for violin and viola / Arnold Cooke. — [s.l.] : Anglo-American Music
Publishers, c2005. — 1 score (27 p.) + 2 parts ; 28 cm.
Cover title. — Includes biographical note.
System number: 013593715

Esser, Karl Michael, Ritter von, 1737-ca. 1795.
[Duets, viola d'amore, viola da gamba]
Three pieces for viola d'amore & viola da gamba or violoncello (1789) /
Karl Michael, Ritter von Esser. Two pieces for violin, viola d'amore & viola
da gamba or violoncello (1789) / Tomaso Carle ; edited by David J. Rhodes.
— [S.l.] : Viola da Gamba Society of Great Britain, c2004. — 2 scores (3,
4 p.) + 5 parts ; 30 cm.
Includes critical commentary.
Pl. no. 191a—191b
System number: 013382402
Also classified at 785.7193

*Tobias, Rudolf, 1873-1918.
[Duet, violins, E minor]
Duo, für zwei Violinen / Rudolf Tobias. — Lilienthal/Bremen : Eres, c2003.
— 1 score (8 p.) + 1 part (4 p.) ; 30 cm.
Part in score format.
Pl. no. Eres 2797
ISMN M202427972
System number: 014629761

785.71921876
Antonii, Giovanni Battista degli, ca. 1660-1698.
[Ricercate, violoncello, op. 1]
Ricercate sopra il violoncello o clavicembalo ; e, Ricercate per il violino /
Giovanni Battista degli Antonii ; edizione della partitura e prefazione a
cura di Marc Vanscheeuwijck. — Sala Bolognese : Forni, 2007. — 1
score (108 p.) + 2 parts ; 30 cm. — Bibliotheca Musica Bononiensis.
Sezione IV ; n. 101
For violin and cello or harpsichord; previously considered to be a work for solo
cello. — Comprises modern edition score and facsimile violin and cello parts. —
1st facsimile is of the violin part of a manuscript held at Biblioteca Estense,
Modena (Ms. Mus. D. 9) ; 2nd facsimile is of the cello part published Bologna,
1687. — Preface and critical report in Italian and English.
ISBN 9788827130087
System number: 013887058

785.719218846
Marchetti, Filippo, 1831-1902.
[Fascinzione. *arr.*]
Fascination : Valzer zingaresco / Filippo Marchetti ; elaborated and
arranged for viola and guitar by Ian Gammie. — St. Albans : Corda
Music Publications, c2004. — 1 score (8 p.) + 2 parts ; 30 cm.
Publ. no. CMP 668-V
System number: 013269271

785.7193
Esser, Karl Michael, Ritter von, 1737-ca. 1795.
[Duets, viola d'amore, viola da gamba]
Three pieces for viola d'amore & viola da gamba or violoncello (1789) /
Karl Michael, Ritter von Esser. Two pieces for violin, viola d'amore &
viola da gamba or violoncello (1789) / Tomaso Carle ; edited by David J.
Rhodes. — [S.l.] : Viola da Gamba Society of Great Britain, c2004. — 2
scores (3, 4 p.) + 5 parts ; 30 cm.
Includes critical commentary.
Pl. no. 191a—191b
System number: 013382402
Primary classification 785.7192

Hertel, Johann Wilhelm, 1727-1789.
[Trios, harp, violin, violoncello. No. 2]
Trio F-Dur : für Harfe (oder Cembalo), Violine (oder Flöte) und
Violoncello / Johann Wilhelm Hertel ; herausgegeben von Johanna Seitz.
— Erstausg. — Magdeburg : Walhall, c2007. — 1 score (14 p.) +
3 parts : 2 facsims. ; 30 cm. — (Collegium Musicum ; Kölner Reihe Alter
Musik)
First edition based on the autograph score from the library of the Conservatoire
Royal in Brussels (shelfmark 6692). — Preface in German and English.
Publ. no. EW 541
System number: 013771125

*Molino, Francesco, 1768-1847.
[Grand trio concertant, no. 1]
Grand trio concertant, op. 30 : for flute or violin, viola, and guitar /
Francesco Molino ; edited by Brian Jeffery. — London : Tecla Editions,
2005. — 1 score (21 p.) + 3 parts ; 31 cm.
Includes editorial notes.
Pl. no. TECLA 0235
ISBN 0948607661 (cased)
ISBN 0948607653 (pbk.)
System number: 013334497
Primary classification 785.44193

785.71931824
Bayliss, Colin.
Bohemian rondo : for string trio : [B127] / Colin Baylis. — Manchester :
Da Capo Music, c2003. — 1 score (15 p.) ; 30 cm.
For violin, viola and violoncello. — Duration: ca. 5:00. — Includes programme
and biographical notes.
Pl. no. DC 570
System number: 013351684

785.7194
An die Musik : 9 classical pieces arranged for string quartet / [arr. by]
John Kember. — London : Schott, c2005. — 1 score (19 p.) + 4 parts ;
31 cm.
Publ. no. ED 12755
Publ. no. S. & Co. 7786
ISMN M220123122
System number: 013192068

Beethoven, Ludwig van, 1770-1827.
[Quartets, strings, no. 1-6, op. 18]
Streichquartette = String quartets, op. 18 / Beethoven ; herausgegeben
von Jonathan Del Mar. — Kassel ; London : Bärenreiter, 2007. — 1
score (xvii, 177 p.) ; 23 cm. + 1 critical commentary (88 p.) ; 24 cm.
Introduction by Barry Cooper and pref. by Jonathan Del Mar in English and
German. — "Urtext."
Publ. no. TP 916
Publ. no. BA 9016
ISMN M006204724 (score)
ISMN M006534715 (commentary)
System number: 013943214

Beethoven, Ludwig van, 1770-1827.
[Symphonies, no. 7, op. 92, A major. Movement 1; *arr.*]
Symphony no 7, movement 1 / Ludwig van Beethoven ; arranged by Carlo
Martelli. — Dover : Broadbent & Dunn, c2002. — 4 parts ; 30 cm. —
Classic string quartet collection
Pl. no. B&D 12933
System number: 013383363

Beethoven, Ludwig van, 1770-1827.
[Symphonies, no. 8, op. 93, F Major. Movement 1; *arr.*]
Symphony no 8, movement 1 / Ludwig van Beethoven ; arranged by Carlo
Martelli. — Dover : Broadbent & Dunn, c2002. — 4 parts ; 30 cm. —
Classic string quartet collection
Pl. no. B&D 12935
System number: 013213498

*Brahms, Johannes, 1833-1897.
[Quartets, strings]
Streichquartette / Johannes Brahms ; herausgegben von Salome Reiser. —
München : G Henle Verlag, 2004. — 1 score (xxiii, 215 p.) : facsims. ;
33 cm. — (Neue Ausgabe sämtlicher Werke. Serie II, Kammermusik /
Johannes Brahms ; Bd. 3.)
"Herausgegeben von der Johannes Brahms Gesamtausgabe … Editionsleitung Kiel
in Verbindung mit der Gesellschaft der Musikfreunde in Wien." — Pref. and critical
commentary in German.
System number: 013465904

Clarke, Rebecca, 1886-1979.
[Comodo e ambile, string quartet]
Two movements for string quartet / Rebecca Clarke. — [New York] :
Oxford University Press, c2004. — 1 score (18 p.) + 4 parts ; 31 cm. —
Oxford music for string quartet
Edited by Christopher Johnson. — "The two movements published here … were
conceived about a year apart as components of distinct larger works"—Editorial
note. — Includes biographical and editorial notes.
ISBN 0193867494
System number: 013062664

*Cooke, Arnold.
[Quartets, strings, no. 2]
String quartet no. 2 / Arnold Cooke. — [s.l.] : Anglo-American Music
Publishers, 2005. — 1 score (75 p.) + 4 parts ; 28 cm.
Cover title. — Includes biographical note. — Duration: 28:00.
System number: 013593823

*Cooke, Arnold.
[Quartets, strings, no. 3]
String quartet no. 3 / Arnold Cooke. — [s.l.] : Anglo-American Music
Publishers, c2005. — 1 score (65 p.) + 4 parts ; 28 cm.
Cover title. — Includes biographical note.
System number: 013593727

*Cooke, Arnold.
[Quartets, strings, no. 4]
String quartet no. 4 / Arnold Cooke. — [s.l.] : Anglo-American Music
Publishers, c2005. — 1 score (64 p.) + 4 parts ; 28 cm.
Cover title. — Includes biographical note.
System number: 013593831

*Cooke, Arnold.
[Quartets, strings, no. 5]
String quartet no. 5 / Arnold Cooke. — [s.l.] : Anglo-American Music
Publishers, c2005. — 1 score (26 p.) + 4 parts ; 28 cm.
Cover title. — Includes biographical note.
System number: 013593651

*Cooke, Arnold.
[Variations and fugue, string quartet]
Variations and fugue : for string quartet : (1945) / Arnold Cooke. — [s.l.] :
Anglo-American Music Publishers, c2005. — 1 score (42 p.) + 4 parts ;
28 cm.
Cover title. — Includes biographical note.
System number: 013593845

*Davies, Peter Maxwell, 1934-
[Naxos quartet, no. 2]
Naxos quartet no. 2 : for string quartet / Peter Maxwell Davies. — London :
Chester Music, c2005. — 1 miniature score ; 19 cm.
Publ. no. CH66594 (score)
ISBN 1844498808
System number: 013190889

*Davies, Peter Maxwell, 1934-
[Naxos quartet, no. 3]
Naxos quartet no. 3 : for string quartet / Peter Maxwell Davies. — London :
Chester Music, c2005. — 1 miniature score (29 p.) ; 19 cm.
Duration: ca. 33:00.
Publ. no. CH67045
ISBN 1846091195
System number: 013314406

Fesca, F. E. (Friedrich Ernst), 1789-1826.
[Quartets, strings]
Sechs ausgewählte Streichquartette / Friedrich Ernst Fesca ;
herausgegeben von Markus Frei-Hauenschild unter Mitarbeit von Felix
Loy. — Kassel : Nagels Verlag, 2005. — 1 score (ix, 233 p.) ; 33 cm. —
(Das Erbe deutscher Musik ; Bd. 112. Abteilung Kammermusik ; Bd. 12.)
Pref. and critical commentary in German.
ISMN M006018116
System number: 013793762

Gilbert, Anthony.
[Quartets, strings, no. 3]
String quartet no. 3 : (1987) / Anthony Gilbert. — London : Schott,
c2007. — 1 score (17 p.) + 4 parts ; 31 cm.
Duration: 7:00.
Pl. no. S&Co.7867
Publ. no. ED 13072
ISMN M001146982
System number: 013771085

Graf, Friedrich Hartmann, 1727-1795.
[Quartets, bassoon, violin, viola, violoncello, B♭ major]
Quartetto VI for bassoon (or cello), violin (or oboe), viola and cello / by
Friedrich Hartmann Graf. — Lancaster : Phylloscopus Publications,
c2004. — 1 score (11 p.) + 4 parts ; 30 cm.
Edited by Chris and Frances Nex.
Publ. no. PP538
ISMN M570166701
System number: 013188898
Primary classification 785.44194

Handel, George Frideric, 1685-1759.
[Acis and Galatea. Heart, the seat of soft delight; *arr.*]
Heart, the seat of soft delight / George Frederick Handel ; arranged by
Carlo Martelli. — Dover : Broadbent & Dunn, c2003. — 4 parts ; 30 cm.
— Classic string quartet collection
Opera excerpt, arr. for string quartet.
Publ. no. B&D 12941
System number: 013167593

Hellawell, Piers, 1956-
The still dancers : (1992) : for string quartet / Piers Hellawell. — Kenley :
Maecenas Music, [ca. 2004], c1992. — 1 score (54 p.) ; 30 cm.
"Three pieces performed in sequence, between other works or individually." —
Commissioned by the Britten Quartet. — Duration: ca. 24:00. — Includes
performance instructions.
System number: 013422557

Mägi, Ester, 1922-
[Quartets, strings, no. 2]
Streichquartett Nr. 2 / Ester Mägi. — Lilienthal : Eres Edition, c2007. —
1 score (35 p.) + 4 parts ; 30 cm. — Eres Estonia edition
Pl. no. Eres 2883
ISMN M202428832
EAN 4030845028835
System number: 013953476

Mozart, Wolfgang Amadeus, 1756-1791.
[Quartets, strings, K. 155-160]
L'autografo dei quartetti "Milanesi" : nella Musikabteilung della
Staatsbibliothek (Preussischer Kulturbesitz) di Berlino = Das Autograph
der "Mailänder" Streichquartette : in der Musikabteilung der
Staatsbibliothek (Preussischer Kulturbesitz) von Berlin : KV 155-160
(134a, 134b, 157-159, 159a) / Wolfgang Amadeus Mozart ; edizione in
facsimile a cura di Giacomo Fornari. — Lucca : Libreria Musicale
Italiana, c2006. — 1 score (various pagings) : ill. ; 25 x 33 cm.
Facsimile of the original ms. — Introduction in Italian, German and English.
System number: 014053348

Mozart, Wolfgang Amadeus, 1756-1791.
[Vocal music. *Selections ; arr.*]
Mozart's choral favourites / arranged for string quartet by William
McConnell. — Laggan Bridge : Spartan Press, c2005. — 1 score (12 p.)
+ 4 parts ; 30 cm.
Includes pref. by the arranger.
Pl. no. SP718
ISMN M579997184
System number: 013203975

On wings of song : 8 popular pieces arranged for string quartet / [arr. by]
Barrie Carson Turner. — London : Schott, c2005. — 1 score (16 p.) +
4 parts ; 31 cm.
Pl. no. S. & Co. 7901
Publ. no. ED 12757
ISMN M220123009
System number: 013192096

Paganini, Nicolò, 1782-1840.
[Quartets, violin, viola, violoncello, guitar, M.S. 35, A major]
Quartetto n. 8 in La maggiore, (M.S. 35), per violino, viola, chitarra e violoncello = Quartet no. 8 in A major (M.S. 35), for violin, viola, guitar and violoncello / Nicolo Paganini ; a cura di Andrea Schiavina. — Bologna : Ut Orpheus Edizioni, c2007. — 1 score (36 p.) + 4 parts ; 31 cm. — (Accademia : musica strumentale e vocale dei secoli XVIII e XIX ; 71)
Edited from the autograph parts kept at the Biblioteca Casanatense, Rome. — Pref. in English and Italian. — "Urtext"—Cover.
Publ. no. ACC 71
ISMN M215314412
System number: 013953477

Pärt, Arvo.
Da pacem Domine : für Streichquartett, 2004/2006 / Arvo Pärt. — 11.09.2006. — Partitur und Stimmen. — Wien : Universal Edition, c2006. — 1 score (4 p.) + 4 parts ; 31 cm.
Duration: 4:15.
Publ. no. UE 33 340
ISBN 9783702432324
ISBN 3702432329
ISMN M008078293
System number: 013812962

*Purcell, Henry, 1659-1695.
[Trio sonatas, violins, continuo, Z. 796, E minor; *arr.*]
Sonata VII in E minor : from set of twelve : for violin, viola/violin & violoncello / Henry Purcell. — London : SJ Music, 2005. — 1 score (6 p.) + 4 parts ; 30 cm. — (Chamber music series)
Originally for 2 violins and continuo.
Publ. no. T2005-1
ISMN M708807780
System number: 013259032

Raff, Joachim, 1822-1882.
[Quartets, strings, no. 4, op. 137, A minor]
Quartett für zwei Violinen, Viola und Violoncello Nr. 4, a-Moll, op. 137 / Joachim Raff ; nach der Erstausgabe von J. Schuberth, 1869, neu herausgegeben von Volker Tosta. — Stuttgart : Edition Nordstern, c2004. — 1 score (x, 63 p.) + 4 parts ; 30 cm. — (Werke / Joachim Raff ; Bd. X/4)
Pref. in German and English; critical report in German. — Limited ed. of 200 copies.
Publ. no. 0110-1370
ISMN M700164669
System number: 014503085

Raff, Joachim, 1822-1882.
[Quartets, strings, no. 8, op. 192, no. 3, C major]
Quartett für zwei Violinen, Viola und Violoncello Nr. 8, C-Dur, op. 192, Nr. 3 : Suite in Kanon-Form / Joachim Raff ; nach der Erstausgabe von C.F. Kahnt, 1876, neu herausgegeben von Volker Tosta. — Stuttgart : Edition Nordstern, c2003. — 1 score (45 p.) + 4 parts ; 30 cm. — (Werke / Joachim Raff ; Bd. X/8)
Pref. in English and German. — Limited ed. of 200 copies.
Publ. no. 0110-1923
Pl. no. 14.07.03
ISMN M700164560
System number: 014503095

Schroeder, Hermann, 1904-1984.
[Quartets, strings, no. 4]
Streichquartette Nr. 4 und 5 / Hermann Schroeder ; herausgegeben von Rainer Mohrs. — Köln : Dohr, 2007. — 1 score (110 p.) + 4 parts : facsims. ; 32 cm. — Denkmäler rheinischer Musik ; Bd. 27, 27a.
Pref. and critical report in German. — Parts issued in a slipcase.
Pl. no. E.D. 21800
Pl. no. E.D. 21801
ISMN M202008003 (score)
ISMN M202008010 (parts)
System number: 014049817

Sheng, Bright, 1955-
[Quartets, strings, no. 4]
String quartet no. 4 : (Silent temple) / Bright Sheng. — New York : G. Schirmer ; Milwaukee, WI : Distributed by Hal Leonard, 2006. — 1 score (21 p.) + 4 parts ; 31 cm.
Duration: 17 min.
Publ. no. ED 4156
Publ. no. HL50484939
ISBN 0634055062
ISBN 978063405506
System number: 014053368

*Sirmen, Maddalena Laura Lombardini, 1745-1818.
[Quartets, strings]
String quartets opus 3 [sic], for 2 violins, viola & violoncello / Maddalena Lombardini-Sirmen. — [S.l.] : SJ Music, c2003. — 1 score (2 v.) + 4 parts (2 v.) ; 30 cm.
The quartets were originally published as 'Sei quartetti a violino I e II, viola et violoncello da Lodovico e Madalena Laura Syrmen, opera III' but are the work of Maddalena Lombardini-Sirmen only and are no longer refered to as her op. 3. — Edited from an edition published by William Napier in London c.1775. — Includes biographical editorial notes.
Publ. no. Q2003-1
Publ. no. Q2003-2
ISMN M708807742 (v. 1)

ISMN M708807759 (v. 2)
System number: 013196163

*Terteryan, A. (Avet), 1929-
[Quartets, strings, no. 2]
Streichquartett Nr. 2 = String quartet no. 2 / Avet Terterjan ; [herausgegeben von Maria Pflüger] — Hamburg : H. Sikorski, c2005. — 1 score (32 p.) + 4 parts ; 30 cm. — (Exempla nova ; 313)
Publ. no. 8513
Pl. no. H.S. 8513
ISMN M003032818
System number: 014629743

*Thoresen, Lasse, 1949-
Pyr aionion : for string quartet / Lasse Thoresen. — Adliswil : Pizzicato Verlag, c2004. — 1 score (24 p.) + 4 parts ; 31 cm.
"Op. 26"—Caption. — Includes performance instructions in English.
Publ. no. PVH 1132
System number: 014629754

Toldrà, Eduardo.
[Quartets, strings, D minor]
Quartet en Do menor : quartet de corda / Eduard Toldrá. — Madrid : Catalana d'editions musicals (C.E.M.), [2007], c1989. — 1 score (30 p.) ; 31 cm.
Duration: 25:10.
Publ. no. C-00049
ISMN M692130109
System number: 013953488

Vaĭnberg, Moiseĭ Samuilovich.
[Quartets, strings, no. 8, op. 66]
Streichquartett Nr. 8, op. 66, für zwei Violinen, Viola und Violoncello = for two violins, viola and violoncello / Mieczyslaw Weinberg (Vainberg, Moisei Samuilovich). — Partitur. — New York ; Hamburg : Peermusic Classical, c2003. — 1 score (24 p.) ; 31 cm.
Preface and biographical notes in German and English.
Publ. no. PCH 3544A
ISMN M500118435
EAN 9790500118435
System number: 014457047

*Vasks, Pēteris, 1946-
[Quartets, strings, no. 4]
4. Streichquartett, für 2 Violinen, Viola und Violoncello = String quartet no. 4, for 2 violins, viola, and violoncello (1999) / Pēteris Vasks. — Mainz ; London : Schott, c2004. — 1 score (36 p.) + 4 parts ; 31 cm.
Duration: 33:00.
Publ. no. ED 9295
Pl. no. 50 273
ISMN M001129299
System number: 013174345

*Vaughan Williams, Ralph, 1872-1958.
[Quartets, strings, C minor]
String quartet in C minor (1898) / Ralph Vaughan Williams. — Score. — London : Faber Music, 2002. — 1 score (38 p.) ; 30 cm. — (The early works / Ralph Vaughan Williams)
First ed., prepared for publication by Bernard Benoliel from the autograph ms. in the British Library. — Includes introd. and editorial notes.
ISBN 0571520855
EAN 9780571520855
System number: 013126578

*Vaughan Williams, Ralph, 1872-1958.
[Quartets, strings, C minor]
String quartet in C minor (1898) / Ralph Vaughan Williams. — Set of parts. — London : Faber Music, 2002. — 4 parts ; 32 cm. — (The early works / Ralph Vaughan Williams)
First ed., prepared for publication by Bernard Benoliel from the autograph ms. in the British Library. — Includes introduction.
ISBN 0571521762
System number: 013126516

*Zimmermann, Anton, 1741-1781.
[Quartets, strings, op. 3. No. 2]
Quartetto in B für 2 Violinen, Viola und Violoncello, op. 3/2 / Anton Zimmerman ; [herausgegeben von] Darina Múdra. — Partitur. — Wien : Doblinger, c2004. — 1 score (19 p.) ; 30 cm. — (Diletto musicale ; 1339)
Vorwort and Revisionsbericht in German.
Publ. no. DM 1339
Pl. no. D.19 048
ISMN M012190486
System number: 014629805

785.71941825
Ullmann, Viktor.
[Variationen und Doppelfuge über ein Thema von Arnold Schönberg; *arr.*]
Variationen und Doppelfuge über ein Thema von Arnold Schönberg
(op. 19/4) : Fassung für Streichquartett, op. 3c = Variations and Double
Fugue on a theme by Arnold Schoenberg (op. 19/4) : version for string
quartet, op. 3c / Viktor Ullmann. — Mainz ; London : Schott, c2005. — 1
score (36 p.) + 4 parts ; 31 cm. — Edition Schott
Originally for piano. — Pref. by Christian Hoesch in German with English, and
French translations.
Publ. no. ED 9182
ISMN M001127158
System number: 013887078

785.71941858
Hedges, Anthony, 1931-
West Oxford walks : op. 143 : for string quartet. Anthony Hedges. —
Beverley : Westfield Music, c2002. — 1 score (15 p.) ; 21 cm.
Duration: 7:15.
System number: 013188413

785.719418844
***Schnittke, Alfred, 1934-1998.**
[Overcoat. Polka; *arr.*]
Polka : Streichquartett = String quartet / Alfred Schnittke ; [arr. by] (Sergej
Dreznin). — Hamburg : Sikorski Musikverlage ; c2005. — 1 score (8 p.) +
4 parts ; 30 cm.
Pl. no. H.S. 2395
ISMN M003034188
System number: 013387829

785.719418846
Tchaikovsky, Peter Ilich, 1840-1893.
[Serenades, string orchestra, op. 48, C major. Valse; *arr.*]
Waltz [from] Serenade for strings / Peter Ilych Tchaikovsky ; arranged by
Carlo Martelli. — Dover : Broadbent & Dunn, c2004. — 4 parts ; 30 cm. —
Classic string quartet collection
Pl. no. B&D 12940
System number: 013383355

785.7195
***Beethoven, Ludwig van, 1770-1827.**
[Sonatas, violin, piano, no. 9, op. 47, A major; *arr.*]
Kreutzer sonata : an anonymous arrangement for string quintet : first
published by Simrock in 1832 : for 2 violins, viola & 2 violoncellos /
Beethoven ; edited by Paul Barritt. — London : SJ Music, 2004. — 1
miniature score (68 p.) ; 21 cm. + 5 parts ; 30 cm. — (Chamber music
series)
Publ. no. SJ Q2004-1
Publ. no. SJ SC2004-2
ISMN M708807766 (parts)
ISMN M708807773 (score)
System number: 013196241

Bruckner, Anton, 1824-1896.
[Quintet, violins, violas, violoncello, F major]
Streichquintett F-Dur ; Intermezzo D-Moll / Anton Bruckner. — Kritische
Neuausg. / unter Berücksichtigung der Arbeiten von Leopold Nowak
vorgelegt von Gerold W. Gruber. — Studienpartitur. — Wien :
Musikwissenschaftlicher Verlag der Internationalen Bruckner-Gesellschaft,
2007. — 1 score (84 p.) ; 24 cm. — (Sämtliche Werke / Anton Bruckner ;
Bd. 13/2)
Series published under the general editorship of the Österreichische
Nationalbibliothek and the Internationale Bruckner-Gesellschaft. — Pref. in German
and English.
System number: 013801996

Cambini, Giuseppe Maria, 1746-1825.
[Quintets, violins, viola, violoncellos, no. 21, C minor]
21. Quintett in c-moll für 2 Violinen, Viola und 2 Violoncelli = 21. quintet
in C minor for two violins, viola and two violoncellos / Giuseppe Cambini ;
nach dem Autograph neu herausgegeben von Bernhard Päuler. — Erstdruck. —
Winterthur : Amadeus, c2006. — 1 score (16 p.) + 5 parts ; 31 cm. —
Edited from the autograph ms. in the Library of Congress, Washington. — Preface in
German and English.
Publ. no. BP 1421
System number: 013887065

Dragonetti, Domenico, 1763-1846.
[Quintets, violin, violas, violoncello, double bass, B♭ major]
Quintett in B-Dur, für Solo-Kontrabass (Solo-Violine), Violine, 2 Violen
und Basso / Domenico Dragonetti ; [herausgegeben von] Nanna Koch ;
[Solostimme durchgesehen von Vladislav Riabokon] — Erstdruck. —
Partitur. — Wien : Doblinger c2006. — 1 score (24 p.) ; 30 cm. — (Diletto
musicale ; 1364)
For double bass (or violin) solo, violin, 2 violas, and violoncello. — Edited from
British Library Add. Ms. 17726. — Pref. in German and English.
Pl. no. D. 19 328
Publ. no. DM 1364
ISMN M012193289
EAN 9790012193289
System number: 013688130

Marco, Tomás, 1942-
La nuit de Bordeaux : aguafuerte goyesco : para guitarra y cuarteto de
cuerda / Tomás Marco. — Valencia : Institució Alfons el Magnànim,
2004. — 1 score (45 p.) + 5 parts ; 31 cm. — Col-lecció partitures ; 5
For guitar with 2 violins, viola, and violoncello.
ISMN M801210012
EAN 9790801210012
System number: 014457028

Thoma, Xaver, 1953-
[Quintets, violins, violas, violoncello, op. 116]
Streichquintett, Opus 116 (xpt), für 2 Violinen, 2 Bratschen und
Violoncello, 1998 / Xaver Paul Thoma. — Erstausg. — Asperg,
Germany : IKURO Edition, c2007. — 1 score (47 p.) ; 31 cm.
Preface in German by the composer.
Pl. no. IKURO 06121
System number: 013953486

***Vaughan Williams, Ralph, 1872-1958.**
[Short pieces]
Nocturne and scherzo (1906) ; Scherzo (1904) : for string quintet (2
violins, 2 violas and cello) / Ralph Vaughan Williams. — Set of parts. —
London : Faber Music, 2002. — 5 parts ; 32 cm. — (The early works /
Ralph Vaughan Williams)
ISBN 0571521754
System number: 013126461

785.7198
Raff, Joachim, 1822-1882.
[Octet, violins (4), violas, violoncellos, op. 176, C major]
Oktett für vier Violinen, zwei Violen und zwei Violoncelli, C-Dur,
op. 176 / Joachim Raff ; nach der Erstausgabe neu herausgegeben von
Volker Tosta. — Stuttgart : Edition Nordstern, c2005. — 1 score (xvi,
85 p.) + 8 parts ; 30 cm. — (Raff Werke ; Bd. XIII/2)
Pref. in German with English translation; critical notes in German. — Limited ed.
of 200 copies.
Publ. no. 0113-1760
ISMN M700164713
System number: 014503110

785.7199
Gorb, Adam, 1958-
Diaspora : 2003 : for string ensemble (33221 players) / Adam Gorb. —
Kenley : Maecenas Music, c2003. — 1 score (32 p.) ; 30 cm.
For 2 solo violins, solo double bass and string ensemble or string orchestra. —
Commissioned by the Goldberg Ensemble. — Duration: ca. 16:00.
System number: 013416719
Also classified at 784.727

Hellawell, Piers, 1956-
Sound carvings from the water's edge : (1996) : for 11 solo strings
(33221) Piers Hellawell. — Kenley : Maecenas Music, c1996. — 1 score
(44 p.) 21 x 30 cm.
For 6 violins, 2 violas, 2 violoncellos, and double bass. — Includes performance
instructions. — Duration: ca. 10:00.
System number: 013416562

Poole, Geoffrey, 1949-
Fragments : (1974 rev. '98) : for 14 solo strings (44321) or multiples /
Geoffrey Poole. — Kenley : Maecenas Music, c1998. — 1 score (36 p.) ;
30 cm.
Duration: ca. 5:00.
System number: 013422512
Also classified at 784.7

785.71991269
LeFanu, Nicola.
Catena : for 11 solo strings : (2000) / Nicola Lefanu. — Kenley, Surrey :
Maecenas Music, [2004?], c2000. — 1 score (33 p.) ; 30 cm.
For 6 violins, 2 violas, 2 violoncellos, and double bass; all instruments play
microtonally at times. — U.A. Fanthorpe's poem Palimpsest ("the original
catalyst for the piece"—programme note) printed on t.p. verso. — Duration:
18:00. — Composer's program note on t.p. verso.
System number: 013193710

785.72192
Boccherini, Luigi, 1743-1805.
[Duets, violins, G. 56-61]
6 duetti per 2 violini = 6 duets for 2 violins = 6 Violinduette : opus 3 : G
56-62 / Luigi Boccherini ; a cura di Rudolf Rasch. — Bologna : Ut
Orpheus Edizioni, 2007. — 1 score (xcviii, 53 p.) : facsims., col. port. ;
32 cm. — (Opera omnia / Luigi Boccherini ; v. 29)
Pref., introduction and critical commentary in Italian, English and German. —
Published in association with Centro Studi Opera Omnia Luigi Boccherini-Onlus
and Stichting - Fondazione Pietro Antonio Locatelli.
Pl. no. BCE 2
ISBN 9788881094608
ISMN M215314436
System number: 013821930

Double act : duets for violin / popular melodies arranged by Marian Hellen. — Buxhall : Kevin Mayhew, 2004. — 1 score (38 p.) ; 30 cm.
Publ. no. 3611816
ISMN M570243136
System number: 013182150

785.72192183

*Zenger, Max, 1837-1911.
[Amor und Psyche. Sonata]
Sonata für zwei Violinen : komponiert im alten Stil für König Ludwig II. von Bayern = Sonata for two violins : composed in ancient style for King Ludwig II of Bavaria / Max Zenger ; herausgegeben von Robert Münster. — Erstausg. — Frankfurt am Main : R. Lienau, c2005. — 1 score (9 p.) ; 31 cm.
"… can be played both as a violin duet and using section strings"—Pref. — From Zenger's opera Amor und Psyche. — Based on the ms. in the Musikabteilung der Bayerischen Staatsbibliothek (Mus. ms. 6954). — Includes pref. in German with English and French translations.
Pl. no. RL 40930
ISBN 9790011409305
ISMN M011409305
System number: 014629800

785.73192

*Benjamin, George.
Viola, viola : for viola duo, 1997 / George Benjamin. — London : Faber Music, c1998. — 1 score (6 leaves) ; 42 cm.
Cover title. — Duration: ca. 9:00.
ISBN 0571519067
System number: 006891403

785.74192

Hedges, Anthony, 1931-
[Dialogues]
Four dialogues : op. 138 : for two cellos / Anthony Hedges. — Beverley : Westfield Music, c2001. — 1 score (11 p.) ; 21 cm.
System number: 013188404

785.74194

*Shchedrin, Rodion Konstantinovich, 1932-
Hamlet ballad : for four-part cello ensemble = für vierstimmiges Celloensemble : (2004) / Rodion Shchedrin. — Mainz ; London : Schott, c2004. — 1 score (15 p.) + 4 parts ; 31 cm. — (Cello-Bibliothek = Cello library ; CB 178)
Publ. no. CB 178
ISMN M001137317
System number: 013565253

785.76192

Seven 16th century duos from the York manuscript : for bass and treble viols / anon. ; edited by Rhiannon Evans. — [S.l.] : Viola da Gamba Society of Great Britain, c2005. — 2 scores (8 p. each) ; 30 cm.
Source: York Minster manuscript M91 (S). — Includes critical commentary.
Pl. no. 203
System number: 013382536

785.76193

Hermansson, Erik.
How do you do Mr. Purcell : TrTB / Erik Hermansson. — [S.l.] : Viola da Gamba Society of Great Britain, c2004. — 3 parts ; 30 cm.
For viols. — Each part includes the full score on the verso. — Includes biographical note.
Pl. no. 202
System number: 013382541

Jenkins, John, 1592-1678.
[Fantasias, viols (3). *Selections*]
3 fantasias à 3 : nos. 10, 11 & 12 : (TrTrB) / John Jenkins ; edited by Virginia Brookes. — [S.l.] : Viola da Gamba Society of Great Britain, c2004. — 1 score (8 p.) + 3 parts ; 30 cm.
For viols. — Source: London, British Library, Add. MS 31428. — Includes critical commentary.
Pl. no. 200
System number: 013382526

Jenkins, John, 1592-1678.
[Fantasias, viols (3). *Selections*]
3 fantasias à 3 : nos. 7, 8 & 9 : (TrTrB) / John Jenkins ; edited by Virginia Brookes. — [S.l.] : Viola da Gamba Society of Great Britain, c2004. — 1 score (14 p.) + 3 parts ; 30 cm.
For viols. — Source: London, British Library, Add. MS 31428. — Includes critical commentary.
Pl. no. 193a—193b
System number: 013382426

785.761931858

*Cooke, Arnold.
[Suites, viols (3)]
Suite for two treble viols and bass viol / Arnold Cooke. — [s.l.] : Anglo-American Music Publishers, c2005. — 1 score (17 p.) + 3 parts ; 28 cm.
Cover title. — Includes biographical note.
System number: 013593801

785.76194

3 In nomines à 4 : (TrTr/TTB) / Parsons, Parsley & Weelkes ; edited by Virginia Brookes. — [S.l.] : Viola da Gamba Society of Great Britain, c2004. — 1 score (11 p.) + 4 parts ; 30 cm.
Includes critical commentary. — Source: Oxford, Bodleian Library, Ms. Mus. Sch. D.212-6.
Pl. no. 198a—198c
System number: 013382510

Lawes, William, 1602-1645.
[Airs, viols (4), VdGS no. 306]
2 aires nos. 306 & 110 : (TrTrBB) / William Lawes ; edited by Gordon Dodd. — [S.l.] : Viola da Gamba Society of Great Britain, c2003. — 1 score (6 p.) + 4 parts ; 30 cm.
For viols. — Includes critical commentary.
Pl. no. 197
System number: 013382498

Lawes, William, 1602-1645.
[Airs, viols (4), VdGS no. 336]
2 aires nos. 336 & 318 : (TrTr/ATB) / William Lawes ; edited by Gordon Dodd. — [S.l.] : Viola da Gamba Society of Great Britain, c2003. — 1 score (8 p.) + 4 parts ; 30 cm.
For viols. — Includes critical commentary.
Pl. no. 196
System number: 013382482

Ward, John, 1571-1638.
[Chamber music. *Selections*]
Consort music of four parts / John Ward ; transcribed and edited by Ian Payne. — London : Stainer and Bell, 2005. — 1 score (xxxviii, 106 p.) : facsims. ; 34 cm. — Musica Britannica ; 83
Fantasias and In nomines for 4 viols, and 6 ayres for 2 bass viols and organ. — Edited from Bibliothèque nationale de France, Fonds du Conservatoire, MS Réserve F.770 (In nomines and "Paris" fantasias), and other sources. — "Published for the Musica Britannica Trust established by the Royal Musical Association." — Pref. in English, French and German; introduction and critical commentary in English only.
ISBN 0852498853
ISMN M220221323
System number: 013216320
Also classified at 785.28193

Wilder, Philip van, d. 1553.
[Chansons. *Selections*]
3 chansons à 4 & à 5 : (TrTr/TTB with text) / Philip Van Wilder ; edited by John Bryan. — [S.l.] : Viola da Gamba Society of Great Britain, c2004. — 2 scores (8, 4 p.) + 5 parts ; 30 cm.
May be performed by voices, viols or a combination. — Source: York Minster Library, Music Manuscript M 91 (S). — French words; English translation printed for reference on verso of front cover.
Pl. no. 201a—201b
Publ. no. 201
System number: 013382531
Primary classification 782.543

785.761941876

Ward, John, 1571-1638.
[Fantasias, viols (4), Meyer 1-6. *Parts*]
Oxford fantasias : and, two-part ayres : for viols and organ / John Ward ; edited by Ian Payne. — London : Stainer & Bell, c2005. — 7 parts ; 30 cm.
"Set for four string parts for the Oxford fantasias corresponding with Musica Britannica, volume LXXXIII, 21-26, and two bass viol and organ parts for the ayres corresponding with Musica Britannica, volume LXXXIII, 27-32"—Cover.
Publ. no. AC221
ISMN M220221484
System number: 013307456
Also classified at 785.28193

785.76195

The amorous hexachord : madrigal fantasies from the Tregian manuscript / Pallavicino, Bianciardi, and Giovannelli ; edited by Hannah Davidson. — [United States] : Viola da Gamba Society of America, 2006. — 1 score (16 p.) + 5 parts ; 28 cm.
For 5 viols. — Edited from the Tregian Manuscript, British Library (MS Egerton 3665). — "Special collections HEX." — Italian words, also printed for reference.
System number: 013646320

*Browne, John, ca. 1608-1691.
[In nomine, viols (5)]
In nomine fantasia & Ayre à 5 : TrTrBB / John Browne ; edited by Virginia Brookes. — [S.l.] : Viola da Gamba Society of Great Britain, c2005. — 1 score (6 p.) + 5 parts ; 30 cm.
For viols. — Cover title. — Source: Oxford, Christ Church, Mus. MS 47308, no.21-22. — Includes critical commentary.
Pl. no. 207
System number: 013424757

*Giovannelli, Ruggiero, ca. 1560-1625.
[Selections]
Three pieces à 5 : TrTrTTB / Ruggiero Giovannelli ; edited by Virginia
Brookes. — [S.l.] : Viola da Gamba Society of Great Britain, c2005. — 1
score (12 p.) + 5 parts ; 30 cm.
For viols (1st and 2nd works) or voices (3rd work). — Cover title. — Sources:
London, British Library, Egerton 3665 f. 199, p. 393 (1st work), Egerton 3665 no.
102, p. 492 (2nd work), London, British Library K.3.1.14 no. XVIII (3rd work). —
Includes critical commentary.
Pl. no. 210
System number: 013441010
Also classified at 782.543

Johnson, Robert, ca. 1500-ca. 1560.
[Knell]
A knell of Johnson / Robert Johnson. Pavan à 5 / Joseph Lupo ; edited by
Virginia Brookes. — [S.l.] : Viola da Gamba Society of Great Britain,
c2004. — 1 score (8 p.) + 5 parts ; 30 cm.
For viols (TrTr/TTT/BB). — Sources: London, British Library, Add 31390, ff25v-26
and Add 22579, f37v; New York Public Library, Drexel 4180-4 f81; Washington,
Folger Shakespeare Library, 408, f19v. — Includes critical commentary.
Pl. no. 199
System number: 013382517

*Milton, John, ca. 1563-1647.
[If that a sinner's sighs, voices (5)]
Two settings of "If that a sinner's sighs" : à 5, TrTrTTB, fully texted : [and]
à 6, TrTrT(with text)TBB / John Milton ; edited by Virginia Brookes. —
[S.l.] : Viola da Gamba Society of Great Britain, c2005. — 1 score (12 p.) +
6 parts ; 30 cm.
Edited for viols (with or without voices). — Cover title. — Includes critical
commentary.
Publ. no. 204
System number: 013441046
Also classified at 782.76196; 782.543

*Sculthorpe, Peter, 1929-
[Djilile, viols (5)]
Djilile : consort music of five parts / Peter Sculthorpe. — [London] : Faber
Music, c1995. — 1 score (7 p.) + 5 parts ; 30 cm.
For 5 viols. — "Based up on an adaptation of an Aboriginal melody from northern
Australia"—Pref. — Duration: ca. 6:30.
System number: 013555103

Wilder, Philip van, d. 1553.
[Chansons. *Selections*]
3 chansons à 4 & 5 : (TrTr/TTB with text) / Philip Van Wilder ; edited by
John Bryan. — [S.l.] : Viola da Gamba Society of Great Britain, c2004. — 2
scores (8, 4 p.) + 5 parts ; 30 cm.
May be performed by voices, viols or a combination. — Source: York Minster
Library, Music Manuscript M 91 (S). — French words; English translation printed
for reference on verso of front cover.
Pl. no. 201a—201b
Publ. no. 201
System number: 013382531
Primary classification 782.543

785.7619518823
Gibbons, Orlando, 1583-1625.
[Pavans, voices (5), H. 30]
Pavane, De la Roye : (TrTrTTB) / Orlando Gibbons ; edited & completed by
Mark Levy. — [S.l.] : Viola da Gamba Society of Great Britain, c2003. — 1
score ([3] p.) + 5 parts ; 30 cm.
For viols. — Edited from London, British Library, Add MSS 30826-8.
Pl. no. 195
System number: 013382472

785.787192
Riehm, Rolf, 1937-
Lamento di Tristano : für zwei Gitarren / Rolf Riehm. — Celle : Moeck,
c1993. — 1 score (30 p.) ; 31 cm. — (Das Gitarren-Repertoire)
For 2 guitars. — Includes program notes and performance instructions in German,
English and French. — Publisher's no.: Edition Moeck Nr. 7031.
Pl. no. 7031
System number: 014053361

Schwaen, Kurt, 1909-2007.
[Fantasia, guitars (2)]
Fantasia für 2 Gitarren / Kurt Schwaen. — Berlin : Edition Margaux, c2005.
— 1 score (11 p.) + 2 parts ; 30 cm.
Pl. no. em 2070
ISBN 9783733303761
ISBN 3733303768
ISMN M203208655
System number: 014599826

Sor, Fernando, 1778-1839.
[Guitar music. 1997]
The new complete works for guitar : re-engraved in eleven volumes /
Fernando Sor ; edited by Brian Jeffery. — 2nd printing with corrections. —
London : Tecla, 2004, c1997. — 1 score (11 v.) ; 31 cm.
"A modern re-engraved edition ... of all Sor's music for guitar solo and for guitar
duet"—Introd. to the series. — Each volume includes notes on the pieces.
Publ. no. 1200
Publ. no. 1201

Publ. no. 1202
Publ. no. 1203
Publ. no. 1204
Publ. no. 1205
Publ. no. 1206
Publ. no. 1207
Publ. no. 1208
Publ. no. 1209
Publ. no. 1210
Publ. no. 1211
ISBN 094860770X (set paperbound)
ISBN 0948607718 (v. 1 paperbound)
ISBN 0948607726 (v. 2 paperbound)
ISBN 0948607734 (v. 3 paperbound)
ISBN 0948607742 (v. 4 paperbound)
ISBN 0948607750 (v. 5 paperbound)
ISBN 0948607769 (v. 6 paperbound)
ISBN 0948607777 (v. 7 paperbound)
ISBN 0948607785 (v. 8 paperbound)
ISBN 0948607793 (v. 9 paperbound)
ISBN 0948607807 (v. 10 paperbound)
ISBN 0948607815 (v. 11 paperbound)
System number: 013334512
Primary classification 787.87

785.795192
Vernier, Jean-Aime, b. 1769.
[Duets, harps, no. 2, op. 30]
Deuxieme duo, op. 30, per 2 arpe = for 2 harps / Jean-Aime Vernier ; a
cura di Anna Pasetti. — Bologna : Ut Orpheus, c2007. — 1 score (43 p.)
+ 2 parts ; 31 cm. — (Magadis : musiche per arpa ; MAG 190)
Preface in Italian and English.
ISMN M215314566
EAN 9790215314566
System number: 014050077

785.8 – WOODWIND ENSEMBLES

785.81858
Gorb, Adam, 1958-
[Suites, woodwinds (1993)]
Suite for winds / Adam Gorb. — Kenley : Maecenas Music, c1995. — 1
score (60 p.) ; 30 cm. — Millennium series for wind bands & ensembles
"The 'official' scoring is for flutes (some doubling piccolos), oboes, clarinets,
saxophones and bassoons, though the composer is happy that directors re-allocate
lines where necessary"—Pref. — Duration: 10:00.
Publ. no. MC0007
System number: 013192928

785.8192
*Ridout, Alan, 1934-1996.
Serenata notturno : for flute and clarinet / Alan Ridout. — Ampleforth :
Emerson Edition, c2005. — 2 scores (8 p. each) : port. ; 28 cm.
Includes biographical note. — Duration: ca. 8:00.
Publ. no. E475
Publ. no. 475
ISMN M570405343
System number: 013460588

785.8193
*Bizet, Georges, 1838-1875.
[Carmen. *Selections; arr.*]
Flexible woodwind trios : Carmen / Georges Bizet ; arr. Karen Evans. —
Laggan Bridge : Spartan Press, c2005. — 1 score (16 p.) + 1 set of parts :
30 cm. port.
May be performed by different combinations of flutes, oboes, clarinets,
saxophones and bassoon. — Cover title. — "Grades 3-7"—Cover. — Includes
biographical note about the arranger.
Pl. no. SP739
ISMN M579997399
System number: 013441187

*Devienne, François, 1759-1803.
[Trios, flutes, violoncello, op. 19. No. 1]
Trio op. 19 no. 1, for flute, flute or violin, and cello or bassoon / by
François Devienne. — Lancaster : Phylloscopus Publications; c2005. —
1 score (6 p.) + 3 parts ; 30 cm.
Edited by Chris and Frances Nex. — New version, replaces PP13 (M570160143).
Publ. no. PP564
ISMN M570166961
System number: 013561743
Primary classification 785.44193

*Duval, Jérôme.
[Trios, flutes, bassoon, op. 2. No. 2]
Trio op. 2 no. 2, for two flutes and bassoon / by Jérôme Duval. —
Lancaster : Phylloscopus Publications, c2005. — 1 score (8 p.) + 3 parts ;
30 cm.
Edited by Chris and Frances Nex. — New version, replaces PP2 (ISMN
M570160020).
Publ. no. PP563
ISMN M570166954
System number: 013560702

Flexible woodwind trios : baroque / arr. Karen Evans. — Laggan Bridge : Spartan Press Music Publishers Ltd., c2005. — 1 score (12 p.) + 1 set of parts : port. ; 30 cm.
May be performed by different combinations of flutes, oboes (including cor anglais), clarinets and saxophones. — "Grades 3-6"—Cover. — Includes biographical note.
Pl. no. SP738
ISMN M579997382
System number: 013376609

Wilson, Andrew, 1960-
Phoenix trio : for flute, oboe and clarinet in B♭ : [opus 46] / by Andrew Wilson. — Lancaster : Phylloscopus Publications, c2004. — 1 score (17 p.) + 3 parts : 30 cm.
Publ. no. PP532
ISMN M570166640
System number: 013188882

785.8199
Gorb, Adam, 1958-
Battle symphony : for woodwind ensemble including saxophones / Adam Gorb. — Kenley : Maecenas Music, c1999. — 1 score (65 p.) ; 30 cm. — Millennium series for wind bands & ensembles
"Op.26 (1997)"—Prelim. — For woodwind "ensembles of quite a wide size range, form one player per part to significantly larger groups."—Prelim. — Duration: 10:00.
Publ. no. MC0053
System number: 013193057
Primary classification 784.89

785.8321921723
The best Christmas flute duet book ever! / selected and edited by Emma Coulthard. — London : Wise, c2005. — 1 score (32 p.) ; 31 cm.
27 Christmas carols and songs arranged for flute duet. — Grades 1-3.
Publ. no. AM982586
ISBN 1846090105
System number: 013312881

785.832192183
Atys, 1715-1784.
[Sonatas, flutes (2), op. 1]
Six sonates en duo : en forme de conversation : pour deux flûtes traversières : Paris s.d. / Atys. — Firenze : Studio per edizioni scelte, 2006. — 1 score (31 p.) ; 34 cm. — (Archivum musicum. L'art de la flûte traversière ; 65)
Reprint. Original published: Paris : L'Auteur, 1754. — Preface in Italian by Marcello Castellani.
ISBN 9788872428221
ISBN 887242822X
System number: 013771072

785.832193
André, Johann Anton, 1775-1842.
[Trios, flutes (3), op. 29, G major]
Trio G-Dur, für 3 Querflöten = Trio G major, for three flutes, opus 29, 1805 / Johann Anton André ; herausgegeben von Peter Thalheimer. — Ilshofen : NotaBene, c2005. — 1 score (34 p.) + 3 parts ; 30 cm.
New edition, edited from a copy of the first edition (Offenbach : Andre, 1805), preserved in the Stiftsbibliothek Heiligenkreuz. — Preface in German and English. — Critical report in German.
Pl. no. NB 1.002.01
Publ. no. 1.002.01
ISMN M700244095
EAN 9790700244095
System number: 014497790

*Moore, Philip, 1943-
[Toccata, adagio & fugue, flutes (3)]
Toccata, adagio & fugue : for three flutes / Philip Moore. — Ampleforth : Emerson Edition, c2005. — 1 score (6 p.) + 3 parts : port. ; 28 cm.
Biographical note on p. [4] of cover. — Duration: ca. 5:00.
Publ. no. E469
Publ. no. 469
ISMN M570405176
System number: 013565446

785.8321941858
Gibbs, Christopher, 1938-
[Forest of Bowland suite; arr.]
Forest of Bowland suite : for two flutes, alto flute and bass flute / by Christopher Gibbs ; arranged by Chris Nex. — Lancaster : Phylloscopus Publications, c1998. — 1 score (11 p.) + 4 parts ; 30 cm.
"Forest of Bowland Suite was originally written in 1994 … the first movement came to him as he was walking on Pendel Hill. The idea grew into a suite for string quartet and a version for wind quartet was made in 1998. The present arrangement for flute quartet was made by Chris Nex with the composer's approval."—Pref.
Publ. no. PP540
ISMN M570166725
System number: 013173876

785.836
*Associated Board of the Royal Schools of Music (Great Britain).
Music medals recorder ensemble pieces. — London : Associated Board of the Royal Schools of Music : sales agent and distributor, Oxford University Press, c2005. — 1 score (5 v.) ; 31 cm. — (Music medals)
"Five volumes of … repertoire for the developing ensemble … original pieces and imaginative arrangements for duets, trios and quartets"—Back cover. — Cover title.
Pl. no. AB 3133 (copper)
Pl. no. AB 3134 (bronze)
Pl. no. AB 3135 (silver)
Pl. no. AB 3136 (gold)
Pl. no. AB 3137 (platinum)
ISBN 1860966020 (copper)
ISBN 1860966039 (bronze)
ISBN 1860966047 (silver)
ISBN 1860966055 (gold)
ISBN 1860966063 (platinum)
System number: 013382222

785.836076
Watts, Sarah.
Red hot treble recorder tutor : [student copy] / Sarah Watts. — Buxhall : Kevin Mayhew, 2004. — 32 p. : ill. ; 21 x 30 cm. + 1 compact disc.
Recorder part(s) for the 23 pieces in the teacher copy, plus two duets and two trios without accompaniment. — Also includes practice patterns, listening exercises, and instructional information.
Publ. no. 3611842
ISMN M570243839
System number: 013182133
Primary classification 788.365076

785.836195
Byrd, William, 1542 or 3-1623.
[Emendemus in melius; arr.]
Emendemus in melius : à 5 / William Byrd. — Chesham : Alex Ayre Music Services, c2005. — 5 parts ; 30 cm.
Arr. for descant, treble, 2 tenor and bass recorders. Originally for voices. — Presumably arranged by Alex Ayre.
Publ. no. C.R.C.S. 1278
System number: 013374803

785.836196
*Mozart, Wolfgang Amadeus, 1756-1791.
[Divertimenti, K270, B♭ major. Selections; arr.]
Divertimento à 6 in C, K. 270. Part II / W.A. Mozart ; recorder arrangement by Alex Ayre. — Chesham : Alex Ayre Music Services, c2005. — 6 parts ; 30 cm. — Chiltern recorder consort series ; 422
Arrangement of the second, third, fourth and fifth movements of Mozart's Divertimento K. 270. — For treble, 2 tenor, bass in F, bass in C and contrabass recorders; originally for 2 oboes, 2 horns, 2 bassoons.
Publ. no. C.R.C.S. 422
System number: 013548612

Mozart, Wolfgang Amadeus, 1756-1791.
[Divertimenti, K270, B♭ major. Allegro molto; arr.]
Divertimento à 6 in C, K. 270 / W.A. Mozart ; recorder arrangement by Alex Ayre. — Chesham : Alex Ayre Music Services, c2005. — 6 parts ; 30 cm. — Chiltern recorder consort series ; 421
Arrangement of the first movement of Mozart's Divertimento K. 270. — For treble, 2 tenor, bass in F, bass in C and contrabass recorders; originally for 2 oboes, 2 horns, 2 bassoons.
Publ. no. C.R.C.S. 421
System number: 013324522

785.836197
Palestrina, Giovanni Pierluigi da, 1525?-1594.
[Motets (1569). Tu es Petrus; arr.]
Tu es petrus : à 7 / Palestrina. — Chesham : Alex Ayre Music Services, c2005. — 7 parts ; 30 cm. — Chiltern recorder consort series ; 1279
Arr. for recorders at either four foot pitch (descant, treble, 3 treble/tenor and 2 bass) or eight foot pitch (treble/tenor, 4 bass in F and 2 bass in C). — Presumably arranged by Alex Ayre.
Publ. no. C.R.C.S. 1279
System number: 013374823

785.85192
Hansell, Philip, 1962-
[Bagatelles, oboe, bassoon (2005)]
Seven bagatelles for oboe and bassoon / by Philip Hansell. — Lancaster ; Phylloscopus Publications, c2005. — 2 scores (8 p.) ; 30 cm.
Publ. no. PP547
ISMN M570166794
System number: 013173894

785.85193
*Aitken, Elizabeth, 1949-
Talisker : where sea meets Skye : for two oboes and cor anglais / by Elizabeth Aitken. — Lancaster : Phylloscopus Publications, c2005. — 1 score (2 p.) + 3 parts ; 30 cm.
Publ. no. PP551
ISMN M570166831
System number: 013472771

Rimsky-Korsakov, Nikolay, 1844-1908.
[Skazka o t͡sare Saltane. Nu, teper', moĭ shmel'; *arr.*]
The flight of the bumblebee / Nikolay Rimsky-Korsakov ; arranged for 2 oboes & cor anglais by John Warrack. — Ampleforth : Emerson Edition, c2003. — 1 score (4 p.) + 3 parts : port. ; 28 cm.
Originally for orchestra. — Cover title. — Duration: ca. 1:40. — Includes biographical note.
Publ. no. 426
System number: 013188151

785.851931825
*Brahms, Johannes, 1833-1897.
[Variationen über ein Thema von Haydn. *Selections; arr.*]
Variations on a theme of Haydn / by Johanness Brahms ; arranged for two oboes and cor anglais by Rachel Broadbent. — Lancaster : Phylloscopus Publications, c2005. — 1 score (7 p.) + 3 parts ; 30 cm.
"Rachel Broadbent has chosen to arrange the Theme, Variations 5, 6 and 7 …"—Pref.
Publ. no. PP562
ISMN M570166947
System number: 013472830

785.851931858
Aitken, Elizabeth, 1949-
Cake dance suite : for two oboes and cor anglais / by Elizabeth Aitken. — Lancaster : Phylloscopus Publications, c2005. — 1 score (5 p.) + 3 parts ; 30 cm.
Publ. no. PP550
ISMN M570166824
System number: 013188905

785.85194
*Eight four-part fantasias : for oboe, oboe & cor anglais and two bassoons / by Simon Ives … [et al.] — Lancaster : Phylloscopus Publications, c2005. — 1 score (22 p.) + 4 parts ; 30 cm.
Works by Simon Ives, Alfonso Ferrabosco, William Byrd, John Bull and John Jenkins. — Edited by Chris and Frances Nex. — Originally for 4 viols. — These 8 fantasias are the same works as those included in Nine fantasias in four parts, edited by Sydney Beck (New York Public Library, 1947). The 9th work is published separately as PP567.
Publ. no. PP566
ISMN M570166985
System number: 013561749

*Ives, Simon, 1600-1662.
Fantasia in four parts (cor anglais and 3 bassoons) / by Simon Ives. — Lancaster : Phylloscopus Publications, c2005. — 1 score (4 p.) + 4 parts ; 30 cm.
Edited by Chris and Frances Nex. — Originally for 4 viols. — Included in Nine fantasias in four parts, edited by Sydney Beck (New York Public Library, 1947). The other 8 works are published in PP566.
Publ. no. PP567
ISMN M570166992
System number: 013561837

785.852193
*McGarr, Peter.
Images of sleep : for three oboes / by Peter McGarr. — Lancaster : Phylloscopus Publications, c2005. — 1 score (4 p.) + 3 parts ; 30 cm.
Publ. no. PP558
ISMN M570166909
System number: 013472911

785.858193
Bratton, John W. (John Walter), 1867-1947.
[Teddy bears' picnic; *arr.*]
The teddy bears' picnic / John W. Bratton ; arranged for three bassoons by Toddy Harman. — Ampleforth : Emerson Edition, [2004?] — 1 score (7 p.) + 3 parts ; 28 cm.
Originally for piano solo; later arranged as a song with words by Jimmy Kennedy. — Includes biographical note.
Publ. no. 464
ISMN M570404650
System number: 013360855

785.858194
*Carr, Gordon, 1943-
Mr. McKie's valediction : for solo bassoon with three companions / Gordon Carr. — Ampleforth : Emerson Edition, c2005. — 1 score (8 p.) + 4 parts : port. ; 28 cm.
For four bassoons. — Includes biographical and programme notes. — Duration: ca. 5:30.
Publ. no. E471
Publ. no. 471
ISMN M570405268
System number: 013460625

Kelly, Bryan.
[Iberian pieces]
Three Iberian pieces : for four bassoons / Bryan Kelly. — Ampleforth : Emerson Edition, c2004. — 1 score (11 p.) + 4 parts : port. ; 28 cm.
Durations: 2:50; 2:00; 2:40.
Publ. no. 448

Publ. no. E448
ISMN M570404704
System number: 013360867

Mozart, Wolfgang Amadeus, 1756-1791.
[Ave verum corpus; *arr.*]
Ave verum corpus : [K.618] / by W.A. Mozart ; arranged for four bassoons by David B. Johnson. — Lancaster : Phylloscopus Publications, c2004. — 4 scores ([2] p. each) ; 30 cm.
Publ. no. PP533
ISMN M570166657
System number: 013178708

785.8581941858
Hermann, Avril.
Fruit salad : three pieces for four bassoons / by Avril Hermann. — Lancaster : Phylloscopus Publications, c2005. — 1 score (8 p.) + 4 parts ; 30 cm.
Publ. no. PP546
ISMN M570166787
System number: 013173898

785.862193
Cowles, Colin.
Group therapy : clarinet trios in popular and jazz styles / by Colin Cowles. — London : Studio Music, c2005. — 1 score (12 p.) + 3 parts ; 30 cm.
11 pieces for clarinet trio. — "A mixture of playing standards between grades two and six"—Cover verso.
ISMN M050065357
System number: 013271638

785.87
*Associated Board of the Royal Schools of Music (Great Britain).
Music medals saxophone ensemble pieces. — London : Associated Board of the Royal Schools of Music : sales agent and distributor, Oxford University Press, c2005. — 1 score (5 v.) ; 31 cm. — (Music medals)
"Five volumes of … repertoire for the developing ensemble … original pieces and imaginative arrangements for duets, trios and quartets"—Back cover. — Cover title.
Pl. no. AB 3138 (copper)
Pl. no. AB 3139 (bronze)
Pl. no. AB 3140 (silver)
Pl. no. AB 3141 (gold)
Pl. no. AB 3142 (platinum)
ISBN 1860096071 (copper)
ISBN 186009660X (bronze)
ISBN 1860096098 (silver)
ISBN 1860096101 (gold)
ISBN 186009611X (platinum)
System number: 013441370

785.87193
Ketley, David F.
Sax a tre : for saxophone trio / David F. Ketley. — Manchester : Da Capo Music, c2005. — 1 score (12 p.) ; 30 cm.
"Scored for Alto in B flat, Tenor in E flat, and Baritone in B flat"—Prelim. — Duration: ca. 10:00. — Includes biographical notes.
Publ. no. DC 629
System number: 013351611

785.87194
Bayliss, Colin.
Lullaby for saxophone quartet : [B134] / Colin Bayliss. — Manchester : Da Capo Music, c2004. — 1 score (5 p.) ; 30 cm.
"This piece is an arrangement of the composer's Christmas Lullaby for SATB choir (B128)"—T.p. verso. — Duration: ca. 3:40. — Includes biographical notes.
Pl. no. DC 618
System number: 013351659

Casken, John.
Nearly distant : for saxophone quartet : (2000) / John Casken. — London : Schott, c2005. — 1 score (22 p.) + 4 parts ; 31 cm.
"Nearly distant draws most of its material from a larger work for saxophone quartet and wind orchestra, Distant variations"—Composer's note. — Duration: 8:00.
Publ. no. ED 12831
Publ. no. S&Co.7766
ISMN M220123184
System number: 013190541

*Harle, John.
Foursquare : for saxophone quartet / John Harle. — London : Chester Music, c2005. — 1 score (19 p.) ; 31 cm.
Each player doubles on more than one saxophone. — Includes composer's note.
Publ. no. CH61574
ISBN 1844499715
System number: 013189099

*Tisné, Antoine.
Labyrinthus sonoris : pour quatuor de saxophones / Antoine Tisné. — Lagny sur Marne : Musik Fabrik, c1998. — 1 score (22 p.) + 4 parts ; 30 cm.
Cover title.
System number: 014629759

785.87198

Peçi, Aleksandër, 1951-
[Mosaical, saxophone (8)]
Mosaical : saxophone ensemble / Aleksandër Peçi. — Tirana : Aelfior
Editions, c2006. — 1 score (60 p.) ; 31 cm.
For 8 saxophones (SSAATTBB).
Pl. no. AED.23406
System number: 014053354

785.9 – BRASS ENSEMBLES

785.9

Richards, Goff.
À la carte : brass band ensemble / by Goff Richards. — Brass band
instrument edition — London : Studio Music, c2005. — 1 score (32 p.) +
12 parts ; 30 cm. — (Studio Music brass ensemble series.)
"A separate set of parts for orchestral brass instruments (M050064275) is also
available. Please note: The two sets are not interchangeable"—Back cover. — For 3
cornets, flugel horn, E flat horn, baritone, 2 trombones, euphonium, E flat bass and 2
percussion.
ISMN M050063841 (set)
ISMN M050063858 (score)
System number: 013188557
Primary classification 785.57

785.9192

Holdom, Colin.
[Studio for brass. Duets]
21 duets / by Colin Holdom. — Bass clef ed. — London : Studio Music,
c2005. — 1 score (22 p.) ; 30 cm.
For 2 bass clef brass instruments. — Contains original pieces and arrangements. —
Supplement to the "Studio for brass" books. — "Intermediate course"—Cover.
ISMN M050064268
System number: 013194551

Holdom, Colin.
[Studio for brass. Duets]
21 duets / by Colin Holdom. — Treble clef ed. — London : Studio Music,
c2004. — 1 score (22 p.) ; 30 cm.
For 2 treble clef brass instruments. — Contains original pieces and arrangements. —
Supplement to the "Studio for brass" books. — "Intermediate course"—Cover.
ISMN M050064251
System number: 013194562

785.9195

Bingham, Judith.
A dream of the past : (1993) : 3 paintings by Millais and a prologue : in
memorium Christoph Delz : for brass quintet / Judith Bingham. — Kenley :
Maecenas Music, c1993. — 1 score (23 p.) ; 30 cm.
For 2 trumpets, horn, trombone and tuba. — Commissioned by the Park Lane Group.
— Reproduced from holograph. — Duration: ca. 15:00
System number: 013193719

Danson, Alan.
Intrada : brass quintet / Alan Danson. — Dover : Broadbent & Dunn, c2001.
— 1 score (4 p.) + 5 parts ; 30 cm.
Pl. no. B&D 10512
System number: 013167570

A medley of rhymes for five brass : brass quintet : traditional / arranged by
Alan Danson. — Dover : Broadbent & Dunn, c2002, c2001. — 1 score
(8 p.) + 5 parts ; 30 cm.
Cover title.
Pl. no. B&D 10513
System number: 013167557

Samuel, Rhian.
Dovey Junction : for brass quintet / by Rhian Samuel. — London : Stainer
& Bell, c2005. — 1 score (8 p.) + 5 parts ; 30 cm.
For 2 trumpets, horn, trombone and tuba. — Includes programme note.
Publ. no. AC224
ISMN M220221552
System number: 013345860

785.91951897

Allen, Michael, 1947-
Alla marcia : for brass quintet / Michael Allen. — Manchester : Da Capo
Music, c2005. — 1 score (18 p.) ; 30 cm.
For 2 trumpets, horn, trombone and tuba. — "This piece was written in 2004 and is
an arrangement of the composer's 'Tuba tune' for organ"—T.p. verso. — Includes
biographical notes. — Duration: ca. 6:00.
Pl. no. DC 624
System number: 013351624

785.94192

Heuschkel, Johann Peter, 1773-1853.
[Duets, horns (2), op. 12]
Six duos pour deux cors = für zwei Hörner : op. 12 / Johann Peter
Heuschkel ; [krit. rev. Neuausgabe von Christian Vitalis] — Partitur und
Stimmen. — Köln : Dohr, c2007. — 1 score (28 p.) + 2 parts (12 p.
each) : 1 facsim. ; 30 cm.
For two horns. — Preface and critical report in German.
Pl. no. E.D. 27436
ISMN M202014363
System number: 013887076

786 – KEYBOARD, MECHANICAL, ELECTROPHONIC, PERCUSSION INSTRUMENTS

786

Byrd, William, 1542 or 3-1623.
[Keyboard music. *Selections*]
Keyboard music II / William Byrd ; transcribed and edited by Alan
Brown. — 3rd, rev. ed. — London : Stainer and Bell, 2004. — xxxiii p.,
217 p. of music : ill., facsims. ; 33 cm. — Musica Britannica ; 28
For unspecified keyboard instrument (probably harpsichord, virginals, or organ).
— Editorial and critical notes in English.
ISBN 0852498861
ISMN M220221330
System number: 013196013

*Lübeck, Vincent, 1654?-1740.
[Keyboard music]
Neue Ausgabe sämtlicher Orgel- und Clavierwerke = New edition of the
complete organ and keyboard works / Vincent Lübeck, Senior & Junior ;
herausgegeben von Siegbert Rampe. — Kassel ; London : Bärenreiter,
c2003-c2004. — 2 v. of music : facsims. ; 24 x 31 cm.
"Bärenreiter Urtext." — Pref. in German and English; critical report in German.
Pl. no. BA 8449—BA 8450
ISMN M006524211 (v. 1)
ISMN M006526048 (v. 2)
System number: 013602725

Rodgers, Richard, 1902-1979.
[Musicals. *Selections; arr.*]
The best of Rodgers and Hart. — Milwaukee, Wis. : Hal Leonard,
[2005?], c1996. — 48 p. ; 31 cm. — EZ play today ; 156
20 songs arr. for organ/piano/electronic keyboard. — Melody lines with note
names, words, registrations and chord symbols. — Music by Richard Rodgers,
words by Lorenz Hart.
Publ. no. HL00100033
ISBN 0793569427
System number: 013323838

Sweelinck, Jan Pieterszoon, 1562-1621.
[Fantasias, keyboard instrument]
Sämtliche Werke für Tasteninstrumente. Band 2, Fantasien = Complete
keyboard works. Volume 2, Fantasias / Jan Pieterszoon Sweelinck ;
herausgegeben von Pieter Dirksen, Harald Vogel. — Wiesbaden :
Breitkopf & Härtel, c2007. — 223 p. of music : facsim. ; 31 cm.
Introductions in German and English.
Pl. no. EB 8742
ISMN M004182727
System number: 014052876

786.165136

Norton, Christopher, 1953-
The easiest way to improvise / Christopher Norton. — London : Boosey
& Hawkes, 2005. — iv, 136 p. ; 21 x 22 cm. + 1 compact disc.
For keyboard. — "A new and innovative approach to improvising, using popular
pieces from the Microjazz series as a starting-point" - p. iv.
ISBN 0851624715
ISMN M060115943
System number: 013213692

786.2 – PIANO

786.2

Associated Board of the Royal Schools of Music (Great Britain).
Selected piano exam pieces : 2005-2006 / The Associated Board of the
Royal Schools of Music. — London : Associated Board of the Royal
Schools of Music , c2004. — 8 v. of music ; 31 cm.
Cover title.
Pl. no. AB 2977-2984
ISBN 1860964095 (grade 1)
ISBN 1860964109 (grade 2)
ISBN 1860964117 (grade 3)
ISBN 1860964125 (grade 4)
ISBN 1860964133 (grade 5)
ISBN 1860964141 (grade 6)
ISBN 186096415X (grade 7)
ISBN 1860964168 (grade 8)
System number: 013281700

*Balakirev, Miliĭ Alekseevich, 1837-1910.
[Islameĭ]
Islamey : Fantaisie orientale / Milij Balakirev ; herausgegeben von Norbert Gertsch. — [München] : G. Henle, c2004. — vi p., 27 p. of music ; 31 cm.
For piano. — "Urtext"—Cover. — Pref. in German, English and French; critical commentary (p. [24]-27) in German and English.
Publ. no. HN 793
Publ. no. 793
ISMN M201807935
EAN 9790201807935
System number: 013115483

Best of gold : the essential collection. — London : Chester Music, c2005. — 96 p. ; 31 cm.
32 pieces for piano, including some arrangements, selected from volumes in the Gold series. — Compiled by Michael Ahmad and Heather Ramage. — Includes biographical notes by Kate Bradley.
Publ. no. CH69245
ISBN 1844497798
System number: 013185953

The best of Richard Clayderman : piano solos. — London : Wise, c2005. — 96 p. of music ; 31 cm.
21 pieces from the repertoire of Richard Clayderman — Mostly arrangements.
Publ. no. AM982861
ISBN 1846090563
System number: 013246716

Brady, Deborah.
Monday's child : a child's blessings / by Deborah Brady ; editor, Margaret Otwell. — Milwaukee, Wis. : Hal Leonard, c2003. — 19 p. of music : port. ; 31 cm. — Hal Leonard student piano library. Composer showcase
"Intermediate piano solos"—T.p. — Includes composer's and biographical notes.
Publ. no. HL00296373
ISBN 0634058347
System number: 013376373

Clark, Sondra, 1941-
Dakota days : five pieces for piano solo / by Sondra Clark ; edited by J. Mark Baker. — Milwaukee, Wis. : Hal Leonard, c2004. — 16 p. of music : port. ; 31 cm. — Hal Leonard student piano library. Composer showcase
"Intermediate piano solos"—T.p. — The score is preceded by unattributed poems for each piece. — Includes composer's and biographical notes. — Durations: 0:54; 1:30; 1:16; 1:23; 1:38.
Publ. no. HL00296521
ISBN 0634084291
System number: 013376149

Classical gold : the essential collection. — London : Chester Music, c2005. — 96 p. of music ; 31 cm.
28 excerpts from symphonies, arranged for piano. — Pref. by Michael Ahmad.
Publ. no. CH68750
ISBN 1844496074
System number: 013292890

Classical masterpieces — London : Wise Publications, c2005. — 160 p. ; 31 cm — I can play that!
"Sixty-nine classical pieces from the world's top composers in easy-to-play piano arrangements, complete with chord symbols"—Cover.
Publ. no. AM92106
ISBN 0711942323
System number: 013320784

*Clementi, Muzio, 1752-1832.
[Keyboard music. *Selections*]
18 composizioni senza numero d'opera, Op-sn 1-18 (WO 2, 3, 5, 8, 10, 13-23), per pianoforte o clavicembalo = 18 compositions without opus number for piano or harpsichord / Muzio Clementi ; a cura di Andrea Coen. — Bologna, Italia : Ut Orpheus, c2004. — xix p., 115 p. of music ; facsims. ; 32 cm. — (Opera omnia / Muzio Clementi ; v. 51)
"Included—The sprig of Shillelah, first modern edition by Barry Cooper." — "Urtext." — Includes pref. and critical notes in Italian and English. Includes thematic index.
Pl. no. MC 51
ISMN M215308817
EAN 9790215308817
System number: 014748278
Also classified at 786.4

*Clementi, Muzio, 1752-1832.
[Monferrinas]
12 monferrine : op. 49, per pianoforte = for piano / [Muzio Clementi] ; a cura di Andrea Coen. — Bologna : Ut Orpheus, c2004. — ix p., 34 p. of music : facsim. ; 30 cm. — (Opera omnia / Muzio Clementi ; v. 49)
Critical matter in Italian. Preface to series in Italian and English. Includes thematic index. — "Urtext."
Publ. no. MC 49
ISMN M215309258
EAN 9790215309258
System number: 014748006

*Clementi, Muzio, 1752-1832.
Musical characteristics : op. 19, per clavicembalo o pianoforte = for harpsichord (piano) / Muzio Clementi ; a cura di Roberto Illiano. — Bologna, Italy : Ut Orpheus, c2004. — xii, 92 p. of music : facsims. ; 32 cm. — (Opera omnia / Muzio Clementi ; vol. 24)
Preludes and cadenzas in the styles of various composers. — Movements first presented as edited by Illiano from ed. published: London : Longman and Broderip, 1787; movements presented again as transcribed from the ms. of the 1807 revision in the Library of Congress, Albrecht 582. — Pref. to series in Italian and English. Critical material in Italian. Includes thematic index. — "Urtext."
Pl. no. MC 24
ISMN M215309050
EAN 9790215309050
System number: 014748001
Primary classification 786.4

*Clementi, Muzio, 1752-1832.
[Progressive sonatinas]
Sonatinas, opus 36 / Clementi ; edited by Jennifer Linn. — New York, NY : G. Schirmer ; Milwaukee, Wis. : distributed by Hal Leonard, c2004. — 72 p. of music : port., ill., facsims. ; 31 cm. + 1 compact disc (digital ; 4 3/4 in.) — Hal Leonard student piano library Schirmer performance editions
Six sonatinas for piano. — Includes biographical and performance notes. — CD contains a performance of the work by the editor.
Publ. no. HL00296466
ISBN 0634073621
System number: 013190994

Colvin, Robert.
The music of Robert Colvin. — [Hartlepool : Robert Colvin,] c2004. — [8] p. : col. ill. ; 21 cm.
Apparently for piano.
System number: 014055809

*Cooke, Arnold.
[Arietta, piano]
Arietta for pianoforte / Arnold Cooke. — [s.l.] : Anglo-American Music Publishers, c2005. — 2 p. ; 28 cm.
Cover title. — Includes biographical note.
System number: 013594075

*Cooke, Arnold.
Intermezzo and capriccio : (1971) : for harpsichord or piano solo / Arnold Cooke. — [s.l.] : Anglo-American Music Publishers, c2005. — 10 p. of music ; 28 cm.
Cover title. — Duration: 1:30. — Includes biographical note.
System number: 013594078
Primary classification 786.4

Duparc, Henri, 1848-1933.
Feuilles volantes : op. 1 : piano solo / Henri Duparc ; edited by David Patrick. — Barnet : Fitzjohn Music Publications, c2005. — 10 p. of music ; 30 cm.
System number: 013214616

Espla, Oscar, 1886-1976.
Romanza antigua : = Romance antique : pour piano / Oscar Esplá. — Paris : Eschig, 2006, c1928. — 4 p. of music ; 30 cm.
Reprint of the 1928 edition.
Publ. no. ME 2030
ISMN M045012229
System number: 013771077

Fauré, Gabriel, 1845-1924.
[Selections; *arr.*]
Fauré gold : the essential collection. — London : Chester Music, c2004. — 95 p. of music ; 31 cm.
25 pieces for piano, including some arrangements. — Compiled by Michael Ahmad. — Includes biographical note.
Publ. no. CH68662
ISBN 1844495949
System number: 013167436

Gershwin, George, 1898-1937.
[Selections; *arr.*]
Gershwin gold : the essential collection. — London : Chester Music, c2005. — 96 p. of music ; 31 cm.
29 pieces for piano, mostly arrangements. — Includes biographical note.
Publ. no. CH70312
ISBN 1846091683
System number: 013332870

Great piano solos : [a wonderful variety of well-known showtunes, jazz and blues classics, film themes, popular songs and classical pieces arranged for solo piano] [The platinum book] — London : Wise Publications, c2004. — 159 p. : 31 cm.
41 pieces, mostly arrangements. — "For the intermediate level pianist"—Back cover.
Publ. no. AM89684
ISBN 0711930554
System number: 013129811

Great piano solos : [a wonderful variety of well-known showtunes, jazz and blues classics, film themes, popular songs and classical pieces arranged for solo piano] The white book. — London : Wise Publications, c2004. — 159 p. : 31 cm.
40 pieces, mostly arrangements. — "For the intermediate level pianist"—Back cover.
Publ. no. AM89692
ISBN 0711930562
System number: 013129812

Great piano solos : the show book. — London : Wise, c2005. — 160 p. of music ; 31 cm.
45 showsongs arranged for piano. — No words. — "For the intermediate level pianist"—Back cover.
Publ. no. AM982806
ISBN 1846090466
System number: 013297731

Hammond, Heather.
Cool piano : funky pieces. 4 / Heather Hammond. — Stowmarket : Kevin Mayhew, c2003. — 31 p. ; 30 cm.
For piano or electronic keyboard. — "The Cool Piano books are progressive and correspond to the grade on the cover"—Back cover.
Publ. no. 3611757
ISMN M570242160
System number: 013201465

Hammond, Heather.
Cool piano : funky pieces. 5 / Heather Hammond. — Stowmarket : Kevin Mayhew, c2003. — 32 p. ; 30 cm.
For piano or electronic keyboard. — "The Cool Piano books are progressive and correspond to the grade on the cover"—Back cover.
Publ. no. 3611758
ISMN M570242177
System number: 013192469

Hammond, Heather.
Cool piano : funky pieces. 6 / Heather Hammond. — Stowmarket : Kevin Mayhew, c2003. — 31 p. ; 30 cm.
For piano or electronic keyboard. — "The Cool Piano books are progressive and correspond to the grade on the cover"—Back cover.
Publ. no. 3611759
ISMN M570242184
System number: 013182142

*Harrison, Sadie, 1965-
Impresa amorosa : for piano : "In virido teneras exurit medulas" / Sadie E. Harrison. — [York] : University of York Music Press, c1997. — [31] p. of music ; 21 x 30 cm.
Reproduction of the composer's ms.
ISMN M570201716
System number: 013433128

Hedges, Anthony, 1931-
Miscellany : op. 152 : six pieces for piano / Anthony Hedges. — Beverley : Westfield Music, c2003. — 23 p. ; 30 cm.
System number: 013188495

Hesketh, Kenneth, 1968-
[Japanese miniatures]
Three Japanese miniatures : for piano : (2002) / Kenneth Hesketh. — Mainz ; Schott, c2004. London : — 16 p. of music ; 31 cm.
Duration: 10:00.
Publ. no. ED 12839
Publ. no. S&Co.7976
ISMN M220123290
System number: 013173243

It's easy to play classical greats. — London : Wise Publications, c2005. — 160 p. ; 31 cm.
"Simplified piano arrangements of 62 classical greats"—Back cover.
Publ. no. AM92082
ISBN 0711942013
System number: 013321736

Kabeláč, Miloslav, 1908-1979.
Cizokrajné motivy = Motive aus fernen Ländern = Motifs from exotic lands : op. 38, piano / Miloslav Kabeláč ; editor, Zdeněk Nouza. — 1. vyd. — Praha : Editio Bärenreiter Praha, c2005. — 27 p. of music : facsim. ; 31 cm. — (Souborné kritické vydání / Miloslav Kabeláč ; řada 5, sv. 4)
Includes programme notes in Czech, German, and English.
Pl. no. H 7906
ISMN M260103412
System number: 013382907

Kember, John.
[On the lighter side. Rock & soul styles]
Rock & soul styles : 18 pieces for piano solo = 18 pièces pour piano = 18 Stücke für Klavier / John Kember. — London : Schott, c2005. — 32 p. ; 31 cm + 1 compact disc.
Includes chord symbols. — Pref. in English, French and German. — CD contains performances of the pieces by the composer.
Publ. no. ED 12789
Publ. no. S&Co. 7989
ISMN M220123146
System number: 013201895

Kember, John.
[On the lighter side. Solo collection]
Solo collection : 15 pieces for piano in blues, spiritual and jazz styles / John Kember. — London : Schott, c2005. — 31 p. ; 31 cm + 1 compact disc. — (On the lighter side)
"15 pieces from three books in the 'On the lighter side' series: '16 pieces' for piano solo ; 'Blues pieces' for piano solo, and '12 spirituals' for piano solo and duet"—Pref. — Performance notes in English, French and German. — Preceding the arrangements of the spirituals are the original tunes with words and chord symbols. — CD contains performances of the pieces by the composer.
Publ. no. ED 12841
Publ. no. S&Co. 7981
ISMN M220123306
System number: 013201919

Kern, Jerome, 1885-1945.
[Songs. *Selections; arr.*]
Jerome Kern classics : for piano solo / arranged by Eugéne Rocherolle ; edited by J. Mark Baker. — Milwaukee, Wis. : Hal Leonard, c2005. — 46 p. ; 31 cm. — Hal Leonard student piano library. Composer showcase
10 songs from musicals arranged for piano. — "Intermediate level"—T.p. — Includes biographical note.
Publ. no. HL00296577
ISBN 063409081X
System number: 013221821

Kirchner, Theodor, 1823-1903.
[Albumblätter, op. 80]
Albumblätter : neun kleine Clavierstücke, op. 80 = Album leaves : nine little piano pieces / Theodor Kirchner ; nach den Quellen herausgegeben von Harry Joelson. — Winterthur : Amadeus, 2005. — 19 p. of music : facsim. ; 31 cm. — (Werke = Works / Theodor Kirchner)
"Rieter-Biedermann published the present Albumblätter (new series) op. 80 in April 1887 in Leipzig"—P. [2] of cover. — Pref. in German and English.
Publ. no. BP 1940
System number: 014659941

Kirchner, Theodor, 1823-1903.
Im Zwielicht : Lieder und Tänze für Klavier, op. 31 = In twilight : songs and dances for piano / Theodor Kirchner ; nach den Quellen herausgegeben von Harry Joelson. — Winterthur : Amadeus, 2004. — 39 p. of music ; 31 cm. — (Werke = Works / Theodor Kirchner)
Includes pref. in English and German.
Publ. no. BP 1297
System number: 014659739

Kirchner, Theodor, 1823-1903.
Legenden : Dichtungen für das Clavier, op. 18 = Legends : poetry for pianoforte / Theodor Kirchner ; nach den Quellen herausgegeben von Harry Joelson. — Winterthur : Amadeus, 2005. — 24 p. of music ; 31 cm. — (Werke = Works / Theodor Kirchner)
Pref. in German and English.
Publ. no. BP 1939
System number: 013806723

Kirchner, Theodor, 1823-1903.
Spielsachen : 14 leichte Klavierstücke : op. 35 = Toys : 14 easy piano pieces / Theodor Kirchner ; herausgegeben von Harry Joelson. — Winterthur : Amadeus, 2004. — 28 p. of music ; 31 cm. — (Werke = Works / Theodor Kirchner)
Includes pref. in English and German.
Publ. no. BP 1316
System number: 014659755

Kirchner, Theodor, 1823-1903.
Still und bewegt : acht Klavierstücke : op. 24 = Tranquil and turbulent : eight piano pieces / Theodor Kirchner ; nach den Quellen herausgegeben von Harry Joelson. — Winterthur : Amadeus, 2004. — 28 p. of music ; 31 cm. — (Werke = Works / Theodor Kirchner)
Includes pref. in English and German.
Publ. no. BP 1323
System number: 014659782

Lepik, Tarmo, 1946-2001.
[Piano music. *Selections*]
Klaverimuusika = Works for piano solo / Tarmo Lepik. — Tallinn : SP Muusikaprojekt, c2006. — 43 p. of music : port. ; 30 cm.
Includes biographical notes in Estonian and English.
Publ. no. SPM 2604
Pl. no. 2604
ISMN M801701381
System number: 013750193

Liszt, Franz, 1811-1886.
[Piano music. *Selections*]
Freie Bearbeitungen. XIII = Free arrangements. XIII / Franz Liszt ; herausgegeben von Péter Bozó, Adrienne Kaczmarczyk. — Budapest : Editio Musica, c2005. — xxxix p., 159 p. of music : facsims. ; 31 cm. — (Neue Ausgabe sämtlicher Werke / Franz Liszt. Serie 2, Freie Bearbeitungen und Transkriptionen für Klavier zu zwei Händen / Bd.13 = New edition of the complete works / Ferenc Liszt. Series 2, Free arrangements and transcriptions for piano solo / v.13)
Piano arrangements of works by other composers. — Pref. in German and English and critical report in English.
Pl. no. Z. 12 402

Publ. no. Z. A 12 402
ISMN M080300312
System number: 013821983

McCreery, Charles.
[Short easy piano pieces]
Ten more short easy piano pieces / Charles McCreery. — Cuddesdon,
Oxford : St. Maur Music, c2005. — 1 score (24 p.) : port. ; 30 cm.
Includes biographical note.
ISMN M900210326
System number: 013313010

*Montague, Stephen.
[Easy pieces]
Five easy pieces : (1998-2003) : piano solo / Stephen Montague. —
Waltham Abbey : United Music Publishers, c2004. — 1 score (6 p.) ; 31 cm.
Includes programme and biographical notes.
ISMN M224404586
System number: 013469015

More essential piano repertoire / editor, Mark Goddard. — Laggan :
Spartan Press, c2004-2005. — 8 v. of music ; 30 cm.
Cover title. — Pl. no.: SP751 (v. 1), SP752 (v. 2), SP753 (v. 3), SP754 (v. 4), SP755
(v. 5), SP756 (v. 6), SP757 (v. 7), SP758 (v. 8).
Pl. no. SP751
Pl. no. SP752
Pl. no. SP753
Pl. no. SP754
Pl. no. SP755
Pl. no. SP756
Pl. no. SP757
Pl. no. SP758
ISMN M579997511 (v. 1)
ISMN M579997528 (v. 2)
ISMN M579997535 (v. 3)
ISMN M579997542 (v. 4)
ISMN M579997559 (v. 5)
ISMN M579997566 (v. 6)
ISMN M579997573 (v. 7)
ISMN M579997580 (v. 8)
System number: 013169232

*Nathan, Simon, 1988 or 9-
Lament : for piano / Simon Nathan. Together with Improvisation on
"Lament" : for piano / Ernest Kaye ; and arranged for organ by Gerald
Barnes. — [New York] : Oxford University Press, c2004. — 8 p. of music ;
31 cm. — Oxford keyboard music
"To the people affected by the fall of the Twin Towers"—Caption. — Includes note
by Ernest Kaye.
ISBN 0193868040
System number: 013122820

A night at the opera for piano : easy-to-play arrangements / arranged by
John Bertalot. — Buxhall : Kevin Mayhew, 2004. — 21 p. ; 31 cm.
11 excerpts from operas by Bizet, Flotow, Gluck, Mozart, Puccini and Verdi.
Publ. no. 3611840
ISMN M570243754
System number: 013159289

Nyman, Michael.
[Selections; arr.]
The piano collection / Michael Nyman. — Wise, 2005. — 96 p. of music ;
31 cm.
25 pieces arranged for piano.
Publ. no. AM984269
ISBN 9781846092398
ISBN 1846092396
System number: 013383402

Opening night : two Souvenirs for solo piano : commissioned to celebrate
the opening of the Bauer & Hieber music shop at 48 Great Marlborough
Street, London, 21st September 2007 / written and performed by Tim
Richards and Huw Watkins. — London : Schott, c2007. — 12 p. of
music ; 31 cm. — Edition Schott
First work includes improvised section with chord symbols.
Publ. no. ED 13211
System number: 014049158

Opera gold : the essential collection. — London : Chester Music, c2005. —
96 p. of music ; 31 cm.
31 excerpts from operas, arranged for piano. — No words.
Publ. no. CH68761
ISBN 1844496082
System number: 013265864

Poole, Geoffrey, 1949-
Schubert's Reliquie / realisation and completion by Geoffrey Poole (1997)
of Schubert's Sonata in C Major, D 840. — Kenley : Maecenas Music,
[2003?], c1999. — 30 p. ; 30 cm.
For piano solo. — "This edition incorporates a number of revisions and
improvements made between 1997 and 2002." — Schubert's original first two
movements are not included in the score. — Includes composer's notes. — Duration:
20:00.
System number: 013422443

*Rachmaninoff, Sergei, 1873-1943.
[Piano music. *Selections*]
Piano compositions. Vol. 1 / Serge Rachmaninoff. — London : Boosey &
Hawkes, c2005. — 103 p. of music ; 31 cm.
"Authentic edition." — Notes on sources in English, French and German.
ISMN M060116490
System number: 013336506

Requiem : the world's most moving music : arranged for solo piano. —
London : Wise Publications, 2005. — 96 p. ; 31 cm.
31 arrangements.
Publ. no. AM982520
ISBN 1844499960
System number: 013265867

*Russian romantic repertoire = Romantische russische Klavierliteratur =
Le répertoire romantique de Russie : level 1 / selected and edited by
Stephen Coombs. — London : Faber Music, 1998. — 40 p. of music ;
31 cm. — Faber piano collection
Approximately grade 4-6 level. — Foreword in English, French and German.
ISBN 0571518931
System number: 006891413

*Schumann, Robert, 1810-1856.
[Album für die Jugend. *Selections*]
Selections from Album for the young : opus 68 / Schumann ; edited by
Jennifer Linn. — New York : G. Schirmer ; Milwaukee, Wis. : distributed
by Hal Leonard, c2005. — 40 p. of music : ill., port., facsims. ; 31 cm. +
1 compact disc (digital ; 4 3/4 in.) — Hal Leonard student piano library
Schirmer performance editions
For piano. — Includes historical and performance notes. — 'Musical rules for
home and life' (from the original edition): p. 36-39. — CD contains
demonstration tracks performed by the editor.
Publ. no. HL00296588
Publ. no. 63009272
ISBN 0634098756
System number: 013440462

*Shchedrin, Rodion Konstantinovich, 1932-
Voprosy : 11 pieces for piano = 11 Stücke für Klavier (2003) / Rodion
Shchedrin. — Mainz ; London : Schott, c2004. — 15 p. of music ; 31 cm.
Preface by the composer in English, German, and French. — "The performer is
free to choose tempo, dynamics, and phrasing"—Prelim. p.
Publ. no. ED 9733
Pl. no. 51 480
ISMN M001136549
ISMN 9790001136549
System number: 014766585

Showstoppers : [24 stage hits] — London : Wise, c2005. — 48 p. of
music ; 31 cm. — Really easy piano
24 songs arranged for piano with interlinear text and chord symbols. —
"Complete with song background notes, and playing hints and tips"—Back cover.
Publ. no. AM982784
ISBN 1846090431
System number: 013299262

Talbot, Joby.
[Once around the sun; arr.]
Once around the sun : for solo piano / Joby Talbot. — London : Chester
Music, c2005. — 70 p. of music ; 31 cm.
12 pieces commissioned over one year by Classic FM and the PRS Foundation for
New Music. — Arr. for piano. Originally for violin, violoncello, piano, harp,
percussion and sound effects. — Includes composer's note.
Publ. no. CH69718
ISBN 1846091594
System number: 013312992

*Terzakis, Dimitri.
Diptychon : zwei Traumdeutungen : für Klavier (2004/05) / Dimitri
Terzakis. — Bad Schwalbach : Edition Gravis, c2005. — 10 p. of music ;
30 cm.
For piano.
Pl. no. EG 954
System number: 014629745

Tsitsaros, Christos.
Songs without words : nine character pieces for piano solo / by Christos
Tsitsaros ; edited by Margaret Otwell. — Milwaukee, Wis. : Hal Leonard,
c2004. — 40 p. of music : port. ; 31 cm. — Hal Leonard student piano
library. Composer showcase
"Late-intermediate piano solos"—T.p. — Includes composer's and biographical
notes.
Publ. no. HL00296506
ISBN 0634078437
System number: 013201186

Van de Vate, Nancy.
Balinese diptych : for solo piano : 2003 / Nancy Van de Vate. — Vienna :
Vienna Masterworks, c2003. — 9 p. of music ; 30 cm.
System number: 014457048

Vivaldi, Antonio, 1678-1741.
[Selections; *arr.*]
Vivaldi gold : the essential collection. — London : Chester Music, c2005.
— 96 p. of music ; 31 cm.
30 pieces arranged for piano by Quentin Thomas and Jerry Lanning. — Includes 4 pieces transcribed for keyboard instrument by J.S. Bach. — Includes biographical note.
Publ. no. CH69234
ISBN 184449778X
System number: 013190759

Wesley, Samuel, 1766-1837.
[Piano music]
Piano music : volume 1 / Samuel Wesley ; edited by Andrew Wells. — London : Redcliffe Edition, c2004. — 53 p. ; 30 cm. — (Works by Samuel Wesley (1766-1837) / edited for practical performance ; general editor: Francis Routh)
ISMN M708046752
System number: 013432959

*Zarębski, Juliusz, 1854-1885.
[Pezzo agitato con un intermezzo amoroso]
Wielka fantazja = Grande fantaisie (Un pezzo agitato con un intermezzo amoroso), JZBO 11 ; Utwór bez tytułu = Piece without title, JZBO 14 : na fortepian = for piano / Juliusz Zarębski ; redakcja Ryszard Daniel Golianek ; opracowanie wykonawcze Andrzej Tatarski. — Poznań : Rhytmos, 2005. — 42 p. of music ; 30 cm.
Pref. and editorial commentary in Polish and English.
ISMN M901333703
System number: 014629793

786.20262
*Schumann, Robert, 1810-1856.
[Waldscenen]
Waldszenen : Opus 82 : Faksimile nach dem Autograph im Besitz der Bibliothèque nationale de France, Paris / Robert Schumann ; Nachwort von Margit L. McCorkle. — München : G. Henle, c2005. — 28 p. of music ; 29 x 37 cm.
For piano. — Reproduces holograph in the Bibliothèque nationale de France (Département de la musique, Ms. 344). — Publisher no. from supplier's information slip. — Postscript in German and English.
Publ. no. HN 3217
ISMN M201832173
System number: 013641757

786.2076
*Grade 8 piano anthology : examination pieces for 2005 and 2006 : from the piano syllabus of the Associated Board of the Royal Schools of Music. — London : Edition Peters, c2004. — 119 p. of music ; 31 cm.
21 pieces with performance notes by Norman Beedie and aural notes by Caroline Evans. — "List A (selection), List B (complete), List C (selection)." — Reprinted from earlier eds.
Publ. no. EP 7777
ISMN M577084848
System number: 013095045

*Heller, Stephen, 1813-1888.
[Etudes faciles. *Selections*]
Selected studies : opus 45 and opus 46 / Heller ; edited by William Westney. — New York : G. Schirmer ; Milwaukee, Wis. : distributed by Hal Leonard, c2005. — 62 p. of music : port. ; 31 cm. + 1 compact disc (digital ; 4 3/4 in.) — Hal Leonard student piano library Schirmer performance editions
For piano. — Includes biographical and performance notes. — CD contains demonstration tracks performed by the editor.
Publ. no. HL00296587
Publ. no. 63009254
ISBN 063409839X
System number: 013434751

*Timakin, E. M.
Essential piano exercises / E.M. Timakin ; editor, Jakša Zlatar. — Laggan Bridge : Spartan Press, 2005. — 3 v. of music ; 30 cm.
Includes biographical notes on the composer and editor. — Cover title. — Pl. no.: SP764 (bk. 1), SP765 (bk. 2), SP766 (bk. 3).
Pl. no. SP764
Pl. no. SP765
Pl. no. SP766
ISMN M579997641 (bk. 1)
ISMN M579997658 (bk. 2)
ISMN M579997665 (bk. 3)
System number: 013441173

Wildman, Peter, 1957-
Rock study : educational solos in pop styles for piano or keyboard / music by Peter Wildman. — Laggan Bridge : Spartan Press, c2005. — 2 v. : port. ; 31 cm + 2 compact discs.
Includes biographical note. — CDs contains demonstration and backing tracks. — Pl. no.: SP791 (bk. 1), SP792 (bk. 2)
Pl. no. SP791
Pl. no. SP792
ISMN M579997917 (bk. 1)
ISMN M579997924 (bk. 2)
System number: 013376536

786.20946
Piano music of Spain. — London : Chester Music, c2004. — 235 p. ; 31 cm.
"This superb three-part collection contains over 40 works by Albeniz, de Falla, Granados, Mompou, Rodrigo and many other outstanding nineteenth and twentieth century composers" — Cover.
Publ. no. CH68288
ISBN 1844495108
System number: 013196854

786.21423
Kember, John.
Sight-reading 2 : piano : a fresh approach = Déchiffrage pour le piano 2 : nouvelle approche = Vom-Blatt-Spielen auf dem Klavier 2 : eine erfrischend neue Methode / John Kember. — London : Schott, c2005. — 62 p. ; 31 cm.
"A progressive approach based on self-learning" — Back cover. — "Grades 2 towards 4" — Back cover. — Instructions in English, French and German.
Publ. no. ED 12791
ISBN 1902455231
ISMN M220123160
System number: 013192084

786.21542
Classic film gold : the essential collection. — London : Chester Music, c2005. — 96 p. ; 31 cm.
Music from films, arranged for piano. — No words.
Publ. no. CH69256
ISBN 1844497801
System number: 013265865

Film songs : 24 screen hits. — London : Wise Publications, 2004. — 48 p. of music ; 31 cm. — Really easy piano
24 songs arranged for piano with interlinear text and chord symbols. — "Complete with song background notes, and playing hints and tips"—Back cover.
Publ. no. AM980441
ISBN 1844495701
System number: 013095248

Great piano solos. The film book. — London : Wise, c2005. — 160 p. of music ; 31 cm.
45 film themes and songs arranged for piano. — No words. — "For the intermediate level pianist"—Back cover.
Publ. no. AM982795
ISBN 1846090458
System number: 013297809

786.21546
TV comedy : themes for solo piano. — London : Chester Music, c2005. — 96 p. ; 31 cm.
"The themes from 35 of the most popular TV comedy shows ever, specially arranged for solo piano complete with chord symbols"—Back cover.
Publ. no. CH68783
ISBN 1844496198
System number: 013321760

TV detective : themes for solo piano. — London : Chester Music, c2005. — 96 p. ; 31 cm.
"The themes from 30 of the most popular TV detective drama series ever, specially arranged for solo piano complete with chord symbols"—Back cover.
Publ. no. CH70004
ISBN 1846090997
System number: 013321762

TV soap & drama : themes for solo piano. — London : Chester Music, c2005. — 96 p. ; 31 cm.
"The themes from 29 of the most popular TV soaps and drama series ever, specially arranged for solo piano complete with chord symbols"—Back cover.
Publ. no. CH68794
ISBN 1844496201
UPC 9781844496204
System number: 013321761

786.21556
Ballet gold : the essential collection. — London : Chester Music, c2004. — 96 p. ; 31 cm.
32 pieces of ballet music, arranged for piano. — Compiled by Michael Ahmad and Heather Ramage.
Publ. no. CH68772
ISBN 1844496090
System number: 013167409

786.21620094237
Cornish folk songs : for piano / researched by Jane Lofthouse ; arranged by Colin Mawby. — Buxhall : Kevin Mayhew, 2004. — 20 p. of music ; 31 cm.
With historical notes to the songs but without words.
Publ. no. 3611838
ISMN M570243761
System number: 013159283

786.2164

Ballads : [24 great songs] — London : Wise Publications, c2005. — 48 p. ; 31 cm. — Really easy piano
24 songs arranged for piano with interlinear text and chord symbols. — "Complete with song background notes, and playing hints and tips"—Back cover.
Publ. no. AM982751
ISBN 1846090407
System number: 013281517

Beatles.
[Songs. *Selections; arr.*]
The Beatles : [23 great hits] — London : Wise, c2005. — 48 p. ; 31 cm. — Really easy piano
23 songs arranged for piano with interlinear text and chord symbols. — Words and music by members of the group. — "Complete with song background notes, and playing hints and tips"—Back cover.
Publ. no. NO91080
ISBN 184609044X
System number: 013281527

Gershwin, George, 1898-1937.
[Songs. *Selections; arr.*]
Easy-to-play Gershwin for piano / arranged by Andrew Wright. — Buxhall : Kevin Mayhew, 2004. — 37 p. 31 cm.
Includes biographical essay.
Publ. no. 3611801
ISMN M570242863
System number: 013159350

Play piano with — Keane, Coldplay, Muse and other great artists. — London : Wise Publications, c2004. — 1 score (56 p.) ; 31 cm. + 1 compact disc.
9 songs for voice and piano, with piano parts taken from the original recordings. — Includes chord symbols. — CD contains full demonstration and backing tracks.
Publ. no. AM91238
ISBN 0711934835
System number: 013101817

786.21643076

Harrison, Mark, 1956-
Blues piano : the complete guide with CD! / by Mark Harrison. — 79 p. : 31 cm. + 1 compact disc. — Hal Leonard keyboard style series
CD contains demonstrations of music examples.
Publ. no. HL00311007
ISBN 0634061690
System number: 006906657

786.2165

Boyd, Bill.
Jazz bits and pieces : original piano solos in various jazz styles / by Bill Boyd. — Milwaukee, Wis. : Hal Leonard, c1990. — 24 p. : port. ; 31 cm. — Hal Leonard student piano library. Composer showcase
"Early-intermediate piano solos"—T.p. — Includes composer's and biographical notes.
Publ. no. HL00290312
ISBN 0793527848
System number: 013376419

Boyd, Bill.
Jazz sketches : original piano solos in various jazz styles / by Bill Boyd. — Milwaukee, WI : Hal Leonard, [2005?], c1996. — 24 p. : 31 cm. — Hal Leonard student piano library. Composer showcase
"Intermediate piano solos"—T.p. — Includes composer's and biographical notes.
Publ. no. HL00220001
ISBN 0793569591
System number: 013376391

Jazz : [24 great songs] — London : Wise, c2005. — 48 p. of music ; 31 cm. — Really easy piano
24 songs and instrumental pieces arranged for piano with interlinear text (where appropriate) and chord symbols. — "Complete with song background notes, and playing hints and tips"—Back cover.
Publ. no. AM982773
ISBN 1846090423
System number: 013281480

More jazz tunes you've always wanted to play : popular jazz songs [arranged] for intermediate piano solo. — London : Chester Music, c2005. — 128 p. of music ; 31 cm.
Includes chord symbols. — 37 songs; no words.
Publ. no. CH70664
ISBN 9781846092404
ISBN 184609240X
System number: 013383532

786.2166

Coldplay (Musical group).
[X&Y]
It's easy to play Coldplay X&Y — London : Wise Publications, c2005. — 1 score (64 p.) ; 31 cm. — It's easy to play
"Easy to read, simplified piano arrangements of all 13 songs from the hit album"—Cover. — For piano with interlinear text and chord symbols. — Words and music by members of the group, arranged by Derek Jones.
Publ. no. AM983477
ISBN 1846091942
System number: 013346020

It's easy to play top 50 hits. — London : Wise Publications, c2005. — 128 p. ; 31 cm. — It's easy to play
34 songs arranged for piano, with interlinear text and chord symbols.
Publ. no. AM92047
ISBN 0711941777
System number: 013359465

Joel, Billy.
[Songs. *Selections*]
Make it easy. Billy Joel. — London : International Music Publications, 2005. — 70 p. ; 31 cm.
"Twenty classic songs in easy-to-play piano arrangements. Complete songs with lyrics, chord symbols and suggested fingerings"—Cover. — Words and music by Billy Joel. — Interlinear text.
Publ. no. 10157A
ISBN 1843288761
ISMN M570218769
System number: 013299330

John, Elton.
[Songs. *Selections*]
Make it easy. Elton John. — London : International Music Publications, 2004. — 55 p. ; 31 cm.
"Twenty classic songs in easy-to-play piano arrangements. Complete songs with lyrics, chord symbols and suggested fingerings"—Cover. — Words and music mostly by Elton John and Bernie Taupin. — Interlinear text.
Publ. no. 10059A
ISBN 1843287587
ISMN M570217588
System number: 013196741

*Norton, Christopher, 1953-
Rock preludes collection : [14 original pieces based on the strong rhythms of rock music for solo piano with playalong CD] / Christopher Norton. — London : Boosey & Hawkes, 2005. — 49 p. of music ; 31 cm. + 1 compact disc (digital ; 4 3/4 in.)
"For intermediate to advanced-level players." — Contains all the pieces from "Rock preludes" and "Rock preludes 2", previously published separately. — CD contains demonstration performances by the composer and backing tracks.
ISBN 0851624758
ISMN M060116384
System number: 013213851

786.21723

Brady, Deborah.
The twelve days of Christmas / by Deborah Brady ; edited by J. Mark Baker. — Milwaukee, Wis. : Hal Leonard, c2004. — 39 p. of music : 31 cm. port., ill. ; — Hal Leonard student piano library. Composer showcase
"Early intermediate/Intermediate piano solos"—T.p. — Includes optional recorder/flute part for "Eleven pipers piping" and optional drum part for "Twelve drummers drumming." — Includes composer's and biographical notes. — Durations: 0:32; 0:52; 1:40; 1:16; 1:33; 1:04; 0:48; 1:54; 1:02; 0:52; 1:14; 1:03; 1:43.
Publ. no. HL00296531
ISBN 0634086480
System number: 013376182

Christmas jazz : six carols for piano solo / arranged by Mike Springer ; edited by J. Mark Baker. — Milwaukee, Wis. : Hal Leonard, c2004. — 23 p. of music : 31 cm. port. ; — Hal Leonard student piano library. Composer showcase
"Intermediate piano solos"—T.p. — Includes biographical note. — Durations: 2:28; 1:29; 3:05; 3:16; 1:56; 1:15.
Publ. no. HL00296525
ISBN 0634084658
System number: 013376380

786.21723165

Jazz at Christmas : piano solo : [elegant jazz arangements of 14 traditional carols] / arranged by Frank Mantooth. — Milwaukee, Wis. : Hal Leonard, c1999. — 55 p.; 31 cm.
No words.
Publ. no. HL00310525
ISBN 0634008587
System number: 013376348

786.21824

Chopin, Frédéric, 1810-1849.
[Rondos, piano]
Ronda, op. 1, 5, 16 = Rondos, opp. 1, 5, 16 / Fryderyk Chopin ; [redakcja tomu, Jan Ekier, Paweł Kamiński, Witalis Raczkiewicz] — Warszawa : Polskie Wydawnictwo Muzyczne, 2005. — 65 p. of music + 1 commentary (12 p. : music ; 31 cm.) — (Wydanie narodowe dzieł Fryderyka Chopina ; 8. Seria A, Utwory wydane za życia ; t. 8)
"Urtext"—Cover. — Includes thematic index. — Performance and source commentary in English.
Pl. no. FWN 8 A VIII
ISBN 8392036557
ISMN M901332850
EAN 9788392036555
System number: 014490560

Parke, Maria F., 1772 or 3-1822.
Divertimento and military rondo : for piano / Maria F. Parke ; edited by
Barbara Harbach. — St. Louis, Mo. : Vivace Press, c2004. — 27 p. of
music ; 30 cm.
Includes pref. and biographical notes on the composer in English.
Publ. no. VIV 1828
UPC 707791018282
System number: 014457036
Primary classification 786.21852

786.2183

Chopin, Frédéric, 1810-1849.
[Sonatas, piano no. 3, op. 58, B minor]
Sonata H-Moll Op. 58 : wydanie faksymilowe rękopisu ze zbiorów
Biblioteki Narodowej w Warszawie (Mus. 232 Cim.) = Sonata in B minor,
op. 58 : facsimile edition of the manuscript held in the National Library in
Warsaw (Mus. 232 Cim.) : A IX/58 / Fryderyk Chopin ; Komitet
redakcyjny = Editorial committee, Jean-Jacques Eigeldinger
(przewodniczący = president), Zofia Chechlińska (redaktor naczelny =
editor in chief) … [et al.] — [Warszawa] : Narodowy Instytut Fryderyka
Chopina : Wydawnictwo Diecezji Pelplińskiej Bernardinum, c2005. — 28
[i.e. 32] p. of music, [1] leaf : facsim. ; 23 x 29 cm. + 1 commentary volume
(51 p. : ill. ; 23 x 29 cm.) — (Dzieła Chopina : wydanie faksymilowe =
Works by Chopin : facsimile edition)
Facsimile of the "autograph Stichvorlage . from the collection of the National
Library" with title: Sonate pour le piano-forte … par F. Chopin … Oeu 58. Cf.
Commentary, p. 12. — Commentary volume, by Zofia Chechlińska and Irena
Poniatowska, has subtitle: Komentarz źródłowy = Source commentary. — Facsimile
and commentary volume issued in a portfolio. — Commentary in Polish, English,
French, German, Spanish, and Japanese.
ISBN 8391741044
ISBN 9788391741047
System number: 013765185

*Clementi, Muzio, 1752-1832.
[Sonatas, op. 13. No. 4-6]
3 sonate op. 13 nn. 4-6 per pianoforte = for piano / Muzio Clementi ; a cura
di Andrea Coen. — Bologna, Italia : Ut Orpheus, c2004. — 1 score (ix,
45 p.) : facsim. ; 30 cm. — (Opera omnia / Muzio Clementi ; v. 19)
Pref. in Italian and English. — "Urtext."
Publ. no. MC 19
ISMN M215309241
EAN 9790215309241
System number: 014747984

*Cooke, Arnold.
[Sonatas, piano, no. 1]
Piano sonata no. 1 / Arnold Cooke. — [Altamonte Springs, FL?] :
Anglo-American Music Publishers, c2005. — 31 p. ; 28 cm.
Cover title. — Includes biographical note.
System number: 013594031

*Cooke, Arnold.
[Sonatas, piano, no. 2]
Piano sonata no. 2 / Arnold Cooke. — Altamonte Springs, FL :
Anglo-American Music Publishers, c2005. — 27 p. ; 28 cm.
Cover title. — Includes biographical note.
System number: 013594039

Febel, Reinhard, 1952-
[Sonatas, piano]
Sieben Sonaten : für Klavier, 2000/02 / Reinhard Febel. — München :
Ricordi, [2005], c2004. — 73 p. of music ; 30 cm.
Performance notes in German. — Duration: 45:00.
Pl. no. Sy. 3591
ISMN M204235919
System number: 013771079

Hedges, Anthony, 1931-
[Sonatas, piano, no. 2, op. 154]
Piano sonata no.2 : op. 154 / Anthony Hedges. — Beverley : Westfield
Music, c2004. — 23 p. ; 30 cm.
System number: 013188474

Hoffmann, E. T. A. (Ernst Theodor Amadeus), 1776-1822.
[Vocal music. *Selections*]
Kleine Vokalkompsitionen und Klaviersonaten / E.T.A. Hoffmann ; aus dem
Nachlaß von Friedrich Schnapp und unter Mitarbeit von Gerhard
Allroggen ; herausgegeben von Alexander Erhard und Thomas Kohlhase.
— Mainz ; London : Schott, c2006. — 1 score (xvii, 203 p.) ; 33 cm. —
(Ausgewählte musikalische Werke / E.T.A. Hoffmann ; Bd. 12a)
Most vocal works for vocal ensemble, with or without piano accompaniment. —
Editorial prefaces and critical commentary in German. — Italian or German words
Publ. no. ETAH 112-10
Publ. no. BSS 43736
System number: 013798962
Primary classification 783

Kaprálová, Vítězslava, 1915-1940.
Sonata appassionata : op. 6 : piano / Vítězslava Kaprálová ; editor
Věroslav Němec. — Praha : Amos, c2006. — 35 p. of music ; 31 cm.
Preface and critical report in Czech and English.
Pl. no. AM 0052
ISMN M660570500
System number: 013771129

*Nicolai, Johann Gottlieb, 1744-1801.
[Sonatas, piano]
24 Klaviersonates in alle toonsoorten : (Zwolle ca 1790) = 24 keyboard
sonatas in all keys / Johann Gottlieb Nicolai ; uitgegeven door Maarten
Engelsman. — Utrecht, The Netherlands : Koninklijke Vereniging voor
Nederlandse Muziekgeschiedenis, 2003. — 103 p. of music ; 30 cm. —
(Muziek uit de Republiek = Music from the Dutch Republic ; 10) —
(Achttiende-eeuwse klaviermuziek = Eighteenth-century keyboard
music ; 10)
Pref. and critical notes in Dutch and English.
Publ. no. MR 10
ISBN 9063751915
System number: 013020245

Parke, Maria F., 1772 or 3-1822.
[Grand sonatas, op. 1. No. 3]
Grand sonata in D major : for solo piano / Maria F. Parke ; edited by
Barbara Harbach. — St. Louis, Mo. : Vivace Press, c2004. — 32 p. of
music ; 30 cm.
Includes pref. and biographical notes in English.
Publ. no. VIV 1833
UPC 707791018336
System number: 014457037

786.21832

Elgar, Edward, 1857-1934.
[Sonatina, piano]
Sonatina : for piano solo / Edward Elgar ; edited by David Patrick. —
Barnet : Fitzjohn Music Publications, c2005. — 6 p. of music ; 30 cm.
System number: 013214664

*Tabakov, Emil.
[Sonatina, piano]
Sonatina za piano = Sonatina for piano / Emil Tabakov. — Sofiia :
Muzika, c2005. — 25 p. of music ; 30 cm.
Includes biographical notes in English.
Publ. no. M.P.H. 2549
Publ. no. 2549
System number: 014629736

786.21852

Parke, Maria F., 1772 or 3-1822.
Divertimento and military rondo : for piano / Maria F. Parke ; edited by
Barbara Harbach. — St. Louis, Mo. : Vivace Press, c2004. — 27 p. of
music ; 30 cm.
Includes pref. and biographical notes on the composer in English.
Publ. no. VIV 1828
UPC 707791018282
System number: 014457036
Also classified at 786.21824

786.21858

*Albéniz, Isaac, 1860-1909.
[Suite española, no. 1]
Suite espagnole : opus 47 / Isaac Albéniz ; herausgegeben von Ullrich
Scheideler ; Fingersatz von Rolf Koenen. — München : G. Henle, c2005.
— vi, 60 p. of music ; 31 cm.
For piano. — "Urtext"—Cover. — Includes pref. in German, English, and French
and critical notes in German and English (p. [51]-60).
Publ. no. 783
Publ. no. HN 783
ISMN M201807836
EAN 9790201807836
System number: 013325842

Bach, Johann Sebastian, 1685-1750.
[Suites violoncello, BWV 1009, C major; *arr.*]
Suite für Violoncello Nr. 3, C-Dur, BWV 1009 / Johann Sebastian Bach ;
für Klavier bearbeitet von Joachim Raff ; nach der Ausgabe von
Rieter-Biedermann ; neu herausgegeben von Volker Tosta. — Stuttgart :
Edition Nordstern, c2003. — 15 p. of music ; 30 cm. — (Werke /
Joachim Raff ; Bd. V/1c)
"Erstmals erschienen im Jahre 1869 unter dem Titel: Sech Sonaten für Violoncell
von J.S. Bach für das Pianoforte bearbeitet, Sonate III in C-Dur." — Pref. in
German and English; critical notes in German. — Limited ed. of 200 copies.
Publ. no. 0105-2173
ISMN M700164058
System number: 014501811

Bach, Johann Sebastian, 1685-1750.
[Suites violoncello, BWV 1012, D major; *arr.*]
Suite für Violoncello Nr. 6, D-Dur, BWV 1012 / Johann Sebastian Bach ;
für Klavier bearbeitet von Joachim Raff ; nach der Ausgabe von
Rieter-Biedermann ; neu herausgegeben von Volker Tosta. — Stuttgart :
Edition Nordstern, c2003. — 16 p. of music ; 30 cm. — (Werke / Joachim
Raff ; Bd. V/1f)
"Erstmals erschienen im Jahre 1869 unter dem Titel: Sech Sonaten für Violoncell
von J.S. Bach für das Pianoforte bearbeitet, Sonate VI in D-Dur." — Pref. in German
and English; critical notes in German. — Limited ed. of 200 copies.
Publ. no. 0105-2176
ISMN M700164157
System number: 014502734

Bach, Johann Sebastian, 1685-1750.
[Suites, violoncello, BWV 1010, E♭ major; *arr.*]
Suite für Violoncello Nr. 4, Es-Dur, BWV 1010 / von Johann Sebastian
Bach ; für Klavier bearbeitet von Joachim Raff ; ... nach der Ausgabe von
Rieter-Biedermann neu herausgegeben von Volker Tosta. — Stuttgart :
Edition Nordstern, c2003. — v p., 15 p. of music ; 30 cm. — (Raff Werke ;
Bd. V/1d)
"Erstmals erschienen im Jahre 1869 unter dem Titel Sechs Sonaten für Violoncell
von J.S. Bach für das Pianoforte bearbeitet Sonate IV in Es-Dur." — Pref. in English
and German. — Limited ed. of 200 copies.
Pl. no. 28.07.03
Publ. no. 0105-2174
ISMN M700164133
System number: 014501816

*Cooke, Arnold.
[Suites, piano, no. 2]
Suite no. 2 for pianoforte / Arnold Cooke. — [s.l.] : Anglo-American Music
Publishers, c2005. — 31 p. ; 28 cm.
Cover title. — Includes biographical note.
System number: 013594067

*Cooke, Arnold.
[Suites, piano, no. 3]
Suite no. 3 for pianoforte / Arnold Cooke. — [s.l.] : Anglo-American Music
Publishers, c2005. — 1 score (17 p.) ; 28 cm.
Cover title. — Includes biographical note.
System number: 013594052

*Montague, Stephen.
Autumn leaves : (2000-2003) : solo piano / Stephen Montague. — London :
United Music Publishers, c2003. — 23 p. of music : ill. ; 31 cm.
The works may be played separately or as a suite. — Includes biographical,
performance and programme notes.
ISMN M224403961
System number: 013063003

Raff, Joachim, 1822-1882.
[Suites, piano, op. 71, C major]
Suite für Klavier Nr. 2, C-Dur, op. 71 / Joachim Raff ; nach der
Originalausgabe des Verlags T.F.A. Kühn neu herausgegeben von Volker
Tosta. — Stuttgart : Edition Nordstern, c2005. — 23 p. of music ; 30 cm. —
(Raff Werke ; Bd. II/2)
Pref. in German with English translation; critical notes in German.   "Erstmals
erschienen in Jahre 1858 unter dem Titel Suite (en Ut majeur) pour piano"—T.p. —
Limited ed. of 200 copies.
Publ. no. 0102-0710
ISMN M700164591
System number: 014501802

Raff, Joachim, 1822-1882.
[Suites, piano, op. 72, E minor]
Suite für Klavier Nr. 3, e-Moll, op. 72 / Joachim Raff ; nach der
Originalausgabe des Verlags T.F.A. Kühn neu herausgegeben von Volker
Tosta. — Stuttgart : Edition Nordstern, c2005. — 29 p. of music ; 30 cm. —
(Raff Werke ; Bd. II/3)
Pref. in German with English translation; critical notes in German. — "Erstmals
erschienen in Jahre 1858 unter dem Titel Suite (en mi mineur) pour piano"—T.p. —
Limited ed. of 200 copies.
Publ. no. 0102-0720
ISMN M700164607
System number: 014501805

*Wagenseil, Georg Christoph, 1715-1777.
[Divertimenti, harpsichord (1761)]
Tre divertimenti per cimbalo : Wie Mozart Klavier spielen lernte— : mit
didaktischem Anhang "Fondamento per il clavicembalo" = How Mozart
learnt to play the piano— / Georg Christoph Wagenseil ; für
Klavier/cembalo herausgegeben von Helga Scholz-Michelitsch. — Wien :
Doblinger, c2005. — 27 p. of music : port. ; 30 cm. — (Diletto musicale ;
1384)
Pref. in German and English.
Publ. no. DM 1384
Pl. no. D. 19 188
ISMN M012191889
System number: 013405077
Primary classification 786.41858

786.2186
Mozart, Wolfgang Amadeus, 1756-1791.
[Concertos, piano, orchestra, K537, D major; *arr.*]
Piano concerto no. 26, K. 537 : "Coronation concerto" : for piano and
orchestra / Wolfgang Amadeus Mozart ; edited and reconstructed by Paul
Badura-Skoda. — New York : G. Schirmer ; Milwaukee, Wis. :
distributed by Hal Leonard, c2004. — 1 score (vii, 63 p.) ; 31 cm. —
Schirmer's library of musical classics ; v. 2045
Arr. for 2 pianos, 4 hands. — Includes pref. by the editor.
Publ. no. HL50483628
ISBN 0634010859
System number: 013211682

786.21872
Handel, George Frideric, 1685-1759.
[Fugues, keyboard, HWV 605-612]
Sechs Fugen HWV 605-610 und Fugen HWV 611, 612 = Six fugues
HWV 605-610 and fugues HWV 611, 612 / Georg Friedrich Händel ;
herausgegeben von Ullrich Scheideler ; Fingersatz von Michael Schneidt.
— München : G. Henle Verlag, c2004. — vi, 44 p. ; 31 cm.
Preface in German, French & English. Notes in English & German.
Publ. no. HN 749
ISMN M201807492
System number: 013246310

786.21874
*Bach, Johann Sebastian, 1685-1750.
[Inventions, harpsichord, BWV 772-786]
Two-part inventions / J.S. Bach ; edited by Christopher Taylor. — New
York, NY : G. Schirmer ; Milwaukee, Wis. : distributed by Hal Leonard,
c2005. — 45 p. of music : port. ; 31 cm. + 1 compact disc (digital ; 4 3/4
in.) — Hal Leonard student piano library Schirmer performance editions
For piano. — Includes biographical and performance notes. — CD contains a
performance of the work by the editor.
Publ. no. HL00296463
ISBN 0634073591
System number: 013191028

786.218846
*Chopin, Frédéric, 1810-1849.
[Waltzes, piano]
Waltzes : piano / Fryderyk Chopin ; edited by Christophe Grabowski. —
New critical ed. — London : Edition Peters, c2006. — xi, 140 p. of
music : facsim. ; 31 cm. — (Complete Chopin : a new critical edition)
"Urtext." — Includes pref. in English, French and German, and critical
commentary in English. — Publisher's no.: Edition Peters no. 7575.
Publ. no. 7575
ISMN M577085579
System number: 013691050

Easy-to-play famous waltzes : piano / arranged [by] Rosalie Bonighton.
— Buxhall : Kevin Mayhew, 2004. — 24 p. ; 31 cm.
Arrangements of 10 waltzes, two each by Brahms, Chopin, Schubert, Johann
Strauss II and Tchaikovsky.
Publ. no. 3611836
ISMN M570243709
System number: 013159307

Kirchner, Theodor, 1823-1903.
[Waltzes, piano, op. 23]
Zwölf Walzer für Klavier, op. 23 = Twelve waltzes for piano / Theodor
Kirchner ; nach den Quellen herausgegeben von Harry Joelson. —
Winterthur : Amadeus, 2005. — 27 p. of music ; 31 cm. — (Werke =
Works / Theodor Kirchner)
Pref. in German and English.
Publ. no. BP 1932
System number: 014659802

786.21888
*Norton, Christopher, 1953-
Latin preludes collection : [14 original pieces based on Latin-American
styles for solo piano with playalong CD] / Christopher Norton. —
London : Boosey & Hawkes, 2005. — 46 p. of music ; 31 cm. + 1
compact disc (digital ; 4 3/4 in.)
"For intermediate to advanced-level players." — Contains all the pieces from
"Latin preludes" and "Latin preludes 2", previously published separately. — CD
contains demonstration performances by the composer and backing tracks.
ISBN 085162474X
ISMN M060116261
System number: 013213840

786.218928
Besses, Antoni.
[Preludi místic, no. 5]
Preludi místic núm. 5 : piano / Antoni Besses. — Berga : Amalgama,
c2003. — 6 p. of music ; 30 cm.
Pl. no. A 1092
ISMN M692110170
System number: 014457002

Besses, Antoni.
[Preludi místic, no. 6]
Preludi místic núm. 6 : piano / Antoni Besses. — Berga : Amalgama, c2003.
— 6 p. of music ; 30 cm.
Pl. no. A 1093
ISMN M692110187
System number: 014457003

Chopin, Frédéric, 1810-1849.
[Preludes, piano]
Préludes / Frédéric Chopin ; herausgegeben von Norbert Müllemann ;
Fingersatz von Hermann Keller. — München : Henle, 2007. — xiv, 71 p.:
col. ill. ; 31 cm. — (Henle Verlag : Publikationen)
New revised edition. — For piano. — Pref. in German, English and French; critical
commentary in German and English.
Publ. no. HN 882
ISMN M201808826
System number: 013943269

Chopin, Frédéric, 1810-1849.
[Preludes, piano]
Préludes / Frédéric Chopin ; herausgegeben von Norbert Müllemann ;
Fingersatz von Hermann Keller. — Studien-Ed. — München : Henle,
c2007. — xx p., 77 p. of music ; 24 cm.
For piano. — Pref. in German, English and French; critical commentary in German
and English.
Publ. no. HN 9882
ISMN M201898827
ISMN 9790201898827
System number: 014049146

Lenot, Jacques.
[Preludes, piano]
24 préludes pour piano / Jacques Lenot. — Paris : L'Oiseau Prophète,
c2006. — 2 v. of music ; 32 cm.
Reproduced from manuscript.
Publ. no. O.P.E. 16
System number: 013771134

786.21894

Homs, Joaquim, 1906-2003.
[Impromptus, piano, no. 7]
Impromptu VII, piano / Joaquim Homs. — Berga : Amalgama, c2004. —
7 p. of music ; 30 cm.
Pl. no. A 1104
ISMN M692110446
System number: 014457018

786.218949

*Burgmüller, Friedrich, 1806-1874.
[Etudes faciles et progressives]
25 progressive studies : opus 100 / Burgmüller ; edited by Margaret Otwell.
— New York, NY : G. Schirmer ; Milwaukee, Wis. : distributed by Hal
Leonard, c2004. — 64 p. of music : port. ; 31 cm. + 1 compact disc (digital ;
4 3/4 in.) — Hal Leonard student piano library Schirmer performance
editions
For piano. — Includes biographical and performance notes. — CD contains a
performance of the work by the editor.
Publ. no. HL00296465
ISBN 0634073613
System number: 013191046

*Liszt, Franz, 1811-1886.
[Piano music. *Selections*]
Etudes d'exécution transcendante : mit = with = avec Grandes etudes 2 & 7
/ Franz Liszt ; nach den Quellen herausgegeben und mit Hinweisen zur
Interpretation versehen von Christian Ubber ; Fingersätze von Detlef Kraus.
— Erste Aufl. = 1st ed. — Wien : Wiener Urtext Edition, c2005. — xxii,
162 p. of music : facsims. ; 31 cm.
For piano. — Includes pref. by the editor in German with English and French
translations and critical commentary in German and English.
Pl. no. UT 50 233
ISBN 3850556409
ISBN 9783850556408
ISMN M500572565
EAN 9790500572565
System number: 013222423

786.218966

Kirchner, Theodor, 1823-1903.
[Nocturnes, piano, op. 28]
Notturnos : 4 Stücke für Klavier : op. 28 = Notturnos : four pieces for piano
/ Theodor Kirchner ; nach den Quellen herausgegeben von Harry Joelson.
— Winterthur : Amadeus, 2004. — 19 p. of music ; 31 cm. — (Werke =
Works / Theodor Kirchner)
Includes pref. in English and German.
Publ. no. BP 1314
System number: 014659748

786.218971587

*Kaye, Ernest.
Wedding march : for piano / Ernest Kaye ; and arranged for organ by
Antony Baldwin. — [New York] : Oxford University Press, c2004. —
6 p. of music ; 31 cm. — Oxford keyboard music
Includes the original version for piano followed by an arrangement for organ. —
Includes biographical notes.
ISBN 0193868032
System number: 013115092

786.2193

*Mach, Elyse.
Learning piano : piece by piece / Elyse Mach. — New York ; Oxford :
Oxford University Press, 2006. — xiii, 274 p. of music : ill., ports. ;
28 cm. + 2 compact discs (digital ; 4 3/4 in.)
CDs contain accompaniments prepared by Philip Keveren.
ISBN 9780195170337
ISBN 0195170334
System number: 013278617

786.4 – HARPSICHORD

786.4

*Clementi, Muzio, 1752-1832.
[Keyboard music. *Selections*]
18 composizioni senza numero d'opera, Op-sn 1-18 (WO 2, 3, 5, 8, 10,
13-23), per pianoforte o clavicembalo = 18 compositions without opus
number for piano or harpsichord / Muzio Clementi ; a cura di Andrea
Coen. — Bologna, Italia : Ut Orpheus, c2004. — xix p., 115 p. of music ;
facsims. ; 32 cm. — (Opera omnia / Muzio Clementi ; v. 51)
"Included—The sprig of Shillelah, first modern edition by Barry Cooper." —
"Urtext." — Includes pref. and critical notes in Italian and English. Includes
thematic index.
Pl. no. MC 51
ISMN M215308817
EAN 9790215308817
System number: 014748278
Primary classification 786.2

*Clementi, Muzio, 1752-1832.
Musical characteristics : op. 19, per clavicembalo o pianoforte = for
harpsichord (piano) / Muzio Clementi ; a cura di Roberto Illiano. —
Bologna, Italy : Ut Orpheus, c2004. — xii, 92 p. of music : facsims. ;
32 cm. — (Opera omnia / Muzio Clementi ; vol. 24)
Preludes and cadenzas in the styles of various composers. — Movements first
presented as edited by Illiano from ed. published: London : Longman and
Broderip, 1787; movements presented again as transcribed from the ms. of the
1807 revision in the Library of Congress, Albrecht 582. — Pref. to series in
Italian and English. Critical material in Italian. Includes thematic index. —
"Urtext."
Pl. no. MC 24
ISMN M215309050
EAN 9790215309050
System number: 014748001
Also classified at 786.2

*Cooke, Arnold.
Intermezzo and capriccio : (1971) : for harpsichord or piano solo / Arnold
Cooke. — [s.l.] : Anglo-American Music Publishers, c2005. — 10 p. of
music ; 28 cm.
Cover title. — Duration: 1:30. — Includes biographical note.
System number: 013594078
Also classified at 786.2

Hasse, Johann Adolf, 1699-1783.
[Concertos, keyboard instrument]
Sei concerti per organo solo / Johann Adolph Hasse ; a cura di Maurizio
Machella. — Padova : Armelin Musica, c2006. — 2 v. of music :
facsims. ; 31 cm. — Antiqui musicae magistri qui adversam fortunam
tulerunt ; 237-238
Keyboard reduction for harpsichord or organ by the composer of a selection from
his 12 concertos in 6 parts, op. 3. — Edited from a score of the 1st ed. published
by I. Walsh in London, ca. 1741?, held at the British Library (f.517.).
Publ. no. AMM 237
Publ. no. AMM 238
System number: 013771094
Primary classification 786.5

Jollage, Charles-Alexandre.
[Pièces de clavecin, 1er livre]
Premier livre de pièces de clavecin : 1738 / Charles Alexandre Jollage. —
Courlay, France : Fuzeau, c2007. — 30 p. ; 30 cm. — Fac-similé
Jean-Marc Fuzeau — (FacsiMusic : Collection FacsiMusic / publiée sous
la direction de Jean Saint-Arroman)
For harpsichord. — Reprint. Originally published: Paris : Labassée, 1738. —
Based on a copy held in the British Library, London (h.60.g.).
Publ. no. 50105
ISMN M049501057

System number: 013943338

*Scarlatti, Alessandro, 1660-1725.
[Harpsichord music. *Selections*]
Dieci pezzi per clavicembalo = Zehn Stücke für Clavierinstrumente /
Alessandro Scarlatti ; herausgegeben von Jörg Jacobi. — Bremen : Edition
Baroque, c2004. — 18 p. of music ; 30 cm.
Edited from a ms. held at the British Library (shelfmark Add. 32587). —
"Alessandro Scarlatti zugeschrieben." — Preface and critical report in German.
Pl. no. eba4012
ISMN M700234522
System number: 013222305

*Trabaci, Giovanni Maria, 1580 (ca.)-1647.
[Ricercate, 2o libro]
Libro secondo (1615) : ricercate & altri varij capricci / Giovanni Maria
Trabaci ; a cura di Armando Carideo. — Castelli : Andromeda Editrice,
c2005. — xxxiv, 133 p. of music : facsims. ; 30 cm. — Tastature ; n. 15
For organ or harpsichord. — Pref. and critical report in Italian and English.
ISBN 9788888643250
ISBN 8888643257
System number: 014629769
Primary classification 786.5

786.41827

*Marcello, Benedetto, 1686-1739.
[Chaconnes, harpsichord, S. C703, C major]
Cioconna stravaganza ; Menuetto per cembalo = für Clavier / Benedetto
Marcello ; herausgegeben und bearbeitet von Jörg Jacobi. — Bremen :
Edition Baroque, c2004. — 31 p. of music ; 30 cm.
For harpsichord. — Edited from mss. held at the British Library (Mus. Add. 31589,
fol. 1-6 and Mus. Add. 29962, fol. 10-17). — Preface in German. — Errata slip
tipped in.
Pl. no. eba4009
ISMN M700234485
System number: 013222373
Also classified at 786.418835

786.4183

Hertel, Johann Wilhelm, 1727-1789.
[Sonatas, harpsichord. *Selections*]
Sei sonate per il cembalo solo / Johann Wilhelm Hertel ; herausgegeben von
Laura Cerutti. — Stuttgart : Cornetto, c2006. — 2 v. of music ; 30 cm.
Twelve sonatas, 6 in each vol. — Edited from mss. in the library of the
Conservatoire Royal, Brussels.
Publ. no. CP422
Publ. no. CP423
ISMN M501003938
ISMN M501003945
System number: 013771123

Rabassa, Pedro, 1683-1767.
[Sonata, harpsichord]
Sonata per a clavicèmbal / Pere Rabassa. — Barcelona : Tritó, 2006. —
20 p. of music ; 23 x 31 cm.
For harpsichord. — Pref., biographical and critical notes in Catalan, Spanish and
English.
Publ. no. TR 521
ISMN M692043478
System number: 013953479

786.41858

Helmont, Charles Joseph van, 1715-1790.
[Pièces de clavecin, op. 1]
Pièces de clavecin, opus I : (Bruxelles, 1737) / Charles-Joseph van
Helmont ; introduction, Robert Wangermée. — Bruxelles :
CEDESOM-ULB, Le Livre Timperman, 2005. — 45 p. of music : facsim. ;
24 x 32 cm. — Musica Bruxellensis ; 3
Suites for harpsichord. — Reprint. Originally published: Bruxelles: Jean Laurent
Krafft, [1737?] — Introduction in French.
ISBN 9077723188
ISBN 9789077723180
System number: 013728837

*Wagenseil, Georg Christoph, 1715-1777.
[Divertimenti, harpsichord (1761)]
Tre divertimenti per cimbalo : Wie Mozart Klavier spielen lernte— : mit
didaktischem Anhang "Fondamento per il clavicembalo" = How Mozart
learnt to play the piano— / Georg Christoph Wagenseil ; für
Klavier/cembalo herausgegeben von Helga Scholz-Michelitsch. — Wien :
Doblinger, c2005. — 27 p. of music : port. ; 30 cm. — (Diletto musicale ;
1384)
Pref. in German and English.
Publ. no. DM 1384
Pl. no. D. 19 188
ISMN M012191889
System number: 013405077
Also classified at 786.21858

786.4186

Bach, Carl Philipp Emanuel, 1714-1788.
[Concertos, harpsichord, H. 242, F major]
Arrangements of orchestral works I / Carl Philipp Emanuel Bach ; edited
by Douglas A. Lee. — Los Altos, Calif. : Packard Humanities Institute,
2007. — xv p., 136 p.: facsims. ; 33 cm. — (Complete works. Series I,
Keyboard music / Carl Philipp Emanuel Bach ; v. 10.1)
The 1st work originally for solo harpsichord, also exists in a version with
orchestral acc. (H. 470), but is not listed in Wq; the 2nd-6th works are
unaccompanied harpsichord versions made by the composer. — Issued in
cooperation with the Bach-Archiv Leipzig, the Sächsische Akademie der
Wissenschaften zu Leipzig, and Harvard University. — Includes prefaces, list of
abbreviations, critical report, commentary, and concordances in English.
ISBN 9781933280271
ISBN 1933280271
System number: 013825297

Bach, Johann Sebastian, 1685-1750.
[Italienisches Konzert]
The Italian concerto : BWV 971 / J. S. Bach. — Urtext performing ed. —
Buxhall : Kevin Mayhew, 2004. — 1 score (22 p.) ; 31 cm.
For solo harpsichord. — Includes unattributed foreword.
Publ. no. 3611848
ISMN M570243952
System number: 013173104

Hertel, Johann Wilhelm, 1727-1789.
[Concertos, harp, string orchestra, F major; *arr.*]
Konzert F-Dur für Harfe oder Cembalo, 2 Violinen, Viola und
Violoncello / Johann Wilhelm Hertel ; herausgegeben von Johanna Seitz ;
Klavierauszug von Burkhard Jäckel. — Magdeburg : Edition Walhall,
c2005. — 1 score (21 p.) + 1 part (13 p.) : facsims. ; 30 cm. —
(Collegium musicum : Kölner Reihe Alter Musik)
Includes pref. in German and English.
Pl. no. EW 428
System number: 013775622
Primary classification 787.95186

786.418835

*Marcello, Benedetto, 1686-1739.
[Chaconnes, harpsichord, S. C703, C major]
Cioconna stravaganza ; Menuetto per cembalo = für Clavier / Benedetto
Marcello ; herausgegeben und bearbeitet von Jörg Jacobi. — Bremen :
Edition Baroque, c2004. — 31 p. of music ; 30 cm.
For harpsichord. — Edited from mss. held at the British Library (Mus. Add.
31589, fol. 1-6 and Mus. Add. 29962, fol. 10-17). — Preface in German. —
Errata slip tipped in.
Pl. no. eba4009
ISMN M700234485
System number: 013222373
Primary classification 786.41827

786.418846

Gavrilin, V. (Valerii).
[Selections]
Val'sy dlià fortepiano i fortepiano v 4 ruki = Waltzes for piano and piano
in four hands / V. Gavrilin. — St. Petersburg : Kompozitor, 2005, c2001.
— 87 p. of music ; 30 cm.
Some works are arrangements of orchestral pieces.
Pl. no. c 3086 k
System number: 013637528
Also classified at 785.6219218846

786.5 – ORGANS

786.5

Bertoldo, Sperindio, ca. 1530-1570.
[Organ music]
Opere per tastiera (Venezia 1591) : con riproduzione in facsimile delle
stampe / Sperindio Bertoldo ; a cura di Luigi Collarile. — Castelli :
Andromeda, 2005. — xxiii p., 63 p. of music : facsims. ; 30 cm. —
Tastature ; n. 16
Includes facsimile reprints of Canzoni francese intavolate per sonar d'organo and
Toccate, ricercari et canzoni francese intavolate per sonar d'organo (both
Venetia : Vincenti, 1591). — Pref. and critical report in Italian and English.
ISBN 8888643354 (pbk.)
EAN 9788888643359
System number: 013887061

Bovet, Guy.
[Esquisses japonaises]
Three Japanese sketches : for organ / Guy Bovet. — [New York] : Oxford
University Press, c2004. — 31 p. of music ; 31 cm. — Oxford music for
organ
T.p. also in Japanese. — The music is based on three Japanese songs, the words
of which are printed in Japansese with English translation preceding each
movement. — Includes composer's and biographical notes.
ISBN 0193866447
System number: 013115370

*Carter, Andrew.
[Organ music. *Selections*]
Organ album / Andrew Carter. — Oxford : Oxford University Press, 2004.
— 40 p. of music ; 31 cm.
Includes composer's note.
ISBN 0193753227
System number: 013062631

*Cooke, Arnold.
[Toccata, organ]
Toccata, & aria : organ solo / Arnold Cooke. — [Alamonte Springs, FL?] :
Anglo-American Music Publishers, c2005. — 14 p. ; 28 cm.
Cover title. — Includes biographical note.
System number: 013594012

Couple the tuba : manuals / Rosalie Bonighton ... [et al.] — Buxhall :
Kevin Mayhew, 2004. — 31 p. of music ; 31 cm.
9 pieces for organ (manuals only) by contemporary composers. — Includes
biographical notes.
Publ. no. 1400359
ISBN 1844171973
ISMN M570242887
System number: 013159882

Elgar, Edward, 1857-1934.
[Carillon; *arr.*]
Carillon, op. 75 ; &, Loughborough memorial chime : organ solo / Edward
Elgar ; arranged & edited by David Patrick. — Barnet : Fitzjohn Music
Publications, c2005. — 13 p. of music ; 30 cm.
Carillon (op. 75) based upon the organ arrangement that Hugh Blair made in 1914.
— Includes editorial notes.
System number: 013196914

*Hancock, Gerre, 1934-
Variations on "Ora labora" : for organ / Gerre Hancock. — [New York] :
Oxford University Press, c2004. — 10 p. of music ; 31 cm. — Oxford music
for organ
Based on the hymn tune 'Ora labora' by Thomas Tertius Noble. — Includes
biographical and composer's notes.
ISBN 0193867613
System number: 013173129

Hasse, Johann Adolf, 1699-1783.
[Concertos, keyboard instrument]
Sei concerti per organo solo / Johann Adolph Hasse ; a cura di Maurizio
Machella. — Padova : Armelin Musica, c2006. — 2 v. of music : facsims. ;
31 cm. — Antiqui musicae magistri qui adversam fortunam tulerunt ;
237-238
Keyboard reduction for harpsichord or organ by the composer of a selection from his
12 concertos in 6 parts, op. 3. — Edited from a score of the 1st ed. published by I.
Walsh in London, ca. 1741?, held at the British Library (f.517.).
Publ. no. AMM 237
Publ. no. AMM 238
System number: 013771094
Also classified at 786.4

Hässler, Johann Wilhelm, 1747-1822.
[Kleine Orgelstücke]
48 kleine Orgelstücke = 48 short organ pieces / Johann Wilhelm Hässler ;
herausgegeben von Volker Choroba. — Mainz : Schott, c2007. — 75 p. of
music ; 31 cm.
Urtext edition based on the first printed edition: Leipzig : Breitkopf & Härtel,
1786-89. — Preface in German and English.
Publ. no. ED 20087
ISMN M001145657
System number: 013771091

Montague, Stephen.
Toccare incandescent : for organ (2003/04) / Stephen Montague. —
Waltham Abbey : United Music Publishers, c2004. — 27 p. of music ; 23 x
31 cm. — UMP organ repertoire series ; no. 45
Duration : ca. 12 min. — Includes programme and biographical notes.
ISMN M224404678
System number: 013383468

*Reincken, Johann Adam, 1623-1722.
[Keyboard music. *Selections*]
Sämtliche Orgelwerke = Complete organ works / Johann Adam Reincken ;
herausgegeben von Pieter Dirksen. — Wiesbaden : Breitkopf & Härtel,
c2005. — 83 p. of music ; 31 cm.
1st-2nd works for organ; 3rd-7th works for harpsichord or organ. — The 5th and 7th
works are dubiously attributed to Reincken; the latter is previously unpublished. —
"Breitkopf Urtext"—Cover. — Pref. in German and English, and critical
commentary in German. — Publisher's no.: Edition Breitkopf 8715.
Pl. no. EB 8715
Publ. no. 8715
ISMN M004182291
System number: 013353334

*Scheidemann, Heinrich, 1596 (ca.)-1663.
[Organ music]
Sämtliche Orgelwerke = Complete organ works / Heinrich Scheidemann ;
herausgegeben von Klaus Beckmann. — Mainz : Schott, c2004. — 3 v. :
facsims. ; 23 x 31 cm. — Meister der Norddeutschen Orgelschule ; Bd.
8-10
Pref. in German and English; critical commentary in German.
Publ. no. ED 9728
Publ. no. ED 9729
Publ. no. ED 9730
ISMN M001136464 (T. 1)
ISMN M001136600 (T. 2)
ISMN M001137218 (T. 3)
System number: 013521876

Strungk, Delphin, 1601-1694.
[Organ music]
Sämtliche Orgelwerke : Choralbearbeitungen, Toccata,
Motettenkolorierungen = Complete organ works : chorale settings,
toccata, motet intabulations / Delphin Strunck ; herausgegeben von Klaus
Beckmann. — Mainz : Schott, c2006. — 76 p. of music : facsims. ; 23 x
31 cm. — (Meister der norddeutschen Orgelschule ; Bd. 14 = Masters of
the north German organ school ; vol. 14)
Preface in German and English ; critical report in German.
Publ. no. ED 20025
ISMN M001144681
System number: 013953484

Three 'storm' pieces : organ solo / edited by David Patrick. — Barnet :
Fitzjohn Music Publications, c2005. — 52 p. of music ; 30 cm.
System number: 013314527

*Trabaci, Giovanni Maria, 1580 (ca.)-1647.
[Ricercate, 2o libro]
Libro secondo (1615) : ricercate & altri varij capricci / Giovanni Maria
Trabaci ; a cura di Armando Carideo. — Castelli : Andromeda Editrice,
c2005. — xxxiv, 133 p. of music : facsims. ; 30 cm. — Tastature ; n. 15
For organ or harpsichord. — Pref. and critical report in Italian and English.
ISBN 9788888643250
ISBN 8888643257
System number: 014629769
Also classified at 786.4

*Vaughan Williams, Ralph, 1872-1958.
[Organ music. *Selections*]
A Vaughan Williams organ album. — Oxford : Oxford University Press,
[2005?], c1964. — 26 p. of music ; 31 cm. — Oxford music for organ
Includes some arrangements. — Reprint. First published: London : Oxford
University Press, 1964.
ISBN 0193850141
ISBN 9780193850149
System number: 013196413

786.51587

Wedding gala : sixteen celebrated pieces for a perfect wedding / selected
and arranged for organ by John Norris. — London : Stainer & Bell,
c2005. — 54 p. ; 31 cm.
Publ. no. H449
ISMN M220221286
System number: 013307472

786.51825

Bach, Johann Christoph Friedrich, 1732-1795.
[Allegretto con variazioni, keyboard instrument, W. XII, 2, G major]
Partita on 'Morgen kommt der Weihnachtsmann' : ('Twinkle, twinkle
little star') : for organ (manuals only) / Johann Christoph Friedrich Bach ;
edited by David Patrick. — Barnet : Fitzjohn Music Publications, c2005.
— 11 p. of music ; 30 cm.
System number: 013243758

*Genesi, Mario G.
L'arte della variazione, per organo / Mario Giuseppe Genesi. —
Bergamo, Italy : Carrara, c2003. — 78 p. of music ; 31 cm. —
(Contemporanei)
Program and biographical notes in Italian and English.
Publ. no. 4658
System number: 014101650

786.51858

*Hakim, Naji, 1955-
Petite suite : for organ / Naji Hakim. — Waltham Abbey : United Music,
c2004. — 11 p. of music ; 31 cm. — UMP organ repertoire series ; no. 44
Programme and biographical notes in English and French.
ISMN M224404548
System number: 013191003

*Martinson, Joel.
Tuba suite : for organ / Joel Martinson. — [New York] : Oxford University Press, c2004. — 20 p. of music ; 31 cm. — Oxford music for organ
Includes composer's and biographical notes. — "In addition to complete performances in a concert setting, this suite may be used as a Prelude-Offertory/Communion-Postlude in a single setting … [or] any movement may be played as a separate voluntary"—Composer's note. — Duration: 5:10 ; 5:00 ; 4:00.
ISBN 0193867621
System number: 013324490

786.51872

*Pott, Francis, 1957-
Introduction, toccata and fugue : for organ / Francis Pott. — Waltham Abbey : United Music Publishers, c2004. — 32 p. of music ; 31 cm. — UMP organ repertoire series ; no. 43
Includes composer's and biographical notes.
ISMN M224403602
System number: 013192631

786.518992

Hassler, Hans Leo, 1564-1612.
[Magnificats, organ. *Selections*]
14 magnificat : (Torino, Biblioteca nazionale Fondo Giordano III, V) / Hans Leo Hassler ; a cura di Aaron Carpenè. — Latina : Levante Libreria, 2006. — xix p., 177 p. of music ; 21 x 30 cm. — Tastature ; TA 17
For organ. — Pref. and notes in Italian and English.
ISBN 8895203003
System number: 013771096

Mills, Alan, 1964-
A wedding postlude : on the chorale Lobe den Herren (Praise to the Lord) : for organ solo / Alan Mills. — Boston, Mass. : ECS Pub., c2006. — 6 p. of music ; 28 cm.
"Suitable for a wide range of church services, not merely weddings"—Program note. — At end: April 1981 (rev. 2001). — Duration: 1:45. — Performance and program notes by the composer on p. [2] of cover; biographical note on p. [4] of cover.
Publ. no. 6516
System number: 014052732

786.59164

*The complete keyboard player 15 showstoppers / based on the best-selling keyboard method by Kenneth Baker. — London : Wise, c2005. — 40 p. of music ; 31 cm.
"Fifteen stage hits arranged for all electronic keyboards. Includes suggested voices, fingering and lyrics, plus chord symbols and charts"—Cover. — Melodies with words and chord symbols. — Compiled by Nick Crispin, music arranged by Paul Honey.
Publ. no. AM983455
ISBN 1846091829
System number: 013432803

786.59166

The complete keyboard player pop hits / based on the best-selling keyboard method by Kenneth Baker. — London : Wise, c2005. — 40 p. of music ; 31 cm.
"Sixteen hit songs arranged for all electronic keyboards. Includes suggested voices, fingering and lyrics, plus chord symbols and charts"—Cover. — Compiled by Nick Crispin, music arranged by Paul Honey.
Publ. no. AM983059
ISBN 1846090938
System number: 013323535

786.591723

The complete keyboard player Christmas favourites / based on the best-selling keyboard method by Kenneth Baker. — London : Wise Publications, c2005. — 39 p. ; 31 cm.
"Seventeen festive songs and carols arranged for all electronic keyboards. Includes suggested voices, fingering and lyrics, plus chord symbols and charts"—Cover. — Compiled by Nick Crispin, music arranged by Paul Honey.
Publ. no. AM983444
ISBN 1846091810
System number: 013323647

786 – KEYBOARD, MECHANICAL, ELECTROPHONIC, PERCUSSION INSTRUMENTS

786.93076

*Richards, Jack, 1947-
Timpani : grades 6 -8 / edited by Jack Richards and Andrew McBirnie. — London : Stainer & Bell, c2004. — 28 p. of music + 1 score (16 p.) ; 31 cm.
"Contains all the material needed for each section of the grades six to eight examinations: tuning tests, pieces, viva voce, sight reading and aural tests"—Back cover. — Some pieces have piano acc. provided in separate score. — At head of title: London College of Music and Media.
Publ. no. H450
ISMN M220221262
System number: 013358034

786.94076

*Richards, Jack, 1947-
Snare drum : grades 5-8 / edited by Jack Richards and Andrew McBirnie ; additional editing by Aidan Geary. — London : Stainer & Bell, c2005. — 47 p. of music + 1 score (16 p.) ; 31 cm.
Some pieces have piano acc. provided in separate score. — At head of title: London College of Music and Media.
Publ. no. H426
ISMN M220219986
System number: 013416586

787.2 – VIOLIN

787.2

Associated Board of the Royal Schools of Music (Great Britain).
Selected violin examination pieces : 2005-2007 / The Associated Board of the Royal Schools of Music. — London : Associated Board of the Royal Schools of Music, c2004. — 5 parts ; 31 cm.
Cover title. — Parts only. Score and parts issued separately & held at British Library shelfmark g.1770.ll/2005-2007.
Pl. no. AB 3001—AB 3005
ISBN 1860964796 (Grade 1, part only)
ISBN 186096480X (Grade 2, part only)
ISBN 1860964818 (Grade 3, part only)
ISBN 1860964826 (Grade 4, part only)
ISBN 1860964834 (Grade 5, part only)
System number: 013281760

Associated Board of the Royal Schools of Music (Great Britain).
Selected violin examination pieces : 2005-2007 / The Associated Board of the Royal Schools of Music. — London : Associated Board of the Royal Schools of Music, c2004. — 7 scores + 7 parts ; 31 cm.
Cover title. — Parts also issued separately. Held at British Library shelfmark g.1770.ll./2005-2007*.
Pl. no. AB 3001—AB 3007
ISBN 1860964729 (Grade 1, score and part)
ISBN 1860964737 (Grade 2, score and part)
ISBN 1860964745 (Grade 3, score and part)
ISBN 1860964753 (Grade 4, score and part)
ISBN 1860964761 (Grade 5, score and part)
ISBN 186096477X (Grade 6, score and part)
ISBN 1860964788 (Grade 7, score and part)
System number: 013281745

*Bach, Johann Sebastian, 1685-1750.
[Jagdkantate. Schafe können sicher weiden; *arr.*]
Sheep may safely graze : aria from secular cantata no. 208 / by J.S. Bach ; arranged for violin (or viola, or 'cello) and pianoforte by Watson Forbes. — Oxford : Oxford University Press, [2005], c1946. — 1 score (7 p.) + 1 part ; 31 cm. — Music for violin
Reprint. Originally published: London : Oxford University Press, 1946.
ISBN 0193850303
System number: 013424681

Blomenkamp, Thomas.
[Kleine Stücke, violin, piano (2002)]
Fünf kleine Stücke für Violine und Klavier, 2002 / Thomas Blomenkamp. — Köln : Dohr, c2007. — 1 score (1 v.) + 1 part ; 30 cm.
Preface and biographical notes in German.
Pl. no. E.D. 27461
ISMN M202014615
System number: 013887062

Clarke, Rebecca, 1886-1979.
[Violin, piano music. *Selections*]
Shorter pieces for violin and piano / Rebecca Clarke. — [New York] : Oxford University Press, c2005. — 1 score (13 p.) + 1 part (4 p.) : facsims ; 31 cm. — Oxford chamber music
Includes pref. in English.
ISBN 0193868628
System number: 013213425

Harizanos, Nickos.
Hesitations : for violin and piano : [op. 32] / Nickos Harizanos. — Manchester : Da Capo Music, c2004. — 1 score (5 p.) ; 30 cm.
Duration: ca. 6:00. — Includes programme and biographical notes.
Pl. no. DC 613
System number: 013351676

*Harrison, Sadie, 1965-
Bavad khair bagi! = May this goodnes last for ever! : for solo violin / Sadie Harrison. — York : University of York Music Press, c2002. — 8 p. of music ; 21 x 30 cm.
The violinist is required to speak Pushto words and make other vocal sounds. — Reproduced from holograph. — Includes programme note, and pronunciation guide.
ISMN M570207060
System number: 013433149

*Hayes, Morgan, 1973-
Opera : for violin and piano / Morgan Hayes. — London : Stainer & Bell,
c2003. — 1 score (11 p.) + 1 part (5 p.) ; 31 cm.
Includes composer's and performance notes. — Duration: ca. 7:00.
Publ. no. H448
ISMN M220221187
System number: 013172399

Hubicki, Margaret.
A posy of pieces : fifteen pieces on open strings for violin and piano / by
Margaret Hubicki. — London : Stainer & Bell, [2005?], c1961. — 1 score
(19 p.) + 1 part (8 p.) ; 31 cm.
Publ. no. H453
ISMN M220221507
System number: 013312983

Lewis, Paul, 1943-
A Somerset garland. for flute, violin or harmonica and piano / by Paul
Lewis. — Dover : Broadbent & Dunn, c2003. — 1 score (15 p.) + 1 part ;
30 cm.
Pl. no. B&D 13206
System number: 013374676
Primary classification 788.32

Lopez-Real, Carlos.
[Dig it. Violin(s)]
Dig it! : 7 cool tunes for violin(s) and piano with optional CD backing /
Carolos Lopez-Real. — Laggan Bridge : Spartan Press, c2005. — 1 score
(22 p.) + 3 parts ; 30 cm + 1 sound disc (digital ; 4 3/4 in.)
Includes optional duo and trio parts — "Grades 3-6"—Cover. — Includes
improvisation sections. — CD contains full demonstrations and backing tracks. —
Mixed instrument ensembles may be created using the other books in the series.
Pl. no. SP735
ISMN M579997351
System number: 013299138

*Maw, Nicholas.
Stanza : for solo violin (1997) / Nicholas Maw. — London : Faber Music,
[2002?], c1997. — 3 p. of music ; 30 cm.
ISBN 0571562930
System number: 006912927

*Rachmaninoff, Sergei, 1873-1943.
[Symphonies, no. 2, op. 27, E minor. Adagio; *arr.*]
Symphony no. 2 : theme from third movment : for violin and piano /
arranged by John York ; violin part edited by Levon Chilingirian. —
London : Boosey & Hawkes, c2004. — 1 score (6 p.) + 1 part ([1] p.) ;
31 cm.
Includes arranger's note.
ISMN M060116179
System number: 013129002

*Samuel, Rhian.
Shards of light : for solo violin / Rhian Samuel. — London : Stainer & Bell,
c2005. — 10 p. of music ; 30 cm.
Publ. no. AC228
ISMN M220221712
System number: 013416342

Sgambati, Giovanni, 1841-1914.
[Violin, piano music. *Selections*]
Quattro pezzi / Giovanni Sgambati ; a cura di Manfred Croci. — Roma :
Boccaccini & Spada, [2006], c2004. — 1 score (26 p.) + 1 part (9 p.) ;
31 cm. — (Giovanni Sgambati. Tutte le opere per violino e pianoforte)
Preface in Italian, English, German and French.
Pl. no. BS. 1763
System number: 014053367

Thistle & minuet : 16 easy pieces from the Scottish Baroque for violin (or
flute or oboe), keyboard, and optional cello (or bassoon) = 16 einfache
Stücke aus der schottischen Barockzeit für Violine (oder Flöte oder Oboe),
Tasteninstrument und Cello (oder Fagott) ad libitum = 16 pièces faciles du
Baroque écossais pour violon (ou flûte ou hautbois), clavier et violoncelle
(ou basson) facultatif / edited by David Johnson. — London : Schott,
c2005. — 1 score (32 p.) + 2 parts ; 31 cm + 1 sound disc (digital ; 4 3/4
in.) — Baroque around the world
Some pieces have an optional part for a second melody instrument. — Pref.,
biographical and historical notes in English, French and German. — CD contains
full demonstrations and backing tracks.
Publ. no. ED 12773
ISBN 1902455193
ISMN M220122965
System number: 013192325
Also classified at 785.28193

*The violin : a collection : new and recent repertoire for violin with piano
accompaniment / Craig Armstrong ... [et al.] — London : Chester Music,
c2005. — 1 score (70 p.) + 1 part (32 p.) ; 31 cm.
Mostly for violin and piano. 4th work (Philip Glass) has organ or piano acc. 7th
(Maxwell Davies) and 12th (Kaija Saariaho) works are for solo violin and 15th
work (Judith Weir) is for 2 violins. 3rd (Malcolm Arnold) and 8th (Falla) works
originally for orchestra, 11th work (Poulenc) originally for piano.
Publ. no. CH69641
ISBN 1844499537
System number: 013193381

*Warshauer, Meira, 1949-
Bracha = (A blessing) : for violin and piano / Meira Warshauer. — [New
York] : Oxford University Press, c2004. — 1 score (4 p.) + 1 part (3 p.) ;
31 cm. — Oxford music for violin
Includes composer's and biographical notes.
ISBN 0193866781
ISBN 9780193866782
System number: 013196406

*Widger, John.
[Jazz, rock 'n' bow. Violin]
Jazz, rock 'n' bow : violin & piano : with optional CD including
performance, rehearsal and backing tracks / music by John Widger. —
Laggan Bridge : Spartan Press, c2005. — 1 score (15 p.) + 1 part (4 p.) ;
30 cm + 1 sound disc (digital ; 4 3/4 in.)
"Grade 1 plus"—T.p. — Publisher's no.: SPCD779 (CD).
Pl. no. SP779
Publ. no. SPCD779
ISMN M579997795
System number: 013441219

787.2076
*Dobbins, Jan.
Strings in step. Violin. Book 1 : with CD / Jan Dobbins. — New ed. —
Oxford : Oxford University Press, c2004. — 62 p. of music : ill. ; 30 cm.
+ 1 compact disc (digital ; 4 3/4 in.)
Tutor for the violin. — CD contains performances of all the pieces and exercises.
— May be used in conjunction with the books for viola and violoncello.
ISBN 0193221381
System number: 013062636

Haughton, Alan, 1950-
Fun club violin : chill-out pieces to enjoy between exams. Violin grade
0-1 / Alan Haughton. — Student copy. — Buxhall : Kevin Mayhew,
2003. — 1 part (12 p.) ; 30 cm. + 1 compact disc.
Another copy (with its own cover) of the violin part supplied with the Teacher
copy. — Cover title.
Publ. no. 3611778
ISMN M570242498
System number: 013182084

Haughton, Alan, 1950-
Fun club violin : chill-out pieces to enjoy between exams. Violin grade
0-1 / Alan Haughton. — Teacher copy. — Buxhall : Kevin Mayhew,
2003. — 1 score (31 p.) + 1 part ; 30 cm. + 1 compact disc.
Publ. no. 3611767
ISMN M570242320
System number: 013182078

Haughton, Alan, 1950-
Fun club violin : chill-out pieces to enjoy between exams. Violin grade
1-2 / Alan Haughton. — Student copy. — Buxhall : Kevin Mayhew,
2003. — 1 part (12 p.) ; 30 cm. + 1 compact disc.
Another copy (with its own cover) of the violin part supplied with the Teacher
copy. — Cover title.
Publ. no. 3611779
ISMN M570242504
System number: 013182061

Haughton, Alan, 1950-
Fun club violin : chill-out pieces to enjoy between exams. Violin grade
1-2 / Alan Haughton. — Teacher copy. — Buxhall : Kevin Mayhew,
2003. — 1 score (30 p.) + 1 part ; 30 cm. + 1 compact disc.
Publ. no. 3611768
ISMN M570242337
System number: 013182066

Haughton, Alan, 1950-
Fun club violin : chill-out pieces to enjoy between exams. Violin grade
2-3 / Alan Haughton. — Student copy. — Buxhall : Kevin Mayhew,
2003. — 1 part (12 p.) ; 30 cm. + 1 compact disc.
Another copy (with its own cover) of the violin part supplied with the Teacher
copy. — Cover title.
Publ. no. 3611780
ISMN M570242511
System number: 013182053

Haughton, Alan, 1950-
Fun club violin : chill-out pieces to enjoy between exams. Violin grade
2-3 / Alan Haughton. — Teacher copy. — Buxhall : Kevin Mayhew,
2003. — 1 score (32 p.) + 1 part ; 30 cm. + 1 compact disc.
Publ. no. 3611769
ISMN M570242344
System number: 013182039

Wohlfahrt, Franz.
[Etüden, violin, op. 45]
Sixty studies for the violin, op. 45 : complete, books I and II / Franz
Wohlfahrt ; edited by Gaston Blay. — New York : G. Schirmer ;
Milwaukee, Wis. : distributed by Hal Leonard, c2004. — 55 p. ; 31 cm.
— Schirmer's library of musical classics ; v. 2046
Reprint of ed. published: New York : G. Schirmer, c1905.
Publ. no. HL50485504
ISBN 0634074032
System number: 013211697

787.21542

Disney greats : violin : [solo arrangements of 15 favorite songs with CD accompaniment] — Milwaukee, Wis. : Hal Leonard, [2005] — 24 p. ; 31 cm + 1 compact disc. — Hal Leonard instrumental play-along
Music from Disney films, musicals and theme parks. — No words.
Publ. no. HL00841941
ISBN 0634085468
System number: 013191561

787.21546

TV hits : playalong for violin. — London : Wise, c2005. — 31 p. of music : ill. 31 cm + 1 sound disc (digital ; 4 3/4 in.) — Guest spot
"Ten classic TV themes in melody line arrangements by Quentin Thomas with specially recorded backing tracks"—Cover. — No words.
Publ. no. AM980573
ISBN 184449618X
System number: 013193409

787.21620941135

Stove, Thomas Gideon.
Running for a fry : and other Shetland fiddle tunes / Thomas Gideon Stove. — Lerwick, Shetland : Shetland Times, c2005. — 44 p. : ill. ; 30 cm + 1 compact disc
Melodies and chord symbols for 24 tunes. — Includes notes on the tunes. — CD contains demonstration tracks.
ISBN 1904746101
System number: 013345843

787.21629163

***Neil, J. Murray.**
The Scots fiddle / J. Murray Neil. — Glasgow : Neil Wilson Publishing, 1999-2004. — 3 v. of music : ill. ; 25 cm.
Unacc. melodies.
ISBN 1897784864 (v. 1)
ISBN 1903238064 (v. 2)
ISBN 1903238684 (v. 3)
System number: 014664031

787.2164

Lloyd Webber, Andrew, 1948-
[Musicals. *Selections; arr.*]
Andrew Lloyd Webber showstoppers : playalong for violin. — London : Wise, c2005. — 32 p. of music ; 31 cm + 1 sound disc (digital ; 4 3/4 in.) — Guest spot
"Ten hit songs in melody line arrangements by Quentin Thomas with specially recorded backing tracks"—Cover. — No words.
Publ. no. AM91953
ISBN 071194069X
System number: 013193460

787.2165

Cullen, David, 1942-
13 ways of getting there : jazzy pieces for violin and piano / David Cullen. — London : Schott, c2005. — 1 score (36 p.) + 1 part (16 p.) ; 31 cm + 1 sound disc (digital ; 4 3/4 in.) — Jazz-it
"Easy to intermediate"—Back cover. — Pref. in English, French and German. — CD contains full demonstrations and backing tracks.
Publ. no. ED 12849
ISMN M220123740
System number: 013312976

Jazzy opera classix : for violin / [arranged by] Darren Fellows. — London : Schott, c2005. — 36 p. ; 31 cm. + 1 sound disc (digital ; 4 3/4 in.)
"Favourite opera themes in jazzy arrangements" — Back cover. — Melody lines with chord symbols. — Piano accompaniments available as PDF files on the CD. — Includes descriptions of the operas in English, French and German. — CD contains full demonstrations and backing tracks.
Publ. no. ED 12826
ISBN 1902455320
ISMN M220123276
System number: 013192197

787.2166

Keane (Musical group).
[Hopes and fears; *arr.*]
Hopes and fears : playalong for violin / Keane. — London : Wise Publications, c2005. — 31 p. ; 31 cm. + 2 compact discs — Guest spot
"Twelve songs from the band's hit album in melody line arrangements by Paul Honey"—Cover. — Melodies only, with chord symbols. — Music by members of the group. — CDs contain full performances and backing tracks.
Publ. no. AM982850
ISBN 1846090555
System number: 013281586

787.2168

Classical favorites : violin : [solo arrangements of 15 great pieces with CD accompaniment] — Milwaukee, Wis. : Hal Leonard, c2005. — 16 p. ; 31 cm. + 1 compact disc — Hal Leonard instrumental play-along
Publ. no. HL00841961
ISBN 0634085670
System number: 013220200

787.2183

Hertel, Johann Christian, 1699-1754.
[Sonatas, violin, continuo, op. 1]
Sonate à violino solo col violone ò cimbalo, opera prima / da Giovanni Christiano Hertelli. — Stuttgart : Cornetto, c2005. — 1 score ([34] p.) : facsims. ; 25 x 35 cm. + 1 compact disc. — Faksimile-Edition Rara
Reprint of the edition: Amsterdam : Le Cene, 1727. — "Diese Faksimile-Ausgabe wurde nach dem Exemplar in der Universität Uppsala angefertigt"—P. [31]
Publ. no. CF470
ISMN M501004416
System number: 013771120

LeBrun, Francesca, 1756-1791.
[Sonatas, violin, harpsichord, op. 2]
Six sonatas for the piano forte or harpsichord with an accompaniment for a violin, op. 2 / by Francesca LeBrun ; edited by Deborah Hayes. — Fayetteville, AR : ClarNan Editions, c2003. — 1 score (xi, 101 p.) + 1 part (29 p.) ; 28 cm.
Edited from the copy of the 1780 London edition held in the music collection of the New York Public Library. — Includes biographical, program, and editorial notes in English. — Errata slip tipped in.
Publ. no. CN47
System number: 014457021

Lonati, Carlo Ambrogio.
[Sonatas, violin, continuo (1701)]
XII sonate a violino solo e basso : ms. Salzburg, Milano 1701 / Carlo Ambrogio Lonati. — Firenze : Studio per edizioni scelte, c2005. — 1 score (125 p.) : 1 port. ; 25 x 31 cm. — Monumenta musicae revocata ; 32
Reproduced from a photocopy in the Paris-Lodron Universität Salzburg of the lost holograph which had been in the Sächsische Landesbibliothek, Dresden (Mus 2020-R-1) before World War II. — Pref. by Christophe Timpe in Italian and German.
ISBN 8872428122
System number: 013750218

***Schmelzer, Johann Heinrich, ca. 1623-1680.**
[Sonatae unarum fidium]
Sonatae unarum fidium seu a violino solo : Nürnberg, 1664 / Johann Heinrich Schmelzer ; transcrizione a cura di Alessandro Bares. — Albese con Cassano, Italia : Musedita ; Stuttgart : Gedruckt in Lizenz von Cornetto-Verlag, c2001. — 1 score (33 p.) + 2 parts ; 30 cm.
For violin and continuo. — Figured bass unrealized. — Edited from the score at the Österreichischer Nationalbibliothek, Wien.
Publ. no. CM548
ISMN M501005192
System number: 014766575

Westhoff, Johann Paul, 1656-1705.
[Sonatas, violin, continuo (1694)]
Sonate per violino e basso continuo : Dresden, 1694 / Johann Paul Westhoff ; transcrizione a cura di Alessandro Bares. — Albese con Cassano : Musedita ; Stuttgart : Cornetto, gedruckt in Lizenz von Musedita, c2005. — 1 score (71 p.) + 2 parts ; 30 cm.
Figured bass unrealized. — Prefatory remarks in Italian, English and French.
Publ. no. CM544
ISMN M501005154
System number: 013887082

787.21858

***Wellesz, Egon, 1885-1974.**
[Suites, violin, piano, op. 56]
Suite für Violine und Klavier, op. 56 (1937, rev. 1957) / Egon Wellesz ; herausgegeben und mit Fingersätzen versehen von David Frühwirth. — Wien : Doblinger, c2003. — 1 score (11 p.) + 1 part (4 p.) ; 30 cm.
Caption title. — Duration: ca. 12:00.
Publ. no. 03 286
Pl. no. D. 19 247
ISMN M012192473
EAN 9790012192473
System number: 013183445

787.2186

***Clement, Franz, 1780-1842.**
[Concertos, violin, orchestra, D major]
Violin concerto in D major : (1805) / Franz Clement ; edited by Clive Brown. — Middleton, Wis. : A-R Editions, c2005. — 1 score (184 p.) : facsims. ; 31 cm. + + 1 piano score (71 p.) + 1 part (31 p.) ; 28 cm. — Recent researches in the music of the nineteenth and early twentieth centuries, 0193-5364 ; 41
Edited from 2 copies of a lithographed edition housed at the British Library, London (GB-Lbl:i100.uu.) and at the Österreichische Nationalbibliothek, Vienna (A-Wn: MS.36456). — Editorial, historical and critical notes in English.
ISBN 0895795698
System number: 013350825
Primary classification 784.272186

Glass, Philip.
[Concertos, violin, orchestra; *arr.*]
Violin concerto : (1987) / Philip Glass ; piano reduction by Charles
Abramovich. — London : Chester Music, c2005. — 1 score (48 p.) +
1 part ; 31 cm.
Publ. no. DU10368
ISBN 1846091462
System number: 013323691

*Seitz, Friedrich, 1848-1918.
[Schüler-Konzerte]
Pupil's concertos nos. 1-5, complete : for violin and piano / Friedrich Seitz ;
edited and fingered by Philipp Mittell. — Milwaukee, Wis. : G Schirmer :
distributed by Hal Leonard, c2005. — 1 score (78 p.) + 1 part (32 p.) ;
31 cm. — Schirmer's library of musical classics ; v. 2054
Publ. no. HL50485872
ISBN 9780634096822 (pbk.)
ISBN 0634096826
System number: 013441065

787.21861524
Vivaldi, Antonio, 1678-1741.
[Cimento dell'armonia e dell'inventione. N. 1-4; *arr.*]
The four seasons : four concertos for violin and orchestra : for violin and
piano reduction / Antonio Vivaldi ; violin part edited by Rok Klopčič ;
piano reduction by Alojz Srebotnjak. — New York : G Schirmer ;
Milwaukee, Wis. : distributed by Hal Leonard, c2004. — 1 score (54 p.) +
1 part ; 31 cm. — Schirmer's library of musical classics ; v. 2047
Includes performance notes. — This ed. previously published in 4 separate nos.:
New York : G. Schirmer, c1978-c1984.
Publ. no. HL50485535
ISBN 0634078976
System number: 013211714

787.218949
Locatelli, Pietro Antonio, 1695-1764.
[Arte del violino. Capricci]
Ventiquattro capricci per violino solo [op. III] / Pietro Antonio Locatelli ; in
base all'edizione a cura di Albert Dunning ; con diteggiature ed esercizi
preparatori di Enzo Porta. — London : Schott, 2005. — cxviii, 68 p. ;
31 cm.
Pref. in Italian, English, German and French.
Publ. no. ED 12709
ISMN M220123108
System number: 013312873

787.3 – VIOLA

787.3
*Terzakis, Dimitri.
Solo für Tanja : (2003) : für Viola solo / Dimitri Terzakis. — Bad
Schwalbach : Edition Gravis, c2004. — 7 leaves of music ; 30 cm.
Duration: ca. 7:00. — Performance notes in German.
Pl. no. EG 891
System number: 014629750

Trapp, Lynn.
Cantilene : for oboe (or English horn, or viola) and organ / Lynn Trapp. —
[New York] : Oxford University Press, c2004. — 1 score (4 p.) + 3 parts ;
31 cm. — Oxford music for organ
Includes biographical note.
ISBN 0193867850
System number: 013115358
Primary classification 788.52

*Widger, John.
[Jazz, rock 'n' bow. Viola]
Jazz, rock 'n' bow : viola & piano : with optional CD including
performance, rehearsal and backing tracks / music by John Widger. —
Laggan Bridge : Spartan Press, c2005. — 1 score (15 p.) + 1 part (4 p.) ; 30
cm + 1 sound disc (digital ; 4 3/4 in.)
"Grade 1 plus"—T.p. — Publisher's no.: SPCD405 (CD).
Pl. no. SP406
Publ. no. SPCD406
ISMN M579994060
System number: 013441227

*Zhou, Long, 1953-
[Wild grass; *arr.*]
Wild grass : for viola / Zhou Long. — [New York] : Oxford University
Press, c2004. — 3 p. of music ; 31 cm. — Oxford music for viola
Originally for violoncello; arranged by the composer for viola. — "The music is
based on the foreword to the poem "Wild Grass" by the father of contemporary
Chinese literature, Lu Hsun"—Pref. — Includes an English translation of the poem's
foreword that may be recited concurrently with the music. — Includes biographical
note.
ISBN 0193868024
System number: 013196402
Also classified at 783.96

787.3076
*Dobbins, Jan.
Strings in step. Viola. Book 1 : with CD / Jan Dobbins. — New ed. —
Oxford : Oxford University Press, c2004. — 62 p. of music : ill. ; 30 cm.
+ 1 compact disc (digital ; 4 3/4 in.)
Tutor for the viola. — CD contains performances of all the pieces and exercises.
— May be used in conjunction with the books for violin and violoncello.
ISBN 019322139X
System number: 013062634

787.31542
Disney greats : viola : [solo arrangements of 15 favorite songs with CD
accompaniment] — Milwaukee, Wis. : Hal Leonard, [2005] — 24 p. ;
31 cm + 1 compact disc. — Hal Leonard instrumental play-along
Music from Disney films, musicals and theme parks. — No words.
Publ. no. HL00841942
ISBN 0634085476
System number: 013191597

787.3168
Classical favorites : viola : [solo arrangements of 15 great pieces with
CD accompaniment] — Milwaukee, Wis. : Hal Leonard, c2005. —
16 p. ; 31 cm. + 1 compact disc. — Hal Leonard instrumental
play-along
Publ. no. HL00841962
ISBN 0634085689
System number: 013220383

787.3183
Benda, Franz, 1709-1786.
[Sonatas, viola, continuo, C minor]
Sonate pour alto et basse continue en do mineur, Lee III-137 / Franz
Benda. — Bruxelles : T. Van Wetteren, 2006. — 1 score ([11] p.) +
2 parts : ill. ; 30 cm.
"…viola version is the original one and was subsequently transcribed for the
violin" [version, Lee III-137]"—Pref. — Figured bass unrealized; includes part
for bass instrument. — Transcribed and edited by Thomas Van Wetteren. —
Reproduced from ms. — Preface in French, Dutch, German and English; includes
postface with bibliographical references.
System number: 014053099

Franck, César, 1822-1890.
[Sonatas, violin, piano, A major; *arr.*]
Sonate für Viola und Klavier A-Dur / César Franck ; [herausgegeben von
Stephanie Gurtner] — Spielpartituren. — Winterthur : Partitura Verlag,
c2007. — 2 scores ; 33 cm.
Arr. by the composer for viola and piano; originally for violin and piano. — Each
playing score emphasizes the appropriate instrumental part. — Preface in
German.
Publ. no. 2612
ISMN M700282066
System number: 013887070

Röntgen, Julius, 1855-1932.
[Sonatas, viola, piano, C minor]
Sonata in C minor for viola and piano, 1924 / Julius Röntgen ; edited by
John Smit. — Amsterdam : Nederlands Muziek Instituut : Donemus,
c2006. — 1 score (38 p.) ; 30 cm. + 1 part ; 37 cm.
Biographical notes in English.
Pl. no. NMI 04.009
System number: 014053364

*Stanford, Charles Villiers, 1852-1924.
[Sonatas, clarinet, piano, op. 129, F major; *arr.*]
Viola sonata, op. 129 / by C.V. Stanford ; the composer's sonata for
clarinet and piano arranged for viola and edited by Henry Waldo Warner
and John White. — London : Stainer & Bell, c2004. — 1 part (11 p.) ;
31 cm.
Viola part, to used with the piano score of the clarinet version. — Note by John
White follows part.
Publ. no. H444
ISMN M220220739
System number: 013123103

787.31858
Sewell, Dominic.
[Suites, viola, op. 38]
Suite for solo viola : [opus 38] / Dominic Sewell. — Dover : Broadbent
& Dunn, c2004. — 7 p. of music ; 30 cm.
Pl. no. B&D 13405
System number: 013383342

787.4 – CELLO

787.4
Botschinsky, Allan, 1940-
Colours for cello : for solo violoncello = für Violoncello solo / Allan
Botschinsky. — Hamburg ; New York : Peermusic Classical, c2005. —
6 p. of music ; 31 cm.
Preface in English and German by the composer.
Pl. no. PCH 3666
Publ. no. 3666
ISMN M500119661
System number: 014457008

*Harvey, Jonathan, 1939-
[Sketches]
Three sketches : for cello : (1989) / Jonathan Harvey. — [London] : Faber
Music, c1989. — 7 p. of music ; 36 cm.
Reproduced from holograph.
ISBN 0571552927
System number: 006891408

Hedges, Anthony, 1931-
[Exchanges, violoncello, piano, no. 2, op. 146]
Exchanges 2 : op. 146 : for cello and piano / Anthony Hedges. — Beverley :
Westfield Music, c2002. — 1 score (14 p.) ; 30 cm.
System number: 013188499

Kurtág, György.
Az hit : für Violoncello solo (1998) / György Kurtág. — Wien ; London :
Universal Edition, c2007. — 3 p. of music ; 31 cm.
"The text that appears below the stave is only for a better understanding and must
not be sung."—P. 2. — Accompanying text in English, German, and Hungarian. —
At end of score: 19.V.1998.
Pl. no. UE 33 372
ISBN 9783702432706
ISBN 3702432701
UPC 803452062097
ISMN M008078460
System number: 013807387

A night at the opera for cello / arranged by Tim Wells. — Buxhall : Kevin
Mayhew, 2004. — 1 score (23 p.) + 1 part ; 31 cm.
With piano acc. — 10 excerpts from operas by Dvořák, Humperdinck, Mozart,
Offenbach, Puccini, Purcell, Sullivan and Verdi.
Publ. no. 3611823
ISMN M570243297
System number: 013159873

*Saariaho, Kaija.
Près : for cello and electronics / Kaija Saariaho. — Rev. 8.04. — London :
Chester Music, [2004], c1998. — 1 score (20 p.) + 1 part (15 p.) ; 31 cm. +
1 computer disc (4 3/4 in.)
Electronic component consists of pre-recorded sound as well as amplification and
various computer-controlled modifications of live violoncello sound. — CD-ROM
contains the software and bears copyright date c2004. — "A second person is needed
to ensure a good mix balance between the different materials"—Composer's note. —
Duration: ca. 18:00. — Includes composer's note, performance note and
biographical note.
Publ. no. CH 61239
Publ. no. CH 61239-01
Publ. no. CH 61239-02
Publ. no. OM24507A
ISBN 1844499340
System number: 013173409

*Saint-Saëns, Camille, 1835-1921.
[Cello, piano music. *Selections*]
The complete shorter works for cello and piano = für Cello und Klavier =
pour violoncelle et piano / Camille Saint-Saëns ; edited by Steven Isserlis &
Sabina Taller Ratner. — London : Faber Music, 1998. — 1 score (48 p.) +
1 part (19 p.) ; 31 cm. — Faber concert repertoire series
Notes and critical commentary in English, German and French.
ISBN 0571518079
System number: 006916073

*Schnittke, Alfred, 1934-1998.
Musica nostalgica : für Violoncello und Klavier = for violoncello and piano
/ Alfred Schnittke. Mit einem Lächeln für Slawa : für Violoncello und
Klavier / Gija Kantscheli = With a smile for Slava : for violoncello and
piano / Giya Kancheli. — Hamburg : Sikorski, c2004. — 1 score (11 p.) +
1 part (4 p.) ; 30 cm. — (Exempla nova ; 281)
Violoncello part of 1st work edited by M. Rostropovich. — Both works dedicated to
Rostropovich.
Publ. no. 1981
Pl. no. H.S. 1981
ISMN M003031538
System number: 013572326

*Terteryan, A. (Avet), 1929-
[Stück, violoncello, piano]
Stück für Violoncello und Klavier / Awet Terterjan. — Hamburg : Sikorski,
[2005, c1968] — 1 score (7 p.) + 1 part (3 p.) ; 30 cm.
Reprint of the edition: Erevan : Hayastan, 1968. — "Autorisierte Kopie"—Stamp on
p. [1]
System number: 014629744

*Widger, John.
Jazz, rock 'n' bow : cello & piano : with optional CD including
performance, rehearsal and backing tracks / music by John Widger. —
Laggan Bridge : Spartan Press, c2005. — 1 score (15 p.) + 1 part (4 p.) ; 30
cm + 1 sound disc (digital ; 4 3/4 in.)
"Grade 1 plus"—T.p. — Publisher's no.: SPCD407 (CD).
Pl. no. SP407
Publ. no. SPCD407
ISMN M579994077
System number: 013441287

787.40905
*Spectrum : for cello : 16 contemporary pieces / compiled by William
Bruce. — London : Associated Board of the Royal Schools of Music,
2004. — 1 score (40 p.) + 1 part ; 31 cm. + 1 compact disc.
Mostly with piano acc. — "With at least one piece at each of the Associated
Board's grades 1-8"—Back cover. — Includes biographical and performance
notes. — CD contains full performances by William Bruce (cello) and Thalia
Myers (piano).
Pl. no. AB 2914
ISBN 1860963730
System number: 013190730

787.41423
*Smith, Doreen, 1931-
Cello sight-reading. Book 1 / Doreen Smith. — Oxford : Oxford
University Press, [2004?], c1992. — 21 p. of music ; 31 cm. — Oxford
music for cello
"One hundred melodies for grades 1 to 5"—Cover.
ISBN 9780193850040
ISBN 0193850044
System number: 013173145

787.41542
Disney greats : cello : [solo arrangements of 15 favorite songs with CD
accompaniment] — Milwaukee, Wis. : Hal Leonard, [2005] — 24 p. ;
31 cm + 1 compact disc. — Hal Leonard instrumental play-along
Music from Disney films, musicals and theme parks. — No words.
Publ. no. HL00841943
ISBN 0634085484
System number: 013191253

787.4168
Classical favorites : cello : [solo arrangements of 15 great pieces with
CD accompaniment] — Milwaukee, Wis. : Hal Leonard, c2005. —
16 p. ; 31 cm. + 1 compact disc. — Hal Leonard instrumental
play-along
Publ. no. HL00841963
ISBN 0634085697
System number: 013220182

787.41723
Cellos for Christmas : 20 Christmas carols for cellos / easy
arrangements by Barrie Carson Turner ; illustrations by John Minnion.
— London : Schott, c2005. — 1 score (32 p.) : ill. ; 31 cm + 1 compact
disc.
Arr. for violoncello with optional second part. — Includes words. — CD contains
piano accompaniments, and full demonstration tracks.
Publ. no. ED 12821
ISMN M220123337
System number: 013335629

787.41827
Routh, Francis.
[Chaconnes, violoncello, string orchestra, op. 51; *arr.*]
Ciacona : (romance) : for violoncello and string orchestra : op. 51 (1989)
/ Franis Routh. — Piano score — London : Redcliffe Edition, [2004?] —
1 score (18 p.) ; 42 cm.
For cello and piano.
ISMN M708045281
System number: 013177057

787.4183
*Bach, Johann Sebastian, 1685-1750.
[Sonatas, viola da gamba, harpsichord]
Sonatas BWV 1027, 1028, 1029 : for violoncello and keyboard / J.S.
Bach ; [violoncello part edited by] Greenhouse & Dillingham. — New
York : G. Schirmer ; Milwaukee, Wis. : distributed by Hal Leonard, 2005.
— 1 score (51 p.) + 1 part (18 p.) ; 31 cm. — Schirmer's library of
musical classics ; v. 2053
Publ. no. HL50485851
ISBN 0634095684
System number: 013374932

*Bennett, Richard Rodney.
[Sonatas, violoncello, piano]
Sonata for violoncello and piano : (1991) / Richard Rodney Bennett. —
London : Novello ; Bury St Edmunds : Music Sales [distributor], c2002.
— 1 score (37 p.) + 1 part ; 30 cm.
Publ. no. NOV 120874
ISBN 0711995133
System number: 013434138

Franck, César, 1822-1890.
[Sonatas, violin, piano, A major; *arr.*]
Sonate für Violoncello und Klavier A-Dur / César Franck ;
[herausgegeben von Stephanie Gurtner] — Spielpartituren. —
Winterthur : Partitura Verlag, c2007. — 2 scores ; 33 cm.
Arr. by the composer for violoncello and piano; originally for violin and piano. —
Each playing score emphasizes the appropriate instrumental part. — Preface in
German.
Publ. no. 2613
ISMN M700282073
System number: 013887071

*McCabe, John, 1939-
[Sonatas, violoncello, piano]
Sonata for violoncello and piano : (1998-9) / John McCabe. — London :
Novello ; Bury St Edmunds : Music Sales [distributor], c2002. — 1 score
(29 p.) + 1 part ; 30 cm.
Includes composer's note.
Publ. no. NOV 121077
ISBN 0711994315
System number: 013434147

Sallinen, Aulis.
[Sonatas, violoncello, piano, op. 86]
Sonata per violoncello e piano, op. 86 : (2004) / Aulis Sallinen. — London :
Novello, c2005. — 1 score (33 p.) + 1 part ; 31 cm.
Publ. no. NOV121253
ISBN 1846092248
System number: 013381902

787.4186

Elgar, Edward, 1857-1934.
[Concertos, violoncello, orchestra, op. 85, E minor; *arr.*]
Concerto in E minor, opus 85, for violoncello and orchestra / Edward Elgar ;
arrangement for violoncello and piano by the composer. — London :
Novello, c2004. — 1 score (34 p.) + 1 part ; 31 cm.
Pref. by Robert Anderson and John Pickard. — Critical commentary follows score.
Publ. no. NOV081334
ISBN 184449862X
System number: 013167669

*Twardowski, Romuald, 1930-
[Concertos, violoncello, orchestra; *arr.*]
Concerto per cello ed orchestra / Romuald Twardowski ; wyciąg
fortepianowy ; opracowanie głosu solowego Tomasz Strahl. — Kraków :
Polskie wydawn. muzyczne, 2005, c1997. — 1 score (38 p.) + 1 part
(17 p.) ; 30 cm.
Acc. arr. for piano. — Duration: ca. 24:00. — Includes biographical and program
notes in Polish and English.
Pl. no. PWM 10 372
ISMN M274001766
EAN 9790274001766
System number: 014629778

787.41896

Boulter, Bryan.
Song without words : for violoncello and piano / Bryan Boulter. —
Manchester : Da Capo Music, c2003. — 1 score (7 p.) ; 30 cm.
Subtitle on caption: "Enrapture". — Duration: ca. 4:00. — Includes biographical and
programme notes.
Pl. no. DC 593
System number: 013351683

787.418966

Barlow, Michael, 1940-
[Nocturnes, violoncello, piano, op. 19]
Nocturne for 'cello and piano / Michael Barlow. — Enfield : Modus Music,
c2005. — 1 score (4 p.) + 1 part ; 30 cm.
Opus 19 (1969/71) — p.2.
Publ. no. MM 326
System number: 013389868

787.6 – VIOLS AND OTHER BOWED STRING INSTRUMENTS

787.65

Hammer, Xaver, 1741-1817.
[Viola da gamba music. *Selections*]
3 pieces for unaccompanied viola da gamba / F.X. Hammer. In diesen
heil'gen Hallen / W.A. Mozart ; anonymous arrangement for
unaccompanied viola da gamba ; edited by David J. Rhodes. — [S.l.] : Viola
da Gamba Society of Great Britain, c2003. — [2] leaves of music ; 30 cm.
Second work is an arrangement of an aria from "Die Zauberflöte." — Includes
critical commentary. — Sources: Germany, Schwerin, Landesbibliothek
Mecklenburg-Vorpommern, (RISM siglum D-Swl) (1st work) ; London, British
Library, Ms. Add. 31697, f.6v (2nd work).
Pl. no. 194
System number: 013382467

787.65183

Graun, Johann Gottlieb, 1702 or 3-1771.
[Sonatas, viola da gamba, continuo, G major]
Solo (Sonata G-Dur) per la viola di gamba / Johann Gottlieb Graun ;
trascrizione a cura di Cristiano Contadin e Monica Pelliciari. — Stuttgart :
Cornetto, gedruckt in Lizenz von Musedita ; Albese con Cassano :
Musedita, c2004. — 1 score (10 p.) + 2 parts ; 30 cm. — (La voce dell'
Ambasciatore. Collana dedicata alla viola da gamba)
Based on a manuscript (Mus.ms.1236) kept in the Hessische Landes- und
Hochschulbibliothek, Darmstadt. — Unfigured bass unrealized. — Prefatory
remarks in Italian, English and French.
Publ. no. CM701
ISMN M501006700
System number: 014167963

Richman, Jacob, d. 1726.
[Sonatas, viola da gamba, continuo, op. 1]
Six sonates à une viole de gambe & basse continue = Sechs Sonaten für
Viola da gamba und Basso continuo / Jacob Richmann ; herausgegeben
von Olaf Tetampel ; Aussetzung des Basso continuo von Jörg Jacobi. —
Bremen : Edition Baroque, c2005. — 1 score (2 v.) + 1 part (2 v.) ; 30 cm.
Figured bass realized. — Critical commentary in German.
Pl. no. eba2131
Pl. no. eba2132
ISMN M700234720
ISMN M700234737
System number: 014488699

787.8 – LUTE, GUITAR, ETC.

787.83

Harling, Wolff Christian von.
[Lute music. *Selections*]
Lautenbuch des Wolff Christian von Harling, ca. 1618 / herausgegeben
von Joachim Lüdtke. — Lübeck : Tree Edition, c2005. — 84 p. of music,
117 p. : facsims. ; 31 cm. + 1 CD-ROM.
Facsimile reproduction of the manuscript held in the Ratsbücherei Lüneburg
(Signatur Mus. ant. pract. 2000). — Pref., critical apparatus, and biographical
notes in German. — Title on CD-ROM: Lüneburg : a dream in bricks. —
CD-ROM contains slide show of photographs of the city of Lüneburg taken by
the editor.
System number: 013605904

Neapolitan lute music / Fabrizio Dentice … [et al.] ; edited by John
Griffiths and Dinko Fabris. — Middleton, Wis. : A-R Editions, c2004.
— xxi p., 181 p. of music, 4 p. of plates : facsims. ; 28 cm. — (Recent
researches in the music of the Renaissance, 0486-123X ; 140)
In tablature and modern notation. — Includes introd. and critical report.
ISBN 0895795663
EAN 9780895795663
System number: 014630266

787.831858

*Handel, George Frideric, 1685-1759.
[Suites, harpsichord, HWV 432, G minor; *arr.*]
Suite in G minor / G.F. Handel ; arranged for archlute by Lynda Sayce. —
Guildford : Lute Society, 2004. — [12] p. of music ; 30 cm.
Originally for harpsichord. — In tablature. — Reprint. Originally published:
[S.l.] : Sul Tasto Editions, 1990.
ISBN 0905655435
System number: 013062225

787.87

Belkadi, Jean Marc, 1959-
Classical themes for electric guitar : 25 solo guitar arrangements / by Jean
Marc Belkadi. — Milwaukee, WI : Hal Leonard, c2004. — 48 p. of
music ; 31 cm + 1 sound disc (digital ; 4 3/4 in.) — Private lessons
(Musicians Institute)
In standard and tablature notation. — Includes historical and biographical notes.
— CD contains demonstration tracks.
Publ. no. HL00695806
ISBN 0634070126
System number: 013167489

Gerhard, Roberto, 1896-1970.
For whom the bell tolls : per a guitarra / Robert Gerhard ; revisio i edicio
de Meirion Bowen i Eugenio Tobalina. — Barcelona : Trito, 2006. — xvi
p., 26 p. of music ; 31 cm.
Preface and biographical notes in Catalan, Spanish, and English.
Publ. no. TR 285
ISMN M692043447
System number: 013887072

Sor, Fernando, 1778-1839.
[Guitar music. 1997]
The new complete works for guitar : re-engraved in eleven volumes /
Fernando Sor ; edited by Brian Jeffery. — 2nd printing with corrections.
— London : Tecla, 2004, c1997. — 1 score (11 v.) ; 31 cm.
"A modern re-engraved edition … of all Sor's music for guitar solo and for guitar
duet"—Introd. to the series. — Each volume includes notes on the pieces.
Publ. no. 1200
Publ. no. 1201
Publ. no. 1202
Publ. no. 1203
Publ. no. 1204
Publ. no. 1205
Publ. no. 1206
Publ. no. 1207
Publ. no. 1208
Publ. no. 1209
Publ. no. 1210
Publ. no. 1211
ISBN 094860770X (set paperbound)
ISBN 0948607718 (v. 1 paperbound)
ISBN 0948607726 (v. 2 paperbound)
ISBN 0948607734 (v. 3 paperbound)
ISBN 0948607742 (v. 4 paperbound)
ISBN 0948607750 (v. 5 paperbound)
ISBN 0948607769 (v. 6 paperbound)
ISBN 0948607777 (v. 7 paperbound)
ISBN 0948607785 (v. 8 paperbound)
ISBN 0948607793 (v. 9 paperbound)

ISBN 0948607807 (v. 10 paperbound)
ISBN 0948607815 (v. 11 paperbound)
System number: 013334512
Also classified at 785.787192

787.87076

Classical guitar miniatures : [a unique collection of beautiful and inspiring pieces for the early stages player] / [compiled] by Tony Skinner and Amanda Cook. — Bexhill : Registry Publications, c2004. — 23 p. ; 30 cm. + 1 compact disc.
Staff notation and guitar tablature in score. — "Music editing and performance notes text by Tony Skinner. Audio performances by Amanda Cook" - T.p. verso.
ISBN 1898466742
System number: 013086497

Early stages classical guitar : [a collection of superb, yet easy to play, pieces] [compiled] by Tony Skinner and Amanda Cook. — Bexhill : Registry Publications, c2004. — 31 p. ; 30 cm. + 1 compact disc. — (Classical guitar)
Staff notation and guitar tablature in score. — Includes biographical and performance notes. — "Music editing and performance notes text by Tony Skinner. Audio performances by Amanda Cook" - T.p. verso.
ISBN 189846670X
System number: 013086496

*Guitare : [France, 1600-1800] : méthodes, dictionnaires et encyclopédies, ouvrages généraux, préfaces d'œuvres / volume réalisé par Caroline Delume. — Courlay, France : J.M. Fuzeau, 2003. — 2 v. : ill., facsims., music ; 33 cm. — Fac-similé Jean-Marc Fuzeau — (Méthodes & traités ; 18. Série I, France, 1600-1800)
Reprints of 17th and 18th century guitar treatises and methods; originally published 1636-1800. — Includes source locations. — Texts in French.
Publ. no. 5877
Publ. no. 5878
ISMN M2306F58775
ISMN M2306F58782
System number: 014790387

Johnson, Chad.
Acoustic guitar : [a complete guide with step-by-step lessons and 45 great acoustic songs] / by Chad Johnson. — [S.l.] : Hal Leonard Europe ; London : Distributed by Music Sales, c2005. — 79 p. : ill. ; 31 cm. + 1 compact disc. — Hal Leonard guitar method
In standard and tablature notation with chord symbols. — CD contains full demonstration and backing tracks.
Publ. no. HLE90002308
ISBN 1844498360
System number: 013265866

Kolb, Tom.
Music theory / Tom Kolb. — Milwaukee, WI : Hal Leonard, c2005. — 104 p.: port ; 31 cm. + 1 compact disc. — Hal Leonard guitar method.
In standard and tablature notation.
Publ. no. HL00695790
ISBN 063406651X
System number: 013299202
Also classified at 781.2

*Ongley, Marc.
Guitar for everyone/ [Marc Ongley] — Teddington : Natural Light, c2002-2004. — 2 v. of music : port., ill. ; 31 cm. + 2 compact discs (digital ; 4 3/4 in.) — Marc Ongley Guitar series
In standard notation with chord symbols. — Includes guitar duets and trios. — CDs contain play-along tracks.
Publ. no. NLPGFE-01
Publ. no. NLPGFE-02
ISBN 0954280202 (bk. 1)
ISBN 0954280210 (bk. 2)
ISMN M900206305 (bk. 1)
ISMN M900206312 (bk. 2)
System number: 014664154

787.871252

Johnson, Chad.
Arpeggio finder : easy-to-use guide to over 1, 300 guitar arpeggios / by Chad Johnson. — Milwaukee, Wis. : Hal Leonard ; c2004. — 95 p. ; 31 cm. — Hal Leonard guitar method
"Supplement to any guitar method"—Cover.
Publ. no. HL00697351
ISBN 0634069217
System number: 012874858

787.87164

Metheny, Pat.
One quiet night / Pat Metheny ; music transcriptions by Masa Takahashi. — Guitar recorded versions. — Milwaukee, Wis. : Hal Leonard, [2003?] — 1 score (88 p.) ; 31 cm. — (Guitar recorded versions)
12 pieces from Pat Metheny's 2003 album "One quiet night." — For guitar in standard and tablature notation, with chord symbols.
Publ. no. HL00690646
ISBN 0634066633
System number: 013280380

787.871643

Blues rock. — Milwaukee, WI : Hal Leonard, [2003?] — 1 score (80 p.) ; 31 cm + 1 compact disc. — Hal Leonard guitar play-along ; 14
8 songs for voice and guitar in standard and tablature notation, with chord symbols. — Words and music by various songwriters. — CD contains full demonstration and backing tracks.
Publ. no. HL00699582
ISBN 0634056344
System number: 013191100
Also classified at 783.2421643; 787.87166; 783.242166

Blues : Guitar play-along. — Milwaukee, WI : Hal Leonard, [2003] — 1 score (53 p.) ; 31 cm + 1 sound disc (digital ; 4 3/4 in.) — Hal Leonard guitar play-along ; 7
7 songs and 1 instrumental piece for voice and guitar in standard and tablature notation, with chord symbols. — Words and music by various songwriters. — CD contains full demonstration and backing tracks.
Publ. no. HL00699575
ISBN 0634056271
System number: 013191092
Primary classification 783.2421643

Koch, Greg.
[Guitar music. *Selections*]
Greg Koch. — Milwaukee, WI : Hal Leonard, [2004?] — 79 p. ; 31 cm + 1 compact disc. — Hal Leonard guitar play-along ; 28
8 songs for guitar in standard and tablature notation, with chord symbols. — CD contains full demonstration and backing tracks.
Publ. no. HL00699646
ISBN 0634079271
System number: 013191097

787.87165

Jazz : guitar play-along. — Milwaukee, WI : Hal Leonard, [2004] — 63 p. of music ; 31 cm + 1 sound disc (digital ; 4 3/4 in.) — Hal Leonard guitar play-along ; 16
8 pieces for guitar in standard and tablature notation, with chord symbols. — CD contains full demonstration and backing tracks.
Publ. no. HL00699584
ISBN 0634056379
System number: 013191073

Metheny, Pat.
Rejoicing / Pat Metheny ; music transcriptions by Alejandro Moro. — Guitar recorded versions. — Milwaukee, WI : Hal Leonard, [2004?] — 71 p. ; 31 cm.
8 pieces from Pat Metheny's 1984 album "Rejoicing." — For guitar(s). — In standard and tablature notation, with chord symbols. — Music by various composers.
Publ. no. HL00690565
ISBN 0634046659
System number: 013169014

787.87165076

Schroedl, Jeff.
Jazz guitar : a comprehensive guide with step-by-step instruction and over 20 great jazz classics / by Jeff Schroedl. — [S.l.] : Hal Leonard Europe ; London : exclusive distributors, Music Sales, c2005. — 80 p. : ill. ; 31 cm + 1 compact disc. — Hal Leonard guitar method
In standard and tablature notation, with chord symbols. — CD contains demonstration and backing tracks.
Publ. no. HLE90002330
ISBN 1844498387
System number: 013358416

787.87166

101 songs for easy guitar. Book 5. — London : Wise Publications, c2005. — 237 p. ; 31 cm.
Melody lines with words and chord symbols.
Publ. no. AM982883
ISBN 184609061X
System number: 013297793
Primary classification 783.242166

The best acoustic guitar songs ever. — [S.l.] : Hal Leonard Europe ; London : exclusive distributors, Music Sales, c2005. — 1 score (239 p.) ; 31 cm. — (Guitar recorded versions)
30 songs for voice and guitar(s), in standard and tablature notation, with chord symbols.
Publ. no. HLE90002451
ISBN 1846090954
System number: 013408007
Primary classification 783.242166

Blues rock. — Milwaukee, WI : Hal Leonard, [2003?] — 1 score (80 p.) ; 31 cm + 1 compact disc. — Hal Leonard guitar play-along ; 14
8 songs for voice and guitar in standard and tablature notation, with chord symbols. — Words and music by various songwriters. — CD contains full demonstration and backing tracks.
Publ. no. HL00699582
ISBN 0634056344
System number: 013191100
Primary classification 787.871643

Clapton, Eric.
[Songs. *Selections*]
Eric Clapton : guitar play-along. — Milwaukee, WI : Hal Leonard, [2004?] — 1 score (56 p.) ; 31 cm + 1 compact disc. — Hal Leonard guitar play-along ; 24
8 songs arranged for voice and guitar in standard and tablature notation, with chord symbols. — Words and music by Eric Clapton and others. — With errata sheet inserted. — CD contains full demonstration and backing tracks.
Publ. no. HL00699649
ISBN 0634080172
System number: 013219768
Also classified at 783.242166

Clapton, Eric.
[Songs. *Selections*]
Play guitar with— Eric Clapton. — London : Wise, [2005], c1997. — 1 score (56 p.) ; 31 cm + 1 sound disc (digital ; 4 3/4 in.) + 1 video disc (digital ; 4 3/4 in.)
Rocks songs with guitar acc. (in tablature and standard notation). — Words and music by Eric Clapton. — CD contains full instrumental performances and backing tracks. — "Includes DVD guitar lesson"—Sticker on cover. — DVD features the song "Layla." — Publisher's no.: AM950862 (t.p.), AM983664 (sticker on back cover).
Publ. no. AM950862
Publ. no. AM983664

ISBN 1846092205 (sticker on back cover)
System number: 013374869
Primary classification 783.242166

Guitar tab : white pages : now! volume 2 : [a giant collection of authentic guitar transcriptions] — [s.l.] : Hal Leonard Europe ; London : exclusive distributors, Music Sales, c2005. — 1 score (1040 p.) ; 28 cm.
150 songs for voice and guitar(s) in standard and tablature notation, with chord symbols. — Spine title: Guitar tab 2 : white pages.
Publ. no. HLE90002297
ISBN 184449814X
System number: 013197181
Primary classification 783.242166

Kiss (Musical group).
[Songs. *Selections*]
Kiss. — Milwaukee, WI : Hal Leonard, [2005] — 1 score (48 p.) ; 31 cm + 1 sound disc (digital ; 4 3/4 in.) — Hal Leonard guitar play-along ; v. 30
8 songs for voice and guitar in standard and tablature notation, with chord symbols. — Words and music by members of the group. — CD contains full demonstration and backing tracks.
Publ. no. HL00699644
ISBN 0634079247
System number: 013383477
Primary classification 783.242166

Lennon, John, 1940-1980.
[Songs. *Selections*]
Lennon & McCartney : guitar play-along. — Milwaukee, WI : Hal Leonard, [2004] — 1 score (46 p.) ; 31 cm + 1 sound disc (digital ; 4 3/4 in.) — Hal Leonard guitar play-along ; 25
8 songs arranged for voice and guitar in standard and tablature notation, with chord symbols. — CD contains full demonstration and backing tracks.
Publ. no. HL00699642
ISBN 0634079220
System number: 013191084
Primary classification 783.242166

Metallica (Musical group).
[Songs. *Selections*]
Play guitar with— Metallica. — London : Wise, [2005], c1997. — 1 score (64 p.) ; 31 cm + 1 sound disc (digital ; 4 3/4 in.) + 1 video disc (digital ; 4 3/4 in.)
6 songs with guitar acc., in tablature and standard notation. — Words and music by members of the group. — CD contains full instrumental performances and backing tracks. — "Includes DVD guitar lesson"—Sticker on cover. — DVD features the song "Enter sandman." — Publisher's no.: AM92559 (inside back cover), AM983642 (sticker on back cover).
Publ. no. AM92559
Publ. no. AM983642
ISBN 1846092183

ISBN 1846092183 (sticker on back cover)
System number: 013374852
Primary classification 783.242166

Muse (Musical group : Great Britain).
[Songs. *Selections*]
Play guitar with— Muse : Stockholm syndrome and other great songs. — London : Wise, [2005], c2004. — 1 score (39 p.) ; 31 cm + 1 sound disc (digital ; 4 3/4 in.) + 1 video disc (digital ; 4 3/4 in.)
5 songs for voice and guitar, in standard and tablature notation, with chord symbols. — Words and music mostly by Matthew Bellamy. — CD contains full instrumental performances and backing tracks. — "Includes DVD guitar lesson"—Sticker on cover. — DVD features the song "Plug in baby." — Publisher's no.: AM981002 (t.p. verso), AM983653 (sticker on back cover).
Publ. no. AM981002
Publ. no. AM983653
ISBN 1844497232 (t.p. verso)
ISBN 1846092191 (sticker on back cover)
System number: 013374879
Primary classification 783.242166

Presley, Elvis, 1935-1977.
[Songs. *Selections*]
Elvis : guitar play-along. — Milwaukee, WI : Hal Leonard, [2004] — 1 score (38 p.) ; 31 cm + 1 sound disc (digital ; 4 3/4 in.) — Hal Leonard guitar play-along ; 26
8 songs arranged for voice and guitar in standard and tablature notation, with chord symbols. — Words and music by Elvis Presley and others. — CD contains full demonstration and backing tracks. — Publisher's no.: HL00699643 (score), 63007869 (CD).
Publ. no. HL00699643
Publ. no. 63007869
ISBN 0634079239
System number: 013219807
Primary classification 783.242166

Satriani, Joe.
Is there love in space? : [guitar/vocal] / Joe Satriani. — New York, NY : Cherry Lane Music Company ; c2004. Milwaukee, Wis. : exclusively distributed by Hal Leonard, — 1 score (112 p.) : port. ; 31 cm. — Play it like it is. Guitar
9 instrumental pieces and 2 songs from Joe Satriani's 2004 album "Is there love in space?" — For guitar(s) in standard and tablature notation, with chord symbols. — Words and music by Joe Satriani; transcribed by Jeff Jacobson and Paul Pappas.
Publ. no. 02500733
ISBN 1575607603
System number: 013191055

Seger, Bob.
[Songs. *Selections*]
Bob Seger. — Milwaukee, WI : Hal Leonard, [2005] — 1 score (64 p.) ; 31 cm + 1 compact disc. — Hal Leonard guitar play-along ; 29
8 songs for voice and guitar in standard and tablature notation, with chord symbols. — CD contains full demonstration and backing tracks.
Publ. no. HL00699647
ISBN 063407931X
System number: 013299275
Also classified at 783.242166

System of a Down (Musical group).
Mezmerize / System of a Down ; music transcriptions by Pete Billmann and David Stocker. — [S.l.] : Sony/ATV Music Publishing ; Milwaukee, Wis. : exclusively distributed by Hal Leonard, c2005. — 1 score (87 p.) ; 31 cm. — (Guitar recorded versions)
11 songs from System of a Down's 2005 album "Mezmerize." — For voice and guitar(s) in standard and tablature notation, with chord symbols. — Words and music by members of the group.
Publ. no. HL00690799
ISBN 142340145X
System number: 013376891
Primary classification 783.242166

787.87166076

Mueller, Michael.
Rock guitar : [learn to play rhythm and lead rock guitar with step-by-step lessons and 68 great rock songs] / by Michael Mueller. — [S.l.] : Hal Leonard Europe ; London : distributed by Music Sales, c2005. — 63 p. : ill. ; 31 cm. + 1 compact disc — Hal Leonard guitar method
In standard and tablature notation, with chord symbols. — CD contains demonstration and backing tracks.
Publ. no. HLE90002319
ISBN 1844498379
System number: 013359589

787.87168

60 progressive solos for classical guitar : featuring the music of the world's greatest composers: Bach, Handel, Mozart, Beethoven, and Brahms / arranged by Mark Phillips. — New York : Cherry Lane Music Co., c2003. — 118 p. ; 31 cm. + 1 compact disc.
In standard and tablature notation. — CD contains a recording of each arrangement.
Publ. no. 02500584
ISBN 1575606283
System number: 006928830

787.87168076

Parkening, Christopher.
The Christopher Parkening guitar method. Vol. 1 : the art and technique of the classical guitar / in collaboration with Jack Marshall and David Brandon. — Rev. ed. — Milwaukee, Wis. : Hal Leonard ; c1999. — 109 p. : ill. ; 31 cm.
Publ. no. HL00695228
ISBN 0793585201
System number: 012874978

Parkening, Christopher.
The Christopher Parkening guitar method. Vol. 2 : the art and technique of the classical guitar / in collaboration with David Brandon. — Milwaukee, Wis. : Hal Leonard ; c1997. — 136 p. : ill. ; 28 cm.
Publ. no. HL00695229
ISBN 079358521X
System number: 012874979

787.871825

*Gammie, Ian.
El lladre reformat : variations on a Catalan folk song : for solo guitar / Ian Gammie. — St. Albans : Corda Music Publications, c2004. — 7 p. of music ; 30 cm. — (Solo and ensemble music for guitars)
Pl. no. CMP 33
System number: 013269154

Urcullu, Leopoldo.
[Thème & variations, guitar, op. 10, E major]
Thème & variations pour guitare, op. 10 / Leopoldo de Urcullu. — Geneva : Philomele Editions, 2005. — 10 p. of music ; 30 cm.
"The theme of the present Variations op. 10 is attributed to Ignaz Pleyel (according to an anonymous manuscript of the early 19th century, belonging to Francisco Herrera)." — "Révision: Johann Gaitzsch"—Caption. — Preface in English, French and German (p. 4-5). — Incorrect publisher number on t.p.
Pl. no. PE 2055
System number: 013887079

787.87193166

Arakawa, Yoichi.
Rock guitar chords and accompaniment : [your ultimate step-by-step manual to rock rhythm-guitar!] / by Yoichi Arakawa. — Torrance, Calif. : Six Strings Music, c2004. — 125 p. : ill. ; 31 cm.
Publ. no. SSM00773
ISBN 1891370138
System number: 006898953

787.9 – HARP

787.95186

Hertel, Johann Wilhelm, 1727-1789.
[Concertos, harp, string orchestra, F major; arr.]
Konzert F-Dur für Harfe oder Cembalo, 2 Violinen, Viola und Violoncello / Johann Wilhelm Hertel ; herausgegeben von Johanna Seitz ; Klavierauszug von Burkhard Jäckel. — Magdeburg : Edition Walhall, c2005. — 1 score (21 p.) + 1 part (13 p.) : facsims. ; 30 cm. — (Collegium musicum : Kölner Reihe Alter Musik)
Includes pref. in German and English.
Pl. no. EW 428
System number: 013775622
Also classified at 786.4186

788.3 – FLUTE, RECORDER, ETC.

788.32

Barton, David, 1983-
On the box : eight pieces on a television theme : for flute and piano / David Barton. — Manchester : Da Capo Music , c2005. — 1 score (15 p.) ; 30 cm.
Includes programme and biographical notes.
Pl. no. DC 640
System number: 013351564

Carlson, Rosalind.
[Forest bell-birds, flute]
Forest bell-birds : for solo flute / by Rosalind Carlson. — Lancaster : Phylloscopus Publications, c2004. — 3 p. ; 30 cm.
Publ. no. PP544
ISMN M570166763
System number: 013173910

Gething, Joseph.
[Flute, piano music. *Selections*]
Themes for flute : flute and piano. Book 1 / Joseph Gething. — Dover : Broadbent & Dunn, c2003. — 1 score (12 p.) + 1 part ; 30 cm.
Cover title.
Pl. no. B&D 13302
ISBN 9790570305155
System number: 013188440

Gething, Joseph.
[Flute, piano music. *Selections*]
Themes for flute : flute and piano. Book 5 / Joseph Gething. — Dover : Broadbent & Dunn, c2003. — 1 score (12 p.) + 1 part ; 30 cm.
Cover title.
Pl. no. B&D 13306
System number: 013213508

Gething, Joseph.
[Flute, piano music. *Selections*]
Themes for flute : flute and piano. Book Four / by Joseph Gething. — Dover : Broadbent & Dunn, c2003. — 1 score (12 p.) + 1 part ; 30 cm.
Pl. no. B&D 13305
System number: 013213520

Gething, Joseph.
[Flute, piano music. *Selections*]
Themes for flute : flute and piano. Book Six / by Joseph Gething. — Dover : Broadbent & Dunn, c2003. — 1 score (12 p.) + 1 part ; 30 cm.
Pl. no. B&D 13307
System number: 013213505

Gething, Joseph.
[Flute, piano music. *Selections*]
Themes for flute : flute and piano. Book Three / by Joseph Gething. — Dover : Broadbent & Dunn, c2003. — 1 score (12 p.) + 1 part ; 30 cm.
Pl. no. B&D 13304
ISBN 9790570305179
System number: 013188420

Gething, Joseph.
[Flute, piano music. *Selections*]
Themes for flute : flute and piano. Book Two / by Joseph Gething. — Dover : Broadbent & Dunn, c2003. — 1 score (12 p.) + 1 part ; 30 cm.
Pl. no. B&D 13303
ISBN 9790570305162
System number: 013188425

Holmes, Chris, composer.
Take off with your flute / Chris Holmes. — Laggan Bridge : Spartan Press, c2004. — 22 p. of music ; 30 cm + 1 sound disc (digital ; 4 3/4 in.)
19 pieces and exercises for flute — Melody lines with chord symbols. — "Grades 0-4"—Cover. — CD contains full performances and backing tracks.
Pl. no. SP784
ISMN M579997849
System number: 013299103

Kabeláč, Miloslav, 1908-1979.
[Malá suita, flute]
Skladby pro flétnu sólo = Kompositionen für Soloflöte = Compositions for flute solo / Miloslav Kabeláč ; [editor, Zdeněk Nouza] — 1. vyd. — Praha : Editio Bärenreiter Praha, c2005. — 23 p. of music : facsim. ; 31 cm. — (Souborné kritické vydání / Miloslav Kabeláč ; řada 4, sv. 5)
Includes program notes in Czech, German, and English.
Pl. no. H 7910
ISMN M260103429
System number: 013385590

*Le Fleming, Antony.
Encounters : for flute and piano / by Antony le Fleming. — Lancaster : Phylloscopus Publications, c2005. — 1 score (14 p.) + 1 part ; 30 cm.
Publ. no. PP553
ISMN M570166855
System number: 013472753

Lewis, Paul, 1943-
A Somerset garland. for flute, violin or harmonica and piano / by Paul Lewis. — Dover : Broadbent & Dunn, c2003. — 1 score (15 p.) + 1 part ; 30 cm.
Pl. no. B&D 13206
System number: 013374676
Also classified at 787.2; 788.82

Lopez-Real, Carlos.
[Dig it. Flute(s)]
Dig it! : 7 cool tunes for flute(s) and piano with optional CD backing / Carolos Lopez-Real. — Laggan Bridge : Spartan Press, c2005. — 1 score (22 p.) + 3 parts , 30 cm + 1 sound disc (digital ; 4 3/4 in.)
Includes optional duo and trio parts — Cover title. — "Grades 3-6"—Cover. — Includes improvisation sections. — CD contains full demonstrations and backing tracks. — Mixed instrument ensembles may be created using the other books in the series.
Pl. no. SP731
ISMN M579997313
System number: 013203784

Marson, John, 1932-2007.
Roundelay : flute and piano / by John Marson. — Dover : Broadbent & Dunn, c2005. — 1 score (8 p.) + 1 part ; 30 cm.
Publ. no. B&D 11823
System number: 013374683

*Moore, Philip, 1943-
Siciliano : flute & piano / Philip Moore. — Ampleforth : Emerson Edition, c2005. — 1 score (3 p.) + 1 part ([1] leaf) : port. ; 28 cm.
Includes biographical and programme notes. — Duration: ca. 2:30.
Publ. no. E468
Publ. no. 468
ISMN M570405022
System number: 013460594

*Warren, Constance, 1905-1984.
[Miniatures, flute, piano]
Two miniatures : for flute & piano / Constance Warren. — Ampleforth : Emerson Edition, c2005. — 1 score (7 p.) + 1 part ([2] p.) : port. ; 28 cm.
Biographical note on back cover. — Duration: ca. 2:30 ; ca. 1:00.
Publ. no. E456
Publ. no. 456
ISMN M570401208
System number: 013565739

Warren, Norman.
Dawn sequence : for oboe (or flute) and piano / by Norman Warren. —
Lancaster : Phylloscopus Publications, c2004. — 1 score (8 p.) + 1 part ;
30 cm.
Publ. no. PP541
ISMN M570166732
System number: 013173866
Also classified at 788.52

*Warren, Norman.
Folksong : oboe (or flute) & piano / Norman Warren. — Ampleforth :
Emerson Edition, c2005. — 1 score (5 p.) + 1 part ([2] p.) : port. ; 28 cm.
Includes biographical and programme notes. — Duration: ca. 4:30.
Publ. no. E470
Publ. no. 470
ISMN M570405015
System number: 013460659
Primary classification 788.52

*Waterhouse, Graham, 1962-
Sicilian air : op. 56, für Flöte und Klavier = for flute and piano / Graham
Waterhouse. — Frankfurt : Zimmermann, c2004. — 1 score (12 p.) + 1 part
(4 p.) ; 31 cm.
Includes biographical and program notes in German, English, and French.
Pl. no. ZM 34970
ISMN M010349701
System number: 013174354

788.32076
*Flûte traversière : France, 1800-1860 : méthodes, traités, périodiques /
sept volumes réalisés par Arlette Biget et Michel Giboureau. — Courlay,
France : Editions Fuzeau, [2005] 1 score (7 v.) : ill. ; 33 cm. —
Méthodes & traités. Série II, France, 1800-1860 — (Fac-similés
Jean-Marc Fuzeau)
Reprints. Originally published c. 1800-c. 1861. — Includes indexes and list of
sources.
Publ. no. 5951—5957
ISMN M230659512
ISMN M230659529
ISMN M230659536
ISMN M230659543
ISMN M230659550
ISMN M230659567
ISMN M230659574
EAN 9790230659512
EAN 9790230659529
EAN 9790230659536
EAN 9790230659543
EAN 9790230659550
EAN 9790230659567
EAN 9790230659574
System number: 013408148

788.321546
TV hits : playalong for flute. — London : Wise, c2005. — 31 p. of music :
31 cm + ill. 1 sound disc (digital ; 4 3/4 in.) — Guest spot
"Ten classic TV themes in melody line arrangements by Quentin Thomas with
specially recorded backing tracks"—Cover. — No words.
Publ. no. AM980518
ISBN 1844496139
System number: 013193417

788.32164
Lloyd Webber, Andrew, 1948-
[Musicals. Selections; arr.]
Andrew Lloyd Webber showstoppers : playalong for flute. — London :
Wise, c2005. — 32 p. of music ; 31 cm + 1 sound disc (digital ; 4 3/4 in.) —
Guest spot
"Ten hit songs in melody line arrangements by Quentin Thomas with specially
recorded backing tracks"—Cover. — No words.
Publ. no. AM91935
ISBN 0711940517
System number: 013193433

788.32165
Cullen, David, 1942-
13 ways of getting there : jazzy pieces for flute and piano / David Cullen. —
London : Schott, c2005. — 1 score (36 p.) + 1 part (15 p.) ; 31 cm + 1 sound
disc (digital ; 4 3/4 in.) — Jazz-it
"Easy to intermediate"—Back cover. — Pref. in English, French and German. — CD
contains full demonstrations and backing tracks.
Publ. no. ED 12845
ISMN M220123702
System number: 013312978

Jazzy opera classix : for flute / [arranged by] Darren Fellows. — London :
Schott, c2005. — 36 p. ; 31 cm. + 1 sound disc (digital ; 4 3/4 in.)
"Favourite opera themes in jazzy arrangements" — Back cover. — Melody lines
with chord symbols. — Piano accompaniments available as PDF files on the CD. —
Includes descriptions of the operas in English, French and German. — CD contains
full demonstrations and backing tracks.
Publ. no. ED 12822
ISBN 1902455282
ISMN M220123238
System number: 013192229

788.32165076
O'Neill, John, 1955-
Developing jazz technique for flute : improvisation, style, special
effects = Technique de jazz pour flûte : improvisation, style, effets
spéciaux = Jazztechnik für Querflöte : Improvisation, Stilistik,
Spezialeffekte / John O'Neill ; traduction Agnès Ausseur ; Übersetzung
Heike Brühl. — London : Schott, c2005. — 88 p. of music + 1 part
(7 p.) : 31 cm + ports. ; 1 sound disc (digital ; 4 3/4 in.)
Chord progressions for the tunes printed as a separate part. — Text in English,
French and German.
Publ. no. ED 12760
ISBN 1902455215
ISMN M220123129
System number: 013382705

788.32166
Keane (Musical group).
[Hopes and fears; arr.]
Hopes and fears : playalong for flute / Keane. — London : Wise
Publications, c2005. — 31 p. ; 31 cm. + 2 compact discs — Guest spot
"Twelve songs from the band's hit album in melody line arrangements by Paul
Honey"—Cover. — Music by members of the group. — CDs contain full
performances and backing tracks.
Publ. no. AM982839
ISBN 1846090547
System number: 013281555

788.32168
Classical favorites : flute : [solo arrangements of 15 great pieces with
CD accompaniment] — Milwaukee, Wis. : Hal Leonard, c2005. —
16 p. ; 31 cm. + 1 compact disc. — Hal Leonard instrumental
play-along
Publ. no. HL00841954
ISBN 0634085603
System number: 013219779

788.32183
*Cooke, Arnold.
[Sonatas, flute, piano]
Sonata for alto flute and piano / Arnold Cooke. — Altamonte Springs,
Fla. : Anglo-American Music Publishers ; [s.l.] : distribution, Worldwide
Music Services International, c2005. — 1 score (26 p.) + 1 part (9 p.) ;
28 cm.
Cover title.
System number: 013440575

Handel, George Frideric, 1685-1759.
[Sonatas, flute, continuo. Selections.]
Sonatas for flute [and continuo] Book 1 / Handel ; flute part edited by
Paul Edmund-Davies ; keyboard realisation by John Alley. — Buxhall :
Kevin Mayhew, 2004. — 1 score (48 p.) + 2 parts ; 31 cm. + 1 compact
disc.
"The Paul Edmund-Davies performing edition". — With separate cello part. —
Includes biographical, historical and performance notes. — 3rd work originally
for recorder and continuo.
Publ. no. 3611825
ISMN M570243488
System number: 013159326

*Handel, George Frideric, 1685-1759.
[Sonatas, flute, continuo. Selections.]
Sonatas for flute [and continuo] Book 3 / Handel ; flute part edited by
Paul Edmund-Davies ; keyboard realisation by John Alley. — Buxhall :
Kevin Mayhew, 2004. — 1 score (45 p.) + 2 parts ; 31 cm. + 1 compact
disc.
"The Paul Edmund-Davies performing edition". — With separate cello part. —
Includes biographical, historical and performance notes. — 1st work originally
for recorder and continuo.
Publ. no. 3611827
ISMN M570243501
System number: 014343469

*Handel, George Frideric, 1685-1759.
[Sonatas, recorder, continuo. Selections.]
Sonatas for flute [and continuo] Book 2 / Handel ; flute part edited by
Paul Edmund-Davies ; keyboard realisation by John Alley. — Buxhall :
Kevin Mayhew, 2004. — 1 score (53 p.) + 2 parts ; 31 cm. + 1 compact
disc.
"The Paul Edmund-Davies performing edition". — With separate cello part. —
Includes biographical, historical and performance notes. — 1st and 2nd works
originally for recorder and continuo.
Publ. no. 3611826
ISMN M570243495
System number: 014343464

Serini, Giovanni Battista, b. ca. 1710.
[Sonatas, flute, continuo, D major]
Sonata no. 1 in D : flute/oboe & piano / Giovanni Battista Serini ; [edited
by Jack Pilgrim] — Ampleforth : Emerson Edition, c2004. — 1 score
(12 p.) + 1 part ; 28 cm.
Originally for flute and continuo.
Publ. no. 432
ISMN M570402175
System number: 013358290
Also classified at 788.52183

788.32185

*Vaughan Williams, Ralph, 1872-1958.
Suite de ballet : for flute and piano / R. Vaughan Williams ; edited by Roy Douglas. — Oxford : Oxford University Press, [2005], c1961. — 1 score (15 p.) + 1 part (5 p.) ; 31 cm.
Reprint. Originally published: London : Oxford University Press, 1961.
ISBN 0193851059
System number: 013433967

788.321858

Lewis, Paul, 1943-
Spring suite : flute, optional 'cello and piano or harmonica and piano / Paul Lewis. — Dover : Broadbent & Dunn, c2003. — 1 score (20 p.) + 2 parts ; 30 cm.
Pl. no. B&D 13205
System number: 013374699
Also classified at 788.821858; 785.24193

788.3218945

Daija, Tish.
[Rhapsody, flute, orchestra; *arr.*]
Rapsodi for flute & orchestra : [arranged for] flute & piano / Tish Daija. — Ampleforth : Emerson Edition, c2004. — 1 score (15 p.) + 1 part : port. ; 28 cm.
Arranged by the composer. — Includes biographical note.
Publ. no. 429a
ISMN M570403165
System number: 013358266

788.33

Carlson, Rosalind.
[Forest bell-birds, piccolo]
Forest bell-birds : for solo piccolo / by Rosalind Carlson. — Lancaster : Phylloscopus Publications, c2004. — 3 p. 30 cm.
Publ. no. PP545
ISMN M570166770
System number: 013173909

Gething, Joseph.
[Piccolo, piano music]
Pieces for piccolo : piccolo and piano / by Joseph Gething. — Dover : Broadbent & Dunn, c2003. — 1 score (12 p.) + 1 part ; 30 cm.
Pl. no. B&D 13301
ISBN 9790570305148
System number: 013188458

788.331858

*Kelly, Bryan.
Globe Theatre suite : for descant recorder or piccolo and piano / by Bryan Kelly ; edited by Atarah Ben-Tovim. — London : Stainer & Bell, c2005. — 1 score (16 p.) + 1 part (8 p.) ; 31 cm.
"The piano part may also be played on the harpsichord or other suitable keyboard instrument"—P. 3.
Publ. no. H452
ISMN M220221392
System number: 013222597
Primary classification 788.3641858

788.36

*Greber, Jakob, 1691-1731.
Fuori di sua capanna : cantata for alto, recorder & continuo ; Sinfonia a flauto solo : symphony for recorder and continuo / Jakob Greber. — Richmond : Green Man Press, c2004. — 2 scores + 2 parts ; 30 cm.
One score contains keyboard realization of continuo part, the other has figured bass only. — Includes continuo part for bass instrument. — Edited from manuscripts in the Santini collection in the Diözesanbibliothek, Münster. — Introduction and editorial notes by Cedric Lee. — Cantata has Italian words, also printed for reference with English translation p. 3.
Publ. no. Gre 1
Pl. no. Gre 1-1—Gre 1-2
System number: 013596869
Primary classification 783.6848

Hedges, Anthony, 1931-
[Concert miniatures, recorder, op. 153]
Three concert miniatures : op. 153 : for recorders and piano / Anthony Hedges. — Beverley : Westfield Music, c2004. — 1 score (16 p.) ; 30 cm.
Movement I for descant recorder, movement II for tenor recorder and movement III for sopranino recorder.
System number: 013188505

788.36076

Fun and games with the recorder : method for the alto recorder. Tune book / [compiled by] Gudrun Heyens and Gerhard Engel ; translated and adapted by Peter Bowman ; with illustrations by John Minnion. — Mainz ; London : Schott , c2004. — 2 scores (2 v.) : ill. ; 31 cm.
"Can be used for both individual and group teaching"—Back cover. — 1st score for 2-4 recorders, 2nd score for recorder and piano (selection of pieces from the 1st score). — Some pieces include optional guitar or percussion. — Includes notes on the composers and the pieces. — Bk. 2 is illustrated by John Minnion and Julie Beech. — Publisher's no.: ED 12704 (bk. 1), ED 12706 (bk. 2).
Publ. no. ED 12704
Publ. no. ED 12706
ISBN 1902455142 (bk. 1)

ISBN 1902455169 (bk. 2)
ISMN M220122583 (bk. 1)
ISMN M220122606 (bk. 2)
System number: 013134305

Watts, Sarah.
Red hot recorder tutor : [student copy] / Sarah Watts. — Buxhall : Kevin Mayhew, 2004. — 31 p. : ill. ; 21 x 30 cm. + 1 compact disc.
Recorder part(s) for 32 pieces, together with practice patterns, clapping and listening exercises, and instructional information.
Publ. no. 3611786
ISMN M570242641
System number: 013182123

Watts, Sarah.
Red hot recorder tutor : teacher copy / Sarah Watts. — Buxhall : Kevin Mayhew, 2004. — 1 score (63 p.) ; 30 cm. + 1 compact disc.
32 pieces for descant recorder(s) with piano accompaniment, including some duets and trios. — Contents entirely different from those of the Red hot treble recorder tutor.
Publ. no. 3611785
ISMN M570242634
System number: 013182101

788.364

*Cooke, Arnold.
[Arietta, recorder, piano]
Arietta : (1986) : for recorder & piano / Arnold Cooke. — [Altamonte Springs, FL?] : Anglo-American Music Publishers, c2005. — 1 score (2 p.) + 1 part ([1] leaf) ; 28 cm.
For descant ("soprano") recorder and piano. — Cover title. — Includes biographical note. — Duration: 1:20.
System number: 013593934

788.364076

Haughton, Alan, 1950-
Fun club descant recorder : chill out pieces to enjoy between exams. Descant recorder grade 0-1 / Alan Haughton. — Student copy. — Buxhall : Kevin Mayhew, 2004. — 1 part (12 p.) ; 30 cm. + 1 compact disc.
For descant recorder with piano acc. — Another copy (with its own cover) of the recorder part supplied with the Teacher copy.
Publ. no. 3611805
ISMN M570242917
System number: 013181995

Haughton, Alan, 1950-
Fun club descant recorder : chill out pieces to enjoy between exams. Descant recorder grade 0-1 / Alan Haughton. — Teacher copy. — Buxhall : Kevin Mayhew, 2004. — 1 score (32 p.) + 1 part ; 30 cm. + 1 compact disc.
For descant recorder with piano acc.
Publ. no. 3611802
ISMN M570242900
System number: 013182000

Haughton, Alan, 1950-
Fun club descant recorder : chill out pieces to enjoy between exams. Descant recorder grade 1-2 / Alan Haughton. — Student copy. — Buxhall : Kevin Mayhew, 2004. — 1 part (12 p.) ; 30 cm. + 1 compact disc.
For descant recorder with piano acc. — Another copy (with its own cover) of the recorder part supplied with the Teacher copy.
Publ. no. 3611806
ISMN M570242931
System number: 013181965

Haughton, Alan, 1950-
Fun club descant recorder : chill out pieces to enjoy between exams. Descant recorder grade 1-2 / Alan Haughton. — Teacher copy. — Buxhall : Kevin Mayhew, 2004. — 1 score (30 p.) + 1 part ; 30 cm. + 1 compact disc.
For descant recorder with piano acc.
Publ. no. 3611803
ISMN M570242924
System number: 013181956

Haughton, Alan, 1950-
Fun club descant recorder : chill out pieces to enjoy between exams. Descant recorder grade 2-3 / Alan Haughton. — Student copy. — Buxhall : Kevin Mayhew, 2004. — 1 part (12 p.) ; 30 cm. + 1 compact disc.
For descant recorder with piano acc. — Another copy (with its own cover) of the recorder part supplied with the Teacher copy.
Publ. no. 3611807
ISMN M570242955
System number: 013181981

Haughton, Alan, 1950-
Fun club descant recorder : chill out pieces to enjoy between exams.
Descant recorder grade 2-3 / Alan Haughton. — Teacher copy. — Buxhall :
Kevin Mayhew, 2004. — 1 score (31 p.) + 1 part ; 30 cm. + 1 compact disc.
For descant recorder with piano acc.
Publ. no. 3611804
ISMN M570242948
System number: 013181989

788.3641858

*Kelly, Bryan.
Globe Theatre suite : for descant recorder or piccolo and piano / by Bryan
Kelly ; edited by Atarah Ben-Tovim. — London : Stainer & Bell, c2005. —
1 score (16 p.) + 1 part (8 p.) ; 31 cm.
"The piano part may also be played on the harpsichord or other suitable keyboard
instrument"—P. 3.
Publ. no. H452
ISMN M220221392
System number: 013222597
Also classified at 788.331858

788.365076

Heyens, Gudrun.
Fun and games with the alto recorder. Teacher's commentary / by Gudrun
Heyens and Gerhard Engel ; translated and adapted by Peter Bowman. —
Mainz ; London : Schott, c2005. — 36 p. : 31 cm.
Publ. no. ED 12707
ISBN 1902455177
ISMN M220122576
ISMN M220122613
System number: 013191815

Heyens, Gudrun.
Fun and games with the alto recorder : method for the alto recorder. Tutor
book 2 / by Gudrun Heyens and Gerhard Engel ; translated and adapted by
Peter Bowman ; with illustrations by Julie Beech and John Minnion. —
Mainz ; London : Schott, c2005. — 1 score (69 p.) : col. ill. ; 31 cm.
Includes solos, duets and trios.
Publ. no. ED 12705
ISBN 1902455150
ISMN M220122590
System number: 013192176

Watts, Sarah.
Red hot treble recorder tutor : [student copy] / Sarah Watts. — Buxhall :
Kevin Mayhew, 2004. — 32 p. : ill. ; 21 x 30 cm. + 1 compact disc.
Recorder part(s) for the 23 pieces in the teacher copy, plus two duets and two trios
without accompaniment. — Also includes practice patterns, listening exercises, and
instructional information.
Publ. no. 3611842
ISMN M570243839
System number: 013182133
Also classified at 785.836076

Watts, Sarah.
Red hot treble recorder tutor : teacher copy / Sarah Watts. — Buxhall :
Kevin Mayhew, 2004. — 1 score (52 p.) ; 30 cm. + 1 compact disc.
23 pieces for treble recorder(s) with piano accompaniment, including three with
optional descant recorder and one with optional descant and tenor. — Contents
entirely different from those of the Red hot recorder tutor.
Publ. no. 3611843
ISMN M570243822
System number: 013201099

788.49 – BAGPIPES

788.49094288

Hill, James, ca. 1811-1853.
The fiddle music of James Hill : a collection of tunes by James Hill and
others, selected from principally local sources and arranged for keyed
Northumbrian smallpipes. — Morpeth : Northumbrian Piper's Society,
c2005. — vi p., 62 p. of music ; 15 x 21 cm.
Contains 94 tunes. — Includes biographical note and notes on the tunes.
ISBN 0902510274
ISMN M708032137
System number: 013299033

788.52 – OBOE

788.52

Addison, John, 1920-1998.
Prologue : oboe & piano / John Addison. — Ampleforth : Emerson Edition,
c2004. — 1 score (3 p.) + 1 part : port. ; 28 cm.
Duration: 1:15. — Includes biographical note.
Publ. no. 462
System number: 013188340

*Baker, Ernest, 1912-
Cantilena : for oboe and piano / Ernest Baker. — London : Chester
Music, [2005] — 1 score (4 p.) + [1] leaf ; 30 cm.
Reprint. Originally published as: Cantilena : for horn (or cello, oboe, clarinet) and
piano, London : J.& W. Chester, 1969.
Publ. no. CH00447
ISBN 1844499804
System number: 013197067

Bullard, Alan, 1947-
Circus skills : [oboe and piano] / Alan Bullard. — Laggan Bridge :
Spartan Press, c2004. — 1 score (15 p.) + 1 part (7 p.) ; 30 cm + 1 sound
disc (digital ; 4 3/4 in.)
"Grades 3-5"—Cover. — CD contains backing tracks.
Pl. no. SP730
ISMN M579997306
System number: 013172410

*Carlson, Rosalind.
Circle of memories : for solo oboe / by Rosalind Calson. — Lancaster :
Phylloscopus Publications, c2005. — 3 p. ; 30 cm.
Publ. no. PP560
ISMN M570166923
System number: 013472889

Graves, Richard, 1926-2002.
Threesome : oboe & piano / Richard Graves. — Ampleforth : Emerson
Edition, c2004. — 1 score (10 p.) + 1 part : port. ; 28 cm.
Duration: 6:00. — Includes biographical note.
Publ. no. 435
System number: 013188399

*Marais, Marin, 1656-1728.
[Pièces de violes, 4e livre. 1ère partie. *Selections; arr.*]
Three old French dances : for oboe and piano / Marin Marais ; [freely
transcribed by Janet Craxton and Alan Richardson] — London : Chester
Music, [2005], c1989. — 1 score (8 p.) + 1 part (3 p.) ; 30 cm.
Originally for viola da gamba and continuo.
Publ. no. CH 01614
ISBN 0711920524
System number: 013182230

Musgrave, Thea.
Niobe : for solo oboe and pre-recorded sound track : (1987) / Thea
Musgrave. — London : Novello, c2005. — 1 score (7 p.) ; 30 cm. + 1
compact disc.
Includes programme note.
Publ. no. NOV36003501
ISBN 1846092361
System number: 013383455

*Tann, Hilary.
Like lightnings : a pastoral for oboe / Hilary Tann. — [New York] :
Oxford University Press, c2005. — 7 p. of music ; 31 cm. — Oxford
music for oboe
Includes biographical, programme and performance notes.
ISBN 0193868520
System number: 013196397

Trapp, Lynn.
Cantilene : for oboe (or English horn, or viola) and organ / Lynn Trapp.
— [New York] : Oxford University Press, c2004. — 1 score (4 p.) +
3 parts ; 31 cm. — Oxford music for organ
Includes biographical note.
ISBN 0193867850
System number: 013115358
Also classified at 788.53; 787.3

Verroust, Stanislas, 1814-1863.
[Capriccios, oboe, piano]
Capriccio : for oboe & piano / Stanislas Verroust ; edited by Myron
Zakopets. — Ampleforth : Emerson Edition, c2004. — 1 score (7 p.) +
1 part ([2] p.) ; 28 cm.
Includes biographical note. — Duration: 4:00.
Publ. no. 458
System number: 013188299

Warren, Norman.
Dawn sequence : for oboe (or flute) and piano / by Norman Warren. —
Lancaster : Phylloscopus Publications, c2004. — 1 score (8 p.) + 1 part ;
30 cm.
Publ. no. PP541
ISMN M570166732
System number: 013173866
Primary classification 788.32

*Warren, Norman.
Folksong : oboe (or flute) & piano / Norman Warren. — Ampleforth :
Emerson Edition, c2005. — 1 score (5 p.) + 1 part ([2] p.) : port. ; 28 cm.
Includes biographical and programme notes. — Duration: ca. 4:30.
Publ. no. E470
Publ. no. 470
ISMN M570405015
System number: 013460659
Also classified at 788.32

788.52076
    *Hautbois : [France, 1800-1860] : méthodes, traités, dictionnaires et
    encyclopédies, ouvrages généraux / volume réalisé par Michel Giboureau.
    — Courlay, France : J.M. Fuzeau, c2003. — 3 v. of music : ill. ; 33 cm. —
    Fac-similé Jean-Marc Fuzeau — (Méthodes & traités ; 14. Série II,
    France, 1800-1860)
    Reprints of works and excerpts of works on the oboe originally published
    1802-1859. — "Volume réalisé par Michel Giboureau." — Includes studies for oboe
    solo and for oboe and continuo.
    Publ. no. 5861—5863
    ISMN M230658614 (v. 1)
    ISMN M230658621 (v. 2)
    ISMN M230668638 (v. 3)
    System number: 014790959

788.52183
    *Poulenc, Francis, 1899-1963.
    [Sonatas, oboe, piano]
    Sonata for oboe and piano / Francis Poulenc ; edited by Millan Sachania. —
    Rev. ed., 2004. — London : Chester Music, c2004. — 1 score (21 p.) +
    1 part (7 p.) ; 31 cm.
    Editor's pref. precedes score.
    Publ. no. CH62711
    ISBN 0711989257
    System number: 013132095

    Serini, Giovanni Battista, b. ca. 1710.
    [Sonatas, flute, continuo, D major]
    Sonata no. 1 in D : flute/oboe & piano / Giovanni Battista Serini ; [edited by
    Jack Pilgrim] — Ampleforth : Emerson Edition, c2004. — 1 score (12 p.) +
    1 part ; 28 cm.
    Originally for flute and continuo.
    Publ. no. 432
    ISMN M570402175
    System number: 013358290
    Primary classification 788.32183

788.521832
    Jacob, Gordon, 1895-1984.
    [Sonatinas, oboe, harpsichord]
    Sonatina for oboe and harpsichord (or piano) / Gordon Jacob. — London :
    Oxford University Press, [2005?], c1963. — 1 score (16 p.) + 1 part ; 31 cm.
    — Oxford music for oboe
    Reprint. Originalaly published: 1963.
    ISBN 0193850869
    System number: 013407967

788.521858
    Milford, Robin, 1903-1959.
    [Suites, oboe, string orchestra, op. 8; arr.]
    Suite in D minor : oboe & piano Robin Milford ; [piano reduction by R.
    Denwood] — Ampleforth : Emerson Edition, c2004. — 1 score (14 p.) +
    1 part (4 p.) : port. ; 28 cm.
    Originally with string orchestra acc. — Cover title. — Duration: 11:00. — Includes
    biographical note.
    Publ. no. E457a
    System number: 013188311

788.521894
    Brod, Henri, 1799-1839.
    [Fantaisie, oboe, piano]
    Fantaisie : oboe & piano / Henri Brod ; edited by Myron Zakopets. —
    Ampleforth : Emerson Edition, c2004. — 1 score (18 p.) + 1 part (7 p.) ;
    28 cm.
    Includes biographical note. — Duration: ca. 15:00.
    Publ. no. 460
    System number: 013188350

    Verroust, Stanislas, 1814-1863.
    Fantaisie sur 'Don Pasquale' : for oboe & piano / Stanislas Verroust ; edited
    by Myron Zakopets. — Ampleforth : Emerson Edition, c2004. — 1 score
    (14 p.) + 1 part (5 p.) ; 28 cm.
    Based on themes from the opera "Don Pasquale" by Donizetti. — Includes
    biographical note. — Duration: ca. 8:30.
    Publ. no. 459
    System number: 013188253

788.53 – COR ANGLAIS

788.53
    *Barret, Apollon Marie-Rose, 1803-1879.
    [Cantilène; arr.]
    Cantilena / by Apollon M.-R. Barret ; arranged for cor anglais and piano by
    professor Myron Zakopets. — Lancaster : Phylloscopus Publications,
    c2005. — 1 score (6 p.) + 1 part ; 30 cm.
    "... the music appears (untitled) in the Barret 'Method', for oboe with bassoon
    accompaniment, in the key of E♭."—Pref.
    Publ. no. PP561
    ISMN M570166930
    System number: 013472844

    Brumby, Colin.
    [Scena; arr.]
    Scena : for cor anglais and strings : version for cor anglais and piano / by
    Colin Brumby. — Lancaster : Phylloscopus Publications, c2004. — 1
    score (15 p.) + 1 part ; 30 cm.
    Publ. no. PP530A
    ISMN M570166626
    System number: 013188776

    Trapp, Lynn.
    Cantilene : for oboe (or English horn, or viola) and organ / Lynn Trapp.
    — [New York] : Oxford University Press, c2004. — 1 score (4 p.) +
    3 parts ; 31 cm. — Oxford music for organ
    Includes biographical note.
    ISBN 0193867850
    System number: 013115358
    Primary classification 788.52

    Wilson, Trevor, composer.
    [Miniatures, English horn, piano]
    Eight miniatures : for cor anglais & piano / Trevor Wilson. —
    Ampleforth : Emerson Edition, c2004. — 1 score (15 p.) + 1 part (7 p.) :
    port. ; 28 cm.
    "Can be performed separately or as a suite of any number and in any
    order"—Back cover. — Duration: ca. 9:00. — Includes biographical note.
    Publ. no. 449
    System number: 013188142

788.58 – BASSOON

788.58
    Carr, Paul.
    [Pieces blue, bassoon, piano (2004)]
    Three pieces blue : for bassoon and piano / by Paul Carr. — Lancaster :
    Phylloscopus Publications, c2004. — 1 score (11 p.) + 1 part ; 30 cm.
    "Three Pieces Blue (for flute and piano) were written in 2001 and were revised in
    2004 to provide a version for bassoon and piano."—Pref.
    Publ. no. PP531
    ISMN M570166633
    System number: 013188797

    Read, Tony, 1935-
    [Scherzetto, bassoon, piano]
    Scherzetto : bassoon & piano / Tony Read. — Ampleforth : Emerson
    Edition, c2005, — 1 score (5 p.) + 1 part (3 p.) : port. ; 28 cm.
    Cover title. — Includes biographical note. — Publisher's no.: 466 (front cover),
    E466 (back cover).
    Publ. no. E466
    ISMN M570404605
    System number: 013360852

    Taylor, Sue.
    Blow the bassoon! Piano accompaniments for book two / a bassoon tutor
    by Sue Taylor. — Laggan : Spartan Press, [2005?], c1994. — 1 score
    (85 p.) ; 30 cm.
    Originally published: Monmouth : Spartan Press, 1994.
    Pl. no. SP298
    System number: 013263948

    *Walker, Robin, 1953-
    Twilight / Robin Walker. — Ampleforth : Emerson Edition, c2005. —
    5 p. of music : port. ; 28 cm.
    For bassoon. — Includes biographical and programme notes. — Duration: ca.
    4:30.
    Publ. no. E473
    Publ. no. 473
    ISMN M570405251
    System number: 013460636

788.58076
    *Basson : France, 1800-1860 : méthodes, traités d'instrumentation,
    dictionnaires, cours de composition, périodiques. — Courlay, France :
    J.M. Fuzeau, 2005. — 4 v. of music : ill. ; 33 cm. — (Méthodes &
    traités ; Série II, France, 1800-1860) — (Fac-similés Jean-Marc
    Fuzeau)
    Reprints of works and excerpts of works on the bassoon originally published
    1803-1859. — Texts in French. — "Volumes réalisés par Michel Giboureau." —
    Includes studies for bassoon solo and duets for two bassoons.
    Publ. no. 5941—5944
    ISMN M230659413 (v. 1)
    ISMN M230659310 (v. 2)
    ISMN M230659437 (v. 3)
    ISMN M230659444 (v. 4)
    System number: 013351080

788.581556
    *Tisné, Antoine.
    Impressions niçoises : (musique de ballet) : pour basson solo / Antoine
    Tisné. — Lagny sur Marne : Musik Fabrik, c1999. — 9 p. of music ;
    30 cm.
    Cover title.
    System number: 014629758

788.581824
Tučapský, Antonín.
Rondo capriccioso : for bassoon & piano / Antonín Tučapský. —
Tewkesbury : Roberton Publications, c2005. — 1 score (15 p.) + 1 part
(4 p.) ; 30 cm.
Includes biographical and programme note.
Pl. no. 95522
ISMN M222261471
System number: 013390435

788.58183
***Aston, Peter.**
[Sonatas, bassoon, piano (2005)]
Sonata for bassoon and piano / by Peter Aston. — Lancaster : Phylloscopus
Publications, c2005. — 1 score (28 p.) + 1 part ; 30 cm.
Composed in 1959 and revised May 2005. — Includes biographical and editorial
notes.
Publ. no. PP569
ISMN M570167012
System number: 013561047

Bayliss, Colin.
[Sonatas, bassoon, piano (2005)]
Sonata for bassoon and piano : [B136] / Colin Bayliss. — Manchester : Da
Capo Music, c2005. — 1 score (15 p.) ; 30 cm.
Duration: ca. 10:00. — Includes programme and biographical notes.
Pl. no. DC 626
System number: 013351618

788.59 – DOUBLE BASSOON

788.59
***Hansell, Philip, 1962-**
So low : for contrabassoon / by Philip Hansell. — Lancaster : Phylloscopus
Publications, c2005. — [2 p.] ; 30 cm.
Includes biographical and programme notes.
Publ. no. PP570
ISMN M570167029
System number: 013561078

788.62 – CLARINET

788.62
***Arnold, Malcolm.**
[You know what sailors are. Scherzetto; arr.]
Scherzetto : for clarinet & piano / Malcolm Arnold. — Buckingham :
Queen's Temple Publications ; Laggan : distributed by Spartan Press, c2001.
— 1 score (4 p.) + 1 part ([2] p.) ; 30 cm.
Originally a clarinet solo in the film "You know what sailors are"; later arranged for
clarinet and orchestra and then for clarinet and piano. — Cover title. — Includes
programme note.
Pl. no. QT43
ISMN M708015437
System number: 013271629

Cropton, Mark.
Ten to go : progressive pieces for B♭ clarinet and piano : with CD
accompaniment / Mark Cropton. — Laggan Bridge : Spartan Press Music
Publishers Ltd., c2005. — 1 score (38 p.) + 1 part (16 p.) ; 30 cm.
CD contains full performances and backing tracks.
Pl. no. SP743
ISMN M579997436
System number: 013376591

Holmes, Chris, composer.
Take off with your B♭ clarinet / Chris Holmes. — Laggan Bridge : Spartan
Press, c2004. — 24 p. of music ; 30 cm + 1 sound disc (digital ; 4 3/4 in.)
20 pieces and exercises for clarinet. — Melody lines with chord symbols. —
"Grades 0-4"—Cover. — CD contains full performances and backing tracks.
Pl. no. SP785
ISMN M579997856
System number: 013299071

Lopez-Real, Carlos.
[Dig it. Clarinet(s)]
Dig it! : 7 cool tunes for clarinet(s) and piano with optional CD backing /
Carolos Lopez-Real. — Laggan Bridge : Spartan Press, c2005. — 1 score
(22 p.) + 3 parts ; 30 cm + 1 sound disc (digital ; 4 3/4 in.)
Includes optional duo and trio parts. — "Grades 3-6"—Cover. — Includes
improvisation sections. — CD contains full demonstrations and backing tracks. —
Mixed instrument ensembles may be created using the other books in the series.
Pl. no. SP732
ISMN M579997320
System number: 013299083

***Pentith, Sybil, 1927-2004.**
Movement : for clarinet & piano / Sybil Pentith. — Ampleforth : Emerson
Edition, c2005. — 1 score (3 p.) + 1 part ([1] leaf) : port. ; 28 cm.
Cover title. — Includes biographical and programme notes. — Duration: ca. 1:45.
Publ. no. E479
Publ. no. 479
ISMN M570405695
System number: 013460664

Roxburgh, Edwin.
Wordsworth miniatures : solo clarinet in B flat / Edwin Roxburgh. —
Waltham Abbey : United Music Publishers, c2003. — 7 p. of music ;
31 cm.
ISMN M224404128
System number: 013222626

Wright, Margot, 1911-2000.
[Improvisation, clarinet]
Improvisation : for solo clarinet / Margot Wright. — Ampleforth :
Emerson Edition, c2005. — [2] p. of music ; port. ; 28 cm.
Duration: 3:30. — Includes biographical note. — Publisher's no.: 397 on t.p.,
E397 on back cover.
Publ. no. E397
ISMN M570402144
System number: 013358203

788.621546
TV hits : playalong for clarinet. — London : Wise Publications, c2005.
— 31 p. : ill. 31 cm. + 1 compact disc — Guest spot
"Ten classic TV themes in melody line arrangements by Quentin Thomas with
specially recorded backing tracks"—Cover.
Publ. no. AM980529
ISBN 1844496147
System number: 013193427

788.62164
The big book of clarinet songs. — [S.l.] : Hal Leonard Europe ;
London : Exclusive distributors, Music Sales, c2005. — 143 p. ; 31 cm.
"128 great songs from jazz and Latin standards to stage, film and chart
hits"—Cover. — Melody lines.
Publ. no. HLE90001034
ISBN 0711982759
System number: 013296654

Lloyd Webber, Andrew, 1948-
[Musicals. Selections; arr.]
Andrew Lloyd Webber showstoppers : playalong for clarinet. —
London : Wise, c2005. — 32 p. of music ; 31 cm + 1 sound disc (digital ;
4 3/4 in.) — Guest spot
"Ten hit songs in melody line arrangements by Quentin Thomas with specially
recorded backing tracks"—Cover. — No words.
Publ. no. AM91937
ISBN 0711940533
System number: 013193475

788.62165
Cullen, David, 1942-
13 ways of getting there : jazzy pieces for clarinet and piano / David
Cullen. — London : Schott, c2005. — 1 score (36 p.) + 1 part (15 p.) ; 31
cm + 1 sound disc (digital ; 4 3/4 in.) — Jazz-it
"Easy to intermediate"—Back cover. — Pref. in English, French and German. —
CD contains full demonstrations and backing tracks.
Publ. no. ED 12846
ISMN M220123719
System number: 013312973

Jazzy opera classix : for clarinet / [arranged by] Darren Fellows. —
London : Schott, c2005. — 36 p. ; 31 cm. + 1 sound disc (digital ; 4 3/4
in.)
"Favourite opera themes in jazzy arrangements" — Back cover. — Melody lines
with chord symbols. — Piano accompaniments available as PDF files on the CD.
— Includes descriptions of the operas in English, French and German. — CD
contains full demonstrations and backing tracks.
Publ. no. ED 12823
ISBN 1902455290
ISMN M220123245
System number: 013192207

788.62166
Keane (Musical group).
[Hopes and fears; arr.]
Hopes and fears : playalong for clarinet / Keane. — London : Wise
Publications, c2005. — 31 p. ; 31 cm. + 2 compact discs. — Guest spot
"Twelve songs from the band's hit album in melody line arrangements by Paul
Honey"—Cover. — Music by members of the group. — CDs contain full
performances and backing tracks.
Publ. no. AM982828
ISBN 1846090539
System number: 013281570

788.62168
Classical favorites : clarinet : [solo arrangements of 15 great pieces with
CD accompaniment] — Milwaukee, Wis. : Hal Leonard, c2005. —
16 p. ; 31 cm. + 1 compact disc. — Hal Leonard instrumental
play-along
Publ. no. HL00841955
ISBN 0634085611
System number: 013220213

788.62186

Gregson, Edward.
[Concertos, clarinet, orchestra; *arr.*]
Clarinet concerto : (1994) / Edward Gregson. — London : Novello, c2005.
— 1 score (62 p.) + 1 part (25 p.) ; 30 cm.
Acc. arr. for piano.
Publ. no. NOV090619
ISBN 1844497623
System number: 013307343

788.621894

Rossini, Gioacchino, 1792-1868.
[Fantasie, clarinet, piano, E♭ major]
Fantaisie per clarinetto e pianoforte / Gioachino Rossini ; a cura di
Margherita Taliercio. — Pavona di Albano Laziale, Roma : Boccaccini &
Spada, c2007. — 1 score (16 p.) + 1 part (4 p.) ; 31 cm. — (Inediti e rarità
Rossiniane)
Pref. by the editor in Italian with English, French, German translations.
Publ. no. BS. 1825
System number: 013802005

788.6218964

*Templeton, Alec, 1910-1963.
[Elegies, saxophone, piano]
Elegie : for tenor saxophone or clarinet & piano / Alec Templeton. —
Ampleforth : Emerson Edition, [2005?] — 1 score (7 p.) + 1 part ([2] p.) :
port. ; 28 cm.
Biographical note on back cover. — Duration: ca. 6:00.
Publ. no. E436
Publ. no. 436
ISMN M570405664
System number: 013565577
Primary classification 788.7418964

788.7 – SAXOPHONE

788.7

Lopez-Real, Carlos.
[Dig it. Saxophone(s)]
Dig it! : 7 cool tunes for saxophone(s) and piano with optional CD backing /
Carolos Lopez-Real. — Laggan Bridge : Spartan Press, c2004. — 1 score
(24 p.) + 6 parts ; 30 cm + 1 sound disc (digital ; 4 3/4 in.)
Includes optional duo and trio parts — Cover title. — "Grades 3-6"—Cover. —
Includes improvisation sections. — CD contains full demonstrations and backing
tracks. — Mixed instrument ensembles may be created using the other books in the
series.
Pl. no. SP733
ISMN M579997337
System number: 013203852

788.73

Bullard, Alan, 1947-
Circus skills : [eight pieces for alto saxophone in E♭ and piano] / Alan
Bullard. — Laggan Bridge : Spartan Press, c2004. — 1 score (15 p.) +
1 part (7 p.) ; 30 cm + 1 compact disc.
"Grades 3-5"—Cover. — CD contains backing tracks.
Pl. no. SP726
ISMN M579997269
System number: 013169171

Cropton, Mark.
Ten to go : progressive pieces for alto saxophone and piano : with CD
accompaniment / Mark Cropton. — Laggan Bridge : Spartan Press, c2004.
— 1 score (41 p.) + 1 part (17 p.) ; 30 cm. 1 compact disc.
CD contains full performances and backing tracks.
Publ. no. SP719
ISMN M579997191
System number: 013169224

Holmes, Chris, composer.
Take off with your [alto] saxophone / Chris Holmes. — Laggan Bridge :
Spartan Press, c2004. — 22 p. of music ; 30 cm + 1 sound disc (digital ; 4
3/4 in.)
19 pieces and exercises for saxophone. — Melody lines with chord symbols. —
"Grades 0-4"—Cover. — CD contains full performances and backing tracks.
Pl. no. SP786
ISMN M579997863
System number: 013299062

Indian melodies : for alto saxophone = Mélodies indiennes : pour saxophon
alto = Indische Melodien : für Alt-Saxophon / [arranged by] Candida
Connolly ; with accompanying CD by Kadri Golpalnath. — London :
Schott, c2005. — 60 p. of music ; 31 cm + ill. ; 1 sound disc (digital ; 4
3/4 in.)
Indian music in western notation. — "Styles/techniques/ornamentation"—Cover. —
Pref. and performance notes in English, French and German.
Publ. no. ED 12733
ISBN 1902455207
ISMN M220123115
System number: 013192424

788.73076

Haughton, Alan, 1950-
Fun club alto sax : chill-out pieces to enjoy between exams. Alto sax
grade 1-2 / Alan Haughton. — Teacher copy. — Buxhall : Kevin
Mayhew, 2004. — 1 score (30 p.) + 1 part ; 30 cm. + 1 compact disc.
For alto saxophone with piano acc.
Publ. no. 3611819
ISMN M570243266
System number: 013201374

788.73136076

Taylor, Dennis, saxophonist.
Amazing phrasing : alto saxophone : 50 ways to improve your
improvisational skills / by Dennis Taylor. — Milwaukee, Wis. : Hal
Leonard, c2005. — 103 p. ; 31 cm. + 1 compact disc
CD contains demonstration and backing tracks.
Publ. no. HL00311108
ISBN 0634074369
System number: 013323568

788.73143

The Boosey woodwind [method] Alto saxophone. Repertoire book C.
— London : Boosey & Hawkes, c2004. — 1 score (43 p.) + 1 part ;
31 cm. — (The Boosey woodwind and brass method)
With keyboard acc. — Series editor: Chris Morgan. — "This book can be used
with stages 1 to 6 of the Boosey Woodwind Method Saxophone Book 2, or by
anyone who is starting the saxophone."—back cover.
ISBN 0851624065
ISMN M060114793
System number: 013192539

788.731546

TV hits : playalong for alto saxophone. — London : Wise, c2005. —
31 p. of music : ill. 31 cm + 1 sound disc (digital ; 4 3/4 in.) — Guest
spot
"Ten classic TV themes in melody line arrangements by Quentin Thomas with
specially recorded backing tracks"—Cover. — No words.
Publ. no. AM980540
ISBN 1844496155
System number: 013193392

788.73164

Lloyd Webber, Andrew, 1948-
[Musicals. *Selections; arr.*]
Andrew Lloyd Webber showstoppers : playalong for alto saxophone. —
London : Wise, c2005. — 32 p. of music ; 31 cm + 1 sound disc (digital ;
4 3/4 in.) — Guest spot
"Ten hit songs in melody line arrangements by Quentin Thomas with specially
recorded backing tracks"—Cover. — No words.
Publ. no. AM91936
ISBN 0711940525
System number: 013193457

788.731643

Penri-Evans, David, 1956-
Bayou blues : (1987) : for E flat alto saxophone and piano / David
Penri-Evans. — Manchester : Da Capo Music, c2005. — 1 score (7 p.) +
1 part ; 30 cm.
Duration: ca. 6:00. — Includes programme and biographical notes.
Pl. no. DC 632
System number: 013351595

788.73165

*Cullen, David, 1942-
13 ways of getting there : jazzy pieces for alto saxophone and piano /
David Cullen. — London : Schott, c2005. — 1 score (36 p.) + 1 part
(15 p.) ; 31 cm + 1 sound disc (digital ; 4 3/4 in.) — Jazz-it
"Easy to intermediate"—Back cover. — Pref. in English, French and German. —
CD contains full demonstrations and backing tracks.
Publ. no. ED 12847
ISMN M220123726
System number: 014521549

Jazzy opera classix : for alto saxophone / [arranged by] Darren Fellows.
— London : Schott, c2005. — 36 p. ; 31 cm. + 1 sound disc (digital ; 4
3/4 in.)
"Favourite opera themes in jazzy arrangements" — Back cover. — Melody lines
with chord symbols. — Piano accompaniments available as PDF files on the CD.
— Includes descriptions of the operas in English, French and German. — CD
contains full demonstrations and backing tracks.
Publ. no. ED 12824
ISBN 1902455304
ISMN M220123252
System number: 013192271

788.73166

Keane (Musical group).
[Hopes and fears; *arr.*]
Hopes and fears : playalong for alto saxophone / Keane. — London : Wise Publications, c2005. — 31 p. ; 31 cm. + 2 compact discs. — Guest spot
"Twelve songs from the band's hit album in melody line arrangements by Paul Honey"—Cover. — Music by members of the group. — CDs contain full performances and backing tracks.
Publ. no. AM982817
ISBN 1846090520
System number: 013281543

788.73168

Classical favorites : alto sax : [solo arrangements of 15 great pieces with CD accompaniment] — Milwaukee, Wis. : Hal Leonard, c2005. — 16 p. ; 31 cm. + 1 compact disc. — Hal Leonard instrumental play-along
Publ. no. HL00841956
ISBN 063408562X
System number: 013220241

788.74165

Cullen, David, 1942-
13 ways of getting there : jazzy pieces for tenor saxophone and piano / David Cullen. — London : Schott, c2005. — 1 score (36 p.) + 1 part (15 p.) ; 31 cm + 1 sound disc (digital ; 4 3/4 in.) — Jazz-it
"Easy to intermediate"—Back cover. — Pref. in English, French and German. — CD contains full demonstrations and backing tracks.
Publ. no. ED 12848
ISMN M220123733
System number: 013313014

Jazzy opera classix : for tenor saxophone / [arranged by] Darren Fellows. — London : Schott, c2005. — 36 p. ; 31 cm. + 1 sound disc (digital ; 4 3/4 in.)
"Favourite opera themes in jazzy arrangements" — Back cover. — Melody lines with chord symbols. — Piano accompaniments available as PDF files on the CD. — Includes descriptions of the operas in English, French and German. — CD contains full demonstrations and backing tracks.
Publ. no. ED 12825
ISBN 1902455312
ISMN M220123269
System number: 013192267

788.74168

Classical favorites : tenor sax : [solo arrangements of 15 great pieces with CD accompaniment] — Milwaukee, Wis. : Hal Leonard, c2005. — 16 p. ; 31 cm. + 1 compact disc. — Hal Leonard instrumental play-along
Publ. no. HL00841957
ISBN 0634085638
System number: 013220257

788.7418964

*Templeton, Alec, 1910-1963.
[Elegies, saxophone, piano]
Elegie : for tenor saxophone or clarinet & piano / Alec Templeton. — Ampleforth : Emerson Edition, [2005?] — 1 score (7 p.) + 1 part ([2] p.) : port. ; 28 cm.
Biographical note on back cover. — Duration: ca. 6:00.
Publ. no. E436
Publ. no. 436
ISMN M570405664
System number: 013565577
Also classified at 788.6218964

788.82 – MOUTH ORGAN

788.82

Lewis, Paul, 1943-
A Somerset garland. for flute, violin or harmonica and piano / by Paul Lewis. — Dover : Broadbent & Dunn, c2003. — 1 score (15 p.) + 1 part ; 30 cm.
Pl. no. B&D 13206
System number: 013374676
Primary classification 788.32

788.82183

*Cooke, Arnold.
[Sonatas, harmonica, piano]
Sonata for harmonica & piano / Arnold Cooke. — [s.l.] : Anglo-American Music Publishers, c2005. — 1 score (25 p.) + 1 part (5 p.) ; 28 cm.
Cover title. — Includes biographical note. — Duration: ca. 3:19.
System number: 013593899

788.821858

Lewis, Paul, 1943-
Spring suite : flute, optional 'cello and piano or harmonica and piano / Paul Lewis. — Dover : Broadbent & Dunn, c2003. — 1 score (20 p.) + 2 parts ; 30 cm.
Pl. no. B&D 13205
System number: 013374699
Primary classification 788.321858

788.86 – ACCORDION

788.86076

Ollila, Jukka.
Harmonikan asteikkosormitus ABC = Accordion scale fingering : standardi- ja melodiabassoharmonikalle = standard- and melody bass accordion / Jukka Ollila. — Tornio : Jukka Ollila, c2007. — 1 score (31 p.) : ill., port. ; 30 cm.
Can be used for the Italian, Swedish and Finnish 5-scale system. — Text in Finnish and English. — Biographical note in Finnish and English on p. [4] of cover.
System number: 013836335

788.92 – TRUMPET

788.92

Holmes, Chris, composer.
Take off with your [B♭] trumpet / Chris Holmes. — Laggan Bridge : Spartan Press, c2004. — 24 p. of music ; 30 cm + 1 sound disc (digital ; 4 3/4 in.)
18 pieces for trumpet. — Melody lines with chord symbols. — "Grades 0-4"—Cover. — CD contains full performances and backing tracks.
Pl. no. SP787
ISMN M579997870
System number: 013203868

Lopez-Real, Carlos.
[Dig it. Trumpet(s)]
Dig it! : 7 cool tunes for trumpet(s) and piano with optional CD backing / Carolos Lopez-Real. — Laggan Bridge : Spartan Press, c2005. — 1 score (22 p.) + 3 parts ; 30 cm + 1 sound disc (digital ; 4 3/4 in.)
Includes optional duo and trio parts — "Grades 3-6"—Cover. — Includes improvisation sections. — CD contains full demonstrations and backing tracks. — Mixed instrument ensembles may be created using the other books in the series.
Pl. no. SP734
ISMN M579997344
System number: 013299125

788.921542

Disney greats : trumpet : [solo arrangements of 15 favorite songs with CD accompaniment] — Milwaukee, Wis. : Hal Leonard, [2005] — 24 p. ; 31 cm + 1 compact disc. — Hal Leonard instrumental play-along
Music from Disney films, musicals and theme parks. — No words.
Publ. no. HL00841938
ISBN 0634085433
System number: 013191587

788.921546

TV hits : playalong for trumpet. — London : Wise, c2005. — 31 p. of music ; ill. 31 cm + 1 sound disc (digital ; 4 3/4 in.) — Guest spot
"Ten classic TV themes in melody line arrangements by Quentin Thomas with specially recorded backing tracks"—Cover. — No words.
Publ. no. AM980562
ISBN 1844496171
System number: 013193400

788.921595

Songs from the sea : for trumpet / arranged by Colin Mawby. — Buxhall : Kevin Mayhew, 2004. — 1 score (23 p.) + 1 part ; 31 cm.
With piano acc. — Without words.
Publ. no. 3611812
ISMN M570243099
System number: 013159343

788.92164

Lloyd Webber, Andrew, 1948-
[Musicals. *Selections; arr.*]
Andrew Lloyd Webber showstoppers : playalong for trumpet. — London : Wise, c2005. — 32 p. of music ; 31 cm + 1 sound disc (digital ; 4 3/4 in.) — Guest spot
"Ten hit songs in melody line arrangements by Quentin Thomas with specially recorded backing tracks"—Cover. — No words.
Publ. no. AM91943
ISBN 0711940592
System number: 013193486

788.92165

Cullen, David, 1942-
13 ways of getting there : jazzy pieces for trumpet and piano = pièces en style de jazz pour trompette et piano = Jazz-Stücke für Trompete und Klavier / David Cullen. — London : Schott, c2005. — 1 score (36 p.) + 1 part (15 p.) ; 31 cm + 1 sound disc (digital ; 4 3/4 in.) — Jazz-it
"Easy to intermediate"—Back cover. — Pref. in English, French and German. — CD contains full demonstrations and backing tracks.
Publ. no. ED 12738
ISMN M220122644
System number: 013192388

Jazzy opera classix : for trumpet / [arranged by] Darren Fellows. —
London : Schott, c2005. — 36 p. ; 31 cm. + 1 sound disc (digital ; 4 3/4
in.)
"Favourite opera themes in jazzy arrangements" — Back cover. — Melody lines
with chord symbols. — Piano accompaniments available as PDF files on the CD. —
Includes descriptions of the operas in English, French and German. — CD contains
full demonstrations and backing tracks.
Publ. no. ED 12761
ISBN 1902455274
ISMN M220123221
System number: 013192282

788.92168
Classical favorites : trumpet : [solo arrangements of 15 great pieces with
CD accompaniment] — Milwaukee, Wis. : Hal Leonard, c2005. — 16 p. ;
31 cm. + 1 compact disc. — Hal Leonard instrumental play-along
Publ. no. HL00841958
ISBN 0634085646
System number: 013219822

788.92183
*Dolar, Janez Krstnik, ca. 1620-1673.
[Sonatas, trumpet, instrumental ensemble, C major; *arr.*]
Sonata à 10 : (Natur-) Trompeten, 3 Posaunen, Streicher, B.c. / Johannes
Baptist Tolar ; edited & arranged by Wolfgang G. Haas ; Orgelauszug. —
Köln : W.G. Haas-Musikverlag, c2004. — 1 score (9 p.) + 3 parts ; 30 cm.
— (Tschechische Barockmusik = Czech Baroque music ; Nr. 75)
Score is for trumpet and organ; parts are for C trumpet, B-flat trumpet, and
violoncello, bassoon, or trombone. — "Europäische Musik: Tschechien,
Kremsler" — Cover. — Includes critical notes in German. — Duration: 6:50.
ISMN M205405465
System number: 014629767

788.93 – TROMBONE

788.93
Bayliss, Colin.
Soliloquy : for solo [alto] trombone : [B137] / Colin Bayliss. —
Manchester : Da Capo Music, c2005. — 1 score (5 p.) ; 30 cm.
Duration: ca. 5:00. — Includes programme and biographical notes.
Pl. no. DC 634
System number: 013351582

Holmes, Chris, composer.
Take off with your B♭ trombone and/or euphonium : [treble clef] / Chris
Holmes. — Laggan Bridge : Spartan Press, c2005. — 24 p. of music ; 30
cm + 1 sound disc (digital ; 4 3/4 in.)
18 pieces for trombone. — Melody lines with chord symbols. — "Grades
0-4"—Cover. — CD contains full performances and backing tracks.
Pl. no. SP789
ISMN M579997894
System number: 013376573
Also classified at 788.975

Holmes, Chris, composer.
Take off with your trombone : [bass clef] / Chris Holmes. — Laggan
Bridge : Spartan Press, c2004. — 24 p. of music ; 30 cm + 1 sound disc
(digital ; 4 3/4 in.)
18 pieces for trombone. — Melody lines with chord symbols. — "Grades
0-4"—Cover. — CD contains full performances and backing tracks.
Pl. no. SP788
ISMN M579997887
System number: 013203884

788.93168
Classical favorites : trombone : [solo arrangements of 15 great pieces with
CD accompaniment] — Milwaukee, Wis. : Hal Leonard, c2005. — 16 p. ;
31 cm. + 1 compact disc. — Hal Leonard instrumental play-along
Publ. no. HL00841960
ISBN 0634085662
System number: 013220279

788.94 – HORN

788.94076
*Cor : [France, 1600-1800] : méthodes, traités, dictionnaires et
encyclopédies, ouvrages généraux / volume réalisé par Jean
Saint-Arroman. — Courlay, France : J.M. Fuzeau, 2003. — 306 p. of
music ; ill. ; 33 cm. — Fac-similé Jean-Marc Fuzeau — (Méthodes &
traités ; 21. Série I, France, 1600-1800)
Reprints of 17th and 18th century horn treatises and methods; originally published
1636-1800. — Texts in French.
Publ. no. 5879
ISMN M2306F58799
System number: 014790370

788.94168
Classical favorites : horn : [solo arrangements of 15 great pieces with CD
accompaniment] — Milwaukee, Wis. : Hal Leonard, c2005. — 16 p. ;
31 cm. + 1 compact disc — Hal Leonard instrumental play-along
Publ. no. HL00841959
ISBN 0634085654
System number: 013220189

788.941856
*Phillips, Craig, 1961-
[Serenade, horn, organ]
Serenade for horn and organ / Craig Phillips. — [New York] : Oxford
University Press, c2004. — 1 score (7 p.) + 1 part ([1] leaf) ; 31 cm. —
Oxford music for horn
Includes biographical note.
ISBN 019386763X
System number: 013114440

788.94186
Mozart, Wolfgang Amadeus, 1756-1791.
[Concertos, horn, orchestra, K. 412, D major; *arr.*]
Horn concerto no. 1 : [arr.] for horn and piano / Wolfgang Amadeus
Mozart ; edited by Barry Tuckwell. — New York : G. Schirmer ;
Milwaukee, Wis. : distributed by Hal Leonard, 2004, c1994. — 1 score
(35 p.) + 1 part ; 31 cm. — Schirmer's library of musical classics ; v.
2048
Includes parts for horn in F and natural horn in D. — Previously published in
"Concertos for horn" (HL50481735).
Publ. no. HL50485603
ISBN 0634081721
System number: 013211728

Mozart, Wolfgang Amadeus, 1756-1791.
[Concertos, horn, orchestra, K. 417, E♭ major; *arr.*]
Horn concerto no. 2 : [arr.] for horn and piano / Wolfgang Amadeus
Mozart ; edited by Barry Tuckwell. — New York : G. Schirmer ;
Milwaukee, Wis. : distributed by Hal Leonard, 2004, c1994. — 1 score
(31 p.) + 1 part ; 31 cm. — Schirmer's library of musical classics ; v.
2049
Includes parts for horn in F and natural horn in E♭. — Previously published in
"Concertos for horn / Mozart" (HL50481735).
Publ. no. HL50485604
ISBN 063408173X
System number: 013211730

Mozart, Wolfgang Amadeus, 1756-1791.
[Concertos, horn, orchestra, K. 447, E♭ major; *arr.*]
Horn concerto no. 3 : [arr.] for horn and piano / Wolfgang Amadeus
Mozart ; edited by Barry Tuckwell. — New York : G. Schirmer ;
Milwaukee, Wis. : distributed by Hal Leonard, 2004, c1994. — 1 score
(31 p.) + 1 part ; 31 cm. — Schirmer's library of musical classics ; v.
2050
Includes parts for horn in F and natural horn in E♭. — Previously published in
"Concertos for horn / Mozart" (HL50481735).
Publ. no. HL50485605
ISBN 0634081748
System number: 013211738

Mozart, Wolfgang Amadeus, 1756-1791.
[Concertos, horn, orchestra, K. 495, E♭ major; *arr.*]
Horn concerto no. 4 : [arr.] for horn and piano / Wolfgang Amadeus
Mozart ; edited by Barry Tuckwell. — New York : G. Schirmer ;
Milwaukee, Wis. : distributed by Hal Leonard, 2004, c1994. — 1 score
(36 p.) + 1 part ; 31 cm. — Schirmer's library of musical classics ; v.
2051
Includes parts for horn in F and natural horn in E♭. — Previously published in
"Concertos for horn / Mozart" (HL50481735).
Publ. no. HL50485606
ISBN 0634081756
System number: 013211776

788.975 – EUPHONIUM, BARITONE, ETC.

788.975
Holmes, Chris, composer.
Take off with your B♭ trombone and/or euphonium : [treble clef] / Chris
Holmes. — Laggan Bridge : Spartan Press, c2005. — 24 p. of music ; 30
cm + 1 sound disc (digital ; 4 3/4 in.)
18 pieces for trombone. — Melody lines with chord symbols. — "Grades
0-4"—Cover. — CD contains full performances and backing tracks.
Pl. no. SP789
ISMN M579997894
System number: 013376573
Primary classification 788.93

788.975186
*Clarke, Nigel, 1960-
[City in the sea; *arr.*]
The city in the sea : (1995) : concerto for euphonium and band / Nigel
Clarke ; piano reduction by Paul Pellay. — Kenley : Maecenas Music,
c1997. — 1 score (29 p.) + 1 part (11 p.) ; 30 cm. — Maecenas
contemporary composers elite edition
Pref. includes note on the history of Dunwich, which inspired the piece. —
Duration: ca. 16:00.
Publ. no. MC0046PR
System number: 013415914

788.98 – TUBA

788.98
Bach, Johann Sebastian, 1685-1750.
[Suites, orchestra, BWV 1067, B minor. Badinerie; *arr.*]
Badinerie / J.S. Bach ; arranged for tuba & piano by John Fletcher. —
Ampleforth : Emerson Edition, c2005. — 1 score (3 p.) + 1 part ([1] leaf) :
port. ; 28 cm.
Originally for flute and orchestra. — Duration: 1:20. — Includes biographical note
on the arranger. — Publisher's no.: 467 on t.p., E467 on back cover.
Publ. no. 467
ISMN M570401314
System number: 013360889

*Bingham, Judith.
Der Spuk : (2001) : a folk-tale from Kleinwalsertal : for tuba solo / Judith
Bingham. — Kenley, Surrey : Maecenas Music, c2001. — 4 p. of music ;
30 cm. — Maecenas contemporary composers elite edition
Duration: ca. 9:00 (without narration). — Includes optional narration to be read
before the performance.
Publ. no. MM0511
System number: 013422345

*Lewis, Anwen.
A— but no : (Aponniad) : (1992) : for tuba and piano / Anwen Lewis. —
Kenley, Surrey : Maecenas Music, c1995. — 1 score (15 p.) + 1 part
(4 p.) ; 30 cm. — Maecenas contemporary composers elite edition
Duration: ca. 8:00. — Includes programme notes.
Publ. no. MM0108
System number: 013422050

796.2
Elgar, Edward, 1857-1934.
[Adieu]
Two piano pieces / Edward Elgar ; edited by David Patrick. — Barnet :
Fitzjohn Music Publications, c2005. — 5 p. of music ; 30 cm.
Includes editorial note.
System number: 013214627

COMPOSER AND TITLE INDEX

—als— l
See **Andre, Mark, 1964- —als— l**

2 aires nos. 306 & 110
See **Lawes, William, 1602-1645.** [Airs, viols
(4), VdGS no. 306] 2 aires nos. 306 & 110

2 aires nos. 336 & 318
See **Lawes, William, 1602-1645.** [Airs, viols
(4), VdGS no. 336] 2 aires nos. 336 & 318

3 chansons à 4 & à 5
See **Wilder, Philip van, d. 1553.** [Chansons.
Selections] 3 chansons à 4 & à 5

3 Duetti à fagotto e viola concerta
See **Giardini, Felice, 1716-1796.** [Duets, viola,
bassoon] 3 Duetti à fagotto e viola concerta

3 fantasias à 3
See **Jenkins, John, 1592-1678.** [Fantasias, viols
(3). *Selections*] 3 fantasias à 3

3 In nomines à 4
3 In nomines à 4 : (TrTr/TTB) / Parsons, Parsley
& Weelkes ; edited by Virginia Brookes. —
Viola da Gamba Society of Great Britain
785.76194   013382510

3 pieces for unaccompanied viola da gamba
See **Hammer, Xaver, 1741-1817.** [Viola da
gamba music. *Selections*] 3 pieces for
unaccompanied viola da gamba

3 sonate op. 13 nn. 4-6 per pianoforte
See **Clementi, Muzio, 1752-1832.** [Sonatas,
op. 13. No. 4-6] 3 sonate op. 13 nn. 4-6 per
pianoforte

4 duets from Orpheus Britannicus
See **Purcell, Henry, 1659-1695.** [Vocal music.
Selections] 4 duets from Orpheus Britannicus

**4. Streichquartett, für 2 Violinen, Viola und
Violoncello**
See **Vasks, Pēteris, 1946-** [Quartets, strings, no.
4] 4. Streichquartett, für 2 Violinen, Viola und
Violoncello

6 duetti per 2 violini
See **Boccherini, Luigi, 1743-1805.** [Duets,
violins, G. 56-61] 6 duetti per 2 violini

8 tunes for Archbishop Parker's psalter
See **Tallis, Thomas, ca. 1505-1585.** [Psalm
tunes] 8 tunes for Archbishop Parker's psalter

12 monferrine
See **Clementi, Muzio, 1752-1832.**
[Monferrinas] 12 monferrine

12 Triosonaten für 2 Violinen und B.c. (1715)
See **Philarmonica, Mrs.** [Sonatas, violins (2),
violoncello, continuo] 12 Triosonaten für 2
Violinen und B.c. (1715)

**13 canzoni strumentali a due e a quattro
strumenti con il basso per l'organo**
See **Ganassi, Giacomo, fl. 1625-1637**
[Vespertina psalmodia (1637) Selections] 13
canzoni strumentali a due e a quattro strumenti
con il basso per l'organo

13 ways of getting there
See **Cullen, David, 1942-** 13 ways of getting
there

14 magnificat
See **Hassler, Hans Leo, 1564-1612.**
[Magnificats, organ. *Selections*] 14 magnificat

**18 composizioni senza numero d'opera, Op-sn
1-18 (WO 2, 3, 5, 8, 10, 13-23), per pianoforte o
clavicembalo**
See **Clementi, Muzio, 1752-1832.** [Keyboard
music. *Selections*] 18 composizioni senza
numero d'opera, Op-sn 1-18 (WO 2, 3, 5, 8, 10,
13-23), per pianoforte o clavicembalo

21 duets
See **Holdom, Colin.** [Studio for brass. Duets] 21
duets

**21. Quintett in c-moll für 2 Violinen, Viola und 2
Violoncelli**
See **Cambini, Giuseppe Maria, 1746-1825.**
[Quintets, violins, viola, violoncellos, no. 21, C
minor] 21. Quintett in c-moll für 2 Violinen,
Viola und 2 Violoncelli

21st century rock
21st century rock : [vol. 5] / compiled by Nick
Crispin ; music arranged by Matt Cowe. —
Guitar tab ed. — Wise Publications
783.242166   013172321

24 Klaviersonaten in alle toonsoorten
See **Nicolai, Johann Gottlieb, 1744-1801.**
[Sonatas, piano] 24 Klaviersonaten in alle
toonsoorten

24 préludes pour piano
See **Lenot, Jacques.** [Preludes, piano] 24
préludes pour piano

25 progressive studies
See **Burgmüller, Friedrich, 1806-1874.** [Etudes
faciles et progressives] 25 progressive studies

48 kleine Orgelstücke
See **Hässler, Johann Wilhelm, 1747-1822.**
[Kleine Orgelstücke] 48 kleine Orgelstücke

60 progressive solos for classical guitar
60 progressive solos for classical guitar :
featuring the music of the world's greatest
composers: Bach, Handel, Mozart, Beethoven,
and Brahms / arranged by Mark Phillips. —
Cherry Lane Music Co.
787.87168   006928830

100 of the greatest love songs ever
100 of the greatest love songs ever : piano,
vocal, guitar. — *Wise*
783.242164   013374970

101 songs for easy guitar.
101 songs for easy guitar. Book 5. — *Wise
Publications*
783.242166   013297793

1.22.03.Acoustic
See **Maroon 5 (Musical group)**
1.22.03.Acoustic

1066
See **Hewitt, Daniel.** 1066

1812 overture
See **Tchaikovsky, Peter Ilich, 1840-1893**
[Overture "1812". Op. 49; *arr.*] 1812 overture

3me messe solennelle : op. 11
See **Guilmant, Alexandre, 1837-1911.** [Masses,
mixed voices, organ, no. 3, op. 11, E♭ major]
3me messe solennelle : op. 11

A Kékszakállú herceg vára
See **Bartók, Béla, 1881-1945.** [Kékszakállú
herceg vára. *English & Hungarian*] A
Kékszakállú herceg vára

À la carte
See **Richards, Goff.** À la carte

A— but no
See **Lewis, Anwen.** A— but no

Abati, Joaquín, *1865-1936.*
See **Luna, Pablo, 1879-1942.** El asombro de
Damasco : zarzuela en dos actos / Pablo Luna ;
libreto, Antonio Paso y Joaquín Abati ; edición
crítica, Miguel Roa.

ABBA (*Musical group*)
See **Andersson, Benny.** [Mamma mia!
Selections; arr.] Mamma mia! : choral
highlights : instrumental pak / arranged by Mac
Huff.

See **Andersson, Benny.** [Mamma mia!
Selections; arr.] Mamma mia! : choral
highlights : SAB / arranged by Mac Huff.

See **Andersson, Benny.** [Mamma mia!
Selections; arr.] Mamma mia! : choral
highlights : SATB / arranged by Mac Huff.

See **Andersson, Benny.** [Mamma mia!
Selections; arr.] Mamma mia! : choral
highlights : SSA / arranged by Mac Huff.

Abramovich, Charles.
See **Glass, Philip.** [Concertos, violin, orchestra;
arr.] Violin concerto : (1987) / Philip Glass ;
piano reduction by Charles Abramovich.

**[Ach Herr, mich armen Sünder (Cantata).
English & German]**
See **Bach, Johann Sebastian, 1685-1750.** [Ach
Herr, mich armen Sünder (Cantata). *English &
German*]

Ach Herr, mich armen Sünder
See **Bach, Johann Sebastian, 1685-1750.** [Ach
Herr, mich armen Sünder (Cantata). *English &
German*] Ach Herr, mich armen Sünder

**[Acis and Galatea. Heart, the seat of soft delight;
arr.]**
See **Handel, George Frideric, 1685-1759** [Acis
and Galatea. Heart, the seat of soft delight; *arr.*]

[Acis and Galatea. O ruddier than the cherry]
See **Handel, George Frideric, 1685-1759.** [Acis
and Galatea. O ruddier than the cherry]

Acoustic guitar
See **Johnson, Chad.** Acoustic guitar

Acteon
See **Charpentier, Marc-Antoine, 1643-1704.**
Acteon

Adagio
See **Sewell, Dominic.** [Adagios, string orchestra,
op. 23] Adagio

Adagio per orchestra (1999)
See **Börtz, Daniel, 1943-** [Adagio, orchestra]
Adagio per orchestra (1999)

[Adagio, orchestra]
See **Börtz, Daniel, 1943-** [Adagio, orchestra]

[Adagios, string orchestra, op. 23]
See **Sewell, Dominic.** [Adagios, string orchestra,
op. 23]

Addison, John, *1920-1998.*
Prologue : oboe & piano / John Addison. —
Emerson Edition
788.52   013188340

Addison, Joseph, *1672-1719.*
See **Sanders, John, 1933-2003.** The firmament : anthem for treble soloist, SATB choir & organ / music by John Sanders.

Adès, Thomas, *1971-*
Asyla : for large orchestra, op. 17 (1997) / Thomas Adès. — *Faber Music*
784.2   006891421

Asyla : for orchestra (1997) / Thomas Adès. — *Faber Music*
784.2   014482452

[Adieu]
See **Elgar, Edward, 1857-1934.** [Adieu]

Adieu, Marie, mon amour
See **Riehm, Rolf, 1937-** Adieu, Marie, mon amour

Adlgasser, Anton Cajetan, *1729-1777.*
Litaniae de venerabili altaris Sacramento : in B-Dur (WV 3/53) : per Soli (SATB), Coro (SATB), Trombone alto solo o Organo solo, 2 Clarini, Timpani, 2 Violini, Basso continuo (Violoncello/Fagotto/Contrabbasso/Organo), 3 Tromboni colla parte voci ad lib. / Anton Cajetan Adlgasser ; herausgegeben von Armin Kircher. — *Erstausg.* — *Carus*
782.522   013353377

Advent antiphons
See **Chilcott, Bob.** Advent antiphons

Advent carol
See **Ledger, Philip.** Advent carol

An Advent carol
See **Voth, Ellen Gilson, 1972-** An Advent carol

An Advent responsory
See **Rose, Barry, 1934-** An Advent responsory

Aecha
See **Warshauer, Meira, 1949-** Aecha

Aesop.
See **McAlister, Clark.** The lion and the mouse : for narrator and woodwind [sic] quintet / music by Clark McAlister ; text by A.J. Wood.

[African Sanctus (Musical work). Lord's prayer; arr.]
See **Fanshawe, David, 1942-** [African Sanctus (Musical work). Lord's prayer; *arr.*]

Ahmad, Michael.
See **Ballet gold :** the essential collection.

See **Best of gold :** the essential collection.

See **Classical gold :** the essential collection.

See **Fauré, Gabriel, 1845-1924.** [Selections; *arr.*] Fauré gold : the essential collection.

Aija bernin pupas
Aija bernin pupas = [Rock my child in feather down : for SAB chorus & piano : Latvian folk song] / arranged by James Hudson. — *Boosey & Hawkes*
782.5421620094796   013361300

[Airs, viols (4), VdGS no. 306]
See **Lawes, William, 1602-1645.** [Airs, viols (4), VdGS no. 306]

[Airs, viols (4), VdGS no. 336]
See **Lawes, William, 1602-1645.** [Airs, viols (4), VdGS no. 336]

Aitken, Elizabeth, *1949-*
Cake dance suite : for two oboes and cor anglais / by Elizabeth Aitken. — *Phylloscopus Publications*
785.851931858   013188905

Talisker : where sea meets Skye : for two oboes and cor anglais / by Elizabeth Aitken. — *Phylloscopus Publications*
785.85193   013472771

Akademie der Künste (Berlin, Germany)
See **Gurre-Lieder :** für Soli, Chor und Orchester : kritischer Bericht / Arnold Schönberg ; [Text] von Jens Peter Jacobsen (deutsch von Robert Franz Arnold) ; herausgegeben von Ulrich Krämer.

Albéniz, Isaac, *1860-1909.*
[Suite española, no. 1] — Suite espagnole : opus 47 / Isaac Albéniz ; herausgegeben von Ullrich Scheideler ; Fingersatz von Rolf Koenen. — *G. Henle*
786.21858   013325842

Albert, Eduard.
See **Fibich, Zdeněk, 1850-1900.** [Štědrý den. *Polyglot*] Štědrý den ; Vodník : melodramy = Der Heilige Abend ; Der Wassermann : Melodramen = Christmas eve ; The water sprite : melodramas : recitazione e piano / Zdeněk Fibich ; text Karel Jaromír Erben ; deutsche Übersetzung Marie Kwaysser und Eduard Albert ; English translation Judith Mabary.

Albinoni, Tomaso, *1671-1750.*
See **Ziani, Pietro Andrea, 1616-1684.** [Sonatas, trumpet, strings, continuo, D major] Sonata à 6 für Trompete, 2 Violinen, 3 Violen & B.c. / Pietro Andrea Ziani ; [herausgegeben von] Konrad Ruhland.

Albrecht, George Alexander, *1935-*
See **Furtwängler, Wilhelm, 1886-1954.** [Symphonies, no. 1, B minor] Sinfonie Nr. 1, H-Moll / Wilhelm Furtwängler ; herausgegeben von George Alexander Albrecht.

See **Furtwängler, Wilhelm, 1886-1954.** [Symphonies, no. 2, E minor] Sinfonie Nr. 2 E-moll / Wilhelm Furtwängler ; herausgegeben von George Alexander Albrecht.

See **Furtwängler, Wilhelm, 1886-1954.** [Symphonies, no. 3, C sharp minor] Sinfonie Nr. 3 cis-moll / Wilhelm Furtwängler ; herausgegeben von George Alexander Albrecht.

See **Furtwängler, Wilhelm, 1886-1954.** [Symphonisches Konzert] Sinfonisches Konzert für Klavier und Orchester / Wilhelm Furtwängler ; herausgegeben von George Alexander Albrecht.

See **Furtwängler, Wilhelm, 1886-1954.** Te Deum : für gemischten Chor, 4 Solostimmen und Orchester / Wilhelm Furtwängler ; herausgegeben von George Alexander Albrecht.

[Album für die Jugend. Selections]
See **Schumann, Robert, 1810-1856.** [Album für die Jugend. *Selections*]

Albumblätter
See **Kirchner, Theodor, 1823-1903.** [Albumblätter, op. 80] Albumblätter

[Albumblätter, op. 80]
See **Kirchner, Theodor, 1823-1903.** [Albumblätter, op. 80]

Alderete Acosta, Igmar.
[Concertos, marimba, orchestra (2004)] — Concierto no. 1 para marimba y orquesta / Igmar Alderete Acosta. — *Junta de Andalucía, Consejería de Cultura*
784.2843186   014053148

Aledort, Andy.
See **Hendrix, Jimi.** Blue wild angel : live at the Isle of Wight / Jimi Hendrix ; music transcriptions Andy Aledort.

Aleotti, Raffaella, *ca. 1570-ca. 1646.*
Sacrae cantiones : quinque, septem, octo & decem vocibus decantandae / Raffaella Aleotti ; edited by C. Ann Carruthers ; introduction by Thomas W. Bridges. — *Broude Trust*
782.526   013750188

Alice - the musical
See **Johnson, Mark.** Alice - the musical

All my trials
All my trials / [arr.] Bob Chilcott. — *Oxford University Press*
782.5253   013083866

All you need is love
See **Lennon, John, 1940-1980.** [All you need is love; *arr.*] All you need is love

[All you need is love; arr.]
See **Lennon, John, 1940-1980.** [All you need is love; *arr.*]

All you who are to mirth inclined
See **Bigler, Dwight.** [All you who are to mirth inclined; *arr.*] All you who are to mirth inclined

[All you who are to mirth inclined; arr.]
See **Bigler, Dwight.** [All you who are to mirth inclined; *arr.*]

The all-time greatest film songs
The all-time greatest film songs : [26 of the best songs from the silver screen : arranged for piano and voice with guitar chord boxes] — *Wise*
783.2421542   013326341

The all-time greatest million-selling singles.
The all-time greatest million-selling singles. — *Wise*
783.242166   013382742

Alla marcia
See **Allen, Michael, 1947-** Alla marcia

Allain, Richard.
Salve Regina : for SSAATTBB chorus / Richard Allain. — *Novello & Co*
782.5324   013360921

See **Portman, Rachel.** [Little prince. Birds; *arr.*] The birds : from The little prince : for SSA and piano / Rachel Portman ; [arr. by Richard Allain]

See **Portman, Rachel.** [Little prince. Lamplighters; *arr.*] The lamplighters : from The little prince ; for SSA and piano / Rachel Portman ; [arr. by Richard Allain]

See **Portman, Rachel.** [Little prince. Look at the stars; *arr.*] Look at the stars : from The little prince ; for SSA and piano / Rachel Portman ; [arr. by Richard Allain]

See **Portman, Rachel.** [Little prince. Roses; *arr.*] The roses : from The little prince : for SSA and piano / Rachel Portman ; [arr. by Richard Allain]

See **Portman, Rachel.** [Little prince. Stars; *arr.*] The stars : from The little prince ; for SSA and piano / Rachel Portman ; [arr. by Richard Allain]

[Allegretto con variazioni, keyboard instrument, W. XII, 2, G major]
See **Bach, Johann Christoph Friedrich, 1732-1795.** [Allegretto con variazioni, keyboard instrument, W. XII, 2, G major]

Alleluia
See **Sametz, Steven, 1954-** Alleluia

Allen, Anita.
See **Hewitt, Daniel.** Henry VIII : the break with Rome.

See **Hewitt, Daniel.** [Henry VIII. *Selections*] Henry VIII : the break with Rome : assembly pack / written by Daniel Dalton ; music [& lyrics] by Dan Hewitt.

See **Hewitt, Daniel.** [Magic tree. *Selections*] The magic tree : a story for Christmas : assembly pack.

See **Hewitt, Daniel.** The Spanish Armada : the invasion of England.

See **Hewitt, Daniel.** [Spanish Armada. *Selections*] The Spanish Armada : the invasion of England : assembly pack.

See **Hewitt, Daniel.** [Trojan horse. *Selections*] The Trojan horse : the fall of Troy : assembly pack.

See **Spencer, Tim.** The ancient Olympics : the legend of Callipateira.

See **Spencer, Tim.** [Ancient Olympics. *Selections*] The ancient Olympics : the Olympic traditions : assembly pack.

See **Spencer, Tim.** [Trafalgar. *Selections*] Trafalgar : Napolean's navy : assembly pack / written by Daniel Dalton ; music [& lyrics] by Tim Spencer.

See **Spencer, Tim.** [Trafalgar. *Selections*] Trafalgar : Nelson's finest hour : assembly pack / written by Daniel Dalton ; musc [& lyrics] by Tim Spencer.

Allen, Chris, *1954-*
See **Grieg, Edvard, 1843-1907.** [Piano music. *Selections; arr.*] A Grieg suite : 3 movements based on Grieg's 'Lyric pieces' arranged for school string ensemble / arranged by Chris Allen.

Allen, Michael, *1947-*
Alla marcia : for brass quintet / Michael Allen. — *Da Capo Music*
785.91951897   013351624

Alley, John.
See **Handel, George Frideric, 1685-1759.** [Sonatas, flute, continuo. *Selections.*] Sonatas for flute [and continuo] Book 1 / Handel ; flute part edited by Paul Edmund-Davies ; keyboard realisation by John Alley.

See **Handel, George Frideric, 1685-1759.** [Sonatas, flute, continuo. *Selections.*] Sonatas for flute [and continuo] Book 3 / Handel ; flute part edited by Paul Edmund-Davies ; keyboard realisation by John Alley.

See **Handel, George Frideric, 1685-1759.** [Sonatas, recorder, continuo. *Selections.*] Sonatas for flute [and continuo] Book 2 / Handel ; flute part edited by Paul Edmund-Davies ; keyboard realisation by John Alley.

Allroggen, Gerhard.
See **Hoffmann, E. T. A. 1776-1822.** [Kreuz an der Ostsee] Zacharias Werners Trauerspiel "Das Kreuz an der Ostsee" : mit der Bühnenmusik von E.T.A. Hoffmann ; Ballettmusik "Arlequin" / E.T.A. Hoffmann ; hrsg. aus dem Nachlaß von Friedrich Schnapp ; unter Mitarbeit von Gerhard Allroggen und Michael Kohlhäufl von Thomas Kohlhase.

See **Hoffmann, E. T. A. 1776-1822.** [Vocal music. *Selections*] Kleine Vokalkompsitionen und Klaviersonaten / E.T.A. Hoffmann ; aus dem Nachlaß von Friedrich Schnapp und unter Mitarbeit von Gerhard Allroggen ; herausgegeben von Alexander Erhard und Thomas Kohlhase.

Alma redemptoris
See **Palestrina, Giovanni Pierluigi da, 1525?-1594.** [Motets (1584 : Voices (4)). *Selections*] Alma redemptoris

Alter Bridge (Musical group)
One day remains / Alter Bridge. — *Hal Leonard*
783.242166   013191642

Altnikol, Johann Christoph, *1719-1759.*
[Mass, D minor] — Missa : Kyrie-Gloria-Messe in d : per soli (SATB), coro (SATB), 2 violini, viola e basso continuo / Johann Christoph Altnickol ; herausgegeben von Clemens Harasim. — *Erstausg.* — *Carus*
782.53232   013887057

Alvarez Quintero, Joaquín, *1873-1944.*
See **Serrano, José, 1873-1941.** El mal de amores ; La mala sombra : sainetes líricos en un acto / José Serrano ; libretos, Joaquín y Serafín Álvarez Quintero ; edición crítica, Miguel Roa.

Amazing phrasing
See **Taylor, Dennis, saxophonist.** Amazing phrasing

America the beautiful
See **Ward, Samuel A., 1847-1903.** [America the beautiful; *arr.*] America the beautiful

[**America the beautiful;** *arr.*]
See **Ward, Samuel A., 1847-1903.** [America the beautiful; *arr.*]

[**American songs**]
Three American songs : SATB / arranged by Jonathan Rathbone. — *Edition Peters*
782.542   013304769

[**Amor und Psyche. Sonata**]
See **Zenger, Max, 1837-1911.** [Amor und Psyche. Sonata]

Amores
See **LeFanu, Nicola.** Amores

The amorous hexachord
The amorous hexachord : madrigal fantasies from the Tregian manuscript / Pallavicino, Bianciardi, and Giovannelli ; edited by Hannah Davidson. — *Viola da Gamba Society of America*
785.76195   013646320

Amos, Tori.
The beekeeper / Tori Amos. — *Amsco Publishing*
783.242166   013323485

An die Musik
An die Musik : 9 classical pieces arranged for string quartet / [arr. by] John Kember. — *Schott*
785.7194   013192068

The ancient Olympics
See **Spencer, Tim.** [Ancient Olympics. *Selections*] The ancient Olympics

See **Spencer, Tim.** The ancient Olympics

[**Ancient Olympics.** *Selections*]
See **Spencer, Tim.** [Ancient Olympics. *Selections*]

And every stone shall cry
See **Chilcott, Bob.** And every stone shall cry

And is it true?
See **Parry, Ben.** And is it true?

[**And peace on earth. Put memory away.** *Vocal score*]
See **Chilcott, Bob.** [And peace on earth. Put memory away. *Vocal score*]

Andante, theme & variations [from] (Duo for guitars, op. 34)
See **Sor, Fernando, 1778-1839.** [Encouragement. *Selections; arr.*] Andante, theme & variations [from] (Duo for guitars, op. 34)

Ander, Owe.
See **Lindblad, Adolf Fredrik, 1801-1878.** [Symphonies, no. 2, D major] Symfoni D-dur = Symphony, D major / Adolf Fredrik Lindblad ; utgiven av Owe Ander.

Anderson, Robert, *1927 Aug. 20-*
See **Elgar, Edward, 1857-1934** [Concertos, violoncello, orchestra, op. 85, E minor; *arr.*] Concerto in E minor, opus 85, for violoncello and orchestra / Edward Elgar ; arrangement for violoncello and piano by the composer.

See **Elgar, Edward, 1857-1934.** The crown of India.

Anderson, Stikkan.
See **Andersson, Benny.** [Mamma mia! *Selections; arr.*] Mamma mia! : choral highlights : instrumental pak / arranged by Mac Huff.

See **Andersson, Benny.** [Mamma mia! *Selections; arr.*] Mamma mia! : choral highlights : SAB / arranged by Mac Huff.

See **Andersson, Benny.** [Mamma mia! *Selections; arr.*] Mamma mia! : choral highlights : SATB / arranged by Mac Huff.

See **Andersson, Benny.** [Mamma mia! *Selections; arr.*] Mamma mia! : choral highlights : SSA / arranged by Mac Huff.

Andersson, Benny.
[Mamma mia! *Selections; arr.*] — Mamma mia! : choral highlights : instrumental pak / arranged by Mac Huff. — *Hal Leonard*
785.594195   013220029

[Mamma mia! *Selections; arr.*] — Mamma mia! : choral highlights : SAB / arranged by Mac Huff. — *Hal Leonard*
782.542   013219992

[Mamma mia! *Selections; arr.*] — Mamma mia! : choral highlights : SATB / arranged by Mac Huff. — *Hal Leonard*
782.542   013219975

[Mamma mia! *Selections; arr.*] — Mamma mia! : choral highlights : SSA / arranged by Mac Huff. — *Hal Leonard*
782.642   013220010

André, Johann Anton, *1775-1842.*
[Trios, flutes (3), op. 29, G major] — Trio G-Dur, für 3 Querflöten = Trio G major, for three flutes, opus 29, 1805 / Johann Anton André ; herausgegeben von Peter Thalheimer. — *NotaBene*
785.832193   014497790

Andre, Mark, *1964-*
—als— I : für Bassklarinette, Violoncello und Klavier, 2001 / Mark André. — *Ricordi*
785.24193   013771071

Andreas, Carolus.
Magnificat & Nunc dimittis : faux-bourdon service : SATB / Carolus Andreas. — *Anglo-American Music Publishers*
782.5326   013594264

Andrée, Elfrida, *1841-1929.*
[Trios, piano, strings, C minor] — Two chamber works / Elfrida Andrée ; edited by Katherine L. Axtell. — *A-R Editions*
785.28193   014746024

Andrée, Elfrida, *1841-1929.* Quartets,
See **Andrée, Elfrida, 1841-1929.** [Trios, piano, strings, C minor] Two chamber works / Elfrida Andrée ; edited by Katherine L. Axtell.

Andrew Lloyd Webber audition songbook
See **Lloyd Webber, Andrew, 1948-** [Musicals. *Selections; arr.*] Andrew Lloyd Webber audition songbook

Andrew Lloyd Webber favorites.
See **Lloyd Webber, Andrew, 1948-** [Musicals.
Selections; arr.] Andrew Lloyd Webber
favorites.

Andrew Lloyd Webber showstoppers
See **Lloyd Webber, Andrew, 1948-** [Musicals.
Selections; arr.] Andrew Lloyd Webber
showstoppers

The angel Gabriel
See **Chilcott, Bob.** The angel Gabriel

The angel Gabriel
The angel Gabriel : for mezzo-soprano with
optional tenor solo, mixed choir (SATB) and
harp / [Basque traditional ; arranged by] Robert
A.M. Ross. — *Oxford University Press*
782.5281723   013472203

The angel Gabriel : for soprano solo, upper
voices (SSAA) and harp / [Basque traditional ;
arranged by] Robert A.M. Ross. — *Oxford
University Press*
782.6281723   013472190

Angelus
See **Davies, Peter Maxwell, 1934-** Angelus

Angelus Silesius, *1624-1677*.
See **Bingham, Judith.** God would be born in
thee : carol for SATB & organ : (2004) / Judith
Bingham ; text, Silesius Angelus.

See **Three carols for Christmas** : for
unaccompanied mixed choir (SATB).

Anglo tango
See **Bayliss, Colin.** Anglo tango

Angstenberger, Hermann.
See **Rathgeber, Valentin, 1682-1750.** [Missale
tum rurale tum civile. Missa brevis, B flat major]
Missa brevis in B : für Soli (SATB), SATB,
Streicher und Orgel / Johann Valentin
Rathgeber ; herausgegeben von Friedrich
Hägele ; Orgelstimme von Hermann
Angstenberger.

**Another reason why I don't keep a gun in the
house**
See **Cipullo, Tom.** Another reason why I don't
keep a gun in the house

Anthem, The priests of the Lord
See **Goddard, Mark.** Anthem, The priests of
the Lord

**Anthology for The musician's guide to theory
and analysis**
Anthology for The musician's guide to theory
and analysis / [compiled by] Jane Piper
Clendinning, Elizabeth West Marvin. — *W.W.
Norton & Co.*
780   001312079

Anthology of Baroque music
Anthology of Baroque music : music in Western
Europe, 1580-1750 / edited by John Walter Hill.
— *W. W. Norton & Co.*
780.9032   013212022

Anthony, James R.
See **Lully, Jean Baptiste, 1632-1687** [Ballets.
Vocal scores. Selections] Ballet des saisons ; Les
amours déguisés ; Ballet royal de Flore /
Jean-Baptiste Lully ; édition [par Ballet des
saisons] de James P. Cassaro ; édition [par Les
amours déguisés] de James R. Anthony et
Rebecca Harris-Warrick ; édition [par Ballet
royal de flore] d'Albert Cohen ; réduction
clavier-chant, Noam A. Krieger.

[Antología (Archivo Musical de Moxos)]
Antología / Archivo Musical de Moxos ;
[transcrita y editada por] Piotr Nawrot. — *1. ed.*
— *Fondo editorial APAC*
780   013043834

Antología
See **[Antología (Archivo Musical de Moxos)]**
Antología

The Anton Webern collection
See **Webern, Anton, 1883-1945.** [Songs.
Selections] The Anton Webern collection

Antonii, Giovanni Battista degli, *ca. 1660-1698*.
[Ricercate, violoncello, op. 1] — Ricercate
sopra il violoncello o clavicembalo ; e, Ricercate
per il violino / Giovanni Battista degli Antonii ;
edizione della partitura e prefazione a cura di
Marc Vanscheeuwijck. — *Forni*
785.71921876   013887058

Anything goes
Anything goes : & three other songs / arranged
by David Nield. — *Novello*
782.542164   013748296

[Apis amata]
See **Fesch, Willem de, 1687-1761.** [Apis amata]

Aquilon et Orithie
See **Rameau, Jean-Philippe, 1683-1764.**
Aquilon et Orithie

Ar gyfer heddiw'r bore'n faban bach
Ar gyfer heddiw'r bore'n faban bach = For us
this Christmas morning : traditional Welsh
folk-song arranged for SSAA choir and piano /
by Jayne Davies ; English text by Rhian Davies.
— *Roberton Publications*
782.6281723   013193235

Arakawa, Yoichi.
Rock guitar chords and accompaniment : [your
ultimate step-by-step manual to rock
rhythm-guitar!] / by Yoichi Arakawa. — *Six
Strings Music*
787.87193166   006898953

Archer, Richard, *1976 or 7-*
Stars of CCTV : guitar tab edition / Hard-Fi. —
Wise Publications
783.242166   013383492

Architechtonia
See **Harrison, Sadie, 1965-** Architechtonia

Archivo Musical de Moxos.
See **Antología** / Archivo Musical de Moxos ;
[transcrita y editada por] Piotr Nawrot.

Are we nearly there yet-?
See **Johnson, Mark** Are we nearly there yet-?

Aresi, Stefano.
See **Porpora, Nicola, 1686-1768.** [Duetti latini
per la passione di Gesù Cristo] Sei duetti latini
sulla passione di nostro signore Gesù Cristo ;
Motetti per Angiola Moro / Nicola Antonio
Porpora ; edizione critica a cura di Stefano
Aresi.

Aria, Hier in meines Vaters Stätte
See **Bach, Johann Sebastian, 1685-1750.**
[Liebster Jesu, mein Verlangen. Hier in meines
Vaters Stätte] Aria, Hier in meines Vaters Stätte

Aria, Leget euch dem Heiland unter
See **Bach, Johann Sebastian, 1685-1750.**
[Himmelskönig, sei willkommen. Leget euch
dem Heiland unter] Aria, Leget euch dem
Heiland unter

Aria, Oh I feel the friendly blow
See **Pepusch, John Christopher, 1667-1752.**
[Death of Dido. Oh I feel the friendly blow]
Aria, Oh I feel the friendly blow

Arietta
See **Cooke, Arnold.** [Arietta, recorder, piano]
Arietta

Arietta for pianoforte
See **Cooke, Arnold.** [Arietta, piano] Arietta for
pianoforte

[Arietta, piano]
See **Cooke, Arnold.** [Arietta, piano]

[Arietta, recorder, piano]
See **Cooke, Arnold.** [Arietta, recorder, piano]

Arioso and scherzo
See **Cooke, Arnold.** Arioso and scherzo

Arise, shine
See **Rutter, John, 1945-** Arise, shine

Armide
See **Lully, Jean Baptiste, 1632-1687** [Armide.
Vocal score] Armide

[Armide. *Vocal score*]
See **Lully, Jean Baptiste, 1632-1687** [Armide.
Vocal score]

Armstrong, Craig.
See **The violin** : a collection : new and recent
repertoire for violin with piano accompaniment /
Craig Armstrong ... [et al.]

Arnold, Malcolm.
[You know what sailors are. Scherzetto; *arr.*] —
Scherzetto : for clarinet & piano / Malcolm
Arnold. — *Queen's Temple Publications*
788.62   013271629

Arnold, Malcolm. Scottish dances.
See **The violin** : a collection : new and recent
repertoire for violin with piano accompaniment /
Craig Armstrong ... [et al.]

Arnold, Robert Franz, *1872-1938*.
See **Gurre-Lieder** : für Soli, Chor und
Orchester : kritischer Bericht / Arnold
Schönberg ; [Text] von Jens Peter Jacobsen
(deutsch von Robert Franz Arnold) ;
herausgegeben von Ulrich Krämer.

Arnold, Samuel, *1740-1802*.
Polly : an opera : (1777) / music by Johann
Christoph Pepusch ; rearrang'd and new airs
compos'd by Samuel Arnold ; libretto by John
Gay ; revis'd by George Colman, the elder ;
edited by Robert Hoskins. — *Artaria Editions*
782.1   013107352

Arpeggio finder
See **Johnson, Chad.** Arpeggio finder

Arrangements of orchestral works I
See **Bach, Carl Philipp Emanuel, 1714-1788**
[Concertos, harpsichord, H. 242, F major]
Arrangements of orchestral works I

[Arte del violino. Capricci]
See **Locatelli, Pietro Antonio, 1695-1764.** [Arte
del violino. Capricci]

L'arte della variazione, per organo
See **Genesi, Mario G.** L'arte della variazione,
per organo

The Arundel choirbook
See **[Lambeth choirbook.]** The Arundel
choirbook

As I went with Tom to Tywyn
As I went with Tom to Tywyn = [Wrth fynd efo
Deio i Dywyn : for unison treble voices &
piano] / arranged by Nigel E. Jones. — *Boosey
& Hawkes*
782.7642162009429   013361287

As it was
See **Grange, Philip.** As it was

As Joseph was a-walking
As Joseph was a-walking : for mixed choir (SATB), oboe and organ / [traditional, arr.] Ian Brentnall. — *Oxford University Press*
782.5281723   013177896

Ascendit Deus
See **Handl, Jacob, 1550-1591.** [Musicum opus, 2. tomus. Ascendit Deus in iubilatione] Ascendit Deus

Ascendo ad Patrem
See **Palestrina, Giovanni Pierluigi da, 1525?-1594.** [Motets (1572). Ascendo ad Patrem] Ascendo ad Patrem

Ascolta i preghi
See **Hasse, Johann Adolf, 1699-1783.** Ascolta i preghi

The ash grove
The ash grove : SSAATTBB : Welsh traditional / arranged by Jonathan Rathbone. — *Edition Peters*
782.542   013304773

Ashbee, Andrew.
See **Jenkins, John, 1592-1678.** [Fantasia-suites, organ, viols (4). *Selections*] Fantasia-suites : for two trebles (violins), two basses (viols) and organ / John Jenkins ; edited by Andrew Ashbee.

Ashcroft, Richard, *1971-*
See [Songs. *Selections*] This is music : the singles 92-98 / The Verve.

El asombro de Damasco
See **Luna, Pablo, 1879-1942.** El asombro de Damasco

Associated Board of the Royal Schools of Music (Great Britain)
Music medals recorder ensemble pieces. — *Associated Board of the Royal Schools of Music :*
785.836   013382222

Music medals saxophone ensemble pieces. — *Associated Board of the Royal Schools of Music :*
785.87   013441370

Selected piano exam pieces : 2005-2006 / The Associated Board of the Royal Schools of Music. — *Associated Board of the Royal Schools of Music*
786.2   013281700

Selected violin examination pieces : 2005-2007 / The Associated Board of the Royal Schools of Music. — *Associated Board of the Royal Schools of Music*
787.2   013281745

Selected violin examination pieces : 2005-2007 / The Associated Board of the Royal Schools of Music. — *Associated Board of the Royal Schools of Music*
787.2   013281760

Aston, Hugh, *b. ca. 1485.*
[Missa Te Deum] — Missa Te deum laudamus / Hugh Aston ; edited by Nick Sandon. — *Antico Edition*
782.53232   013087141

Aston, Michael, arranger.
See **Walton, William, 1902-1983.** Duets for children / William Walton ; edited by Michael Aston.

Aston, Peter
If ye love me : for mixed voices and organ / Peter Aston. — *Encore Publications*
782.5265   013199443

Aston, Peter.
[Sonatas, bassoon, piano (2005)] — Sonata for bassoon and piano / by Peter Aston. — *Phylloscopus Publications*
788.58183   013561047

Asyla
See **Adès, Thomas, 1971-** Asyla

Athalia
See **Handel, George Frideric, 1685-1759** Athalia

Athlete (Musical group)
Tourist / Athlete. — *Wise Publications*
783.242166   013382614

Atys, *1715-1784.*
[Sonatas, flutes (2), op. 1] — Six sonates en duo : en forme de conversation : pour deux flûtes traversières : Paris s.d. / Atys. — *Studio per edizioni scelte*
785.832192183   013771072

Audelay, John, *fl. 1426.*
See **Boyle, Rory.** Flower of all : a carol of the Incarnation : SSAA chorus / Rory Boyle ; text, John Audelay, c.1426 (adapted).

Auden, W. H. *1907-1973.*
See **D'Amico, Matteo, 1955-** The entertainment of the senses : cabaret musicale per voce e strumenti (2005) / Matteo D'Amico ; su testi di W.H. Auden and Ch. Kallman.

Audition songs for female singers.
Audition songs for female singers. R&B anthems : nine great songs ideal for auditions. — *Wise*
783.6421643   013441494

Audition songs for male singers.
Audition songs for male singers. R&B anthems : ten great songs ideal for auditions. — *Wise*
783.2421643   013434068

Audition songs for male singers. The rat pack : Frank Sinatra, Dean Martin, Sammy Davis, jr. : ten great songs ideal for auditions. — *Wise*
783.842164   013441477

Audition songs.
Audition songs. Number one hits. — *Wise Publications*
783.642166   013268771

Audition sourcebook
Audition sourcebook : female singers : a collection of 22 songs covering eight different vocal styles : arranged for piano, voice and guitar, with sound-alike backing tracks on 2 CDs. — *Wise Publications*
783.242164   013281431

Audition sourcebook : male singers : a collection of 22 songs : covering seven different vocal styles : arranged for piano, voice and guitar, with sound-alike backing tracks on 2 CDs. — *Wise*
783.242164   013374888

Aue!
See **Marshall, Christopher, 1956-** Aue!

Augsbach, Horst.
See **Quantz, Johann Joachim, 1697-1773.** [Concertos, flute, string orchestra, QV 5:149, F major] Flötenkonzert in F : Concerto QV 5:149, per flauto traverso, 2 violini, viola e basso continuo (violoncello, contrabbasso, cembalo) / Johann Joachim Quantz ; Generalbassaussetzung von Siegfried Petrenz.

Un' aura amorosa
See **Mozart, Wolfgang Amadeus, 1756-1791** [Così fan tutte. Aura amorosa; *arr.*] Un' aura amorosa

Ausgewählte Bassmotetten für Bass und B.c.
See **Leonarda, Isabella, 1620-1704.** [Motets, bass, continuo. *Selections*] Ausgewählte Bassmotetten für Bass und B.c.

Ausseur, Agnès.
See **O'Neill, John, 1955-** Developing jazz technique for flute : improvisation, style, special effects = Technique de jazz pour flûte : improvisation, style, effets spéciaux = Jazztechnik für Querflöte : Improvisation, Stilistik, Spezialeffekte / John O'Neill ; traduction Agnès Ausseur ; Übersetzung Heike Brühl.

L'autografo dei quartetti "Milanesi"
See **Mozart, Wolfgang Amadeus, 1756-1791.** [Quartets, strings, K. 155-160] L'autografo dei quartetti "Milanesi"

Autreau, Jacques, *1657?-1745.*
See **Rameau, Jean-Philippe, 1683-1764.** [Platée. *Vocal score*] Platée : ballet bouffon en un prologue et trois actes : version 1749, version 1745 (compléments) / [musique de Jean-Philippe Rameau] ; livret de Jacques Autreau ; révisé par Adrien-Joseph Valois d'Orville et Balot de Sovot ; édition de M. Elizabeth C. Barlet ; réduction clavier-chant de François Saint-Yves.

Autumn leaves
See **Montague, Stephen.** Autumn leaves

Ave Regina coelorum
See **Hasse, Johann Adolf, 1699-1783.** Ave Regina coelorum

Ave verum corpus
See **Mozart, Wolfgang Amadeus, 1756-1791** [Ave verum corpus; *arr.*] Ave verum corpus

[Ave verum corpus; *arr.*]
See **Mozart, Wolfgang Amadeus, 1756-1791** [Ave verum corpus; *arr.*]

Awayday
See **Gorb, Adam, 1958-** Awayday

Axtell, Katherine Leigh.
See **Andrée, Elfrida, 1841-1929.** [Trios, piano, strings, C minor] Two chamber works / Elfrida Andrée ; edited by Katherine L. Axtell.

Ayre, Alex.
See **Byrd, William, 1542 or 3-1623.** [Emendemus in melius; *arr.*] Emendemus in melius : à 5 / William Byrd.

See **Mozart, Wolfgang Amadeus, 1756-1791** [Divertimenti, K270, B♭ major. Allegro molto; *arr.*] Divertimento à 6 in C, K. 270 / W.A. Mozart ; recorder arrangement by Alex Ayre.

See **Mozart, Wolfgang Amadeus, 1756-1791** [Divertimenti, K270, B♭ major. *Selections; arr.*] Divertimento à 6 in C, K. 270. Part II / W.A. Mozart ; recorder arrangement by Alex Ayre.

See **Palestrina, Giovanni Pierluigi da, 1525?-1594.** [Motets (1569). Tu es Petrus; *arr.*] Tu es petrus : à 7 / Palestrina.

Az hit
See **Kurtág, György.** Az hit

Azioni musicali
See **Badings, Henk, 1907-1987.** Azioni musicali

Bacchus bagatelles
See **Grange, Philip.** Bacchus bagatelles

Bach, Carl Philipp Emanuel, *1714-1788*
[Concertos, harpsichord, H. 242, F major] — Arrangements of orchestral works I / Carl Philipp Emanuel Bach ; edited by Douglas A. Lee. — *Packard Humanities Institute*
786.4186   013825297

[Concertos, oboe, string orchestra, H. 466, B♭ major] — Oboe concertos / Carl Philipp Emanuel Bach ; edited by Janet K. Page. — *Packard Humanities Institute*
784.72852186   013810205

Bach, Carl Philipp Emanuel, *1714-1788*.
[Fantasien, violin, keyboard instrument, H. 536, F minor; *arr.*] — I sentimenti di Carl Philipp Emanuel Bach : (1982) : trascrizione per flauto, arpa ed archi della Clavier-Fantasie con accompagnemento di un violino (1787) = Transkription für Flöte, Harfe und Streicher der Clavier-Fantasie mit Begleitung einer Violine (1787) = transcription for flute, harp, and strings of the Clavier-Fantasie with violin accompaniment (1787) / [composed by C.P.E. Bach ; arr. by] Hans Werner Henze. — *Schott*
784.724   014457017

Bach, Carl Philipp Emanuel, *1714-1788*. Concertos,
See **Bach, Carl Philipp Emanuel, 1714-1788** [Concertos, oboe, string orchestra, H. 466, B♭ major] Oboe concertos / Carl Philipp Emanuel Bach ; edited by Janet K. Page.

Bach, Carl Philipp Emanuel, *1714-1788* Concertos,
See **Bach, Carl Philipp Emanuel, 1714-1788** [Concertos, harpsichord, H. 242, F major] Arrangements of orchestral works I / Carl Philipp Emanuel Bach ; edited by Douglas A. Lee.

Bach, Johann Christoph Friedrich, *1732-1795*.
[Allegretto con variazioni, keyboard instrument, W. XII, 2, G major] — Partita on 'Morgen kommt der Weihnachtsmann' : ('Twinkle, twinkle little star') : for organ (manuals only) / Johann Christoph Friedrich Bach ; edited by David Patrick. — *Fitzjohn Music Publications*
786.51825   013243758

Bach, Johann Ludwig, *1677-1731*. O Herr, ich bin dein Knecht.
See **Musik am Meininger Hofe** / herausgegeben von Ulrike Feld und Ulrich Leisinger.

Bach, Johann Sebastian, *1685-1750*.
[Ach Herr, mich armen Sünder (Cantata). *English & German*] — Ach Herr, mich armen Sünder : BWV 135/BC A 100 : Kantate zum 3. Sonntag nach Trinitatis für Soli (ATB), Chor (SATB), Zink, Posaune, 2 oboen, 2 Violinen, Viola und Basso continuo = Ah Lord, spare thou this sinner : cantata for the third Sunday after Trinity for soli (ATB), choir (SATB), cornett, trombone, 2 oboes, 2 violins, viola, and basso continuo / Johann Sebastian Bach ; herausgegeben von Wolfram Ensslin ; English version by Henry S. Drinker. — *Urtext.* — *Carus*
782.524   013714858

[Gott, der Herr, ist Sonn' und Schild. *English & German*] — Gott der Herr ist Sonn und Schild : BWV 79 / BC 184 : Kantate zum Reformationsfest : für Soli (SAB), Chor (SATB), 2 Hörner, Pauken, 2 Traversflöten ad libitum, 2 Oboen, 2 Violinen, Viola und Basso continuo = God the Lord is sun and shield : cantata for the Reformation Festival : for soli (SAB), choir (SATB), 2 horns, timpani, 2 flutes ad libitum, 2 oboes, 2 violins, viola and basso continuo / Johann Sebastian Bach ; herausgegeben von Uwe Wolf ; English version by Jutta and Vernon Wicker and Catherine Winkworth. — *Carus*
782.524   013714792

[Herr Gott, dich loben wir (Cantata). *English & German*] — Herr Gott, dich loben wir : BWV 16/BC A 23 : Kantate zum Neujahrstag für Soli (ATB), Chor (SATB), Corno da caccia, 2 Oboen, Oboe da caccia (Violetta), 2 Violinen, Viola und Basso continuo = Lord God, Thy praise we sing : cantata for New Year's Day for soli (ATB), choir (SATB), corno da caccia, 2 oboes, oboe da caccia (violetta), 2 violins, viola, and basso continuo / Johann Sebastian Bach ; herausgegeben von Michael Märker ; English version by Henry S. Drinker. — *Carus*
782.524   013714778

[Himmel lacht, die Erde jubilieret. *English & German*] — Der Himmel lacht! Die Erde jubilieret : BWV 31 / BC A 55b, Kantate zum ersten Ostertag : für Soli (STB), Chor (SSATB), 3 Trompeten, Pauken, Oboe, 2 Oboen ad lib., Taille ad lib., Fagott ad lib., 2 Violinen, 2 Violen und Basso continuo = The heavens laugh, the earth exults in gladness : cantata for Easter Sunday : for soli (STB), choir (SSATB), 3 trumpets, timpani, oboe, 2 oboes ad lib., taille ad lib., bassoon ad lib., 2 violins, 2 violas and basso continuo / Johann Sebastian Bach ; herausgegeben von Michael Märker ; English version by Henry S. Drinker. — *Carus*
782.5241727   013714787

[Himmelskönig, sei willkommen. Leget euch dem Heiland unter] — Aria, Leget euch dem Heiland unter : from cantata BWV 182 : for alto, recorder (or flute) and continuo / J.S. Bach. — *Green Man Press*
783.6842   013597019

[Inventions, harpsichord, BWV 772-786] — Two-part inventions / J.S. Bach ; edited by Christopher Taylor. — *G. Schirmer*
786.21874   013191028

[Italienisches Konzert] — The Italian concerto : BWV 971 / J. S. Bach. — *Urtext performing ed.* — *Kevin Mayhew*
786.4186   013173104

[Jagdkantate. Schafe können sicher weiden; *arr.*] — Sheep may safely graze : aria from secular cantata no. 208 / by J.S. Bach ; arranged for violin (or viola, or 'cello) and pianoforte by Watson Forbes. — *Oxford University Press*
787.2   013424681

[Liebster Jesu, mein Verlangen. Hier in meines Vaters Stätte] — Aria, Hier in meines Vaters Stätte : from cantata BWV 32 : for bass, violin and basso continuo / J.S. Bach. — *Green Man Press*
783.8925   013596985

[Lobet Gott in seinen Reichen. *English & German*] — Himmelfahrtsoratorium : Lobet Gott in seinen Reichen : BWV 11/BC D 9 : Oratorium Festo Ascensionis Christi : für Soli (SATB), Chor (SATB), 3 Trompeten, Pauken, 2 Traversflöten, 2 Oboen, 2 Violinen, Viola und Basso continuo = Oratorio for Ascension Day : Praise God on high in heaven : for soli (SATB), choir (SATB), 3 trumpets, timpani, 2 flutes, 2 oboes, 2 violins, viola, and basso continuo / Johann Sebastian Bach ; herausgegeben von Ulrich Leisinger ; English version by Henry S. Drinker. — *Urtext.* — *Carus*
782.523   013714772

[Masses, BWV 232, B minor] — Messe in h-Moll, BWV 232 : mit Sanctus in D-Dur (1724), BWV 232 / Johann Sebastian Bach ; commentary by Christoph Wolff. — *Limitierte ed.* — *Bärenreiter*
782.53232   014048771

[Sonatas, viola da gamba, harpsichord] — Sonatas BWV 1027, 1028, 1029 : for violoncello and keyboard / J.S. Bach ; [violoncello part edited by] Greenhouse & Dillingham. — *G. Schirmer*
787.4183   013374932

[Suites violoncello, BWV 1009, C major; *arr.*] — Suite für Violoncello Nr. 3, C-Dur, BWV 1009 / Johann Sebastian Bach ; für Klavier bearbeitet von Joachim Raff ; nach der Ausgabe von Rieter-Biedermann ; neu herausgegeben von Volker Tosta. — *Edition Nordstern*
786.21858   014501811

[Suites violoncello, BWV 1012, D major; *arr.*] — Suite für Violoncello Nr. 6, D-Dur, BWV 1012 / Johann Sebastian Bach ; für Klavier bearbeitet von Joachim Raff ; nach der Ausgabe von Rieter-Biedermann ; neu herausgegeben von Volker Tosta. — *Edition Nordstern*
786.21858   014502734

[Suites, orchestra, BWV 1067, B minor. Badinerie; *arr.*] — Badinerie / J.S. Bach ; arranged for tuba & piano by John Fletcher. — *Emerson Edition*
788.98   013360889

[Suites, violoncello, BWV 1010, E♭ major; *arr.*] — Suite für Violoncello Nr. 4, Es-Dur, BWV 1010 / von Johann Sebastian Bach ; für Klavier bearbeitet von Joachim Raff ; ... nach der Ausgabe von Rieter-Biedermann neu herausgegeben von Volker Tosta. — *Edition Nordstern*
786.21858   014501816

[Wachet auf, ruft uns die Stimme (Cantata). Wachet auf, ruft uns die Stimme; *arr.*] — Sleepers wake : SSATTBB / J.S. Bach ; arranged by Ben Parry. — *Edition Peters*
782.525   013305901

[Weihnachts-Oratorium. *English & German*] — Weihnachtsoratorium : Oratorium tempore nativitatis Christi : BWV 248 : für Soli (SSATB), Chor (SATB), 3 Trompeten, Pauken, 2 Hörner, 2 Querflöten, 2 Oboen/Oboen d'amore, 2 Oboen da caccia, 2 Violinen, Viola und Basso continuo : Urtext = Christmas oratorio : for soli (SSATB), choir (SATB), 3 trumpets, timpani, 2 horns, 2 flutes, 2 oboes/oboes d'amore, 2 oboes da caccia, 2 violins, viola, and basso continuo / Johann Sebastian Bach ; herausgegeben von Klaus Hofmann ; English version by Henry S. Drinker. — *Carus*
782.5231723   013714886

[Weihnachts-Oratorium. Bereite dich Zion, mit zärtlichen Trieben; *arr. English & German*] — Prepare thyself, Zion : unison treble / J. S. Bach ; arranged by B. Wayne Bisbee. — *Boosey & Hawkes*
782.6625   013243843

[Wir müssen durch viel Trübsal in das Reich Gottes eingehen. *English & German*] — Wir müssen durch viel Trübsal in das Reich Gottes eingehen : BWV 146/BC A 70 : Kantate zum Sonntag Jubilate für Soli (SATB), Chor (SATB), Traversflöte, 2 Oboen/Oboen d'amore, Taille, 2 Violinen, Viola, obligate Orgel und Basso continuo = Through bitter tribulation we enter into God's kingdom : cantata for the third Sunday after Easter for soli (STB), choir (SATB), flute, 2 oboes/oboes d'amore, taille, 2 violins, viola, organ obbligato, and basso continuo / Johann Sebastian Bach ; herausgegeben von Anja Morgenstern ; English version by Henry S. Drinker. — *Urtext.* — *Carus*
782.524   013714867

See **60 progressive solos for classical guitar :** featuring the music of the world's greatest composers: Bach, Handel, Mozart, Beethoven, and Brahms / arranged by Mark Phillips.

See **Riehm, Rolf, 1937-** Adieu, Marie, mon amour : drei Liebeslieder in den Tod : nach Klavierstücken von Johann Sebastian Bach : für Bratsche und Akkordeon, 2002-2003 / Rolf Riehm.

See **Vivaldi, Antonio**, *1678-1741* [Selections; *arr.*] Vivaldi gold : the essential collection.

Bach, Johann Sebastian, *1685-1750.*
Jagdkantate.
See **Flexible woodwind trios :** baroque / arr. Karen Evans.

Bach, Johann Sebastian, *1685-1750.* **O Ewigkeit, du Donnerwort (Cantata),**
See **Roxburgh, Edwin.** The beginning of sorrows : soprano solo, off-stage vocal quartet, divided SATB choir / Edwin Roxburgh.

Bach, Johann Sebastian, *1685-1750.* **Suites,**
See **Flexible woodwind trios :** baroque / arr. Karen Evans.

Bach-Archiv Leipzig.
See **Bach, Carl Philipp Emanuel, 1714-1788** [Concertos, harpsichord, H. 242, F major] Arrangements of orchestral works I / Carl Philipp Emanuel Bach ; edited by Douglas A. Lee.

See **Bach, Carl Philipp Emanuel, 1714-1788** [Concertos, oboe, string orchestra, H. 466, B♭ major] Oboe concertos / Carl Philipp Emanuel Bach ; edited by Janet K. Page.

Backofen, Johann Georg Heinrich, *1768-1839.*
[Concertantes, basset horn, harp, violoncello, op. 7, F major] — Concertante, op. 7/8, per arpa, corno di bassetto (o viola) e violoncello ad libitum = for harp, basset-horn (or viola) and violoncello and libitum / Heinrich Backofen ; a cura di Anna Pasetti. — *Ut Orpheus*
785.44193186   013887059

Bacon, Ernst, *1898-1990.* **Cherubic pilgrim.**
See **Three carols for Christmas :** for unaccompanied mixed choir (SATB).

Badinerie
See **Bach, Johann Sebastian, 1685-1750.** [Suites, orchestra, BWV 1067, B minor. Badinerie; *arr.*] Badinerie

Badings, Henk, *1907-1987.*
Azioni musicali : per duodeci strumenti, TWEC: HHB-1, 1980 / Henk Badings. — *Floricor Editions*
785.42199   014599804

Badoaro, Giacomo, *1602-1654.*
See **Monteverdi, Claudio, 1567-1643.** [Ritorno d'Ulisse in patria] Il ritorno di Ulisse in patria : Ms. Wien, partitura / Claudio Monteverdi .

Badura-Skoda, Paul.
See **Mozart, Wolfgang Amadeus, 1756-1791** [Concertos, piano, orchestra, K537, D major; *arr.*] Piano concerto no. 26, K. 537 : "Coronation concerto" : for piano and orchestra / Wolfgang Amadeus Mozart ; edited and reconstructed by Paul Badura-Skoda.

[Bagatelles, oboe, bassoon (2005)]
See **Hansell, Philip, 1962-** [Bagatelles, oboe, bassoon (2005)]

Bahá'u'lláh, *1817-1892.*
See **Thoresen, Lasse, 1949-** Yá kafi, yá shafi : for two choirs, 1996 / Lasse Thoresen ; text, Bahá'u'lláh.

Bahha, Nor Eddine.
See **Rawlins, Robert.** Jazzology : the encyclopedia of jazz theory for all musicians / by Robert Rawlins and Nor Eddine Bahha ; edited by Barrett Tagliarino.

Bailey, Judith, *1941-*
[Concertos, wind ensemble, op. 20] — Concerto for ten wind instruments, op. 20 : for two flutes, two oboes, two clarinets in B♭, two bassoons and two horns in F / by Judith Bailey. — *Phylloscopus Publications*
785.43199186   013472741

Bainbridge, Simon, *1952-*
Eichá : (Lamentation) : for mezzo-soprano solo, SATB chorus and wind ensemble : (1997) / Simon Bainbridge. — *Novello*
782.524   013434131

Baker, Ernest, *1912-*
Cantilena : for oboe and piano / Ernest Baker. — *Chester Music*
788.52   013197067

Baker, H. W. Sir, *1821-1877.*
See **Vaughan Williams, Ralph, 1872-1958** [Fantasia on Greensleeves; *arr*] Greensleeves : or, The king of love : a choral setting for female voice choir and piano or orchestra of "Fantasia on Greensleeves" / by R. Vaughan Williams ; arranged by Philip Lane.

See **Vaughan Williams, Ralph, 1872-1958** [Fantasia on Greensleeves; *arr*] Greensleeves : or, The king of love : a choral setting for mixed voice choir and piano or orchestra of "Fantasia on Greensleeves" / by R. Vaughan Williams ; arranged by Philip Lane.

Baker, J. Mark.
See **Brady, Deborah.** The toymaker's workshop : for one piano, four hands / by Deborah Brady ; edited by J. Mark Baker.

See **Brady, Deborah.** The twelve days of Christmas / by Deborah Brady ; edited by J. Mark Baker.

See **Christmas jazz :** six carols for piano solo / arranged by Mike Springer ; edited by J. Mark Baker.

See **Clark, Sondra, 1941-** Dakota days : five pieces for piano solo / by Sondra Clark ; edited by J. Mark Baker.

See **Kern, Jerome, 1885-1945.** [Songs. Selections; *arr.*] Jerome Kern classics : for piano solo / arranged by Eugéne Rocherolle ; edited by J. Mark Baker.

See **Six songs from John Gay's The beggar's opera** / arranged for piano trio by Nancy O'Neill Breth and Jean Goberman ; edited by J. Mark Baker.

Baker, Kenneth.
See **The complete keyboard player 15 showstoppers** / based on the best-selling keyboard method by Kenneth Baker.

See **The complete keyboard player Christmas favourites** / based on the best-selling keyboard method by Kenneth Baker.

See **The complete keyboard player pop hits** / based on the best-selling keyboard method by Kenneth Baker.

Baker, Richard, *1972-*
To keep a true Lent : SATTBB (with T solo) a cappella / Richard Baker. — *Oxford University Press*
782.5265   013213405

Baker, Theodore, *1851-1934.*
See **Rentz, Earlene.** Lo, how a rose e'er blooming = (Es ist ein' Ros' entsprungen) : for mixed choir (SATB), flute and piano / [from Alte Catholische Geistliche Kirchengesang' (1599) harmonized by Michael Praetorius (1609) ; arranged by] Earlene Rentz.

See **Rentz, Earlene.** Lo, how a rose e'er blooming = (Es ist ein' Ros' entsprungen) : for upper voices (SA), flute and piano / [from Alte Catholische Geistliche Kirchengesang' (1599) harmonized by Michael Praetorius (1609) ; arranged by] Earlene Rentz.

Balaguer, Víctor, *1824-1901.*
See **Pedrell, Felipe, 1841-1922.** Los Pirineus : ópera en tres actos / Felipe Pedrell ; libreto, Victor Balaguer ; edición crítica, Francesc Cortes y Edmon Colomer.

Balakirev, Miliĭ Alekseevich, *1837-1910.*
[Islameĭ] — Islamey : Fantaisie orientale / Milij Balakirev ; herausgegeben von Norbert Gertsch. — *G. Henle*
786.2   013115483

Balázs, Béla, *1884-1949.*
See **Bartók, Béla, 1881-1945.** [Kékszakállú herceg vára. English & Hungarian] A Kékszakállú herceg vára : opera egy felvonásban szövegét írta Balázs Béla = Duke Bluebeard's castle : opera in one act to the libretto by Béla Balázs / Béla Bartók.

Baldwin, Antony, *1957-*
God be in my head : for unaccompanied mixed choir (SATB) / Antony Baldwin. — *Oxford University Press*
782.5265   013212297

See **Kaye, Ernest.** Wedding march : for piano / Ernest Kaye ; and arranged for organ by Antony Baldwin.

Balinese diptych
See **Van de Vate, Nancy.** Balinese diptych

Ballads
Ballads : [24 great songs] — *Wise Publications*
786.2164   013281517

Ballet des saisons
See **Lully, Jean Baptiste, 1632-1687** [Ballets. Vocal scores. Selections] Ballet des saisons

Ballet gold
Ballet gold : the essential collection. — *Chester Music*
786.21556   013167409

[Ballets. Selections]
See **Schmelzer, Johann Heinrich, ca. 1623-1680.** [Ballets. Selections]

[Ballets. Vocal scores. Selections]
See **Lully, Jean Baptiste, 1632-1687** [Ballets. Vocal scores. Selections]

Balletti à 4 für 2 Violinen, Violetta (Viola), Violone & B.c.
See **Schmelzer, Johann Heinrich, ca. 1623-1680.** [Ballets. Selections] Balletti à 4 für 2 Violinen, Violetta (Viola), Violone & B.c.

Balletti à 5 für 2 Violinen, 3 Violen & B.c.
See **Schmelzer, Johann Heinrich, ca. 1623-1680.** [Ballets. Selections] Balletti à 5 für 2 Violinen, 3 Violen & B.c.

Ballot de Sovot, d. 1761.
See **Rameau, Jean-Philippe, 1683-1764.** [Platée. Vocal score] Platée : ballet bouffon en un prologue et trois actes : version 1749, version 1745 (compléments) / [musique de Jean-Philippe Rameau] ; livret de Jacques Autreau ; révisé par Adrien-Joseph Valois d'Orville et Balot de Sovot ; édition de M. Elizabeth C. Barlet ; réduction clavier-chant de François Saint-Yves.

A baptism hymn
See **White, Nicholas.** A baptism hymn

Il Barbiere di Siviglia
See **Rossini, Gioacchino, 1792-1868** [Barbiere di Siviglia. Sinfonia; *arr.*] Il Barbiere di Siviglia

[Barbiere di Siviglia. Sinfonia; *arr.*]
See **Rossini, Gioacchino, 1792-1868** [Barbiere di Siviglia. Sinfonia; *arr.*]

Bares, Alessandro, *1970-*
See **Buchner, Philipp Friedrich, 1614-1669.** Harmonia instrumentalis : 12 sonate per 2 violini, fagotto e basso continuo, op. 5, Würzburg 1664 / Philipp Friedrich Buchner ; trascrizione a cura di Alessandro Bares.

See **Ganassi, Giacomo, fl. 1625-1637** [Vespertina psalmodia (1637) Selections] 13 canzoni strumentali a due e a quattro strumenti con il basso per l'organo : estratte da: Vespertina psalmodia in totius anni solemnitates— : Venezia, 1637 / Giacomo Ganassi ; trascrizione a cura di Alessandro Bares.

See **Schmelzer, Johann Heinrich, ca. 1623-1680.** Sacro-profanus concentus musicus : fidium aliorumque instrumentorum : 13 sonate a 2, 4, 5, 6, 7, e 8 strumenti, Nürnberg, 1662 / Johann Heinrich Schmelzer ; a cura di Alessandro Bares.

See **Schmelzer, Johann Heinrich, ca. 1623-1680.** [Sonatae unarum fidium] Sonatae unarum fidium seu a violino solo : Nürnberg, 1664 / Johann Heinrich Schmelzer ; transcrizione a cura di Alessandro Bares.

See **Vierdanck, Johann, ca. 1605-1646.** [Capricci, Canzoni und Sonaten] Capricci, Canzoni und Sonaten : [mit 2, 3, 4 und 5 Instrumenten ohne und mit dem Basso continuo], Rostock 1641 / Johann Vierdanck ; trascrizione a cura di Alessandro Bares.

See **Westhoff, Johann Paul, 1656-1705.** [Sonatas, violin, continuo (1694)] Sonate per violino e basso continuo : Dresden, 1694 / Johann Paul Westhoff ; trascrizione a cura di Alessandro Bares.

Baring-Gould, S. *1834-1924.*
See **The angel Gabriel** : for mezzo-soprano with optional tenor solo, mixed choir (SATB) and harp / [Basque traditional ; arranged by] Robert A.M. Ross.

See **The angel Gabriel** : for soprano solo, upper voices (SSAA) and harp / [Basque traditional ; arranged by] Robert A.M. Ross.

See **Chilcott, Bob.** The angel Gabriel / Bob Chilcott.

Baring-Gould, S. *1834-1924*
See **Ledger, Philip.** Advent carol : for unison voices and keyboard / Philip Ledger.

Barlow, Jeremy, *1939-*
See **Thistle & minuet** : 16 easy pieces from the Scottish Baroque for violin (or flute or oboe), keyboard, and optional cello (or bassoon) = 16 einfache Stücke aus der schottischen Barockzeit für Violine (oder Flöte oder Oboe), Tasteninstrument und Cello (oder Fagott) ad libitum = 16 pièces faciles du Baroque écossais pour violon (ou flûte ou hautbois), clavier et violoncelle (ou basson) facultatif / edited by David Johnson.

Barlow, Michael, *1940-*
[Nocturnes, violoncello, piano, op. 19] — Nocturne for 'cello and piano / Michael Barlow. — *Modus Music*
787.418966 013389868

Barnes, Gerald.
See **Nathan, Simon, 1988 or 9-** Lament : for piano / Simon Nathan. Together with Improvisation on "Lament" : for piano / Ernest Kaye ; and arranged for organ by Gerald Barnes.

Barratier, Christophe.
See **Coulais, Bruno.** [Choristes. *Vocal score.* Selections] Les choristes : piano, chant (choeurs), paroles.

Barret, Apollon Marie-Rose, *1803-1879.*
[Cantilène; *arr.*] — Cantilena / by Apollon M.-R. Barret ; arranged for cor anglais and piano by professor Myron Zakopets. — *Phylloscopus Publications*
788.53 013472844

Barritt, Paul.
See **Beethoven, Ludwig van, 1770-1827.** [Sonatas, violin, piano, no. 9, op. 47, A major; *arr.*] Kreutzer sonata : an anonymous arrangement for string quintet : first published by Simrock in 1832 : for 2 violins, viola & 2 violoncellos / Beethoven ; edited by Paul Barritt.

Barry, Darrol.
See **A Christmas lullaby** / arranged for flugel horn and brass band by Darrol Barry.

See **Saint-Saëns, Camille, 1835-1921.** [Carnaval des animaux. Cygne; *arr.*] The swan : from Carnival of the animals : grade 2 / Saint-Saëns ; arr. Darrol Barry.

Bartholomäus, Helge.
See **Giardini, Felice, 1716-1796.** [Duets, viola, bassoon] 3 Duetti à fagotto e viola concerta / Felice de Giardini ; herausgegeben von Helge Bartholomäus.

Bartlet, M. Elizabeth C. *1948-*
See **Rameau, Jean-Philippe, 1683-1764.** [Platée. *Vocal score*] Platée : ballet bouffon en un prologue et trois actes : version 1749, version 1745 (compléments) / [musique de Jean-Philippe Rameau] ; livret de Jacques Autreau ; révisé par Adrien-Joseph Valois d'Orville et Balot de Sovot ; édition de M. Elizabeth C. Barlet ; réduction clavier-chant de François Saint-Yves.

Bartlett, Keith.
Christmas cancan / Keith Bartlett. — *United Music Publishers*
784.68188417230834 013416246

Cossack capers / Keith Bartlett. — *United Music Publishers*
784.680834 013416287

Jingle jangle jungle / Keith Bartlett. — *United Music Publishers*
784.680834 013416318

Mystical march / Keith Bartlett. — *United Music Publishers*
784.6818970834 013416262

Sing a song o' conga / Keith Bartlett. — *United Music Publishers*
784.6818880834 013416191

Viva Mexico / Keith Bartlett. — *United Music Publishers*
784.680834 013416308

Bartók, Béla, *1881-1945.*
[Kékszakállú herceg vára. *English & Hungarian*] — A Kékszakállú herceg vára : opera egy felvonásban szövegét írta Balázs Béla = Duke Bluebeard's castle : opera in one act to the libretto by Béla Balázs / Béla Bartók. — *Bartók Records*
782.10265 014586910

See **Shchedrin, Rodion Konstantinovich, 1932-** [Vologodskie svireli] Shepherd's pipes of Vologda : for oboe, cor anglais, horn and string orchestra = Hirtenklänge aus Wologda : für Oboe, Englisch Horn, Horn und Streichorchester : Hommage à Bartók (1995) / Rodion Shchedrin.

Bartók, Peter, *1924-*
See **Bartók, Béla, 1881-1945.** [Kékszakállú herceg vára. *English & Hungarian*] A Kékszakállú herceg vára : opera egy felvonásban szövegét írta Balázs Béla = Duke Bluebeard's castle : opera in one act to the libretto by Béla Balázs / Béla Bartók.

Bartoli, Giuseppe, *1739-1801.*
Messa a tre voci con stromenti / Giuseppe Bartoli. — *Erstausg. / — Dohr*
782.53232 013887060

Barton, David, *1983-*
On the box : eight pieces on a television theme : for flute and piano / David Barton. — *Da Capo Music*
788.32 013351564

[Pieces, piano, flutes (2) (2004)] — Two pieces for flute duet and piano / David Barton. — *Da Capo Music*
785.26193 013351600

Basson
Basson : France, 1800-1860 : méthodes, traités d'instrumentation, dictionnaires, cours de composition, périodiques. — *J.M. Fuzeau*
788.58076 013351080

Bates, Katharine Lee, *1859-1929.*
See **Ward, Samuel A., 1847-1903.** [America the beautiful; *arr.*] America the beautiful : for mixed chorus (SATB) and organ / [Samuel A. Ward ; arranged by] Mack Wilberg.

Battaglia per espugnare Amore
See **Mazzocchi, D. 1592-1665.** [Musiche sacre, e morali. Battaglia per espugnare Amore] Battaglia per espugnare Amore

The battle hymn of the Republic
See **Steffe, William, ca. 1830-1890.** The battle hymn of the Republic

Battle of Britain
See **Hewitt, Daniel.** Battle of Britain

The Battle of Britain
See **Hewitt, Daniel.** [Battle of Britain. *Selections*] The Battle of Britain

[Battle of Britain. *Selections*]
See **Hewitt, Daniel.** [Battle of Britain. *Selections*]

Battle symphony
See **Gorb, Adam, 1958-** Battle symphony

Bauer & Hieber (*Firm*)
See **Opening night** : two Souvenirs for solo piano : commissioned to celebrate the opening of the Bauer & Hieber music shop at 48 Great Marlborough Street, London, 21st September 2007 / written and performed by Tim Richards and Huw Watkins.

Bauer, Astrid.
See **Rheinberger, Josef, 1839-1901.** [Chamber music. *Selections*] Kammermusik V / [Josef Gabriel Rheinberger] ; vorgelegt von Astrid Bauer.

Bauni, Axel, *1961-*
See **Ullmann, Viktor.** [Songs] Sämtliche Lieder für Singstimme und Klavier = Complete songs for voice and piano / Viktor Ullmann ; herausgegeben von Axel Bauni und Christian Hoesch.

Bavad khair bagi!
See **Harrison, Sadie, 1965-** Bavad khair bagi!

Bayerische Staatsbibliothek.
See **Legrenzi, Giovanni, 1626-1690.** [Dal calore agitato] Two cantatas from the Munich ms. : for bass and basso continuo / Giovanni Legrenzi ; edited by Barbara Sachs.

Bayford, Frank.
Echoes from a golden time : opus 95 : seven songs to poems from the Greek Anthology : for soprano and piano / translated by Forrest Reid ; [music by] Frank Bayford. — *Modus Music*
783.6642   013373629

Bayliss, Colin.
Anglo tango : for tango band : (violin, double bass, guitar, bandoneon and piano) : [B126] / Colin Bayliss. — *Da Capo Music*
785.2819518885   013351688

Bohemian rondo : for string trio : [B127] / Colin Baylis. — *Da Capo Music*
785.71931824   013351684

Epilogue : for string orchestra : [B139] / Colin Bayliss. — *Da Capo Music*
784.7   013351513

[Grumpy tunes; *arr.*] — Grumpy tunes : arranged for recorder and guitar : [B79a] / Colin Bayliss. — *Da Capo Music*
785.44192   013351677

Lullaby for saxophone quartet : [B134] / Colin Bayliss. — *Da Capo Music*
785.87194   013351659

Soliloquy : for solo [alto] trombone : [B137] / Colin Bayliss. — *Da Capo Music*
788.93   013351582

[Sonatas, bassoon, piano (2005)] — Sonata for bassoon and piano : [B136] / Colin Bayliss. — *Da Capo Music*
788.58183   013351618

Bayou blues
See **Penri-Evans, David, 1956-** Bayou blues

Be joyful!
See **Cousins, Mervyn.** Be joyful!

Be music, night
See **Ellingboe, Bradley.** Be music, night

Be still, my soul
See **Sibelius, Jean, 1865-1957.** [Finlandia. Hymni; *arr.*] Be still, my soul

Be strong and of good courage
See **Goddard, Mark.** Be strong and of good courage

Beach, H. H. A., Mrs., *1867-1944.*
[Song of liberty; *arr.*] — A song of liberty : for high voice and piano, op. 49 / by Amy Beach. — *Masters Music Publications*
783.342   014497795

Bean, Shirley.
See **Martinez, Marianne, 1744-1812.** [Concertos, harpsichord, orchestra, G major] Concerto in G major for piano and orchestra / by Marianna Martines ; edited by Shirley Bean.

See **Martinez, Marianne, 1744-1812.** [Isacco, figura del Redentore. Ouverture] Overture to the oratorio Isacco figura del Redentore (1782) / by Marianna Martines ; edited by Shirley Bean.

See **Martinez, Marianne, 1744-1812.** [Symphony, C major] Sinfonia in C major, (Ouverture), (1770) / by Marianna Martines ; edited by Shirley Bean and Karen Fremar.

The Beatles
See **Beatles.** [Songs. *Selections*] The Beatles

Beatles love songs
See **Lennon, John, 1940-1980.** [Songs. *Selections*] Beatles love songs

Beatles.
[Songs. *Selections; arr.*] — The Beatles : [23 great hits] — *Wise*
786.2164   013281527

[Songs. *Selections*] — Play bass with— The Beatles. — *Wise Publications*
783.242166   013190805

[Songs. *Selections*] — The Beatles : note-for-note. — *Wise*
783.242166   013432684

See **Lennon, John, 1940-1980.** [All you need is love; *arr.*] All you need is love : the 1967 #1 pop hit by The Beatles : [for 2-part and piano] / words and music by John Lennon and Paul McCartney ; arranged by Alan Billingsley.

See **Lennon, John, 1940-1980.** [All you need is love; *arr.*] All you need is love : the 1967 #1 pop hit by The Beatles : [for SAB and piano] / words and music by John Lennon and Paul McCartney ; arranged by Alan Billingsley.

See **Lennon, John, 1940-1980.** [All you need is love; *arr.*] All you need is love : the 1967 #1 pop hit by The Beatles : [for SATB and piano] / words and music by John Lennon and Paul McCartney ; arranged by Alan Billingsley.

See **Lennon, John, 1940-1980.** [Songs. *Selections*] Beatles love songs / words and music by John Lennon and Paul McCartney ; arranged by Ed Lojeski ; recorded by The Beatles.

Beavers, Kevin, *1971-*
[Wandlebury Ring. *Vocal score*] — Wandlebury Ring : for voice and string quartet / words by Andrew Sofer ; music by Kevin E. Beavers. — *Oxford University Press*
783.6642   013115468

Beck.
Guero / Beck ; music transcriptions by Pete Billmann, Addi Booth and David Stocker. — *Hal Leonard*
783.242166   013383507

Sea change / Beck ; music transcriptions by Andrew Moore, David Stocker, and Jeff Story. — *Hal Leonard*
783.242166   006906656

Beckmann, Klaus.
See **Scheidemann, Heinrich, 1596 (ca.)-1663.** [Organ music] Sämtliche Orgelwerke = Complete organ works / Heinrich Scheidemann ; herausgegeben von Klaus Beckmann.

See **Strungk, Delphin, 1601-1694.** [Organ music] Sämtliche Orgelwerke : Choralbearbeitungen, Toccata, Motettenkolorierungen = Complete organ works : chorale settings, toccata, motet intabulations / Delphin Strunck ; herausgegeben von Klaus Beckmann.

Bedingfield, Natasha.
Unwritten / Natasha Bedingfield. — *International Music Publications*
783.242166   013185871

Bee Gees.
[Songs. *Selections*] — Number ones : piano, vocal, guitar / Bee Gees. — *Hal Leonard*
783.242166   013222066

Beech, Julie.
See **Fun and games with the recorder** : method for the alto recorder. Tune book / [compiled by] Gudrun Heyens and Gerhard Engel ; translated and adapted by Peter Bowman ; with illustrations by John Minnion.

See **Heyens, Gudrun.** Fun and games with the alto recorder : method for the alto recorder. Tutor book 2 / by Gudrun Heyens and Gerhard Engel ; translated and adapted by Peter

Bowman ; with illustrations by Julie Beech and John Minnion.

Beedie, Norman.
See **Grade 8 piano anthology** : examination pieces for 2005 and 2006 : from the piano syllabus of the Associated Board of the Royal Schools of Music.

The beekeeper
See **Amos, Tori.** The beekeeper

Beethoven, Ludwig van, *1770-1827.*
[Concertos, violin, orchestra, op. 61, D major; *arr.*] — Klavierkonzert Opus 61a : nach dem Violinkonzert Opus 61 = Piano concerto op. 61a : after the Violin concerto op. 61 / Ludwig van Beethoven ; herausgegeben von Hans-Werner Küthen ; Fingersatz von Klaus Schilde ; Klavierauszug von Jürgen Sommer ; Kadenzen vom Komponisten. — *G. Henle*
785.62192186   013364364

[Quartets, strings, no. 1-6, op. 18] — Streichquartette = String quartets, op. 18 / Beethoven ; herausgegeben von Jonathan Del Mar. — *Bärenreiter*
785.7194   013943214

[Sonatas, violin, piano, no. 9, op. 47, A major; *arr.*] — Kreutzer sonata : an anonymous arrangement for string quintet : first published by Simrock in 1832 : for 2 violins, viola & 2 violoncellos / Beethoven ; edited by Paul Barritt. — *SJ Music*
785.7195   013196241

Beethoven, Ludwig van, *1770-1827*
[Symphonies, no. 7, op. 92, A major. Movement 1; *arr.*] — Symphony no 7, movement 1 / Ludwig van Beethoven ; arranged by Carlo Martelli. — *Broadbent & Dunn*
785.7194   013383363

[Symphonies, no. 8, op. 93, F Major. Movement 1; *arr.*] — Symphony no 8, movement 1 / Ludwig van Beethoven ; arranged by Carlo Martelli. — *Broadbent & Dunn*
785.7194   013213498

Beethoven, Ludwig van, *1770-1827* Sonatas,
See **An die Musik** : 9 classical pieces arranged for string quartet / [arr. by] John Kember.

Begelman, Danny.
See **The end of all things to come** / Mudvayne ; transcribed by Danny Begelman, Bill LaFleur and Greg Tribbett.

[Beggar's opera. *Selections; arr.*]
Six songs from John Gay's The beggar's opera / arranged for piano trio by Nancy O'Neill Breth and Jean Goberman ; edited by J. Mark Baker. — *Hal Leonard*
785.28193   013220496

Beggar's opera.
See **Arnold, Samuel, 1740-1802.** Polly : an opera : (1777) / music by Johann Christoph Pepusch ; rearrang'd and new airs compos'd by Samuel Arnold ; libretto by John Gay ; revis'd by George Colman, the elder ; edited by Robert Hoskins. — *Artaria Editions*

The beginning of sorrows
See **Roxburgh, Edwin.** The beginning of sorrows

Behold, I tell you a mystery
See **Carey, Paul, 1954-** Behold, I tell you a mystery

Belkadi, Jean Marc, *1959-*
Classical themes for electric guitar : 25 solo guitar arrangements / by Jean Marc Belkadi. — *Hal Leonard*
787.87   013167489

Bella dama di nome santa
See **Scarlatti, Alessandro, 1660-1725.** Bella dama di nome santa

Bellamy, Matthew.
See [**Songs.** *Selections*] The best of Muse.

See [**Songs.** *Selections*] Play bass with— Muse.

See [**Songs.** *Selections*] Play guitar with— Muse : Stockholm syndrome and other great songs.

Bellini, Vincenzo, *1801-1835.*
I Capuleti e i Montecchi / Vincenzo Bellini ; tragedia lirica in due atti di Felice Romani ; a cura di Claudio Toscani. — *Ricordi*
782.1   014682330

Bělský, Vratislav.
See **Michna z Otradovic, Adam, ca. 1600-1676.** [Officium vespertinum. *Selections*] Officium vespertinum : Compositiones ad honorem B.M.V. ; Falsi burdoni / [Adam Michna z Otradovic] ; ed., Vratislav Bělský, Jiři Sehnal.

Bemmann, Katrin.
See **Heinichen, Johann David, 1683-1729.** [Masses, S. 5, D major] Missa Nr. 9 in D : für Soli SATB, Chor SATB, 2 flauti, 2 oboi, fagotto, 2 corni, 2 trombe, timpani, 2 violini, viola, violoncello, contrabasso, organo / Johann David Heinichen.

Ben-Tovim, Atarah.
See **Kelly, Bryan.** Globe Theatre suite : for descant recorder or piccolo and piano / by Bryan Kelly ; edited by Atarah Ben-Tovim.

Benda, Franz, *1709-1786.*
[Sonatas, viola, continuo, C minor] — Sonate pour alto et basse continue en do mineur, Lee III-137 / Franz Benda. — *T. Van Wetteren*
787.3183   014053099

Bendetto Marcello
See **Raff, Joachim, 1822-1882.** [Benedetto Marcello. *Vocal score*] Bendetto Marcello

[**Benedetto Marcello.** *Vocal score*]
See **Raff, Joachim, 1822-1882.** [Benedetto Marcello. *Vocal score*]

Benjamin, George.
Viola, viola : for viola duo, 1997 / George Benjamin. — *Faber Music*
785.73192   006891403

Bennett, Richard Rodney.
Missa brevis / Richard Rodney Bennett. — *Novello*
782.53232   013218330

[Sonatas, violoncello, piano] — Sonata for violoncello and piano : (1991) / Richard Rodney Bennett. — *Novello*
787.4183   013434138

Time : for SAATTBB / Richard Rodney Bennett. — *Novello*
782.542   013497176

Bennett, Richard Rodney. Country dances,
See **The violin** : a collection : new and recent repertoire for violin with piano accompaniment / Craig Armstrong … [et al.]

Benoliel, Bernard, *1943-*
See **Vaughan Williams, Ralph, 1872-1958.** [Quartets, strings, C minor] String quartet in C minor (1898) / Ralph Vaughan Williams.

See **Vaughan Williams, Ralph, 1872-1958.** [Quintets, piano, clarinet, horn, violin, violoncello, D major] Quintet in D major (1898), for clarinet, horn, violin, cello and piano / Ralph Vaughan Williams.

See **Vaughan Williams, Ralph, 1872-1958.** [Quintets, piano, violin, viola, violoncello,

double bass, C minor] Piano quintet in C minor (1903), for violin, viola, cello, double bass and piano / Ralph Vaughan Williams.

Bentivogli, Abbate.
See **Mazzocchi, D. 1592-1665.** [Musiche sacre, e morali. Cangia miio cor] Cangia mio cor : si dee fuggire il diletto dannoso / Domenico Mazzocchi ; [words by] Abbate Bentivogli.

Bergquist, Peter.
See **The complete motets** [of] Orlando di Lasso : afterword, addenda and corrigenda, indexes / edited by Peter Bergquist.

See **Lasso, Orlando di, 1532-1594.** [Motets. *Selections*] Motets for three to twelve voices from Magnum Opus Musicum (Munich, 1604) / Orlando di Lasso ; edited by Peter Bergquist.

Berke, Dietrich.
See **Schubert, Franz, 1797-1828.** [Vocal music. *Selections*] Mehrstimmige Gesänge für gemischte Stimmen. Teil b / [Franz Schubert] ; vorgelegt von Dietrich Berke und Michael Kube.

Bernier, Nicolas, *1665-1734.*
[Cantates françoises, 2e livre. Diane et Endimion] — Diane et Endimion : cantata for soprano, bass & continuo / Nicolas Bernier. — *Green Man Press*
783.1248   013596964

Bertalot, John.
See **A night at the opera for piano** : easy-to-play arrangements / arranged by John Bertalot.

Bertaux, Betty.
See **Wondrous love** : SSA a capella [sic] / arr. by Betty Bertaux.

Bertoldo, Sperindio, ca. *1530-1570.*
[Organ music] — Opere per tastiera (Venezia 1591) : con riproduzione in facsimile delle stampe / Sperindio Bertoldo ; a cura di Luigi Collarile. — *Andromeda*
786.5   013887061

Bertolusi, Vincenzo, ca. *1550-1607 or 8.*
[Sacrae cantiones, libro 1o] — Sacrarum cantionum : 1601 / Vincentius Bertholusius ; edgivet af = herausgegeben von = edited by Ole Kongsted. — *Capella Hafniensis Editions*
782.526   013581664

Besses, Antoni.
[Preludi místic, no. 5] — Preludi místic núm. 5 : piano / Antoni Besses. — *Amalgama*
786.218928   014457002

[Preludi místic, no. 6] — Preludi místic núm. 6 : piano / Antoni Besses. — *Amalgama*
786.218928   014457003

The best acoustic guitar songs ever.
The best acoustic guitar songs ever. — *Hal Leonard Europe*
783.242166   013408007

The best Christmas flute duet book ever!
The best Christmas flute duet book ever! / selected and edited by Emma Coulthard. — *Wise*
785.8321921723   013312881

The best of 1000 UK number one hits.
The best of 1000 UK number one hits. Early years : [from 1952 to 1974 : arranged for piano, voice and guitar] — *Wise Publications*
783.242166   013129814

The best of Bobby Darin
See **Darin, Bobby.** [Songs. *Selections*] The best of Bobby Darin

Best of gold
Best of gold : the essential collection. — *Chester Music*
786.2   013185953

The best of Richard Clayderman
The best of Richard Clayderman : piano solos. — *Wise*
786.2   013246716

The best of Rodgers and Hart.
See **Rodgers, Richard, 1902-1979** [Musicals. *Selections; arr.*] The best of Rodgers and Hart.

Best of swing
Best of swing : 10 swing classics / [arranged and produced by Mark Taylor and Jim Roberts] — *Hal Leonard Europe*
781.654   013323811

Best of Train
See **Train (Musical group)** [Songs. *Selections*] Best of Train

Bethlehem
See **Ledger, Philip.** Bethlehem

Betjeman, John, *1906-1984.*
See **Parry, Ben.** And is it true? : SATB / Ben Parry ; [words by John Betjeman]

Bewitched
See **Rodgers, Richard, 1902-1979** [Musicals. *Vocal scores. Selections*] Bewitched

Bianciardi, Francesco, *1572?-1607.* Madrigals,
See **The amorous hexachord** : madrigal fantasies from the Tregian manuscript / Pallavicino, Bianciardi, and Giovannelli ; edited by Hannah Davidson.

Biba, Otto.
See **Salieri, Antonio, 1750-1825.** Salve regina : für vierstimmigen gemischten Chor, 2 Violinen, Viola, Bass und Orgel / Antonio Salieri ; revidiert und herausgegeben von Otto Biba ; Continuofassung von Wolfgang Fürlinger.

Biber, Heinrich Ignaz Franz, *1644-1704.*
Chi la dura la vince (Wer ausharrt, siegt) : Dramma musicale in drei Akten / Heinrich Franz Biber ; Text von Francesco Maria Raffaelini (?) ; Einführung von Sibylle Dahms. — *Selke Verlag*
782.1   013120293

O dulcis Jesu : geistliches Konzert : canto solo, violino discordato e basso continuo / Heinrich Ignaz Franz Biber? ; herausgegeben von Wolfram Steude. — *Erstausg.* — *Carus*
783.6724   013771073

Bible.
See **Vacchi, Fabio, 1949-** Voce d'altra voce : per due recitanti, grande coro misto e orchestra, 2005 / Fabio Vacchi. — *Ricordi*

Biblioteka Narodowa (Poland).
See **Chopin, Frédéric, 1810-1849.** [Sonatas, piano no. 3, op. 58, B minor] Sonata H-Moll Op. 58 : wydanie faksymilowe rękopisu ze zbiorów Biblioteki Narodowej w Warszawie (Mus. 232 Cim.) = Sonata in B minor, op. 58 : facsimile edition of the manuscript held in the National Library in Warsaw (Mus. 232 Cim.) : A IX/58 / Fryderyk Chopin ; Komitet redakcyjny = Editorial committee, Jean-Jacques Eigeldinger (przewodniczący = president), Zofia Chechlińska (redaktor naczelny = editor in chief) … [et al.]

Bibliothèque nationale de France.
See **Schumann, Robert, 1810-1856.** [Waldscenen] Waldszenen : Opus 82 : Faksimile nach dem Autograph im Besitz der Bibliothèque nationale de France, Paris / Robert Schumann ; Nachwort von Margit L. McCorkle.

See **Tropaire séquentiaire prosaire prosulaire de Moissac :** (troisième quart du XIe siècle) : Manuscrit Paris, Bibliothèque nationale de France, n.a.l. 1871 / édition, introduction et index par Marie-Noël Colette ; analyse de l'écriture et de la décoration par Marie-Thérèse Gousset.

The big acoustic guitar chord songbook.
The big acoustic guitar chord songbook. Female. — *Wise Publications*
783.642166   006914459

The big book of clarinet songs.
The big book of clarinet songs. — *Hal Leonard Europe*
788.62164   013296654

The big book of Irish songs.
The big book of Irish songs. piano, vocal, guitar. — *Hal Leonard*
783.242162009415   012874857

The big book of piano songs
The big book of piano songs : piano, vocal, guitar. — *Hal Leonard Europe*
783.242164   013358425

The big guitar chord songbook.
The big guitar chord songbook. Classic rock. — *Wise Publications*
783.242166   013203906

Bigler, Dwight.
[All you who are to mirth inclined; *arr.*] — All you who are to mirth inclined : for mixed choir (SATB), brass quintet and piano (with optional percussion) / [traditional English carol, arr.] Dwight Bigler. — *Oxford University Press*
782.5281723   013115013

Bill Evans
See **Evans, Bill, 1929-1980.** [Selections; *arr.*] Bill Evans

Billingsley, Alan.
See **Lennon, John, 1940-1980.** [All you need is love; *arr.*] All you need is love : the 1967 #1 pop hit by The Beatles : [for 2-part and piano] / words and music by John Lennon and Paul McCartney ; arranged by Alan Billingsley.

See **Lennon, John, 1940-1980.** [All you need is love; *arr.*] All you need is love : the 1967 #1 pop hit by The Beatles : [for SAB and piano] / words and music by John Lennon and Paul McCartney ; arranged by Alan Billingsley.

See **Lennon, John, 1940-1980.** [All you need is love; *arr.*] All you need is love : the 1967 #1 pop hit by The Beatles : [for SATB and piano] / words and music by John Lennon and Paul McCartney ; arranged by Alan Billingsley.

Billmann, Pete.
See **Beck.** Guero / Beck ; music transcriptions by Pete Billmann, Addi Booth and David Stocker.

See **Good news for people who love bad news :** guitar recorded versions / by Modest Mouse ; music transcriptions by Pete Billmann, Addi Booth and Jeff Story.

See **In your honor /** Foo Fighters ; music transcriptions by Pete Billmann and David Stocker.

See **Mezmerize /** System of a Down ; music transcriptions by Pete Billmann and David Stocker.

See **One day remains /** Alter Bridge.

Bingham, Judith.
A dream of the past : (1993) : 3 paintings by Millais and a prologue : in memorium Christoph Delz : for brass quintet / Judith Bingham. — *Maecenas Music*
785.9195   013193719

God would be born in thee : carol for SATB & organ : (2004) / Judith Bingham ; text, Silesius Angelus. — *Maecenas Music*
782.5281723   013193696

In nomine : anthem after Taverner for SATB choir unaccompanied : (2005) / Judith Bingham. — *Maecenas Music*
782.5265   013416593

Our faith is a light : anthem for SATB and organ : (2004) / Judith Bingham. — *Maecenas Music*
782.5265   013193889

Der Spuk : (2001) : a folk-tale from Kleinwalsertal : for tuba solo / Judith Bingham. — *Maecenas Music*
788.98   013422345

The temple at Karnak : (1996) : [for orchestra] / Judith Bingham. — *Maecenas, Music*
784.2   013193680

Binney, Malcolm.
Brasser : an overture / Malcolm Binney. — *Maecenas Music*
784.818926   013422221

Charivari / Malcolm Binney. — *Maecenas Music*
784.81858   013421618

Civitas / Malcolm Binney. — *Maecenas Music*
784.8   013422238

Emerald breeze : for wind orchestra / Malcolm Binney. — *Maecenas Music*
784.8   013192940

London pageant : a British concert march for the millennium / Malcolm Binney. — *Maecenas Music*
784.81897   013192902

Overture Saturnalia / Malcolm Binney. — *Maecenas Music*
784.818926   013192992

Binyon, Laurence, 1869-1943.
See **Tavener, John.** Exhortation and Kohima : for unaccompanied choir and semichorus SATB/SATB / John Tavener.

The birds
See **Portman, Rachel.** [Little prince. Birds; *arr.*] The birds

A birthday offering
See **Lilburn, Douglas, 1915-2001.** A birthday offering

Bisbee, B. Wayne.
I never ate a cloud : unison treble [voices & piano] / by B. Wayne Bisbee — *Boosey & Hawkes*
782.7642   013312813

Night song : 2-pt treble / [music by] B. Wayne Bisbee. — *Boosey & Hawkes*
782.6642   013243862

See **Bach, Johann Sebastian, 1685-1750.** [Weihnachts-Oratorium. Bereite dich Zion, mit zärtlichen Trieben; *arr. English & German*] Prepare thyself, Zion : unison treble / J. S. Bach ; arranged by B. Wayne Bisbee.

See **Nursery songs for young choirs :** unison treble / arranged by B. Wayne Bisbee.

Bizet, Georges, *1838-1875.*
[*Carmen. Selections; arr.*] — Flexible woodwind trios : Carmen / Georges Bizet ; arr. Karen Evans. — *Spartan Press*
785.8193   013441187

Bizet, Georges, *1838-1875*. Pêcheurs de perles.
See **On wings of song :** 8 popular pieces arranged for string quartet / [arr. by] Barrie Carson Turner.

Blackburn, Bonnie J.
See **Josquin, des Prez, d. 1521.** [Motets. *Selections*] Motets on non-biblical texts. I, De domino Jesu Christo. 1 / Josquin des Prez ; edited by Bonnie J. Blackburn.

Blackford, Richard, *1954-*
On another's sorrow / words by Willam [sic] Blake ; music by Richard Blackford. — *Novello & Co*
782.5265   013582444

Blackwell, David.
See **Pierpont, James, 1822-1893.** [Jingle bells; *arr.*] Jingle, bells / J. Pierpont ; arranged by David Blackwell.

Blair, Hugh, *1862-1932*.
See **Elgar, Edward, 1857-1934.** [Carillon; *arr.*] Carillon, op. 75 ; &, Loughborough memorial chime : organ solo / Edward Elgar ; arranged & edited by David Patrick.

[Blake songs]
See **Vaughan Williams, Ralph, 1872-1958.** [Blake songs]

Blake, William, *1757-1827*.
See **Blackford, Richard, 1954-** On another's sorrow / words by Willam [sic] Blake ; music by Richard Blackford.

See **Carey, Paul, 1954-** A cradle song : for upper voices (SA) and piano or harp / Paul Carey.

See **Vaughan Williams, Ralph, 1872-1958.** [Blake songs] Ten Blake songs : for voice and oboe / Ralph Vaughan Williams.

Blaut, Stephan.
See **Handel, George Frideric, 1685-1759** Athalia : oratorio in three parts : HWV 52 / Georg Friedrich Händel ; herausgegeben von Stephan Blaut.

See **Theile, Johann, 1646-1724.** [Vocal music. *Selections*] Weltliche Arien und Canzonetten / Johann Theile ; herausgegeben von Stephan Blaut.

Blay, Gaston.
See **Wohlfahrt, Franz.** [Etüden, violin, op. 45] Sixty studies for the violin, op. 45 : complete, books I and II / Franz Wohlfahrt ; edited by Gaston Blay.

Blomenkamp, Thomas.
[Kleine Stücke, violin, piano (2002)] — Fünf kleine Stücke für Violine und Klavier, 2002 / Thomas Blomenkamp. — *Dohr*
787.2   013887062

Blomhert, Bastiaan.
See **Martin, Frank, 1890-1974.** [Ouverture et foxtrot, pianos (2); *arr.*] Concerto pour les instruments à vent et le piano (1924) / Frank Martin ; edition realized by Bastiaan Blomhert.

Blow the bassoon!
See **Taylor, Sue.** Blow the bassoon!

Blue wild angel
See **Hendrix, Jimi.** Blue wild angel

Blueberry blues
See **Cunliffe, Simon.** Blueberry blues

Blues
Blues : Guitar play-along. — *Hal Leonard*
783.2421643
013191092

Blues piano
Blues piano : the complete guide with CD! / by Mark Harrison.
786.21643076
006906657

Blues rock.
Blues rock. — *Hal Leonard*
787.871643
013191100

Bluesy jazz
Bluesy jazz : 10 jazz favorites / [arranged and produced by Mark Taylor] — *Hal Leonard Europe*
781.651643
013219947

The boar's head carol
The boar's head carol : SSAATTBB / English traditional ; arranged by Ben Parry. — *Edition Peters*
782.5281723
013304423

Bobby Darin
See **Darin, Bobby.** [Songs. *Selections*] Bobby Darin

Boccherini, Luigi, *1743-1805.*
[Duets, violins, G. 56-61] — 6 duetti per 2 violini = 6 duets for 2 violins = 6 Violinduette : opus 3 : G 56-62 / Luigi Boccherini ; a cura di Rudolf Rasch. — *Ut Orpheus Edizioni*
785.72192
013821930

Body, Jack, *1944-*
[Lullabies, voices] — Five lullabies : choir / Jack Body. — *Waiteata Music Press*
782.5
013728819

[Melodies, orchestra] — Melodies for orchestra / Jack Body. — *Waiteata Music Press*
784.2
013728860

Bohemian rondo
See **Bayliss, Colin.** Bohemian rondo

Bon Jovi (Musical group)
Have a nice day / Bon Jovi. — *Guitar tab ed. — Wise*
783.242166
013395868

Bonar, Horatius, *1808-1889.*
See **Rose, Barry, *1934-*** Here, O my Lord : SATB and organ / [music by] Barry Rose ; [words by] Horatius Bonar.

See **Rose, Barry, *1934-*** Here, O my Lord : unis. with descant & organ / [music by] Barry Rose ; [words by] Horatius Bonar.

Bonastre, Francesc.
See **La misa policoral en Cataluña en la segunda mitad del siglo XVII** / introducción, estudio y transcripción, Francesc Bonastre.

Bonighton, Rosalie.
See **Couple the tuba** : manuals / Rosalie Bonighton ... [et al.]

See **Easy-to-play famous waltzes** : piano / arranged [by] Rosalie Bonighton.

The Boosey woodwind [method]
The Boosey woodwind [method] Alto saxophone. Repertoire book C. — *Boosey & Hawkes*
788.73143
013192539

Booth, Addi.
See **1.22.03.Acoustic** : guitar recorded versions / Maroon 5 ; music transcriptions by Addi Booth.

See **Beck.** Guero / Beck ; music transcriptions by Pete Billmann, Addi Booth and David Stocker.

See **Good news for people who love bad news** : guitar recorded versions / by Modest

Mouse ; music transcriptions by Pete Billmann, Addi Booth and Jeff Story.

See **Start something** / Lostprophets ; music transcriptions by Addi Booth and David Stocker.

See **Vai, Steve.** Eat 'em and smile / David Lee Roth ; music transcriptions by Addi Booth.

Booth, Barton, *1681-1733.*
See **Pepusch, John Christopher, *1667-1752.*** [Death of Dido. Oh I feel the friendly blow] Aria, Oh I feel the friendly blow : from The death of Dido : for soprano, recorder, strings and continuo / J.C. Pepusch.

Börtz, Daniel, *1943-*
[Adagio, orchestra] — Adagio per orchestra (1999) / Daniel Börtz. — *Gehrmans Musikförlag*
784.2
014457005

Pipor och klockor / Daniel Börtz. — *Gehrmans*
784.2836
014457007

The bossy king
See **Davies, Niki.** The bossy king

[Botschaften für die Königin von Saba]
See **Henze, Hans Werner, *1926-*** [Botschaften für die Königin von Saba]

Botschinsky, Allan, *1940-*
Colours for cello : for solo violoncello = für Violoncello solo / Allan Botschinsky. — *Peermusic Classical*
787.4
014457008

Boublil, Alain.
See **Schönberg, Claude-Michel.** [Misérables. *Vocal score. English. Selections*] Les Misérables : Boublil and Schönberg's legendary musical : in concert : piano, vocal, guitar / music by Claude-Michel Schönberg.

See **Schönberg, Claude-Michel.** [Musicals. *Vocal scores. Selections*] The Boublil-Schönberg collection : show hits : twelve great show songs, ideal for auditions.

The Boublil-Schönberg collection
See **Schönberg, Claude-Michel.** [Musicals. *Vocal scores. Selections*] The Boublil-Schönberg collection

Bouissou, Sylvie.
See **Rameau, Jean-Philippe, *1683-1764.*** Hippolyte et Aricie : tragédie en cinq actes : version 1757 ; version 1742 (compléments) / [musique de Jean Philippe Rameau] ; livret de Simon-Joseph Pellegrin ; édition de Sylvie Bouissou.

Boulez, Pierre, *1925-*
See **Serei, Zsolt.** L'ombre sur les structures pliées : hommage à Pierre Boulez : pour deux clarinettes et cinq instruments à cordes = for two clarinets and five strings / Serei Zsolt.

Boulter, Bryan.
Song without words : for violoncello and piano / Bryan Boulter. — *Da Capo Music*
787.41896
013351683

Bouvard, François, *1683-1760.*
La feste de Cloris : cantata for soprano, violin, flute, oboe, bassoon & continuo / François Bouvard. — *Green Man Press*
783.6648
013596823

Bovet, Guy.
[Esquisses japonaises] — Three Japanese sketches : for organ / Guy Bovet. — *Oxford University Press*
786.5
013115370

Bowen, Meirion.
See **Gerhard, Roberto, *1896-1970.*** For whom the bell tolls : per a guitarra / Robert Gerhard ; revisio i edicio de Meirion Bowen i Eugenio Tobalina.

Bowman, Peter, *1952-*
See **Fun and games with the recorder** : method for the alto recorder. Tune book / [compiled by] Gudrun Heyens and Gerhard Engel ; translated and adapted by Peter Bowman ; with illustrations by John Minnion.

See **Heyens, Gudrun.** Fun and games with the alto recorder : method for the alto recorder. Tutor book 2 / by Gudrun Heyens and Gerhard Engel ; translated and adapted by Peter Bowman ; with illustrations by Julie Beech and John Minnion.

See **Heyens, Gudrun.** Fun and games with the alto recorder. Teacher's commentary / Gudrun Heyens and Gerhard Engel ; translated and adapted by Peter Bowman.

The boy king
See **Spencer, Tim.** [Boy king. *Selections*] The boy king

See **Spencer, Tim.** The boy king

[Boy king. *Selections*]
See **Spencer, Tim.** [Boy king. *Selections*]

Boyd, Anne, *1946-*
[Concertos, flute, string orchestra] — Concerto for flute and strings / Anne Boyd. — *University of York Music Press*
784.72832186
013430702

Meditations on a Chinese character : for ensemble / Anne Boyd. — *University of York Music Press*
783.8642
013430714

Boyd, Bill.
Jazz bits and pieces : original piano solos in various jazz styles / by Bill Boyd. — *Hal Leonard*
786.2165
013376419

Jazz sketches : original piano solos in various jazz styles / by Bill Boyd. — *Hal Leonard*
786.2165
013376391

Boyle, Rory.
Flower of all : a carol of the Incarnation : SSAA chorus / Rory Boyle ; text, John Audelay, c.1426 (adapted). — *Novello Publishing*
782.628
013434226

Bozó, Péter.
See **Liszt, Franz, *1811-1886.*** [Piano music. *Selections*] Freie Bearbeitungen. XIII = Free arrangements. XIII / Franz Liszt ; herausgegeben von Péter Bozó, Adrienne Kaczmarczyk.

Bracha
See **Warshauer, Meira, *1949-*** Bracha

Bradley, Kate.
See **Best of gold** : the essential collection.

Brady, Deborah.
Monday's child : a child's blessings / by Deborah Brady ; editor, Margaret Otwell. — *Hal Leonard*
786.2
013376373

The toymaker's workshop : for one piano, four hands / by Deborah Brady ; edited by J. Mark Baker. — *Hal Leonard*
785.62192
013376406

The twelve days of Christmas / by Deborah Brady ; edited by J. Mark Baker. — *Hal Leonard*
786.21723
013376182

Brahms, Johannes, *1833-1897.*
[Concertos, violin, orchestra, op. 77, D major]
— Violinkonzert D-Dur Opus 77 / Johannes
Brahms ; herausgegeben von Linda Correll
Roesner und Michael Struck. — *G. Henle Verlag*
784.272186   013474479

[Quartets, strings] — Streichquartette / Johannes
Brahms ; herausgegben von Salome Reiser. —
G. Henle Verlag
785.7194   013465904

[Symphonies, no. 3, op. 90, F major] —
Symphonie Nr. 3, F-Dur, Opus 90 / Johannes
Brahms ; herausgegeben von Robert Pascall. —
G. Henle
784.2184   013428349

[Variationen über ein Thema von Haydn.
Selections; arr.] — Variations on a theme of
Haydn / by Johanness Brahms ; arranged for two
oboes and cor anglais by Rachel Broadbent. —
Phylloscopus Publications
785.851931825   013472830

Brandon, David.
See **Parkening, Christopher.** The Christopher
Parkening guitar method. Vol. 1 : the art and
technique of the classical guitar / in
collaboration with Jack Marshall and David
Brandon.

See **Parkening, Christopher.** The Christopher
Parkening guitar method. Vol. 2 : the art and
technique of the classical guitar / in
collaboration with David Brandon.

Brasser
See **Binney, Malcolm.** Brasser

Bratton, John W. *1867-1947.*
[Teddy bears' picnic; *arr.*] — The teddy bears'
picnic / John W. Bratton ; arranged for three
bassoons by Toddy Harman. — *Emerson Edition*
785.858193   013360855

Bremner, Robert, *d. 1789.*
See **Thistle & minuet** : 16 easy pieces from the
Scottish Baroque for violin (or flute or oboe),
keyboard, and optional cello (or bassoon) = 16
einfache Stücke aus der schottischen Barockzeit
für Violine (oder Flöte oder Oboe),
Tasteninstrument und Cello (oder Fagott) ad
libitum = 16 pièces faciles du Baroque écossais
pour violon (ou flûte ou hautbois), clavier et
violoncelle (ou basson) facultatif / edited by
David Johnson.

Brentnall, Ian, *1961-*
See **As Joseph was a-walking** : for mixed choir
(SATB), oboe and organ / [traditional, arr.] Ian
Brentnall.

Breth, Nancy O'Neill.
See **Six songs from John Gay's The beggar's
opera** / arranged for piano trio by Nancy
O'Neill Breth and Jean Goberman ; edited by J.
Mark Baker.

Brett, Philip.
See **Byrd, William,** 1542 or 3-1623. [Psalmes,
sonets, and songs] Psalmes, sonets and songs
(1588) / [William Byrd] ; edited by Jeremy
Smith.

See **Byrd, William,** 1542 or 3-1623. [Songs of
sundrie natures] Songs of sundrie natures (1589)
/ [William Byrd] ; edited by David Mateer.

Bridges, Thomas Whitney, *1930-*
See **Aleotti, Raffaella,** ca. 1570-ca. 1646.
Sacrae cantiones : quinque, septem, octo &
decem vocibus decantandae / Raffaella Aleotti ;
edited by C. Ann Carruthers ; introduction by
Thomas W. Bridges.

Bridgewater breeze
See **Gorb, Adam,** 1958- Bridgewater breeze

Brikner, Eryk, *1705-1760.*
[Completorium (RISM A/II 300.033.575)] —
Completorium : a canto & basso obligato, alto &
tenore ad libitum, due violini con organo ;
Hymnus pro festis apostolorum : a canto, alto,
tenore, basso con organo / Eryk Brikner ;
opracowanie i wstęp Aleksandra Patalas. —
Wyd. 1. — Klasztor OO. Paulinów Jasna Góra
782.526   013887063

Brikner, Eryk, *1705-1760.* **Hymnus pro festis
apostolorum.**
See **Brikner, Eryk,** 1705-1760. [Completorium
(RISM A/II 300.033.575)] Completorium : a
canto & basso obligato, alto & tenore ad libitum,
due violini con organo ; Hymnus pro festis
apostolorum : a canto, alto, tenore, basso con
organo / Eryk Brikner ; opracowanie i wstęp
Aleksandra Patalas.

British Library. *Additional 17802-5.*
See **The Gyffard partbooks I** / transcribed and
edited by David Mateer.

Broadbent, Jason.
See **The big acoustic guitar chord songbook.**
Female.

See **The big guitar chord songbook.** Classic
rock.

Broadbent, Rachel.
See **Brahms, Johannes,** 1833-1897.
[Variationen über ein Thema von Haydn.
Selections; arr.] Variations on a theme of Haydn
/ by Johanness Brahms ; arranged for two oboes
and cor anglais by Rachel Broadbent.

Brod, Henri, *1799-1839.*
[Fantaisie, oboe, piano] — Fantaisie : oboe &
piano / Henri Brod ; edited by Myron Zakopets.
— *Emerson Edition*
788.521894   013188350

Brooker, Gary.
[Whiter shade of pale; *arr.*] — A whiter shade of
pale : grade 3 / Gary Brooker ; arr. Kit Turnbull.
— *Studio Music*
784.8   013359070

Brookes, Katherine.
The gunpowder plot : remember, remember the
5th of November. — *Maplewood Education*
782.14083   013390750

Happy Christmas Tommy : the Christmas
miracle of 1914. — *Maplewood Education*
782.141723083   013390785

[Happy Christmas Tommy. *Selections*] — Happy
Christmas Tommy : the Christmas miracle of
1914 : assembly pack. — *Maplewood
Education :*
782.7421723   013587523

Perfect pirates : the story of Anne Bonny &
Mary Read. — *Maplewood Education*
782.14083   013390755

Pompeii : the rain of fire / written by Katherine
Brookes ; music by Katherine Brookes. —
Maplewood Education :
782.14083   013587134

[Pompeii. *Selections*] — Pompeii : escape from
the cloud : assembly pack / written by Katherine
Brookes ; music by Katherine Brookes. —
Educational Musicals
782.7   013587016

[Pompeii. *Selections*] — Pompeii : life in a
Roman town : assembly pack / written by
Katherine Brookes ; music by Katherine
Brookes. — *Educational Musicals*
782.7   013587020

The Saxon king : the story of Sutton Hoo. —
Maplewood Education :
782.14083   013587305

See **Christmas selection 1** : a collection of
songs from Educational Musicals' Christmas
shows.

See **Christmas selection 2** : a collection of
songs from our Christmas shows.

See **Hewitt, Daniel.** World wars I & II : a
collection of wars songs from Educational
Musicals shows / [music & lyrics by Daniel
Hewitt & Katherine Brookes]

Brookes, Virginia.
See **3 in nomines à 4** : (TrTr/TTB) / Parsons,
Parsley & Weelkes ; edited by Virginia Brookes.

See **Browne, John,** ca. 1608-1691. [In nomine,
viols (5)] In nomine fantasia & Ayre à 5 :
TrTrBB / John Browne ; edited by Virginia
Brookes.

See **Giovannelli, Ruggiero,** ca. 1560-1625.
[Selections] Three pieces à 5 : TrTrTTB /
Ruggiero Giovannelli ; edited by Virginia
Brookes.

See **Jenkins, John,** 1592-1678. [Fantasias, viols
(3). *Selections*] 3 fantasias à 3 : nos. 10, 11 &
12 : (TrTrB) / John Jenkins ; edited by Virginia
Brookes.

See **Jenkins, John,** 1592-1678. [Fantasias, viols
(3). *Selections*] 3 fantasias à 3 : nos. 7, 8 & 9 :
(TrTrB) / John Jenkins ; edited by Virginia
Brookes.

See **Johnson, Robert,** ca. 1500-ca. 1560.
[Knell] A knell of Johnson / Robert Johnson.
Pavan à 5 / Joseph Lupo ; edited by Virginia
Brookes.

See **Milton, John,** ca. 1563-1647. [If that a
sinner's sighs, voices (5)] Two settings of "If
that a sinner's sighs" : à 5, TrTrTTB, fully
texted : [and] à 6, TrTrT(with text)TBB / John
Milton ; edited by Virginia Brookes.

Brother bear (Motion picture)
See **Collins, Phil.** Brother bear : piano, vocal,
guitar / [words and music by Phil Collins] —
Walt Disney Music Co.

See **Collins, Phil.** [Look through my eyes; *arr.*]
Look through my eyes : from Walt Disney
Pictures' Brother Bear : SAB / words and music
by Phil Collins ; arranged by Ed Lojeski. —
Walt Disney Music Company

See **Collins, Phil.** [Look through my eyes; *arr.*]
Look through my eyes : from Walt Disney
Pictures' Brother Bear : SATB / words and
music by Phil Collins ; arranged by Ed Lojeski.
— *Walt Disney Music Company*

Brother bear
See **Collins, Phil.** Brother bear

Brouwer, Leo, *1939-*
Pictures at another exhibition : for horn, violin
and piano / Leo Brouwer. — *Chester Music*
785.25193   013182227

Brown, Alan, *1941-*
See **Byrd, William,** 1542 or 3-1623. [Keyboard
music. *Selections*] Keyboard music II / William
Byrd ; transcribed and edited by Alan Brown.

Brown, Clive, *1947-*
See **Clement, Franz,** 1780-1842. [Concertos,
violin, orchestra, D major] Violin concerto in D
major : (1805) / Franz Clement ; edited by Clive
Brown.

Brown, George Mackay.
See **Davies, Peter Maxwell,** 1934- Sea elegy :
for SATB soli, chorus and orchestra : (1998) /
Peter Maxwell Davies ; words by George
Mackay Brown.

Browne, John, ca. 1608-1691.
[In nomine, viols (5)] — In nomine fantasia &
Ayre à 5 : TrTrBB / John Browne ; edited by
Virginia Brookes. — *Viola da Gamba Society of
Great Britain*
785.76195   013424757

Browne, John, ca. 1608-1691. Ayre,
See **Browne, John, ca. 1608-1691.** [In nomine,
viols (5)] In nomine fantasia & Ayre à 5 :
TrTrBB / John Browne ; edited by Virginia
Brookes.

Bruce, William, 1957-
See **Spectrum :** for cello : 16 contemporary
pieces / compiled by William Bruce.

Bruckner, Anton, 1824-1896.
[Masses, no. 3, F minor] — Messe f-Moll /
[Anton Bruckner] — *Kritische Neuausgabe / —
Musikwissenschaftlicher Verlag der
Internationalen Bruckner-Gesellschaft*
782.53232   014654474

[Quintet, violins, violas, violoncello, F major]
— Streichquintett F-Dur ; Intermezzo D-Moll /
Anton Bruckner. — *Kritische Neuausg. / —
Musikwissenschaftlicher Verlag der
Internationalen Bruckner-Gesellschaft*
785.7195   013801996

[Symphonies, no. 2, C minor] — II. Symphonie,
C-Moll : Fassung von 1872 / Anton Bruckner ;
vorgelegt von William Carragan. —
*Musikwissenschaftlicher Verlag der
Internationalen Bruckner-Gesellschaft*
784.2184   013622832

Bruckner, Anton, 1824-1896. Intermezzo,
See **Bruckner, Anton, 1824-1896.** [Quintet,
violins, violas, violoncello, F major]
Streichquintett F-Dur ; Intermezzo D-Moll /
Anton Bruckner.

Brühl, Heike.
See **O'Neill, John, 1955-** Developing jazz
technique for flute : improvisation, style, special
effects = Technique de jazz pour flûte :
improvisation, style, effets spéciaux =
Jazztechnik für Querflöte : Improvisation,
Stilistik, Spezialeffekte / John O'Neill ;
traduction Agnès Ausseur ; Übersetzung Heike
Brühl.

Brumby, Colin.
Scena : for cor anglais and strings / by Colin
Brumby. — *Phylloscopus Publications*
784.72853   013188736

[Scena; *arr.*] — Scena : for cor anglais and
strings : version for cor anglais and piano / by
Colin Brumby. — *Phylloscopus Publications*
788.53   013188776

Brunner, David L., 1953-
Painted memories : 2-pt treble / [music by]
David L. Brunner. — *Boosey & Hawkes*
782.7642   013243919

Bryan, John, 1952-
See **Wilder, Philip van, d. 1553.** [Chansons.
Selections] 3 chansons à 4 & à 5 : (TrTr/TTB
with text) / Philip Van Wilder ; edited by John
Bryan.

Buchner, Philipp Friedrich, 1614-1669.
Harmonia instrumentalis : 12 sonate per 2
violini, fagotto e basso continuo, op. 5,
Würzburg 1664 / Philipp Friedrich Buchner ;
trascrizione a cura di Alessandro Bares. —
Musedita
785.24194   014599810

Buckley, Jeff, 1966-1997.
[Songs. *Selections*] — Jeff Buckley : arranged
for piano [sic] — *Wise*
783.242164   013441950

Bugeilio'r gwenith gwyn
Bugeilio'r gwenith gwyn = Watching the white
wheat : traditional Welsh folk-song arranged for
SSA choir, solo voice and piano / by Jayne
Davies ; English text by Rhian Davies. —
Roberton Publications
782.64216209429   013193376

Bullard, Alan, 1947-
Circus skills : [eight pieces for alto saxophone in
E♭ and piano] / Alan Bullard. — *Spartan Press*
788.73   013169171

Circus skills : [oboe and piano] / Alan Bullard.
— *Spartan Press*
788.52   013172410

Burgmüller, Friedrich, 1806-1874.
[Etudes faciles et progressives] — 25
progressive studies : opus 100 / Burgmüller ;
edited by Margaret Otwell. — *G. Schirmer*
786.218949   013191046

The burning babe
See **Dicie, Don Michael.** The burning babe

Burns, Alison.
See **Raining bliss and benison :** a collection of
folk carols arranged for voices / compiled and
arranged by Alison Burns ; illustrations by
Denise Zygadlo.

Burns, Robert, 1759-1796.
See **My love is like a red, red rose :** SATB /
Scottish traditional ; arranged by Jonathan
Rathbone ; words by Robert Burns.

See **The white cockade :** Jacobite song arranged
for male voice choir with accompaniment of
snare drum and two piccolos / by Bryan Davies.

Burrows, Donald, 1945-
See **Handel, George Frideric, 1685-1759**
[Samson. *Vocal score*] Samson : an oratorio for
soloists (3 sopranos, alto, 2 tenors, 2 basses; or
soprano, alto tenor and bass), mixed chorus and
orchestra / music by George Frideric Handel ;
words by Newburgh Hamilton, after John
Milton's Samson Agonistes ; edited by Donald
Burrows ; vocal score.

Burt, Phil.
See **Junior praise /** compiled by Phil Burt, Peter
Horrobin and Greg Leavers.

Buschmann, Eberhard, bassoonist.
See **Rosetti, Antonio, ca. 1750-1792.** [Partitas,
woodwinds, horns (3), violone, M. B18, F
major] Partita in F-Dur für 2 Flöten, 2 Oboen, 2
Klarinetten, 3 Hörner, 2 Fagotte und Kontrabass,
RWV B18 = Partita in F major for 2 flutes, 2
oboes, 2 clarinets, 3 horns, 2 bassoons and
double-bass / Antonio Rosetti ; herausgegeben
von Eberhard Buschmann.

Bushes and briars
Bushes and briars : alto solo, SSATTBB :
English traditional / arranged by Ben Parry. —
Edition Peters
782.542   013304845

Butchart, David S.
See **Striggio, Alessandro, 1536 or 7-1592.**
[Madrigals, voices (5), book 1] Il primo libro di
madrigali a cinque voci / Alessandro Striggio ;
edited by David Butchart.

Buxtehude, Dietrich, 1637-1707.
[Laudate pueri] — Laudate pueri Dominum :
chiaccona für 2 Soprane, 6 Gamben (oder andere
Streicher) und B.c., BuxWV 69 = chiaconna für
2 sopranos, 6 viols (or other strings) and b.c. /
Dieterich Buxtehude ; Generalbassaussetzung
von Dankwart von Zadow ; herausgegeben von
Günter und Leonore Zadow. — *Edition
Güntersberg*
783.126648   013887064

By purling streams
See **Croft, William, 1678-1727.** By purling
streams

By your word, O God
See **Schelat, David.** By your word, O God

Byrd, William, 1542 or 3-1623.
[Emendemus in melius; *arr.*] — Emendemus in
melius : à 5 / William Byrd. — *Alex Ayre Music
Services*
785.836195   013374803

[Keyboard music. *Selections*] — Keyboard
music II / William Byrd ; transcribed and edited
by Alan Brown. — *3rd, rev. ed.* — *Stainer and
Bell*
786   013196013

[Psalmes, sonets, and songs] — Psalmes, sonets
and songs (1588) / [William Byrd] ; edited by
Jeremy Smith. — *Stainer & Bell*
782.542   013063061

[Songs of sundrie natures] — Songs of sundrie
natures (1589) / [William Byrd] ; edited by
David Mateer. — *Stainer & Bell*
782.542   013201995

Cake dance suite
See **Aitken, Elizabeth, 1949-** Cake dance suite

Caldara, Antonio, 1670-1736.
[Clori, mia bella Clori] — Cantata, Clori, mia
bella Clori : for contralto, flute, oboe & basso
continuo / Antonio Caldara ; edited by Gail
Hennessy. — *Green Man Press*
783.6848   013589459

Cambini, Giuseppe Maria, 1746-1825.
[Quintets, violins, viola, violoncellos, no. 21, C
minor] — 21. Quintett in c-moll für 2 Violinen,
Viola und 2 Violoncelli = 21. quintet in C minor
for two violins, viola and two violoncellos /
Giuseppe Cambini ; nach dem Autograph
herausgegeben von Bernhard Päuler. —
Erstdruck. — *Amadeus*
785.7195   013887065

Campion, Thomas, 1567-1620.
See **Davies, Bryan.** [Never weather beaten sail,
men's voices] Never weather beaten sail /
[words by] Thomas Campion ; [setting by]
Bryan Davies.

See **Davies, Bryan.** [Never weather beaten sail,
mixed voices] Never weather beaten sail /
[words by] Thomas Campion ; [setting by]
Bryan Davies.

Campra, André, 1660-1744.
[Cantates françoises, livre 1. Femmes] — Les
femmes : cantata for bass, two violins &
continuo / André Campra. — *Green Man Press*
783.8948   013597179

Cancionero poético-musical hispánico de Lisboa
Cancionero poético-musical hispánico de Lisboa
/ introducción y edición crítica de Mariano
Lambea y Lola Josa. — *Sociedad Española de
Musicología*
782.543   013647252

Cangia mio cor
See **Mazzocchi, D. 1592-1665.** [Musiche sacre,
e morali. Cangia miio cor] Cangia mio cor

Canovacci
See **McAlister, Clark.** Canovacci

Cantare con silenzio
See **Sciarrino, Salvatore.** Cantare con silenzio

A cantata & two canzonettas
See **Legrenzi, Giovanni, 1626-1690.** [Cantate e
canzonette. *Selections*] A cantata & two
canzonettas

Cantata, Clori, mia bella Clori
See **Caldara, Antonio, 1670-1736.** [Clori, mia bella Clori] Cantata, Clori, mia bella Clori

[Cantatas, bass, continuo. *Selections*]
See **Cesti, Antonio, 1623-1669.** [Cantatas, bass, continuo. *Selections*]

[Cantatas, book 3. Tircis et Climene]
See **Montéclair, Michel Pignolet de, 1667-1737.** [Cantatas, book 3. Tircis et Climene]

[Cantatas, op. 8]
See **Stanley, John, 1712-1786.** [Cantatas, op. 8]

[Cantatas. *Selections*]
See **Handel, George Frideric, 1685-1759.** [Cantatas. *Selections*]

See **Scarlatti, Alessandro, 1660-1725.** [Cantatas. *Selections*]

See **Telemann, Georg Philipp, 1681-1767.** [Cantatas. *Selections*]

[Cantate e canzonette. *Selections*]
See **Legrenzi, Giovanni, 1626-1690.** [Cantate e canzonette. *Selections*]

[Cantates françoises, 2e livre. Diane et Endimion]
See **Bernier, Nicolas, 1665-1734.** [Cantates françoises, 2e livre. Diane et Endimion]

[Cantates françoises, livre 1. Femmes]
See **Campra, André, 1660-1744.** [Cantates françoises, livre 1. Femmes]

[Cantates françoises, livre 2. Léandre et Héro]
See **Clérambault, Louis-Nicolas, 1676-1749.** [Cantates françoises, livre 2. Léandre et Héro]

[Cantates françoises, livre 3. Mort d'Hercule]
See **Clérambault, Louis-Nicolas, 1676-1749.** [Cantates françoises, livre 3. Mort d'Hercule]

Canti d'ombre
See **Vacchi, Fabio, 1949-** Canti d'ombre

Cantica nova
Cantica nova : 18 new motets for choirs. — *Oxford University Press*
782.526   013062771

Cantilena
See **Barret, Apollon Marie-Rose, 1803-1879.** [Cantilène; *arr.*] Cantilena
See **Baker, Ernest, 1912-** Cantilena

Cantilene
See **Trapp, Lynn.** Cantilene

[Cantilène; *arr.*]
See **Barret, Apollon Marie-Rose, 1803-1879.** [Cantilène; *arr.*]

Cantiones quatuor vocum
See **Crecquillon, Thomas, d. 1557?** [Chansons, voices (4). *Selections*] Cantiones quatuor vocum

Cantiones quinque vocum (Munich, 1597)
See **Lasso, Orlando di, 1532-1594.** [Motets. *Selections.*] Cantiones quinque vocum (Munich, 1597)

Cantiones sacrae
Cantiones sacrae : madrigalian motets from Jacobean England / edited by Ross W. Duffin. — *A-R Editions*
782.526   013379210

[Canzonettas, violin, continuo acc.]
See **Fesch, Willem de, 1687-1761.** [Canzonettas, violin, continuo acc.]

[Canzonette ed arie, violin, continuo acc.]
See **Fesch, Willem de, 1687-1761.** [Canzonette ed arie, violin, continuo acc.]

[Capricci, Canzoni und Sonaten]
See **Vierdanck, Johann, ca. 1605-1646.** [Capricci, Canzoni und Sonaten]

Capricci, Canzoni und Sonaten
See **Vierdanck, Johann, ca. 1605-1646.** [Capricci, Canzoni und Sonaten] Capricci, Canzoni und Sonaten

Capriccio
See **Routh, Francis.** Capriccio
See **Verroust, Stanislas, 1814-1863.** [Capriccios, oboe, piano] Capriccio

[Capriccio sinfonico]
See **Puccini, Giacomo, 1858-1924.** [Capriccio sinfonico]

Capriccio sinfonico
See **Puccini, Giacomo, 1858-1924.** [Capriccio sinfonico] Capriccio sinfonico

[Capriccios, oboe, piano]
See **Verroust, Stanislas, 1814-1863.** [Capriccios, oboe, piano]

Capricornus, Samuel, d. 1665.
Theatrum musicum : quod per duodecim scenas seu sacras cantiones / aperuit Samuel Capricornus. — *Cornetto-Verlag*
782.524   013521766

I Capuleti e i Montecchi
See **Bellini, Vincenzo, 1801-1835.** I Capuleti e i Montecchi

Carbonell i Saurí, Albert, *1972-*
Seqüències : sis petites peces per a clarinet, violí, violoncel i piano / Albert Carbonell i Saurí. — *Institució Alfons el Magnànim :*
785.24194   014457010

Carden, Allen D., *1792-1859.*
See **The Missouri harmony :** or, a choice collection of psalm tunes, hymns, and anthems / [compiled] by Wings of Song.

Cardone, Francesco, *16th cent.* **Canto llano & Contrapunto sobre el Canto llano.**
See **Neapolitan lute music** / Fabrizio Dentice … [et al.] ; edited by John Griffiths and Dinko Fabris.

Careless love
Careless love / Madeleine Peyroux. — *Wise*
783.242164   013376154

Carey, Paul, *1954-*
Behold, I tell you a mystery : for unaccompanied mixed choir (SATB) / Paul Carey. — *Oxford University Press*
782.5265   013472331

A cradle song : for upper voices (SA) and piano or harp / Paul Carey. — *Oxford University Press*
782.642   013174157

A million miracles : a Celtic prayer for mixed choir (SATB) and piano / Paul Carey. — *Oxford University Press*
782.5265   013324499

See **Il est né le divin enfant :** for unaccompanied mixed choir (SATB) / traditional French ; arr. Paul Carey.

Carillon, op. 75
See **Elgar, Edward, 1857-1934.** [Carillon; *arr.*] Carillon, op. 75

[Carillon; *arr.*]
See **Elgar, Edward, 1857-1934.** [Carillon; *arr.*]

Carle, Tomaso. Trios,
See **Esser, Karl Michael, Ritter von, 1737-ca. 1795.** [Duets, viola d'amore, viola da gamba] Three pieces for viola d'amore & viola da gamba or violoncello (1789) / Karl Michael, Ritter von Esser. Two pieces for violin, viola d'amore & viola da gamba or violoncello (1789) / Tomaso Carle ; edited by David J. Rhodes.

Carlson, Kent.
See **Fenaroli, Fedele, 1730-1818.** Stabat mater : for soprano, alto, strings & basso continuo / Fedele Fenaroli ; edited by Alejandro Garri ; assisted by Kent Carlson.

See **Graun, Johann Gottlieb, 1702 or 3-1771** [Concertos, viola da gamba, string orchestra, A major] Concerto in A major for viola da gamba, strings & basso continuo / Johann Gottlieb Graun ; edited by Alejandro Garri ; assisted by Kent Carlson.

See **Hasse, Johann Adolf, 1699-1783.** Ascolta i preghi : (Psalm 42:9, 10) : motet for 2 sopranos and basso continuo / Johann A. Hasse ; edited by Alejandro Garri ; assisted by Kent Carlson.

See **Hasse, Johann Adolf, 1699-1783.** Ave Regina coelorum : Marian antiphon for alto, 2 oboes, strings & basso continuo / Johann A. Hasse ; edited by Alejandro Garri ; assisted by Kent Carlson.

See **Herbst, Johann Andreas, 1588-1666** Lobet, ihr Knechte des Herrn : (Psalm 113) : motet for tenor, baritone, bass, 2 violins & basso continuo / Johann Andreas Herbst ; edited by Alejandro Garri ; assisted by Kent Carlson.

See **Herbst, Johann Andreas, 1588-1666.** Erbarm' dich mein, o Herre Gott : (Psalm 51) : Miserere for baritone or bass, strings & basso continuo ; edited by Alejandro Garri, assited by Kent Carlson.

See **Werner, Gregor Joseph, 1695-1766.** [Salve Regina, voices (4), violins (2), organ, B♭ major] Salve Regina : in B-flat major : for mixed choir, two violins and organ / by Gregor Joseph Werner ; edited by Alejandro Garri ; assisted by Kent Carlson.

Carlson, Rosalind.
Circle of memories : for solo oboe / by Rosalind Calson. — *Phylloscopus Publications*
788.52   013472889

[Forest bell-birds, flute] — Forest bell-birds : for solo flute / by Rosalind Carlson. — *Phylloscopus Publications*
788.32   013173910

[Forest bell-birds, piccolo] — Forest bell-birds : for solo piccolo / by Rosalind Carlson. — *Phylloscopus Publications*
788.33   013173909

Carlton, Vanessa.
Harmonium : piano, vocal, guitar / Vanessa Carlton. — *Hal Leonard*
783.242166   013335640

[Carmen. *Selections; arr.*]
See **Bizet, Georges, 1838-1875.** [Carmen. *Selections; arr.*]

[Carnaval des animaux. Cygne; *arr.*]
See **Saint-Saëns, Camille, 1835-1921.** [Carnaval des animaux. Cygne; *arr.*]

Carol medley
Carol medley : Deck the halls ; I saw three ships ; We wish you a merry Christmas ; The holly and the ivy ; The first nowell ; Past three o'clock : SSAATTBB (with optional organ part) / arranged by Jonathan Rathbone. — *Edition Peters*
782.5241723   013304437

Carols
See **Rutter, John, 1945-** [Carols. *Selections*]
Carols

[Carols, mixed voices, orchestra. *Vocal score*]
See **Warlock, Peter, 1894-1930.** [Carols, mixed
voices, orchestra. *Vocal score*]

[Carols. *Selections*]
See **Rutter, John, 1945-** [Carols. *Selections*]

Carpenè, Aaron.
See **Hassler, Hans Leo, 1564-1612.**
[Magnificats, organ. *Selections*] 14 magnificat :
(Torino, Biblioteca nazionale Fondo Giordano
III, V) / Hans Leo Hassler ; a cura di Aaron
Carpenè.

Carr, Gordon, *1943-*
Mr. McKie's valediction : for solo bassoon with
three companions / Gordon Carr. — *Emerson
Edition*
785.858194   013460625

Carr, Paul.
Diverting Sundays : for wind quintet / by Paul
Carr. — *Phylloscopus Publications*
785.43195   013188715

[Pieces blue, bassoon, piano (2004)] — Three
pieces blue : for bassoon and piano / by Paul
Carr. — *Phylloscopus Publications*
788.58   013188797

See **The big guitar chord songbook.** Classic
rock.

Carragan, William.
See **Bruckner, Anton, 1824-1896.**
[Symphonies, no. 2, C minor] II. Symphonie,
C-Moll : Fassung von 1872 / Anton Bruckner ;
vorgelegt von William Carragan.

Carroll, Fergal.
Song of Lir : [2004] : for symphonic wind band /
Fergal Carroll. — *Maecenas Music*
784.8   013192951

Carroll, Lewis, *1832-1898.* **Alice's adventures in
Wonderland.**
See **Johnson, Mark.** Alice - the musical : a
children's musical with up to eighteen songs, in
two acts / by Mark and Helen Johnson ; based
on the original story of 'Alice's adventures in
Wonderland', by Lewis Carroll, retold in song
and dance, drama and narrative.

Carruthers, C. Ann.
See **Aleotti, Raffaella, ca. 1570-ca. 1646.**
Sacrae cantiones : quinque, septem, octo &
decem vocibus decantandae / Raffaella Aleotti ;
edited by C. Ann Carruthers ; introduction by
Thomas W. Bridges.

Carter, Andrew.
O mistress mine / Andrew Carter. — *Oxford
University Press*
782.542   013134168

[Organ music. *Selections*] — Organ album /
Andrew Carter. — *Oxford University Press*
786.5   013062631

Carter, Richard, composer.
See **Praetorius, Bartholomeus, ca. 1590-1623.**
[Newe liebliche Paduanen und Galliarden]
Pavans and galliards in five parts = Newe
liebliche Paduanen und Galliarden mit fünff
Stimmen, 1616 / Bartholomeus Praetorius ;
[Bearbeitung und Herausgabe, Richard Carter]

Case, John Carol.
See **Sing solo contralto** / edited by Constance
Shacklock ; general editor, John Carol Case.

See **Sing solo tenor** / edited by Robert Tear ;
general editor, John Carol Case.

Casken, John.
Nearly distant : for saxophone quartet : (2000) /
John Casken. — *Schott*
785.87194   013190541

Casken, John. Distant variations.
See **Casken, John.** Nearly distant : for
saxophone quartet : (2000) / John Casken.

Cassaro, James P.
See **Lully, Jean Baptiste, 1632-1687** [Ballets.
Vocal scores. Selections] Ballet des saisons ; Les
amours déguisés ; Ballet royal de Flore /
Jean-Baptiste Lully ; édition [par Ballet des
saisons] de James P. Cassaro ; édition [par Les
amours déguisés] de James R. Anthony et
Rebecca Harris-Warrick ; édition [par Ballet
royal de flore] d'Albert Cohen ; réduction
clavier-chant, Noam A. Krieger.

Castellani, Marcello.
See **Atys, 1715-1784.** [Sonatas, flutes (2), op. 1]
Six sonates en duo : en forme de conversation :
pour deux flûtes traversières : Paris s.d. / Atys.

Catena
See **LeFanu, Nicola.** Catena

Cather, Willa, *1873-1947.* **My Antonia.**
See **Larsen, Libby.** My Ántonia : seven songs
for high voice and piano / Libby Larsen ; based
on the novel by Willa Cather ; text adapted by
Libby Larsen.

Catholic Church.
Tropaire séquentiaire prosaire prosulaire de
Moissac : (troisième quart du XIe siècle) :
Manuscrit Paris, Bibliothèque nationale de
France, n.a.l. 1871 / édition, introduction et
index par Marie-Noël Colette ; analyse de
l'écriture et de la décoration par Marie-Thérèse
Gousset. — *Société Française de Musicologie*
782.3222   013822688

Cavaccio, Giovanni, *ca. 1556-1626.*
[Music, voices (4)] — Musica a quattro voci :
Venezia 1597 / Giovanni Cavaccio ; a cura di
Daniele Salvatore. — *Ut Orpheus*
785.14   014167958

Cavallini, Ivano.
See **Puliti, Gabriello, b. ca. 1575.** Ghirlanda
odorifera : (1612) / Gabriello Puliti ;
transkribiral in revidiral = transcription and
revision by Ivano Cavallini.

Cellavenia, Francesco, *d. 1567.* **Missa Quem
dicunt homines.**
See **Tres missae super "Quem dicunt
homines"** / edidit Harry Elzinga.

Cello sight-reading.
See **Smith, Doreen, 1931-** Cello sight-reading.

[Cello, piano music. *Selections*]
See **Saint-Saëns, Camille, 1835-1921.** [Cello,
piano music. *Selections*]

Cellos for Christmas
Cellos for Christmas : 20 Christmas carols for
cellos / easy arrangements by Barrie Carson
Turner ; illustrations by John Minnion. — *Schott*
787.41723   013335629

Centorio, Marco Antonio, *d. 1638.*
Messa a sei voci / Marco Antonio Centorio ; a
cura di Marco Romagnoli. — *Libreria Musicale
Italiana*
782.53232   013688124

Centro di musicologia "Walter Stauffer".
See **Il codice rossiano 215** : madrigali, ballate,
una caccia, un rotondello / edizione critica e
studio introduttivo a cura di Tiziana Sucato.

**Centro Studi Opera Omnia Luigi
Boccherini-Onlus.**
See **Boccherini, Luigi, 1743-1805.** [Duets,
violins, G. 56-61] 6 duetti per 2 violini = 6 duets
for 2 violins = 6 Violinduette : opus 3 : G 56-62
/ Luigi Boccherini ; a cura di Rudolf Rasch.

Cerutti, Laura.
See **Hertel, Johann Wilhelm, 1727-1789.**
[Sonatas, harpsichord. *Selections*] Sei sonate per
il cembalo solo / Johann Wilhelm Hertel ;
herausgegeben von Laura Cerutti.

Cesti, Antonio, *1623-1669.*
[Cantatas, bass, continuo. *Selections*] — Four
cantatas for bass / Antonio Cesti ; a critical
performing edition edited by Barbara Sachs. —
Green Man Press
783.8948   013597096

Cesti, Antonio, *1623-1669.* **Chino la fronte.**
See **Cesti, Antonio, 1623-1669.** [Cantatas, bass,
continuo. *Selections*] Four cantatas for bass /
Antonio Cesti ; a critical performing edition
edited by Barbara Sachs.

[Chaconnes, harpsichord, S. C703, C major]
See **Marcello, Benedetto, 1686-1739.**
[Chaconnes, harpsichord, S. C703, C major]

[Chaconnes, violoncello, string orchestra, op. 51]
See **Routh, Francis.** [Chaconnes, violoncello,
string orchestra, op. 51]

**[Chaconnes, violoncello, string orchestra, op. 51;
arr.]**
See **Routh, Francis.** [Chaconnes, violoncello,
string orchestra, op. 51; *arr.*]

[Chamber music. *Selections*]
See **Rheinberger, Josef, 1839-1901.** [Chamber
music. *Selections*]

See **Ward, John, 1571-1638.** [Chamber music.
Selections]

[Chansons, voices (4). *Selections*]
See **Crecquillon, Thomas, d. 1557?** [Chansons,
voices (4). *Selections*]

[Chansons. *Selections*]
See **Wilder, Philip van, d. 1553.** [Chansons.
Selections]

Chapí, Ruperto, *1851-1909.*
La venta de Don Quijote : comedia lírica en un
acto / Ruperto Chapí ; libreto, Carlos Fernández
Shaw ; edición crítica Manuel Moreno-Buendia.
— *Instituto Complutense de Ciencias Musicales*
782.1   014679578

Chapple, Brian. For Latin lovers.
See **The violin** : a collection : new and recent
repertoire for violin with piano accompaniment /
Craig Armstrong … [et al.]

Charivari
See **Binney, Malcolm.** Charivari

Charles, Ray, *1930-2004.*
[Songs. *Selections*] — Ray : essential piano
songs : transcribed for piano, voice & guitar. —
Wise
783.242164   013199575

See **Play piano with— Ray Charles.**

Charlie is my darlin'
Charlie is my darlin' : SSAATTBB : Scottish
traditional / arranged by Ben Parry. — *Edition
Peters*
782.542   013304863

Charpentier, Marc-Antoine, *1643-1704.*
Acteon : H. 481 ; Acteon changé en biche, H.
481a / M.-A. Charpentier. — *Éditions des
Abbesses*
782.1   013728836

Charpentier, Marc-Antoine, *1643-1704.* **Acteon changé en biche.**
See **Charpentier, Marc-Antoine, 1643-1704.** Acteon : H. 481 ; Acteon changé en biche, H. 481a / M.-A. Charpentier.

Chechlińska, Zofia.
See **Chopin, Frédéric, 1810-1849.** [Sonatas, piano no. 3, op. 58, B minor] Sonata H-Moll Op. 58 : wydanie faksymilowe rękopisu ze zbiorów Biblioteki Narodowej w Warszawie (Mus. 232 Cim.) = Sonata in B minor, op. 58 : facsimile edition of the manuscript held in the National Library in Warsaw (Mus. 232 Cim.) : A IX/58 / Fryderyk Chopin ; Komitet redakcyjny = Editorial committee, Jean-Jacques Eigeldinger (przewodniczący = president), Zofia Chechlińska (redaktor naczelny = editor in chief) ... [et al.]

Chesterton, Frances, *1875-1938.*
See **Wilberg, Mack.** How far is it to Bethlehem? : for mixed choir (SATB), 2 flutes, and harp or piano / [English carol ; arranged by] Mack Wilberg.

Chi la dura la vince (Wer ausharrt, siegt)
See **Biber, Heinrich Ignaz Franz, 1644-1704.** Chi la dura la vince (Wer ausharrt, siegt)

Chi sà dove è speranza?
Chi sà dove è speranza? : cantata for soprano, oboe or recorder and continuo : an anonymous cantata from a manuscript in the Santini collection, Münster / attrib. A.D. Lignani. — *Green Man Press*
783.6648   013596854

Chilcott, Bob.
Advent antiphons : for SATB double choir a cappella / Bob Chilcott. — *Oxford University Press*
782.53261722   013382226

And every stone shall cry : SATB unaccompanied / Bob Chilcott. — *Oxford University Press*
782.5281723   013225229

[And peace on earth. Put memory away. *Vocal score*] — Put memory away : SATB and piano / Bob Chilcott. — *Oxford University Press*
782.5281723   013225234

The angel Gabriel / Bob Chilcott. — *Oxford University Press*
782.6281723   013084329

The dove and the olive leaf : for mixed choir (SATB), soprano saxophone (or B♭ clarinet) and piano / Bob Chilcott. — *Oxford University Press*
782.5265   013521812

The isle is full of noises : SAATB with divisions, unaccompanied / Bob Chilcott. — *Oxford University Press*
782.542   013132075

Now thank we : for mixed choir (SATB), soprano descant, and organ / Bob Chilcott. — *Oxford University Press*
782.5265   013515526

You and me : SATB unaccompanied / Bob Chilcott. — *Oxford University Press*
782.542   013225225

See **All my trials /** [arr.] Bob Chilcott.

See **World carols for choirs :** 31 carols for mixed voices / edited and compiled by Bob Chilcott & Susan Knight.

[Child of our time. *Selections; arr.*]
See **Tippett, Michael, 1905-1998.** [Child of our time. *Selections; arr.*]

Child, William, *1606?-1697.*
Sing we merrily : anthem for seven voices (SSAATTBB) with organ accompaniment / William Child. — *Anglo-American Music Publishers*
782.5265   013594302

[Children's corner. Little shepherd; *arr.*]
See **Debussy, Claude, 1862-1918** [Children's corner. Little shepherd; *arr.*]

Children's songs
Children's songs : piano, vocal, guitar. — *Hal Leonard*
782.742   013219922

Child's carol
See **Lewis, Paul, 1943-** Child's carol

Chilingirian, Levon.
See **Rachmaninoff, Sergei, 1873-1943.** [Symphonies, no. 2, op. 27, E minor. Adagio; *arr.*] Symphony no. 2 : theme from third movment : for violin and piano / arranged by John York ; violin part edited by Levon Chilingirian.

Chinese folk songs
See **Zhou, Long, 1953-** Chinese folk songs

Chopin, Frédéric, *1810-1849.*
[Concertos, piano, orchestra, no. 1, op. 11, E minor] — Koncert e-moll op. 11 na fortepian i orkiestrę = Concerto in E minor op. 11 for piano and orchestra / Fryderyk Chopin ; [redakcja tomu, Jan Ekier, Paweł Kamiński] — *Polskie Wydawnictwo Muzyczne*
784.262186   014490787

[Concertos, piano, orchestra, no. 1, op. 11, E minor] — Koncert e-moll op. 11 na fortepian i orkiestrę : wersja historyczna = Concerto in E minor op. 11 for piano and orchestra : historical version / Fryderyk Chopin ; [redakcja tomu, Jan Ekier, Paweł Kamiński] — *Fundacja Wydania Narodowego Dzieł Fryderyka Chopina*
784.262186   014490802

[Concertos, piano, orchestra, no. 2, op. 21, F minor] — Koncert f-moll op. 21 na fortepian i orkiestrę = Concerto in F minor op. 21 for piano and orchestra / Fryderyk Chopin ; [redakcja tomu, Jan Ekier, Paweł Kamiński] — *Wydanie Narodowe*
784.262186   014490798

[Concertos, piano, orchestra, no. 2, op. 21, F minor] — Koncert f-moll op. 21 na fortepian i orkiestrę : wersja historyczna = Concerto in F minor op. 21 for piano and orchestra : historical version / Fryderyk Chopin ; [redakcja tomu, Jan Ekier, Paweł Kamiński] — *Fundacja Wydania Narodowego Dzieł Fryderyka Chopina*
784.262186   014490807

[Preludes, piano] — Préludes / Frédéric Chopin ; herausgegeben von Norbert Müllemann ; Fingersatz von Hermann Keller. — *Henle*
786.218928   013943269

[Preludes, piano] — Préludes / Frédéric Chopin ; herausgegeben von Norbert Müllemann ; Fingersatz von Hermann Keller. — *Studien-Ed. — Henle*
786.218928   014049146

[Rondos, piano] — Ronda, op. 1, 5, 16 = Rondos, opp. 1, 5, 16 / Fryderyk Chopin ; [redakcja tomu, Jan Ekier, Paweł Kamiński, Witalis Raczkiewicz] — *Polskie Wydawnictwo Muzyczne*
786.21824   014490560

[Sonatas, piano no. 3, op. 58, B minor] — Sonata H-Moll Op. 58 : wydanie faksymilowe rękopisu ze zbiorów Biblioteki Narodowej w Warszawie (Mus. 232 Cim.) = Sonata in B minor, op. 58 : facsimile edition of the

manuscript held in the National Library in Warsaw (Mus. 232 Cim.) : A IX/58 / Fryderyk Chopin ; Komitet redakcyjny = Editorial committee, Jean-Jacques Eigeldinger (przewodniczący = president), Zofia Chechlińska (redaktor naczelny = editor in chief) ... [et al.] — *Narodowy Instytut Fryderyka Chopina :*
786.2183   013765185

[Waltzes, piano] — Waltzes : piano / Fryderyk Chopin ; edited by Christophe Grabowski. — *New critical ed. — Edition Peters*
786.218846   013691050

Chopin, Frédéric, *1810-1849.* **Mazurkas,**
See **On wings of song :** 8 popular pieces arranged for string quartet / [arr. by] Barrie Carson Turner.

[Choral music]
See **Schreker, Franz, 1878-1934.** [Choral music]

[Choral music. *Selections*]
See **Moeran, E. J. 1894-1950.** [Choral music. *Selections*]

See **Purcell, Henry, 1659-1695.** [Choral music. *Selections*]

See **Sviridov, Georgiĭ Vasil'evich, 1915-1998.** [Choral music. *Selections*]

Choristes (Motion picture)
See **Coulais, Bruno.** [Choristes. *Vocal score. Selections*] Les choristes : piano, chant (choeurs), paroles. — *Éditions Galatée :*

Les choristes
See **Coulais, Bruno.** [Choristes. *Vocal score. Selections*] Les choristes

[Choristes. *Vocal score. Selections*]
See **Coulais, Bruno.** [Choristes. *Vocal score. Selections*]

Choroba, Volker.
See **Hässler, Johann Wilhelm, 1747-1822.** [Kleine Orgelstücke] 48 kleine Orgelstücke = 48 short organ pieces / Johann Wilhelm Hässler ; herausgegeben von Volker Choroba.

Choruses, Sacred (Mixed voices) with organ.
See **Cantica nova :** 18 new motets for choirs.

Chorwerk
See **Schreker, Franz, 1878-1934.** [Choral music] Chorwerk

Chosen
See **MacMillan, James, 1959-** Chosen

Christe, Jesu, pastor bone
See **Taverner, John, 1495 (ca.)-1545.** Christe, Jesu, pastor bone

Christie, William
See **Charpentier, Marc-Antoine, 1643-1704.** Acteon : H. 481 ; Acteon changé en biche, H. 481a / M.-A. Charpentier.

Christmas cancan
See **Bartlett, Keith.** Christmas cancan

[Christmas carols, op. 77]
See **Swayne, Giles.** [Christmas carols, op. 77]

Christmas in Saint Petersburg
See **Crescenz, Valerie Showers.** Christmas in Saint Petersburg

Christmas jazz
Christmas jazz : six carols for piano solo / arranged by Mike Springer ; edited by J. Mark Baker. — *Hal Leonard*
786.21723   013376380

A Christmas lullaby
A Christmas lullaby / arranged for flugel horn and brass band by Darrol Barry. — *Studio Music*
784.928971723   013376806

Christmas selection 1
Christmas selection 1 : a collection of songs from Educational Musicals' Christmas shows. — *Maplewood Education : Educational Musicals*
782.7421723   013587517

Christmas selection 2
Christmas selection 2 : a collection of songs from our Christmas shows. — *Maplewood Education : Educational Musicals*
782.7421723   013587493

Christopher Columbus
See **Hewitt, Daniel.** [Christopher Columbus. *Selections*] Christopher Columbus

[Christopher Columbus. *Selections*]
See **Hewitt, Daniel.** [Christopher Columbus. *Selections*]

The Christopher Parkening guitar method.
See **Parkening, Christopher.** The Christopher Parkening guitar method.

Church hymnary.
Church hymnary. — *4th ed.* — *Canterbury Press*
782.527   013217828

Church hymnary. — *4th ed.* — *published on behalf of The Church Hymnary Trust by Canterbury Press*
782.527   013432918

Church, Charlotte, *1986-*
Selections from Prelude : the best of Charlotte Church. — *Chester Music*
783.242   013312897

Ciacona
See **Routh, Francis.** [Chaconnes, violoncello, string orchestra, op. 51] Ciacona

See **Routh, Francis.** [Chaconnes, violoncello, string orchestra, op. 51; *arr.*] Ciacona

Ciampoli, Giovanni Battista, *1590-1643.*
See **Mazzocchi, D. 1592-1665.** [Musiche sacre, e morali. Colombella, che di latte] Colombella, che di latte : sopra Maria, e Giesù / Domenico Mazzocchi ; [words by] Monsignor Ciampoli.

Ciao bella, ciao
Ciao bella, ciao : SSAATTBB : Italian traditional / arranged by Ben Parry. — *Edition Peters*
782.542   013304873

[Cimento dell'armonia e dell'inventione. N. 1-4; *arr.*]
See **Vivaldi, Antonio, 1678-1741** [Cimento dell'armonia e dell'inventione. N. 1-4; *arr.*]

Cioconna stravaganza
See **Marcello, Benedetto, 1686-1739.** [Chaconnes, harpsichord, S. C703, C major] Cioconna stravaganza

Cipullo, Tom.
Another reason why I don't keep a gun in the house : songs on poems of Billy Collins : for voice and piano / Tom Cipullo. — *Oxford University Press*
783.6642   013115549

Circle of memories
See **Carlson, Rosalind.** Circle of memories

The circle of time
See **Voth, Ellen Gilson.** The circle of time

Circus skills
See **Bullard, Alan, 1947-** Circus skills

The city in the sea
See **Clarke, Nigel, 1960-** [City in the sea; *arr.*] The city in the sea

[City in the sea; *arr.*]
See **Clarke, Nigel, 1960-** [City in the sea; *arr.*]

Civitas
See **Binney, Malcolm.** Civitas

Cizokrajné motivy
See **Kabeláč, Miloslav, 1908-1979.** Cizokrajné motivy

Clapton, Eric.
[Songs. *Selections*] — Eric Clapton : guitar play-along. — *Hal Leonard*
787.87166   013219768

[Songs. *Selections*] — Play guitar with— Eric Clapton. — *Wise*
783.242166   013374869

Clarinet concerto
See **Gregson, Edward.** [Concertos, clarinet, orchestra; *arr.*] Clarinet concerto

Clark, Derek J.
See **Scarborough Fair** : English folk song : arranged for female voice choir and piano / by Derek J. Clark.

See **Scarborough Fair** : English folk song : arranged for male voice choir and piano / by Derek J. Clark.

See **Scarborough Fair** : English folk song : arranged for mixed voice choir and piano / by Derek J. Clark.

Clark, Sondra, *1941-*
Dakota days : five pieces for piano solo / by Sondra Clark ; edited by J. Mark Baker. — *Hal Leonard*
786.2   013376149

Clarke, Nigel, *1960-*
[City in the sea; *arr.*] — The city in the sea : (1995) : concerto for euphonium and band / Nigel Clarke ; piano reduction by Paul Pellay. — *Maecenas Music*
788.975186   013415914

Clarke, Rebecca, *1886-1979.*
[Comodo e ambile, string quartet] — Two movements for string quartet / Rebecca Clarke. — *Oxford University Press*
785.7194   013062664

[Violin, piano music. *Selections*] — Shorter pieces for violin and piano / Rebecca Clarke. — *Oxford University Press*
787.2   013213425

Clarke, Rebecca, *1886-1979.* Adagio,
See **Clarke, Rebecca, *1886-1979.*** [Comodo e ambile, string quartet] Two movements for string quartet / Rebecca Clarke.

Clarke, Rebecca, *1886-1979.* Chinese puzzle.
See **Clarke, Rebecca, 1886-1979.** [Violin, piano music. *Selections*] Shorter pieces for violin and piano / Rebecca Clarke.

Clash (Musical group)
[Songs. *Selections*] — Play guitar with— The Clash. — *Wise*
783.242166   013432677

Classic film gold
Classic film gold : the essential collection. — *Chester Music*
786.21542   013265865

Classic FM (*Radio station : London, England*)
See **Talbot, Joby.** [Once around the sun; *arr.*] Once around the sun : for solo piano / Joby Talbot.

Classical favorites
Classical favorites : alto sax : [solo arrangements of 15 great pieces with CD accompaniment] — *Hal Leonard*
788.73168   013220241

Classical favorites : cello : [solo arrangements of 15 great pieces with CD accompaniment] — *Hal Leonard*
787.4168   013220182

Classical favorites : clarinet : [solo arrangements of 15 great pieces with CD accompaniment] — *Hal Leonard*
788.62168   013220213

Classical favorites : flute : [solo arrangements of 15 great pieces with CD accompaniment] — *Hal Leonard*
788.32168   013219779

Classical favorites : horn : [solo arrangements of 15 great pieces with CD accompaniment] — *Hal Leonard*
788.94168   013220189

Classical favorites : tenor sax : [solo arrangements of 15 great pieces with CD accompaniment] — *Hal Leonard*
788.74168   013220257

Classical favorites : trombone : [solo arrangements of 15 great pieces with CD accompaniment] — *Hal Leonard*
788.93168   013220279

Classical favorites : trumpet : [solo arrangements of 15 great pieces with CD accompaniment] — *Hal Leonard*
788.92168   013219822

Classical favorites : viola : [solo arrangements of 15 great pieces with CD accompaniment] — *Hal Leonard*
787.3168   013220383

Classical favorites : violin : [solo arrangements of 15 great pieces with CD accompaniment] — *Hal Leonard*
787.2168   013220200

Classical gold
Classical gold : the essential collection. — *Chester Music*
786.2   013292890

Classical guitar miniatures
Classical guitar miniatures : [a unique collection of beautiful and inspiring pieces for the early stages player] / [compiled] by Tony Skinner and Amanda Cook. — *Registry Publications*
787.87076   013086497

Classical masterpieces
Classical masterpieces — *Wise Publications*
786.2   013320784

Classical themes for electric guitar
See **Belkadi, Jean Marc, 1959-** Classical themes for electric guitar

Clayderman, Richard.
See **The best of Richard Clayderman** : piano solos.

Clement, Franz, *1780-1842.*
[Concertos, violin, orchestra, D major] — Violin concerto in D major : (1805) / Franz Clement ; edited by Clive Brown. — *A-R Editions*
784.272186   013350825

Clementi, Muzio, *1752-1832.*
[Concerto, piano, orchestra, C major] — Concerto in do maggiore, op-sn 30, per clavicembalo (pianoforte) e orchestra = for harpsichord (piano) and orchestra / [Muzio Clementi] ; a cura di Luca Sala. — *Ut Orpheus*
784.262186   014748297

[Keyboard music. *Selections*] — 18 composizioni senza numero d'opera, Op-sn 1-18

(WO 2, 3, 5, 8, 10, 13-23), per pianoforte o clavicembalo = 18 compositions without opus number for piano or harpsichord / Muzio Clementi ; a cura di Andrea Coen. — *Ut Orpheus*
786.2   014748278

[Monferrinas] — 12 monferrine : op. 49, per pianoforte = for piano / [Muzio Clementi] ; a cura di Andrea Coen. — *Ut Orpheus*
786.2   014748006

Musical characteristics : op. 19, per clavicembalo o pianoforte = for harpsichord (piano) / Muzio Clementi ; a cura di Roberto Illiano. — *Ut Orpheus*
786.4   014748001

[Progressive sonatinas] — Sonatinas, opus 36 / Clementi ; edited by Jennifer Linn. — *G. Schirmer*
786.2   013190994

[Sonatas, op. 13. No. 4-6] — 3 sonate op. 13 nn. 4-6 per pianoforte = for piano / Muzio Clementi ; a cura di Andrea Coen. — *Ut Orpheus*
786.2183   014747984

[Symphonies, T. 35, D major] — Sinfonia n. 4 in re maggiore, op-sn 37 (WO 35) / [Muzio Clementi] ; a cura di Manuel De Col e Massimiliano Sala. — *Ut Orpheus*
784.2184   014748291

Clementi, Muzio, *1752-1832*. Sprig of Shillelah.
See **Clementi, Muzio, 1752-1832. [Keyboard music. *Selections*]** 18 composizioni senza numero d'opera, Op-sn 1-18 (WO 2, 3, 5, 8, 10, 13-23), per pianoforte o clavicembalo = 18 compositions without opus number for piano or harpsichord / Muzio Clementi ; a cura di Andrea Coen.

Clendinning, Jane Piper.
See **Anthology for The musician's guide to theory and analysis** / [compiled by] Jane Piper Clendinning, Elizabeth West Marvin.

Clérambault, Louis-Nicolas, *1676-1749*.
[Cantates françoises, livre 2. Léandre et Héro] — Leandre et Hero : cantata for soprano, flute, violin & continuo / Louis-Nicolas Clérambault. — *Green Man Press*
783.6648   013596908

[Cantates françoises, livre 3. Mort d'Hercule] — La mort d'Hercule : cantata for bass, violin & continuo / Louis-Nicolas Clérambault. — *Green Man Press*
783.8948   013596900

Clerk, John, Sir, *1676-1755*.
See **Thistle & minuet** : 16 easy pieces from the Scottish Baroque for violin (or flute or oboe), keyboard, and optional cello (or bassoon) = 16 einfache Stücke aus der schottischen Barockzeit für Violine (oder Flöte oder Oboe), Tasteninstrument und Cello (oder Fagott) ad libitum = 16 pièces faciles du Baroque écossais pour violon (ou flûte ou hautbois), clavier et violoncelle (ou basson) facultatif / edited by David Johnson.

Cliff, Tony.
Crackers at Christmas : male voice choir (TTBB) with piano accompaniment / [lyrics & music] Tony Cliff. — *Tony Cliff Music*
782.8421723   013216368

The wreck of the Anson : male voice choir (TTBB) with piano accompaniment / [lyrics and music] Tony Cliff. — *Tony Cliff Music*
782.842   013216375

[Clori, mia bella Clori]
See **Caldara, Antonio, 1670-1736. [Clori, mia bella Clori]**

Coates, Dan.
See **Popular sheet music hits** : easy piano ; arranged by Dan Coates.

[Codice Rossi 215.]
Il codice rossiano 215 : madrigali, ballate, una caccia, un rotondello / edizione critica e studio introduttivo a cura di Tiziana Sucato. — *Edizioni ETS*
782.543   013224000

Il codice rossiano 215
See **[Codice Rossi 215.] Il codice rossiano 215**

Coen, Andrea.
See **Clementi, Muzio, 1752-1832. [Keyboard music. *Selections*]** 18 composizioni senza numero d'opera, Op-sn 1-18 (WO 2, 3, 5, 8, 10, 13-23), per pianoforte o clavicembalo = 18 compositions without opus number for piano or harpsichord / Muzio Clementi ; a cura di Andrea Coen.

See **Clementi, Muzio, 1752-1832.** [Monferrinas] 12 monferrine : op. 49, per pianoforte = for piano / [Muzio Clementi] ; a cura di Andrea Coen.

See **Clementi, Muzio, 1752-1832. [Sonatas, op. 13. No. 4-6]** 3 sonate op. 13 nn. 4-6 per pianoforte = for piano / Muzio Clementi ; a cura di Andrea Coen.

Cohen, Albert, *1929-*
See **Lully, Jean Baptiste, 1632-1687 [Ballets. *Vocal scores. Selections*]** Ballet des saisons ; Les amours déguisés / Jean-Baptiste Lully ; édition [par Ballet des saisons] de James P. Cassaro ; édition [par Les amours déguisés] de James R. Anthony et Rebecca Harris-Warrick ; édition [par Ballet royal de flore] d'Albert Cohen ; réduction clavier-chant, Noam A. Krieger.

Colahan, Arthur.
Galway Bay : SSAATTBB / Arthur Colohan [sic] ; arranged by Jonathan Rathbone. — *Edition Peters*
782.542   013304928

Coldplay (Musical group)
Coldplay live 2003. — *Wise*
783.242166   013297924

X&Y : guitar tab edition / Coldplay. — *Wise Publications*
783.242166   013226461

X&Y : [piano/vocal transcriptions] / Coldplay. — *Wise Publications*
783.242166   013226469

[X&Y] — It's easy to play Coldplay X&Y — *Wise Publications*
786.2166   013346020

[X&Y; *arr.*] — Play guitar with— Coldplay : X&Y. — *Wise*
783.242166   013371830

Coldplay live 2003.
See **Coldplay (Musical group)** Coldplay live 2003.

Cole, Peter, *1941-*
See **Rommereim, John Christian.** I look for you early : for mixed choir (SATB), organ and optional alto saxophone / John Christian Rommereim.

Colette, Marie-Noëlle.
See **Tropaire séquentiaire prosaire prosulaire de Moissac** : (troisième quart du XIe siècle) : Manuscrit Paris, Bibliothèque nationale de France, n.a.l. 1871 / édition, introduction et index par Marie-Noël Colette ; analyse de l'écriture et de la décoration par Marie-Thérèse Gousset.

Collarile, Luigi.
See **Bertoldo, Sperindio, ca. 1530-1570.** [Organ music] Opere per tastiera (Venezia 1591) : con riproduzione in facsimile delle stampe / Sperindio Bertoldo ; a cura di Luigi Collarile.

Collected choral music.
See **Moeran, E. J. 1894-1950. [Choral music. *Selections*]** Collected choral music.

Collins, Billy.
See **Cipullo, Tom.** Another reason why I don't keep a gun in the house : songs on poems of Billy Collins : for voice and piano / Tom Cipullo.

Collins, Phil.
Brother bear : piano, vocal, guitar / [words and music by Phil Collins] — *Walt Disney Music Co.*
783.2421542   006906655

[Look through my eyes; *arr.*] — Look through my eyes : from Walt Disney Pictures' Brother Bear : SAB / words and music by Phil Collins ; arranged by Ed Lojeski. — *Walt Disney Music Company*
782.5421542   013194161

[Look through my eyes; *arr.*] — Look through my eyes : from Walt Disney Pictures' Brother Bear : SATB / words and music by Phil Collins ; arranged by Ed Lojeski. — *Walt Disney Music Company*
782.5421542   013194143

Colman, George, *1732-1794*.
See **Arnold, Samuel, 1740-1802.** Polly : an opera : (1777) / music by Johann Christoph Pepusch ; rearrang'd and new airs compos'd by Samuel Arnold ; libretto by John Gay ; revis'd by George Colman, the elder ; edited by Robert Hoskins.

Colombella, che di latte
See **Mazzocchi, D. 1592-1665. [Musiche sacre, e morali. Colombella, che di latte]** Colombella, che di latte

Colomer, Edmon.
See **Pedrell, Felipe, 1841-1922.** Los Pirineus : ópera en tres actos / Felipe Pedrell ; libreto, Victor Balaguer ; edición crítica, Francesc Cortes y Edmon Colomer.

Colorful sutra banner
See **Ye, Xiaogang.** Colorful sutra banner

Colours for cello
See **Botschinsky, Allan, 1940-** Colours for cello

Colum, Padraic, *1881-1972*.
See **She moved thro' the fair** : ATTBarBB / Irish traditional ; arranged by Jonathan Rathbone ; [words by Padraic Colum]

Colvin, Robert.
The music of Robert Colvin. — *Robert Colvin,]*
786.2   014055809

Come on let's celebrate!
See **Hardwick, John.** Come on let's celebrate!

[Comodo e ambile, string quartet]
See **Clarke, Rebecca, 1886-1979. [Comodo e ambile, string quartet]**

The complete history of Western music (abridged)
See **Snyder, Audrey.** The complete history of Western music (abridged)

The complete keyboard player 15 showstoppers
The complete keyboard player 15 showstoppers / based on the best-selling keyboard method by Kenneth Baker. — *Wise*
786.59164   013432803

The complete keyboard player Christmas favourites
The complete keyboard player Christmas favourites / based on the best-selling keyboard method by Kenneth Baker. — *Wise Publications*
786.591723   013323647

The complete keyboard player pop hits
The complete keyboard player pop hits / based on the best-selling keyboard method by Kenneth Baker. — *Wise*
786.59166   013323535

Complete mission praise
Complete mission praise / compiled by Peter Horrobin and Greg Leavers — *Music ed.* — *Collins*
782.527   013028169

The complete motets [of] Orlando di Lasso
The complete motets [of] Orlando di Lasso : afterword, addenda and corrigenda, indexes / edited by Peter Bergquist. — *A-R Editions*
782.526   013801796

The complete shorter works for cello and piano
See **Saint-Saëns, Camille, 1835-1921.** [Cello, piano music. *Selections*] The complete shorter works for cello and piano

Complete songs
See **Duparc, Henri, 1848-1933.** [Songs] Complete songs

Complete wind chamber music
See **Michael, David Moritz, 1751-1827.** [Wind music] Complete wind chamber music

[Completorium (RISM A/II 300.033.575)]
See **Brikner, Eryk, 1705-1760.** [Completorium (RISM A/II 300.033.575)]

Completorium
See **Brikner, Eryk, 1705-1760.** [Completorium (RISM A/II 300.033.575)] Completorium

[Concert miniatures, recorder, op. 153]
See **Hedges, Anthony, 1931-** [Concert miniatures, recorder, op. 153]

Concertante, op. 7/8, per arpa, corno di bassetto (o viola) e violoncello ad libitum
See **Backofen, Johann Georg Heinrich, 1768-1839.** [Concertantes, basset horn, harp, violoncello, op. 7, F major] Concertante, op. 7/8, per arpa, corno di bassetto (o viola) e violoncello ad libitum

[Concertantes, basset horn, harp, violoncello, op. 7, F major]
See **Backofen, Johann Georg Heinrich, 1768-1839.** [Concertantes, basset horn, harp, violoncello, op. 7, F major]

Concerti a quattro da chiesa, cioè due violini, alto viola, violoncello e basso continuo, opera seconda
See **Dall'Abaco, Evaristo Felice, 1675-1742.** [Concerti da chiesa] Concerti a quattro da chiesa, cioè due violini, alto viola, violoncello e basso continuo, opera seconda

[Concerti da chiesa]
See **Dall'Abaco, Evaristo Felice, 1675-1742.** [Concerti da chiesa]

[Concerti grossi, no. 4]
See **Schnittke, Alfred, 1934-1998.** [Concerti grossi, no. 4]

Concerti per cembalo n. 5 e n. 6 per clavicembalo, violino I, violino II, viola e basso
See **Galuppi, Baldassare, 1706-1785.** [Concertos, harpsichord, string orchestra, C minor] Concerti per cembalo n. 5 e n. 6 per clavicembalo, violino I, violino II, viola e basso

Concertino a 4 stromenti, für Oboe, Klarinette (B), Fagott und Basso continuo
See **Stulick, Matthäus Nikolaus.** [Concertino, woodwinds, continuo, B♭ major] Concertino a 4 stromenti, für Oboe, Klarinette (B), Fagott und Basso continuo

[Concertino, woodwinds, continuo, B♭ major]
See **Stulick, Matthäus Nikolaus.** [Concertino, woodwinds, continuo, B♭ major]

Concerto (1924), for piano solo, 2 trumpets, strings and timpani
See **Lambert, Constant, 1905-1951.** [Concertos, piano, instrumental ensemble, (1924)] Concerto (1924), for piano solo, 2 trumpets, strings and timpani

[Concerto da camera]
See **Torelli, Giuseppe, 1658-1709.** [Concerto da camera]

Concerto da camera per due violini, violone e clavicembalo, op. 2
See **Torelli, Giuseppe, 1658-1709.** [Concerto da camera] Concerto da camera per due violini, violone e clavicembalo, op. 2

Concerto for flute and strings
See **Boyd, Anne, 1946-** [Concertos, flute, string orchestra] Concerto for flute and strings

Concerto for ten wind instruments, op. 20
See **Bailey, Judith, 1941-** [Concertos, wind ensemble, op. 20] Concerto for ten wind instruments, op. 20

[Concerto grosso]
See **Gudmundsen-Holmgreen, Pelle.** [Concerto grosso]

Concerto grosso (1990, rev. 2006)
See **Gudmundsen-Holmgreen, Pelle.** [Concerto grosso] Concerto grosso (1990, rev. 2006)

Concerto grosso Nr. 4— Sinfonie Nr. 5
See **Schnittke, Alfred, 1934-1998.** [Concerti grossi, no. 4] Concerto grosso Nr. 4— Sinfonie Nr. 5

Concerto in A major for viola da gamba, strings & basso continuo
See **Graun, Johann Gottlieb, 1702 or 3-1771** [Concertos, viola da gamba, string orchestra, A major] Concerto in A major for viola da gamba, strings & basso continuo

Concerto in A minor à 4 stromenti, c.1710
See **Fesch, Willem de, 1687-1761.** [Concertos, violins (2), string orchestra] Concerto in A minor à 4 stromenti, c.1710

Concerto in do maggiore, op-sn 30, per clavicembalo (pianoforte) e orchestra
See **Clementi, Muzio, 1752-1832.** [Concerto, piano, orchestra, C major] Concerto in do maggiore, op-sn 30, per clavicembalo (pianoforte) e orchestra

Concerto in E minor, opus 85, for violoncello and orchestra
See **Elgar, Edward, 1857-1934** [Concertos, violoncello, orchestra, op. 85, E minor; *arr.*] Concerto in E minor, opus 85, for violoncello and orchestra

Concerto in G major for piano and orchestra
See **Martinez, Marianne, 1744-1812.** [Concertos, harpsichord, orchestra, G major] Concerto in G major for piano and orchestra

Concerto in G-Dur für 2 Violinen, Viola und Basso continuo
See **Telemann, Georg Philipp, 1681-1767.** [Concertos, violins (2), viola, continuo, TWV 43:G8, G major] Concerto in G-Dur für 2 Violinen, Viola und Basso continuo

Concerto in re maggiore, per archi e cembalo, F. XI, no. 30
See **Vivaldi, Antonio, 1678-1741.** [Concertos, string orchestra, RV 121, D major] Concerto in re maggiore, per archi e cembalo, F. XI, no. 30

Concerto per cello ed orchestra
See **Twardowski, Romuald, 1930-** [Concertos, violoncello, orchestra; *arr.*] Concerto per cello ed orchestra

Concerto per flauto ed archi
See **Porpora, Nicola, 1686-1768.** [Concertos, flute, string orchestra, D major] Concerto per flauto ed archi

Concerto per violino e orchestra, 1998/99
See **Fedele, Ivan.** [Concertos, violin, orchestra, (1999)] Concerto per violino e orchestra, 1998/99

Concerto pour les instruments à vent et le piano (1924)
See **Martin, Frank, 1890-1974.** [Ouverture et foxtrot, pianos (2); *arr.*] Concerto pour les instruments à vent et le piano (1924)

Concerto pour piano et orchestre no. 1
See **Peçi, Aleksandër, 1951-** [Concertos, piano, orchestra, no. 1] Concerto pour piano et orchestre no. 1

Concerto Shēng Shēng Bù Shí
See **Grange, Philip.** [Concertos, clarinet, band] Concerto Shēng Shēng Bù Shí

[Concerto, piano, orchestra, C major]
See **Clementi, Muzio, 1752-1832.** [Concerto, piano, orchestra, C major]

[Concertos, clarinet, band]
See **Grange, Philip.** [Concertos, clarinet, band]

[Concertos, clarinet, orchestra; *arr.*]
See **Gregson, Edward.** [Concertos, clarinet, orchestra; *arr.*]

[Concertos, flute, string orchestra]
See **Boyd, Anne, 1946-** [Concertos, flute, string orchestra]

[Concertos, flute, string orchestra, D major]
See **Porpora, Nicola, 1686-1768.** [Concertos, flute, string orchestra, D major]

[Concertos, flute, string orchestra, QV 5:149, F major]
See **Quantz, Johann Joachim, 1697-1773.** [Concertos, flute, string orchestra, QV 5:149, F major]

[Concertos, harp, string orchestra, F major; *arr.*]
See **Hertel, Johann Wilhelm, 1727-1789.** [Concertos, harp, string orchestra, F major; *arr.*]

[Concertos, harpsichord, H. 242, F major]
See **Bach, Carl Philipp Emanuel, 1714-1788** [Concertos, harpsichord, H. 242, F major]

[Concertos, harpsichord, orchestra, G major]
See **Martinez, Marianne, 1744-1812.** [Concertos, harpsichord, orchestra, G major]

[Concertos, harpsichord, string orchestra, C minor]
See **Galuppi, Baldassare, 1706-1785.** [Concertos, harpsichord, string orchestra, C minor]

[Concertos, horn, orchestra, K. 495, E♭ major. Rondo; *arr.*]
See **Mozart, Wolfgang Amadeus, 1756-1791** [Concertos, horn, orchestra, K. 495, E♭ major. Rondo; *arr.*]

[Concertos, keyboard instrument]
See **Hasse, Johann Adolf, 1699-1783.** [Concertos, keyboard instrument]

[Concertos, marimba, orchestra (2004)]
See **Alderete Acosta, Igmar.** [Concertos, marimba, orchestra (2004)]

[Concertos, oboe, string orchestra, H. 466, B♭, major]
See **Bach, Carl Philipp Emanuel, 1714-1788** [Concertos, oboe, string orchestra, H. 466, B♭, major]

[Concertos, piano, instrumental ensemble, (1924)]
See **Lambert, Constant, 1905-1951.** [Concertos, piano, instrumental ensemble, (1924)]

[Concertos, piano, orchestra, no. 1]
See **Lindberg, Magnus, 1958-** [Concertos, piano, orchestra, no. 1]

See **Peçi, Aleksandër, 1951-** [Concertos, piano, orchestra, no. 1]

[Concertos, piano, orchestra, no. 1, op. 11, E minor]
See **Chopin, Frédéric, 1810-1849.** [Concertos, piano, orchestra, no. 1, op. 11, E minor]

[Concertos, piano, orchestra, no. 2, op. 21, F minor]
See **Chopin, Frédéric, 1810-1849.** [Concertos, piano, orchestra, no. 2, op. 21, F minor]

[Concertos, string orchestra, RV 121, D major]
See **Vivaldi, Antonio, 1678-1741.** [Concertos, string orchestra, RV 121, D major]

[Concertos, string quartet, band]
See **Schulhoff, Ervín, 1894-1942.** [Concertos, string quartet, band]

[Concertos, viola da gamba, string orchestra, A major]
See **Graun, Johann Gottlieb, 1702 or 3-1771** [Concertos, viola da gamba, string orchestra, A major]

[Concertos, violin, orchestra]
See **Maw, Nicholas.** [Concertos, violin, orchestra]

[Concertos, violin, orchestra, (1999)]
See **Fedele, Ivan.** [Concertos, violin, orchestra, (1999)]

[Concertos, violin, orchestra, D major]
See **Clement, Franz, 1780-1842.** [Concertos, violin, orchestra, D major]

[Concertos, violin, orchestra, op. 61, D major; *arr.*]
See **Beethoven, Ludwig van, 1770-1827.** [Concertos, violin, orchestra, op. 61, D major; *arr.*]

[Concertos, violin, orchestra, op. 77, D major]
See **Brahms, Johannes, 1833-1897.** [Concertos, violin, orchestra, op. 77, D major]

[Concertos, violin, orchestra; *arr.*]
See **Glass, Philip.** [Concertos, violin, orchestra; *arr.*]

[Concertos, violins (2), string orchestra]
See **Fesch, Willem de, 1687-1761.** [Concertos, violins (2), string orchestra]

[Concertos, violins (2), viola, continuo, TWV 43:G8, G major]
See **Telemann, Georg Philipp, 1681-1767.** [Concertos, violins (2), viola, continuo, TWV 43:G8, G major]

[Concertos, violoncello, orchestra, op. 85, E minor; *arr.*]
See **Elgar, Edward, 1857-1934** [Concertos, violoncello, orchestra, op. 85, E minor; *arr.*]

[Concertos, violoncello, orchestra; *arr.*]
See **Twardowski, Romuald, 1930-** [Concertos, violoncello, orchestra; *arr.*]

[Concertos, wind ensemble, op. 20]
See **Bailey, Judith, 1941-** [Concertos, wind ensemble, op. 20]

Concierto no. 1 para marimba y orquesta
See **Alderete Acosta, Igmar.** [Concertos, marimba, orchestra (2004)] Concierto no. 1 para marimba y orquesta

[Confessions. *Selections*]
See **Usher.** [Confessions. *Selections*]

Confirma hoc Deus
See **Palestrina, Giovanni Pierluigi da, 1525?-1594.** [Offertories, voices (5). Confirma hoc Deus] Confirma hoc Deus

Connolly, Candida.
See **Indian melodies :** for alto saxophone = Mélodies indiennes : pour saxophon alto = Indische Melodien : für Alt-Saxophon / [arranged by] Candida Connolly ; with accompanying CD by Kadri Golpalnath.

Consolation II
See **Lachenmann, Helmut.** [Consolation, no. 2] Consolation II

[Consolation, no. 2]
See **Lachenmann, Helmut.** [Consolation, no. 2]

Consort music of four parts
See **Ward, John, 1571-1638.** [Chamber music. *Selections*] Consort music of four parts

Contadin, Cristiano.
See **Graun, Johann Gottlieb, 1702 or 3-1771.** [Sonatas, viola da gamba, continuo, G major] Solo (Sonata G-Dur) per la viola di gamba / Johann Gottlieb Graun ; trascrizione a cura di Cristiano Contadin e Monica Pelliciari.

[Contemplations]
See **Hedges, Anthony, 1931-** [Contemplations]

Cook, Amanda.
See **Classical guitar miniatures :** [a unique collection of beautiful and inspiring pieces for the early stages player] / [compiled] by Tony Skinner and Amanda Cook.

See **Early stages classical guitar :** [a collection of superb, yet easy to play, pieces] [compiled] by Tony Skinner and Amanda Cook.

Cooke, Arnold.
[Arietta, piano] — Arietta for pianoforte / Arnold Cooke. — *Anglo-American Music Publishers*
786.2   013594075

[Arietta, recorder, piano] — Arietta : (1986) : for recorder & piano / Arnold Cooke. — *Anglo-American Music Publishers*
788.364   013593934

Arioso and scherzo : for French horn & strings (violin, 2 violas & cello) / Arnold Cooke. — *Anglo-American Music Publishers*
785.45195   013593736

[Divertimenti, piano, flute, oboe, violin, violoncello] — Divertimento for flute, oboe, violin, cello and piano / Arnold Cooke. — *Anglo-American Music Publishers*
785.24195   013593668

[Divertimenti, recorder, string quartet] — Divertimento for treble recorder and string quartet / Arnold Cooke. — *Anglo-American Music Publishers*
785.44195   013593661

[Duet, violin, viola] — Duo for violin and viola / Arnold Cooke. — *Anglo-American Music Publishers*
785.7192   013593715

Fanfare : four trumpets [and timpani] / Arnold Cooke. — *Anglo-American Music Publishers*
785.5719518924   013593963

Intermezzo and capriccio : (1971) : for harpsichord or piano solo / Arnold Cooke. — *Anglo-American Music Publishers*
786.4   013594078

[Octet, woodwinds, horn, strings] — Octet : (Passacaglia & fugue) / Arnold Cooke. — *Anglo-American Music Publishers*
785.42198   013593949

[Quartets, strings, no. 2] — String quartet no. 2 / Arnold Cooke. — *Anglo-American Music Publishers*
785.7194   013593823

[Quartets, strings, no. 3] — String quartet no. 3 / Arnold Cooke. — *Anglo-American Music Publishers*
785.7194   013593727

[Quartets, strings, no. 4] — String quartet no. 4 / Arnold Cooke. — *Anglo-American Music Publishers*
785.7194   013593831

[Quartets, strings, no. 5] — String quartet no. 5 / Arnold Cooke. — *Anglo-American Music Publishers*
785.7194   013593651

[Quintets, clarinet, flute, harp, violin, violoncello] — Quintet for harp, flute, clarinet, violin and violoncello / Arnold Cooke. — *Anglo-American Music Publishers*
785.44195   013440594

[Septets, bassoon, clarinet, horn, violin, viola, violoncello, double bass] — Septet for clarinet, horn, bassoon, violin, viola, violoncello and contrabass / Arnold Cooke. — *Anglo-American Music Publishers*
785.42197   013440636

[Sonatas, flute, harp] — Sonata for flute and harp : (1988) / Arnold Cooke. — *Anglo-American Music Publishers*
785.44192183   013440553

[Sonatas, flute, piano] — Sonata for alto flute and piano / Arnold Cooke. — *Anglo-American Music Publishers*
788.32183   013440575

[Sonatas, harmonica, piano] — Sonata for harmonica & piano / Arnold Cooke. — *Anglo-American Music Publishers*
788.82183   013593899

[Sonatas, piano, no. 1] — Piano sonata no. 1 / Arnold Cooke. — *Anglo-American Music Publishers*
786.2183   013594031

[Sonatas, piano, no. 2] — Piano sonata no. 2 / Arnold Cooke. — *Anglo-American Music Publishers*
786.2183   013594039

[Suites, piano, no. 2] — Suite no. 2 for pianoforte / Arnold Cooke. — *Anglo-American Music Publishers*
786.21858   013594067

[Suites, piano, no. 3] — Suite no. 3 for pianoforte / Arnold Cooke. — *Anglo-American Music Publishers*
786.21858   013594052

[Suites, viols (3)] — Suite for two treble viols and bass viol / Arnold Cooke. — *Anglo-American Music Publishers*
785.761931858   013593801

[Toccata, organ] — Toccata, & aria : organ solo / Arnold Cooke. — *Anglo-American Music Publishers*
786.5   013594012

[Variations and fugue, string quartet] — Variations and fugue : for string quartet : (1945) / Arnold Cooke. — *Anglo-American Music Publishers*
785.7194   013593845

Cooke, Arnold. Aria,
See **Cooke, Arnold.** [Toccata, organ] Toccata, & aria : organ solo / Arnold Cooke.

Cool piano
See **Hammond, Heather.** Cool piano

Coombs, Stephen, *1960-*
See **Russian romantic repertoire** = Romantische russische Klavierliteratur = Le répertoire romantique de Russie : level 1 / selected and edited by Stephen Coombs.

Cooper, Barry
See **Beethoven, Ludwig van, 1770-1827.** [Quartets, strings, no. 1-6, op. 18] Streichquartette = String quartets, op. 18 / Beethoven ; herausgegeben von Jonathan Del Mar.

See **Clementi, Muzio, 1752-1832.** [Keyboard music. *Selections*] 18 composizioni senza numero d'opera, Op-sn 1-18 (WO 2, 3, 5, 8, 10, 13-23), per pianoforte o clavicembalo = 18 compositions without opus number for piano or harpsichord / Muzio Clementi ; a cura di Andrea Coen.

Cor
Cor : [France, 1600-1800] : méthodes, traités, dictionnaires et encyclopédies, ouvrages généraux / volume réalisé par Jean Saint-Arroman. — *J.M. Fuzeau*
788.94076   014790370

Corneille, Pierre, *1606-1684.* **Horace.**
See **Portugal, Marcos Antônio da Fonseca, 1762-1830.** Gli Orazi e i Curiazi : partitura dell'opera in facsimile, edizione del libretto / [libretto di] Simeone Antonio Sografi ; [musica di] Marco Portogallo. Catalogo cronologico degli spettacoli a Venezia (1797-1815) / a cura di Maria Giovanna Miggiani.

Cornish folk songs
Cornish folk songs : for piano / researched by Jane Lofthouse ; arranged by Colin Mawby. — *Kevin Mayhew*
786.21620094237   013159283

Corrente
See **Lindberg, Magnus, 1958-** Corrente

Cortès, Francesc.
See **Pedrell, Felipe, 1841-1922.** Los Pirineus : ópera en tres actos / Felipe Pedrell ; libreto, Victor Balaguer ; edición crítica, Francesc Cortes y Edmon Colomer.

[Così fan tutte. Aura amorosa; arr.]
See **Mozart, Wolfgang Amadeus, 1756-1791** [Così fan tutte. Aura amorosa; arr.]

Cossack capers
See **Bartlett, Keith.** Cossack capers

Cottrau, Teodoro, *1827-1879.* **Santa Lucia;**
See **On wings of song :** 8 popular pieces arranged for string quartet / [arr. by] Barrie Carson Turner.

Coulais, Bruno.
[Choristes. *Vocal score. Selections*] — Les choristes : piano, chant (choeurs), paroles. — *Éditions Galatée :*
782.71542   013376913

Coulthard, Emma.
See **The best Christmas flute duet book ever!** / selected and edited by Emma Coulthard.

Couple the tuba
Couple the tuba : manuals / Rosalie Bonighton … [et al.] — *Kevin Mayhew*
786.5   013159882

Cousins, Mervyn.
Be joyful! : for sopranos (with divisions) and piano (or organ) / Mervyn Cousins. — *Encore Publications*
782.6265   013299044

Coventry carol
Coventry carol : SSAATTBB / arranged by Jonathan Rathbone. — *Edition Peters*
782.5281723   013304460

The Coventry carol
See **Swayne, Giles.** The Coventry carol

Cowe, Matt.
See **21st century rock :** [vol. 5] / compiled by Nick Crispin ; music arranged by Matt Cowe.

See **The essential nü metal playlist.**

Cowles, Colin,
[Suites, harpsichord, saxophones (4)] — Suite for harpsichord and saxophone quartet / by Colin Cowles. — *Spartan Press*
785.261951858   013169102

Cowles, Colin.
Group therapy : clarinet trios in popular and jazz styles / by Colin Cowles. — *Studio Music*
785.862193   013271638

Cox, David Vassall, *1916-1997.*
See **Timmermann, Leni, 1901-** [Weihnachtslieder] Three Christmas carols = Drei Weihnachtslieder : gemischter Chor und Orgel (Klavier) / Leni Timmermann.

Crackers at Christmas
See **Cliff, Tony.** Crackers at Christmas

A cradle song
See **Carey, Paul, 1954-** A cradle song

Cranmer, Damian.
See **A selection of Italian arias, c.1600-c.1800.** Volume II / edition prepared by Damian Cranmer ; English translations by Dorothy Richardson ; edition supervised by Michael Pilkington.

Crawford, Lisa.
See **Royer, Pancrace, 1705-1755.** Le pouvoir de l'Amour / Pancrace Royer ; édition de Lisa Goode Crawford ; avec la collaboration de Gérard Geay.

Craxton, Janet.
See **Marais, Marin, 1656-1728.** [Pièces de violes, 4e livre. 1ère partie. *Selections; arr.*] Three old French dances : for oboe and piano / Marin Marais ; [freely transcribed by Janet Craxton and Alan Richardson]

Crecquillon, Thomas, *d. 1557?*
[Chansons, voices (4). *Selections*] — Cantiones quatuor vocum / edidit Laura Youens and Barton Hudson ; editrix verborum Mary Beth Winn. — *American Institute of Musicology*
782.543   013718133

Crescenz, Valerie Showers.
Christmas in Saint Petersburg : for unaccompanied mixed choir (SSAATTBB) / Valerie Showers Crescenz. — *Oxford University Press*
782.5421723   013472185

Crossing the bar : for mixed chorus (SATB) and piano / Valerie Showers Crescenz. — *Oxford University Press*
782.542   013472291

Cresswell, Helen.
See **Lewis, Paul, 1943-** Child's carol : for two-part choir or two solo voices with piano or harp / words by Helen Cresswell ; music by Paul Lewis.

Crispin, Nick.
See **21st century rock :** [vol. 5] / compiled by Nick Crispin ; music arranged by Matt Cowe.

See **The best of 1000 UK number one hits.** Early years : [from 1952 to 1974 : arranged for piano, voice and guitar]

See **The big acoustic guitar chord songbook. Female.**

See **The big guitar chord songbook.** Classic rock.

See **The complete keyboard player 15 showstoppers** / based on the best-selling keyboard method by Kenneth Baker.

See **The complete keyboard player Christmas favourites** / based on the best-selling keyboard method by Kenneth Baker.

See **The complete keyboard player pop hits** / based on the best-selling keyboard method by Kenneth Baker.

See **Essential film songs :** the ultimate modern-day movie songbook. Take 2.

See **The essential nü metal playlist.**

See **Play piano with— Ray Charles.**

Croci, Manfred.
See **Sgambati, Giovanni, 1841-1914.** [Violin, piano music. *Selections*] Quattro pezzi / Giovanni Sgambati ; a cura di Manfred Croci.

Croft, William, *1678-1727.*
By purling streams : (a song with hautboy) : for soprano, oboe/flute and continuo / William Croft. — *Green Man Press*
783.6642   013430526

[How charming is beauty] — Songs with violins : for bass, two violins and basso continuo / William Croft. — *Green Man Press*
783.8942   013597294

[Musicus apparatus academicus. With noise of cannon. With noise of cannon] — With noise of cannon : from the ode : for bass, two violins and basso continuo / William Croft. — *Green Man Press*
783.8942   013430857

Croft, William, *1678-1727.* **Lost is my love.**
See **Croft, William, 1678-1727.** [How charming is beauty] Songs with violins : for bass, two violins and basso continuo / William Croft.

Crook, David, *1957-*
See **Lasso, Orlando di, 1532-1594.** [Motets. *Selections.*] Cantiones quinque vocum (Munich, 1597) / Orlando and Ferdinand di Lasso. Cantiones sacrae sex vocibus (Munich, 1601) / Orlando and Rudolph di Lasso ; [both] edited by David Crook.

Cropton, Mark.
Ten to go : progressive pieces for alto saxophone and piano : with CD accompaniment / Mark Cropton. — *Spartan Press*
788.73   013169224

Ten to go : progressive pieces for B♭ clarinet and piano : with CD accompaniment / Mark Cropton. — *Spartan Press Music Publishers Ltd.*
788.62   013376591

Crossing the bar
See **Crescenz, Valerie Showers.** Crossing the bar

Crossman, Samuel, *1624?-1684.*
See **Shephard, Richard, 1949-** Lord, I have loved the habitation of thy house : for mixed voices and organ / Richard Shephard.

A crown of glory
See **Rutter, John, 1945-** A crown of glory

The crown of India.
See **Elgar, Edward, 1857-1934.** The crown of India.

La cucaracha
La cucaracha : SSAATTBB : Mexican traditional / arranged by Jonathan Rathbone. — *Edition Peters*
782.542   013304936

Cullen, David, *1942-*
13 ways of getting there : jazzy pieces for alto saxophone and piano / David Cullen. — *Schott*
788.73165   014521549

13 ways of getting there : jazzy pieces for clarinet and piano / David Cullen. — *Schott*
788.62165   013312973

13 ways of getting there : jazzy pieces for flute and piano / David Cullen. — *Schott*
788.32165   013312978

13 ways of getting there : jazzy pieces for tenor saxophone and piano / David Cullen. — *Schott*
788.74165   013313014

13 ways of getting there : jazzy pieces for trumpet and piano = pièces en style de jazz pour trompette et piano = Jazz-Stücke für Trompete und Klavier / David Cullen. — *Schott*
788.92165   013192388

13 ways of getting there : jazzy pieces for violin and piano / David Cullen. — *Schott*
787.2165   013312976

Cummings, William Hayman, *1831-1915.*
[Hark! the herald angels sing; *arr.*] — Hark! the herald angels sing : for mixed choir (SATB) and organ / [arranged by] Mack Wilberg. — *Oxford University Press*
782.5281723   013515341

Cunliffe, Simon.
Blueberry blues / Simon Cunliffe. — *Spartan Press*
785   013516041

Let's rumba / Simon Cunliffe. — *Spartan Press*
785   013516079

[Cuopre tal volta il cielo]
See **Handel, George Frideric, 1685-1759.** [Cuopre tal volta il cielo]

Cuopre tal volto il cielo
See **Handel, George Frideric, 1685-1759.** [Cuopre tal volta il cielo] Cuopre tal volto il cielo

Cure (Musical group)
The Cure : guitar tab edition / The Cure. — *Wise Publications*
783.242166   013185954

The Cure
See **Cure (Musical group)** The Cure

Cwm Rhondda
See **Hughes, John, 1873-1932.** [Cwm Rhondda; *arr.*] Cwm Rhondda

[Cwm Rhondda; *arr.*]
See **Hughes, John, 1873-1932.** [Cwm Rhondda; *arr.*]

Czerny, Carl, *1791-1857.*
[Ouverture charactéristique et brillante] — Ouverture brillante : piano duet, (op. 54) / Carl Czerny ; edited by David Patrick. — *Fitzjohn Music Publications*
785.62192   013214605

Da pacem Domine
See **Pärt, Arvo.** Da pacem Domine

Dahlhaus, Carl, *1928-1989.*
See **Dokumente und Texte zu "Tannhäuser und der Sängerkrieg auf Wartburg" /** herausgegeben von Peter Jost ; Reinschrift des Textbuches mit Varianten herausgegeben von Cristina Urcheuguía.

Dahms, Sibylle
See **Biber, Heinrich Ignaz Franz, 1644-1704.** Chi la dura la vince (Wer ausharrt, siegt) : Dramma musicale in drei Akten / Heinrich Franz Biber ; Text von Francesco Maria Raffaelini (?) ; Einfürhung von Sibylle Dahms.

Daija, Tish.
[Rhapsody, flute, orchestra; *arr.*] — Rapsodi for flute & orchestra : [arranged for] flute & piano / Tish Daija. — *Emerson Edition*
788.3218945   013358266

Dakota days
See **Clark, Sondra, 1941-** Dakota days

[Dal calore agitato]
See **Legrenzi, Giovanni, 1626-1690.** [Dal calore agitato]

Dall'Abaco, Evaristo Felice, *1675-1742.*
[Concerti da chiesa] — Concerti a quattro da chiesa, cioè due violini, alto viola, violoncello e basso continuo, opera seconda : Amsterdam s.d. / Evaristo Felice Dall'Abaco. — *Studio per edizioni scelte*
784.71858   013688127

Dalton, Daniel.
See **Brookes, Katherine.** The gunpowder plot : remember, remember the 5th of November.

See **Hewitt, Daniel.** 1066 : the Battle of Hastings / written by Daniel Dalton ; music [& lyrics] by Dan Hewitt.

See **Hewitt, Daniel.** [Christopher Columbus. *Selections*] Christopher Columbus : voyage to the end of the world : assembly pack / written by Daniel Dalton ; music [& lyrics] by Dan Hewitt.

See **Hewitt, Daniel.** Henry VIII : the break with Rome.

See **Hewitt, Daniel.** [Henry VIII. *Selections*] Henry VIII : Henry and Anne Boleyn : assembly pack / written by Daniel Dalton ; music [& lyrics] by Dan Hewitt.

See **Hewitt, Daniel.** [Henry VIII. *Selections*] Henry VIII : the break with Rome : assembly pack / written by Daniel Dalton ; music [& lyrics] by Dan Hewitt.

See **Hewitt, Daniel.** [Magic tree. *Selections*] The magic tree : a story for Christmas : assembly pack.

See **Hewitt, Daniel.** The Spanish Armada : the invasion of England.

See **Hewitt, Daniel.** [Spanish Armada. *Selections*] The Spanish Armada : the invasion of England : assembly pack.

See **Hewitt, Daniel.** The Trojan horse : the fall of Troy.

See **Hewitt, Daniel.** [Trojan horse. *Selections*] The Trojan horse : the fall of Troy : assembly pack.

See **Spencer, Tim.** The ancient Olympics : the legend of Callipateira.

See **Spencer, Tim.** [Ancient Olympics. *Selections*] The ancient Olympics : the Olympic traditions : assembly pack.

See **Spencer, Tim.** [Ancient Olympics. *Selections*] The ancient Olympics : the story of Callipateira : assembly pack / written by Daniel Dalton ; music [& lyrics] by Tim Spencer.

See **Spencer, Tim.** Trafalgar : Nelson's finest hour / written by Daniel Dalton ; music [& lyrics] by Tim Spencer.

See **Spencer, Tim.** [Trafalgar. *Selections*] Trafalgar : Napolean's navy : assembly pack / written by Daniel Dalton ; music [& lyrics] by Tim Spencer.

See **Spencer, Tim.** [Trafalgar. *Selections*] Trafalgar : Nelson's finest hour : assembly pack / written by Daniel Dalton ; musc [& lyrics] by Tim Spencer.

D'Amico, Matteo, *1955-*
The entertainment of the senses : cabaret musicale per voce e strumenti (2005) / Matteo D'Amico ; su testi di W.H. Auden and Ch. Kallman. — *Ricordi*
783.442   013688128

Danny boy
Danny boy : SSAATTBB : Irish traditional / arranged by Jonathan Rathbone. — *Edition Peters*
782.542   013304902

Danson, Alan.
Intrada : brass quintet / Alan Danson. — *Broadbent & Dunn*
785.9195   013167570

See **A medley of rhymes for five brass :** brass quintet : traditional / arranged by Alan Danson.

Dante Alighieri, *1265-1321.*
See **Davies, Peter Maxwell, 1934-** Il rozzo martello : for unaccompanied choir SATB / words by Dante and Michelangelo ; music by Peter Maxwell Davies.

Darin, Bobby.
[Songs. *Selections*] — The best of Bobby Darin : [a selection of his biggest hits, arranged for piano, voice and guitar] — *Wise Publications*
783.242164   013220435

[Songs. *Selections*] — Bobby Darin : 15 timeless classics : piano/vocal arrangements with guitar chord boxes. — *International Music Publications*
783.242164   013226555

Dark Horse Records.
See **Harrison, George, 1943-2001.** [Songs. *Selections*] The Dark Horse years : 1976-1992 / George Harrison.

The Dark Horse years
See **Harrison, George, 1943-2001.** [Songs. *Selections*] The Dark Horse years

Daucé, Sébastien.
See **Charpentier, Marc-Antoine, 1643-1704.** Acteon : H. 481 ; Acteon changé en biche, H. 481a / M.-A. Charpentier.

David of the white rock
David of the white rock : SSAATTBB : Welsh traditional / arranged by Ben Parry. — *Edition Peters*
782.542   013304919

David, Jonathan, *1965-*
Now sleeps the crimson petal : for unaccompanied mixed chorus (SSAATTBB) / Jonathan David. — *Oxford University Press*
782.542   013472278

Davidson, Hannah.
See **The amorous hexachord** : madrigal fantasies from the Tregian manuscript / Pallavicino, Bianciardi, and Giovannelli ; edited by Hannah Davidson.

Davies, Aneirin Talfan.
See **Hughes, Arwel, 1909-1988.** [Dewi Sant. O dyred, Dewi. *Vocal score. English & Welsh*] O dyred, Dewi : cytgan i leisiau SSA allan o'r oratorio Dewi Sant = Come hither, David : chorus for SSA voices from the oratorio Saint David / Arwel Hughes.

Davies, Bryan.
Kolokolchik = The little bell : Russian folk song for tenor solo and male voice choir with balalaikas (opotional) and tubular bell / arranged by Bryan Davies ; [English words by Leon Wiltshire] — *Roberton Publications, a part of Goodmusic Publishing*
782.842   013486514

[Never weather beaten sail, men's voices] — Never weather beaten sail / [words by] Thomas Campion ; [setting by] Bryan Davies. — *Roberton Publications, a part of Goodmusic Publishing*
782.825   013373045

[Never weather beaten sail, mixed voices] — Never weather beaten sail / [words by] Thomas Campion ; [setting by] Bryan Davies. — *Roberton Publications, a part of Goodmusic Publishing*
782.525   013373029

See **Drake, Ervin.** [I believe; *arr.*] I believe : arranged for male voice choir (TTBB) with piano accompaniment and optional string bass / Words & music by Ervin Drake … [et al.] ; arranged by Bryan Davies.

See **The white cockade** : Jacobite song arranged for male voice choir with accompaniment of snare drum and two piccolos / by Bryan Davies.

Davies, Jayne
See **Ar gyfer heddiw'r bore'n faban bach** = For us this Christmas morning : traditional Welsh folk-song arranged for SSAA choir and piano / by Jayne Davies ; English text by Rhian Davies.

See **Bugeilio'r gwenith gwyn** = Watching the white wheat : traditional Welsh folk-song arranged for SSA choir, solo voice and piano / by Jayne Davies ; English text by Rhian Davies.

See **Deryn y bwn o'r banna'** = The bittern : traditional Welsh folk-song arranged for SSAA choir, solo voice and piano and bottle (optional) / by Jayne Davies ; English text by Rhian Davies.

See **Y gelynnen** = The holly : traditional Welsh folk-song arranged for female voice choir and piano / by Jayne Davies ; English text by Rhian Davies.

See **Y g'loman** = The dove : traditional Welsh folk-song arranged for SSAA choir, solo voice, flute and piano / by Jayne Davies ; English text by Rhian Davies.

See **Lisa Lân** = Lisa fair : traditional Welsh folk-song arranged for SSAA choir and piano / by Jayne Davies ; English text by Rhian Davies.

Davies, Niki.
The bossy king : a new nativity musical / by Niki Davies. — *Out of the Ark Music*
782.141723083   013272406

Humph the camel : an amusing new nativity musical / by Niki Davies. — *Out of the Ark Music*
782.141723083   013272400

Ralph the reindeer : an original Christmas musical / by Niki Davies. — *Out of the Ark Music*
782.141723083   013272403

The sleepy shepherd : a great new nativity musical / by Niki Davies ; edited by Mark and Helen Johnson. — *Out of the Ark Music*
782.141723083   013272373

Snowman at sunset : a delightful new Christmas musical / by Niki Davies ; edited by Mark and Helen Johnson. — *Out of the Ark Music*
782.141723083   013272426

Toby's Christmas drum: a simple new Christmas musical / by Niki Davies. — *Out of the Ark Music*
782.141723083   013270981

Whoops-a-daisy angel : a short nativity musical / by Niki Davies ; edited by Mark and Helen Johnson. — *Out of the Ark Music*
782.141723083   013270971

Davies, Peter Maxwell, 1934-
Angelus : for mixed chorus, SATB (2003) / Peter Maxwell Davies. — *Schott*
782.5   013381830

[Glasses of wine] — Two glasses of wine : for instrumental ensemble / Peter Maxwell Davies. — *Chester Music*
785.34196   013190640

[Naxos quartet, no. 2] — Naxos quartet no. 2 : for string quartet / Peter Maxwell Davies. — *Chester Music*
785.7194   013190889

[Naxos quartet, no. 3] — Naxos quartet no. 3 : for string quartet / Peter Maxwell Davies. — *Chester Music*
785.7194   013314406

Il rozzo martello : for unaccompanied choir SATB / words by Dante and Michelangelo ; music by Peter Maxwell Davies. — *Chester Music*
782.542   006937452

Sea elegy : for SATB soli, chorus and orchestra : (1998) / Peter Maxwell Davies ; words by George Mackay Brown. — *Chester Music*
782.542   013203926

[Songs for a mad king. *Vocal score*] — Eight songs for a mad king : music-theatre work for male voice and ensemble / Peter Maxwell Davies ; text by Randolph Stow and George III ; vocal score. — *Boosey & Hawkes*
783.8   013194613

Spinning Jenny : a portrait of Leigh, Lancashire c.1948 : for orchestra / Peter Maxwell Davies. — *Chester Music*
784.2   013281644

Swinton jig : on a nineteenth century Lancashire fiddle tune : for orchestra / Peter Maxwell Davies. — *Chester Music*
784.21825   013213654

[Symphonies, no. 7] — Symphony no. 7 / Peter Maxwell Davies. — *Boosey & Hawkes*
784.2184   013194597

Temenos, with mermaids and angels : for flute and orchestra / Peter Maxwell Davies. — *Chester Music*
784.2832   013190880

[Trio, piano, strings] — Piano trio : a voyage to Fair Isle : for violin, cello and piano / Peter Maxwell Davies. — *Chester Music*
785.28193   013346047

Davies, Peter Maxwell, 1934- Mrs. Linklater's tune.
See **The violin** : a collection : new and recent repertoire for violin with piano accompaniment / Craig Armstrong … [et al.]

Davies, Rhian, 1961-
See **Ar gyfer heddiw'r bore'n faban bach** = For us this Christmas morning : traditional Welsh folk-song arranged for SSAA choir and piano / by Jayne Davies ; English text by Rhian Davies.

See **Bugeilio'r gwenith gwyn** = Watching the white wheat : traditional Welsh folk-song arranged for SSA choir, solo voice and piano / by Jayne Davies ; English text by Rhian Davies.

See **Deryn y bwn o'r banna'** = The bittern : traditional Welsh folk-song arranged for SSAA choir, solo voice and piano and bottle (optional) / by Jayne Davies ; English text by Rhian Davies.

See **Y gelynnen** = The holly : traditional Welsh folk-song arranged for female voice choir and piano / by Jayne Davies ; English text by Rhian Davies.

See **Y g'loman** = The dove : traditional Welsh folk-song arranged for SSAA choir, solo voice, flute and piano / by Jayne Davies ; English text by Rhian Davies.

See **Lisa Lân** = Lisa fair : traditional Welsh folk-song arranged for SSAA choir and piano / by Jayne Davies ; English text by Rhian Davies.

Davis, Sammy, 1925-1990
See **Audition songs for male singers.** The rat pack : Frank Sinatra, Dean Martin, Sammy Davis, jr. : ten great songs ideal for auditions.

Dawn sequence
See **Warren, Norman.** Dawn sequence

Day by day
See **Godfrey, Philip, 1964-** Day by day

Day, Doris, 1924-
See **Doris Day :** 15 timeless classics : piano/vocal arrangements with guitar chord boxes.

De Col, Manuel, 1968-
See **Clementi, Muzio, 1752-1832.** [Symphonies, T. 35, D major] Sinfonia n. 4 in re maggiore, op-sn 37 (WO 35) / [Muzio Clementi] ; a cura di Manuel De Col e Massimiliano Sala.

De Wald, Frank K.
If you were coming in the fall : 2-part treble / [music] by Frank K. DeWald. — *Boosey & Hawkes*
782.642   013361318

Dean, James, arranger.
See **Songbird** : chord songbook.

Dear Lord and father of mankind
See **Parnell, Andrew.** Dear Lord and father of mankind

[Death of Dido. Oh I feel the friendly blow]
See **Pepusch, John Christopher, 1667-1752.** [Death of Dido. Oh I feel the friendly blow]

Debussy, Claude, 1862-1918
[Children's corner. Little shepherd; *arr.*] — The little shepherd : from Children's corner : grade 3 / Claude Debussy ; arr. Rodney Newton. — *Studio Music*
784.8   013382631

[Fantaisie, piano, orchestra] — Fantaisie pour piano et orchestre (2e version) / Claude Debussy ; édition de Jean-Pierre Marty ; avec la collaboration de Denis Herlin et Edmond Lemaître. — *Durand*
784.2621894   013801751

[Rêverie (Piano work); *arr.*] — Rêverie / Debussy ; arranged for oboe solo and wind band by Rob Wiffin. — *Studio Music*
784.82852   013359017

Debussy, Claude, *1862-1918.* **Preludes,**
See **Leyendecker, Ulrich, 1946-** Pensées sur un prélude : Debussy-Variationen : für Orchester = Debussy-variations : for orchestra / Ulrich Leyendecker.

The definitive Paul Simon songbook.
See **Simon, Paul, 1941-** [Songs. *Selections*] The definitive Paul Simon songbook.

Del Mar, Jonathan.
See **Beethoven, Ludwig van, 1770-1827.** [Quartets, strings, no. 1-6, op. 18] Streichquartette = String quartets, op. 18 / Beethoven ; herausgegeben von Jonathan Del Mar.

Delibes, Léo, *1836-1891.* **Sylvia.**
See **On wings of song :** 8 popular pieces arranged for string quartet / [arr. by] Barrie Carson Turner.

Dellaborra, Mariateresa.
See **Stradella, Alessandro, 1639-1682.** La forza dell'amor paterno / Alessandro Stradella ; a cura di Mariateresa Dellaborra, Carolyn Gianturco.

Delume, Caroline.
See **Guitare :** [France, 1600-1800] : méthodes, dictionnaires et encyclopédies, ouvrages généraux, préfaces d'œuvres / volume réalisé par Caroline Delume.

Y delyn aur
Y delyn aur : alaw gymreig : [arranged for SATB double chorus] / arr. John Hearne. — *Longship*
782.52709429   013440356

Denny, Thomas Arthur, *1949-*
See **Schubert, Franz, 1797-1828.** Fierabras / Franz Schubert.

Dentice, Fabrizio, *16th cent.* **Lute music.**
See **Neapolitan lute music** / Fabrizio Dentice … [et al.] ; edited by John Griffiths and Dinko Fabris.

Denwood, Russell.
See **Milford, Robin, 1903-1959.** [Suites, oboe, string orchestra, op. 8; *arr.*] Suite in D minor : oboe & piano Robin Milford ; [piano reduction by R. Denwood]

Deryn y bwn o'r banna'
Deryn y bwn o'r banna' = The bittern : traditional Welsh folk-song arranged for SSAA choir, solo voice and piano and bottle (optional) / by Jayne Davies ; English text by Rhian Davies. — *Roberton Publications*
782.64216209429   013193361

Deuxieme duo, op. 30, per 2 arpe
See **Vernier, Jean-Aime, b. 1769.** [Duets, harps, no. 2, op. 30] Deuxieme duo, op. 30, per 2 arpe

Developing jazz technique for flute
See **O'Neill, John, 1955-** Developing jazz technique for flute

Devienne, François, *1759-1803.*
[Trios, flutes, violoncello, op. 19. No. 1] — Trio op. 19 no. 1, for flute, flute or violin, and cello or bassoon / by François Devienne. — *Phylloscopus Publications;*
785.44193   013561743

DeWald, Frank K.
Summer's farewell : [for SSA voices, viola or horn & piano] / by Frank K. DeWald. — *Boosey & Hawkes*
782.642   013312827

[Dewi Sant. O dyred, Dewi. *Vocal score.* **English & Welsh]**
See **Hughes, Arwel, 1909-1988.** [Dewi Sant. O dyred, Dewi. *Vocal score. English & Welsh*]

[Dialogues]
See **Hedges, Anthony, 1931-** [Dialogues]

Diamond, Eileen.
Let's make music fun. The blue songbook / Eileen Diamond. — *International Music Publications*
782.742   013039915

Let's make music fun. The green songbook / Eileen Diamond. — *International Music Publications*
782.742   013039917

Let's make music fun. The red songbook / Eileen Diamond. — *International Music Publications*
782.742   013039914

Let's make music fun. The yellow songbook / Eileen Diamond. — *International Music Publications*
782.742   013039916

Diane et Endimion
See **Bernier, Nicolas, 1665-1734.** [Cantates françoises, 2e livre. Diane et Endimion] Diane et Endimion

Diaspora
See **Gorb, Adam, 1958-** Diaspora

Dicie, Don Michael.
The burning babe : a Christmas anthem for unaccompanied mixed choir (SATB) / Don Michael Dicie. — *Oxford University Press*
782.52651723   013472523

Gloria in excelsis : for unaccompanied mixed choir (SATB) / Don Michael Dicie. — *Oxford University Press*
782.53232   013115451

[Nineteenth-century hymns. Marching to Zion] — Three nineteenth-century hymns. 3, Marching to Zion : for lower voices (TTBB) and piano / [arranged by] Don Michael Dicie. — *Oxford University Press*
782.827   013472346

[Nineteenth-century hymns. My faith looks up to Thee] — Three nineteenth-century hymns. 1, My faith looks up to Thee : for lower voices (TTBB) and piano / [arranged by] Don Michael Dicie. — *Oxford University Press*
782.827   013472357

[Nineteenth-century hymns. The church in the wildwood] — Three nineteenth-century hymns. 2, The church in the wildwood : for lower voices (TTBB) and piano / [arranged by] Don Michael Dicie. — *Oxford University Press*
782.827   013472351

Songs of comfort : for high voice and keyboard / Don Michael Dicie. — *Oxford University Press*
783.6642   013115541

See **He is born :** [a setting of "Il est né"] : for mixed choir (SATB) and keyboard, with optional flute and oboe / [traditional French melody arr.] Don Michael Dicie.

See **Masters in this hall :** for two-part choir (equal or unequal voices), flute, oboe and keyboard / [traditional French carol, arr.] Don Michael Dicie.

See **Masters in this hall :** for two-part choir (equal or unequal voices), flute, oboe and strings / [traditional French carol, arr.] Don Michael Dicie.

Dick, Arthur.
See **The essential nü metal playlist.**

See **[Songs. Selections]** Play guitar with— The Clash.

See **[X&Y; arr.]** Play guitar with— Coldplay : X&Y.

Dickinson, Emily, *1830-1886.*
See **De Wald, Frank K.** If you were coming in the fall : 2-part treble / [music] by Frank K. DeWald.

Dieci pezzi per clavicembalo
See **Scarlatti, Alessandro, 1660-1725.** [Harpsichord music. *Selections*] Dieci pezzi per clavicembalo

Diehl, Gunther.
See **Weill, Kurt, 1900-1950.** Der Protagonist : ein Akt Oper : op. 15 / Musik von Kurt Weill ; Text von Georg Kaiser ; edited by Gunther Diehl and Jürgen Selk.

Dies sanctificatus
See **Palestrina, Giovanni Pierluigi da, 1525?-1594.** [Motets (1563). Dies sanctificatus] Dies sanctificatus

Dig it!
See **Lopez-Real, Carlos.** [Dig it. Clarinet(s)] Dig it!

See **Lopez-Real, Carlos.** [Dig it. Flute(s)] Dig it!

See **Lopez-Real, Carlos.** [Dig it. Saxophone(s)] Dig it!

See **Lopez-Real, Carlos.** [Dig it. Trumpet(s)] Dig it!

See **Lopez-Real, Carlos.** [Dig it. Violin(s)] Dig it!

[Dig it. Clarinet(s)]
See **Lopez-Real, Carlos.** [Dig it. Clarinet(s)]

[Dig it. Flute(s)]
See **Lopez-Real, Carlos.** [Dig it. Flute(s)]

[Dig it. Saxophone(s)]
See **Lopez-Real, Carlos.** [Dig it. Saxophone(s)]

[Dig it. Trumpet(s)]
See **Lopez-Real, Carlos.** [Dig it. Trumpet(s)]

[Dig it. Violin(s)]
See **Lopez-Real, Carlos.** [Dig it. Violin(s)]

Dillingham, Kate.
See **Bach, Johann Sebastian, 1685-1750.** [Sonatas, viola da gamba, harpsichord] Sonatas BWV 1027, 1028, 1029 : for violoncello and keyboard / J.S. Bach ; [violoncello part edited by] Greenhouse & Dillingham.

DiPietro, Joe.
See **Roberts, Jimmy.** [I love you, you're perfect, now change. *Vocal score. Selections*] I love you, you're perfect, now change : vocal selections / [book and lyrics by Joe Dipietro ; music by Jimmy Roberts ; with Jordan Leeds … [et al.]]

Diptychon
See **Terzakis, Dimitri.** Diptychon

Dirksen, Pieter.
See **Reincken, Johann Adam, 1623-1722.** [Keyboard music. *Selections*] Sämtliche Orgelwerke = Complete organ works / Johann Adam Reincken ; herausgegeben von Pieter Dirksen.

See **Sweelinck, Jan Pieterszoon, 1562-1621.** [Fantasias, keyboard instrument] Sämtliche Werke für Tasteninstrumente. Band 2, Fantasien = Complete keyboard works. Volume 2, Fantasias / Jan Pieterszoon Sweelinck ; herausgegeben von Pieter Dirksen, Harald Vogel.

Disney greats
Disney greats : cello : [solo arrangements of 15 favorite songs with CD accompaniment] — *Hal Leonard*
787.41542   013191253

Disney greats : trumpet : [solo arrangements of 15 favorite songs with CD accompaniment] — *Hal Leonard*
788.921542   013191587

Disney greats : viola : [solo arrangements of 15 favorite songs with CD accompaniment] — *Hal Leonard*
787.31542   013191597

Disney greats : violin : [solo arrangements of 15 favorite songs with CD accompaniment] — *Hal Leonard*
787.21542   013191561

[Divertimenti, H. IV, 1-11.]
See **Haydn, Joseph, 1732-1809.** [Divertimenti, H. IV, 1-11.]

[Divertimenti, harpsichord (1761)]
See **Wagenseil, Georg Christoph, 1715-1777.** [Divertimenti, harpsichord (1761)]

[Divertimenti, K270, B♭ major. *Selections; arr.*]
See **Mozart, Wolfgang Amadeus, 1756-1791** [Divertimenti, K270, B♭ major. *Selections; arr.*]

[Divertimenti, K270, B♭ major. Allegro molto; *arr.*]
See **Mozart, Wolfgang Amadeus, 1756-1791** [Divertimenti, K270, B♭ major. Allegro molto; *arr.*]

[Divertimenti, piano, flute, oboe, violin, violoncello]
See **Cooke, Arnold.** [Divertimenti, piano, flute, oboe, violin, violoncello]

[Divertimenti, recorder, string quartet]
See **Cooke, Arnold.** [Divertimenti, recorder, string quartet]

[Divertimenti, winds (2005)]
See **Lorriman, Howard.** [Divertimenti, winds (2005)]

[Divertimenti, winds, op. 22]
See **Gál, Hans, 1890-1987.** [Divertimenti, winds, op. 22]

Divertimento
See **Lewis, Paul, 1943-** Divertimento

Divertimento à 6 in C, K. 270
See **Mozart, Wolfgang Amadeus, 1756-1791** [Divertimenti, K270, B♭ major. Allegro molto; *arr.*] Divertimento à 6 in C, K. 270

Divertimento à 6 in C, K. 270.
See **Mozart, Wolfgang Amadeus, 1756-1791** [Divertimenti, K270, B♭ major. *Selections; arr.*] Divertimento à 6 in C, K. 270.

Divertimento and military rondo
See **Parke, Maria F., 1772 or 3-1822.** Divertimento and military rondo

Divertimento for flute, oboe, violin, cello and piano
See **Cooke, Arnold.** [Divertimenti, piano, flute, oboe, violin, violoncello] Divertimento for flute, oboe, violin, cello and piano

Divertimento for treble recorder and string quartet
See **Cooke, Arnold.** [Divertimenti, recorder, string quartet] Divertimento for treble recorder and string quartet

Divertimento for wind nonet
See **Lorriman, Howard.** [Divertimenti, winds (2005)] Divertimento for wind nonet

Divertimento, op. 22, octet for woodwind and brass
See **Gál, Hans, 1890-1987.** [Divertimenti, winds, op. 22] Divertimento, op. 22, octet for woodwind and brass

Diverting Sundays
See **Carr, Paul.** Diverting Sundays

Dix, W. Chatterton *1837-1898*.
See **Nixon, June.** Harvest carol / text: W. Chatterton Dix ; music: June Dixon.

Dixon, Jon, *1928-*
See **Palestrina, Giovanni Pierluigi da, 1525?-1594.** [Hymni totius anni. Conditor alme siderum] Two hymns for Advent and Christmas / Giovanni Pierluigi da Palestrina ; transcribed and edited by Jon Dixon.

See **Palestrina, Giovanni Pierluigi da, 1525?-1594.** [Hymni totius anni. Veni Creator Spiritus] Veni Creator Spiritus : SAT(T)B / Giovanni Pierluigi da Palestrina ; transcribed and edited by Jon Dixon.

See **Palestrina, Giovanni Pierluigi da, 1525?-1594.** [Masses, book 3. Missa de Beata Virgine] Missa de Beata Virgine : [SSATTB] / Giovanni Pierluigi da Palestrina ; transcribed and edited by Jon Dixon.

See **Palestrina, Giovanni Pierluigi da, 1525?-1594.** Missa confitebor tibi Domine : [SATB+SATB] / Giovanni Pierluigi da Palestrina ; transcribed and edited by Jon Dixon.

See **Palestrina, Giovanni Pierluigi da, 1525?-1594.** Missa fratres ego enim accepi : [SATB+SATB] / Giovanni Pierluigi da Palestrina ; transcribed and edited by Jon Dixon.

See **Palestrina, Giovanni Pierluigi da, 1525?-1594.** Missa Hodie Christus natus est : [SSAB+ATTB] / Giovanni Pierluigi da Palestrina ; transcribed and edited by Jon Dixon.

See **Palestrina, Giovanni Pierluigi da, 1525?-1594.** [Missa Laudate Dominum omnes gentes] Missa Laudate Domine : [SATB+SATB] / Giovanni Pierluigi da Palestrina ; transcribed and edited by Jon Dixon.

See **Palestrina, Giovanni Pierluigi da, 1525?-1594.** [Motets (1563). Dies sanctificatus] Dies sanctificatus : SATB / Giovanni Pierluigi da Palestrina ; transcribed and edited by Jon Dixon.

See **Palestrina, Giovanni Pierluigi da, 1525?-1594.** [Motets (1563). Veni sponsa Christi] Veni sponsa Christi : SATB / Giovanni Pierluigi da Palestrina ; transcribed and edited by Jon Dixon.

See **Palestrina, Giovanni Pierluigi da, 1525?-1594.** [Motets (1569). Stella, quam viderant Magi] Stella quam viderant Magi : SATTB / Giovanni Pierluigi da Palestrina ; transcribed and edited by Jon Dixon.

See **Palestrina, Giovanni Pierluigi da, 1525?-1594.** [Motets (1572). Ascendo ad Patrem] Ascendo ad Patrem : (SATTB) / Giovanni Pierluigi da Palestrina ; transcribed and edited by Jon Dixon.

See **Palestrina, Giovanni Pierluigi da, 1525?-1594.** [Motets (1572). Domine, in virtute tua] Domine, in virtute tua : (SATB+SATB) / Giovanni Pierluigi da Palestrina ; transcribed and edited by Jon Dixon.

See **Palestrina, Giovanni Pierluigi da, 1525?-1594.** [Motets (1572). Laudate Dominum omnes gentes] Laudate Dominum omnes gentes : (SATB+SATB) / Giovanni Pierluigi da Palestrina ; transcribed and edited by Jon Dixon.

See **Palestrina, Giovanni Pierluigi da, 1525?-1594.** [Motets (1572). Laudate pueri] Laudate pueri Dominum : SATB+SATB / Giovanni Pierluigi da Palestrina ; transcribed and edited by Jon Dixon.

See **Palestrina, Giovanni Pierluigi da, 1525?-1594.** [Motets (1575). Haec dies] Haec dies : SSATTB / Giovanni Pierluigi da Palestrina ; transcribed and edited by Jon Dixon.

See **Palestrina, Giovanni Pierluigi da, 1525?-1594.** [Motets (1575). Hodie Christus natus est] Hodie Christus natus est : (SSAB+ATTB) / Giovanni Pierluigi da Palestrina ; transcribed and edited by Jon Dixon.

See **Palestrina, Giovanni Pierluigi da, 1525?-1594.** [Motets (1575). Inclytae Sanctae Virginis Catherinae] Inclytae Sanctae Virginis Catherinae : SAATB / Giovanni Pierluigi da Palestrina ; transcribed and edited by Jon Dixon.

See **Palestrina, Giovanni Pierluigi da, 1525?-1594.** [Motets (1575). Jubilate Deo omnis terra, voices (8)] Iubilate Deo : SATB+SATB / Giovanni Pierluigi da Palestrina ; transcribed and edited by Jon Dixon.

See **Palestrina, Giovanni Pierluigi da, 1525?-1594.** [Motets (1575). Rex pacificus] Rex pacificus : SAATTB / Giovanni Pierluigi da Palestrina ; transcribed and edited by Jon Dixon.

See **Palestrina, Giovanni Pierluigi da, 1525?-1594.** [Motets (1584 : Voices (4)). *Selections*] Alma redemptoris ; Ave Regina ; and, Salve Regina : SSSA / Giovanni Pierluigi da Palestrina ; transcribed and edited by Jon Dixon.

See **Palestrina, Giovanni Pierluigi da, 1525?-1594.** [Offertories, voices (5). Confirma hoc Deus] Confirma hoc Deus : (SATTB) / Giovanni Pierluigi da Palestrina ; transcribed and edited by Jon Dixon.

See **Palestrina, Giovanni Pierluigi da, 1525?-1594.** [Offertories, voices (5). *Selections*] Four offertories for Sundays in Advent / Giovanni Pierluigi da Palestrina ; transcribed and edited by Jon Dixon.

See **Palestrina, Giovanni Pierluigi da, 1525?-1594.** [Offertories, voices (5). Tui sunt coeli] Offertory at the third mass of Christmas : Tui sunt coeli : SATTB / Giovanni Pierluigi da Palestrina ; transcribed and edited by Jon Dixon.

See **Palestrina, Giovanni Pierluigi da, 1525?-1594.** [Stabat Mater, voices (8)] Stabat Mater dolorosa : SATB+SATB / Giovanni Pierluigi da Palestrina ; transcribed and edited by Jon Dixon.

See **Tallis, Thomas, ca. 1505-1585.** Gaude gloriosa Dei Mater : S(S)A(A)TTBB / Thomas Tallis ; transcribed and edited by Jon Dixon.

See **Tallis, Thomas, ca. 1505-1585.** [Lamentations, no. 1] Lamentations I & II / Thomas Tallis ; transcribed and edited by Jon Dixon.

See **Tallis, Thomas, ca. 1505-1585.** [Magnificat, voices (5)] Magnificat and Nunc dimittis : SAT(T)BB / Thomas Tallis ; transcribed and edited by Jon Dixon.

See **Tallis, Thomas, ca. 1505-1585.** [Masses, voices (4)] Mass for four voices / Thomas Tallis ; transcribed and edited by Jon Dixon.

See **Tallis, Thomas, ca. 1505-1585.** [Miserere nostri] Miserere nostri ; & Loquebantur variis linguis : SSAATBB / Thomas Tallis ; transcribed and edited by Jon Dixon.

See **Tallis, Thomas, ca. 1505-1585.** [Missa Salve intemerata virgo] Mass, Salve intemerata / Thomas Tallis ; transcribed and edited by Jon Dixon.

See **Tallis, Thomas, ca. 1505-1585.** [Psalm tunes] 8 tunes for Archbishop Parker's psalter / Thomas Tallis ; transcribed and edited by Jon Dixon.

Djilile
See **Sculthorpe, Peter, 1929-** [Djilile, percussion] Djilile

See **Sculthorpe, Peter, 1929-** [Djilile, viols (5)] Djilile

[Djilile, percussion]

See **Sculthorpe, Peter, 1929-** [Djilile, percussion]

[Djilile, viols (5)]

See **Sculthorpe, Peter, 1929-** [Djilile, viols (5)]

Dmitriev, Alexander I., *1961-*
[Songs of Mary] — Two songs of Mary : for unaccompanied mixed choir (SATB) / Alexander Dmitriev. — *Oxford University Press*
782.5281723   013177881

Dobbins, Jan.
Strings in step. Viola. Book 1 : with CD / Jan Dobbins. — *New ed.* — *Oxford University Press*
787.3076   013062634

Strings in step. Violin. Book 1 : with CD / Jan Dobbins. — *New ed.* — *Oxford University Press*
787.2076   013062636

Dodd, Gordon.
See **Lawes, William, 1602-1645.** [Airs, viols (4), VdGS no. 306] 2 aires nos. 306 & 110 : (TrTrBB) / William Lawes ; edited by Gordon Dodd.

See **Lawes, William, 1602-1645.** [Airs, viols (4), VdGS no. 336] 2 aires nos. 336 & 318 : (TrTr/ATB) / William Lawes ; edited by Gordon Dodd.

Dodgson, Stephen, *1924-*
[Partitas, winds (1994)] — Partita for ten wind instruments : flute 1, flute 2 & piccolo, 2 oboes, 2 clarinets in B♭, 2 horns in F and 2 bassoons / by Stephen Dodgson. — *Phylloscopus Publications*
785.431991854   013188929

Pieces of eight : [1997] : for wind octet : two oboes, two clarinets in B♭, two horns in F and two bassoons / by Stephen Dodgson. — *Phylloscopus Publications*
785.43198   013173888

Windbag : five occasional pieces for ten occasional players (2 flutes, 2 oboes, 2 clarinets in B♭, 2 horns in F and 2 bassoons / by Stephen Dodgson. — *Phylloscopus Publications*
785.43199   013561027

Döge, Klaus.
See **Dvořák, Antonín, 1841-1904.** [Stabat Mater, op. 58, D major] Stabat mater : für Soli, Chor und Orchester = for soloists, chorus and orchestra : op. 58 / Antonín Dvořák ; herausgegeben von Klaus Döge.

See **Dvořák, Antonín, 1841-1904.** [Stabat Mater, op. 58, D major. *Vocal score*] Stabat Mater für Soli, Chor und Orchester, op. 58 = for soloists, chorus and orchestra / Antonín Dvořák ; Klavierauszug von Josef Zubatý ; herausgegeben von Klaus Döge.

See **Dvořák, Antonín, 1841-1904.** [Symphonies, no. 8, op. 88, G major] Symphonie Nr. 8, G dur, op. 88 = Symphony no. 8 in G major, op. 88 / Antonín Dvořák ; herausgegeben von Klaus Döge.

Dokumente und Texte zu "Tannhäuser und der Sängerkrieg auf Wartburg"
Dokumente und Texte zu "Tannhäuser und der Sängerkrieg auf Wartburg" / herausgegeben von Peter Jost ; Reinschrift des Textbuches mit Varianten herausgegeben von Cristina Urcheuguía. — *Schott*
782.1   013825606

Dolar, Janez Krstnik, *ca. 1620-1673.*
[Sonatas, trumpet, instrumental ensemble, C major] — Sonata à 10 : (Natur-) Trompete C/B, 3 Posaunen, 2 Violinen, 3 Violen, Violoncello, Orgel (Cembalo) / Johannes Babtist Tolar ; edited & arranged by Wolfgang G. Haas. — *W.G. Haas-Musikverlag*
785.25199183   014629766

[Sonatas, trumpet, instrumental ensemble, C major; *arr.*] — Sonata à 10 : (Natur-) Trompeten, 3 Posaunen, Streicher, B.c. / Johannes Baptist Tolar ; edited & arranged by Wolfgang G. Haas ; Orgelauszug. — *W.G. Haas-Musikverlag*
788.92183   014629767

Domine, in virtute tua
See **Palestrina, Giovanni Pierluigi da, 1525?-1594.** [Motets (1572). Domine, in virtute tua] Domine, in virtute tua

Dominus illuminatio mea
See **Tunder, Franz, 1614-1667.** Dominus illuminatio mea

Donizetti, Gaetano, *1797-1848.*
Piccola composizione : per clarinetto ed orchestra / Gaetano Donizetti ; a cura di Pietro Spada. — *Boccaccini & Spada*
784.2862   013771075

Donizetti, Gaetano, *1797-1848* Don Pasquale.
See **Verroust, Stanislas, 1814-1863.** Fantaisie sur 'Don Pasquale' : for oboe & piano / Stanislas Verroust ; edited by Myron Zakopets.

Donne, John, *1572-1631.*
See **Sanders, John, 1933-2003.** Requiem : for unaccompanied mixed voices (SSAATTBB) / John Sanders.

Don't believe the truth
See **Oasis (Musical group)** Don't believe the truth

Don't know why
See **Harris, Jesse, 1969-** [Don't know why; *arr.*] Don't know why

[Don't know why; *arr.*]
See **Harris, Jesse, 1969-** [Don't know why; *arr.*]

Doris Day
Doris Day : 15 timeless classics : piano/vocal arrangements with guitar chord boxes. — *International Music Publications*
783.242164   013226543

Double act
Double act : duets for piano / popular melodies arranged by Marian Hellen. — *Kevin Mayhew*
785.62192   013201432

Double act : duets for violin / popular melodies arranged by Marian Hellen. — *Kevin Mayhew*
785.72192   013182150

Double concerto
See **Routh, Francis.** Double concerto

Douglas, Roy, *1907-*
See **Vaughan Williams, Ralph, 1872-1958.** [Old Hundredth Psalm tune; *arr.*] The Old Hundreth Psalm tune : (All people that on earth do dwell) / R. Vaughan Williams (arr.) ; rescored by Roy Douglas for mixed choir (SATB), congregation, 3 trumpets, organ and optional timpani.

See **Vaughan Williams, Ralph, 1872-1958.** Suite de ballet : for flute and piano / R. Vaughan Williams ; edited by Roy Douglas.

The dove and the olive leaf
See **Chilcott, Bob.** The dove and the olive leaf

Doves (Musical group)
Some cities / Doves. — *Guitar tab ed.* — *International Music Publications*
783.242166   013299322

Dovey Junction
See **Samuel, Rhian.** Dovey Junction

Dow, Daniel, *1732-1783.*
See **Thistle & minuet :** 16 easy pieces from the Scottish Baroque for violin (or flute or oboe), keyboard, and optional cello (or bassoon) = 16 einfache Stücke aus der schottischen Barockzeit für Violine (oder Flöte oder Oboe), Tasteninstrument und Cello (oder Fagott) ad libitum = 16 pièces faciles du Baroque écossais pour violon (ou flûte ou hautbois), clavier et violoncelle (ou basson) facultatif / edited by David Johnson.

[Down by the Salley Gardens; *arr.*]
The Salley Gardens : SATB / Irish traditional ; arranged by Ben Parry ; [words by W.B. Yeats] — *Edition Peters*
782.542   013305005

Down Hilo
See **Wegener, Margaret, 1920-** [Down Hilo; *arr.*] Down Hilo

[Down Hilo; *arr.*]
See **Wegener, Margaret, 1920-** [Down Hilo; *arr.*]

Dragonetti, Domenico, *1763-1846.*
[Quintets, violin, violas, violoncello, double bass, B♭, major] — Quintett in B-Dur, für Solo-Kontrabass (Solo-Violine), Violine, 2 Violen und Basso / Domenico Dragonetti ; [herausgegeben von] Nanna Koch ; [Solostimme durchgesehen von Vladislav Riabokon] — *Erstdruck.* — *Doblinger*
785.7195   013688130

Drake, Ervin.
[I believe; *arr.*] — I believe : arranged for male voice choir (TTBB) with piano accompaniment and optional string bass / Words & music by Ervin Drake … [et al.] ; arranged by Bryan Davies. — *Roberton Publications, a part of Goodmusic Publishing*
782.842   013373024

The dream catcher
See **Spencer, Tim.** [Dream catcher. *Selections*] The dream catcher

See **Spencer, Tim.** The dream catcher

[Dream catcher. *Selections*]
See **Spencer, Tim.** [Dream catcher. *Selections*]

A dream of the past
See **Bingham, Judith.** A dream of the past

Dreamworld
See **Townsend, Declan.** Dreamworld

Drei Gedichte von Günter Grass
See **Heider, Werner, 1930-** [Gedichte von Günter Grass] Drei Gedichte von Günter Grass

Drei Lieder
See **Ullmann, Viktor.** [Herbst] Drei Lieder

Dreznin, Sergei.
See **Schnittke, Alfred, 1934-1998.** [Overcoat. Polka; *arr.*] Polka : Streichquartett = String quartet / Alfred Schnittke ; [arr. by] (Sergej Dreznin).

Drinker, Henry Sandwith, *1880-1965.*
See **Bach, Johann Sebastian, 1685-1750.** [Ach Herr, mich armen Sünder (Cantata). *English & German*] Ach Herr, mich armen Sünder : BWV 135/BC A 100 : Kantate zum 3. Sonntag nach Trinitatis für Soli (ATB), Chor (SATB), Zink, Posaune, 2 oboen, 2 Violinen, Viola und Basso continuo = Ah Lord, spare thou this sinner : cantata for the third Sunday after Trinity for soli (ATB), choir (SATB), cornett, trombone, 2 oboes, 2 violins, viola, and basso continuo / Johann Sebastian Bach ; herausgegeben von Wolfram Ensslin ; English version by Henry S. Drinker.

See **Bach, Johann Sebastian, 1685-1750.** [Herr Gott, dich loben wir (Cantata). *English & German*] Herr Gott, dich loben wir : BWV 16/BC A 23 : Kantate zum Neujahrstag für Soli (ATB), Chor (SATB), Corno da caccia, 2 Oboen, Oboe da caccia (Violetta), 2 Violinen, Viola und Basso continuo = Lord God, Thy praise we sing : cantata for New Year's Day for soli (ATB), choir (SATB), corno da caccia, 2 oboes, oboe da caccia (violetta), 2 violins, viola, and basso continuo / Johann Sebastian Bach ; herausgegeben von Michael Märker ; English version by Henry S. Drinker.

See **Bach, Johann Sebastian, 1685-1750.** [Himmel lacht, die Erde jubilieret. *English & German*] Der Erde jubilieret : BWV 31 / BC A 55b, Kantate zum ersten Ostertag : für Soli (STB), Chor (SSATB), 3 Trompeten, Pauken, Oboe, 2 Oboen ad lib, Taille ad lib., Fagot ad lib., 2 Violinen, 2 Violen und Basso continuo = The heavens laugh, the earth exults in gladness : cantata for Easter Sunday : for soli (STB), choir (SSATB), 3 trumpets, timpani, oboe, 2 oboes ad lib., taille ad lib., bassoon ad lib., 2 violins, 2 violas and basso continuo / Johann Sebastian Bach ; herausgegeben von Michael Märker ; English version by Henry S. Drinker.

See **Bach, Johann Sebastian, 1685-1750.** [Lobet Gott in seinen Reichen. *English & German*] Himmelfahrtsoratorium : Lobet Gott in seinen Reichen : BWV 11/BC D 9 : Oratorium Festo Ascensionis Christi : für Soli (SATB), Chor (SATB), 3 Trompeten, Pauken, 2 Traversföten, 2 Oboen, 2 Violinen, Viola und Basso continuo = Oratorio for Ascension Day : Praise God on high in heaven : for soli (SATB), choir (SATB), 3 trumpets, timpani, 2 flutes, 2 oboes, 2 violins, viola, and basso continuo / Johann Sebastian Bach ; herausgegeben von Ulrich Leisinger ; English version by Henry S. Drinker.

See **Bach, Johann Sebastian, 1685-1750.** [Weihnachts-Oratorium. *English & German*] Weihnachtsoratorium : Oratorium tempore nativitatis Christi : BWV 248 : für Soli (SSATB), Chor (SATB), 3 Trompeten, Pauken, 2 Hörner, 2 Querflöten, 2 Oboen/Oboen d'amore, 2 Oboen da caccia, 2 Violinen, Viola und Basso continuo : Urtext = Christmas oratorio : for soli (SSATB), choir (SATB), 3 trumpets, timpani, 2 horns, 2 flutes, 2 oboes/oboes d'amore, 2 oboes da caccia, 2 violins, viola, and basso continuo / Johann Sebastian Bach ; herausgegeben von Klaus Hofmann ; English version by Henry S. Drinker.

See **Bach, Johann Sebastian, 1685-1750.** [Wir müssen durch viel Trübsal in das Reich Gottes eingehen. *English & German*] Wir müssen durch viel Trübsal in das Reich Gottes eingehen : BWV 146/BC A 70 : Kantate zum Sonntag Jubilate für Soli (SATB), Chor (SATB), Traversflöte, 2 Oboen/Oboen d'amore, Taille, 2 Violinen, Viola, obligate Orgel und Basso continuo = Through bitter tribulation we enter into God's kingdom : cantata for the third Sunday after Easter for soli (STB), choir (SATB), flute, 2 oboes/oboes d'amore, taille, 2 violins, viola, organ obbligato, and basso continuo / Johann Sebastian Bach ; herausgegeben von Anja Morgenstern ; English version by Henry S. Drinker.

Duae sonatae a 5 für 2 Violinen, 3 Violen & B.c.
See **Schmelzer, Johann Heinrich, ca. 1623-1680.** [Sonatas, violins (2), viols (3), continuo, (1676)] Duae sonatae a 5 für 2 Violinen, 3 Violen & B.c.

Duddell, Joe, *1972-*
Parallel lines : for tuned percussion and piano : (1999) / Joe Duddell. — *Schott*
785.39192   013173234

Dudley-Smith, Timothy.
See **Ledger, Philip.** Lie still and slumber : two lullabies for Christmas : for mixed voices and keyboard / Philip Ledger.

Duerme negrito
See **Neaum, Michael.** Duerme negrito

[Duet, violin, viola]
See **Cooke, Arnold.** [Duet, violin, viola]

[Duet, violins, E minor]
See **Tobias, Rudolf, 1873-1918.** [Duet, violins, E minor]

Duets for children
See **Walton, William, 1902-1983.** Duets for children

[Duets, harps, no. 2, op. 30]
See **Vernier, Jean-Aime, b. 1769.** [Duets, harps, no. 2, op. 30]

[Duets, horns (2), op. 12]
See **Heuschkel, Johann Peter, 1773-1853.** [Duets, horns (2), op. 12]

[Duets, soprano, bass, continuo]
See **Jeffreys, George, ca. 1610-1685.** [Duets, soprano, bass, continuo]

[Duets, viola d'amore, viola da gamba]
See **Esser, Karl Michael, 1737-ca. 1795.** [Duets, viola d'amore, viola da gamba]

[Duets, viola, bassoon]
See **Giardini, Felice, 1716-1796.** [Duets, viola, bassoon]

[Duets, violins, G. 56-61]
See **Boccherini, Luigi, 1743-1805.** [Duets, violins, G. 56-61]

[Duetti latini per la passione di Gesù Cristo]
See **Porpora, Nicola, 1686-1768.** [Duetti latini per la passione di Gesù Cristo]

Duffin, Ross W.
See **Cantiones sacrae :** madrigalian motets from Jacobean England / edited by Ross W. Duffin.

Duffy, Stephen, composer.
See **Williams, Robbie.** Intensive care : piano, vocal, guitar / Robbie Williams.

Dunning, Albert.
See **Locatelli, Pietro Antonio, 1695-1764.** [Arte del violino. Capricci] Ventiquattro capricci per violino solo [op. III] / Pietro Antonio Locatelli ; in base all'edizione a cura di Albert Dunning ; con diteggiature ed esercizi preparatori di Enzo Porta.

Duo for violin and viola
See **Cooke, Arnold.** [Duet, violin, viola] Duo for violin and viola

Duo, für zwei Violinen
See **Tobias, Rudolf, 1873-1918.** [Duet, violins, E minor] Duo, für zwei Violinen

Duparc, Henri, *1848-1933.*
Feuilles volantes : op. 1 : piano solo / Henri Duparc ; edited by David Patrick. — *Fitzjohn Music Publications*
786.2   013214616

[Songs] — Complete songs : with texts in English, German and French : high voice = Hohe Stimme = voix élevées / Henri Duparc ; edited by Roger Nichols. — *Edition Peters*
783.342   013312852

[Songs] — Complete songs : with texts in English, German and French : medium/low voice = Mittlere/Tiefe Stimme = voix moyennes/graves / Henri Duparc ; edited by Roger Nichols. — *Edition Peters*
783.442   013643025

Dürr, Walther.
See **Schulz, J. A. P. 1747-1800.** Lieder im Volkston / Johann Abraham Peter Schulz ; herausgegeben von Walther Dürr und Stefanie Steiner unter Mitarbeit von Michael Kohlhäufl.

Duval, Jérôme.
[Trios, flutes, bassoon, op. 2. No. 2] — Trio op. 2 no. 2, for two flutes and bassoon / by Jérôme Duval. — *Phylloscopus Publications*
785.8193   013560702

Dve basni I.A. Krylova, dlia metstso-soprano, zhenskogo khora (metstso-soprano) i orkestra, soch. 4
See **Shostakovich, Dmitriĭ Dmitrievich, 1906-1975.** [Vocal music. *Selections*] Dve basni I.A. Krylova, dlia metstso-soprano, zhenskogo khora (metstso-soprano) i orkestra, soch. 4

Dvořák, Antonín, *1841-1904.*
[Masses, B. 175, D major. *Vocal score*] — Mass in D major : op. 86 : for soprano, alto, tenor and bass soloists, SATB and organ, or SATB (with optional soloists) and orchestra = Mše D dur / Antonín Dvořák ; edited by Michael Pilkington. — *Novello*
782.53232   013528269

[Sonatina, violin, piano, op. 100, G major; *arr.*] — Sonatina in G, op. 100 / by Anton Dvořák ; arranged for flute, two oboes, two clarinets in B♭, two horns in F and two bassoons by David King. — *Phylloscopus Publications*
785.431991832   013472992

[Stabat Mater, op. 58, D major] — Stabat mater : für Soli, Chor und Orchester = for soloists, chorus and orchestra : op. 58 / Antonín Dvořák ; herausgegeben von Klaus Döge. — *Breitkopf & Härtel*
782.53235   013113504

[Stabat Mater, op. 58, D major. *Vocal score*] — Stabat Mater für Soli, Chor und Orchester, op. 58 = for soloists, chorus and orchestra / Antonín Dvořák ; Klavierauszug von Josef Zubatý ; herausgegeben von Klaus Döge. — *Breitkopf & Härtel*
782.532351726   013111497

[Symphonies, no. 8, op. 88, G major] — Symphonie Nr. 8, G dur, op. 88 = Symphony no. 8 in G major, op. 88 / Antonín Dvořák ; herausgegeben von Klaus Döge. — *Breitkopf & Härtel*
784.2184   013113516

[Symphonies, no. 9, op. 95, E minor. Largo; *arr.*] — Largo from New World symphony : SSAATTBB / Antonín Dvořák ; arranged by Jonathan Rathbone. — *Edition Peters*
782.5   013305848

Dvořák, Antonín, *1841-1904.* **Masses,**
See **Dvořák, Antonín,** *1841-1904.* [Masses, B. 175, D major. *Vocal score*] Mass in D major : op. 86 : for soprano, alto, tenor and bass soloists, SATB and organ, or SATB (with optional soloists) and orchestra = Mše D dur / Antonín Dvořák ; edited by Michael Pilkington.

Dynamic duos
Dynamic duos : the best duets ever! : the most memorable vocal duets of all time. — *Wise*
783.1242164   013432696

Early one morning
Early one morning : grade 1.5 / traditional ; arr. Duncan Stubbs. — *Studio Music*
784.8   013358958

Early stages classical guitar
Early stages classical guitar : [a collection of superb, yet easy to play, pieces] [compiled] by Tony Skinner and Amanda Cook. — *Registry Publications*
787.87076   013086496

The easiest way to improvise
See **Norton, Christopher,** *1953-* The easiest way to improvise

Easterbrook, Giles.
See **Lambert, Constant,** *1905-1951.* [Concertos, piano, instrumental ensemble, (1924)] Concerto (1924), for piano solo, 2 trumpets, strings and timpani / Constant Lambert ; edited, arranged and orchestrated from the composer's original 2 piano score by Edward Shipley and Giles Easterbrook.

[Easy pieces]
See **Montague, Stephen.** [Easy pieces]

Easy-to-play famous waltzes
Easy-to-play famous waltzes : piano / arranged [by] Rosalie Bonighton. — *Kevin Mayhew*
786.218846   013159307

Easy-to-play Gershwin for piano
See **Gershwin, George,** *1898-1937.* [Songs. *Selections; arr.*] Easy-to-play Gershwin for piano

Eat 'em and smile
See **Vai, Steve.** Eat 'em and smile

Ebb, Fred.
See **Kander, John.** [Kiss of the spider woman. *Vocal score. Selections*] Kiss of the spider woman : the musical : [vocal selections] / book by Terrence McNally ; music by John Kander ; lyrics by Fred Ebb ; based on the novel by Manuel Puig.

Eberlin, Johann Ernst, *1702-1762.*
Missa septimi toni : für Soli, SATB, Streicher und Orgel / Johann Ernst Eberlin ; herausgegeben von Konrad Führlinger und Friedrich Hägele. — *Erstausg.* — *Butz*
782.53232   013887067

Echoes from a golden time
See **Bayford, Frank.** Echoes from a golden time

Ecstatic architecture
See **Lim, Liza,** *1966-* Ecstatic architecture

Edmonds, J. M.
See **Tavener, John.** Exhortation and Kohima : for unaccompanied choir and semichorus SATB/SATB / John Tavener.

Edmund-Davies, Paul.
See **Handel, George Frideric,** *1685-1759.* [Sonatas, flute, continuo. *Selections.*] Sonatas for flute [and continuo] Book 1 / Handel ; flute part edited by Paul Edmund-Davies ; keyboard realisation by John Alley.

See **Handel, George Frideric,** *1685-1759.* [Sonatas, flute, continuo. *Selections.*] Sonatas for flute [and continuo] Book 3 / Handel ; flute part edited by Paul Edmund-Davies ; keyboard realisation by John Alley.

See **Handel, George Frideric,** *1685-1759.* [Sonatas, recorder, continuo. *Selections.*] Sonatas for flute [and continuo] Book 2 / Handel ; flute part edited by Paul Edmund-Davies ; keyboard realisation by John Alley.

Edwards, Warwick.
See **Haydn, Joseph,** *1732-1809.* [Songs, violin, continuo acc. *Selections*] Volksliedbearbeitungen Nr. 269-364 : Schottische und Walisische Lieder für George Thomson / Joseph Haydn ; herausgegeben von Marjorie Rycroft in Verbindung von Warwick Edwards und Kirsteen McCue.

Egressy, Béni, *1814-1851.*
See **Erkel, Ferenc.** [Hunyadi László] Hunyadi László : opera négy felvonásban = opera in four acts / [Erkel Ferenc] ; szöveg Benjámin Egressy ; közreadja Katalin Szacsvai-Kim ; bevezetés Tibor Tallián, Katalin Szacsvai-Kim.

Egyptian selection 1
See **Spencer, Tim.** Egyptian selection 1

Eichá
See **Bainbridge, Simon,** *1952-* Eichá

Eight four-part fantasias
Eight four-part fantasias : for oboe, oboe & cor anglais and two bassoons / by Simon Ives ... [et al.] — *Phylloscopus Publications*
785.85194   013561749

Eight miniatures
See **Wilson, Trevor, composer.** [Miniatures, English horn, piano] Eight miniatures

Eight songs for a mad king
See **Davies, Peter Maxwell,** *1934-* [Songs for a mad king. *Vocal score*] Eight songs for a mad king

Ekier, Jan.
See **Chopin, Frédéric,** *1810-1849.* [Concertos, piano, orchestra, no. 1, op. 11, E minor] Koncert e-moll op. 11 na fortepian i orkiestrę = Concerto in E minor op. 11 for piano and orchestra / Fryderyk Chopin ; [redakcja tomu, Jan Ekier, Paweł Kamiński]

See **Chopin, Frédéric,** *1810-1849.* [Concertos, piano, orchestra, no. 1, op. 11, E minor] Koncert e-moll op. 11 na fortepian i orkiestrę : wersja historyczna = Concerto in E minor op. 11 for piano and orchestra : historical version / Fryderyk Chopin ; [redakcja tomu, Jan Ekier, Paweł Kamiński]

See **Chopin, Frédéric,** *1810-1849.* [Concertos, piano, orchestra, no. 2, op. 21, F minor] Koncert f-moll op. 21 na fortepian i orkiestrę = Concerto in F minor op. 21 for piano and orchestra / Fryderyk Chopin ; [redakcja tomu, Jan Ekier, Paweł Kamiński]

See **Chopin, Frédéric,** *1810-1849.* [Concertos, piano, orchestra, no. 2, op. 21, F minor] Koncert f-moll op. 21 na fortepian i orkiestrę : wersja historyczna = Concerto in F minor op. 21 for piano and orchestra : historical version / Fryderyk Chopin ; [redakcja tomu, Jan Ekier, Paweł Kamiński]

See **Chopin, Frédéric,** *1810-1849.* [Rondos, piano] Ronda, op. 1, 5, 16 = Rondos, opp. 1, 5, 16 / Fryderyk Chopin ; [redakcja tomu, Jan Ekier, Paweł Kamiński, Witalis Raczkiewicz]

Elegie
See **Templeton, Alec,** *1910-1963.* [Elegies, saxophone, piano] Elegie

Elegie für grosses Orchester WoO 48, urpsrünglicher, dritter Satz aus der Symphonie Nr. 10 "Zur Herbstzeit," op. 213
See **Raff, Joachim,** *1822-1882.* [Elegy, orchestra, WoO 48, C minor] Elegie für grosses Orchester WoO 48, urpsrünglicher, dritter Satz aus der Symphonie Nr. 10 "Zur Herbstzeit," op. 213

[Elegies, saxophone, piano]
See **Templeton, Alec,** *1910-1963.* [Elegies, saxophone, piano]

[Elegy, orchestra, WoO 48, C minor]
See **Raff, Joachim,** *1822-1882.* [Elegy, orchestra, WoO 48, C minor]

Elements
See **Gorb, Adam,** *1958-* Elements

Elfyn, Menna.
See **Tann, Hilary.** Wings of the grasses : for voice and oboe (or other melody instrument) / words by Menna Elfyn ; music by Hilary Tann.

Elgar, Edward, *1857-1934.*
[Adieu] — Two piano pieces / Edward Elgar ; edited by David Patrick. — *Fitzjohn Music Publications*
796.2   013214627

[Carillon; *arr.*] — Carillon, op. 75 ; &, Loughborough memorial chime : organ solo / Edward Elgar ; arranged & edited by David Patrick. — *Fitzjohn Music Publications*
786.5   013196914

Elgar, Edward, *1857-1934*
[Concertos, violoncello, orchestra, op. 85, E minor; *arr.*] — Concerto in E minor, opus 85, for violoncello and orchestra / Edward Elgar ; arrangement for violoncello and piano by the composer. — *Novello*
787.4186   013167669

Elgar, Edward, *1857-1934.*
The crown of India. — *Elgar Society Edition Ltd. in association with Novello*
782.15   013173848

[Rapid stream, voices (2)] — The rapid stream ; The woodland stream / Edward Elgar ; edited by David Patrick. — *Fitzjohn Music Publications*
782.742   013214639

[Sonatina, piano] — Sonatina : for piano solo / Edward Elgar ; edited by David Patrick. — *Fitzjohn Music Publications*
786.21832   013214664

Elgar, Edward, *1857-1934.* **Memorial chime;**
See **Elgar, Edward,** *1857-1934.* [Carillon; *arr.*] Carillon, op. 75 ; &, Loughborough memorial chime : organ solo / Edward Elgar ; arranged & edited by David Patrick.

Elgar, Edward, *1857-1934.* **Mina,**
See **Elgar, Edward,** *1857-1934.* [Adieu] Two piano pieces / Edward Elgar ; edited by David Patrick.

Elgar, Edward, *1857-1934.* **Woodland stream,**
See **Elgar, Edward,** *1857-1934.* [Rapid stream, voices (2)] The rapid stream ; The woodland stream / Edward Elgar ; edited by David Patrick.

Ellerby, Martin, *1957-*
Paris sketches : homages for band : [1994 rev. 2004] / Martin Ellerby. — *10th anniversay ed.* — *Maecenas Music*
784.8   013193019

Ellingboe, Bradley.
Be music, night : for unaccompanied mixed
choir (SSAATTBB) / words by Kenneth
Patchen ; music by Bradley Ellingboe. —
Oxford University Press
782.542   013472304

Elliott, Charlotte, *1789-1871*.
See **Stewart, Richard N.** Just as I am : for
unaccompanied mixed choir (SATB) / Richard
N. Stewart.

See **Stewart, Richard N.** [Just as I am. *Spanish*]
Tal como soy = (Just as I am) : for
unaccompanied mixed choir (SATB) / Richard
N. Stewart.

Ellis, John Steven.
See **Tann, Hilary.** Wales, our land : for mixed
choir (SATB) and flute, with optional piano /
Hilary Tann.

Elsner, Józef, *1769-1854*.
[Masses, F major] — Missa F a canto, alto,
tenore, basso, due violini, viole, bassi
(violoncello et basso), due clarinetti, due corni
con organo / Józef Elsner ; opracowanie, Hubert
Prochota ; wstęp, Remigiusz Pośpiech ;
[redaktor, Irena Stachel] — *Polskie Wydawn.
Muzyczne*
782.53232   013887068

[Vespers, D major] — Nieszpory = Vespers : ex
Officio majori Beatae Virginis Mariae ad
Vesperas : a canto, alto, tenore, basso, due
violini, viola, bassi (violoncello et basso), due
flauti, due clarinetti, due corni, due clarini,
timpani con organo / Jozef Elsner ; opracowanie
Hubert Prochota ; wstęp Remigiusz Pośpiech. —
Wyd. 1. — Klasztor OO. Paulinów Jasna Góra
782.5325   013887069

Elvis
See **Presley, Elvis, 1935-1977.** [Songs.
Selections] Elvis

Elvis Presley greats.
Elvis Presley greats. — *Hal Leonard*
783.242166   013383571

Elzinga, Harry.
See **Tres missae super "Quem dicunt
homines"** / edidit Harry Elzinga.

Embrace (Musical group)
Out of nothing / Embrace. — *Guitar tab ed. —
International Music Publications*
783.242166   013158969

Emendemus in melius
See **Byrd, William, 1542 or 3-1623.**
[Emendemus in melius; *arr.*] Emendemus in
melius

[Emendemus in melius; *arr.*]
See **Byrd, William, 1542 or 3-1623.**
[Emendemus in melius; *arr.*]

Emerald breeze
See **Binney, Malcolm.** Emerald breeze

Employment
See **Kaiser Chiefs (Musical group)**
Employment

Encounters
See **Le Fleming, Antony.** Encounters

[Encouragement. *Selections; arr.*]
See **Sor, Fernando, 1778-1839.**
[Encouragement. *Selections; arr.*]

The end of all things to come
See **Mudvayne (Musical group)** The end of all
things to come

Engel, Gerhard.
See **Fun and games with the recorder** : method
for the alto recorder. Tune book / [compiled by]
Gudrun Heyens and Gerhard Engel ; translated
and adapted by Peter Bowman ; with
illustrations by John Minnion.

See **Heyens, Gudrun.** Fun and games with the
alto recorder : method for the alto recorder.
Tutor book 2 / by Gudrun Heyens and Gerhard
Engel ; translated and adapted by Peter
Bowman ; with illustrations by Julie Beech and
John Minnion.

See **Heyens, Gudrun.** Fun and games with the
alto recorder. Teacher's commentary / by
Gudrun Heyens and Gerhard Engel ; translated
and adapted by Peter Bowman.

Engelsman, Maarten.
See **Nicolai, Johann Gottlieb, 1744-1801.**
[Sonatas, piano] 24 Klaviersonates in alle
toonsoorten : (Zwolle ca 1790) = 24 keyboard
sonatas in all keys / Johann Gottlieb Nicolai ;
uitgegeven door Maarten Engelsman.

[English cantatas. *Selections*]
See **Pepusch, John Christopher, 1667-1752.**
[English cantatas. *Selections*]

[English songs]
See **Fesch, Willem de, 1687-1761.** [English
songs]

Ensslin, Wolfram, *1967-*
See **Bach, Johann Sebastian, 1685-1750.** [Ach
Herr, mich armen Sünder (Cantata). *English &
German*] Ach Herr, mich armen Sünder : BWV
135/BC A 100 : Kantate zum 3. Sonntag nach
Trinitatis für Soli (ATB), Chor (SATB), Zink,
Posaune, 2 oboen, 2 Violinen, Viola und Basso
continuo = Ah Lord, spare thou this sinner :
cantata for the third Sunday after Trinity for soli
(ATB), choir (SATB), cornett, trombone, 2
oboes, 2 violins, viola, and basso continuo /
Johann Sebastian Bach ; herausgegeben von
Wolfram Ensslin ; English version by Henry S.
Drinker.

The entertainment of the senses
See **D'Amico, Matteo, 1955-** The entertainment
of the senses

Epilogue
See **Bayliss, Colin.** Epilogue

Epitaph for Grace
See **Grylls, Richard G.** Epitaph for Grace

Erbarm' dich mein, o Herre Gott
See **Herbst, Johann Andreas, 1588-1666.**
Erbarm' dich mein, o Herre Gott

Erben, Karel Jaromír, *1811-1870*.
See **Fibich, Zdeněk, 1850-1900.** [Štědrý den.
Polyglot] Štědrý den ; Vodník : melodramy =
Der Heilige Abend ; Der Wassermann :
Melodramen = Christmas eve ; The water sprite :
melodramas : recitazione e piano / Zdeněk
Fibich ; text Karel Jaromír Erben ; deutsche
Übersetzung Marie Kwaysser und Eduard
Albert ; English translation Judith Mabary.

Erhard, Alexander.
See **Hoffmann, E. T. A. 1776-1822.** [Vocal
music. *Selections*] Kleine Vokalkompsitionen
und Klaviersonaten / E.T.A. Hoffmann ; aus dem
Nachlaß von Friedrich Schnapp und unter
Mitarbeit von Gerhard Allroggen ;
herausgegeben von Alexander Erhard und
Thomas Kohlhase.

Eric Clapton
See **Clapton, Eric.** [Songs. *Selections*] Eric
Clapton

Erinnerung an Marienbad
See **Spohr, Louis, 1784-1859** Erinnerung an
Marienbad

Erkel, Ferenc.
[Hunyadi László] — Hunyadi László : opera
négy felvonásban = opera in four acts / [Erkel
Ferenc] ; szöveg Benjámin Egressy ; közreadja
Katalin Szacsvai-Kim ; bevezetés Tibor Tallián,
Katalin Szacsvai-Kim. — *Rózsavölgyi és Társa
kiadása*
782.1   013688162

Erskine, Frances, Lady, *d. 1776*.
See **Fesch, Willem de, 1687-1761.** [Canzonette
ed arie, violin, continuo acc.] Lady Erskine
canzonettas : for soprano, violin or flute and
basso continuo : c.1730 / Willem de Fesch ; on
poems by Paolo Rolli and others ; edited by
Robert L. Tusler.

Es ist ein Ros entsprungen;
See **Rentz, Earlene.** Lo, how a rose e'er
blooming = (Es ist ein' Ros' entsprungen) : for
mixed choir (SATB), flute and piano / [from
Alte Catholiche Geistliche Kirchengesang'
(1599) harmonized by Michael Praetorius
(1609) ; arranged by] Earlene Rentz. — *Oxford
University Press*

Es ist ein Ros' entsprungen;
See **Rentz, Earlene.** Lo, how a rose e'er
blooming = (Es ist ein' Ros' entsprungen) : for
upper voices (SA), flute and piano / [from Alte
Catholische Geistliche Kirchengesang' (1599)
harmonized by Michael Praetorius (1609) ;
arranged by] Earlene Rentz. — *Oxford
University Press*

Escudero, Francisco, *1912-2002*.
Evocación en Icíar : preludio matinal / Francisco
Escudero. — *1a ed. — Tritó :*
784.218928   013710068

[Nocturne, orchestra] — Nocturno / Francisco
Escudero. — *1a ed. — Tritó : Eresbil*
784.218966   013710094

Poème symphonique / Francisco Escudero. —
1a ed. — Tritó :
784.21843   013710090

[Prelude, orchestra] — Preludio / Francisco
Escudero. — *1a ed. — Tritó :*
784.218928   013710105

El sueño de un bailarín : poema coreográfico /
Francisco Escudero. — *1a ed. — Tritó : Eresbil*
784.21556   013710053

[Symphonies, no. 5] — Quinta sinfonía : Ultreia
/ Francisco Escudero. — *1a ed. — Tritó :
Eresbil*
782.4184   013710076

Espla, Oscar, *1886-1976*.
Romanza antigua : = Romance antique : pour
piano / Oscar Esplá. — *Eschig*
786.2   013771077

[Esquisses japonaises]
See **Bovet, Guy.** [Esquisses japonaises]

Essential film songs
Essential film songs : the ultimate modern-day
movie songbook. Take 2. — *Wise Publications*
783.2421542   013169092

Essential jazz classics
Essential jazz classics : 10 essential jazz classics
/ arranged and produced by Mark Taylor. — *Hal
Leonard Europe*
781.65   013357996

The essential nü metal playlist.
The essential nü metal playlist. — *Wise
Publications*
783.242166   013139688

Essential piano exercises
See **Timakin, E. M.** Essential piano exercises

Essential piano songs.
Essential piano songs. Book 2 : [a superb collection of 22 exceptional songs by some of the world's greatest songwriters] — *Wise*
783.242164   013292865

Esser, Karl Michael, Ritter von, *1737-ca. 1795.*
[Duets, viola d'amore, viola da gamba] — Three pieces for viola d'amore & viola da gamba or violoncello (1789) / Karl Michael, Ritter von Esser. Two pieces for violin, viola d'amore & viola da gamba or violoncello (1789) / Tomaso Carle ; edited by David J. Rhodes. — *Viola da Gamba Society of Great Britain*
785.7192   013382402

Esteve, Pablo.
Los jardineros de Aranjuez : (1768) : zarzuela en dos actos / Pablo Esteve y Grimau ; estudio y edición crítica de Juan Pablo Fernández-Cortés. — *Universidad de Granada*
782.12   013335030

Esto mihi in Deum protectorem
See **Pitkin, Jonathan, 1978-** Esto mihi in Deum protectorem

Estonian wedding song
Estonian wedding song : for mixed chorus (SATB) and piano / [Estonian folk song, arr.] Theron Kirk. — *Oxford University Press*
782.5421587   013324505

Etudes d'exécution transcendante
See **Liszt, Franz, 1811-1886.** [Piano music. *Selections*] Etudes d'exécution transcendante

[Etudes faciles et progressives]
See **Burgmüller, Friedrich, 1806-1874.** [Etudes faciles et progressives]

[Etudes faciles. *Selections*]
See **Heller, Stephen, 1813-1888.** [Etudes faciles. *Selections*]

Eulogy
See **Turnage, Mark-Anthony.** Eulogy

Evans, Bill, *1929-1980.*
[Selections; *arr.*] — Bill Evans : 10 original compositions / arranged and produced by Mark Taylor. — *TRO The Richmond Organization*
781.65   013335910

Evans, Caroline, pianist.
See **Grade 8 piano anthology** : examination pieces for 2005 and 2006 : from the piano syllabus of the Associated Board of the Royal Schools of Music.

Evans, Karen, flutist.
See **Bizet, Georges, 1838-1875.** [Carmen. *Selections; arr.*] Flexible woodwind trios : Carmen / Georges Bizet ; arr. Karen Evans.

See **Flexible woodwind trios** : baroque / arr. Karen Evans.

Evans, Peter *1953-*
See **Sting (Musician).** [Songs. *Selections*] Sting for guitar tab / [Compiled by Peter Evans]; [words & music by Sting]

Evans, Rhiannon.
See **Seven 16th century duos from the York manuscript** : for bass and treble viols / anon. ; edited by Rhiannon Evans.

An evening prayer
See **Gordon, Andrew, composer.** An evening prayer

The evening watch
See **McCabe, John, 1939-** The evening watch

Evocación en Icíar
See **Escudero, Francisco, 1912-2002.** Evocación en Icíar

Exchanges 2
See **Hedges, Anthony, 1931-** [Exchanges, violoncello, piano, no. 2, op. 146] Exchanges 2

[Exchanges, violoncello, piano, no. 2, op. 146]
See **Hedges, Anthony, 1931-** [Exchanges, violoncello, piano, no. 2, op. 146]

Exhortation and Kohima
See **Tavener, John.** Exhortation and Kohima

Eye to the telescope
See **Tunstall, KT.** Eye to the telescope

Ezquerro Esteban, Antonio.
See **Música instrumental en las catedrales españolas en la época ilustrada** : conciertos, versos y sonatas, para chirimía, flauta y bajón—con violines y/u órgano—, de La Seo y El Pilar de Zaragoza / estudio y edición, Antonio Ezquerro Esteban.

Fabris, Dinko.
See **Neapolitan lute music** / Fabrizio Dentice … [et al.] ; edited by John Griffiths and Dinko Fabris.

[Fairy queen. *Selections*]
See **Purcell, Henry, 1659-1695.** [Fairy queen. *Selections*]

[Fairy queen. *Plaint*]
See **Purcell, Henry, 1659-1695.** [Fairy queen. Plaint]

Falla, Manuel de, *1876-1946.* Amor brujo.
See **The violin** : a collection : new and recent repertoire for violin with piano accompaniment / Craig Armstrong … [et al.]

Fanfare
See **Cooke, Arnold.** Fanfare

Fanning, David
See **Russian operatic arias for baritone** : 19th and 20th-century repertoire : complete with translations and guidance on pronunciation / selected and edited by David Fanning ; singing translations by Martin Pickard.

See **Russian operatic arias for tenor** : 19th and 20th century repertoire complete with translations and guidance on pronunciation / selected and edited by David Fanning ; singing translations by Alexander Wells.

Fanshawe, David, *1942-*
[African Sanctus (Musical work). Lord's prayer; *arr.*] — The Lord's prayer : from African sanctus / vocal arrangement by the composer, David Fanshawe ; brass band arrangement by Liz Lane. — *Studio Music*
784.9   013382672

Fantaisie
See **Brod, Henri, 1799-1839.** [Fantaisie, oboe, piano] Fantaisie

Fantaisie per clarinetto e pianoforte
See **Rossini, Gioacchino, 1792-1868** [Fantaisie, clarinet, piano, E♭ major] Fantaisie per clarinetto e pianoforte

Fantaisie pour piano et orchestre (2e version)
See **Debussy, Claude, 1862-1918** [Fantaisie, piano, orchestra] Fantaisie pour piano et orchestre (2e version)

Fantaisie sur 'Don Pasquale'
See **Verroust, Stanislas, 1814-1863.** Fantaisie sur 'Don Pasquale'

[Fantaisie, oboe, piano]
See **Brod, Henri, 1799-1839.** [Fantaisie, oboe, piano]

[Fantaisie, piano, orchestra]
See **Debussy, Claude, 1862-1918** [Fantaisie, piano, orchestra]

Fantasia für 2 Gitarren
See **Schwaen, Kurt, 1909-2007.** [Fantasia, guitars (2)] Fantasia für 2 Gitarren

Fantasia in four parts (cor anglais and 3 bassoons)
See **Ives, Simon, 1600-1662** Fantasia in four parts (cor anglais and 3 bassoons)

[Fantasia on Greensleeves; *arr.*]
See **Vaughan Williams, Ralph, 1872-1958** [Fantasia on Greensleeves; *arr.*]

[Fantasia on Greensleeves; *arr*]
See **Vaughan Williams, Ralph, 1872-1958** [Fantasia on Greensleeves; *arr*]

[Fantasia, guitars (2)]
See **Schwaen, Kurt, 1909-2007.** [Fantasia, guitars (2)]

Fantasia-suites
See **Jenkins, John, 1592-1678.** [Fantasia-suites, organ, viols (4). *Selections*] Fantasia-suites

[Fantasia-suites, organ, viols (4). *Selections*]
See **Jenkins, John, 1592-1678.** [Fantasia-suites, organ, viols (4). *Selections*]

[Fantasias, keyboard instrument]
See **Sweelinck, Jan Pieterszoon, 1562-1621.** [Fantasias, keyboard instrument]

[Fantasias, viols (3). *Selections*]
See **Jenkins, John, 1592-1678.** [Fantasias, viols (3). *Selections*]

[Fantasias, viols (4), Meyer 1-6. *Parts*]
See **Ward, John, 1571-1638.** [Fantasias, viols (4), Meyer 1-6. *Parts*]

Fantasie
See **Franckenstein, Clemens von, 1875-1942.** [Fantasien, orchestra, op. 15] Fantasie

[Fantasie, clarinet, piano, E♭ major]
See **Rossini, Gioacchino, 1792-1868** [Fantaisie, clarinet, piano, E♭ major]

[Fantasien, orchestra, op. 15]
See **Franckenstein, Clemens von, 1875-1942.** [Fantasien, orchestra, op. 15]

[Fantasien, violin, keyboard instrument, H. 536, F minor; *arr.*]
See **Bach, Carl Philipp Emanuel, 1714-1788.** [Fantasien, violin, keyboard instrument, H. 536, F minor; *arr.*]

The fantastic big book of children's songs.
The fantastic big book of children's songs. — *Hal Leonard*
782.742   013129773

Farjeon, Eleanor, *1881-1965.*
See **People, look east** : upper-voices and organ / Besançon melody arr. Barry Rose ; [words by] Eleanor Farjeon.

Fascination
See **Marchetti, Filippo, 1831-1902.** [Fascinzione. *arr.*] Fascination

[Fascinzione. *arr.*]
See **Marchetti, Filippo, 1831-1902.** [Fascinzione. *arr.*]

Father and son
Father and son : + 9 smash hits. — *Wise Publications*
783.242166   013178698

Fauré gold
See **Fauré, Gabriel, 1845-1924.** [Selections; *arr.*] Fauré gold

Fauré, Gabriel, 1845-1924.
[Selections; *arr.*] — Fauré gold : the essential collection. — *Chester Music*
786.2   013167436

Favorite standards
Favorite standards : piano, vocal, guitar. — *Hal Leonard*
783.242164   013219842

[Favourite quartettos. No. 5]
See **Graf, Friedrich Hartmann, 1727-1795** [Favourite quartettos. No. 5]

Fayrfax, Robert, 1464-1521.
See **The Arundel choirbook** : London, Lambeth Palace Library, MS 1 : a facsimile and introduction / introduction by David Skinner.

Febel, Reinhard, 1952-
Die Masken des Pierrot : für Frauenstimme und Klavier, 2003 / Reinhard Febel. — *Ricordi*
783.6   013771078

[Sonatas, piano] — Sieben Sonaten : für Klavier, 2000/02 / Reinhard Febel. — *Ricordi*
786.2183   013771079

Fedele, Ivan.
[Concertos, violin, orchestra, (1999)] — Concerto per violino e orchestra, 1998/99 / Ivan Fedele. — *Edizioni Suvini Zerboni*
784.272186   013771080

La fée aux roses
See **Halévy, F., 1799-1862.** La fée aux roses

Feeder (Musical group)
Pushing the senses / Feeder. — *Guitar tab ed.* — *Wise*
783.242166   013201234

Feel the spirit.
Feel the spirit. Volume two : twenty-eight arrangements for mixed chorus / by Moses Hogan ; with a foreword by Craig Jessop. — *Hal Leonard*
782.5253   013222168

Les fées du Rhin
See **Offenbach, Jacques, 1819-1880.** [Rheinnixen. *Vocal score*] Les fées du Rhin

Feld, Ulrike.
See **Musik am Meininger Hofe** / herausgegeben von Ulrike Feld und Ulrich Leisinger.

Fellows, Darren.
See **Jazzy opera classix** : for alto saxophone / [arranged by] Darren Fellows.

See **Jazzy opera classix** : for clarinet / [arranged by] Darren Fellows.

See **Jazzy opera classix** : for flute / [arranged by] Darren Fellows.

See **Jazzy opera classix** : for tenor saxophone / [arranged by] Darren Fellows.

See **Jazzy opera classix** : for trumpet / [arranged by] Darren Fellows.

See **Jazzy opera classix** : for violin / [arranged by] Darren Fellows.

Les femmes
See **Campra, André, 1660-1744.** [Cantates françoises, livre 1. Femmes] Les femmes

Fenaroli, Fedele, 1730-1818.
Stabat mater : for soprano, alto, strings & basso continuo / Fedele Fenaroli ; edited by Alejandro Garri ; assisted by Kent Carlson. — *First ed.* — *Garri Editions*
782.532351726   013771081

Fendt, Leopold.
See **Guggumos, Gallus, 16th cent.** [Motets, voices (4-6), continuo (1612). *Selections*] Mottecta, Venedig 1612. Heft 1, Motetten zu vier Stimmen mit b.c. / Gallus Guggumos ; herausgegeben von Leopold Fendt.

See **Guggumos, Gallus, 16th cent.** [Motets, voices (4-6), continuo (1612). *Selections*] Mottecta, Venedig 1612. Heft 2, Motetten zu fünf Stimmen mit B.c. / Gallus Guggumos ; herausgegeben von Leopold Fendt.

Fernández Shaw, Carlos, 1865-1911.
See **Chapí, Ruperto, 1851-1909.** La venta de Don Quijote : comedia lírica en un acto / Ruperto Chapí ; libreto, Carlos Fernández Shaw ; edición crítica Manuel Moreno-Buendia.

Fernández-Cortés, Juan Pablo.
See **Esteve, Pablo.** Los jardineros de Aranjuez : (1768) : zarzuela en dos actos / Pablo Esteve y Grimau ; estudio y edición crítica de Juan Pablo Fernández-Cortés.

Ferster, Piotr.
See **Pieśni i hymny Piwnicy pod Baranami** / [wybór piosenek Piotr Ferster, Marek Pacuła]

Fesca, F. E. 1789-1826.
[Quartets, strings. *Selections*] — Sechs ausgewählte Streichquartette / Friedrich Ernst Fesca ; herausgegeben von Markus Frei-Hauenschild unter Mitarbeit von Felix Loy. — *Nagels Verlag*
785.7194   013793762

Fesch, Willem de, 1687-1761.
[Apis amata] — Two solo cantatas / Willem de Fesch ; edited by Robert L. Tusler. — *Donemus*
783.6848   014747929

[Canzonettas, violin, continuo acc.] — Miss Ashe canzonettas : for soprano, violin or flute, mandoline and basso continuo : c.1734 / Willem de Fesch ; on poems by Paolo Rolli, Pietro Metastasio and others ; edited by Robert L. Tusler. — *Donemus*
783.6642   014747661

[Canzonette ed arie, violin, continuo acc.] — Lady Erskine canzonettas : for soprano, violin or flute and basso continuo : c.1730 / Willem de Fesch ; on poems by Paolo Rolli and others ; edited by Robert L. Tusler. — *Donemus*
783.6642   014747651

[Concertos, violins (2), string orchestra] — Concerto in A minor à 4 stromenti, c.1710 / Willem de Fesch ; edited by Robert L. Tusler. — *Donemus*
784.724186   014747956

[English songs] — VI English songs : for soprano, violins, flutes and basso continuo : 1748 / Willem de Fesch ; edited by Robert L. Tusler. — *Donemus*
783.342   014747718

[New English songs] — VI new English songs : for soprano, violin or flute and basso continuo : 1749 / Willem de Fesch ; edited by Robert L. Tusler. — *Donemus*
783.6642   014747723

[Songs. *Selections*] — Matthew Prior songs : for voice and basso continuo : 1741 / Willem de Fesch ; based on 'Lyric Poems' by Matthew Prior ; edited by Robert L. Tusler. — *Donemus*
783.242   014747680

[Songs. *Selections*] — Miscellaneous songs : for soprano, violin or flute, and basso continuo : 1748-53 / Willem de Fesch ; edited by Robert L. Tusler. — *Donemus*
783.6642   014747925

[Tempest] — The Tempest songs, or, The enchanted island : for soprano, small ensemble and basso continuo : 1745 / Willem de Fesch ; edited by Robert L. Tusler. — *Donemus*
783.6642   014747698

Temple of love : for voice, two obligato instruments and basso continuo : 1753 / Willem de Fesch ; edited by Robert L. Tusler. — *Donemus*
783.242   014747725

Fesch, Willem de, 1687-1761. Alla medisima.
See **Fesch, Willem de, 1687-1761.** [Apis amata] Two solo cantatas / Willem de Fesch ; edited by Robert L. Tusler.

La feste de Cloris
See **Bouvard, François, 1683-1760.** La feste de Cloris

Feuilles volantes
See **Duparc, Henri, 1848-1933.** Feuilles volantes

Fibich, Zdeněk, 1850-1900.
[Štědrý den. *Polyglot*] — Štědrý den ; Vodník : melodramy = Der Heilige Abend ; Der Wassermann : Melodramen = Christmas eve ; The water sprite : melodramas : recitazione e piano / Zdeněk Fibich ; text Karel Jaromír Erben ; deutsche Übersetzung Marie Kwaysser und Eduard Albert ; English translation Judith Mabary. — *Amos Editio*
783.96   013114862

Fibich, Zdeněk, 1850-1900. Vodník.
See **Fibich, Zdeněk, 1850-1900.** [Štědrý den. *Polyglot*] Štědrý den ; Vodník : melodramy = Der Heilige Abend ; Der Wassermann : Melodramen = Christmas eve ; The water sprite : melodramas : recitazione e piano / Zdeněk Fibich ; text Karel Jaromír Erben ; deutsche Übersetzung Marie Kwaysser und Eduard Albert ; English translation Judith Mabary.

Ficino, Marsilio, 1433-1499.
See **Davies, Peter Maxwell, 1934-** Angelus : for mixed chorus, SATB (2003) / Peter Maxwell Davies.

The fiddle music of James Hill
See **Hill, James, ca. 1811-1853.** The fiddle music of James Hill

Fiedler, Eric F.
See **Telemann, Georg Philipp, 1681-1767.** Jesu, wirst du bald erscheinen : Kantate zum 26. Sonntag nach Trinitatis, für Sopran-, Tenor- und Bass-Solo, vierstimmigen gemischten Chor, Zink, 3 Posaunen, 2 Oboen, Streicher und Basso continuo, TWV 1:988 / Georg Philipp Telemann ; herausgegeben von Arno Paduch und Eric F. Fiedler.

See **Telemann, Georg Philipp, 1681-1767.** [Wo soll ich fliehen hin?, TVWV 1:1724] Wo soll ich fliehen hin? : Kantate zum 22. Sonntag nach Trinitatis für Bariton-Solo, Flauto traverso, Oboe, Fagotto, Violine, Viola und Basso continuo, TVWV 1:1724 / Georg Philipp Telemann ; herausgegeben von Eric F. Fiedler.

Fierabras
See **Schubert, Franz, 1797-1828.** Fierabras

Fifteenth-century liturgical music V,
Fifteenth-century liturgical music V, Settings of the Sanctus and Agnus dei / transcribed and edited by Peter Wright. — *Published for the British Academy :*
782.53232   013701476

Figaro ; Cantate zum Geburts oder Namensfeste einer Mutter
See **Novak, Janez Krstnik, ca. 1756-1833.** Figaro ; Cantate zum Geburts oder Namensfeste einer Mutter

Filippi, Daniele V.
See **Palestrina, Giovanni Pierluigi da, 1525?-1594.** [Motets (1563)] Motecta festorum totius anni cum communi sanctorum quaternis vocibus / Giovanni Pierluigi da Palestrina ; edizione critica a cura di Daniele V. Filippi.

Film songs
Film songs : 24 screen hits. — *Wise Publications*
786.21542   013095248

Filthy/Gorgeous
Filthy/Gorgeous : + 9 smash hits. — *Wise Publications*
783.242166   013201212

Final straw
See **Snow Patrol (Musical group)** Final straw

A fine romance
A fine romance : & four other songs / arranged by David Nield. — *Novello*
782.542164   013748338

[Finlandia. Hymni; *arr.*]
See **Sibelius, Jean, 1865-1957.** [Finlandia. Hymni; *arr.*]

Finnissy, Michael.
Keroiylu : oboe, bassoon and piano = Oboe, Fagott und Klavier, 1981 / Michael Finnissy. — *Tre Media*
785.26193   013771082

The firmament
See **Sanders, John, 1933-2003.** The firmament

Fisherman Peter
Fisherman Peter : a South Carolina spiritual for unaccompanied choir (SATB) / arranged by Robert J. Powell. — *Oxford University Press*
782.5253   013472242

Five cantatas with recorder
See **Pepusch, John Christopher, 1667-1752.** [English cantatas. *Selections*] Five cantatas with recorder

Five easy pieces
See **Montague, Stephen.** [Easy pieces] Five easy pieces

Five folk songs
See **Gilmore, Bernard, 1937-** [Folksongs] Five folk songs

Five lullabies
See **Body, Jack, 1944-** [Lullabies, voices] Five lullabies

Five songs
See **Kaye, Ernest.** [Songs. *Selections*] Five songs

Five spirituals
See **Tippett, Michael, 1905-1998.** [Child of our time. *Selections; arr.*] Five spirituals

Five- and six-part Masses
See **Ludford, Nicholas, ca. 1490-1557.** [Vocal music. *Selections*] Five- and six-part Masses

Un flambeau, Jeannette, Isabelle
Un flambeau, Jeannette, Isabelle : SSAATTBB / French traditional ; arranged by Mark Williams. — *Edition Peters*
782.5281723   013304730

Flatman, Thomas, *1637-1688.*
See **Purcell, Henry, 1659-1695.** [Choral music. *Selections*] Royal welcome songs. Part II / Henry Purcell ; edited under the supervision of the Purcell Society by Bruce Wood.

Fletcher, Giles, *1549?-1611.*
See **Bennett, Richard Rodney.** Time : for SAATTBB / Richard Rodney Bennett.

Fletcher, John, *1941-*
See **Bach, Johann Sebastian, 1685-1750.** [Suites, orchestra, BWV 1067, B minor. Badinerie; *arr.*] Badinerie / J.S. Bach ; arranged for tuba & piano by John Fletcher.

Flexible woodwind trios
See **Bizet, Georges, 1838-1875.** [Carmen. *Selections; arr.*] Flexible woodwind trios

Flexible woodwind trios
Flexible woodwind trios : baroque / arr. Karen Evans. — *Spartan Press Music Publishers Ltd.*
785.8193   013376609

The flight of song
See **Skempton, Howard, 1947-** The flight of song

The flight of the bumblebee
See **Rimsky-Korsakov, Nikolay, 1844-1908.** [Skazka o t͡sare Saltane. Nu, teper', moĭ shmel'; *arr.*] The flight of the bumblebee

Florentz, Jean-Louis.
Requiem de la vierge : conte liturgique pour l'assomption de Marie : pour soprano, tenor, baryton, chœur d'enfants, chœur mixte et orchestre, opus 7, [1986-1988] / Jean-Louis Florentz. — *Ricordi*
782.53238   013762688

Flötenkonzert in F
See **Quantz, Johann Joachim, 1697-1773.** [Concertos, flute, string orchestra, QV 5:149, F major] Flötenkonzert in F

Flower of all
See **Boyle, Rory.** Flower of all

Flûte traversière
Flûte traversière : France, 1800-1860 : méthodes, traités, périodiques / sept volumes réalisés par Arlette Biget et Michel Giboureau. — *Editions Fuzeau*
788.32076   013408148

[Flute, piano music. *Selections*]
See **Gething, Joseph.** [Flute, piano music. *Selections*]

Folds, Ben, *1966-*
Songs for Silverman : piano transcriptions, vocal / Ben Folds. — *BMG Publications*
783.242166   013383512

Folk rock
Folk rock : guitar play-along. — *Hal Leonard*
783.242166   013222766

Folksong
See **Warren, Norman.** Folksong

[Folksongs]
See **Gilmore, Bernard, 1937-** [Folksongs]

Folle cor
See **Mazzocchi, D. 1592-1665.** [Musiche sacre, e morali. Folle cor] Folle cor

Foo Fighters (Musical group)
In your honor / Foo Fighters ; music transcriptions by Pete Billmann and David Stocker. — *Wise*
783.242166   013395944

The fool on the hill
See **Lennon, John, 1940-1980.** [Fool on the hill; *arr.*] The fool on the hill

[Fool on the hill; *arr.*]
See **Lennon, John, 1940-1980.** [Fool on the hill; *arr.*]

For all thy saints, O Lord
See **Lole, Simon.** For all thy saints, O Lord

For whom the bell tolls
See **Gerhard, Roberto, 1896-1970.** For whom the bell tolls

Forbes, Watson.
See **Bach, Johann Sebastian, 1685-1750.** [Jagdkantate. Schafe können sicher weiden; *arr.*] Sheep may safely graze : aria from secular cantata no. 208 / by J.S. Bach ; arranged for violin (or viola, or 'cello) and pianoforte by Watson Forbes.

Forest bell-birds
See **Carlson, Rosalind.** [Forest bell-birds, flute] Forest bell-birds
See **Carlson, Rosalind.** [Forest bell-birds, piccolo] Forest bell-birds

[Forest bell-birds, flute]
See **Carlson, Rosalind.** [Forest bell-birds, flute]

[Forest bell-birds, piccolo]
See **Carlson, Rosalind.** [Forest bell-birds, piccolo]

Forest music
See **McAlister, Clark.** Forest music

Forest of Bowland suite
See **Gibbs, Christopher, 1938-** [Forest of Bowland suite; *arr.*] Forest of Bowland suite

[Forest of Bowland suite; *arr.*]
See **Gibbs, Christopher, 1938-** [Forest of Bowland suite; *arr.*]

Fornari, Giacomo.
See **Mozart, Wolfgang Amadeus, 1756-1791.** [Quartets, strings, K. 155-160] L'autografo dei quartetti "Milanesi" : nella Musikabteilung della Staatsbibliothek (Preussischer Kulturbesitz) di Berlino = Das Autograph der "Mailänder" Streichquartette : in der Musikabteilung der Staatsbibliothek (Preussischer Kulturbesitz) von Berlin : KV 155-160 (134a, 134b, 157-159, 159a) / Wolfgang Amadeus Mozart ; edizione in facsimile a cura di Giacomo Fornari.

La forza dell'amor paterno
See **Stradella, Alessandro, 1639-1682.** La forza dell'amor paterno

Foster, Stephen Collins, *1826-1864.*
[Songs. *Selections; arr.*] Seven songs of Stephen Foster : for voice and piano / in versions by Warren Michel Swenson. — *Oxford University Press*
783.6642   013103270

[Songs. *Selections; arr.*] — Stephen Foster medley : SSAATTBB / music by Stephen Foster ; arranged by Jonathan Rathbone. — *Edition Peters*
782.542   013305049

Four cantatas for bass
See **Cesti, Antonio, 1623-1669.** [Cantatas, bass, continuo. *Selections*] Four cantatas for bass

Four cantatas from Rome, 1707
See **Handel, George Frideric, 1685-1759.**
[Cantatas. *Selections*] Four cantatas from Rome,
1707

Four Christmas carols
See **Swayne, Giles.** [Christmas carols, op. 77]
Four Christmas carols

Four dialogues
See **Hedges, Anthony, 1931-** [Dialogues] Four
dialogues

Four offertories for Sundays in Advent
See **Palestrina, Giovanni Pierluigi da,
1525?-1594.** [Offertories, voices (5). *Selections*]
Four offertories for Sundays in Advent

The four seasons
See **Vivaldi, Antonio, 1678-1741** [Cimento
dell'armonia e dell'inventione. N. 1-4; *arr.*] The
four seasons

Four seasons
See **Zhou, Long, 1953-** Four seasons

The four seasons in the Fairy queen
See **Purcell, Henry, 1659-1695.** [Fairy queen.
Selections] The four seasons in the Fairy queen

Four songs
See **Previn, André, 1929-** [Songs (2004)] Four
songs

Four symphonies
See **Zimmermann, Anton, 1741-1781.**
[Symphonies. *Selections*] Four symphonies

Foursquare
See **Harle, John.** Foursquare

Fragments
See **Poole, Geoffrey, 1949-** Fragments

Francis, of Assisi, Saint, *1182-1226*
See **Gubaĭdulina, Sofʻia Asgatovna.**
Sonnengesang = The canticle of the sun :
revidierte Fassung 5/1998 / Sofia Gubaidulina.

Franck, César, *1822-1890.*
[Sonatas, violin, piano, A major; *arr.*] — Sonate
für Viola und Klavier A-Dur / César Franck ;
[herausgegeben von Stephanie Gurtner] —
Partitura Verlag
787.3183   013887070

[Sonatas, violin, piano, A major; *arr.*] — Sonate
für Violoncello und Klavier A-Dur / César
Franck ; [herausgegeben von Stephanie Gurtner]
— *Partitura Verlag*
787.4183   013887071

Franckenstein, Clemens von, *1875-1942.*
[Fantasien, orchestra, op. 15] — Fantasie :
Nachtstimmung / Clemens von Franckenstein.
Symphonische Phantasie über ein Gedicht von
Edgar Steiger : ("Ibsen-Phantasie") / August
Reuss. Nachtstück / Felix vom Rath ;
herausgegeben von Stephan Hörner. —
Breitkopf & Härtel
784.21894   014620316

Franklin, Cary John.
A Navaho prayer : SATB a cappella / [music] by
Cary John Franklin. — *Boosey & Hawkes*
782.525   013361391

Franz Ferdinand (Musical group)
You could have it so much better / [Franz
Ferdinand] — *Guitar tab ed.* — *Wise
Publications*
783.242166   013440051

Französischer Jahrgang
See **Telemann, Georg Philipp, 1681-1767.**
[Cantatas. *Selections*] Französischer Jahrgang

Frei-Hauenschild, Markus.
See **Fesca, F. E. 1789-1826.** [Quartets, strings.
Selections] Sechs ausgewählte Streichquartette /
Friedrich Ernst Fesca ; herausgegeben von
Markus Frei-Hauenschild unter Mitarbeit von
Felix Loy.

Freie Bearbeitungen.
See **Liszt, Franz, 1811-1886.** [Piano music.
Selections] Freie Bearbeitungen.

Fremar, Karen.
See **Martinez, Marianne, 1744-1812.**
[Symphony, C major] Sinfonia in C major,
(Ouverture), (1770) / by Marianna Martines ;
edited by Shirley Bean and Karen Fremar.

Friesenhagen, Andreas.
See **Haydn, Joseph, 1732-1809.** [Divertimenti,
H. IV, 1-11.] Trios für Blas- und
Streichinstrumente / Joseph Haydn ;
herausgegeben von Andreas Friesenhagen.

From a river's edge
See **Ramsey, Andrea.** From a river's edge

From me flows what you call time
See **Takemitsu, Tōru.** From me flows what you
call time

From Nourlangie
See **Sculthorpe, Peter, 1929-** [From Nourlangie;
arr.] From Nourlangie

[From Nourlangie; *arr.*]
See **Sculthorpe, Peter, 1929-** [From Nourlangie;
arr.]

From the shadows
See **Woolrich, John.** From the shadows

Frühwirth, David.
See **Wellesz, Egon, 1885-1974.** [Suites, violin,
piano, op. 56] Suite für Violine und Klavier,
op. 56 (1937, rev. 1957) / Egon Wellesz ;
herausgegeben und mit Fingersätzen versehen
von David Frühwirth.

Fruit salad
See **Hermann, Avril.** Fruit salad

Fun and games with the alto recorder
See **Heyens, Gudrun.** Fun and games with the
alto recorder

Fun and games with the alto recorder.
See **Heyens, Gudrun.** Fun and games with the
alto recorder.

Fun and games with the recorder
Fun and games with the recorder : method for
the alto recorder. Tune book / [compiled by]
Gudrun Heyens and Gerhard Engel ; translated
and adapted by Peter Bowman ; with
illustrations by John Minnion. — *Schott*
788.36076   013134305

Fun club alto sax
See **Haughton, Alan, 1950-** Fun club alto sax

Fun club descant recorder
See **Haughton, Alan, 1950-** Fun club descant
recorder

Fun club violin
See **Haughton, Alan, 1950-** Fun club violin

Fünf Botschaften für die Königin von Saba
See **Henze, Hans Werner, 1926-** [Botschaften
für die Königin von Saba] Fünf Botschaften für
die Königin von Saba

Fünf kleine Stücke für Violine und Klavier, 2002
See **Blomenkamp, Thomas.** [Kleine Stücke,
violin, piano (2002)] Fünf kleine Stücke für
Violine und Klavier, 2002

Fuori di sua capanna
See **Greber, Jakob, 1691-1731.** Fuori di sua
capanna

Fürlinger, Wolfgang.
See **Eberlin, Johann Ernst, 1702-1762.** Missa
septimi toni : für Soli, SATB, Streicher und
Orgel / Johann Ernst Eberlin ; herausgegeben
von Konrad Führlinger und Friedrich Hägele.

See **Salieri, Antonio, 1750-1825.** Salve regina :
für vierstimmigen gemischten Chor, 2 Violinen,
Viola, Bass und Orgel / Antonio Salieri ;
revidiert und herausgegeben von Otto Biba ;
Continuofassung von Wolfgang Fürlinger.

Furrer, Beat, *1954-*
Stimmen : für Chor und 4 Schlagzeuger : 1996 /
Beat Furrer. — *Bärenreiter*
782.5   013771069

Furtwängler, Wilhelm, *1886-1954.*
[Symphonies, no. 1, B minor] — Sinfonie Nr. 1,
H-Moll / Wilhelm Furtwängler ; herausgegeben
von George Alexander Albrecht. — *Ries &
Erler*
784.2184   014655929

[Symphonies, no. 2, E minor] — Sinfonie Nr. 2
E-moll / Wilhelm Furtwängler ; herausgegeben
von George Alexander Albrecht. — *Ries &
Erler*
784.2184   013570939

[Symphonies, no. 3, C sharp minor] — Sinfonie
Nr. 3 cis-moll / Wilhelm Furtwängler ;
herausgegeben von George Alexander Albrecht.
— *Ries & Erler*
784.2184   013599651

[Symphonisches Konzert] — Sinfonisches
Konzert für Klavier und Orchester / Wilhelm
Furtwängler ; herausgegeben von George
Alexander Albrecht. — *Ries & Erler*
784.262186   014658035

Te Deum : für gemischten Chor, 4 Solostimmen
und Orchester / Wilhelm Furtwängler ;
herausgegeben von George Alexander Albrecht.
— *Ries & Erler*
782.5325   014658145

Fuzelier, M. *1672-1752.*
See **Bernier, Nicolas, 1665-1734.** [Cantates
françoises, 2e livre. Diane et Endimion] Diane et
Endimion : cantata for soprano, bass & continuo
/ Nicolas Bernier.

Gabriel's message
Gabriel's message : SSAATTBB / arranged by
Jonathan Rathbone. — *Edition Peters*
782.5281723   013304479

Gaitzsch, J.
See **Urcullu, Leopoldo.** [Thème & variations,
guitar, op. 10, E major] Thème & variations pour
guitare, op. 10 / Leopoldo de Urcullu.

Gál, Hans, *1890-1987.*
[Divertimenti, winds, op. 22] — Divertimento,
op. 22, octet for woodwind and brass / Hans Gál.
— *Maecenas Contemporary Composers*
785.431981852   013322060

Galuppi, Baldassare, *1706-1785.*
[Concertos, harpsichord, string orchestra, C
minor] — Concerti per cembalo n. 5 e n. 6 per
clavicembalo, violino I, violino II, viola e basso
/ Baldassare Galuppi, detto il Buranello ; a cura
di Rita Peiretti ; prefazione di Alberto Iesuè. —
Associazione clavicembalistica bolognese
784.7264186   013647815

Galuppi, Baldassare, *1706-1785.* Concertos,
See **Galuppi, Baldassare, 1706-1785.**
[Concertos, harpsichord, string orchestra, C
minor] Concerti per cembalo n. 5 e n. 6 per
clavicembalo, violino I, violino II, viola e basso
/ Baldassare Galuppi, detto il Buranello ; a cura
di Rita Peiretti ; prefazione di Alberto Iesuè.

Galway Bay
See **Colahan, Arthur.** Galway Bay

Gammie, Ian.
El lladre reformat : variations on a Catalan folk
song : for solo guitar / Ian Gammie. — *Corda
Music Publications*
787.871825 013269154

Ganassi, Giacomo, *fl. 1625-1637*
[Vespertina psalmodia (1637) Selections] — 13
canzoni strumentali a due e a quattro strumenti
con il basso per l'organo : estratte da: Vespertina
psalmodia in totius anni solemnitates— :
Venezia, 1637 / Giacomo Ganassi ; trascrizione
a cura di Alessandro Bares. — *Musedita*
785.25193 013688132

García Lorca, Federico, *1898-1936.*
See **Henze, Hans Werner, 1926-** El rey de
Harlem : imaginäres Theater I : für Mezzosopran
und kleines Ensemble = imaginary theatre I : for
mezzo soprano and small ensemble / Hans
Werner Henze ; Dichtung von Federico Garcia
Lorca.

Garri, Alejandro.
See **Fenaroli, Fedele, 1730-1818.** Stabat mater :
for soprano, alto, strings & basso continuo /
Fedele Fenaroli ; edited by Alejandro Garri ;
assisted by Kent Carlson.

See **Graun, Johann Gottlieb, 1702 or 3-1771**
[Concertos, viola da gamba, string orchestra, A
major] Concerto in A major for viola da gamba,
strings & basso continuo / Johann Gottlieb
Graun ; edited by Alejandro Garri ; assisted by
Kent Carlson.

See **Hasse, Johann Adolf, 1699-1783.** Ascolta i
preghi : (Psalm 42:9, 10) : motet for 2 sopranos
and basso continuo / Johann A. Hasse ; edited
by Alejandro Garri ; assisted by Kent Carlson.

See **Hasse, Johann Adolf, 1699-1783.** Ave
Regina coelorum : Marian antiphon for alto, 2
oboes, strings & basso continuo / Johann A.
Hasse ; edited by Alejandro Garri ; assisted by
Kent Carlson.

See **Herbst, Johann Andreas, 1588-1666**
Lobet, ihr Knechte des Herrn : (Psalm 113) :
motet for tenor, baritone, bass, 2 violins & basso
continuo / Johann Andreas Herbst ; edited by
Alejandro Garri ; assisted by Kent Carlson.

See **Herbst, Johann Andreas, 1588-1666.**
Erbarm' dich mein, o Herre Gott : (Psalm 51) :
Miserere for baritone or bass, strings & basso
continuo ; edited by Alejandro Garri, assited by
Kent Carlson.

See **Werner, Gregor Joseph, 1695-1766.** [Salve
Regina, voices (4), violins (2), organ, B♭ major]
Salve Regina : in B-flat major : for mixed choir,
two violins and organ / by Gregor Joseph
Werner ; edited by Alejandro Garri ; assisted by
Kent Carlson.

Gaslight Square II
See **Samuel, Rhian.** Gaslight Square II

Gaude gloriosa Dei Mater
See **Tallis, Thomas, ca. 1505-1585.** Gaude
gloriosa Dei Mater

Gavrilin, V.
[Selections] — Val'sy dlïa fortepiano i
fortepiano v 4 ruki = Waltzes for piano and
piano in four hands / V. Gavrilin. — *Kompozitor*
786.418846 013637528

Gay, John, *1685-1732.*
See **Arnold, Samuel, 1740-1802.** Polly : an
opera : (1777) / music by Johann Christoph
Pepusch ; rearrang'd and new airs compos'd by
Samuel Arnold ; libretto by John Gay ; revis'd
by George Colman, the elder ; edited by Robert
Hoskins.

See **Six songs from John Gay's The beggar's
opera /** arranged for piano trio by Nancy
O'Neill Breth and Jean Goberman ; edited by J.
Mark Baker.

Geary, Aidan.
See **Richards, Jack, 1947-** Snare drum : grades
5-8 / edited by Jack Richards and Andrew
McBirnie ; additional editing by Aidan Geary.

Geay, Gérard.
See **Royer, Pancrace, 1705-1755.** Le pouvoir de
l'Amour / Pancrace Royer ; édition de Lisa
Goode Crawford ; avec la collaboration de
Gérard Geay.

Gedge, David.
See **The violin** : a collection : new and recent
repertoire for violin with piano accompaniment /
Craig Armstrong ... [et al.]

[Gedichte von Günter Grass]
See **Heider, Werner, 1930-** [Gedichte von
Günter Grass]

Geistliche Gesänge.
See **Rheinberger, Josef, 1839-1901** [Vocal
music. Selections] Geistliche Gesänge.

Y gelynnen
Y gelynnen = The holly : traditional Welsh
folk-song arranged for female voice choir and
piano / by Jayne Davies ; English text by Rhian
Davies. — *Roberton Publications*
782.64216209429 013193204

Genesi, Mario G.
L'arte della variazione, per organo / Mario
Giuseppe Genesi. — *Carrara*
786.51825 014101650

George King of Great Britain, *1738-1820.*
See **Davies, Peter Maxwell, 1934-** [Songs for a
mad king. Vocal score] Eight songs for a mad
king : music-theatre piece for male voice and
ensemble / Peter Maxwell Davies ; text by
Randolph Stow and George III ; vocal score.

Gerhard, Roberto, *1896-1970.*
For whom the bell tolls : per a guitarra / Robert
Gerhard ; revisio i edicio de Meirion Bowen i
Eugenio Tobalina. — *Trito*
787.87 013887072

Gershwin gold
See **Gershwin, George, 1898-1937.** [Selections;
arr.] Gershwin gold

Gershwin, George, *1898-1937.*
[Selections; *arr.*] — Gershwin gold : the
essential collection. — *Chester Music*
786.2 013332870

[Songs. *Selections; arr.*] — Easy-to-play
Gershwin for piano / arranged by Andrew
Wright. — *Kevin Mayhew*
786.2164 013159350

Gertsch, Norbert.
See **Balakirev, Milïï Alekseevich, 1837-1910.**
[Islameĭ] Islamey : Fantaisie orientale / Milij
Balakirev ; herausgegeben von Norbert Gertsch.

Get lifted
See **Legend, John.** Get lifted

Gething, Joseph.
[Flute, piano music. *Selections*] — Themes for
flute : flute and piano. Book 1 / Joseph Gething.
— *Broadbent & Dunn*
788.32 013188440

[Flute, piano music. *Selections*] — Themes for
flute : flute and piano. Book 5 / Joseph Gething.
— *Broadbent & Dunn*
788.32 013213508

[Flute, piano music. *Selections*] — Themes for
flute : flute and piano. Book Four / by Joseph
Gething. — *Broadbent & Dunn*
788.32 013213520

[Flute, piano music. *Selections*] — Themes for
flute : flute and piano. Book Six / by Joseph
Gething. — *Broadbent & Dunn*
788.32 013213505

[Flute, piano music. *Selections*] — Themes for
flute : flute and piano. Book Three / by Joseph
Gething. — *Broadbent & Dunn*
788.32 013188420

[Flute, piano music. *Selections*] — Themes for
flute : flute and piano. Book Two / by Joseph
Gething. — *Broadbent & Dunn*
788.32 013188425

[Piccolo, piano music] — Pieces for piccolo :
piccolo and piano / by Joseph Gething. —
Broadbent & Dunn
788.33 013188458

Gettysburg
See **Hewitt, Daniel.** Gettysburg

Ghirlanda odorifera
See **Puliti, Gabriello, b. ca. 1575.** Ghirlanda
odorifera

Ghostwatch
See **Hearne, John, 1937-** [Ghostwatch ; *arr.*]
Ghostwatch

[Ghostwatch ; *arr.*]
See **Hearne, John, 1937-** [Ghostwatch ; *arr.*]

Gianturco, Carolyn.
See **Stradella, Alessandro, 1639-1682.** La forza
dell'amor paterno / Alessandro Stradella ; a cura
di Mariateresa Dellaborra, Carolyn Gianturco.

Giardini, Felice, *1716-1796.*
[Duets, viola, bassoon] — 3 Duetti à fagotto e
viola concerta / Felice de Giardini ;
herausgegeben von Helge Bartholomäus. —
Erstdruck — *Hofmeister*
785.44192 013887073

Gibbons, Orlando, *1583-1625.*
[Pavans, voices (5), H. 30] — Pavane, De la
Roye : (TrTrTTB) / Orlando Gibbons ; edited &
completed by Mark Levy. — *Viola da Gamba
Society of Great Britain*
785.7619518823 013382472

[Song 13; *arr.*] — With grateful hearts :
meditation for Remembrance Sunday : for mixed
voices and organ / [Orlando Gibbons ; arr.]
Philip Ledger. — *Encore Publications*
782.5265 013225245

Gibbs, Christopher, *1938-*
[Forest of Bowland suite; *arr.*] — Forest of
Bowland suite : for two flutes, alto flute and
bass flute / by Christopher Gibbs ; arranged by
Chris Nex. — *Phylloscopus Publications*
785.8321941858 013173876

Giboureau, Michel.
See **Basson** : France, 1800-1860 : méthodes,
traités d'instrumentation, dictionnaires, cours de
composition, périodiques.

See **Flûte traversière** : France, 1800-1860 : méthodes, traités, périodiques / sept volumes réalisés par Arlette Biget et Michel Giboureau.

See **Hautbois** : [France, 1800-1860] : méthodes, traités, dictionnaires et encyclopédies, ouvrages généraux / volume réalisé par Michel Giboureau.

Gift of love
See **Ledger, Philip.** Gift of love

Gilbert, Anthony.
Moonfaring : for cello and percussion (1983-1986) / Anthony Gilbert. — *Schott*
785.58192   013771084

Os : for oboe and vibraphone : [2002 revision] / Anthony Gilbert. — *University of York Music Press*
785.56192   013430853

[Quartets, strings, no. 3] — String quartet no. 3 : (1987) / Anthony Gilbert. — *Schott*
785.7194   013771085

Unrise : for ten wind (2001) / Anthony Gilbert. — *University of York Music Press*
785.43199   013430756

Gilmore, Bernard, *1937-*
[Folksongs] — Five folk songs : for soprano and symphonic wind band : (1966) / Bernard Gilmore. — *Maecenas Music*
783.6642   013192859

Giordani, Giuseppe, *1751-1798.*
Veni sponsa Christi : antifona / Giuseppe Giordani (Giordaniello) ; edizione critica a cura di Ugo Gironacci e Italo Vescovo. — *Libreria Musicale Italiana*
782.625   013949593

Giovannelli, Ruggiero, *ca. 1560-1625.*
[Selections] — Three pieces à 5 : TrTrTTB / Ruggiero Giovannelli ; edited by Virginia Brookes. — *Viola da Gamba Society of Great Britain*
785.76195   013441010

Giovannelli, Ruggiero, *ca. 1560-1625.* **Madrigals,**
See **The amorous hexachord** : madrigal fantasies from the Tregian manuscript / Pallavicino, Bianciardi, and Giovannelli ; edited by Hannah Davidson.

Gironacci, Ugo.
See **Giordani, Giuseppe,** *1751-1798.* Veni sponsa Christi : antifona / Giuseppe Giordani (Giordaniello) ; edizione critica a cura di Ugo Gironacci e Italo Vescovo.

I giuochi d'Agrigento
See **Paisiello, Giovanni,** *1740-1816.* I giuochi d'Agrigento

Give almes of thy goods
See **Tye, Christopher,** *1497?-1572.* Give almes of thy goods

Glass, Philip.
[Concertos, violin, orchestra; *arr.*] — Violin concerto : (1987) / Philip Glass ; piano reduction by Charles Abramovich. — *Chester Music*
787.2186   013323691

Glass, Philip. Knee 2.
See **The violin** : a collection : new and recent repertoire for violin with piano accompaniment / Craig Armstrong ... [et al.]

[Glasses of wine]
See **Davies, Peter Maxwell,** *1934-* [Glasses of wine]

Glinka, Mikhail Ivanovich, *1804-1857.*
See **Uspenskiĭ , Vladislav Aleksandrovich.** Tokkata-fantaziiā : na temu M.I. Glinki : dlià dvukh fortepiano v vosem' ruk = Toccata-fantasy : to M.I. Glinka : for two pianos in eight hands / Vladislav Uspenskiĭ .

Globe Theatre suite
See **Kelly, Bryan.** Globe Theatre suite

Globokar, Vinko, *1934-*
Métamorphoses parallèles : für Viola, Klavier und Live-Elektronik, 2005 / Vinko Globokar. — *Ricordi*
785.2998193   013771088

Y g'loman
Y g'loman = The dove : traditional Welsh folk-song arranged for SSAA choir, solo voice, flute and piano / by Jayne Davies ; English text by Rhian Davies. — *Roberton Publications*
782.64216209429   013193354

Gloria in excelsis
See **Dicie, Don Michael.** Gloria in excelsis

Glory to God
Glory to God : Englische Chormusik aus fünf Jahrhunderten / herausgegeben von Hans Wülfing für den Landesverband ev. Kirchenchöre im Rheinland in Zusammenarbeit mit dem Verband ev. Kirchenchöre Deutschlands. — *Oxford University Press*
782.522   013312902

Glover, Denis, *1912-1980.*
See **Chilcott, Bob.** You and me : SATB unaccompanied / Bob Chilcott.

Goberman, Jean.
See **Six songs from John Gay's The beggar's opera** / arranged for piano trio by Nancy O'Neill Breth and Jean Goberman ; edited by J. Mark Baker.

God be in my head
See **Baldwin, Antony,** *1957-* God be in my head

God be with you till we meet again
See **Rose, Barry,** *1934-* God be with you till we meet again

God would be born in thee
See **Bingham, Judith.** God would be born in thee

Goddard, Mark.
Anthem, The priests of the Lord : for SATB and organ / music by Mark Goddard ; text from Leviticus. — *Spartan Press*
782.5265   013263962

Be strong and of good courage : an anthem for St. Barnabas Day : SATB with STB soloists [and organ] / music by Mark Goddard. — *Spartan Press*
782.5265   013482277

See **More essential piano repertoire** / editor, Mark Goddard.

Godfrey, Philip, *1964-*
Day by day : [a prayer of St. Richard of Chichester] : for mixed voices (SATB) and piano or organ / Philip Godfrey. — *Encore Publications*
782.5265   013416377

May the road rise with you : a choral blessing / music: Philip Godfrey ; words: a Gaelic blessing. — *Encore Publications*
782.5265   013416371

Gogol-Suite
See **Schnittke, Alfred,** *1934-1998.* Gogol-Suite

Gogol', Nikolaĭ Vasil'evich, *1809-1852.* **Mertvye dushi.**
See **Schnittke, Alfred,** *1934-1998.* Gogol-Suite : Suite aus der Bühnenmusik zum Schauspiel "Die Revisionsliste" von Nikolai Gogol = Suite from the music to a production of "The dead souls register" by Nikolai Gogol / Alfred Schnittke ; Zusammenstellung, Gennadi Rozhdestvensky.

Going north
See **Musgrave, Thea.** Going north

The golden city
See **Spencer, Tim.** The golden city

Goldrich, Zina.
[Songs. *Selections*] — Songbook : volume 1 / Goldrich and Heisler ; lyrics by Marcy Heisler ; music by Zina Goldrich. — *2nd ed.* — *Marcy and Zina Co.*
783.242164   013212015

Golianek, Ryszard Daniel.
See **Zarębski, Juliusz,** *1854-1885.* [Pezzo agitato con un intermezzo amoroso] Wielka fantazja = Grande fantaisie (Un pezzo agitato con un intermezzo amoroso), JZBO 11 ; Utwór bez tytułu = Piece without title, JZBO 14 : na fortepian = for piano / Juliusz Zarębski ; redakcja Ryszard Daniel Golianek ; opracowanie wykonawcze Andrzej Tatarski.

González Marín, Luis Antonio.
See **Música para exequias en tiempo de Felipe IV** / estudio y edición, Luis Antonio Gonzáles Marín.

Good Christian men, rejoice
See **[In dulci jubilo]** Good Christian men, rejoice

Good news for people who love bad news
See **Modest Mouse (Musical group)** Good news for people who love bad news

Goode, David, organist.
Like as the hart : for sopranos (with solo parts) and organ / David Goode. — *Encore Publications*
782.6294   013182240

Goodison, Jack.
See **Jack Goodison's collection of local & traditional carols** / [collected and compiled by Jack Goodison]

Gopalnath, Kadiri.
See **Indian melodies** : for alto saxophone = Mélodies indiennes : pour saxophon alto = Indische Melodien : für Alt-Saxophon / [arranged by] Candida Connolly ; with accompanying CD by Kadri Golpalnath.

Gorb, Adam, *1958-*
Awayday : (1996) / Adam Gorb. — *Maecenas Music*
784.8   013193029

Battle symphony : for woodwind ensemble including saxophones / Adam Gorb. — *Maecenas Music*
784.89   013193057

Bridgewater breeze : [1996] / Adam Gorb. — *Maecenas Music*
784.81858   013193076

Diaspora : 2003 : for string ensemble (33221 players) / Adam Gorb. — *Maecenas Music*
785.7199   013416719

Elements : (1998) : suite for solo percussion and wind ensemble / Adam Gorb. — *Maecenas Music*
785.321991858   013422352

Over hill, over dale / Adam Gorb. — *Maecenas Music*
784.8   013193107

[Suites, woodwinds (1993)] — Suite for winds / Adam Gorb. — *Maecenas Music*
785.81858   013192928

[Symphonies, no. 1, C] — Symphony no. 1 in C : for 12 wind & double bass / Adam Gorb. — *Maecenas Music*
785.42199184   013422267

Towards Nirvana : (2002) : for wind orchestra / Adam Gorb. — *Maecenas Music*
784.8   013422427

Weimar : (2000) : for large ensemble / Adam Gorb. — *Maecenas Music*
785.32199   013422553

Gorb, Adam, *1958-* Suites,
See **Gorb, Adam, *1958-*** Bridgewater breeze : [1996] / Adam Gorb.

Gordon, Andrew, composer.
An evening prayer : for unison treble choir and organ / Andrew Gordon. — *Oxford University Press*
782.76265   013525131

Gott der Herr ist Sonn und Schild
See **Bach, Johann Sebastian, 1685-1750.** [Gott, der Herr, ist Sonn' und Schild. *English & German*] Gott der Herr ist Sonn und Schild

Gott ist gegenwärtig
See **Herzogenberg, Heinrich von, 1843-1900.** Gott ist gegenwärtig

[Gott, der Herr, ist Sonn' und Schild. *English & German*]
See **Bach, Johann Sebastian, 1685-1750.** [Gott, der Herr, ist Sonn' und Schild. *English & German*]

Gould, Glenn.
See **Wagner, Richard, 1813-1883.** [Meistersinger von Nürnberg. Vorspiel; *arr.*] Die Meistersinger von Nürnberg : (Vorspiel) = (Prelude) / Richard Wagner ; in einer Transkription für Klavier zu zwei Händen oder für zwei Klaviere zu vier Händen von Glenn Gould ; herausgegeben von Carl Morey.

Gousset, Marie-Thérèse.
See **Tropaire séquentiaire prosaire prosulaire de Moissac :** (troisième quart du XIe siècle) : Manuscrit Paris, Bibliothèque nationale de France, n.a.l. 1871 / édition, introduction et index par Marie-Noël Colette ; analyse de l'écriture et de la décoration par Marie-Thérèse Gousset.

Grabowski, Christophe.
See **Chopin, Frédéric, 1810-1849.** [Waltzes, piano] Waltzes : piano / Fryderyk Chopin ; edited by Christophe Grabowski.

Grade 8 piano anthology
Grade 8 piano anthology : examination pieces for 2005 and 2006 : from the piano syllabus of the Associated Board of the Royal Schools of Music. — *Edition Peters*
786.2076   013095045

Graf, Friedrich Hartmann, *1727-1795*
[Favourite quartettos. No. 5] — Quartetto V for bassoon (or cello), violin 1 (or oboe) violin 2 and cello / by Friedrich Hartmann Graf. — *Phylloscopus Publications*
785.44194   013188895

Graf, Friedrich Hartmann, *1727-1795*.
[Quartets, bassoon, violin, viola, violoncello, B♭ major] — Quartetto VI for bassoon (or cello), violin (or oboe), viola and cello / by Friedrich Hartmann Graf. — *Phylloscopus Publications*
785.44194   013188898

Graffito sul mare
See **Sciarrino, Salvatore.** Graffito sul mare

Grainer, Ron.
[Tales of the unexpected. Theme; *arr.*] — Tales of the unexpected : grade 1.5 / Ron Grainer ; arr. Rodney Newton. — *Studio Music*
784.8   013359115

Gran duo
See **Lindberg, Magnus, 1958-** Gran duo

Granade, John Adam, *1763?-1807*.
See **Moore, William, d. 1825.** [Sweet rivers; *arr.*] Sweet rivers : for lower voices (TBB) and piano / William Moore ; arr. Reginald Unterseher.

Grand octetto op. 33
See **St.-Lubin, Léon de.** [Octet, op. 33, E minor] Grand octetto op. 33

Grand quintette
See **Kreutzer, Rodolphe, 1766-1831.** [Quintets, oboe, violins, viola, violoncello, C major] Grand quintette

Grand sonata in D major
See **Parke, Maria F., 1772 or 3-1822.** [Grand sonatas, op. 1. No. 3] Grand sonata in D major

[Grand sonatas, op. 1. No. 3]
See **Parke, Maria F., 1772 or 3-1822.** [Grand sonatas, op. 1. No. 3]

[Grand trio concertant, no. 1]
See **Molino, Francesco, 1768-1847.** [Grand trio concertant, no. 1]

Grand trio concertant, op. 30
See **Molino, Francesco, 1768-1847.** [Grand trio concertant, no. 1] Grand trio concertant, op. 30

Grande, Miguel, *1940-*
See **Ordoñez, Carlos d', 1734-1786.** [Symphonies. *Selections*] Sinfonías ; Concierto para violín en re mayor / Carlos Ordóñez ; edición crítica Miguel Simarro Grande [y] Ángel Oliver.

Grange, Philip.
As it was : (1985) / Philip Grange ; words, Edward Thomas. — *Maecenas Music*
783.6642   013422451

Bacchus bagatelles : (1993) : six short pieces for wind quintet / Philip Grange. — *Maecenas Music*
785.43195   013422538

[Concertos, clarinet, band] — Concerto Shēng Shēng Bù Shí : for solo clarinet radical & symphonic wind band / Philip Grange. — *Maecenas Music*
784.82862186   013422379

Grass, Günter, *1927-*
See **Heider, Werner, 1930-** [Gedichte von Günter Grass] Drei Gedichte von Günter Grass : (2003) : für mittlere Stimme (Mezzosopran/Bariton) und Klavier = for medium voice (mezzo-soprano/baritone) and piano / Werner Heider.

Graun, Johann Gottlieb, *1702 or 3-1771*
[Concertos, viola da gamba, string orchestra, A major] — Concerto in A major for viola da gamba, strings & basso continuo / Johann Gottlieb Graun ; edited by Alejandro Garri ; assisted by Kent Carlson. — *1st ed.* — *Garri Editions*
784.72765186   013750191

Graun, Johann Gottlieb, *1702 or 3-1771*.
[Sonatas, viola da gamba, continuo, G major] — Solo (Sonata G-Dur) per la viola di gamba / Johann Gottlieb Graun ; trascrizione a cura di Cristiano Contadin e Monica Pelliciari. — *Cornetto, gedruckt in Lizenz von Musedita*
787.65183   014167963

Graves, Richard, *1926-2002*.
Threesome : oboe & piano / Richard Graves. — *Emerson Edition*
788.52   013188399

Gray, David, *1970-*
Life in slow motion / David Gray. — *Wise Publications*
783.242166   013371790

Great jazz standards
Great jazz standards : 10 jazz standards / arranged and produced by Mark Taylor. — *Hal Leonard Europe*
781.65   013212159

Great piano solos
Great piano solos : [a wonderful variety of well-known showtunes, jazz and blues classics, film themes, popular songs and classical pieces arranged for solo piano] [The platinum book] — *Wise Publications*
786.2   013129811

Great piano solos : [a wonderful variety of well-known showtunes, jazz and blues classics, film themes, popular songs and classical pieces arranged for solo piano] The white book. — *Wise Publications*
786.2   013129812

Great piano solos : the show book. — *Wise*
786.2   013297731

Great piano solos.
Great piano solos. The film book. — *Wise*
786.21542   013297809

Great songs of the 60s for guitar
Great songs of the 60s for guitar : [thirty songs that defined an era] — *Hal Leonard Europe*
783.242166   013130716

Great songs of the 70s
Great songs of the 70s : for guitar : [thirty songs that defined an era] — *Hal Leonard Europe*
783.242166   013130717

Great women! Great songs!
Great women! Great songs! [36 classic hits from some of the greatest female artists of all time! : arranged for piano, voice and guitar, complete with lyrics and guitar chord boxes] — *Wise*
783.642164   013220473

Greatest hits
See **Twain, Shania.** Greatest hits

Greber, Jakob, *1691-1731*.
Fuori di sua capanna : cantata for alto, recorder & continuo ; Sinfonia a flauto solo : symphony for recorder and continuo / Jakob Greber. — *Green Man Press*
783.6848   013596869

Greber, Jakob, *1691-1731*. Sinfonia,
See **Greber, Jakob, 1691-1731.** Fuori di sua capanna : cantata for alto, recorder & continuo ; Sinfonia a flauto solo : symphony for recorder and continuo / Jakob Greber.

Greek selection 1
See **Hewitt, Daniel.** Greek selection 1

Greene, Maurice, *1696-1755*
Phoebe : a pastoral opera / Maurice Greene ;
edited by H. Diack Johnstone. — *Stainer and
Bell*
782.1   013195981

Greenhouse, Bernard, *1916-*
See **Bach, Johann Sebastian, 1685-1750.**
[Sonatas, viola da gamba, harpsichord] Sonatas
BWV 1027, 1028, 1029 : for violoncello and
keyboard / J.S. Bach ; [violoncello part edited
by] Greenhouse & Dillingham.

Greensleeves
See **Vaughan Williams, Ralph, 1872-1958**
[Fantasia on Greensleeves; *arr.*] Greensleeves

See **Vaughan Williams, Ralph, 1872-1958**
[Fantasia on Greensleeves; *arr*] Greensleeves

Gregson, Edward.
[Concertos, clarinet, orchestra; *arr.*] — Clarinet
concerto : (1994) / Edward Gregson. — *Novello*
788.62186   013307343

A Grieg suite
See **Grieg, Edvard, 1843-1907.** [Piano music.
Selections; arr.] A Grieg suite

Grieg, Edvard, *1843-1907.*
[Piano music. *Selections; arr.*] — A Grieg suite :
3 movements based on Grieg's 'Lyric pieces'
arranged for school string ensemble / arranged
by Chris Allen. — *Spartan Press*
784.71858   013482658

Griffiths, John, *1952 Dec.-*
See **Neapolitan lute music** / Fabrizio Dentice ...
[et al.] ; edited by John Griffiths and Dinko
Fabris.

Group therapy
See **Cowles, Colin.** Group therapy

Gruber, Franz Xaver, *1787-1863.*
[Stille Nacht, heilige Nacht; *arr.*] — Silent
night : for tenor solo and men's choir (TTBB),
unaccompanied / [Franz Gruber ; arranged by]
Mack Wilberg. — *Oxford University Press*
782.8281723   013472433

[Stille Nacht, heilige Nacht; *arr.*] — Silent
night : SSAATTBB / Franz Gruber ; arranged by
Jonathan Rathbone. — *Edition Peters*
782.5281723   013304669

[Stille Nacht, heilige Nacht; *arr.*] — Stille
nacht : SATB : [music by Franz Gruber] ;
arranged by Jonathan Rathbone. — *Edition
Peters*
782.5281723   013304656

Gruber, Gernot.
See **Haydn, Joseph, 1732-1809** [Symphonies.
Selections.] Londoner Sinfonien. 1. Folge /
Joseph Haydn ; herausgegeben von Robert von
Zahn und Gernot Gruber.

Gruber, Gerold W.
See **Bruckner, Anton, 1824-1896.** [Quintet,
violins, violas, violoncello, F major]
Streichquintett F-Dur ; Intermezzo D-Moll /
Anton Bruckner.

Grumpy tunes
See **Bayliss, Colin.** [Grumpy tunes; *arr.*]
Grumpy tunes

[Grumpy tunes; *arr.*]
See **Bayliss, Colin.** [Grumpy tunes; *arr.*]

Grylls, Richard G.
Epitaph for Grace : for unaccompanied mixed
voice choir / by Richard G. Grylls. — *Roberton
Publications, a part of Goodmusic Publishing*
782.5   013373072

A royal nursery muddley : traditional tunes
arranged for unaccompanied mixed voice choir /
by Richard G. Grylls. — *Roberton Publications,
a part of Goodmusic Publishing*
782.5   013373074

Gubaĭdulina, Sof́ia Asgatovna.
Sonnengesang = The canticle of the sun :
revidierte Fassung 5/1998 / Sofia Gubaidulina.
— *Sikorski Musikverlage*
782.522   013688147

Gudmundsen-Holmgreen, Pelle.
[Concerto grosso] — Concerto grosso (1990,
rev. 2006) : for strygekvartet og symfonisk
ensemble / Pelle Gudmundsen-Holmgreen. —
Samfundet til udgivelse af dansk musik
784.24186   013711552

Guero
See **Beck.** Guero

Guerrero, Francisco, *1528?-1599.*
[Motets. *Selections*] — Motetes de tempore et
alia : LXXVI-CVII / Francisco Guerrero ;
introducción, estudio y transcripción, Josep M.
Llorens i Cisteró ; semitonía y estructuras
modales, Karl H. Müller-Lancé. — *Consejo
Superior de Investigaciones Científicas,
Institución "Milà i Fontanals", Departamento
de Musicología*
782.526   013812163

Guggumos, Gallus, *16th cent.*
[Motets, voices (4-6), continuo (1612).
Selections] — Mottecta, Venedig 1612. Heft 1,
Motetten zu vier Stimmen mit b.c. / Gallus
Guggumos ; herausgegeben von Leopold Fendt.
— *Cornetto-Verlag*
782.526   014646420

[Motets, voices (4-6), continuo (1612).
Selections] — Mottecta, Venedig 1612. Heft 2,
Motetten zu fünf Stimmen mit B.c. / Gallus
Guggumos ; herausgegeben von Leopold Fendt.
— *Cornetto-Verlag*
782.526   014646432

Guggumos, Gallus, *fl. 1612.* **Veni sponsa Christi.**
See **Guggumos, Gallus, 16th cent.** [Motets,
voices (4-6), continuo (1612). *Selections*]
Mottecta, Venedig 1612. Heft 1, Motetten zu
vier Stimmen mit b.c. / Gallus Guggumos ;
herausgegeben von Leopold Fendt.

Guillaume, de Machaut, *ca. 1300-1377.*
Hoquetus David.
See **Gilbert, Anthony.** [Quartets, strings, no. 3]
String quartet no. 3 : (1987) / Anthony Gilbert.

Guilmant, Alexandre, *1837-1911.*
[Masses, mixed voices, organ, no. 3, op. 11, E♭
major] — 3me messe solennelle : op. 11 : für
Soli, Chor und Orgel / Felix-Alexandre
Guilmant ; herausgegeben von Martin Sokoll. —
Butz
782.53232   013887074

Guinjoan, Joan.
In tribulatione mea invocavi Dominum : per a
cor i orquestra / Joan Guinjoan. — *1a ed.* —
Tritó
782.5294   013711562

Guitar for everyone
See **Ongley, Marc.** Guitar for everyone

[Guitar music. 1997]
See **Sor, Fernando, 1778-1839.** [Guitar music.
1997]

Guitar tab
Guitar tab : white pages : now! volume 2 : [a
giant collection of authentic guitar
transcriptions] — *Hal Leonard Europe*
783.242166   013197181

Guitare
Guitare : [France, 1600-1800] : méthodes,
dictionnaires et encyclopédies, ouvrages
généraux, préfaces d'œuvres / volume réalisé par
Caroline Delume. — *J.M. Fuzeau*
787.87076   014790387

The gunpowder plot
See **Brookes, Katherine.** The gunpowder plot

Gurre-Lieder
Gurre-Lieder : für Soli, Chor und Orchester :
kritischer Bericht / Arnold Schönberg ; [Text]
von Jens Peter Jacobsen (deutsch von Robert
Franz Arnold) ; herausgegeben von Ulrich
Krämer. — *Schott Musik International*
782.524   013821946

Gurtner, Stephanie.
See **Franck, César, 1822-1890.** [Sonatas, violin,
piano, A major; *arr.*] Sonate für Viola und
Klavier A-Dur / César Franck ; [herausgegeben
von Stephanie Gurtner]

See **Franck, César, 1822-1890.** [Sonatas, violin,
piano, A major; *arr.*] Sonate für Violoncello und
Klavier A-Dur / César Franck ; [herausgegeben
von Stephanie Gurtner]

The Gyffard partbooks I
The Gyffard partbooks I / transcribed and edited
by David Mateer. — *Published for the British
Academy by Stainer and Bell*
782.522   013815039

Gyffard, Philip.
See **The Gyffard partbooks I** / transcribed and
edited by David Mateer.

Haas, Robert, *1886-1960.*
See **Bruckner, Anton, 1824-1896.** [Masses, no.
3, F minor] Messe f-Moll / [Anton Bruckner]

Haas, Wolfgang G.
See **Dolar, Janez Krstnik, ca. 1620-1673.**
[Sonatas, trumpet, instrumental ensemble, C
major] Sonata à 10 : (Natur-) Trompete C/B, 3
Posaunen, 2 Violinen, 3 Violen, Violoncello,
Orgel (Cembalo) / Johannes Babtist Tolar ;
edited & arranged by Wolfgang G. Haas.

See **Dolar, Janez Krstnik, ca. 1620-1673.**
[Sonatas, trumpet, instrumental ensemble, C
major; *arr.*] Sonata à 10 : (Natur-) Trompeten, 3
Posaunen, Streicher, B.c. / Johannes Baptist
Tolar ; edited & arranged by Wolfgang G. Haas ;
Orgelauszug.

Haec dies
See **Palestrina, Giovanni Pierluigi da,
1525?-1594.** [Motets (1575). Haec dies] Haec
dies

Hägele, Friedrich.
See **Eberlin, Johann Ernst, 1702-1762.** Missa
septimi toni : für Soli, SATB, Streicher und
Orgel / Johann Ernst Eberlin ; herausgegeben
von Konrad Führlinger und Friedrich Hägele.

See **Rathgeber, Valentin, 1682-1750.** [Missale
tum rurale tum civile. Missa brevis, B flat major]
Missa brevis in B : für Soli (SATB), SATB,
Streicher und Orgel / Johann Valentin
Rathgeber ; herausgegeben von Friedrich
Hägele ; Orgelstimme von Hermann
Angstenberger.

Hagels, Bert.
See **Wilms, J. W. 1772-1847.** [Symphonies, no. 5, op. 52, D major] Sinfonie D-Dur, op. 52 / Johann Wilhelm Wilms ; herausgegeben von Bert Hagels.

Hailey, Christopher.
See **Schreker, Franz, 1878-1934.** [Choral music] Chorwerk / Franz Schreker ; Gesamtausgabe herausgegeben von Christopher Hailey, Iris Pfeiffer.

Hakim, Naji, *1955-*
Petite suite : for organ / Naji Hakim. — *United Music*
786.51858   013191003

[Rhapsody, organs (2)] — Rhapsody for organ duet / Naji Hakim. — *United Music Publishers*
785.6519218945   013383464

Halévy, F., *1799-1862.*
La fée aux roses : opéra-comique en trois actes / Fromental Halévy ; paroles d'Eugène Scribe et de Henri V. de Saint-Georges ; edité par Peter Kaiser. — *Musik-Edition Lucie Galland*
782.1   013801715

Hall, Pauline, *1924-*
Mixed doubles : piano time duets. Book 2 / Pauline Hall. — *New ed.* — *Oxford University Press*
785.62192   013190557

Hamilton, Henry, *1853?-1918.*
See **Elgar, Edward, 1857-1934.** The crown of India.

Hamilton, Newburgh, *fl. 1712-1759.*
See **Handel, George Frideric, 1685-1759** [Samson. *Vocal score*] Samson : an oratorio for soloists (3 sopranos, alto, 2 tenors, 2 basses; or soprano, alto tenor and bass), mixed chorus and orchestra / music by George Frideric Handel ; words by Newburgh Hamilton, after John Milton's Samson Agonistes ; edited by Donald Burrows ; vocal score.

Hamlet ballad
See **Shchedrin, Rodion Konstantinovich, 1932-** Hamlet ballad

Hammer, Xaver, *1741-1817.*
[Viola da gamba music. *Selections*] — 3 pieces for unaccompanied viola da gamba / F.X. Hammer. In diesen heil'gen Hallen / W.A. Mozart ; anonymous arrangement for unaccompanied viola da gamba ; edited by David J. Rhodes. — *Viola da Gamba Society of Great Britain*
787.65   013382467

Hammerstein, Oscar, *1895-1960.*
See **Rodgers, Richard, 1902-1979.** [Sound of music. My favorite things; *arr.*] My favorite things : from The sound of music : SSA / lyrics by Oscar Hammerstein II ; music by Richard Rodgers ; arranged by Mac Huff.

See **Rodgers, Richard, 1902-1979.** [Sound of music. *Vocal score. Selections; arr.*] The sound of music / Rodgers and Hammerstein.

Hammond, Heather.
Cool piano : funky pieces. 4 / Heather Hammond. — *Kevin Mayhew*
786.2   013201465

Cool piano : funky pieces. 5 / Heather Hammond. — *Kevin Mayhew*
786.2   013192469

Cool piano : funky pieces. 6 / Heather Hammond. — *Kevin Mayhew*
786.2   013182142

Hancock, Gerre, *1934-*
Variations on "Ora labora" : for organ / Gerre Hancock. — *Oxford University Press*
786.5   013173129

Hancock, Herbie, *1940-*
[Selections; *arr.*] — Herbie Hancock : 9 jazz classics / arranged and produced by Mark Taylor. — *Hal Leonard Europe*
781.65   013383268

Handel, George Frideric, *1685-1759*
[Acis and Galatea. Heart, the seat of soft delight; *arr.*] — Heart, the seat of soft delight / George Frederick Handel ; arranged by Carlo Martelli. — *Broadbent & Dunn*
785.7194   013167593

Handel, George Frideric, *1685-1759.*
[Acis and Galatea. O ruddier than the cherry] — O ruddier than the cherry : recitative and aria from Acis and Galatea (HWV 49a) : for bass, recorder, two violins & continuo / G.F. Handel. — *Green Man Press*
783.8942   013597596

Handel, George Frideric, *1685-1759*
[Athalia : oratorio in three parts : HWV 52 / Georg Friedrich Händel ; herausgegeben von Stephan Blaut. — *Bärenreiter*
782.523   013772192

Handel, George Frideric, *1685-1759.*
[Cantatas. *Selections*] — Four cantatas from Rome, 1707 : for soprano and basso continuo / G.F. Handel. — *Green Man Press*
783.6648   013597568

[Cuopre tal volta il cielo] — Cuopre tal volto il cielo : (HWV 98) : Italian cantata for bass, 2 violins and basso continuo / G.F. Handel. — *Green Man Press*
783.8948   013589492

Handel, George Frideric, *1685-1759*
[Fugues, keyboard, HWV 605-612] — Sechs Fugen HWV 605-610 und Fugen HWV 611, 612 = Six fugues HWV 605-610 and fugues HWV 611, 612 / Georg Friedrich Händel ; herausgegeben von Ullrich Scheideler ; Fingersatz von Michael Schneidt. — *G. Henle Verlag*
786.21872   013246310

Handel, George Frideric, *1685-1759.*
Languia di bocca lusinghiera : (HWV 123) : recitative and aria for soprano, oboe, violin and basso continuo / G.F. Handel. — *2nd ed.* — *Green Man Press*
783.6642   013597586

[Messiah. *Chorus score*] — Handel's Messiah from scratch / [edited by David Meacock] — *Alto ed.* — *Artemis Editions*
782.523   006920515

[Messiah. *Chorus score*] — Handel's Messiah from scratch / [edited by David Meacock] — *Bass ed.* — *Artemis Editions*
782.523   006920500

[Messiah. *Chorus score*] — Handel's Messiah from scratch / [edited by David Meacock] — *Soprano ed.* — *Artemis Editions*
782.523   006920529

[Messiah. *Chorus score*] — Handel's Messiah from scratch / [edited by David Meacock] — *Tenor ed.* — *Artemis Editions*
782.523   006920502

[Nell' Africane selve] — Nell' Africane selve (HWV 136a) ; Dalla guerra amorosa (HWV 102[a]) : Italian cantatas for bass and basso continuo / G.F. Handel. — *Green Man Press*
783.8948   013597552

Handel, George Frideric, *1685-1759*
[Samson. *Vocal score*] — Samson : an oratorio for soloists (3 sopranos, alto, 2 tenors, 2 basses; or soprano, alto tenor and bass), mixed chorus and orchestra / music by George Frideric Handel ; words by Newburgh Hamilton, after John Milton's Samson Agonistes ; edited by Donald Burrows ; vocal score. — *Novello*
782.523   013433587

Handel, George Frideric, *1685-1759.*
[Sonatas, flute, continuo. *Selections.*] — Sonatas for flute [and continuo] Book 1 / Handel ; flute part edited by Paul Edmund-Davies ; keyboard realisation by John Alley. — *Kevin Mayhew*
788.32183   013159326

[Sonatas, flute, continuo. *Selections.*] — Sonatas for flute [and continuo] Book 3 / Handel ; flute part edited by Paul Edmund-Davies ; keyboard realisation by John Alley. — *Kevin Mayhew*
788.32183   014343469

[Sonatas, recorder, continuo. *Selections.*] — Sonatas for flute [and continuo] Book 2 / Handel ; flute part edited by Paul Edmund-Davies ; keyboard realisation by John Alley. — *Kevin Mayhew*
788.32183   014343464

Spande ancor a mio dispetto : (HWV 165) : Italian cantata for bass, 2 violins and basso continuo / G.F. Handel. — *Green Man Press*
783.8948   013597541

[Suites, harpsichord, HWV 432, G minor; *arr.*] — Suite in G minor / G.F. Handel ; arranged for archlute by Lynda Sayce. — *Lute Society*
787.831858   013062225

Handel, George Frideric, *1685-1759.* Aure soavi e liete.
See **Handel, George Frideric, 1685-1759.** [Cantatas. *Selections*] Four cantatas from Rome, 1707 : for soprano and basso continuo / G.F. Handel.

Handel, George Frideric, *1685-1759.* Dalla guerra amorosa,
See **Handel, George Frideric, 1685-1759.** [Nell' Africane selve] Nell' Africane selve (HWV 136a) ; Dalla guerra amorosa (HWV 102[a]) : Italian cantatas for bass and basso continuo / G.F. Handel.

Handel, George Frideric, *1685-1759.* Menzognere speranze.
See **Handel, George Frideric, 1685-1759.** [Cantatas. *Selections*] Four cantatas from Rome, 1707 : for soprano and basso continuo / G.F. Handel.

Handel, George Frideric, *1685-1759.* Sonatas,
See **Handel, George Frideric, 1685-1759.** [Sonatas, flute, continuo. *Selections.*] Sonatas for flute [and continuo] Book 1 / Handel ; flute part edited by Paul Edmund-Davies ; keyboard realisation by John Alley.

See **Handel, George Frideric, 1685-1759.** [Sonatas, flute, continuo. *Selections.*] Sonatas for flute [and continuo] Book 3 / Handel ; flute part edited by Paul Edmund-Davies ; keyboard realisation by John Alley.

See **Handel, George Frideric, 1685-1759.** [Sonatas, recorder, continuo. *Selections.*] Sonatas for flute [and continuo] Book 2 / Handel ; flute part edited by Paul Edmund-Davies ; keyboard realisation by John Alley.

Handel, George Frideric, *1685-1759* Solomon.
See **Flexible woodwind trios :** baroque / arr. Karen Evans.

Handel's Messiah from scratch
See **Handel, George Frideric, 1685-1759.**
[Messiah. *Chorus score*] Handel's Messiah from scratch

Handl, Jacob, *1550-1591*.
[Musicum opus, 2. tomus. Ascendit Deus in iubilatione] — Ascendit Deus : motet for the Feast of Ascension : SSSAA / Jakob Handl. — *Anglo-American Music Publishers :*
782.626   013594209

Der Handschuh
See **Waterhouse, Graham, 1962-** Der Handschuh

Hansell, Kathleen Kuzmick, *1941-*
See **Verdi, Giuseppe, 1813-1901.** Stiffelio / Giuseppe Verdi ; libretto (in three acts) by Francesco Maria Piave ; edited by Kathleen Kuzmick Hansell.

Hansell, Philip, *1962-*
[Bagatelles, oboe, bassoon (2005)] — Seven bagatelles for oboe and bassoon / by Philip Hansell. — *Phylloscopus Publications*
785.85192   013173894

So low : for contrabassoon / by Philip Hansell. — *Phylloscopus Publications*
788.59   013561078

Happy Christmas Tommy
See **Brookes, Katherine.** Happy Christmas Tommy

See **Brookes, Katherine.** [Happy Christmas Tommy. *Selections*] Happy Christmas Tommy

[Happy Christmas Tommy. *Selections*]
See **Brookes, Katherine.** [Happy Christmas Tommy. *Selections*]

Happy songs
Happy songs : twenty-three of the greatest feel-good songs of all time : arranged for piano, voice and guitar. — *Wise Publications*
783.242166   013371778

Harasim, Clemens, *1974-*
See **Altnikol, Johann Christoph, 1719-1759.**
[Mass, D minor] Missa : Kyrie-Gloria-Messe in d : per soli (SATB), coro (SATB), 2 violini, viola e basso continuo / Johann Christoph Altnickol ; herausgegeben von Clemens Harasim.

Harbach, Barbara.
See **Parke, Maria F., 1772 or 3-1822.**
Divertimento and military rondo : for piano / Maria F. Parke ; edited by Barbara Harbach.

See **Parke, Maria F., 1772 or 3-1822.** [Grand sonatas, op. 1. No. 3] Grand sonata in D major : for solo piano / Maria F. Parke ; edited by Barbara Harbach.

Hard-Fi (*Musical group*)
See **Archer, Richard, 1976 or 7-** Stars of CCTV : guitar tab edition / Hard-Fi.

Hardwick, John.
Come on let's celebrate! : 20 songs and talks for all occasions / John Hardwick. — *Kevin Mayhew*
782.725   013173251

Hardy, Thomas, *1840-1928*
See **Rathbone, Jonathan.** The oxen : SAATTBB / Jonathan Rathbone ; [words by Thomas Hardy]

Harizanos, Nickos.
Hesitations : for violin and piano : [op. 32] / Nickos Harizanos. — *Da Capo Music*
787.2   013351676

Hark! the herald angels sing
See **Cummings, William Hayman, 1831-1915.**
[Hark! the herald angels sing; *arr.*] Hark! the herald angels sing

[Hark! the herald angels sing; *arr.*]
See **Cummings, William Hayman, 1831-1915.**
[Hark! the herald angels sing; *arr.*]

Harle, John.
Foursquare : for saxophone quartet / John Harle. — *Chester Music*
785.87194   013189099

Harling, Wolff Christian von.
[Lute music. *Selections*] — Lautenbuch des Wolff Christian von Harling, ca. 1618 / herausgegeben von Joachim Lüdtke. — *Tree Edition*
787.83   013605904

Harman, Toddy.
See **Bratton, John W. 1867-1947.** [Teddy bears' picnic; *arr.*] The teddy bears' picnic / John W. Bratton ; arranged for three bassoons by Toddy Harman.

Harmonia instrumentalis
See **Buchner, Philipp Friedrich, 1614-1669.**
Harmonia instrumentalis

Harmonikan asteikkosormitus ABC
See **Ollila, Jukka.** Harmonikan asteikkosormitus ABC

Harmonium
See **Carlton, Vanessa.** Harmonium

[Harpsichord music. *Selections*]
See **Scarlatti, Alessandro, 1660-1725.**
[Harpsichord music. *Selections*]

Harris, Jesse, *1969-*
[Don't know why; *arr.*] — Don't know why / words and music by Jesse Harris ; arranged by Paris Rutherford ; recorded by Norah Jones. — *Hal Leonard*
782.542164   013222721

Harris-Warrick, Rebecca.
See **Lully, Jean Baptiste, 1632-1687** [Ballets. *Vocal scores. Selections*] Ballet des saisons ; Les amours déguisés ; Ballet royal de Flore / Jean-Baptiste Lully ; édition [par Ballet des saisons] de James P. Cassaro ; édition [par Les amours déguisés] de James R. Anthony et Rebecca Harris-Warrick ; édition [par Ballet royal de flore] d'Albert Cohen ; réduction clavier-chant, Noam A. Krieger.

Harrison, Derek
See **Scarlatti, Alessandro, 1660-1725.** Bella dama di nome santa : Tu sei quella : cantata for alto, recorder, two violins and continuo / Alessandro Scarlatti ; edited by Derek Harrison.

Harrison, George, *1943-2001*.
[Songs. *Selections*] — The Dark Horse years : 1976-1992 / George Harrison. — *Hal Leonard*
783.242166   013383584

Harrison, Mark, *1956-*
Blues piano : the complete guide with CD! / by Mark Harrison.
786.21643076   006906657

Harrison, Pamela, *1915-1990*.
Octetto pastorale : for wind octet (2 oboes, 2 clarinets in A, 2 horns in F and 2 bassoons) / by Pamela Harrison. — *Phylloscopus Publications*
785.43198   013173924

Harrison, Sadie, *1965-*
Architechtonia : for solo violoncello and ensemble / Sadie Harrison. — *University of York Music Press*
785.32199   013433162

Bavad khair bagi! = May this goodnes last for ever! : for solo violin / Sadie Harrison. — *University of York Music Press*
787.2   013433149

Impresa amorosa : for piano : "In virido teneras exurit medulas" / Sadie E. Harrison. — *University of York Music Press*
786.2   013433128

Hart, Barry.
Jesus is alive! : a simple Easter musical for key stage 1 / O'Gorman & Hart. — *Kevin Mayhew*
782.141727083   013159205

Hart, Lorenz, *1895-1943*.
See **Rodgers, Richard, 1902-1979** [Musicals. *Selections; arr.*] The best of Rodgers and Hart.

See **Rodgers, Richard, 1902-1979** [Musicals. *Selections; arr.*] Rodgers & Hart favorites : 10 Rodgers & Hart favorites / arranged and produced by Mark Taylor.

See **Rodgers, Richard, 1902-1979** [Musicals. *Vocal scores. Selections*] Bewitched : the greatest songs of Rodgers & Hart.

See **Rodgers, Richard, 1902-1979** [Musicals. *Vocal scores. Selections*] Rodgers and Hart : a musical anthology : piano-vocal.

See **Rodgers, Richard, 1902-1979.** [Musicals. *Selections; arr.*] Rodgers & Hart classics : 10 Rodgers & Hart classics / arranged and produced by Mark Taylor.

Hartoin, Benoît.
See **Charpentier, Marc-Antoine, 1643-1704.**
Acteon : H. 481 ; Acteon changé en biche, H. 481a / M.-A. Charpentier.

Harvest carol
See **Nixon, June.** Harvest carol

Harvey, Jonathan, *1939-*
[Sketches] — Three sketches : for cello : (1989) / Jonathan Harvey. — *Faber Music*
787.4   006891408

Hasse, Johann Adolf, *1699-1783*.
Ascolta i preghi : (Psalm 42:9, 10) : motet for 2 sopranos and basso continuo / Johann A. Hasse ; edited by Alejandro Garri ; assisted by Kent Carlson. — *First ed.* — *Garri Editions*
782.526   013771092

Ave Regina coelorum : Marian antiphon for alto, 2 oboes, strings & basso continuo / Johann A. Hasse ; edited by Alejandro Garri ; assisted by Kent Carlson. — *1st ed.* — *Garri Editions*
783.8624   013771093

[Concertos, keyboard instrument] — Sei concerti per organo solo / Johann Adolph Hasse ; a cura di Maurizio Machella. — *Armelin Musica*
786.5   013771094

[Salve regina, soprano, alto, orchestra, E♭ major] — Salve regina Es-Dur für Sopran, Alt und Instrumente, 1766 : Facsimile nach der Handschrift des Komponisten / Johann Adolph Hasse. — *Edition Kemel*
783.1225   013887075

Hassler, Hans Leo, *1564-1612*.
[Magnificats, organ. *Selections*] — 14 magnificat : (Torino, Biblioteca nazionale Fondo Giordano III, V) / Hans Leo Hassler ; a cura di Aaron Carpenè. — *Levante Libreria*
786.518992   013771096

See **Strungk, Delphin, 1601-1694.** [Organ music] Sämtliche Orgelwerke : Choralbearbeitungen, Toccata, Motettenkolorierungen = Complete organ works : chorale settings, toccata, motet intabulations / Delphin Strunck ; herausgegeben von Klaus Beckmann.

Hässler, Johann Wilhelm, *1747-1822.*
[Kleine Orgelstücke] — 48 kleine Orgelstücke = 48 short organ pieces / Johann Wilhelm Hässler ; herausgegeben von Volker Choroba. — *Schott*
786.5   013771091

Hatfield, Stephen.
See **J'ai vû le loup** : SSA a cappella / arranged by Stephen Hatfield.

See **O sapo** : SSATB a cappella : [Brazilian folk song] / arranged by Stephen Hatfield.

See **The scarlet cover** : SATB a cappella / arranged by Stephen Hatfield.

Haughton, Alan, *1950-*
Fun club alto sax : chill-out pieces to enjoy between exams. Alto sax grade 1-2 / Alan Haughton. — *Kevin Mayhew*
788.73076   013201374

Fun club descant recorder : chill out pieces to enjoy between exams. Descant recorder grade 0-1 / Alan Haughton. — *Kevin Mayhew*
788.364076   013181995

Fun club descant recorder : chill out pieces to enjoy between exams. Descant recorder grade 0-1 / Alan Haughton. — *Kevin Mayhew*
788.364076   013182000

Fun club descant recorder : chill out pieces to enjoy between exams. Descant recorder grade 1-2 / Alan Haughton. — *Kevin Mayhew*
788.364076   013181956

Fun club descant recorder : chill out pieces to enjoy between exams. Descant recorder grade 1-2 / Alan Haughton. — *Kevin Mayhew*
788.364076   013181965

Fun club descant recorder : chill out pieces to enjoy between exams. Descant recorder grade 2-3 / Alan Haughton. — *Kevin Mayhew*
788.364076   013181981

Fun club descant recorder : chill out pieces to enjoy between exams. Descant recorder grade 2-3 / Alan Haughton. — *Kevin Mayhew*
788.364076   013181989

Fun club violin : chill-out pieces to enjoy between exams. Violin grade 0-1 / Alan Haughton. — *Kevin Mayhew*
787.2076   013182078

Fun club violin : chill-out pieces to enjoy between exams. Violin grade 0-1 / Alan Haughton. — *Kevin Mayhew*
787.2076   013182084

Fun club violin : chill-out pieces to enjoy between exams. Violin grade 1-2 / Alan Haughton. — *Kevin Mayhew*
787.2076   013182061

Fun club violin : chill-out pieces to enjoy between exams. Violin grade 1-2 / Alan Haughton. — *Kevin Mayhew*
787.2076   013182066

Fun club violin : chill-out pieces to enjoy between exams. Violin grade 2-3 / Alan Haughton. — *Kevin Mayhew*
787.2076   013182039

Fun club violin : chill-out pieces to enjoy between exams. Violin grade 2-3 / Alan Haughton. — *Kevin Mayhew*
787.2076   013182053

Hautbois
Hautbois : [France, 1800-1860] : méthodes, traités, dictionnaires et encyclopédies, ouvrages généraux / volume réalisé par Michel Giboureau. — *J.M. Fuzeau*
788.52076   014790959

Have a nice day
See **Bon Jovi (Musical group)** Have a nice day

Hawes, Andrew, *1954-*
See **Hawes, Patrick.** Tres amores : double SATB choir / words by Andrew Hawes ; music by Patrick Hawes.

Hawes, Patrick.
Tres amores : double SATB choir / words by Andrew Hawes ; music by Patrick Hawes. — *Novello & Co*
782.542   013582428

Hawick Callants Club.
See **The Hawick songs** : a complete collection / edited by Ian W. Seeley.

The Hawick songs
The Hawick songs : a complete collection / edited by Ian W. Seeley. — *Rev. and enl.* [ed.] — *Hawick Callants' Club*
783.242094137   013201857

Hawkins, John, Sir, *1719-1789.*
See **Stanley, John,** *1712-1786.* [Cantatas, op. 8] Six cantata's, for a voice and instruments / set to musick by John Stanley.

Hawkshaw, Paul, *1950-*
See **Bruckner, Anton,** *1824-1896.* [Masses, no. 3, F minor] Messe f-Moll / [Anton Bruckner]

Haydn, Joseph, *1732-1809.*
[Divertimenti, H. IV, 1-11.] — Trios für Blas- und Streichinstrumente / Joseph Haydn ; herausgegeben von Andreas Friesenhagen. — *G. Henle*
785.13   014730851

Haydn, Joseph, *1732-1809*
[Sieben letzten Worte unseres Erlösers am Kreuze. *English. Vocal score*] — Passion : the seven words of our Saviour on the cross / Joseph Haydn ; vocal score. — *Novello*
782.5231726   013190863

Haydn, Joseph, *1732-1809.*
[Songs, violin, continuo acc. *Selections*] — Volksliedbearbeitungen Nr. 269-364 : Schottische und Walisische Lieder für George Thomson / Joseph Haydn ; herausgegeben von Marjorie Rycroft in Verbindung von Warwick Edwards und Kirsteen McCue. — *G. Henle*
783.242162009411   014710566

Haydn, Joseph, *1732-1809*
[Symphonies. *Selections.*] — Londoner Sinfonien. 1. Folge / Joseph Haydn ; herausgegeben von Robert von Zahn und Gernot Gruber. — *G. Henle*
784.2184   013581255

Haydn, Joseph, *1732-1809.* **Divertimenti,**
See **Haydn, Joseph,** *1732-1809.* [Divertimenti, H. IV, 1-11.] Trios für Blas- und Streichinstrumente / Joseph Haydn ; herausgegeben von Andreas Friesenhagen.

Haydn, Joseph, *1732-1809* **Adagios,**
See **An die Musik** : 9 classical pieces arranged for string quartet / [arr. by] John Kember.

Haydn, Joseph, *1732-1809* **Symphonies,**
See **Haydn, Joseph,** *1732-1809* [Symphonies. *Selections.*] Londoner Sinfonien. 1. Folge / Joseph Haydn ; herausgegeben von Robert von Zahn und Gernot Gruber.

Haydn, Michael, *1737-1806.*
[Missa pro defunctis, MH 838] — Requiem in B-Dur, MH 838 : Faksimile der autographen Partitur aus dem Besitz der Österreichischen Nationalbibliothek ; Faksimile des Partitur-Erstdrucks (Leipzig, Ambros Kühnel) aus dem Besitz der Bayerischen Staatsbibliothek München / Johann Michael Haydn ; vorgelegt und kommentiert von Manfred Hermann Schmid. — *Strube Verlag*
782.53238   013771097

Hayes, Deborah.
See **LeBrun, Francesca,** *1756-1791.* [Sonatas, violin, harpsichord, op. 2] Six sonatas for the piano forte or harpsichord with an accompaniment for a violin, op. 2 / by Francesca LeBrun ; edited by Deborah Hayes.

Hayes, Morgan, *1973-*
Opera : for violin and piano / Morgan Hayes. — *Stainer & Bell*
787.2   013172399

He is born
He is born : [a setting of "Il est né"] : for mixed choir (SATB) and keyboard, with optional flute and oboe / [traditional French melody arr.] Don Michael Dicie. — *Oxford University Press*
782.5281723   013177891

Head, Michael, *1900-1976.*
[Psalms. I will lift up mine eyes; *arr.*] — I will lift up mine eyes : Psalm 121 ; for mixed voice choir with organ or piano / by Michael Head ; arranged by Antonín Tučapský. — *Roberton Publications, a part of Goodmusic Publishing*
782.5294   013554436

[Psalms. Make a joyful noise unto the Lord; *arr.*] — Make a joyful noise unto the Lord : Psalm 100 : (SATB) / Michael Head ; arranged by Antonín Tučapský. — *Roberton Publications, a part of Goodmusic Publishing*
782.5294   013554372

Hearne, John, *1937-*
[Ghostwatch ; *arr.*] — Ghostwatch : [originally] for brass quintet : arranged for wind quintet / John Hearne. — *Longship*
785.43195   013440381

See **Y delyn aur** : alaw gymreig : [arranged for SATB double chorus] / arr. John Hearne.

See **Steffe, William,** *ca. 1830-1890.* The battle hymn of the Republic / [attributed to] William Steffe ; arr. John Hearne.

Heart, the seat of soft delight
See **Handel, George Frideric,** *1685-1759* [Acis and Galatea. Heart, the seat of soft delight; *arr.*] Heart, the seat of soft delight

Hedges, Anthony, *1931-*
[Concert miniatures, recorder, op. 153] — Three concert miniatures : op. 153 : for recorders and piano / Anthony Hedges. — *Westfield Music*
788.36   013188505

[Contemplations] — Three contemplations : op. 149 : for soprano, flute, cello & piano / Anthony Hedges. — *Westfield Music*
783.6642   013188532

[Dialogues] — Four dialogues : op. 138 : for two cellos / Anthony Hedges. — *Westfield Music*
785.74192   013188404

[Exchanges, violoncello, piano, no. 2, op. 146] — Exchanges 2 : op. 146 : for cello and piano / Anthony Hedges. — *Westfield Music*
787.4   013188499

Miscellany : op. 152 : six pieces for piano / Anthony Hedges. — *Westfield Music*
786.2   013188495

[Sonatas, piano, no. 2, op. 154] — Piano sonata no.2 : op. 154 / Anthony Hedges. — *Westfield Music*
786.2183   013188474

West Oxford walks : op. 143 : for string quartet. Anthony Hedges. — *Westfield Music*
785.71941858   013188413

Heider, Werner, *1930-*
[Gedichte von Günter Grass] — Drei Gedichte von Günter Grass : (2003) : für mittlere Stimme (Mezzosopran/Bariton) und Klavier = for medium voice (mezzo-soprano/baritone) and piano / Werner Heider. — *Edition Gravis*
783.6742   013771099

Heifetz, Jascha, *1901-1987.*
See **The violin** : a collection : new and recent repertoire for violin with piano accompaniment / Craig Armstrong … [et al.]

Heimat
See **Terteryan, A. 1929-** [Rodina. *Russian & Armenian*] Heimat

Heinichen, Johann David, *1683-1729.*
[Masses, S. 5, D major] — Missa Nr. 9 in D : für Soli SATB, Chor SATB, 2 flauti, 2 oboi, fagotto, 2 corni, 2 trombe, timpani, 2 violini, viola, violoncello, contrabasso, organo / Johann David Heinichen. — *Erstausg.* / — *Carus-Verlag*
782.53232   013635330

Heisler, Marcey.
See **Goldrich, Zina.** [Songs. *Selections*] Songbook : volume 1 / Goldrich and Heisler ; lyrics by Marcy Heisler ; music by Zina Goldrich.

Hellawell, Piers, *1956-*
The Hilliard songbook : (1995) : (in two volumes) / Piers Hellawell ; text: Treatise upon the art of limning, by Nicholas Hilliard. — *Maecenas Music*
782.5   013416604

Inside story : violin & viola soli and orchestra (1999) / Piers Hellawell. — *Maecenas Music*
784.24   013416609

Quem quæritis : (1995) : [cantata] for soprano and five players : clarinet in B♭, bass clarinet, viola, 'cello and double bass / Piers Hellawell. — *Maecenas Music*
783.6624   013422567

Sound carvings from the water's edge : (1996) : for 11 solo strings (33221) Piers Hellawell. — *Maecenas Music*
785.7199   013416562

The still dancers : (1992) : for string quartet / Piers Hellawell. — *Maecenas Music*
785.7194   013422557

Hellen, Marian.
See **Double act** : duets for piano / popular melodies arranged by Marian Hellen.

See **Double act** : duets for violin / popular melodies arranged by Marian Hellen.

Heller, Stephen, *1813-1888.*
[Etudes faciles. *Selections*] — Selected studies : opus 45 and opus 46 / Heller ; edited by William Westney. — *G. Schirmer*
786.2076   013434751

Heller, Stephen, *1813-1888.* Etudes progressives.
See **Heller, Stephen, 1813-1888.** [Etudes faciles. *Selections*] Selected studies : opus 45 and opus 46 / Heller ; edited by William Westney.

Hellinck, Lupus, *d. 1541.* Missa Quem dicunt homines.
See **Tres missae super "Quem dicunt homines"** / edidit Harry Elzinga.

Helmont, Charles Joseph van, *1715-1790.*
[Pièces de clavecin, op. 1] — Pièces de clavecin, opus I : (Bruxelles, 1737) / Charles-Joseph van Helmont ; introduction, Robert Wangermée. — *CEDESOM-ULB, Le Livre Timperman*
786.41858   013728837

Hendrix, Jimi.
Blue wild angel : live at the Isle of Wight / Jimi Hendrix ; music transcriptions Andy Aledort. — *Experience Hendrix*
783.242166   013382751

Hennessy, Gail.
See **Caldara, Antonio, 1670-1736.** [Clori, mia bella Clori] Cantata, Clori, mia bella Clori : for contralto, flute, oboe & basso continuo / Antonio Caldara ; edited by Gail Hennessy.

Henrici, Christian Friedrich, *1700-1764.*
See **Bach, Johann Sebastian, 1685-1750.** [Weihnachts-Oratorium. Bereite dich Zion, mit zärtlichen Trieben; *arr. English & German*] Prepare thyself, Zion : unison treble / J. S. Bach ; arranged by B. Wayne Bisbee.

Henry VIII
See **Hewitt, Daniel.** Henry VIII

See **Hewitt, Daniel.** [Henry VIII. *Selections*] Henry VIII

[Henry VIII. *Selections*]
See **Hewitt, Daniel.** [Henry VIII. *Selections*]

Henze, Hans Werner, *1926-*
[Botschaften für die Königin von Saba] — Fünf Botschaften für die Königin von Saba = Five messages for the Queen of Saba : (2004) / Hans Werner Henze. — *Chester Music*
784.2   013323716

El rey de Harlem : imaginäres Theater I : für Mezzosopran und kleines Ensemble = imaginary theatre I : for mezzo soprano and small ensemble / Hans Werner Henze ; Dichtung von Federico Garcia Lorca. — *Schott*
783.6742   014406572

See **Bach, Carl Philipp Emanuel, 1714-1788.** [Fantasien, violin, keyboard instrument, H. 536, F minor; *arr.*] I sentimenti di Carl Philipp Emanuel Bach : (1982) : trascrizione per flauto, arpa ed archi della Clavier-Fantasie con accompagnemento di un violino (1787) = Transkription für Flöte, Harfe und Streicher der Clavier-Fantasie mit Begleitung einer Violine (1787) = transcription for flute, harp, and strings of the Clavier-Fantasie with violin accompaniment (1787) / [composed by C.P.E. Bach ; arr. by] Hans Werner Henze.

Herbie Hancock
See **Hancock, Herbie, 1940-** [Selections; *arr.*] Herbie Hancock

[Herbst]
See **Ullmann, Viktor.** [Herbst]

Herbst, Johann Andreas, *1588-1666.*
Erbarm' dich mein, o Herre Gott : (Psalm 51) : Miserere for baritone or bass, strings & basso continuo ; edited by Alejandro Garri, assited by Kent Carlson. — *1st ed.* — *Garri Editions*
783.88294   013771118

Herbst, Johann Andreas, *1588-1666*
Lobet, ihr Knechte des Herrn : (Psalm 113) : motet for tenor, baritone, bass, 2 violins & basso continuo / Johann Andreas Herbst ; edited by Alejandro Garri ; assisted by Kent Carlson. — *1st ed.* — *Garri Editions*
783.1326   013771119

Here, O my Lord
See **Rose, Barry, 1934-** Here, O my Lord

Here's a health
See **Wiffin, R. K.** Here's a health

Herlin, Denis.
See **Debussy, Claude, 1862-1918** [Fantaisie, piano, orchestra] Fantaisie pour piano et orchestre (2e version) / Claude Debussy ; édition de Jean-Pierre Marty ; avec la collaboration de Denis Herlin et Edmond Lemaître.

Hermann, Avril.
Fruit salad : three pieces for four bassoons / by Avril Hermann. — *Phylloscopus Publications*
785.8581941858   013173898

Hermansson, Erik.
How do you do Mr. Purcell : TrTB / Erik Hermansson. — *Viola da Gamba Society of Great Britain*
785.76193   013382541

Hero und Leander
See **Terzakis, Dimitri.** Hero und Leander

[Herr Gott, dich loben wir (Cantata). *English & German*]
See **Bach, Johann Sebastian, 1685-1750.** [Herr Gott, dich loben wir (Cantata). *English & German*]

Herr Gott, dich loben wir
See **Bach, Johann Sebastian, 1685-1750.** [Herr Gott, dich loben wir (Cantata). *English & German*] Herr Gott, dich loben wir

Herrick, Robert, *1591-1674.*
See **Baker, Richard, 1972-** To keep a true Lent : SATTBB (with T solo) a cappella / Richard Baker.

Hertel, Johann Christian, *1699-1754.*
[Sonatas, violin, continuo, op. 1] — Sonate à violino solo col violone ò cimbalo, opera prima / da Giovanni Cristiano Hertelli. — *Cornetto*
787.2183   013771120

Hertel, Johann Wilhelm, *1727-1789.*
[Concertos, harp, string orchestra, F major; *arr.*] — Konzert F-Dur für Harfe oder Cembalo, 2 Violinen, Viola und Violoncello / Johann Wilhelm Hertel ; herausgegeben von Johanna Seitz ; Klavierauszug von Burkhard Jäckel. — *Edition Walhall*
787.95186   013775622

Jesu, meine Freude : Kantate für Sopran und Tenor solo, 4 st. gem. Chor SSTB, 2 Trompeten, 2 Hörner, Pauken, 2 Flöten, 2 Oboen, Fagott, Streichorchester und Generalbass / Johann Wilhelm Hertel; herausgegeben von Norbert Klose. — *Erstausg.* — *Renaissance Musikverlag*
782.524   013771121

[Sonatas, harpsichord. *Selections*] — Sei sonate per il cembalo solo / Johann Wilhelm Hertel ; herausgegeben von Laura Cerutti. — *Cornetto*
786.4183   013771123

[Trios, harp, violin, violoncello. No. 2] — Trio F-Dur : für Harfe (oder Cembalo), Violine (oder Flöte) und Violoncello / Johann Wilhelm Hertel ; herausgegeben von Johanna Seitz. — *Erstausg.* — *Walhall*
785.7193   013771125

Herzogenberg, Heinrich von, *1843-1900.*
Gott ist gegenwärtig : Choralkantate op. 106 : Gemeindegesang, Chor SATB, 2 Trompeten, 3 Posaunen, Pauken, 2 Violinen, Viola, 2 Violoncelli, Kontrabass, Orgel / Heinrich von Herzogenberg ; Text, Gerhard Tersteegen ; vorgelegt und revidiert von Konrad Klek. — *Carus*
782.524   013771126

Hesitations
See **Harizanos, Nickos.** Hesitations

Hesketh, Kenneth, *1968-*
[Japanese miniatures] — Three Japanese
miniatures : for piano : (2002) / Kenneth
Hesketh. — *Schott*
786.2   013173243

Heuschkel, Johann Peter, *1773-1853.*
[Duets, horns (2), op. 12] — Six duos pour deux
cors = für zwei Hörner : op. 12 / Johann Peter
Heuschkel] ; [krit. rev. Neuausgabe von Christian
Vitalis] — *Dohr*
785.94192   013887076

Hewitt, Daniel.
1066 : the Battle of Hastings / written by Daniel
Dalton ; music [& lyrics] by Dan Hewitt. —
Educational Musicals
782.14083   013587029

Battle of Britain : a story of the few. —
Maplewood Education
782.14083   013390765

[Battle of Britain. *Selections*] — The Battle of
Britain : their finest hour : assembly pack /
written by Anthony James ; music [& lyrics] by
Dan[iel] Hewitt. — *Maplewood Education :*
782.7   013587396

[Christopher Columbus. *Selections*] —
Christopher Columbus : voyage to the end of the
world : assembly pack / written by Daniel
Dalton ; music [& lyrics] by Dan Hewitt. —
Maplewood Education : Educational Musicals
782.7   013587439

Gettysburg : brothers at war. — *Maplewood
Education*
782.14083   013390730

Greek selection 1 : a collection of songs from
Educational Musicals' Greek shows / [music &
lyrics by Daniel Hewitt & Tim Spencer] —
Maplewood Education :
782.742   013587341

Henry VIII : the break with Rome. — *2nd ed.* —
Maplewood Education
782.14083   013390722

[Henry VIII. *Selections*] — Henry VIII : Henry
and Anne Boleyn : assembly pack / written by
Daniel Dalton ; music [& lyrics] by Dan Hewitt.
— *Educational Musicals*
782.7   013587013

[Henry VIII. *Selections*] — Henry VIII : the
break with Rome : assembly pack / written by
Daniel Dalton ; music [& lyrics] by Dan Hewitt.
— *Maplewood Education : Educational
Musicals*
782.7   013587425

The magic tree : a story for Christmas. —
Maplewood Education
782.141723083   013390726

[Magic tree. *Selections*] — The magic tree : a
story for Christmas : assembly pack. —
Maplewood Education :
782.7421723   013587069

Saint Nicholas : the real Santa Claus. — *2nd ed.*
— *Maplewood Education*
782.141723083   013390759

[Saint Nicholas. *Selections*] — Saint Nicholas :
the real Santa Claus : assembly pack. —
Maplewood Education : Educational Musicals
782.7421723   013587060

The Spanish Armada : the invasion of England.
— *2nd ed.* — *Maplewood Education*
782.14083   013390715

[Spanish Armada. *Selections*] — The Spanish
Armada : the invasion of England : assembly

pack. — *Maplewood Education : Educational
Musicals*
782.7   013587402

The Trojan horse : the fall of Troy. —
Maplewood Education
782.14083   013390719

[Trojan horse. *Selections*] — The Trojan horse :
the fall of Troy : assembly pack. — *Maplewood
Education :*
782.7   013587435

Tudor selection 1 : a collection of songs from
Educational Musicals' Tudor shows / [music and
lyrics by Daniel Hewitt] — *Maplewood
Education :*
782.742   013587323

The valley of the kings : the power of the Sun
God. — *2nd ed.* — *Maplewood Education*
782.14083   013390789

World wars I & II : a collection of wars songs
from Educational Musicals shows / [music &
lyrics by Daniel Hewitt & Katherine Brookes]
— *Maplewood Education :*
782.742   013587347

See **Christmas selection 1 :** a collection of
songs from Educational Musicals' Christmas
shows.

See **Christmas selection 2 :** a collection of
songs from our Christmas shows.

See **Spencer, Tim.** Egyptian selection 1 : a
collection of songs from Educational Musicals'
Egyptian shows / [music & lyrics by Tim
Spencer and Daniel Hewitt]

Heyens, Gudrun.
Fun and games with the alto recorder : method
for the alto recorder. Tutor book 2 / by Gudrun
Heyens and Gerhard Engel ; translated and
adapted by Peter Bowman ; with illustrations by
Julie Beech and John Minnion. — *Schott*
788.365076   013192176

Fun and games with the alto recorder. Teacher's
commentary / by Gudrun Heyens and Gerhard
Engel ; translated and adapted by Peter
Bowman. — *Schott*
788.365076   013191815

See **Fun and games with the recorder :** method
for the alto recorder. Tune book / [compiled by]
Gudrun Heyens and Gerhard Engel ; translated
and adapted by Peter Bowman ; with
illustrations by John Minnion.

Heyink, Rainer.
See **Longueval, Antoine de, fl. 1498-1525.**
Passio Domini nostri Jesu Christi : zu 4 Stimmen
/ Antoine de Longueval ; herausgegeben von
Rainer Heyink.

Hildegard, Saint, *1098-1179.*
[Symphonia armonie celestium revelationum] —
Symphonia harmoniae caelestium revelationum :
Dendermonde, St.-Pieters & Paulusabdij, ms.
Cod. 9 / Hildegard of Bingen ; introduction,
Peter van Poucke. — *Alamire*
782.3222   014763129

Hill, David, *1957-*
See **The Novello short anthems collection :**
five centuries of anthems for smaller mixed
voice choirs, a cappella or with organ
accompaniment / selected & edited with a
preface by David Hill.

Hill, James, *ca. 1811-1853.*
The fiddle music of James Hill : a collection of
tunes by James Hill and others, selected from
principally local sources and arranged for keyed
Northumbrian smallpipes. — *Northumbrian
Piper's Society*
788.49094288   013299033

Hill, John Walter, *1942-*
See **Anthology of Baroque music :** music in
Western Europe, 1580-1750 / edited by John
Walter Hill.

The Hilliard songbook
See **Hellawell, Piers, 1956-** The Hilliard
songbook

Hilliard, Nicholas, *1537 (ca.)-1619.* **Treatise
concerning the arte of limning.**
See **Hellawell, Piers, 1956-** The Hilliard
songbook : (1995) : (in two volumes) / Piers
Hellawell ; text: Treatise upon the art of limning,
by Nicholas Hilliard.

Der Himmel lacht! Die Erde jubilieret
See **Bach, Johann Sebastian, 1685-1750.**
[Himmel lacht, die Erde jubilieret. *English &
German*] Der Himmel lacht! Die Erde jubilieret

[Himmel lacht, die Erde jubilieret. *English &
German*]
See **Bach, Johann Sebastian, 1685-1750.**
[Himmel lacht, die Erde jubilieret. *English &
German*]

Himmelfahrtsoratorium
See **Bach, Johann Sebastian, 1685-1750.**
[Lobet Gott in seinen Reichen. *English &
German*] Himmelfahrtsoratorium

**[Himmelskönig, sei willkommen. Leget euch dem
Heiland unter]**
See **Bach, Johann Sebastian, 1685-1750.**
[Himmelskönig, sei willkommen. Leget euch
dem Heiland unter]

Hind, John, *1916-*
[Shakespearean songs] — Two Shakespearean
songs : for SSA and piano / by John Hind. —
Novello
782.642   013173213

Hindemith, Paul, *1895-1963.*
[Kammermusik, no. 1] — Konzertante
Kammermusiken I / Paul Hindemith ;
herausgegeben von Giselher Schubert. — *Schott*
784.3   013822607

Hindemith, Paul, *1895-1963.* **Kammermusik,**
See **Hindemith, Paul, 1895-1963.**
[Kammermusik, no. 1] Konzertante
Kammermusiken I / Paul Hindemith ;
herausgegeben von Giselher Schubert.

Hippolyte et Aricie
See **Rameau, Jean-Philippe, 1683-1764.**
Hippolyte et Aricie

Hitchcock, H. Wiley *1923-2007.*
See **Charpentier, Marc-Antoine, 1643-1704.**
Acteon : H. 481 ; Acteon changé en biche, H.
481a / M.-A. Charpentier.

Hoadly, John, *1711-1776.*
See **Greene, Maurice, 1696-1755** Phoebe : a
pastoral opera / Maurice Greene ; edited by H.
Diack Johnstone.

Hochstein, Wolfgang.
See **Rheinberger, Josef, 1839-1901**
[Instrumental music. *Selections*] Orgelkonzerte /
[Josef Gabriel Rheinberger] ; vorgelegt von
Wolfgang Hochstein.

Hodie Christus natus est
See **Palestrina, Giovanni Pierluigi da,
1525?-1594.** [Motets (1575). Hodie Christus
natus est] Hodie Christus natus est

Hoekstra, Gerald R.
See **Le rossignol musical des chansons :**
(Antwerp, 1597) / edited by Gerald R. Hoekstra.

Hoesch, Christian.
See **Ullmann, Viktor.** [Songs] Sämtliche Lieder für Singstimme und Klavier = Complete songs for voice and piano / Viktor Ullmann ; herausgegeben von Axel Bauni und Christian Hoesch.

See **Ullmann, Viktor.** [Variationen und Doppelfuge über ein Thema von Arnold Schönberg; *arr.*] Variationen und Doppelfuge über ein Thema von Arnold Schönberg (op. 19/4) : Fassung für Streichquartett, op. 3c = Variations and Double Fugue on a theme by Arnold Schoenberg (op. 19/4) : version for string quartet, op. 3c / Viktor Ullmann.

Höfer, Karlheinz.
See **Romberg, Andreas, 1767-1821.** Der Messias : Kantate in drei Teilen : für Soli, Chor und Orchester, nach Friedrich Gottlieb Klopstocks "Messias" : WoO, zweite Fassung (1802) / Andreas Romberg ; vorgelegt von Karlheinz Höfer und Klaus G. Werner.

Hoffmann, E. T. A. 1776-1822.
[Kreuz an der Ostsee] — Zacharias Werners Trauerspiel "Das Kreuz an der Ostsee" : mit der Bühnenmusik von E.T.A. Hoffmann ; Ballettmusik "Arlequin" / E.T.A. Hoffmann ; hrsg. aus dem Nachlaß von Friedrich Schnapp ; unter Mitarbeit von Gerhard Allroggen und Michael Kohlhäufl von Thomas Kohlhase. — *Schott*
782.51552   013798965

[Vocal music. *Selections*] — Kleine Vokalkompositionen und Klaviersonaten / E.T.A. Hoffmann ; aus dem Nachlaß von Friedrich Schnapp und unter Mitarbeit von Gerhard Allroggen ; herausgegeben von Alexander Erhard und Thomas Kohlhase. — *Schott*
783   013798962

Hoffmann, E. T. A. 1776-1822. Arlequin.
See **Hoffmann, E. T. A. 1776-1822.** [Kreuz an der Ostsee] Zacharias Werners Trauerspiel "Das Kreuz an der Ostsee" : mit der Bühnenmusik von E.T.A. Hoffmann ; Ballettmusik "Arlequin" / E.T.A. Hoffmann ; hrsg. aus dem Nachlaß von Friedrich Schnapp ; unter Mitarbeit von Gerhard Allroggen und Michael Kohlhäufl von Thomas Kohlhase.

Hoffmann, E. T. A. 1776-1822. Sonatas,
See **Hoffmann, E. T. A. 1776-1822.** [Vocal music. *Selections*] Kleine Vokalkompositionen und Klaviersonaten / E.T.A. Hoffmann ; aus dem Nachlaß von Friedrich Schnapp und unter Mitarbeit von Gerhard Allroggen ; herausgegeben von Alexander Erhard und Thomas Kohlhase.

Hofmann, Klaus, *1939-*
See **Bach, Johann Sebastian, 1685-1750.** [Weihnachts-Oratorium. *English & German*] Weihnachtsoratorium : Oratorium tempore nativitatis Christi : BWV 248 : für Soli (SSATB), Chor (SATB), 3 Trompeten, Pauken, 2 Hörner, 2 Querflöten, 2 Oboen/Oboen d'amore, 2 Oboen da caccia, 2 Violinen, Viola und Basso continuo : Urtext = Christmas oratorio : for soli (SSATB), choir (SATB), 3 trumpets, timpani, 2 horns, 2 flutes, 2 oboes/oboes d'amore, 2 oboes da caccia, 2 violins, viola, and basso continuo / Johann Sebastian Bach ; herausgegeben von Klaus Hofmann ; English version by Henry S. Drinker.

Hogan, Moses.
See **Feel the spirit.** Volume two : twenty-eight arrangements for mixed chorus / by Moses Hogan ; with a foreword by Craig Jessop.

Holdom, Colin.
[Studio for brass. Duets] — 21 duets / by Colin Holdom. — *Bass clef ed.* — *Studio Music*
785.9192   013194551

[Studio for brass. Duets] — 21 duets / by Colin Holdom. — *Treble clef ed.* — *Studio Music*
785.9192   013194562

Holiday, Billie, *1915-1959.*
See **You're the voice :** Billie Holliday.

Holliday, Lucy.
See **Audition songs.** Number one hits.

Holmes, Chris, composer
Take off with your [alto] saxophone / Chris Holmes. — *Spartan Press*
788.73   013299062

Take off with your B♭ clarinet / Chris Holmes. — *Spartan Press*
788.62   013299071

Take off with your B♭ trombone and/or euphonium : [treble clef] / Chris Holmes. — *Spartan Press*
788.93   013376573

Take off with your [B♭] trumpet / Chris Holmes. — *Spartan Press*
788.92   013203868

Take off with your flute / Chris Holmes. — *Spartan Press*
788.32   013299103

Take off with your trombone : [bass clef] / Chris Holmes. — *Spartan Press*
788.93   013203884

Holmes, Oliver Wendell, 1809-1894.
See **Wilberg, Mack.** Thou gracious God, whose mercy lends : for mixed choir (SATBarB) and piano / [English folk tune ; arranged by] Mack Wilberg.

Homer Odyssey.
See **Monteverdi, Claudio, 1567-1643.** [Ritorno d'Ulisse in patria] Il ritorno di Ulisse in patria : Ms. Wien, partitura / Claudio Monteverdi .

Homs, Joaquim, 1906-2003.
[Impromptus, piano, no. 7] — Impromptu VII, piano / Joaquim Homs. — *Amalgama*
786.21894   014457018

Honey, Paul, *1963-*
See **The complete keyboard player 15 showstoppers** / based on the best-selling keyboard method by Kenneth Baker.

See **The complete keyboard player Christmas favourites** / based on the best-selling keyboard method by Kenneth Baker.

See **The complete keyboard player pop hits** / based on the best-selling keyboard method by Kenneth Baker.

See **Essential film songs :** the ultimate modern-day movie songbook. Take 2.

See **[Hopes and fears; *arr.*]** Hopes and fears : playalong for alto saxophone / Keane.

See **[Hopes and fears; *arr.*]** Hopes and fears : playalong for clarinet / Keane.

See **[Hopes and fears; *arr.*]** Hopes and fears : playalong for flute / Keane.

See **[Hopes and fears; *arr.*]** Hopes and fears : playalong for violin / Keane.

See **[Hopes and fears; *arr.*]** Play piano with — Keane : Hopes and fears.

Honey, Paul.
See **Play piano with— Ray Charles.**

Hopes and fears
See **Keane (Musical group)** [Hopes and fears; *arr.*] Hopes and fears

[Hopes and fears; *arr.*]
[Hopes and fears; *arr.*]

Hopkins, John H. *1820-1891.*
[We three kings of Orient are; *arr.*] — We three kings : SATB / [words and music by J. H. Hopkins] ; arranged by Jonathan Rathbone. — *Edition Peters*
782.5281723   013304743

[We three kings of Orient are; *arr.*] — We three kings : TTBB / John Henry Hopkins ; arranged by Jonathan Rathbone. — *Edition Peters*
782.8281723   013304747

Horace Silver
See **Silver, Horace, 1928-** [Selections; *arr.*] Horace Silver

Horn concerto, rondo
See **Mozart, Wolfgang Amadeus, 1756-1791** [Concertos, horn, orchestra, K. 495, E♭ major. Rondo; *arr.*] Horn concerto, rondo

Horn, Paul, *1922-*
See **Ryba, Jakub Jan, 1765-1815.** [Missa pastoralis, C major] Missa pastoralis in C : in Nativitate Domini in nocte : per soli SATB, coro SATB, fagotto solo, clarino solo, 2 violini e basso continuo / Jakub Jan Ryba ; herausgegeben von Karlheinz Ostermann ; Generalbassaussetzung von Paul Horn.

Hörner, Stephan.
See **Franckenstein, Clemens von, 1875-1942.** [Fantasien, orchestra, op. 15] Fantasie : Nachtstimmung / Clemens von Franckenstein. Symphonische Phantasie über ein Gedicht von Edgar Steiger : ("Ibsen-Phantasie") / August Reuss. Nachtstück / Felix vom Rath ; herausgegeben von Stephan Hörner.

Horrobin, Peter J.
See **Complete mission praise** / compiled by Peter Horrobin and Greg Leavers

Horrobin, Peter.
See **Junior praise** / compiled by Phil Burt, Peter Horrobin and Greg Leavers.

Hoskins, Robert H. B.
See **Arnold, Samuel, 1740-1802.** Polly : an opera : (1777) / music by Johann Christoph Pepusch ; rearrang'd and new airs compos'd by Samuel Arnold ; libretto by John Gay ; revis'd by George Colman, the elder ; edited by Robert Hoskins.

Hoskins, Robert.
See **Linley, Thomas, 1733-1795.** [Robinson Crusoe. *Vocal score*] The pantomine [or rather, pantomime] of Robinson Crusoe : (1781) / Thomas Linley ; wordbook by Richard Brinsley Sheridan ; edited by Robert Hoskins.

Hot fuss
See **Killers (Musical group)** Hot fuss

[How charming is beauty]
See **Croft, William, 1678-1727.** [How charming is beauty]

How do you do Mr. Purcell
See **Hermansson, Erik.** How do you do Mr. Purcell

How far is it to Bethlehem?
See **Wilberg, Mack.** How far is it to Bethlehem?

How many bards
See **Richardson, Michael.** How many bards

Howe, Julia Ward, *1819-1910.*
See **Steffe, William, ca. 1830-1890.** The battle hymn of the Republic / [attributed to] William Steffe ; arr. John Hearne.

Huber, Christine, *1963-*
See **Furrer, Beat, 1954-** Stimmen : für Chor und 4 Schlagzeuger : 1996 / Beat Furrer.

Hubicki, Margaret.
A posy of pieces : fifteen pieces on open strings for violin and piano / by Margaret Hubicki. — *Stainer & Bell*
787.2   013312983

Hudson, Barton.
See **Crecquillon, Thomas, d. 1557?** [Chansons, voices (4). *Selections*] Cantiones quatuor vocum / edidit Laura Youens and Barton Hudson ; editrix verborum Mary Beth Winn.

Hudson, James W.
See **Aija bernin pupas** = [Rock my child in feather down : for SAB chorus & piano : Latvian folk song] / arranged by James Hudson.

Huff, Mac.
See **Andersson, Benny.** [Mamma mia! *Selections; arr.*] Mamma mia! : choral highlights : instrumental pak / arranged by Mac Huff.

See **Andersson, Benny.** [Mamma mia! *Selections; arr.*] Mamma mia! : choral highlights : SAB / arranged by Mac Huff.

See **Andersson, Benny.** [Mamma mia! *Selections; arr.*] Mamma mia! : choral highlights : SATB / arranged by Mac Huff.

See **Andersson, Benny.** [Mamma mia! *Selections; arr.*] Mamma mia! : choral highlights : SSA / arranged by Mac Huff.

See **Lennon, John, 1940-1980.** [Fool on the hill; *arr.*] The fool on the hill : [for SAB and piano] / words and music by John Lennon and Paul McCartney ; recorded by Sergio Mendes ; arranged by Mac Huff.

See **Lennon, John, 1940-1980.** [Fool on the hill; *arr.*] The fool on the hill : [for SATB and piano] / words and music by John Lennon and Paul McCartney ; recorded by Sergio Mendes ; arranged by Mac Huff.

See **Lennon, John, 1940-1980.** [Fool on the hill; *arr.*] The fool on the hill : [for SSA and piano] / words and music by John Lennon and Paul McCartney ; recorded by Sergio Mendes ; arranged by Mac Huff.

See **Rodgers, Richard, 1902-1979.** [Sound of music. My favorite things; *arr.*] My favorite things : from The sound of music : SSA / lyrics by Oscar Hammerstein II ; music by Richard Rodgers ; arranged by Mac Huff.

Hughes, Arwel, *1909-1988.*
[Dewi Sant. O dyred, Dewi. *Vocal score. English & Welsh*] — O dyred, Dewi : cytgan i leisiau SSA allan o'r oratorio Dewi Sant = Come hither, David : chorus for SSA voices from the oratorio Saint David / Arwel Hughes. — *Aureus*
782.625   013173362

See **Hughes, John, 1873-1932.** [Cwm Rhondda; *arr.*] Cwm Rhondda : i leisiau merched a phiano = for female voices and piano / John Hughes (Llanilltud Faerdref) ; trefnwyd gan Arwel Hughes.

Hughes, John, *1873-1932.*
[Cwm Rhondda; *arr.*] — Cwm Rhondda : i leisiau merched a phiano = for female voices and piano / John Hughes (Llanilltud Faerdref) ; trefnwyd gan Arwel Hughes. — *Aureus Publishing*
782.627   013382379

Hugo, Victor, *1802-1885* Misérables.
See **Schönberg, Claude-Michel.** [Misérables. *Vocal score. English. Selections*] Les Misérables : Boublil and Schönberg's legendary musical : in concert : piano, vocal, guitar / music by Claude-Michel Schönberg.

Humph the camel
See **Davies, Niki.** Humph the camel

Humphreys, Samuel, *1698?-1738.*
See **Handel, George Frideric, 1685-1759** Athalia : oratorio in three parts : HWV 52 / Georg Friedrich Händel ; herausgegeben von Stephan Blaut.

[Hunyadi László]
See **Erkel, Ferenc.** [Hunyadi László]

Hunyadi László
See **Erkel, Ferenc.** [Hunyadi László] Hunyadi László

Hurel, Philippe, *1955-*
[Phonus] — Phonus, ou, La voix du faune : pour flûte et orchestre / Philippe Hurel. — *Lemoine*
784.2832   014835204

Hymn to Mary
See **Þorkell Sigurbjörnsson, 1938-** Hymn to Mary

[Hymni totius anni. Conditor alme siderum]
See **Palestrina, Giovanni Pierluigi da, 1525?-1594.** [Hymni totius anni. Conditor alme siderum]

[Hymni totius anni. Veni Creator Spiritus]
See **Palestrina, Giovanni Pierluigi da, 1525?-1594.** [Hymni totius anni. Veni Creator Spiritus]

I believe
See **Drake, Ervin.** [I believe; *arr.*] I believe

[I believe; arr.]
See **Drake, Ervin.** [I believe; *arr.*]

I don't know how to love him
See **Lloyd Webber, Andrew, 1948-** [Jesus Christ superstar. I don't know how to love him; *arr.*] I don't know how to love him

I don't want to talk about it
See **Whitten, Danny.** [I don't want to talk about it; *arr.*] I don't want to talk about it

[I don't want to talk about it; arr.]
See **Whitten, Danny.** [I don't want to talk about it; *arr.*]

I look for you early
See **Rommereim, John Christian.** I look for you early

I love you, you're perfect, now change
See **Roberts, Jimmy.** [I love you, you're perfect, now change. *Vocal score. Selections*] I love you, you're perfect, now change

[I love you, you're perfect, now change. Vocal score. Selections]
See **Roberts, Jimmy.** [I love you, you're perfect, now change. *Vocal score. Selections*]

I never ate a cloud
See **Bisbee, B. Wayne.** I never ate a cloud

I sing of a maiden
See **Wiggins, Christopher.** I sing of a maiden

I want Jesus to walk with me
I want Jesus to walk with me / [arr.] Roderick Williams. — *Oxford University Press*
782.5253   013083861

I will lift up mine eyes
See **Head, Michael, 1900-1976.** [Psalms. I will lift up mine eyes; *arr.*] I will lift up mine eyes

[Iberian pieces]
See **Kelly, Bryan.** [Iberian pieces]

Ibn Gabirol, *11th cent.*
See **Rommereim, John Christian.** I look for you early : for mixed choir (SATB), organ and optional alto saxophone / John Christian Rommereim.

[If that a sinner's sighs, voices (5)]
See **Milton, John, ca. 1563-1647.** [If that a sinner's sighs, voices (5)]

If ye love me
See **Aston, Peter** If ye love me

If you were coming in the fall
See **De Wald, Frank K.** If you were coming in the fall

[Ihr Hirten Bethlehems]
See **Zechner, Georg, 1716-1778.** [Ihr Hirten Bethlehems]

II. Symphonie, C-Moll
See **Bruckner, Anton, 1824-1896.** [Symphonies, no. 2, C minor] II. Symphonie, C-Moll

Il est né le divin enfant
Il est né le divin enfant : for unaccompanied mixed choir (SATB) / traditional French ; arr. Paul Carey. — *Oxford University Press*
782.5281723   013212287

Illiano, Roberto.
See **Clementi, Muzio, 1752-1832.** Musical characteristics : op. 19, per clavicembalo o pianoforte = for harpsichord (piano) / Muzio Clementi ; a cura di Roberto Illiano.

Im Zwielicht
See **Kirchner, Theodor, 1823-1903.** Im Zwielicht

Images of sleep
See **McGarr, Peter.** Images of sleep

Impresa amorosa
See **Harrison, Sadie, 1965-** Impresa amorosa

Impressions niçoises
See **Tisné, Antoine.** Impressions niçoises

Impromptu VII, piano
See **Homs, Joaquim, 1906-2003.** [Impromptus, piano, no. 7] Impromptu VII, piano

[Impromptus, piano, no. 7]
See **Homs, Joaquim, 1906-2003.** [Impromptus, piano, no. 7]

Improvisation
See **Wright, Margot, 1911-2000.** [Improvisation, clarinet] Improvisation

[Improvisation, clarinet]
See **Wright, Margot, 1911-2000.** [Improvisation, clarinet]

In between dreams
See **Johnson, Jack, 1975-** In between dreams

[In dulci jubilo]
Good Christian men, rejoice : German carol In dulci jubilo arranged for mixed voices & organ / arranged by Philip Ledger. — *Encore Publications*
782.5281723   013382719

In memoriam magistri
See **Tippett, Michael, 1905-1998.** In memoriam magistri

In nomine
See **Bingham, Judith.** In nomine

In nomine fantasia & Ayre à 5
See **Browne, John, ca. 1608-1691.** [In nomine, viols (5)] In nomine fantasia & Ayre à 5

[In nomine, viols (5)]
See **Browne, John, ca. 1608-1691.** [In nomine, viols (5)]

In tribulatione mea invocavi Dominum
See **Guinjoan, Joan.** In tribulatione mea invocavi Dominum

In your honor
See **Foo Fighters (Musical group)** In your honor

Inclytae Sanctae Virginis Catherinae
See **Palestrina, Giovanni Pierluigi da, 1525?-1594.** [Motets (1575). Inclytae Sanctae Virginis Catherinae] Inclytae Sanctae Virginis Catherinae

Indian melodies
Indian melodies : for alto saxophone = Mélodies indiennes : pour saxophone alto = Indische Melodien : für Alt-Saxophon / [arranged by] Candida Connolly ; with accompanying CD by Kadri Golpalnath. — *Schott*
788.73 013192424

Infant holy, infant lowly
Infant holy, infant lowly : for mixed choir (SATB) and organ / [Polish carol ; arr.] Mack Wilberg. — *Oxford University Press*
782.5281723 013126609

Ingegneri, Marc Antonio, 1535 or 6-1592.
[Madrigals, voices (5), book 5] — V libro di madrigali a 5 voci / Marc'Antonio Ingegneri ; a cura di Gloria Joriini e Marco Mangani. — *Libreria musicale italiana*
782.543 013707583

Inside story
See **Hellawell, Piers, 1956-** Inside story

Institución Milá y Fontanals. *Departamento de Musicología.*
See **Música instrumental en las catedrales españolas en la época ilustrada** : conciertos, versos y sonatas, para chirimía, oboe, flauta y bajón—con violines y/u órgano—, de La Seo y El Pilar de Zaragoza / estudio y edición, Antonio Ezquerro Esteban.

[Instrumental music. Selections]
See **Rheinberger, Josef, 1839-1901** [Instrumental music. *Selections*]

Intensive care
See **Williams, Robbie.** Intensive care

Intermezzo and capriccio
See **Cooke, Arnold.** Intermezzo and capriccio

Internationale Bruckner-Gesellschaft.
See **Bruckner, Anton, 1824-1896.** [Masses, no. 3, F minor] Messe f-Moll / [Anton Bruckner]

See **Bruckner, Anton, 1824-1896.** [Quintet, violins, violas, violoncello, F major] Streichquintett F-Dur ; Intermezzo D-Moll / Anton Bruckner.

See **Bruckner, Anton, 1824-1896.** [Symphonies, no. 2, C minor] II. Symphonie, C-Moll : Fassung von 1872 / Anton Bruckner ; vorgelegt von William Carragan.

Internationale Schubert-Gesellschaft.
See **Schubert, Franz, 1797-1828.** Fierabras / Franz Schubert.

Intrada
See **Danson, Alan.** Intrada

Introduction, toccata and fugue
See **Pott, Francis, 1957-** Introduction, toccata and fugue

[Inventions, harpsichord, BWV 772-786]
See **Bach, Johann Sebastian, 1685-1750.** [Inventions, harpsichord, BWV 772-786]

Is God, our endless day
See **Larsen, Libby.** Is God, our endless day

Is there love in space?
See **Satriani, Joe.** Is there love in space?

[Isacco, figura del Redentore. Ouverture]
See **Martinez, Marianne, 1744-1812.** [Isacco, figura del Redentore. Ouverture]

[Islameĭ]
See **Balakirev, Miliĭ Alekseevich, 1837-1910.** [Islameĭ]

Islamey
See **Balakirev, Miliĭ Alekseevich, 1837-1910.** [Islameĭ] Islamey

The isle is full of noises
See **Chilcott, Bob.** The isle is full of noises

Isserlis, Steven, 1958-
See **Saint-Saëns, Camille, 1835-1921.** [Cello, piano music. *Selections*] The complete shorter works for cello and piano = für Cello und Klavier = pour violoncelle et piano / Camille Saint-Saëns ; edited by Steven Isserlis & Sabina Taller Ratner.

Istituto italiano Antonio Vivaldi.
See **Paisiello, Giovanni, 1740-1816.** I giuochi d'Agrigento / [libretto di] Alessandro Pepoli ; [musica di] Giovanni Paisiello ; saggio introduttivo a cura di Lorenzo Mattei.

See **Portugal, Marcos Antônio da Fonseca, 1762-1830.** Gli Orazi e i Curiazi : partitura dell'opera in facsimile, edizione del libretto / [libretto di] Simeone Antonio Sografi ; [musica di] Marco Portogallo. Catalogo cronologico degli spettacoli a Venezia (1797-1815) / a cura di Maria Giovanna Miggiani.

See **Vivaldi, Antonio, 1678-1741.** [Concertos, string orchestra, RV 121, D major] Concerto in re maggiore, per archi e cembalo, F. XI, no. 30 / Antonio Vivaldi ; a cura di Gian Francesco Malipiero.

It was Christmas to us
It was Christmas to us : carol singing in Bamford through the 20th century / words, music and historical notes researched and transcribed by Joanna and Peter Mackey ; introduction by Ian Russell. — *Bamford Community Arts and Crafts*
782.5281723 013178364

The Italian concerto
See **Bach, Johann Sebastian, 1685-1750.** [Italienisches Konzert] The Italian concerto

[Italienisches Konzert]
See **Bach, Johann Sebastian, 1685-1750.** [Italienisches Konzert]

It's a baby!
See **Johnson, Mark** It's a baby!

It's a party!
See **Johnson, Mark** It's a party!

It's easy to play classical greats.
It's easy to play classical greats. — *Wise Publications*
786.2 013321736

It's easy to play top 50 hits.
It's easy to play top 50 hits. — *Wise Publications*
786.2166 013359465

Iubilate Deo
See **Palestrina, Giovanni Pierluigi da, 1525?-1594.** [Motets (1575). Jubilate Deo omnis terra, voices (8)] Iubilate Deo

Ives, Simon, 1600-1662
Fantasia in four parts (cor anglais and 3 bassoons) / by Simon Ives. — *Phylloscopus Publications*
785.85194 013561837

See **Eight four-part fantasias** : for oboe, oboe & cor anglais and two bassoons / by Simon Ives … [et al.]

IAkubov, Manashir.
See **Shostakovich, Dmitriĭ Dmitrievich, 1906-1975.** [Vocal music. *Selections*] Dve basni I.A. Krylova, dlía metsso-soprano, zhenskogo khora (metsso-soprano) i orkestra, soch. 4 ; Shest' romansov na slova íaponskikh poètov, dl ía tenora s orkestrom, soch. 21 ; Tri romansa na slova A.S. Pushkina, dlía basa i kamernogo orkestra, soch. 46a / Dmitriĭ Shostakovich ; obshchaía redaktsiía i poíasnitel'naía stat'ía Manashira IAkubova.

Jack Goodison's collection of local & traditional carols
Jack Goodison's collection of local & traditional carols / [collected and compiled by Jack Goodison] — *4th ed., fully rev. and augm. — Forgefolk on behalf of Rolling Stock Company*
782.528 013358302

Jäckel, Burkhard.
See **Hertel, Johann Wilhelm, 1727-1789.** [Concertos, harp, string orchestra, F major; *arr.*] Konzert F-Dur für Harfe oder Cembalo, 2 Violinen, Viola und Violoncello / Johann Wilhelm Hertel ; herausgegeben von Johanna Seitz ; Klavierauszug von Burkhard Jäckel.

Jackman, Andrew Pryce.
See **Swing low, sweet chariot** / [arr.] Andrew Pryce Jackman.

Jackman, Jeremy.
Wedding responses : for upper voices (divisi) / by Jeremy Jackman. — *Stainer & Bell*
782.632231587 013307563

Jackson, Gabriel, 1962-
Magnificat and Nunc dimittis : (Truro service) : SATB a cappella / Gabriel Jackson. — *Oxford University Press*
782.5326 013213389

Jackson, William, 1730-1803.
[Songs, op. 16. When fond, you Damon's charms recite] — When fond, you Damon's charms recite : op. 16 no. 7 (c. 1793) : song with obbligato viola da gamba / William Jackson ; edited by David J. Rhodes. — *Viola da Gamba Society of Great Britain*
783.342 013382414

Jacob, Gordon, 1895-1984.
[Sonatinas, oboe, harpsichord] — Sonatina for oboe and harpsichord (or piano) / Gordon Jacob. — *Oxford University Press*
788.521832 013407967

Jacobean salute
See **Waterhouse, Graham, 1962-** Jacobean salute

Jacobi, Jörg.
See **Marcello, Benedetto, 1686-1739.** [Chaconnes, harpsichord, S. C703, C major] Cioconna stravaganza ; Menuetto per cembalo = für Clavier / Benedetto Marcello ; herausgegeben und bearbeitet von Jörg Jacobi.

See **Riehman, Jacob, d. 1726.** [Sonatas, viola da gamba, continuo, op. 1] Six sonates à une viole de gambe & basse continue = Sechs Sonaten für Viola da gamba und Basso continuo / Jacob Richmann ; herausgegeben von Olaf Tetampel ; Aussetzung des Basso continuo von Jörg Jacobi.

See **Scarlatti, Alessandro, 1660-1725.** [Harpsichord music. *Selections*] Dieci pezzi per clavicembalo = Zehn Stücke für Clavierinstrumente / Alessandro Scarlatti ; herausgegeben von Jörg Jacobi.

Jacobsen, J. P. *1847-1885.*
See **Gurre-Lieder : für Soli, Chor und Orchester : kritischer Bericht / Arnold Schönberg ; [Text] von Jens Peter Jacobsen (deutsch von Robert Franz Arnold) ; herausgegeben von Ulrich Krämer.**

Jacobson, Jeff.
See **Johnson, Jack, 1975-** In between dreams / Jack Johnson ; transcribed by Jeff Jacobson.

See **Satriani, Joe.** Is there love in space? : [guitar/vocal] / Joe Satriani.

See **St Anger** / Metallica ; arranged by Jeff Jacobson.

Jäderlund, Ann.
See **Salonen, Esa-Pekka, 1958-** [Sēnger till text av Ann Jäderlund] Two songs from Kalender röd : for unaccompanied choir SSAATTBB / Esa-Pekka Salonen ; poems by Ann Jäderlund.

[Jagdkantate. Schafe können sicher weiden; *arr.*]
See **Bach, Johann Sebastian, 1685-1750.** [Jagdkantate. Schafe können sicher weiden; *arr.*]

J'ai vû le loup
J'ai vû le loup : SSA a cappella / arranged by Stephen Hatfield. — *Boosey & Hawkes*
782.64216200944   013243898

James, Anthony.
See **Brookes, Katherine.** The gunpowder plot : remember, remember the 5th of November.

See **Brookes, Katherine.** Happy Christmas Tommy : the Christmas miracle of 1914.

See **Brookes, Katherine.** [Happy Christmas Tommy. *Selections*] Happy Christmas Tommy : the Christmas miracle of 1914 : assembly pack.

See **Brookes, Katherine.** Perfect pirates : the story of Anne Bonny & Mary Read.

See **Brookes, Katherine.** Pompeii : the rain of fire / written by Katherine Brookes ; music by Katherine Brookes.

See **Brookes, Katherine.** [Pompeii. *Selections*] Pompeii : escape from the cloud : assembly pack / written by Katherine Brookes ; music by Katherine Brookes.

See **Brookes, Katherine.** The Saxon king : the story of Sutton Hoo.

See **Hewitt, Daniel.** 1066 : the Battle of Hastings / written by Daniel Dalton ; music [& lyrics] by Dan Hewitt.

See **Hewitt, Daniel.** Battle of Britain : a story of the few.

See **Hewitt, Daniel.** [Battle of Britain. *Selections*] The Battle of Britain : their finest hour : assembly pack / written by Anthony James ; music [& lyrics] by Dan[iel] Hewitt.

See **Hewitt, Daniel.** [Christopher Columbus. *Selections*] Christopher Columbus : voyage to

the end of the world : assembly pack / written by Daniel Dalton ; music [& lyrics] by Dan Hewitt.

See **Hewitt, Daniel.** Gettysburg : brothers at war.

See **Hewitt, Daniel.** Henry VIII : the break with Rome.

See **Hewitt, Daniel.** [Henry VIII. *Selections*] Henry VIII : Henry and Anne Boleyn : assembly pack / written by Daniel Dalton ; music [& lyrics] by Dan Hewitt.

See **Hewitt, Daniel.** [Henry VIII. *Selections*] Henry VIII : the break with Rome : assembly pack / written by Daniel Dalton ; music [& lyrics] by Dan Hewitt.

See **Hewitt, Daniel.** The magic tree : a story for Christmas.

See **Hewitt, Daniel.** [Magic tree. *Selections*] The magic tree : a story for Christmas : assembly pack.

See **Hewitt, Daniel.** Saint Nicholas : the real Santa Claus.

See **Hewitt, Daniel.** [Saint Nicholas. *Selections*] Saint Nicholas : the real Santa Claus : assembly pack.

See **Hewitt, Daniel.** The Spanish Armada : the invasion of England.

See **Hewitt, Daniel.** [Spanish Armada. *Selections*] The Spanish Armada : the invasion of England : assembly pack.

See **Hewitt, Daniel.** The Trojan horse : the fall of Troy.

See **Hewitt, Daniel.** [Trojan horse. *Selections*] The Trojan horse : the fall of Troy : assembly pack.

See **Hewitt, Daniel.** The valley of the kings : the power of the Sun God.

See **Spencer, Tim.** The ancient Olympics : the legend of Callipateira.

See **Spencer, Tim.** [Ancient Olympics. *Selections*] The ancient Olympics : the Olympic traditions : assembly pack.

See **Spencer, Tim.** [Ancient Olympics. *Selections*] The ancient Olympics : the story of Callipateira : assembly pack / written by Daniel Dalton ; music [& lyrics] by Tim Spencer.

See **Spencer, Tim.** The boy king : the legend of Tutankhamun.

See **Spencer, Tim.** [Boy king. *Selections*] The boy king : the legend of Tutankhamun : assembly pack / written by Anthony James ; music [& lyrics] by Tim Spencer.

See **Spencer, Tim.** The dream catcher : the plains indians of North America.

See **Spencer, Tim.** [Dream catcher. *Selections*] The dream catcher : the Plains Indians of North America : assembly pack.

See **Spencer, Tim.** The golden city : the lost empire of the Aztecs.

See **Spencer, Tim.** The lucky Viking : the discovery of America.

See **Spencer, Tim.** [Lucky Viking. *Selections*] The lucky Viking : the discovery of America : assembly pack / written by Anthony James ; music [& lyrics] by Tim Spencer.

See **Spencer, Tim.** Monster of the maze : the story of Theseus and the Minotaur.

See **Spencer, Tim.** [Monster of the maze. *Selections*] Monster of the maze : the story of Theseus and the Minotaur : assembly pack.

See **Spencer, Tim.** The ship of dreams : the voyage of the RMS Titanic.

See **Spencer, Tim.** The star child : the Christmas story.

See **Spencer, Tim.** Trafalgar : Nelson's finest hour / written by Daniel Dalton ; music [& lyrics] by Tim Spencer.

See **Spencer, Tim.** [Trafalgar. *Selections*] Trafalgar : Napolean's navy : assembly pack / written by Daniel Dalton ; music [& lyrics] by Tim Spencer.

See **Spencer, Tim.** [Trafalgar. *Selections*] Trafalgar : Nelson's finest hour : assembly pack / written by Daniel Dalton ; musc [& lyrics] by Tim Spencer.

See **Spencer, Tim.** The Victorian historian : a journey to Victorian Britain.

See **Spencer, Tim.** [Victorian historian. *Selections*] The Victorian historian : history is boring? : assembly pack / written by Anthony James ; music [& lyrics] by Tim Spencer.

See **Spencer, Tim.** [Victorian historian. *Selections*] The Victorian historian : rogues, railways & royalty: assembly pack.

See **Spencer, Tim.** The warrior queen : Boudica and the Romans.

See **Spencer, Tim.** [Warrior queen. *Selections*] The warrior queen : Boudica and the Romans : assembly pack.

See **Spencer, Tim.** [Warrior queen. *Selections*] The warrior queen : the Romans in Britannia : assembly pack / written by Anthony James ; music [& lyrics] by Tim Spencer.

Japanese lullaby
See **Neaum, Michael.** Japanese lullaby

[Japanese miniatures]
See **Hesketh, Kenneth, 1968-** [Japanese miniatures]

Los jardineros de Aranjuez
See **Esteve, Pablo.** Los jardineros de Aranjuez

Jazz
Jazz : [24 great songs] — *Wise*
786.2165   013281480
Jazz : guitar play-along. — *Hal Leonard*
787.87165   013191073

Jazz at Christmas
Jazz at Christmas : piano solo : [elegant jazz arangements of 14 traditional carols] / arranged by Frank Mantooth. — *Hal Leonard*
786.21723165   013376348

Jazz bits and pieces
See **Boyd, Bill.** Jazz bits and pieces

Jazz guitar
See **Schroedl, Jeff.** Jazz guitar

Jazz in three
Jazz in three : 9 jazz waltzes / arranged and produced by Mark Taylor. — *Hal Leonard Europe*
784.18846165   013335922

Jazz sketches
See **Boyd, Bill.** Jazz sketches

Jazz, rock 'n' bow
See **Widger, John.** Jazz, rock 'n' bow

See **Widger, John.** [Jazz, rock 'n' bow. Viola] Jazz, rock 'n' bow

See **Widger, John.** [Jazz, rock 'n' bow. Violin] Jazz, rock 'n' bow

[Jazz, rock 'n' bow. Viola]
See **Widger, John.** [Jazz, rock 'n' bow. Viola]

[Jazz, rock 'n' bow. Violin]
See **Widger, John.** [Jazz, rock 'n' bow. Violin]

Jazzology
See **Rawlins, Robert.** Jazzology

Jazzy opera classix
Jazzy opera classix : for alto saxophone / [arranged by] Darren Fellows. — *Schott*
788.73165   013192271

Jazzy opera classix : for clarinet / [arranged by] Darren Fellows. — *Schott*
788.62165   013192207

Jazzy opera classix : for flute / [arranged by] Darren Fellows. — *Schott*
788.32165   013192229

Jazzy opera classix : for tenor saxophone / [arranged by] Darren Fellows. — *Schott*
788.74165   013192267

Jazzy opera classix : for trumpet / [arranged by] Darren Fellows. — *Schott*
788.92165   013192282

Jazzy opera classix : for violin / [arranged by] Darren Fellows. — *Schott*
787.2165   013192197

Jeff Buckley
See **Buckley, Jeff, 1966-1997.** [Songs. *Selections*] Jeff Buckley

Jeffery, Brian.
See **Molino, Francesco, 1768-1847.** [Grand trio concertant, no. 1] Grand trio concertant, op. 30 : for flute or violin, viola, and guitar / Francesco Molino ; edited by Brian Jeffery.

See **Sor, Fernando, 1778-1839.** [Guitar music. 1997] The new complete works for guitar : re-engraved in eleven volumes / Fernando Sor ; edited by Brian Jeffery.

Jeffreys, George, ca. 1610-1685.
[Duets, soprano, bass, continuo] — Three dialogues : for soprano, bass and continuo / George Jeffreys. — *Green Man Press*
783.1242   013597274

[Songs. *Selections*] — Three devotional songs : solo bass with bass continuo / George Jeffreys. — *Green Man Press*
783.8925   013597217

[With notes that are both loud and sweet] — Two duets for basses : for voices and basso continuo / Jeffreys & Purcell. — *Green Man Press*
783.128925   013597245

Jeffreys, George, ca. 1610-1685. Heu, me miseram.
See **Jeffreys, George, ca. 1610-1685.** [Duets, soprano, bass, continuo] Three dialogues : for soprano, bass and continuo / George Jeffreys.

Jeffreys, George, ca. 1610-1685. O quam suave.
See **Jeffreys, George, ca. 1610-1685.** [Songs. *Selections*] Three devotional songs : solo bass with bass continuo / George Jeffreys.

Jeffreys, George, ca. 1610-1685. Why sigh you swayne.
See **Jeffreys, George, ca. 1610-1685.** [Duets, soprano, bass, continuo] Three dialogues : for soprano, bass and continuo / George Jeffreys.

Jenkins, John, *1592-1678*.
[Fantasia-suites, organ, viols (4). *Selections*] — Fantasia-suites : for two trebles (violins), two basses (viols) and organ / John Jenkins ; edited by Andrew Ashbee. — *Stainer & Bell*
785.281951858   013182170

[Fantasias, viols (3). *Selections*] — 3 fantasias à 3 : nos. 10, 11 & 12 : (TrTrB) / John Jenkins ; edited by Virginia Brookes. — *Viola da Gamba Society of Great Britain*
785.76193   013382526

[Fantasias, viols (3). *Selections*] — 3 fantasias à 3 : nos. 7, 8 & 9 : (TrTrB) / John Jenkins ; edited by Virginia Brookes. — *Viola da Gamba Society of Great Britain*
785.76193   013382426

Jenkins, Stephan.
See **Carlton, Vanessa.** Harmonium : piano, vocal, guitar / Vanessa Carlton.

Jennings, Elizabeth, *1926-2001*.
See **Chilcott, Bob.** [And peace on earth. Put memory away. *Vocal score*] Put memory away : SATB and piano / Bob Chilcott.

See **Chilcott, Bob.** You and me : SATB unaccompanied / Bob Chilcott.

Jerusalem
See **Parry, C. Hubert H. 1848-1918.** [Jerusalem; *arr.*] Jerusalem

[Jerusalem; *arr.*]
See **Parry, C. Hubert H. 1848-1918.** [Jerusalem; *arr.*]

Jessop, Craig D.
See **Feel the spirit.** Volume two : twenty-eight arrangements for mixed chorus / by Moses Hogan ; with a foreword by Craig Jessop.

Jesu, meine Freude
See **Hertel, Johann Wilhelm, 1727-1789.** Jesu, meine Freude

Jesu, wirst du bald erscheinen
See **Telemann, Georg Philipp, 1681-1767.** Jesu, wirst du bald erscheinen

[Jesus Christ superstar. I don't know how to love him; *arr.*]
See **Lloyd Webber, Andrew, 1948-** [Jesus Christ superstar. I don't know how to love him; *arr.*]

Jesus is alive!
See **Hart, Barry.** Jesus is alive!

Jesus, Jesus, rest your head
Jesus, Jesus, rest your head : for unaccompanied mixed choir (SATB) with baritone solo / [American folk carol ; arranged by] Lester Seigel. — *Oxford University Press*
782.5281723   013126600

Jeux d'été
See **McAlister, Clark.** Jeux d'été

Jindra, MaryAnn.
See **Larsen, Libby.** Lord, before this fleeting season : an anthem for mixed choir (SATB), unaccompanied : for the First Sunday of Advent (A, B, C) / text by MaryAnn Jindra ; music by Libby Larsen.

Jingle bells
See **Pierpont, James, 1822-1893.** [Jingle bells; *arr.*] Jingle bells

[Jingle bells; *arr.*]
See **Pierpont, James, 1822-1893.** [Jingle bells; *arr.*]

Jingle jangle jungle
See **Bartlett, Keith.** Jingle jangle jungle

Jingle, bells
See **Pierpont, James, 1822-1893.** [Jingle bells; *arr.*] Jingle, bells

Joel, Billy.
[Songs. *Selections*] — Make it easy. Billy Joel. — *International Music Publications*
786.2166   013299330

Joelson-Strohbach, Harry.
See **Kirchner, Theodor, 1823-1903.** [Albumblätter, op. 80] Albumblätter : neun kleine Clavierstücke, op. 80 = Album leaves : nine little piano pieces / Theodor Kirchner ; nach den Quellen herausgegeben von Harry Joelson.

See **Kirchner, Theodor, 1823-1903.** Im Zwielicht : Lieder und Tänze für Klavier, op. 31 = In twilight : songs and dances for piano / Theodor Kirchner ; nach den Quellen herausgegeben von Harry Joelson.

See **Kirchner, Theodor, 1823-1903.** Legenden : Dichtungen für das Clavier, op. 18 = Legends : poetry for pianoforte / Theodor Kirchner ; nach den Quellen herausgegeben von Harry Joelson.

See **Kirchner, Theodor, 1823-1903.** [Nocturnes, piano, op. 28] Notturnos : 4 Stücke für Klavier : op. 28 = Notturnos : four pieces for piano / Theodor Kirchner ; nach den Quellen herausgegeben von Harry Joelson.

See **Kirchner, Theodor, 1823-1903.** Spielsachen : 14 leichte Klavierstücke : op. 35 = Toys : 14 easy piano pieces / Theodor Kirchner ; herausgegeben von Harry Joelson.

See **Kirchner, Theodor, 1823-1903.** Still und bewegt : acht Klavierstücke : op. 24 = Tranquil and turbulent : eight piano pieces / Theodor Kirchner ; nach den Quellen herausgegeben von Harry Joelson.

See **Kirchner, Theodor, 1823-1903.** [Waltzes, piano, op. 23] Zwölf Walzer für Klavier, op. 23 = Twelve waltzes for piano / Theodor Kirchner ; nach den Quellen herausgegeben von Harry Joelson.

John, Elton.
[Songs. *Selections*] — Make it easy. Elton John. — *International Music Publications*
786.2166   013196741

[Songs. *Selections*] — The piano transcriptions / Elton John. — *Wise*
783.242166   013326340

Johnson, Chad.
Acoustic guitar : [a complete guide with step-by-step lessons and 45 great acoustic songs] / by Chad Johnson. — *Hal Leonard Europe*
787.87076   013265866

Arpeggio finder : easy-to-use guide to over 1, 300 guitar arpeggios / by Chad Johnson. — *Hal Leonard*
787.871252   012874858

Johnson, Christopher, *1947-*
See **Clarke, Rebecca, 1886-1979.** [Comodo e ambile, string quartet] Two movements for string quartet / Rebecca Clarke.

Johnson, David B., *1942-*
See **Sor, Fernando, 1778-1839.** [Encouragement. *Selections; arr.*] Andante, theme & variations [from] (Duo for guitars, op. 34) / by Fernando Sor; arranged for wind quintet by David B. Johnson.

Johnson, David B., bassoonist.
See **Mozart, Wolfgang Amadeus, 1756-1791** [Ave verum corpus; *arr.*] Ave verum corpus : [K.618] / by W.A. Mozart ; arranged for four bassoons by David B. Johnson.

Johnson, David, *1942 Oct. 27-*
See **Thistle & minuet** : 16 easy pieces from the Scottish Baroque for violin (or flute or oboe), keyboard, and optional cello (or bassoon) = 16 einfache Stücke aus der schottischen Barockzeit für Violine (oder Flöte oder Oboe), Tasteninstrument und Cello (oder Fagott) ad libitum = 16 pièces faciles du Baroque écossais pour violon (ou flûte ou hautbois), clavier et violoncelle (ou basson) facultatif / edited by David Johnson.

Johnson, Helen
See **Johnson, Mark** Are we nearly there yet-? : another great nativity musical / by Mark and Helen Johnson.

See **Johnson, Mark** It's a baby! : 9 new nativity songs for 3-7 year olds / by Mark and Helen Johnson.

See **Johnson, Mark** It's a party! : a great new nativity musical / by Mark and Helen Johnson.

See **Johnson, Mark** Moving on : a brilliant new musical for primary schools / by Mark and Helen Johnson.

See **Johnson, Mark** Songs for every assembly : 15 great new songs for the whole year through / by Mark and Helen Johnson.

Johnson, Helen.
See **Davies, Niki.** The sleepy shepherd : a great new nativity musical / by Niki Davies ; edited by Mark and Helen Johnson.

See **Davies, Niki.** Snowman at sunset : a delightful new Christmas musical / by Niki Davies ; edited by Mark and Helen Johnson.

See **Davies, Niki.** Toby's Christmas drum: a simple new Christmas musical / by Niki Davies.

See **Davies, Niki.** Whoops-a-daisy angel : a short nativity musical / by Niki Davies ; edited by Mark and Helen Johnson.

See **Johnson, Mark.** Alice - the musical : a children's musical with up to eighteen songs, in two acts / by Mark and Helen Johnson ; based on the original story of 'Alice's adventures in Wonderland', by Lewis Carroll, retold in song and dance, drama and narrative.

Johnson, Jack, *1975-*
In between dreams / Jack Johnson ; transcribed by Jeff Jacobson. — *Cherry Lane Music*
783.242166   013382270

Johnson, Mark
Are we nearly there yet-? : another great nativity musical / by Mark and Helen Johnson. — *Out of the Ark Music*
782.141723083   013272448

It's a baby! : 9 new nativity songs for 3-7 year olds / by Mark and Helen Johnson. — *Out of the Ark Music*
782.7421723   013270802

It's a party! : a great new nativity musical / by Mark and Helen Johnson. — *Out of the Ark Music*
782.141723083   013272440

Moving on : a brilliant new musical for primary schools / by Mark and Helen Johnson. — *Out of the Ark Music*
782.14083   013277136

Songs for every assembly : 15 great new songs for the whole year through / by Mark and Helen Johnson. — *Out of the Ark Music*
782.725   013272453

Johnson, Mark.
Alice - the musical : a children's musical with up to eighteen songs, in two acts / by Mark and Helen Johnson ; based on the original story of 'Alice's adventures in Wonderland', by Lewis Carroll, retold in song and dance, drama and narrative. — *Out of the Ark Music*
782.14083   013271525

See **Davies, Niki.** The sleepy shepherd : a great new nativity musical / by Niki Davies ; edited by Mark and Helen Johnson.

See **Davies, Niki.** Snowman at sunset : a delightful new Christmas musical / by Niki Davies ; edited by Mark and Helen Johnson.

See **Davies, Niki.** Toby's Christmas drum: a simple new Christmas musical / by Niki Davies.

See **Davies, Niki.** Whoops-a-daisy angel : a short nativity musical / by Niki Davies ; edited by Mark and Helen Johnson.

Johnson, Robert, *ca. 1500-ca. 1560.*
[Knell] — A knell of Johnson / Robert Johnson. Pavan a 5 / Joseph Lupo ; edited by Virginia Brookes. — *Viola da Gamba Society of Great Britain*
785.76195   013382517

Johnson, Robert, *d. 1938.*
Robert Johnson complete : piano, vocal, guitar. — *Hal Leonard*
783.2421643   006936059

Johnstone, H. Diack.
See **Greene, Maurice,** *1696-1755* Phoebe : a pastoral opera / Maurice Greene ; edited by H. Diack Johnstone.

Jollage, Charles-Alexandre.
[Pièces de clavecin, 1er livre] — Premier livre de pièces de clavecin : 1738 / Charles Alexandre Jollage. — *Fuzeau*
786.4   013943338

Jón Arason, Bishop of Hólar, *1484-1550.*
See **Þorkell Sigurbjörnsson,** *1938-* Hymn to Mary = (Maríukvæði) / Þorkell Sigurbjörnsson.

Jones, Derek, arranger.
See **The best of 1000 UK number one hits.** Early years : [from 1952 to 1974 : arranged for piano, voice and guitar]

See **Essential film songs** : the ultimate modern-day movie songbook. Take 2.

See **[X&Y]** It's easy to play Coldplay X&Y

Jones, Kelly.
See **Language, sex, violence, other?** / Stereophonics.

Jones, Nesta Wyn.
See **Samuel, Rhian.** Pan ddaw ust y nos : i gôr SATB & organ / [alaw] Rhian Samuel ; [geiriau gan] Nesta Wyn Jones.

Jones, Nigel E.
See **As I went with Tom to Tywyn** = [Wrth fynd efo Deio i Dywyn : for unison treble voices & piano] / arranged by Nigel E. Jones.

See **Little cuckoo** = (Cwcw fach) : SATB a cappella / arranged by Nigel E. Jones.

See **Lullaby** = (Suo-gân) : 3-part treble / arranged by Nigel E. Jones.

Jones, Norah, *1979-*
See **Harris, Jesse,** *1969-* [Don't know why; arr.] Don't know why / words and music by Jesse Harris ; arranged by Paris Rutherford ; recorded by Norah Jones.

Jordan, Stephanie.
See **Stravinsky, Igor,** *1882-1971.* [Svadebka. French & Russian] Les noces = (Svadebka) : scènes chorégraphiques russes avec chant et musique : for four pianos, percussion and voices in a revised and corrected edition based upon relevant autograph and printed sources / composées par Igor Stravinsky ; French text by C.-F. Ramuz ; edited by Margarita Mazo ; associate editor, Millan Sachania.

Joriini, Gloria.
See **Ingegneri, Marc Antonio,** *1535 or 6-1592.* [Madrigals, voices (5), book 5] V libro di madrigali a 5 voci / Marc'Antonio Ingegneri ; a cura di Gloria Joriini e Marco Mangani.

Josa, Lola.
See **Cancionero poético-musical hispánico de Lisboa** / introducción y edición crítica de Mariano Lambea y Lola Josa.

Joshua fought the battle of Jericho
Joshua fought the battle of Jericho : SSAATTBB / arranged by Jonathan Rathbone. — *Edition Peters*
782.5253   013305728

Josquin, des Prez, *d. 1521.*
[Motets. *Selections*] — Motets on non-biblical texts. I, De domino Jesu Christo. 1 / Josquin des Prez ; edited by Bonnie J. Blackburn. — *Koninklijke Vereniging voor Nederlandse Muziekgeschiedenis*
782.526   013949874

Josquin, des Prez, *d. 1521*
[Motets. *Selections*] — "Si placet" parts for motets by Josquin and his contemporaries / edited by Stephanie P. Schlagel. — *A-R Editions*
782.526   013801801

Jost, Peter, *1960-*
See **Dokumente und Texte zu "Tannhäuser und der Sängerkrieg auf Wartburg"** / herausgegeben von Peter Jost ; Reinschrift des Textbuches mit Varianten herausgegeben von Cristina Urcheuguía.

Joy to the world
See **Mason, Lowell,** *1792-1872.* [Modern Psalmist. Antioch; *arr.*] Joy to the world

Jubilate Deo
See **Mozart, Wolfgang Amadeus,** *1756-1791.* Jubilate Deo

Judd, Cristle Collins.
See **Zarlino, Gioseffo,** *1517-1590.* [Motets. *Selections*] Motets from 1549 / Gioseffo Zarlino ; edited by Cristle Collins Judd.

Julian, of Norwich, *b. 1343.*
See **Larsen, Libby.** Is God, our endless day : an anthem for mixed choir (SATB), unaccompanied : for Trinity Sunday (A, B, C), Third Sunday after the Epiphany (A), Last Sunday after the Epiphany (C) / text by Julian of Norwich ; music by Libby Larsen.

Julian, of Norwich, *b. 1343.* **Revelations of divine love.**
See **Bingham, Judith.** Our faith is a light : anthem for SATB and organ : (2004) / Judith Bingham.

Junior praise
Junior praise / compiled by Phil Burt, Peter Horrobin and Greg Leavers. — *Combined music ed.* — *Collins*
782.725   012878554

Just as I am
See **Stewart, Richard N.** Just as I am

[Just as I am. *Spanish*]
See **Stewart, Richard N.** [Just as I am. *Spanish*]

Just classic rock real book.
Just classic rock real book. — *C edition fakebook.* — *International Music Publications*
783.242166   013189085

Kabeláč, Miloslav, *1908-1979*.
Cizokrajné motivy = Motive aus fernen Ländern = Motifs from exotic lands : op. 38, piano / Miloslav Kabeláč ; editor, Zdeněk Nouza. — *1. vyd.* — *Editio Bärenreiter Praha*
786.2   013382907

[Malá suita, flute] — Skladby pro flétnu sólo = Kompositionen für Soloflöte = Compositions for flute solo / Miloslav Kabeláč ; [editor, Zdeněk Nouza]. — *1. vyd.* — *Editio Bärenreiter Praha*
788.32   013385590

Kabeláč, Miloslav, *1908-1979* Improvizace na vlastní téma.
See **Kabeláč, Miloslav, 1908-1979.** [Malá suita, flute] Skladby pro flétnu sólo = Kompositionen für Soloflöte = Compositions for flute solo / Miloslav Kabeláč ; [editor, Zdeněk Nouza]

Kaczmarczyk, Adrienne.
See **Liszt, Franz, 1811-1886.** [Piano music. *Selections*] Freie Bearbeitungen. XIII = Free arrangements. XIII / Franz Liszt ; herausgegeben von Péter Bozó, Adrienne Kaczmarczyk.

Kaiser Chiefs (Musical group)
Employment : guitar tab ed. / Kaiser Chiefs. — *Wise Publications*
783.242166   013297794

Kaiser, Georg, *1878-1945*
See **Weill, Kurt, 1900-1950.** Der Protagonist : ein Akt Oper : op. 15 / Musik von Kurt Weill ; Text von Georg Kaiser ; edited by Gunther Diehl and Jürgen Selk.

Kaiser, Peter.
See **Halévy, F., 1799-1862.** La fée aux roses : opéra-comique en trois actes / Fromental Halévy ; paroles d'Eugène Scribe et de Henri V. de Saint-Georges ; edité par Peter Kaiser.

Kallman, Chester, *1921-1975*.
See **D'Amico, Matteo, 1955-** The entertainment of the senses : cabaret musicale per voce e strumenti (2005) / Matteo D'Amico ; su testi di W.H. Auden and Ch. Kallman.

Kalsons, Romualds.
[Symphonies, chamber orchestra, no. 1] — Sinfonie für Kammerorchester, 1981 / Romualds Kalsons. — *Sikorski*
784.3184   013762794

Kamiński, Paweł, *1958-*
See **Chopin, Frédéric, 1810-1849.** [Concertos, piano, orchestra, no. 1, op. 11, E minor] Koncert e-moll op. 11 na fortepian i orkiestrę = Concerto in E minor op. 11 for piano and orchestra / Fryderyk Chopin ; [redakcja tomu, Jan Ekier, Paweł Kamiński]

See **Chopin, Frédéric, 1810-1849.** [Concertos, piano, orchestra, no. 1, op. 11, E minor] Koncert e-moll op. 11 na fortepian i orkiestrę : wersja historyczna = Concerto in E minor op. 11 for piano and orchestra : historical version / Fryderyk Chopin ; [redakcja tomu, Jan Ekier, Paweł Kamiński]

See **Chopin, Frédéric, 1810-1849.** [Concertos, piano, orchestra, no. 2, op. 21, F minor] Koncert f-moll op. 21 na fortepian i orkiestrę = Concerto in F minor op. 21 for piano and orchestra / Fryderyk Chopin ; [redakcja tomu, Jan Ekier, Paweł Kamiński]

See **Chopin, Frédéric, 1810-1849.** [Concertos, piano, orchestra, no. 2, op. 21, F minor] Koncert

f-moll op. 21 na fortepian i orkiestrę : wersja historyczna = Concerto in F minor op. 21 for piano and orchestra : historical version / Fryderyk Chopin ; [redakcja tomu, Jan Ekier, Paweł Kamiński]

See **Chopin, Frédéric, 1810-1849.** [Rondos, piano] Ronda, op. 1, 5, 16 = Rondos, opp. 1, 5, 16 / Fryderyk Chopin ; [redakcja tomu, Jan Ekier, Paweł Kamiński, Witalis Raczkiewicz]

Kammermusik V
See **Rheinberger, Josef, 1839-1901.** [Chamber music. *Selections*] Kammermusik V

[Kammermusik, no. 1]
See **Hindemith, Paul, 1895-1963.** [Kammermusik, no. 1]

Kancheli, Giia. Mit einem Lächeln für Slawa.
See **Schnittke, Alfred, 1934-1998.** Musica nostalgica : für Violoncello und Klavier = for violoncello and piano / Alfred Schnittke. Mit einem Lächeln für Slawa : für Violoncello und Klavier / Gija Kantscheli = With a smile for Slava : for violoncello and piano / Giya Kancheli.

Kander, John.
[Kiss of the spider woman. *Vocal score. Selections*] — Kiss of the spider woman : the musical : [vocal selections] / book by Terrence McNally ; music by John Kander ; lyrics by Fred Ebb ; based on the novel by Manuel Puig. — *Carlin America*
783.242164   013381892

Kaprálová, Vítězslava, *1915-1940*.
Sonata appassionata : op. 6 : piano / Vítězslava Kaprálová ; editor Věroslav Němec. — *Amos*
786.2183   013771129

Karolic, Dragan.
See **Leonarda, Isabella, 1620-1704.** [Motets, bass, continuo. *Selections*] Ausgewählte Bassmotetten für Bass und B.c. = Selected bass motets for bass and b.c. / Isabella Leonarda ; [edited by Dragan Karolic]

Kaye, Ernest.
[Songs. *Selections*] — Five songs : for voice and piano / Ernest Kaye. — *Oxford University Press*
783.6642   013434221

Wedding march : for piano / Ernest Kaye ; and arranged for organ by Antony Baldwin. — *Oxford University Press*
786.218971587   013115092

Kaye, Ernest. Improvisation on lament.
See **Nathan, Simon, 1988 or 9-** Lament : for piano / Simon Nathan. Together with Improvisation on "Lament" : for piano / Ernest Kaye ; and arranged for organ by Gerald Barnes.

Kaye, Ernest. Wedding march;
See **Kaye, Ernest.** Wedding march : for piano / Ernest Kaye ; and arranged for organ by Antony Baldwin.

Keane (Musical group)
[Hopes and fears; *arr.*] — Hopes and fears : playalong for alto saxophone / Keane. — *Wise Publications*
788.73166   013281543

[Hopes and fears; *arr.*] — Hopes and fears : playalong for clarinet / Keane. — *Wise Publications*
788.62166   013281570

[Hopes and fears; *arr.*] — Hopes and fears : playalong for flute / Keane. — *Wise Publications*
788.32166   013281555

[Hopes and fears; *arr.*] — Hopes and fears : playalong for violin / Keane. — *Wise Publications*
787.2166   013281586

[Hopes and fears; *arr.*] — Play piano with — Keane : Hopes and fears. — *Wise*
783.242166   013193365

Keane (*Musical group*)
See **Play piano with — Keane, Coldplay, Muse and other great artists.**

Keats, John, *1795-1821*.
See **Musgrave, Thea.** Going north : for children's chorus and two clarinets / Thea Musgrave.

See **Richardson, Michael.** How many bards : [for SATB voices, oboe (or violin) & piano] / Michael Richardson.

See **Richardson, Michael.** How many bards : SSA / [music by] Michael Richardson.

Kecat dhe ujku
See **Peçi, Aleksandër, 1951-** Kecat dhe ujku

Keck, Jean-Christophe.
See **Offenbach, Jacques, 1819-1880.** [Rheinnixen. *Vocal score*] Les fées du Rhin = Die Rheinnixen : opéra romantique en 4 actes (1864 / Jacques Offenbach ; livret de Jacques Offenbach et Charles Nuitter ; adaptation allemande par Alfred von Wolzogen ; partition chant-piano [par Jean-Yves Aizic avec la collaboration de Dominik Rahmer, Jean-Christophe Keck]

[Kékszakállú herceg vára. *English & Hungarian*]
See **Bartók, Béla, 1881-1945.** [Kékszakállú herceg vára. *English & Hungarian*]

Keller, Hermann, *1885-1967*.
See **Chopin, Frédéric, 1810-1849.** [Preludes, piano] Préludes / Frédéric Chopin ; herausgegeben von Norbert Müllemann ; Fingersatz von Hermann Keller.

Kellhuber, Martin.
See **Zelenka, Johann Dismas, 1679-1745.** Missa Sanctae Caeciliae : für Soprano, Alt, Tenor, Bass, Chor, 2 Oboen, Fagott, Streicher & B.c. / Jan Dismas Zelenka ; herausgegeben von Martin Kellhuber.

Kelly, Bryan.
Globe Theatre suite : for descant recorder or piccolo and piano / by Bryan Kelly ; edited by Atarah Ben-Tovim. — *Stainer & Bell*
788.3641858   013222597

[Iberian pieces] — Three Iberian pieces : for four bassoons / Bryan Kelly. — *Emerson Edition*
785.858194   013360867

Kentucky canticles : Magnificat and Nunc dimittis for SATB and organ / Bryan Kelly. — *Stainer & Bell*
782.5326   013307559

Kelly, Thomas Alexander Erskine, Earl of, *1732-1781*.
See **Thistle & minuet** : 16 easy pieces from the Scottish Baroque for violin (or flute or oboe), keyboard, and optional cello (or bassoon) = 16 einfache Stücke aus der schottischen Barockzeit für Violine (oder Flöte oder Oboe), Tasteninstrument und Cello (oder Fagott) ad libitum = 16 pièces faciles du Baroque écossais pour violon (ou flûte ou hautbois), clavier et violoncelle (ou basson) facultatif / edited by David Johnson.

Kember, John.
On the lighter side : duet collection : 10 pieces for piano duet in Latin, spiritual and jazz styles / John Kember. — *Schott*
785.62192   013192400

[On the lighter side. Rock & soul styles] — Rock & soul styles : 18 pieces for piano solo = 18 pièces pour piano = 18 Stücke für Klavier / John Kember. — *Schott*
786.2   013201895

[On the lighter side. Solo collection] — Solo collection : 15 pieces for piano in blues, spiritual and jazz styles / John Kember. — *Schott*
786.2   013201919

Sight-reading 2 : piano : a fresh approach = Déchiffrage pour le piano 2 : nouvelle approche = Vom-Blatt-Spielen auf dem Klavier 2 : eine erfrischend neue Methode / John Kember. — *Schott*
786.21423   013192084

Sight-singing 2 : a fresh approach = Déchiffrage pour le chant 2 : nouvelle approche = Vom-Blatt-Singen 2 : eine erfrischend neue Methode / John Kember. — *Schott*
783.21423   013191850

See An die Musik : 9 classical pieces arranged for string quartet / [arr. by] John Kember.

Kennedy, Michael, *1926-*
See **Vaughan Williams, Ralph,** *1872-1958.* [Quintets, piano, violin, viola, violoncello, double bass, C minor] Piano quintet in C minor (1903), for violin, viola, cello, double bass and piano / Ralph Vaughan Williams.

Kentucky canticles
See **Kelly, Bryan.** Kentucky canticles

Kern, Jerome, *1885-1945.*
[Songs. *Selections; arr.*] — Jerome Kern classics : for piano solo / arranged by Eugéne Rocherolle ; edited by J. Mark Baker. — *Hal Leonard*
786.2   013221821

Keroiylu
See **Finnissy, Michael.** Keroiylu

Kesselman, Lee R.
[Nights in armor. No. 1, Merlin's riddle] — Merlin's riddle (no. 1 from "Nights in Armor") / Lee R. Kesselman. — *Boosey & Hawkes*
782.542   013213621

Kethe, William, *d. 1608?*
See **Vaughan Williams, Ralph,** *1872-1958.* [Old Hundredth Psalm tune; *arr.*] The Old Hundreth Psalm tune : (All people that on earth do dwell) / R. Vaughan Williams (arr.) ; rescored by Roy Douglas for mixed choir (SATB), congregation, 3 trumpets, organ and optional timpani.

Ketley, David F.
Sax a tre : for saxophone trio / David F. Ketley. — *Da Capo Music*
785.87193   013351611

Keveren, Phillip.
See **Mach, Elyse.** Learning piano : piece by piece / Elyse Mach.

Key, Francis Scott, *1779-1843.*
See **The star-spangled banner** : for mixed chorus, unaccompanied / arranged by Jerry Rubino.

[Keyboard music]
See **Lübeck, Vincent,** *1654?-1740.* [Keyboard music]

Keyboard music II
See **Byrd, William,** *1542 or 3-1623.* [Keyboard music. *Selections*] Keyboard music II

[Keyboard music. *Selections*]
See **Byrd, William,** *1542 or 3-1623.* [Keyboard music. *Selections*]

See **Clementi, Muzio,** *1752-1832.* [Keyboard music. *Selections*]

See **Reincken, Johann Adam,** *1623-1722.* [Keyboard music. *Selections*]

Killers (Musical group)
Hot fuss / The Killers. — *Guitar recorded versions.* — *Wise Publications*
783.242166   013169025

Kim-Szacsvai, Katalin.
See **Erkel, Ferenc.** [Hunyadi László] Hunyadi László : opera négy felvonásban = opera in four acts / [Erkel Ferenc] ; szöveg Benjámin Egressy ; közreadja Katalin Szacsvai-Kim ; bevezetés Tibor Tallián, Katalin Szacsvai-Kim.

King Priam
See **Tippett, Michael,** *1905-1998.* [King Priam. *German & English*] King Priam

[King Priam. *German & English*]
See **Tippett, Michael,** *1905-1998.* [King Priam. *German & English*]

King, David.
See **Dvořák, Antonín,** *1841-1904.* [Sonatina, violin, piano, op. 100, G major; *arr.*] Sonatina in G, op. 100 / by Anton Dvořák ; arranged for flute, two oboes, two clarinets in B♭, two horns in F and two bassoons by David King.

King's Singers (*Vocal group***)**
See **King's Singers Christmas.**

King's Singers Christmas.
King's Singers Christmas. — *Hal Leonard*
782.5281723   013222165

Kipling, Rudyard, *1865-1936.*
See **Vaughan Williams, Ralph,** *1872-1958.* [Song of thanksgiving. *Vocal score*] A song of thanksgiving : for soprano solo, speaker, chorus and orchestra / R. Vaughan Williams ; vocal score.

Kircher, Armin.
See **Adlgasser, Anton Cajetan,** *1729-1777.* Litaniae de venerabili altaris Sacramento : in B-Dur (WV 3/53) : per Soli (SATB), Coro (SATB), Trombone alto solo o Organo solo, 2 Clarini, Timpani, 2 Violini, Basso continuo (Violoncello/Fagotto/Contrabbasso/Organo), 3 Tromboni colla parte voci ad lib. / Anton Cajetan Adlgasser ; herausgegeben von Armin Kircher.

Kirchner, Theodor, *1823-1903.*
[Albumblätter, op. 80] — Albumblätter : neun kleine Clavierstücke, op. 80 = Album leaves : nine little piano pieces / Theodor Kirchner ; nach den Quellen herausgegeben von Harry Joelson. — *Amadeus*
786.2   014659941

Im Zwielicht : Lieder und Tänze für Klavier, op. 31 = In twilight : songs and dances for piano / Theodor Kirchner ; nach den Quellen herausgegeben von Harry Joelson. — *Amadeus*
786.2   014659739

Legenden : Dichtungen für das Clavier, op. 18 = Legends : poetry for pianoforte / Theodor Kirchner ; nach den Quellen herausgegeben von Harry Joelson. — *Amadeus*
786.2   013806723

[Nocturnes, piano, op. 28] — Notturnos : 4 Stücke für Klavier : op. 28 = Notturnos : four pieces for piano / Theodor Kirchner ; nach den Quellen herausgegeben von Harry Joelson. — *Amadeus*
786.218966   014659748

Spielsachen : 14 leichte Klavierstücke : op. 35 = Toys : 14 easy piano pieces / Theodor Kirchner ; herausgegeben von Harry Joelson. — *Amadeus*
786.2   014659755

Still und bewegt : acht Klavierstücke : op. 24 = Tranquil and turbulent : eight piano pieces / Theodor Kirchner ; nach den Quellen herausgegeben von Harry Joelson. — *Amadeus*
786.2   014659782

[Waltzes, piano, op. 23] — Zwölf Walzer für Klavier, op. 23 = Twelve waltzes for piano / Theodor Kirchner ; nach den Quellen herausgegeben von Harry Joelson. — *Amadeus*
786.218846   014659802

Kirk, Theron, *1919-1999.*
See **Estonian wedding song** : for mixed chorus (SATB) and piano / [Estonian folk song, arr.] Theron Kirk.

Kiss (Musical group)
[Songs. *Selections*] — Kiss. — *Hal Leonard*
783.242166   013383477

Kiss of the spider woman
See **Kander, John.** [Kiss of the spider woman. *Vocal score. Selections*] Kiss of the spider woman

[Kiss of the spider woman. *Vocal score. Selections*]
See **Kander, John.** [Kiss of the spider woman. *Vocal score. Selections*]

Kiss.
See **Kiss (Musical group)** [Songs. *Selections*] Kiss.

Klaverimuusika
See **Lepik, Tarmo,** *1946-2001.* [Piano music. *Selections*] Klaverimuusika

Klavierkonzert Opus 61a
See **Beethoven, Ludwig van,** *1770-1827.* [Concertos, violin, orchestra, op. 61, D major; *arr.*] Klavierkonzert Opus 61a

[Kleine Orgelstücke]
See **Hässler, Johann Wilhelm,** *1747-1822.* [Kleine Orgelstücke]

Eine kleine Snailmusik
See **Larsen, Libby.** Eine kleine Snailmusik

[Kleine Stücke, violin, piano (2002)]
See **Blomenkamp, Thomas.** [Kleine Stücke, violin, piano (2002)]

Kleine Vokalkompsitionen und Klaviersonaten
See **Hoffmann, E. T. A. 1776-1822.** [Vocal music. *Selections*] Kleine Vokalkompsitionen und Klaviersonaten

Klek, Konrad.
See **Herzogenberg, Heinrich von,** *1843-1900.* Gott ist gegenwärtig : Choralkantate op. 106 : Gemeindegesang, Chor SATB, 2 Trompeten, 3 Posaunen, Pauken, 2 Violinen, Viola, 2 Violoncelli, Kontrabass, Orgel / Heinrich von Herzogenberg ; Text, Gerhard Tersteegen ; vorgelegt und revidiert von Konrad Klek.

Klitheu tragjik
See **Peçi, Aleksandër,** *1951-* Klitheu tragjik

Klöckner, Dieter.
See **Schermar-Bibliothek Ulm Ms. 237** : Brugge? ca. 1515-1540 : unedierte Stücke und Unikate. Stücke zu 4 Stimmen / herausgegeben von Dieter Klöckner.

See **Schermar-Bibliothek Ulm Ms. 237** : Brugge? ca. 1515-1540 : unedierte Stücke und Unikate. Stücke zu 5 und 6 Stimmen / herausgegeben von Dieter Klöckner.

Klopčič, Rok.
See **Vivaldi, Antonio, 1678-1741** [Cimento dell'armonia e dell'inventione. N. 1-4; arr.] The four seasons : four concertos for violin and orchestra : for violin and piano reduction / Antonio Vivaldi ; violin part edited by Rok Klopčič ; piano reduction by Alojz Srebotnjak.

Klopstock, Friedrich Gottlieb, 1724-1803.
See **Romberg, Andreas, 1767-1821.** Der Messias : Kantate in drei Teilen : für Soli, Chor und Orchester, nach Friedrich Gottlieb Klopstocks "Messias" : WoO, zweite Fassung (1802) / Andreas Romberg ; vorgelegt von Karlheinz Höfer und Klaus G. Werner.

Klose, Norbert, musician.
See **Hertel, Johann Wilhelm, 1727-1789.** Jesu, meine Freude : Kantate für Sopran und Tenor solo, 4 st. gem. Chor SSTB, 2 Trompeten, 2 Hörner, Pauken, 2 Flöten, 2 Oboen, Fagott, Streichorchester und Generalbass / Johann Wilhelm Hertel; herausgegeben von Norbert Klose.

See **Loewe, Carl, 1796-1869** Was Gott tut, das ist wohlgetan : Kantate für Solisten SAB, 4 st. gem. Chor SATB, und Kammerorchester (2 Klarinetten, 2 Fagotti und Streicher) / Carl Loewe ; herausgegeben von Norbert Klose.

[Knell]
See **Johnson, Robert, ca. 1500-ca. 1560.**
[Knell]

A knell of Johnson
See **Johnson, Robert, ca. 1500-ca. 1560.**
[Knell] A knell of Johnson

Knight, Susan
See **World carols for choirs :** 31 carols for mixed voices / edited and compiled by Bob Chilcott & Susan Knight.

Knouse, Nola Reed.
See **Michael, David Moritz, 1751-1827.** [Wind music] Complete wind chamber music / David Moritz Michael ; edited by Nola Reed Knouse.

Koch, Greg.
[Guitar music. Selections] — Greg Koch. — Hal Leonard
787.871643   013191097

Koch, Nanna, 1963-
See **Dragonetti, Domenico, 1763-1846.** [Quintets, violin, violas, violoncello, double bass, B♭ major] Quintett in B-Dur, für Solo-Kontrabass (Solo-Violine), Violine, 2 Violen und Basso / Domenico Dragonetti ; [herausgegeben von] Nanna Koch ; [Solostimme durchgesehen von Vladislav Riabokon]

Kochański, Paweł.
See **The violin :** a collection : new and recent repertoire for violin with piano accompaniment / Craig Armstrong ... [et al.]

Koenen, Rolf, 1946-
See **Albéniz, Isaac, 1860-1909.** [Suite española, no. 1] Suite espagnole : opus 47 / Isaac Albéniz ; herausgegeben von Ullrich Scheideler ; Fingersatz von Rolf Koenen.

Kohlhase, Thomas.
See **Hoffmann, E. T. A. 1776-1822.** [Kreuz an der Ostsee] Zacharias Werners Trauerspiel "Das Kreuz an der Ostsee" : mit der Bühnenmusik von E.T.A. Hoffmann ; Ballettmusik "Arlequin" / E.T.A. Hoffmann ; hrsg. aus dem Nachlaß von Friedrich Schnapp ; unter Mitarbeit von Gerhard Allroggen und Michael Kohlhäufl von Thomas Kohlhase.

See **Hoffmann, E. T. A. 1776-1822.** [Vocal music. Selections] Kleine Vokalkompsitionen und Klaviersonaten / E.T.A. Hoffmann ; aus dem Nachlaß von Friedrich Schnapp und unter Mitarbeit von Gerhard Allroggen ; herausgegeben von Alexander Erhard und Thomas Kohlhase.

See **Zelenka, Johann Dismas, 1679-1745.** [O magnum mysterium] Motetto pro nativitate I, ZWV 171 : Dormi nate, dormi Deus : per alto solo, 2 flauti traversi o flauti a becco (ad lib.), 2 violini, viola e basso continuo / Jan Dismas Zelenka ; Erstausgabe herausgegeben von Thomas Kohlhase.

See **Zelenka, Johann Dismas, 1679-1745.** [Pro quos criminis] Motetto pro nativitate II, ZWV 172 : Dormi, Deus incarnate : per tenore solo, 2 flauti a becco, 2 flauti traversi, 2 violini, viola e basso continuo / Jan Dismas Zelenka ; herausgegeben von Thomas Kohlhase.

Kohlhäufl, Michael.
See **Hoffmann, E. T. A. 1776-1822.** [Kreuz an der Ostsee] Zacharias Werners Trauerspiel "Das Kreuz an der Ostsee" : mit der Bühnenmusik von E.T.A. Hoffmann ; Ballettmusik "Arlequin" / E.T.A. Hoffmann ; hrsg. aus dem Nachlaß von Friedrich Schnapp ; unter Mitarbeit von Gerhard Allroggen und Michael Kohlhäufl von Thomas Kohlhase.

See **Schulz, J. A. P. 1747-1800.** Lieder im Volkston / Johann Abraham Peter Schulz ; herausgegeben von Walther Dürr und Stefanie Steiner unter Mitarbeit von Michael Kohlhäufl.

Köhs, Andreas.
See **Telemann, Georg Philipp, 1681-1767.** [Cantatas. Selections] Französischer Jahrgang : Kantaten von Neujahr bis zum Sonntag Sexagesimae und dem Fest Mariae Reinigung / Georg Philipp Telemann ; herausgegeben von Ute Poetzsch-Seban.

Kolb, Tom.
Music theory / Tom Kolb. — Hal Leonard
787.87076   013299202

Kolokolchik
See **Davies, Bryan.** Kolokolchik

Koncert e-moll op. 11 na fortepian i orkiestrę
See **Chopin, Frédéric, 1810-1849.** [Concertos, piano, orchestra, no. 1, op. 11, E minor] Koncert e-moll op. 11 na fortepian i orkiestrę

Koncert f-moll op. 21 na fortepian i orkiestrę
See **Chopin, Frédéric, 1810-1849.** [Concertos, piano, orchestra, no. 2, op. 21, F minor] Koncert f-moll op. 21 na fortepian i orkiestrę

Kongsted, Ole, 1943-
See **Bertolusi, Vincenzo, ca. 1550-1607 or 8.** [Sacrae cantiones, libro 1o] Sacrarum cantionum : 1601 / Vincentius Bertholusius ; edgivet af = herausgegeben von = edited by Ole Kongsted.

Konrad, Ulrich.
See **Mozart, Wolfgang Amadeus, 1756-1791.** [Symphonies, K. 551, C major] Sinfonie in C, KV 551 : "Jupiter" / Wolfgang Amadeus Mozart ; Ulrich Konrad, commentary.

Konzert F-Dur für Harfe oder Cembalo, 2 Violinen, Viola und Violoncello
See **Hertel, Johann Wilhelm, 1727-1789.** [Concertos, harp, string orchestra, F major; arr.] Konzert F-Dur für Harfe oder Cembalo, 2 Violinen, Viola und Violoncello

Konzert pro smyčcovy kvartet a dechový orchestr
See **Schulhoff, Ervín, 1894-1942.** [Concertos, string quartet, band] Konzert pro smyčcovy kvartet a dechový orchestr

Konzertante Kammermusiken 1
See **Hindemith, Paul, 1895-1963.** [Kammermusik, no. 1] Konzertante Kammermusiken 1

Kostujak, Wolfgang, 1968-
See **Telemann, Georg Philipp, 1681-1767.** [Concertos, violins (2), viola, continuo, TWV 43:G8, G major] Concerto in G-Dur für 2 Violinen, Viola und Basso continuo = Concerto in G major for 2 violins, viola and basso continuo, TWV 43:G8 / Georg Philipp Telemann ; herausgegeben von Bernhard Päuler ; Continuo-Aussetzung von Wolfgang Kostujak.

Kotnowska, Jadwiga.
See **Thistle & minuet :** 16 easy pieces from the Scottish Baroque for violin (or flute or oboe), keyboard, and optional cello (or bassoon) = 16 einfache Stücke aus der schottischen Barockzeit für Violine (oder Flöte oder Oboe), Tasteninstrument und Cello (oder Fagott) ad libitum = 16 pièces faciles du Baroque écossais pour violon (ou flûte ou hautbois), clavier et violoncelle (ou basson) facultatif / edited by David Johnson.

Kozeluch, Leopold, 1747-1818.
See **Thomson, Mr. 1757-1851.** [Select collection of original Scotish airs] Scottish songs : for George Thomson : 32 schottische Lieder für 1-2 Singstimmen, Violine, Violoncello und Klavier / [music by] Ignaz Pleyel] ; [edited by] Marjorie Rycroft.

Kramer, Ulrich.
See **Gurre-Lieder :** für Soli, Chor und Orchester : kritischer Bericht / Arnold Schönberg ; [Text] von Jens Peter Jacobsen (deutsch von Robert Franz Arnold) ; herausgegeben von Ulrich Krämer.

Kraus, Detlef, 1919-2008.
See **Liszt, Franz, 1811-1886.** [Piano music. Selections] Etudes d'exécution transcendante : mit = with = avec Grandes etudes 2 & 7 / Franz Liszt ; nach den Quellen herausgegeben und mit Hinweisen zur Interpretation versehen von Christian Ubber ; Fingersätze von Detlef Kraus.

Kraus, Georg.
See **Strauss, Johann, 1825-1899.** [Nachtigall-Polka; arr.] Nachtigall-Polka : op. 222 / Johann Strauss (Sohn) ; [herausgegeben von] Isabella Sommer.

Kremers, Klaus-Norbert, 1962-
See **Bartoli, Giuseppe, 1739-1801.** Messa a tre voci con stromenti / Giuseppe Bartoli.

Kretzmer, Herbert.
See **Schönberg, Claude-Michel.** [Misérables. Vocal score. English. Selections] Les Misérables : Boublil and Schönberg's legendary musical : in concert : piano, vocal, guitar / music by Claude-Michel Schönberg.

Kreutzer sonata
See **Beethoven, Ludwig van, 1770-1827.** [Sonatas, violin, piano, no. 9, op. 47, A major; arr.] Kreutzer sonata

Kreutzer, Rodolphe, 1766-1831.
[Quintets, oboe, violins, viola, violoncello, C major] — Grand quintette : for oboe, two violins, viola and cello / by Rodolphe Kreutzer. — Phylloscopus Publications
785.44195   013188886

[Kreuz an der Ostsee]
See **Hoffmann, E. T. A. 1776-1822.** [Kreuz an der Ostsee]

Krieger, Noam A.
See **Lully, Jean Baptiste, 1632-1687** [Armide. *Vocal score*] Armide : tragédie en musique / Jean-Baptiste Lully ; édition de Lois Rosow ; réduction clavier-chant, Noam A. Krieger.

See **Lully, Jean Baptiste, 1632-1687** [Ballets. *Vocal scores. Selections*] Ballet des saisons ; Les amours déguisés ; Ballet royal de Flore / Jean-Baptiste Lully ; édition [par Ballet des saisons] de James P. Cassaro ; édition [par Les amours déguisés] de James R. Anthony et Rebecca Harris-Warrick ; édition [par Ballet royal de flore] d'Albert Cohen ; réduction clavier-chant, Noam A. Krieger.

See **Lully, Jean Baptiste, 1632-1687.** [Monsieur de Pourceaugnac. *Vocal score*] Monsieur de Pourceaugnac : (Le divertissement de Chambord) ; Le bourgeois gentilhomme : comédie-ballet / Jean-Baptiste Lully/Molière ; [Monsieur de Pourceaugnac] édition de Jérôme de La Gorce ; [Le bourgeois gentilhomme] édition de Herbert Schneider ; réduction clavier-chant, Noam A. Krieger.

Krouwel, Juliet.
Slow down Moses! : for SATB (unaccompanied) / words by Cecily Taylor [based on Exodus 18:13-18] ; music by Juliet Krouwel. — *Stainer & Bell*
782.5253   013222612

Krstulović, Zoran.
See **Novak, Janez Krstnik, ca. 1756-1833.** Figaro ; Cantate zum Geburts oder Namensfeste einer Mutter / Janez Krstnik Novak ; transkribirala in revidirala = transcription and critical edition by Aleš Nagode (Figaro), Zoran Krstulović (Cantate).

Krylov, Ivan Andreevich, *1768-1844*
See **Shostakovich, Dmitrii Dmitrievich, 1906-1975.** [Vocal music. *Selections*] Dve basni I.A. Krylova, dli︠a︡ met︠s︡so-soprano, zhenskogo khora (met︠s︡so-soprano) i orkestra, soch. 4 ; Shest' romansov na slova i︠a︡ponskikh poėtov, dl i︠a︡ tenora s orkestrom, soch. 21 ; Tri romansa na slova A.S. Pushkina, dli︠a︡ basa i kamernogo orkestra, soch. 46a / Dmitrii Shostakovich ; obshchai︠a︡ redakt︠s︡ii︠a︡ i poi︠a︡snitel'nai︠a︡ stat'i︠a︡ Manashira I︠A︡kubova.

Kube, Michael, *1968-*
See **Schubert, Franz, 1797-1828.** [Vocal music. *Selections*] Mehrstimmige Gesänge für gemischte Stimmen. Teil b / [Franz Schubert] ; vorgelegt von Dietrich Berke und Michael Kube.

Küchler, Johann, *1738-1790*
[Quartets, clarinet, bassoon, violin, viola, op. 1. No. 2] — Quatuor concertant op. 1, no. 2, for clarinet in B♭, or oboe, violin, viola and bassoon or cello / by Johann Küchler. — *Phylloscopus Publications*
785.44194   013189015

Kupelwieser, Josef.
See **Schubert, Franz, 1797-1828.** Fierabras / Franz Schubert.

Kurpiński, Karol, *1785-1857*.
[Nocturnes, bassoon, horn, viola, op. 16] — Nocturne, op. 16 : for viola, horn in F and bassoon / by C. Kurpinsky. — *Phylloscopus Publications*
785.4219318966   013472925

[Kurskie pesni]
See **Sviridov, Georgii Vasil'evich, 1915-1998.** [Kurskie pesni]

Kurskie pesni
See **Sviridov, Georgii Vasil'evich, 1915-1998.** [Kurskie pesni] Kurskie pesni

Kurtág, György.
Az hit : für Violoncello solo (1998) / György Kurtág. — *Universal Edition*
787.4   013807387

Küthen, Hans-Werner.
See **Beethoven, Ludwig van, 1770-1827.** [Concertos, violin, orchestra, op. 61, D major; *arr.*] Klavierkonzert Opus 61a : nach dem Violinkonzert Opus 61 = Piano concerto op. 61a : after the Violin concerto op. 61 / Ludwig van Beethoven ; herausgegeben von Hans-Werner Küthen ; Fingersatz von Klaus Schilde ; Klavierauszug von Jürgen Sommer ; Kadenzen vom Komponisten.

Kwaysser, Marie.
See **Fibich, Zdeněk, 1850-1900.** [Štědrý den. *Polyglot*] Štědrý den ; Vodník : melodramy = Der Heilige Abend ; Der Wassermann : Melodramen = Christmas eve ; The water sprite : melodramas : recitazione e piano / Zdeněk Fibich ; text Karel Jaromír Erben ; deutsche Übersetzung Marie Kwaysser und Eduard Albert ; English translation Judith Mabary.

La Gorce, Jérôme de.
See **Lully, Jean Baptiste, 1632-1687.** [Monsieur de Pourceaugnac. *Vocal score*] Monsieur de Pourceaugnac : (Le divertissement de Chambord) ; Le bourgeois gentilhomme : comédie-ballet / Jean-Baptiste Lully/Molière ; [Monsieur de Pourceaugnac] édition de Jérôme de La Gorce ; [Le bourgeois gentilhomme] édition de Herbert Schneider ; réduction clavier-chant, Noam A. Krieger.

Labyrinthus sonoris
See **Tisné, Antoine.** Labyrinthus sonoris

Lachenmann, Helmut.
[Consolation, no. 2] — Consolation II : (Wessobrunner Gebet) : für 16 Singstimmen / Helmut Lachenmann. — *Breitkopf & Härtel*
782.5   014798262

Nun : Musik für Flöte, Posaune, Männerstimmen und Orchester : Neufassung 2003 = Music for flute, trombone, male voices, and orchestra : revised version 2003 / Helmut Lachenmann. — *Breitkopf & Härtel*
783.188   014457020

Lady Erskine canzonettas
See **Fesch, Willem de, 1687-1761.** [Canzonette ed arie, violin, continuo acc.] Lady Erskine canzonettas

LaFleur, Bill.
See **The end of all things to come** / Mudvayne ; transcribed by Danny Begelman, Bill LaFleur and Greg Tribbett.

Lambea Castro, Mariano.
See **Cancionero poético-musical hispánico de Lisboa** / introducción y edición crítica de Mariano Lambea y Lola Josa.

Lambert, Constant, *1905-1951*.
[Concertos, piano, instrumental ensemble, (1924)] — Concerto (1924), for piano solo, 2 trumpets, strings and timpani / Constant Lambert ; edited, arranged and orchestrated from the composer's original 2 piano score by Edward Shipley and Giles Easterbrook. — *Maecenas Music*
784.3262186   013422549

Prize fight : (1924 rev. '27) : ballet in one act for small orchestra / Constant Lambert. — *Maecenas Music*
784.21556   013193732

[Lambeth choirbook.]
The Arundel choirbook : London, Lambeth Palace Library, MS 1 : a facsimile and introduction / introduction by David Skinner. — *Roxburghe Club*
782.53232   013216740

Lament
See **Nathan, Simon, 1988 or 9-** Lament

Lamentations I & II
See **Tallis, Thomas, ca. 1505-1585.** [Lamentations, no. 1] Lamentations I & II

[Lamentations, no. 1]
See **Tallis, Thomas, ca. 1505-1585.** [Lamentations, no. 1]

[Lamento d'Arianna (Aria)]
See **Monteverdi, Claudio, 1567-1643.** [Lamento d'Arianna (Aria)]

Lamento d'Arianna, and addendum
See **Monteverdi, Claudio, 1567-1643.** [Lamento d'Arianna (Aria)] Lamento d'Arianna, and addendum

Lamento di Tristano
See **Riehm, Rolf, 1937-** Lamento di Tristano

The lamplighters
See **Portman, Rachel.** [Little prince. Lamplighters; *arr.*] The lamplighters

Landesverband Evangelischer Kirchenchöre in Rheinland.
See **Glory to God** : Englische Chormusik aus fünf Jahrhunderten / herausgegeben von Hans Wülfing für den Landesverband ev. Kirchenchöre im Rheinland in Zusammenarbeit mit dem Verband ev. Kirchenchöre Deutschlands.

Lane, Liz.
See **Fanshawe, David, 1942-** [African Sanctus (Musical work). Lord's prayer; *arr.*] The Lord's prayer : from African sanctus / vocal arrangement by the composer, David Fanshawe ; brass band arrangement by Liz Lane.

Lane, Philip.
See **Vaughan Williams, Ralph, 1872-1958** [Fantasia on Greensleeves; *arr*] Greensleeves : or, The king of love : a choral setting for female voice choir and piano or orchestra of "Fantasia on Greensleeves" / by R. Vaughan Williams ; arranged by Philip Lane.

See **Vaughan Williams, Ralph, 1872-1958** [Fantasia on Greensleeves; *arr.*] Greensleeves : or, The king of love : a choral setting for mixed voice choir and piano or orchestra of "Fantasia on Greensleeves" / by R. Vaughan Williams ; arranged by Philip Lane.

Lange, Robert John.
See **Twain, Shania.** Greatest hits / Shania Twain.

Language, sex, violence, other?
See **Stereophonics.** Language, sex, violence, other?

Languia di bocca lusinghiera
See **Handel, George Frideric, 1685-1759.** Languia di bocca lusinghiera

Lanning, Jerry.
See **Vivaldi, Antonio, 1678-1741** [Selections; *arr.*] Vivaldi gold : the essential collection.

Largo from New World symphony
See **Dvořák, Antonín, 1841-1904.** [Symphonies, no. 9, op. 95, E minor. Largo; *arr.*] Largo from New World symphony

Larkin, Philip.
See **Previn, André, 1929-** [Songs (2004)] Four songs : for tenor and piano / André Previn ; texts by Philip Larkin and William Carlos Williams.

Larsen, Libby.
Is God, our endless day : an anthem for mixed choir (SATB), unaccompanied : for Trinity Sunday (A, B, C), Third Sunday after the Epiphany (A), Last Sunday after the Epiphany (C) / text by Julian of Norwich ; music by Libby Larsen. — *Oxford University Press*
782.5265   013472561

Eine kleine Snailmusik : for upper voices and contrabass / Libby Larsen. — *Oxford University Press*
782.7642   013196364

Lord, before this fleeting season : an anthem for mixed choir (SATB), unaccompanied : for the First Sunday of Advent (A, B, C) / text by MaryAnn Jindra ; music by Libby Larsen. — *Oxford University Press*
782.52651722   013472556

My Ántonia : seven songs for high voice and piano / Libby Larsen ; based on the novel by Willa Cather ; text adapted by Libby Larsen. — *Oxford University Press*
783.6642   013062653

[Trios, piano, strings] — Trio for violin, cello and piano / Libby Larsen. — *Oxford University Press*
785.28193   013324497

A young nun singing : for unaccompanied upper voices (SSA) / Libby Larsen. — *Oxford University Press*
782.642   013472566

Lasso, Orlando di, *1532-1594*.
[Motets. *Selections.*] — Cantiones quinque vocum (Munich, 1597) / Orlando and Ferdinand di Lasso. Cantiones sacrae sex vocibus (Munich, 1601) / Orlando and Rudolph di Lasso ; [both] edited by David Crook. — *A-R Editions*
782.526   013801776

[Motets. *Selections*] — Motets for three to twelve voices from Magnum Opus Musicum (Munich, 1604) / Orlando di Lasso ; edited by Peter Bergquist. — *A-R Editions*
782.526   013801786

[Mottetta typis nondum uspiam excusa] — Mottetta, sex vocum, typis nondum uspiam excusa (Munich, 1582) / edited by Rebecca Wagner Oettinger. — *A-R Editions*
782.526   013294495

See **Strungk, Delphin, 1601-1694.** [Organ music] Sämtliche Orgelwerke : Choralbearbeitungen, Toccata, Motettenkolorierungen = Complete organ works : chorale settings, toccata, motet intabulations / Delphin Strunck ; herausgegeben von Klaus Beckmann.

Lassus, Ferdinand de, *ca. 1560-1609*. Motets.
See **Lasso, Orlando di, 1532-1594.** [Motets. *Selections.*] Cantiones quinque vocum (Munich, 1597) / Orlando and Ferdinand di Lasso. Cantiones sacrae sex vocibus (Munich, 1601) / Orlando and Rudolph di Lasso ; [both] edited by David Crook.

The last rose of summer
The last rose of summer : for upper voices (SSA), flute and piano / [Irish air ; arr.] Earlene Rentz. — *Oxford University Press*
782.642   013050493

Latin preludes collection
See **Norton, Christopher, 1953-** Latin preludes collection

Laudate Dominum omnes gentes
See **Palestrina, Giovanni Pierluigi da, 1525?-1594.** [Motets (1572). Laudate Dominum omnes gentes] Laudate Dominum omnes gentes

|Laudate pueri|
See **Buxtehude, Dietrich, 1637-1707.** [Laudate pueri]

Laudate pueri Dominum
See **Buxtehude, Dietrich, 1637-1707.** [Laudate pueri] Laudate pueri Dominum

See **Palestrina, Giovanni Pierluigi da, 1525?-1594.** [Motets (1572). Laudate pueri] Laudate pueri Dominum

Lautenbuch des Wolff Christian von Harling, ca. 1618
See **Harling, Wolff Christian von.** [Lute music. *Selections*] Lautenbuch des Wolff Christian von Harling, ca. 1618

LAWA
See **Sadler, Kathryn.** LAWA

Lawes, William, *1602-1645*.
[Airs, viols (4), VdGS no. 306] — 2 aires nos. 306 & 110 : (TrTrBB) / William Lawes ; edited by Gordon Dodd. — *Viola da Gamba Society of Great Britain*
785.76194   013382498

[Airs, viols (4), VdGS no. 336] — 2 aires nos. 336 & 318 : (TrTr/ATB) / William Lawes ; edited by Gordon Dodd. — *Viola da Gamba Society of Great Britain*
785.76194   013382482

Lawes, William, *1602-1645*. Airs,
See **Lawes, William, 1602-1645.** [Airs, viols (4), VdGS no. 306] 2 aires nos. 306 & 110 : (TrTrBB) / William Lawes ; edited by Gordon Dodd.

See **Lawes, William, 1602-1645.** [Airs, viols (4), VdGS no. 336] 2 aires nos. 336 & 318 : (TrTr/ATB) / William Lawes ; edited by Gordon Dodd.

Le Fleming, Antony.
Encounters : for flute and piano / by Antony le Fleming. — *Phylloscopus Publications*
788.32   013472753

Le Huray, Peter.
See **Wilkinson, fl. 1579-1596.** O Lord, my God : verse anthem for SS/AATB with organ and/or viols / Thomas Wylkinson ; edited by Peter le Huray.

See **Wilkinson, fl. 1579-1596.** Praise the Lord, O ye his servants : verse anthem for SAATB with organ and/or viols / Thomas Wylkinson ; edited by Peter le Huray.

See **Wilkinson, fl. 1579-1596.** Preserve me, O Lord : verse anthem for SSATB with organ and/or viols / Thomas Wylkinson ; edited by Peter le Huray.

Le Valois d'Orville, Adrien-Joseph.
See **Rameau, Jean-Philippe, 1683-1764.** [Platée. *Vocal score*] Platée : ballet bouffon en un prologue et trois actes : version 1749, version 1745 (compléments) / [musique de Jean-Philippe Rameau] ; livret de Jacques Autreau ; révisé par Adrien-Joseph Valois d'Orville et Balot de Sovot ; édition de M. Elizabeth C. Barlet ; réduction clavier-chant de François Saint-Yves.

Leandre et Hero
See **Clérambault, Louis-Nicolas, 1676-1749.** [Cantates françoises, livre 2. Léandre et Héro] Leandre et Hero

Learning piano
See **Mach, Elyse.** Learning piano

Leavers, Greg.
See **Complete mission praise** / compiled by Peter Horrobin and Greg Leavers

See **Junior praise** / compiled by Phil Burt, Peter Horrobin and Greg Leavers.

Leavitt, Peggy.
See **Bisbee, B. Wayne.** Night song : 2-pt treble / [music by] B. Wayne Bisbee.

LeBrun, Francesca, *1756-1791*.
[Sonatas, violin, harpsichord, op. 2] — Six sonatas for the piano forte or harpsichord with an accompaniment for a violin, op. 2 / by Francesca LeBrun ; edited by Deborah Hayes. — *ClarNan Editions*
787.2183   014457021

Ledger, Philip.
Advent carol : for unison voices and keyboard / Philip Ledger. — *Encore Publications*
782.5281722   013382713

Bethlehem : for unison voices & keyboard [and percussion] / Philip Ledger ; words by Richard Pomfret. — *Encore Publications*
782.5281723   013225249

Gift of love : for solo, upper voices (SSA) & keyboard / Philip Ledger & David Miller ; words by Richard Pomfret. — *Encore Publications*
782.6265   013220448

Lie still and slumber : two lullabies for Christmas : for mixed voices and keyboard / Philip Ledger. — *Encore Publications*
782.5251723   013382722

See **Gibbons, Orlando, 1583-1625.** [Song 13; *arr.*] With grateful hearts : meditation for Remembrance Sunday : for mixed voices and organ / [Orlando Gibbons ; arr.] Philip Ledger.

See **Good Christian men, rejoice :** German carol In dulci jubilo arranged for mixed voices & organ / arranged by Philip Ledger.

Ledger, Philip. Hush you, my baby.
See **Ledger, Philip.** Lie still and slumber : two lullabies for Christmas : for mixed voices and keyboard / Philip Ledger.

Lee, Cedric.
See **Bach, Johann Sebastian, 1685-1750.** [Himmelskönig, sei willkommen. Leget euch dem Heiland unter] Aria, Leget euch dem Heiland unter : from cantata BWV 182 : for alto, recorder (or flute) and continuo / J.S. Bach.

See **Bach, Johann Sebastian, 1685-1750.** [Liebster Jesu, mein Verlangen. Hier in meines Vaters Stätte] Aria, Hier in meines Vaters Stätte : from cantata BWV 32 : for bass, violin and basso continuo / J.S. Bach.

See **Bernier, Nicolas, 1665-1734.** [Cantates françoises, 2e livre. Diane et Endimion] Diane et Endimion : cantata for soprano, bass & continuo / Nicolas Bernier.

See **Bouvard, François, 1683-1760.** La feste de Cloris : cantata for soprano, violin, flute, oboe, bassoon & continuo / François Bouvard.

See **Campra, André, 1660-1744.** [Cantates françoises, livre 1. Femmes] Les femmes : cantata for bass, two violins & continuo / André Campra.

See **Chi sà dove è speranza? :** cantata for soprano, oboe or recorder and continuo : an anonymous cantata from a manuscript in the Santini collection, Münster / attrib. A.D. Lignani.

See **Clérambault, Louis-Nicolas, 1676-1749.** [Cantates françoises, livre 2. Léandre et Héro] Leandre et Hero : cantata for soprano, flute, violin & continuo / Louis-Nicolas Clérambault.

See **Clérambault, Louis-Nicolas, 1676-1749.** [Cantates françoises, livre 3. Mort d'Hercule] La mort d'Hercule : cantata for bass, violin & continuo / Louis-Nicolas Clérambault.

See **Croft, William, 1678-1727.** By purling streams : (a song with hautboy) : for soprano, oboe/flute and continuo / William Croft.

See **Croft, William, 1678-1727.** [How charming is beauty] Songs with violins : for bass, two violins and basso continuo / William Croft.

See **Croft, William, 1678-1727.** [Musicus apparatus academicus. With noise of cannon. With noise of cannon] With noise of cannon : from the ode : for bass, two violins and basso continuo / William Croft.

See **Greber, Jakob, 1691-1731.** Fuori di sua capanna : cantata for alto, recorder & continuo ; Sinfonia a flauto solo : symphony for recorder and continuo / Jakob Greber.

See **Handel, George Frideric, 1685-1759.** [Acis and Galatea. O ruddier than the cherry] O ruddier than the cherry : recitative and aria from Acis and Galatea (HWV 49a) : for bass, recorder, two violins & continuo / G.F. Handel.

See **Handel, George Frideric, 1685-1759.** [Cantatas. *Selections*] Four cantatas from Rome, 1707 : for soprano and basso continuo / G.F. Handel.

See **Handel, George Frideric, 1685-1759.** [Cuopre tal volta il cielo] Cuopre tal volto il cielo : (HWV 98) : Italian cantata for bass, 2 violins and basso continuo / G.F. Handel.

See **Handel, George Frideric, 1685-1759.** Languia di bocca lusinghiera : (HWV 123) : recitative and aria for soprano, oboe, violin and basso continuo / G.F. Handel.

See **Handel, George Frideric, 1685-1759.** [Nell' Africane selve] Nell' Africane selve (HWV 136a) ; Dalla guerra amorosa (HWV 102[a]) : Italian cantatas for bass and basso continuo / G.F. Handel.

See **Handel, George Frideric, 1685-1759.** Spande ancor a mio dispetto : (HWV 165) : Italian cantata for bass, 2 violins and basso continuo / G.F. Handel.

See **Jeffreys, George, ca. 1610-1685.** [Duets, soprano, bass, continuo] Three dialogues : for soprano, bass and continuo / George Jeffreys.

See **Jeffreys, George, ca. 1610-1685.** [Songs. *Selections*] Three devotional songs : solo bass with bass continuo / George Jeffreys.

See **Jeffreys, George, ca. 1610-1685.** [With notes that are both loud and sweet] Two duets for basses : for voices and basso continuo / Jeffreys & Purcell.

See **Legrenzi, Giovanni, 1626-1690.** [Cantate e canzonette. *Selections*] A cantata & two canzonettas : for bass and basso continuo / Giovanni Legrenzi.

See **Legrenzi, Giovanni, 1626-1690.** [Cantate e canzonette. *Selections*] Three cantatas for bass and basso continuo / Giovanni Legrenzi.

See **Luzzaschi, Luzzasco, d. 1607.** [Madrigali per cantare et sonare. O dolcezze] O dolcezze amarissime d'amore : a tre soprani / Luzzasco Luzzaschi.

See **Mazzocchi, D. 1592-1665.** [Musiche sacre, e morali. Battaglia per espugnare Amore] Battaglia per espugnare Amore : concerto à 3 : for two sopranos, bass and basso continuo / Domenico Mazzocchi.

See **Mazzocchi, D. 1592-1665.** [Musiche sacre, e morali. Cangia miio cor] Cangia mio cor : si dee fuggire il diletto dannoso / Domenico Mazzocchi ; [words by] Abbate Bentivogli.

See **Mazzocchi, D. 1592-1665.** [Musiche sacre, e morali. Colombella, che di latte] Colombella, che di latte : sopra Maria, e Giesù / Domenico Mazzocchi ; [words by] Monsignor Ciampoli.

See **Mazzocchi, D. 1592-1665.** [Musiche sacre, e morali. Folle cor] Folle cor : breve è la vita nostra : aria a tre soprani / Domenico Mazzocchi ; [words by] Ottavio Tronsarelli.

See **Mazzocchi, D. 1592-1665.** [Musiche sacre, e morali. Piangete occhi, piangete] Piangete occhi, piangete : dovemo piangere la Passione di N. S. / Domenico Mazzocchi ; [words by] Girolamo Preti.

See **Mazzocchi, D. 1592-1665.** [Musiche sacre, e morali. Signor, non sotto l'ombra] Signor, non sotto l'ombra : eccitamento alle virtù / Domenico Mazzocchi ; [words by] Torquato Tasso.

See **Mazzocchi, D. 1592-1665.** [Songs. *Selections*] Three songs for solo bass / Domenico Mazzocchi.

See **Montéclair, Michel Pignolet de, 1667-1737.** [Cantatas, book 3. Tircis et Climene] Tircis et Climene : cantata for soprano, bass, violin/flute & continuo / M P de Montéclair.

See **Pepusch, John Christopher, 1667-1752.** [Death of Dido. Oh I feel the friendly blow] Aria, Oh I feel the friendly blow : from The death of Dido : for soprano, recorder, strings and continuo / J.C. Pepusch.

See **Pepusch, John Christopher, 1667-1752.** [English cantatas. *Selections*] Five cantatas with recorder : for soprano or tenor, recorder and continuo / J.C. Pepusch.

See **Purcell, Henry, 1659-1695.** [Fairy queen. Plaint] O, O let me weep! : for soprano, oboe (or recorder) and continuo : from Orpheus Britannicus / Henry Purcell.

See **Purcell, Henry, 1659-1695.** [Fairy queen. *Selections*] The four seasons in the Fairy queen : for soprano, alto, tenor, and bass solos, strings and continuo : from Orpheus Britannicus / Henry Purcell.

See **Purcell, Henry, 1659-1695.** [Soft notes and gently rais'd accent] Two songs with flutes : from Orpheus Britannicus / Henry Purcell.

See **Purcell, Henry, 1659-1695.** [Songs. *Selections*] Songs for bass solo : from Orpheus Britannicus / Henry Purcell.

See **Purcell, Henry, 1659-1695.** [Vocal music. *Selections*] 4 duets from Orpheus Britannicus : for soprano and bass with basso continuo / Henry Purcell.

See **Purcell, Henry, 1659-1695.** [Vocal music. *Selections*] Three songs with hautboys : from Orpheus Britannicus / Henry Purcell.

See **Rameau, Jean-Philippe, 1683-1764.** Aquilon et Orithie : cantata : for bass, violin & basso continuo / Jean-Philippe Rameau.

See **Rameau, Jean-Philippe, 1683-1764.** Thétis : cantata for bass, violin & basso continuo / Jean-Philippe Rameau.

Lee, Douglas A.
See **Bach, Carl Philipp Emanuel, 1714-1788** [Concertos, harpsichord, H. 242, F major] Arrangements of orchestral works I / Carl Philipp Emanuel Bach ; edited by Douglas A. Lee.

Leeds, Jordan.
See **Roberts, Jimmy.** [I love you, you're perfect, now change. *Vocal score. Selections*] I love you, you're perfect, now change : vocal selections / [book and lyrics by Joe Dipietro ; music by Jimmy Roberts ; with Jordan Leeds … [et al.]]

Leeson, Jane Eliza.
See **Tadman-Robins, Hilary.** Loving shepherd : for soprano solo, two-part upper voices and organ or piano / Hilary Tadman-Robins.

LeFanu, Nicola.
Amores : (2003) : 5 songs without words for horn and strings (33221 players min) / Nicola LeFanu. — *Maecenas Music*
784.728941896   013193882

Catena : for 11 solo strings : (2000) / Nicola Lefanu. — *Maecenas Music*
785.71991269   013193710

Lefébure-Wély, Louis James Alfred, *1817-1870*. Organiste moderne.
See **Three 'storm' pieces :** organ solo / edited by David Patrick.

Lefebvre de Saint-Marc, Charles Hugues, *1698-1769*.
See **Royer, Pancrace, 1705-1755.** Le pouvoir de l'Amour / Pancrace Royer ; édition de Lisa Goode Crawford ; avec la collaboration de Gérard Geay.

Legend, John.
Get lifted / John Legend ; piano/vocal arrangements by John Nicholas. — *Cherry Lane Music Company*
783.242164   013359497

Legenden
See **Kirchner, Theodor, 1823-1903.** Legenden

Legends of the bear
See **Wood, Gareth.** Legends of the bear

Legnani, Angelo Domenico, *1663-1700*.
See **Chi sà dove è speranza? :** cantata for soprano, oboe or recorder and continuo : an anonymous cantata from a manuscript in the Santini collection, Münster / attrib. A.D. Lignani.

Legrenzi, Giovanni, *1626-1690*.
[Cantate e canzonette. *Selections*] — A cantata & two canzonettas : for bass and basso continuo / Giovanni Legrenzi. — *Green Man Press*
783.8948   013597373

[Cantate e canzonette. *Selections*] — Three cantatas for bass and basso continuo / Giovanni Legrenzi. — *Green Man Press*
783.8948   013597308

[Dal calore agitato] — Two cantatas from the Munich ms. : for bass and basso continuo / Giovanni Legrenzi ; edited by Barbara Sachs. — *Green Man Press*
783.8948   013597388

Legrenzi, Giovanni, *1626-1690*. A piè d'eccelso monte.
See **Legrenzi, Giovanni, 1626-1690.** [Dal calore agitato] Two cantatas from the Munich ms. : for bass and basso continuo / Giovanni Legrenzi ; edited by Barbara Sachs.

Leibl, Carl, *1784-1870*.
[Masses, no. 3, E♭ major. *Vocal score*] — Messe Nr. 3 Es-Dur / Carl Leibl ; herausgegeben von Eberhard Metternich ; mit einem einführenden Text von Oliver Sperling ; Klavierauszug. — *Erstdruck.* — *Dohr*
782.53232   013801668

Leisinger, Ulrich.
See **Bach, Johann Sebastian, 1685-1750.** [Lobet Gott in seinen Reichen. *English & German*] Himmelfahrtsoratorium : Lobet Gott in seinen Reichen : BWV 11/BC D 9 : Oratorium Festo Ascensionis Christi : für Soli (SATB), Chor (SATB), 3 Trompeten, Pauken, 2 Traversflöten, 2 Oboen, 2 Violinen, Viola und Basso continuo = Oratorio for Ascension Day : Praise God on high in heaven : for soli (SATB), choir (SATB), 3 trumpets, timpani, 2 flutes, 2 oboes, 2 violins, viola, and basso continuo / Johann Sebastian Bach ; herausgegeben von Ulrich Leisinger ; English version by Henry S. Drinker.

See **Musik am Meininger Hofe** / herausgegeben von Ulrike Feld und Ulrich Leisinger.

Leland, John, *1754-1841.*
See **White, B. F. 1800-1879.** [O when shall I see Jesus; *arr.*] The morning trumpet : for unaccompanied lower voices / B.F. White ; arr. Mack Wilberg.

Lemaître, Edmond.
See **Debussy, Claude, 1862-1918** [Fantaisie, piano, orchestra] Fantaisie pour piano et orchestre (2e version) / Claude Debussy ; édition de Jean-Pierre Marty ; avec la collaboration de Denis Herlin et Edmond Lemaître.

Lemmens, Jaak Nikolaas, *1823-1881*. Grand fantasia.
See **Three 'storm' pieces** : organ solo / edited by David Patrick.

Lennon & McCartney
See **Lennon, John, 1940-1980.** [Songs. Selections] Lennon & McCartney

Lennon, John, *1940-1980*.
[All you need is love; *arr.*] — All you need is love : the 1967 #1 pop hit by The Beatles : [for 2-part and piano] / words and music by John Lennon and Paul McCartney ; arranged by Alan Billingsley. — *Hal Leonard*
782.542166   013211851

[All you need is love; *arr.*] — All you need is love : the 1967 #1 pop hit by The Beatles : [for SAB and piano] / words and music by John Lennon and Paul McCartney ; arranged by Alan Billingsley. — *Hal Leonard*
782.542166   013211842

[All you need is love; *arr.*] — All you need is love : the 1967 #1 pop hit by The Beatles : [for SATB and piano] / words and music by John Lennon and Paul McCartney ; arranged by Alan Billingsley. — *Hal Leonard*
782.542166   013211833

[Fool on the hill; *arr.*] — The fool on the hill : [for SAB and piano] / words and music by John Lennon and Paul McCartney ; recorded by Sergio Mendes ; arranged by Mac Huff. — *Hal Leonard*
782.542   013211808

[Fool on the hill; *arr.*] — The fool on the hill : [for SATB and piano] / words and music by John Lennon and Paul McCartney ; recorded by Sergio Mendes ; arranged by Mac Huff. — *Hal Leonard*
782.542   013211798

[Fool on the hill; *arr.*] — The fool on the hill : [for SSA and piano] / words and music by John Lennon and Paul McCartney ; recorded by Sergio Mendes ; arranged by Mac Huff. — *Hal Leonard*
782.642   013211827

[Songs. *Selections*] — Beatles love songs / words and music by John Lennon and Paul McCartney ; arranged by Ed Lojeski ; recorded by The Beatles. — *Hal Leonard*
782.542166   013220387

[Songs. *Selections*] — Beatles love songs / words and music by John Lennon and Paul McCartney ; arranged by Ed Lojeski ; recorded by The Beatles. — *Hal Leonard*
782.542166   013222742

[Songs. *Selections*] — Lennon & McCartney : guitar play-along. — *Hal Leonard*
783.242166   013191084

[Songs. *Selections*] — Ticket to ride : a collection of Lennon and McCartney arrangements / The Swingle Singers. — *Contemporary A Cappella Publishing*
782.542166   013222593

See **Play piano with— John Lennon … [et al.]**

See **[Songs. *Selections*] The Beatles : note-for-note.**

See **[Songs. *Selections*] Play bass with— The Beatles.**

Lenot, Jacques.
[Preludes, piano] — 24 préludes pour piano / Jacques Lenot. — *L'Oiseau Prophète*
786.218928   013771134

Leonarda, Isabella, *1620-1704*.
[Motets, bass, continuo. *Selections*] — Ausgewählte Bassmotetten für Bass und B.c. = Selected bass motets for bass and b.c. / Isabella Leonarda ; [edited by Dragan Karolic] — *Moderne kritische Ed.* — *Furore*
783.8926   013623496

Vespro a cappella della Beata Vergine e motetti concertati : opera ottava (1678) / Isabella Leonarda ; a cura di Paolo Monticelli. — *Libreria Musicale Italiana*
782.526   013739259

Leonardo, da Vinci, *1452-1519*.
See **Furrer, Beat, 1954-** Stimmen : für Chor und 4 Schlagzeuger : 1996 / Beat Furrer.

Lepik, Tarmo, *1946-2001*.
[Piano music. *Selections*] — Klaverimuusika = Works for piano solo / Tarmo Lepik. — *SP Muusikaprojekt*
786.2   013750193

Leroy-Biget, Arlette.
See **Flûte traversière** : France, 1800-1860 : méthodes, traités, périodiques / sept volumes réalisés par Arlette Biget et Michel Giboureau.

Let's make music fun.
See **Diamond, Eileen.** Let's make music fun.

Let's rumba
See **Cunliffe, Simon.** Let's rumba

Levin, Robert D.
See **Mozart, Wolfgang Amadeus, 1756-1791.** [Masses, K. 427, C minor] Missa in c, KV 427 (417a), per soli (SSTB), coro (SATB), flauto, 2 oboi, 2 fagotti, 2 corni, 2 clarini, 3 tromboni, timpani, 2 violini, viola e basso continuo (Violoncello / contrabbasso, organo) / Wolfgang Amadeus Mozart ; ergänzt und herausgegeben von Robert D. Levin.

Levy, Mark.
See **Gibbons, Orlando, 1583-1625.** [Pavans, voices (5), H. 30] Pavane, De la Roye : (TrTrTTB) / Orlando Gibbons ; edited & completed by Mark Levy.

Lewis, Anwen.
A— but no : (Aponniad) : (1992) : for tuba and piano / Anwen Lewis. — *Maecenas Music*
788.98   013422050

Lewis, Paul, *1943-*
Child's carol : for two-part choir or two solo voices with piano or harp / words by Helen Cresswell ; music by Paul Lewis. — *Roberton Publications, a part of Goodmusic Publishing*
782.6281723   013373065

Divertimento : flute, viola & harp / by Paul Lewis. — *Broadbent & Dunn*
785.441931852   013167535

[Rosa Mundi; *arr.*] — Rosa Mundi : a vocalise for vocal sextet or mixed voice choir (SSATBarB) / by Paul Lewis. — *Roberton Publications, a part of Goodmusic Publishing*
782.5   013373054

A Somerset garland. for flute, violin or harmonica and piano / by Paul Lewis. — *Broadbent & Dunn*
788.32   013374676

Spring suite : flute, optional 'cello and piano or harmonica and piano / Paul Lewis. — *Broadbent & Dunn*
788.321858   013374699

Leyendecker, Ulrich, *1946-*
Pensées sur un prélude : Debussy-Variationen : für Orchester = Debussy-variations : for orchestra / Ulrich Leyendecker. — *H. Sikorski*
784.21825   013750198

Liani, Davide, *1921-2005*.
See **Schütz, Heinrich, 1585-1672.** [Psalmen Davids (1619). 100. Psalm. *Italian & German*] Salmo 100 : per doppio coro a voci miste o per coro e quartetto di ottoni : Lodi al Signore = "Jauchzet dem Herren" / Heinrich Schütz ; revisione e versione italiana di Davide Liani.

Liberto, Giuseppe.
Missa "Pie Iesu Domine" : in exsequiis Ioannis Pauli PP. II / Giuseppe Liberto. — *Libreria editrice vaticana*
782.53232   013750206

Te Deum laudamus / Giuseppe Liberto. — *Libreria Editrice Vaticana*
782.5324   013750207

Libro secondo (1615)
See **Trabaci, Giovanni Maria, 1580 (ca.)-1647.** [Ricercate, 2o libro] Libro secondo (1615)

[Lichfield Service]
See **Vann, Stanley.** [Lichfield Service]

Lie still and slumber
See **Ledger, Philip.** Lie still and slumber

[Liebster Jesu, mein Verlangen. Hier in meines Vaters Stätte]
See **Bach, Johann Sebastian, 1685-1750.** [Liebster Jesu, mein Verlangen. Hier in meines Vaters Stätte]

Lieder im Volkston
See **Schulz, J. A. P. 1747-1800.** Lieder im Volkston

Life in slow motion
See **Gray, David, 1970-** Life in slow motion

[Light and water]
See **Samuel, Rhian.** [Light and water]

Like as the hart
See **Goode, David, organist.** Like as the hart

Like lightnings
See **Tann, Hilary.** Like lightnings

Lilburn, Douglas, *1915-2001*.
A birthday offering : orchestra / Douglas Lilburn. — *Waiteata Music Press*
784.2   013731870

Lim, Liza, *1966-*
Ecstatic architecture : for large orchestra,
2002-2004 / Liza Lim. — *Ricordi*
784.2   013771131

Lindberg, Magnus, *1958-*
[Concertos, piano, orchestra, no. 1] — Piano
concerto, 1990, revised 1994 : for piano and
orchestra / Magnus Lindberg. — *Edition
Wilhelm Hansen*
784.262186   013750211

Corrente : for chamber ensemble : 1992 /
Magnus Lindberg. — *Chester Music*
785.32199   013222829

Gran duo : for woodwind and brass / Magnus
Lindberg. — *Boosey & Hawkes*
785.43199   013214771

Lindblad, Adolf Fredrik, *1801-1878.*
[Symphonies, no. 2, D major] — Symfoni
D-dur = Symphony, D major / Adolf Fredrik
Lindblad ; utgiven av Owe Ander. — *Edition
Reimers*
784.2184   014619868

Linley, Thomas, *1733-1795.*
[Robinson Crusoe. *Vocal score*] — The
pantomine [or rather, pantomime] of Robinson
Crusoe : (1781) / Thomas Linley ; wordbook by
Richard Brinsley Sheridan ; edited by Robert
Hoskins. — *Artaria Editions*
782.14   013750212

Linn, Jennifer.
See **Clementi, Muzio, 1752-1832.** [Progressive
sonatinas] Sonatinas, opus 36 / Clementi ; edited
by Jennifer Linn.

See **Schumann, Robert, 1810-1856.** [Album für
die Jugend. *Selections*] Selections from Album
for the young : opus 68 / Schumann ; edited by
Jennifer Linn.

The lion and the mouse
See **McAlister, Clark.** The lion and the mouse

Lions and oxen
See **Martinson, Joel.** Lions and oxen

Lisa Lân
Lisa Lân = Lisa fair : traditional Welsh
folk-song arranged for SSAA choir and piano /
by Jayne Davics ; English text by Rhian Davies.
— *Roberton Publications*
782.64216209429   013193393

Liszt, Franz, *1811-1886.*
[Piano music. *Selections*] — Etudes d'exécution
transcendante : mit = with = avec Grandes
etudes 2 & 7 / Franz Liszt ; nach den Quellen
herausgegeben und mit Hinweisen zur
Interpretation versehen von Christian Ubber ;
Fingersätze von Detlef Kraus. — *Erste Aufl.* —
Wiener Urtext Edition
786.218949   013222423

[Piano music. *Selections*] — Freie
Bearbeitungen. XIII = Free arrangements. XIII /
Franz Liszt ; herausgegeben von Péter Bozó,
Adrienne Kaczmarczyk. — *Editio Musica*
786.2   013821983

Liszt, Franz, *1811-1886.* **Études d'exécution
transcendante.**
See **Liszt, Franz, 1811-1886.** [Piano music.
Selections] Etudes d'exécution transcendante :
mit = with = avec Grandes etudes 2 & 7 / Franz
Liszt ; nach den Quellen herausgegeben und mit
Hinweisen zur Interpretation versehen von
Christian Ubber ; Fingersätze von Detlef Kraus.

Litaniae de venerabili altaris Sacramento
See **Adlgasser, Anton Cajetan, 1729-1777.**
Litaniae de venerabili altaris Sacramento

Little cuckoo
Little cuckoo = (Cwcw fach) : SATB a cappella /
arranged by Nigel E. Jones. — *Boosey &
Hawkes*
782.542162009429   013243888

[Little prince. Birds; *arr.***]**
See **Portman, Rachel.** [Little prince. Birds; *arr.*]

[Little prince. Lamplighters; *arr.***]**
See **Portman, Rachel.** [Little prince.
Lamplighters; *arr.*]

[Little prince. Look at the stars; *arr.***]**
See **Portman, Rachel.** [Little prince. Look at
the stars; *arr.*]

[Little prince. Roses; *arr.***]**
See **Portman, Rachel.** [Little prince. Roses;
arr.]

[Little prince. Stars; *arr.***]**
See **Portman, Rachel.** [Little prince. Stars; *arr.*]

The little shepherd
See **Debussy, Claude, 1862-1918** [Children's
corner. Little shepherd; *arr.*] The little shepherd

Little suite for strings
See **Sculthorpe, Peter, 1929-** Little suite for
strings

Live with me, and be my love
See **Unterseher, Reginald.** Live with me, and be
my love

Liza Minnelli
Liza Minnelli : 15 timeless classics : piano/vocal
arrangements with guitar chord boxes. —
International Music Publications
783.242164   013226564

El lladre reformat
See **Gammie, Ian.** El lladre reformat

Llorens, José M.
See **Guerrero, Francisco, 1528?-1599.** [Motets.
Selections] Motetes de tempore et alia :
LXXVI-CVII / Francisco Guerrero ;
introducción, estudio y transcripción, Josep M.
Llorens i Cisteró ; semitonía y estructuras
modales, Karl H. Müller-Lancé.

Lloyd Webber, Andrew, *1948-*
[Jesus Christ superstar. I don't know how to love
him; *arr.*] — I don't know how to love him :
grade 2 / Tim Rice & Andrew Lloyd Webber ;
arr. Rob Wiffin. — *Studio Music*
784.8   013376747

[Musicals. *Selections; arr.*] — Andrew Lloyd
Webber audition songbook : ten great show
songs, ideal for auditions. — *Female ed.* —
Wise
783.642   013222757

[Musicals. *Selections; arr.*] — Andrew Lloyd
Webber audition songbook : ten great show
songs, ideal for auditions. — *Male ed.* — *Wise*
783.842   013220095

[Musicals. *Selections; arr.*] — Andrew Lloyd
Webber favorites. — *Hal Leonard*
783.242164   013383285

[Musicals. *Selections; arr.*] — Andrew Lloyd
Webber showstoppers : playalong for alto
saxophone. — *Wise*
788.73164   013193457

[Musicals. *Selections; arr.*] — Andrew Lloyd
Webber showstoppers : playalong for clarinet.
— *Wise*
788.62164   013193475

[Musicals. *Selections; arr.*] — Andrew Lloyd
Webber showstoppers : playalong for flute. —
Wise
788.32164   013193433

[Musicals. *Selections; arr.*] — Andrew Lloyd
Webber showstoppers : playalong for trumpet.
— *Wise*
788.92164   013193486

[Musicals. *Selections; arr.*] — Andrew Lloyd
Webber showstoppers : playalong for violin. —
Wise
787.2164   013193460

Lo, how a rose e'er blooming
See **Rentz, Earlene.** Lo, how a rose e'er
blooming

Lobe den Herren;
See **Mills, Alan, 1964-** A wedding postlude : on
the chorale Lobe den Herren (Praise to the
Lord) : for organ solo / Alan Mills. — *ECS Pub.*

[Lobet Gott in seinen Reichen. *English &
German***]**
See **Bach, Johann Sebastian, 1685-1750.**
[Lobet Gott in seinen Reichen. *English &
German*]

Lobet, ihr Knechte des Herrn
See **Herbst, Johann Andreas, 1588-1666**
Lobet, ihr Knechte des Herrn

Locatelli, Pietro Antonio, *1695-1764.*
[Arte del violino. Capricci] — Ventiquattro
capricci per violino solo [op. III] / Pietro
Antonio Locatelli ; in base all'edizione a cura di
Albert Dunning ; con diteggiature ed esercizi
preparatori di Enzo Porta. — *Schott*
787.218949   013312873

Loch Lomond
Loch Lomond : tenor solo & SSAATBB :
Scottish traditional / arranged by Jonathan
Rathbone. — *Edition Peters*
782.542   013304945

Lockwood, Robert In the bleak mid-winter.
See **Three carols for Christmas :** for
unaccompanied mixed choir (SATB).

Loewe, Carl, *1796-1869*
Was Gott tut, das ist wohlgetan : Kantate für
Solisten SAB, 4 st. gem. Chor SATB, und
Kammerorchester (2 Klarinetten, 2 Fagotti und
Streicher) / Carl Loewe ; herausgegeben von
Norbert Klose. — *Erstausgabe.* — *Renaissance
Musikverlag*
782.524   013750217

Lofthouse, Jane.
See **Cornish folk songs :** for piano / researched
by Jane Lofthouse ; arranged by Colin Mawby.

Lojeski, Ed.
See **Collins, Phil.** [Look through my eyes; *arr.*]
Look through my eyes : from Walt Disney
Pictures' Brother Bear : SAB / words and music
by Phil Collins ; arranged by Ed Lojeski.

See **Collins, Phil.** [Look through my eyes; *arr.*]
Look through my eyes : from Walt Disney
Pictures' Brother Bear : SATB / words and
music by Phil Collins ; arranged by Ed Lojeski.

See **Lennon, John, 1940-1980.** [Songs.
Selections] Beatles love songs / words and
music by John Lennon and Paul McCartney ;
arranged by Ed Lojeski ; recorded by The
Beatles.

Lole, Simon.
For all thy saints, O Lord / music: Simon Lole ;
words: Richard Mant. — *Encore Publications*
782.527   013416381

My beloved is mine / music: Simon Lole ;
words: Francis Quarles. — *Encore Publications*
782.5265   013416520

A Sarum blessing / Simon Lole ; words: Sarum
Breviary. — *Encore Publications*
782.5265   013416538

Ubi caritas et amor / Simon Lole. — *Encore Publications*
782.626   013416531

Lonati, Carlo Ambrogio.
[Sonatas, violin, continuo (1701)] — XII sonate a violino solo e basso : ms. Salzburg, Milano 1701 / Carlo Ambrogio Lonati. — *Studio per edizioni scelte*
787.2183   013750218

London College of Music and Media (*Great Britain*)
See **Richards, Jack, 1947-** Snare drum : grades 5-8 / edited by Jack Richards and Andrew McBirnie ; additional editing by Aidan Geary.

See **Richards, Jack, 1947-** Timpani : grades 6 -8 / edited by Jack Richards and Andrew McBirnie.

London pageant
See **Binney, Malcolm.** London pageant

Londoner Sinfonien.
See **Haydn, Joseph, 1732-1809** [Symphonies. *Selections.*] Londoner Sinfonien.

Longfellow, Henry Wadsworth, *1807-1882*.
See **Skempton, Howard, 1947-** The flight of song : SATB a cappella / Howard Skempton.

Longueval, Antoine de, *fl. 1498-1525*.
Passio Domini nostri Jesu Christi : zu 4 Stimmen / Antoine de Longueval ; herausgegeben von Rainer Heyink. — *Möseler*
782.523   013714764

Look at the stars
See **Portman, Rachel.** [Little prince. Look at the stars; *arr.*] Look at the stars

Look through my eyes
See **Collins, Phil.** [Look through my eyes; *arr.*] Look through my eyes

[Look through my eyes; *arr.*]
See **Collins, Phil.** [Look through my eyes; *arr.*]

Lopez-Real, Carlos.
[Dig it. Clarinet(s)] — Dig it! : 7 cool tunes for clarinet(s) and piano with optional CD backing / Carolos Lopez-Real. — *Spartan Press*
788.62   013299083

[Dig it. Flute(s)] — Dig it! : 7 cool tunes for flute(s) and piano with optional CD backing / Carolos Lopez-Real. — *Spartan Press*
788.32   013203784

[Dig it. Saxophone(s)] — Dig it! : 7 cool tunes for saxophone(s) and piano with optional CD backing / Carolos Lopez-Real. — *Spartan Press*
788.7   013203852

[Dig it. Trumpet(s)] — Dig it! : 7 cool tunes for trumpet(s) and piano with optional CD backing / Carolos Lopez-Real. — *Spartan Press*
788.92   013299125

[Dig it. Violin(s)] — Dig it! : 7 cool tunes for violin(s) and piano with optional CD backing / Carolos Lopez-Real. — *Spartan Press*
787.2   013299138

The Lord at first did Adam make
See **Mills, Alan, 1964-** The Lord at first did Adam make

The Lord is risen
See **Rose, Barry, 1934-** The Lord is risen

Lord of all hopefulness
Lord of all hopefulness : for SATB chorus and organ / [arranged by] Barry Rose (2002). — *Novello & Co*
782.527   013505674

Lord, before this fleeting season
See **Larsen, Libby.** Lord, before this fleeting season

Lord, I have loved the habitation of thy house
See **Shephard, Richard, 1949-** Lord, I have loved the habitation of thy house

[Lord's prayer (1982). *Slavonic & English*]
See **Tavener, John.** [Lord's prayer (1982). *Slavonic & English*]

The Lord's prayer
See **Fanshawe, David, 1942-** [African Sanctus (Musical work). Lord's prayer; *arr.*] The Lord's prayer

See **Tavener, John.** [Lord's prayer (1982). *Slavonic & English*] The Lord's prayer

Lorriman, Howard.
[Divertimenti, winds (2005)] — Divertimento for wind nonet : (flute, 2 oboes, 2 clarinets in B♭, 2 horns in F & 2 bassoons) / by Howard Lorriman. — *Phylloscopus Publications*
785.431991852   013561727

Lostprophets (Musical group)
Start something / Lostprophets ; music transcriptions by Addi Booth and David Stocker. — *Hal Leonard*
783.242166   013169064

Love divine
Love divine : a collection of Victorian & Edwardian anthems : for mixed voice chorus / selected & edited by Barry Rose. — *Novello*
782.5265   013201787

Love songs
Love songs : piano, vocal, guitar. — *Hal Leonard*
783.242164   013219936

Loving shepherd
See **Tadman-Robins, Hilary.** Loving shepherd

Lowry, Robert, *1826-1899*. Marching to Zion.
See **Dicie, Don Michael.** [Nineteenth-century hymns. Marching to Zion] Three nineteenth-century hymns. 3, Marching to Zion : for lower voices (TTBB) and piano / [arranged by] Don Michael Dicie.

Loy, Felix.
See **Fesca, F. E. 1789-1826.** [Quartets, strings. *Selections*] Sechs ausgewählte Streichquartette / Friedrich Ernst Fesca ; herausgegeben von Markus Frei-Hauenschild unter Mitarbeit von Felix Loy.

Lu, Xun, *1881-1936*.
See **Zhou, Long, 1953-** [Wild grass; *arr.*] Wild grass : for viola / Zhou Long.

Lübeck, Vincent, *1654?-1740*.
[Keyboard music] — Neue Ausgabe sämtlicher Orgel- und Clavierwerke = New edition of the complete organ and keyboard works / Vincent Lübeck, Senior & Junior ; herausgegeben von Siegbert Rampe. — *Bärenreiter*
786   013602725

Lübeck, Vincent, *1684-1755*.
See **Lübeck, Vincent, 1654?-1740.** [Keyboard music] Neue Ausgabe sämtlicher Orgel- und Clavierwerke = New edition of the complete organ and keyboard works / Vincent Lübeck, Senior & Junior ; herausgegeben von Siegbert Rampe.

The lucky Viking
See **Spencer, Tim.** [Lucky Viking. *Selections*] The lucky Viking

See **Spencer, Tim.** The lucky Viking

[Lucky Viking. *Selections*]
See **Spencer, Tim.** [Lucky Viking. *Selections*]

Ludford, Nicholas, *ca. 1490-1557*.
[Vocal music. *Selections*] — Five- and six-part Masses ; and, Magnificat / [Nicholas Ludford] ; transcribed and edited by David Skinner. — *Published for the British Academy by Stainer and Bell*
782.53232   013433942

See **The Arundel choirbook** : London, Lambeth Palace Library, MS 1 : a facsimile and introduction / introduction by David Skinner.

Lüdtke, Joachim.
See **Harling, Wolff Christian von.** [Lute music. *Selections*] Lautenbuch des Wolff Christian von Harling, ca. 1618 / herausgegeben von Joachim Lüdtke.

Luk'ianchenko, P. V.
See **Sviridov, Georgiĭ Vasil'evich, 1915-1998.** [Kurskie pesni] Kurskie pesni ; Kurskie pesni ; Tri starinnye pesni kurskoĭ gubernii / Georgiĭ Sviridov ; tom podgotovlen P. V. Luk'ianchenko.

[Lullabies, voices]
See **Body, Jack, 1944-** [Lullabies, voices]

Lullaby
Lullaby = (Suo-gân) : 3-part treble / arranged by Nigel E. Jones. — *Boosey & Hawkes*
782.6642162009429   013243902

Lullaby for saxophone quartet
See **Bayliss, Colin.** Lullaby for saxophone quartet

Lullay, my liking
See **Pott, Francis, 1957-** Lullay, my liking

Lully, Jean Baptiste, *1632-1687*
[Armide. *Vocal score*] — Armide : tragédie en musique / Jean-Baptiste Lully ; édition de Lois Rosow ; réduction clavier-chant, Noam A. Krieger. — *G. Olms*
782.1   013775736

[Ballets. *Vocal scores. Selections*] — Ballet des saisons ; Les amours déguisés ; Ballet royal de Flore / Jean-Baptiste Lully ; édition [par Ballet des saisons] de James P. Cassaro ; édition [par Les amours déguisés] de James R. Anthony et Rebecca Harris-Warrick ; édition [par Ballet royal de flore] d'Albert Cohen ; réduction clavier-chant, Noam A. Krieger. — *G. Olms*
784.31556   013775846

Lully, Jean Baptiste, *1632-1687*.
[Monsieur de Pourceaugnac. *Vocal score*] — Monsieur de Pourceaugnac : (Le divertissement de Chambord) ; Le bourgeois gentilhomme : comédie-ballet / Jean-Baptiste Lully/Molière ; [Monsieur de Pourceaugnac] édition de Jérôme de La Gorce ; [Le bourgeois gentilhomme] édition de Herbert Schneider ; réduction clavier-chant, Noam A. Krieger. — *Georg Olms*
784.31556   013949776

Lully, Jean Baptiste, *1632-1687* Amours déguisés.
See **Lully, Jean Baptiste, 1632-1687** [Ballets. *Vocal scores. Selections*] Ballet des saisons ; Les amours déguisés ; Ballet royal de Flore / Jean-Baptiste Lully ; édition [par Ballet des saisons] de James P. Cassaro ; édition [par Les amours déguisés] de James R. Anthony et Rebecca Harris-Warrick ; édition [par Ballet royal de flore] d'Albert Cohen ; réduction clavier-chant, Noam A. Krieger.

Lully, Jean Baptiste, *1632-1687* **Bourgeois gentilhomme.**
See **Lully, Jean Baptiste, 1632-1687.**
[Monsieur de Pourceaugnac. *Vocal score*]
Monsieur de Pourceaugnac : (Le divertissement de Chambord) ; Le bourgeois gentilhomme : comédie-ballet / Jean-Baptiste Lully/Molière ; [Monsieur de Pourceaugnac] édition de Jérôme de La Gorce ; [Le bourgeois gentilhomme] édition de Herbert Schneider ; réduction clavier-chant, Noam A. Krieger.

Luna, Pablo, *1879-1942.*
El asombro de Damasco : zarzuela en dos actos / Pablo Luna ; libreto, Antonio Paso y Joaquín Abati ; edición crítica, Miguel Roa. — *Instituto Complutense de Ciencias Musicales*
782.12   014679583

Lupo, Joseph, *d. 1616.* **Pavan,**
See **Johnson, Robert, ca. 1500-ca. 1560.**
[Knell] A knell of Johnson / Robert Johnson. Pavan à 5 / Joseph Lupo ; edited by Virginia Brookes.

[**Lute music.** *Selections*]
See **Harling, Wolff Christian von.** [Lute music. *Selections*]

Lutosławski, Witold, *1913-1994.* **Recitativo e arioso.**
See **The violin** : a collection : new and recent repertoire for violin with piano accompaniment / Craig Armstrong … [et al.]

Luzzaschi, Luzzasco, *d. 1607.*
[Madrigali per cantare et sonare. O dolcezze] — O dolcezze amarissime d'amore : a tre soprani / Luzzasco Luzzaschi. — *Green Man Press*
783.136643   013613916

[Madrigals. *Selections*] — Il quarto libro de' madrigali a cinque voci (Ferrara, 1594) ; and, Madrigals published only in anthologies, 1583-1604 / Luzzasco Luzzaschi ; edited by Anthony Newcomb. — *A-R Editions*
782.543   014630289

Luzzaschi, Luzzasco, *d. 1607.* **Madrigals,**
See **Luzzaschi, Luzzasco,** *d. 1607.* [Madrigals. *Selections*] Il quarto libro de' madrigali a cinque voci (Ferrara, 1594) ; and, Madrigals published only in anthologies, 1583-1604 / Luzzasco Luzzaschi ; edited by Anthony Newcomb.

[**Má vlast. Vltava;** *arr.*]
See **Smetana, Bedřich, 1824-1884.** [Má vlast. Vltava; *arr.*]

Mabary, Judith.
See **Fibich, Zdeněk, 1850-1900.** [Štědrý den. *Polyglot*] Štědrý den ; Vodník : melodramy = Der Heilige Abend ; Der Wassermann = Christmas eve ; The water sprite : melodramas : recitazione e piano / Zdeněk Fibich ; text Karel Jaromír Erben ; deutsche Übersetzung Marie Kwaysser und Eduard Albert ; English translation Judith Mabary.

Macbeth.
See **Verdi, Giuseppe, 1813-1901.** [Macbeth. Ballo] Macbeth.

[**Macbeth. Ballo**]
See **Verdi, Giuseppe, 1813-1901.** [Macbeth. Ballo]

MacDonald, Malcolm, *1948-*
See **Rachmaninoff, Sergei, 1873-1943.** [Orchestra music. *Selections*] Symphonic dances ; 5 études-tableaux ; Vocalise [2 versions] / Serge Rachmaninoff.

See **Rachmaninoff, Sergei, 1873-1943.** [Symphonies, no. 3, op. 44, A minor] Symphony no.3, op. 44 / Serge Rachmaninoff.

Mach, Elyse.
Learning piano : piece by piece / Elyse Mach. — *Oxford University Press*
786.2193   013278617

Machella, Maurizio.
See **Hasse, Johann Adolf, 1699-1783.** [Concertos, keyboard instrument] Sei concerti per organo solo / Johann Adolph Hasse ; a cura di Maurizio Machella.

Mackay, Charles, *1814-1889.*
See **Elgar, Edward, 1857-1934.** [Rapid stream, voices (2)] The rapid stream ; The woodland stream / Edward Elgar ; edited by David Patrick.

Mackey, Joanna.
See **It was Christmas to us** : carol singing in Bamford through the 20th century / words, music and historical notes researched and transcribed by Joanna and Peter Mackey ; introduction by Ian Russell.

MacMillan, James, *1959-*
Chosen : for SAATTB and organ / James MacMillan ; words by Michael Symmons Roberts. — *Boosey & Hawkes*
782.5265   013192577

[**Madrigali per cantare et sonare. O dolcezze**]
See **Luzzaschi, Luzzasco, d. 1607.** [Madrigali per cantare et sonare. O dolcezze]

[**Madrigals, voices (5), book 1**]
See **Striggio, Alessandro, 1536 or 7-1592.** [Madrigals, voices (5), book 1]

[**Madrigals, voices (5), book 5**]
See **Ingegneri, Marc Antonio, 1535 or 6-1592.** [Madrigals, voices (5), book 5]

[**Madrigals.** *Selections*]
See **Luzzaschi, Luzzasco, d. 1607.** [Madrigals. *Selections*]

Maffei, Andrea, *1798-1885.*
See **Verdi, Giuseppe, 1813-1901.** I masnadieri : a tragic opera (in four acts) = melodramma (in quattro atti) / Giuseppe Verdi ; libretto by Andrea Maffei ; edited by Roberta Montemorra Marvin.

Mägi, Ester, *1922-*
[Quartets, strings, no. 2] — Streichquartett Nr. 2 / Ester Mägi. — *Eres Edition*
785.7194   013953476

Magic flute
See **Mozart, Wolfgang Amadeus, 1756-1791** [Zauberflöte. Ouverture; *arr.*] Magic flute

The magic tree
See **Hewitt, Daniel.** [Magic tree. *Selections*] The magic tree

See **Hewitt, Daniel.** The magic tree

[**Magic tree.** *Selections*]
See **Hewitt, Daniel.** [Magic tree. *Selections*]

Magnificat & Nunc dimittis
See **Andreas, Carolus.** Magnificat & Nunc dimittis

See **O'Regan, Tarik.** Magnificat & Nunc dimittis

Magnificat
See **Rathbone, Jonathan.** Magnificat

[**Magnificat and Nunc dimittis (Collegium Regale)**]
See **Whitbourn, James.** [Magnificat and Nunc dimittis (Collegium Regale)]

[**Magnificat and Nunc dimittis (Ripon Service)**]
See **Vann, Stanley.** [Magnificat and Nunc dimittis (Ripon Service)]

Magnificat and Nunc dimittis
See **Jackson, Gabriel, 1962-** Magnificat and Nunc dimittis

See **Tallis, Thomas, ca. 1505-1585.** [Magnificat, voices (5)] Magnificat and Nunc dimittis

See **Vann, Stanley.** [Lichfield Service] Magnificat and Nunc dimittis

See **Vann, Stanley.** [Magnificat and Nunc dimittis (Ripon Service)] Magnificat and Nunc dimittis

See **Walton, William, 1902-1983.** Magnificat and Nunc dimittis

See **Whitbourn, James.** [Magnificat and Nunc dimittis (Collegium Regale)] Magnificat and Nunc dimittis

[**Magnificat, voices (5)**]
See **Tallis, Thomas, ca. 1505-1585.** [Magnificat, voices (5)]

[**Magnificats, organ.** *Selections*]
See **Hassler, Hans Leo, 1564-1612.** [Magnificats, organ. *Selections*]

Make a joyful noise unto the Lord
See **Head, Michael, 1900-1976.** [Psalms. Make a joyful noise unto the Lord; *arr.*] Make a joyful noise unto the Lord

Make it easy.
See **Joel, Billy.** [Songs. *Selections*] Make it easy.

See **John, Elton.** [Songs. *Selections*] Make it easy.

Make we merry
See **Parry, Ben.** Make we merry

El mal de amores
See **Serrano, José, 1873-1941.** El mal de amores

[**Malá suita, flute**]
See **Kabeláč, Miloslav, 1908-1979.** [Malá suita, flute]

Malipiero, Gian Francesco, *1882-1973.*
See **Vivaldi, Antonio, 1678-1741.** [Concertos, string orchestra, RV 121, D major] Concerto in re maggiore, per archi e cembalo, F. XI, no. 30 / Antonio Vivaldi ; a cura di Gian Francesco Malipiero.

Mamma mia!
See **Andersson, Benny.** [Mamma mia! *Selections; arr.*] Mamma mia!

[**Mamma mia!** *Selections; arr.*]
See **Andersson, Benny.** [Mamma mia! *Selections; arr.*]

Mammarella, Alberto.
See **Tortamano, Nicola.** [Masses. *Selections*] Messa a due cori e messe a quattro voci con basso continuo / Nicola Tortamano ; edizione critica a cura di Alberto Mammarella.

Mangani, Marco.
See **Ingegneri, Marc Antonio, 1535 or 6-1592.** [Madrigals, voices (5), book 5] V libro di madrigali a 5 voci / Marc'Antonio Ingegneri ; a cura di Gloria Joriini e Marco Mangani.

Mant, Richard, *1776-1848.*
See **Lole, Simon.** For all thy saints, O Lord / music: Simon Lole ; words: Richard Mant.

Mantooth, Frank.
See **Jazz at Christmas** : piano solo : [elegant jazz arrangements of 14 traditional carols] / arranged by Frank Mantooth.

Marais, Marin, *1656-1728.*
[Pièces de violes, 4e livre. 1ère partie.
Selections; arr.] — Three old French dances :
for oboe and piano / Marin Marais ; [freely
transcribed by Janet Craxton and Alan
Richardson] — *Chester Music*
788.52   013182230

Marcello, Benedetto, *1686-1739.*
[Chaconnes, harpsichord, S. C703, C major] —
Cioconna stravaganza ; Menuetto per cembalo =
für Clavier / Benedetto Marcello ;
herausgegeben und bearbeitet von Jörg Jacobi.
— *Edition Baroque*
786.41827   013222373

Marcello, Benedetto, *1686-1739.* Minuets,
See **Marcello, Benedetto, 1686-1739.**
[Chaconnes, harpsichord, S. C703, C major]
Cioconna stravaganza ; Menuetto per cembalo =
für Clavier / Benedetto Marcello ;
herausgegeben und bearbeitet von Jörg Jacobi.

Marchetti, Filippo, *1831-1902.*
[Fascinzione. *arr.*] — Fascination : Valzer
zingaresco / Filippo Marchetti ; elaborated and
arranged for viola and guitar by Ian Gammie. —
Corda Music Publications
785.719218846   013269271

Marco, Tomás, *1942-*
La nuit de Bordeaux : aguafuerte goyesco : para
guitarra y cuarteto de cuerda / Tomás Marco. —
Institució Alfons el Magnànim
785.7195   014457028

Märker, Michael.
See **Bach, Johann Sebastian, 1685-1750.** [Herr
Gott, dich loben wir (Cantata). *English &
German*] Herr Gott, dich loben wir : BWV
16/BC A 23 : Kantate zum Neujahrstag für Soli
(ATB), Chor (SATB), Corno da caccia, 2 Oboen,
Oboe da caccia (Violetta), 2 Violinen, Viola und
Basso continuo = Lord God, Thy praise we
sing : cantata for New Year's Day for soli
(ATB), choir (SATB), corno da caccia, 2 oboes,
oboe da caccia (violetta), 2 violins, viola, and
basso continuo / Johann Sebastian Bach ;
herausgegeben von Michael Märker ; English
version by Henry S. Drinker.

See **Bach, Johann Sebastian, 1685-1750.**
[Himmel lacht, die Erde jubilieret. *English &
German*] Der Himmel lacht! Die Erde jubilieret :
BWV 31 / BC A 55b, Kantate zum ersten
Ostertag : für Soli (STB), Chor (SSATB), 3
Trompeten, Pauken, Oboe, 2 Oboen ad lib, Taille
ad lib., Fagott ad lib., 2 Violinen, 2 Violen und
Basso continuo = The heavens laugh, the earth
exults in gladness : cantata for Easter Sunday :
for soli (STB), choir (SSATB), 3 trumpets,
timpani, oboe, 2 oboes ad lib., taille ad lib.,
bassoon ad lib., 2 violins, 2 violas and basso
continuo / Johann Sebastian Bach ;
herausgegeben von Michael Märker ; English
version by Henry S. Drinker.

Maroon 5 (Musical group)
1.22.03.Acoustic : guitar recorded versions /
Maroon 5 ; music transcriptions by Addi Booth.
— *Hal Leonard*
783.242166   013383808

Marr, Johnny, *1963-*
See **[Songs]** The Smiths : complete chord
songbook : every song recorded by The Smiths.

Marr, Johnny.
See **[Songs. *Selections*]** Play guitar with— The
Smiths.

See **[Songs. *Selections*]** The singles collection /
The Smiths.

Marshall, Christopher, *1956-*
Aue! : for wind orchestra / Christopher
Marshall. — *Maecenas Music*
784.8   013422114

Marshall, Jack.
See **Parkening, Christopher.** The Christopher
Parkening guitar method. Vol. 1 : the art and
technique of the classical guitar / in
collaboration with Jack Marshall and David
Brandon.

Marson, John, *1932-2007*
Roundelay : flute and piano / by John Marson.
— *Broadbent & Dunn*
788.32   013374683

Martelli, Carlo.
See **Beethoven, Ludwig van, 1770-1827**
[Symphonies, no. 7, op. 92, A major. Movement
1; *arr.*] Symphony no 7, movement 1 / Ludwig
van Beethoven ; arranged by Carlo Martelli.

See **Beethoven, Ludwig van, 1770-1827**
[Symphonies, no. 8, op. 93, F Major. Movement
1; *arr.*] Symphony no 8, movement 1 / Ludwig
van Beethoven ; arranged by Carlo Martelli.

See **Handel, George Frideric, 1685-1759** [Acis
and Galatea. Heart, the seat of soft delight; *arr.*]
Heart, the seat of soft delight / George
Frederick Handel ; arranged by Carlo Martelli.

See **Tchaikovsky, Peter Ilich, 1840-1893**
[Serenades, string orchestra, op. 48, C major.
Valse; *arr.*] Waltz [from] Serenade for strings /
Peter Ilych Tchaikovsky ; arranged by Carlo
Martelli.

Martin, Christine, *1961-*
See **Schubert, Franz, 1797-1828.** Fierabras /
Franz Schubert.

Martin, Dean, *1917-1995*
See **Audition songs for male singers.** The rat
pack : Frank Sinatra, Dean Martin, Sammy
Davis, jr. : ten great songs ideal for auditions.

Martin, Frank, *1890-1974.*
[Ouverture et foxtrot, pianos (2); *arr.*] —
Concerto pour les instruments à vent et le piano
(1924) / Frank Martin ; edition realized by
Bastiaan Blomhert. — *Floricor Editions*
784.8186   014406581

Martinaitis, A. *1950-*
Paskutinių sodų muzika : obojui, violončelei,
fortepijonui ir mušamiesiems = Music of the last
gardens : for oboe, cello, piano and percussion :
1979 / Algirdas Martinaitis ; leidini redagavo
Julius Andrejevas. — *Muzikos informacijos ir
leidybos centras*
785.34194   013771132

Martinez, Marianne, *1744-1812.*
[Concertos, harpsichord, orchestra, G major] —
Concerto in G major for piano and orchestra / by
Marianna Martines ; edited by Shirley Bean. —
ClarNan Editions
784.3262186   014457031

[Isacco, figura del Redentore. Ouverture] —
Overture to the oratorio Isacco figura del
Redentore (1782) / by Marianna Martines ;
edited by Shirley Bean. — *ClarNan Editions*
784.218926   014457029

[Symphony, C major] — Sinfonia in C major,
(Ouverture), (1770) / by Marianna Martines ;
edited by Shirley Bean and Karen Fremar. —
ClarNan Editions
784.3184   014457030

Martinson, Joel.
Lions and oxen : for unison voices (with
optional divisi), oboe and organ / words by
Thomas H. Troeger ; music by Joel Martinson.
— *Oxford University Press*
782.5251723   013115654

Tuba suite : for organ / Joel Martinson. —
Oxford University Press
786.51858   013324490

Marty, Jean-Pierre.
See **Debussy, Claude, 1862-1918** [Fantaisie,
piano, orchestra] Fantaisie pour piano et
orchestre (2e version) / Claude Debussy ; édition
de Jean-Pierre Marty ; avec la collaboration de
Denis Herlin et Edmond Lemaître.

Marvin, Elizabeth West, *1955-*
See **Anthology for The musician's guide to
theory and analysis** / [compiled by] Jane Piper
Clendinning, Elizabeth West Marvin.

Marvin, Roberta Montemorra.
See **Verdi, Giuseppe, 1813-1901. I masnadieri :
a tragic opera (in four acts) = melodramma (in
quattro atti) / Giuseppe Verdi ; libretto by
Andrea Maffei ; edited by Roberta Montemorra
Marvin.

Maschat, Alexander.
See **Righini, Vincenzo, 1756-1812.** [Partita,
woodwinds, horns (2), E♭ major] Serenade
Es-Dur für zwei Oboen, zwei Klarinetten in B,
zwei Hörner in Es (F) und zwei Fagotte /
Vincenzo Righini ; Herausgeber, Alexander
Maschat.

Die Masken des Pierrot
See **Febel, Reinhard, 1952-** Die Masken des
Pierrot

I masnadieri
See **Verdi, Giuseppe, 1813-1901.** I masnadieri

Mason, Lowell, *1792-1872.*
[Modern Psalmist. Antioch; *arr.*] — Joy to the
world : for mixed choir (SATB) and keyboard /
['Antioch' by Lowell Mason ; arranged by]
Mack Wilberg. — *Oxford University Press*
782.5281723   013472421

Mason, Lowell, *1792-1872.* Olivet.
See **Dicie, Don Michael.** [Nineteenth-century
hymns. My faith looks up to Thee] Three
nineteenth-century hymns. 1, My faith looks up
to Thee : for lower voices (TTBB) and piano /
[arranged by] Don Michael Dicie.

Mass for four voices
See **Tallis, Thomas, ca. 1505-1585.** [Masses,
voices (4)] Mass for four voices

Mass in D major
See **Dvořák, Antonín, 1841-1904.** [Masses, B.
175, D major. *Vocal score*] Mass in D major

[Mass, D minor]
See **Altnikol, Johann Christoph, 1719-1759.**
[Mass, D minor]

Mass, Salve intemerata
See **Tallis, Thomas, ca. 1505-1585.** [Missa
Salve intemerata virgo] Mass, Salve intemerata

[Masses (1583). Missa O quam gloriosum]
See **Victoria, Tomás Luis de, ca. 1548-1611.**
[Masses (1583). Missa O quam gloriosum]

[Masses, B. 175, D major. *Vocal score*]
See **Dvořák, Antonín, 1841-1904.** [Masses, B.
175, D major. *Vocal score*]

[Masses, book 3. Missa de Beata Virgine]
See **Palestrina, Giovanni Pierluigi da,
1525?-1594.** [Masses, book 3. Missa de Beata
Virgine]

[Masses, BWV 232, B minor]
 See **Bach, Johann Sebastian, 1685-1750.**
 [Masses, BWV 232, B minor]

[Masses, D major (RISM A/II 300.033.496)]
 See **Żebrowski, Marcin Józef.** [Masses, D major (RISM A/II 300.033.496)]

[Masses, F major]
 See **Elsner, Józef, 1769-1854.** [Masses, F major]

[Masses, K. 427, C minor]
 See **Mozart, Wolfgang Amadeus, 1756-1791.** [Masses, K. 427, C minor]

[Masses, mixed voices, organ, no. 3, op. 11, E♭ major]
 See **Guilmant, Alexandre, 1837-1911.** [Masses, mixed voices, organ, no. 3, op. 11, E♭ major]

[Masses, no. 3, E♭ major. *Vocal score*]
 See **Leibl, Carl, 1784-1870.** [Masses, no. 3, E♭ major. *Vocal score*]

[Masses, no. 3, F minor]
 See **Bruckner, Anton, 1824-1896.** [Masses, no. 3, F minor]

[Masses, S. 5, D major]
 See **Heinichen, Johann David, 1683-1729.** [Masses, S. 5, D major]

[Masses, voices (4)]
 See **Tallis, Thomas, ca. 1505-1585.** [Masses, voices (4)]

[Masses. *Selections*]
 See **Tortamano, Nicola.** [Masses. *Selections*]

Masters in this hall
 Masters in this hall : for two-part choir (equal or unequal voices), flute, oboe and keyboard / [traditional French carol, arr.] Don Michael Dicie. — *Oxford University Press*
 782.5281723   013177983

 Masters in this hall : for two-part choir (equal or unequal voices), flute, oboe and strings / [traditional French carol, arr.] Don Michael Dicie. — *Oxford University Press*
 782.5281723   013196381

Masters in this hall
 See **Wilberg, Mack.** Masters in this hall

Mateer, David.
 See **Byrd, William, 1542 or 3-1623.** [Songs of sundrie natures] Songs of sundrie natures (1589) / [William Byrd] ; edited by David Mateer.

 See **The Gyffard partbooks I** / transcribed and edited by David Mateer.

Materassi, Marco.
 See **Dall'Abaco, Evaristo Felice, 1675-1742.** [Concerti da chiesa] Concerti a quattro da chiesa, cioè due violini, alto viola, violoncello e basso continuo, opera seconda : Amsterdam s.d. / Evaristo Felice Dall'Abaco.

Mattei, Lorenzo.
 See **Paisiello, Giovanni, 1740-1816.** I giuochi d'Agrigento / [libretto di] Alessandro Pepoli ; [musica di] Giovanni Paisiello ; saggio introduttivo a cura di Lorenzo Mattei.

Matthew Prior songs
 See **Fesch, Willem de, 1687-1761.** [Songs. *Selections*] Matthew Prior songs

Maw, Nicholas.
 [Concertos, violin, orchestra] — Violin concerto / Nicholas Maw. — *Faber Music*
 784.272186   006914457

 Stanza : for solo violin (1997) / Nicholas Maw. — *Faber Music*
 787.2   006912927

Mawby, Colin.
 See **Cornish folk songs** : for piano / researched by Jane Lofthouse ; arranged by Colin Mawby.

 See **Songs from the sea** : for trumpet / arranged by Colin Mawby.

May the road rise with you
 See **Godfrey, Philip, 1964-** May the road rise with you

Mazo, Margarita.
 See **Stravinsky, Igor, 1882-1971.** [Svadebka. *French & Russian*] Les noces = (Svadebka) : scènes chorégraphiques russes avec chant et musique : for four pianos, percussion and voices in a revised and corrected edition based upon relevant autograph and printed sources / composées par Igor Stravinsky ; French text by C.-F. Ramuz ; edited by Margarita Mazo ; associate editor, Millan Sachania.

Mazzocchi, D. *1592-1665.*
 [Musiche sacre, e morali. Battaglia per espugnare Amore] — Battaglia per espugnare Amore : concerto à 3 : for two sopranos, bass and basso continuo / Domenico Mazzocchi. — *Green Man Press*
 783.1342   013597082

 [Musiche sacre, e morali. Cangia miio cor] — Cangia mio cor : si dee fuggire il diletto dannoso / Domenico Mazzocchi ; [words by] Abbate Bentivogli. — *Green Man Press*
 783.126625   013613877

 [Musiche sacre, e morali. Colombella, che di latte] — Colombella, che di latte : sopra Maria, e Giesù / Domenico Mazzocchi ; [words by] Monsignor Ciampoli. — *Green Man Press*
 783.126625   013613882

 [Musiche sacre, e morali. Folle cor] — Folle cor : breve è la vita nostra : aria a tre soprani / Domenico Mazzocchi ; [words by] Ottavio Tronsarelli. — *Green Man Press*
 783.136642   013613865

 [Musiche sacre, e morali. Piangete occhi, piangete] — Piangete occhi, piangete : dovemo piangere la Passione di N. S. / Domenico Mazzocchi ; [words by] Girolamo Preti. — *Green Man Press*
 783.126625   013613855

 [Musiche sacre, e morali. Signor, non sotto l'ombra] — Signor, non sotto l'ombra : eccitamento alle virtù / Domenico Mazzocchi ; [words by] Torquato Tasso. — *Green Man Press*
 783.126625   013613872

 [Songs. *Selections*] — Three songs for solo bass / Domenico Mazzocchi. — *Green Man Press*
 783.8942   013597053

Mazzocchi, D. *1592-1665.* Dialoghi e sonetti.
 See **Mazzocchi, D. 1592-1665.** [Songs. *Selections*] Three songs for solo bass / Domenico Mazzocchi.

McAlister, Clark.
 Canovacci : [2002] : commedia for winds / Clark McAlister. — *Maecenas*
 784.8   013422223

 Forest music : [1991] : for wind octet / Clark McAlister. — *Maecenas Music*
 785.43198   013193628

 Jeux d'été : [1989 rev. 1990] : for ten wind instruments / Clark McAlister. — *Maecenas Music*
 785.43199   013193616

 The lion and the mouse : for narrator and woodwind [sic] quintet / music by Clark McAlister ; text by A.J. Wood. — *Maecenas Music*
 785.43195   013193651

McBirnie, Andrew, *1971-*
 See **Richards, Jack, 1947-** Snare drum : grades 5-8 / edited by Jack Richards and Andrew McBirnie ; additional editing by Aidan Geary.

 See **Richards, Jack, 1947-** Timpani : grades 6-8 / edited by Jack Richards and Andrew McBirnie.

McCabe, John, *1939-*
 The evening watch : for SATB and organ / John McCabe. — *Novello & Co*
 782.542   013498327

 [Sonatas, violoncello, piano] — Sonata for violoncello and piano : (1998-9) / John McCabe. — *Novello*
 787.4183   013434147

 [Songs of the garden. *Vocal score*] — Songs of the garden : [for SATB soloists, SATB choir, brass quintet and organ : (2004) / John McCabe ; [vocal score] — *Novello*
 782.548   013202052

McCartney, Paul Songs.
 See **Lennon, John, 1940-1980.** [Songs. *Selections*] Beatles love songs / words and music by John Lennon and Paul McCartney ; arranged by Ed Lojeski ; recorded by The Beatles.

McCartney, Paul.
 See **Lennon, John, 1940-1980.** [All you need is love; *arr.*] All you need is love : the 1967 #1 pop hit by The Beatles : [for 2-part and piano] / words and music by John Lennon and Paul McCartney ; arranged by Alan Billingsley.

 See **Lennon, John, 1940-1980.** [All you need is love; *arr.*] All you need is love : the 1967 #1 pop hit by The Beatles : [for SAB and piano] / words and music by John Lennon and Paul McCartney ; arranged by Alan Billingsley.

 See **Lennon, John, 1940-1980.** [All you need is love; *arr.*] All you need is love : the 1967 #1 pop hit by The Beatles : [for SATB and piano] / words and music by John Lennon and Paul McCartney ; arranged by Alan Billingsley.

 See **Lennon, John, 1940-1980.** [Fool on the hill; *arr.*] The fool on the hill : [for SAB and piano] / words and music by John Lennon and Paul McCartney ; recorded by Sergio Mendes ; arranged by Mac Huff.

 See **Lennon, John, 1940-1980.** [Fool on the hill; *arr.*] The fool on the hill : [for SATB and piano] / words and music by John Lennon and Paul McCartney ; recorded by Sergio Mendes ; arranged by Mac Huff.

 See **Lennon, John, 1940-1980.** [Fool on the hill; *arr.*] The fool on the hill : [for SSA and piano] / words and music by John Lennon and Paul McCartney ; recorded by Sergio Mendes ; arranged by Mac Huff.

 See **Lennon, John, 1940-1980.** [Songs. *Selections*] Lennon & McCartney : guitar play-along.

 See **Lennon, John, 1940-1980.** [Songs. *Selections*] Ticket to ride : a collection of Lennon and McCartney arrangements / The Swingle Singers.

 See **[Songs. *Selections*]** The Beatles : note-for-note.

 See **[Songs. *Selections*]** Play bass with— The Beatles.

McCartney, Paul. Songs.
 See **Lennon, John, 1940-1980.** [Songs. *Selections*] Beatles love songs / words and music by John Lennon and Paul McCartney ; arranged by Ed Lojeski ; recorded by The Beatles.

McConnell, William, *1931-*
See **Mozart, Wolfgang Amadeus, 1756-1791**
[Vocal music. *Selections ; arr.*] Mozart's choral
favourites / arranged for string quartet by
William McConnell.

McCorkle, Margit L.
See **Schumann, Robert, 1810-1856.**
[Waldscenen] Waldszenen : Opus 82 : Faksimile
nach dem Autograph im Besitz der Bibliothèque
nationale de France, Paris / Robert Schumann ;
Nachwort von Margit L. McCorkle.

McCrae, Kevin.
See **Thistle & minuet** : 16 easy pieces from the
Scottish Baroque for violin (or flute or oboe),
keyboard, and optional cello (or bassoon) = 16
einfache Stücke aus der schottischen Barockzeit
für Violine (oder Flöte oder Oboe),
Tasteninstrument und Cello (oder Fagott) ad
libitum = 16 pièces faciles du Baroque écossais
pour violon (ou flûte ou hautbois), clavier et
violoncelle (ou basson) facultatif / edited by
David Johnson.

McCreery, Charles.
[Short easy piano pieces] — Ten more short easy
piano pieces / Charles McCreery. — *St. Maur
Music*
786.2   013313010

McCue, Kirsteen.
See **Haydn, Joseph, 1732-1809.** [Songs, violin,
continuo acc. *Selections*]
Volksliedbearbeitungen Nr. 269-364 :
Schottische und Walisische Lieder für George
Thomson / Joseph Haydn ; herausgegeben von
Marjorie Rycroft in Verbindung von Warwick
Edwards und Kirsteen McCue.

McDermott, Michael, *1955-*
See **Mozart, Wolfgang Amadeus, 1756-1791**
[Concertos, horn, orchestra, K. 495, E♭ major.
Rondo; *arr.*] Rondo from Horn concerto in E flat
(K.495) : grade 3 / Mozart ; arr. Michael
McDermott.

McDowall, Cecilia.
Regina caeli : SATB (with divisions) a cappella /
Cecilia McDowall. — *Oxford University Press*
782.5271727   013213418

McDowell, Laura Pollie.
See **Payen, Nicolas, ca. 1512-ca. 1559.** [Vocal
music. *Selections*] Motets and chansons /
Nicolas Payen ; edited by Laura Pollie
McDowell.

McFly (Musical group)
Room on the 3rd floor / McFly. — *Wise
Publications*
783.242166   013190707

Wonderland / McFly. — *Wise*
783.242166   013374982

McGarr, Peter.
Images of sleep : for three oboes / by Peter
McGarr. — *Phylloscopus Publications*
785.852193   013472911

McGibbon, William, *ca. 1690-1756.*
See **Thistle & minuet** : 16 easy pieces from the
Scottish Baroque for violin (or flute or oboe),
keyboard, and optional cello (or bassoon) = 16
einfache Stücke aus der schottischen Barockzeit
für Violine (oder Flöte oder Oboe),
Tasteninstrument und Cello (oder Fagott) ad
libitum = 16 pièces faciles du Baroque écossais
pour violon (ou flûte ou hautbois), clavier et
violoncelle (ou basson) facultatif / edited by
David Johnson.

McNally, Terrence.
See **Kander, John.** [Kiss of the spider woman.
Vocal score. Selections] Kiss of the spider
woman : the musical : [vocal selections] / book
by Terrence McNally ; music by John Kander ;
lyrics by Fred Ebb ; based on the novel by
Manuel Puig.

McNamara, Danny.
See **Out of nothing** / Embrace.

McNeff, Stephen.
Moving parts : (1991 rev. 2003) : for concert
band / Stephen McNeff. — *Maecenas Music*
784.8   013193087

Rant! : [2002] : for concert band / Stephen
McNeff. — *Maecenas Music*
784.8   013192983

Wasteland wind music 2 : (2001) : for concert
band / Stephen McNeff. — *Maecenas Music*
784.8   013193003

Meacock, David.
See **Handel, George Frideric, 1685-1759.**
[Messiah. *Chorus score*] Handel's Messiah from
scratch / [edited by David Meacock]

Meditations on a Chinese character
See **Boyd, Anne, 1946-** Meditations on a
Chinese character

A medley of rhymes for five brass
A medley of rhymes for five brass : brass
quintet : traditional / arranged by Alan Danson.
— *Broadbent & Dunn*
785.9195   013167557

Mehrstimmige Gesänge für gemischte Stimmen.
See **Schubert, Franz, 1797-1828.** [Vocal music.
Selections] Mehrstimmige Gesänge für
gemischte Stimmen.

Die Meistersinger von Nürnberg
See **Wagner, Richard, 1813-1883.**
[Meistersinger von Nürnberg. Vorspiel; *arr.*] Die
Meistersinger von Nürnberg

[Meistersinger von Nürnberg. Vorspiel; *arr.*]
See **Wagner, Richard, 1813-1883.**
[Meistersinger von Nürnberg. Vorspiel; *arr.*]

Melodies for orchestra
See **Body, Jack, 1944-** [Melodies, orchestra]
Melodies for orchestra

[Melodies, orchestra]
See **Body, Jack, 1944-** [Melodies, orchestra]

Men of Harlech
Men of Harlech : grade 1.5 / traditional ; arr.
Rodney Newton. — *Studio Music*
784.8   013359131

Mendelssohn-Bartholdy, Felix, *1809-1847*
[Overtures. *Selections*] — Ouvertüren 1 / Felix
Mendelssohn Bartholdy ; herausgegeben von
Christian Martin Schmidt. — *Breitkopf & Härtel*
784.218926   013798492

Mendelssohn-Bartholdy, Felix, *1809-1847.*
See **Cummings, William Hayman, 1831-1915.**
[Hark! the herald angels sing; *arr.*] Hark! the
herald angels sing : for mixed choir (SATB) and
organ / [arranged by] Mack Wilberg.

Mendelssohn-Bartholdy, Felix, *1809-1847*
Gesange,
See **On wings of song** : 8 popular pieces
arranged for string quartet / [arr. by] Barrie
Carson Turner.

Mendes, Sergio.
See **Lennon, John, 1940-1980.** [Fool on the
hill; *arr.*] The fool on the hill : [for SAB and
piano] / words and music by John Lennon and
Paul McCartney ; recorded by Sergio Mendes ;
arranged by Mac Huff.

See **Lennon, John, 1940-1980.** [Fool on the
hill; *arr.*] The fool on the hill : [for SATB and
piano] / words and music by John Lennon and
Paul McCartney ; recorded by Sergio Mendes ;
arranged by Mac Huff.

See **Lennon, John, 1940-1980.** [Fool on the
hill; *arr.*] The fool on the hill : [for SSA and
piano] / words and music by John Lennon and
Paul McCartney ; recorded by Sergio Mendes ;
arranged by Mac Huff.

Mengal, Martin-Joseph, *1784-1851.*
[Quintets, winds, no. 2] — Wind quintet after
Mozart : for flute, oboe, clarinet in B♭, horn in E♭
& F and bassoon / by Martin Joseph Mengal
(l'aîné). — *New, rev. ed.* — *Phylloscopus
Publications*
785.43195   013472984

Merlin's riddle (no. 1 from "Nights in Armor")
See **Kesselman, Lee R.** [Nights in armor. No. 1,
Merlin's riddle] Merlin's riddle (no. 1 from
"Nights in Armor")

**Messa a due cori e messe a quattro voci con
basso continuo**
See **Tortamano, Nicola.** [Masses. *Selections*]
Messa a due cori e messe a quattro voci con
basso continuo

Messa a sei voci
See **Centorio, Marco Antonio, d. 1638.** Messa
a sei voci

Messa a tre voci con stromenti
See **Bartoli, Giuseppe, 1739-1801.** Messa a tre
voci con stromenti

Messe f-Moll
See **Bruckner, Anton, 1824-1896.** [Masses, no.
3, F minor] Messe f-Moll

Messe in h-Moll, BWV 232
See **Bach, Johann Sebastian, 1685-1750.**
[Masses, BWV 232, B minor] Messe in h-Moll,
BWV 232

Messe Nr. 3 Es-Dur
See **Leibl, Carl, 1784-1870.** [Masses, no. 3, E♭
major. *Vocal score*] Messe Nr. 3 Es-Dur

[Messiah. *Chorus score*]
See **Handel, George Frideric, 1685-1759.**
[Messiah. *Chorus score*]

Der Messias
See **Romberg, Andreas, 1767-1821.** Der
Messias

Metallica (Musical group)
St Anger / Metallica ; arranged by Jeff Jacobson.
— *Cherry Lane Music Company*
783.242166   012875197

[Songs. *Selections*] — Play guitar with—
Metallica. — *Wise*
783.242166   013374852

Métamorphoses parallèles
See **Globokar, Vinko, 1934-** Métamorphoses
parallèles

Metastasio, Pietro, *1698-1782.*
See **Fesch, Willem de, 1687-1761.**
[Canzonettas, violin, continuo acc.] Miss Ashe
canzonettas : for soprano, violin or flute,
mandoline and basso continuo : c.1734 / Willem
de Fesch ; on poems by Paolo Rolli, Pietro
Metastasio and others ; edited by Robert L.
Tusler.

Metheny, Pat.
One quiet night / Pat Metheny ; music
transcriptions by Masa Takahashi. — *Guitar
recorded versions.* — *Hal Leonard*
787.87164   013280380

Rejoicing / Pat Metheny ; music transcriptions
by Alejandro Moro. — *Guitar recorded
versions.* — *Hal Leonard*
787.87165   013169014

Metternich, Eberhard.
See **Leibl, Carl, 1784-1870.** [Masses, no. 3, E♭
major. *Vocal score*] Messe Nr. 3 Es-Dur / Carl
Leibl ; herausgegeben von Eberhard
Metternich ; mit einem einführenden Text von
Oliver Sperling ; Klavierauszug.

[Mexican pictures. Spanish]
See **Wood, Gareth.** [Mexican pictures. Spanish]

Meyer, Lesley Hopwood.
[Nunc gaudet Maria; *arr.*] — Nunc gaudet
Maria : for upper voices (SSAA), harp and drum
/ Lesley Hopwood Meyer ; arranged by Robert
A.M. Ross. — *Oxford University Press*
782.6251723   013472173

Mezmerize
See **System of a Down (Musical group)**
Mezmerize

Miceli, Sergio, *1944-*
See **Morricone, Ennio.** Neodiscanto : per voce
recitante, pianoforte e percussioni / Ennio
Morricone ; [testo di Sergio Miceli]

Michael, David Moritz, *1751-1827.*
[Wind music] — Complete wind chamber music
/ David Moritz Michael ; edited by Nola Reed
Knouse. — *Published for the American
Musicological Society by A-R Editions*
785.43   013802028

Michael, David Moritz, *1751-1827.* Partitas.
See **Michael, David Moritz, 1751-1827.** [Wind
music] Complete wind chamber music / David
Moritz Michael ; edited by Nola Reed Knouse.

Michelangelo Buonarroti, *1475-1564.*
See **Davies, Peter Maxwell, 1934-** Angelus : for
mixed chorus, SATB (2003) / Peter Maxwell
Davies.

See **Davies, Peter Maxwell, 1934-** Il rozzo
martello : for unaccompanied choir SATB /
words by Dante and Michelangelo ; music by
Peter Maxwell Davies.

Michna z Otradovic, Adam, *ca. 1600-1676.*
[Officium vespertinum. *Selections*] — Officium
vespertinum : Compositiones ad honorem
B.M.V. ; Falsi burdoni / [Adam Michna z
Otradovic] ; ed., Vratislav Bělský, Jiří Sehnal.
— *1. vyd.* — *Editio Bärenreiter Praha*
782.324   014764427

Miggiani, Maria Giovanna.
See **Portugal, Marcos Antônio da Fonseca,
1762-1830.** Gli Orazi e i Curiazi : partitura
dell'opera in facsimile, edizione del libretto /
[libretto di] Simeone Antonio Sografi ; [musica
di] Marco Portogallo. Catalogo cronologico
degli spettacoli a Venezia (1797-1815) / a cura
di Maria Giovanna Miggiani.

Milford, Robin, *1903-1959.*
[Suites, oboe, string orchestra, op. 8; *arr.*] —
Suite in D minor : oboe & piano Robin Milford ;
[piano reduction by R. Denwood] — *Emerson
Edition*
788.521858   013188311

The miller of Dee
The miller of Dee : SSAATTBB : English
traditional / arranged by Mark Williams. —
Edition Peters
782.542   013304961

Miller, David, *1962-*
See **Ledger, Philip.** Gift of love : for solo, upper
voices (SSA) & keyboard / Philip Ledger &
David Miller ; words by Richard Pomfret.

A million miracles
See **Carey, Paul, 1954-** A million miracles

Mills, Alan, *1964-*
The Lord at first did Adam make : for SATB
chorus unaccompanied / Alan Mills. — *ECS
Pub.*
782.5281723   014052735

A wedding postlude : on the chorale Lobe den
Herren (Praise to the Lord) : for organ solo /
Alan Mills. — *ECS Pub.*
786.518992   014052732

Milner, Edward.
See **Tippett, Michael, 1905-1998.** [Child of our
time. *Selections; arr.*] Five spirituals : from A
child of our time / Michael Tippett ; arr. by
Edward Milner for male voice choir.

Milsom, John, *1953-*
See **Tye, Christopher, 1497?-1572.** Give almes
of thy goods / Christopher Tye ; edited by John
Milsom.

Milton, John, *ca. 1563-1647.*
[If that a sinner's sighs, voices (5)] — Two
settings of "If that a sinner's sighs" : à 5,
TrTrTTB, fully texted : [and] à 6, TrTrT(with
text)TBB / John Milton ; edited by Virginia
Brookes. — *Viola da Gamba Society of Great
Britain*
785.76195   013441046

Milton, John, *1608-1674* Samson Agonistes.
See **Handel, George Frideric, 1685-1759**
[Samson. *Vocal score*] Samson : an oratorio for
soloists (3 sopranos, alto, 2 tenors, 2 basses; or
soprano, alto tenor and bass), mixed chorus and
orchestra / music by George Frideric Handel ;
words by Newburgh Hamilton, after John
Milton's Samson Agonistes ; edited by Donald
Burrows ; vocal score.

**Milton, John, *ca. 1563-1647.* If that a sinner's
sighs,**
See **Milton, John, ca. 1563-1647.** [If that a
sinner's sighs, voices (5)] Two settings of "If
that a sinner's sighs" : à 5, TrTrTTB, fully
texted : [and] à 6, TrTrT(with text)TBB / John
Milton ; edited by Virginia Brookes.

Minato, Niccolò.
See **Stradella, Alessandro, 1639-1682.** La forza
dell'amor paterno / Alessandro Stradella ; a cura
di Mariateresa Dellaborra, Carolyn Gianturco.

[Miniatures, English horn, piano]
See **Wilson, Trevor,** [Miniatures, English horn,
piano]

[Miniatures, flute, piano]
See **Warren, Constance, 1905-1984.**
[Miniatures, flute, piano]

Minnelli, Liza.
See **Liza Minnelli :** 15 timeless classics :
piano/vocal arrangements with guitar chord
boxes.

Minnion, John.
See **Fun and games with the recorder :** method
for the alto recorder. Tune book / [compiled by]
Gudrun Heyens and Gerhard Engel ; translated
and adapted by Peter Bowman ; with
illustrations by John Minnion.

See **Heyens, Gudrun.** Fun and games with the
alto recorder : method for the alto recorder.
Tutor book 2 / by Gudrun Heyens and Gerhard
Engel ; translated and adapted by Peter
Bowman ; with illustrations by Julie Beech and
John Minnion.

Minuet
See **Pezold, Christian, 1677-1733** [Suites,
harpsichord, G major. Menuet alternativement;
arr.] Minuet

**La misa policoral en Cataluña en la segunda
mitad del siglo XVII**
La misa policoral en Cataluña en la segunda
mitad del siglo XVII / introducción, estudio y
transcripción, Francesc Bonastre. — *Consejo
Superior de Investigaciones Científicas,
Institución "Milà i Fontanals", Departamento
de Musicología*
782.53232   013812474

Miscellaneous songs
See **Fesch, Willem de, 1687-1761.** [Songs.
Selections] Miscellaneous songs

Miscellany
See **Hedges, Anthony, 1931-** Miscellany

**Misere d-Moll, ZWV 56, für Soli (SATB), Chor
(SATB), 2 Oboen, 3 Posaunen, 2 Violinen, 2
Violen und Basso continuo**
See **Zelenka, Johann Dismas, 1679-1745.**
[Miserere, ZWV 56, D minor] Misere d-Moll,
ZWV 56, für Soli (SATB), Chor (SATB), 2
Oboen, 3 Posaunen, 2 Violinen, 2 Violen und
Basso continuo

[Miserere nostri]
See **Tallis, Thomas, ca. 1505-1585.** [Miserere
nostri]

Miserere nostri
See **Tallis, Thomas, ca. 1505-1585.** [Miserere
nostri] Miserere nostri

[Miserere, ZWV 56, D minor]
See **Zelenka, Johann Dismas, 1679-1745.**
[Miserere, ZWV 56, D minor]

Miss Ashe canzonettas
See **Fesch, Willem de, 1687-1761.**
[Canzonettas, violin, continuo acc.] Miss Ashe
canzonettas

Missa
See **Altnikol, Johann Christoph, 1719-1759.**
[Mass, D minor] Missa

Missa brevis
See **Bennett, Richard Rodney.** Missa brevis

Missa brevis in B
See **Rathgeber, Valentin, 1682-1750.** [Missale
tum rurale tum civile. Missa brevis, B flat major]
Missa brevis in B

Missa brevis pro defunctis
See **Moryto, Stanisław, 1947-** Missa brevis pro
defunctis

Missa confitebor tibi Domine
See **Palestrina, Giovanni Pierluigi da,
1525?-1594.** Missa confitebor tibi Domine

Missa de Beata Virgine
See **Palestrina, Giovanni Pierluigi da,
1525?-1594.** [Masses, book 3. Missa de Beata
Virgine] Missa de Beata Virgine

Missa Dum complerentur (SAATTB)
See **Victoria, Tomás Luis de, ca. 1548-1611.**
[Missae, Psalmi, Magnificat, ad Virginem Dei
Matrem salutiones, aliaque. Missa Dum
complerentur] Missa Dum complerentur
(SAATTB)

Missa ex D a canto, basso, due violini, due clarini ad libitum con organo
See **Żebrowski, Marcin Józef.** [Masses, D major (RISM A/II 300.033.496)] Missa ex D a canto, basso, due violini, due clarini ad libitum con organo

Missa F a canto, alto, tenore, basso, due violini, viole, bassi (violoncello et basso), due clarinetti, due corni con organo
See **Elsner, Józef, 1769-1854.** [Masses, F major] Missa F a canto, alto, tenore, basso, due violini, viole, bassi (violoncello et basso), due clarinetti, due corni con organo

Missa fratres ego enim accepi
See **Palestrina, Giovanni Pierluigi da, 1525?-1594.** Missa fratres ego enim accepi

Missa Hodie Christus natus est
See **Palestrina, Giovanni Pierluigi da, 1525?-1594.** Missa Hodie Christus natus est

Missa in c, KV 427 (417a), per soli (SSTB), coro (SATB), flauto, 2 oboi, 2 fagotti, 2 corni, 2 clarini, 3 tromboni, timpani, 2 violini, viola e basso continuo (Violoncello / contrabbasso, organo)
See **Mozart, Wolfgang Amadeus, 1756-1791.** [Masses, K. 427, C minor] Missa in c, KV 427 (417a), per soli (SSTB), coro (SATB), flauto, 2 oboi, 2 fagotti, 2 corni, 2 clarini, 3 tromboni, timpani, 2 violini, viola e basso continuo (Violoncello / contrabbasso, organo)

[Missa in honorem Sancti Stephani]
See **Zechlin, Ruth, 1926-2007.** [Missa in honorem Sancti Stephani]

Missa in honorem Sancti Stephanie
See **Zechlin, Ruth, 1926-2007.** [Missa in honorem Sancti Stephani] Missa in honorem Sancti Stephanie

Missa Laudate Domine
See **Palestrina, Giovanni Pierluigi da, 1525?-1594.** [Missa Laudate Dominum omnes gentes] Missa Laudate Domine

[Missa Laudate Dominum omnes gentes]
See **Palestrina, Giovanni Pierluigi da, 1525?-1594.** [Missa Laudate Dominum omnes gentes]

Missa Nr. 9 in D
See **Heinichen, Johann David, 1683-1729.** [Masses, S. 5, D major] Missa Nr. 9 in D

Missa O Quam gloriosum (SATB)
See **Victoria, Tomás Luis de, ca. 1548-1611.** [Masses (1583). Missa O quam gloriosum] Missa O Quam gloriosum (SATB)

Missa pastoralis
See **Żebrowski, Marcin Józef.** Missa pastoralis

Missa pastoralis in C
See **Ryba, Jakub Jan, 1765-1815.** [Missa pastoralis, C major] Missa pastoralis in C

[Missa pastoralis, C major]
See **Ryba, Jakub Jan, 1765-1815.** [Missa pastoralis, C major]

Missa "Pie Iesu Domine"
See **Liberto, Giuseppe.** Missa "Pie Iesu Domine"

[Missa pro defunctis, MH 838]
See **Haydn, Michael, 1737-1806.** [Missa pro defunctis, MH 838]

[Missa Salve intemerata virgo]
See **Tallis, Thomas, ca. 1505-1585.** [Missa Salve intemerata virgo]

Missa Sanctae Caeciliae
See **Zelenka, Johann Dismas, 1679-1745.** Missa Sanctae Caeciliae

Missa septimi toni
See **Eberlin, Johann Ernst, 1702-1762.** Missa septimi toni

[Missa Te Deum]
See **Aston, Hugh, b. ca. 1485.** [Missa Te Deum]

Missa Te deum laudamus
See **Aston, Hugh, b. ca. 1485.** [Missa Te Deum] Missa Te deum laudamus

[Missae, Psalmi, Magnificat, ad Virginem Dei Matrem salutiones, aliaque. Missa Dum complerentur]
See **Victoria, Tomás Luis de, ca. 1548-1611.** [Missae, Psalmi, Magnificat, ad Virginem Dei Matrem salutiones, aliaque. Missa Dum complerentur]

[Missale tum rurale tum civile. Missa brevis, B flat major]
See **Rathgeber, Valentin, 1682-1750.** [Missale tum rurale tum civile. Missa brevis, B flat major]

The Missouri harmony
The Missouri harmony : or, a choice collection of psalm tunes, hymns, and anthems / [compiled] by Wings of Song. — *2005 ed.* — *Missouri Historical Society Press*
782.527   013307548

Mitchell, Joni.
[Songs. *Selections*] — The very best of Joni Mitchell. — *Wise Publications*
783.2421640264   013222822

Mittell, Philipp, b. 1865.
See **Seitz, Friedrich, 1848-1918.** [Schüler-Konzerte] Pupil's concertos nos. 1-5, complete : for violin and piano / Friedrich Seitz ; edited and fingered by Philipp Mittell.

Mixed doubles
See **Hall, Pauline, 1924-** Mixed doubles

[Modern Psalmist. Antioch; *arr.*]
See **Mason, Lowell, 1792-1872.** [Modern Psalmist. Antioch; *arr.*]

Modest Mouse (Musical group)
Good news for people who love bad news : guitar recorded versions / by Modest Mouse ; music transcriptions by Pete Billmann, Addi Booth and Jeff Story. — *Hal Leonard*
783.242166   013222187

Moeran, E. J. 1894-1950.
[Choral music. *Selections*] — Collected choral music. Volume five, church music / E.J. Moeran ; edited by John Talbot. — *Centenary ed.* — *Thames Publishing*
782.525   013167658

[Choral music. *Selections*] — Collected choral music. Volume four, unison voices / E.J. Moeran ; edited by John Talbot. — *Centenary ed.* — *Thames Publishing*
782.542   013167517

[Choral music. *Selections*] — Collected choral music. Volume three, male voices / E.J. Moeran ; edited by John Talbot. — *Centenary ed.* — *Thames Publishing*
782.842   012965820

[Choral music. *Selections*] — Collected choral music. Volume two, female (and treble) voices / E.J. Moeran ; edited by John Talbot. — *Centenary ed.* — *Thames Publishing*
782.642   012965821

Moesus, Johannes.
See **Rosetti, Antonio, ca. 1750-1792.** [Simphonie concertante, M. C14, D major] Sinfonia concertante für zwei Violinen und Orchester in D-Dur RWV C14 = Sinfonia concertante for two violins and orchestra in D major / Antonio Rosetti ; herausgegeben von Johannes Moesus.

See **Rosetti, Antonio, ca. 1750-1792.** [Symphonies, M. A21, D major] Sinfonie Nr. 26 in D-dur = Symphony no. 26 in D major : RWV A21 / Antonio Rosetti ; herausgegeben von Johannes Moesus.

Mohr, Joseph, *1792-1848*.
See **Gruber, Franz Xaver, 1787-1863.** [Stille Nacht, heilige Nacht; *arr.*] Silent night : for tenor solo and men's choir (TTBB), unaccompanied / [Franz Gruber ; arranged by] Mack Wilberg.

Mohrs, Rainer.
See **Schroeder, Hermann, 1904-1984.** [Quartets, strings, no. 4] Streichquartette Nr. 4 und 5 / Hermann Schroeder ; herausgegeben von Rainer Mohrs.

Die Moldau
See **Smetana, Bedřich, 1824-1884.** [Má vlast. Vltava; *arr.*] Die Moldau

Molière, *1622-1673*.
See **Lully, Jean Baptiste, 1632-1687.** [Monsieur de Pourceaugnac. *Vocal score*] Monsieur de Pourceaugnac : (Le divertissement de Chambord) ; Le bourgeois gentilhomme : comédie-ballet / Jean-Baptiste Lully/Molière ; [Monsieur de Pourceaugnac] édition de Jérôme de La Gorce ; [Le bourgeois gentilhomme] édition de Herbert Schneider ; réduction clavier-chant, Noam A. Krieger.

Molino, Francesco, *1768-1847*.
[Grand trio concertant, no. 1] — Grand trio concertant, op. 30 : for flute or violin, viola, and guitar / Francesco Molino ; edited by Brian Jeffery. — *Tecla Editions*
785.44193   013334497

Monday's child
See **Brady, Deborah.** Monday's child

[Monferrinas]
See **Clementi, Muzio, 1752-1832.** [Monferrinas]

Monsieur de Pourceaugnac
See **Lully, Jean Baptiste, 1632-1687.** [Monsieur de Pourceaugnac. *Vocal score*] Monsieur de Pourceaugnac

[Monsieur de Pourceaugnac. *Vocal score*]
See **Lully, Jean Baptiste, 1632-1687.** [Monsieur de Pourceaugnac. *Vocal score*]

Monster of the maze
See **Spencer, Tim.** Monster of the maze

See **Spencer, Tim.** [Monster of the maze. *Selections*] Monster of the maze

[Monster of the maze. *Selections*]
See **Spencer, Tim.** [Monster of the maze. *Selections*]

Montague, Stephen.
Autumn leaves : (2000-2003) : solo piano / Stephen Montague. — *United Music Publishers*
786.21858   013063003

[Easy pieces] — Five easy pieces : (1998-2003) : piano solo / Stephen Montague. — *United Music Publishers*
786.2   013469015

Toccare incandescent : for organ (2003/04) / Stephen Montague. — *United Music Publishers*
786.5   013383468

Montéclair, Michel Pignolet de, *1667-1737*.
[Cantatas, book 3. Tircis et Climene] — Tircis et Climene : cantata for soprano, bass, violin/flute & continuo / M P de Monteclair. — *Green Man Press*
783.1248   013596837

Monteverdi, Claudio, *1567-1643*.
[Lamento d'Arianna (Aria)] — Lamento d'Arianna, and addendum : for soprano & basso continuo / Claudio Monteverdi ; edited by Barbara Sachs. — *Green Man Press*
783.6642   013589497

[Ritorno d'Ulisse in patria] — Il ritorno di Ulisse in patria : Ms. Wien, partitura / Claudio Monteverdi . — *Studio per edizioni scelte*
782.1   013771133

Monticelli, Paolo.
See **Leonarda, Isabella, 1620-1704.** Vespro a cappella della Beata Vergine e motetti concertati : opera ottava (1678) / Isabella Leonarda ; a cura di Paolo Monticelli.

Moon, Frank.
See **The big acoustic guitar chord songbook.** Female.

Moonfaring
See **Gilbert, Anthony.** Moonfaring

Moore, Andrew, arranger.
See **Beck.** Sea change / Beck ; music transcriptions by Andrew Moore, David Stocker, and Jeff Story.

Moore, Philip, *1943-*
Siciliano : flute & piano / Philip Moore. — *Emerson Edition*
788.32   013460594

[Toccata, adagio & fugue, flutes (3)] — Toccata, adagio & fugue : for three flutes / Philip Moore. — *Emerson Edition*
785.832193   013565446

Moore, Thomas, *1779-1852*.
See **Oft in the stilly night** : traditional Irish song for female voice choir (SSA), solo voice and piano / words by Thomas Moore ; arranged by Michael Neaum.

Moore, William, *d. 1825*.
[Sweet rivers; *arr.*] — Sweet rivers : for lower voices (TBB) and piano / William Moore ; arr. Reginald Unterseher. — *Oxford University Press*
782.8253   013196353

More essential piano repertoire
More essential piano repertoire / editor, Mark Goddard. — *Spartan Press*
786.2   013169232

More jazz tunes you've always wanted to play
More jazz tunes you've always wanted to play : popular jazz songs [arranged] for intermediate piano solo. — *Chester Music*
786.2165   013383532

Moreno-Buendía, Manuel, *1932-*
See **Chapí, Ruperto, 1851-1909.** La venta de Don Quijote : comedia lírica en un acto / Ruperto Chapí ; libreto, Carlos Fernández Shaw ; edición crítica Manuel Moreno-Buendia.

Morey, Carl.
See **Wagner, Richard, 1813-1883.** [Meistersinger von Nürnberg. Vorspiel; *arr.*] Die Meistersinger von Nürnberg : (Vorspiel) = (Prelude) / Richard Wagner ; in einer Transkription für Klavier zu zwei Händen oder für zwei Klaviere zu vier Händen von Glenn Gould ; herausgegeben von Carl Morey.

Morgan, Chris, *1952-*
See **The Boosey woodwind [method]** Alto saxophone. Repertoire book C.

Morgenstern, Anja.
See **Bach, Johann Sebastian, 1685-1750.** [Wir müssen durch viel Trübsal in das Reich Gottes eingehen. *English & German*] Wir müssen durch viel Trübsal in das Reich Gottes eingehen : BWV 146/BC A 70 : Kantate zum Sonntag Jubilate für Soli (SATB), Chor (SATB), Traversflöte, 2 Oboen/Oboen d'amore, Taille, 2 Violinen, Viola, obligate Orgel und Basso continuo = Through bitter tribulation we enter into God's kingdom : cantata for the third Sunday after Easter for soli (STB), choir (SATB), flute, 2 oboes/oboes d'amore, taille, 2 violins, viola, organ obbligato, and basso continuo / Johann Sebastian Bach ; herausgegeben von Anja Morgenstern ; English version by Henry S. Drinker.

The morning trumpet
See **White, B. F. 1800-1879.** [O when shall I see Jesus; *arr.*] The morning trumpet

Moro, Alejandro.
See **Metheny, Pat.** Rejoicing / Pat Metheny ; music transcriptions by Alejandro Moro.

Moro, Angiola.
See **Porpora, Nicola, 1686-1768.** [Duetti latini per la passione di Gesù Cristo] Sei duetti latini sulla passione di nostro signore Gesù Cristo ; Motetti per Angiola Moro / Nicola Antonio Porpora ; edizione critica a cura di Stefano Aresi.

Morricone, Ennio.
Neodiscanto : per voce recitante, pianoforte e percussioni / Ennio Morricone ; [testo di Sergio Miceli] — *Edizioni Curci*
783.96   014050067

Morris, Christopher, *1922-*
See **Vaughan Williams, Ralph, 1872-1958.** [Organ music. *Selections*] A Vaughan Williams organ album.

Morris, William, *1834-1896*.
See **Masters in this hall** : for two-part choir (equal or unequal voices), flute, oboe and strings / [traditional French carol, arr.] Don Michael Dicie.

See **Wilberg, Mack.** Masters in this hall : for mixed choir (SATB) and piano / [French carol ; arranged by] Mack Wilberg.

Morris, William, *1834-1896*
See **Masters in this hall** : for two-part choir (equal or unequal voices), flute, oboe and keyboard / [traditional French carol, arr.] Don Michael Dicie.

Morrissey.
See [**Songs**] The Smiths : complete chord songbook : every song recorded by The Smiths.

See [**Songs. *Selections***] Play guitar with— The Smiths.

See [**Songs. *Selections***] The singles collection / The Smiths.

La mort d'Hercule
See **Clérambault, Louis-Nicolas, 1676-1749.** [Cantates françoises, livre 3. Mort d'Hercule] La mort d'Hercule

Moryto, Stanisław, *1947-*
Missa brevis pro defunctis : na chór mieszany a cappella / Stanisław Moryto. — *s.n.*]
782.53238   013810172

Mosaical
See **Peçi, Aleksandër, 1951-** [Mosaical, saxophones (8)] Mosaical

[**Mosaical, saxophones (8)**]
See **Peçi, Aleksandër, 1951-** [Mosaical, saxophones (8)]

The most beautiful songs ever
The most beautiful songs ever : piano, vocal, guitar. — *Hal Leonard Europe*
783.242164   013220402

Motecta festorum totius anni cum communi sanctorum quaternis vocibus
See **Palestrina, Giovanni Pierluigi da, 1525?-1594.** [Motets (1563)] Motecta festorum totius anni cum communi sanctorum quaternis vocibus

Motetes de tempore et alia
See **Guerrero, Francisco, 1528?-1599.** [Motets. *Selections*] Motetes de tempore et alia

[**Motets (1563)**]
See **Palestrina, Giovanni Pierluigi da, 1525?-1594.** [Motets (1563)]

[**Motets (1563). Dies sanctificatus**]
See **Palestrina, Giovanni Pierluigi da, 1525?-1594.** [Motets (1563). Dies sanctificatus]

[**Motets (1563). Veni sponsa Christi**]
See **Palestrina, Giovanni Pierluigi da, 1525?-1594.** [Motets (1563). Veni sponsa Christi]

[**Motets (1569). Stella, quam viderant Magi**]
See **Palestrina, Giovanni Pierluigi da, 1525?-1594.** [Motets (1569). Stella, quam viderant Magi]

[**Motets (1569). Tu es Petrus; *arr.***]
See **Palestrina, Giovanni Pierluigi da, 1525?-1594.** [Motets (1569). Tu es Petrus; *arr.*]

[**Motets (1572). Ascendo ad Patrem**]
See **Palestrina, Giovanni Pierluigi da, 1525?-1594.** [Motets (1572). Ascendo ad Patrem]

[**Motets (1572). Domine, in virtute tua**]
See **Palestrina, Giovanni Pierluigi da, 1525?-1594.** [Motets (1572). Domine, in virtute tua]

[**Motets (1572). Laudate Dominum omnes gentes**]
See **Palestrina, Giovanni Pierluigi da, 1525?-1594.** [Motets (1572). Laudate Dominum omnes gentes]

[**Motets (1572). Laudate pueri**]
See **Palestrina, Giovanni Pierluigi da, 1525?-1594.** [Motets (1572). Laudate pueri]

[**Motets (1575). Haec dies**]
See **Palestrina, Giovanni Pierluigi da, 1525?-1594.** [Motets (1575). Haec dies]

[**Motets (1575). Hodie Christus natus est**]
See **Palestrina, Giovanni Pierluigi da, 1525?-1594.** [Motets (1575). Hodie Christus natus est]

[Motets (1575). Inclytae Sanctae Virginis Catherinae]
See **Palestrina, Giovanni Pierluigi da, 1525?-1594.** [Motets (1575). Inclytae Sanctae Virginis Catherinae]

[Motets (1575). Jubilate Deo omnis terra, voices (8)]
See **Palestrina, Giovanni Pierluigi da, 1525?-1594.** [Motets (1575). Jubilate Deo omnis terra, voices (8)]

[Motets (1575). Rex pacificus]
See **Palestrina, Giovanni Pierluigi da, 1525?-1594.** [Motets (1575). Rex pacificus]

[Motets (1584 : Voices (4)). *Selections*]
See **Palestrina, Giovanni Pierluigi da, 1525?-1594.** [Motets (1584 : Voices (4)). *Selections*]

Motets and chansons
See **Payen, Nicolas, ca. 1512-ca. 1559.** [Vocal music. *Selections*] Motets and chansons

Motets for three to twelve voices from Magnum Opus Musicum (Munich, 1604)
See **Lasso, Orlando di, 1532-1594.** [Motets. *Selections*] Motets for three to twelve voices from Magnum Opus Musicum (Munich, 1604)

Motets from 1549
See **Zarlino, Gioseffo, 1517-1590.** [Motets. *Selections*] Motets from 1549

Motets on non-biblical texts.
See **Josquin, des Prez, d. 1521.** [Motets. *Selections*] Motets on non-biblical texts.

[Motets, bass, continuo. *Selections*]
See **Leonarda, Isabella, 1620-1704.** [Motets, bass, continuo. *Selections*]

[Motets, voices (4-6), continuo (1612). *Selections*]
See **Guggumos, Gallus, 16th cent.** [Motets, voices (4-6), continuo (1612). *Selections*]

[Motets. *Selections.*]
See **Lasso, Orlando di, 1532-1594.** [Motets. *Selections.*]

[Motets. *Selections*]
See **Guerrero, Francisco, 1528?-1599.** [Motets. *Selections*]

See **Josquin, d. 1521.** [Motets. *Selections*]

See **Josquin, d. 1521** [Motets. *Selections*]

See **Lasso, Orlando di, 1532-1594.** [Motets. *Selections*]

See **Zarlino, Gioseffo, 1517-1590.** [Motets. *Selections*]

Motetto pro nativitate I, ZWV 171
See **Zelenka, Johann Dismas, 1679-1745.** [O magnum mysterium] Motetto pro nativitate I, ZWV 171

Motetto pro nativitate II, ZWV 172
See **Zelenka, Johann Dismas, 1679-1745.** [Pro quos criminis] Motetto pro nativitate II, ZWV 172

Motor motus
See **Peçi, Aleksandër, 1951-** Motor motus

Mottecta, Venedig 1612.
See **Guggumos, Gallus, 16th cent.** [Motets, voices (4-6), continuo (1612). *Selections*] Mottecta, Venedig 1612.

[Mottetta typis nondum uspiam excusa]
See **Lasso, Orlando di, 1532-1594.** [Mottetta typis nondum uspiam excusa]

Mottetta, sex vocum, typis nondum uspiam excusa (Munich, 1582)
See **Lasso, Orlando di, 1532-1594.** [Mottetta typis nondum uspiam excusa] Mottetta, sex vocum, typis nondum uspiam excusa (Munich, 1582)

Mouton, Jean, d. 1522.
[Noe, noe, noe psallite noe] — Noe, noe, psallite noe : motet for the season of Christmas : SATB / Jean Mouton. — *Anglo-American Music Publishers*
782.5261723   013594406

Movement
See **Pentith, Sybil, 1927-2004.** Movement

Moving on
See **Johnson, Mark** Moving on

Moving parts
See **McNeff, Stephen.** Moving parts

Mozart, Wolfgang Amadeus, *1756-1791*
[Ave verum corpus; *arr.*] — Ave verum corpus / Mozart ; arranged for four euphoniums and brass band by Philip Sparke. — *Studio Music*
784.928975   013376831

[Ave verum corpus; *arr.*] — Ave verum corpus : [K.618] / by W.A. Mozart ; arranged for four bassoons by David B. Johnson. — *Phylloscopus Publications*
785.858194   013178708

[Concertos, horn, orchestra, K. 412, D major; *arr.*] — Horn concerto no. 1 : [arr.] for horn and piano / Wolfgang Amadeus Mozart ; edited by Barry Tuckwell. — *G. Schirmer*
788.94186   013211728

[Concertos, horn, orchestra, K. 417, E♭, major; *arr.*] — Horn concerto no. 2 : [arr.] for horn and piano / Wolfgang Amadeus Mozart ; edited by Barry Tuckwell. — *G. Schirmer*
788.94186   013211730

[Concertos, horn, orchestra, K. 447, E♭, major; *arr.*] — Horn concerto no. 3 : [arr.] for horn and piano / Wolfgang Amadeus Mozart ; edited by Barry Tuckwell. — *G. Schirmer*
788.94186   013211738

[Concertos, horn, orchestra, K. 495, E♭, major. Rondo; *arr.*] — Horn concerto, rondo : TTBB / Mozart ; arranged by Jonathan Rathbone. — *Edition Peters*
782.8   013305805

[Concertos, horn, orchestra, K. 495, E♭, major. Rondo; *arr.*] — Rondo from Horn concerto in E flat (K.495) : grade 3 / Mozart ; arr. Michael McDermott. — *Studio Music*
784.81824   013390596

[Concertos, horn, orchestra, K. 495, E♭, major; *arr.*] — Horn concerto no. 4 : [arr.] for horn and piano / Wolfgang Amadeus Mozart ; edited by Barry Tuckwell. — *G. Schirmer*
788.94186   013211776

[Concertos, piano, orchestra, K537, D major; *arr.*] — Piano concerto no. 26, K. 537 : "Coronation concerto" : for piano and orchestra / Wolfgang Amadeus Mozart ; edited and reconstructed by Paul Badura-Skoda. — *G. Schirmer*
786.2186   013211682

[Così fan tutte. Aura amorosa; *arr.*] — Un' aura amorosa : from Cosi fan tutte : T solo & SSAATBB / Mozart ; arranged by Jonathan Rathbone. — *Edition Peters*
782.542   013305913

[Divertimenti, K270, B♭, major. *Selections; arr.*] — Divertimento à 6 in C, K. 270. Part II / W.A. Mozart ; recorder arrangement by Alex Ayre. — *Alex Ayre Music Services*
785.836196   013548612

[Divertimenti, K270, B♭, major. Allegro molto; *arr.*] — Divertimento à 6 in C, K. 270 / W.A. Mozart ; recorder arrangement by Alex Ayre. — *Alex Ayre Music Services*
785.836196   013324522

Mozart, Wolfgang Amadeus, *1756-1791*.
Jubilate Deo : motet for SATB and organ / attributed to W.A.Mozart ; edited by David Patrick. — *Fitzjohn Music*
782.526   013359697

[Masses, K. 427, C minor] — Missa in c, KV 427 (417a), per soli (SSTB), coro (SATB), flauto, 2 oboi, 2 fagotti, 2 corni, 2 clarini, 3 tromboni, timpani, 2 violini, viola e basso continuo (Violoncello / contrabbasso, organo) / Wolfgang Amadeus Mozart ; ergänzt und herausgegeben von Robert D. Levin. — *Carus*
782.53232   013728835

[Quartets, strings, K. 155-160] — L'autografo dei quartetti "Milanesi" : nella Musikabteilung della Staatsbibliothek (Preussischer Kulturbesitz) di Berlino = Das Autograph der "Mailänder" Streichquartette : in der Musikabteilung der Staatsbibliothek (Preussischer Kulturbesitz) von Berlin : KV 155-160 (134a, 134b, 157-159, 159a) / Wolfgang Amadeus Mozart ; edizione in facsimile a cura di Giacomo Fornari. — *Libreria Musicale Italiana*
785.7194   014053348

[Sinfonie concertanti, violin, viola, orchestra, K. 364, E♭, major; *arr.*] — Sinfonia concertante für Violine, Viola und Orchester, Es-dur, KV 364 = Sinfonia concertante in E♭ major for violin, viola and orchestra, K. 364 / Wolfgang Amadeus Mozart ; herausgegeben von Wolf-Dieter Seiffert ; Klavierauszug von Siegfried Petrenz ; Fingersatz und Strichbezeichnung von Frank Peter Zimmermann [und] Tabea Zimmermann ; piano reduction. — *G. Henle*
785.28193   013945442

Mozart, Wolfgang Amadeus, *1756-1791*
[Symphonies, K. 550, G minor. Molto allegro; *arr.*] — Symphony no. 40 : (movement 1) : SSAATTBB : Mozart ; arranged by Jonathan Rathbone. — *Edition Peters*
782.5   013305906

Mozart, Wolfgang Amadeus, *1756-1791*.
[Symphonies, K. 551, C major] — Sinfonie in C, KV 551 : "Jupiter" / Wolfgang Amadeus Mozart ; Ulrich Konrad, commentary. — *Bärenreiter*
784.2184   014491849

Mozart, Wolfgang Amadeus, *1756-1791*
[Vocal music. *Selections ; arr.*] — Mozart's choral favourites / arranged for string quartet by William McConnell. — *Spartan Press*
785.7194   013203975

[Zauberflöte. Ouverture; *arr.*] — Magic flute : overture : SSAATTBB / Mozart ; arranged by Ben Parry. — *Edition Peters*
782.5   013305892

Mozart, Wolfgang Amadeus, *1756-1791* Ave verum corpus
See **An die Musik :** 9 classical pieces arranged for string quartet / [arr. by] John Kember.

See **Mozart, Wolfgang Amadeus, 1756-1791** [Vocal music. *Selections ; arr.*] Mozart's choral favourites / arranged for string quartet by William McConnell.

Mozart, Wolfgang Amadeus, *1756-1791* Exsultate, jubilate.
See **An die Musik :** 9 classical pieces arranged for string quartet / [arr. by] John Kember.

See **Mozart, Wolfgang Amadeus, 1756-1791** [Vocal music. *Selections ; arr.*] Mozart's choral favourites / arranged for string quartet by William McConnell.

Mozart, Wolfgang Amadeus, *1756-1791*
Quintets,
　　See **An die Musik : 9 classical pieces arranged for string quartet** / [arr. by] John Kember.

Mozart, Wolfgang Amadeus, *1756-1791*
Requiem,
　　See **Mozart, Wolfgang Amadeus, 1756-1791** [Vocal music. *Selections ; arr.*] Mozart's choral favourites / arranged for string quartet by William McConnell.

Mozart, Wolfgang Amadeus, *1756-1791* **Sonatas,**
　　See **Mengal, Martin-Joseph, 1784-1851.** [Quintets, winds, no. 2] Wind quintet after Mozart : for flute, oboe, clarinet in B♭, horn in E♭ & F and bassoon / by Martin Joseph Mengal (l'aîné).

Mozart, Wolfgang Amadeus, *1756-1791* **Zauberflöte.**
　　See **Hammer, Xaver, 1741-1817.** [Viola da gamba music. *Selections*] 3 pieces for unaccompanied viola da gamba / F.X. Hammer. In diesen heil'gen Hallen / W.A. Mozart ; anonymous arrangement for unaccompanied viola da gamba ; edited by David J. Rhodes.

Mozart's choral favourites
　　See **Mozart, Wolfgang Amadeus, 1756-1791** [Vocal music. *Selections ; arr.*] Mozart's choral favourites

Mr. McKie's valediction
　　See **Carr, Gordon, 1943-** Mr. McKie's valediction

Mraz, Jason.
　　Waiting for my rocket to come / Jason Mraz ; transcribed by Paul Pappas. — *Cherry Lane Music Co.*
　　783.242166　　　　　　　　013382309

Múdra, Darina.
　　See **Zimmermann, Anton, 1741-1781.** [Quartets, strings, op. 3. No. 2] Quartetto in B für 2 Violinen, Viola und Violoncello, op. 3/2 / Anton Zimmerman ; [herausgegeben von] Darina Múdra.

Mudvayne (Musical group)
　　The end of all things to come / Mudvayne ; transcribed by Danny Begelman, Bill LaFleur and Greg Tribbett. — *Zomba Music*
　　783.242166　　　　　　　　013376127

Mueller, Michael.
　　Rock guitar : [learn to play rhythm and lead rock guitar with step-by-step lessons and 68 great rock songs] / by Michael Mueller. — *Hal Leonard Europe*
　　787.87166076　　　　　　　013359589

Müllemann, Norbert.
　　See **Chopin, Frédéric, 1810-1849.** [Preludes, piano] Préludes / Frédéric Chopin ; herausgegeben von Norbert Müllemann ; Fingersatz von Hermann Keller.

Müller-Lancé, Karl H.
　　See **Guerrero, Francisco, 1528?-1599.** [Motets. *Selections*] Motetes de tempore et alia : LXXVI-CVII / Francisco Guerrero ; introducción, estudio y transcripción, Josep M. Llorens i Cisteró ; semitonía y estructuras modales, Karl H. Müller-Lancé.

Münster, Robert, *1928-*
　　See **Zenger, Max, 1837-1911.** [Amor und Psyche. Sonata] Sonata für zwei Violinen : komponiert im alten Stil für König Ludwig II. von Bayern = Sonata for two violins : composed in ancient style for King Ludwig II of Bavaria / Max Zenger ; herausgegeben von Robert Münster.

Musaeus, Grammaticus. Hero and Leander.
　　See **Terzakis, Dimitri.** Hero und Leander : 2002/03 : Rapsodia für 1 Sprecher, Viola, Klavier und Tonband / Dimitri Terzakis ; nach Texten von Ovid und Friedrich Schiller.

Muse (Musical group : Great Britain)
　　[Songs. *Selections*] — Play bass with— Muse. — *Wise*
　　783.242166　　　　　　　　013173839

　　[Songs. *Selections*] — Play guitar with— Muse : Stockholm syndrome and other great songs. — *Wise*
　　783.242166　　　　　　　　013374879

　　[Songs. *Selections*] — The best of Muse. — *Guitar tab ed.* — *Wise*
　　783.242166　　　　　　　　013221817

Musgrave, Thea.
　　Going north : for children's chorus and two clarinets / Thea Musgrave. — *Novello*
　　782.742　　　　　　　　013383451

　　Niobe : for solo oboe and pre-recorded sound track : (1987) / Thea Musgrave. — *Novello*
　　788.52　　　　　　　　013383455

Music medals recorder ensemble pieces.
　　See **Associated Board of the Royal Schools of Music (Great Britain)** Music medals recorder ensemble pieces.

Music medals saxophone ensemble pieces.
　　See **Associated Board of the Royal Schools of Music (Great Britain)** Music medals saxophone ensemble pieces.

The music of Robert Colvin.
　　See **Colvin, Robert.** The music of Robert Colvin.

Music theory
　　See **Kolb, Tom.** Music theory

Music, David W., *1949-*
　　See **A selection of shape-note folk hymns :** from Southern United States tune books, 1816-61 / edited by David W. Music.

[Music, voices (4)]
　　See **Cavaccio, Giovanni, ca. 1556-1626.** [Music, voices (4)]

Musica a quattro voci
　　See **Cavaccio, Giovanni, ca. 1556-1626.** [Music, voices (4)] Musica a quattro voci

Música instrumental en las catedrales españolas en la época ilustrada
　　Música instrumental en las catedrales españolas en la época ilustrada : conciertos, versos y sonatas, para chirimía, oboe, flauta y bajón—con violines y/u órgano—, de La Seo y El Pilar de Zaragoza / estudio y edición, Antonio Ezquerro Esteban. — *Consejo Superior de Investigaciones Científicas, Institución "Milà i Fontanals, " Departamento de Musicología*
　　784　　　　　　　　013796771

Musica nostalgica
　　See **Schnittke, Alfred, 1934-1998.** Musica nostalgica

Música para exequias en tiempo de Felipe IV
　　Música para exequias en tiempo de Felipe IV / estudio y edición, Luis Antonio Gonzáles Marín. — *Consejo Superior de Investigaciones Científicas, Institución "Milà i Fontanals, " Departamento de Musicología*
　　782.525　　　　　　　　013812414

Musical characteristics
　　See **Clementi, Muzio, 1752-1832.** Musical characteristics

[Musicals. *Selections; arr.*]
　　See **Lloyd Webber, Andrew, 1948-** [Musicals. *Selections; arr.*]

　　See **Rodgers, Richard, 1902-1979.** [Musicals. *Selections; arr.*]

　　See **Rodgers, Richard, 1902-1979** [Musicals. *Selections; arr.*]

[Musicals. *Vocal scores. Selections*]
　　See **Rodgers, Richard, 1902-1979** [Musicals. *Vocal scores. Selections*]

　　See **Schönberg, Claude-Michel.** [Musicals. *Vocal scores. Selections*]

[Musiche sacre, e morali. Battaglia per espugnare Amore]
　　See **Mazzocchi, D. 1592-1665.** [Musiche sacre, e morali. Battaglia per espugnare Amore]

[Musiche sacre, e morali. Cangia miio cor]
　　See **Mazzocchi, D. 1592-1665.** [Musiche sacre, e morali. Cangia miio cor]

[Musiche sacre, e morali. Colombella, che di latte]
　　See **Mazzocchi, D. 1592-1665.** [Musiche sacre, e morali. Colombella, che di latte]

[Musiche sacre, e morali. Folle cor]
　　See **Mazzocchi, D. 1592-1665.** [Musiche sacre, e morali. Folle cor]

[Musiche sacre, e morali. Piangete occhi, piangete]
　　See **Mazzocchi, D. 1592-1665.** [Musiche sacre, e morali. Piangete occhi, piangete]

[Musiche sacre, e morali. Signor, non sotto l'ombra]
　　See **Mazzocchi, D. 1592-1665.** [Musiche sacre, e morali. Signor, non sotto l'ombra]

[Musicum opus, 2. tomus. Ascendit Deus in iubilatione]
　　See **Handl, Jacob, 1550-1591.** [Musicum opus, 2. tomus. Ascendit Deus in iubilatione]

[Musicus apparatus academicus. With noise of cannon. With noise of cannon]
　　See **Croft, William, 1678-1727.** [Musicus apparatus academicus. With noise of cannon. With noise of cannon]

Musik am Meininger Hofe
　　Musik am Meininger Hofe / herausgegeben von Ulrike Feld und Ulrich Leisinger. — *Friedrich Hofmeister*
　　782.52417293　　　　　　014660514

Muslim songs of the British Isles
　　Muslim songs of the British Isles / arranged for schools by Abdal Hakim Murad [Timothy J. Winter] — *Quilliam Press*
　　782.54217700941　　　　013190270

My Ántonia
　　See **Larsen, Libby.** My Ántonia

My beloved is mine
　　See **Lole, Simon.** My beloved is mine

My favorite things
See **Rodgers, Richard, 1902-1979.** [Sound of music. My favorite things; *arr.*] My favorite things

My Lord, what a mornin'
My Lord, what a mornin' : TTBB : spiritual / arranged by Mark Williams. — *Edition Peters*
782.8253   013305738

My love is like a red, red rose
My love is like a red, red rose : SATB / Scottish traditional ; arranged by Jonathan Rathbone ; words by Robert Burns. — *Edition Peters*
782.542   013304980

My love's an arbutus
My love's an arbutus : traditional Irish melody arranged for SSA choir, solo voice and piano / by Michael Neaum. — *Roberton Publications*
782.64216209415   013193614

Mystical march
See **Bartlett, Keith.** Mystical march

Mythic Trevithick!
See **Richards, Goff.** Mythic Trevithick!

Nachtigall-Polka
See **Strauss, Johann, 1825-1899.** [Nachtigall-Polka; *arr.*] Nachtigall-Polka

[Nachtigall-Polka; *arr.*]
See **Strauss, Johann, 1825-1899.** [Nachtigall-Polka; *arr.*]

Nagode, Aleš.
See **Novak, Janez Krstnik, ca. 1756-1833.** Figaro ; Cantate zum Geburts oder Namensfeste einer Mutter / Janez Krstnik Novak ; transkribirala in revidirala = transcription and critical edition by Aleš Nagode (Figaro), Zoran Krstulović (Cantate).

Natel, Jean-Marc.
See **Schönberg, Claude-Michel.** [Misérables. *Vocal score. English. Selections*] Les Misérables : Boublil and Schönberg's legendary musical : in concert : piano, vocal, guitar / music by Claude-Michel Schönberg.

Nathan, Simon, *1988 or 9-*
Lament : for piano / Simon Nathan. Together with Improvisation on "Lament" : for piano / Ernest Kaye ; and arranged for organ by Gerald Barnes. — *Oxford University Press*
786.2   013122820

Nation shall speak peace unto nation
See **Rose, Barry, 1934-** Nation shall speak peace unto nation

A Navaho prayer
See **Franklin, Cary John.** A Navaho prayer

Nawrot, Piotr.
See **Antología** / Archivo Musical de Moxos ; [transcrita y editada por] Piotr Nawrot.

Naxos quartet no. 2
See **Davies, Peter Maxwell, 1934-** [Naxos quartet, no. 2] Naxos quartet no. 2

Naxos quartet no. 3
See **Davies, Peter Maxwell, 1934-** [Naxos quartet, no. 3] Naxos quartet no. 3

[Naxos quartet, no. 2]
See **Davies, Peter Maxwell, 1934-** [Naxos quartet, no. 2]

[Naxos quartet, no. 3]
See **Davies, Peter Maxwell, 1934-** [Naxos quartet, no. 3]

Neale, J. M. *1818-1866.*
See **Good Christian men, rejoice** : German carol In dulci jubilo arranged for mixed voices & organ / arranged by Philip Ledger.

Neapolitan lute music
Neapolitan lute music / Fabrizio Dentice ... [et al.] ; edited by John Griffiths and Dinko Fabris. — *A-R Editions*
787.83   014630266

Nearly distant
See **Casken, John.** Nearly distant

Neaum, Michael.
Duerme negrito : traditional Cuban song arranged for SSAA choir and soloist with piano / by Michael Neaum. — *Roberton Publications, a part of Goodmusic Publishing*
782.642162097291   013373083

Japanese lullaby : for choir of female voices with soloists and piano accompaniment / [traditional] ; arranged by Michael Neaum. — *Roberton Publications, a part of Goodmusic Publishing*
782.642   013373016

See **My love's an arbutus** : traditional Irish melody arranged for SSA choir, solo voice and piano / by Michael Neaum.

See **Oft in the stilly night** : traditional Irish song for female voice choir (SSA), solo voice and piano / words by Thomas Moore ; arranged by Michael Neaum.

See **Rosseter, Philip, 1567 or 8-1623.** [What then is love but mourning?; *arr.*] What, then, is love but mourning? / by Philip Rosseter ; arranged for unaccompanied female voice choir (SSA) by Michael Neaum.

See **She's like the swallow** : traditional Newfoundland song for SSAA choir and piano / arranged by Michael Neaum.

See **Two French folksongs** : for female voice choir (SSA), soloists and piano / arranged by Michael Neaum.

See **The Virgin Mary had a baby boy** / [West Indian] ; arranged by Michael Neaum for three-part female voice choir and piano.

Neil Sedaka
See **Sedaka, Neil.** [Songs. *Selections*] Neil Sedaka

Neil, J. Murray.
The Scots fiddle / J. Murray Neil. — *Neil Wilson Publishing*
787.21629163   014664031

[Nell' Africane selve]
See **Handel, George Frideric, 1685-1759.** [Nell' Africane selve]

Nell' Africane selve (HWV 136a)
See **Handel, George Frideric, 1685-1759.** [Nell' Africane selve] Nell' Africane selve (HWV 136a)

Němec, Věroslav.
See **Kaprálová, Vítězslava, 1915-1940.** Sonata appassionata : op. 6 : piano / Vítězslava Kaprálová ; editor Věroslav Němec.

Neodiscanto
See **Morricone, Ennio.** Neodiscanto

Neubauer, Franz Christoph, *1750-1795.*
[Trios, flute, violin, viola, op. 14. No. 1] — Trio op. 14, no. 1, for flute, violin or flute and viola / by Franz Christoph Neubauer. — *Phylloscopus Publications*
785.44193   013188891

Neue Ausgabe sämtlicher Orgel- und Clavierwerke
See **Lübeck, Vincent, 1654?-1740.** [Keyboard music] Neue Ausgabe sämtlicher Orgel- und Clavierwerke

Neufeld, Ken.
Veni, Sancte Spiritus : para coro mixto / Kenneth Neufeld. — *Piles*
782.525   014053349

Neukomm, Sigismund, Ritter von, *1778-1858.* Grandes études,
See **Three 'storm' pieces** : organ solo / edited by David Patrick.

Never weather beaten sail
See **Davies, Bryan.** [Never weather beaten sail, men's voices] Never weather beaten sail

See **Davies, Bryan.** [Never weather beaten sail, mixed voices] Never weather beaten sail

[Never weather beaten sail, men's voices]
See **Davies, Bryan.** [Never weather beaten sail, men's voices]

[Never weather beaten sail, mixed voices]
See **Davies, Bryan.** [Never weather beaten sail, mixed voices]

The new complete works for guitar
See **Sor, Fernando, 1778-1839.** [Guitar music. 1997] The new complete works for guitar

The new crooners
The new crooners : [22 spectacular songs from the greatest male vocalists of the 21st century : arranged for piano, voice & guitar] — *Wise*
783.242164   013432776

The new divas
The new divas : [22 stunning songs from the greatest female vocalists of the 21st century : arranged for piano, voice & guitar] — *Wise Publications*
783.642164   013432793

[New English songs]
See **Fesch, Willem de, 1687-1761.** [New English songs]

Newcomb, Anthony, *1943-*
See **Luzzaschi, Luzzasco, d. 1607.** [Madrigals. *Selections*] Il quarto libro de' madrigali a cinque voci (Ferrara, 1594) ; and, Madrigals published only in anthologies, 1583-1604 / Luzzasco Luzzaschi ; edited by Anthony Newcomb.

[Newe liebliche Paduanen und Galliarden]
See **Praetorius, Bartholomeus, ca. 1590-1623.** [Newe liebliche Paduanen und Galliarden]

Newton, Rodney Stephen.
See **Debussy, Claude, 1862-1918** [Children's corner. Little shepherd; *arr.*] The little shepherd : from Children's corner : grade 3 / Claude Debussy ; arr. Rodney Newton.

See **Grainer, Ron.** [Tales of the unexpected. Theme; *arr.*] Tales of the unexpected : grade 1.5 / Ron Grainer ; arr. Rodney Newton.

See **Men of Harlech** : grade 1.5 / traditional ; arr. Rodney Newton.

Nex, C. M. M.
See **Devienne, François, 1759-1803.** [Trios, flutes, violoncello, op. 19. No. 1] Trio op. 19 no. 1, for flute, flute or violin, and cello or bassoon / by François Devienne.

See **Duval, Jérôme.** [Trios, flutes, bassoon, op. 2. No. 2] Trio op. 2 no. 2, for two flutes and bassoon / by Jérôme Duval.

See **Eight four-part fantasias** : for oboe, oboe & cor anglais and two bassoons / by Simon Ives ... [et al.]

See **Gibbs, Christopher, 1938-** [Forest of Bowland suite; *arr.*] Forest of Bowland suite : for two flutes, alto flute and bass flute / by Christopher Gibbs ; arranged by Chris Nex.

See **Graf, Friedrich Hartmann, 1727-1795** [Favourite quartettos. No. 5] Quartetto V for bassoon (or cello), violin 1 (or oboe) violin 2 and cello / by Friedrich Hartmann Graf.

See **Graf, Friedrich Hartmann, 1727-1795.** [Quartets, bassoon, violin, viola, violoncello, B♭ major] Quartetto VI for bassoon (or cello), violin (or oboe) viola and cello / by Friedrich Hartmann Graf.

See **Ives, Simon, 1600-1662** Fantasia in four parts (cor anglais and 3 bassoons) / by Simon Ives.

See **Kreutzer, Rodolphe, 1766-1831.** [Quintets, oboe, violins, viola, violoncello, C major] Grand quintette : for oboe, two violins, viola and cello / by Rodolphe Kreutzer.

See **Küchler, Johann, 1738-1790** [Quartets, clarinet, bassoon, violin, viola, op. 1. No. 2] Quatuor concertant op. 1, no. 2, for clarinet in B♭ or oboe, violin, viola and bassoon or cello / by Johann Küchler.

See **Kurpiński, Karol, 1785-1857.** [Nocturnes, bassoon, horn, viola, op. 16] Nocturne, op. 16 : for viola, horn in F and bassoon / by C. Kurpinsky.

See **Mengal, Martin-Joseph, 1784-1851.** [Quintets, winds, no. 2] Wind quintet after Mozart : for flute, oboe, clarinet in B♭, horn in E♭ & F and bassoon / by Martin Joseph Mengal (l'aîné).

See **Neubauer, Franz Christoph, 1750-1795.** [Trios, flute, violin, viola, op. 14. No. 1] Trio op. 14, no. 1, for flute, violin or flute and viola / by Franz Christoph Neubauer.

See **Spohr, Louis, 1784-1859** Erinnerung an Marienbad : (waltz, op. 89) : for flute, clarinet 1 in A (or oboe), clarinet 2 in A, horns 1 & 2 in D (or in F), bassoon, violins 1 & 2, viola and bassi / by Louis Spohr.

See **St.-Lubin, Léon de.** [Octet, op. 33, E minor] Grand octetto op. 33 : for flute, clarinet in A, horn in E, D & G (part in F included), bassoon, viola, cello, double bass and piano / by Léon de Saint-Lubin ; [edited by Chris & Frances Nex]

See **Wranitzky, Paul, 1756-1808.** [Quintets, flute, oboe, violas, violoncello, op. 3. No. 1] Quintet in F, op. III no. 1 : for flute, oboe, two violas and cello / by Paul Wranitzky.

Nex, F. H.
See **Devienne, François, 1759-1803.** [Trios, flutes, violoncello, op. 19. No. 1] Trio op. 19 no. 1, for flute, flute or violin, and cello or bassoon / by François Devienne.

See **Duval, Jérôme.** [Trios, flutes, bassoon, op. 2. No. 2] Trio op. 2 no. 2, for two flutes and bassoon / by Jérôme Duval.

See **Eight four-part fantasias :** for oboe, oboe & cor anglais and two bassoons / by Simon Ives … [et al.]

See **Graf, Friedrich Hartmann, 1727-1795** [Favourite quartettos. No. 5] Quartetto V for bassoon (or cello), violin 1 (or oboe) violin 2 and cello / by Friedrich Hartmann Graf.

See **Graf, Friedrich Hartmann, 1727-1795.** [Quartets, bassoon, violin, viola, violoncello, B♭ major] Quartetto VI for bassoon (or cello), violin (or oboe), viola and cello / by Friedrich Hartmann Graf.

See **Ives, Simon, 1600-1662** Fantasia in four parts (cor anglais and 3 bassoons) / by Simon Ives.

See **Kreutzer, Rodolphe, 1766-1831.** [Quintets, oboe, violins, viola, violoncello, C major] Grand quintette : for oboe, two violins, viola and cello / by Rodolphe Kreutzer.

See **Küchler, Johann, 1738-1790** [Quartets, clarinet, bassoon, violin, viola, op. 1. No. 2] Quatuor concertant op. 1, no. 2, for clarinet in B♭ or oboe, violin, viola and bassoon or cello / by Johann Küchler.

See **Kurpiński, Karol, 1785-1857.** [Nocturnes, bassoon, horn, viola, op. 16] Nocturne, op. 16 : for viola, horn in F and bassoon / by C. Kurpinsky.

See **Mengal, Martin-Joseph, 1784-1851.** [Quintets, winds, no. 2] Wind quintet after Mozart : for flute, oboe, clarinet in B♭, horn in E♭ & F and bassoon / by Martin Joseph Mengal (l'aîné).

See **Neubauer, Franz Christoph, 1750-1795.** [Trios, flute, violin, viola, op. 14. No. 1] Trio op. 14, no. 1, for flute, violin or flute and viola / by Franz Christoph Neubauer.

See **Spohr, Louis, 1784-1859** Erinnerung an Marienbad : (waltz, op. 89) : for flute, clarinet 1 in A (or oboe), clarinet 2 in A, horns 1 & 2 in D (or in F), bassoon, violins 1 & 2, viola and bassi / by Louis Spohr.

See **St.-Lubin, Léon de.** [Octet, op. 33, E minor] Grand octetto op. 33 : for flute, clarinet in A, horn in E, D & G (part in F included), bassoon, viola, cello, double bass and piano / by Léon de Saint-Lubin ; [edited by Chris & Frances Nex]

See **Wranitzky, Paul, 1756-1808.** [Quintets, flute, oboe, violas, violoncello, op. 3. No. 1] Quintet in F, op. III no. 1 : for flute, oboe, two violas and cello / by Paul Wranitzky.

Nicholas, Grant.
See **Pushing the senses** / Feeder.

Nicholas, John, *1960-*
See **Legend, John.** Get lifted / John Legend ; piano/vocal arrangements by John Nicholas.

Nichols, Roger.
See **Duparc, Henri, 1848-1933.** [Songs] Complete songs : with texts in English, German and French : high voice = Hohe Stimme = voix élevées / Henri Duparc ; edited by Roger Nichols.

See **Duparc, Henri, 1848-1933.** [Songs] Complete songs : with texts in English, German and French : medium/low voice = Mittlere/Tiefe Stimme = voix moyennes/graves / Henri Duparc ; edited by Roger Nichols.

Nicolai, Johann Gottlieb, *1744-1801.*
[Sonatas, piano] — 24 Klaviersonates in alle toonsoorten : (Zwolle ca 1790) = 24 keyboard sonatas in all keys / Johann Gottlieb Nicolai ; uitgegeven door Maarten Engelsman. — *Koninklijke Vereniging voor Nederlandse Muziekgeschiedenis*
786.2183   013020245

Nield, David, musician.
See **Anything goes :** & three other songs / arranged by David Nield.

See **A fine romance :** & four other songs / arranged by David Nield.

See **Smoke gets in your eyes :** & five other songs / arranged by David Nield.

Nieszpory
See **Elsner, Józef, 1769-1854.** [Vespers, D major] Nieszpory

A night at the opera for cello
A night at the opera for cello / arranged by Tim Wells. — *Kevin Mayhew*
787.4   013159873

A night at the opera for piano
A night at the opera for piano : easy-to-play arrangements / arranged by John Bertalot. — *Kevin Mayhew*
786.2   013159289

Night song
See **Bisbee, B. Wayne.** Night song

[Nights in armor. No. 1, Merlin's riddle]
See **Kesselman, Lee R.** [Nights in armor. No. 1, Merlin's riddle]

[Nineteenth-century hymns. Marching to Zion]
See **Dicie, Don Michael.** [Nineteenth-century hymns. Marching to Zion]

[Nineteenth-century hymns. My faith looks up to Thee]
See **Dicie, Don Michael.** [Nineteenth-century hymns. My faith looks up to Thee]

[Nineteenth-century hymns. The church in the wildwood]
See **Dicie, Don Michael.** [Nineteenth-century hymns. The church in the wildwood]

Niobe
See **Musgrave, Thea.** Niobe

Nixon, June.
Harvest carol / text: W. Chatterton Dix ; music: June Dixon. — *Encore Publications*
782.52815246   013382725

Noble, T. Tertius *1867-1953.* Ora labora.
See **Hancock, Gerre, 1934-** Variations on "Ora labora" : for organ / Gerre Hancock.

Nobody knows / Deep river (medley)
Nobody knows / Deep river (medley) : soprano solo, TTBB : spiritual / arranged by Jonathan Rathbone. — *Edition Peters*
782.5253   013305751

Les noces
See **Stravinsky, Igor, 1882-1971.** [Svadebka. *French & Russian*] Les noces

Nocturne and scherzo (1906)
See **Vaughan Williams, Ralph, 1872-1958.** [Short pieces] Nocturne and scherzo (1906)

Nocturne for 'cello and piano
See **Barlow, Michael, 1940-** [Nocturnes, violoncello, piano, op. 19] Nocturne for 'cello and piano

Nocturne, op. 16
See **Kurpiński, Karol, 1785-1857.** [Nocturnes, bassoon, horn, viola, op. 16] Nocturne, op. 16

[Nocturne, orchestra]
See **Escudero, Francisco, 1912-2002.** [Nocturne, orchestra]

[Nocturnes, bassoon, horn, viola, op. 16]
See **Kurpiński, Karol, 1785-1857.** [Nocturnes, bassoon, horn, viola, op. 16]

[Nocturnes, piano, op. 28]
See **Kirchner, Theodor, 1823-1903.** [Nocturnes, piano, op. 28]

[Nocturnes, violoncello, piano, op. 19]
See **Barlow, Michael, 1940-** [Nocturnes, violoncello, piano, op. 19]

Nocturno
See **Escudero, Francisco, 1912-2002.** [Nocturne, orchestra] Nocturno

[Noe, noe, noe psallite noe]
See Mouton, Jean, d. 1522. [Noe, noe, noe psallite noe]

Noe, noe, psallite noe
See Mouton, Jean, d. 1522. [Noe, noe, noe psallite noe] Noe, noe, psallite noe

[Nonet, woodwinds, horn, strings, op. 30]
See Waterhouse, Graham, 1962- [Nonet, woodwinds, horn, strings, op. 30]

Nonett, op. 30, für Flöte (Piccolo), Oboe, Klarinette, Horn, Fagott, Violine, Viola, Violoncello, Kontrabass
See Waterhouse, Graham, 1962- [Nonet, woodwinds, horn, strings, op. 30] Nonett, op. 30, für Flöte (Piccolo), Oboe, Klarinette, Horn, Fagott, Violine, Viola, Violoncello, Kontrabass

Nootka paddle song
Nootka paddle song : (no. 1 from "Northwest trilogy") : SATB a cappella / arranged by Imant Raminsh. — *Boosey & Hawkes*
782.542162009711   013243880

Norris, John, arranger
See Wedding gala : sixteen celebrated pieces for a perfect wedding / selected and arranged for organ by John Norris.

Norton, Christopher, *1953-*
The easiest way to improvise / Christopher Norton. — *Boosey & Hawkes*
786.165136   013213692

Latin preludes collection : [14 original pieces based on Latin-American styles for solo piano with playalong CD] / Christopher Norton. — *Boosey & Hawkes*
786.21888   013213840

Rock preludes collection : [14 original pieces based on the strong rhythms of rock music for solo piano with playalong CD] / Christopher Norton. — *Boosey & Hawkes*
786.2166   013213851

Notturnos
See Kirchner, Theodor, 1823-1903. [Nocturnes, piano, op. 28] Notturnos

Nouza, Zdeněk.
See Kabeláč, Miloslav, 1908-1979. Cizokrajné motivy = Motive aus fernen Ländern = Motifs from exotic lands : op. 38, piano / Miloslav Kabeláč ; editor, Zdeněk Nouza.

See Kabeláč, Miloslav, 1908-1979. [Malá suita, flute] Skladby pro flétnu sólo = Kompositionen für Soloflöte = Compositions for flute solo / Miloslav Kabeláč ; [editor, Zdeněk Nouza]

Novak, Janez Krstnik, *ca. 1756-1833.*
Figaro ; Cantate zum Geburts oder Namensfeste einer Mutter / Janez Krstnik Novak ; transkribirala in revidirala = transcription and critical edition by Aleš Nagode (Figaro), Zoran Krstulović (Cantate). — *Slovenska akademija znanosti in umetnosti*
782.1   014663614

Novak, Janez Krstnik, *ca. 1756-1833.* Cantate zum Geburts oder Namensfeste einer Mutter.
See Novak, Janez Krstnik, ca. 1756-1833. Figaro ; Cantate zum Geburts oder Namensfeste einer Mutter / Janez Krstnik Novak ; transkribirala in revidirala = transcription and critical edition by Aleš Nagode (Figaro), Zoran Krstulović (Cantate).

The Novello short anthems collection
The Novello short anthems collection : five centuries of anthems for smaller mixed voice choirs, a cappella or with organ accompaniment / selected & edited with a preface by David Hill. — *Novello*
782.5265   013335704

Now sleeps the crimson petal
See David, Jonathan, 1965- Now sleeps the crimson petal

Now thank we
See Chilcott, Bob. Now thank we

Nowak, Leopold, *1904-1991.*
See Bruckner, Anton, 1824-1896. [Masses, no. 3, F minor] Messe f-Moll / [Anton Bruckner]

Nowak, Leopold, *1904-1991*
See Bruckner, Anton, 1824-1896. [Quintet, violins, violas, violoncello, F major] Streichquintett F-Dur ; Intermezzo D-Moll / Anton Bruckner.

La nuit de Bordeaux
See Marco, Tomás, 1942- La nuit de Bordeaux

Nuitter, Charles, *1828-1899.*
See Offenbach, Jacques, 1819-1880. [Rheinnixen. *Vocal score*] Les fées du Rhin = Die Rheinnixen : opéra romantique en 4 actes (1864 / Jacques Offenbach) ; livret de Jacques Offenbach et Charles Nuitter ; adaptation allemande par Alfred von Wolzogen ; partition chant-piano [par Jean-Yves Aizic avec la collaboration de Dominik Rahmer, Jean-Christophe Keck]

Number ones
See Bee Gees. [Songs. *Selections*] Number ones

Nun
See Lachenmann, Helmut. Nun

Nunc gaudet Maria
See Meyer, Lesley Hopwood. [Nunc gaudet Maria; *arr.*] Nunc gaudet Maria

[Nunc gaudet Maria; *arr.*]
See Meyer, Lesley Hopwood. [Nunc gaudet Maria; *arr.*]

Nursery songs for young choirs
Nursery songs for young choirs : unison treble / arranged by B. Wayne Bisbee. — *Boosey & Hawkes*
782.7642   013243822

Nyman, Michael.
[Selections; *arr.*] — The piano collection / Michael Nyman. — *Wise*
786.2   013383402

Nyman, Michael. Miserere paraphrase.
See The violin : a collection : new and recent repertoire for violin with piano accompaniment / Craig Armstrong … [et al.]

O
See Rice, Damien. O

O come, let us sing unto the Lord
See Piccolo, Anthony, 1946- O come, let us sing unto the Lord

O come, o come Emmanuel
See [Veni Emmanuel.] O come, o come Emmanuel

O dolcezze amarissime d'amore
See Luzzaschi, Luzzasco, d. 1607. [Madrigali per cantare et sonare. O dolcezze] O dolcezze amarissime d'amore

O dulcis Jesu
See Biber, Heinrich Ignaz Franz, 1644-1704. O dulcis Jesu

O dyred, Dewi
See Hughes, Arwel, 1909-1988. [Dewi Sant. O dyred, Dewi. *Vocal score. English & Welsh*] O dyred, Dewi

[O Herr hilf]
See Wecker, Georg Kaspar, 1632-1695. [O Herr hilf]

O Herr hilf! O Herr, laß wohl gelingen!
See Wecker, Georg Kaspar, 1632-1695. [O Herr hilf] O Herr hilf! O Herr, laß wohl gelingen!

O Lord, my God
See Wilkinson, fl. 1579-1596. O Lord, my God

[O magnum mysterium]
See Zelenka, Johann Dismas, 1679-1745. [O magnum mysterium]

O mistress mine
See Carter, Andrew. O mistress mine

See Willcocks, David, 1919- O mistress mine

O ruddier than the cherry
See Handel, George Frideric, 1685-1759. [Acis and Galatea. O ruddier than the cherry] O ruddier than the cherry

[O when shall I see Jesus; *arr.*]
See White, B. F. 1800-1879. [O when shall I see Jesus; *arr.*]

O, O let me weep!
See Purcell, Henry, 1659-1695. [Fairy queen. Plaint] O, O let me weep!

Oasis (Musical group)
Don't believe the truth / Oasis. — *Guitar tab ed.* — *Wise Publications*
783.242166   013390011

Don't believe the truth / Oasis. — *Wise Publications*
783.242166   013383522

Oboe concertos
See Bach, Carl Philipp Emanuel, 1714-1788 [Concertos, oboe, string orchestra, H. 466, B♭ major] Oboe concertos

Och, Laura.
See Dall'Abaco, Evaristo Felice, 1675-1742. [Concerti da chiesa] Concerti a quattro da chiesa, cioè due violini, alto viola, violoncello e basso continuo, opera seconda : Amsterdam s.d. / Evaristo Felice Dall'Abaco.

Octet
See Cooke, Arnold. [Octet, woodwinds, horn, strings] Octet

[Octet, op. 33, E minor]
See St.-Lubin, Léon de. [Octet, op. 33, E minor]

[Octet, violins (4), violas, violoncellos, op. 176, C major]
See Raff, Joachim, 1822-1882. [Octet, violins (4), violas, violoncellos, op. 176, C major]

[Octet, woodwinds, horn, strings]
See Cooke, Arnold. [Octet, woodwinds, horn, strings]

Octetto pastorale
See Harrison, Pamela, 1915-1990. Octetto pastorale

Oettinger, Rebecca Wagner.
See Lasso, Orlando di, 1532-1594. [Mottetta typis nondum uspiam excusa] Mottetta, sex vocum, typis nondum uspiam excusa (Munich, 1582) / edited by Rebecca Wagner Oettinger.

Offenbach, Jacques, *1819-1880.*
[Rheinnixen. *Vocal score*] — Les fées du Rhin = Die Rheinnixen : opéra romantique en 4 actes (1864 / Jacques Offenbach ; livret de Jacques Offenbach et Charles Nuitter ; adaptation allemande par Alfred von Wolzogen ; partition chant-piano [par Jean-Yves Aizic avec la collaboration de Dominik Rahmer, Jean-Christophe Keck] — *Boosey & Hawkes :*
782.1   013598594

Offenbach, Jacques, *1819-1880* **Contes d'Hoffmann.**
See **On wings of song :** 8 popular pieces arranged for string quartet / [arr. by] Barrie Carson Turner.

[Offertories, voices (5). *Selections***]**
See **Palestrina, Giovanni Pierluigi da, 1525?-1594.** [Offertories, voices (5). *Selections*]

[Offertories, voices (5). Confirma hoc Deus]
See **Palestrina, Giovanni Pierluigi da, 1525?-1594.** [Offertories, voices (5). Confirma hoc Deus]

[Offertories, voices (5). Tui sunt coeli]
See **Palestrina, Giovanni Pierluigi da, 1525?-1594.** [Offertories, voices (5). Tui sunt coeli]

Offertory at the third mass of Christmas
See **Palestrina, Giovanni Pierluigi da, 1525?-1594.** [Offertories, voices (5). Tui sunt coeli] Offertory at the third mass of Christmas

Officium vespertinum
See **Michna z Otradovic, Adam, ca. 1600-1676.** [Officium vespertinum. *Selections*] Officium vespertinum

[Officium vespertinum. *Selections***]**
See **Michna z Otradovic, Adam, ca. 1600-1676.** [Officium vespertinum. *Selections*]

Oft in the stilly night
Oft in the stilly night : traditional Irish song for female voice choir (SSA), solo voice and piano / words by Thomas Moore ; arranged by Michael Neaum. — *Roberton Publications*
782.64216209415   013192689

O'Gorman, Denis.
See **Hart, Barry.** Jesus is alive! : a simple Easter musical for key stage 1 / O'Gorman & Hart.

Oktett für vier Violinen, zwei Violen und zwei Violoncelli, C-Dur, op. 176
See **Raff, Joachim, 1822-1882.** [Octet, violins (4), violas, violoncellos, op. 176, C major] Oktett für vier Violinen, zwei Violen und zwei Violoncelli, C-Dur, op. 176

Okun, Milton.
See **Legend, John.** Get lifted / John Legend ; piano/vocal arrangements by John Nicholas.

See **Mraz, Jason.** Waiting for my rocket to come / Jason Mraz ; transcribed by Paul Pappas.

[Old Hundredth Psalm tune; *arr.***]**
See **Vaughan Williams, Ralph, 1872-1958.** [Old Hundredth Psalm tune; *arr.*]

The Old Hundreth Psalm tune
See **Vaughan Williams, Ralph, 1872-1958.** [Old Hundredth Psalm tune; *arr.*] The Old Hundreth Psalm tune

Oliver, Angel, *1937-*
See **Ordoñez, Carlos d', 1734-1786.** [Symphonies. *Selections*] Sinfonías ; Concierto para violín en re mayor / Carlos Ordóñez ; edición crítica Miguel Simarro Grande [y] Ángel Oliver.

Ollila, Jukka.
Harmonikan asteikkosormitus ABC = Accordion scale fingering : standardi- ja melodiabassoharmonikalle = standard- and melody bass accordion / Jukka Ollila. — *Jukka Ollila*
788.86076   013836335

L'ombre sur les structures pliées
See **Serei, Zsolt.** L'ombre sur les structures pliées

On another's sorrow
See **Blackford, Richard, 1954-** On another's sorrow

On the box
See **Barton, David, 1983-** On the box

On the lighter side
See **Kember, John.** On the lighter side

[On the lighter side. Rock & soul styles]
See **Kember, John.** [On the lighter side. Rock & soul styles]

[On the lighter side. Solo collection]
See **Kember, John.** [On the lighter side. Solo collection]

On wings of song
On wings of song : 8 popular pieces arranged for string quartet / [arr. by] Barrie Carson Turner. — *Schott*
785.7194   013192096

Once around the sun
See **Talbot, Joby.** [Once around the sun; *arr.*] Once around the sun

[Once around the sun; *arr.***]**
See **Talbot, Joby.** [Once around the sun; *arr.*]

One day remains
See **Alter Bridge (Musical group)** One day remains

One quiet night
See **Metheny, Pat.** One quiet night

O'Neill, John, *1955-*
Developing jazz technique for flute : improvisation, style, special effects = Technique de jazz pour flûte : improvisation, style, effets spéciaux = Jazztechnik für Querflöte : Improvisation, Stilistik, Spezialeffekte / John O'Neill ; traduction Agnès Ausseur ; Übersetzung Heike Brühl. — *Schott*
788.32165076   013382705

Ongley, Marc.
Guitar for everyone/ [Marc Ongley] — *Natural Light*
787.87076   014664154

Onslow, Georges, *1784-1853.*
[Quintets, piano, violin, viola, violoncello, double bass, op. 70, B minor] — Quintet in B minor, opus 70 : for piano, violin, viola, cello & double bass/cello / George Onslow. — *SJ Music*
785.28195   013394887

Opening night
Opening night : two Souvenirs for solo piano : commissioned to celebrate the opening of the Bauer & Hieber music shop at 48 Great Marlborough Street, London, 21st September 2007 / written and performed by Tim Richards and Huw Watkins. — *Schott*
786.2   014049158

Opera
See **Hayes, Morgan, 1973-** Opera

Opera gold
Opera gold : the essential collection. — *Chester Music*
786.2   013265864

Opere per tastiera (Venezia 1591)
See **Bertoldo, Sperindio, ca. 1530-1570.** [Organ music] Opere per tastiera (Venezia 1591)

Gli Orazi e i Curiazi
See **Portugal, Marcos Antônio da Fonseca, 1762-1830.** Gli Orazi e i Curiazi

Orchestervorspiel E-Dur
See **Rott, Hans, 1858-1884.** [Vorspiele, orchestra, E major] Orchestervorspiel E-Dur

[Orchestra music. *Selections***]**
See **Rachmaninoff, Sergei, 1873-1943.** [Orchestra music. *Selections*]

Ordoñez, Carlos d', *1734-1786.*
[Symphonies. *Selections*] — Sinfonías ; Concierto para violín en re mayor / Carlos Ordóñez ; edición crítica Miguel Simarro Grande [y] Ángel Oliver. — *Instituto Complutense de Ciencias Musicales*
784.2184   014679359

Ordoñez, Carlos d', *1734-1786.* **Concerto,**
See **Ordoñez, Carlos d', 1734-1786.** [Symphonies. *Selections*] Sinfonías ; Concierto para violín en re mayor / Carlos Ordóñez ; edición crítica Miguel Simarro Grande [y] Ángel Oliver.

O'Regan, Tarik.
Magnificat & Nunc dimittis : variations for choir : [for SATB (divisi) ripieno choir and SATB concertante choir (four or eight soloists) with solo soprano saxophone or violoncello] / Tarik O'Regan. — *Novello*
782.5326   013173392

O'Regan, Tarik. Nunc dimittis.
See **O'Regan, Tarik.** Magnificat & Nunc dimittis : variations for choir : [for SATB (divisi) ripieno choir and SATB concertante choir (four or eight soloists) with solo soprano saxophone or violoncello] / Tarik O'Regan.

Organ album
See **Carter, Andrew.** [Organ music. *Selections*] Organ album

[Organ music]
See **Bertoldo, Sperindio, ca. 1530-1570.** [Organ music]

See **Scheidemann, Heinrich, 1596 (ca.)-1663.** [Organ music]

See **Strungk, Delphin, 1601-1694.** [Organ music]

[Organ music. *Selections***]**
See **Carter, Andrew.** [Organ music. *Selections*]

See **Vaughan Williams, Ralph, 1872-1958.** [Organ music. *Selections*]

Orgelkonzerte
See **Rheinberger, Josef, 1839-1901** [Instrumental music. *Selections*] Orgelkonzerte

Os
See **Gilbert, Anthony.** Os

Ostermann, Karlheinz.
See **Ryba, Jakub Jan, 1765-1815.** [Missa pastoralis, C major] Missa pastoralis in C : in Nativitate Domini in nocte : per soli SATB, coro SATB, fagotto solo, clarino solo, 2 violini e basso continuo / Jakub Jan Ryba ; herausgegeben von Karlheinz Ostermann ; Generalbassaussetzung von Paul Horn.

Oswald, James, *1710-1769.*
See **Thistle & minuet** : 16 easy pieces from the Scottish Baroque for violin (or flute or oboe), keyboard, and optional cello (or bassoon) = 16 einfache Stücke aus der schottischen Barockzeit für Violine (oder Flöte oder Oboe), Tasteninstrument und Cello (oder Fagott) ad libitum = 16 pièces faciles du Baroque écossais pour violon (ou flûte ou hautbois), clavier et violoncelle (ou basson) facultatif / edited by David Johnson.

Otwell, Margaret.
See **Brady, Deborah.** Monday's child : a child's blessings / by Deborah Brady ; editor, Margaret Otwell.

See **Burgmüller, Friedrich, 1806-1874.** [Etudes faciles et progressives] 25 progressive studies : opus 100 / Burgmüller ; edited by Margaret Otwell.

See **Tsitsaros, Christos.** Songs without words : nine character pieces for piano solo / by Christos Tsitsaros ; edited by Margaret Otwell.

Our faith is a light
See **Bingham, Judith.** Our faith is a light

Out of nothing
See **Embrace (Musical group)** Out of nothing

Ouverture brillante
See **Czerny, Carl, 1791-1857.** [Ouverture charactéristique et brillante] Ouverture brillante

|Ouverture charactéristique et brillante|
See **Czerny, Carl, 1791-1857.** [Ouverture charactéristique et brillante]

|Ouverture et foxtrot, pianos (2); arr.|
See **Martin, Frank, 1890-1974.** [Ouverture et foxtrot, pianos (2); arr.]

Ouvertüren I
See **Mendelssohn-Bartholdy, Felix, 1809-1847** [Overtures. *Selections*] Ouvertüren I

Over hill, over dale
See **Gorb, Adam, 1958-** Over hill, over dale

Over, Berthold.
See **Rheinberger, Josef, 1839-1901** [Vocal music. *Selections*] Geistliche Gesänge. 1 : für Solostimmen bzw. Frauenchor mit Begleitung / [Josef Gabriel Rheinberger] ; vorgelegt von Berthold Over.

|Overcoat. Polka; arr.|
See **Schnittke, Alfred, 1934-1998.** [Overcoat. Polka; arr.]

|Overture "1812". Op. 49; arr.|
See **Tchaikovsky, Peter Ilich, 1840-1893** [Overture "1812". Op. 49; arr.]

Overture Saturnalia
See **Binney, Malcolm.** Overture Saturnalia

Overture to the oratorio Isacco figura del Redentore (1782)
See **Martinez, Marianne, 1744-1812.** [Isacco, figura del Redentore. Ouverture] Overture to the oratorio Isacco figura del Redentore (1782)

|Overtures. *Selections*|
See **Mendelssohn-Bartholdy, Felix, 1809-1847** [Overtures. *Selections*]

Ovid, *43 B.C.-17 or 18 A.D.*
See **Terzakis, Dimitri.** Hero und Leander : 2002/03 : Rapsodia für 1 Sprecher, Viola, Klavier und Tonband / Dimitri Terzakis ; nach Texten von Ovid und Friedrich Schiller.

The oxen
See **Rathbone, Jonathan.** The oxen

Oxford fantasias
See **Ward, John, 1571-1638.** [Fantasias, viols (4), Meyer 1-6. *Parts*] Oxford fantasias

Pacuła, Marek.
See **Pieśni i hymny Piwnicy pod Baranami** / [wybór piosenek Piotr Ferster, Marek Pacuła]

Paderborner Gesangbuch (1609)
See **Rentz, Earlene.** Lo, how a rose e'er blooming = (Es ist ein' Ros' entsprungen) : for mixed choir (SATB), flute and piano / [from Alte Catholische Geistliche Kirchengesang' (1599) harmonized by Michael Praetorius (1609) ; arranged by] Earlene Rentz. — *Oxford University Press*

See **Rentz, Earlene.** Lo, how a rose e'er blooming = (Es ist ein' Ros' entsprungen) : for upper voices (SA), flute and piano / [from Alte Catholische Geistliche Kirchengesang' (1599) harmonized by Michael Praetorius (1609) ; arranged by] Earlene Rentz. — *Oxford University Press*

Paduch, Arno.
See **Telemann, Georg Philipp, 1681-1767.** Jesu, wirst du bald erscheinen : Kantate zum 26. Sonntag nach Trinitatis, für Sopran-, Tenor- und Bass-Solo, vierstimmigen gemischten Chor, Zink, 3 Posaunen, 2 Oboen, Streicher und Basso continuo, TWV 1:988 / Georg Philipp Telemann ; herausgegeben von Arno Paduch und Eric F. Fiedler.

Paganini, Nicolò, *1782-1840.*
[Quartets, violin, viola, violoncello, guitar, M.S. 35, A major] — Quartetto n. 8 in La maggiore, (M.S. 35), per violino, viola, chitarra e violoncello = Quartet no. 8 in A major (M.S. 35), for violin, viola, guitar and violoncello / Nicolo Paganini ; a cura di Andrea Schiavina. — *Ut Orpheus Edizioni*
785.7194   013953477

Page, Janet Kathleen, *1957-*
See **Bach, Carl Philipp Emanuel, 1714-1788** [Concertos, oboe, string orchestra, H. 466, B♭ major] Oboe concertos / Carl Philipp Emanuel Bach ; edited by Janet K. Page.

Painted memories
See **Brunner, David L., 1953-** Painted memories

Paisiello, Giovanni, *1740-1816.*
I giuochi d'Agrigento / [libretto di] Alessandro Pepoli ; [musica di] Giovanni Paisiello ; saggio introduttivo a cura di Lorenzo Mattei. — *Ricordi*
782.1   013801677

Palestrina, Giovanni Pierluigi da, *1525?-1594.*
[Hymni totius anni. Conditor alme siderum] — Two hymns for Advent and Christmas / Giovanni Pierluigi da Palestrina ; transcribed and edited by Jon Dixon. — *JOED Music*
782.527   013526329

[Hymni totius anni. Veni Creator Spiritus] — Veni Creator Spiritus : SAT(T)B / Giovanni Pierluigi da Palestrina ; transcribed and edited by Jon Dixon. — *JOED Music*
782.52617293   013498084

[Masses, book 3. Missa de Beata Virgine] — Missa de Beata Virgine : [SSATTB] / Giovanni Pierluigi da Palestrina ; transcribed and edited by Jon Dixon. — *JOED Music*
782.53232   013498043

Missa confitebor tibi Domine : [SATB+SATB] / Giovanni Pierluigi da Palestrina ; transcribed and edited by Jon Dixon. — *JOED Music*
782.53232   013498037

Missa fratres ego enim accepi : [SATB+SATB] / Giovanni Pierluigi da Palestrina ; transcribed and edited by Jon Dixon. — *JOED Music*
782.53232   013498057

Missa Hodie Christus natus est : [SSAB+ATTB] / Giovanni Pierluigi da Palestrina ; transcribed and edited by Jon Dixon. — *JOED Music*
782.53232   013498024

[Missa Laudate Dominum omnes gentes] — Missa Laudate Domine : [SATB+SATB] / Giovanni Pierluigi da Palestrina ; transcribed and edited by Jon Dixon. — *JOED Music*
782.53232   013498052

[Motets (1563)] — Motecta festorum totius anni cum communi sanctorum quaternis vocibus / Giovanni Pierluigi da Palestrina ; edizione critica a cura di Daniele V. Filippi. — *ETS*
782.526   013224013

[Motets (1563). Dies sanctificatus] — Dies sanctificatus : SATB / Giovanni Pierluigi da Palestrina ; transcribed and edited by Jon Dixon. — *JOED Music*
782.5261723   013498138

[Motets (1563). Veni sponsa Christi] — Veni sponsa Christi : SATB / Giovanni Pierluigi da Palestrina ; transcribed and edited by Jon Dixon. — *JOED Music*
782.526   013498095

[Motets (1569). Stella, quam viderant Magi] — Stella quam viderant Magi : SATTB / Giovanni Pierluigi da Palestrina ; transcribed and edited by Jon Dixon. — *JOED Music*
782.5261724   013498144

[Motets (1569). Tu es Petrus; arr.] — Tu es petrus : à 7 / Palestrina. — *Alex Ayre Music Services*
785.836197   013374823

[Motets (1572). Ascendo ad Patrem] — Ascendo ad Patrem : (SATTB) / Giovanni Pierluigi da Palestrina ; transcribed and edited by Jon Dixon. — *JOED Music*
782.5261728   013526318

[Motets (1572). Domine, in virtute tua] — Domine, in virtute tua : (SATB+SATB) / Giovanni Pierluigi da Palestrina ; transcribed and edited by Jon Dixon. — *JOED Music*
782.526   013498156

[Motets (1572). Laudate Dominum omnes gentes] — Laudate Dominum omnes gentes : (SATB+SATB) / Giovanni Pierluigi da Palestrina ; transcribed and edited by Jon Dixon. — *JOED Music*
782.5294   013526028

[Motets (1572). Laudate pueri] — Laudate pueri Dominum : SATB+SATB / Giovanni Pierluigi da Palestrina ; transcribed and edited by Jon Dixon. — *JOED Music*
782.5294   013526040

[Motets (1575). Haec dies] — Haec dies : SSATTB / Giovanni Pierluigi da Palestrina ; transcribed and edited by Jon Dixon. — *JOED Music*
782.5261727   013498077

[Motets (1575). Hodie Christus natus est] — Hodie Christus natus est : (SSAB+ATTB) / Giovanni Pierluigi da Palestrina ; transcribed and edited by Jon Dixon. — *JOED Music*
782.5261723   013498063

[Motets (1575). Inclytae Sanctae Virginis Catherinae] — Inclytae Sanctae Virginis Catherinae : SAATB / Giovanni Pierluigi da Palestrina ; transcribed and edited by Jon Dixon. — *JOED Music*
782.526   013498151

[Motets (1575). Jubilate Deo omnis terra, voices (8)] — Iubilate Deo : SATB+SATB / Giovanni

Pierluigi da Palestrina ; transcribed and edited by Jon Dixon. — *JOED Music*
782.5294   013498162

[Motets (1575). Rex pacificus] — Rex pacificus : SAATTB / Giovanni Pierluigi da Palestrina ; transcribed and edited by Jon Dixon. — *JOED Music*
782.5261723   013498111

[Motets (1584 : Voices (4)). *Selections*] — Alma redemptoris ; Ave Regina ; and, Salve Regina : SSSA / Giovanni Pierluigi da Palestrina ; transcribed and edited by Jon Dixon. — *JOED Music*
782.626   013498068

[Offertories, voices (5). *Selections*] — Four offertories for Sundays in Advent / Giovanni Pierluigi da Palestrina ; transcribed and edited by Jon Dixon. — *JOED Music*
782.532351722   013526296

[Offertories, voices (5). Confirma hoc Deus] — Confirma hoc Deus : (SATTB) / Giovanni Pierluigi da Palestrina ; transcribed and edited by Jon Dixon. — *JOED Music*
782.5323517293   013526326

[Offertories, voices (5). Tui sunt coeli] — Offertory at the third mass of Christmas : Tui sunt coeli : SATTB / Giovanni Pierluigi da Palestrina ; transcribed and edited by Jon Dixon. — *JOED Music*
782.532351723   013498103

[Stabat Mater, voices (8)] — Stabat Mater dolorosa : SATB+SATB / Giovanni Pierluigi da Palestrina ; transcribed and edited by Jon Dixon. — *JOED Music*
782.532351726   013526308

Palestrina, Giovanni Pierluigi da, *1525?-1594*. Hymni totius anni.
See **Palestrina, Giovanni Pierluigi da, 1525?-1594.** [Hymni totius anni. Conditor alme siderum] Two hymns for Advent and Christmas / Giovanni Pierluigi da Palestrina ; transcribed and edited by Jon Dixon.

Pallavicino, Benedetto, *ca. 1551-1601*. Madrigals,
See **The amorous hexachord :** madrigal fantasies from the Tregian manuscript / Pallavicino, Bianciardi, and Giovannelli ; edited by Hannah Davidson.

Palmer, Ray, *1808-1887*.
See **Dicie, Don Michael.** [Nineteenth-century hymns. My faith looks up to Thee] Three nineteenth-century hymns. 1, My faith looks up to Thee : for lower voices (TTBB) and piano / [arranged by] Don Michael Dicie.

Pan ddaw ust y nos
See **Samuel, Rhian.** Pan ddaw ust y nos

The pantomine [or rather, pantomime] of Robinson Crusoe
See **Linley, Thomas, 1733-1795.** [Robinson Crusoe. *Vocal score*] The pantomine [or rather, pantomime] of Robinson Crusoe

Panufnik, Roxanna, *1968-*
Westminster mass : for soprano, mixed choir, tubular bells, harp and organ : (1997) / Roxanna Panufnik. — *Universal Edition*
782.53232   014053350

Pappas, Paul.
See **Mraz, Jason.** Waiting for my rocket to come / Jason Mraz ; transcribed by Paul Pappas.

See **Satriani, Joe.** Is there love in space? : [guitar/vocal] / Joe Satriani.

Paradies, Pietro Domenico, *1707-1791*. Sicilienne
See **An die Musik :** 9 classical pieces arranged for string quartet / [arr. by] John Kember.

Parallel lines
See **Duddell, Joe, 1972-** Parallel lines

Paris sketches
See **Ellerby, Martin, 1957-** Paris sketches

Parke, Maria F., *1772 or 3-1822*.
Divertimento and military rondo : for piano / Maria F. Parke ; edited by Barbara Harbach. — *Vivace Press*
786.21852   014457036

[Grand sonatas, op. 1. No. 3] — Grand sonata in D major : for solo piano / Maria F. Parke ; edited by Barbara Harbach. — *Vivace Press*
786.2183   014457037

Parkening, Christopher.
The Christopher Parkening guitar method. Vol. 1 : the art and technique of the classical guitar / in collaboration with Jack Marshall and David Brandon. — *Rev. ed.* — *Hal Leonard*
787.87168076   012874978

The Christopher Parkening guitar method. Vol. 2 : the art and technique of the classical guitar / in collaboration with David Brandon. — *Hal Leonard*
787.87168076   012874979

Parker, Andrew.
See **Victoria, Tomás Luis de, ca. 1548-1611.** [Masses (1583). Missa O quam gloriosum] Missa O Quam gloriosum (SATB) ; Motet, O quam gloriosum est regnum (SATB) / Tomás Luis de Victoria ; transcribed and edited by Andrew Parker.

See **Victoria, Tomás Luis de, ca. 1548-1611.** [Missae, Psalmi, Magnificat, ad Virginem Dei Matrem salutiones, aliaque. Missa Dum complerentur] Missa Dum complerentur (SAATTB) ; Motet, Dum complerentur dies Pentecostes (SSATB) / Tomás Luis de Victoria ; transcribed and edited by Andrew Parker.

Parker, Matthew, *1504-1575*.
See **Tallis, Thomas, ca. 1505-1585.** [Psalm tunes] 8 tunes for Archbishop Parker's psalter / Thomas Tallis ; transcribed and edited by Jon Dixon.

Parnell, Andrew.
Dear Lord and father of mankind : for two-part upper voices and organ / Andrew Parnell. — *Encore Publications*
782.6265   013220445

Preces and responses / words, The Book of common prayer ; music, Andrew Parnell. — *Encore Publications*
782.6326   013220461

Parry, Ben.
And is it true? : SATB / Ben Parry ; [words by John Betjeman] — *Edition Peters*
782.5281723   013304402

Make we merry : SSAATTBB / Ben Parry. — *Edition Peters*
782.52651722   013304583

See **Bach, Johann Sebastian, 1685-1750.** [Wachet auf, ruft uns die Stimme (Cantata). Wachet auf, ruft uns die Stimme; *arr.*] Sleepers wake : SSATTBB / J.S. Bach ; arranged by Ben Parry.

See **The boar's head carol :** SSAATTBB / English traditional ; arranged by Ben Parry.

See **Bushes and briars :** alto solo, SSATTBB : English traditional / arranged by Ben Parry.

See **Charlie is my darlin' :** SSAATTBB : Scottish traditional / arranged by Ben Parry.

See **Ciao bella, ciao :** SSAATTBB : Italian traditional / arranged by Ben Parry.

See **David of the white rock :** SSAATTBB : Welsh traditional / arranged by Ben Parry.

See **Mozart, Wolfgang Amadeus, 1756-1791** [Zauberflöte. Ouverture; *arr.*] Magic flute : overture : SSAATTBB / Mozart ; arranged by Ben Parry.

See **Pierpont, James, 1822-1893.** [Jingle bells; *arr.*] Jingle bells : SSAATTBB / arranged by Ben Parry.

See **The Salley Gardens :** SATB / Irish traditional ; arranged by Ben Parry ; [words by W.B. Yeats]

See **Star of the County Down :** SSAATTBB / Irish traditional ; arranged by Ben Parry.

See **Viel Freuden mit sich bringet :** SSAATTBB / German traditional ; arranged by Ben Parry.

Parry, C. Hubert H. *1848-1918*.
[Jerusalem; *arr.*] — Jerusalem / Hubert Parry ; arranged for wind band by Rob Wiffin. — *Studio Music*
784.8   013390607

Parsley, Osbert, *1511-1585*. In nomine,
See **3 In nomines à 4 :** (TrTr/TTB) / Parsons, Parsley & Weelkes ; edited by Virginia Brookes.

Pärt, Arvo.
Da pacem Domine : für Streichquartett, 2004/2006 / Arvo Pärt. — *11.09.2006.* — *Universal Edition*
785.7194   013812962

Partita for ten wind instruments
See **Dodgson, Stephen, 1924-** [Partitas, winds (1994)] Partita for ten wind instruments

Partita in F-Dur für 2 Flöten, 2 Oboen, 2 Klarinetten, 3 Hörner, 2 Fagotte und Kontrabass, RWV B18 = Partita in F major for 2 flutes, 2 oboes, 2 clarinets, 3 horns, 2 bassoons and double-bass
See **Rosetti, Antonio, ca. 1750-1792.** [Partitas, woodwinds, horns (3), violone, M. B18, F major] Partita in F-Dur für 2 Flöten, 2 Oboen, 2 Klarinetten, 3 Hörner, 2 Fagotte und Kontrabass, RWV B18 = Partita in F major for 2 flutes, 2 oboes, 2 clarinets, 3 horns, 2 bassoons and double-bass

Partita on 'Morgen kommt der Weihnachtsmann'
See **Bach, Johann Christoph Friedrich, 1732-1795.** [Allegretto con variazioni, keyboard instrument, W. XII, 2, G major] Partita on 'Morgen kommt der Weihnachtsmann'

[Partita, woodwinds, horns (2), E♭ major]
See **Righini, Vincenzo, 1756-1812.** [Partita, woodwinds, horns (2), E♭ major]

[Partitas, winds (1994)]
See **Dodgson, Stephen, 1924-** [Partitas, winds (1994)]

[Partitas, woodwinds, horns (3), violone, M. B18, F major]
See **Rosetti, Antonio, ca. 1750-1792.** [Partitas, woodwinds, horns (3), violone, M. B18, F major]

Pascall, Robert.
See **Brahms, Johannes, 1833-1897.** [Symphonies, no. 3, op. 90, F major] Symphonie Nr. 3, F-Dur, Opus 90 / Johannes Brahms ; herausgegeben von Robert Pascall.

Pasetti, Anna, *1967-*
See **Backofen, Johann Georg Heinrich, 1768-1839.** [Concertantes, basset horn, harp, violoncello, op. 7, F major] Concertante, op. 7/8, per arpa, corno di bassetto (o viola) e violoncello ad libitum = for harp, basset-horn (or viola) and violoncello and libitum / Heinrich Backofen ; a cura di Anna Pasetti.

See **Vernier, Jean-Aime, b. 1769.** [Duets, harps, no. 2, op. 30] Deuxieme duo, op. 30, per 2 arpe = for 2 harps / Jean-Aime Vernier ; a cura di Anna Pasetti.

Paskutinių sodų muzika
See **Martinaitis, A. 1950-** Paskutinių sodų muzika

Paso, Antonio, *1870-1958.*
See **Luna, Pablo, 1879-1942.** El asombro de Damasco : zarzuela en dos actos / Pablo Luna ; libreto, Antonio Paso y Joaquín Abati ; edición crítica, Miguel Roa.

Pasquini, Ercole. Jubilate Deo omnis terra.
See **Aleotti, Raffaella, ca. 1570-ca. 1646.** Sacrae cantiones : quinque, septem, octo & decem vocibus decantandae / Raffaella Aleotti ; edited by C. Ann Carruthers ; introduction by Thomas W. Bridges.

Passio Domini nostri Jesu Christi
See **Longueval, Antoine de, fl. 1498-1525.** Passio Domini nostri Jesu Christi

Passion
See **Haydn, Joseph, 1732-1809** [Sieben letzten Worte unseres Erlösers am Kreuze. *English. Vocal score*] Passion

Patalas, Aleksandra.
See **Brikner, Eryk, 1705-1760.** [Completorium (RISM A/II 300.033.575)] Completorium : a canto & basso obligato, alto & tenore ad libitum, due violini con organo ; Hymnus pro festis apostolorum : a canto, alto, tenore, basso con organo / Eryk Brikner ; opracowanie i wstęp Aleksandra Patalas.

Patchen, Kenneth, *1911-1972.*
See **Ellingboe, Bradley.** Be music, night : for unaccompanied mixed choir (SSAATTBB) / words by Kenneth Patchen ; music by Bradley Ellingboe.

Patrick, David, *1934-*
See **Bach, Johann Christoph Friedrich, 1732-1795.** [Allegretto con variazioni, keyboard instrument, W. XII, 2, G major] Partita on 'Morgen kommt der Weihnachtsmann' : ('Twinkle, twinkle little star') : for organ (manuals only) / Johann Christoph Friedrich Bach ; edited by David Patrick.

See **Czerny, Carl, 1791-1857.** [Ouverture charactéristique et brillante] Ouverture brillante : piano duet, (op. 54) / Carl Czerny ; edited by David Patrick.

See **Duparc, Henri, 1848-1933.** Feuilles volantes : op. 1 : piano solo / Henri Duparc ; edited by David Patrick.

See **Elgar, Edward, 1857-1934.** [Adieu] Two piano pieces / Edward Elgar ; edited by David Patrick.

See **Elgar, Edward, 1857-1934.** [Carillon; *arr.*] Carillon, op. 75 ; &, Loughborough memorial chime : organ solo / Edward Elgar ; arranged & edited by David Patrick.

See **Elgar, Edward, 1857-1934.** [Rapid stream, voices (2)] The rapid stream ; The woodland stream / Edward Elgar ; edited by David Patrick.

See **Elgar, Edward, 1857-1934.** [Sonatina, piano] Sonatina : for piano solo / Edward Elgar ; edited by David Patrick.

See **Mozart, Wolfgang Amadeus, 1756-1791.** Jubilate Deo : motet for SATB and organ / attributed to W.A.Mozart ; edited by David Patrick.

See **Three 'storm' pieces** : organ solo / edited by David Patrick.

Päuler, Bernhard.
See **Cambini, Giuseppe Maria, 1746-1825.** [Quintets, violins, viola, violoncellos, no. 21, C minor] 21. Quintett in c-moll für 2 Violinen, Viola und 2 Violoncelli = 21. quintet in C minor for two violins, viola and two violoncellos / Giuseppe Cambini ; nach dem Autograph herausgegeben von Bernhard Päuler.

See **Telemann, Georg Philipp, 1681-1767.** [Concertos, violins (2), viola, continuo, TWV 43:G8, G major] Concerto in G-Dur für 2 Violinen, Viola und Basso continuo = Concerto in G major for 2 violins, viola and basso continuo, TWV 43:G8 / Georg Philipp Telemann ; herausgegeben von Bernhard Päuler ; Continuo-Aussetzung von Wolfgang Kostujak.

Paulinus Saint, *d. 802.*
See **Lole, Simon.** Ubi caritas et amor / Simon Lole.

Pavane, De la Roye
See **Gibbons, Orlando, 1583-1625.** [Pavans, voices (5), H. 30] Pavane, De la Roye

Pavans and galliards in five parts
See **Praetorius, Bartholomeus, ca. 1590-1623.** [Newe liebliche Paduanen und Galliarden] Pavans and galliards in five parts

[Pavans, voices (5), H. 30]
See **Gibbons, Orlando, 1583-1625.** [Pavans, voices (5), H. 30]

Payen, Nicolas, *ca. 1512-ca. 1559.*
[Vocal music. *Selections*] — Motets and chansons / Nicolas Payen ; edited by Laura Pollie McDowell. — *A-R Editions*
782.526   013693493

Payne, Ian.
See **Ward, John, 1571-1638.** [Chamber music. *Selections*] Consort music of four parts / John Ward ; transcribed and edited by Ian Payne.

See **Ward, John, 1571-1638.** [Fantasias, viols (4), Meyer 1-6. *Parts*] Oxford fantasias : and, two-part ayres : for viols and organ / John Ward ; edited by Ian Payne.

Peace like a river
Peace like a river : for mixed chorus (SATB) and organ / [African-American spiritual ; arranged by] Mack Wilberg. — *Oxford University Press*
782.5253   013483999

Peace on earth, goodwill to men
See **Rogers, Wayland.** Peace on earth, goodwill to men

Pearce, Malcolm, musician.
See **Tomorrow shall be my dancing day** : SATB and organ / [English trad. arr.] Malcolm Pearce.

Peçi, Aleksandër, *1951-*
[Concertos, piano, orchestra, no. 1] — Concerto pour piano et orchestre no. 1 / Aleksander Peci. — *Aelfior Editions*
784.262186   014053351

Kecat dhe ujku : Ballet : symphony orchestra / Aleksandër Peçi. — *Aelfior Editions*
784.21556   014053352

Klitheu tragjik : clarinet, string orchestra / Aleksandër Peçi. — *Aelfior Editions*
784.72862   014053353

[Mosaical, saxophones (8)] — Mosaical : saxophone ensemble / Aleksandër Peçi. — *Aelfior Editions*
785.87198   014053354

Motor motus : string orchestra / Aleksandër Peçi. — *Aelfior Editions*
784.7   014053355

Pizzicato brillante : string orchestra / Aleksandër Peçi. — *Aelfior Editions*
784.7   014053356

[Symphonies, no. 1] — Symphonie no. 1 / Aleksander Peçi. — *Aelfior Editions*
784.2184   014053357

Pedrell, Felipe, *1841-1922.*
Los Pirineus : ópera en tres actos / Felipe Pedrell ; libreto, Victor Balaguer ; edición crítica, Francesc Cortes y Edmon Colomer. — *Instituto Complutense de Ciencias Musicales*
782.1   014679497

Peiretti, Rita.
See **Galuppi, Baldassare, 1706-1785.** [Concertos, harpsichord, string orchestra, C minor] Concerti per cembalo n. 5 e n. 6 per clavicembalo, violino I, violino II, viola e basso / Baldassare Galuppi, detto il Buranello ; a cura di Rita Peiretti ; prefazione di Alberto Iesuè.

Pellay, Paul.
See **Clarke, Nigel, 1960-** [City in the sea; *arr.*] The city in the sea : (1995) : concerto for euphonium and band / Nigel Clarke ; piano reduction by Paul Pellay.

Pellegrin, M. l'abbé *1663-1745*
See **Rameau, Jean-Philippe, 1683-1764.** Hippolyte et Aricie : tragédie en cinq actes : version 1757 ; version 1742 (compléments) / [musique de Jean Philippe Rameau] ; livret de Simon-Joseph Pellegrin ; édition de Sylvie Bouissou.

Pelliciari, Monica.
See **Graun, Johann Gottlieb, 1702 or 3-1771.** [Sonatas, viola da gamba, continuo, G major] Solo (Sonata G-Dur) per la viola di gamba / Johann Gottlieb Graun ; trascrizione a cura di Cristiano Contadin e Monica Pelliciari.

Penri-Evans, David, *1956-*
Bayou blues : (1987) : for E flat alto saxophone and piano / David Penri-Evans. — *Da Capo Music*
788.731643   013351595

Pensées sur un prélude
See **Leyendecker, Ulrich, 1946-** Pensées sur un prélude

Pentith, Sybil, *1927-2004.*
Movement : for clarinet & piano / Sybil Pentith. — *Emerson Edition*
788.62   013460664

People who help us
People who help us : 12 original songs from Out of the Ark Music. — *Out of the Ark Music*
782.742   013269312

People, look east
People, look east : upper-voices and organ / Besançon melody arr. Barry Rose ; [words by] Eleanor Farjeon. — *Novello & Co*
782.6281722   013506279

Pepoli, Alessandro Ercole, conte, *1757-1796.*
See **Paisiello, Giovanni, 1740-1816.** I giuochi d'Agrigento / [libretto di] Alessandro Pepoli ; [musica di] Giovanni Paisiello ; saggio introduttivo a cura di Lorenzo Mattei.

Pepusch, John Christopher, *1667-1752.*
[Death of Dido. Oh I feel the friendly blow] —
Aria, Oh I feel the friendly blow : from The
death of Dido : for soprano, recorder, strings and
continuo / J.C. Pepusch. — *Green Man Press*
783.6642   013589506

[English cantatas. *Selections*] — Five cantatas
with recorder : for soprano or tenor, recorder and
continuo / J.C. Pepusch. — *Green Man Press*
783.348   013590950

See **Arnold, Samuel, 1740-1802.** Polly : an
opera : (1777) / music by Johann Christoph
Pepusch ; rearrang'd and new airs compos'd by
Samuel Arnold ; libretto by John Gay ; revis'd
by George Colman, the elder ; edited by Robert
Hoskins.

Perfect pirates
See **Brookes, Katherine.** Perfect pirates

Perrin, Jacques, *1941-*
See **Coulais, Bruno.** [Choristes. *Vocal score.*
Selections] Les choristes : piano, chant
(choeurs), paroles.

Peter Warlock Society.
See **Warlock, Peter, 1894-1930.** [Songs.
Selections] Songs 1920-1923 : medium voice /
Peter Warlock ; edited by Michael Pilkington.

See **Warlock, Peter, 1894-1930.** [Songs.
Selections] Songs 1923-1926 : medium voice /
Peter Warlock ; edited by Michael Pilkington.

See **Warlock, Peter, 1894-1930.** [Songs.
Selections] Songs 1923-1928 : high voice / Peter
Warlock ; edited by Michael Pilkington.

See **Warlock, Peter, 1894-1930.** [Songs.
Selections] Songs 1927-1928 : medium voice /
Peter Warlock ; edited by Michael Pilkington.

See **Warlock, Peter, 1894-1930.** [Songs.
Selections] Songs 1928-1930 : medium voice /
Peter Warlock ; edited by Michael Pilkington.

Petite suite
See **Hakim, Naji, 1955-** Petite suite

Petrenz, Siegfried.
See **Mozart, Wolfgang Amadeus, 1756-1791.**
[Sinfonie concertanti, violin, viola, orchestra, K.
364, E♭, major; *arr.*] Sinfonia concertante für
Violine, Viola und Orchester, Es-dur, KV 364 =
Sinfonia concertante in E♭ major for violin, viola
and orchestra, K. 364 / Wolfgang Amadeus
Mozart ; herausgegeben von Wolf-Dieter
Seiffert ; Klavierauszug von Siegfried Petrenz ;
Fingersatz und Strichbezeichnung von Frank
Peter Zimmermann [und] Tabea Zimmermann ;
piano reduction.

See **Quantz, Johann Joachim, 1697-1773.**
[Concertos, flute, string orchestra, QV 5:149, F
major] Flötenkonzert in F : Concerto QV 5:149,
per flauto traverso, 2 violini, viola e basso
continuo (violoncello, contrabbasso, cembalo) /
Johann Joachim Quantz ; Generalbassaussetzung
von Siegfried Petrenz.

Petrie, Robert, *1767-1830.*
See **Thistle & minuet :** 16 easy pieces from the
Scottish Baroque for violin (or flute or oboe),
keyboard, and optional cello (or bassoon) = 16
einfache Stücke aus der schottischen Barockzeit
für Violine (oder Flöte oder Oboe),
Tasteninstrument und Cello (oder Fagott) ad
libitum = 16 pièces faciles du Baroque écossais
pour violon (ou flûte ou hautbois), clavier et
violoncelle (ou basson) facultatif / edited by
David Johnson.

Peyroux, Madeleine.
See **Careless love** / Madeleine Peyroux.

Pezold, Christian, *1677-1733*
[Suites, harpsichord, G major. Menuet
alternativement; *arr.*] — Minuet : from the Anna
Magdalena notebook : grade 1 / J.S. Bach [or
rather, Christian Pezold] ; arr. Kit Turnbull. —
Studio Music
784.818835   013359647

[Pezzo agitato con un intermezzo amoroso]
See **Zarębski, Juliusz, 1854-1885.** [Pezzo
agitato con un intermezzo amoroso]

Pfeiffer, Iris.
See **Schreker, Franz, 1878-1934.** [Choral
music] Chorwerk / Franz Schreker ;
Gesamtausgabe herausgegeben von Christopher
Hailey, Iris Pfeiffer.

Pflüger, Maria.
See **Terteryan, A. 1929-** [Quartets, strings, no.
2] Streichquartett Nr. 2 = String quartet no. 2 /
Avet Terterjan ; [herausgegeben von Maria
Pflüger]

Phalèse, Pierre, *ca. 1550-1629.*
See **Le rossignol musical des chansons :**
(Antwerp, 1597) / edited by Gerald R. Hoekstra.

Philarmonica, Mrs.
[Sonatas, violins (2), violoncello, continuo] —
12 Triosonaten für 2 Violinen und B.c. (1715) =
12 trio sonatas for 2 violins and b.c. (1715) / by
Mrs. Philarmonica ; edited by Elke Martha
Umbach. — *Furore Verlag*
785.28194183   013031307

Philarmonica, Mrs. Divertimenti da camera.
See **Philarmonica, Mrs.** [Sonatas, violins (2),
violoncello, continuo] 12 Triosonaten für 2
Violinen und B.c. (1715) = 12 trio sonatas for 2
violins and b.c. (1715) / by Mrs. Philarmonica ;
edited by Elke Martha Umbach.

Phillips, Craig, *1961-*
[Serenade, horn, organ] — Serenade for horn
and organ / Craig Phillips. — *Oxford University
Press*
788.941856   013114440

Phillips, Mark, *1947-*
See **60 progressive solos for classical guitar :**
featuring the music of the world's greatest
composers: Bach, Handel, Mozart, Beethoven,
and Brahms / arranged by Mark Phillips.

Phoebe
See **Greene, Maurice, 1696-1755** Phoebe

Phoenix trio
See **Wilson, Andrew, 1960-** Phoenix trio

[Phonus]
See **Hurel, Philippe, 1955-** [Phonus]

Phonus, ou, La voix du faune
See **Hurel, Philippe, 1955-** [Phonus] Phonus,
ou, La voix du faune

Piangete occhi, piangete
See **Mazzocchi, D. 1592-1665.** [Musiche sacre,
e morali. Piangete occhi, piangete] Piangete
occhi, piangete

The piano collection
See **Nyman, Michael.** [Selections; *arr.*] The
piano collection

Piano compositions.
See **Rachmaninoff, Sergei, 1873-1943.** [Piano
music. *Selections*] Piano compositions.

Piano concerto, 1990, revised 1994
See **Lindberg, Magnus, 1958-** [Concertos,
piano, orchestra, no. 1] Piano concerto, 1990,
revised 1994

[Piano music]
See **Wesley, Samuel, 1766-1837.** [Piano music]

Piano music
See **Wesley, Samuel, 1766-1837.** [Piano music]
Piano music

Piano music of Spain.
Piano music of Spain. — *Chester Music*
786.20946   013196854

[Piano music. *Selections; arr.*]
See **Grieg, Edvard, 1843-1907.** [Piano music.
Selections; arr.]

[Piano music. *Selections*]
See **Lepik, Tarmo, 1946-2001.** [Piano music.
Selections]

See **Liszt, Franz, 1811-1886.** [Piano music.
Selections]

See **Rachmaninoff, Sergei, 1873-1943.** [Piano
music. *Selections*]

**Piano quintet in C minor (1903), for violin, viola,
cello, double bass and piano**
See **Vaughan Williams, Ralph, 1872-1958.**
[Quintets, piano, violin, viola, violoncello,
double bass, C minor] Piano quintet in C minor
(1903), for violin, viola, cello, double bass and
piano

Piano sonata no. 1
See **Cooke, Arnold.** [Sonatas, piano, no. 1]
Piano sonata no. 1

Piano sonata no. 2
See **Cooke, Arnold.** [Sonatas, piano, no. 2]
Piano sonata no. 2

Piano sonata no.2
See **Hedges, Anthony, 1931-** [Sonatas, piano,
no. 2, op. 154] Piano sonata no.2

The piano transcriptions
See **John, Elton.** [Songs. *Selections*] The piano
transcriptions

Piano trio
See **Davies, Peter Maxwell, 1934-** [Trio, piano,
strings] Piano trio

Piave, Francesco Maria, *1810-1876.*
See **Verdi, Giuseppe, 1813-1901.** Stiffelio /
Giuseppe Verdi ; libretto (in three acts) by
Francesco Maria Piave ; edited by Kathleen
Kuzmick Hansell.

Piccola composizione
See **Donizetti, Gaetano, 1797-1848.** Piccola
composizione

Piccolo, Anthony, *1946-*
O come, let us sing unto the Lord = (Venite,
exultemus Domino) / Anthony Piccolo ; [words],
Psalm 95:1-7. — *Oxford University Press*
782.5294   013441837

[Piccolo, piano music]
See **Gething, Joseph.** [Piccolo, piano music]

Pickard, John, *1963-*
See **Elgar, Edward, 1857-1934** [Concertos,
violoncello, orchestra, op. 85.] Concerto in E
minor, opus 85, for violoncello and orchestra /
Edward Elgar ; arrangement for violoncello and
piano by the composer.

Pickard, Martin.
See **Russian operatic arias for baritone :** 19th
and 20th-century repertoire : complete with
translations and guidance on pronunciation /
selected and edited by David Fanning ; singing
translations by Martin Pickard.

Pictures at another exhibition
See **Brouwer, Leo, 1939-** Pictures at another
exhibition

[Pieces blue, bassoon, piano (2004)]
See **Carr, Paul.** [Pieces blue, bassoon, piano (2004)]

[Pièces de clavecin, 1er livre]
See **Jollage, Charles-Alexandre.** [Pièces de clavecin, 1er livre]

[Pièces de clavecin, op. 1]
See **Helmont, Charles Joseph van, 1715-1790.** [Pièces de clavecin, op. 1]

Pièces de clavecin, opus I
See **Helmont, Charles Joseph van, 1715-1790.** [Pièces de clavecin, op. 1] Pièces de clavecin, opus I

[Pièces de violes, 4e livre. 1ère partie. *Selections; arr.*]
See **Marais, Marin, 1656-1728.** [Pièces de violes, 4e livre. 1ère partie. *Selections; arr.*]

Pieces for piccolo
See **Gething, Joseph.** [Piccolo, piano music] Pieces for piccolo

Pieces of eight
See **Dodgson, Stephen, 1924-** Pieces of eight

[Pieces, piano, flutes (2) (2004)]
See **Barton, David, 1983-** [Pieces, piano, flutes (2) (2004)]

Pierpont, James, 1822-1893.
[Jingle bells; *arr.*] — Jingle bells : for two-part or mixed chorus and piano / [James Pierpont ; arranged by] Reginald Unterseher. — *Oxford University Press*
782.5421723   013515374

[Jingle bells; *arr.*] — Jingle bells : SATB / arranged by Jonathan Rathbone. — *Edition Peters*
782.5421723   013304552

[Jingle bells; *arr.*] — Jingle bells : SSAATTBB / arranged by Ben Parry. — *Edition Peters*
782.5421723   013304535

[Jingle bells; *arr.*] — Jingle, bells / J. Pierpont ; arranged by David Blackwell. — *Oxford University Press*
782.5421723   013173829

Pieśni i hymny Piwnicy pod Baranami
Pieśni i hymny Piwnicy pod Baranami / [wybór piosenek Piotr Ferster, Marek Pacuła] — *Piwnica pod Baranami*
783.42709438   013739029

Piglet's big movie (Motion picture)
See **Piglet's big movie** / featuring new songs by Carly Simon. — *Walt Disney Music Co. :*

Piglet's big movie
Piglet's big movie / featuring new songs by Carly Simon. — *Walt Disney Music Co. :*
783.2421542   006914468

Pilgrim, Jack.
See **Serini, Giovanni Battista, b. ca. 1710.** [Sonatas, flute, continuo, D major] Sonata no. 1 in D : flute/oboe & piano / Giovanni Battista Serini ; [edited by Jack Pilgrim]

Pilkington, Michael.
See **Dvořák, Antonín, 1841-1904.** [Masses, B. 175, D major. *Vocal score*] Mass in D major : op. 86 : for soprano, alto, tenor and bass soloists, SATB and organ, or SATB (with optional soloists) and orchestra = Mše D dur / Antonín Dvořák ; edited by Michael Pilkington.

See **A selection of Italian arias, c.1600-c.1800.** Volume II / edition prepared by Damian Cranmer ; English translations by Dorothy Richardson ; edition supervised by Michael Pilkington.

See **Warlock, Peter, 1894-1930.** [Songs. *Selections*] Songs 1920-1923 : medium voice / Peter Warlock ; edited by Michael Pilkington.

See **Warlock, Peter, 1894-1930.** [Songs. *Selections*] Songs 1923-1926 : medium voice / Peter Warlock ; edited by Michael Pilkington.

See **Warlock, Peter, 1894-1930.** [Songs. *Selections*] Songs 1923-1928 : high voice / Peter Warlock ; edited by Michael Pilkington.

See **Warlock, Peter, 1894-1930.** [Songs. *Selections*] Songs 1927-1928 : medium voice / Peter Warlock ; edited by Michael Pilkington.

See **Warlock, Peter, 1894-1930.** [Songs. *Selections*] Songs 1928-1930 : medium voice / Peter Warlock ; edited by Michael Pilkington.

Pipor och klockor
See **Börtz, Daniel, 1943-** Pipor och klockor

Los Pirineus
See **Pedrell, Felipe, 1841-1922.** Los Pirineus

Pitkin, Jonathan, *1978-*
Esto mihi in Deum protectorem : SATB (with divisions) a cappella / Jonathan Pitkin. — *Oxford University Press*
782.526   013213412

Pitts, W. S. *1830-1918*. Church in the wildwood.
See **Dicie, Don Michael.** [Nineteenth-century hymns. The church in the wildwood] Three nineteenth-century hymns. 2, The church in the wildwood : for lower voices (TTBB) and piano / [arranged by] Don Michael Dicie.

Pizzicato brillante
See **Peçi, Aleksandër, 1951-** Pizzicato brillante

Platée
See **Rameau, Jean-Philippe, 1683-1764.** [Platée. *Vocal score*] Platée

[Platée. *Vocal score*]
See **Rameau, Jean-Philippe, 1683-1764.** [Platée. *Vocal score*]

Play bass with— Muse.
See **Muse (Musical group : Great Britain)** [Songs. *Selections*] Play bass with— Muse.

Play guitar with— 20 rock classics.
Play guitar with— 20 rock classics. — *Wise*
783.242166   013299265

Play guitar with— Coldplay
See **Coldplay (Musical group)** [X&Y; *arr.*] Play guitar with— Coldplay

Play guitar with— Eric Clapton.
See **Clapton, Eric.** [Songs. *Selections*] Play guitar with— Eric Clapton.

Play guitar with— Metallica.
See **Metallica (Musical group)** [Songs. *Selections*] Play guitar with— Metallica.

Play guitar with— Muse
See **Muse (Musical group : Great Britain)** [Songs. *Selections*] Play guitar with— Muse

Play guitar with— The Clash.
See **Clash (Musical group)** [Songs. *Selections*] Play guitar with— The Clash.

Play guitar with— The Smiths.
See **Smiths (Musical group)** [Songs. *Selections*] Play guitar with— The Smiths.

Play guitar with— U2
See **U2 (Musical group)** [Songs. *Selections*] Play guitar with— U2

Play guitar with— Velvet Revolver, U2, Jeff Buckley, the Killers, Jet and Razorlight.
Play guitar with— Velvet Revolver, U2, Jeff Buckley, the Killers, Jet and Razorlight. — *Wise Publications*
783.242166   013191043

Play piano with — Keane
See **Keane (Musical group)** [Hopes and fears; *arr.*] Play piano with — Keane

Play piano with — Keane, Coldplay, Muse and other great artists.
Play piano with — Keane, Coldplay, Muse and other great artists. — *Wise Publications*
786.2164   013101817

Play piano with— John Lennon … [et al.]
Play piano with— John Lennon … [et al.] — *Wise*
783.242166   013432731

Play piano with— Ray Charles.
Play piano with— Ray Charles. — *Wise*
783.242164   013201608

Pleyel, Ignaz, 1757-1831.
See **Thomson, Mr. 1757-1851.** [Select collection of original Scotish airs] Scottish songs : for George Thomson : 32 schottische Lieder für 1-2 Singstimmen, Violine, Violoncello und Klavier / [music by] Ignaz Pleyel ; [edited by] Marjorie Rycroft.

See **Urcullu, Leopoldo.** [Thème & variations, guitar, op. 10, E major] Thème & variations pour guitare, op. 10 / Leopoldo de Urcullu.

Poème symphonique
See **Escudero, Francisco, 1912-2002.** Poème symphonique

Poetzsch-Seban, Ute.
See **Telemann, Georg Philipp, 1681-1767.** [Cantatas. *Selections*] Französischer Jahrgang : Kantaten von Neujahr bis zum Sonntag Sexagesimae und dem Fest Mariae Reinigung / Georg Philipp Telemann ; herausgegeben von Ute Poetzsch-Seban.

Polka
See **Schnittke, Alfred, 1934-1998.** [Overcoat. Polka; *arr.*] Polka

Polly
See **Arnold, Samuel, 1740-1802.** Polly

Polska pieśń wielogłosowa XVI i początku XVII wieku
Polska pieśń wielogłosowa XVI i początku XVII wieku / zebrał i przygotował do druku = edited by Piotr Poźniak ; transkrypcja i opracowanie tekstów staropolskich = old Polish texts transcribed and annotated by Wacław Walecki. — *Instytut Sztuki Polskiej Akademii Nauk*
782.527   013277659

Pomfret, Richard.
See **Ledger, Philip.** Bethlehem : for unison voices & keyboard [and percussion] / Philip Ledger ; words by Richard Pomfret.

See **Ledger, Philip.** Gift of love : for solo, upper voices (SSA) & keyboard / Philip Ledger & David Miller ; words by Richard Pomfret.

Pompeii
See **Brookes, Katherine.** Pompeii

See **Brookes, Katherine.** [Pompeii. *Selections*] Pompeii

[Pompeii. *Selections*]
See **Brookes, Katherine.** [Pompeii. *Selections*]

Poniatowska, Irena.
See **Chopin, Frédéric, 1810-1849.** [Sonatas, piano no. 3, op. 58, B minor] Sonata H-Moll Op. 58 : wydanie faksymilowe rękopisu ze zbiorów Biblioteki Narodowej w Warszawie (Mus. 232 Cim.) = Sonata in B minor, op. 58 : facsimile edition of the manuscript held in the National Library in Warsaw (Mus. 232 Cim.) : A IX/58 / Fryderyk Chopin ; Komitet redakcyjny = Editorial committee, Jean-Jacques Eigeldinger (przewodniczący = president), Zofia Chechlińska (redaktor naczelny = editor in chief) … [et al.]

Pooh's heffalump movie (Motion picture)
See **Pooh's heffalump movie** / [featuring new songs by Carly Simon] — *Disneytoon studios :*

Pooh's heffalump movie
Pooh's heffalump movie / [featuring new songs by Carly Simon] — *Disneytoon studios :*
783.2421542   013376143

Poole, Geoffrey, *1949-*
Fragments : (1974 rev. '98) : for 14 solo strings (44321) or multiples / Geoffrey Poole. — *Maecenas Music*
785.7199   013422512

Schubert's Reliquie / realisation and completion by Geoffrey Poole (1997) of Schubert's Sonata in C Major, D 840. — *Maecenas Music*
786.2   013422443

Popular sheet music hits
Popular sheet music hits : easy piano ; arranged by Dan Coates. — *International Music Publications*
783.242164   013046772

Porpora, Nicola, *1686-1768*.
[Concertos, flute, string orchestra, D major] — Concerto per flauto ed archi / Niccolò Porpora ; a cura di Pietro Spada. — *Boccaccini & Spada*
784.72832186   014053358

[Duetti latini per la passione di Gesù Cristo] — Sei duetti latini sulla passione di nostro signore Gesù Cristo ; Motetti per Angiola Moro / Nicola Antonio Porpora ; edizione critica a cura di Stefano Aresi. — *ETS*
783.1226   013224213

Porpora, Nicola, *1686-1768*. Placida surge Aurora.
See **Porpora, Nicola, 1686-1768.** [Duetti latini per la passione di Gesù Cristo] Sei duetti latini sulla passione di nostro signore Gesù Cristo ; Motetti per Angiola Moro / Nicola Antonio Porpora ; edizione critica a cura di Stefano Aresi.

Porta, Enzo.
See **Locatelli, Pietro Antonio, 1695-1764.** [Arte del violino. Capricci] Ventiquattro capricci per violino solo [op. III] / Pietro Antonio Locatelli ; in base all'edizione a cura di Albert Dunning ; con diteggiature ed esercizi preparatori di Enzo Porta.

Portman, Rachel.
[Little prince. Birds; *arr.*] — The birds : from The little prince : for SSA and piano / Rachel Portman ; [arr. by Richard Allain] — *Chester Music*
782.642   013213576

[Little prince. Lamplighters; *arr.*] — The lamplighters : from The little prince ; for SSA and piano / Rachel Portman ; [arr. by Richard Allain] — *Chester Music*
782.642   013213662

[Little prince. Look at the stars; *arr.*] — Look at the stars : from The little prince ; for SSA and

piano / Rachel Portman ; [arr. by Richard Allain] — *Chester Music*
782.642   013213587

[Little prince. Roses; *arr.*] — The roses : from The little prince : for SSA and piano / Rachel Portman ; [arr. by Richard Allain] — *Chester Music*
782.642   013213598

[Little prince. Stars; *arr.*] — The stars : from The little prince ; for SSA and piano / Rachel Portman ; [arr. by Richard Allain] — *Chester Music*
782.642   013213592

Portugal, Marcos Antônio da Fonseca, *1762-1830*.
Gli Orazi e i Curiazi : partitura dell'opera in facsimile, edizione del libretto / [libretto di] Simeone Antonio Sografi ; [musica di] Marco Portogallo. Catalogo cronologico degli spettacoli a Venezia (1797-1815) / a cura di Maria Giovanna Miggiani. — *Ricordi*
782.1   014661287

Pośpiech, Remigiusz.
See **Elsner, Józef, 1769-1854.** [Masses, F major] Missa F a canto, alto, tenore, basso, due violini, viole, bassi (violoncello et basso), due clarinetti, due corni con organo / Józef Elsner ; opracowanie, Hubert Prochota ; wstęp, Remigiusz Pośpiech ; [redaktor, Irena Stachel]

See **Żebrowski, Marcin Józef.** [Masses, D major (RISM A/II 300.033.496)] Missa ex D a canto, basso, due violini, due clarini ad libitum con organo / Marcin Józef Żebrowski ; opracowanie i wstęp Remigiusz Pośpiech.

See **Żebrowski, Marcin Józef.** Missa pastoralis : a canto, basso, due violini, due clarini con organo / Marcin Józef Żebrowski ; opracowanie i wstęp Remigiusz Pośpiech ; [redaktor, Irena Stachel]

A posy of pieces
See **Hubicki, Margaret.** A posy of pieces

Pott, Francis, *1957-*
Introduction, toccata and fugue : for organ / Francis Pott. — *United Music Publishers*
786.51872   013192631

Lullay, my liking : for SATB chorus / Francis Pott. — *Novello*
785.281723   013313841

Poucke, Peter van.
See **Hildegard, Saint, 1098-1179.** [Symphonia armonie celestium revelationum] Symphonia harmoniae caelestium revelationum : Dendermonde, St.-Pieters & Paulusabdij, ms. Cod. 9 / Hildegard of Bingen ; introduction, Peter van Poucke.

Poulenc, Francis, *1899-1963*.
[Sonatas, oboe, piano] — Sonata for oboe and piano / Francis Poulenc ; edited by Millan Sachania. — *Rev. ed., 2004.* — *Chester Music*
788.52183   013132095

Poulenc, Francis, *1899-1963*. Mouvements perpétuels;
See **The violin** : a collection : new and recent repertoire for violin with piano accompaniment / Craig Armstrong … [et al.]

Le pouvoir de l'Amour
See **Royer, Pancrace, 1705-1755.** Le pouvoir de l'Amour

Powell, Robert J.
See **Fisherman Peter** : a South Carolina spiritual for unaccompanied choir (SATB) / arranged by Robert J. Powell.

Poźniak, Piotr.
See **Polska pieśń wielogłosowa XVI i początku XVII wieku** / zebrał i przygotował do druku = edited by Piotr Poźniak ; transkrypcja i opracowanie tekstów staropolskich = old Polish texts transcribed and annotated by Wacław Walecki.

Praetorius, Bartholomeus, *ca. 1590-1623*.
[Newe liebliche Paduanen und Galliarden] — Pavans and galliards in five parts = Newe lieblische Paduanen und Galliarden mit fünff Stimmen, 1616 / Bartholomeus Praetorius ; [Bearbeitung und Herausgabe, Richard Carter] — *Cornetto, Lizenzausgabe von Oriana*
785.151882   014629729

Praetorius, Michael, *1571-1621*. Musae Sioniae,
See **Rentz, Earlene.** Lo, how a rose e'er blooming = (Es ist ein' Ros' entsprungen) : for mixed choir (SATB), flute and piano / [from Alte Catholische Geistliche Kirchengesang' (1599) harmonized by Michael Praetorius (1609) ; arranged by] Earlene Rentz.

See **Rentz, Earlene.** Lo, how a rose e'er blooming = (Es ist ein' Ros' entsprungen) : for upper voices (SA), flute and piano / [from Alte Catholische Geistliche Kirchengesang' (1599) harmonized by Michael Praetorius (1609) ; arranged by] Earlene Rentz.

Praise the Lord, O ye his servants
See **Wilkinson, fl. 1579-1596.** Praise the Lord, O ye his servants

Prayer for the healing of the sick
See **Tavener, John.** Prayer for the healing of the sick

Preces and responses
See **Parnell, Andrew.** Preces and responses

[Prelude, orchestra]
See **Escudero, Francisco, 1912-2002.** [Prelude, orchestra]

Préludes
See **Chopin, Frédéric, 1810-1849.** [Preludes, piano] Préludes

[Preludes, piano]
See **Chopin, Frédéric, 1810-1849.** [Preludes, piano]

See **Lenot, Jacques.** [Preludes, piano]

Preludi místic núm. 5
See **Besses, Antoni.** [Preludi místic, no. 5] Preludi místic núm. 5

Preludi místic núm. 6
See **Besses, Antoni.** [Preludi místic, no. 6] Preludi místic núm. 6

[Preludi místic, no. 5]
See **Besses, Antoni.** [Preludi místic, no. 5]

[Preludi místic, no. 6]
See **Besses, Antoni.** [Preludi místic, no. 6]

Preludio
See **Escudero, Francisco, 1912-2002.** [Prelude, orchestra] Preludio

Premier livre de pièces de clavecin
See **Jollage, Charles-Alexandre.** [Pièces de clavecin, 1er livre] Premier livre de pièces de clavecin

Prepare thyself, Zion
See **Bach, Johann Sebastian, 1685-1750.** [Weihnachts-Oratorium. Bereite dich Zion, mit zärtlichen Trieben; *arr. English & German*] Prepare thyself, Zion

Près
See **Saariaho, Kaija.** Près

Preserve me, O Lord
See **Wilkinson, fl. 1579-1596.** Preserve me, O Lord

Presley, Elvis, *1935-1977.*
[Songs. *Selections*] — Elvis : guitar play-along. — *Hal Leonard*
783.242166   013219807

See **Elvis Presley greats.**

Preti, Girolamo, *1582-1626.*
See **Mazzocchi, D. 1592-1665.** [Musiche sacre, e morali. Piangete occhi, piangete] Piangete occhi, piangete : dovemo piangere la Passione di N. S. / Domenico Mazzocchi ; [words by] Girolamo Preti.

Previn, André, *1929-*
[Songs (2004)] — Four songs : for tenor and piano / André Previn ; texts by Philip Larkin and William Carlos Williams. — *G. Schirmer*
783.8742   013376711

Il primo libro de madrigali a cinque voci
See **Striggio, Alessandro, 1536 or 7-1592.** [Madrigals, voices (5), book 1] Il primo libro de madrigali a cinque voci

Prior, Matthew, *1664-1721.*
See **Fesch, Willem de, 1687-1761.** [Songs. *Selections*] Matthew Prior songs : for voice and basso continuo : 1741 / Willem de Fesch ; based on 'Lyric Poems' by Matthew Prior ; edited by Robert L. Tusler.

Prize fight
See **Lambert, Constant, 1905-1951.** Prize fight

[Pro quos criminis]
See **Zelenka, Johann Dismas, 1679-1745.** [Pro quos criminis]

Prochota, Hubert.
See **Elsner, Józef, 1769-1854.** [Masses, F major] Missa F a canto, alto, tenore, basso, due violini, viole, bassi (violoncello et basso), due clarinetti, due corni con organo / Józef Elsner ; opracowanie, Hubert Prochota ; wstęp, Remigiusz Pośpiech ; [redaktor, Irena Stachel]

See **Elsner, Józef, 1769-1854.** [Vespers, D major] Nieszpory = Vespers : ex Officio majori Beatae Virginis Mariae ad Vesperas : a canto, alto, tenore, basso, due violini, viola, bassi (violoncello et basso), due flauti, due clarinetti, due corni, due clarini, timpani con organo / Jozef Elsner ; opracowanie Hubert Prochota ; wstęp Remigiusz Pośpiech.

[Progressive sonatinas]
See **Clementi, Muzio, 1752-1832.** [Progressive sonatinas]

Prologue & canzona
See **Vine, Carl, 1954-** Prologue & canzona

Prologue
See **Addison, John, 1920-1998.** Prologue

Der Protagonist
See **Weill, Kurt, 1900-1950.** Der Protagonist

Psalm 124: a song of deliverance
See **Shields, Valerie.** Psalm 124: a song of deliverance

[Psalm tunes]
See **Tallis, Thomas, ca. 1505-1585.** [Psalm tunes]

[Psalmen Davids (1619). 100. Psalm. *Italian & German***]**
See **Schütz, Heinrich, 1585-1672.** [Psalmen Davids (1619). 100. Psalm. *Italian & German*]

Psalmes, sonets and songs (1588)
See **Byrd, William, 1542 or 3-1623.** [Psalmes, sonets, and songs] Psalmes, sonets and songs (1588)

[Psalmes, sonets, and songs]
See **Byrd, William, 1542 or 3-1623.** [Psalmes, sonets, and songs]

[Psalms. I will lift up mine eyes; arr.]
See **Head, Michael, 1900-1976.** [Psalms. I will lift up mine eyes; arr.]

[Psalms. Make a joyful noise unto the Lord; arr.]
See **Head, Michael, 1900-1976.** [Psalms. Make a joyful noise unto the Lord; arr.]

Puccini, Giacomo, *1858-1924.*
[Capriccio sinfonico] — Capriccio sinfonico / Giacomo Puccini ; a cura di Pietro Spada. — *Boccaccini & Spada*
784.2   014694866

Puig, Manuel Beso de la mujer araña.
See **Kander, John.** [Kiss of the spider woman. *Vocal score. Selections*] Kiss of the spider woman : the musical : [vocal selections] / book by Terrence McNally ; music by John Kander ; lyrics by Fred Ebb ; based on the novel by Manuel Puig.

Puliti, Gabriello, b. ca. 1575.
Ghirlanda odorifera : (1612) / Gabriello Puliti ; transkribiral in revidiral = transcription and revision by Ivano Cavallini. — *Slovenska akademija znanosti in umetnosti*
783.1343   014663578

Pupil's concertos nos. 1-5, complete
See **Seitz, Friedrich, 1848-1918.** [Schüler-Konzerte] Pupil's concertos nos. 1-5, complete

Purcell Society.
See **Purcell, Henry, 1659-1695.** [Choral music. *Selections*] Royal welcome songs. Part II / Henry Purcell ; edited under the supervision of the Purcell Society by Bruce Wood.

Purcell, Henry, *1659-1695.*
[Choral music. *Selections*] — Royal welcome songs. Part II / Henry Purcell ; edited under the supervision of the Purcell Society by Bruce Wood. — *[New ed.]* — *Novello*
782.542   013213667

[Fairy queen. *Selections*] — The four seasons in the Fairy queen : for soprano, alto, tenor, and bass solos, strings and continuo : from Orpheus Britannicus / Henry Purcell. — *Green Man Press*
783.342   013597526

[Fairy queen. Plaint] — O, O let me weep! : for soprano, oboe (or recorder) and continuo : from Orpheus Britannicus / Henry Purcell. — *Green Man Press*
783.6642   013597510

[Soft notes and gently rais'd accent] — Two songs with flutes : from Orpheus Britannicus / Henry Purcell. — *Green Man Press*
783.1242   013589523

[Songs. *Selections*] — Songs for bass solo : from Orpheus Britannicus / Henry Purcell. — *Green Man Press*
783.8942   013590938

[Trio sonatas, violins, continuo, Z. 796, E minor; *arr.*] — Sonata VII in E minor : from set of twelve : for violin, viola/violin & violoncello / Henry Purcell. — *SJ Music*
785.7194   013259032

[Vocal music. *Selections*] — 4 duets from Orpheus Britannicus : for soprano and bass with basso continuo / Henry Purcell. — *Green Man Press*
783.1242   013589515

[Vocal music. *Selections*] — Three songs with hautboys : from Orpheus Britannicus / Henry Purcell. — *Green Man Press*
783.342   013597487

Purcell, Henry, *1659-1695.* **Awake, ye dead.**
See **Jeffreys, George, ca. 1610-1685.** [With notes that are both loud and sweet] Two duets for basses : for voices and basso continuo / Jeffreys & Purcell.

Purcell, Henry, *1659-1695.* **How pleasant is this flow'ry plain.**
See **Purcell, Henry, 1659-1695.** [Soft notes and gently rais'd accent] Two songs with flutes : from Orpheus Britannicus / Henry Purcell.

Pushing the senses
See **Feeder (Musical group)** Pushing the senses

Pushkin, Aleksandr Sergeevich, *1799-1837*
See **Shostakovich, Dmitriĭ Dmitrievich, 1906-1975.** [Vocal music. *Selections*] Dve basni I.A. Krylova, dlià metsso-soprano, zhenskogo khora (metsso-soprano) i orkestra, soch. 4 ; Shest' romansov na slova iāponskikh poėtov, dlià tenora s orkestrom, soch. 21 ; Tri romansa na slova A.S. Pushkina, dlià basa i kamernogo orkestra, soch. 46a / Dmitriĭ Shostakovich ; obshchaià redaktsiià i poiàsnitel'naià stat'ià Manashira ĬAkubova.

Put memory away
See **Chilcott, Bob.** [And peace on earth. Put memory away. *Vocal score*] Put memory away

Pyr aionion
See **Thoresen, Lasse, 1949-** Pyr aionion

Quantz, Johann Joachim, *1697-1773.*
[Concertos, flute, string orchestra, QV 5:149, F major] — Flötenkonzert in F : Concerto QV 5:149, per flauto traverso, 2 violini, viola e basso continuo (violoncello, contrabbasso, cembalo) / Johann Joachim Quantz ; Generalbassaussetzung von Siegfried Petrenz. — *Erstausg. / — Carus*
784.72832186   013953478

Quarles, Francis, *1592-1644.*
See **Lole, Simon.** My beloved is mine / music: Simon Lole ; words: Francis Quarles.

Quartet
See **Samuel, Rhian.** [Light and water] Quartet

Quartet en Do menor
See **Toldrà, Eduardo.** [Quartets, strings, D minor] Quartet en Do menor

[Quartets, bassoon, violin, viola, violoncello, B♭ major]
See **Graf, Friedrich Hartmann, 1727-1795.** [Quartets, bassoon, violin, viola, violoncello, B♭ major]

[Quartets, clarinet, bassoon, violin, viola, op. 1. No. 2]
See **Küchler, Johann, 1738-1790** [Quartets, clarinet, bassoon, violin, viola, op. 1. No. 2]

[Quartets, strings]
See **Brahms, Johannes, 1833-1897.** [Quartets, strings]

See **Sirmen, Maddalena Laura Lombardini, 1745-1818.** [Quartets, strings]

[Quartets, strings, C minor]
See **Vaughan Williams, Ralph, 1872-1958.** [Quartets, strings, C minor]

[Quartets, strings, D minor]
See Toldrà, Eduardo. [Quartets, strings, D minor]

[Quartets, strings, K. 155-160]
See Mozart, Wolfgang Amadeus, 1756-1791. [Quartets, strings, K. 155-160]

[Quartets, strings, no. 1-6, op. 18]
See Beethoven, Ludwig van, 1770-1827. [Quartets, strings, no. 1-6, op. 18]

[Quartets, strings, no. 2]
See Cooke, Arnold. [Quartets, strings, no. 2]

See Mägi, Ester, 1922- [Quartets, strings, no. 2]

See Terteryan, A. 1929- [Quartets, strings, no. 2]

[Quartets, strings, no. 3]
See Cooke, Arnold. [Quartets, strings, no. 3]

See Gilbert, Anthony. [Quartets, strings, no. 3]

[Quartets, strings, no. 4]
See Cooke, Arnold. [Quartets, strings, no. 4]

See Schroeder, Hermann, 1904-1984. [Quartets, strings, no. 4]

See Sheng, Bright, 1955- [Quartets, strings, no. 4]

See Vasks, Pēteris, 1946- [Quartets, strings, no. 4]

[Quartets, strings, no. 4, op. 137, A minor]
See Raff, Joachim, 1822-1882. [Quartets, strings, no. 4, op. 137, A minor]

[Quartets, strings, no. 5]
See Cooke, Arnold. [Quartets, strings, no. 5]

[Quartets, strings, no. 8, op. 192, no. 3, C major]
See Raff, Joachim, 1822-1882. [Quartets, strings, no. 8, op. 192, no. 3, C major]

[Quartets, strings, no. 8, op. 66]
See Vaïnberg, Moiseĭ Samuilovich. [Quartets, strings, no. 8, op. 66]

[Quartets, strings, op. 3. No. 2]
See Zimmermann, Anton, 1741-1781. [Quartets, strings, op. 3. No. 2]

[Quartets, strings. *Selections*]
See Fesca, F. E. 1789-1826. [Quartets, strings. *Selections*]

[Quartets, violin, viola, violoncello, guitar, M.S. 35, A major]
See Paganini, Nicolò, 1782-1840. [Quartets, violin, viola, violoncello, guitar, M.S. 35, A major]

Quartett für zwei Violinen, Viola und Violoncello Nr. 4, a-Moll, op. 137
See Raff, Joachim, 1822-1882. [Quartets, strings, no. 4, op. 137, A minor] Quartett für zwei Violinen, Viola und Violoncello Nr. 4, a-Moll, op. 137

Quartett für zwei Violinen, Viola und Violoncello Nr. 8, C-Dur, op. 192, Nr. 3
See Raff, Joachim, 1822-1882. [Quartets, strings, no. 8, op. 192, no. 3, C major] Quartett für zwei Violinen, Viola und Violoncello Nr. 8, C-Dur, op. 192, Nr. 3

Quartetto in B für 2 Violinen, Viola und Violoncello, op. 3/2
See Zimmermann, Anton, 1741-1781. [Quartets, strings, op. 3. No. 2] Quartetto in B für 2 Violinen, Viola und Violoncello, op. 3/2

Quartetto n. 8 in La maggiore, (M.S. 35), per violino, viola, chitarra e violoncello
See Paganini, Nicolò, 1782-1840. [Quartets, violin, viola, violoncello, guitar, M.S. 35, A major] Quartetto n. 8 in La maggiore, (M.S. 35), per violino, viola, chitarra e violoncello

Quartetto V for bassoon (or cello), violin 1 (or oboe) violin 2 and cello
See Graf, Friedrich Hartmann, 1727-1795 [Favourite quartettos. No. 5] Quartetto V for bassoon (or cello), violin 1 (or oboe) violin 2 and cello

Quartetto VI for bassoon (or cello), violin (or oboe), viola and cello
See Graf, Friedrich Hartmann, 1727-1795. [Quartets, bassoon, violin, viola, violoncello, B♭ major] Quartetto VI for bassoon (or cello), violin (or oboe), viola and cello

Il quarto libro de' madrigali a cinque voci (Ferrara, 1594)
See Luzzaschi, Luzzasco, d. 1607. [Madrigals. *Selections*] Il quarto libro de' madrigali a cinque voci (Ferrara, 1594)

Quattro pezzi
See Sgambati, Giovanni, 1841-1914. [Violin, piano music. *Selections*] Quattro pezzi

Quatuor concertant op. 1, no. 2, for clarinet in B♭ or oboe, violin, viola and bassoon or cello
See Küchler, Johann, 1738-1790 [Quartets, clarinet, bassoon, violin, viola, op. 1. No. 2] Quatuor concertant op. 1, no. 2, for clarinet in B♭ or oboe, violin, viola and bassoon or cello

Quem pastores laudavere
Quem pastores laudavere : SSAATTBB / German 14th century ; arranged by Jonathan Rathbone. — *Edition Peters*
782.5281723   013304633

Quem quæritis
See Hellawell, Piers, 1956- Quem quæritis

Quilliam, William Henry, *1856-1932.*
See Muslim songs of the British Isles / arranged for schools by Abdal Hakim Murad [Timothy J. Winter]

Quinault, Philippe, *1635-1688.*
See Lully, Jean Baptiste, 1632-1687 [Armide. *Vocal score*] Armide : tragédie en musique / Jean-Baptiste Lully ; édition de Lois Rosow ; réduction clavier-chant, Noam A. Krieger.

Quinta sinfonía
See Escudero, Francisco, 1912-2002. [Symphonies, no. 5] Quinta sinfonía

Quintet for flute, oboe, clarinet, horn & bassoon
See Wolstenholme, W. 1865-1931. [Quintets, winds] Quintet for flute, oboe, clarinet, horn & bassoon

Quintet for harp, flute, clarinet, violin and violoncello
See Cooke, Arnold. [Quintets, clarinet, flute, harp, violin, violoncello] Quintet for harp, flute, clarinet, violin and violoncello

Quintet in B minor, opus 70
See Onslow, Georges, 1784-1853. [Quintets, piano, violin, viola, violoncello, double bass, op. 70, B minor] Quintet in B minor, opus 70

Quintet in D major (1898), for clarinet, horn, violin, cello and piano
See Vaughan Williams, Ralph, 1872-1958. [Quintets, piano, clarinet, horn, violin, violoncello, D major] Quintet in D major (1898), for clarinet, horn, violin, cello and piano

Quintet in F, op. III no. 1
See Wranitzky, Paul, 1756-1808. [Quintets, flute, oboe, violas, violoncello, op. 3. No. 1] Quintet in F, op. III no. 1

[Quintet, violins, violas, violoncello, F major]
See Bruckner, Anton, 1824-1896. [Quintet, violins, violas, violoncello, F major]

[Quintets, clarinet, flute, harp, violin, violoncello]
See Cooke, Arnold. [Quintets, clarinet, flute, harp, violin, violoncello]

[Quintets, flute, oboe, violas, violoncello, op. 3. No. 1]
See Wranitzky, Paul, 1756-1808. [Quintets, flute, oboe, violas, violoncello, op. 3. No. 1]

[Quintets, oboe, violins, viola, violoncello, C major]
See Kreutzer, Rodolphe, 1766-1831. [Quintets, oboe, violins, viola, violoncello, C major]

[Quintets, piano, clarinet, horn, violin, violoncello, D major]
See Vaughan Williams, Ralph, 1872-1958. [Quintets, piano, clarinet, horn, violin, violoncello, D major]

[Quintets, piano, violin, viola, violoncello, double bass, C minor]
See Vaughan Williams, Ralph, 1872-1958. [Quintets, piano, violin, viola, violoncello, double bass, C minor]

[Quintets, piano, violin, viola, violoncello, double bass, op. 70, B minor]
See Onslow, Georges, 1784-1853. [Quintets, piano, violin, viola, violoncello, double bass, op. 70, B minor]

[Quintets, violin, violas, violoncello, double bass, B♭ major]
See Dragonetti, Domenico, 1763-1846. [Quintets, violin, violas, violoncello, double bass, B♭ major]

[Quintets, violins, viola, violoncellos, no. 21, C minor]
See Cambini, Giuseppe Maria, 1746-1825. [Quintets, violins, viola, violoncellos, no. 21, C minor]

[Quintets, violins, violas, violoncello, op. 116]
See Thoma, Xaver, 1953- [Quintets, violins, violas, violoncello, op. 116]

[Quintets, winds]
See Wolstenholme, W. 1865-1931. [Quintets, winds]

[Quintets, winds, no. 2]
See Mengal, Martin-Joseph, 1784-1851. [Quintets, winds, no. 2]

Quintett in B-Dur, für Solo-Kontrabass (Solo-Violine), Violine, 2 Violen und Basso
See Dragonetti, Domenico, 1763-1846. [Quintets, violin, violas, violoncello, double bass, B♭ major] Quintett in B-Dur, für Solo-Kontrabass (Solo-Violine), Violine, 2 Violen und Basso

Quittez, pasteurs
See Sutton, Tim, composer. Quittez, pasteurs

Rabassa, Pedro, *1683-1767.*
[Sonata, harpsichord] — Sonata per a clavicèmbal / Pere Rabassa. — *Tritó*
786.4183   013953479

Raccolta Foà-Giordano.
See Hassler, Hans Leo, 1564-1612. [Magnificats, organ. *Selections*] 14 magnificat : (Torino, Biblioteca nazionale Fondo Giordano III, V) / Hans Leo Hassler ; a cura di Aaron Carpenè.

Rachmaninoff, Sergei, *1873-1943*.
[Orchestra music. *Selections*] — Symphonic dances ; 5 études-tableaux ; Vocalise [2 versions] / Serge Rachmaninoff. — *Boosey & Hawkes*
784.2   013194634

[Piano music. *Selections*] — Piano compositions. Vol. 1 / Serge Rachmaninoff. — *Boosey & Hawkes*
786.2   013336506

[Symphonic dances; *arr.*] — Symphonic dances, op. 45 : 2 pianos, 4 hands / Serge Rachmaninoff. — *Definitive ed.* — *Boosey & Hawkes*
785.62192   013312836

[Symphonies, no. 2, op. 27, E minor. Adagio; *arr.*] — Symphony no. 2 : theme from third movment : for violin and piano / arranged by John York ; violin part edited by Levon Chilingirian. — *Boosey & Hawkes*
787.2   013129002

[Symphonies, no. 3, op. 44, A minor] — Symphony no.3, op. 44 / Serge Rachmaninoff. — *Boosey & Hawkes*
784.2184   013095150

Rachmaninoff, Sergei, *1873-1943*.
Études-tableaux.
See **Rachmaninoff, Sergei, *1873-1943*.** [Orchestra music. *Selections*] Symphonic dances ; 5 études-tableaux ; Vocalise [2 versions] / Serge Rachmaninoff.

Racine, Jean, *1639-1699*
See **Handel, George Frideric, 1685-1759** Athalia : oratorio in three parts : HWV 52 / Georg Friedrich Händel ; herausgegeben von Stephan Blaut.

Raczkiewicz, Witalis.
See **Chopin, Frédéric, 1810-1849.** [Rondos, piano] Ronda, op. 1, 5, 16 = Rondos, opp. 1, 5, 16 / Fryderyk Chopin ; [redakcja tomu, Jan Ekier, Paweł Kamiński, Witalis Raczkiewicz]

Raedt, Pierkin de. Missa Quem dicunt homines.
See **Tres missae super "Quem dicunt homines"** / edidit Harry Elzinga.

Raff, Joachim, *1822-1882*.
[Benedetto Marcello. *Vocal score*] — Bendetto Marcello : (Kunst und Liebe) : lyrische Oper in drei Aufzugen : WoO 46 / Joachim Raff ; Text vom Komponisten ; nach dem Autograph herausgegeben von Volker Tosta ; Klavierauszug. — *Edition Nordstern*
782.1   014503175

[Elegy, orchestra, WoO 48, C minor] — Elegie für grosses Orchester WoO 48, urpsrünglicher, dritter Satz aus der Symphonie Nr. 10 "Zur Herbstzeit, " op. 213 / Joachim Raff ; Erstausgabe nach dem Autograph des Komponisten herausgegeben von Volker Tosta. — *Edition Nordstern*
784.218964   014503139

[Octet, violins (4), violas, violoncellos, op. 176, C major] — Oktett für vier Violinen, zwei Violen und zwei Violoncelli, C-Dur, op. 176 / Joachim Raff ; nach der Erstausgabe neu herausgegeben von Volker Tosta. — *Edition Nordstern*
785.7198   014503110

[Quartets, strings, no. 4, op. 137, A minor] — Quartett für zwei Violinen, Viola und Violoncello Nr. 4, a-Moll, op. 137 / Joachim Raff ; nach der Erstausgabe von J. Schuberth, 1869, neu herausgegeben von Volker Tosta. — *Edition Nordstern*
785.7194   014503085

[Quartets, strings, no. 8, op. 192, no. 3, C major] — Quartett für zwei Violinen, Viola und Violoncello Nr. 8, C-Dur, op. 192, Nr. 3 : Suite

in Kanon-Form / Joachim Raff ; nach der Erstausgabe von C.F. Kahnt, 1876, neu herausgegeben von Volker Tosta. — *Edition Nordstern*
785.7194   014503095

[Suites, piano, op. 71, C major] — Suite für Klavier Nr. 2, C-Dur, op. 71 / Joachim Raff ; nach der Originalausgabe des Verlags T.F.A. Kühn neu herausgegeben von Volker Tosta. — *Edition Nordstern*
786.21858   014501802

[Suites, piano, op. 72, E minor] — Suite für Klavier Nr. 3, e-Moll, op. 72 / Joachim Raff ; nach der Originalausgabe des Verlags T.F.A. Kühn neu herausgegeben von Volker Tosta. — *Edition Nordstern*
786.21858   014501805

[Suites, violin, orchestra, op. 180, G minor] — Suite für Violine und Orchester g-Moll, op. 180 / Joachim Raff ; nach der Erstausgabe neu herausgegeben von Volker Tosta. — *Edition Nordstern*
784.2721858   014503121

See **Bach, Johann Sebastian, 1685-1750.** [Suites violoncello, BWV 1009, C major; *arr.*] Suite für Violoncello Nr. 3, C-Dur, BWV 1009 / Johann Sebastian Bach ; für Klavier bearbeitet von Joachim Raff ; nach der Ausgabe von Rieter-Biedermann ; neu herausgegeben von Volker Tosta.

See **Bach, Johann Sebastian, 1685-1750.** [Suites violoncello, BWV 1012, D major; *arr.*] Suite für Violoncello Nr. 6, D-Dur, BWV 1012 / Johann Sebastian Bach ; für Klavier bearbeitet von Joachim Raff ; nach der Ausgabe von Rieter-Biedermann ; neu herausgegeben von Volker Tosta.

See **Bach, Johann Sebastian, 1685-1750.** [Suites, violoncello, BWV 1010, E♭ major; *arr.*] Suite für Violoncello Nr. 4, Es-Dur, BWV 1010 / von Johann Sebastian Bach ; für Klavier bearbeitet von Joachim Raff ; ... nach der Ausgabe von Rieter-Biedermann neu herausgegeben von Volker Tosta.

Raffaelini, Francesco Maria.
See **Biber, Heinrich Ignaz Franz, 1644-1704.** Chi la dura la vince (Wer ausharrt, siegt) : Dramma musicale in drei Akten / Heinrich Franz Biber ; Text von Francesco Maria Raffaelini (?) ; Einfürhung von Sibylle Dahms.

Rahmer, Dominik.
See **Offenbach, Jacques, 1819-1880.** [Rheinnixen. *Vocal score*] Les fées du Rhin = Die Rheinnixen : opéra romantique en 4 actes (1864 / Jacques Offenbach ; livret de Jacques Offenbach et Charles Nuitter ; adaptation allemande par Alfred von Wolzogen ; partition chant-piano [par Jean-Yves Aizic avec la collaboration de Dominik Rahmer, Jean-Christophe Keck]

Raining bliss and benison
Raining bliss and benison : a collection of folk carols arranged for voices / compiled and arranged by Alison Burns ; illustrations by Denise Zygadlo. — *Little Egg*
782.5281723   013383307

Ralph the reindeer
See **Davies, Niki.** Ralph the reindeer

Ramage, Heather.
See **Ballet gold : the essential collection.**

See **Best of gold : the essential collection.**

Rameau, Jean-Philippe, *1683-1764*.
Aquilon et Orithie : cantata : for bass, violin & basso continuo / Jean-Philippe Rameau. — *Green Man Press*
783.8948   013596876

Hippolyte et Aricie : tragédie en cinq actes : version 1757 ; version 1742 (compléments) / [musique de Jean Philippe Rameau] ; livret de Simon-Joseph Pellegrin ; édition de Sylvie Bouissou. — *Société Jean-Philippe Rameau*
782.1   013822163

[Platée. *Vocal score*] — Platée : ballet bouffon en un prologue et trois actes : version 1749, version 1745 (compléments) / [musique de Jean-Philippe Rameau] ; livret de Jacques Autreau ; révisé par Adrien-Joseph Valois d'Orville et Balot de Sovot ; édition de M. Elizabeth C. Barlet ; réduction clavier-chant de François Saint-Yves. — *Société Jean-Philippe Rameau*
782.1   013376540

Thétis : cantata for bass, violin & basso continuo / Jean-Philippe Rameau. — *Green Man Press*
783.8948   013596888

Raminsh, Imant, *1943-* Northwest trilogy.
See **Nootka paddle song :** (no. 1 from "Northwest trilogy") : SATB a cappella / arranged by Imant Raminsh.

See **Sunset :** (no. 3 from "Northwest trilogy") : SATB a cappella / arranged by Imant Raminsh.

Rampe, Siegbert.
See **Lübeck, Vincent, 1654?-1740.** [Keyboard music] Neue Ausgabe sämtlicher Orgel- und Clavierwerke = New edition of the complete organ and keyboard works / Vincent Lübeck, Senior & Junior ; herausgegeben von Siegbert Rampe.

Ramsay, A. B. *1872-1955*.
See **Wilberg, Mack.** Whence is that goodly fragrance flowing? : for mixed choir (SATB) and piano / [French carol ; arranged by] Mack Wilberg.

Ramsey, Andrea.
From a river's edge : treble voices / [words & music by] Andrea Ramsey. — *Boosey & Hawkes*
782.6647   013243914

Ramuz, C. F. *1878-1947*
See **Stravinsky, Igor, 1882-1971.** [Svadebka. *French & Russian*] Les noces = (Svadebka) : scènes chorégraphiques russes avec chant et musique : for four pianos, percussion and voices in a revised and corrected edition based upon relevant autograph and printed sources / composées par Igor Stravinsky ; French text by C.-F. Ramuz ; edited by Margarita Mazo ; associate editor, Millan Sachania.

Rankin, Jeremiah Eames, *1828-1904*.
See **Rose, Barry, 1934-** God be with you till we meet again : unis. voices & org. / Barry Rose.

Rant!
See **McNeff, Stephen.** Rant!

The rapid stream
See **Elgar, Edward, 1857-1934.** [Rapid stream, voices (2)] The rapid stream

[Rapid stream, voices (2)]
See **Elgar, Edward, 1857-1934.** [Rapid stream, voices (2)]

Rapsodi for flute & orchestra
See **Daija, Tish.** [Rhapsody, flute, orchestra; *arr.*] Rapsodi for flute & orchestra

Rasch, Rudolf, *1945-*
  See **Boccherini, Luigi, 1743-1805.** [Duets, violins, G. 56-61] 6 duetti per 2 violini = 6 duets for 2 violins = 6 Violinduette : opus 3 : G 56-62 / Luigi Boccherini ; a cura di Rudolf Rasch.

Rathbone, Jonathan.
  Magnificat : SSAATTBB / Jonathan Rathbone. — *Edition Peters*
  782.5326   013304565

  The oxen : SAATTBB / Jonathan Rathbone ; [words by Thomas Hardy] — *Edition Peters*
  782.5281723   013304621

  Running wild : ATBarBB / Jonathan Rathbone. — *Edition Peters*
  782.51655   013305895

  See **The ash grove** : SSAATTBB : Welsh traditional / arranged by Jonathan Rathbone.

  See **Carol medley** : Deck the halls ; I saw three ships ; We wish you a merry Christmas ; The holly and the ivy ; The first nowell ; Past three o'clock : SSAATTBB (with optional organ part) / arranged by Jonathan Rathbone.

  See **Colahan, Arthur.** Galway Bay : SSAATTBB / Arthur Colohan [sic] ; arranged by Jonathan Rathbone.

  See **Coventry carol** : SSAATTBB / arranged by Jonathan Rathbone.

  See **La cucaracha** : SSAATTBB : Mexican traditional / arranged by Jonathan Rathbone.

  See **Danny boy** : SSAATTBB : Irish traditional / arranged by Jonathan Rathbone.

  See **Dvořák, Antonín, 1841-1904.** [Symphonies, no. 9, op. 95, E minor. Largo; *arr.*] Largo from New World symphony : SSAATTBB / Antonín Dvořák ; arranged by Jonathan Rathbone.

  See **Foster, Stephen Collins, 1826-1864.** [Songs. *Selections; arr.*] Stephen Foster medley : SSAATTBB / music by Stephen Foster ; arranged by Jonathan Rathbone.

  See **Gabriel's message** : SSAATTBB / arranged by Jonathan Rathbone.

  See **Gruber, Franz Xaver, 1787-1863.** [Stille Nacht, heilige Nacht; *arr.*] Silent night : SSAATTBB / Franz Gruber ; arranged by Jonathan Rathbone.

  See **Gruber, Franz Xaver, 1787-1863.** [Stille Nacht, heilige Nacht; *arr.*] Stille nacht : SATB : [music by Franz Gruber] ; arranged by Jonathan Rathbone.

  See **Hopkins, John H. 1820-1891.** [We three kings of Orient are; *arr.*] We three kings : SATB / [words and music by J. H. Hopkins] ; arranged by Jonathan Rathbone.

  See **Hopkins, John H. 1820-1891.** [We three kings of Orient are; *arr.*] We three kings : TTBB / John Henry Hopkins ; arranged by Jonathan Rathbone.

  See **Joshua fought the battle of Jericho** : SSAATTBB / arranged by Jonathan Rathbone.

  See **Loch Lomond** : tenor solo & SSAATBB : Scottish traditional / arranged by Jonathan Rathbone.

  See **Mozart, Wolfgang Amadeus, 1756-1791** [Concertos, horn, orchestra, K. 495, E♭ major. Rondo; *arr.*] Horn concerto, rondo : TTBB / Mozart ; arranged by Jonathan Rathbone.

  See **Mozart, Wolfgang Amadeus, 1756-1791** [Così fan tutte. Aura amorosa; *arr.*] Un' aura amorosa : from Così fan tutte : T solo & SSAATTBB / Mozart ; arranged by Jonathan Rathbone.

  See **Mozart, Wolfgang Amadeus, 1756-1791** [Symphonies, K. 550, G minor. Molto allegro; *arr.*] Symphony no. 40 : (movement 1) : SSAATTBB : Mozart ; arranged by Jonathan Rathbone.

  See **My love is like a red, red rose** : SATB / Scottish traditional ; arranged by Jonathan Rathbone ; words by Robert Burns.

  See **Nobody knows / Deep river (medley)** : soprano solo, TTBB : spiritual / arranged by Jonathan Rathbone.

  See **O come, o come Emmanuel** : SSAATTBB : arranged by Jonathan Rathbone.

  See **Pierpont, James, 1822-1893.** [Jingle bells; *arr.*] Jingle bells : SATB / arranged by Jonathan Rathbone.

  See **Quem pastores laudavere** : SSAATTBB / German 14th century ; arranged by Jonathan Rathbone.

  See **Rossini, Gioacchino, 1792-1868** [Barbiere di Siviglia. Sinfonia; *arr.*] Il Barbiere di Siviglia : overture : SSAATTBB / music by Gioachino Rossini ; arranged by Jonathan Rathbone.

  See **Sakkijarven polkka** : SSAATTBB / Finnish traditional ; arranged by Jonathan Rathbone.

  See **She moved thro' the fair** : ATTBarBB / Irish traditional ; arranged by Jonathan Rathbone ; [words by Padraic Colum]

  See **Skye boat song** : SSAATTBB / Scottish traditional ; arranged by Jonathan Rathbone.

  See **Smetana, Bedřich, 1824-1884.** [Má vlast. Vltava; *arr.*] Die Moldau : SSAATTBB = Vltava / Bedřich Smetana ; arranged by Jonathan Rathbone.

  See **Tchaikovsky, Peter Ilich, 1840-1893** [Overture "1812". Op. 49; *arr.*] 1812 overture : SSAATTBB / Tchaikovsky ; arranged by Jonathan Rathbone.

  See **Three American songs** : SATB / arranged by Jonathan Rathbone.

  See **Three folk songs** : The oak and the ash ; Swing low, sweet chariot ; Nine hundred miles : SATB / arranged by Jonathan Rathbone.

  See **The twelve days of Christmas** : SSAATTBB / arranged by Jonathan Rathbone.

  See **Vem kan segla förutan vind?** : SSAATTBB / Swedish traditional ; arranged by Jonathan Rathbone.

  See **Waltzing Matilda** : SSAATTBB : Australian traditional / arranged by Jonathan Rathbone.

  See **What child is this?** : SSAATTBB / arranged by Jonathan Rathbone.

  See **What shall we do with the drunken sailor?** : SSAATTBB : English traditional / arranged by Jonathan Rathbone.

Rathgeber, Valentin, 1682-1750.
  [Missale tum rurale tum civile. Missa brevis, B flat major] — Missa brevis in B : für Soli (SATB), SATB, Streicher und Orgel / Johann Valentin Rathgeber ; herausgegeben von Friedrich Hägele ; Orgelstimme von Hermann Angstenberger. — *Butz*
  782.53232   013953480

Ratner, Sabina Teller.
  See **Saint-Saëns, Camille, 1835-1921.** [Cello, piano music. *Selections*] The complete shorter works for cello and piano = für Cello und Klavier = pour violoncelle et piano / Camille Saint-Saëns ; edited by Steven Isserlis & Sabina Taller Ratner.

Rawlins, Robert.
  Jazzology : the encyclopedia of jazz theory for all musicians / by Robert Rawlins and Nor Eddine Bahha ; edited by Barrett Tagliarino. — *Hal Leonard*
  781.65076   013358435

Ray (Motion picture : 2004)
  See **Charles, Ray, 1930-2004.** [Songs. *Selections*] Ray : essential piano songs : transcribed for piano, voice & guitar. — *Wise*

Ray
  See **Charles, Ray, 1930-2004.** [Songs. *Selections*] Ray

Read, Tony, 1935-
  [Scherzetto, bassoon, piano] — Scherzetto : bassoon & piano / Tony Read. — *Emerson Edition*
  788.58   013360852

Red Hot Chili Peppers (Musical group)
  [Songs. *Selections*] — Red Hot Chili Peppers : guitar chord songbook : [50 songs : includes complete lyrics, chord symbols & guitar chord diagrams] — *Hal Leonard*
  783.242166   013336122

Red Hot Chili Peppers
  See **Red Hot Chili Peppers (Musical group)** [Songs. *Selections*] Red Hot Chili Peppers

Red hot recorder tutor
  See **Watts, Sarah.** Red hot recorder tutor

Red hot treble recorder tutor
  See **Watts, Sarah.** Red hot treble recorder tutor

Reed, Edith M. G. 1886-1933.
  See **Infant holy, infant lowly** : for mixed choir (SATB) and organ / [Polish carol ; arr.] Mack Wilberg.

Regina caeli
  See **McDowall, Cecilia.** Regina caeli

Registry of Guitar Tutors.
  See **Classical guitar miniatures** : [a unique collection of beautiful and inspiring pieces for the early stages player] / [compiled] by Tony Skinner and Amanda Cook.

  See **Early stages classical guitar** : [a collection of superb, yet easy to play, pieces] [compiled] by Tony Skinner and Amanda Cook.

Reid, Forrest, 1875-1947.
  See **Bayford, Frank.** Echoes from a golden time : opus 95 : seven songs to poems from the Greek Anthology : for soprano and piano / translated by Forrest Reid ; [music by] Frank Bayford.

Reid, John, 1721-1807.
  See **Thistle & minuet** : 16 easy pieces from the Scottish Baroque for violin (or flute or oboe), keyboard, and optional cello (or bassoon) = 16 einfache Stücke aus der schottischen Barockzeit für Violine (oder Flöte oder Oboe), Tasteninstrument und Cello (oder Fagott) ad libitum = 16 pièces faciles du Baroque écossais pour violon (ou flûte ou hautbois), clavier et violoncelle (ou basson) facultatif / edited by David Johnson.

Reincken, Johann Adam, 1623-1722.
  [Keyboard music. *Selections*] — Sämtliche Orgelwerke = Complete organ works / Johann Adam Reincken ; herausgegeben von Pieter Dirksen. — *Breitkopf & Härtel*
  786.5   013353334

Reiser, Salome.
  See **Brahms, Johannes, 1833-1897.** [Quartets, strings] Streichquartette / Johannes Brahms ; herausgegben von Salome Reiser.

Rejoice and be merry
See **Rutter, John, 1945-** [Rejoice and be merry.
Vocal score] Rejoice and be merry

[Rejoice and be merry. *Vocal score*]
See **Rutter, John, 1945-** [Rejoice and be merry.
Vocal score]

Rejoicing
See **Metheny, Pat.** Rejoicing

Rentz, Earlene.
Lo, how a rose e'er blooming = (Es ist ein' Ros'
entsprungen) : for mixed choir (SATB), flute and
piano / [from Alte Catholische Geistliche
Kirchengesang' (1599) harmonized by Michael
Praetorius (1609) ; arranged by] Earlene Rentz.
— *Oxford University Press*
782.5281723   013472538
Lo, how a rose e'er blooming = (Es ist ein' Ros'
entsprungen) : for upper voices (SA), flute and
piano / [from Alte Catholische Geistliche
Kirchengesang' (1599) harmonized by Michael
Praetorius (1609) ; arranged by] Earlene Rentz.
— *Oxford University Press*
782.6281723   013472544
See **The last rose of summer : for upper voices
(SSA), flute and piano** / [Irish air ; arr.] Earlene
Rentz.

Requiem
Requiem : the world's most moving music :
arranged for solo piano. — *Wise Publications*
786.2   013265867

Requiem
See **Rutter, John, 1945-** Requiem

See **Sanders, John, 1933-2003.** Requiem

Requiem de la vierge
See **Florentz, Jean-Louis.** Requiem de la vierge

Requiem in B-Dur, MH 838
See **Haydn, Michael, 1737-1806.** [Missa pro
defunctis, MH 838] Requiem in B-Dur, MH 838

Respighi, Ottorino, *1879-1936.*
See **Rachmaninoff, Sergei, 1873-1943.**
[Orchestra music. *Selections*] Symphonic
dances ; 5 études-tableaux ; Vocalise [2
versions] / Serge Rachmaninoff.

**Reuss, August, *1871-1935.* Symphonische
Phantasie über ein Gedicht von Edgar Steiger.**
See **Franckenstein, Clemens von, 1875-1942.**
[Fantasien, orchestra, op. 15] Fantasie :
Nachtstimmung / Clemens von Franckenstein.
Symphonische Phantasie über ein Gedicht von
Edgar Steiger : ("Ibsen-Phantasie") / August
Reuss. Nachtstück / Felix vom Rath ;
herausgegeben von Stephan Hörner.

[Rêverie (Piano work); *arr.*]
See **Debussy, Claude, 1862-1918** [Rêverie
(Piano work); *arr.*]

Rêverie
See **Debussy, Claude, 1862-1918** [Rêverie
(Piano work); *arr.*] Rêverie

Rex pacificus
See **Palestrina, Giovanni Pierluigi da,
1525?-1594.** [Motets (1575). Rex pacificus] Rex
pacificus

El rey de Harlem
See **Henze, Hans Werner, 1926-** El rey de
Harlem

Rhapsody for organ duet
See **Hakim, Naji, 1955-** [Rhapsody, organs (2)]
Rhapsody for organ duet

[Rhapsody, flute, orchestra; *arr.*]
See **Daija, Tish.** [Rhapsody, flute, orchestra;
arr.]

[Rhapsody, organs (2)]
See **Hakim, Naji, 1955-** [Rhapsody, organs (2)]

Rheinberger, Josef, *1839-1901.*
[Chamber music. *Selections*] — Kammermusik
V / [Josef Gabriel Rheinberger] ; vorgelegt von
Astrid Bauer. — *Carus-Verlag*
785   013949572

Rheinberger, Josef, *1839-1901*
[Instrumental music. *Selections*] —
Orgelkonzerte / [Josef Gabriel Rheinberger] ;
vorgelegt von Wolfgang Hochstein. — *Carus*
784.265186   013836215

[Vocal music. *Selections*] — Geistliche Gesänge.
I : für Solostimmen bzw. Frauenchor mit
Begleitung / [Josef Gabriel Rheinberger] ;
vorgelegt von Berthold Over. — *Carus*
780   013534196

Rheinberger, Josef, *1839-1901* Concertos,
See **Rheinberger, Josef, 1839-1901**
[Instrumental music. *Selections*] Orgelkonzerte /
[Josef Gabriel Rheinberger] ; vorgelegt von
Wolfgang Hochstein.

[Rheinnixen. *Vocal score*]
See **Offenbach, Jacques, 1819-1880.**
[Rheinnixen. *Vocal score*]

Rhodes, David J., *1955-*
See **Esser, Karl Michael, Ritter von, 1737-ca.
1795.** [Duets, viola d'amore, viola da gamba]
Three pieces for viola d'amore & viola da
gamba or violoncello (1789) / Karl Michael,
Ritter von Esser. Two pieces for violin, viola
d'amore & viola da gamba or violoncello (1789)
/ Tomaso Carle ; edited by David J. Rhodes.

See **Hammer, Xaver, 1741-1817.** [Viola da
gamba music. *Selections*] 3 pieces for
unaccompanied viola da gamba / F.X. Hammer.
In diesen heil'gen Hallen / W.A. Mozart ;
anonymous arrangement for unaccompanied
viola da gamba ; edited by David J. Rhodes.

See **Jackson, William, 1730-1803.** [Songs,
op. 16. When fond, you Damon's charms recite]
When fond, you Damon's charms recite : op. 16
no. 7 (c. 1793) : song with obbligato viola da
gamba / William Jackson ; edited by David J.
Rhodes.

Riabokon, Vladislav.
See **Dragonetti, Domenico, 1763-1846.**
[Quintets, violin, violas, violoncello, double
bass, B♭ major] Quintett in B-Dur, für
Solo-Kontrabass (Solo-Violine), Violine, 2
Violen und Basso / Domenico Dragonetti ;
[herausgegeben von] Nanna Koch ; [Solostimme
durchgesehen von Vladislav Riabokon]

Rice, Damien.
O / Damien Rice. — *Guitar tab ed.* — *Faber*
782.421660263   013086203

Ricercate sopra il violoncello o clavicembalo
See **Antonii, Giovanni Battista degli, ca.
1660-1698.** [Ricercate, violoncello, op. 1]
Ricercate sopra il violoncello o clavicembalo

[Ricercate, 2o libro]
See **Trabaci, Giovanni Maria, 1580 (ca.)-1647.**
[Ricercate, 2o libro]

[Ricercate, violoncello, op. 1]
See **Antonii, Giovanni Battista degli, ca.
1660-1698.** [Ricercate, violoncello, op. 1]

**Richafort, Jean, *fl. 1507-1548.* Quem dicunt
homines.**
See **Tres missae super "Quem dicunt
homines"** / edidit Harry Elzinga.

Richard, of Chichester, Saint, *1197 or 8-1253.*
See **Godfrey, Philip, 1964-** Day by day : [a
prayer of St. Richard of Chichester) : for mixed
voices (SATB) and piano or organ / Philip
Godfrey.

Richards, Alison.
See **Under Filk Wood : a songbook created for
Interaction, the 2005 World Science Fiction
Convention, held in Glasgow, Scotland** /
compiled by Alison Richards.

Richards, Goff.
À la carte : brass band ensemble / by Goff
Richards. — *Studio Music*
785.57   013188557

À la carte : orchestral brass ensemble / Goff
Richards. — *Studio Music*
785.57   013188547

Mythic Trevithick! / by Goff Richards. — *Studio
Music*
784.9   013190979

Richards, Jack, *1947-*
Snare drum : grades 5-8 / edited by Jack
Richards and Andrew McBirnie ; additional
editing by Aidan Geary. — *Stainer & Bell*
786.94076   013416586

Timpani : grades 6 -8 / edited by Jack Richards
and Andrew McBirnie. — *Stainer & Bell*
786.93076   013358034

Richards, Tim, pianist. Southern discomfort.
See **Opening night : two Souvenirs for solo
piano** : commissioned to celebrate the opening
of the Bauer & Hieber music shop at 48 Great
Marlborough Street, London, 21st September
2007 / written and performed by Tim Richards
and Huw Watkins.

Richardson, Alan, *1904-1978.*
See **Marais, Marin, 1656-1728.** [Pièces de
violes, 4e livre. 1ère partie. *Selections; arr.*]
Three old French dances : for oboe and piano /
Marin Marais ; [freely transcribed by Janet
Craxton and Alan Richardson]

Richardson, Dorothy.
See **A selection of Italian arias, c.1600-c.1800.**
Volume II / edition prepared by Damian
Cranmer ; English translations by Dorothy
Richardson ; edition supervised by Michael
Pilkington.

Richardson, Michael.
How many bards : [for SATB voices, oboe (or
violin) & piano] / Michael Richardson. —
Boosey & Hawkes
782.542   013213606

How many bards : SSA / [music by] Michael
Richardson. — *Boosey & Hawkes*
782.642   013243892

Rideout, Bonnie.
See **Thistle & minuet : 16 easy pieces from the
Scottish Baroque for violin (or flute or oboe),
keyboard, and optional cello (or bassoon)** = 16
einfache Stücke aus der schottischen Barockzeit
für Violine (oder Flöte oder Oboe),
Tasteninstrument und Cello (oder Fagott) ad
libitum = 16 pièces faciles du Baroque écossais
pour violon (ou flûte ou hautbois), clavier et
violoncelle (ou basson) facultatif / edited by
David Johnson.

Riders to the sea
See **Vaughan Williams, Ralph, 1872-1958.**
[Riders to the sea. *Vocal score*] Riders to the sea

[Riders to the sea. *Vocal score*]
See **Vaughan Williams, Ralph, 1872-1958.**
[Riders to the sea. *Vocal score*]

Ridout, Alan, *1934-1996.*
Serenata notturno : for flute and clarinet / Alan Ridout. — *Emerson Edition*
785.8192   013460588

Riedel, Leonhard.
See **Zechner, Georg,** 1716-1778. [Ihr Hirten Bethlehems] Weihnachtskantate Ihr Hirten Bethlehems : soprano, alto, tenore e basso, 2 corni, 2 violini, 2 viole e basso continuo / Johann Georg Zechner.

Riehm, Rolf, *1937-*
Adieu, Marie, mon amour : drei Liebeslieder in den Tod : nach Klavierstücken von Johann Sebastian Bach : für Bratsche und Akkordeon, 2002-2003 / Rolf Riehm. — *Ricordi*
785.44192   014053359

Lamento di Tristano : für zwei Gitarren / Rolf Riehm. — *Moeck*
785.787192   014053361

Riehman, Jacob, *d. 1726.*
[Sonatas, viola da gamba, continuo, op. 1] — Six sonates à une viole de gambe & basse continue = Sechs Sonaten für Viola da gamba und Basso continuo / Jacob Richmann ; herausgegeben von Olaf Tetampel ; Aussetzung des Basso continuo von Jörg Jacobi. — *Edition Baroque*
787.65183   014488699

Righini, Vincenzo, *1756-1812.*
[Partita, woodwinds, horns (2), E♭ major] — Serenade Es-Dur für zwei Oboen, zwei Klarinetten in B, zwei Hörner in Es (F) und zwei Fagotte / Vincenzo Righini ; Herausgeber, Alexander Maschat. — *Erstausg.* — *Accolade*
785.43198   013953481

Rights, Douglas L. *1891-1956.*
See **Rogers, Wayland.** Peace on earth, goodwill to men : SATB a cappella / [music] by Wayland Rogers.

Rimsky-Korsakov, Nikolay, *1844-1908.*
[Skazka o t͡sare Saltane. Nu, teper', moĭ shmel'; *arr.*] — The flight of the bumblebee / Nikolay Rimsky-Korsakov ; arranged for 2 oboes & cor anglais by John Warrack. — *Emerson Edition*
785.85193   013188151

Rinckart, Martin, *1586-1649.*
See **Chilcott, Bob.** Now thank we : for mixed choir (SATB), soprano descant, and organ / Bob Chilcott.

Rinuccini, Ottavio, *1562-1621.*
See **Monteverdi, Claudio,** 1567-1643. [Lamento d'Arianna (Aria)] Lamento d'Arianna, and addendum : for soprano & basso continuo / Claudio Monteverdi ; edited by Barbara Sachs.

Rise up, my love
See **Skempton, Howard,** 1947- Rise up, my love

Il ritorno di Ulisse in patria
See **Monteverdi, Claudio,** 1567-1643. [Ritorno d'Ulisse in patria] Il ritorno di Ulisse in patria

[Ritorno d'Ulisse in patria]
See **Monteverdi, Claudio,** 1567-1643. [Ritorno d'Ulisse in patria]

Roa, Miguel.
See **Luna, Pablo,** 1879-1942. El asombro de Damasco : zarzuela en dos actos / Pablo Luna ; libreto, Antonio Paso y Joaquín Abati ; edición crítica, Miguel Roa.

See **Serrano, José,** 1873-1941. El mal de amores ; La mala sombra : sainetes líricos en un acto / José Serrano ; libretos, Joaquín y Serafín Álvarez Quintero ; edición crítica, Miguel Roa.

Robert Johnson complete
See **Johnson, Robert,** d. 1938. Robert Johnson complete

Roberts, Jim, *1958-*
See **Best of swing** : 10 swing classics / [arranged and produced by Mark Taylor and Jim Roberts]

Roberts, Jimmy.
[I love you, you're perfect, now change. *Vocal score. Selections*] — I love you, you're perfect, now change : vocal selections / [book and lyrics by Joe Dipietro ; music by Jimmy Roberts ; with Jordan Leeds ... [et al.]] — *Expanded ed.* — *Williamson Music*
782.14   013383297

Roberts, Michael Symmons, *1963-*
See **MacMillan, James,** 1959- Chosen : for SAATTB and organ / James MacMillan ; words by Michael Symmons Roberts.

[Robinson Crusoe. *Vocal score*]
See **Linley, Thomas,** 1733-1795. [Robinson Crusoe. *Vocal score*]

Rocherolle, Eugénie R.
See **Kern, Jerome,** 1885-1945. [Songs. *Selections; arr.*] Jerome Kern classics : for piano solo / arranged by Eugéne Rocherolle ; edited by J. Mark Baker.

Rock & soul styles
See **Kember, John.** [On the lighter side. Rock & soul styles] Rock & soul styles

Rock guitar
See **Mueller, Michael.** Rock guitar

Rock guitar chords and accompaniment
See **Arakawa, Yoichi.** Rock guitar chords and accompaniment

Rock preludes collection
See **Norton, Christopher,** 1953- Rock preludes collection

Rock study
See **Wildman, Peter,** 1957- Rock study

Rock study duets
See **Wildman, Peter,** 1957- Rock study duets

Rodgers & Hart classics
See **Rodgers, Richard,** 1902-1979. [Musicals. *Selections; arr.*] Rodgers & Hart classics

Rodgers and Hart
See **Rodgers, Richard,** 1902-1979 [Musicals. *Vocal scores. Selections*] Rodgers and Hart

Rodgers, Dorothy F., *1909-*
See **Rodgers, Richard,** 1902-1979 [Musicals. *Vocal scores. Selections*] Rodgers and Hart : a musical anthology : piano-vocal.

Rodgers, Richard, *1902-1979*
[Musicals. *Selections; arr.*] — The best of Rodgers and Hart. — *Hal Leonard*
786   013323838

Rodgers, Richard, *1902-1979.*
[Musicals. *Selections; arr.*] — Rodgers & Hart classics : 10 Rodgers & Hart classics / arranged and produced by Mark Taylor. — *Williamson Music*
782.14   013323820

Rodgers, Richard, *1902-1979*
[Musicals. *Selections; arr.*] — Rodgers & Hart favorites : 10 Rodgers & Hart favorites / arranged and produced by Mark Taylor. — *Williamson Music*
782.14   013323827

[Musicals. *Vocal scores. Selections*] — Bewitched : the greatest songs of Rodgers & Hart. — *Chappell/Intersong*
783.242164   013323785

[Musicals. *Vocal scores. Selections*] — Rodgers and Hart : a musical anthology : piano-vocal. — *Hal Leonard*
783.242164   013323664

Rodgers, Richard, *1902-1979.*
[Sound of music. *Vocal score. Selections; arr.*] — The sound of music / Rodgers and Hammerstein. — *Williamson Music*
783.242164   013382301

[Sound of music. My favorite things; *arr.*] — My favorite things : from The sound of music : SSA / lyrics by Oscar Hammerstein II ; music by Richard Rodgers ; arranged by Mac Huff. — *Williamson Music*
782.642164   013424061

[Rodina. *Russian & Armenian*]
See **Terteryan, A.** 1929- [Rodina. *Russian & Armenian*]

Roesner, Linda Correll, *1940-*
See **Brahms, Johannes,** 1833-1897. [Concertos, violin, orchestra, op. 77, D major] Violinkonzert D-Dur Opus 77 / Johannes Brahms ; herausgegeben von Linda Correll Roesner und Michael Struck.

Rogers, Wayland.
Peace on earth, goodwill to men : SATB a cappella / [music] by Wayland Rogers. — *Boosey & Hawkes*
782.5251723   013243906

Rolli, Paolo, *1687-1765.*
See **Fesch, Willem de,** 1687-1761. [Canzonettas, violin, continuo acc.] Miss Ashe canzonettas : for soprano, violin or flute, mandoline and basso continuo : c.1734 / Willem de Fesch ; on poems by Paolo Rolli, Pietro Metastasio and others ; edited by Robert L. Tusler.

See **Fesch, Willem de,** 1687-1761. [Canzonette ed arie, violin, continuo acc.] Lady Erskine canzonettas : for soprano, violin or flute and basso continuo : c.1730 / Willem de Fesch ; on poems by Paolo Rolli and others ; edited by Robert L. Tusler.

Rollins, Sonny.
[Selections; *arr.*] — Sonny Rollins : 10 jazz classics / arranged and produced by Mark Taylor. — *Hal Leonard*
781.65   013335917

Romagnoli, Marco.
See **Centorio, Marco Antonio,** d. 1638. Messa a sei voci / Marco Antonio Centorio ; a cura di Marco Romagnoli.

Romansy i pesni
See **Sviridov, Georgiĭ Vasil'evich,** 1915-1998. [Songs. *Selections*] Romansy i pesni

Romanza antigua
See **Espla, Oscar,** 1886-1976. Romanza antigua

Romberg, Andreas, *1767-1821.*
Der Messias : Kantate in drei Teilen : für Soli, Chor und Orchester, nach Friedrich Gottlieb Klopstocks "Messias" : WoO, zweite Fassung (1802) / Andreas Romberg ; vorgelegt von Karlheinz Höfer und Klaus G. Werner. — *F. Noetzel*
782.524   014763138

Romer, Bernhard.
See **Tunder, Franz, 1614-1667.** Dominus illuminatio mea : (Ps. 27, 1-3) : Geistliches Konzert für Solo (A), Chor (SSATB), 2 Violinen und Basso continuo / Franz Tunder ; herausgegeben von Bernhard Römer.

Rommereim, John Christian.
I look for you early : for mixed choir (SATB), organ and optional alto saxophone / John Christian Rommereim. — *Oxford University Press*
782.5265   013324503

Ronda, op. 1, 5, 16
See **Chopin, Frédéric, 1810-1849.** [Rondos, piano] Ronda, op. 1, 5, 16

Rondo capriccioso
See **Tučapský, Antonín.** Rondo capriccioso

Rondo from Horn concerto in E flat (K.495)
See **Mozart, Wolfgang Amadeus, 1756-1791** [Concertos, horn, orchestra, K. 495, E♭ major. Rondo; *arr.*] Rondo from Horn concerto in E flat (K.495)

[Rondos, piano]
See **Chopin, Frédéric, 1810-1849.** [Rondos, piano]

Röntgen, Julius, 1855-1932.
[Sonatas, viola, piano, C minor] — Sonata in C minor for viola and piano, 1924 / Julius Röntgen ; edited by John Smit. — *Nederlands Muziek Instituut :*
787.3183   014053364

Room on the 3rd floor
See **McFly (Musical group)** Room on the 3rd floor

Roper, E. Stanley 1878-1953.
See **Vaughan Williams, Ralph, 1872-1958.** [Organ music. *Selections*] A Vaughan Williams organ album.

Rosa Mundi
See **Lewis, Paul, 1943-** [Rosa Mundi; *arr.*] Rosa Mundi

[Rosa Mundi; *arr.*]
See **Lewis, Paul, 1943-** [Rosa Mundi; *arr.*]

Rose, Barry, 1934-
An Advent responsory : I look from afar : for SSAA chorus / Barry Rose. — *Novello & Co*
782.62921722   013506231

God be with you till we meet again : unis. voices & org. / Barry Rose. — *Novello & Co*
782.725   013506226

Here, O my Lord : SATB and organ / [music by] Barry Rose ; [words by] Horatius Bonar. — *Novello & Co*
782.525   013505660

Here, O my Lord : unis. with descant & organ / [music by] Barry Rose ; [words by] Horatius Bonar. — *Novello & Co*
782.525   013505667

The Lord is risen : (2005) : SATB chorus and organ / Barry Rose. — *Novello & Co*
782.525   013505682

Nation shall speak peace unto nation : SSATBarB / Barry Rose ; words from the Book of Micah. — *Novello & Co*
782.525   013506278

Watts's cradle hymn : SSA and organ / Barry Rose. — *Novello & Co*
782.627   013506274

See **Lord of all hopefulness :** for SATB chorus and organ / [arranged by] Barry Rose (2002).

See **Love divine :** a collection of Victorian & Edwardian anthems : for mixed voice chorus / selected & edited by Barry Rose.

See **People, look east :** upper-voices and organ / Besançon melody arr. Barry Rose ; [words by] Eleanor Farjeon.

See **Still, still, still :** for SAA chorus and organ / [arranged by] Barry Rose (1999).

The roses
See **Portman, Rachel.** [Little prince. Roses; *arr.*] The roses

Rosetti, Antonio, ca. 1750-1792.
[Partitas, woodwinds, horns (3), violone, M. B18, F major] — Partita in F-Dur für 2 Flöten, 2 Oboen, 2 Klarinetten, 3 Hörner, 2 Fagotte und Kontrabass, RWV B18 = Partita in F major for 2 flutes, 2 oboes, 2 clarinets, 3 horns, 2 bassoons and double-bass / Antonio Rosetti ; herausgegeben von Eberhard Buschmann. — *Amadeus*
785.420991858   014763916

[Simphonie concertante, M. C14, D major] — Sinfonia concertante für zwei Violinen und Orchester in D-Dur RWV C14 = Sinfonia concertante for two violins and orchestra in D major / Antonio Rosetti ; herausgegeben von Johannes Moesus. — *Amadeus*
784.24   014764138

[Symphonies, M. A21, D major] — Sinfonie Nr. 26 in D-dur = Symphony no. 26 in D major : RWV A21 / Antonio Rosetti ; herausgegeben von Johannes Moesus. — *Amadeus :*
784.2814   014763892

Rosow, Lois.
See **Lully, Jean Baptiste, 1632-1687** [Armide. *Vocal score*] Armide : tragédie en musique / Jean-Baptiste Lully ; édition de Lois Rosow ; réduction clavier-chant, Noam A. Krieger.

Ross, Robert A. M.
See **The angel Gabriel :** for mezzo-soprano with optional tenor solo, mixed choir (SATB) and harp / [Basque traditional ; arranged by] Robert A.M. Ross.

See **The angel Gabriel :** for soprano solo, upper voices (SSAA) and harp / [Basque traditional ; arranged by] Robert A.M. Ross.

See **Meyer, Lesley Hopwood.** [Nunc gaudet Maria; *arr.*] Nunc gaudet Maria : for upper voices (SSAA), harp and drum / Lesley Hopwood Meyer ; arranged by Robert A.M. Ross.

Rosseter, Philip, 1567 or 8-1623.
[What then is love but mourning?; *arr.*] — What, then, is love but mourning? / by Philip Rosseter ; arranged for unaccompanied female voice choir (SSA) by Michael Neaum. — *Roberton Publications*
782.642   013193607

Rossetti, Christina Georgina, 1830-1894.
See **Three carols for Christmas :** for unaccompanied mixed choir (SATB).

See **Voth, Ellen Gilson, 1972-** An Advent carol : for mixed choir (SATB) and keyboard / Ellen Gilson Voth.

See **Voth, Ellen Gilson, 1972-** An Advent carol : for upper voices (SSA) and keyboard / Ellen Gilson Voth.

Rossetti, Dante Gabriel, 1828-1882.
See **Vaughan Williams, Ralph, 1872-1958** [Willow-wood. *Vocal score*] Willow-wood : cantata for baritone solo, soprano and alto chorus (ad lib.) and orchestra / by Ralph Vaughan Williams.

Le rossignol musical des chansons
Le rossignol musical des chansons : (Antwerp, 1597) / edited by Gerald R. Hoekstra. — *A-R Editions*
782.543   014630302

Rossini, Gioacchino, 1792-1868
[Barbiere di Siviglia. Sinfonia; *arr.*] — Il Barbiere di Siviglia : overture : SSAATTBB / music by Gioachino Rossini ; arranged by Jonathan Rathbone. — *Edition Peters*
782.5   013305815

[Fantasie, clarinet, piano, E♭ major] — Fantaisie per clarinetto e pianoforte / Gioachino Rossini ; a cura di Margherita Taliercio. — *Boccaccini & Spada*
788.621894   013802005

Rostropovich, Mstislav, 1927-2007.
See **Schnittke, Alfred, 1934-1998.** Musica nostalgica : für Violoncello und Klavier = for violoncello and piano / Alfred Schnittke. Mit einem Lächeln für Slawa : für Violoncello und Klavier / Gija Kantscheli = With a smile for Slava : for violoncello and piano / Giya Kancheli.

Roth, David Lee, 1955-
See **Vai, Steve.** Eat 'em and smile / David Lee Roth ; music transcriptions by Addi Booth.

Rott, Hans, 1858-1884.
[Vorspiele, orchestra, E major] — Orchestervorspiel E-Dur / Hans Rott ; herausgegeben von Johannes Volker Schmidt. — *Ries & Erler*
784.218926   013953482

Roundelay
See **Marson, John, 1932-2007** Roundelay

Routh, Francis.
Capriccio : op. 62 (1995) / Francis Routh. — *Redcliffe Edition*
784.2   013175818

[Chaconnes, violoncello, string orchestra, op. 51] — Ciacona : (romance) : for violoncello and string orchestra : op. 51 (1989) / Franis Routh. — *Redcliffe Edition*
784.72741827   013176950

[Chaconnes, violoncello, string orchestra, op. 51; *arr.*] — Ciacona : (romance) : for violoncello and string orchestra : op. 51 (1989) / Franis Routh. — *Redcliffe Edition*
787.41827   013177057

[Concertos, instrumental ensemble, no. 1, op. 41] — Concerto for ensemble I : op. 41 (1981) / Francis Routh. — *Redcliffe Edition*
785.24196   013176131

[Concertos, instrumental ensemble, no. 2, op. 44] — Concerto for ensemble II : op. 44 (1983) / Francis Routh. — *Redcliffe Edition*
785.24196   013176159

[Concertos, instrumental ensemble, no. 3, op. 55] — Concerto for ensemble III : op. 55 (1991) / Francis Routh. — *Redcliffe Edition*
785.22196   013176186

[Concertos, instrumental ensemble, no. 4, op. 67] — Concerto for ensemble IV : suite for Tblisi : op. 67 (1997/2002) / Francis Routh. — *Redcliffe Edition*
785.22196   013176282

Double concerto : for violin, violoncello and orchestra : op. 19 (1970) / Francis Routh. — *Redcliffe Edition*
784.24186   013174254

Roxburgh, Edwin.
The beginning of sorrows : soprano solo, off-stage vocal quartet, divided SATB choir / Edwin Roxburgh. — *United Music Publishers*
782.525   013222641

Wordsworth miniatures : solo clarinet in B flat / Edwin Roxburgh. — *United Music Publishers*
788.62   013222626

Roxburghe Club.
See The Arundel choirbook : London, Lambeth Palace Library, MS 1 : a facsimile and introduction / introduction by David Skinner.

A royal nursery muddley
See Grylls, Richard G. A royal nursery muddley

Royal welcome songs.
See Purcell, Henry, 1659-1695. [Choral music. *Selections*] Royal welcome songs.

Royer, Pancrace, *1705-1755.*
Le pouvoir de l'Amour / Pancrace Royer ; édition de Lisa Goode Crawford ; avec la collaboration de Gérard Geay. — *Éditions du Centre de Musique Baroque*
782.1   013825410

Rozhdestvenskiĭ, Gennadiĭ.
See Schnittke, Alfred, 1934-1998. Gogol-Suite : Suite aus der Bühnenmusik zum Schauspiel "Die Revisionsliste" von Nikolai Gogol = Suite from the music to a production of "The dead souls register" by Nikolai Gogol / Alfred Schnittke ; Zusammenstellung, Gennadi Rozhdestvensky.

Il rozzo martello
See Davies, Peter Maxwell, 1934- Il rozzo martello

Rubino, Jerry.
See The star-spangled banner : for mixed chorus, unaccompanied / arranged by Jerry Rubino.

Rufer, Josef, *1893-1985*
See Gurre-Lieder : für Soli, Chor und Orchester : kritischer Bericht / Arnold Schönberg ; [Text] von Jens Peter Jacobsen (deutsch von Robert Franz Arnold) ; herausgegeben von Ulrich Krämer.

Ruhland, Konrad.
See Schmelzer, Johann Heinrich, ca. 1623-1680. [Ballets. *Selections*] Balletti à 4 für 2 Violinen, Violetta (Viola), Violone & B.c. / Johann Heinrich Schmelzer.

See Schmelzer, Johann Heinrich, ca. 1623-1680. [Ballets. *Selections*] Balletti à 5 für 2 Violinen, 3 Violen & B.c. / Johann Heinrich Schmelzer.

See Schmelzer, Johann Heinrich, ca. 1623-1680. [Trio sonatas, violin, viola da gamba, continuo, D minor] Sonata â due für Violine, Viola da gamba & B.c. / Johann Heinrich Schmelzer ; herausgegeben von Christian Zincke.

See Ziani, Pietro Andrea, 1616-1684. [Sonatas, trumpet, strings, continuo, D major] Sonata à 6 für Trompete, 2 Violinen, 3 Violen & B.c. / Pietro Andrea Ziani ; [herausgegeben von] Konrad Ruhland.

Running for a fry
See Stove, Thomas Gideon. Running for a fry

Running wild
See Rathbone, Jonathan. Running wild

Russell, Ian.
See It was Christmas to us : carol singing in Bamford through the 20th century / words, music and historical notes researched and transcribed by Joanna and Peter Mackey ; introduction by Ian Russell.

Russian operatic arias for baritone
Russian operatic arias for baritone : 19th and 20th-century repertoire : complete with translations and guidance on pronunciation / selected and edited by David Fanning ; singing translations by Martin Pickard. — *Edition Peters*
783.8842   013335808

Russian operatic arias for tenor
Russian operatic arias for tenor : 19th and 20th century repertoire complete with translations and guidance on pronunciation / selected and edited by David Fanning ; singing translations by Alexander Wells. — *Edition Peters*
783.8742   013191206

Russian romantic repertoire
Russian romantic repertoire = Romantische russische Klavierliteratur = Le répertoire romantique de Russie : level 1 / selected and edited by Stephen Coombs. — *Faber Music*
786.2   006891413

Rutherford, Paris.
See Harris, Jesse, 1969- [Don't know why; *arr.*] Don't know why / words and music by Jesse Harris ; arranged by Paris Rutherford ; recorded by Norah Jones.

Rutter, John, *1945-*
Arise, shine / John Rutter. — *Oxford University Press*
782.5265   013084325

[Carols. *Selections*] — Carols : 10 carols for mixed voices / John Rutter. — *Oxford University Press*
782.5281723   013382232

A crown of glory / John Rutter. — *Oxford University Press*
782.5265   013084314

[Rejoice and be merry. *Vocal score*] — Rejoice and be merry / John Rutter. — *Oxford University Press*
782.5281723   013084320

Requiem : for soprano solo, mixed choir and instrumental ensemble with organ / John Rutter. — *Version with ensemble.* — *Oxford University Press*
782.53238   013122746

Wedding canticle : (Blessed are all they that fear the Lord) / John Rutter. — *Oxford University Press*
782.52951587   013122839

[Wings of the morning. *Vocal score*] — Wings of the morning / John Rutter. — *Oxford University Press*
782.5265   013084308

Ryba, Jakub Jan, *1765-1815.*
[Missa pastoralis, C major] — Missa pastoralis in C : in Nativitate Domini in nocte : per soli SATB, coro SATB, fagotto solo, clarino solo, 2 violini e basso continuo / Jakub Jan Ryba ; herausgegeben von Karlheinz Ostermann ; Generalbassaussetzung von Paul Horn. — *Erstausg.* — *Carus*
782.53232   013832392

Rycroft, Marjorie.
See Haydn, Joseph, 1732-1809. [Songs, violin, continuo acc. *Selections*] Volksliedbearbeitungen Nr. 269-364 : Schottische und Walisische Lieder für George Thomson / Joseph Haydn ; herausgegeben von Marjorie Rycroft in Verbindung von Warwick Edwards und Kirsteen McCue.

See Thomson, Mr. 1757-1851. [Select collection of original Scotish airs] Scottish songs : for George Thomson : 32 schottische Lieder für 1-2 Singstimmen, Violine, Violoncello und Klavier / [music by] Ignaz Pleyel] ; [edited by] Marjorie Rycroft.

Saariaho, Kaija.
Près : for cello and electronics / Kaija Saariaho. — *Chester Music*
787.4   013173409

Saariaho, Kaija. Nocturne,
See The violin : a collection : new and recent repertoire for violin with piano accompaniment / Craig Armstrong ... [et al.]

Sachania, Millan.
See Poulenc, Francis, 1899-1963. [Sonatas, oboe, piano] Sonata for oboe and piano / Francis Poulenc ; edited by Millan Sachania.

See Stravinsky, Igor, 1882-1971. [Svadebka. French & Russian] Les noces = (Svadebka) : scènes chorégraphiques russes avec chant et musique : for four pianos, percussion and voices in a revised and corrected edition based upon relevant autograph and printed sources / composées par Igor Stravinsky ; French text by C.-F. Ramuz ; edited by Margarita Mazo ; associate editor, Millan Sachania.

Sachs, Barbara.
See Cesti, Antonio, 1623-1669. [Cantatas, bass, continuo. *Selections*] Four cantatas for bass / Antonio Cesti ; a critical performing edition edited by Barbara Sachs.

See Legrenzi, Giovanni, 1626-1690. [Dal calore agitato] Two cantatas from the Munich ms. : for bass and basso continuo / Giovanni Legrenzi ; edited by Barbara Sachs.

See Monteverdi, Claudio, 1567-1643. [Lamento d'Arianna (Aria)] Lamento d'Arianna, and addendum : for soprano & basso continuo / Claudio Monteverdi ; edited by Barbara Sachs.

See Scarlatti, Alessandro, 1660-1725. [Cantatas. *Selections*] Three cantatas with recorders : for soprano, two recorders & continuo / Alessandro Scarlatti ; edited by Barbara Sachs.

Sächsische Akademie der Wissenschaften zu Leipzig.
See Mendelssohn-Bartholdy, Felix, 1809-1847 [Overtures. *Selections*] Ouvertüren I / Felix Mendelssohn Bartholdy ; herausgegeben von Christian Martin Schmidt.

Sacrae cantiones
See Aleotti, Raffaella, ca. 1570-ca. 1646. Sacrae cantiones

[Sacrae cantiones, libro 1o]
See Bertolusi, Vincenzo, ca. 1550-1607 or 8. [Sacrae cantiones, libro 1o]

Sacrarum cantionum
See Bertolusi, Vincenzo, ca. 1550-1607 or 8. [Sacrae cantiones, libro 1o] Sacrarum cantionum

Sacro-profanus concentus musicus
See Schmelzer, Johann Heinrich, ca. 1623-1680. Sacro-profanus concentus musicus

Sadler, Kathryn.
LAWA : (Love Art Wisdom Adventure) : 4-part treble voices a cappella / [words & music by] Kathryn Sadler. — *Boosey & Hawkes*
782.6625   013324488

Saint Nicholas
See **Hewitt, Daniel.** Saint Nicholas

See **Hewitt, Daniel.** [Saint Nicholas. *Selections*] Saint Nicholas

[Saint Nicholas. *Selections*]
See **Hewitt, Daniel.** [Saint Nicholas. *Selections*]

Saint-Arroman, Jean.
See **Jollage, Charles-Alexandre.** [Pièces de clavecin, 1er livre] Premier livre de pièces de clavecin : 1738 / Charles Alexandre Jollage.

Saint-Exupéry, Antoine de, *1900-1944*. Petit prince.
See **Portman, Rachel.** [Little prince. Birds; *arr.*] The birds : from The little prince : for SSA and piano / Rachel Portman ; [arr. by Richard Allain]

See **Portman, Rachel.** [Little prince. Lamplighters; *arr.*] The lamplighters : from The little prince ; for SSA and piano / Rachel Portman ; [arr. by Richard Allain]

See **Portman, Rachel.** [Little prince. Look at the stars; *arr.*] Look at the stars : from The little prince ; for SSA and piano / Rachel Portman ; [arr. by Richard Allain]

See **Portman, Rachel.** [Little prince. Roses; *arr.*] The roses : from The little prince : for SSA and piano / Rachel Portman ; [arr. by Richard Allain]

See **Portman, Rachel.** [Little prince. Stars; *arr.*] The stars : from The little prince ; for SSA and piano / Rachel Portman ; [arr. by Richard Allain]

Saint-Georges, Henri, *1801?-1875*
See **Halévy, F., *1799-1862*.** La fée aux roses : opéra-comique en trois actes / Fromental Halévy ; paroles d'Eugène Scribe et de Henri V. de Saint-Georges ; edité par Peter Kaiser.

Saint-Saëns, Camille, *1835-1921*.
[Carnaval des animaux. Cygne; *arr.*] — The swan : from Carnival of the animals : grade 2 / Saint-Saëns ; arr. Darrol Barry. — *Studio Music*
784.8   013359053

[Cello, piano music. *Selections*] — The complete shorter works for cello and piano = für Cello und Klavier = pour violoncelle et piano / Camille Saint-Saëns ; edited by Steven Isserlis & Sabina Taller Ratner. — *Faber Music*
787.4   006916073

Saint-Saëns, Camille, *1835-1921*. Allegro appassionato,
See **Saint-Saëns, Camille, 1835-1921.** [Cello, piano music. *Selections*] The complete shorter works for cello and piano = für Cello und Klavier = pour violoncelle et piano / Camille Saint-Saëns ; edited by Steven Isserlis & Sabina Taller Ratner.

Saint-Yves, François.
See **Rameau, Jean-Philippe, 1683-1764.** Hippolyte et Aricie : tragédie en cinq actes : version 1757 ; version 1742 (compléments) / [musique de Jean Philippe Rameau] ; livret de Simon-Joseph Pellegrin ; édition de Sylvie Bouissou.

See **Rameau, Jean-Philippe, 1683-1764.** [Platée. *Vocal score*] Platée : ballet bouffon en un prologue et trois actes : version 1749, version 1745 (compléments) / [musique de Jean-Philippe Rameau] ; livret de Jacques Autreau ; révisé par Adrien-Joseph Valois d'Orville et Balot de Sovot ; édition de M. Elizabeth C. Barlet ; réduction clavier-chant de François Saint-Yves.

Sakkijarven polkka
Sakkijarven polkka : SSAATTBB / Finnish traditional ; arranged by Jonathan Rathbone. — *Edition Peters*
782.542   013304996

Sala, Luca.
See **Clementi, Muzio, 1752-1832.** [Concerto, piano, orchestra, C major] Concerto in do maggiore, op-sn 30, per clavicembalo (pianoforte) e orchestra = for harpsichord (piano) and orchestra / [Muzio Clementi] ; a cura di Luca Sala.

Sala, Massimiliano.
See **Clementi, Muzio, 1752-1832.** [Symphonies, T. 35, D major] Sinfonia n. 4 in re maggiore, op-sn 37 (WO 35) / [Muzio Clementi] ; a cura di Manuel De Col e Massimiliano Sala.

Salieri, Antonio, *1750-1825*.
Salve regina : für vierstimmigen gemischten Chor, 2 Violinen, Viola, Bass und Orgel / Antonio Salieri ; revidiert und herausgegeben von Otto Biba ; Continuofassung von Wolfgang Fürlinger. — *Erstdruck*. — *Alfred Coppenrath*
782.5324   014666999

The Salley Gardens
See **[Down by the Salley Gardens;]** The Salley Gardens

Sallinen, Aulis.
[Sonatas, violoncello, piano, op. 86] — Sonata per violoncello e piano, op. 86 : (2004) / Aulis Sallinen. — *Novello*
787.4183   013381902

Salmo 100
See **Schütz, Heinrich, 1585-1672.** [Psalmen Davids (1619). 100. Psalm. *Italian & German*] Salmo 100

Salonen, Esa-Pekka, *1958-*
[Sånger till text av Ann Jäderlund] — Two songs from Kalender röd : for unaccompanied choir SSAATTBB / Esa-Pekka Salonen ; poems by Ann Jäderlund. — *Chester Music*
782.542   013173422

Salvatore, Daniele.
See **Cavaccio, Giovanni, ca. 1556-1626.** [Music, voices (4)] Musica a quattro voci : Venezia 1597 / Giovanni Cavaccio ; a cura di Daniele Salvatore.

Salve Regina
See **Allain, Richard.** Salve Regina

Salve regina
See **Salieri, Antonio, 1750-1825.** Salve regina

Salve Regina
See **Werner, Gregor Joseph, 1695-1766.** [Salve Regina, voices (4), violins (2), organ, B♭ major] Salve Regina

Salve regina Es-Dur für Sopran, Alt und Instrumente, 1766 : Facsimile nach der Handschrift des Komponisten
See **Hasse, Johann Adolf, 1699-1783.** [Salve regina, soprano, alto, orchestra, E♭ major] Salve regina Es-Dur für Sopran, Alt und Instrumente, 1766 : Facsimile nach der Handschrift des Komponisten

[Salve regina, soprano, alto, orchestra, E♭ major]
See **Hasse, Johann Adolf, 1699-1783.** [Salve regina, soprano, alto, orchestra, E♭ major]

[Salve Regina, voices (4), violins (2), organ, B♭ major]
See **Werner, Gregor Joseph, 1695-1766.** [Salve Regina, voices (4), violins (2), organ, B♭ major]

Salzburger Museum Carolino Augusteum.
See **Biber, Heinrich Ignaz Franz, 1644-1704.** Chi la dura la vince (Wer ausharrt, siegt) : Dramma musicale in drei Akten / Heinrich Franz Biber ; Text von Francesco Maria Raffaelini (?) ; Einfürhung von Sibylle Dahms.

Sametz, Steven, *1954-*
Alleluia : for mixed choir (SA, TB, or SATB) and handbells with optional harp or keyboard / Steven Sametz. — *Oxford University Press*
782.5265   013472367

Samson
See **Handel, George Frideric, 1685-1759** [Samson. *Vocal score*] Samson

[Samson. *Vocal score*]
See **Handel, George Frideric, 1685-1759** [Samson. *Vocal score*]

Sämtliche Lieder für Singstimme und Klavier
See **Ullmann, Viktor.** [Songs] Sämtliche Lieder für Singstimme und Klavier

Sämtliche Orgelwerke
See **Reincken, Johann Adam, 1623-1722.** [Keyboard music. *Selections*] Sämtliche Orgelwerke

See **Scheidemann, Heinrich, 1596 (ca.)-1663.** [Organ music] Sämtliche Orgelwerke

See **Strungk, Delphin, 1601-1694.** [Organ music] Sämtliche Orgelwerke

Sämtliche Werke für Tasteninstrumente.
See **Sweelinck, Jan Pieterszoon, 1562-1621.** [Fantasias, keyboard instrument] Sämtliche Werke für Tasteninstrumente.

Samuel, Rhian.
Dovey Junction : for brass quintet / by Rhian Samuel. — *Stainer & Bell*
785.9195   013345860

Gaslight Square II : for piano duet / Rhian Samuel. — *Stainer & Bell*
785.62192   013280257

[Light and water] — Quartet : light and water : for piano and strings / Rhian Samuel. — *Stainer & Bell*
785.281941   013050614

Pan ddaw ust y nos : i gôr SATB & organ / [alaw] Rhian Samuel ; [geiriau gan] Nesta Wyn Jones. — *Stainer & Bell*
782.542   013237465

Serenade duo : for two pianos / Rhian Samuel. — *Stainer & Bell*
785.62192   013213368

Shards of light : for solo violin / Rhian Samuel. — *Stainer & Bell*
787.2   013416342

Trinity : three songs for high voice, flute and piano / to texts by Anne Stevenson ; by Rhian Samuel. — *Stainer & Bell*
783.342   013213374

Sanders, John, *1933-2003*.
The firmament : anthem for treble soloist, SATB choir & organ / music by John Sanders. — *Anglo-American Music Publishers* :
782.5265   013594323

Requiem : for unaccompanied mixed voices (SSAATTBB) / John Sanders. — *Encore Publications*
782.53238   013222726

Sandon, Nick.
See **Aston, Hugh, b. ca. 1485.** [Missa Te Deum] Missa Te deum laudamus / Hugh Aston ; edited by Nick Sandon.

[Sānger till text av Ann Jäderlund]
See **Salonen, Esa-Pekka**, 1958- [Sānger till text av Ann Jäderlund]

O sapo
O sapo : SSATB a cappella : [Brazilian folk song] / arranged by Stephen Hatfield. — *Boosey & Hawkes*
782.54216200981   013361311

Sarton, May, *1912-1995.*
See **Larsen, Libby.** Eine kleine Snailmusik : for upper voices and contrabass / Libby Larsen.

A Sarum blessing
See **Lole, Simon.** A Sarum blessing

Sas, Ágnes.
See **Zimmermann, Anton**, 1741-1781. [Symphonies. *Selections*] Four symphonies / Anton Zimmermann ; edited by János Bali and Péter Halász ; introduced by Péter Halász.

Satriani, Joe.
Is there love in space? : [guitar/vocal] / Joe Satriani. — *Cherry Lane Music Company*
787.87166   013191055

Savile, Jeremy. Here's a health unto his majesty.
See **Wiffin, R. K.** Here's a health / Rob Wiffin.

Sax a tre
See **Ketley, David F.** Sax a tre

The Saxon king
See **Brookes, Katherine.** The Saxon king

Sayce, Lynda.
See **Handel, George Frideric**, 1685-1759. [Suites, harpsichord, HWV 432, G minor; *arr.*] Suite in G minor / G.F. Handel ; arranged for archlute by Lynda Sayce.

Scarborough Fair
Scarborough Fair : English folk song : arranged for female voice choir and piano / by Derek J. Clark. — *Roberton Publications*
782.642   013193334

Scarborough Fair : English folk song : arranged for male voice choir and piano / by Derek J. Clark. — *Roberton Publications*
782.842   013193324

Scarborough Fair : English folk song : arranged for mixed voice choir and piano / by Derek J. Clark. — *Roberton Publications*
782.542   013193327

Scarlatti, Alessandro, *1660-1725.*
Bella dama di nome santa : Tu sei quella : cantata for alto, recorder, two violins and continuo / Alessandro Scarlatti ; edited by Derek Harrison. — *Green Man Press*
783.6848   013612367

[Cantatas. *Selections*] — Three cantatas with recorders : for soprano, two recorders & continuo / Alessandro Scarlatti ; edited by Barbara Sachs. — *Green Man Press*
783.6648   013612380

[Harpsichord music. *Selections*] — Dieci pezzi per clavicembalo = Zehn Stücke für Clavierinstrumente / Alessandro Scarlatti ; herausgegeben von Jörg Jacobi. — *Edition Baroque*
786.4   013222305

Scarlatti, Alessandro, *1660-1725.* **Augellin vago e canoro.**
See **Scarlatti, Alessandro**, 1660-1725. [Cantatas. *Selections*] Three cantatas with recorders : for soprano, two recorders & continuo / Alessandro Scarlatti ; edited by Barbara Sachs.

The scarlet cover
The scarlet cover : SATB a cappella / arranged by Stephen Hatfield. — *Boosey & Hawkes*
782.525   013243883

Scena
See **Brumby, Colin.** Scena

See **Brumby, Colin.** [Scena; *arr.*] Scena

[Scena; *arr.*]
See **Brumby, Colin.** [Scena; *arr.*]

Schächer, Raimund.
See **Wecker, Georg Kaspar**, 1632-1695. [O Herr hilf] O Herr hilf! O Herr, laß wohl gelingen! : (1695) : geistliches Konzert zum 1. Advent für Sopran I, Sopran II (Tenor), Alt, Baß, 2 Violinen, 2 Violen und B.c. / Georg Caspar Wecker ; herausgegeben von Raimund Schächer.

Scheideler, Ullrich.
See **Albéniz, Isaac**, 1860-1909. [Suite española, no. 1] Suite espagnole : opus 47 / Isaac Albéniz ; herausgegeben von Ullrich Scheideler ; Fingersatz von Rolf Koenen.

See **Handel, George Frideric**, 1685-1759 [Fugues, keyboard, HWV 605-612] Sechs Fugen HWV 605-610 und Fugen HWV 611, 612 = Six fugues HWV 605-610 and fugues HWV 611, 612 / Georg Friedrich Händel ; herausgegeben von Ullrich Scheideler ; Fingersatz von Michael Schneidt.

Scheidemann, Heinrich, *1596 (ca.)-1663.*
[Organ music] — Sämtliche Orgelwerke = Complete organ works / Heinrich Scheidemann ; herausgegeben von Klaus Beckmann. — *Schott*
786.5   013521876

Schelat, David.
By your word, O God : for two-part choir and organ / David Schelat. — *Oxford University Press*
782.5265   013472216

Schermar-Bibliothek (*Ulm, Germany*).
See **Schermar-Bibliothek Ulm Ms. 237 :** Brugge? ca. 1515-1540 : unedierte Stücke und Unikate. Stücke zu 4 Stimmen / herausgegeben von Dieter Klöckner.

See **Schermar-Bibliothek Ulm Ms. 237 :** Brugge? ca. 1515-1540 : unedierte Stücke und Unikate. Stücke zu 5 und 6 Stimmen / herausgegeben von Dieter Klöckner.

Schermar-Bibliothek Ulm Ms. 237
Schermar-Bibliothek Ulm Ms. 237 : Brugge? ca. 1515-1540 : unedierte Stücke und Unikate. Stücke zu 4 Stimmen / herausgegeben von Dieter Klöckner. — *Cornetto*
782.526   014766586

Schermar-Bibliothek Ulm Ms. 237 : Brugge? ca. 1515-1540 : unedierte Stücke und Unikate. Stücke zu 5 und 6 Stimmen / herausgegeben von Dieter Klöckner. — *Cornetto*
782.526   014766587

Scherzetto
See **Arnold, Malcolm.** [You know what sailors are. Scherzetto; *arr.*] Scherzetto

See **Read, Tony**, 1935- [Scherzetto, bassoon, piano] Scherzetto

[Scherzetto, bassoon, piano]
See **Read, Tony**, 1935- [Scherzetto, bassoon, piano]

Schiavina, Andrea.
See **Paganini, Nicolò**, 1782-1840. [Quartets, violin, viola, violoncello, guitar, M.S. 35, A major] Quartetto n. 8 in La maggiore, (M.S. 35), per violino, viola, chitarra e violoncello = Quartet no. 8 in A major (M.S. 35), for violin, viola, guitar and violoncello / Nicolo Paganini ; a cura di Andrea Schiavina.

Schilde, Klaus.
See **Beethoven, Ludwig van**, 1770-1827. [Concertos, violin, orchestra, op. 61, D major; *arr.*] Klavierkonzert Opus 61a : nach dem Violinkonzert Opus 61 = Piano concerto op. 61a : after the Violin concerto op. 61 / Ludwig van Beethoven ; herausgegeben von Hans-Werner Küthen ; Fingersatz von Klaus Schilde ; Klavierauszug von Jürgen Sommer ; Kadenzen vom Komponisten.

Schiller, Friedrich, *1759-1805.*
See **Terzakis, Dimitri.** Hero und Leander : 2002/03 : Rapsodia für 1 Sprecher, Viola, Klavier und Tonband / Dimitri Terzakis ; nach Texten von Ovid und Friedrich Schiller.

See **Waterhouse, Graham**, 1962- Der Handschuh : Ballade von Friedrich Schiller : für Sprechstimme und Violoncello = The glove : a ballad by Friedrich Schiller : for speaking voice and violoncello / Graham Waterhouse.

Schiller, Friedrich, *1759-1805.* **Räuber.**
See **Verdi, Giuseppe**, 1813-1901. I masnadieri : a tragic opera (in four acts) = melodramma (in quattro atti) / Giuseppe Verdi ; libretto by Andrea Maffei ; edited by Roberta Montemorra Marvin.

Schlagel, Stephanie P.
See **Josquin, des Prez**, d. 1521 [Motets. *Selections*] "Si placet" parts for motets by Josquin and his contemporaries / edited by Stephanie P. Schlagel.

Schlegel, Kathrina von.
See **Sibelius, Jean**, 1865-1957. [Finlandia. Hymni; *arr.*] Be still, my soul : for mixed choir (SATB) and organ / [Jean Sibelius ; arr. by] Mack Wilberg.

Schmelzer, Johann Heinrich, *ca. 1623-1680.*
[Ballets. *Selections*] — Balletti à 4 für 2 Violinen, Violetta (Viola), Violone & B.c. / Johann Heinrich Schmelzer. — *Erstausg.* — *Edition Walhall*
785.281941858   014766568

[Ballets. *Selections*] — Balletti à 5 für 2 Violinen, 3 Violen & B.c. / Johann Heinrich Schmelzer. — *Erstausg.* — *Edition Walhall*
785.281951858   014766569

Sacro-profanus concentus musicus : fidium aliorumque instrumentorum : 13 sonate a 2, 4, 5, 6, 7, e 8 strumenti, Nürnberg, 1662 / Johann Heinrich Schmelzer ; a cura di Alessandro Bares. — *Musedita*
785.22183   014766573

[Sonatae unarum fidium] — Sonatae unarum fidium seu a violino solo : Nürnberg, 1664 / Johann Heinrich Schmelzer ; transcrizione a cura di Alessandro Bares. — *Musedita*
787.2183   014766575

[Sonatas, violins (2), viols (3), continuo, (1676)] — Duae sonatae a 5 für 2 Violinen, 3 Violen & B.c. / Johann Heinrich Schmelzer. — *Erstausg.* — *Walhall*
785.28196   014766570

[Trio sonatas, violin, viola da gamba, continuo, D minor] — Sonata â due für Violine, Viola da gamba & B.c. / Johann Heinrich Schmelzer ; herausgegeben von Christian Zincke. — *Erstausg.* — *Edition Walhall*
785.28193183   014766574

Schmid, Manfred Hermann.
See **Haydn, Michael, 1737-1806.** [Missa pro defunctis, MH 838] Requiem in B-Dur, MH 838 : Faksimile der autographen Partitur aus dem Besitz der Österreichischen Nationalbibliothek ; Faksimile des Partitur-Erstdrucks (Leipzig, Ambros Kühnel) aus dem Besitz der Bayerischen Staatsbibliothek München / Johann Michael Haydn ; vorgelegt und kommentiert von Manfred Hermann Schmid.

Schmidt, Christian Martin.
See **Mendelssohn-Bartholdy, Felix, 1809-1847.** [Overtures. *Selections*] Ouvertüren I / Felix Mendelssohn Bartholdy ; herausgegeben von Christian Martin Schmidt.

Schmidt, Johannes Volker.
See **Rott, Hans, 1858-1884.** [Vorspiele, orchestra, E major] Orchestervorspiel E-Dur / Hans Rott ; herausgegeben von Johannes Volker Schmidt.

Schnapp, Friedrich.
See **Hoffmann, E. T. A. 1776-1822.** [Kreuz an der Ostsee] Zacharias Werners Trauerspiel "Das Kreuz an der Ostsee" : mit der Bühnenmusik von E.T.A. Hoffmann ; Ballettmusik "Arlequin" / E.T.A. Hoffmann ; hrsg. aus dem Nachlaß von Friedrich Schnapp ; unter Mitarbeit von Gerhard Allroggen und Michael Kohlhäufl von Thomas Kohlhase.

See **Hoffmann, E. T. A. 1776-1822.** [Vocal music. *Selections*] Kleine Vokalkompsitionen und Klaviersonaten / E.T.A. Hoffmann ; aus dem Nachlaß von Friedrich Schnapp und unter Mitarbeit von Gerhard Allroggen ; herausgegeben von Alexander Erhard und Thomas Kohlhase.

Schneider, Herbert, 1941-
See **Lully, Jean Baptiste, 1632-1687.** [Monsieur de Pourceaugnac. *Vocal score*] Monsieur de Pourceaugnac : (Le divertissement de Chambord) ; Le bourgeois gentilhomme : comédie-ballet / Jean-Baptiste Lully/Molière ; [Monsieur de Pourceaugnac] édition de Jérôme de La Gorce ; [Le bourgeois gentilhomme] édition de Herbert Schneider ; réduction clavier-chant, Noam A. Krieger.

Schnittke, Alfred, 1934-1998.
[Concerti grossi, no. 4] — Concerto grosso Nr. 4— Sinfonie Nr. 5 = Concerto grosso no. 4— Symphony no. 5 / Alfred Schnittke. — *Hans Sikorski*
784.2184   013571403

Gogol-Suite : Suite aus der Bühnenmusik zum Schauspiel "Die Revisionsliste" von Nikolai Gogol = Suite from the music to a production of "The dead souls register" by Nikolai Gogol / Alfred Schnittke ; Zusammenstellung, Gennadi Rozhdestvensky. — *Sikorski*
784.21858   013577535

Musica nostalgica : für Violoncello und Klavier = for violoncello and piano / Alfred Schnittke. Mit einem Lächeln für Slawa : für Violoncello und Klavier / Gija Kantscheli = With a smile for Slava : for violoncello and piano / Giya Kancheli. — *Sikorski*
787.4   013572326

[Overcoat. Polka; *arr.*] — Polka : Streichquartett = String quartet / Alfred Schnittke ; [arr. by] (Sergej Dreznin). — *Sikorski Musikverlage*
785.719418844   013387829

Schoenberg, Arnold, 1874-1951. Gurrelieder.
See **Gurre-Lieder :** für Soli, Chor und Orchester : kritischer Bericht / Arnold Schönberg ; [Text] von Jens Peter Jacobsen (deutsch von Robert Franz Arnold) ; herausgegeben von Ulrich Krämer.

Schoenberg, Arnold, 1874-1951. Kleine Klavierstücke.
See **Ullmann, Viktor.** [Variationen und Doppelfuge über ein Thema von Arnold Schönberg; *arr.*] Variationen und Doppelfuge über ein Thema von Arnold Schönberg (op. 19/4) : Fassung für Streichquartett, op. 3c = Variations and Double Fugue on a theme by Arnold Schoenberg (op. 19/4) : version for string quartet, op. 3c / Viktor Ullmann.

Scholz-Michelitsch, Helga.
See **Wagenseil, Georg Christoph, 1715-1777.** [Divertimenti, harpsichord (1761)] Tre divertimenti per cimbalo : Wie Mozart Klavier spielen lernte— : mit didaktischem Anhang "Fondamento per il clavicembalo" = How Mozart learnt to play the piano— / Georg Christoph Wagenseil ; für Klavier/cembalo herausgegeben von Helga Scholz-Michelitsch.

Schönberg, Claude-Michel.
[Misérables. *Vocal score. English. Selections*] — Les Misérables : Boublil and Schönberg's legendary musical : in concert : piano, vocal, guitar / music by Claude-Michel Schönberg. — *Alain Boublil Music*
782.140264   006936060

[Musicals. *Vocal scores. Selections*] — The Boublil-Schönberg collection : show hits : twelve great show songs, ideal for auditions. — *Female ed.* — *Wise*
783.642   013432817

[Musicals. *Vocal scores. Selections*] — The Boublil-Schönberg collection : show hits : twelve great show songs, ideal for auditions. — *Male ed.* — *Wise*
783.842   013432662

Schreker, Franz, 1878-1934.
[Choral music] — Chorwerk / Franz Schreker ; Gesamtausgabe herausgegeben von Christopher Hailey, Iris Pfeiffer. — *Carus*
782.5   013565245

Schroeder, Hermann, 1904-1984.
[Quartets, strings, no. 4] — Streichquartette Nr. 4 und 5 / Hermann Schroeder ; herausgegeben von Rainer Mohrs. — *Dohr*
785.7194   014049817

Schroeder, Hermann, 1904-1984. Quartets,
See **Schroeder, Hermann, 1904-1984.** [Quartets, strings, no. 4] Streichquartette Nr. 4 und 5 / Hermann Schroeder ; herausgegeben von Rainer Mohrs.

Schroedl, Jeff.
Jazz guitar : a comprehensive guide with step-by-step instruction and over 20 great jazz classics / by Jeff Schroedl. — *Hal Leonard Europe*
787.87165076   013358416

Schubert, Franz, 1797-1828.
Fierabras / Franz Schubert. — *Bärenreiter*
782.1   013777720

[Vocal music. *Selections*] — Mehrstimmige Gesänge für gemischte Stimmen. Teil b / [Franz Schubert] ; vorgelegt von Dietrich Berke und Michael Kube. — *Bärenreiter*
783.12   013798568

Schubert, Franz, 1797-1828. Sonatas,
See **Poole, Geoffrey, 1949-** Schubert's Reliquie / realisation and completion by Geoffrey Poole (1997) of Schubert's Sonata in C Major, D 840.

Schubert, Franz, 1797-1828 An die Musik
See **An die Musik :** 9 classical pieces arranged for string quartet / [arr. by] John Kember.

Schubert, Franz, 1797-1828 Marches militaires.
See **On wings of song :** 8 popular pieces arranged for string quartet / [arr. by] Barrie Carson Turner.

Schubert, Franz, 1797-1828 Rosamunde.
See **An die Musik :** 9 classical pieces arranged for string quartet / [arr. by] John Kember.

Schubert, Giselher.
See **Hindemith, Paul, 1895-1963.** [Kammermusik, no. 1] Konzertante Kammermusiken I / Paul Hindemith ; herausgegeben von Giselher Schubert.

Schubert's Reliquie
See **Poole, Geoffrey, 1949-** Schubert's Reliquie

[Schüler-Konzerte]
See **Seitz, Friedrich, 1848-1918.** [Schüler-Konzerte]

Schulhoff, Ervín, 1894-1942.
[Concertos, string quartet, band] — Konzert pro smyčcovy kvartet a dechový orchestr = Konzert für Streichquartett und Bläser-Ensemble = Concerto for string quartet and wind ensemble : 1930 / Erwin Schulhoff. — *Praha :*
784.2186   013953483

Schulz, J. A. P. 1747-1800.
Lieder im Volkston / Johann Abraham Peter Schulz ; herausgegeben von Walther Dürr und Stefanie Steiner unter Mitarbeit von Michael Kohlhäufl. — *Henle*
783.242   013801647

Schumann, Robert, 1810-1856.
[Album für die Jugend. *Selections*] — Selections from Album for the young : opus 68 / Schumann ; edited by Jennifer Linn. — *G. Schirmer*
786.2   013440462

[Waldscenen] — Waldszenen : Opus 82 : Faksimile nach dem Autograph im Besitz der Bibliothèque nationale de France, Paris / Robert Schumann ; Nachwort von Margit L. McCorkle. — *G. Henle*
786.20262   013641757

Schumann, Robert, 1810-1856 Kinderscenen.
See **On wings of song :** 8 popular pieces arranged for string quartet / [arr. by] Barrie Carson Turner.

Schürmann, Georg Caspar, 1672 or 3-1751. Aber über das Haus Davids.
See **Musik am Meininger Hofe /** herausgegeben von Ulrike Feld und Ulrich Leisinger.

Schütz, Heinrich, 1585-1672.
[Psalmen Davids (1619). 100. Psalm. *Italian & German*] — Salmo 100 : per doppio coro a voci miste e quartetto di ottoni : Lodi al Signore = "Jauchzet dem Herren" / Heinrich Schütz ; revisione e versione italiana di Davide Liani. — *Pizzicato edizioni musicali*
782.5294   014766580

Schwaen, Kurt, 1909-2007.
[Fantasia, guitars (2)] — Fantasia für 2 Gitarren / Kurt Schwaen. — *Edition Margaux*
785.787192   014599826

Sciarrino, Salvatore.
Cantare con silenzio : per voci, flauto, risonanze e percussori, 1999 / Salvatore Sciarrino. — *Ricordi*
783.1642   014053365

Graffito sul mare : per trio e orchestra, 2003 / Salvatore Sciarrino. — *Ricordi*
784.24   014053366

Scissor Sisters.
Scissor Sisters. — *International Music Publications*
783.242166   013265863

Scissor Sisters.
See **Scissor Sisters.** Scissor Sisters.

The Scots fiddle
See **Neil, J. Murray.** The Scots fiddle

Scottish songs
See **Thomson, Mr. 1757-1851.** [Select collection of original Scotish airs] Scottish songs

Scribe, Eugène, *1791-1861.*
See **Halévy, F., 1799-1862.** La fée aux roses : opéra-comique en trois actes / Fromental Halévy ; paroles d'Eugène Scribe et de Henri V. de Saint-Georges ; edité par Peter Kaiser.

Sculthorpe, Peter, *1929-*
[Djilile, percussion] — Djilile : arranged for percussion ensemble : (1981/90) / Peter Sculthorpe. — *Faber Music*
785.68194   013555083

[Djilile, viols (5)] — Djilile : consort music of five parts / Peter Sculthorpe. — *Faber Music*
785.76195   013555103

[From Nourlangie; *arr.*] — From Nourlangie : for piano quartet / Peter Sculthorpe. — *Faber Music*
785.28194   006917878

Little suite for strings : for string orchestra : (1983) / Peter Sculthorpe. — *Faber Music*
784.71858   013555388

Sea change
See **Beck.** Sea change

Sea elegy
See **Davies, Peter Maxwell, 1934-** Sea elegy

Seal (Musician)
[Songs. *Selections*] — Seal best : 1991-2004. — *Wise Publications*
783.242166   013178685

Seal best
See **Seal (Musician)** [Songs. *Selections*] Seal best

Sechs ausgewählte Streichquartette
See **Fesca, F. E. 1789-1826.** [Quartets, strings. *Selections*] Sechs ausgewählte Streichquartette

Sedaka, Neil.
[Songs. *Selections*] — Neil Sedaka : 15 timeless classics : piano/vocal arrangements with guitar chord boxes. — *International Music Publications*
783.242164   013226509

Seeger, Pete, *1919-*
Where have all the flowers gone? : for SATB choir & piano / words and music by Pete Seeger ; arranged by Mark G. Sirett. — *Boosey & Hawkes*
782.542   013312787

Where have all the flowers gone? : three part treble voices & piano / words and music by Pete Seeger ; arranged by Mark G. Sirett. — *Boosey & Hawkes*
782.7642   013312821

Seeley, Ian W.
See **The Hawick songs :** a complete collection / edited by Ian W. Seeley.

Seger, Bob.
[Songs. *Selections*] — Bob Seger. — *Hal Leonard*
787.87166   013299275

Sehnal, Jiří.
See **Michna z Otradovic, Adam, ca. 1600-1676.** [Officium vespertinum. *Selections*] Officium vespertinum : Compositiones ad honorem B.M.V. ; Falsi burdoni / [Adam Michna z Otradovic] ; ed., Vratislav Bělský, Jiří Sehnal.

Sei concerti per organo solo
See **Hasse, Johann Adolf, 1699-1783.** [Concertos, keyboard instrument] Sei concerti per organo solo

Sei duetti latini sulla passione di nostro signore Gesù Cristo
See **Porpora, Nicola, 1686-1768.** [Duetti latini per la passione di Gesù Cristo] Sei duetti latini sulla passione di nostro signore Gesù Cristo

Sei sonate per il cembalo solo
See **Hertel, Johann Wilhelm, 1727-1789.** [Sonatas, harpsichord. *Selections*] Sei sonate per il cembalo solo

Seiffert, Wolf-Dieter.
See **Mozart, Wolfgang Amadeus, 1756-1791.** [Sinfonie concertanti, violin, viola, orchestra, K. 364, E♭ major; *arr.*] Sinfonie concertante für Violine, Viola und Orchester, Es-dur, KV 364 = Sinfonia concertante in E♭ major for violin, viola and orchestra, K. 364 / Wolfgang Amadeus Mozart ; herausgegeben von Wolf-Dieter Seiffert ; Klavierauszug von Siegfried Petrenz ; Fingersatz und Strichbezeichnung von Frank Peter Zimmermann [und] Tabea Zimmermann ; piano reduction.

Seigel, Lester.
See **Jesus, Jesus, rest your head :** for unaccompanied mixed choir (SATB) with baritone solo / [American folk carol ; arranged by] Lester Seigel.

Seitz, Friedrich, *1848-1918.*
[Schüler-Konzerte] — Pupil's concertos nos. 1-5, complete : for violin and piano / Friedrich Seitz ; edited and fingered by Philipp Mittell. — *G. Schirmer :*
787.2186   013441065

Seitz, Johanna.
See **Hertel, Johann Wilhelm, 1727-1789.** [Concertos, harp, string orchestra, F major; *arr.*] Konzert F-Dur für Harfe oder Cembalo, 2 Violinen, Viola und Violoncello / Johann Wilhelm Hertel ; herausgegeben von Johanna Seitz ; Klavierauszug von Burkhard Jäckel.

See **Hertel, Johann Wilhelm, 1727-1789.** [Trios, harp, violin, violoncello. No. 2] Trio F-Dur : für Harfe (oder Cembalo), Violine (oder Flöte) und Violoncello / Johann Wilhelm Hertel ; herausgegeben von Johanna Seitz.

[Select collection of original Scotish airs]
See **Thomson, 1757-1851.** [Select collection of original Scotish airs]

Selected piano exam pieces
See **Associated Board of the Royal Schools of Music (Great Britain)** Selected piano exam pieces

Selected studies
See **Heller, Stephen, 1813-1888.** [Etudes faciles. *Selections*] Selected studies

Selected violin examination pieces
See **Associated Board of the Royal Schools of Music (Great Britain)** Selected violin examination pieces

A selection of Italian arias, c.1600-c.1800.
A selection of Italian arias, c.1600-c.1800. Volume II / edition prepared by Damian Cranmer ; English translations by Dorothy Richardson ; edition supervised by Michael Pilkington. — *Associated Board of the Royal Schools of Music*
783.5420945   013307377

A selection of Italian arias, c.1600-c.1800. Volume II / edition prepared by Damian Cranmer ; English translations by Dorothy Richardson ; edition supervised by Michael Pilkington. — *Associated Board of the Royal Schools of Music*
783.3420945   013307384

A selection of shape-note folk hymns
A selection of shape-note folk hymns : from Southern United States tune books, 1816-61 / edited by David W. Music. — *A-R Editions*
782.527   014619892

[Selections]
See **Gavrilin, V.** [Selections]

See **Giovannelli, Ruggiero, ca. 1560-1625.** [Selections]

Selections from Album for the young
See **Schumann, Robert, 1810-1856.** [Album für die Jugend. *Selections*] Selections from Album for the young

Selections from Confessions
See **Usher.** [Confessions. *Selections*] Selections from Confessions

Selections from Prelude
See **Church, Charlotte, 1986-** Selections from Prelude

[Selections; *arr.*]
See **Evans, Bill, 1929-1980.** [Selections; *arr.*]

See **Fauré, Gabriel, 1845-1924.** [Selections; *arr.*]

See **Gershwin, George, 1898-1937.** [Selections; *arr.*]

See **Hancock, Herbie, 1940-** [Selections; *arr.*]

See **Nyman, Michael.** [Selections; *arr.*]

See **Rollins, Sonny.** [Selections; *arr.*]

See **Silver, Horace, 1928-** [Selections; *arr.*]

See **Vivaldi, Antonio, 1678-1741** [Selections; *arr.*]

Selk, Jürgen.
See **Weill, Kurt, 1900-1950.** Der Protagonist : ein Akt Oper : op. 15 / Musik von Kurt Weill ; Text von Georg Kaiser ; edited by Gunther Diehl and Jürgen Selk.

I sentimenti di Carl Philipp Emanuel Bach
See **Bach, Carl Philipp Emanuel, 1714-1788.** [Fantasien, violin, keyboard instrument, H. 536, F minor; *arr.*] I sentimenti di Carl Philipp Emanuel Bach

Septet for clarinet, horn, bassoon, violin, viola, violoncello and contrabass
See **Cooke, Arnold.** [Septets, bassoon, clarinet, horn, violin, viola, violoncello, double bass] Septet for clarinet, horn, bassoon, violin, viola, violoncello and contrabass

[Septets, bassoon, clarinet, horn, violin, viola, violoncello, double bass]
See **Cooke, Arnold.** [Septets, bassoon, clarinet, horn, violin, viola, violoncello, double bass]

Seqüències
See **Carbonell i Saurí, Albert, 1972-** Seqüències

Serebrier, José, *1938-*
Tango in blue = Tango in azul : for orchestra / José Serebrier. — *PeerMusic Classical*
784.218885   014457045

Serei, Zsolt.
L'ombre sur les structures pliées : hommage à Pierre Boulez : pour deux clarinettes et cinq instruments à cordes = for two clarinets and five strings / Serei Zsolt. — *Editio Musica*
785.44197   014766582

Serenade duo
See **Samuel, Rhian.** Serenade duo

Serenade Es-Dur für zwei Oboen, zwei Klarinetten in B, zwei Hörner in Es (F) und zwei Fagotte
See **Righini, Vincenzo, 1756-1812.** [Partita, woodwinds, horns (2), E♭ major] Serenade Es-Dur für zwei Oboen, zwei Klarinetten in B, zwei Hörner in Es (F) und zwei Fagotte

Serenade for horn and organ
See **Phillips, Craig, 1961-** [Serenade, horn, organ] Serenade for horn and organ

[Serenade, horn, organ]
See **Phillips, Craig, 1961-** [Serenade, horn, organ]

[Serenades, string orchestra, op. 48, C major. Valse; *arr.*]
See **Tchaikovsky, Peter Ilich, 1840-1893** [Serenades, string orchestra, op. 48, C major. Valse; *arr.*]

Serenata notturno
See **Ridout, Alan, 1934-1996.** Serenata notturno

Serini, Giovanni Battista, *b. ca. 1710.*
[Sonatas, flute, continuo, D major] — Sonata no. 1 in D : flute/oboe & piano / Giovanni Battista Serini ; [edited by Jack Pilgrim] — *Emerson Edition*
788.32183   013358290

Serrano, José, *1873-1941.*
El mal de amores ; La mala sombra : sainetes líricos en un acto / José Serrano ; libretos, Joaquín y Serafín Álvarez Quintero ; edición crítica, Miguel Roa. — *Instituto Complutense de Ciencias Musicales*
782.1   014679490

Serrano, José, *1873-1941.* **Mala sombra.**
See **Serrano, José, 1873-1941.** El mal de amores ; La mala sombra : sainetes líricos en un acto / José Serrano ; libretos, Joaquín y Serafín Álvarez Quintero ; edición crítica, Miguel Roa.

Seven 16th century duos from the York manuscript
Seven 16th century duos from the York manuscript : for bass and treble viols / anon. ; edited by Rhiannon Evans. — *Viola da Gamba Society of Great Britain*
785.76192   013382536

Seven bagatelles for oboe and bassoon
See **Hansell, Philip, 1962-** [Bagatelles, oboe, bassoon (2005)] Seven bagatelles for oboe and bassoon

Seven songs of Stephen Foster
See **Foster, Stephen Collins, 1826-1864.** [Songs. *Selections; arr.*] Seven songs of Stephen Foster

Severino, Giovanni Antonio, *fl. 1579-1601.* **Fantasia,**
See **Neapolitan lute music** / Fabrizio Dentice ... [et al.] ; edited by John Griffiths and Dinko Fabris.

Sewell, Dominic.
[Adagios, string orchestra, op. 23] — Adagio : opus 23 / Dominic Sewell. — *Broadbent & Dunn*
784.7   013167651

[Suites, viola, op. 38] — Suite for solo viola : [opus 38] / Dominic Sewell. — *Broadbent & Dunn*
787.31858   013383342

Sgambati, Giovanni, *1841-1914.*
[Violin, piano music. *Selections*] — Quattro pezzi / Giovanni Sgambati ; a cura di Manfred Croci. — *Boccaccini & Spada*
787.2   014053367

Sgambati, Giovanni, *1841-1914.* **Berceuse,**
See **Sgambati, Giovanni, 1841-1914.** [Violin, piano music. *Selections*] Quattro pezzi / Giovanni Sgambati ; a cura di Manfred Croci.

Shacklock, Constance.
See **Sing solo contralto** / edited by Constance Shacklock ; general editor, John Carol Case.

Shaftel, Matthew R.
See **Webern, Anton, 1883-1945.** [Songs. *Selections*] The Anton Webern collection : early vocal music, 1899-1909 / [Anton Webern] ; ed. by Matthew R. Shaftel.

Shakespeare, William, *1564-1616.*
See **Carter, Andrew.** O mistress mine / Andrew Carter.

See **Chilcott, Bob.** The isle is full of noises : SAATB with divisions, unaccompanied / Bob Chilcott.

See **Fesch, Willem de, 1687-1761.** [Tempest] The Tempest songs, or, The enchanted island : for soprano, small ensemble and basso continuo, 1745 / Willem de Fesch ; edited by Robert L. Tusler.

See **Unterseher, Reginald.** Live with me, and be my love : for mixed chorus (SATB) and piano / Reginald Unterseher.

See **Vaughan Williams, Ralph, 1872-1958.** [Song of thanksgiving. *Vocal score*] A song of thanksgiving : for soprano solo, speaker, chorus and orchestra / R. Vaughan Williams ; vocal score.

See **Willcocks, David, 1919-** O mistress mine : SATB a cappella / David Willcocks.

Shakespeare, William, *1564-1616*
See **Hind, John, 1916-** [Shakespearean songs] Two Shakespearean songs : for SSA and piano / by John Hind.

[Shakespearean songs]
See **Hind, John, 1916-** [Shakespearean songs]

Shards of light
See **Samuel, Rhian.** Shards of light

Shchedrin, Rodion Konstantinovich, *1932-*
Hamlet ballad : for four-part cello ensemble = für vierstimmiges Celloensemble : (2004) / Rodion Shchedrin. — *Schott*
785.74194   013565253

[Vologodskie svireli] — Shepherd's pipes of Vologda : for oboe, cor anglais, horn and string orchestra = Hirtenklänge aus Wologda : für Oboe, Englisch Horn, Horn und Streichorchester : Hommage à Bartók (1995) / Rodion Shchedrin. — *Schott*
784.724   013587082

Voprosy : 11 pieces for piano = 11 Stücke für Klavier (2003) / Rodion Shchedrin. — *Schott*
786.2   014766585

She moved thro' the fair
She moved thro' the fair : ATTBarBB / Irish traditional ; arranged by Jonathan Rathbone ; [words by Padraic Colum] — *Edition Peters*
782.542   013305020

Sheep may safely graze
See **Bach, Johann Sebastian, 1685-1750.** [Jagdkantate. Schafe können sicher weiden; *arr.*] Sheep may safely graze

Shellard, Martin.
See **[X&Y; *arr.*]** Play guitar with— Coldplay : X&Y.

Sheng, Bright, *1955-*
[Quartets, strings, no. 4] — String quartet no. 4 : (Silent temple) / Bright Sheng. — *G. Schirmer*
785.7194   014053368

Shephard, Richard, *1949-*
Lord, I have loved the habitation of thy house : for mixed voices and organ / Richard Shephard. — *Encore Publications*
782.5265   013192606

Shepherd's pipes of Vologda
See **Shchedrin, Rodion Konstantinovich, 1932-** [Vologodskie svireli] Shepherd's pipes of Vologda

Sheridan, Richard Brinsley, *1751-1816.*
See **Linley, Thomas, 1733-1795.** [Robinson Crusoe. *Vocal score*] The pantomine [or rather, pantomime] of Robinson Crusoe : (1781) / Thomas Linley ; wordbook by Richard Brinsley Sheridan ; edited by Robert Hoskins.

She's like the swallow
She's like the swallow : traditional Newfoundland song for SSAA choir and piano / arranged by Michael Neaum. — *Roberton Publications, a part of Goodmusic Publishing*
782.642   013193600

Shields, Valerie.
Psalm 124: a song of deliverance : [for unison treble voices, SAB chorus & piano] / by Valerie Shields. — *Boosey & Hawkes*
782.5294   013312831

The ship of dreams
See **Spencer, Tim.** The ship of dreams

Shipley, Edward.
See **Lambert, Constant, 1905-1951.** [Concertos, piano, instrumental ensemble, (1924)] Concerto (1924), for piano solo, 2 trumpets, strings and timpani / Constant Lambert ; edited, arranged and orchestrated from the composer's original 2 piano score by Edward Shipley and Giles Easterbrook.

Shiraz, Hovhannes, *1915-1984.*
See **Terteryan, A. 1929-** [Rodina. *Russian & Armenian*] Heimat : vokalsinfonischer Zyklus für Sopran, Bariton und Orchester (1957) / Awet Terterjan.

[Short easy piano pieces]
See **McCreery, Charles.** [Short easy piano pieces]

[Short pieces]
See **Vaughan Williams, Ralph, 1872-1958.** [Short pieces]

[Short songs]
See **Steele, Douglas, 1910-** [Short songs]

Shorter pieces for violin and piano
See **Clarke, Rebecca, 1886-1979.** [Violin, piano music. *Selections*] Shorter pieces for violin and piano

Shostakovich, Dmitriĭ Dmitrievich, *1906-1975*.
[Vocal music. *Selections*] — Dve basni I.A. Krylova, dl︠i︡a met︠s︡so-soprano, zhenskogo khora (met︠s︡so-soprano) i orkestra, soch. 4 ; Shest' romansov na slova ︠i︡aponskikh poėtov, dl︠i︡a tenora s orkestrom, soch. 21 ; Tri romansa na slova A.S. Pushkina, dl︠i︡a basa i kamernogo orkestra, soch. 46a / Dmitriĭ Shostakovich ; obshcha︠i︡a redakt︠s︡i︠i︡a i po︠i︡asnitel'na︠i︡a stat'︠i︡a Manashira ︠I︡Akubova. — *Izd-vo "DSCH"*
783.242   013821897

Showstoppers
Showstoppers : [24 stage hits] — *Wise*
786.2   013299262

"Si placet" parts for motets by Josquin and his contemporaries
See **Josquin, des Prez, d. 1521** [Motets. *Selections*] "Si placet" parts for motets by Josquin and his contemporaries

Sibelius, Jean, *1865-1957*.
[Finlandia. Hymni; *arr.*] — Be still, my soul : for mixed choir (SATB) and organ / [Jean Sibelius ; arr. by] Mack Wilberg. — *Oxford University Press*
782.527   013571345

Sicilian air
See **Waterhouse, Graham, 1962-** Sicilian air

Siciliano
See **Moore, Philip, 1943-** Siciliano

[Sieben letzten Worte unseres Erlösers am Kreuze. *English. Vocal score*]
See **Haydn, Joseph, 1732-1809** [Sieben letzten Worte unseres Erlösers am Kreuze. *English. Vocal score*]

Sieben Sonaten
See **Febel, Reinhard, 1952-** [Sonatas, piano] Sieben Sonaten

Sight-reading 2
See **Kember, John.** Sight-reading 2

Sight-singing 2
See **Kember, John.** Sight-singing 2

Signor, non sotto l'ombra
See **Mazzocchi, D. 1592-1665.** [Musiche sacre, e morali. Signor, non sotto l'ombra] Signor, non sotto l'ombra

Silent night
See **Gruber, Franz Xaver, 1787-1863.** [Stille Nacht, heilige Nacht; *arr.*] Silent night

Silver, Horace, *1928-*
[Selections; *arr.*] — Horace Silver : [10 hard bop classics] / arranged and produced by Mark Taylor. — *Hal Leonard*
781.65   013381861

Simon, Carly.
See **Piglet's big movie** / featuring new songs by Carly Simon.

See **Pooh's heffalump movie** / [featuring new songs by Carly Simon]

Simon, Paul, *1941-*
[Songs. *Selections*] — The definitive Paul Simon songbook. — *Amsco*
783.242164   013265854

[Simphonie concertante, M. C14, D major]
See **Rosetti, Antonio, ca. 1750-1792.** [Simphonie concertante, M. C14, D major]

Sinatra, Frank, *1915-1998*
See **Audition songs for male singers.** The rat pack : Frank Sinatra, Dean Martin, Sammy Davis, jr. : ten great songs ideal for auditions.

Sinfonia concertante für Violine, Viola und Orchester, Es-dur, KV 364
See **Mozart, Wolfgang Amadeus, 1756-1791.** [Sinfonie concertanti, violin, viola, orchestra, K. 364, E♭ major; *arr.*] Sinfonia concertante für Violine, Viola und Orchester, Es-dur, KV 364

Sinfonia concertante für zwei Violinen und Orchester in D-Dur RWV C14
See **Rosetti, Antonio, ca. 1750-1792.** [Simphonie concertante, M. C14, D major] Sinfonia concertante für zwei Violinen und Orchester in D-Dur RWV C14

Sinfonia in C major, (Ouverture), (1770)
See **Martinez, Marianne, 1744-1812.** [Symphony, C major] Sinfonia in C major, (Ouverture), (1770)

Sinfonia n. 4 in re maggiore, op-sn 37 (WO 35)
See **Clementi, Muzio, 1752-1832.** [Symphonies, T. 35, D major] Sinfonia n. 4 in re maggiore, op-sn 37 (WO 35)

Sinfonías
See **Ordoñez, Carlos d', 1734-1786.** [Symphonies. *Selections*] Sinfonías

[Sinfonie concertanti, violin, viola, orchestra, K. 364, E♭ major; *arr.*]
See **Mozart, Wolfgang Amadeus, 1756-1791.** [Sinfonie concertanti, violin, viola, orchestra, K. 364, E♭ major; *arr.*]

Sinfonie D-Dur, op. 52
See **Wilms, J. W. 1772-1847.** [Symphonies, no. 5, op. 52, D major] Sinfonie D-Dur, op. 52

Sinfonie für Kammerorchester, 1981
See **Kalsons, Romualds.** [Symphonies, chamber orchestra, no. 1] Sinfonie für Kammerorchester, 1981

Sinfonie in C, KV 551
See **Mozart, Wolfgang Amadeus, 1756-1791.** [Symphonies, K. 551, C major] Sinfonie in C, KV 551

Sinfonie Nr. 1, H-Moll
See **Furtwängler, Wilhelm, 1886-1954.** [Symphonies, no. 1, B minor] Sinfonie Nr. 1, H-Moll

Sinfonie Nr. 2 E-moll
See **Furtwängler, Wilhelm, 1886-1954.** [Symphonies, no. 2, E minor] Sinfonie Nr. 2 E-moll

Sinfonie Nr. 26 in D-dur
See **Rosetti, Antonio, ca. 1750-1792.** [Symphonies, M. A21, D major] Sinfonie Nr. 26 in D-dur

Sinfonie Nr. 3 cis-moll
See **Furtwängler, Wilhelm, 1886-1954.** [Symphonies, no. 3, C sharp minor] Sinfonie Nr. 3 cis-moll

Sinfonie Nr. 4 für grosses Sinfonieorchester
See **Terteryan, A. 1929-** [Symphonies, no. 4] Sinfonie Nr. 4 für grosses Sinfonieorchester

Sinfonie Nr. 7 für grosses Sinfonieorchester
See **Terteryan, A. 1929-** [Symphonies, no. 7] Sinfonie Nr. 7 für grosses Sinfonieorchester

Sinfonisches Konzert für Klavier und Orchester
See **Furtwängler, Wilhelm, 1886-1954.** [Symphonisches Konzert] Sinfonisches Konzert für Klavier und Orchester

Sing a song o' conga
See **Bartlett, Keith.** Sing a song o' conga

Sing solo contralto
Sing solo contralto / edited by Constance Shacklock ; general editor, John Carol Case. — *Oxford University Press*
783.6842   013173224

Sing solo tenor
Sing solo tenor / edited by Robert Tear ; general editor, John Carol Case. — *Oxford University Press*
783.8742   013172270

Sing we merrily
See **Child, William, 1606?-1697.** Sing we merrily

The singles collection
See **(Musician) Smiths (Musical group)** [Songs. *Selections*] The singles collection

Sirett, Mark, *1952-*
See **Seeger, Pete, 1919-** Where have all the flowers gone? : for SATB choir & piano / words and music by Pete Seeger ; arranged by Mark G. Sirett.

See **Seeger, Pete, 1919-** Where have all the flowers gone? : three part treble voices & piano / words and music by Pete Seeger ; arranged by Mark G. Sirett.

Sirmen, Maddalena Laura Lombardini, *1745-1818*.
[Quartets, strings] — String quartets opus 3 [sic], for 2 violins, viola & violoncello / Maddalena Lombardini-Sirmen. — *SJ Music*
785.7194   013196163

Six cantata's, for a voice and instruments
See **Stanley, John, 1712-1786.** [Cantatas, op. 8] Six cantata's, for a voice and instruments

Six chord songbook
Six chord songbook : hits collection. — *Wise Publications*
783.242166   013185211

Six duos pour deux cors
See **Heuschkel, Johann Peter, 1773-1853.** [Duets, horns (2), op. 12] Six duos pour deux cors

Six sonatas for the piano forte or harpsichord with an accompaniment for a violin, op. 2
See **LeBrun, Francesca, 1756-1791.** [Sonatas, violin, harpsichord, op. 2] Six sonatas for the piano forte or harpsichord with an accompaniment for a violin, op. 2

Six sonates à une viole de gambe & basse continue
See **Riehman, Jacob, d. 1726.** [Sonatas, viola da gamba, continuo, op. 1] Six sonates à une viole de gambe & basse continue

Six sonates en duo
See **Atys, 1715-1784.** [Sonatas, flutes (2), op. 1] Six sonates en duo

Six songs from John Gay's The beggar's opera
See **[Beggar's opera.]** Six songs from John Gay's The beggar's opera

[Skazka o t︠s︡are Saltane. Nu, teper', moĭ shmel'; *arr.*]
See **Rimsky-Korsakov, Nikolay, 1844-1908.** [Skazka o t︠s︡are Saltane. Nu, teper', moĭ shmel'; *arr.*]

Skempton, Howard, *1947-*
The flight of song : SATB a cappella / Howard Skempton. — *Oxford University Press*
782.542   013243774

Rise up, my love : SATB a cappella / Howard Skempton. — *Oxford University Press*
782.5265   013213402

[Sketches]
See **Harvey, Jonathan, 1939-** [Sketches]

Skinner, David.
See **The Arundel choirbook** : London, Lambeth Palace Library, MS 1 : a facsimile and introduction / introduction by David Skinner.

See **Ludford, Nicholas, ca. 1490-1557.** [Vocal music. *Selections*] Five- and six-part Masses ; and, Magnificat / [Nicholas Ludford] ; transcribed and edited by David Skinner.

See **Taverner, John, 1495 (ca.)-1545.** Christe, Jesu, pastor bone / John Taverner ; edited by David Skinner.

Skinner, Tony, *1960-*
See **Classical guitar miniatures** : [a unique collection of beautiful and inspiring pieces for the early stages player] / [compiled] by Tony Skinner and Amanda Cook.

See **Early stages classical guitar** : [a collection of superb, yet easy to play, pieces] [compiled] by Tony Skinner and Amanda Cook.

Skladby pro flétnu sólo
See **Kabeláč, Miloslav, 1908-1979.** [Malá suita, flute] Skladby pro flétnu sólo

Skye boat song
Skye boat song : SSAATTBB / Scottish traditional ; arranged by Jonathan Rathbone. — *Edition Peters*
782.542   013305026

Skyrider
See **Sparke, Philip.** Skyrider

Sleepers wake
See **Bach, Johann Sebastian, 1685-1750.** [Wachet auf, ruft uns die Stimme (Cantata). Wachet auf, ruft uns die Stimme; *arr.*] Sleepers wake

The sleepy shepherd
See **Davies, Niki.** The sleepy shepherd

Slow down Moses!
See **Krouwel, Juliet.** Slow down Moses!

Smetana, Bedřich, *1824-1884.*
[Má vlast. Vltava; *arr.*] — Die Moldau : SSAATTBB = Vltava / Bedřich Smetana ; arranged by Jonathan Rathbone. — *Edition Peters*
782.5   013305784

Smit, John.
See **Röntgen, Julius, 1855-1932.** [Sonatas, viola, piano, C minor] Sonata in C minor for viola and piano, 1924 / Julius Röntgen ; edited by John Smit.

Smith, Alan, *1930-*
There is no rose : SATB, unaccompanied / Alan Smith. — *Oxford University Press*
782.5251723   013668630

Smith, Doreen, *1931-*
Cello sight-reading. Book 1 / Doreen Smith. — *Oxford University Press*
787.41423   013173145

See **Smith, Doreen, 1931-** Cello sight-reading. Book 1 / Doreen Smith.

Smith, Jeremy L., *1962-*
See **Byrd, William, 1542 or 3-1623.** [Psalmes, sonets, and songs] Psalmes, sonets and songs (1588) / [William Byrd] ; edited by Jeremy Smith.

Smith, John Stafford, *1750-1836.* To Anacreon in heaven.
See **The star-spangled banner** : for mixed chorus, unaccompanied / arranged by Jerry Rubino.

Smiths (Musical group)
[Songs] — The Smiths : complete chord songbook : every song recorded by The Smiths. — *Wise Publications*
783.242166   013359293

[Songs. *Selections*] — Play guitar with— The Smiths. — *Wise*
783.242166   013336526

[Songs. *Selections*] — The singles collection / The Smiths. — *Wise*
783.242166   013383555

The Smiths
See **Smiths (Musical group)** [Songs] The Smiths

Smoke gets in your eyes
Smoke gets in your eyes : & five other songs / arranged by David Nield. — *Novello*
782.542164   013323734

Snare drum
See **Richards, Jack, 1947-** Snare drum

Snow Patrol (Musical group)
Final straw / Snow Patrol. — *Guitar tab ed.* — *International Music Publications*
783.242166   013262486

Snowman at sunset
See **Davies, Niki.** Snowman at sunset

Snyder, Audrey.
The complete history of Western music (abridged) / arranged by Audrey Snyder ; additional words and music by Audrey Snyder. — *Hal Leonard*
782.542   013221833

The complete history of Western music (abridged) / arranged by Audrey Snyder ; additional words and music by Audrey Snyder. — *Hal Leonard*
782.542   013221839

So low
See **Hansell, Philip, 1962-** So low

Sochineniia dlia khora bez soprovozhdeniia
See **Sviridov, Georgiĭ Vasil'evich, 1915-1998.** [Choral music. *Selections*] Sochineniia dlia khora bez soprovozhdeniia

Sofer, Andrew, *1964-*
See **Beavers, Kevin, 1971-** [Wandlebury Ring. *Vocal score*] Wandlebury Ring : for voice and string quartet / words by Andrew Sofer ; music by Kevin E. Beavers.

[Soft notes and gently rais'd accent]
See **Purcell, Henry, 1659-1695.** [Soft notes and gently rais'd accent]

Sografi, Antonio Simone, *1759-1818.*
See **Portugal, Marcos Antônio da Fonseca, 1762-1830.** Gli Orazi e i Curiazi : partitura dell'opera in facsimile, edizione del libretto / [libretto di] Simeone Antonio Sografi ; [musica di] Marco Portogallo. Catalogo cronologico degli spettacoli a Venezia (1797-1815) / a cura di Maria Giovanna Miggiani.

Sokoll, Martin.
See **Guilmant, Alexandre, 1837-1911.** [Masses, mixed voices, organ, no. 3, op. 11, E♭ major] 3me messe solennelle : op. 11 : für Soli, Chor und Orgel / Felix-Alexandre Guilmant ; herausgegeben von Martin Sokoll.

Soliloquy
See **Bayliss, Colin.** Soliloquy

Solo (Sonata G-Dur) per la viola di gamba
See **Graun, Johann Gottlieb, 1702 or 3-1771.** [Sonatas, viola da gamba, continuo, G major] Solo (Sonata G-Dur) per la viola di gamba

Solo collection
See **Kember, John.** [On the lighter side. Solo collection] Solo collection

Solo für Tanja
See **Terzakis, Dimitri.** Solo für Tanja

Some cities
See **Doves (Musical group)** Some cities

A Somerset garland.
See **Lewis, Paul, 1943-** A Somerset garland.

Sommer, Isabella.
See **Strauss, Johann, 1825-1899.** [Nachtigall-Polka; *arr.*] Nachtigall-Polka : op. 222 / Johann Strauss (Sohn) ; [herausgegeben von] Isabella Sommer.

Sommer, Jürgen.
See **Beethoven, Ludwig van, 1770-1827.** [Concertos, violin, orchestra, op. 61, D major; *arr.*] Klavierkonzert Opus 61a : nach dem Violinkonzert Opus 61 = Piano concerto op. 61a : after the Violin concerto op. 61 / Ludwig van Beethoven ; herausgegeben von Hans-Werner Küthen ; Fingersatz von Klaus Schilde ; Klavierauszug von Jürgen Sommer ; Kadenzen vom Komponisten.

Sonata à 10
See **Dolar, Janez Krstnik, ca. 1620-1673.** [Sonatas, trumpet, instrumental ensemble, C major] Sonata à 10

See **Dolar, Janez Krstnik, ca. 1620-1673.** [Sonatas, trumpet, instrumental ensemble, C major; *arr.*] Sonata à 10

Sonata à 6 für Trompete, 2 Violinen, 3 Violen & B.c.
See **Ziani, Pietro Andrea, 1616-1684.** [Sonatas, trumpet, strings, continuo, D major] Sonata à 6 für Trompete, 2 Violinen, 3 Violen & B.c.

Sonata â due für Violine, Viola da gamba & B.c.
See **Schmelzer, Johann Heinrich, ca. 1623-1680.** [Trio sonatas, violin, viola da gamba, continuo, D minor] Sonata â due für Violine, Viola da gamba & B.c.

Sonata appassionata
See **Kaprálová, Vítězslava, 1915-1940.** Sonata appassionata

Sonata for alto flute and piano
See **Cooke, Arnold.** [Sonatas, flute, piano] Sonata for alto flute and piano

Sonata for bassoon and piano
See **Aston, Peter.** [Sonatas, bassoon, piano (2005)] Sonata for bassoon and piano

See **Bayliss, Colin.** [Sonatas, bassoon, piano (2005)] Sonata for bassoon and piano

Sonata for flute and harp
See **Cooke, Arnold.** [Sonatas, flute, harp] Sonata for flute and harp

Sonata for harmonica & piano
See **Cooke, Arnold.** [Sonatas, harmonica, piano] Sonata for harmonica & piano

Sonata for oboe and piano
See **Poulenc, Francis, 1899-1963.** [Sonatas, oboe, piano] Sonata for oboe and piano

Sonata for violoncello and piano
See **Bennett, Richard Rodney.** [Sonatas, violoncello, piano] Sonata for violoncello and piano

See **McCabe, John, 1939-** [Sonatas, violoncello, piano] Sonata for violoncello and piano

Sonata für zwei Violinen
See **Zenger, Max, 1837-1911.** [Amor und Psyche. Sonata] Sonata für zwei Violinen

Sonata H-Moll Op. 58
See **Chopin, Frédéric, 1810-1849.** [Sonatas, piano no. 3, op. 58, B minor] Sonata H-Moll Op. 58

Sonata in C minor for viola and piano, 1924
See **Röntgen, Julius, 1855-1932.** [Sonatas, viola, piano, C minor] Sonata in C minor for viola and piano, 1924

Sonata no. 1 in D
See **Serini, Giovanni Battista, b. ca. 1710.** [Sonatas, flute, continuo, D major] Sonata no. 1 in D

Sonata per a clavicèmbal
See **Rabassa, Pedro, 1683-1767.** [Sonata, harpsichord] Sonata per a clavicèmbal

Sonata per violoncello e piano, op. 86
See **Sallinen, Aulis.** [Sonatas, violoncello, piano, op. 86] Sonata per violoncello e piano, op. 86

Sonata VII in E minor
See **Purcell, Henry, 1659-1695.** [Trio sonatas, violins, continuo, Z. 796, E minor; *arr.*] Sonata VII in E minor

[Sonata, harpsichord]
See **Rabassa, Pedro, 1683-1767.** [Sonata, harpsichord]

[Sonatae unarum fidium]
See **Schmelzer, Johann Heinrich, ca. 1623-1680.** [Sonatae unarum fidium]

Sonatae unarum fidium seu a violino solo
See **Schmelzer, Johann Heinrich, ca. 1623-1680.** [Sonatae unarum fidium] Sonatae unarum fidium seu a violino solo

Sonatas BWV 1027, 1028, 1029
See **Bach, Johann Sebastian, 1685-1750.** [Sonatas, viola da gamba, harpsichord] Sonatas BWV 1027, 1028, 1029

Sonatas for flute [and continuo]
See **Handel, George Frideric, 1685-1759.** [Sonatas, flute, continuo. *Selections.*] Sonatas for flute [and continuo]

See **Handel, George Frideric, 1685-1759.** [Sonatas, recorder, continuo. *Selections.*] Sonatas for flute [and continuo]

[Sonatas, bassoon, piano (2005)]
See **Aston, Peter.** [Sonatas, bassoon, piano (2005)]

See **Bayliss, Colin.** [Sonatas, bassoon, piano (2005)]

[Sonatas, clarinet, piano, op. 129, F major; *arr.*]
See **Stanford, Charles Villiers, 1852-1924.** [Sonatas, clarinet, piano, op. 129, F major; *arr.*]

[Sonatas, flute, continuo, D major]
See **Serini, Giovanni Battista, b. ca. 1710.** [Sonatas, flute, continuo, D major]

[Sonatas, flute, continuo. *Selections.*]
See **Handel, George Frideric, 1685-1759.** [Sonatas, flute, continuo. *Selections.*]

[Sonatas, flute, harp]
See **Cooke, Arnold.** [Sonatas, flute, harp]

[Sonatas, flute, piano]
See **Cooke, Arnold.** [Sonatas, flute, piano]

[Sonatas, flutes (2), op. 1]
See **Atys, 1715-1784.** [Sonatas, flutes (2), op. 1]

[Sonatas, harmonica, piano]
See **Cooke, Arnold.** [Sonatas, harmonica, piano]

[Sonatas, harpsichord. *Selections*]
See **Hertel, Johann Wilhelm, 1727-1789.** [Sonatas, harpsichord. *Selections*]

[Sonatas, oboe, piano]
See **Poulenc, Francis, 1899-1963.** [Sonatas, oboe, piano]

[Sonatas, op. 13. No. 4-6]
See **Clementi, Muzio, 1752-1832.** [Sonatas, op. 13. No. 4-6]

[Sonatas, piano]
See **Febel, Reinhard, 1952-** [Sonatas, piano]

See **Nicolai, Johann Gottlieb, 1744-1801.** [Sonatas, piano]

[Sonatas, piano no. 3, op. 58, B minor]
See **Chopin, Frédéric, 1810-1849.** [Sonatas, piano no. 3, op. 58, B minor]

[Sonatas, piano, no. 1]
See **Cooke, Arnold.** [Sonatas, piano, no. 1]

[Sonatas, piano, no. 2]
See **Cooke, Arnold.** [Sonatas, piano, no. 2]

[Sonatas, piano, no. 2, op. 154]
See **Hedges, Anthony, 1931-** [Sonatas, piano, no. 2, op. 154]

[Sonatas, recorder, continuo. *Selections.*]
See **Handel, George Frideric, 1685-1759.** [Sonatas, recorder, continuo. *Selections.*]

[Sonatas, trumpet, instrumental ensemble, C major]
See **Dolar, Janez Krstnik, ca. 1620-1673.** [Sonatas, trumpet, instrumental ensemble, C major]

[Sonatas, trumpet, instrumental ensemble, C major; *arr.*]
See **Dolar, Janez Krstnik, ca. 1620-1673.** [Sonatas, trumpet, instrumental ensemble, C major; *arr.*]

[Sonatas, trumpet, strings, continuo, D major]
See **Ziani, Pietro Andrea, 1616-1684.** [Sonatas, trumpet, strings, continuo, D major]

[Sonatas, viola da gamba, continuo, G major]
See **Graun, Johann Gottlieb, 1702 or 3-1771.** [Sonatas, viola da gamba, continuo, G major]

[Sonatas, viola da gamba, continuo, op. 1]
See **Riehman, Jacob, d. 1726.** [Sonatas, viola da gamba, continuo, op. 1]

[Sonatas, viola da gamba, harpsichord]
See **Bach, Johann Sebastian, 1685-1750.** [Sonatas, viola da gamba, harpsichord]

[Sonatas, viola, continuo, C minor]
See **Benda, Franz, 1709-1786.** [Sonatas, viola, continuo, C minor]

[Sonatas, viola, piano, C minor]
See **Röntgen, Julius, 1855-1932.** [Sonatas, viola, piano, C minor]

[Sonatas, violin, continuo (1694)]
See **Westhoff, Johann Paul, 1656-1705.** [Sonatas, violin, continuo (1694)]

[Sonatas, violin, continuo (1701)]
See **Lonati, Carlo Ambrogio.** [Sonatas, violin, continuo (1701)]

[Sonatas, violin, continuo, op. 1]
See **Hertel, Johann Christian, 1699-1754.** [Sonatas, violin, continuo, op. 1]

[Sonatas, violin, harpsichord, op. 2]
See **LeBrun, Francesca, 1756-1791.** [Sonatas, violin, harpsichord, op. 2]

[Sonatas, violin, piano, A major; *arr.*]
See **Franck, César, 1822-1890.** [Sonatas, violin, piano, A major; *arr.*]

[Sonatas, violin, piano, no. 9, op. 47, A major; *arr.*]
See **Beethoven, Ludwig van, 1770-1827.** [Sonatas, violin, piano, no. 9, op. 47, A major; *arr.*]

[Sonatas, violins (2), violoncello, continuo]
See **Philarmonica,** [Sonatas, violins (2), violoncello, continuo]

[Sonatas, violins (2), viols (3), continuo, (1676)]
See **Schmelzer, Johann Heinrich, ca. 1623-1680.** [Sonatas, violins (2), viols (3), continuo, (1676)]

[Sonatas, violoncello, piano]
See **Bennett, Richard Rodney.** [Sonatas, violoncello, piano]

See **McCabe, John, 1939-** [Sonatas, violoncello, piano]

[Sonatas, violoncello, piano, op. 86]
See **Sallinen, Aulis.** [Sonatas, violoncello, piano, op. 86]

Sonate à violino solo col violone ò cimbalo, opera prima
See **Hertel, Johann Christian, 1699-1754.** [Sonatas, violin, continuo, op. 1] Sonate à violino solo col violone ò cimbalo, opera prima

Sonate für Viola und Klavier A-Dur
See **Franck, César, 1822-1890.** [Sonatas, violin, piano, A major; *arr.*] Sonate für Viola und Klavier A-Dur

Sonate für Violoncello und Klavier A-Dur
See **Franck, César, 1822-1890.** [Sonatas, violin, piano, A major; *arr.*] Sonate für Violoncello und Klavier A-Dur

Sonate per violino e basso continuo
See **Westhoff, Johann Paul, 1656-1705.** [Sonatas, violin, continuo (1694)] Sonate per violino e basso continuo

Sonate pour alto et basse continue en do mineur, Lee III-137
See **Benda, Franz, 1709-1786.** [Sonatas, viola, continuo, C minor] Sonate pour alto et basse continue en do mineur, Lee III-137

Sonatina
See **Elgar, Edward, 1857-1934.** [Sonatina, piano] Sonatina

Sonatina for oboe and harpsichord (or piano)
See **Jacob, Gordon, 1895-1984.** [Sonatinas, oboe, harpsichord] Sonatina for oboe and harpsichord (or piano)

Sonatina in G, op. 100
See **Dvořák, Antonín, 1841-1904.** [Sonatina, violin, piano, op. 100, G major; *arr.*] Sonatina in G, op. 100

Sonatina za piano
See **Tabakov, Emil.** [Sonatina, piano] Sonatina za piano

[Sonatina, piano]
See **Elgar, Edward, 1857-1934.** [Sonatina, piano]

See **Tabakov, Emil.** [Sonatina, piano]

[Sonatina, violin, piano, op. 100, G major; *arr.*]
See **Dvořák, Antonín, 1841-1904.** [Sonatina, violin, piano, op. 100, G major; *arr.*]

[Sonatinas, oboe, harpsichord]
See **Jacob, Gordon, 1895-1984**. [Sonatinas, oboe, harpsichord]

Sonatinas, opus 36
See **Clementi, Muzio, 1752-1832**. [Progressive sonatinas] Sonatinas, opus 36

[Song 13; *arr.*]
See **Gibbons, Orlando, 1583-1625**. [Song 13; *arr.*]

A song of liberty
See **Beach, H. H. A., Mrs., 1867-1944**. [Song of liberty; *arr.*] A song of liberty

[Song of liberty; *arr.*]
See **Beach, H. H. A., 1867-1944**. [Song of liberty; *arr.*]

Song of Lir
See **Carroll, Fergal**. Song of Lir

A song of thanksgiving
See **Vaughan Williams, Ralph, 1872-1958**. [Song of thanksgiving. *Vocal score*] A song of thanksgiving

[Song of thanksgiving. *Vocal score*]
See **Vaughan Williams, Ralph, 1872-1958**. [Song of thanksgiving. *Vocal score*]

Song without words
See **Boulter, Bryan**. Song without words

Songbird
Songbird : chord songbook. — *Wise Publications*
783.242164   013085454

[Songs]
[Songs]
See **Duparc, Henri, 1848-1933**. [Songs]

See **Ullmann, Viktor**. [Songs]

[Songs (2004)]
See **Previn, André, 1929-** [Songs (2004)]

Songs 1920-1923
See **Warlock, Peter, 1894-1930**. [Songs. Selections] Songs 1920-1923

Songs 1923-1926
See **Warlock, Peter, 1894-1930**. [Songs. Selections] Songs 1923-1926

Songs 1923-1928
See **Warlock, Peter, 1894-1930**. [Songs. Selections] Songs 1923-1928

Songs 1927-1928
See **Warlock, Peter, 1894-1930**. [Songs. Selections] Songs 1927-1928

Songs 1928-1930
See **Warlock, Peter, 1894-1930**. [Songs. Selections] Songs 1928-1930

[Songs for a mad king. *Vocal score*]
See **Davies, Peter Maxwell, 1934-** [Songs for a mad king. *Vocal score*]

Songs for bass solo
See **Purcell, Henry, 1659-1695**. [Songs. Selections] Songs for bass solo

Songs for every assembly
See **Johnson, Mark** Songs for every assembly

Songs for Silverman
See **Folds, Ben, 1966-** Songs for Silverman

Songs from the sea
Songs from the sea : for trumpet / arranged by Colin Mawby. — *Kevin Mayhew*
788.921595   013159343

Songs of comfort
See **Dicie, Don Michael**. Songs of comfort

[Songs of Mary]
See **Dmitriev, Alexander I., 1961-** [Songs of Mary]

[Songs of sundrie natures]
See **Byrd, William, 1542 or 3-1623**. [Songs of sundrie natures]

Songs of sundrie natures (1589)
See **Byrd, William, 1542 or 3-1623**. [Songs of sundrie natures] Songs of sundrie natures (1589)

Songs of the garden
See **McCabe, John, 1939-** [Songs of the garden. *Vocal score*] Songs of the garden

[Songs of the garden. *Vocal score*]
See **McCabe, John, 1939-** [Songs of the garden. *Vocal score*]

Songs with violins
See **Croft, William, 1678-1727**. [How charming is beauty] Songs with violins

Songs without words
See **Tsitsaros, Christos**. Songs without words

[Songs, op. 16. When fond, you Damon's charms recite]
See **Jackson, William, 1730-1803**. [Songs, op. 16. When fond, you Damon's charms recite]

[Songs, violin, continuo acc. *Selections*]
See **Haydn, Joseph, 1732-1809**. [Songs, violin, continuo acc. *Selections*]

[Songs. *Selections; arr.*]
See **Foster, Stephen Collins, 1826-1864**. [Songs. *Selections; arr.*]

See **Gershwin, George, 1898-1937**. [Songs. *Selections; arr.*]

[Songs. *Selections*]
[Songs. *Selections*]
See **Buckley, Jeff, 1966-1997**. [Songs. Selections]

See **Charles, Ray, 1930-2004**. [Songs. Selections]

See **Clapton, Eric**. [Songs. *Selections*]

See **Darin, Bobby**. [Songs. *Selections*]

See **Fesch, Willem de, 1687-1761**. [Songs. Selections]

See **Harrison, George, 1943-2001**. [Songs. Selections]

See **Jeffreys, George, ca. 1610-1685**. [Songs. Selections]

See **Joel, Billy**. [Songs. *Selections*]

See **John, Elton**. [Songs. *Selections*]

See **Kaye, Ernest**. [Songs. *Selections*]

See **Lennon, John, 1940-1980**. [Songs. Selections]

See **Mazzocchi, D. 1592-1665**. [Songs. Selections]

See **Presley, Elvis, 1935-1977**. [Songs. Selections]

See **Purcell, Henry, 1659-1695**. [Songs. Selections]

See **Seal** [Songs. *Selections*]

See **Sedaka, Neil**. [Songs. *Selections*]

See **Simon, Paul, 1941-** [Songs. *Selections*]

See **Sting** [Songs. *Selections*]

See **Sviridov, Georgiĭ Vasil'evich, 1915-1998**. [Songs. *Selections*]

See **Warlock, Peter, 1894-1930**. [Songs. Selections]

See **Webern, Anton, 1883-1945**. [Songs. Selections]

Sonnengesang = The canticle of the sun : revidierte Fassung 5/1998
See **Gubaĭdulina, Sofía Asgatovna**. Sonnengesang = The canticle of the sun : revidierte Fassung 5/1998

Sonny Rollins
See **Rollins, Sonny**. [Selections; *arr.*] Sonny Rollins

Sor, Fernando, *1778-1839.*
[Encouragement. *Selections; arr.*] — Andante, theme & variations [from] (Duo for guitars, op. 34) / by Fernando Sor ; arranged for wind quintet by David B. Johnson. — *Phylloscopus Publications*
785.43195   013173919

[Guitar music. 1997] — The new complete works for guitar : re-engraved in eleven volumes / Fernando Sor ; edited by Brian Jeffery. — *2nd printing with corrections.* — *Tecla*
787.87   013334512

Sound carvings from the water's edge
See **Hellawell, Piers, 1956-** Sound carvings from the water's edge

The sound of music
See **Rodgers, Richard, 1902-1979**. [Sound of music. *Vocal score. Selections; arr.*] The sound of music

[Sound of music. *Vocal score. Selections; arr.*]
See **Rodgers, Richard, 1902-1979**. [Sound of music. *Vocal score. Selections; arr.*]

[Sound of music. My favorite things; *arr.*]
See **Rodgers, Richard, 1902-1979**. [Sound of music. My favorite things; *arr.*]

A South Yorkshire suite
See **Walker, Robert, 1946-** A South Yorkshire suite

Southwell, Robert, Saint, *1561?-1595.*
See **Dicie, Don Michael**. The burning babe : a Christmas anthem for unaccompanied mixed choir (SATB) / Don Michael Dicie.

Souvestre, Émile, *1806-1854.* Pasteur.
See **Verdi, Giuseppe, 1813-1901**. Stiffelio / Giuseppe Verdi ; libretto (in three acts) by Francesco Maria Piave ; edited by Kathleen Kuzmick Hansell.

Spada, Pietro, *1935-*
See **Donizetti, Gaetano, 1797-1848**. Piccola composizione : per clarinetto ed orchestra / Gaetano Donizetti ; a cura di Pietro Spada.

See **Porpora, Nicola, 1686-1768**. [Concertos, flute, string orchestra, D major] Concerto per flauto ed archi / Niccolò Porpora ; a cura di Pietro Spada.

See **Puccini, Giacomo, 1858-1924**. [Capriccio sinfonico] Capriccio sinfonico / Giacomo Puccini ; a cura di Pietro Spada.

See **Verdi, Giuseppe, 1813-1901**. [Macbeth. Ballo] Macbeth. Ballet : (1865) / [Giuseppe Verdi] ; a cura di Pietro Spada.

Spande ancor a mio dispetto
See **Handel, George Frideric, 1685-1759**. Spande ancor a mio dispetto

The Spanish Armada
See **Hewitt, Daniel**. [Spanish Armada. *Selections*] The Spanish Armada

See **Hewitt, Daniel**. The Spanish Armada

[Spanish Armada. *Selections*]
See **Hewitt, Daniel**. [Spanish Armada. *Selections*]

Spanish picture
See **Wood, Gareth.** [Mexican pictures. Spanish]
Spanish picture

Sparke, Philip.
Skyrider : [concert march] / by Philip Sparke. —
Studio Music
784.81897   013407857

See **Mozart, Wolfgang Amadeus, 1756-1791**
[Ave verum corpus; *arr.*] Ave verum corpus /
Mozart ; arranged for four euphoniums and
brass band by Philip Sparke.

Spectrum
Spectrum : for cello : 16 contemporary pieces /
compiled by William Bruce. — *Associated
Board of the Royal Schools of Music*
787.40905   013190730

Spencer, Tim.
The ancient Olympics : the legend of
Callipateira. — *Maplewood Education :*
782.14083   013587294

[Ancient Olympics. *Selections*] — The ancient
Olympics : the Olympic traditions : assembly
pack. — *Maplewood Education :*
782.7   013586998

[Ancient Olympics. *Selections*] — The ancient
Olympics : the story of Callipateira : assembly
pack / written by Daniel Dalton ; music [&
lyrics] by Tim Spencer. — *Educational Musicals*
782.7   013587006

The boy king : the legend of Tutankhamun. —
2nd ed. — Maplewood Education
782.14083   013390813

[Boy king. *Selections*] — The boy king : the
legend of Tutankhamun : assembly pack /
written by Anthony James ; music [& lyrics] by
Tim Spencer. — *Maplewood Education :*
782.7   013587415

The dream catcher : the plains indians of North
America. — *2nd ed. — Maplewood Education*
782.41083   013390705

[Dream catcher. *Selections*] — The dream
catcher : the Plains Indians of North America :
assembly pack. — *Maplewood Education :*
782.7   013587532

Egyptian selection 1 : a collection of songs from
Educational Musicals' Egyptian shows / [music
& lyrics by Tim Spencer and Daniel Hewitt] —
Maplewood Education :
782.742   013587354

The golden city : the lost empire of the Aztecs.
— *2nd ed. — Maplewood Education*
782.14083   013390718

The lucky Viking : the discovery of America. —
2nd ed. — Maplewood Education
782.14083   013390817

[Lucky Viking. *Selections*] — The lucky
Viking : the discovery of America : assembly
pack / written by Anthony James ; music [&
lyrics] by Tim Spencer. — *Educational Musicals*
782.7   013587391

Monster of the maze : the story of Theseus and
the Minotaur. — *2nd ed. — Maplewood
Education*
782.14083   013390808

[Monster of the maze. *Selections*] — Monster of
the maze : the story of Theseus and the
Minotaur : assembly pack. — *Maplewood
Education :*
782.7   013587420

The ship of dreams : the voyage of the RMS
Titanic. — *Maplewood Education*
782.14083   013390712

The star child : the Christmas story. — *2nd ed.
— Maplewood Education*
782.141723083   013390742

Trafalgar : Nelson's finest hour / written by
Daniel Dalton ; music [& lyrics] by Tim
Spencer. — *Maplewood Education :*
782.14083   013587097

[Trafalgar. *Selections*] — Trafalgar : Napolean's
navy : assembly pack / written by Daniel
Dalton ; music [& lyrics] by Tim Spencer. —
Educational Musicals
782.7   013586933

[Trafalgar. *Selections*] — Trafalgar : Nelson's
finest hour : assembly pack / written by Daniel
Dalton ; musc [& lyrics] by Tim Spencer. —
Maplewood Education :
782.7   013587002

The Victorian historian : a journey to Victorian
Britain. — *2nd ed. — Maplewood Education*
782.14083   013390670

[Victorian historian. *Selections*] — The
Victorian historian : history is boring? :
assembly pack / written by Anthony James ;
music [& lyrics] by Tim Spencer. — *Maplewood
Education :*
782.7   013587074

[Victorian historian. *Selections*] — The
Victorian historian : rogues, railways & royalty:
assembly pack. — *Maplewood Education :*
782.7   013587081

The warrior queen : Boudica and the Romans.
— *2nd ed. — Maplewood Education*
782.14083   013390707

[Warrior queen. *Selections*] — The warrior
queen : Boudica and the Romans : assembly
pack. — *Maplewood Education :*
782.7   013587444

[Warrior queen. *Selections*] — The warrior
queen : the Romans in Britannia : assembly pack
/ written by Anthony James ; music [& lyrics] by
Tim Spencer. — *Educational Musicals*
782.7   013586988

See **Christmas selection 1 :** a collection of
songs from Educational Musicals' Christmas
shows.

See **Christmas selection 2 :** a collection of
songs from our Christmas shows.

See **Hewitt, Daniel.** Greek selection 1 : a
collection of songs from Educational Musicals'
Greek shows / [music & lyrics by Daniel Hewitt
& Tim Spencer]

Sperling, Oliver, 1965-
See **Leibl, Carl, 1784-1870.** [Masses, no. 3, E♭
major. *Vocal score*] Messe Nr. 3 Es-Dur / Carl
Leibl ; herausgegeben von Eberhard
Metternich ; mit einem einführenden Text von
Oliver Sperling ; Klavierauszug.

Spielsachen
See **Kirchner, Theodor, 1823-1903.**
Spielsachen

Spiniello, Pasquale.
See **Torelli, Giuseppe, 1658-1709.** [Concerto da
camera] Concerto da camera per due violini,
violone e clavicembalo, op. 2 : Bologna, 1686 /
Giuseppe Torelli ; trascizione a cura di Pasquale
Spiniello.

Spinning Jenny
See **Davies, Peter Maxwell, 1934-** Spinning
Jenny

Spohr, Louis, 1784-1859
Erinnerung an Marienbad : (waltz, op. 89) : for
flute, clarinet 1 in A (or oboe), clarinet 2 in A,
horns 1 & 2 in D (or in F), bassoon, violins 1 &
2, viola and bassi / by Louis Spohr. —
Phylloscopus Publications
785.4219918846   013173883

Spring suite
See **Lewis, Paul, 1943-** Spring suite

Springer, Mike.
See **Christmas jazz :** six carols for piano solo /
arranged by Mike Springer ; edited by J. Mark
Baker.

Der Spuk
See **Bingham, Judith.** Der Spuk

Srebotnjak, Alojz.
See **Vivaldi, Antonio, 1678-1741** [Cimento
dell'armonia e dell'inventione. N. 1-4; *arr.*] The
four seasons : four concertos for violin and
orchestra : for violin and piano reduction /
Antonio Vivaldi ; violin part edited by Rok
Klopčič ; piano reduction by Alojz Srebotnjak.

St Anger
See **Metallica (Musical group)** St Anger

St.-Lubin, Léon de.
[Octet, op. 33, E minor] — Grand octetto
op. 33 : for flute, clarinet in A, horn in E, D & G
(part in F included), bassoon, viola, cello,
double bass and piano / by Léon de
Saint-Lubin ; [edited by Chris & Frances Nex]
— *Phylloscopus Publications*
785.22198   013561009

**St.-Pieters & Paulusabdij (*Dendermonde,
Belgium*).**
See **Hildegard, Saint, 1098-1179.** [Symphonia
armonie celestium revelationum] Symphonia
harmoniae caelestium revelationum :
Dendermonde, St.-Pieters & Paulusabdij, ms.
Cod. 9 / Hildegard of Bingen ; introduction,
Peter van Poucke.

Stabat mater
See **Dvořák, Antonín, 1841-1904.** [Stabat
Mater, op. 58, D major] Stabat mater

See **Fenaroli, Fedele, 1730-1818.** Stabat mater

Stabat Mater dolorosa
See **Palestrina, Giovanni Pierluigi da,
1525?-1594.** [Stabat Mater, voices (8)] Stabat
Mater dolorosa

**Stabat Mater für Soli, Chor und Orchester,
op. 58**
See **Dvořák, Antonín, 1841-1904.** [Stabat
Mater, op. 58, D major. *Vocal score*] Stabat
Mater für Soli, Chor und Orchester, op. 58

[Stabat Mater, op. 58, D major]
See **Dvořák, Antonín, 1841-1904.** [Stabat
Mater, op. 58, D major]

[Stabat Mater, op. 58, D major. *Vocal score*]
See **Dvořák, Antonín, 1841-1904.** [Stabat
Mater, op. 58, D major. *Vocal score*]

[Stabat Mater, voices (8)]
See **Palestrina, Giovanni Pierluigi da,
1525?-1594.** [Stabat Mater, voices (8)]

Stachel, Irena.
See **Elsner, Józef, 1769-1854.** [Masses, F major]
Missa F a canto, alto, tenore, basso, due violini,
viole, bassi (violoncello et basso), due clarinetti,
due corni con organo / Józef Elsner ;
opracowanie, Hubert Prochota ; wstęp,
Remigiusz Pośpiech ; [redaktor, Irena Stachel]

See **Żebrowski, Marcin Józef.** Missa pastoralis :
a canto, basso, due violini, due clarini con
organo / Marcin Józef Żebrowski ; opracowanie i
wstęp Remigiusz Pośpiech ; [redaktor, Irena
Stachel]

Stanford, Charles Villiers, *1852-1924.*
[Sonatas, clarinet, piano, op. 129, F major; *arr.*]
— Viola sonata, op. 129 / by C.V. Stanford ; the
composer's sonata for clarinet and piano
arranged for viola and edited by Henry Waldo
Warner and John White. — *Stainer & Bell*
787.3183   013123103

Stanley, John, *1712-1786.*
[Cantatas, op. 8] — Six cantata's, for a voice
and instruments / set to musick by John Stanley.
— *JPH Publications*
783.348   013312779

Stanton, Frank L. *1895-1932.*
See **Beach, H. H. A., Mrs.,** *1867-1944.* [Song of
liberty; *arr.*] A song of liberty : for high voice
and piano, op. 49 / by Amy Beach.

Stanza
See **Maw, Nicholas.** Stanza

The star child
See **Spencer, Tim.** The star child

Star of the County Down
Star of the County Down : SSAATTBB / Irish
traditional ; arranged by Ben Parry. — *Edition
Peters*
782.542   013305040

[Star-spangled banner (Song); *arr.*]
The star-spangled banner : for mixed chorus,
unaccompanied / arranged by Jerry Rubino. —
Oxford University Press
782.54215990973   013196283

The star-spangled banner
See **[Star-spangled banner (Song);]** The
star-spangled banner

Starry night
See **Willcocks, David,** *1919-* Starry night

The stars
See **Portman, Rachel.** [Little prince. Stars; *arr.*]
The stars

Stars of CCTV
See **Archer, Richard,** *1976 or 7-* Stars of CCTV

Start something
See **Lostprophets (Musical group)** Start
something

Štědrý den
See **Fibich, Zdeněk,** *1850-1900.* [Štědrý den.
Polyglot] Štědrý den

[Štědrý den. *Polyglot*]
See **Fibich, Zdeněk,** *1850-1900.* [Štědrý den.
Polyglot]

Steele, Douglas, *1910-*
[Short songs] — Three short songs : for either
solo voice, or unison voices, with piano /
Douglas Steele. — *Encore Publications*
783.242   013358905

Steffe, William, *ca. 1830-1890.*
The battle hymn of the Republic / [attributed to]
William Steffe ; arr. John Hearne. — *Longship*
782.527   013440370

Steffen, Albert, *1884-1963.*
See **Ullmann, Viktor.** [Herbst] Drei Lieder : für
Singstimme und Streichtrio = for voice and
string trio (1943) / Viktor Ullmann ; nach Texten
von Georg Trakl und Albert Steffen.

Steiner, Stefanie.
See **Schulz, J. A. P.** *1747-1800.* Lieder im
Volkston / Johann Abraham Peter Schulz ;
herausgegeben von Walther Dürr und Stefanie
Steiner unter Mitarbeit von Michael Kohlhäufl.

Stella quam viderant Magi
See **Palestrina, Giovanni Pierluigi da,**
1525?-1594. [Motets (1569). Stella, quam
viderant Magi] Stella quam viderant Magi

Stephan, Rudolf.
See **Gurre-Lieder** : für Soli, Chor und
Orchester : kritischer Bericht / Arnold
Schönberg ; [Text] von Jens Peter Jacobsen
(deutsch von Robert Franz Arnold) ;
herausgegeben von Ulrich Krämer.

Stephen Foster medley
See **Foster, Stephen Collins,** *1826-1864.*
[Songs. *Selections; arr.*] Stephen Foster medley

Stereophonics.
Language, sex, violence, other? / Stereophonics.
— *Guitar tab ed.* — *Wise*
783.242166   013297754

Steude, Wolfram.
See **Biber, Heinrich Ignaz Franz,** *1644-1704.*
O dulcis Jesu : geistliches Konzert : canto solo,
violino discordato e basso continuo / Heinrich
Ignaz Franz Biber? ; herausgegeben von
Wolfram Steude.

Stevenson, Anne, *1933 Jan. 3-*
See **Samuel, Rhian.** Trinity : three songs for
high voice, flute and piano / to texts by Anne
Stevenson ; by Rhian Samuel.

Stewart, Richard N.
Just as I am : for unaccompanied mixed choir
(SATB) / Richard N. Stewart. — *Oxford
University Press*
782.5265   013472140

[Just as I am. *Spanish*] — Tal como soy = (Just
as I am) : for unaccompanied mixed choir
(SATB) / Richard N. Stewart. — *Oxford
University Press*
782.5265   013472571

Stiffelio
See **Verdi, Giuseppe,** *1813-1901.* Stiffelio

The still dancers
See **Hellawell, Piers,** *1956-* The still dancers

Still und bewegt
See **Kirchner, Theodor,** *1823-1903.* Still und
bewegt

Still, still, still
Still, still, still : for SAA chorus and organ /
[arranged by] Barry Rose (1999). — *Novello &
Co*
782.6281723   013506277

Stille nacht
See **Gruber, Franz Xaver,** *1787-1863.* [Stille
Nacht, heilige Nacht; *arr.*] Stille nacht

[Stille Nacht, heilige Nacht; *arr.*]
See **Gruber, Franz Xaver,** *1787-1863.* [Stille
Nacht, heilige Nacht; *arr.*]

Stimmen
See **Furrer, Beat,** *1954-* Stimmen

Sting (Musician)
[Songs. *Selections*] — The singles collection /
Sting. — *Wise Publications*
783.2421660264   013383548

Sting (Musician).
[Songs. *Selections*] — Sting for guitar tab /
[Compiled by Peter Evans]; [words & music by
Sting] — *Wise Publications*
783.242166   013202148

Sting for guitar tab
See **Sting (Musician).** [Songs. *Selections*] Sting
for guitar tab

Stocker, David.
See **Beck.** Guero / Beck ; music transcriptions
by Pete Billmann, Addi Booth and David
Stocker.

See **Beck.** Sea change / Beck ; music
transcriptions by Andrew Moore, David Stocker,
and Jeff Story.

See **In your honor** / Foo Fighters ; music
transcriptions by Pete Billmann and David
Stocker.

See **Mezmerize** / System of a Down ; music
transcriptions by Pete Billmann and David
Stocker.

See **[Songs. *Selections* |** Best of Train / music
transcriptions by David Stocker.

See **Start something** / Lostprophets ; music
transcriptions by Addi Booth and David Stocker.

Stone, Thomas, *1957-*
See **Gilmore, Bernard,** *1937-* [Folksongs] Five
folk songs : for soprano and symphonic wind
band : (1966) / Bernard Gilmore.

Story, Jeffrey.
See **Beck.** Sea change / Beck ; music
transcriptions by Andrew Moore, David Stocker,
and Jeff Story.

See **Good news for people who love bad
news** : guitar recorded versions / by Modest
Mouse ; music transcriptions by Pete Billmann,
Addi Booth and Jeff Story.

Stove, Thomas Gideon.
Running for a fry : and other Shetland fiddle
tunes / Thomas Gideon Stove. — *Shetland
Times*
787.21620941135   013345843

Stow, Randolph, *1935-*
See **Davies, Peter Maxwell,** *1934-* [Songs for a
mad king. *Vocal score*] Eight songs for a mad
king : music-theatre work for male voice and
ensemble / Peter Maxwell Davies ; text by
Randolph Stow and George III ; vocal score.

Stradella, Alessandro, *1639-1682.*
La forza dell'amor paterno / Alessandro
Stradella ; a cura di Mariateresa Dellaborra,
Carolyn Gianturco. — *ETS*
782.1   013825578

Strahl, Tomasz.
See **Twardowski, Romuald,** *1930-* [Concertos,
violoncello, orchestra; *arr.*] Concerto per cello
ed orchestra / Romuald Twardowski ; wyciąg
fortepianowy ; opracowanie głosu solowego
Tomasz Strahl.

Strauss, Johann, *1825-1899.*
[Nachtigall-Polka; *arr.*] — Nachtigall-Polka :
op. 222 / Johann Strauss (Sohn) ;
[herausgegeben von] Isabella Sommer. —
Doblinger
784.218844   013587599

Stravinsky, Igor, *1882-1971.*
[Svadebka. *French & Russian*] — Les noces =
(Svadebka) : scènes chorégraphiques russes avec
chant et musique : for four pianos, percussion
and voices in a revised and corrected edition
based upon relevant autograph and printed
sources / composées par Igor Stravinsky ;
French text by C.-F. Ramuz ; edited by
Margarita Mazo ; associate editor, Millan
Sachania. — *Chester Music*
782.51556   013383538

Streichquartett Nr. 2
See **Terteryan, A.** *1929-* [Quartets, strings, no.
2] Streichquartett Nr. 2

See **Mägi, Ester,** *1922-* [Quartets, strings, no. 2]
Streichquartett Nr. 2

Streichquartett Nr. 8, op. 66, für zwei Violinen, Viola und Violoncello

    See **Vaĭnberg, Moiseĭ Samuilovich.** [Quartets, strings, no. 8, op. 66] Streichquartett Nr. 8, op. 66, für zwei Violinen, Viola und Violoncello

Streichquartette

    See **Beethoven, Ludwig van, 1770-1827.** [Quartets, strings, no. 1-6, op. 18] Streichquartette

    See **Brahms, Johannes, 1833-1897.** [Quartets, strings] Streichquartette

Streichquartette Nr. 4 und 5

    See **Schroeder, Hermann, 1904-1984.** [Quartets, strings, no. 4] Streichquartette Nr. 4 und 5

Streichquintett F-Dur

    See **Bruckner, Anton, 1824-1896.** [Quintet, violins, violas, violoncello, F major] Streichquintett F-Dur

Streichquintett, Opus 116 (xpt), für 2 Violinen, 2 Bratschen und Violoncello, 1998

    See **Thoma, Xaver, 1953-** [Quintets, violins, violas, violoncello, op. 116] Streichquintett, Opus 116 (xpt), für 2 Violinen, 2 Bratschen und Violoncello, 1998

Striggio, Alessandro, *1536 or 7-1592*.

    [Madrigals, voices (5), book 1] — Il primo libro de madrigali a cinque voci / Alessandro Striggio ; edited by David Butchart. — *A-R Editions*

    782.543   013703139

String quartet in C minor (1898)

    See **Vaughan Williams, Ralph, 1872-1958.** [Quartets, strings, C minor] String quartet in C minor (1898)

String quartet no. 2

    See **Cooke, Arnold.** [Quartets, strings, no. 2] String quartet no. 2

String quartet no. 3

    See **Cooke, Arnold.** [Quartets, strings, no. 3] String quartet no. 3

    See **Gilbert, Anthony.** [Quartets, strings, no. 3] String quartet no. 3

String quartet no. 4

    See **Cooke, Arnold.** [Quartets, strings, no. 4] String quartet no. 4

    See **Sheng, Bright, 1955-** [Quartets, strings, no. 4] String quartet no. 4

String quartet no. 5

    See **Cooke, Arnold.** [Quartets, strings, no. 5] String quartet no. 5

String quartets opus 3 [sic], for 2 violins, viola & violoncello

    See **Sirmen, Maddalena Laura Lombardini, 1745-1818.** [Quartets, strings] String quartets opus 3 [sic], for 2 violins, viola & violoncello

Strings in step.

    See **Dobbins, Jan.** Strings in step.

Struck, Michael.

    See **Brahms, Johannes, 1833-1897.** [Concertos, violin, orchestra, op. 77, D major] Violinkonzert D-Dur Opus 77 / Johannes Brahms ; herausgegeben von Linda Correll Roesner und Michael Struck.

Strungk, Delphin, *1601-1694*.

    [Organ music] — Sämtliche Orgelwerke : Choralbearbeitungen, Toccata, Motettenkolorierungen = Complete organ works : chorale settings, toccata, motet intabulations / Delphin Strunck ; herausgegeben von Klaus Beckmann. — *Schott*

    786.5   013953484

Struther, Jan, *1901-1953*.

    See **Lord of all hopefulness** : for SATB chorus and organ / [arranged by] Barry Rose (2002).

Stubbs, Duncan.

    See **Early one morning** : grade 1.5 / traditional ; arr. Duncan Stubbs.

Stück für Violoncello und Klavier

    See **Terteryan, A. 1929-** [Stück, violoncello, piano] Stück für Violoncello und Klavier

[Stück, violoncello, piano]

    See **Terteryan, A. 1929-** [Stück, violoncello, piano]

[Studio for brass. Duets]

    See **Holdom, Colin.** [Studio for brass. Duets]

Stulick, Matthäus Nikolaus.

    [Concertino, woodwinds, continuo, B♭ major] — Concertino a 4 stromenti, für Oboe, Klarinette (B), Fagott und Basso continuo = Concertino a 4 stromenti, for oboe, clarinet (B♭), bassoon and basso continuo / Matthäus Nicolaus Stulick ; herausgegeben von Hans-Peter Vogel. — *Erstdruck 1st ed.* — *Thomi-Berg*

    785.26194   014053369

Sucato, Tiziana.

    See **Il codice rossiano 215** : madrigali, ballate, una caccia, un rotondello / edizione critica e studio introduttivo a cura di Tiziana Sucato.

El sueño de un bailarín

    See **Escudero, Francisco, 1912-2002.** El sueño de un bailarín

Suite de ballet

    See **Vaughan Williams, Ralph, 1872-1958.** Suite de ballet

Suite espagnole

    See **Albéniz, Isaac, 1860-1909.** [Suite española, no. 1] Suite espagnole

[Suite española, no. 1]

    See **Albéniz, Isaac, 1860-1909.** [Suite española, no. 1]

Suite for harpsichord and saxophone quartet

    See **Cowles, Colin,** [Suites, harpsichord, saxophones (4)] Suite for harpsichord and saxophone quartet

Suite for solo viola

    See **Sewell, Dominic.** [Suites, viola, op. 38] Suite for solo viola

Suite for two treble viols and bass viol

    See **Cooke, Arnold.** [Suites, viols (3)] Suite for two treble viols and bass viol

Suite for winds

    See **Gorb, Adam, 1958-** [Suites, woodwinds (1993)] Suite for winds

Suite für Klavier Nr. 2, C-Dur, op. 71

    See **Raff, Joachim, 1822-1882.** [Suites, piano, op. 71, C major] Suite für Klavier Nr. 2, C-Dur, op. 71

Suite für Klavier Nr. 3, e-Moll, op. 72

    See **Raff, Joachim, 1822-1882.** [Suites, piano, op. 72, E minor] Suite für Klavier Nr. 3, e-Moll, op. 72

Suite für Violine und Klavier, op. 56 (1937, rev. 1957)

    See **Wellesz, Egon, 1885-1974.** [Suites, violin, piano, op. 56] Suite für Violine und Klavier, op. 56 (1937, rev. 1957)

Suite für Violine und Orchester g-Moll, op. 180

    See **Raff, Joachim, 1822-1882.** [Suites, violin, orchestra, op. 180, G minor] Suite für Violine und Orchester g-Moll, op. 180

Suite für Violoncello Nr. 3, C-Dur, BWV 1009

    See **Bach, Johann Sebastian, 1685-1750.** [Suites violoncello, BWV 1009, C major; *arr.*] Suite für Violoncello Nr. 3, C-Dur, BWV 1009

Suite für Violoncello Nr. 4, Es-Dur, BWV 1010

    See **Bach, Johann Sebastian, 1685-1750.** [Suites, violoncello, BWV 1010, E♭ major; *arr.*] Suite für Violoncello Nr. 4, Es-Dur, BWV 1010

Suite für Violoncello Nr. 6, D-Dur, BWV 1012

    See **Bach, Johann Sebastian, 1685-1750.** [Suites violoncello, BWV 1012, D major; *arr.*] Suite für Violoncello Nr. 6, D-Dur, BWV 1012

Suite in D minor

    See **Milford, Robin, 1903-1959.** [Suites, oboe, string orchestra, op. 8; *arr.*] Suite in D minor

Suite in G minor

    See **Handel, George Frideric, 1685-1759.** [Suites, harpsichord, HWV 432, G minor; *arr.*] Suite in G minor

Suite no. 2 for pianoforte

    See **Cooke, Arnold.** [Suites, piano, no. 2] Suite no. 2 for pianoforte

Suite no. 3 for pianoforte

    See **Cooke, Arnold.** [Suites, piano, no. 3] Suite no. 3 for pianoforte

[Suites violoncello, BWV 1009, C major; *arr.*]

    See **Bach, Johann Sebastian, 1685-1750.** [Suites violoncello, BWV 1009, C major; *arr.*]

[Suites violoncello, BWV 1012, D major; *arr.*]

    See **Bach, Johann Sebastian, 1685-1750.** [Suites violoncello, BWV 1012, D major; *arr.*]

[Suites, harpsichord, G major. Menuet alternativement; *arr.*]

    See **Pezold, Christian, 1677-1733** [Suites, harpsichord, G major. Menuet alternativement; *arr.*]

[Suites, harpsichord, HWV 432, G minor; *arr.*]

    See **Handel, George Frideric, 1685-1759.** [Suites, harpsichord, HWV 432, G minor; *arr.*]

[Suites, harpsichord, saxophones (4)]

    See **Cowles, Colin,** [Suites, harpsichord, saxophones (4)]

[Suites, oboe, string orchestra, op. 8; *arr.*]

    See **Milford, Robin, 1903-1959.** [Suites, oboe, string orchestra, op. 8; *arr.*]

[Suites, orchestra, BWV 1067, B minor. Badinerie; *arr.*]

    See **Bach, Johann Sebastian, 1685-1750.** [Suites, orchestra, BWV 1067, B minor. Badinerie; *arr.*]

[Suites, piano, no. 2]

    See **Cooke, Arnold.** [Suites, piano, no. 2]

[Suites, piano, no. 3]

    See **Cooke, Arnold.** [Suites, piano, no. 3]

[Suites, piano, op. 71, C major]

    See **Raff, Joachim, 1822-1882.** [Suites, piano, op. 71, C major]

[Suites, piano, op. 72, E minor]

    See **Raff, Joachim, 1822-1882.** [Suites, piano, op. 72, E minor]

[Suites, viola, op. 38]
See **Sewell, Dominic.** [Suites, viola, op. 38]

[Suites, violin, orchestra, op. 180, G minor]
See **Raff, Joachim, 1822-1882.** [Suites, violin, orchestra, op. 180, G minor]

[Suites, violin, piano, op. 56]
See **Wellesz, Egon, 1885-1974.** [Suites, violin, piano, op. 56]

[Suites, violoncello, BWV 1010, E♭ major; arr.]
See **Bach, Johann Sebastian, 1685-1750.** [Suites, violoncello, BWV 1010, E♭ major; arr.]

[Suites, viols (3)]
See **Cooke, Arnold.** [Suites, viols (3)]

[Suites, woodwinds (1993)]
See **Gorb, Adam, 1958-** [Suites, woodwinds (1993)]

Summer's farewell
See **DeWald, Frank K.** Summer's farewell

Sumsion, Herbert.
See **Vaughan Williams, Ralph, 1872-1958.** [Organ music. *Selections*] A Vaughan Williams organ album.

Sunset
Sunset : (no. 3 from "Northwest trilogy") : SATB a cappella / arranged by Imant Raminsh. — *Boosey & Hawkes*
782.542162009711   013243875

Sutton, Tim, composer.
Quittez, pasteurs : for SATB chorus and organ / Tim Sutton. — *Novello*
785.281723   013313838

[Svadebka. *French & Russian*]
See **Stravinsky, Igor, 1882-1971.** [Svadebka. *French & Russian*]

Sviridov, Georgiĭ Vasil'evich, *1915-1998*.
[Choral music. *Selections*] — Sochineniiä dlä khora bez soprovozhdeniiä / Georgiĭ Sviridov ; tom podgotovlen K. A. Titarenko. — *Natsional'nyĭ Sviridovskiĭ Fond*
782.5   014750711

[Kurskie pesni] — Kurskie pesni ; Kurskie pesni ; Tri starinnye pesni kurskoĭ gubernii / Georgiĭ Sviridov ; tom podgotovlen P. V. Luk'iänchenko. — *Natsional'nyĭ Sviridovskiĭ Fond*
782.548   014750500

[Songs. *Selections*] — Romansy i pesni : dlä golosa i fortepiano / Georgiĭ Sviridov ; tom podgotovlen K. A. Titarenko. — *Natsional'nyĭ Sviridovskiĭ Fond*
783.242   014750606

Sviridov, Georgiĭ Vasil'evich, *1915-1998*.
Starinnye pesni kurskoĭ gubernii.
See **Sviridov, Georgiĭ Vasil'evich, 1915-1998.** [Kurskie pesni] Kurskie pesni ; Kurskie pesni ; Tri starinnye pesni kurskoĭ gubernii / Georgiĭ Sviridov ; tom podgotovlen P. V. Luk'iänchenko.

The swan
See **Saint-Saëns, Camille, 1835-1921.** [Carnaval des animaux. Cygne; arr.] The swan

Swayne, Giles.
[Christmas carols, op. 77] — Four Christmas carols : op. 77 / Giles Swayne. — *Novello*
782.5281723   013336027

The Coventry carol : op. 77 no. 4 : (2005) : for SATB chorus and piano / Giles Swayne. — *Novello & Co*
782.5281723   013526387

Sweelinck, Jan Pieterszoon, *1562-1621*.
[Fantasias, keyboard instrument] — Sämtliche Werke für Tasteninstrumente. Band 2, Fantasien = Complete keyboard works. Volume 2, Fantasias / Jan Pieterszoon Sweelinck ; herausgegeben von Pieter Dirksen, Harald Vogel. — *Breitkopf & Härtel*
786   014052876

Sweet rivers
See **Moore, William, d. 1825.** [Sweet rivers; arr.] Sweet rivers

[Sweet rivers; arr.]
See **Moore, William, d. 1825.** [Sweet rivers; arr.]

Swenson, Warren, *1937-*
See **Foster, Stephen Collins, 1826-1864.** [Songs. *Selections; arr.*] Seven songs of Stephen Foster : for voice and piano / in versions by Warren Michel Swenson.

Swing low, sweet chariot
Swing low, sweet chariot / [arr.] Andrew Pryce Jackman. — *Oxford University Press*
782.5253   013084260

Swingle Singers.
See **Lennon, John, 1940-1980.** [Songs. *Selections*] Ticket to ride : a collection of Lennon and McCartney arrangements / The Swingle Singers.

Swinton jig
See **Davies, Peter Maxwell, 1934-** Swinton jig

Symfoni D-dur
See **Lindblad, Adolf Fredrik, 1801-1878.** [Symphonies, no. 2, D major] Symfoni D-dur

[Symphonia armonie celestium revelationum]
See **Hildegard, 1098-1179.** [Symphonia armonie celestium revelationum]

Symphonia harmoniae caelestium revelationum
See **Hildegard, Saint, 1098-1179.** [Symphonia armonie celestium revelationum] Symphonia harmoniae caelestium revelationum

Symphonic dances
See **Rachmaninoff, Sergei, 1873-1943.** [Orchestra music. *Selections*] Symphonic dances

Symphonic dances, op. 45
See **Rachmaninoff, Sergei, 1873-1943.** [Symphonic dances; arr.] Symphonic dances, op. 45

[Symphonic dances; arr.]
See **Rachmaninoff, Sergei, 1873-1943.** [Symphonic dances; arr.]

Symphonie no. 1
See **Peçi, Aleksandër, 1951-** [Symphonies, no. 1] Symphonie no. 1

Symphonie Nr. 3, F-Dur, Opus 90
See **Brahms, Johannes, 1833-1897.** [Symphonies, no. 3, op. 90, F major] Symphonie Nr. 3, F-Dur, Opus 90

Symphonie Nr. 8, G dur, op. 88
See **Dvořák, Antonín, 1841-1904.** [Symphonies, no. 8, op. 88, G major] Symphonie Nr. 8, G dur, op. 88

[Symphonies, chamber orchestra, no. 1]
See **Kalsons, Romualds.** [Symphonies, chamber orchestra, no. 1]

[Symphonies, K. 550, G minor. Molto allegro; arr.]
See **Mozart, Wolfgang Amadeus, 1756-1791** [Symphonies, K. 550, G minor. Molto allegro; arr.]

[Symphonies, K. 551, C major]
See **Mozart, Wolfgang Amadeus, 1756-1791.** [Symphonies, K. 551, C major]

[Symphonies, M. A21, D major]
See **Rosetti, Antonio, ca. 1750-1792.** [Symphonies, M. A21, D major]

[Symphonies, no. 1]
See **Peçi, Aleksandër, 1951-** [Symphonies, no. 1]

[Symphonies, no. 1, B minor]
See **Furtwängler, Wilhelm, 1886-1954.** [Symphonies, no. 1, B minor]

[Symphonies, no. 1, C]
See **Gorb, Adam, 1958-** [Symphonies, no. 1, C]

[Symphonies, no. 2, C minor]
See **Bruckner, Anton, 1824-1896.** [Symphonies, no. 2, C minor]

[Symphonies, no. 2, D major]
See **Lindblad, Adolf Fredrik, 1801-1878.** [Symphonies, no. 2, D major]

[Symphonies, no. 2, E minor]
See **Furtwängler, Wilhelm, 1886-1954.** [Symphonies, no. 2, E minor]

[Symphonies, no. 2, op. 27, E minor. Adagio; arr.]
See **Rachmaninoff, Sergei, 1873-1943.** [Symphonies, no. 2, op. 27, E minor. Adagio; arr.]

[Symphonies, no. 3, C sharp minor]
See **Furtwängler, Wilhelm, 1886-1954.** [Symphonies, no. 3, C sharp minor]

[Symphonies, no. 3, op. 44, A minor]
See **Rachmaninoff, Sergei, 1873-1943.** [Symphonies, no. 3, op. 44, A minor]

[Symphonies, no. 3, op. 90, F major]
See **Brahms, Johannes, 1833-1897.** [Symphonies, no. 3, op. 90, F major]

[Symphonies, no. 4]
See **Terteryan, A. 1929-** [Symphonies, no. 4]

[Symphonies, no. 5]
See **Escudero, Francisco, 1912-2002.** [Symphonies, no. 5]

[Symphonies, no. 5, op. 52, D major]
See **Wilms, J. W. 1772-1847.** [Symphonies, no. 5, op. 52, D major]

[Symphonies, no. 7]
See **Davies, Peter Maxwell, 1934-** [Symphonies, no. 7]

See **Terteryan, A. 1929-** [Symphonies, no. 7]

[Symphonies, no. 7, op. 92, A major. Movement 1; arr.]
See **Beethoven, Ludwig van, 1770-1827** [Symphonies, no. 7, op. 92, A major. Movement 1; arr.]

[Symphonies, no. 8, op. 88, G major]
See **Dvořák, Antonín, 1841-1904.** [Symphonies, no. 8, op. 88, G major]

[Symphonies, no. 8, op. 93, F Major. Movement 1; arr.]
See **Beethoven, Ludwig van, 1770-1827** [Symphonies, no. 8, op. 93, F Major. Movement 1; arr.]

[Symphonies, no. 9, op. 95, E minor. Largo; arr.]
See **Dvořák, Antonín, 1841-1904.** [Symphonies, no. 9, op. 95, E minor. Largo; arr.]

[Symphonies, T. 35, D major]
See **Clementi, Muzio, 1752-1832.** [Symphonies, T. 35, D major]

[Symphonies. *Selections.*]
See **Haydn, Joseph, 1732-1809** [Symphonies. *Selections.*]

[Symphonies. *Selections*]
See **Ordoñez, Carlos d', 1734-1786.** [Symphonies. *Selections*]

See **Zimmermann, Anton, 1741-1781.** [Symphonies. *Selections*]

[Symphonisches Konzert]
See **Furtwängler, Wilhelm, 1886-1954.** [Symphonisches Konzert]

Symphony no 7, movement 1
See **Beethoven, Ludwig van, 1770-1827** [Symphonies, no. 7, op. 92, A major. Movement 1; *arr.*] Symphony no 7, movement 1

Symphony no 8, movement 1
See **Beethoven, Ludwig van, 1770-1827** [Symphonies, no. 8, op. 93, F Major. Movement 1; *arr.*] Symphony no 8, movement 1

Symphony no. 1 in C
See **Gorb, Adam, 1958-** [Symphonies, no. 1, C] Symphony no. 1 in C

Symphony no. 2
See **Rachmaninoff, Sergei, 1873-1943.** [Symphonies, no. 2, op. 27, E minor. Adagio; *arr.*] Symphony no. 2

Symphony no. 40
See **Mozart, Wolfgang Amadeus, 1756-1791** [Symphonies, K. 550, G minor. Molto allegro; *arr.*] Symphony no. 40

Symphony no. 7
See **Davies, Peter Maxwell, 1934-** [Symphonies, no. 7] Symphony no. 7

Symphony no.3, op. 44
See **Rachmaninoff, Sergei, 1873-1943.** [Symphonies, no. 3, op. 44, A minor] Symphony no.3, op. 44

[Symphony, C major]
See **Martinez, Marianne, 1744-1812.** [Symphony, C major]

Synge, J. M. *1871-1909.*
See **Vaughan Williams, Ralph, 1872-1958.** [Riders to the sea. *Vocal score*] Riders to the sea / [based on the play by] J.M. Synge ; set to music by R. Vaughan Williams.

System of a Down (Musical group)
Mezmerize / System of a Down ; music transcriptions by Pete Billmann and David Stocker. — *Sony/ATV Music Publishing*
783.242166   013376891

Szkladányi, Péter.
See **Zimmermann, Anton, 1741-1781.** [Symphonies. *Selections*] Four symphonies / Anton Zimmermann ; edited by János Bali and Péter Halász ; introduced by Péter Halász.

Tabakov, Emil.
[Sonatina, piano] — Sonatina za piano = Sonatina for piano / Emil Tabakov. — *Muzika*
786.21832   014629736

Tadman-Robins, Hilary.
Loving shepherd : for soprano solo, two-part upper voices and organ or piano / Hilary Tadman-Robins. — *Encore Publications*
782.6265   013382732

Tagliarino, Barrett.
See **Rawlins, Robert.** Jazzology : the encyclopedia of jazz theory for all musicians / by Robert Rawlins and Nor Eddine Bahha ; edited by Barrett Tagliarino.

Takahashi, Masa.
See **Metheny, Pat.** One quiet night / Pat Metheny ; music transcriptions by Masa Takahashi.

Take off with your [alto] saxophone
See **Holmes, Chris, composer** Take off with your [alto] saxophone

Take off with your [B♭] trumpet
See **Holmes, Chris, composer** Take off with your [B♭] trumpet

Take off with your B♭ clarinet
See **Holmes, Chris, composer** Take off with your B♭ clarinet

Take off with your B♭ trombone and/or euphonium
See **Holmes, Chris, composer** Take off with your B♭ trombone and/or euphonium

Take off with your flute
See **Holmes, Chris, composer** Take off with your flute

Take off with your trombone
See **Holmes, Chris, composer** Take off with your trombone

Takemitsu, Tōru.
From me flows what you call time : for five percussionists and orchestra / Tōru Takemitsu. — *Schott Japan*
784.268   013015917

Tal como soy
See **Stewart, Richard N.** [Just as I am. *Spanish*] Tal como soy

Talbot, Joby.
[Once around the sun; *arr.*] — Once around the sun : for solo piano / Joby Talbot. — *Chester Music*
786.2   013312992

Talbot, Joby. Vanishing point.
See **The violin :** a collection : new and recent repertoire for violin with piano accompaniment / Craig Armstrong ... [et al.]

Talbot, John, *1941-*
See **Moeran, E. J. 1894-1950.** [Choral music. *Selections*] Collected choral music. Volume five, church music / E.J. Moeran ; edited by John Talbot.

See **Moeran, E. J. 1894-1950.** [Choral music. *Selections*] Collected choral music. Volume four, unison voices / E.J. Moeran ; edited by John Talbot.

See **Moeran, E. J. 1894-1950.** [Choral music. *Selections*] Collected choral music. Volume three, male voices / E.J. Moeran ; edited by John Talbot.

See **Moeran, E. J. 1894-1950.** [Choral music. *Selections*] Collected choral music. Volume two, female (and treble) voices / E.J. Moeran ; edited by John Talbot.

Tales of the unexpected
See **Grainer, Ron.** [Tales of the unexpected. Theme; *arr.*] Tales of the unexpected

[Tales of the unexpected. Theme; *arr.*]
See **Grainer, Ron.** [Tales of the unexpected. Theme; *arr.*]

Taliercio, Margherita.
See **Rossini, Gioacchino, 1792-1868** [Fantasie, clarinet, piano, E♭, major] Fantaisie per clarinetto e pianoforte / Gioachino Rossini ; a cura di Margherita Taliercio.

Talisker
See **Aitken, Elizabeth, 1949-** Talisker

Tallis, Thomas, *ca. 1505-1585.*
Gaude gloriosa Dei Mater : S(S)A(A)TTBB / Thomas Tallis ; transcribed and edited by Jon Dixon. — *[Rev. ed.]* — *JOED Music*
782.526   013525907

[Lamentations, no. 1] — Lamentations I & II / Thomas Tallis ; transcribed and edited by Jon Dixon. — *[Rev. ed.]* — *JOED Music*
782.53241726   013525975

[Magnificat, voices (5)] — Magnificat and Nunc dimittis : SAT(T)BB / Thomas Tallis ; transcribed and edited by Jon Dixon. — *[Rev. ed.]* — *JOED Music*
782.526   013525924

[Masses, voices (4)] — Mass for four voices / Thomas Tallis ; transcribed and edited by Jon Dixon. — *[Rev. ed.]* — *JOED Music*
782.53232   013525964

[Miserere nostri] — Miserere nostri ; & Loquebantur variis linguis : SSAATBB / Thomas Tallis ; transcribed and edited by Jon Dixon. — *JOED Music*
782.526   013525881

[Missa Salve intemerata virgo] — Mass, Salve intemerata / Thomas Tallis ; transcribed and edited by Jon Dixon. — *[Rev. ed.]* — *JOED Music*
782.53232   013526358

[Psalm tunes] — 8 tunes for Archbishop Parker's psalter / Thomas Tallis ; transcribed and edited by Jon Dixon. — *JOED Music*
782.5294   013525858

Tallis, Thomas, *ca. 1505-1585.* Lamentations,
See **Tallis, Thomas, ca. 1505-1585.** [Lamentations, no. 1] Lamentations I & II / Thomas Tallis ; transcribed and edited by Jon Dixon.

Tallis, Thomas, *ca. 1505-1585.* Loquebantur variis linguis.
See **Tallis, Thomas, ca. 1505-1585.** [Miserere nostri] Miserere nostri ; & Loquebantur variis linguis : SSAATBB / Thomas Tallis ; transcribed and edited by Jon Dixon.

Tallis, Thomas, *ca. 1505-1585.* Nunc dimittis,
See **Tallis, Thomas, ca. 1505-1585.** [Magnificat, voices (5)] Magnificat and Nunc dimittis : SAT(T)BB / Thomas Tallis ; transcribed and edited by Jon Dixon.

Tango in blue
See **Serebrier, José, 1938-** Tango in blue

Tango Toulouse
See **Waterhouse, Graham, 1962-** Tango Toulouse

Tann, Hilary.
Like lightnings : a pastoral for oboe / Hilary Tann. — *Oxford University Press*
788.52   013196397

Wales, our land : for mixed choir (SATB) and flute, with optional piano / Hilary Tann. — *Oxford University Press*
782.5   013062310

Wings of the grasses : for voice and oboe (or other melody instrument) / words by Menna Elfyn ; music by Hilary Tann. — *Oxford University Press*
783.442   013114973

Tasso, Torquato, *1544-1595.*
See **Mazzocchi, D. 1592-1665.** [Musiche sacre, e morali. Signor, non sotto l'ombra] Signor, non sotto l'ombra : eccitamento alle virtù / Domenico Mazzocchi ; [words by] Torquato Tasso.

Tasso, Torquato, *1544-1595* **Gerusalemme liberata.**
See **Lully, Jean Baptiste, 1632-1687** [Armide. *Vocal score*] Armide : tragédie en musique / Jean-Baptiste Lully ; édition de Lois Rosow ; réduction clavier-chant, Noam A. Krieger.

Tatarski, Andrzej.
See **Zarębski, Juliusz, 1854-1885.** [Pezzo agitato con un intermezzo amoroso] Wielka fantazja = Grande fantaisie (Un pezzo agitato con un intermezzo amoroso), JZBO 11 ; Utwór bez tytułu = Piece without title, JZBO 14 : na fortepian = for piano / Juliusz Zarębski ; redakcja Ryszard Daniel Golianek ; opracowanie wykonawcze Andrzej Tatarski.

Taupin, Bernie.
See **John, Elton.** [Songs. *Selections*] Make it easy. Elton John.

See **John, Elton.** [Songs. *Selections*] The piano transcriptions / Elton John.

Tavener, John.
Exhortation and Kohima : for unaccompanied choir and semichorus SATB/SATB / John Tavener. — *Chester Music*
782.542   013201804

[Lord's prayer (1982). *Slavonic & English*] — The Lord's prayer : versions in English and Slavonic : (1982) : for SATB chorus / John Tavener. — *Chester Music*
782.5295   013222679

Prayer for the healing of the sick : for SATB chorus and bass solo / John Tavener. — *Chester Music*
782.5265   013190774

Tavener, John. Fragment for the Virgin.
See **The violin** : a collection : new and recent repertoire for violin with piano accompaniment / Craig Armstrong … [et al.]

Taverner, John, *1495 (ca.)-1545.*
Christe, Jesu, pastor bone / John Taverner ; edited by David Skinner. — *Oxford University Press*
782.526   013424001

Taverner, John, *1495 (ca.)-1545.* **Missa Gloria tibi Trinitas.**
See **Bingham, Judith.** In nomine : anthem after Taverner for SATB choir unaccompanied : (2005) / Judith Bingham.

Taylor, Cecily.
See **Krouwel, Juliet.** Slow down Moses! : for SATB (unaccompanied) / words by Cecily Taylor [based on Exodus 18:13-18] ; music by Juliet Krouwel.

Taylor, Christopher, *1970-*
See **Bach, Johann Sebastian, 1685-1750.** [Inventions, harpsichord, BWV 772-786] Two-part inventions / J.S. Bach ; edited by Christopher Taylor.

Taylor, Dennis, saxophonist.
Amazing phrasing : alto saxophone : 50 ways to improve your improvisational skills / by Dennis Taylor. — *Hal Leonard*
788.73136076   013323568

Taylor, Mark *1950-*
See **Best of swing** : 10 swing classics / [arranged and produced by Mark Taylor and Jim Roberts]

See **Bluesy jazz** : 10 jazz favorites / [arranged and produced by Mark Taylor]

See **Essential jazz classics** : 10 essential jazz classics / arranged and produced by Mark Taylor.

See **Evans, Bill, 1929-1980.** [Selections; *arr.*] Bill Evans : 10 original compositions / arranged and produced by Mark Taylor.

See **Great jazz standards** : 10 jazz standards / arranged and produced by Mark Taylor.

See **Hancock, Herbie, 1940-** [Selections; *arr.*] Herbie Hancock : 9 jazz classics / arranged and produced by Mark Taylor.

See **Jazz in three** : 9 jazz waltzes / arranged and produced by Mark Taylor.

See **Rodgers, Richard, 1902-1979** [Musicals. *Selections; arr.*] Rodgers & Hart favorites : 10 Rodgers & Hart favorites / arranged and produced by Mark Taylor.

See **Rodgers, Richard, 1902-1979.** [Musicals. *Selections; arr.*] Rodgers & Hart classics : 10 Rodgers & Hart classics / arranged and produced by Mark Taylor.

See **Rollins, Sonny.** [Selections; *arr.*] Sonny Rollins : 10 jazz classics / arranged and produced by Mark Taylor.

See **Silver, Horace, 1928-** [Selections; *arr.*] Horace Silver : [10 hard bop classics] / arranged and produced by Mark Taylor.

Taylor, Stainton de B. *1903-1975.*
See **Vaughan Williams, Ralph, 1872-1958.** [Organ music. *Selections*] A Vaughan Williams organ album.

Taylor, Sue.
Blow the bassoon! Piano accompaniments for book two / a bassoon tutor by Sue Taylor. — *Spartan Press*
788.58   013263948

Tchaikovsky, Peter Ilich, *1840-1893*
[Overture "1812". Op. 49; *arr.*] — 1812 overture : SSAATTBB / Tchaikovsky ; arranged by Jonathan Rathbone. — *Edition Peters*
782.5   013305764

[Serenades, string orchestra, op. 48, C major. Valse; *arr.*] — Waltz [from] Serenade for strings / Peter Ilych Tchaikovsky ; arranged by Carlo Martelli. — *Broadbent & Dunn*
785.719418846   013383355

Te Deum
See **Furtwängler, Wilhelm, 1886-1954.** Te Deum

Te Deum laudamus
See **Liberto, Giuseppe.** Te Deum laudamus

Tear, Robert.
See **Sing solo tenor** / edited by Robert Tear ; general editor, John Carol Case.

The teddy bears' picnic
See **Bratton, John W. 1867-1947.** [Teddy bears' picnic; *arr.*] The teddy bears' picnic

[Teddy bears' picnic; *arr.*]
See **Bratton, John W. 1867-1947.** [Teddy bears' picnic; *arr.*]

Telemann, Georg Philipp, *1681-1767.*
[Cantatas. *Selections*] — Französischer Jahrgang : Kantaten von Neujahr bis zum Sonntag Sexagesimae und dem Fest Mariae Reinigung / Georg Philipp Telemann ; herausgegeben von Ute Poetzsch-Seban. — *Bärenreiter*
782.524   013798608

[Concertos, violins (2), viola, continuo, TWV 43:G8, G major] — Concerto in G-Dur für 2 Violinen, Viola und Basso continuo = Concerto in G major for 2 violins, viola and basso continuo, TWV 43:G8 / Georg Philipp Telemann ; herausgegeben von Bernhard

Päuler ; Continuo-Aussetzung von Wolfgang Kostujak. — *Erstdruck.* — *Amadeus*
785.28194   013953485

Jesu, wirst du bald erscheinen : Kantate zum 26. Sonntag nach Trinitatis, für Sopran-, Tenor- und Bass-Solo, vierstimmigen gemischten Chor, Zink, 3 Posaunen, 2 Oboen, Streicher und Basso continuo, TWV 1:988 / Georg Philipp Telemann ; herausgegeben von Arno Paduch und Eric F. Fiedler. — *Habsburger Verlag*
782.524   014655745

[Wo soll ich fliehen hin?, TVWV 1:1724] — Wo soll ich fliehen hin? : Kantate zum 22. Sonntag nach Trinitatis für Bariton-Solo, Flauto traverso, Oboe, Fagotto, Violine, Viola und Basso continuo, TVWV 1:1724 / Georg Philipp Telemann ; herausgegeben von Eric F. Fiedler. — *Habsburger Verlag*
783.8824   014655646

Temenos, with mermaids and angels
See **Davies, Peter Maxwell, 1934-** Temenos, with mermaids and angels

[Tempest]
See **Fesch, Willem de, 1687-1761.** [Tempest]

The Tempest songs, or, The enchanted island
See **Fesch, Willem de, 1687-1761.** [Tempest] The Tempest songs, or, The enchanted island

The temple at Karnak
See **Bingham, Judith.** The temple at Karnak

Temple of love
See **Fesch, Willem de, 1687-1761.** Temple of love

Templeton, Alec, *1910-1963.*
[Elegies, saxophone, piano] — Elegie : for tenor saxophone or clarinet & piano / Alec Templeton. — *Emerson Edition*
788.7418964   013565577

Ten Blake songs
See **Vaughan Williams, Ralph, 1872-1958.** [Blake songs] Ten Blake songs

Ten more short easy piano pieces
See **McCreery, Charles.** [Short easy piano pieces] Ten more short easy piano pieces

Ten to go
See **Cropton, Mark.** Ten to go

Tennyson, Alfred Tennyson, Baron, *1809-1892.*
See **Crescenz, Valerie Showers.** Crossing the bar : for mixed chorus (SATB) and piano / Valerie Showers Crescenz.

See **David, Jonathan, 1965-** Now sleeps the crimson petal : for unaccompanied mixed chorus (SSAATTBB) / Jonathan David.

See **Kesselman, Lee R.** [Nights in armor. No. 1, Merlin's riddle] Merlin's riddle (no. 1 from "Nights in Armor") / Lee R. Kesselman.

Tersteegen, Gerhard, *1697-1769.*
See **Herzogenberg, Heinrich von, 1843-1900.** Gott ist gegenwärtig : Choralkantate op. 106 : Gemeindegesang, Chor SATB, 2 Trompeten, 3 Posaunen, Pauken, 2 Violinen, Viola, 2 Violoncelli, Kontrabass, Orgel / Heinrich von Herzogenberg ; Text, Gerhard Tersteegen ; vorgelegt und revidiert von Konrad Klek.

Terteryan, A. *1929-*
[Quartets, strings, no. 2] — Streichquartett Nr. 2 = String quartet no. 2 / Avet Terterjan ; [herausgegeben von Maria Pflüger] — *H. Sikorski*
785.7194   014629743

[Rodina. *Russian & Armenian*] — Heimat : vokalsinfonischer Zyklus für Sopran, Bariton

und Orchester (1957) / Awet Terterjan. —
Sikorski
783.6647   014629740

[Stück, violoncello, piano] — Stück für
Violoncello und Klavier / Awet Terterjan. —
Sikorski
787.4   014629744

[Symphonies, no. 4] — Sinfonie Nr. 4 für
grosses Sinfonieorchester = Symphony no. 4 for
full symphony orchestra (1976) / Awet Terterjan.
— *Sikorski*
784.2184   014629741

[Symphonies, no. 7] — Sinfonie Nr. 7 für
grosses Sinfonieorchester = Symphony no. 7 for
full symphony orchestra (1987) / Awet Terterjan.
— *Sikorski*
784.2184   014629742

Terzakis, Dimitri.
Diptychon : zwei Traumdeutungen : für Klavier
(2004/05) / Dimitri Terzakis. — *Edition Gravis*
786.2   014629745

Hero und Leander : 2002/03 : Rapsodia für 1
Sprecher, Viola, Klavier und Tonband / Dimitri
Terzakis ; nach Texten von Ovid und Friedrich
Schiller. — *Edition Gravis*
783.9618945   013015978

Solo für Tanja : (2003) : für Viola solo / Dimitri
Terzakis. — *Edition Gravis*
787.3   014629750

Visionen : Die Schalen des Zorns : für
gemischten Chor und Viola ad libitum = for
mixed chorus and viola ad libitum (2004) /
Dimitri Terzakis. — *Edition Gravis*
782.525   014629751

Tetampel, Olaf.
See **Riehman, Jacob, d. 1726.** [Sonatas, viola
da gamba, continuo, op. 1] Six sonates à une
viole de gambe & basse continue = Sechs
Sonaten für Viola da gamba und Basso continuo
/ Jacob Richmann ; herausgegeben von Olaf
Tetampel ; Aussetzung des Basso continuo von
Jörg Jacobi.

Thalheimer, Peter.
See **André, Johann Anton, 1775-1842.** [Trios,
flutes (3), op. 29, G major] Trio G-Dur, für 3
Querflöten = Trio G major, for three flutes, opus
29, 1805 / Johann Anton André ; herausgegeben
von Peter Thalheimer.

Thamm, Stephan.
See **Zelenka, Johann Dismas, 1679-1745.**
[Miserere, ZWV 56, D minor] Misere d-Moll,
ZWV 56, für Soli (SATB), Chor (SATB), 2
Oboen, 3 Posaunen, 2 Violinen, 2 Violen und
Basso continuo / Jan Dismas Zelenka ;
herausgegeben von Stephan Thamm.

Theatrum musicum
See **Capricornus, Samuel, d. 1665.** Theatrum
musicum

Theile, Johann, *1646-1724*.
[Vocal music. *Selections*] — Weltliche Arien
und Canzonetten / Johann Theile ;
herausgegeben von Stephan Blaut. — *Friedrich
Hofmeister*
783.42   014660605

Thème & variations pour guitare, op. 10
See **Urcullu, Leopoldo.** [Thème & variations,
guitar, op. 10, E major] Thème & variations pour
guitare, op. 10

[Thème & variations, guitar, op. 10, E major]
See **Urcullu, Leopoldo.** [Thème & variations,
guitar, op. 10, E major]

Themes for flute
See **Gething, Joseph.** [Flute, piano music.
Selections] Themes for flute

There is no rose
See **Smith, Alan, 1930-** There is no rose

Thétis
See **Rameau, Jean-Philippe, 1683-1764.** Thétis

This is music
See **Verve (Musical group)** [Songs. *Selections*]
This is music

Thistle & minuet
Thistle & minuet : 16 easy pieces from the
Scottish Baroque for violin (or flute or oboe),
keyboard, and optional cello (or bassoon) = 16
einfache Stücke aus der schottischen Barockzeit
für Violine (oder Flöte oder Oboe),
Tasteninstrument und Cello (oder Fagott) ad
libitum = 16 pièces faciles du Baroque écossais
pour violon (ou flûte ou hautbois), clavier et
violoncelle (ou basson) facultatif / edited by
David Johnson. — *Schott*
787.2   013192325

Thoma, Xaver, *1953-*
[Quintets, violins, violas, violoncello, op. 116]
— Streichquintett, Opus 116 (xpt), für 2
Violinen, 2 Bratschen und Violoncello, 1998 /
Xaver Paul Thoma. — *Erstausg.* — *IKURO
Edition*
785.7195   013953486

Thomas, Edward, *1878-1917*
See **Grange, Philip.** As it was : (1985) / Philip
Grange ; words, Edward Thomas.

Thomas, Quentin, *1972-*
See **Lloyd Webber, Andrew, 1948-** [Musicals.
Selections; arr.] Andrew Lloyd Webber
showstoppers : playalong for alto saxophone.

See **Lloyd Webber, Andrew, 1948-** [Musicals.
Selections; arr.] Andrew Lloyd Webber
showstoppers : playalong for clarinet.

See **Lloyd Webber, Andrew, 1948-** [Musicals.
Selections; arr.] Andrew Lloyd Webber
showstoppers : playalong for flute.

See **Lloyd Webber, Andrew, 1948-** [Musicals.
Selections; arr.] Andrew Lloyd Webber
showstoppers : playalong for trumpet.

See **Lloyd Webber, Andrew, 1948-** [Musicals.
Selections; arr.] Andrew Lloyd Webber
showstoppers : playalong for violin.

See **TV hits** : playalong for alto saxophone.

See **TV hits** : playalong for clarinet.

See **TV hits** : playalong for flute.

See **TV hits** : playalong for trumpet.

See **TV hits** : playalong for violin.

See **Vivaldi, Antonio, 1678-1741** [Selections;
arr.] Vivaldi gold : the essential collection.

Thomson, Mr. *1757-1851*.
[Select collection of original Scotish airs] —
Scottish songs : for George Thomson : 32
schottische Lieder für 1-2 Singstimmen, Violine,
Violoncello und Klavier / [music by] Ignaz
Pleyel] ; [edited by] Marjorie Rycroft. —
Erstdruck. — *Doblinger*
783.242   014050890

See **Haydn, Joseph, 1732-1809.** [Songs, violin,
continuo acc. *Selections*]
Volksliedbearbeitungen Nr. 269-364 :
Schottische und Walisische Lieder für George
Thomson / Joseph Haydn ; herausgegeben von
Marjorie Rycroft in Verbindung von Warwick
Edwards und Kirsteen McCue.

Thoresen, Lasse, *1949-*
Pyr aionion : for string quartet / Lasse Thoresen.
— *Pizzicato Verlag*
785.7194   014629754

Yá kafi, yá shafi : for two choirs, 1996 / Lasse
Thoresen ; text, Bahá'u'lláh. — *Pizzicato
Verlag*
782.5   014629755

Thou gracious God, whose mercy lends
See **Wilberg, Mack.** Thou gracious God, whose
mercy lends

Three American songs
Three American songs : SATB / arranged by
Jonathan Rathbone. — *Edition Peters*
782.542   013304769

Three cantatas for bass and basso continuo
See **Legrenzi, Giovanni, 1626-1690.** [Cantate e
canzonette. *Selections*] Three cantatas for bass
and basso continuo

Three cantatas with recorders
See **Scarlatti, Alessandro, 1660-1725.**
[Cantatas. *Selections*] Three cantatas with
recorders

Three carols
See **Warlock, Peter, 1894-1930.** [Carols, mixed
voices, orchestra. *Vocal score*] Three carols

Three carols for Christmas
Three carols for Christmas : for unaccompanied
mixed choir (SATB). — *Oxford University Press*
782.5281723   013177887

Three Christmas carols
See **Timmermann, Leni, 1901-**
[Weihnachtslieder] Three Christmas carols

Three concert miniatures
See **Hedges, Anthony, 1931-** [Concert
miniatures, recorder, op. 153] Three concert
miniatures

Three contemplations
See **Hedges, Anthony, 1931-** [Contemplations]
Three contemplations

Three devotional songs
See **Jeffreys, George, ca. 1610-1685.** [Songs.
Selections] Three devotional songs

Three dialogues
See **Jeffreys, George, ca. 1610-1685.** [Duets,
soprano, bass, continuo] Three dialogues

Three folk songs
Three folk songs : The oak and the ash ; Swing
low, sweet chariot ; Nine hundred miles : SATB /
arranged by Jonathan Rathbone. — *Edition
Peters*
782.542   013304758

Three Iberian pieces
See **Kelly, Bryan.** [Iberian pieces] Three Iberian
pieces

Three Japanese miniatures
See **Hesketh, Kenneth, 1968-** [Japanese
miniatures] Three Japanese miniatures

Three Japanese sketches
See **Bovet, Guy.** [Esquisses japonaises] Three
Japanese sketches

Three nineteenth-century hymns.
See **Dicie, Don Michael.** [Nineteenth-century
hymns. Marching to Zion] Three
nineteenth-century hymns.

See **Dicie, Don Michael.** [Nineteenth-century
hymns. My faith looks up to Thee] Three
nineteenth-century hymns.

See **Dicie, Don Michael.** [Nineteenth-century
hymns. The church in the wildwood] Three
nineteenth-century hymns.

Three old French dances
See **Marais, Marin, 1656-1728.** [Pièces de
violes, 4e livre. 1ère partie. *Selections; arr.*]
Three old French dances

Three pieces à 5
See **Giovannelli, Ruggiero, ca. 1560-1625.**
[Selections] Three pieces à 5

Three pieces blue
See **Carr, Paul.** [Pieces blue, bassoon, piano
(2004)] Three pieces blue

**Three pieces for viola d'amore & viola da gamba
or violoncello (1789)**
See **Esser, Karl Michael, Ritter von, 1737-ca.
1795.** [Duets, viola d'amore, viola da gamba]
Three pieces for viola d'amore & viola da
gamba or violoncello (1789)

Three short songs
See **Steele, Douglas, 1910-** [Short songs] Three
short songs

Three sketches
See **Harvey, Jonathan, 1939-** [Sketches] Three
sketches

Three songs for solo bass
See **Mazzocchi, D. 1592-1665.** [Songs.
Selections] Three songs for solo bass

Three songs with hautboys
See **Purcell, Henry, 1659-1695.** [Vocal music.
Selections] Three songs with hautboys

Three 'storm' pieces
Three 'storm' pieces : organ solo / edited by
David Patrick. — *Fitzjohn Music Publications*
786.5   013314527

Threesome
See **Graves, Richard, 1926-2002.** Threesome

Ticket to ride
See **Lennon, John, 1940-1980.** [Songs.
Selections] Ticket to ride

Timakin, E. M.
Essential piano exercises / E.M. Timakin ;
editor, Jakša Zlatar. — *Spartan Press*
786.2076   013441173

Time
See **Bennett, Richard Rodney.** Time

Timmermann, Leni, 1901-
[Weihnachtslieder] — Three Christmas carols =
Drei Weihnachtslieder : gemischter Chor und
Orgel (Klavier) / Leni Timmermann. —
Bergischer Musikverlag
782.5281723   013019535

Timpani
See **Richards, Jack, 1947-** Timpani

Timpe, Christoph.
See **Lonati, Carlo Ambrogio.** [Sonatas, violin,
continuo (1701)] XII sonate a violino solo e
basso : ms. Salzburg, Milano 1701 / Carlo
Ambrogio Lonati.

Tippett, Michael, 1905-1998.
[Child of our time. *Selections; arr.*] — Five
spirituals : from A child of our time / Michael
Tippett ; arr. by Edward Milner for male voice
choir. — *Schott*
782.8253   013173808

In memoriam magistri : for flute, clarinet and
string quartet : (1971) / Michael Tippett. —
Schott
785.44196   013381848

[King Priam. *German & English*] — King
Priam : opera in three acts : (1958-61) / Michael

Tippett ; text by the composer. — *New rev. ed.*
— *Schott*
782.1   013382330

Tircis et Climene
See **Montéclair, Michel Pignolet de,
1667-1737.** [Cantatas, book 3. Tircis et Climene]
Tircis et Climene

Tisné, Antoine.
Impressions niçoises : (musique de ballet) : pour
basson solo / Antoine Tisné. — *Musik Fabrik*
788.581556   014629758

Labyrinthus sonoris : pour quatuor de
saxophones / Antoine Tisné. — *Musik Fabrik*
785.87194   014629759

Titarenko, K.
See **Sviridov, Georgiĭ Vasil'evich, 1915-1998.**
[Choral music. *Selections*] Sochineniĭa dlĭa
khora bez soprovozhdeniĭa / Georgiĭ Sviridov ;
tom podgotovlen K. A. Titarenko.

See **Sviridov, Georgiĭ Vasil'evich, 1915-1998.**
[Songs. *Selections*] Romansy i pesni : dlĭa
golosa i fortepiano / Georgiĭ Sviridov ; tom
podgotovlen K. A. Titarenko.

To keep a true Lent
See **Baker, Richard, 1972-** To keep a true Lent

Tobalina, Eugenio.
See **Gerhard, Roberto, 1896-1970.** For whom
the bell tolls : per a guitarra / Robert Gerhard ;
revisio i edicio de Meirion Bowen i Eugenio
Tobalina.

Tobias, Rudolf, 1873-1918.
[Duet, violins, E minor] — Duo, für zwei
Violinen / Rudolf Tobias. — *Eres*
785.7192   014629761

Toby's Christmas drum
See **Davies, Niki.** Toby's Christmas drum

Toccare incandescent
See **Montague, Stephen.** Toccare incandescent

Toccata, & aria
See **Cooke, Arnold.** [Toccata, organ] Toccata, &
aria

Toccata, adagio & fugue
See **Moore, Philip, 1943-** [Toccata, adagio &
fugue, flutes (3)] Toccata, adagio & fugue

[Toccata, adagio & fugue, flutes (3)]
See **Moore, Philip, 1943-** [Toccata, adagio &
fugue, flutes (3)]

[Toccata, organ]
See **Cooke, Arnold.** [Toccata, organ]

Tokkata-fantaziĭa
See **Uspenskiĭ , Vladislav Aleksandrovich.**
Tokkata-fantaziĭa

Toldrà, Eduardo.
[Quartets, strings, D minor] — Quartet en Do
menor : quartet de corda / Eduard Toldrá. —
Catalana d'editions musicals (C.E.M.)
785.7194   013953488

Tomorrow shall be my dancing day
Tomorrow shall be my dancing day : SATB and
organ / [English trad. arr.] Malcolm Pearce. —
Oxford University Press
782.5281723   013225210

Top of the charts.
Top of the charts. — *International Music
Publications*
783.242166   013307375

Torelli, Giuseppe, 1658-1709.
[Concerto da camera] — Concerto da camera
per due violini, violone e clavicembalo, op. 2 :
Bologna, 1686 / Giuseppe Torelli ; trascizione a
cura di Pasquale Spiniello. — *Musedita*
785.28194   014456961

Tortamano, Nicola.
[Masses. *Selections*] — Messa a due cori e
messe a quattro voci con basso continuo / Nicola
Tortamano ; edizione critica a cura di Alberto
Mammarella. — *Libreria Musicale Italiana*
782.53232   014629768

Tortamano, Nicola. Libro primo.
See **Tortamano, Nicola.** [Masses. *Selections*]
Messa a due cori e messe a quattro voci con
basso continuo / Nicola Tortamano ; edizione
critica a cura di Alberto Mammarella.

Toscani, Claudio.
See **Bellini, Vincenzo, 1801-1835.** I Capuleti e i
Montecchi / Vincenzo Bellini ; tragedia lirica in
due atti di Felice Romani ; a cura di Claudio
Toscani.

Tosta, Volker.
See **Bach, Johann Sebastian, 1685-1750.**
[Suites violoncello, BWV 1009, C major; *arr.*]
Suite für Violoncello Nr. 3, C-Dur, BWV 1009 /
Johann Sebastian Bach ; für Klavier bearbeitet
von Joachim Raff ; nach der Ausgabe von
Rieter-Biedermann ; neu herausgegeben von
Volker Tosta.

See **Bach, Johann Sebastian, 1685-1750.**
[Suites violoncello, BWV 1012, D major; *arr.*]
Suite für Violoncello Nr. 6, D-Dur, BWV 1012 /
Johann Sebastian Bach ; für Klavier bearbeitet
von Joachim Raff ; nach der Ausgabe von
Rieter-Biedermann ; neu herausgegeben von
Volker Tosta.

See **Bach, Johann Sebastian, 1685-1750.**
[Suites, violoncello, BWV 1010, E♭ major; *arr.*]
Suite für Violoncello Nr. 4, Es-Dur, BWV 1010 /
von Johann Sebastian Bach ; für Klavier
bearbeitet von Joachim Raff ; … nach der
Ausgabe von Rieter-Biedermann neu
herausgegeben von Volker Tosta.

See **Raff, Joachim, 1822-1882.** [Benedetto
Marcello. *Vocal score*] Bendetto Marcello :
(Kunst und Liebe) : lyrische Oper in drei
Aufzugen : WoO 46 / Joachim Raff ; Text vom
Komponisten ; nach dem Autograph
herausgegeben von Volker Tosta ;
Klavierauszug.

See **Raff, Joachim, 1822-1882.** [Elegy,
orchestra, WoO 48, C minor] Elegie für grosses
Orchester WoO 48, urprsünglicher, dritter Satz
aus der Symphonie Nr. 10 "Zur Herbstzeit, "
op. 213 / Joachim Raff ; Erstausgabe nach dem
Autograph des Komponisten herausgegeben von
Volker Tosta.

See **Raff, Joachim, 1822-1882.** [Octet, violins
(4), violas, violoncellos, op. 176, C major]
Oktett für vier Violinen, zwei Violen und zwei
Violoncelli, C-Dur, op. 176 / Joachim Raff ;
nach der Erstausgabe neu herausgegeben von
Volker Tosta.

See **Raff, Joachim, 1822-1882.** [Quartets,
strings, no. 4, op. 137, A minor] Quartett für
zwei Violinen, Viola und Violoncello Nr. 4,
a-Moll, op. 137 / Joachim Raff ; nach der
Erstausgabe von J. Schuberth, 1869, neu
herausgegeben von Volker Tosta.

See **Raff, Joachim, 1822-1882.** [Quartets,
strings, no. 8, op. 192, no. 3, C major] Quartett
für zwei Violinen, Viola und Violoncello Nr. 8,
C-Dur, op. 192, Nr. 3 : Suite in Kanon-Form /
Joachim Raff ; nach der Erstausgabe von C.F.
Kahnt, 1876, neu herausgegeben von Volker
Tosta.

See **Raff, Joachim, 1822-1882.** [Suites, piano, op. 71, C major] Suite für Klavier Nr. 2, C-Dur, op. 71 / Joachim Raff ; nach der Originalausgabe des Verlags T.F.A. Kühn neu herausgegeben von Volker Tosta.

See **Raff, Joachim, 1822-1882.** [Suites, piano, op. 72, E minor] Suite für Klavier Nr. 3, e-Moll, op. 72 / Joachim Raff ; nach der Originalausgabe des Verlags T.F.A. Kühn neu herausgegeben von Volker Tosta.

See **Raff, Joachim, 1822-1882.** [Suites, violin, orchestra, op. 180, G minor] Suite für Violine und Orchester g-Moll, op. 180 / Joachim Raff ; nach der Erstausgabe neu herausgegeben von Volker Tosta.

Tóth, Lőrinc, *1814-1903*. Két László.
See **Erkel, Ferenc.** [Hunyadi László] Hunyadi László : opera négy felvonásban = opera in four acts / [Erkel Ferenc] ; szöveg Benjámin Egressy ; közreadja Katalin Szacsvai-Kim ; bevezetés Tibor Tallián, Katalin Szacsvai-Kim.

Tourist
See **Athlete (Musical group)** Tourist

Towards Nirvana
See **Gorb, Adam, 1958-** Towards Nirvana

Townsend, Declan.
Dreamworld = Taidhreamh : [1994] / Declan Townsend. — *Maecenas Music*
784.8   013192918

The toymaker's workshop
See **Brady, Deborah.** The toymaker's workshop

Trabaci, Giovanni Maria, *1580 (ca.)-1647*.
[Ricercate, 2o libro] — Libro secondo (1615) : ricercate & altri varij capricci / Giovanni Maria Trabaci ; a cura di Armando Carideo. — *Andromeda Editrice*
786.5   014629769

Trafalgar
See **Spencer, Tim.** Trafalgar

See **Spencer, Tim.** [Trafalgar. *Selections*] Trafalgar

[Trafalgar. *Selections*]
See **Spencer, Tim.** [Trafalgar. *Selections*]

Train (Musical group)
[Songs. *Selections*] — Best of Train / music transcriptions by David Stocker. — *Guitar recorded versions.* — *Hal Leonard*
783.242166   013167704

Trakl, Georg, *1887-1914*.
See **Ullmann, Viktor.** [Herbst] Drei Lieder : für Singstimme und Streichtrio = for voice and string trio (1943) / Viktor Ullmann ; nach Texten von Georg Trakl und Albert Steffen.

Trapp, Joseph, *1679-1747*.
See **Croft, William, 1678-1727.** [Musicus apparatus academicus. With noise of cannon. With noise of cannon] With noise of cannon : from the ode : for bass, two violins and basso continuo / William Croft.

Trapp, Lynn.
Cantilene : for oboe (or English horn, or viola) and organ / Lynn Trapp. — *Oxford University Press*
788.52   013115358

Tre divertimenti per cimbalo
See **Wagenseil, Georg Christoph, 1715-1777.** [Divertimenti, harpsichord (1761)] Tre divertimenti per cimbalo

Tremonti, Mark.
See **One day remains** / Alter Bridge.

Tres amores
See **Hawes, Patrick.** Tres amores

Tres missae super "Quem dicunt homines"
Tres missae super "Quem dicunt homines" / edidit Harry Elzinga. — *American Institute of Musicology*
782.53232   013718230

Tribbett, Greg.
See **The end of all things to come** / Mudvayne ; transcribed by Danny Begelman, Bill LaFleur and Greg Tribbett.

Trinity
See **Samuel, Rhian.** Trinity

Trio F-Dur
See **Hertel, Johann Wilhelm, 1727-1789.** [Trios, harp, violin, violoncello. No. 2] Trio F-Dur

Trio for violin, cello and piano
See **Larsen, Libby.** [Trios, piano, strings] Trio for violin, cello and piano

Trio G-Dur, für 3 Querflöten
See **André, Johann Anton, 1775-1842.** [Trios, flutes (3), op. 29, G major] Trio G-Dur, für 3 Querflöten

Trio op. 14, no. 1, for flute, violin or flute and viola
See **Neubauer, Franz Christoph, 1750-1795.** [Trios, flute, violin, viola, op. 14. No. 1] Trio op. 14, no. 1, for flute, violin or flute and viola

Trio op. 19 no. 1, for flute, flute or violin, and cello or bassoon
See **Devienne, François, 1759-1803.** [Trios, flutes, violoncello, op. 19. No. 1] Trio op. 19 no. 1, for flute, flute or violin, and cello or bassoon

Trio op. 2 no. 2, for two flutes and bassoon
See **Duval, Jérôme.** [Trios, flutes, bassoon, op. 2. No. 2] Trio op. 2 no. 2, for two flutes and bassoon

[Trio sonatas, violin, viola da gamba, continuo, D minor]
See **Schmelzer, Johann Heinrich, ca. 1623-1680.** [Trio sonatas, violin, viola da gamba, continuo, D minor]

[Trio sonatas, violins, continuo, Z. 796, E minor; arr.]
See **Purcell, Henry, 1659-1695.** [Trio sonatas, violins, continuo, Z. 796, E minor; arr.]

[Trio, piano, strings]
See **Davies, Peter Maxwell, 1934-** [Trio, piano, strings]

Trios für Blas- und Streichinstrumente
See **Haydn, Joseph, 1732-1809.** [Divertimenti, H. IV, 1-11.] Trios für Blas- und Streichinstrumente

[Trios, flute, violin, viola, op. 14. No. 1]
See **Neubauer, Franz Christoph, 1750-1795.** [Trios, flute, violin, viola, op. 14. No. 1]

[Trios, flutes (3), op. 29, G major]
See **André, Johann Anton, 1775-1842.** [Trios, flutes (3), op. 29, G major]

[Trios, flutes, bassoon, op. 2. No. 2]
See **Duval, Jérôme.** [Trios, flutes, bassoon, op. 2. No. 2]

[Trios, flutes, violoncello, op. 19. No. 1]
See **Devienne, François, 1759-1803.** [Trios, flutes, violoncello, op. 19. No. 1]

[Trios, harp, violin, violoncello. No. 2]
See **Hertel, Johann Wilhelm, 1727-1789.** [Trios, harp, violin, violoncello. No. 2]

[Trios, piano, strings]
See **Larsen, Libby.** [Trios, piano, strings]

[Trios, piano, strings, C minor]
See **Andrée, Elfrida, 1841-1929.** [Trios, piano, strings, C minor]

Troeger, Thomas H.
See **Martinson, Joel.** Lions and oxen : for unison voices (with optional divisi), oboe and organ / words by Thomas H. Troeger ; music by Joel Martinson.

The Trojan horse
See **Hewitt, Daniel.** The Trojan horse

See **Hewitt, Daniel.** [Trojan horse. *Selections*] The Trojan horse

[Trojan horse. *Selections*]
See **Hewitt, Daniel.** [Trojan horse. *Selections*]

Tronsarelli, Ottavio, *d. 1646*.
See **Mazzocchi, D. 1592-1665.** [Musiche sacre, e morali. Folle cor] Folle cor : breve è la vita nostra : aria a tre soprani / Domenico Mazzocchi ; [words by] Ottavio Tronsarelli.

Tropaire séquentiaire prosaire prosulaire de Moissac
See **Catholic Church.** Tropaire séquentiaire prosaire prosulaire de Moissac

Tropi proprii missae
Tropi proprii missae / editor Hana Vlhova-Wörner. — *Editio Bärenreiter*
782.53235   014629770

Troutbeck, J. *1832-1899*.
See **Bach, Johann Sebastian, 1685-1750.** [Weihnachts-Oratorium. Bereite dich Zion, mit zärtlichen Trieben; arr. English & German] Prepare thyself, Zion : unison treble / J. S. Bach ; arranged by B. Wayne Bisbee.

Tsitsaros, Christos.
Songs without words : nine character pieces for piano solo / by Christos Tsitsaros ; edited by Margaret Otwell. — *Hal Leonard*
786.2   013201186

Tu es petrus
See **Palestrina, Giovanni Pierluigi da, 1525?-1594.** [Motets (1569). Tu es Petrus; arr.] Tu es petrus

Tuba suite
See **Martinson, Joel.** Tuba suite

Tučapský, Antonín.
Rondo capriccioso : for bassoon & piano / Antonín Tučapský. — *Roberton Publications*
788.581824   013390435

See **Head, Michael, 1900-1976.** [Psalms. I will lift up mine eyes; arr.] I will lift up mine eyes : Psalm 121 ; for mixed voice choir with organ or piano / by Michael Head ; arranged by Antonín Tučapský.

See **Head, Michael, 1900-1976.** [Psalms. Make a joyful noise unto the Lord; arr.] Make a joyful noise unto the Lord : Psalm 100 : (SATB) / Michael Head ; arranged by Antonín Tučapský.

Tuckwell, Barry.
See **Mozart, Wolfgang Amadeus, 1756-1791** [Concertos, horn, orchestra, K. 412, D major; arr.] Horn concerto no. 1 : [arr.] for horn and piano / Wolfgang Amadeus Mozart ; edited by Barry Tuckwell.

See **Mozart, Wolfgang Amadeus, 1756-1791** [Concertos, horn, orchestra, K. 417, E♭ major; arr.] Horn concerto no. 2 : [arr.] for horn and piano / Wolfgang Amadeus Mozart ; edited by Barry Tuckwell.

See **Mozart, Wolfgang Amadeus, 1756-1791**
[Concertos, horn, orchestra, K. 447, E♭ major;
arr.] Horn concerto no. 3 : [arr.] for horn and
piano / Wolfgang Amadeus Mozart ; edited by
Barry Tuckwell.

See **Mozart, Wolfgang Amadeus, 1756-1791**
[Concertos, horn, orchestra, K. 495, E♭ major;
arr.] Horn concerto no. 4 : [arr.] for horn and
piano / Wolfgang Amadeus Mozart ; edited by
Barry Tuckwell.

Tudor selection 1
See **Hewitt, Daniel.** Tudor selection 1

Tunder, Franz, *1614-1667*.
Dominus illuminatio mea : (Ps. 27, 1-3) :
Geistliches Konzert für Solo (A), Chor
(SSATB), 2 Violinen und Basso continuo / Franz
Tunder ; herausgegeben von Bernhard Römer.
— *Ostinato*
782.524   014629772

Tunstall, KT.
Eye to the telescope / KT Tunstall. — *Wise
Publications*
783.242166   013326342

Turnage, Mark-Anthony.
Eulogy : for solo viola and eight instruments /
Mark-Anthony Turnage. — *Boosey & Hawkes*
785.22199   013213736

Turnbull, Kit.
See **Brooker, Gary.** [Whiter shade of pale; *arr.*]
A whiter shade of pale : grade 3 / Gary Brooker ;
arr. Kit Turnbull.

See **Pezold, Christian, 1677-1733** [Suites,
harpsichord, G major. Menuet alternativement;
arr.] Minuet : from the Anna Magdalena
notebook : grade 1 / J.S. Bach [or rather,
Christian Pezold] ; arr. Kit Turnbull.

See **Whitten, Danny.** [I don't want to talk about
it; *arr.*] I don't want to talk about it : grade 1.5 /
Danny Whitten ; arr. Kit Turnbull.

Turner, Barrie Carson, *1951-*
See **Cellos for Christmas** : 20 Christmas carols
for cellos / easy arrangements by Barrie Carson
Turner ; illustrations by John Minnion.

See **On wings of song** : 8 popular pieces
arranged for string quartet / [arr. by] Barrie
Carson Turner.

Tusler, Robert L.
See **Fesch, Willem de, 1687-1761.** [Apis amata]
Two solo cantatas / Willem de Fesch ; edited by
Robert L. Tusler.

See **Fesch, Willem de, 1687-1761.**
[Canzonettas, violin, continuo acc.] Miss Ashe
canzonettas : for soprano, violin or flute,
mandoline and basso continuo : c.1734 / Willem
de Fesch ; on poems by Paolo Rolli, Pietro
Metastasio and others ; edited by Robert L.
Tusler.

See **Fesch, Willem de, 1687-1761.** [Canzonette
ed arie, violin, continuo acc.] Lady Erskine
canzonettas : for soprano, violin or flute and
basso continuo : c.1730 / Willem de Fesch ; on
poems by Paolo Rolli and others ; edited by
Robert L. Tusler.

See **Fesch, Willem de, 1687-1761.** [Concertos,
violins (2), string orchestra] Concerto in A
minor à 4 stromenti, c.1710 / Willem de Fesch ;
edited by Robert L. Tusler.

See **Fesch, Willem de, 1687-1761.** [English
songs] VI English songs : for soprano, violins,
flutes and basso continuo : 1748 / Willem de
Fesch ; edited by Robert L. Tusler.

See **Fesch, Willem de, 1687-1761.** [New
English songs] VI new English songs : for
soprano, violin or flute and basso continuo :

1749 / Willem de Fesch ; edited by Robert L.
Tusler.

See **Fesch, Willem de, 1687-1761.** [Songs.
Selections] Matthew Prior songs : for voice and
basso continuo : 1741 / Willem de Fesch ; based
on 'Lyric Poems' by Matthew Prior ; edited by
Robert L. Tusler.

See **Fesch, Willem de, 1687-1761.** [Songs.
Selections] Miscellaneous songs : for soprano,
violin or flute, and basso continuo : 1748-53 /
Willem de Fesch ; edited by Robert L. Tusler.

See **Fesch, Willem de, 1687-1761.** [Tempest]
The Tempest songs, or, The enchanted island :
for soprano, small ensemble and basso continuo,
1745 / Willem de Fesch ; edited by Robert L.
Tusler.

See **Fesch, Willem de, 1687-1761.** Temple of
love : for voice, two obligato instruments and
basso continuo : 1753 / Willem de Fesch ; edited
by Robert L. Tusler.

TV classics
TV classics : piano, vocal, guitar. — *Hal
Leonard*
783.2421546   013220396

TV comedy
TV comedy : themes for solo piano. — *Chester
Music*
786.21546   013321760

TV detective
TV detective : themes for solo piano. — *Chester
Music*
786.21546   013321762

TV hits
TV hits : playalong for alto saxophone. — *Wise*
788.731546   013193392

TV hits : playalong for clarinet. — *Wise
Publications*
788.621546   013193427

TV hits : playalong for flute. — *Wise*
788.321546   013193417

TV hits : playalong for trumpet. — *Wise*
788.921546   013193400

TV hits : playalong for violin. — *Wise*
787.21546   013193409

TV soap & drama
TV soap & drama : themes for solo piano. —
Chester Music
786.21546   013321761

Twain, Shania.
Greatest hits / Shania Twain. — *Wise
Publications*
783.242166   013167493

Twardowski, Romuald, *1930-*
[Concertos, violoncello, orchestra; *arr.*] —
Concerto per cello ed orchestra / Romuald
Twardowski ; wyciąg fortepianowy ;
opracowanie głosu solowego Tomasz Strahl. —
Polskie wydawn. muzyczne
787.4186   014629778

The twelve days of Christmas
See **Brady, Deborah.** The twelve days of
Christmas

The twelve days of Christmas
The twelve days of Christmas : SSAATTBB /
arranged by Jonathan Rathbone. — *Edition
Peters*
782.5421723   013304685

Twilight
See **Walker, Robin, 1953-** Twilight

Two cantatas from the Munich ms.
See **Legrenzi, Giovanni, 1626-1690.** [Dal
calore agitato] Two cantatas from the Munich
ms.

Two chamber works
See **Andrée, Elfrida, 1841-1929.** [Trios, piano,
strings, C minor] Two chamber works

Two duets for basses
See **Jeffreys, George, ca. 1610-1685.** [With
notes that are both loud and sweet] Two duets
for basses

Two French folksongs
Two French folksongs : for female voice choir
(SSA), soloists and piano / arranged by Michael
Neaum. — *Roberton Publications*
782.6421620944   013193595

Two glasses of wine
See **Davies, Peter Maxwell, 1934-** [Glasses of
wine] Two glasses of wine

Two hymns for Advent and Christmas
See **Palestrina, Giovanni Pierluigi da,
1525?-1594.** [Hymni totius anni. Conditor alme
siderum] Two hymns for Advent and Christmas

Two miniatures
See **Warren, Constance, 1905-1984.**
[Miniatures, flute, piano] Two miniatures

Two movements for string quartet
See **Clarke, Rebecca, 1886-1979.** [Comodo e
ambile, string quartet] Two movements for
string quartet

Two piano pieces
See **Elgar, Edward, 1857-1934.** [Adieu] Two
piano pieces

Two pieces for flute duet and piano
See **Barton, David, 1983-** [Pieces, piano, flutes
(2) (2004)] Two pieces for flute duet and piano

Two settings of "If that a sinner's sighs"
See **Milton, John, ca. 1563-1647.** [If that a
sinner's sighs, voices (5)] Two settings of "If
that a sinner's sighs"

Two Shakespearean songs
See **Hind, John, 1916-** [Shakespearean songs]
Two Shakespearean songs

Two solo cantatas
See **Fesch, Willem de, 1687-1761.** [Apis amata]
Two solo cantatas

Two songs from Kalender röd
See **Salonen, Esa-Pekka, 1958-** [Sänger till text
av Ann Jäderlund] Two songs from Kalender röd

Two songs of Mary
See **Dmitriev, Alexander I., 1961-** [Songs of
Mary] Two songs of Mary

Two songs with flutes
See **Purcell, Henry, 1659-1695.** [Soft notes and
gently rais'd accent] Two songs with flutes

Two-part inventions
See **Bach, Johann Sebastian, 1685-1750.**
[Inventions, harpsichord, BWV 772-786]
Two-part inventions

Tye, Christopher, 1497?-1572.
Give almes of thy goods / Christopher Tye ;
edited by John Milsom. — *Oxford University
Press*
782.5265   013424016

Tyssen, Amherst D. *1843-1930*.
See **Muslim songs of the British Isles /**
arranged for schools by Abdal Hakim Murad
[Timothy J. Winter]

U2 (Musical group)
[Songs. *Selections*] — Play guitar with— U2 : (1984-1987). — *Wise*
783.242166   013190592

[Songs. *Selections*] — U2 : the piano collection : twenty hit songs from one of the world's best rock bands specially arranged for piano, voice and guitar. — *Wise Publications*
783.242166   013395771

Ubber, Christian.
See **Liszt, Franz, 1811-1886.** [Piano music. *Selections*] Etudes d'exécution transcendante : mit = with = avec Grandes etudes 2 & 7 / Franz Liszt ; nach den Quellen herausgegeben und mit Hinweisen zur Interpretation versehen von Christian Ubber ; Fingersätze von Detlef Kraus.

Ubi caritas et amor
See **Lole, Simon.** Ubi caritas et amor

Ullmann, Viktor.
[Herbst] — Drei Lieder : für Singstimme und Streichtrio = for voice and string trio (1943) / Viktor Ullmann ; nach Texten von Georg Trakl und Albert Steffen. — *Schott*
783.442   013510089

[Songs] — Sämtliche Lieder für Singstimme und Klavier = Complete songs for voice and piano / Viktor Ullmann ; herausgegeben von Axel Bauni und Christian Hoesch. — *Schott*
783.242   013887077

[Variationen und Doppelfuge über ein Thema von Arnold Schönberg; *arr.*] — Variationen und Doppelfuge über ein Thema von Arnold Schönberg (op. 19/4) : Fassung für Streichquartett, op. 3c = Variations and Double Fugue on a theme by Arnold Schoenberg (op. 19/4) : version for string quartet, op. 3c / Viktor Ullmann. — *Schott*
785.71941825   013887078

Ullmann, Viktor. Lieder der Tröstung.
See **Ullmann, Viktor.** [Herbst] Drei Lieder : für Singstimme und Streichtrio = for voice and string trio (1943) / Viktor Ullmann ; nach Texten von Georg Trakl und Albert Steffen.

Ulvaeus, Björn.
See **Andersson, Benny.** [Mamma mia! *Selections; arr.*] Mamma mia! : choral highlights : instrumental pak / arranged by Mac Huff.

See **Andersson, Benny.** [Mamma mia! *Selections; arr.*] Mamma mia! : choral highlights : SAB / arranged by Mac Huff.

See **Andersson, Benny.** [Mamma mia! *Selections; arr.*] Mamma mia! : choral highlights : SATB / arranged by Mac Huff.

See **Andersson, Benny.** [Mamma mia! *Selections; arr.*] Mamma mia! : choral highlights : SSA / arranged by Mac Huff.

Umbach, Elke Martha, *1960-*
See **Philarmonica, Mrs.** [Sonatas, violins (2), violoncello, continuo] 12 Triosonaten für 2 Violinen und B.c. (1715) = 12 trio sonatas for 2 violins and b.c. (1715) / by Mrs. Philarmonica ; edited by Elke Martha Umbach.

Under Filk Wood
Under Filk Wood : a songbook created for Interaction, the 2005 World Science Fiction Convention, held in Glasgow, Scotland / compiled by Alison Richards. — *Beccon Publications*
783.242164   013280373

Università di Pavia. *Dipartimento di scienze musicologiche e paleografico-filologiche.*
See **Palestrina, Giovanni Pierluigi da, 1525?-1594.** [Motets (1563)] Motecta festorum totius anni cum communi sanctorum quaternis vocibus / Giovanni Pierluigi da Palestrina ; edizione critica a cura di Daniele V. Filippi.

See **Porpora, Nicola, 1686-1768.** [Duetti latini per la passione di Gesù Cristo] Sei duetti latini sulla passione di nostro signore Gesù Cristo ; Motetti per Angiola Moro / Nicola Antonio Porpora ; edizione critica a cura di Stefano Aresi.

Unrise
See **Gilbert, Anthony.** Unrise

Unterseher, Reginald.
Live with me, and be my love : for mixed chorus (SATB) and piano / Reginald Unterseher. — *Oxford University Press*
782.542   013472311

See **Moore, William, d. 1825.** [Sweet rivers; *arr.*] Sweet rivers : for lower voices (TBB) and piano / William Moore ; arr. Reginald Unterseher.

See **Pierpont, James, 1822-1893.** [Jingle bells; *arr.*] Jingle bells : for two-part or mixed chorus and piano / [James Pierpont ; arranged by] Reginald Unterseher.

Unwritten
See **Bedingfield, Natasha.** Unwritten

Urcheuguía, Cristina.
See **Dokumente und Texte zu "Tannhäuser und der Sängerkrieg auf Wartburg" /** herausgegeben von Peter Jost ; Reinschrift des Textbuches mit Varianten herausgegeben von Cristina Urcheuguía.

Urcullu, Leopoldo.
[Thème & variations, guitar, op. 10, E major] — Thème & variations pour guitare, op. 10 / Leopoldo de Urcullu. — *Philomele Editions*
787.871825   013887079

Usher.
[Confessions. *Selections*] — Selections from Confessions : piano/vocal/guitar / Usher. — *EMI Music Publishing*
783.242166   013191618

Uspenskiĭ, Vladislav Aleksandrovich.
Tokkata-fantaziia : na temu M.I. Glinki : dlia dvukh fortepiano v vosem' ruk = Toccata-fantasy : to M.I. Glinka : for two pianos in eight hands / Vladislav Uspenskiĭ. — *Kompozitor*
785.6219218947   013887081

V libro di madrigali a 5 voci
See **Ingegneri, Marc Antonio, 1535 or 6-1592.** [Madrigals, voices (5), book 5] V libro di madrigali a 5 voci

Vacchi, Fabio, *1949-*
Canti d'ombre : per grande orchestra, 2004 / Fabio Vacchi. — *Ricordi*
784.2   014053371

Voce d'altra voce : per due recitanti, grande coro misto e orchestra, 2005 / Fabio Vacchi. — *Ricordi*
782.524   014053372

Vai, Steve.
Eat 'em and smile / David Lee Roth ; music transcriptions by Addi Booth. — *Hal Leonard*
783.242166   013222589

Vaĭnberg, Moiseĭ Samuilovich.
[Quartets, strings, no. 8, op. 66] — Streichquartett Nr. 8, op. 66, für zwei Violinen, Viola und Violoncello = for two violins, viola and violoncello / Mieczyslaw Weinberg (Vainberg, Moisei Samuilovich). — *Peermusic Classical*
785.7194   014457047

The valley of the kings
See **Hewitt, Daniel.** The valley of the kings

Val'sy dlia fortepiano i fortepiano v 4 ruki
See **Gavrilin, V.** [Selections] Val'sy dlia fortepiano i fortepiano v 4 ruki

Van de Vate, Nancy.
Balinese diptych : for solo piano : 2003 / Nancy Van de Vate. — *Vienna Masterworks*
786.2   014457048

Vann, Stanley.
[Lichfield Service] — Magnificat and Nunc dimittis : (the Lichfield Service) : for men's voices (ATB divisi) / Stanley Vann. — *Anglo-American Music Publishers*
782.8326   013196878

[Magnificat and Nunc dimittis (Ripon Service)] — Magnificat and Nunc dimittis : (Ripon Cathedral) : SATB with organ / Stanley Vann. — *Anglo-American Music Publishers*
782.5326   013594285

Vanscheeuwijck, Marc.
See **Antonii, Giovanni Battista degli, ca. 1660-1698.** [Ricercate, violoncello, op. 1] Ricercate sopra il violoncello o clavicembalo ; e, Ricercate per il violino / Giovanni Battista degli Antonii ; edizione della partitura e prefazione a cura di Marc Vanscheeuwijck.

[Variationen über ein Thema von Haydn. *Selections; arr.*]
See **Brahms, Johannes, 1833-1897.** [Variationen über ein Thema von Haydn. *Selections; arr.*]

Variationen und Doppelfuge über ein Thema von Arnold Schönberg (op. 19/4)
See **Ullmann, Viktor.** [Variationen und Doppelfuge über ein Thema von Arnold Schönberg; *arr.*] Variationen und Doppelfuge über ein Thema von Arnold Schönberg (op. 19/4)

[Variationen und Doppelfuge über ein Thema von Arnold Schönberg; *arr.*]
See **Ullmann, Viktor.** [Variationen und Doppelfuge über ein Thema von Arnold Schönberg; *arr.*]

Variations and fugue
See **Cooke, Arnold.** [Variations and fugue, string quartet] Variations and fugue

[Variations and fugue, string quartet]
See **Cooke, Arnold.** [Variations and fugue, string quartet]

Variations on a theme of Haydn
See **Brahms, Johannes, 1833-1897.** [Variationen über ein Thema von Haydn. *Selections; arr.*] Variations on a theme of Haydn

Variations on "Ora labora"
See **Hancock, Gerre, 1934-** Variations on "Ora labora"

Vartolo, Sergio.
See **Monteverdi, Claudio, 1567-1643.** [Ritorno d'Ulisse in patria] Il ritorno di Ulisse in patria : Ms. Wien, partitura / Claudio Monteverdi.

Vasks, Pēteris, *1946-*
[Quartets, strings, no. 4] — 4. Streichquartett, für 2 Violinen, Viola und Violoncello = String quartet no. 4, for 2 violins, viola, and violoncello (1999) / Pēteris Vasks. — *Schott*
785.7194   013174345

A Vaughan Williams organ album.
See **Vaughan Williams, Ralph, 1872-1958.**
[Organ music. *Selections*] A Vaughan Williams organ album.

Vaughan Williams, Ralph, *1872-1958.*
[Blake songs] — Ten Blake songs : for voice and oboe / Ralph Vaughan Williams. — *Oxford University Press*
783.342   013094158

Vaughan Williams, Ralph, *1872-1958*
[Fantasia on Greensleeves; *arr.*] — Greensleeves : or, The king of love : a choral setting for mixed voice choir and piano or orchestra of "Fantasia on Greensleeves" / by R. Vaughan Williams ; arranged by Philip Lane. — *Roberton Publications*
782.542   013193252

[Fantasia on Greensleeves; *arr*] — Greensleeves : or, The king of love : a choral setting for female voice choir and piano or orchestra of "Fantasia on Greensleeves" / by R. Vaughan Williams ; arranged by Philip Lane. — *Roberton Publications*
782.642   013193259

Vaughan Williams, Ralph, *1872-1958.*
[Old Hundredth Psalm tune; *arr.*] — The Old Hundreth Psalm tune : (All people that on earth do dwell) / R. Vaughan Williams (arr.) ; rescored by Roy Douglas for mixed choir (SATB), congregation, 3 trumpets, organ and optional timpani. — *Oxford University Press*
782.527   013280400

[Organ music. *Selections*] — A Vaughan Williams organ album. — *Oxford University Press*
786.5   013196413

[Quartets, strings, C minor] — String quartet in C minor (1898) / Ralph Vaughan Williams. — *Faber Music*
785.7194   013126516

[Quartets, strings, C minor] — String quartet in C minor (1898) / Ralph Vaughan Williams. — *Faber Music*
785.7194   013126578

[Quintets, piano, clarinet, horn, violin, violoncello, D major] — Quintet in D major (1898), for clarinet, horn, violin, cello and piano / Ralph Vaughan Williams. — *Faber Music*
785.22195   013126445

[Quintets, piano, violin, viola, violoncello, double bass, C minor] — Piano quintet in C minor (1903), for violin, viola, cello, double bass and piano / Ralph Vaughan Williams. — *Faber Music*
785.28195   013126521

[Riders to the sea. *Vocal score*] — Riders to the sea / [based on the play by] J.M. Synge ; set to music by R. Vaughan Williams. — *Oxford University Press*
782.1   013199387

[Short pieces] — Nocturne and scherzo (1906) ; Scherzo (1904) : for string quintet (2 violins, 2 violas and cello) / Ralph Vaughan Williams. — *Faber Music*
785.7195   013126461

[Song of thanksgiving. *Vocal score*] — A song of thanksgiving : for soprano solo, speaker, chorus and orchestra / R. Vaughan Williams ; vocal score. — *Oxford University Press*
782.542   013050462

Suite de ballet : for flute and piano / R. Vaughan Williams ; edited by Roy Douglas. — *Oxford University Press*
788.32185   013433967

Vaughan Williams, Ralph, *1872-1958*
[Willow-wood. *Vocal score*] — Willow-wood : cantata for baritone solo, soprano and alto chorus (ad lib.) and orchestra / by Ralph Vaughan Williams. — *Stainer & Bell*
783.8848   013190675

Vaughan Williams, Ralph, *1872-1958.* **Ballade and scherzo,**
See **Vaughan Williams, Ralph, 1872-1958.**
[Short pieces] Nocturne and scherzo (1906) ; Scherzo (1904) : for string quintet (2 violins, 2 violas and cello) / Ralph Vaughan Williams.

Vaughan, Henry, *1621-1695.*
See **McCabe, John, 1939-** The evening watch : for SATB and organ / John McCabe.

Velvet Underground (*Musical group***)**
See **Play guitar with— Velvet Revolver, U2, Jeff Buckley, the Killers, Jet and Razorlight.**

Vem kan segla förutan vind?
Vem kan segla förutan vind? : SSAATTBB / Swedish traditional ; arranged by Jonathan Rathbone. — *Edition Peters*
782.542   013305058

Veni Creator Spiritus
See **Palestrina, Giovanni Pierluigi da, 1525?-1594.** [Hymni totius anni. Veni Creator Spiritus] Veni Creator Spiritus

[Veni Emmanuel.]
O come, o come Emmanuel : SSAATTBB : arranged by Jonathan Rathbone. — *Edition Peters*
782.52651722   013304602

Veni sponsa Christi
See **Giordani, Giuseppe, 1751-1798.** Veni sponsa Christi

See **Palestrina, Giovanni Pierluigi da, 1525?-1594.** [Motets (1563). Veni sponsa Christi] Veni sponsa Christi

Veni, Sancte Spiritus
See **Neufeld, Ken.** Veni, Sancte Spiritus

La venta de Don Quijote
See **Chapí, Ruperto, 1851-1909.** La venta de Don Quijote

Ventiquattro capricci per violino solo [op. III]
See **Locatelli, Pietro Antonio, 1695-1764.** [Arte del violino. Capricci] Ventiquattro capricci per violino solo [op. III]

Verdi, Giuseppe, *1813-1901.*
[Macbeth. Ballo] — Macbeth. Ballet : (1865) / [Giuseppe Verdi] ; a cura di Pietro Spada. — *Boccaccini & Spada*
784.21556   014876376

I masnadieri : a tragic opera (in four acts) = melodramma (in quattro atti) / Giuseppe Verdi ; libretto by Andrea Maffei ; edited by Roberta Montemorra Marvin. — *University of Chicago Press*
782.1   013122497

Stiffelio / Giuseppe Verdi ; libretto (in three acts) by Francesco Maria Piave ; edited by Kathleen Kuzmick Hansell. — *University of Chicago Press*
782.1   013122506

Vernier, Jean-Aime, *b. 1769.*
[Duets, harps, no. 2, op. 30] — Deuxieme duo, op. 30, per 2 arpe = for 2 harps / Jean-Aime Vernier ; a cura di Anna Pasetti. — *Ut Orpheus*
785.795192   014050077

Verroust, Stanislas, *1814-1863.*
[Capriccios, oboe, piano] — Capriccio : for oboe & piano / Stanislas Verroust ; edited by Myron Zakopets. — *Emerson Edition*
788.52   013188299

Fantaisie sur 'Don Pasquale' : for oboe & piano / Stanislas Verroust ; edited by Myron Zakopets. — *Emerson Edition*
788.521894   013188253

Versuche über einen Marsch
See **Wengler, Marcel, 1946-** Versuche über einen Marsch

Verve (Musical group)
[Songs. *Selections*] — This is music : the singles 92-98 / The Verve. — *Guitar tab ed.* — *International Music Publications*
783.242166   013172276

Vescovo, Italo, *1953-*
See **Giordani, Giuseppe, 1751-1798.** Veni sponsa Christi : antifona / Giuseppe Giordani (Giordaniello) ; edizione critica a cura di Ugo Gironacci e Italo Vescovo.

[Vespers, D major]
See **Elsner, Józef, 1769-1854.** [Vespers, D major]

[Vespertina psalmodia (1637) Selections]
See **Ganassi, Giacomo, fl. 1625-1637**
[Vespertina psalmodia (1637) Selections]

Vespro a cappella della Beata Vergine e motetti concertati
See **Leonarda, Isabella, 1620-1704.** Vespro a cappella della Beata Vergine e motetti concertati

VI English songs
See **Fesch, Willem de, 1687-1761.** [English songs] VI English songs

VI new English songs
See **Fesch, Willem de, 1687-1761.** [New English songs] VI new English songs

Victoria, Tomás Luis de, *ca. 1548-1611.*
[Masses (1583). Missa O quam gloriosum] — Missa O Quam gloriosum (SATB) ; Motet, O quam gloriosum est regnum (SATB) / Tomás Luis de Victoria ; transcribed and edited by Andrew Parker. — *Novello*
782.53232   013335998

[Missae, Psalmi, Magnificat, ad Virginem Dei Matrem salutiones, aliaque. Missa Dum complerentur] — Missa Dum complerentur (SAATTB) ; Motet, Dum complerentur dies Pentecostes (SSATB) / Tomás Luis de Victoria ; transcribed and edited by Andrew Parker. — *Novello*
782.53232   013335980

Victoria, Tomás Luis de, *ca. 1548-1611.* **Motets**
See **Victoria, Tomás Luis de, ca. 1548-1611.** [Masses (1583). Missa O quam gloriosum] Missa O Quam gloriosum (SATB) ; Motet, O quam gloriosum est regnum (SATB) / Tomás Luis de Victoria ; transcribed and edited by Andrew Parker.

See **Victoria, Tomás Luis de, ca. 1548-1611.** [Missae, Psalmi, Magnificat, ad Virginem Dei Matrem salutiones, aliaque. Missa Dum complerentur] Missa Dum complerentur (SAATTB) ; Motet, Dum complerentur dies Pentecostes (SSATB) / Tomás Luis de Victoria ; transcribed and edited by Andrew Parker.

The Victorian historian
See **Spencer, Tim.** The Victorian historian

See **Spencer, Tim.** [Victorian historian. *Selections*] The Victorian historian

[Victorian historian. *Selections*]
See Spencer, Tim. [Victorian historian. *Selections*]

Viel Freuden mit sich bringet
Viel Freuden mit sich bringet : SSAATTBB / German traditional ; arranged by Ben Parry. — *Edition Peters*
782.542   013305072

Vierdanck, Johann, *ca. 1605-1646.*
[Capricci, Canzoni und Sonaten] — Capricci, Canzoni und Sonaten : [mit 2, 3, 4 und 5 Instrumenten ohne und mit dem Basso continuo], Rostock 1641 / Johann Vierdanck ; trascrizione a cura di Alessandro Bares. — *Musedita*
785   014599831

Vine, Carl, *1954-*
Prologue & canzona : for string orchestra (1985-6) / Carl Vine. — *Faber Music*
784.7   006915011

[Viola da gamba music. *Selections*]
See Hammer, Xaver, 1741-1817. [Viola da gamba music. *Selections*]

Viola sonata, op. 129
See Stanford, Charles Villiers, 1852-1924. [Sonatas, clarinet, piano, op. 129, F major; *arr.*] Viola sonata, op. 129

Viola, viola
See Benjamin, George. Viola, viola

The violin
The violin : a collection : new and recent repertoire for violin with piano accompaniment / Craig Armstrong ... [et al.] — *Chester Music*
787.2   013193381

Violin concerto
See Maw, Nicholas. [Concertos, violin, orchestra] Violin concerto

See Glass, Philip. [Concertos, violin, orchestra; *arr.*] Violin concerto

Violin concerto in D major
See Clement, Franz, 1780-1842. [Concertos, violin, orchestra, D major] Violin concerto in D major

[Violin, piano music. *Selections*]
See Clarke, Rebecca, 1886-1979. [Violin, piano music. *Selections*]

See Sgambati, Giovanni, 1841-1914. [Violin, piano music. *Selections*]

Violinkonzert D-Dur Opus 77
See Brahms, Johannes, 1833-1897. [Concertos, violin, orchestra, op. 77, D major] Violinkonzert D-Dur Opus 77

The Virgin Mary had a baby boy
The Virgin Mary had a baby boy / [West Indian] ; arranged by Michael Neaum for three-part female voice choir and piano. — *Roberton Publications, a part of Goodmusic Publishing*
782.6281723   013192676

Visionen
See Terzakis, Dimitri. Visionen

Vitalis, Christian, *1976-*
See Heuschkel, Johann Peter, 1773-1853. [Duets, horns (2), op. 12] Six duos pour deux cors = für zwei Hörner : op. 12 / Johann Peter Heuschkel ; [krit. rev. Neuausgabe von Christian Vitalis]

Viva Mexico
See Bartlett, Keith. Viva Mexico

Vivaldi gold
See Vivaldi, Antonio, 1678-1741 [Selections; *arr.*] Vivaldi gold

Vivaldi, Antonio, *1678-1741*
[Cimento dell'armonia e dell'inventione. N. 1-4; *arr.*] — The four seasons : four concertos for violin and orchestra : for violin and piano reduction / Antonio Vivaldi ; violin part edited by Rok Klopčič ; piano reduction by Alojz Srebotnjak. — *G. Schirmer*
787.21861524   013211714

Vivaldi, Antonio, *1678-1741.*
[Concertos, string orchestra, RV 121, D major] — Concerto in re maggiore, per archi e cembalo, F. XI, no. 30 / Antonio Vivaldi ; a cura di Gian Francesco Malipiero. — *Ricordi*
                                            014649911

Vivaldi, Antonio, *1678-1741*
[Selections; *arr.*] — Vivaldi gold : the essential collection. — *Chester Music*
786.2   013190759

Vlhová-Wörner, Hana.
See Tropi proprii missae / editor Hana Vlhova-Wörner.

[Vocal music. *Selections*]
See Hoffmann, E. T. A. 1776-1822. [Vocal music. *Selections*]

See Ludford, Nicholas, ca. 1490-1557. [Vocal music. *Selections*]

See Payen, Nicolas, ca. 1512-ca. 1559. [Vocal music. *Selections*]

See Purcell, Henry, 1659-1695. [Vocal music. *Selections*]

See Rheinberger, Josef, 1839-1901 [Vocal music. *Selections*]

See Schubert, Franz, 1797-1828. [Vocal music. *Selections*]

See Shostakovich, Dmitriĭ Dmitrievich, 1906-1975. [Vocal music. *Selections*]

See Theile, Johann, 1646-1724. [Vocal music. *Selections*]

[Vocal music. *Selections* ; *arr.*]
See Mozart, Wolfgang Amadeus, 1756-1791 [Vocal music. *Selections* ; *arr*]

Voce d'altra voce
See Vacchi, Fabio, 1949- Voce d'altra voce

Vogel, Hans-Peter.
See Stulick, Matthäus Nikolaus. [Concertino, woodwinds, continuo, B♭, major] Concertino a 4 stromenti, für Oboe, Klarinette (B), Fagott und Basso continuo = Concertino a 4 stromenti, for oboe, clarinet (B♭), bassoon and basso continuo / Matthäus Nicolaus Stulick ; herausgegeben von Hans-Peter Vogel.

Vogel, Harald.
See Sweelinck, Jan Pieterszoon, 1562-1621. [Fantasias, keyboard instrument] Sämtliche Werke für Tasteninstrumente. Band 2, Fantasien = Complete keyboard works. Volume 2, Fantasias / Jan Pieterszoon Sweelinck ; herausgegeben von Pieter Dirksen, Harald Vogel.

Voisenon, abbé de *1708-1775.*
See Royer, Pancrace, 1705-1755. Le pouvoir de l'Amour / Pancrace Royer ; édition de Lisa Goode Crawford ; avec la collaboration de Gérard Geay.

Volksliedbearbeitungen Nr. 269-364
See Haydn, Joseph, 1732-1809. [Songs, violin, continuo acc. *Selections*] Volksliedbearbeitungen Nr. 269-364

[Vologodskie svireli]
See Shchedrin, Rodion Konstantinovich, 1932- [Vologodskie svireli]

Vom Rath, Felix, *1866-1905.* Nachtstück.
See Franckenstein, Clemens von, 1875-1942. [Fantasien, orchestra, op. 15] Fantasie : Nachtstimmung / Clemens von Franckenstein. Symphonische Phantasie über ein Gedicht von Edgar Steiger : ("Ibsen-Phantasie") / August Reuss. Nachtstück / Felix vom Rath ; herausgegeben von Stephan Hörner.

Voprosy
See Shchedrin, Rodion Konstantinovich, 1932- Voprosy

[Vorspiele, orchestra, E major]
See Rott, Hans, 1858-1884. [Vorspiele, orchestra, E major]

Voss, Egon.
See Dokumente und Texte zu "Tannhäuser und der Sängerkrieg auf Wartburg" / herausgegeben von Peter Jost ; Reinschrift des Textbuches mit Varianten herausgegeben von Cristina Urcheuguía.

Voth, Ellen Gilson, *1972-*
An Advent carol : for mixed choir (SATB) and keyboard / Ellen Gilson Voth. — *Oxford University Press*
782.5281722   013472156

An Advent carol : for upper voices (SSA) and keyboard / Ellen Gilson Voth. — *Oxford University Press*
782.6281722   013472165

Voth, Ellen Gilson.
The circle of time : for unaccompanied mixed choir (SSAATTBB) with solo voices / Ellen Gilson Voth. — *Oxford University Press*
782.5   013472230

[Wachet auf, ruft uns die Stimme (Cantata). Wachet auf, ruft uns die Stimme; *arr.*]
See Bach, Johann Sebastian, 1685-1750. [Wachet auf, ruft uns die Stimme (Cantata). Wachet auf, ruft uns die Stimme; *arr.*]

Wagenseil, Georg Christoph, *1715-1777.*
[Divertimenti, harpsichord (1761)] — Tre divertimenti per cimbalo : Wie Mozart Klavier spielen lernte : mit didaktischem Anhang "Fondamento per il clavicembalo" = How Mozart learnt to play the piano— / Georg Christoph Wagenseil ; für Klavier/cembalo herausgegeben von Helga Scholz-Michelitsch. — *Doblinger*
786.41858   013405077

Wagner, Richard, *1813-1883.*
[Meistersinger von Nürnberg. Vorspiel; *arr.*] — Die Meistersinger von Nürnberg : (Vorspiel) = (Prelude) / Richard Wagner ; in einer Transkription für Klavier zu zwei Händen oder für zwei Klaviere zu vier Händen von Glenn Gould ; herausgegeben von Carl Morey. — *Schott*
785.62192   013176594

Waiting for my rocket to come
See Mraz, Jason. Waiting for my rocket to come

[Waldscenen]
See Schumann, Robert, 1810-1856. [Waldscenen]

Waldszenen
See Schumann, Robert, 1810-1856. [Waldscenen] Waldszenen

Walecki, Wacław.
See **Polska pieśń wielogłosowa XVI i początku XVII wieku** / zebrał i przygotował do druku = edited by Piotr Poźniak ; transkrypcja i opracowanie tekstów staropolskich = old Polish texts transcribed and annotated by Wacław Walecki.

Wales, our land
See **Tann, Hilary.** Wales, our land

Walker, Robert, *1946-*
A South Yorkshire suite / Robert Walker. — *Maecenas Music*
784.91858   013193564

Walker, Robin, *1953-*
Twilight / Robin Walker. — *Emerson Edition*
788.58   013460636

Walt Disney Pictures
See **Disney greats :** trumpet : [solo arrangements of 15 favorite songs with CD accompaniment]

Walt Disney Pictures.
See **Collins, Phil.** [Look through my eyes; *arr.*] Look through my eyes : from Walt Disney Pictures' Brother Bear : SAB / words and music by Phil Collins ; arranged by Ed Lojeski.

See **Collins, Phil.** [Look through my eyes; *arr.*] Look through my eyes : from Walt Disney Pictures' Brother Bear : SATB / words and music by Phil Collins ; arranged by Ed Lojeski.

See **Disney greats :** cello : [solo arrangements of 15 favorite songs with CD accompaniment]

See **Disney greats :** viola : [solo arrangements of 15 favorite songs with CD accompaniment]

See **Disney greats :** violin : [solo arrangements of 15 favorite songs with CD accompaniment]

See **Piglet's big movie** / featuring new songs by Carly Simon.

See **Pooh's heffalump movie** / [featuring new songs by Carly Simon]

Walton, William, *1902-1983.*
Duets for children / William Walton ; edited by Michael Aston. — *Oxford University Press*
785.62192   013174177

Magnificat and Nunc dimittis : SATB / William Walton. — *Oxford University Press*
782.5326   013432739

Waltz [from] Serenade for strings
See **Tchaikovsky, Peter Ilich, 1840-1893** [Serenades, string orchestra, op. 48, C major. Valse; *arr.*] Waltz [from] Serenade for strings

Waltzes
See **Chopin, Frédéric, 1810-1849.** [Waltzes, piano] Waltzes

[Waltzes, piano]
See **Chopin, Frédéric, 1810-1849.** [Waltzes, piano]

[Waltzes, piano, op. 23]
See **Kirchner, Theodor, 1823-1903.** [Waltzes, piano, op. 23]

Waltzing Matilda
Waltzing Matilda : SSAATTBB : Australian traditional / arranged by Jonathan Rathbone. — *Edition Peters*
782.542   013305700

Wandlebury Ring
See **Beavers, Kevin, 1971-** [Wandlebury Ring. *Vocal score*] Wandlebury Ring

[Wandlebury Ring. *Vocal score*]
See **Beavers, Kevin, 1971-** [Wandlebury Ring. *Vocal score*]

Wangermée, Robert.
See **Helmont, Charles Joseph van, 1715-1790.** [Pièces de clavecin, op. 1] Pièces de clavecin, opus I : (Bruxelles, 1737) / Charles-Joseph van Helmont ; introduction, Robert Wangermée.

Ward, John, *1571-1638.*
[Chamber music. *Selections*] — Consort music of four parts / John Ward ; transcribed and edited by Ian Payne. — *Stainer and Bell*
785.76194   013216320

[Fantasias, viols (4), Meyer 1-6. *Parts*] — Oxford fantasias : and, two-part ayres : for viols and organ / John Ward ; edited by Ian Payne. — *Stainer & Bell*
785.761941876   013307456

Ward, John, *1571-1638.* **Ayres.**
See **Ward, John, 1571-1638.** [Fantasias, viols (4), Meyer 1-6. *Parts*] Oxford fantasias : and, two-part ayres : for viols and organ / John Ward ; edited by Ian Payne.

Ward, Samuel A., *1847-1903.*
[America the beautiful; *arr.*] — America the beautiful : for mixed chorus (SATB) and organ / [Samuel A. Ward ; arranged by] Mack Wilberg. — *Oxford University Press*
782.54215990973   013472297

Warlock, Peter, *1894-1930.*
[Carols, mixed voices, orchestra. *Vocal score*] — Three carols / by Peter Warlock. — *Oxford University Press*
782.5281723   013424586

[Songs. *Selections*] — Songs 1920-1923 : medium voice / Peter Warlock ; edited by Michael Pilkington. — *Thames Publishing, in association with the Peter Warlock Society*
783.442   013173934

[Songs. *Selections*] — Songs 1923-1926 : medium voice / Peter Warlock ; edited by Michael Pilkington. — *Thames Publishing, in association with the Peter Warlock Society*
783.442   013173995

[Songs. *Selections*] — Songs 1923-1928 : high voice / Peter Warlock ; edited by Michael Pilkington. — *Thames Publishing, in association with the Peter Warlock Society*
783.342   013173999

[Songs. *Selections*] — Songs 1927-1928 : medium voice / Peter Warlock ; edited by Michael Pilkington. — *Thames Publishing, in association with the Peter Warlock Society*
783.442   013214749

[Songs. *Selections*] — Songs 1928-1930 : medium voice / Peter Warlock ; edited by Michael Pilkington. — *Thames Publishing, in association with the Peter Warlock Society*
783.442   013214763

Warner, Henry Waldo.
See **Stanford, Charles Villiers, 1852-1924.** [Sonatas, clarinet, piano, op. 129, F major; *arr.*] Viola sonata, op. 129 / by C.V. Stanford ; the composer's sonata for clarinet and piano arranged for viola and edited by Henry Waldo Warner and John White.

Warrack, John.
See **Rimsky-Korsakov, Nikolay, 1844-1908.** [Skazka o tsare Saltane. Nu, teper', moi shmel'; *arr.*] The flight of the bumblebee / Nikolay Rimsky-Korsakov ; arranged for 2 oboes & cor anglais by John Warrack.

Warren, Constance, *1905-1984.*
[Miniatures, flute, piano] — Two miniatures : for flute & piano / Constance Warren. — *Emerson Edition*
788.32   013565739

Warren, Norman.
Dawn sequence : for oboe (or flute) and piano / by Norman Warren. — *Phylloscopus Publications*
788.32   013173866

Folksong : oboe (or flute) & piano / Norman Warren. — *Emerson Edition*
788.52   013460659

The warrior queen
See **Spencer, Tim.** The warrior queen

See **Spencer, Tim.** [Warrior queen. *Selections*] The warrior queen

[Warrior queen. *Selections*]
See **Spencer, Tim.** [Warrior queen. *Selections*]

Warshauer, Meira, *1949-*
Aecha = Lamentations : for violin, cello and piano / Meira Warshauer. — *Oxford University Press*
785.28193   013062978

Bracha = (A blessing) : for violin and piano / Meira Warshauer. — *Oxford University Press*
787.2   013196406

Was Gott tut, das ist wohlgetan
See **Loewe, Carl, 1796-1869** Was Gott tut, das ist wohlgetan

Wasteland wind music 2
See **McNeff, Stephen.** Wasteland wind music 2

Waterhouse, Graham, *1962-*
Der Handschuh : Ballade von Friedrich Schiller : für Sprechstimme und Violoncello = The glove : a ballad by Friedrich Schiller : for speaking voice and violoncello / Graham Waterhouse. — *Heinrichshofen*
783.96   013953489

Jacobean salute : op. 34 : für Bläserquintett, Streichquartett und Kontrabass = for wind quintet, string quartet and double bass / Graham Waterhouse. — *R. Lienau*
785.42199   013176618

[Nonet, woodwinds, horn, strings, op. 30] — Nonett, op. 30, für Flöte (Piccolo), Oboe, Klarinette, Horn, Fagott, Violine, Viola, Violoncello, Kontrabass = for flute (piccolo), oboe, clarinet, horn, bassoon, violin, viola, violoncello, double bass / Graham Waterhouse. — *R. Lienau*
785.42199   013176633

Sicilian air : op. 56, für Flöte und Klavier = for flute and piano / Graham Waterhouse. — *Zimmermann*
788.32   013174354

Tango Toulouse : for violin, clarinet in B♭, violoncello and piano = für Violine, Klarinette in B, Violoncello und Klavier / Graham Waterhouse. — *Hofmeister*
785.2419418885   013953490

Watkins, Huw, *1976-* **Fanfare.**
See **Opening night :** two Souvenirs for solo piano : commissioned to celebrate the opening of the Bauer & Hieber music shop at 48 Great Marlborough Street, London, 21st September 2007 / written and performed by Tim Richards and Huw Watkins.

Watts, Isaac, *1674-1748.*
See **Dicie, Don Michael.** [Nineteenth-century hymns. Marching to Zion] Three nineteenth-century hymns. 3, Marching to Zion : for lower voices (TTBB) and piano / [arranged by] Don Michael Dicie.

See **Ledger, Philip.** Lie still and slumber : two lullabies for Christmas : for mixed voices and keyboard / Philip Ledger.

See **Mason, Lowell, 1792-1872.** [Modern Psalmist. Antioch; *arr.*] Joy to the world : for mixed choir (SATB) and keyboard / ['Antioch' by Lowell Mason ; arranged by] Mack Wilberg.

See **Rose, Barry, 1934-** Watts's cradle hymn : SSA and organ / Barry Rose.

Watts, Sarah.
Red hot recorder tutor : [student copy] / Sarah Watts. — *Kevin Mayhew*
788.36076   013182123

Red hot recorder tutor : teacher copy / Sarah Watts. — *Kevin Mayhew*
788.36076   013182101

Red hot treble recorder tutor : [student copy] / Sarah Watts. — *Kevin Mayhew*
788.365076   013182133

Red hot treble recorder tutor : teacher copy / Sarah Watts. — *Kevin Mayhew*
788.365076   013201099

Watts's cradle hymn
See **Rose, Barry, 1934-** Watts's cradle hymn

We three kings
See **Hopkins, John H. 1820-1891.** [We three kings of Orient are; *arr.*] We three kings

[We three kings of Orient are; *arr.*]
See **Hopkins, John H. 1820-1891.** [We three kings of Orient are; *arr.*]

Webern, Anton, 1883-1945.
[Songs. *Selections*] — The Anton Webern collection : early vocal music, 1899-1909 / [Anton Webern] ; ed. by Matthew R. Shaftel. — *Carl Fischer*
783.242   014688074

Wecker, Georg Kaspar, 1632-1695.
[O Herr hilf] — O Herr hilf! O Herr, laß wohl gelingen! : (1695) : geistliches Konzert zum 1. Advent für Sopran I, Sopran II (Tenor), Alt, Baß, 2 Violinen, 2 Violen und B.c. / Georg Caspar Wecker ; herausgegeben von Raimund Schächer. — *Erstausg.* — *Cornetto-Verlag*
782.5261722   014629780

Wedding canticle
See **Rutter, John, 1945-** Wedding canticle

Wedding gala
Wedding gala : sixteen celebrated pieces for a perfect wedding / selected and arranged for organ by John Norris. — *Stainer & Bell*
786.51587   013307472

Wedding march
See **Kaye, Ernest.** Wedding march

A wedding postlude
See **Mills, Alan, 1964-** A wedding postlude

Wedding responses
See **Jackman, Jeremy.** Wedding responses

Weelkes, Thomas, 1575 (ca.)-1623. In nomine,
See **3 In nomines à 4 :** (TrTr/TTB) / Parsons, Parsley & Weelkes ; edited by Virginia Brookes.

Wegener, Margaret, 1920-
[Down Hilo; *arr.*] — Down Hilo : fantasy for small orchestra based on two sea-shanties / Margaret Wegener. — *Da Capo Music*
784.31894   013351570

[Weihnachts-Oratorium. *English & German*]
See **Bach, Johann Sebastian, 1685-1750.**
[Weihnachts-Oratorium. *English & German*]

[Weihnachts-Oratorium. Bereite dich Zion, mit zärtlichen Trieben; *arr. English & German*]
See **Bach, Johann Sebastian, 1685-1750.**
[Weihnachts-Oratorium. Bereite dich Zion, mit zärtlichen Trieben; *arr. English & German*]

Weihnachtskantate Ihr Hirten Bethlehems
See **Zechner, Georg, 1716-1778.** [Ihr Hirten Bethlehems] Weihnachtskantate Ihr Hirten Bethlehems

[Weihnachtslieder]
See **Timmermann, Leni, 1901-** [Weihnachtslieder]

Weihnachtsoratorium
See **Bach, Johann Sebastian, 1685-1750.**
[Weihnachts-Oratorium. *English & German*] Weihnachtsoratorium

Weill, Kurt, 1900-1950.
Der Protagonist : ein Akt Oper : op. 15 / Musik von Kurt Weill ; Text von Georg Kaiser ; edited by Gunther Diehl and Jürgen Selk. — *Kurt Weill Foundation for Music :*
782.1   013813360

Weimar
See **Gorb, Adam, 1958-** Weimar

Weir, Judith. Rain and mist are on the moutain, I'd better buy some shoes.
See **The violin :** a collection : new and recent repertoire for violin with piano accompaniment / Craig Armstrong … [et al.]

Wellesz, Egon, 1885-1974.
[Suites, violin, piano, op. 56] — Suite für Violine und Klavier, op. 56 (1937, rev. 1957) / Egon Wellesz ; herausgegeben und mit Fingersätzen versehen von David Frühwirth. — *Doblinger*
787.21858   013183445

Wells, Alexander.
See **Russian operatic arias for tenor :** 19th and 20th century repertoire complete with translations and guidance on pronunciation / selected and edited by David Fanning ; singing translations by Alexander Wells.

Wells, Andrew.
See **Wesley, Samuel, 1766-1837.** [Piano music] Piano music : volume 1 / Samuel Wesley ; edited by Andrew Wells.

Wells, Tim.
See **A night at the opera for cello** / arranged by Tim Wells.

Weltliche Arien und Canzonetten
See **Theile, Johann, 1646-1724.** [Vocal music. *Selections*] Weltliche Arien und Canzonetten

Wengler, Marcel, 1946-
Versuche über einen Marsch : (1981 rev. '98) : for wind orchestra / Marcel Wengler. — *Maecenas Music*
784.8   013422366

Werner, Friedrich Ludwig Zacharias, 1768-1823. Kreuz an der Ostsee.
See **Hoffmann, E. T. A. 1776-1822.** [Kreuz an der Ostsee] Zacharias Werners Trauerspiel "Das Kreuz an der Ostsee" : mit der Bühnenmusik von E.T.A. Hoffmann ; Ballettmusik "Arlequin" / E.T.A. Hoffmann ; hrsg. aus dem Nachlaß von Friedrich Schnapp ; unter Mitarbeit von Gerhard Allroggen und Michael Kohlhäufl von Thomas Kohlhase.

Werner, Gregor Joseph, 1695-1766.
[Salve Regina, voices (4), violins (2), organ, B♭ major] — Salve Regina : in B-flat major : for mixed choir, two violins and organ / by Gregor Joseph Werner ; edited by Alejandro Garri ; assisted by Kent Carlson. — *1st ed.* — *Garri Editions*
782.526   014629781

Werner, Klaus-Günter, 1951-
See **Romberg, Andreas, 1767-1821.** Der Messias : Kantate in drei Teilen : für Soli, Chor und Orchester, nach Friedrich Gottlieb Klopstocks "Messias" : WoO, zweite Fassung (1802) / Andreas Romberg ; vorgelegt von Karlheinz Höfer und Klaus G. Werner.

Wesley, Charles, 1707-1788.
See **Cummings, William Hayman, 1831-1915.** [Hark! the herald angels sing; *arr.*] Hark! the herald angels sing : for mixed choir (SATB) and organ / [arranged by] Mack Wilberg.

Wesley, Samuel, 1766-1837.
[Piano music] — Piano music : volume 1 / Samuel Wesley ; edited by Andrew Wells. — *Redcliffe Edition*
786.2   013432959

West End hit songs
West End hit songs : twenty-nine hit songs from London's most successful stage musicals : arranged for piano, voice and guitar, complete with lyrics and chord symbols. — *Wise*
783.242164   013312999

West End love songs
West End love songs : thirty-four of the best romantic songs from London's most successful stage musicals : arranged for piano, voice and guitar, complete with lyrics and chord symbols. — *Wise*
783.242164   013307269

West End show hits.
West End show hits. — *Wise*
783.242164   013307364

West Oxford walks
See **Hedges, Anthony, 1931-** West Oxford walks

Westhoff, Johann Paul, 1656-1705.
[Sonatas, violin, continuo (1694)] — Sonate per violino e basso continuo : Dresden, 1694 / Johann Paul Westhoff ; trascrizione a cura di Alessandro Bares. — *Musedita*
787.2183   013887082

Westminster mass
See **Panufnik, Roxanna, 1968-** Westminster mass

Westney, William.
See **Heller, Stephen, 1813-1888.** [Etudes faciles. *Selections*] Selected studies : opus 45 and opus 46 / Heller ; edited by William Westney.

Wetteren, Thomas van.
See **Benda, Franz, 1709-1786.** [Sonatas, viola, continuo, C minor] Sonate pour alto et basse continue en do mineur, Lee III-137 / Franz Benda.

What child is this?
What child is this? : SSAATTBB / arranged by Jonathan Rathbone. — *Edition Peters*
782.5281723   013304755

What shall we do with the drunken sailor?
What shall we do with the drunken sailor? : SSAATTBB : English traditional / arranged by Jonathan Rathbone. — *Edition Peters*
782.5421595   013305710

[What then is love but mourning?; *arr.*]
See **Rosseter, Philip, 1567 or 8-1623.** [What then is love but mourning?; *arr.*]

What, then, is love but mourning?
See **Rosseter, Philip, 1567 or 8-1623.** [What then is love but mourning?; *arr.*] What, then, is love but mourning?

When fond, you Damon's charms recite

See **Jackson, William, 1730-1803.** [Songs, op. 16. When fond, you Damon's charms recite] When fond, you Damon's charms recite

Whence is that goodly fragrance flowing?

See **Wilberg, Mack.** Whence is that goodly fragrance flowing?

Where have all the flowers gone?

See **Seeger, Pete, 1919-** Where have all the flowers gone?

Whitbourn, James.

[Magnificat and Nunc dimittis (Collegium Regale)] — Magnificat and Nunc dimittis : Collegium regale : for tenor solo, SATB choir, organ and optional tam-tam / James Whitbourn. — *Chester Music*
782.5326   013222158

The white cockade

The white cockade : Jacobite song arranged for male voice choir with accompaniment of snare drum and two piccolos / by Bryan Davies. — *Roberton Publications, a part of Goodmusic Publishing*
782.842   013486508

The White Russian

See **Wiffin, R. K.** The White Russian

White, B. F. *1800-1879.*

[O when shall I see Jesus; *arr.*] — The morning trumpet : for unaccompanied lower voices / B.F. White ; arr. Mack Wilberg. — *Oxford University Press*
782.827   013196342

White, John, *1938-*

See **Stanford, Charles Villiers, 1852-1924.** [Sonatas, clarinet, piano, op. 129, F major; *arr.*] Viola sonata, op. 129 / by C.V. Stanford ; the composer's sonata for clarinet and piano arranged for viola and edited by Henry Waldo Warner and John White.

White, Nicholas.

A baptism hymn : for unison choir, soprano descant and keyboard / Nicholas White. — *Oxford University Press*
782.52651582   013472208

A whiter shade of pale

See **Brooker, Gary.** [Whiter shade of pale; *arr.*] A whiter shade of pale

[Whiter shade of pale; *arr.*]

See **Brooker, Gary.** [Whiter shade of pale; *arr.*]

Whitten, Danny.

[I don't want to talk about it; *arr.*] — I don't want to talk about it : grade 1.5 / Danny Whitten ; arr. Kit Turnbull. — *Studio Music*
784.8   013359661

Whittier, John Greenleaf, *1807-1892.*

See **Parnell, Andrew.** Dear Lord and father of mankind : for two-part upper voices and organ / Andrew Parnell.

Whoops-a-daisy angel

See **Davies, Niki.** Whoops-a-daisy angel

Wicker, Jutta.

See **Bach, Johann Sebastian, 1685-1750.** [Gott, der Herr, ist Sonn' und Schild. *English & German*] Gott der Herr ist Sonn und Schild : BWV 79 / BC 184 : Kantate zum Reformationsfest : für Soli (SAB), Chor (SATB), 2 Hörner, Pauken, 2 Traversflöten ad libitum, 2 Oboen, 2 Violinen, Viola und Basso continuo = God the Lord is sun and shield : cantata for the Reformation Festival : for soli (SAB), choir (SATB), 2 horns, timpani, 2 flutes ad libitum, 2 oboes, 2 violins, viola and basso continuo / Johann Sebastian Bach ; herausgegeben von Uwe Wolf ; English version by Jutta and Vernon Wicker and Catherine Winkworth.

Widger, John.

Jazz, rock 'n' bow : cello & piano : with optional CD including performance, rehearsal and backing tracks / music by John Widger. — *Spartan Press*
787.4   013441287

[Jazz, rock 'n' bow. Viola] — Jazz, rock 'n' bow : viola & piano : with optional CD including performance, rehearsal and backing tracks / music by John Widger. — *Spartan Press*
787.3   013441227

[Jazz, rock 'n' bow. Violin] — Jazz, rock 'n' bow : violin & piano : with optional CD including performance, rehearsal and backing tracks / music by John Widger. — *Spartan Press*
787.2   013441219

Wielka fantazja

See **Zarębski, Juliusz, 1854-1885.** [Pezzo agitato con un intermezzo amoroso] Wielka fantazja

Wiffin, R. K.

Here's a health / Rob Wiffin. — *Studio Music*
784.8   013416628

The White Russian / Rob Wiffin. — *Studio Music*
784.8   013390561

See **Debussy, Claude, 1862-1918** [Rêverie (Piano work); *arr.*] Rêverie / Debussy ; arranged for oboe solo and wind band by Rob Wiffin.

See **Lloyd Webber, Andrew, 1948-** [Jesus Christ superstar. I don't know how to love him; *arr.*] I don't know how to love him : grade 2 / Tim Rice & Andrew Lloyd Webber ; arr. Rob Wiffin.

See **Parry, C. Hubert H. 1848-1918.** [Jerusalem; *arr.*] Jerusalem / Hubert Parry ; arranged for wind band by Rob Wiffin.

Wiggins, Christopher.

I sing of a maiden : SSA and organ / Christopher Wiggins. — *Oxford University Press*
782.6281723   013243540

Wilberg, Mack.

How far is it to Bethlehem? : for mixed choir (SATB), 2 flutes, and harp or piano / [English carol ; arranged by] Mack Wilberg. — *Oxford University Press*
782.5281723   013472428

Masters in this hall : for mixed choir (SATB) and piano / [French carol ; arranged by] Mack Wilberg. — *Oxford University Press*
782.5281723   013472417

Thou gracious God, whose mercy lends : for mixed choir (SATBarB) and piano / [English folk tune ; arranged by] Mack Wilberg. — *Oxford University Press*
782.5265   013472378

Whence is that goodly fragrance flowing? : for mixed choir (SATB) and piano / [French carol ;

arranged by] Mack Wilberg. — *Oxford University Press*
782.5281723   013472410

See **Cummings, William Hayman, 1831-1915.** [Hark! the herald angels sing; *arr.*] Hark! the herald angels sing : for mixed choir (SATB) and organ / [arranged by] Mack Wilberg.

See **Gruber, Franz Xaver, 1787-1863.** [Stille Nacht, heilige Nacht; *arr.*] Silent night : for tenor solo and men's choir (TTBB), unaccompanied / [Franz Gruber ; arranged by] Mack Wilberg.

See **Infant holy, infant lowly :** for mixed choir (SATB) and organ / [Polish carol ; arr.] Mack Wilberg.

See **Mason, Lowell, 1792-1872.** [Modern Psalmist. Antioch; *arr.*] Joy to the world : for mixed choir (SATB) and keyboard / ['Antioch' by Lowell Mason ; arranged by] Mack Wilberg.

See **Peace like a river :** for mixed chorus (SATB) and organ / [African-American spiritual ; arranged by] Mack Wilberg.

See **Sibelius, Jean, 1865-1957.** [Finlandia. Hymni; *arr.*] Be still, my soul : for mixed choir (SATB) and organ / [Jean Sibelius ; arr. by] Mack Wilberg.

See **Ward, Samuel A., 1847-1903.** [America the beautiful; *arr.*] America the beautiful : for mixed chorus (SATB) and organ / [Samuel A. Ward ; arranged by] Mack Wilberg.

See **White, B. F. 1800-1879.** [O when shall I see Jesus; *arr.*] The morning trumpet : for unaccompanied lower voices / B.F. White ; arr. Mack Wilberg.

Wilbur, Richard, *1921-*

See **Chilcott, Bob.** And every stone shall cry : SATB unaccompanied / Bob Chilcott.

Wild grass

See **Zhou, Long, 1953-** [Wild grass; *arr.*] Wild grass

[Wild grass; *arr.*]

See **Zhou, Long, 1953-** [Wild grass; *arr.*]

Wilder, Philip van, *d. 1553.*

[Chansons. *Selections*] — 3 chansons à 4 & à 5 : (TrTr/TTB with text) / Philip Van Wilder ; edited by John Bryan. — *Viola da Gamba Society of Great Britain*
782.543   013382531

Wildman, Peter, *1957-*

Rock study : educational solos in pop styles for piano or keyboard / music by Peter Wildman. — *Spartan Press*
786.2076   013376536

Rock study duets : educational duets in pop styles for piano or keyboard / music by Peter Wildman. — *Spartan Press*
785.62192   013376539

Wilkinson, *fl. 1579-1596.*

O Lord, my God : verse anthem for SS/AATB with organ and/or viols / Thomas Wylkinson ; edited by Peter le Huray. — *Anglo-American Music Publishers*
782.5265   013594681

Praise the Lord, O ye his servants : verse anthem for SAATB with organ and/or viols / Thomas Wylkinson ; edited by Peter le Huray. — *Anglo-American Music Publishers*
782.5265   013594684

Preserve me, O Lord : verse anthem for SSATB with organ and/or viols / Thomas Wylkinson ; edited by Peter le Huray. — *Anglo-American Music Publishers*
782.5265   013594691

Willcocks, Anne.
See **Willcocks, David, 1919-** Starry night : SATB (with divisions) and organ / David Willcocks.

Willcocks, David, *1919-*
O mistress mine : SATB a cappella / David Willcocks. — *Oxford University Press*
782.542   013243525

Starry night : SATB (with divisions) and organ / David Willcocks. — *Oxford University Press*
782.5281723   013243536

Williams, Mark.
See **Un flambeau, Jeannette, Isabelle :** SSAATTBB / French traditional ; arranged by Mark Williams.

See **The miller of Dee : SSAATTBB** : English traditional / arranged by Mark Williams.

See **My Lord, what a mornin' : TTBB :** spiritual / arranged by Mark Williams.

Williams, Robbie.
Intensive care : piano, vocal, guitar / Robbie Williams. — *Wise*
783.242166   013395834

Williams, Roderick.
See **I want Jesus to walk with me** / [arr.] Roderick Williams.

Williams, William Carlos, *1883-1963*.
See **Previn, André, 1929-** [Songs (2004)] Four songs : for tenor and piano / André Previn ; texts by Philip Larkin and William Carlos Williams.

Williams, William, *1717-1791*.
See **Y delyn aur :** alaw gymreig : [arranged for SATB double chorus] / arr. John Hearne.

Willow-wood
See **Vaughan Williams, Ralph, 1872-1958** [Willow-wood. *Vocal score*] Willow-wood

[Willow-wood. *Vocal score*]
See **Vaughan Williams, Ralph, 1872-1958** [Willow-wood. *Vocal score*]

Wilms, J. W. *1772-1847*.
[Symphonies, no. 5, op. 52, D major] — Sinfonie D-Dur, op. 52 / Johann Wilhelm Wilms ; herausgegeben von Bert Hagels. — *Ries & Erler*
784.2184   014629783

Wilson, Andrew, *1960-*
Phoenix trio : for flute, oboe and clarinet in B♭ : [opus 46] / by Andrew Wilson. — *Phylloscopus Publications*
785.8193   013188882

Wilson, Trevor, composer.
[Miniatures, English horn, piano] — Eight miniatures : for cor anglais & piano / Trevor Wilson. — *Emerson Edition*
788.53   013188142

Wiltshire, Leon.
See **Davies, Bryan.** Kolokolchik = The little bell : Russian folk song for tenor solo and male voice choir with balalaikas (opotional) and tubular bell / arranged by Bryan Davies ; [English words by Leon Wiltshire]

[Wind music]
See **Michael, David Moritz, 1751-1827.** [Wind music]

Wind quintet after Mozart
See **Mengal, Martin-Joseph, 1784-1851.** [Quintets, winds, no. 2] Wind quintet after Mozart

Windbag
See **Dodgson, Stephen, 1924-** Windbag

Wings of Song (*Not-for-Profit Corporation*)
See **The Missouri harmony :** or, a choice collection of psalm tunes, hymns, and anthems / [compiled] by Wings of Song.

Wings of the grasses
See **Tann, Hilary.** Wings of the grasses

Wings of the morning
See **Rutter, John, 1945-** [Wings of the morning. *Vocal score*] Wings of the morning

[Wings of the morning. *Vocal score*]
See **Rutter, John, 1945-** [Wings of the morning. *Vocal score*]

Winkworth, Catherine, *1827-1878*.
See **Bach, Johann Sebastian, 1685-1750.** [Gott, der Herr, ist Sonn' und Schild. *English & German*] Gott der Herr ist Sonn und Schild : BWV 79 / BC 184 : Kantate zum Reformationsfest : für Soli (SAB), Chor (SATB), 2 Hörner, Pauken, 2 Traversflöten ad libitum, 2 Oboen, 2 Violinen, Viola und Basso continuo = God the Lord is sun and shield : cantata for the Reformation Festival : for soli (SAB), choir (SATB), 2 horns, timpani, 2 flutes ad libitum, 2 oboes, 2 violins, viola and basso continuo / Johann Sebastian Bach ; herausgegeben von Uwe Wolf ; English version by Jutta and Vernon Wicker and Catherine Winkworth.

Winn, Mary Beth.
See **Crecquillon, Thomas, d. 1557?** [Chansons, voices (4). *Selections*] Cantiones quatuor vocum / edidit Laura Youens and Barton Hudson ; editrix verborum Mary Beth Winn.

Winter, T. J.
See **Muslim songs of the British Isles /** arranged for schools by Abdal Hakim Murad [Timothy J. Winter]

Wir müssen durch viel Trübsal in das Reich Gottes eingehen
See **Bach, Johann Sebastian, 1685-1750.** [Wir müssen durch viel Trübsal in das Reich Gottes eingehen. *English & German*] Wir müssen durch viel Trübsal in das Reich Gottes eingehen

[Wir müssen durch viel Trübsal in das Reich Gottes eingehen. *English & German*]
See **Bach, Johann Sebastian, 1685-1750.** [Wir müssen durch viel Trübsal in das Reich Gottes eingehen. *English & German*]

With grateful hearts
See **Gibbons, Orlando, 1583-1625.** [Song 13; *arr.*] With grateful hearts

With noise of cannon
See **Croft, William, 1678-1727.** [Musicus apparatus academicus. With noise of cannon. With noise of cannon] With noise of cannon

[With notes that are both loud and sweet]
See **Jeffreys, George, ca. 1610-1685.** [With notes that are both loud and sweet]

Wo soll ich fliehen hin?
See **Telemann, Georg Philipp, 1681-1767.** [Wo soll ich fliehen hin?, TVWV 1:1724] Wo soll ich fliehen hin?

[Wo soll ich fliehen hin?, TVWV 1:1724]
See **Telemann, Georg Philipp, 1681-1767.** [Wo soll ich fliehen hin?, TVWV 1:1724]

Wohlfahrt, Franz.
[Etüden, violin, op. 45] — Sixty studies for the violin, op. 45 : complete, books I and II / Franz Wohlfahrt ; edited by Gaston Blay. — *G. Schirmer*
787.2076   013211697

Wolf, Uwe, *1961-*
See **Bach, Johann Sebastian, 1685-1750.** [Gott, der Herr, ist Sonn' und Schild. *English & German*] Gott der Herr ist Sonn und Schild : BWV 79 / BC 184 : Kantate zum Reformationsfest : für Soli (SAB), Chor (SATB), 2 Hörner, Pauken, 2 Traversflöten ad libitum, 2 Oboen, 2 Violinen, Viola und Basso continuo = God the Lord is sun and shield : cantata for the Reformation Festival : for soli (SAB), choir (SATB), 2 horns, timpani, 2 flutes ad libitum, 2 oboes, 2 violins, viola and basso continuo / Johann Sebastian Bach ; herausgegeben von Uwe Wolf ; English version by Jutta and Vernon Wicker and Catherine Winkworth.

Wolff, Christoph.
See **Bach, Johann Sebastian, 1685-1750.** [Masses, BWV 232, B minor] Messe in h-Moll, BWV 232 : mit Sanctus in D-Dur (1724), BWV 232 / Johann Sebastian Bach ; commentary by Christoph Wolff.

Wolstenholme, W. *1865-1931*.
[Quintets, winds] — Quintet for flute, oboe, clarinet, horn & bassoon / William Wolstenholme. — *Emerson Edition*
785.43195   013360897

Wolzogen, Alfred, Freiherr von, *1823-1883*.
See **Offenbach, Jacques, 1819-1880.** [Rheinnixen. *Vocal score*] Les fées du Rhin = Die Rheinnixen : opéra romantique en 4 actes (1864 / Jacques Offenbach ; livret de Jacques Offenbach et Charles Nuitter ; adaptation allemande par Alfred von Wolzogen ; partition chant-piano [par Jean-Yves Aizic avec la collaboration de Dominik Rahmer, Jean-Christophe Keck]

Wonderland
See **McFly (Musical group)** Wonderland

Wondrous love
Wondrous love : SSA a capella [sic] / arr. by Betty Bertaux. — *Boosey & Hawkes*
782.627   013243922

Wood, A. J., *1960-*
See **McAlister, Clark.** The lion and the mouse : for narrator and woodwind [sic] quintet / music by Clark McAlister ; text by A.J. Wood.

Wood, Bruce, *1945-*
See **Purcell, Henry, 1659-1695.** [Choral music. *Selections*] Royal welcome songs. Part II / Henry Purcell ; edited under the supervision of the Purcell Society by Bruce Wood.

Wood, Gareth.
Legends of the bear : for wind orchestra / Gareth Wood. — *Maecenas Music*
784.81858   013422589

[Mexican pictures. Spanish] — Spanish picture : from Three Mexican pictures / Gareth Wood. — *Maecenas Music*
784.8   013422274

Woolrich, John.
From the shadows : five pieces for chamber ensemble of eleven players (1994) / John Woolrich. — *Faber Music*
785.32199   013243713

Wordsworth miniatures
See **Roxburgh, Edwin.** Wordsworth miniatures

Wordsworth, William, *1770-1850*.
See **Roxburgh, Edwin.** Wordsworth miniatures : solo clarinet in B flat / Edwin Roxburgh.

World carols for choirs
World carols for choirs : 31 carols for mixed
voices / edited and compiled by Bob Chilcott &
Susan Knight. — *Oxford University Press*
782.528   013334443

World wars I & II
See **Hewitt, Daniel.** World wars I & II

The world's greatest artists and bands
The world's greatest artists and bands : chord
songbook : a selection of fifty-five songs from
the album. — *Wise Publications*
783.242166   013265847

Worrell, Bill.
See **Brunner, David L., 1953-** Painted
memories : 2-pt treble / [music by] David L.
Brunner.

Wranitzky, Paul, 1756-1808.
[Quintets, flute, oboe, violas, violoncello, op. 3.
No. 1] — Quintet in F, op. III no. 1 : for flute,
oboe, two violas and cello / by Paul Wranitzky.
— *Phylloscopus Publications*
785.44195   013472931

The wreck of the Anson
See **Cliff, Tony.** The wreck of the Anson

Wright, Andrew, 1955-
See **Gershwin, George, 1898-1937.** [Songs.
Selections; arr.] Easy-to-play Gershwin for
piano / arranged by Andrew Wright.

Wright, Margot, 1911-2000.
[Improvisation, clarinet] — Improvisation : for
solo clarinet / Margot Wright. — *Emerson
Edition*
788.62   013358203

Wright, Nicholas, 1940-
See **Portman, Rachel.** [Little prince. Birds; arr.]
The birds : from The little prince : for SSA and
piano / Rachel Portman ; [arr. by Richard Allain]

See **Portman, Rachel.** [Little prince.
Lamplighters; arr.] The lamplighters : from The
little prince ; for SSA and piano / Rachel
Portman ; [arr. by Richard Allain]

See **Portman, Rachel.** [Little prince. Look at
the stars; arr.] Look at the stars : from The little
prince ; for SSA and piano / Rachel Portman ;
[arr. by Richard Allain]

See **Portman, Rachel.** [Little prince. Roses;
arr.] The roses : from The little prince : for SSA
and piano / Rachel Portman ; [arr. by Richard
Allain]

See **Portman, Rachel.** [Little prince. Stars; arr.]
The stars : from The little prince ; for SSA and
piano / Rachel Portman ; [arr. by Richard Allain]

Wright, Peter, 1953-
See **Fifteenth-century liturgical music V,**
Settings of the Sanctus and Agnus dei /
transcribed and edited by Peter Wright.

Wülfing, Hans.
See **Glory to God :** Englische Chormusik aus
fünf Jahrhunderten / herausgegeben von Hans
Wülfing für den Landesverband ev.
Kirchenchöre im Rheinland in Zusammenarbeit
mit dem Verband ev. Kirchenchöre
Deutschlands.

X&Y
See **Coldplay (Musical group)** X&Y

[X&Y; arr.]
[X&Y; *arr.*]

XII sonate a violino solo e basso
See **Lonati, Carlo Ambrogio.** [Sonatas, violin,
continuo (1701)] XII sonate a violino solo e
basso

Yá kafi, yá shafi
See **Thoresen, Lasse, 1949-** Yá kafi, yá shafi

Ye, Xiaogang.
Colorful sutra banner : for piano trio, opus 58
(2006) / Xiaogang Ye. — *Schott*
785.28193   013953491

Yeats, W. B. *1865-1939*
See **The Salley Gardens :** SATB / Irish
traditional ; arranged by Ben Parry ; [words by
W.B. Yeats]

York, John, *1949-*
See **Rachmaninoff, Sergei, 1873-1943.**
[Symphonies, no. 2, op. 27, E minor. Adagio;
arr.] Symphony no. 2 : theme from third
movment : for violin and piano / arranged by
John York ; violin part edited by Levon
Chilingirian.

Þorkell Sigurbjörnsson, *1938-*
Hymn to Mary = (Maríukvæði) / Þorkell
Sigurbjörnsson. — *Oxford University Press*
782.5265   013359691

You and me
See **Chilcott, Bob.** You and me

You could have it so much better
See **Franz Ferdinand (Musical group)** You
could have it so much better

You know what sailors are (Motion picture)
See **Arnold, Malcolm.** [You know what sailors
are. Scherzetto; *arr.*] Scherzetto : for clarinet &
piano / Malcolm Arnold. — *Queen's Temple
Publications*

[You know what sailors are. Scherzetto; *arr.*]
See **Arnold, Malcolm.** [You know what sailors
are. Scherzetto; *arr.*]

Youens, Laura.
See **Crecquillon, Thomas, d. 1557?** [Chansons,
voices (4). *Selections*] Cantiones quatuor vocum
/ edidit Laura Youens and Barton Hudson ;
editrix verborum Mary Beth Winn.

A young nun singing
See **Larsen, Libby.** A young nun singing

Young, J. Freeman *1820-1885.*
See **Gruber, Franz Xaver, 1787-1863.** [Stille
Nacht, heilige Nacht; *arr.*] Silent night : for
tenor solo and men's choir (TTBB),
unaccompanied / [Franz Gruber ; arranged by]
Mack Wilberg.

You're the voice
You're the voice : Billie Holliday. —
International Music Publications
783.242165   013086205

**Zacharias Werners Trauerspiel "Das Kreuz an
der Ostsee"**
See **Hoffmann, E. T. A. 1776-1822.** [Kreuz an
der Ostsee] Zacharias Werners Trauerspiel "Das
Kreuz an der Ostsee"

Zadow, Dankwart von.
See **Buxtehude, Dietrich, 1637-1707.** [Laudate
pueri] Laudate pueri Dominum : chiaccona für 2
Soprane, 6 Gamben (oder andere Streicher) und
B.c., BuxWV 69 = chiaconna for 2 sopranos, 6
viols (or other strings) and b.c. / Dieterich
Buxtehude ; Generalbassaussetzung von
Dankwart von Zadow ; herausgegeben von
Günter und Leonore Zadow.

Zahn, Robert von.
See **Haydn, Joseph, 1732-1809** [Symphonies.
Selections.] Londoner Sinfonien. 1. Folge /
Joseph Haydn ; herausgegeben von Robert von
Zahn und Gernot Gruber.

Zakopets, Myron.
See **Barret, Apollon Marie-Rose, 1803-1879.**
[Cantilène; *arr.*] Cantilena / by Apollon M.-R.
Barret ; arranged for cor anglais and piano by
professor Myron Zakopets.

See **Brod, Henri, 1799-1839.** [Fantaisie, oboe,
piano] Fantaisie : oboe & piano / Henri Brod ;
edited by Myron Zakopets.

See **Verroust, Stanislas, 1814-1863.**
[Capriccios, oboe, piano] Capriccio : for oboe &
piano / Stanislas Verroust ; edited by Myron
Zakopets.

See **Verroust, Stanislas, 1814-1863.** Fantaisie
sur 'Don Pasquale' : for oboe & piano /
Stanislas Verroust ; edited by Myron Zakopets.

Zarębski, Juliusz, *1854-1885.*
[Pezzo agitato, con un intermezzo amoroso] —
Wielka fantazja = Grande fantaisie (Un pezzo
agitato con un intermezzo amoroso), JZBO 11 ;
Utwór bez tytułu = Piece without title, JZBO
14 : na fortepian = for piano / Juliusz Zarębski ;
redakcja Ryszard Daniel Golianek ; opracowanie
wykonawcze Andrzej Tatarski. — *Rhytmos*
786.2   014629793

Zarębski, Juliusz, *1854-1885.* Utwór,
See **Zarębski, Juliusz, 1854-1885.** [Pezzo
agitato con un intermezzo amoroso] Wielka
fantazja = Grande fantaisie (Un pezzo agitato
con un intermezzo amoroso), JZBO 11 ; Utwór
bez tytułu = Piece without title, JZBO 14 : na
fortepian = for piano / Juliusz Zarębski ;
redakcja Ryszard Daniel Golianek ; opracowanie
wykonawcze Andrzej Tatarski.

Zarlino, Gioseffo, *1517-1590.*
[Motets. *Selections*] — Motets from 1549 /
Gioseffo Zarlino ; edited by Cristle Collins Judd.
— *A-R Editions*
782.526   013888152

[Zauberflöte. Ouverture; *arr.*]
See **Mozart, Wolfgang Amadeus, 1756-1791**
[Zauberflöte. Ouverture; *arr.*]

Żebrowski, Marcin Józef.
[Masses, D major (RISM A/II 300.033.496)] —
Missa ex D a canto, basso, due violini, due
clarini ad libitum con organo / Marcin Józef
Żebrowski ; opracowanie i wstęp Remigiusz
Pośpiech. — *Wyd. 1.* — *Klasztor OO. Paulinów
Jasna Góra*
782.53232   013953492

Missa pastoralis : a canto, basso, due violini, due
clarini con organo / Marcin Józef Żebrowski ;
opracowanie i wstęp Remigiusz Pośpiech ;
[redaktor, Irena Stachel] — *Klasztor OO.
Paulinów Jasna Góra*
782.53232   013953493

Zechlin, Ruth, *1926-2007.*
[Missa in honorem Sancti Stephani] — Missa in
honorem Sancti Stephanie : für 4 Solisten,
4-16-stimmigen Chor, grosses Orchester und
Orgel / Ruth Zechlin. — *Manuskript-Edition.* —
Ries & Erler
782.53232   014629795

Zechner, Georg, *1716-1778.*
[Ihr Hirten Bethlehems] — Weihnachtskantate
Ihr Hirten Bethlehems : soprano, alto, tenore e
basso, 2 corni, 2 violini, 2 viole e basso continuo
/ Johann Georg Zechner. — *Erstausg. /* — *Carus*
782.5241723   013832409

Zelenka, Johann Dismas, *1679-1745.*
[Miserere, ZWV 56, D minor] — Misere d-Moll,
ZWV 56, für Soli (SATB), Chor (SATB), 2
Oboen, 3 Posaunen, 2 Violinen, 2 Violen und
Basso continuo / Jan Dismas Zelenka ;
herausgegeben von Stephan Thamm. — *Ortus*
782.5294   013775682

Missa Sanctae Caeciliae : für Soprano, Alt, Tenor, Bass, Chor, 2 Oboen, Fagott, Streicher & B.c. / Jan Dismas Zelenka ; herausgegeben von Martin Kellhuber. — *Erstausg.* — *Edition Walhall*
782.53232   013631618

[O magnum mysterium] — Motetto pro nativitate I, ZWV 171 : Dormi nate, dormi Deus : per alto solo, 2 flauti traversi o flauti a becco (ad lib.), 2 violini, viola e basso continuo / Jan Dismas Zelenka ; Erstausgabe herausgegeben von Thomas Kohlhase. — *Carus*
783.68241723   013641968

[Pro quos criminis] — Motetto pro nativitate II, ZWV 172 : Dormi, Deus incarnate : per tenore solo, 2 flauti a becco, 2 flauti traversi, 2 violini, viola e basso continuo / Jan Dismas Zelenka ; herausgegeben von Thomas Kohlhase. — *Erstausg.* — *Carus*
783.87241723   013641972

Zenger, Max, *1837-1911*.
[Amor und Psyche. Sonata] — Sonata für zwei Violinen : komponiert im alten Stil für König Ludwig II. von Bayern = Sonata for two violins : composed in ancient style for King Ludwig II of Bavaria / Max Zenger ; herausgegeben von Robert Münster. — *Erstausg.* — *R. Lienau*
785.72192183   014629800

Zhou, Long, *1953-*
Chinese folk songs : for string orchestra / Zhou Long. — *Oxford University Press*
784.7   013115382

Four seasons : for unaccompanied treble chorus (SSAA) / Zhou Long. — *Oxford University Press*
782.642   013115222

[Wild grass; *arr.*] — Wild grass : for viola / Zhou Long. — *Oxford University Press*
787.3   013196402

Ziani, Pietro Andrea, *1616-1684*.
[Sonatas, trumpet, strings, continuo, D major] — Sonata à 6 für Trompete, 2 Violinen, 3 Violen & B.c. / Pietro Andrea Ziani ; [herausgegeben von] Konrad Ruhland. — *Erstausg.* — *Edition Walhall*
785.22197   014629801

Zimmermann, Anton, *1741-1781*.
[Quartets, strings, op. 3. No. 2] — Quartetto in B für 2 Violinen, Viola und Violoncello, op. 3/2 / Anton Zimmerman ; [herausgegeben von] Darina Múdra. — *Doblinger*
785.7194   014629805

[Symphonies. *Selections*] — Four symphonies / Anton Zimmermann ; edited by János Bali and Péter Halász ; introduced by Péter Halász. —

Magyar Tudományos Akadémia Zenetudományi Intézet
784.2184   014629804

Zimmermann, Frank Peter.
See **Mozart, Wolfgang Amadeus, 1756-1791.** [Sinfonie concertanti, violin, viola, orchestra, K. 364, E♭ major; *arr.*] Sinfonia concertante für Violine, Viola und Orchester, Es-dur, KV 364 = Sinfonia concertante in E♭ major for violin, viola and orchestra, K. 364 / Wolfgang Amadeus Mozart ; herausgegeben von Wolf-Dieter Seiffert ; Klavierauszug von Siegfried Petrenz ; Fingersatz und Strichbezeichnung von Frank Peter Zimmermann [und] Tabea Zimmermann ; piano reduction.

Zlatar, Jakša.
See **Timakin, E. M.** Essential piano exercises / E.M. Timakin ; editor, Jakša Zlatar.

Zubatý, Josef, *1855-1931*.
See **Dvořák, Antonín, 1841-1904.** [Stabat Mater, op. 58, D major. *Vocal score*] Stabat Mater für Soli, Chor und Orchester, op. 58 = for soloists, chorus and orchestra / Antonín Dvořák ; Klavierauszug von Josef Zubatý ; herausgegeben von Klaus Döge.

Zwölf Walzer für Klavier, op. 23
See **Kirchner, Theodor, 1823-1903.** [Waltzes, piano, op. 23] Zwölf Walzer für Klavier, op. 23

SUBJECT INDEX

Accordion
Accordion 788.86076
Accordion, Instruction and study 788.86076

Advent music
Advent music 782.5261722
Advent music 782.5265
Advent music 782.52651722
Advent music 782.527
Advent music 782.5281722
Advent music 782.5281723
Advent music 782.532351722
Advent music 782.53261722
Advent music 782.6281722
Advent music 782.62921722

Agnus Dei (Music)
Agnus Dei (Music), 15th century 782.53232

Alternative metal (Music)
Alternative metal (Music) 783.242166

Alto trombone music
Alto trombone music 788.93

Anthems
Anthems 782.5265
Anthems 782.52651582
Anthems 782.52651722
Anthems 782.52651723
Anthems 782.52951587
Anthems 782.542
Anthems 782.6265
Anthems 782.642
Anthems 782.76265

Antiphons (Music)
Antiphons (Music) 782.526
Antiphons (Music) 782.53261722
Antiphons (Music) 782.625
Antiphons (Music) 783.8624

Ariadne (Greek mythology)
Ariadne (Greek mythology) 783.6642

Arpeggios
Arpeggios 787.871252

Ascension Day music
Ascension Day music 782.523

Ascensiontide
Ascensiontide 782.5261728
Ascensiontide 782.626

Ballate
Ballate 782.543

Ballets
Ballets 782.1
Ballets 782.51552
Ballets 782.51556
Ballets 784.21556
Ballets 784.31556
Ballets 785.281941858
Ballets 785.281951858
Ballets 786.21556
Ballets 788.581556

Band music
Band music 784.8
Band music 784.89

Band music, Arranged
Band music, Arranged 784.8
Band music, Arranged 784.818835

Baptism
Baptism 782.52651582

Bassoon
Bassoon 788.58076
Bassoon, Instruction and study 788.58076

Bassoon and oboe music
Bassoon and oboe music 785.85192

Bassoon and piano music
Bassoon and piano music 788.58

Bassoon and piano music, Arranged
Bassoon and piano music, Arranged 788.58

Bassoon and viola music
Bassoon and viola music 785.44192

Bassoon music
Bassoon music 788.58
Bassoon music 788.581556

Bassoon music (Bassoons (2))
Bassoon music (Bassoons (2)) 788.58076

Blues (Music)
Blues (Music) 781.651643
Blues (Music) 783.2421643

Blues (Music) 783.242165
Blues (Music) 785
Blues (Music) 787.871643
Blues (Music) 788.731643
Blues (Music), 1931-1940 783.2421643
Blues (Music), Instruction and study 786.21643076

Brass band music
Brass band music 784.9

Brass band music, Arranged
Brass band music, Arranged 784.9

Brass ensembles
Brass ensembles 785.57

Brass instrument music (Brass instruments (2))
Brass instrument music (Brass instruments (2)) 785.9192

Brass instrument music (Brass instruments (2)), Arranged
Brass instrument music (Brass instruments (2)), Arranged 785.9192

Brass quintets (Horn, trombone, trumpets (2), tuba)
Brass quintets (Horn, trombone, trumpets (2), tuba) 785.9195
Brass quintets (Horn, trombone, trumpets (2), tuba) 785.91951897

Cacce (Part songs)
Cacce (Part songs) 782.543

Cancans
Cancans 784.68188417230834

Canons, fugues, etc. (Bassoons (2), English horn, oboe), Arranged
Canons, fugues, etc. (Bassoons (2), English horn, oboe), Arranged 785.85194

Canons, fugues, etc. (Bassoons (2), oboes (2)), Arranged
Canons, fugues, etc. (Bassoons (2), oboes (2)), Arranged 785.85194

Canons, fugues, etc. (Bassoons (3), English horn), Arranged
Canons, fugues, etc. (Bassoons (3), English horn), Arranged 785.85194

Canons, fugues, etc. (Flutes (3))
Canons, fugues, etc. (Flutes (3)) 785.832193

Canons, fugues, etc. (Organ)
Canons, fugues, etc. (Organ) 786.5
Canons, fugues, etc. (Organ) 786.51872

Canons, fugues, etc. (Piano)
Canons, fugues, etc. (Piano) 786.21872

Canons, fugues, etc. (String quartet)
Canons, fugues, etc. (String quartet) 785.7194

Canons, fugues, etc. (String quartet), Arranged
Canons, fugues, etc. (String quartet), Arranged 785.71941825

Cantatas, Sacred
Cantatas, Sacred 782.524
Cantatas, Sacred 782.5241723
Cantatas, Sacred 782.5241727
Cantatas, Sacred 782.52417293
Cantatas, Sacred 782.5281723
Cantatas, Sacred 783.6842
Cantatas, Sacred 783.8925
Cantatas, Sacred 787.2

Cantatas, Sacred (Women's voices)
Cantatas, Sacred (Women's voices) 783.126648

Cantatas, Secular
Cantatas, Secular 782.1
Cantatas, Secular 782.524
Cantatas, Secular 782.548
Cantatas, Secular 783.1248
Cantatas, Secular 783.6848

Canzonets (Part songs), Italian
Canzonets (Part songs), Italian 783

Carols
Carols 782.5241723
Carols 782.528
Carols 782.52815246
Carols 782.5281722
Carols 782.5281723
Carols 782.6281723
Carols 782.8281723
Carols 785.8321921723
Carols 786.21723

Carols 786.21723165
Carols 787.41723

Carols, English
Carols, English 782.5281722
Carols, English 782.5281723
Carols, English 782.628
Carols, English 782.6281722
Carols, English 782.6281723
Carols, English 785.281723
Carols, English 786.591723
Carols, English, Sheffield (England) 782.528

Carols, French
Carols, French 782.5281723
Carols, French 785.281723

Carols, German
Carols, German 782.6281723

Carols, Welsh
Carols, Welsh 782.6281723

Chaconnes (Harpsichord)
Chaconnes (Harpsichord) 786.41827

Chaconnes (Violoncello with string orchestra)
Chaconnes (Violoncello with string orchestra) 784.72741827
Chaconnes (Violoncello with string orchestra) 787.41827

Chamber music
Chamber music 784

Chamber orchestra music
Chamber orchestra music 784.3
Chamber orchestra music 784.31894

Children's songs
Children's songs 782.725
Children's songs 782.742
Children's songs 782.7421723

Children's songs, English
Children's songs, English 782.742
Children's songs, English 782.7421723

Chorale preludes
Chorale preludes 786.518992

Choruses (Mixed voices)
Choruses (Mixed voices) 782.5281723

Choruses (Mixed voices), Unaccompanied
Choruses (Mixed voices), Unaccompanied 782.527

Choruses, Sacred
Choruses, Sacred 782.5

Choruses, Sacred (Children's voices) with organ
Choruses, Sacred (Children's voices) with organ 782.76265

Choruses, Sacred (Children's voices) with piano
Choruses, Sacred (Children's voices) with piano 782.71542

Choruses, Sacred (Children's voices, 2 parts) with organ
Choruses, Sacred (Children's voices, 2 parts) with organ 782.626

Choruses, Sacred (Equal voices)
Choruses, Sacred (Equal voices) 782.54217700941

Choruses, Sacred (Equal voices) with instrumental ensemble
Choruses, Sacred (Equal voices) with instrumental ensemble 782.725

Choruses, Sacred (Men's voices), Unaccompanied
Choruses, Sacred (Men's voices), Unaccompanied 782.8253
Choruses, Sacred (Men's voices), Unaccompanied 782.8326

Choruses, Sacred (Men's voices, 2 parts) with handbells
Choruses, Sacred (Men's voices, 2 parts) with handbells 782.5265

Choruses, Sacred (Men's voices, 3 parts) with piano
Choruses, Sacred (Men's voices, 3 parts) with piano 782.8253

Choruses, Sacred (Men's voices, 4 parts) with piano
Choruses, Sacred (Men's voices, 4 parts) with piano 782.827

Choruses, Sacred (Men's voices, 4 parts), Unaccompanied
Choruses, Sacred (Men's voices, 4 parts), Unaccompanied   782.825
Choruses, Sacred (Men's voices, 4 parts), Unaccompanied   782.8253
Choruses, Sacred (Men's voices, 4 parts), Unaccompanied   782.827
Choruses, Sacred (Men's voices, 4 parts), Unaccompanied   782.8281723

Choruses, Sacred (Mixed voices)
Choruses, Sacred (Mixed voices)   782.528

Choruses, Sacred (Mixed voices) with brass band
Choruses, Sacred (Mixed voices) with brass band   784.9

Choruses, Sacred (Mixed voices) with brass ensemble
Choruses, Sacred (Mixed voices) with brass ensemble   782.5281723

Choruses, Sacred (Mixed voices) with chamber orchestra
Choruses, Sacred (Mixed voices) with chamber orchestra   782.524

Choruses, Sacred (Mixed voices) with continuo
Choruses, Sacred (Mixed voices) with continuo   782.525

Choruses, Sacred (Mixed voices) with instrumental ensemble
Choruses, Sacred (Mixed voices) with instrumental ensemble   782.522
Choruses, Sacred (Mixed voices) with instrumental ensemble   782.524
Choruses, Sacred (Mixed voices) with instrumental ensemble   782.5241723
Choruses, Sacred (Mixed voices) with instrumental ensemble   782.52417293
Choruses, Sacred (Mixed voices) with instrumental ensemble   782.526
Choruses, Sacred (Mixed voices) with instrumental ensemble   782.5265
Choruses, Sacred (Mixed voices) with instrumental ensemble   782.527
Choruses, Sacred (Mixed voices) with instrumental ensemble   782.5281723
Choruses, Sacred (Mixed voices) with instrumental ensemble   782.5294
Choruses, Sacred (Mixed voices) with instrumental ensemble   782.52951587
Choruses, Sacred (Mixed voices) with instrumental ensemble   782.53232
Choruses, Sacred (Mixed voices) with instrumental ensemble   782.53238
Choruses, Sacred (Mixed voices) with instrumental ensemble   782.5324

Choruses, Sacred (Mixed voices) with instrumental ensemble, Arranged
Choruses, Sacred (Mixed voices) with instrumental ensemble, Arranged   782.5281723

Choruses, Sacred (Mixed voices) with orchestra
Choruses, Sacred (Mixed voices) with orchestra   782.524
Choruses, Sacred (Mixed voices) with orchestra   782.5281723
Choruses, Sacred (Mixed voices) with orchestra   782.5294
Choruses, Sacred (Mixed voices) with orchestra   782.53232
Choruses, Sacred (Mixed voices) with orchestra   782.53235
Choruses, Sacred (Mixed voices) with orchestra   782.532351726
Choruses, Sacred (Mixed voices) with orchestra   782.5325

Choruses, Sacred (Mixed voices) with organ
Choruses, Sacred (Mixed voices) with organ   782.522
Choruses, Sacred (Mixed voices) with organ   782.526
Choruses, Sacred (Mixed voices) with organ   782.5265
Choruses, Sacred (Mixed voices) with organ   782.527
Choruses, Sacred (Mixed voices) with organ   782.5281723

Choruses, Sacred (Mixed voices) with piano
Choruses, Sacred (Mixed voices) with piano   782.522
Choruses, Sacred (Mixed voices) with piano   782.5281723

Choruses, Sacred (Mixed voices) with piano   782.5294
Choruses, Sacred (Mixed voices) with piano   783.12

Choruses, Sacred (Mixed voices) with saxophone
Choruses, Sacred (Mixed voices) with saxophone   782.5326

Choruses, Sacred (Mixed voices) with string orchestra
Choruses, Sacred (Mixed voices) with string orchestra   782.526
Choruses, Sacred (Mixed voices) with string orchestra   782.5261722

Choruses, Sacred (Mixed voices) with violoncello
Choruses, Sacred (Mixed voices) with violoncello   782.5326

Choruses, Sacred (Mixed voices) with wind ensemble
Choruses, Sacred (Mixed voices) with wind ensemble   782.524

Choruses, Sacred (Mixed voices), Unaccompanied
Choruses, Sacred (Mixed voices), Unaccompanied   782.5
Choruses, Sacred (Mixed voices), Unaccompanied   782.522
Choruses, Sacred (Mixed voices), Unaccompanied   782.525
Choruses, Sacred (Mixed voices), Unaccompanied   782.526
Choruses, Sacred (Mixed voices), Unaccompanied   782.52617293
Choruses, Sacred (Mixed voices), Unaccompanied   782.5265
Choruses, Sacred (Mixed voices), Unaccompanied   782.527
Choruses, Sacred (Mixed voices), Unaccompanied   782.53232
Choruses, Sacred (Mixed voices), Unaccompanied   782.5326
Choruses, Sacred (Mixed voices), Unaccompanied   783.12

Choruses, Sacred (Mixed voices, 2 parts) with handbells
Choruses, Sacred (Mixed voices, 2 parts) with handbells   782.5265

Choruses, Sacred (Mixed voices, 2 parts) with organ
Choruses, Sacred (Mixed voices, 2 parts) with organ   782.5265

Choruses, Sacred (Mixed voices, 3 parts) with continuo
Choruses, Sacred (Mixed voices, 3 parts) with continuo   782.526

Choruses, Sacred (Mixed voices, 4 parts)
Choruses, Sacred (Mixed voices, 4 parts)   782.528
Choruses, Sacred (Mixed voices, 4 parts)   782.5281723

Choruses, Sacred (Mixed voices, 4 parts) with continuo
Choruses, Sacred (Mixed voices, 4 parts) with continuo   782.324
Choruses, Sacred (Mixed voices, 4 parts) with continuo   782.526

Choruses, Sacred (Mixed voices, 4 parts) with harp
Choruses, Sacred (Mixed voices, 4 parts) with harp   782.5281723

Choruses, Sacred (Mixed voices, 4 parts) with keyboard instrument
Choruses, Sacred (Mixed voices, 4 parts) with keyboard instrument   782.5251723
Choruses, Sacred (Mixed voices, 4 parts) with keyboard instrument   782.5281722
Choruses, Sacred (Mixed voices, 4 parts) with keyboard instrument   782.5281723

Choruses, Sacred (Mixed voices, 4 parts) with orchestra
Choruses, Sacred (Mixed voices, 4 parts) with orchestra   782.5265

Choruses, Sacred (Mixed voices, 4 parts) with organ
Choruses, Sacred (Mixed voices, 4 parts) with organ   782.324
Choruses, Sacred (Mixed voices, 4 parts) with organ   782.525
Choruses, Sacred (Mixed voices, 4 parts) with organ   782.5253

Choruses, Sacred (Mixed voices, 4 parts) with organ
Choruses, Sacred (Mixed voices, 4 parts) with organ   782.526
Choruses, Sacred (Mixed voices, 4 parts) with organ   782.5265
Choruses, Sacred (Mixed voices, 4 parts) with organ   782.527
Choruses, Sacred (Mixed voices, 4 parts) with organ   782.52815246
Choruses, Sacred (Mixed voices, 4 parts) with organ   782.5281723
Choruses, Sacred (Mixed voices, 4 parts) with organ   782.5294
Choruses, Sacred (Mixed voices, 4 parts) with organ   782.53232
Choruses, Sacred (Mixed voices, 4 parts) with organ   782.5326
Choruses, Sacred (Mixed voices, 4 parts) with organ   782.542
Choruses, Sacred (Mixed voices, 4 parts) with organ   782.54215990973
Choruses, Sacred (Mixed voices, 4 parts) with organ   785.281723

Choruses, Sacred (Mixed voices, 4 parts) with piano
Choruses, Sacred (Mixed voices, 4 parts) with piano   782.5253
Choruses, Sacred (Mixed voices, 4 parts) with piano   782.5265
Choruses, Sacred (Mixed voices, 4 parts) with piano   782.5281723
Choruses, Sacred (Mixed voices, 4 parts) with piano   782.5294
Choruses, Sacred (Mixed voices, 4 parts) with piano   782.52951587
Choruses, Sacred (Mixed voices, 4 parts) with piano   782.542

Choruses, Sacred (Mixed voices, 4 parts), Unaccompanied
Choruses, Sacred (Mixed voices, 4 parts), Unaccompanied   782.523
Choruses, Sacred (Mixed voices, 4 parts), Unaccompanied   782.525
Choruses, Sacred (Mixed voices, 4 parts), Unaccompanied   782.5251723
Choruses, Sacred (Mixed voices, 4 parts), Unaccompanied   782.5253
Choruses, Sacred (Mixed voices, 4 parts), Unaccompanied   782.526
Choruses, Sacred (Mixed voices, 4 parts), Unaccompanied   782.5261723
Choruses, Sacred (Mixed voices, 4 parts), Unaccompanied   782.5265
Choruses, Sacred (Mixed voices, 4 parts), Unaccompanied   782.52651722
Choruses, Sacred (Mixed voices, 4 parts), Unaccompanied   782.52651723
Choruses, Sacred (Mixed voices, 4 parts), Unaccompanied   782.5271727
Choruses, Sacred (Mixed voices, 4 parts), Unaccompanied   782.5281723
Choruses, Sacred (Mixed voices, 4 parts), Unaccompanied   782.5294
Choruses, Sacred (Mixed voices, 4 parts), Unaccompanied   782.5295
Choruses, Sacred (Mixed voices, 4 parts), Unaccompanied   782.53232
Choruses, Sacred (Mixed voices, 4 parts), Unaccompanied   782.53238
Choruses, Sacred (Mixed voices, 4 parts), Unaccompanied   782.5326
Choruses, Sacred (Mixed voices, 4 parts), Unaccompanied   785.281723

Choruses, Sacred (Mixed voices, 5 parts) with continuo
Choruses, Sacred (Mixed voices, 5 parts) with continuo   782.526

Choruses, Sacred (Mixed voices, 5 parts) with organ
Choruses, Sacred (Mixed voices, 5 parts) with organ   782.5265

Choruses, Sacred (Mixed voices, 5 parts) with piano
Choruses, Sacred (Mixed voices, 5 parts) with piano   782.5265

Choruses, Sacred (Mixed voices, 5 parts), Unaccompanied
Choruses, Sacred (Mixed voices, 5 parts), Unaccompanied   782.5253
Choruses, Sacred (Mixed voices, 5 parts), Unaccompanied   782.526

Choruses, Sacred (Mixed voices, 5 parts),
Unaccompanied 782.5261724
Choruses, Sacred (Mixed voices, 5 parts),
Unaccompanied 782.5261728
Choruses, Sacred (Mixed voices, 5 parts),
Unaccompanied 782.5265
Choruses, Sacred (Mixed voices, 5 parts),
Unaccompanied 782.53232
Choruses, Sacred (Mixed voices, 5 parts),
Unaccompanied 782.532351722
Choruses, Sacred (Mixed voices, 5 parts),
Unaccompanied 782.532351723
Choruses, Sacred (Mixed voices, 5 parts),
Unaccompanied 782.5323517293
Choruses, Sacred (Mixed voices, 5 parts),
Unaccompanied 782.53241726

**Choruses, Sacred (Mixed voices, 6 parts) with
organ**
Choruses, Sacred (Mixed voices, 6 parts) with
organ 782.5265

**Choruses, Sacred (Mixed voices, 6 parts),
Unaccompanied**
Choruses, Sacred (Mixed voices, 6 parts),
Unaccompanied 782.525
Choruses, Sacred (Mixed voices, 6 parts),
Unaccompanied 782.526
Choruses, Sacred (Mixed voices, 6 parts),
Unaccompanied 782.5261723
Choruses, Sacred (Mixed voices, 6 parts),
Unaccompanied 782.5261727
Choruses, Sacred (Mixed voices, 6 parts),
Unaccompanied 782.5265
Choruses, Sacred (Mixed voices, 6 parts),
Unaccompanied 782.53232

**Choruses, Sacred (Mixed voices, 7 parts),
Unaccompanied**
Choruses, Sacred (Mixed voices, 7 parts),
Unaccompanied 782.525
Choruses, Sacred (Mixed voices, 7 parts),
Unaccompanied 782.526

**Choruses, Sacred (Mixed voices, 8 parts) with
organ**
Choruses, Sacred (Mixed voices, 8 parts) with
organ 782.5265

**Choruses, Sacred (Mixed voices, 8 parts),
Unaccompanied**
Choruses, Sacred (Mixed voices, 8 parts),
Unaccompanied 782.5
Choruses, Sacred (Mixed voices, 8 parts),
Unaccompanied 782.5241723
Choruses, Sacred (Mixed voices, 8 parts),
Unaccompanied 782.5253
Choruses, Sacred (Mixed voices, 8 parts),
Unaccompanied 782.526
Choruses, Sacred (Mixed voices, 8 parts),
Unaccompanied 782.5261723
Choruses, Sacred (Mixed voices, 8 parts),
Unaccompanied 782.52651722
Choruses, Sacred (Mixed voices, 8 parts),
Unaccompanied 782.52709429
Choruses, Sacred (Mixed voices, 8 parts),
Unaccompanied 782.5281723
Choruses, Sacred (Mixed voices, 8 parts),
Unaccompanied 782.5294
Choruses, Sacred (Mixed voices, 8 parts),
Unaccompanied 782.53232
Choruses, Sacred (Mixed voices, 8 parts),
Unaccompanied 782.532351726
Choruses, Sacred (Mixed voices, 8 parts),
Unaccompanied 782.53238
Choruses, Sacred (Mixed voices, 8 parts),
Unaccompanied 782.5324
Choruses, Sacred (Mixed voices, 8 parts),
Unaccompanied 782.5326
Choruses, Sacred (Mixed voices, 8 parts),
Unaccompanied 782.53261722

**Choruses, Sacred (Unison) with instrumental
ensemble**
Choruses, Sacred (Unison) with instrumental
ensemble 782.5251723
Choruses, Sacred (Unison) with instrumental
ensemble 782.5281723

**Choruses, Sacred (Unison) with keyboard
instrument**
Choruses, Sacred (Unison) with keyboard
instrument 782.52651582
Choruses, Sacred (Unison) with keyboard
instrument 782.5281722

Choruses, Sacred (Unison) with organ
Choruses, Sacred (Unison) with organ 782.525

Choruses, Sacred (Unison) with piano
Choruses, Sacred (Unison) with piano 782.6625
Choruses, Sacred (Unison) with piano, Juvenile
782.725

Choruses, Sacred (Women's voices)
Choruses, Sacred (Women's voices) 780

Choruses, Sacred (Women's voices) with harp
Choruses, Sacred (Women's voices) with harp
782.6251723

**Choruses, Sacred (Women's voices) with
instrumental ensemble**
Choruses, Sacred (Women's voices) with
instrumental ensemble 782.6251723
Choruses, Sacred (Women's voices) with
instrumental ensemble 782.6281723

**Choruses, Sacred (Women's voices) with
orchestra**
Choruses, Sacred (Women's voices) with
orchestra 782.625

Choruses, Sacred (Women's voices) with organ
Choruses, Sacred (Women's voices) with organ
782.6265
Choruses, Sacred (Women's voices) with organ
782.627
Choruses, Sacred (Women's voices) with organ
782.6281722
Choruses, Sacred (Women's voices) with organ
782.6281723
Choruses, Sacred (Women's voices) with organ
782.6294

Choruses, Sacred (Women's voices) with piano
Choruses, Sacred (Women's voices) with piano
782.6265

**Choruses, Sacred (Women's voices),
Unaccompanied**
Choruses, Sacred (Women's voices),
Unaccompanied 782.627
Choruses, Sacred (Women's voices),
Unaccompanied 782.62921722
Choruses, Sacred (Women's voices),
Unaccompanied 782.6625

**Choruses, Sacred (Women's voices), with
keyboard instrument**
Choruses, Sacred (Women's voices), with
keyboard instrument 782.6265

**Choruses, Sacred (Women's voices, 2 parts) with
handbells**
Choruses, Sacred (Women's voices, 2 parts) with
handbells 782.5265

**Choruses, Sacred (Women's voices, 2 parts) with
harp**
Choruses, Sacred (Women's voices, 2 parts) with
harp 782.6281723

**Choruses, Sacred (Women's voices, 2 parts) with
organ**
Choruses, Sacred (Women's voices, 2 parts) with
organ 782.626
Choruses, Sacred (Women's voices, 2 parts) with
organ 782.6265

**Choruses, Sacred (Women's voices, 2 parts) with
piano**
Choruses, Sacred (Women's voices, 2 parts) with
piano 782.6281723

**Choruses, Sacred (Women's voices, 3 parts) with
keyboard instrument**
Choruses, Sacred (Women's voices, 3 parts) with
keyboard instrument 782.6281722

**Choruses, Sacred (Women's voices, 3 parts) with
organ**
Choruses, Sacred (Women's voices, 3 parts) with
organ 782.6265
Choruses, Sacred (Women's voices, 3 parts) with
organ 782.6281723
Choruses, Sacred (Women's voices, 3 parts) with
organ 782.642

**Choruses, Sacred (Women's voices, 3 parts) with
piano**
Choruses, Sacred (Women's voices, 3 parts) with
piano 782.625
Choruses, Sacred (Women's voices, 3 parts) with
piano 782.6265
Choruses, Sacred (Women's voices, 3 parts) with
piano 782.627
Choruses, Sacred (Women's voices, 3 parts) with
piano 782.6281723
Choruses, Sacred (Women's voices, 3 parts) with
piano 782.642

**Choruses, Sacred (Women's voices, 3 parts),
Unaccompanied**
Choruses, Sacred (Women's voices, 3 parts),
Unaccompanied 782.6326

**Choruses, Sacred (Women's voices, 4 parts) with
harp**
Choruses, Sacred (Women's voices, 4 parts) with
harp 782.6281723

**Choruses, Sacred (Women's voices, 4 parts) with
piano**
Choruses, Sacred (Women's voices, 4 parts) with
piano 782.6281723

**Choruses, Sacred (Women's voices, 4 parts),
Unaccompanied**
Choruses, Sacred (Women's voices, 4 parts),
Unaccompanied 782.626
Choruses, Sacred (Women's voices, 4 parts),
Unaccompanied 782.628
Choruses, Sacred (Women's voices, 4 parts),
Unaccompanied 782.632231587

**Choruses, Sacred (Women's voices, 5 parts),
Unaccompanied**
Choruses, Sacred (Women's voices, 5 parts),
Unaccompanied 782.626

Choruses, Sacred, with instrumental ensemble
Choruses, Sacred, with instrumental ensemble
782.522
Choruses, Sacred, with instrumental ensemble
782.5281723

Choruses, Sacred, with piano
Choruses, Sacred, with piano 782.5281723

Choruses, Secular
Choruses, Secular 782.5

**Choruses, Secular (Children's voices) with
instrumental ensemble**
Choruses, Secular (Children's voices) with
instrumental ensemble 782.742
Choruses, Secular (Children's voices) with
instrumental ensemble 782.7642

Choruses, Secular (Children's voices) with piano
Choruses, Secular (Children's voices) with piano
782.71542
Choruses, Secular (Children's voices) with piano
782.7642
Choruses, Secular (Children's voices) with piano
782.7642162009429

**Choruses, Secular (Children's voices, 2 parts)
with piano**
Choruses, Secular (Children's voices, 2 parts)
with piano 782.742

**Choruses, Secular (Children's voices, 3 parts)
with double bass**
Choruses, Secular (Children's voices, 3 parts)
with double bass 782.7642

**Choruses, Secular (Children's voices, 3 parts)
with piano**
Choruses, Secular (Children's voices, 3 parts)
with piano 782.7642

**Choruses, Secular (Equal voices) with
instrumental ensemble**
Choruses, Secular (Equal voices) with
instrumental ensemble 782.6642

**Choruses, Secular (Men's voices) with
instrumental ensemble**
Choruses, Secular (Men's voices) with
instrumental ensemble 782.842

Choruses, Secular (Men's voices) with piano
Choruses, Secular (Men's voices) with piano
782.842

**Choruses, Secular (Men's voices, 2 parts) with
piano**
Choruses, Secular (Men's voices, 2 parts) with
piano 782.5421723

**Choruses, Secular (Men's voices, 4 parts) with
piano**
Choruses, Secular (Men's voices, 4 parts) with
piano 782.842
Choruses, Secular (Men's voices, 4 parts) with
piano 782.8421723

**Choruses, Secular (Men's voices, 4 parts),
Unaccompanied**
Choruses, Secular (Men's voices, 4 parts),
Unaccompanied 782.8
Choruses, Secular (Men's voices, 4 parts),
Unaccompanied 782.842

Choruses, Secular (Mixed voices) with flute
Choruses, Secular (Mixed voices) with flute
782.5

Choruses, Secular (Mixed voices) with instrumental ensemble

Choruses, Secular (Mixed voices) with instrumental ensemble 782.51556
Choruses, Secular (Mixed voices) with instrumental ensemble 782.542
Choruses, Secular (Mixed voices) with instrumental ensemble 782.548
Choruses, Secular (Mixed voices) with instrumental ensemble 783.42

Choruses, Secular (Mixed voices) with orchestra

Choruses, Secular (Mixed voices) with orchestra 782.524
Choruses, Secular (Mixed voices) with orchestra 782.542

Choruses, Secular (Mixed voices) with percussion

Choruses, Secular (Mixed voices) with percussion 782.5
Choruses, Secular (Mixed voices) with percussion 782.54216200981

Choruses, Secular (Mixed voices) with piano

Choruses, Secular (Mixed voices) with piano 782.5421723
Choruses, Secular (Mixed voices) with piano 783.12

Choruses, Secular (Mixed voices) with string orchestra

Choruses, Secular (Mixed voices) with string orchestra 782.542

Choruses, Secular (Mixed voices), Unaccompanied

Choruses, Secular (Mixed voices), Unaccompanied 782.5
Choruses, Secular (Mixed voices), Unaccompanied 782.542
Choruses, Secular (Mixed voices), Unaccompanied 782.542166

Choruses, Secular (Mixed voices, 2 parts) with piano

Choruses, Secular (Mixed voices, 2 parts) with piano 782.542166

Choruses, Secular (Mixed voices, 3 parts) with piano

Choruses, Secular (Mixed voices, 3 parts) with piano 782.542
Choruses, Secular (Mixed voices, 3 parts) with piano 782.5421542
Choruses, Secular (Mixed voices, 3 parts) with piano 782.5421620094796
Choruses, Secular (Mixed voices, 3 parts) with piano 782.542166

Choruses, Secular (Mixed voices, 3 parts), Unaccompanied

Choruses, Secular (Mixed voices, 3 parts), Unaccompanied 782.542166

Choruses, Secular (Mixed voices, 4 parts) with organ

Choruses, Secular (Mixed voices, 4 parts) with organ 782.542

Choruses, Secular (Mixed voices, 4 parts) with piano

Choruses, Secular (Mixed voices, 4 parts) with piano 782.542
Choruses, Secular (Mixed voices, 4 parts) with piano 782.5421542
Choruses, Secular (Mixed voices, 4 parts) with piano 782.5421587
Choruses, Secular (Mixed voices, 4 parts) with piano 782.542164
Choruses, Secular (Mixed voices, 4 parts) with piano 782.542166

Choruses, Secular (Mixed voices, 4 parts), Unaccompanied

Choruses, Secular (Mixed voices, 4 parts), Unaccompanied 782.5
Choruses, Secular (Mixed voices, 4 parts), Unaccompanied 782.542
Choruses, Secular (Mixed voices, 4 parts), Unaccompanied 782.542162009429
Choruses, Secular (Mixed voices, 4 parts), Unaccompanied 782.542162009711
Choruses, Secular (Mixed voices, 4 parts), Unaccompanied 782.542164
Choruses, Secular (Mixed voices, 4 parts), Unaccompanied 782.542166
Choruses, Secular (Mixed voices, 4 parts), Unaccompanied 782.5421723

Choruses, Secular (Mixed voices, 5 parts), Unaccompanied

Choruses, Secular (Mixed voices, 5 parts), Unaccompanied 782.51655
Choruses, Secular (Mixed voices, 5 parts), Unaccompanied 782.542

Choruses, Secular (Mixed voices, 6 parts) with orchestra

Choruses, Secular (Mixed voices, 6 parts) with orchestra 782.542

Choruses, Secular (Mixed voices, 6 parts), Unaccompanied

Choruses, Secular (Mixed voices, 6 parts), Unaccompanied 782.5
Choruses, Secular (Mixed voices, 6 parts), Unaccompanied 782.542

Choruses, Secular (Mixed voices, 7 parts), Unaccompanied

Choruses, Secular (Mixed voices, 7 parts), Unaccompanied 782.542

Choruses, Secular (Mixed voices, 8 parts), Unaccompanied

Choruses, Secular (Mixed voices, 8 parts), Unaccompanied 782.5
Choruses, Secular (Mixed voices, 8 parts), Unaccompanied 782.5241723
Choruses, Secular (Mixed voices, 8 parts), Unaccompanied 782.542
Choruses, Secular (Mixed voices, 8 parts), Unaccompanied 782.5421595
Choruses, Secular (Mixed voices, 8 parts), Unaccompanied 782.54215990973
Choruses, Secular (Mixed voices, 8 parts), Unaccompanied 782.5421723

Choruses, Secular (Mixed voices, 4 parts), Unaccompanied

Choruses, Secular (Mixed voices, 4 parts), Unaccompanied 782.542

Choruses, Secular (Mixed voices, 8 parts), Unaccompanied

Choruses, Secular (Mixed voices, 8 parts), Unaccompanied 782.5421723

Choruses, Secular (Unison) with piano

Choruses, Secular (Unison) with piano 782.542
Choruses, Secular (Unison) with piano 783.242

Choruses, Secular (Women's voices) with instrumental ensemble

Choruses, Secular (Women's voices) with instrumental ensemble 782.642
Choruses, Secular (Women's voices) with instrumental ensemble 782.64216209429

Choruses, Secular (Women's voices) with piano

Choruses, Secular (Women's voices) with piano 782.642
Choruses, Secular (Women's voices) with piano 782.6647

Choruses, Secular (Women's voices, 2 parts) with harp

Choruses, Secular (Women's voices, 2 parts) with harp 782.642

Choruses, Secular (Women's voices, 2 parts) with piano

Choruses, Secular (Women's voices, 2 parts) with piano 782.5421723
Choruses, Secular (Women's voices, 2 parts) with piano 782.642
Choruses, Secular (Women's voices, 2 parts) with piano 782.64216209429

Choruses, Secular (Women's voices, 3 parts) with piano

Choruses, Secular (Women's voices, 3 parts) with piano 782.642
Choruses, Secular (Women's voices, 3 parts) with piano 782.64216209415
Choruses, Secular (Women's voices, 3 parts) with piano 782.64216209429
Choruses, Secular (Women's voices, 3 parts) with piano 782.6421620944
Choruses, Secular (Women's voices, 3 parts) with piano 782.642164
Choruses, Secular (Women's voices, 3 parts) with piano 782.6642162009429

Choruses, Secular (Women's voices, 3 parts), Unaccompanied

Choruses, Secular (Women's voices, 3 parts), Unaccompanied 782.642
Choruses, Secular (Women's voices, 3 parts), Unaccompanied 782.64216200944

Choruses, Secular (Women's voices, 4 parts) with piano

Choruses, Secular (Women's voices, 4 parts) with piano 782.642
Choruses, Secular (Women's voices, 4 parts) with piano 782.64216209429
Choruses, Secular (Women's voices, 4 parts) with piano 782.642162097291

Choruses, Secular (Women's voices, 4 parts), Unaccompanied

Choruses, Secular (Women's voices, 4 parts), Unaccompanied 782.642

Choruses, Secular, with piano

Choruses, Secular, with piano 782.542

Christmas music

Christmas music 782.141723083
Christmas music 782.5231723
Christmas music 782.5241723
Christmas music 782.5251723
Christmas music 782.526
Christmas music 782.5261723
Christmas music 782.52651723
Christmas music 782.527
Christmas music 782.528
Christmas music 782.5281723
Christmas music 782.53232
Christmas music 782.532351723
Christmas music 782.5421723
Christmas music 782.6251723
Christmas music 782.6281723
Christmas music 782.7421723
Christmas music 782.8281723
Christmas music 782.8421723
Christmas music 783.68241723
Christmas music 783.87241723
Christmas music 784.68188417230834
Christmas music 784.928971723
Christmas music 785.8321921723
Christmas music 786.21723
Christmas music 786.591723

Church music

Church music, 17th century, Catalonia 782.53232

Clarinet and flute music

Clarinet and flute music 785.8192

Clarinet and piano music

Clarinet and piano music 788.62
Clarinet and piano music 788.62165
Clarinet and piano music 788.621894
Clarinet and piano music 788.7418964

Clarinet and piano music, Arranged

Clarinet and piano music, Arranged 788.62

Clarinet music

Clarinet music 788.62

Clarinet music, Arranged

Clarinet music, Arranged 788.621546
Clarinet music, Arranged 788.62164
Clarinet music, Arranged 788.62165
Clarinet music, Arranged 788.62166
Clarinet music, Arranged 788.62168

Clarinet with orchestra

Clarinet with orchestra 784.2862

Clarinet with string orchestra

Clarinet with string orchestra 784.72862

Clarinets (2) with string ensemble

Clarinets (2) with string ensemble 785.44197

Concerti grossi

Concerti grossi 784.24186

Concertos

Concertos 784

Concertos (Band), Arranged

Concertos (Band), Arranged 784.8186

Concertos (Clarinet with band)

Concertos (Clarinet with band) 784.82862186

Concertos (Clarinet)

Concertos (Clarinet) 788.62186

Concertos (Euphonium with band)

Concertos (Euphonium with band) 788.975186

Concertos (Flute with string orchestra)

Concertos (Flute with string orchestra) 784.72832186

Concertos (Harp with string orchestra)

Concertos (Harp with string orchestra) 787.95186

Concertos (Harpsichord with string orchestra)

Concertos (Harpsichord with string orchestra) 784.7264186
Concertos (Harpsichord with string orchestra) 787.95186

Concertos (Harpsichord)
Concertos (Harpsichord) 784.262186
Concertos (Horn)
Concertos (Horn) 788.94186
Concertos (Marimba)
Concertos (Marimba) 784.2843186
Concertos (Oboe with string orchestra)
Concertos (Oboe with string orchestra) 784.72852186
Concertos (Organ)
Concertos (Organ) 784.265186
Concertos (Piano with instrumental ensemble)
Concertos (Piano with instrumental ensemble) 784.3
Concertos (Piano with instrumental ensemble) 784.3262186
Concertos (Piano)
Concertos (Piano) 784.262186
Concertos (Piano) 784.3262186
Concertos (Piano) 785.62192186
Concertos (Piano) 786.2186
Concertos (String orchestra)
Concertos (String orchestra)
Concertos (String quartet with band)
Concertos (String quartet with band) 784.2186
Concertos (Viola da gamba with string orchestra)
Concertos (Viola da gamba with string orchestra) 784.72765186
Concertos (Violin and violoncello)
Concertos (Violin and violoncello) 784.24186
Concertos (Violin with string orchestra)
Concertos (Violin with string orchestra) 787.21861524
Concertos (Violin)
Concertos (Violin) 784.2184
Concertos (Violin) 784.272186
Concertos (Violin) 787.2186
Concertos (Violins (2) with string orchestra)
Concertos (Violins (2) with string orchestra) 784.724186
Concertos (Violoncello with instrumental ensemble)
Concertos (Violoncello with instrumental ensemble) 784.3
Concertos (Violoncello)
Concertos (Violoncello) 787.4186
Concertos (Wind ensemble)
Concertos (Wind ensemble) 785.43199186
Contemporary Christian music
Contemporary Christian music 782.527
Contemporary Christian music 782.725
Contrabassoon music
Contrabassoon music 788.59
Crusoe, Robinson (Fictitious character)
Crusoe, Robinson (Fictitious character) 782.14
Dance music
Dance music 786.4
Easter music
Easter music 782.141727083
Easter music 782.5261727
Easter music 782.5271727
Electric guitar music (Heavy metal)
Electric guitar music (Heavy metal) 783.242166
Electric guitar music (Rock)
Electric guitar music (Rock) 783.242166
Electronic and violoncello music
Electronic and violoncello music 787.4
Electronic keyboard
Electronic keyboard 785.62192
Electronic keyboard 786.2076
Electronic keyboard music
Electronic keyboard music 786.2
Electronic keyboard music 786.2076
Electronic keyboard music (4 hands)
Electronic keyboard music (4 hands) 785.62192
Electronic keyboard music, Arranged
Electronic keyboard music, Arranged 786
Electronic keyboard music, Arranged 786.59164
Electronic keyboard music, Arranged 786.59166
Electronic keyboard music, Arranged 786.591723
Electronic music
Electronic music 788.52
Electronic organ music, Arranged
Electronic organ music, Arranged 786
English horn and organ music
English horn and organ music 788.52
English horn and piano music
English horn and piano music 788.53
English horn and piano music, Arranged
English horn and piano music, Arranged 788.53
English horn with string ensemble
English horn with string ensemble 784.72853
English horn with string orchestra
English horn with string orchestra 784.72853
English horn with string orchestra 788.53
English horn, horn, oboe with string orchestra
English horn, horn, oboe with string orchestra 784.724
Epiphany music
Epiphany music 782.5261724
Epiphany music 782.5265
Euphonium music
Euphonium music 788.93
Euphoniums (4) with brass band, Arranged
Euphoniums (4) with brass band, Arranged 784.928975
Fanfares
Fanfares 785.5719518924
Fanfares 786.2
Fantasia
Fantasia 784.31894
Fiddle tunes
Fiddle tunes 787.21620941135
Fiddle tunes, Scotland 787.21629163
Flügelhorn with brass band
Flügelhorn with brass band 784.928971723
Flute
Flute 788.32076
Flute 788.32165076
Flute, Instruction and study 788.32076
Flute and harp with string orchestra, Arranged
Flute and harp with string orchestra, Arranged 784.724
Flute and piano music
Flute and piano music 788.32
Flute and piano music 788.32165
Flute and piano music 788.52
Flute music
Flute music 788.32
Flute music (Flutes (2)), Arranged
Flute music (Flutes (2)), Arranged 785.8321921723
Flute music, Arranged
Flute music, Arranged 788.321546
Flute music, Arranged 788.32164
Flute music, Arranged 788.32165
Flute music, Arranged 788.32166
Flute music, Arranged 788.32168
Flute with orchestra
Flute with orchestra 784.2832
Flute with orchestra 788.3218945
Folk music
Folk music, Cornwall 786.21620094237
Folk music, India 788.73
Folk music, Northumberland 788.49094288
Folk music, Scotland 787.21629163
Folk music, Shetland 787.21620941135
Folk songs
Folk songs 783.6642
Folk songs, Germany 783.242
Folk songs, Scotland 783.242
Folk songs, Catalan
Folk songs, Catalan 787.871825
Folk songs, English
Folk songs, English 782.542
Folk songs, English 782.642
Folk songs, English 782.842
Folk songs, English, Australia 782.542
Folk songs, English, British Columbia 782.542162009711
Folk songs, English, Canada 782.642
Folk songs, English, England 782.542
Folk songs, English, Ireland 782.542
Folk songs, English, Ireland 782.642
Folk songs, English, Ireland 782.64216209415
Folk songs, English, Ireland 783.242162009415
Folk songs, English, Mexico 782.542
Folk songs, English, Scotland 782.542
Folk songs, English, Scotland 783.242162009411
Folk songs, English, United States 782.542
Folk songs, English, Wales 782.542
Folk songs, English, Wales 783.242162009411
Folk songs, Estonian
Folk songs, Estonian 782.5421587
Folk songs, Finnish
Folk songs, Finnish 782.542
Folk songs, French
Folk songs, French 782.64216200944
Folk songs, French 782.6421620944
Folk songs, Italian
Folk songs, Italian 782.542
Folk songs, Latvian
Folk songs, Latvian 782.5421620094796
Folk songs, Portuguese
Folk songs, Portuguese, Brazil 782.54216200981
Folk songs, Russian
Folk songs, Russian 782.548
Folk songs, Scots
Folk songs, Scots, Scotland 783.242162009411
Folk songs, Spanish
Folk songs, Spanish, Cuba 782.642162097291
Folk songs, Swedish
Folk songs, Swedish 782.542
Folk songs, Welsh
Folk songs, Welsh 782.542
Folk songs, Welsh 782.542162009429
Folk songs, Welsh 782.6281723
Folk songs, Welsh 782.64216209429
Folk songs, Welsh 782.6642162009429
Folk songs, Welsh 782.7642162009429
Folk songs, Welsh, Wales 783.242162009411
Folk-rock music
Folk-rock music 783.242166
Funeral music
Funeral music 782.52417293
Funeral music, Spain 782.525
Galliards
Galliards 785.151882
Glees, catches, rounds, etc
Glees, catches, rounds, etc 782.5281723
Glees, catches, rounds, etc 782.742
Gloria in excelsis Deo (Music)
Gloria in excelsis Deo (Music) 782.53232
Good Friday music
Good Friday music 782.5231726
Gregorian chants
Gregorian chants 782.3222
Gregorian chants 782.53235
Guitar
Guitar 787.87076
Guitar 787.871252
Guitar 787.87165076
Guitar 787.87166076
Guitar 787.87168076
Guitar 787.87193166
Guitar, Instruction and study 787.87076
Guitar, Instruction and study 787.87168076
Guitar music
Guitar music 787.87
Guitar music 787.87076
Guitar music 787.87164
Guitar music 787.87168076
Guitar music 787.871825
Guitar music (Blues)
Guitar music (Blues) 783.2421643
Guitar music (Blues) 787.871643
Guitar music (Guitars (2))
Guitar music (Guitars (2)) 785.787192
Guitar music (Guitars (2)) 787.87
Guitar music (Jazz)
Guitar music (Jazz) 787.87165
Guitar music (Rock)
Guitar music (Rock) 782.421660263
Guitar music (Rock) 783.242166
Guitar music (Rock) 787.871643
Guitar music (Rock) 787.87166
Guitar music (Rock) 787.87193166
Guitar music, Arranged
Guitar music, Arranged 787.87
Guitar music, Arranged 787.87168
Harmonica and piano music
Harmonica and piano music 788.32
Harp music (Harps (2))
Harp music (Harps (2)) 785.795192
Harpsichord music
Harpsichord music 786
Harpsichord music 786.2
Harpsichord music 786.4
Harpsichord music 786.41827
Harpsichord music 786.41858
Harpsichord music 786.4186
Harpsichord music 786.5

Harpsichord music, Arranged
Harpsichord music, Arranged 786.4186
Heavy metal (Music)
Heavy metal (Music) 783.242166
Heavy metal (Music), 1991-2000 783.242166
Heavy metal (Music), 2001-2010 783.242166
Hercules (Roman mythology)
Hercules (Roman mythology) 783.8948
Hero (Greek mythology)
Hero (Greek mythology) 783.6648
Holy Week music
Holy Week music 782.522
Horn (Musical instrument)
Horn (Musical instrument) 788.94076
Horn (Musical instrument), Instruction and study
788.94076
Horn and organ music
Horn and organ music 788.941856
Horn music (Horns (2))
Horn music (Horns (2)) 785.94192
Horn music (Horns (2)) 788.94076
Horn music, Arranged
Horn music, Arranged 788.94168
Horn with string orchestra
Horn with string orchestra 784.728941896
Hymns
Hymns 782.527
Hymns 782.5271727
Hymns, English
Hymns, English 782.527
Hymns, English 782.627
Hymns, English 782.827
Hymns, English, Southern States 782.527
Hymns, English, United States 782.527
Hymns, English, United States 782.627
Hymns, English, Wales 782.627
Hymns, English, Juvenile 782.725
Hymns, German
Hymns, German 780
Hymns, Latin
Hymns, Latin 780
Hymns, Latin 782.526
Hymns, Latin 782.527
Hymns, Polish
Hymns, Polish 782.527
Hymns, Polish 783.42709438
Hymns, Welsh
Hymns, Welsh 782.52709429
Hymns, Welsh 782.627
Improvisation (Music)
Improvisation (Music) 786.165136
Improvisation (Music) 787.87165076
Improvisation (Music) 788.73136076
In nomine (Music)
In nomine (Music) 785.76194
Incidental music
Incidental music 782.51552
Incidental music 783.6642
Incidental music 784.21858
Instrumental ensembles
Instrumental ensembles 784.3
Instrumental ensembles 785
Instrumental ensembles 785.22183
Instrumental ensembles 785.32199
Instrumental ensembles 785.42199
Instrumental ensembles 785.4219918846
Instrumental ensembles 785.57
Instrumental music
Instrumental music, Spain 784
Instrumental music, 16th century, Naples 787.83
Intabulations (Organ)
Intabulations (Organ) 786.5
Islamic music
Islamic music, British Isles 782.54217700941
Jacobites
Jacobites 782.842
Jazz
Jazz 781.65
Jazz 781.651643
Jazz 781.654
Jazz 784.18846165
Jazz 786.2165
Jazz 787.2165
Jazz 787.87165
Jazz 788.32165
Jazz 788.62165
Jazz 788.73165
Jazz 788.74165
Jazz 788.92165

Jazz, Instruction and study 781.65076
Jazz music
Jazz music 788.32165076
Jazz vocals
Jazz vocals 782.51655
Jazz vocals 783.242165
Keyboard instrument
Keyboard instrument 786.165136
Keyboard instrument music
Keyboard instrument music 786
Keyboard instrument music 786.2
Keyboard instrument music 786.5
Keyboard instruments
Keyboard instruments, Instruction and study
786.41858
Lamentations of Jeremiah (Music)
Lamentations of Jeremiah (Music)
782.53241726
Leander (Greek mythology)
Leander (Greek mythology) 783.6648
Litanies (Music)
Litanies (Music) 782.522
Lord's prayer (Music)
Lord's prayer (Music) 782.526
Lord's prayer (Music) 782.5295
Lord's prayer (Music) 784.9
Love songs
Love songs 783.242164
Lullabies
Lullabies 782.5251723
Lullabies 782.642
Lullabies, Japanese
Lullabies, Japanese 782.642
Lullabies, Welsh
Lullabies, Welsh 782.6642162009429
Lute music
Lute music 787.83
Lute music, 16th century 787.83
Madrigals, English
Madrigals, English 785.76195
Madrigals, Italian
Madrigals, Italian 782.543
Madrigals, Italian 783.1343
Madrigals, Italian 783.136643
Magnificat (Music)
Magnificat (Music) 782.53232
Magnificat (Music) 782.5325
Magnificat (Music) 782.5326
Magnificat (Music) 782.8326
Magnificat (Music) 786.518992
Marches
Marches 785.91951897
Marches (Band)
Marches (Band) 784.8
Marches (Band) 784.81897
Marches (Band), Arranged
Marches (Band), Arranged 784.81897
Marches (Organ), Arranged
Marches (Organ), Arranged 786.218971587
Marches (Percussion ensemble)
Marches (Percussion ensemble), Juvenile
784.6818970834
Marches (Piano)
Marches (Piano) 786.218971587
Masques with music
Masques with music 782.15
Masques with music 783.6642
Masses
Masses 780
Masses 782.53232
Masses, 17th century 782.53232
Masses, Unaccompanied
Masses, Unaccompanied 782.53232
Memorial music
Memorial music 782.542
Microtonal music
Microtonal music 785.71991269
Minuets
Minuets 784.818835
Minuets 786.41827
Monferrinas
Monferrinas 786.2
Monologues with music (Instrumental ensemble)
Monologues with music (Instrumental ensemble)
783.96
Monologues with music (Instrumental ensemble)
783.9618945

Monologues with music (Instrumental ensemble)
785.43195
Monologues with music (Orchestra)
Monologues with music (Orchestra) 783.96
Monologues with music (Piano)
Monologues with music (Piano) 783.96
Monologues with music (Viola)
Monologues with music (Viola) 787.3
Monologues with music (Violoncello)
Monologues with music (Violoncello) 783.96
Motets
Motets 780
Motets 782.526
Motets 782.5261722
Motets 782.5261723
Motets 782.5261724
Motets 782.5261727
Motets 782.5261728
Motets 782.52617293
Motets 782.5294
Motets 782.53232
Motets 782.532351722
Motets 782.532351723
Motets 782.5323517293
Motets 782.626
Motets 783.1226
Motets 783.1242
Motets 783.1326
Motets 783.8925
Motets 783.8926
Motets 785.836195
Motets 785.836197
Motion picture music
Motion picture music 782.71542
Motion picture music 783.2421542
Motion picture music 783.242164
Motion picture music 786.21542
Motion picture music 787.21542
Motion picture music 787.31542
Motion picture music 787.41542
Motion picture music 788.62
Motion picture music 788.921542
Motion picture music, Arranged
Motion picture music, Arranged 782.5421542
Motion picture music, Arranged 786.21542
Music
Music, Catalonia 782.53232
Music, Moxos 780
Music, 17th century 780.9032
Music, 18th century 780.9032
Music, 18th century, Meiningen 782.52417293
Music, Facsimiles 782.1
Music theory
Music theory 781.65076
Music theory 787.87076
Musical
Musical, Juvenile 782.141723083
Musical analysis
Musical analysis 780
Musical instruments
Musical instruments 781.65076
Musicals
Musicals 782.14
Musicals 782.14083
Musicals 782.141723083
Musicals 782.542
Musicals 782.642
Musicals 782.642164
Musicals 782.7
Musicals 782.7421723
Musicals 783.242164
Musicals 783.642
Musicals 783.842
Musicals 785.594195
Musicals 786
Musicals 786.2
Musicals 786.59164
Musicals 787.2164
Musicals 788.32164
Musicals 788.62164
Musicals 788.73164
Musicals 788.92164
Musicals, Excerpts 782.140264
Musicals, Juvenile 782.14083
Musicals, Juvenile 782.141723083
Musicals, Juvenile 782.41083
National songs
National songs, United States 782.54215990973
Niobe (Greek mythology)
Niobe (Greek mythology) 788.52

Nonets (Bassoon, clarinet, flute, horn, oboe, violin, viola, violoncello, double bass)
Nonets (Bassoon, clarinet, flute, horn, oboe, violin, viola, violoncello, double bass)
785.42199

Northumbrian small pipe music, Arranged
Northumbrian small pipe music, Arranged
788.49094288

Nunc dimittis (Music)
Nunc dimittis (Music)   782.5326
Nunc dimittis (Music)   782.8326

Nursery rhymes, English
Nursery rhymes, English   782.7642

Oboe
Oboe   788.52076
Oboe, Instruction and study   788.52076

Oboe and continuo music
Oboe and continuo music   788.52076

Oboe and electronic music
Oboe and electronic music   788.52

Oboe and organ music
Oboe and organ music   788.52

Oboe and organ music, Arranged
Oboe and organ music, Arranged   785

Oboe and piano music
Oboe and piano music   788.32
Oboe and piano music   788.52
Oboe and piano music   788.521894

Oboe and piano music, Arranged
Oboe and piano music, Arranged   788.52

Oboe and vibraphone music
Oboe and vibraphone music   785.56192

Oboe music
Oboe music   788.52

Oboe with band, Arranged
Oboe with band, Arranged   784.82852

Oboe with string orchestra
Oboe with string orchestra   788.521858

Octets (Bassoon, clarinet, flute, horn, violin, viola, violoncello, double bass)
Octets (Bassoon, clarinet, flute, horn, violin, viola, violoncello, double bass)   785.42198

Octets (Piano, bassoon, clarinet, flute, horn, viola, violoncello, double bass)
Octets (Piano, bassoon, clarinet, flute, horn, viola, violoncello, double bass)   785.22198

Offertories (Music)
Offertories (Music)   782.532351722
Offertories (Music)   782.532351723

Operas
Operas   782.1
Operas   782.10265
Operas   782.5
Operas   782.542
Operas   782.642
Operas   783.342
Operas   783.3420945
Operas   783.5420945
Operas   783.6642
Operas   783.8742
Operas   783.8842
Operas   784.21556
Operas   785.28193
Operas   785.62192
Operas   785.7194
Operas   785.72192183
Operas   785.8193
Operas   785.85193
Operas   786.2
Operas   787.2165
Operas   787.4
Operas   787.65
Operas   788.32165
Operas   788.521894
Operas   788.62165
Operas   788.73165
Operas   788.74165
Operas   788.92165
Operas, 19th century, Russia   783.8742
Operas, 20th century, Russia   783.8742

Oratorios
Oratorios   782.523
Oratorios   782.5231723
Oratorios   782.5231726
Oratorios   782.625
Oratorios   782.6625
Oratorios   782.8253
Oratorios   784.218926

Orchestral music
Orchestral music   784.2
Orchestral music   784.21556
Orchestral music   784.21825
Orchestral music   784.218885
Orchestral music   784.218926
Orchestral music   784.218928
Orchestral music   784.218964
Orchestral music   784.218966
Orchestral music   784.724

Orchestral music, Arranged
Orchestral music, Arranged   784.2
Orchestral music, Arranged   784.21825
Orchestral music, Arranged   784.218844

Organ music
Organ music   786
Organ music   786.5
Organ music   786.51858
Organ music   786.51872
Organ music   786.518992
Organ music, 21st century   786.5

Organ music (Organs (2))
Organ music (Organs (2))   785.6519218945

Organ music, Arranged
Organ music, Arranged   786.2
Organ music, Arranged   786.5
Organ music, Arranged   786.51587

Overtures
Overtures   784.218926

Overtures (Band)
Overtures (Band)   784.818926

Pantomimes with music
Pantomimes with music   782.14

Part songs
Part songs   782.642

Part songs, English
Part songs, English   782.542
Part songs, English   782.642
Part songs, English   782.7642

Part songs, German
Part songs, German   783

Part songs, Italian
Part songs, Italian   782.543
Part songs, Italian   783.1343

Part songs, Polish
Part songs, Polish   782.527

Part songs, Sacred
Part songs, Sacred   782.542

Passion music
Passion music   780
Passion music   782.523

Pastoral music (Secular)
Pastoral music (Secular)   782.1

Patriotic music
Patriotic music   783.342
Patriotic music, United States   782.54215990973

Pavans
Pavans   785.151882
Pavans   785.76195
Pavans   785.7619518823

Pentecost Festival music
Pentecost Festival music   782.52617293
Pentecost Festival music   782.5323517293

Percussion and piano music
Percussion and piano music   785.39192

Percussion and violoncello music
Percussion and violoncello music   785.58192

Percussion ensembles
Percussion ensembles   785.68194
Percussion ensembles, Juvenile   784.680834
Percussion ensembles, Juvenile   784.68188417230834
Percussion ensembles, Juvenile   784.6818880834

Percussion with orchestra
Percussion with orchestra   784.268

Piano
Piano   785.62192
Piano   786.2076
Piano   786.21643076
Piano   786.218949
Piano   786.2193
Piano, Examinations, questions, etc, Great Britain   786.2
Piano, Instruction and study   786.2076
Piano, Instruction and study   786.21423
Piano, Instruction and study   786.2193

Piano music
Piano music   786.2
Piano music   786.20262
Piano music   786.2076
Piano music   786.2165
Piano music   786.21723
Piano music   786.21858
Piano music   786.21874
Piano music   786.218846
Piano music   786.21888
Piano music   786.218928
Piano music   786.21894
Piano music   786.218949
Piano music   786.218966
Piano music   786.4
Piano music   786.418846
Piano music   796.2
Piano music, 19th century, Russia   786.2
Piano music, 19th century, Spain   786.20946
Piano music, 20th century, Spain   786.20946
Piano music, Juvenile   786.2

Piano music (4 hands)
Piano music (4 hands)   785.62192

Piano music (4 hands), Arranged
Piano music (4 hands), Arranged   785.62192

Piano music (Blues)
Piano music (Blues)   786.21643076

Piano music (Jazz)
Piano music (Jazz)   786.2165
Piano music (Jazz)   786.21723165

Piano music (Pianos (2))
Piano music (Pianos (2))   785.62192
Piano music (Pianos (2))   786.418846

Piano music (Pianos (2)), Arranged
Piano music (Pianos (2)), Arranged   785.62192

Piano music (Pianos (2), 8 hands)
Piano music (Pianos (2), 8 hands)
785.6219218947

Piano music (Rock)
Piano music (Rock)   786.2
Piano music (Rock)   786.2166

Piano music, Arranged
Piano music, Arranged   785.62192
Piano music, Arranged   786
Piano music, Arranged   786.2
Piano music, Arranged   786.21542
Piano music, Arranged   786.21546
Piano music, Arranged   786.21556
Piano music, Arranged   786.21620094237
Piano music, Arranged   786.2164
Piano music, Arranged   786.2165
Piano music, Arranged   786.2166
Piano music, Arranged   786.21723
Piano music, Arranged   786.218846

Piano quartets
Piano quartets   785.28193
Piano quartets   785.281941

Piano quartets, Arranged
Piano quartets, Arranged   785.28194

Piano trios
Piano trios   785.28193

Piano trios, Arranged
Piano trios, Arranged   785.28193

Piano with orchestra
Piano with orchestra   784.2621894

Piano, saxophone, percussion with orchestra
Piano, saxophone, percussion with orchestra
784.24

Piccolo and piano music
Piccolo and piano music   788.33

Piccolo music
Piccolo music   788.33

Polkas
Polkas   784.218844
Polkas   785.719418844

Polyphonic chansons
Polyphonic chansons   782.526
Polyphonic chansons   782.543

Popular instrumental music
Popular instrumental music   782.14
Popular instrumental music   786.2
Popular instrumental music   786.21542
Popular instrumental music   786.2164
Popular instrumental music   786.2165
Popular instrumental music   787.2
Popular instrumental music   787.21542
Popular instrumental music   787.2164
Popular instrumental music   787.3
Popular instrumental music   787.31542
Popular instrumental music   787.4
Popular instrumental music   787.41542
Popular instrumental music   788.32164

Popular instrumental music   788.62164
Popular instrumental music   788.73164
Popular instrumental music   788.921542
Popular instrumental music   788.92164
Popular instrumental music, 2001-2010
                                    787.87164
Popular instrumental music, 2001-2010
                                    788.32166
Popular instrumental music, 2001-2010
                                    788.62166
Popular instrumental music, 2001-2010
                                    788.73166

Popular music
Popular music   782.742
Popular music   783.1242164
Popular music   783.242
Popular music   783.2421542
Popular music   783.2421546
Popular music   783.242164
Popular music   783.242166
Popular music   783.642164
Popular music   783.642166
Popular music   783.842164
Popular music   786
Popular music   786.21542
Popular music   786.2164
Popular music   786.2166
Popular music   786.59164
Popular music   786.591723
Popular music   787.87076
Popular music, Ireland   783.242162009415
Popular music, 1911-1920   782.542164
Popular music, 1921-1930   782.542164
Popular music, 1931-1940   782.542164
Popular music, 1961-1970   782.542166
Popular music, 1961-1970   783.242164
Popular music, 1961-1970   783.242166
Popular music, 1961-1970   786.2164
Popular music, 1971-1980   782.542
Popular music, 1971-1980   782.642
Popular music, 1971-1980   783.242164
Popular music, 1971-1980   783.242166
Popular music, 1971-1980   785.594195
Popular music, 1981-1990   783.242166
Popular music, 1991-2000   783.242164
Popular music, 1991-2000   783.242166
Popular music, 1991-2000   786.2164
Popular music, 2001-2010   782.5421542
Popular music, 2001-2010   782.542164
Popular music, 2001-2010   783.242164
Popular music, 2001-2010   783.242166
Popular music, 2001-2010   783.642164
Popular music, 2001-2010   787.87166

Priam (Greek mythology)
Priam (Greek mythology)   782.1

Propers (Music)
Propers (Music)   782.53235

Psalms (Music)
Psalms (Music)   782.324
Psalms (Music)   782.524
Psalms (Music)   782.526
Psalms (Music)   782.5265
Psalms (Music)   782.527
Psalms (Music)   782.5294
Psalms (Music)   782.52951587
Psalms (Music)   782.5325
Psalms (Music)   782.542
Psalms (Music)   782.6294
Psalms (Music)   783.126648
Psalms (Music)   783.1326
Psalms (Music)   783.88294
Psalms (Music)   783.8925

Quartets (Bassoon, clarinet, oboe, continuo)
Quartets (Bassoon, clarinet, oboe, continuo)
                                    785.26194

Quartets (Bassoon, clarinet, violin, viola)
Quartets (Bassoon, clarinet, violin, viola)
                                    785.44194

Quartets (Bassoon, oboe, viola, violoncello)
Quartets (Bassoon, oboe, viola, violoncello)
                                    785.44194

Quartets (Bassoon, oboe, violin, viola)
Quartets (Bassoon, oboe, violin, viola)
                                    785.44194

Quartets (Bassoon, oboe, violin, violoncello)
Quartets (Bassoon, oboe, violin, violoncello)
                                    785.44194

Quartets (Bassoon, violin, viola, violoncello)
Quartets (Bassoon, violin, viola, violoncello)
                                    785.44194

Quartets (Bassoon, violins (2), continuo)
Quartets (Bassoon, violins (2), continuo)
                                    785.24194

Quartets (Bassoon, violins (2), violoncello)
Quartets (Bassoon, violins (2), violoncello)
                                    785.44194

Quartets (Clarinet, violin, viola, violoncello)
Quartets (Clarinet, violin, viola, violoncello)
                                    785.44194

Quartets (Guitar, violin, viola, violoncello)
Quartets (Guitar, violin, viola, violoncello)
                                    785.7194

Quartets (Harpsichord, violins (2), violone)
Quartets (Harpsichord, violins (2), violone)
                                    785.28194

Quartets (Oboe, viola, violoncellos (2))
Quartets (Oboe, viola, violoncellos (2))
                                    785.44194

Quartets (Oboe, violin, viola, violoncello)
Quartets (Oboe, violin, viola, violoncello)
                                    785.44194

Quartets (Oboe, violin, violoncellos (2))
Quartets (Oboe, violin, violoncellos (2))
                                    785.44194

Quartets (Piano, clarinet, viola, violoncello)
Quartets (Piano, clarinet, viola, violoncello)
                                    785.24194

Quartets (Piano, clarinet, violin, violoncello)
Quartets (Piano, clarinet, violin, violoncello)
                                    785.2419418885

Quartets (Piano, oboe, percussion, violoncello)
Quartets (Piano, oboe, percussion, violoncello)
                                    785.34194

Quartets (Unspecified instruments (4))
Quartets (Unspecified instruments (4))   782.526
Quartets (Unspecified instruments (4))   785.14

Quartets (Violins (2), viola, continuo)
Quartets (Violins (2), viola, continuo)785.28194
Quartets (Violins (2), viola, continuo)
                                    785.281941858

Quartets (Violins (2), violoncello, continuo)
Quartets (Violins (2), violoncello, continuo)
                                    785.28194183

Quintets (Bandoneon, piano, guitar, violin, double bass)
Quintets (Bandoneon, piano, guitar, violin,
double bass)   785.2819518885

Quintets (Clarinet, flute, harp, violin, violoncello)
Quintets (Clarinet, flute, harp, violin,
violoncello)   785.44195

Quintets (Flute, oboe, violas (2), violoncello)
Quintets (Flute, oboe, violas (2), violoncello)
                                    785.44195

Quintets (Guitar, violins (2), viola, violoncello)
Quintets (Guitar, violins (2), viola, violoncello)
                                    785.7195

Quintets (Harpsichord, saxophones (4))
Quintets (Harpsichord, saxophones (4))
                                    785.261951858

Quintets (Horn, violin, violas (2), violoncello)
Quintets (Horn, violin, violas (2), violoncello)
                                    785.45195

Quintets (Oboe, violins (2), viola, violoncello)
Quintets (Oboe, violins (2), viola, violoncello)
                                    785.44195

Quintets (Organ, violins (2), viole da gamba (2))
Quintets (Organ, violins (2), viole da gamba (2))
785.281951858

Quintets (Piano, clarinet, horn, violin, violoncello)
Quintets (Piano, clarinet, horn, violin,
violoncello)   785.22195

Quintets (Piano, flute, oboe, violin, violoncello)
Quintets (Piano, flute, oboe, violin, violoncello)
                                    785.24195

Quintets (Piano, violin, viola, violoncello, double bass)
Quintets (Piano, violin, viola, violoncello,
double bass)   785.28195

Quintets (Recorder, violins (2), viola, violoncello)
Quintets (Recorder, violins (2), viola,
violoncello)   785.44195

Quintets (Trumpets (4), timpani)
Quintets (Trumpets (4), timpani)
                                    785.5719518924

Quintets (Unspecified instruments (4), continuo)
Quintets (Unspecified instruments (4), continuo)
785.25193

Quintets (Unspecified instruments (5))
Quintets (Unspecified instruments (5))   782.526
Quintets (Unspecified instruments (5))
                                    785.151882

Quintets (Violins (2), violas (2), violoncello)
Quintets (Violins (2), violas (2), violoncello)
                                    785.7195

Rap (Music)
Rap (Music)   783.242164

Rat Pack (Entertainers)
Rat Pack (Entertainers)   783.842164

Recorded accompaniments
Recorded accompaniments   782.523

Recorded accompaniments (Clarinet)
Recorded accompaniments (Clarinet)   788.62
Recorded accompaniments (Clarinet) 788.62164
Recorded accompaniments (Clarinet) 788.62165

Recorded accompaniments (Euphonium)
Recorded accompaniments (Euphonium) 788.93

Recorded accompaniments (Flute)
Recorded accompaniments (Flute)   788.32
Recorded accompaniments (Flute)   788.321546
Recorded accompaniments (Flute)   788.32164
Recorded accompaniments (Flute)   788.32165

Recorded accompaniments (Guitar)
Recorded accompaniments (Guitar) 783.242166

Recorded accompaniments (Oboe)
Recorded accompaniments (Oboe)   788.52

Recorded accompaniments (Piano)
Recorded accompaniments (Piano)   783.242164
Recorded accompaniments (Piano)   783.242166
Recorded accompaniments (Piano)   785.62192
Recorded accompaniments (Piano)   786.2166
Recorded accompaniments (Piano)   786.21888

Recorded accompaniments (Saxophone)
Recorded accompaniments (Saxophone)   788.7
Recorded accompaniments (Saxophone) 788.73
Recorded accompaniments (Saxophone)
                                    788.73076
Recorded accompaniments (Saxophone)
                                    788.731546
Recorded accompaniments (Saxophone)
                                    788.73164
Recorded accompaniments (Saxophone)
                                    788.73165
Recorded accompaniments (Saxophone)
                                    788.74165

Recorded accompaniments (Trombone)
Recorded accompaniments (Trombone) 788.93

Recorded accompaniments (Trumpet)
Recorded accompaniments (Trumpet)   788.92
Recorded accompaniments (Trumpet)
                                    788.921546
Recorded accompaniments (Trumpet)788.92164
Recorded accompaniments (Trumpet)788.92165

Recorded accompaniments (Viola)
Recorded accompaniments (Viola)   787.3

Recorded accompaniments (Violin)
Recorded accompaniments (Violin)   787.2
Recorded accompaniments (Violin)   787.21546
Recorded accompaniments (Violin)   787.2164
Recorded accompaniments (Violin)   787.2165

Recorded accompaniments (Violoncello)
Recorded accompaniments (Violoncello) 787.4

Recorded accompaniments (Voice)
Recorded accompaniments (Voice)   783.642
Recorded accompaniments (Voice) 783.6421643
Recorded accompaniments (Voice)   783.842
Recorded accompaniments (Voice) 783.842164

Recorder
Recorder   788.36076
Recorder   788.365076

Recorder (Musical instrument)
Recorder (Musical instrument), Juvenile
                                    788.36076
Recorder (Musical instrument), Juvenile
                                    788.365076

Recorder and continuo music
Recorder and continuo music   783.6848

Recorder and guitar music
Recorder and guitar music   785.44192

Recorder and piano music
Recorder and piano music   788.36
Recorder and piano music   788.36076
Recorder and piano music   788.364
Recorder and piano music   788.364076
Recorder and piano music   788.365076

Recorder and piano music, Arranged
Recorder and piano music, Arranged 788.36076

Recorder choir music
Recorder choir music 788.365076
Recorder ensembles
Recorder ensembles 785.836
Recorder ensembles, Arranged
Recorder ensembles, Arranged 788.36076
Recorder with orchestra
Recorder with orchestra 784.2836
Regina Caeli laetare (Music)
Regina Caeli laetare (Music) 782.5265
Remembrance Sunday
Remembrance Sunday 782.5265
Requiems
Requiems 782.53238
Responses (Music)
Responses (Music) 782.62921722
Responses (Music) 782.632231587
Responses (Music) 782.6326
Rhapsodies (Music)
Rhapsodies (Music) 783.9618945
Rhapsodies (Music) 785.6519218945
Rhythm and blues music
Rhythm and blues music 783.2421643
Rhythm and blues music 783.6421643
Rock music
Rock music 782.421660263
Rock music 783.242164
Rock music 783.242166
Rock music 783.642166
Rock music 786.2166
Rock music 787.871643
Rock music 787.87166
Rock music, 1951-1960 783.242166
Rock music, 1961-1970 782.542
Rock music, 1961-1970 782.542166
Rock music, 1961-1970 782.642
Rock music, 1961-1970 783.2421640264
Rock music, 1961-1970 783.242166
Rock music, 1971-1980 783.2421640264
Rock music, 1971-1980 783.242166
Rock music, 1971-1980 787.87166
Rock music, 1981-1990 783.242166
Rock music, 1981-1990 783.2421660264
Rock music, 1991-2000 783.242166
Rock music, 1991-2000 783.2421660264
Rock music, 2001-2010 783.242166
Rock music, 2001-2010 786.2166
Rock music, 2001-2010 786.59166
Rock music, 2001-2010 787.2166
Rock music, 2001-2010 787.87166
Rock music, 2001-2010 788.32166
Rock music, 2001-2010 788.62166
Rock music, 2001-2010 788.73166
Romances (Music)
Romances (Music) 787.4
Rondos (Band), Arranged
Rondos (Band), Arranged 784.81824
Rondos (Bassoon and piano)
Rondos (Bassoon and piano) 788.581824
Rondos (Piano)
Rondos (Piano) 786.21824
Rondos (Piano) 786.21852
Rondos (String trio)
Rondos (String trio) 785.71931824
Rumbas
Rumbas 785
Sacred monologues with music (Chorus with viola)
Sacred monologues with music (Chorus with viola) 782.525
Sacred monologues with music (Chorus)
Sacred monologues with music (Chorus) 782.525
Sacred musicals
Sacred musicals, Juvenile 782.141727083
Sacred songs
Sacred songs 780
Sacred songs (High voice) with instrumental ensemble
Sacred songs (High voice) with instrumental ensemble 783.87241723
Sacred songs (High voice) with keyboard instrument
Sacred songs (High voice) with keyboard instrument 783.6642
Sacred songs (Low voice) with continuo
Sacred songs (Low voice) with continuo 783.8925

Sacred songs (Low voice) with continuo 783.8926
Sacred songs (Low voice) with instrumental ensemble
Sacred songs (Low voice) with instrumental ensemble 783.68241723
Sacred songs (Low voice) with instrumental ensemble 783.6842
Sacred songs (Low voice) with instrumental ensemble 783.88294
Sacred songs (Low voice) with instrumental ensemble 783.8925
Sacred songs (Medium voice) with instrumental ensemble
Sacred songs (Medium voice) with instrumental ensemble 783.88294
Sacred songs (Medium voice) with string orchestra
Sacred songs (Medium voice) with string orchestra 783.1226
Sacred songs with piano
Sacred songs with piano 783.242
Sacred vocal duets
Sacred vocal duets 780
Sacred vocal duets with chamber orchestra
Sacred vocal duets with chamber orchestra 782.532351726
Sacred vocal duets with continuo
Sacred vocal duets with continuo 782.526
Sacred vocal duets with continuo 783.1226
Sacred vocal duets with continuo 783.1242
Sacred vocal duets with continuo 783.126625
Sacred vocal duets with continuo 783.128925
Sacred vocal duets with harp
Sacred vocal duets with harp 782.6281723
Sacred vocal duets with orchestra
Sacred vocal duets with orchestra 783.1225
Sacred vocal duets with piano
Sacred vocal duets with piano 782.6281723
Sacred vocal ensembles, Unaccompanied
Sacred vocal ensembles, Unaccompanied 782.526
Sacred vocal music
Sacred vocal music, 16th century 782.522
Sacred vocal music, 17th century, England 782.526
Sacred vocal music, 19th century, Southern States 782.527
Sacred vocal trios
Sacred vocal trios 780
Sacred vocal trios with instrumental ensemble
Sacred vocal trios with instrumental ensemble 783.1326
Sainetes
Sainetes 782.1
Saint Cecilia's Day
Saint Cecilia's Day 782.53232
Salve Regina (Music)
Salve Regina (Music) 782.526
Salve Regina (Music) 782.5324
Salve Regina (Music) 783.1225
Salve Regina (Music) 783.8926
Sanctus (Music)
Sanctus (Music), 15th century 782.53232
Saxophone
Saxophone 788.73136076
Saxophone and piano music
Saxophone and piano music 788.7
Saxophone and piano music 788.73
Saxophone and piano music 788.73076
Saxophone and piano music 788.73143
Saxophone and piano music 788.731643
Saxophone and piano music 788.73165
Saxophone and piano music 788.74165
Saxophone and piano music 788.7418964
Saxophone ensembles
Saxophone ensembles 785.87
Saxophone music
Saxophone music 788.73
Saxophone music, Arranged
Saxophone music, Arranged 788.73
Saxophone music, Arranged 788.731546
Saxophone music, Arranged 788.73164
Saxophone music, Arranged 788.73165
Saxophone music, Arranged 788.73166
Saxophone music, Arranged 788.73168
Saxophone music, Arranged 788.74165
Saxophone music, Arranged 788.74168

Science fiction
Science fiction 783.242164
Sea songs
Sea songs 782.5421595
Sea songs 788.921595
Seasons
Seasons 782.642
September 11 Terrorist Attacks, 2001
September 11 Terrorist Attacks, 2001 786.2
Septets (Bassoon, clarinet, horn, violin, viola, violoncello, double bass)
Septets (Bassoon, clarinet, horn, violin, viola, violoncello, double bass) 785.42197
Septets (Clarinets (2), violins (3), viola, violoncello)
Septets (Clarinets (2), violins (3), viola, violoncello) 785.44197
Septets (Trumpet, violins (2), violas (3), continuo)
Septets (Trumpet, violins (2), violas (3), continuo) 785.22197
Sequences (Music)
Sequences (Music) 782.5
Service books (Music)
Service books (Music) 782.53232
Sextets (Clarinet, flute, violins (2), viola, violoncello)
Sextets (Clarinet, flute, violins (2), viola, violoncello) 785.44196
Sextets (Piano, clarinet, flute, marimba, violin, violoncello)
Sextets (Piano, clarinet, flute, marimba, violin, violoncello) 785.34196
Sextets (Piano, clarinet, guitar, violin, viola, violoncello)
Sextets (Piano, clarinet, guitar, violin, viola, violoncello) 785.24196
Sextets (Piano, clarinet, horn, violin, viola, violoncello)
Sextets (Piano, clarinet, horn, violin, viola, violoncello) 785.22196
Sextets (Piano, clarinet, trumpet, violin, viola, violoncello)
Sextets (Piano, clarinet, trumpet, violin, viola, violoncello) 785.22196
Sextets (Unspecified instruments (6))
Sextets (Unspecified instruments (6)) 782.526
Sextets (Violins (2), violas (2), viola da gamba, continuo)
Sextets (Violins (2), violas (2), viola da gamba, continuo) 785.28196
Sextets (Violins (2), viols (3), continuo)
Sextets (Violins (2), viols (3), continuo) 785.28196
Shape-note hymnals
Shape-note hymnals 782.527
Sight-reading (Music)
Sight-reading (Music) 786.21423
Sight-reading (Music) 787.41423
Sight-singing
Sight-singing 783.21423
Snare drum
Snare drum 786.94076
Snare drum and piano music
Snare drum and piano music 786.94076
Snare drum music
Snare drum music 786.94076
Solo cantatas, Sacred (High voice)
Solo cantatas, Sacred (High voice) 783.6624
Solo cantatas, Sacred (High voice) 783.6724
Solo cantatas, Sacred (High voice) 783.87241723
Solo cantatas, Sacred (Low voice)
Solo cantatas, Sacred (Low voice) 783.68241723
Solo cantatas, Sacred (Low voice) 783.8624
Solo cantatas, Sacred (Medium voice)
Solo cantatas, Sacred (Medium voice) 783.6724
Solo cantatas, Sacred (Medium voice) 783.8824
Solo cantatas, Secular (High voice)
Solo cantatas, Secular (High voice) 783.348
Solo cantatas, Secular (High voice) 783.6648
Solo cantatas, Secular (High voice) with instrumental ensemble
Solo cantatas, Secular (High voice) with instrumental ensemble 783.348
Solo cantatas, Secular (High voice) with instrumental ensemble 783.6648

Solo cantatas, Secular (Low voice)
  Solo cantatas, Secular (Low voice)   783.6848
  Solo cantatas, Secular (Low voice)   783.8948
Solo cantatas, Secular (Low voice) with continuo
  Solo cantatas, Secular (Low voice) with continuo
    783.8948
Solo cantatas, Secular (Low voice) with instrumental ensemble
  Solo cantatas, Secular (Low voice) with
    instrumental ensemble   783.6848
Solo cantatas, Secular (Medium voice)
  Solo cantatas, Secular (Medium voice) 783.8848
Sonatas (Alto flute and piano)
  Sonatas (Alto flute and piano)   788.32183
Sonatas (Bassoon and piano)
  Sonatas (Bassoon and piano)   788.58183
Sonatas (Flute and harp)
  Sonatas (Flute and harp)   785.44192183
Sonatas (Flute and piano), Arranged
  Sonatas (Flute and piano), Arranged 788.32183
Sonatas (Flutes (2))
  Sonatas (Flutes (2))   785.832192183
Sonatas (Harmonica and piano)
  Sonatas (Harmonica and piano)   788.82183
Sonatas (Harpsichord)
  Sonatas (Harpsichord)   786.4183
Sonatas (Oboe and harpsichord)
  Sonatas (Oboe and harpsichord)   788.521832
Sonatas (Oboe and piano)
  Sonatas (Oboe and piano)   788.52183
  Sonatas (Oboe and piano)   788.521832
Sonatas (Oboe and piano), Arranged
  Sonatas (Oboe and piano), Arranged 788.32183
Sonatas (Piano)
  Sonatas (Piano)   783
  Sonatas (Piano)   786.2
  Sonatas (Piano)   786.2183
  Sonatas (Piano)   786.21832
Sonatas (Trumpet with instrumental ensemble)
  Sonatas (Trumpet with instrumental ensemble)
    785.25199183
  Sonatas (Trumpet with instrumental ensemble)
    788.92183
Sonatas (Viola and continuo)
  Sonatas (Viola and continuo)   787.3183
Sonatas (Viola and piano)
  Sonatas (Viola and piano)   787.3183
Sonatas (Viola and piano), Arranged
  Sonatas (Viola and piano), Arranged 787.3183
Sonatas (Viola da gamba and continuo)
  Sonatas (Viola da gamba and continuo)
    787.65183
Sonatas (Viola da gamba and harpsichord)
  Sonatas (Viola da gamba and harpsichord)
    787.4183
Sonatas (Violin and continuo)
  Sonatas (Violin and continuo)   787.2183
Sonatas (Violin and harpsichord)
  Sonatas (Violin and harpsichord)   787.2183
Sonatas (Violin and piano)
  Sonatas (Violin and piano)   787.2183
Sonatas (Violins (2))
  Sonatas (Violins (2))   785.72192183
Sonatas (Violoncello and harpsichord)
  Sonatas (Violoncello and harpsichord) 787.4183
Sonatas (Violoncello and piano)
  Sonatas (Violoncello and piano)   787.4183
Sonatas (Violoncello and piano), Arranged
  Sonatas (Violoncello and piano), Arranged
    787.4183
Song cycles
  Song cycles   783.6642
  Song cycles   783.6647
Song of Solomon (Music)
  Song of Solomon (Music)   782.526
Songs
  Songs   783.242164
Songs (High voice) with band
  Songs (High voice) with band   783.6642
Songs (High voice) with continuo
  Songs (High voice) with continuo   783.342
  Songs (High voice) with continuo   783.6642
Songs (High voice) with instrumental ensemble
  Songs (High voice) with instrumental ensemble
    783.342
  Songs (High voice) with instrumental ensemble
    783.6642

Songs (High voice) with instrumental ensemble
    783.8642
Songs (High voice) with oboe
  Songs (High voice) with oboe   783.342
Songs (High voice) with orchestra
  Songs (High voice) with orchestra   783.6647
Songs (High voice) with orchestra, Arranged
  Songs (High voice) with orchestra, Arranged
    784.2
Songs (High voice) with piano
  Songs (High voice) with piano   783.342
  Songs (High voice) with piano   783.3420945
  Songs (High voice) with piano   783.6642
  Songs (High voice) with piano   783.8742
Songs (High voice) with piano, Arranged
  Songs (High voice) with piano, Arranged
    783.342
Songs (Low voice) with chamber orchestra, Arranged
  Songs (Low voice) with chamber orchestra,
    Arranged   783.242
Songs (Low voice) with continuo
  Songs (Low voice) with continuo   783.6848
  Songs (Low voice) with continuo   783.8942
  Songs (Low voice) with continuo   783.8948
Songs (Low voice) with instrumental ensemble
  Songs (Low voice) with instrumental ensemble
    783.342
  Songs (Low voice) with instrumental ensemble
    783.6848
  Songs (Low voice) with instrumental ensemble
    783.8942
  Songs (Low voice) with instrumental ensemble
    783.8948
Songs (Low voice) with piano
  Songs (Low voice) with piano   783.442
  Songs (Low voice) with piano   783.5420945
Songs (Medium voice) with instrumental ensemble
  Songs (Medium voice) with instrumental
    ensemble   783.442
  Songs (Medium voice) with instrumental
    ensemble   783.6742
  Songs (Medium voice) with instrumental
    ensemble   783.8
Songs (Medium voice) with oboe
  Songs (Medium voice) with oboe   783.442
Songs (Medium voice) with orchestra
  Songs (Medium voice) with orchestra 783.6647
Songs (Medium voice) with piano
  Songs (Medium voice) with piano   783.442
  Songs (Medium voice) with piano   783.6
  Songs (Medium voice) with piano   783.6742
  Songs (Medium voice) with piano   783.6842
  Songs (Medium voice) with piano   783.8842
Songs (Medium voice) with unspecified instrument
  Songs (Medium voice) with unspecified
    instrument   783.442
Songs with continuo
  Songs with continuo   783.242
Songs with instrumental ensemble
  Songs with instrumental ensemble   783.242
  Songs with instrumental ensemble
    783.242162009411
  Songs with instrumental ensemble   783.42
  Songs with instrumental ensemble   783.442
Songs with orchestra
  Songs with orchestra   783.242
Songs with piano
  Songs with piano   783
  Songs with piano   783.242
  Songs with piano   783.242094137
  Songs with piano   783.242164
  Songs with piano   783.6642
Songs with violin
  Songs with violin   787.2
Songs without words (Instrumental music)
  Songs without words (Instrumental music)
    784.728941896
Songs, English
  Songs, English, Borders   783.242094137
  Songs, English, Scotland   783.242
  Songs, English, Scotland   783.242162009411
  Songs, English, Wales   783.242162009411
Songs, German
  Songs, German   783.242
Songs, Polish
  Songs, Polish   783.42709438

Songs, Scots
  Songs, Scots, Borders   783.242094137
  Songs, Scots, Scotland 783.242162009411
Songs, Welsh
  Songs, Welsh, Wales   783.242162009411
Soul music
  Soul music   783.242164
  Soul music   786.2
Spirituals (Songs)
  Spirituals (Songs)   782.5253
  Spirituals (Songs)   782.542
  Spirituals (Songs)   782.8253
  Spirituals (Songs)   786.2
Stabat Mater dolorosa (Music)
  Stabat Mater dolorosa (Music)   782.53235
  Stabat Mater dolorosa (Music) 782.532351726
String ensembles
  String ensembles   785.7199
  String ensembles   785.71991269
String octets (Violins (4), violas (2), violoncellos (2))
  String octets (Violins (4), violas (2), violoncellos
    (2))   785.7198
String orchestra music
  String orchestra music   784.7
  String orchestra music   784.71858
  String orchestra music   785.7199
String quartets
  String quartets   785.7194
  String quartets   785.719418844
String quartets (Violin, viola, violoncellos (2))
  String quartets (Violin, viola, violoncellos (2))
    785.44194
String quartets (Violins (2), violoncellos (2))
  String quartets (Violins (2), violoncellos (2))
    785.44194
String quartets (Violoncellos (4))
  String quartets (Violoncellos (4)) 785.74194
String quartets (Viols (4))
  String quartets (Viols (4))   782.543
  String quartets (Viols (4))   785.76194
  String quartets (Viols (4)) 785.761941876
String quartets, Arranged
  String quartets, Arranged   785.7194
  String quartets, Arranged 785.719418846
String quintets (Violin, violas (2), violoncello, double bass)
  String quintets (Violin, violas (2), violoncello,
    double bass)   785.7195
String quintets (Violins (2), viola, violoncellos (2))
  String quintets (Violins (2), viola, violoncellos
    (2))   785.7195
String quintets (Violins (2), violas (2), violoncello
  String quintets (Violins (2), violas (2),
    violoncello   785.7195
String quintets (Violins (2), violas (2), violoncello)
  String quintets (Violins (2), violas (2),
    violoncello)   785.7195
String quintets (Viols (5))
  String quintets (Viols (5))   782.543
  String quintets (Viols (5))   785.76195
  String quintets (Viols (5)) 785.7619518823
String quintets, Arranged
  String quintets, Arranged   785.7195
String sextets (Viols (6))
  String sextets (Viols (6))   785.76195
String trios (Violin, viola d'amore, viola da gamba)
  String trios (Violin, viola d'amore, viola da
    gamba)   785.7192
String trios (Violin, viola d'amore, violoncello)
  String trios (Violin, viola d'amore, violoncello)
    785.7192
String trios (Violins (2), violoncello)
  String trios (Violins (2), violoncello) 785.13
String trios (Viols (3))
  String trios (Viols (3))   785.76193
Suites
  Suites   788.98
Suites (Archlute), Arranged
  Suites (Archlute), Arranged   787.831858
Suites (Band)
  Suites (Band)   784.81858
Suites (Bassoon, clarinets (2), flute, horns (2))
  Suites (Bassoon, clarinets (2), flute, horns (2))
    785.43

Suites (Bassoon, clarinets (2), flute, horns (2), oboe, trumpet)
Suites (Bassoon, clarinets (2), flute, horns (2), oboe, trumpet)   785.431981852

Suites (Bassoon, clarinets (2), horns (2))
Suites (Bassoon, clarinets (2), horns (2))   785.43

Suites (Bassoon, clarinets (2), horns (2), trumpet)
Suites (Bassoon, clarinets (2), horns (2), trumpet)   785.43

Suites (Bassoons (2), clarinets (2), flute, horns (2), oboes (2))
Suites (Bassoons (2), clarinets (2), flute, horns (2), oboes (2))   785.431991852

Suites (Bassoons (2), clarinets (2), horns (2))
Suites (Bassoons (2), clarinets (2), horns (2))   785.43

Suites (Bassoons (2), clarinets (2), horns (2), trumpet)
Suites (Bassoons (2), clarinets (2), horns (2), trumpet)   785.43

Suites (Bassoons (4))
Suites (Bassoons (4))   785.8581941858

Suites (Brass band)
Suites (Brass band)   784.91858

Suites (English horn and piano)
Suites (English horn and piano)   788.53

Suites (English horn, oboes (2))
Suites (English horn, oboes (2))   785.851931858

Suites (Flute and piano)
Suites (Flute and piano)   788.32185
Suites (Flute and piano)   788.321858

Suites (Flute)
Suites (Flute)   788.32

Suites (Flutes (4)), Arranged
Suites (Flutes (4)), Arranged   785.8321941858

Suites (Harmonica and piano)
Suites (Harmonica and piano)   788.321858

Suites (Harpsichord)
Suites (Harpsichord)   786.41858

Suites (Harpsichord, saxophones (4))
Suites (Harpsichord, saxophones (4))   785.261951858

Suites (Instrumental ensemble)
Suites (Instrumental ensemble)   785.420991858

Suites (Oboe and piano)
Suites (Oboe and piano)   788.52

Suites (Oboe with string orchestra)
Suites (Oboe with string orchestra)   788.521858

Suites (Orchestra)
Suites (Orchestra)   782.15
Suites (Orchestra)   784.21858

Suites (Organ)
Suites (Organ)   786.51858

Suites (Organ, violin, violoncello with string orchestra), Arranged
Suites (Organ, violin, violoncello with string orchestra), Arranged   784.265186

Suites (Organ, violins (2), viole da gamba (2))
Suites (Organ, violins (2), viole da gamba (2))   785.281951858

Suites (Organ, viols (4))
Suites (Organ, viols (4))   785.281951858

Suites (Percussion with instrumental ensemble)
Suites (Percussion with instrumental ensemble)   785.321991858

Suites (Piano)
Suites (Piano)   786.21852
Suites (Piano)   786.21858
Suites (Piano)   786.41858

Suites (Piano), Arranged
Suites (Piano), Arranged   786.21858

Suites (Piccolo and piano)
Suites (Piccolo and piano)   788.3641858

Suites (Recorder and piano)
Suites (Recorder and piano)   788.3641858

Suites (String orchestra)
Suites (String orchestra)   784.71858

Suites (String orchestra), Arranged
Suites (String orchestra), Arranged   784.71858

Suites (String quartet)
Suites (String quartet)   785.7194
Suites (String quartet)   785.71941858

Suites (Viola)
Suites (Viola)   787.31858

Suites (Violin and piano)
Suites (Violin and piano)   787.21858

Suites (Violin with orchestra)
Suites (Violin with orchestra)   784.2721858

Suites (Violins (2), viola, continuo)
Suites (Violins (2), viola, continuo)   785.281941858

Suites (Violins (2), violas (2), continuo)
Suites (Violins (2), violas (2), continuo)   785.281951858

Suites (Violins (2), viols (2), continuo)
Suites (Violins (2), viols (2), continuo)   785.281951858

Suites (Viols (3))
Suites (Viols (3))   785.761931858

Suites (Wind ensemble)
Suites (Wind ensemble)   785.431991854

Suites (Woodwind ensemble)
Suites (Woodwind ensemble)   785.81858

Swing (Music)
Swing (Music)   781.654
Swing (Music)   785

Symphonic poems
Symphonic poems   782.527
Symphonic poems   784.21843
Symphonic poems   784.21894

Symphonies
Symphonies   782.4184
Symphonies   782.5
Symphonies   784.2184
Symphonies   784.2814
Symphonies   785.7194
Symphonies   786.2
Symphonies   787.2

Symphonies (Chamber orchestra)
Symphonies (Chamber orchestra)   784.3184

Symphonies (Instrumental ensemble)
Symphonies (Instrumental ensemble)   785.42199184

Symphonies (String orchestra)
Symphonies (String orchestra)   784.2184

Tangos
Tangos   784.218885
Tangos   785.2419418885
Tangos   785.2819518885

Te Deum laudamus (Music)
Te Deum laudamus (Music)   782.5324
Te Deum laudamus (Music)   782.5325

Television music
Television music   783.2421546
Television music   786.21546
Television music   787.21546
Television music   788.321546
Television music   788.621546
Television music   788.731546
Television music   788.921546

Theater
Theater, 19th century, Venice   782.1

Timpani
Timpani   786.93076

Timpani and piano music
Timpani and piano music   786.93076

Timpani music
Timpani music   786.93076

Toccatas
Toccatas   785.6219218947
Toccatas   785.832193
Toccatas   786.5
Toccatas   786.51872

Trinity Sunday music
Trinity Sunday music   782.5265

Trio sonatas (Violin, viola da gamba, continuo)
Trio sonatas (Violin, viola da gamba, continuo)   785.28193183

Trio sonatas (Violins (2), continuo)
Trio sonatas (Violins (2), continuo)   780
Trio sonatas (Violins (2), continuo)   785.28194183

Trios (Basset horn, harp, violoncello)
Trios (Basset horn, harp, violoncello)   785.44193186

Trios (Bassoon, flute, violin)
Trios (Bassoon, flute, violin)   785.44193

Trios (Bassoon, horn, viola)
Trios (Bassoon, horn, viola)   785.4219318966

Trios (Flute, guitar, viola)
Trios (Flute, guitar, viola)   785.44193

Trios (Flute, harp, viola)
Trios (Flute, harp, viola)   785.441931852

Trios (Flute, violin, viola)
Trios (Flute, violin, viola)   785.44193

Trios (Flute, violin, violoncello)
Trios (Flute, violin, violoncello)   785.13
Trios (Flute, violin, violoncello)   785.44193

Trios (Flutes (2), viola)
Trios (Flutes (2), viola)   785.44193

Trios (Flutes (2), violoncello)
Trios (Flutes (2), violoncello)   785.13
Trios (Flutes (2), violoncello)   785.44193

Trios (Guitar, violin, viola)
Trios (Guitar, violin, viola)   785.44193

Trios (Harp, violin, violoncello)
Trios (Harp, violin, violoncello)   785.7193

Trios (Horn, violin, violoncello)
Trios (Horn, violin, violoncello)   785.13

Trios (Organ, viole da gamba (2))
Trios (Organ, viole da gamba (2))   785.76194

Trios (Organ, viols (2))
Trios (Organ, viols (2))   785.761941876

Trios (Piano, bass clarinet, violoncello)
Trios (Piano, bass clarinet, violoncello)   785.24193

Trios (Piano, bassoon, oboe)
Trios (Piano, bassoon, oboe)   785.26193

Trios (Piano, electronics, viola)
Trios (Piano, electronics, viola)   785.2998193

Trios (Piano, flute, violoncello)
Trios (Piano, flute, violoncello)   788.321858

Trios (Piano, flutes (2))
Trios (Piano, flutes (2))   785.26193

Trios (Piano, horn, violin)
Trios (Piano, horn, violin)   785.25193

Trios (Trombone, violin, continuo)
Trios (Trombone, violin, continuo)   785.25193

Trios (Violin, viola, continuo)
Trios (Violin, viola, continuo)   785.25193

Trios (Violins (2), continuo)
Trios (Violins (2), continuo)   787.2

Trombone music
Trombone music   788.93

Trombone music, Arranged
Trombone music, Arranged   788.93168

Tropes (Music)
Tropes (Music)   782.3222
Tropes (Music)   782.53235

Trumpet and organ music, Arranged
Trumpet and organ music, Arranged   788.92183

Trumpet and piano music
Trumpet and piano music   788.92
Trumpet and piano music   788.92165

Trumpet and piano music, Arranged
Trumpet and piano music, Arranged   788.921595

Trumpet music
Trumpet music   788.92
Trumpet music   788.921542

Trumpet music, Arranged
Trumpet music, Arranged   788.921546
Trumpet music, Arranged   788.92164
Trumpet music, Arranged   788.92165
Trumpet music, Arranged   788.92168

Trumpet with instrumental ensemble
Trumpet with instrumental ensemble   785.25199183
Trumpet with instrumental ensemble   788.92183

Tuba and piano music
Tuba and piano music   788.98

Tuba and piano music, Arranged
Tuba and piano music, Arranged   788.98

Tuba music
Tuba music   788.98

Variations (English horn, oboes (2)), Arranged
Variations (English horn, oboes (2)), Arranged   785.851931825

Variations (Guitar)
Variations (Guitar)   787.871825

Variations (Orchestra)
Variations (Orchestra)   784.21825

Variations (Organ)
Variations (Organ)   786.5
Variations (Organ)   786.51825

Variations (Piano)
Variations (Piano)   786.2

Variations (String quartet)
Variations (String quartet)   785.7194

Variations (String quartet), Arranged
Variations (String quartet), Arranged   785.71941825

Veni Sancte Spiritus (Music)
Veni Sancte Spiritus (Music)   782.525
Vespers (Music)
Vespers (Music)   782.324
Vespers (Music)   782.526
Vespers (Music)   782.5325
Villancicos (Music)
Villancicos (Music)   780
Viol music (Viols (2))
Viol music (Viols (2))   785.76192
Viola
Viola   787.3076
Viola and accordion music
Viola and accordion music   785.44192
Viola and guitar music, Arranged
Viola and guitar music, Arranged
                                            785.719218846
Viola and organ music
Viola and organ music   788.52
Viola and piano music
Viola and piano music   787.3
Viola da gamba music
Viola da gamba music   787.65
Viola da gamba music, Arranged
Viola da gamba music, Arranged   787.65
Viola d'amore and viola da gamba music
Viola d'amore and viola da gamba music
                                               785.7192
Viola d'amore and violoncello music
Viola d'amore and violoncello music   785.7192
Viola music
Viola music   787.3
Viola music   787.31542
Viola music (Violas (2))
Viola music (Violas (2))   785.73192
Viola music, Arranged
Viola music, Arranged   787.3
Viola music, Arranged   787.3168
Viola with instrumental ensemble
Viola with instrumental ensemble   785.22199
Violin
Violin   787.2076
Violin   787.218949
Violin, Examinations, questions, etc, Great
Britain   787.2
Violin and continuo music
Violin and continuo music   787.2
Violin and organ music
Violin and organ music   785
Violin and organ music, Arranged
Violin and organ music, Arranged   785
Violin and piano music
Violin and piano music   787.2
Violin and piano music   787.2076
Violin and piano music   787.2165
Violin and piano music   787.2186
Violin and piano music   788.32
Violin and piano music, Arranged
Violin and piano music, Arranged   785
Violin and piano music, Arranged   787.2
Violin and viola music
Violin and viola music   785.7192
Violin and viola with orchestra
Violin and viola with orchestra   784.24
Violin and viola with orchestra   785.28193
Violin and violoncello music
Violin and violoncello music   785.71921876
Violin choir music
Violin choir music   785.72192183
Violin music
Violin music   787.2
Violin music   787.21542
Violin music   787.218949
Violin music (Violins (2))
Violin music (Violins (2))   785.7192
Violin music (Violins (2))   785.72192
Violin music (Violins (2))   787.2
Violin music (Violins (2)), Arranged
Violin music (Violins (2)), Arranged 785.72192
Violin music, Arranged
Violin music, Arranged   787.21546
Violin music, Arranged   787.2164
Violin music, Arranged   787.2165
Violin music, Arranged   787.2166

Violin music, Arranged   787.2168
Violins (2) with orchestra
Violins (2) with orchestra   784.24
Violins (2), double bass with string ensemble
Violins (2), double bass with string ensemble
                                               785.7199
Violins (2), double bass with string orchestra
Violins (2), double bass with string orchestra
                                               785.7199
Violoncello
Violoncello   787.41423
Violoncello and organ music, Arranged
Violoncello and organ music, Arranged   785
Violoncello and piano music
Violoncello and piano music   787.4
Violoncello and piano music   787.41896
Violoncello and piano music   787.418966
Violoncello and piano music, 21st century
                                              787.40905
Violoncello and piano music, Arranged
Violoncello and piano music, Arranged   787.4
Violoncello music
Violoncello music   783.96
Violoncello music   787.4
Violoncello music   787.41542
Violoncello music   787.41723
Violoncello music, 21st century   787.40905
Violoncello music (Violoncellos (2))
Violoncello music (Violoncellos (2)) 785.74192
Violoncello music, Arranged
Violoncello music, Arranged   787.4168
Violoncello with instrumental ensemble
Violoncello with instrumental ensemble
                                              785.32199
Vocal duets with continuo
Vocal duets with continuo   783.1242
Vocal duets with continuo   783.1248
Vocal duets with instrumental ensemble
Vocal duets with instrumental ensemble
                                               783.1242
Vocal duets with instrumental ensemble
                                               783.1248
Vocal duets with instrumental ensemble 783.242
Vocal duets with instrumental ensemble
                                          783.242162009411
Vocal duets with instrumental ensemble   783.42
Vocal duets with orchestra
Vocal duets with orchestra   783.6647
Vocal duets with piano
Vocal duets with piano   783
Vocal duets with piano   783.12
Vocal duets with piano   783.1242164
Vocal duets with piano   783.242
Vocal ensembles, Unaccompanied
Vocal ensembles, Unaccompanied   782.5
Vocal music
Vocal music, 17th century, Portugal   782.543
Vocal octets with orchestra
Vocal octets with orchestra   783.188
Vocal quartets with continuo
Vocal quartets with continuo   782.543
Vocal quartets with instrumental ensemble
Vocal quartets with instrumental ensemble
                                                783.42
Vocal sextets with electronics
Vocal sextets with electronics   783.1642
Vocal sextets with instrumental ensemble
Vocal sextets with instrumental ensemble
                                               783.1642
Vocal trios with continuo
Vocal trios with continuo   783.1342
Vocal trios with continuo   783.136642
Vocal trios with continuo   783.136643
Vocalises (Voices (6)), Unaccompanied
Vocalises (Voices (6)), Unaccompanied   782.5
Vocalises (Voices(2)) with chamber orchestra
Vocalises (Voices(2)) with chamber orchestra
                                              785.32199
Vocalises (Voices(2)) with instrumental ensemble
Vocalises (Voices(2)) with instrumental
ensemble   785.32199
Waltzes
Waltzes   784.18846165
Waltzes   785.4219918846

Waltzes   785.719218846
Waltzes   785.719418846
Waltzes   786.218846
Waltzes   786.418846
Wedding music
Wedding music   782.52951587
Wedding music   782.5421587
Wedding music   782.632231587
Wedding music   786.218971587
Wedding music   786.51587
Wedding music   786.518992
Wind ensembles
Wind ensembles   785.43199
Wind nonets (Bassoons (2), clarinets (2), flute, horns (2), oboes (2)), Arranged
Wind nonets (Bassoons (2), clarinets (2), flute,
horns (2), oboes (2)), Arranged   785.431991832
Wind octets (Bassoons (2), clarinets (2) horns (2) oboes (2))
Wind octets (Bassoons (2), clarinets (2) horns (2)
oboes (2))   785.43198
Wind octets (Bassoons (2), clarinets (2), horns (2), oboes (2))
Wind octets (Bassoons (2), clarinets (2), horns
(2), oboes (2))   785.43198
Wind quintets (Bassoon, clarinet, flute, horn, oboe)
Wind quintets (Bassoon, clarinet, flute, horn,
oboe)   785.43195
Wind quintets (Bassoon, clarinet, flute, horn, oboe), Arranged
Wind quintets (Bassoon, clarinet, flute, horn,
oboe), Arranged   785.43195
Wine
Wine   785.34196
Woodwind ensembles
Woodwind ensembles   784.89
Woodwind octets (Saxophones (8))
Woodwind octets (Saxophones (8))   785.87198
Woodwind quartets (bassoons (4))
Woodwind quartets (bassoons (4))   785.858194
Woodwind quartets (Bassoons (4))
Woodwind quartets (Bassoons (4))   785.858194
Woodwind quartets (Bassoons (4)), Arranged
Woodwind quartets (Bassoons (4)), Arranged
                                             785.858194
Woodwind quartets (Saxophones (4))
Woodwind quartets (Saxophones (4)) 785.87194
Woodwind quintets (Recorders (5)), Arranged
Woodwind quintets (Recorders (5)), Arranged
                                             785.836195
Woodwind septets (Recorders (7)), Arranged
Woodwind septets (Recorders (7)), Arranged
                                             785.836197
Woodwind sextets (Recorders (6)), Arranged
Woodwind sextets (Recorders (6)), Arranged
                                             785.836196
Woodwind trios (Bassoon, flutes (2))
Woodwind trios (Bassoon, flutes (2)) 785.44193
Woodwind trios (Bassoon, flutes (2)) 785.8193
Woodwind trios (Bassoons (3)), Arranged
Woodwind trios (Bassoons (3)), Arranged
                                             785.858193
Woodwind trios (Clarinet, flute, oboe)
Woodwind trios (Clarinet, flute, oboe) 785.8193
Woodwind trios (Clarinets (3))
Woodwind trios (Clarinets (3))   785.862193
Woodwind trios (English horn, oboes (2))
Woodwind trios (English horn, oboes (2))
                                              785.85193
Woodwind trios (English horn, oboes (2)), Arranged
Woodwind trios (English horn, oboes (2)),
Arranged   785.85193
Woodwind trios (Flutes (3))
Woodwind trios (Flutes (3))   785.832193
Woodwind trios (Oboes (3))
Woodwind trios (Oboes (3))   785.852193
Woodwind trios (Saxophones (3)
Woodwind trios (Saxophones (3)   785.87193
Woodwind trios, Arranged
Woodwind trios, Arranged   785.8193
Zarzuelas
Zarzuelas   782.12